THE KING'S REFORMATION

THE
KING'S REFORMATION
HENRY VIII AND THE REMAKING
OF THE ENGLISH CHURCH

G.W. BERNARD

Yale University Press
New Haven and London

For information about this and other Yale University Press publications, please contact:
U.S. Office: sales.press@yale.edu   yalebooks.com
Europe Office: sales@yaleup.co.uk   www.yaleup.co.uk

Set in Sabon by SNP Best-set Typesetter Ltd, Hong Kong
Printed in Great Britain by St Edmundsbury Press Ltd, Bury St Edmunds

Library of Congress Control Number: 2005932989

ISBN 0–300–10908–3

A catalogue record for this book is available from the British Library.

10 9 8 7 6 5 4 3 2 1

Published with assistance from the foundation established in memory of Oliver Baty
Cunningham of the Class of 1917, Yale College.

Contents

Illustrations

Preface

The claim of this book is encapsulated in its title—that Henry VIII was largely responsible for the break with Rome and for subsequent religious changes which together have had such a lasting impact. But to support such a claim is by no means as straightforward as might at first appear. We know what we know about the past from surviving sources. Those for the reign of Henry VIII are plentiful, ranging from chronicles, government papers, drafts of legislation, royal proclamations, letters to and from the king and leading councillors, noblemen and gentry, interrogations of those caught up in dissent and rebellion, and many letters from foreign ambassadors in England, reporting back to their masters, especially those of Eustace Chapuys, imperial ambassador. Most of these have been edited and summarised in the volumes of *Letters and Papers of Henry VIII*. While such editions are enormously helpful, I have gone back as far as practicable to the precise wordings in the original manuscripts. But even these are difficult to interpret. They were not written with the modern historian in mind. Their writers' purposes may have coloured what they wrote. Chapuys, for example, may in his fortnightly despatches have exaggerated opposition to the break with Rome, while the lawyer MP Edward Hall, looking back in his *Chronicle*, may have offered too sympathetic an impression of royal policy. That does not make their testimony worthless; it means rather that what they wrote must be read carefully, in an ever-questioning spirit. In this book I have attempted to share my explorations in the sources, setting out the evidence in detail, quoting at some length, not simply to convey the vivid phraseology of Tudor writers, but so that readers can assess for themselves how far my presentation of the sources rings true. And since history is not just a dialogue between historians and their sources, but also a dialogue, sometimes a debate, or even an argument, between historians, I have tried to give due weight to interpretations other than my own, showing where I think they fall short, but again offering readers enough from which they can make up their own minds. All that explains the length and the detail of this book, as I try not just to give an account but to show how and why I have come to the arguments that I set forward here.

I have gained enormously from the stimulus of teaching, and this book is dedicated to the generations of students who have taken my Special Subject. My book has been prepared against the background of chronic underfunding and increasing bureaucratisation of higher education. I am therefore greatly indebted to the Leverhulme Trust for the award of a Senior Research Fellowship which allowed me the space in which to question current orthodoxies, to the Arts and Humanities Research Board for an award under its research leave scheme which at a crucial stage gave me uninterrupted time in which to write, and to the University of Southampton for study leave. I also wish to thank the British Academy for grants enabling study in the Haus-, Hof- und Staatsarchiv in Vienna, and the British Library and Public Record Office in London. I am grateful too to the staff of the Public Record Office, the British Library and the Bodleian Library, Oxford, for all their assistance. I thank Cambridge University Press, Chicago University Press and Ashgate Publishing for permission to draw on material from earlier publications. I owe much to the encouragement and stimulus of friends, notably Kevin Sharpe, Alan Thacker, David Katz, Alastair Duke, Richard Hoyle, Penry Williams, Steve Gunn and the late Jennifer Loach. Robert Baldock and Tom Buhler at Yale University Press and an anonymous reader offered very helpful suggestions. I thank Anne Borg warmly for reading the proofs. Above all for the labour of reading and commenting invaluably on many drafts, I am especially grateful to Cliff Davies, Peter Gwyn, the late T.B. Pugh, Greg Walker and Mark Stoyle.

George Bernard
April 2004

Prologue

In the late 1520s, Henry VIII, by then king of England for nearly two decades, came to believe that his marriage to Catherine of Aragon, whom he had wed soon after coming to the throne in 1509, had been null and void from the very beginning. And he set about vindicating his new conviction, trying, but in the end failing, to secure an annulment from the pope, and then cutting loose from papal jurisdiction. How and why Henry brought about the break with Rome, what it meant for the church in England, especially for the monasteries, and how far and with what effect there was dissent, opposition and resistance from within the church and beyond are the questions that this book seeks to explore.

The Pilgrimage of Grace, 1536–37

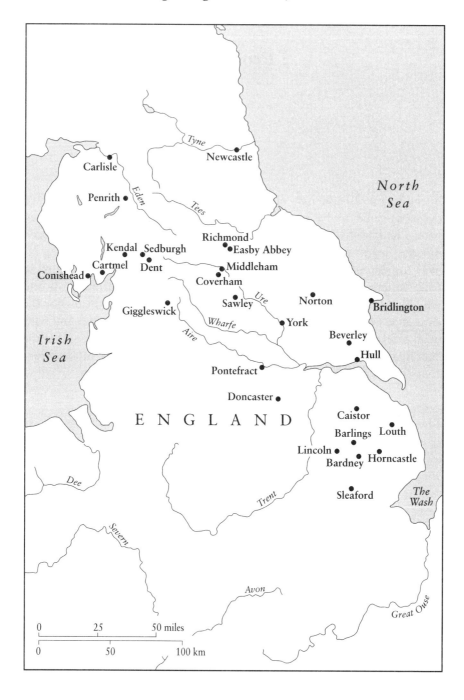

Tyne

Newcastle

Carlisle

North Sea

Penrith

Eden

Tees

Richmond

Kendal Sedburgh
Easby Abbey

Cartmel Dent
Middleham

Conishead
Coverham

Ure

Sawley
Norton

Irish Sea

Giggleswick
Wharfe
York

Bridlington

Aire

Beverley

Hull

Pontefract

Doncaster

E N G L A N D

Caistor

Barlings Louth

Lincoln

Bardney Horncastle

Dee

Trent

Sleaford

The Wash

Severn

Avon

Great Ouse

0	25	50 miles
0	50	100 km

1

The Divorce

The Origins of the Divorce

How Henry arrived at the momentous conviction that his marriage was against the law of God is the first conundrum that we must resolve. Was the king persuaded by others—by John Longland, bishop of Lincoln and one of his confessors, or by John Stokesley, then a theologian but later to be bishop of London, or by various 'well learned' divines?[1] On such accounts, Henry, married to Catherine for more than a decade, was approached by theologians and churchmen who told him that his marriage was damnable. It is, perhaps, just thinkable that close counsellors would see it as their duty to inform the king that what he was doing was wicked, though, given that the king had been married for many years, it is not easy to explain why they should only now discover that his marriage was evil. A more plausible explanation is that the observers from whose remarks these interpretations are drawn were in various ways misled. Longland, Stokesley and several other churchmen were from an early stage to become heavily and publicly involved in the presentation of the king's case. That does not mean, however, that they had put the idea in the king's head in the first place—though it might explain why those looking on from outside thought that they had.

Catherine of Aragon put all the blame on Thomas Wolsey, the king's long-serving and closest counsellor. He had maliciously 'kindled this fire' because she had 'wondered at' his 'high pride & vainglory', abhorred his 'voluptuous life, and abominable lechery', and had 'little regard' for his 'presumptuous power and tyranny'. Catherine also accused Wolsey of 'malice' against her nephew, the Emperor Charles V, 'whom I perfectly know you hate worse than a scorpion, because he would not satisfy your ambition, and make you pope by force'.[2] That was how the

chronicler Edward Hall reported it. According to Bishop Fisher's earliest biographer, Wolsey, 'doubting that her words about the king might
hap in time to be occasion of withdrawing his high favour now borne
towards him', consequently questioned the validity of Catherine's marriage. He persuaded Longland—'who being a timorous man and fearing
his great power, [did] as the cardinal commanded him'—to admonish
the king when hearing his confession.[3] Many others saw Wolsey as
responsible for the king's doubts about his marriage: Mendoza, the
Spanish ambassador in May 1527,[4] Polydore Vergil,[5] More's biographer
William Roper[6] and, later, John Foxe[7] and Nicholas Harpsfield.[8] In such
a scenario, Cardinal Wolsey, playing the part of a vengeful royal minister, questioned the king's marriage because the queen had criticised
him, and because the queen's nephew had failed to make him pope. It
is a superficially attractive picture, yet it lacks plausibility. It would have
been a highly risky manoeuvre for Wolsey. And if the cardinal had
indeed been seeking to damage the queen, there might have been other
methods—for example, accusing her of some trumped-up charges of
corruption, or heresy or even adultery—that did not directly bring in
the king. Moreover, the sources that place the responsibility upon
Wolsey do not do so unquestioningly. Hall quotes Catherine's attack—
but also reports Wolsey's response, that he was 'not the beginner, nor
the mover of the doubt, and that it was sore against his will, that ever
the marriage should come in question'.[9] And, intriguingly, Harpsfield,
who still concluded that 'it is most credible that the said cardinal was
the first author and incenser of this divorce', because Catherine accused
him of it, nevertheless included a different account. He had heard Dr
Draycott, Wolsey's chaplain and chancellor, tell how he had himself
asked Wolsey about it all. Wolsey had insisted that 'the king broke the
matter to him first, and never left urging of him until he had won him
to give his consent to others that were the chief setters forth of the
divorce between the king and queen Katherine'.[10] And Wolsey allegedly
later came to regret having agreed to it. On this account, it was Henry
who first broached the matter with Wolsey, not the other way about.
That in turn raises the possibility that, when in May 1527 Wolsey summoned the king, declaring that *he* had come to be troubled in his mind
and conscience over a matter touching the king's soul, he may not have
been telling the truth, but simply putting on a public performance in
which the king appeared as if swayed by his minister. For Henry would
have had good reasons to avoid openly presenting himself as the first
mover: his case would sound disinterested and thus more convincing if
others were seen to be responsible for it.

Henry's official justification for calling his marriage into question was (as Wolsey put it in December 1527) that his doubts arose both from his own assiduous study and learning, and from his discussions with many theologians.[11] The instructions prepared for Henry's ambassadors to Charles V stress this. The king some years past had noticed while reading in the Bible the severe penalty inflicted by God on those who married the widows of their brothers. He began to be troubled in his conscience and came to think that the sudden deaths of his male children had been a divine judgment upon his marriage. The more he studied the matter, the more clearly it appeared to him that he had broken a divine law. He called together learned canon lawyers to know their opinion on the dispensation: several pronounced it invalid. He then consulted bishops and the most learned men in human and divine law.[12] Such an account presents the canon lawyers as tending to endorse the conclusion to which the king was already moving. That sounds more plausible than any account which has the divines telling an unsuspecting king that his marriage was not just technically illegal but damnable in the eyes of God.[13] But if Henry's account of how he came to doubt the validity of his marriage is essentially true, it does not contain the whole truth. It presents a troubled king reflecting on God's purpose in allowing his male children to die very young, and coming to the conclusion that there was something intrinsically flawed in his marriage. Yet this account omits a crucial point—there is no place within it for Anne Boleyn.

Henry had married Catherine in 1509, very quickly after his accession to the throne, seemingly of his own volition, though possibly responding to his father's deathbed wishes. Hall says that 'the king was moved, by some of his council, that it should be honourable and profitable to his realm' for him to marry Catherine: 'by reason of which motion, the king being young, and not understanding the law of God', he did so. That Hall writes '*some* of his council' hints that others were less enthusiastic; and in 1529 Bishop Nicholas West of Ely would recall that Archbishop Warham and Bishop Foxe of Winchester disagreed over it.[14] But the most plausible reading is that the young Henry married Catherine because he believed that it was the right course of action to take.

There were several pregnancies, but Catherine famously failed to give Henry a male heir. There was a stillborn girl in early 1510; a boy, Henry, who died in early 1511 after fifty-two days; a miscarriage in September 1513; a boy who died very soon after birth in December 1514; a miscarriage in autumn 1517; a stillborn child in November 1518. Only

Mary, born on 18 February 1516, survived. How badly did Henry take the lack of a male heir? In 1519 he vowed to lead a crusade against the Turk in person if, by the mercy of God, he had a male heir.[15] Some historians have claimed that fearful concern over the succession dominated Henry's foreign policy in the early 1520s, with the king anxious to see Mary married off first to Charles V, then to King Francis of France, thus ensuring a peaceful transmission of authority. Others, with more reason, have seen such negotiations as purely tactical in the tangled diplomacy of the day.[16]

From the start Henry was an unfaithful husband. As early as 1510 he was reported as courting the sister of Edward Stafford, third duke of Buckingham, which led to an angry scene between king and duke. By early 1514 Elizabeth Blount, one of Catherine's ladies-in-waiting, had become his mistress. Henry had a son by her in 1519: Henry Fitzroy, created duke of Richmond in 1525.[17]

In the early 1520s Mary Boleyn, daughter of Sir Thomas Boleyn, one of the king's more important servants, was his mistress. She was already married, to William Carey, but it is possible, as Anthony Hoskins has argued, that her two children, Catherine, born 1524, and Henry, born 1526, were the king's, not Carey's. John Hale, vicar of Isleworth, would much later confess that he had been shown the young Master Carey, and told that he was the king's son by Anne Boleyn's sister.[18]

Then Anne Boleyn won Henry's heart, possibly as early as 1526, though precise and specific information on the circumstances and the timing is hard to find. That Henry was passionately in love emerges from his undated love letters. (If he wrote them during the epidemic of sweating sickness that kept them apart, that dates them to 1528, but some may be earlier.) This reinforces the case that it was Henry himself who came to the view that his first marriage was null and void, for nothing induces a man to question his marriage more than falling in love with another woman. In that sense, Anne Boleyn was undoubtedly responsible for Henry's assertion that his first marriage had always been null and void.

Anne Boleyn

But was she responsible in a more direct and active sense? One of the most common claims made for Anne Boleyn, who would eventually become Henry VIII's second queen, is that, unlike other women whom the king had pursued, including her elder sister Mary, she refused to sleep with Henry unless he made an honest woman of her. Only, it is held, if Henry put aside Catherine of Aragon, his queen, and formally married Anne would she yield to his entreaties. 'Either because of virtue or ambition,' writes Professor Jack Scarisbrick in his classic biography of Henry VIII, 'Anne refused to become his mistress and thus to follow the conventional, inconspicuous path of her sister; and the more she resisted, the more, apparently, did Henry prize her'; 'the king . . . had . . . fallen in love with one who would give herself entirely to him only if he would give himself entirely to her'.[19] Diarmaid MacCulloch, biographer of Thomas Cranmer, endorses this view, writing of Anne's 'nearly six years of keeping Henry from his heart's desire'.[20]

What contemporary evidence is there in support of this tenacious assumption about Anne's supposed resistance to a supposedly lascivious king? The earliest appears to be Reginald Pole's jibe in *De unitate*, printed in 1536. Pole, younger son of Margaret, countess of Salisbury, had studied theology and was on the verge of making a brilliant career in the church in the early 1530s when his unwillingness to support the king over his divorce led him into exile. In 1536 he denounced the king, and his evidence must therefore be read cautiously. Berating Henry, 'miserably burning with passion for love of a girl', Pole went on:

> she, indeed, has said that she will make herself available to you on one condition alone. You must reject your wife whose place she desires to hold. This modest woman does not want to be your concubine. She wants to be your wife. I believe that she learned from the example of her sister . . . how quickly you can have your fill of concubines. This woman . . . desired to be joined to you by an indissoluble bond. She desired to remain with you perpetually.

At first glance, Pole seems to support the legend, even to be its source. But if on his account it was Anne who first insisted on becoming the king's wife, it was Henry who readily agreed to her demand:

> And in this passionate longing you responded mutually. In fact you actually surpassed her so that you thought it would be the greatest achievement of your fortunes, the height of happiness, if your legitimate and just wife were cast out of your marriage and it were permitted you to be united with this woman in matrimony and to live with her forever.

Henry unhesitatingly agreed to Anne's condition. Their abstinence from full sexual relations was thus a mutual decision. Pole's account is in no sense evidence that it was Anne who resisted the king's advances for six years. And Pole's testimony, while interesting, is not wholly compelling. He wants to have Anne insisting on marriage, but Henry wanting marriage even more than she did. That produces a tension between the lascivious Henry, the image of the king that Pole most wishes to present, and Henry as the devoted and faithful lover seeking perpetual marriage.[21]

But that in turn prompts a different counter-suggestion against the standard view: that over the years it was not Anne who held Henry back, but rather that it was Henry himself who refrained from sleeping with his beloved. Closely read, the love letters that Henry wrote Anne in the years 1527–28 support such a hypothesis. In one of these letters, he wrote:

> I desire also, if at any time I have offended you, that you will give me the same absolution that you ask, assuring you that henceforth my heart shall be devoted to you only. *I wish my body could also be*. God can do it if he pleases, to whom I pray once a day that it may be, and hope at length to be heard.[22]

It is God, not Anne, that Henry sees as the arbiter of his desires. What exactly Henry was praying to God that he should do we shall shortly consider. In another letter Henry encouraged Anne to trust that 'you and I would shortly have our desired end, more to my heart's ease and quietness of mind than anything in the world. My letter is written with the hand of him which desireth as much to be yours *as you do to have him*.'[23] The wording implies restraint by Henry, who excuses himself for not immediately meeting Anne's desires, which he wants as much as she does. Once again what the end that they desired was is not spelled out. Again Henry referred to an end that they sought when he begged her not to be distressed at his absence when she was ill: whoever fights against fortune is often the further from his end, insisted the king.[24] On another occasion Henry informed Anne of what joy it was to him to learn of her 'conformableness to reason' and 'of the suppressing of your inutile vain thoughts and fantasies with the bridle of reason'. In that way to them both would come 'the greatest quietness that may be in this world'.[25] Once again it is Henry who is emphasising reason and the suppression of fantasies; and it is Anne's 'conformableness to reason'—her acceptance of what the king wanted her to accept – that Henry is joyously acknowledging. And the tone of the king's delight at Anne's 'conformableness' hints that a little earlier she had been less conformable.

Before looking at what the king was hoping for, it is necessary first to emphasise that Henry's letters make it clear that their relationship was not confined to written expressions of love. In one letter, Henry wished himself specially an evening in his sweetheart's arms, 'whose pretty dukkys [breasts] he trusted shortly to kiss'.[26] In another, he wished that she was in his arms or he in hers, 'for I think it long since I kissed you'.[27] Such intimacy raises considerable difficulties for the conventional image of Anne refusing to sleep with the king until she was his queen. This view would have Anne locked in passionate embrace with the king, allowing Henry to kiss her breasts, and yet sufficiently determined and strong to prevent him from enjoying full sexual relations with her. That is perhaps a somewhat implausible image of Henry VIII: and it is puzzling that it has left no echoes in the love letters. And yet it seems very likely that they did stop short of regular sexual intercourse, since it was not until early 1533 that Anne became pregnant. Indeed, in December 1529, if Chapuys, the imperial ambassador, is to be believed, Anne complained to Henry that 'jay este desja long temps en attente' (she had already been waiting a long time) and that instead she could 'estre preveue de quelque bon party dont jeusse desja eu des enfants quest le principal soulas que lon puysse avore en ce monde' (she could have made a good marriage and already had children, which is the greatest comfort to be had in this world).[28]

So was it not Anne but Henry who held back? Why should the king have abstained? That can only be understood in the context of what he was seeking to achieve. From 1527 Henry would assert that his marriage to Catherine of Aragon had been invalid—against canon law—from the start. If that claim were accepted, then Henry would be free to marry as if for the first time, and he would be able to make his beloved Anne Boleyn not his mistress but rather his queen and, in due course, the mother of his legitimate children. But in the pursuit of the annulment of his first marriage, Henry had to be very careful. Already in 1528 Pope Clement suspected that Henry wanted an annulment only for private reasons and that his mistress was pregnant.[29] In June 1529, at the time when Cardinal Wolsey and Campeggio were trying the king's divorce suit, du Bellay, the French ambassador, keen for diplomatic reasons that Henry should repudiate Queen Catherine, Emperor Charles V's aunt, very much feared that for some time past the king had come very near Anne—'ce roy ait approche bien pres de Mademoiselle Anne'—and it was not therefore surprising that they wanted to hasten the divorce: 'car si le ventre croist, tout sera gaste' (if the belly grows, all will be spoilt). If Anne became pregnant, that, the French ambassador opined, would ruin Henry's cause.[30] In seeking an annulment the way he did, Henry was staking a claim to the high moral ground. A visibly pregnant Anne would destroy his case. It would also affect public opinion in England, which was suspicious of his motives. It is interesting that the lawyer and MP Edward Hall in his *Chronicle* noted how 'surely the most part of the lay people of England, which knew not the law of God, sore murmured at the matter, and much the more, because there was a gentle woman in the court, called Anne Boleyn'. Queen Catherine's ladies claimed that 'she so enticed the king, and brought him in such amours, that only for her sake and occasion, he would be divorced from his Queen'. For Hall, 'this was the foolish communication of people, contrary to the truth'. And he insisted that the king was not sleeping with Anne in these years, adding immediately after his mention of Anne the words 'whom the king much favoured in all honesty, and surely none otherwise, as all the world well knew after'. 'Honesty' in this context is a synonym for sexually chaste.[31] Henry, then, had good reason to hold back.

But if Henry did not sleep with Anne Boleyn in the years after 1527, that does not mean that he had never slept with her. A more plausible scenario is that Henry and Anne did indeed sleep together when their relationship began. But at some point Henry became convinced that his marriage to Catherine was invalid, embarked on what proved to be a long road to securing his divorce, and consequently held back from further sexual intercourse with Anne until all was resolved. For such a hypothesis there is some suggestive evidence. In autumn 1527 Henry sent one of his minor servants, William Knight, to the pope, without first consulting Cardinal Wolsey. What Knight was asked to obtain was not only an annulment of Henry's marriage with Catherine of Aragon, but also a further papal bull granting him permission to marry. Knight took with him a draft for this desired permissive bull. It has often been remarked that it would allow the king to marry a woman with whose sister he had already had intercourse, and that this was an allusion to the king's earlier relationship with Mary Boleyn, Anne's sister. But it has not been so clearly noticed that the draft bull also allowed the king to marry even one with whom he had himself had intercourse already.[32] However bold and reckless Henry's ambitions may have been, he had often, as here, also shown a curiously painstaking attention to detail. He was confident not only that the pope would grant him the annulment that he sought, but also that he would remove any obstacles in canon law to his planned future marriage. Because he believed that all this could be quickly sorted out, he was prepared, for the time being, to defer further sexual gratification. And it was precisely that evident abstinence which allowed Pole—and most modern historians—to surmise that it was Anne who was holding him back.

Henry's Campaign for the Divorce

What Henry asserted was that his marriage to Catherine had always been invalid: it should never have been permitted. Catherine had previously married Henry's brother, Arthur, in November 1501; Arthur had died in April 1502. That marriage had created, Henry claimed, an irremediable impediment to Henry's subsequent marriage to Catherine. That there was a potential problem was obvious, and for that reason a dispensation had straight away been sought from the pope to enable Henry to marry his brother's widow. Such permission had been duly forthcoming, in a bull issued by Pope Julius II on 26 December 1503 and received in November 1504. But the prospective marriage then fell foul of the tangles of Henry VII's diplomacy and it was not till after his death in 1509 that Henry VIII married Catherine. Nearly two decades later Henry now claimed that he should never have been allowed to do so.

The first public, dated evidence of Henry's objections is from May 1527. Wolsey, speaking as a cardinal and papal legate, announced that he had come to be troubled by the king's marriage and deployed a series of arguments, which we shall shortly consider, against the marriage. But after a brief hearing the case was adjourned, with leading theologians named to elucidate the matter. Perhaps Henry hoped that the changed international situation following the sack of Rome by Charles V's troops would ease his quest. That summer Wolsey schemed to summon cardinals to Avignon and elect him papal deputy during the captivity of the pope: that, he hoped in vain, would allow him to set in train procedures by which Henry would secure what he wanted.[33] At the same time, but unknown to Wolsey, Henry sent his secretary William Knight to the pope in order to secure a dispensation allowing him to marry Anne Boleyn, despite the impediments created by the fact that Anne's sister, Mary, had been his mistress.[34] These manoeuvres were unsuccessful: Knight returned with a papal bull, but it was conditional on Henry's first marriage being proved invalid.[35]

Next, in late 1527 and early 1528, by means of the king's Italian agent Gregory Casale, and his close servants Stephen Gardiner and Edward Foxe, who were sent to Rome in February 1528, Henry and Wolsey sought a decretal commission from the pope. Such a commission would

declare what the law was. It would also name judges who were allotted the simple task of judging whether the facts of the case were what
Henry claimed. If they were, these judges were empowered to deliver
their verdict. Crucially, the decretal commission empowered the named
judges to deliver a final verdict. From their pronouncement, no appeal
was possible.[36] A draft bull prepared for the pope to sign illustrates what
Henry and Wolsey wanted: it appointed Wolsey judge, stated that the
papal dispensation enabling Henry to marry had been granted on false
grounds, and empowered Wolsey to enquire into the matter and pronounce.[37] Clearly such a legal procedure would give Henry what he
wanted. Gardiner and Foxe worked hard on the pope. At first they
obtained various inadequate arrangements: inadequate because whatever verdict was given would still require ultimate papal approval.[38] In
June Gardiner finally succeeded in persuading Clement VII to issue a
secret decretal commission to Cardinals Wolsey and Campeggio to
examine the facts and decide the validity of the king's marriage without
any possibility of appeal.[39] Then Gardiner worked hard to persuade
Campeggio actually to set off for England.[40] By September, Campeggio
was on his way, and Henry must have become more hopeful of an early
resolution of the matter, the more so if Pope Clement also, as Henry
would claim in 1534, at the same time sent him a brief 'noted with his
own hand wherein he did also approve the justice of the kings cause'
and promised that he would never 'advoke the case out of England'.[41]
But the pope was changing his mind, and he instructed Campeggio—
despite the decretal commission—not to pronounce any definite verdict
and instead to prolong the matter as long as possible; indeed, he hoped
that Henry might be persuaded to give up his quest for a divorce.[42] On
his arrival in October,[43] Campeggio did exactly as the pope instructed,
having first tried but failed to persuade Catherine to retire to a nunnery,
which offered an alternative way of ending the marriage.[44] Within a few
weeks, Henry had realised that Campeggio was reluctant to follow the
procedure set out in the decretal commission. In November Wolsey was
instructing Casale in Rome to complain that the pope had granted
Campeggio a commission but then had told him not to use it: Campeggio had, Wolsey said, followed an entirely different course, namely
trying to persuade both Henry and Catherine not to divorce. Henry was
not at all pleased.[45]

And then Catherine wrecked the king's plans by producing further
documentation, the so-called Spanish brief, a papal brief that had permitted her marriage. Its instant effect was technically to invalidate all
the commissions that Clement VII had granted to Campeggio and
Wolsey and that Campeggio had brought with him.[46] (Its effects on the

substance of Henry's case we shall consider a little later.) Sir Francis Bryan and Peter Vannes were accordingly sent to Rome to obtain fresh commissions and to see whether this Spanish brief was a forgery.[47] But by April 1529 Pope Clement was quite settled in his unwillingness—or inability—to meet Henry's desires. He could not imagine, he disingenuously informed one of his advisers, how any hope had arisen that he might revoke Julius II's bulls.[48] He wrote to Henry that he would be glad to do what he desired but that he could not declare Julius's bull false without hearing both sides, given his position and responsibility to God. He had to act according to justice. In his own hand he added that he was very anxious to oblige Henry.[49] When he received this letter, dated 21 April, the king must have realised, if he had not already done so, that his efforts to secure an annulment from the pope had run into the sands, and that the matter would not be resolved by Wolsey and Campeggio in England.

In these early months of 1529 Henry received repeated reports from Rome that his cause was increasingly hopeless. Many of Henry's agents cast doubt upon the loyalty of Cardinal Campeggio. Campeggio's agreement was indispensable if Wolsey and he were jointly and definitively to pronounce on the king's marriage. Doubts about Campeggio's reliability in turn cast a shadow over Wolsey, not least since the broad plan of having the matter resolved by the two legates was one to which Wolsey was deeply committed. On 9 January Francis Bryan, whom the king had sent to Italy, reported his encounter with Governor Umberto de Gambara of Bologna. The latter

> swore many great oaths, that and if he were in my Lord legates place, he would have given judgment on your side long or this time; and also he said, he marvels why that my said Lords legates did not give judgment with Your Grace, for he swore to me that he knew well that they had commission of the Pope to judge your cause; and further he said, that whatsoever they did judge for Your Grace, that he was sure the Pope would affirm it.

This is just what Henry would have wanted the legates to do.[50] Bryan wrote directly to Henry expressing further doubts about Campeggio: 'and, Sir, it is here in every man's mouth, that Cardinal Campeggio is, heart body and soul, good Imperial, and that men reckon, for your purpose, there could not have been sent a worse.' The pope was and would remain 'good Imperial'.[51] In late March Stephen Gardiner wrote pessimistically to the king; at the same time Bryan wrote, 'totally of desperation', saying that the pope would do nothing for Henry.[52] It may have been in response to these letters that the king berated Campeggio, as Campeggio reported in early April: Henry, he wrote, seemingly sympathised with Lutheran-inspired attacks on church property in Germany and criticised wickedness at Rome.[53] Meanwhile Bryan once more wrote pessimistically to Henry. He and the royal agents in Rome, Gardiner, Peter Vannes and Gregory Casale, had done as much as they thought could be done; but the king would see clearly that the pope would do nothing for him. Ominously Bryan added, 'and who so ever hath made your grace believe that he would do for you in this cause, hath not, as I think, done your grace the best service.' Bryan said how sorry he was to give such news, 'but if I should not write this, I should not do my duty. I would to God my former letter might have been lies, but I feared ever this end.' It is not clear whether Bryan's target was Campeggio or Wolsey: it seems more likely that it was Campeggio. Probably before he received this letter Henry had written to Bryan defending Campeggio against earlier warnings.[54] In early May Bryan responded by telling Henry bluntly, 'and where as your grace writes unto us, that the Cardinal Campeggio says he is your servant, and that he will do for your grace in all things; sir, his fair words that he says to your grace is because he would have the Bishopric of D[urham]' (then vacant). Bryan assured Henry that Campeggio[55]

> hath written hither to the pope, that he . . . never promised nothing to your grace particularly, but in general words, and bids the Pope trust thereto, for he never did nor never will do, and bad the pope stick fast him self, for of him he said he should be sure. Sir, all that is told you there, that the pope will do for your grace in this cause, I insure you they tell you the gloss, and not the text.

At some point Bryan also told Henry how Francis I, king of France, had cast doubt upon Campeggio's loyalty. Francis had asked Bryan about the progress of Henry's divorce, and added, 'well, there be some that the King my brother doth trust in that matter that would it should never take effect'—intending Campeggio, it seems, a deduction that Francis had apparently made from his conversation with the legate when he had been on his way to England in autumn 1528. Our knowledge of Bryan's report comes not from any surviving letter from Bryan, but from the account that the duke of Suffolk gave of the 'secret charge' Henry VIII had given him in May 1529. By then Henry was becoming increasingly suspicious of Campeggio and sent Suffolk to pursue Bryan's report directly with Francis I. Francis confirmed what he had told Bryan.

What happened next shows that Henry VIII had begun to mistrust not just Campeggio but also Thomas Wolsey. Suffolk, after asking Francis about Campeggio, went on, astonishingly, to ask Francis's opinion about Wolsey's devotion to the king's cause. His response was opaque. When he had seen Wolsey, 'as far as I could perceive in him, he would the divorce should go forth and take effect, for he loved not the Queen'. Francis then offered to 'speak frankly'. His advice was that Henry 'shall have good regard, and not to put so much trust in no man, whereby he may be deceived, as nigh as he can'; and he should 'look substantially upon his matters him self', as he heard the king was doing. Francis went on, Suffolk added, to say that Wolsey

> had a marvellous intelligence with the Pope, and in Rome, and also with the Cardinal Campeggio. Wherefore, seeing that he hath such intelligence with them, which have not minded to advance your matter, he thinketh it shall be the more needy for your Grace to have the better regard to your said affair.

In effect Francis was reinforcing the suspicion that was already in Henry's mind and that had prompted him to send Suffolk to consult with the French king.[56]

Eventually the two legates held a trial at Blackfriars, beginning on 31 May 1529.[57] On 16 June Catherine, challenging the authority of the court, and the competence of Campeggio and Wolsey as judges, appealed to Rome.[58] Henry—disingenuously, indeed brazenly—declared that, given 'the great love that he had had for her and still had at that time', he desired more than anything else that the marriage should be declared valid.[59] Campeggio, curiously, despite Catherine's appeal, allowed the case to continue. Catherine's advocates made their orations. Bishop Fisher, Catherine's leading counsellor, declared that no power whether human or divine could dissolve this marriage—'hoc matrimonium regis et reginae nulla potestate humana vel divina potest dissolvi'—an opinion for which he would lay down his life—'pro qua sententia asseruit etiam se animam positurum'—and in support of which he produced a book.[60] Several witnesses testified on behalf of the king. But it had become clear to Henry that he would not succeed in this forum. What he and Wolsey now tried hard to avoid was an advocation of the case to Rome, since that would place everything in the hands of the pope and his cardinals, over whom Henry's influence was small. Campeggio's adjournment of the court at the end of July was itself no blow to Henry's interests (and was not unexpected).[61] What mattered

was the attitude of the pope. And there Henry's hopes of a straightforward granting of his divorce were fast disappearing.

Henry's Case for the Divorce

On what did Henry build his case for a divorce? The true reason may
well have been his passion for Anne Boleyn, but the public reasons were
grounded on canon law. From the start, Henry was heavily involved in
the elaboration of his own case. But from the start, too, opinions were
sought from churchmen and from scholars. Efforts were made to inform
and to persuade. There was a national and international public opinion
to which the king was in effect appealing. Indeed, he discussed the issues
himself with those whom he hoped to persuade. That he was the guiding
force does not, of course, mean that others did not contribute crucial
arguments and interpretations.

   Most importantly, a series of compilations of precedents and biblical
and patristic quotations was made, justifying Henry's position and
dealing with objections, as Virginia Murphy has shown. In this labour,
Henry was much involved. 'It is likely that Henry oversaw the preparation and approved the contents of these works, for signs of his influence and involvement are found in a number of treatises', Murphy
writes, noting that 'he actually wrote an early version of one tract
himself'.[62] As early as 1527 a book was prepared which the king called
'librum nostrum'.[63] A fragment in the Public Record Office[64] refers back
to an earlier 'iustum volumen', most probably, Murphy suggests, the
volume that was prepared for a group of bishops and scholars in
November 1527, and presented to the pope in March 1528.[65] The PRO
manuscript was the next version of the king's case, probably begun in
early 1528, and constantly in the making that year. Writing to Anne
Boleyn, Henry referred to 'my book' on which he had spent above four
hours that day.[66] There was much compilation and revision. All the
arguments showing the insufficiency of the king's marriage were then
collected into one volume, said to be 'by the king's labour and study
written'.[67] This became, in a revised form, the submission that Henry
made to the legatine court in 1529. A copy of that book—Murphy refers
to it as 'Henricus octavus'—has been found in Trinity College, Cambridge (MS B.15.19): it begins with an address from Henry to Wolsey
and Campeggio, and then argues Henry's case for the divorce.[68] An
enhanced version was printed in Latin as *Censurae academiarum* in
1530 (or 1531), and translated by Thomas Cranmer as the *Determination of the Universities* in 1531.[69]

Who was involved in the composition of these works? Henry clearly took a prominent part himself. From the start many churchmen and scholars were consulted on the issues. The king assembled a number of learned men—we should say experts—at Hampton Court in November 1527 to give their opinions; a book was later read at York Place in Cardinal Wolsey's chamber in the presence of bishops and learned men. And from an early point a small number of churchmen are found to be deeply involved: their names read as a roll-call of future bishops. Stephen Gardiner, the king's secretary, in whose hand part of the PRO manuscript of 1528 was written, was despatched to Rome in February of that year in order to present the king's book to the pope, and to press the pope to take the procedural measures necessary to resolve the matter. He was accompanied by Edward Foxe, a fellow of King's College, Cambridge, and Wolsey's secretary since 1527. Foxe returned by May and reported on their audiences with the pope.[70] John Stokesley (described by the French ambassador as dean of the chapel in September 1529)[71] was sent to France as an ambassador, with Anne Boleyn's brother, to declare his opinion on the king's 'great matter', and to consult the doctors of Paris in October, doing his best to obtain opinions favourable to the king.[72] Stokesley also sent detailed instructions to Richard Croke, Henry's agent in Italy, on the authors whose works he was to study in Rome.[73] Stokesley was then sent to northern Italy in spring 1530, securing the opinions of the theologians of the university of Bologna,[74] lobbying the senate in Venice,[75] arguing at Padua.[76] Thomas Cranmer was sent to Rome and Bologna in summer 1531.[77]

Others appear to have offered their comments more independently, notably Robert Wakefield in 1527: he seems to have studied the question from his own interest and then offered to share his findings with the king—though, according to Pace, he was reluctant to meddle without first securing the king's express licence and commandment.[78] A Hebrew scholar, a royal chaplain since 1523[79] and one of the priests serving the Bridgettine nunnery at Syon, Wakefield initially took the queen's side, but was persuaded to take the king's side first by Edward Foxe, and then by Henry himself, with whom he had an audience and who commissioned him to write a book in reply to John Fisher, bishop of Rochester, who stood by the queen.[80] Later Foxe out of jealousy told the king that it was John Stokesley, not Wakefield, who laboured on this book; but Stokesley admitted to the king that the book was Wakefield's.[81] It was directly to Henry that Wakefield wrote offering to defend the king's cause in all the universities in Christendom. And, as we shall see, Wakefield may have offered the king some helpfully loose translations from Hebrew.

Cardinal Wolsey was greatly involved in the detailed diplomacy of the divorce. He appears also to have collected books relating to the divorce, asking monasteries to send volumes in their libraries that might be useful to the king's cause. These books, many of them from St Albans—where Wolsey was abbot—found their way into the king's library after the cardinal's death. Many more books would be acquired from monastic libraries in 1530–31: for example, payments were recorded to a servant of Reading Abbey on 29 November 1530 for delivering books to Hampton Court, to a servant of Ramsey Abbey on 27 January 1531 for transporting books to the king, and to the abbot of Gloucester on 17 February 1531 for bringing books to Westminster.[82]

It is very hard to pinpoint influences on particular arguments, and we should be careful about attributing ideas to particular individuals here. For example, in 1535 Stokesley—excusing his reluctance to write up the sermon he had just delivered in support of the king's divorce—explained that much of what he had just said was in the king's book that Foxe, Nicholas de Burgo and he had made before he went abroad on embassy (in October 1529), and that Cranmer later translated with additions and changes, in order to prove the invalidity of the first marriage.[83] Clearly this refers to 'Henricus octavus', as Murphy says.[84] But should one suppose that Stokesley alone was the author of its arguments or the instigator of the policies it contained? That would need much more detailed proof. Some parts of the draft for 'Henricus octavus' in the PRO, section C, are in Gardiner's hand.[85] But that cannot itself prove that they represent Gardiner's intellectual contribution.

All in all, it makes most sense to see the king's case as a team effort, with the king as a very active captain. After all, the basic ideas were, as we shall shortly see, straightforward enough; what scholars doubtless contributed was the wealth of detailed illustrative material drawn from the Bible and the church fathers. It is interesting that Cardinal Campeggio formed the impression that Henry had so diligently studied the matter that he knew more than a great theologian and jurist.[86] In December 1528 the French ambassador du Bellay reported how the king had talked about the divorce: the king needed no lawyer, he understood the case so well.[87]

And Henry personally attempted to win men over. Thomas More's biographer has left vivid accounts of Henry's efforts to persuade More, outlining his case to him in September 1527 while walking in the gallery at Hampton Court. This was the first time that More heard it said that the king's marriage was fundamentally unlawful. Henry 'laid the Bible open before me and there showed me the words that moved his highness and diverse other erudite persons so to think'. Henry asked More's opinion, More told him (though More does not say what he said), and Henry 'commanded me to commune further' with Edward Foxe and 'to read a book with him that then was in the making for that matter'. More read it, and told Henry his opinion. Later, after Henry had appointed him lord chancellor, he again attempted to persuade More, asking him to consider his great matter, to discuss it with his advisors, naming Thomas Cranmer, Edward Lee, Edward Foxe and Dr Nicholas de Burgo.[88] Thanks to More's biographer, we know of these efforts. It is likely that there were many more, and probably more successful, persuasions of others in the king's service.

*   *   *

Henry used two distinct arguments in support of his case. The boldest was the claim that a marriage between a man and the widow of his deceased brother was against divine law. The words of Leviticus were cited: 'thou shalt not uncover the nakedness of thy brother's wife: it is thy brother's nakedness' (18:16); 'if a man shall take his brother's wife, it is an impurity: he hath uncovered his brother's nakedness: they shall be childless' (20:21). Such prohibitions were absolute: no pope could dispense from them. But there were many problems with this line of attack. It would be easy to reply, as Bishop Fisher did, that the Levitical prohibition applied only if both brothers were alive, not if the married brother died.[89] If sterility was indeed the punishment for incest, the tricky point here was that Catherine had not been barren, simply that she had not had a surviving male child. So the Levitical prohibition was rewritten: 'for who so marrieth his brother's wife doth a thing that is unlawful, he shall be without sons or heirs male.'[90] It is likely that Robert Wakefield, or possibly John Stokesley, discovered this reading,[91] substituting 'filiis' (sons) for 'liberis' (children), and then translating 'filiis' as 'heirs'; Cranmer's later translation would slant it further as 'male heirs'. In fact, the Hebrew term refers loosely to 'barrenness', and not to 'filiis', much less to 'male heirs', an anachronistic concept alien to Old Testament society.[92]

A further problem was that there were contrary instructions in Deuteronomy: 'when brethren dwell together, and one of them dieth without children, the wife of the deceased shall not marry to another; but his brother shall take her, and raise up seed for his brother' (25:6). If anything, these seemed more definite than the words of Leviticus. And

since—as Fisher countered, possibly following John Clerk—Deuteronomy clearly in some circumstances required marriage to a brother's
widow, the practice could not be absolutely against divine law, as the
king claimed.[93] Henry thus faced the challenge of reconciling Leviticus
and Deuteronomy. He wished to see Leviticus as an absolute and time-
less barrier, while dismissing Deuteronomy as merely local and super-
seded, a collection of secondary laws.[94] The best way seemed to be to
argue that the practice of levirate marriage apparently commanded by
Deuteronomy had been no more than a ceremonial law of the Jews. Not
only that, it was moreover one that they had abandoned since the fall
of Jerusalem. If Henry could indeed show that the Jews themselves had
abandoned the practice, that would be a further weapon in his
armoury.[95] Accordingly, English agents in Italy made contact with
Italian Jews, notably Elijah Menahem Halfan, rabbi and doctor in
Venice; Francesco Giorgi, a Venetian theologian and the leading Christian cabbalist; and Marco Raphael, a Venetian convert to Christianity.
Plans were afoot in late 1530 to bring Raphael to England; the imperialists tried hard to prevent it; but by January 1531 he was there, twice
seeing the king (though first suggesting bigamy, and then restricting levirate marriages to occasions when the raising up of seed for the dead
brother was an unimpeachable motive), and remaining for three years
(including accompanying Henry when he met Francis, king of France,
in autumn 1532). It turned out that it was the Ashkenazi Jews who no
longer practised levirate marriage but rather resorted to a ceremony
releasing surviving brothers from the duty of succeeding their dead
brother. For Sephardi Jews, however, levirate marriage remained very
much a living custom. Some Italian Jews and converts consequently
wrote against the king, including Rabbi Jacob Mantino of Modena. And
then the claim that the Jews no longer practised levirate marriage was
dramatically disproved in Rome: a Jew living there had been compelled
by Jewish law to marry the widow of his brother (though the event may
have been specially staged).[96]

   The interpretation of Leviticus and Deuteronomy gave rise to an international debate, especially in 1530 to 31 when European universities
were consulted. The role of university opinions was there from the start,
as Richard Wakefield's offer—as early as 1527—to defend the king's
cause in all the universities of Christendom shows.[97] The duke of
Norfolk would in October 1529 insist that the king had from the very
beginning submitted the matter to the consideration of ecclesiastics,
doctors in theology and other learned persons.[98] Hall says that in the
winter of 1528/29 Archbishop Warham sent for 'the famous doctors of

both the universities to Lambeth and there were every day disputations, and communings of this matter'.[99] In June 1529 Campeggio reported that they were consulting the theologians of the university of Paris.[100] It did not (despite what is so often said) need Thomas Cranmer to suggest the idea. But when it became clear in late 1529 that the matter would not be speedily resolved by the pope, it was the more necessary to secure university support for Henry's case and to deploy that endorsement in justification. In August 1529 du Bellay, the French ambassador, reported that Henry and Wolsey very much wanted him to go to France to get the opinions of learned men there on the divorce, not least their reactions to Catherine's defence.[101]

Henry did secure several opinions broadly in his favour, especially from French and some Italian universities: Angers (where the canon lawyers supported him), Bologna, Bourges, Ferrara, Orléans, Padua, Paris, Toulouse and Vicenza. But Alcala, Louvain, Marburg, Salamanca, Valladolid and the theologians of Angers were for Catherine. And Harpsfield could pointedly ask about the other universities of France and Italy: where were Florence and Pisa; where were the Spanish universities; what of Germany, Poland and Bohemia; what of Scotland?[102] Doubtless some academics were browbeaten into offering favourable verdicts. Reginald Pole noted that 'many times they be led by affections' and 'with how great difficulty the universities were brought to the king's party'.[103] What Henry wanted was, of course, support, not the fruits of the disinterested pursuit of scholarly truth. When, briefly in December 1529, it looked as if what the doctors of the university of Paris would say would fall short of his expectations, Henry was heard to say rather sharply that he did not care for the opinion of the Paris doctors, nor that of those of other universities, and that he knew how to act—in other words, that he would do what he needed to do even without their support.[104] But soon afterwards Henry was able to claim that the most distinguished men in that university had voted in his favour.[105]

And, all the same, Henry did secure a good deal of academic support. His case, though problematic, was not impossible. But there was one awkward feature. It was generally agreed that the nature of the first marriage was crucial. If Arthur had consummated his marriage with Catherine, then no pope could allow his brother to marry her after she had become a widow. For example, the university of Cambridge declared on 16 February 1530 that 'we affirm that it is forbidden to christians even now by divine and natural law to marry the wife of one's brother deceased without issue, the woman having been known to the first man through carnal copulation'.[106] It was this point that had convinced Richard Wakefield, who had begun by taking Catherine's part but changed sides when he learned that Arthur had consummated his marriage to her.[107] It was this that swayed the 'divines' at the time of the legatine trial: according to Edward Hall, they 'were all of opinion, that the marriage was against the law of God, if she were carnally known by the first brother'.[108] It was this that persuaded Cuthbert Tunstal, so he said. Initially, he had told Catherine that her matter was just, but that judgment, offered when Campeggio was in England, had referred only to the validity of the papal bull and brief. Further questions had then arisen and been debated in the leading universities of Christendom, especially Bologna, and their conclusion had been that, on the death of a brother who had consummated his marriage, no papal dispensation could allow the surviving brother to marry the deceased brother's widow 'because it was forbidden by the law of god'. The pope, Tunstal maintained, had never denied that principle; and had indeed, at Marseilles in 1527, even offered to find in the king's favour. That principle had also been the basis of the decretal commission that Campeggio had brought with him to England: if he found that Arthur had consummated his marriage to Catherine, then no pope could rightly allow Henry to marry her. It was such reasoning that had led Tunstal, he said, to alter his opinion.[109]

But if Arthur had not consummated his marriage, then—it was widely agreed—the matter *was* open to papal resolution. The theologians and canon lawyers of the university of Angers were divided, the canon lawyers favouring Henry, the theologians Catherine; but both explicitly stated that the Levitical prohibition applied *only* if the first marriage was consummated. The difficulty here was that Catherine throughout insisted, repeatedly and on oath, that her first marriage had not been consummated and that Henry had found her a virgin. In October 1528, in confession with Cardinal Campeggio, she declared that she had slept with Arthur no more than seven nights, and that he had left her intact and uncorrupted.[110] Catherine denied consummation publicly and embarrassingly at the legatine trial in June 1529. Privately, in October 1529, she wrote to the pope that she would accept whatever Henry said on oath about her virginity. That was a challenge to which Henry never rose. We know of it from Clement's reply, noting that 'the Queen herself affirms in her mandate, that she was not known by Arthur . . . and you yourself know better, . . . she is prepared to stand freely by your oath'.[111] It was also known to William Peto, provincial of the Observant Franciscans, who (according to Sir George Throckmorton, a Warwickshire gentleman and member of the reformation parliament) told Henry after preaching a sermon before him on Easter Day 1532 that Catherine had denied that there had been any carnal knowledge between Prince Arthur and her, and had received the sacrament to the contrary: she was so virtuous, Peto said, that she deserved credence.[112] According to Chapuys, the imperial ambassador, in December 1529 the queen told Henry that he himself knew perfectly well that the principal cause for the divorce did not exist 'cart yl lavoit trouve pucelle'—for he had found her a virgin—as he had owned, she claimed, on more than one occasion, an outburst that—if we believe Chapuys—prompted the king to leave downcast.[113] In July 1531 Chapuys reported how Henry had berated the queen for her obstinacy in taking an oath that Arthur had not consummated his marriage, and telling all the world; Henry defiantly asserted that he would produce good witnesses to show that the opposite was true.[114] In April 1533 Henry would—if Chapuys is to be believed—admit that he had often said that Catherine was a virgin when he married her; but he claimed it had been said in jest, adding that a man jesting and feasting says many things that are not true.[115]

Given Catherine's insistence that Henry found her a virgin, witnesses were called upon to testify that Arthur did consummate his marriage. George Talbot, fourth earl of Shrewsbury, said that he had taken the prince to his bedchamber, and supposed that he had consummated his marriage just as he himself had done, having been the same age, fifteen and a half, when he married. Other witnesses testified to stained bedsheets and to Arthur's boasts about his inflamed member and his declaration 'I have been this night in the midst of Spain', a hot country.[116] After Arthur died, Catherine thought she might be pregnant and accordingly Henry VII waited for almost half a year before creating his younger son prince of Wales.[117] Not all the witnesses called upon testified in the way Henry would have preferred, however: Nicholas West, bishop of Ely, declared how he doubted that the marriage had been consummated, since Catherine had often told him that she had not been carnally known by Arthur.[118] Yet it is interesting that Chapuys was at first by no means convinced by Catherine's denial, fearing it would not stand up in a court of law: that Arthur and Catherine's marriage had not been consummated was 'presque improbable' (almost improbable) he wrote in February 1531.[119] The balance of probability was against her since she slept several nights with Prince Arthur. And the queen's oath could not outweigh the testimony of witnesses.[120] That Catherine's father had joined with Henry VII in 1503 in seeking a papal dispensation that allowed for the possibility that the first marriage had been consummated also told against her.[121] But in April 1531 the archbishop of Toledo found a letter among earlier diplomatic correspondence in which Ferdinand, Catherine's father, affirmed Catherine's virginity on the death of her first husband, and explained that the dispensation was only being asked for in this form to satisfy the importunity of the English, not because it was necessary.[122] And by September Chapuys could claim that the king knew for certain that the queen was a virgin when she had come to his bed and that that could be proven.[123]

As the debates went on, Henry, led by Thomas Cranmer, came to argue that consummation was not the crux. Even the mere fact of betrothal and marriage created an impediment—of public honesty—that was itself divinely imposed and therefore not open to papal dispensation. That novelty of Cranmer's—to extend the Levitical prohibitions to unconsummated first marriages—greatly assisted Henry's arguments, and it was inserted into the king's book. Cranmer was again explicitly consulted over this point in late 1537. He was asked 'whether marriage contracted and solemnised in lawful age per verba de presenti (by the words of those present) and without carnal copulation be matrimony before god or not'—which precisely describes the status of Catherine and Arthur's marriage if it had not been consummated. 'This matrimony contracted per verba de presenti is perfect matrimony before god', Cranmer pronounced.[124] In September 1531 Edward Foxe returned from Paris where he had worked as hard as possible to persuade the university to determine that, even if Prince Arthur had not consummated his marriage to the queen, the pope could still not issue a dispensation allowing the second marriage, on the grounds that it was verbal consent, and not consummation, that made a marriage. The king had sent Foxe to secure such a determination, accepting that Catherine was indeed a virgin when he married her.[125]

While, then, much turned on whether Arthur had consummated his marriage, nonetheless Henry's case here essentially rested on the principle that no one—no pope—could permit him to marry his deceased brother's widow.

*   *   *

But from the start Henry had also tried to secure the annulment on much more technical grounds. If he could show that the dispensation granted by Julius II in December 1503 was in some ways flawed, then he could argue that the permission it had appeared to grant was void and his marriage had never been legal. So Henry and his advisers used a range of technical arguments against the particular dispensation granted by Julius. It did not give a sufficient cause: it referred only to the marriage as promoting peace between Spain and England, which was both historically inaccurate, since the two powers were already at peace, and frivolous, since marriages were not to be made for such reasons. It was out of date, since both Isabella of Castile and Henry VII, mentioned as seeking it, had died before the marriage took place. Moreover, it was wrong to say that Henry VIII had sought the dispensation, as the bull alleged, since he was not of age at the time. On coming of age in June 1505, Henry had protested against the dispensation and did not consent to it. The bull was unclear whether Arthur had consummated his marriage with Catherine: it said 'forsan' (perhaps) which was too vague. Moreover, it did not follow the usual form and style.[126]

Such objections were partly destroyed by the production by Catherine of a further brief in November 1528, which added 'and other reasons' to the causes of the dispensation and implied that the first marriage was consummated. That brief was dismissed as a forgery by Henry.

There was a further level of technical objection to the dispensation that has been brilliantly elaborated by Jack Scarisbrick. Julius II's bull dispensed from the impediment of affinity, created by the consummation of a union previously announced by betrothal and subsequently marked by marriage. It did not, however, explicitly dispense from the impediment of public honesty, the impediment created by a betrothal. Yet if Arthur had not consummated his marriage, then no impediment of affinity existed, only the impediment of public honesty. If the papal dispensation did not cover this, it was invalid. Wolsey pointed this out as early as June 1527: if Arthur had not known Catherine, as Catherine very stiffly and obstinately maintained, then while there was no affinity between them, nonetheless

> in that she was married in facie ecclesiae [according to ecclesiastical procedures], and contracted per verba de presenti [by the words of those present], there did arise impedimentum publicae honestatis [the impediment of public honesty], which is no less impedimentum ad dirimendum matrimonium [an impediment to the marriage] than affinity, whereof the bull maketh no express mention.[127]

In May 1528 Wolsey instructed Gardiner, then at Rome, to consult as to what would happen if Catherine—renouncing all benefit from Julius's dispensation—simply insisted that she was not known by Arthur: would Julius II's bull then be invalid because it did not mention de publica honestate, only cum affinitate cuius modi?[128] Scarisbrick originally claimed that this approach, which he saw as Wolsey's line, might well have worked, but that it was rejected by the king, who favoured relying on the principle laid down in the verses in Leviticus.[129] In fact, such a line of argument was repeatedly used, but along both with the other technical objections and with the more principled case against the marriage, as in the first hearing of the case by Wolsey in May 1527 or as in a summary, in Vannes's hand, of reasons which should persuade the pope to pronounce for the king.[130] According to Chapuys, the king himself once told Catherine that he was content that she defended herself on the grounds that she was not known by Arthur: she was not his wife for all that, he added, since the bull did not dispense *super impedimento publicae honestatis*.[131]

But the difficulty of such a tactic was that it was not necessarily a winning move. As Catherine's counsel argued at the legatine trial in 1529, 'if Henry is permitted [by the dispensation] to marry his brother's wife in spite of the fact that his brother may have known her by carnal copula, is he not permitted all the more to marry her if she had only been married and not so known?'[132] And if it failed, it would leave Henry the more exposed. It meant accepting that Catherine came to Henry a virgin, which, as we have seen, many authorities saw as making the marriage fall outside the Levitical prohibition. So too open and definite a commitment to this argument could weaken the king's position if he needed to press on along Levitical lines.

And the great weakness of all the technical arguments with which Henry bombarded the pope was that the obvious way of resolving any technical deficiency was not by declaring the marriage null and void but by issuing fresh and more perfect dispensations. As Fisher especially argued, 'the continuance of so long space, had made the marriage honest'.[133] In October 1529 Clement VII offered a further dispensation to satisfy Henry's conscience.[134] As Scarisbrick has conceded, the principle of *supplet ecclesia* (let the church provide) would have made good any defects in Julius II's bull.[135] Campeggio, in his first private discussion with Henry, said that if the king had any scruple, he could have a new dispensation.[136] That the papal dispensation had been negligently granted may have been true, as even Bishop Fisher conceded; but, as he pointed out, that did not matter if it were done in good faith.

*   *   *

Thus Henry's cases in canon law were not strong. One challenged papal authority as such and thus raised complex and controversial questions, while being dependent on the unprovable question of whether Arthur had indeed consummated his marriage to Catherine. The others were more technical and aimed at exploiting loopholes in Julius II's dispensations. The latter approach might, perhaps, have succeeded if the current pope, Clement VII, had been a free agent. Popes and their canon lawyers had long found ways of meeting the demands of secular rulers by creative interpretation of laws and conventions. But the pope's attitude was very much conditioned by Italian power politics and by his relationships with Charles V and Francis I. That was more complex than just a matter of his dependence on Charles, as is often said: a more convincing elaboration has been offered by Peter Gwyn.[137] What would have suited Henry was a state of enmity between the pope and emperor, but with the emperor not so threatening as to intimidate the pope completely, and a corresponding show of unity among the principal Italian city-states that might stiffen the pope's resolve. The flourishing of the League of Cognac in spring 1528 was Henry's opportunity, but it collapsed in the summer. Thus in June Clement, as we have seen, had been willing to grant a secret decretal commission by which two commissioners, Cardinals Campeggio and Wolsey, would ascertain the facts—whether Arthur had married Catherine and consummated his marriage—and then pronounce finally on them without appeal; but by the autumn he was much more reluctant, not least since the Venetians showed themselves unreliable allies for the papacy by refusing to relinquish Ravenna, which they had just recaptured after the city had spent nearly two decades under papal control.[138] Consequently Clement now instructed Cardinal Campeggio to destroy the earlier document and not to proceed to a judgment, but rather to try to persuade Henry to abandon the divorce. In June du Bellay, the French ambassador, presciently told Wolsey that by sending Campeggio, and then delaying him on his journey, the pope could wait to see what happened in Italy.[139] By December, if not by August, 1528, Clement was sure that it was better to deal with Charles than to expect much from the heterogeneous coalition against him.[140] Clement's subsequent reluctance to challenge Charles V led directly to the inconclusive legatine trial. On his behalf in December 1528 Giovanni Baptista Sanga, a much-trusted papal adviser, informed Campeggio of the pope's dilemma: Clement had every wish to please the king but was hindered by powerful reasons from setting in train procedures that would produce the result which the king sought. The pope believed that it would be impossible for him to do anything that would offend Charles V more than this, though he added that he would not be influenced by that consideration if the reasonableness of the king's desire were evident.[141] And that last comment is important. Henry's case—principled or technical—just was not sufficiently compelling for Clement, given contemporary power politics, to concede to the king what he wanted.

The Challenge to Papal Authority

Right from the beginning Henry's attitudes had raised questions about papal authority. To cite Leviticus and present it as a prohibition that no pope could lift was implicitly to challenge papal power. To seek support from university theologians and canon lawyers was also in a sense to qualify the plenitude of papal power. As Chapuys reported in February 1530, Henry was so firmly convinced of his case for a divorce that he could not be firmer; the leading authorities in Christendom agreed with him; moreover, he hoped to have his judgment confirmed by the majority of the universities in Christendom, 'questoint celles que devront juger de ce affere, non point le papee' (who were those who should judge in this matter, in no way the pope).[142] How much Henry's position challenged papal power from the start is neatly illustrated by Bishop Fisher's response when asked his opinion in June 1527. Fisher found the authorities that he consulted conflicting, but he believed the answer was nonetheless straightforward. Given the fullness of the authority granted by Jesus to St Peter, and thence to the popes, it would be for the pope, Fisher declared, to offer dispensations. And it was, Fisher added, the responsibility of the pope to clarify ambiguous passages of scripture, after hearing the opinions of the best divines. Henry's assertion that the words of Leviticus constituted a divine prohibition that nothing could override effectively denied that the pope possessed any such discretionary powers or that the pope was the arbiter when the scriptures were unclear.[143]

In support of this interpretation of Henry's attitudes is Virginia Murphy's conclusion based on a close study of the series of treatises produced on the king's behalf from 1527 that

> from the opening stages of the divorce, Henry favoured a more uncompromising position than has been supposed, one which, in the longer perspective, made the likelihood of coming to terms with the Pope short of a divorce all that much more remote, if it did not put it entirely out of the question.[144]

Indeed, Murphy has elsewhere written that Henry's 'uncompromising position' was 'one which inevitably set him on a course of confrontation with the papacy'.[145] What is important here is the recognition that Henry's stand was potentially radical from the start: the logic that would produce the break with Rome was already there in 1527. 'The king's books from this period ... make it clear that from the outset Henry endorsed the line of argument which always contained an implicit challenge to the pope's dispensing power.'[146] 'As early as 1527 the king had come to the conclusion that his marriage contravened a divine law from which the pope could not dispense.'[147] This was not, then, a reaction to the discovery of the Spanish brief in autumn 1528, as has been supposed;[148] nor was it a policy only adopted after the failure of the legatine trial in 1529, let alone only after the rise of Thomas Cromwell, whether Cromwell is seen as rising in 1530, as Geoffrey Elton came to claim, [149] or not till 1532, as Elton first claimed.[150] Murphy's argument is powerful, and it undermines suggestions that Henry did not know what to do until someone else, whether Cromwell or Edward Foxe, later told him,[151] and any interpretation that contrasts, as Elton did, 'the pointlessness of all these arguments about the Levitical law and so forth' with 'a new line moving powerfully towards a policy of ignoring Rome altogether and settling the whole affair in the realm, effectively by royal authority'.[152] That 'new line' was present from the very beginning, as Murphy's explorations make plain.

But when Murphy goes on to make a sharp difference between such a position, seen as adopted by Henry, and the more technical objections to the marriage, raised, she says, by Wolsey, she misleads. She suggests that the version of the king's book presented to the pope in March 1528 was more moderate than earlier versions of the king's case, and attributes that to Wolsey's participation in its preparation. 'The cardinal is generally believed to have preferred the more cautious approach centring on the dispensation.' The French ambassador remarked in 1528 that Wolsey would rather 'declare the dispensation ill-founded' than deny that the pope could dispense and thus 'subvert his power which is infinite'.[153] But Murphy has here misunderstood the document she cites. Du Bellay was reporting conversations he had had with Cardinal Campeggio, and in particular a long discussion in which Campeggio—not Wolsey—had made the point that to say that the pope could not have dispensed in this case was to subvert his power, which was infinite. Wolsey, grasping Campeggio's point, tried to exploit it: he tried to put the issue across to him so that Campeggio would feel compelled to recognise that the original dispensation had been ill-grounded, rather than denying it and then risk falling into the awkwardness of an open and principled challenge to papal authority. Wolsey was raising the possibility of a principled denial of papal power as a threat intended to persuade Campeggio to declare the dispensation technically flawed.[154] All that this reveals of Wolsey's own attitudes is his negotiating skill, in trying to extract what he wanted—the king's divorce—by whatever means seemed most likely to secure it. Of course, Wolsey would rather see the pope declare the dispensation invalid than get involved in a principled challenge to papal power, which would not necessarily, and certainly not immediately, provide the king with his divorce. But it was not because he did not grasp, or because he rejected, the king's Levitical arguments. It is important here to recognise how tactical Wolsey was being: he was not following his own preferences.[155] Murphy has misunderstood Peter Gwyn's argument that Wolsey was very likely responsible for the plan to secure a decretal commission from the pope. She reads it as supporting her view that Henry's Levitical arguments made Wolsey uneasy: Wolsey, she says, preferred to concentrate on the technical faults in the dispensation granted by Julius II. But what Gwyn suggests is not that Wolsey was embarrassed by any challenge implied in the Levitical arguments to papal authority, but rather that he thought that a technical approach offered the best chance of early success.[156] The weakness in Murphy's often penetrating analysis is that it is not sufficient to examine just the treatises prepared by and for the king: they have to be set in the general context of negotiations, diplomacy and trials. 'Significantly,' Murphy writes of one of the earliest royal propagandists, 'Wakefield does not base his case on any alleged insufficiency of the original dispensation.'[157] But it is not of significance that such theoretical writings, from the earliest in 1527 to the drafts of 1528 and early 1529, do not deal with the technical objections to the various papal bulls and briefs.[158] That was done in different ways, most particularly in the legal hearings, at which they were raised in great detail. And it would be wrong to see Henry as the theoretician—'Henry and his supporters continuing to advance exclusively the Levitical argument in 1528 and early 1529'[159]—and Wolsey as the practical politician. Henry was much involved, as correspondence shows, in the minutiae of negotiations over the technical details of the bulls and the legal hearings.

And Wolsey was quite prepared to threaten the papacy, to draw attention to the incalculable broader implications of the king's stand: he quickly grasped what the Levitical approach might lead to. Immediately in May 1527 he criticised Fisher's defence of papal powers of dispensation: on Fisher's arguments, he said, the pope could allow everything, something that Wolsey saw as self-evidently wrong.[160] In late August/early September 1527, while at Compiègne, he had long discussions with Giovanni Stafileo, sometime dean of the Rota (the supreme court at Rome), who, Wolsey reported, 'being by me ripely instructed of the facts', had changed his opinion and now 'expressly affirmeth that the pope's dispensation is clearly void and nought, as well for that, that the impediment of affinite, in primo gradu, is de jure divino; as also that the pope can not, nisi clave errante, dispense with the same', and had now written 'a great book right substantially and clerkly handled' to that effect, 'furnished plentiously with the decrees and authorities of the law'. He would be willing to come to England to defend his opinions. Wolsey was here persuading a senior papal official of the strength of Henry's claim that affinity was a divine impediment against which popes were powerless. This was the principled argument, based on Leviticus, that Henry was developing; not some technical illegality. And here Wolsey was using all his powers of persuasion to put it forward.[161] In February 1528, in instructions for Gardiner and Foxe, Wolsey defended the king against any misapprehension that he had 'set on foot this cause not from fear of his succession but out of a vain affection or undue love to a gentlewoman of not so excellent qualities': the king's desire, Wolsey declared, was grounded upon justice. Since this matrimony was contrary to God's law, the king's conscience was grievously offended. Once more Wolsey was endorsing the boldest claim—the king's marriage was contrary to God's law.[162] When Wolsey discussed the matter with Campeggio in October 1528, after the cardinal's arrival in England, Wolsey's objections, Campeggio stated, were always founded on the invalidity of the marriage—not, one might note, the technical invalidity of the dispensation.[163] Perhaps, who knows, Wolsey was less keen on the divorce than Henry: after all, it did not personally concern him. He may well have privately disapproved; he may have hoped that the king's passion for Anne would cool, making it unnecessary. Meanwhile it undoubtedly complicated his diplomatic activities. Yet Wolsey saw himself above all as the king's servant. In so delicate a matter he was most unlikely to have done anything other than to serve his master as best he could. It is striking how fervently he expressed his loyalty to the king when Henry seemed to suspect him of doubting his 'secret matter': 'there is nothing earthly that I covet so much, as the advancing thereof';[164] 'which to bring to pass is my continual study and ardent desire, ready to expone my body, life and blood for the achieving of the same'.[165] And while Wolsey indeed made the technical objections to the original bull, which did not dispense from the impediment of public honesty, he did so as a tactical and polemical response to Catherine's insistence that Arthur had not consummated their marriage, Wolsey's purpose being to show that even this line of argument would not help the queen.[166] It is very difficult to find any evidence to support the claim that Henry and Wolsey significantly differed over the divorce. Wolsey, as Gwyn has shown, worked tirelessly to secure the conditions he thought necessary to obtain the divorce: it is misleading to say that he 'persisted in misreading the situation to a quite astonishing degree'.[167] But Henry, briefly suspicious in spring 1527, came, by early 1529— unfairly—to doubt the commitment of his minister; and in any case he saw that attacking Wolsey might be an excellent means of putting pressure on the pope.

*　　*　　*

Henry's attitude from the start was that he was right and that his marriage should be annulled. He sought the public approval of the pope, not the pope's adjudication or arbitration. In all the tortuous diplomacy, the king's underlying assumption was that the pope should and would give him what he wanted. And, from a much earlier stage than has generally been recognised, Henry was threatening the pope that he would, if necessary, seek what he needed elsewhere.[168] Once the king had decided that he needed an annulment of his marriage, he and his agents persistently spoke of what might happen if he were denied this. What they said was essentially the same thing, and the paraphrases and quotations that follow repeat them again and again. But that very repetitiousness makes, and reinforces, the case that Henry was consistent and determined to get his way. These threats have not received the attention they deserve. They strongly suggested that it would be Wolsey who would pay the price of papal refusal to satisfy the king, and, beyond Wolsey's fate, they hinted at ever greater threats to papal authority within England.

　　Wolsey, writing to Casale in December 1527, instructed him to warn the pope that the nobility, and indeed the whole nation, wished for an heir, and to remind him that no one had till then shown himself as good a defender of the apostolic see against the Lutherans as Henry VIII.[169] It would never be in Wolsey's power to continue to serve the pope if the pope did not comply, and Wolsey's life would be shortened.[170] Writing directly to Clement, Wolsey made the threat quite explicit: if he desired Henry and England to remain devoted to him, then he had to send a decretal commission in the amplest and strongest form.[171] Wolsey insisted later that month that the king could not allow the case to be referred to a place to which his subjects could not have access, given the wars in Italy. Such objections were practical, not principled; but at the end of the letter Wolsey instructed Casale to remind the pope that, if he insisted on simply sending a legate to inquire about the facts while reserving sentence to himself, the king could not agree to such a procedure without the greatest prejudice to the jurisdiction of the church, and Wolsey went on to write vaguely and menacingly of grave dangers.[172] Similarly, in instructions prepared in January 1528 for Giovanni Stafileo, sent to Rome as joint ambassador of Henry VIII and Francis I, practical objections to the determination of the king's case anywhere but England were followed by a threat: the king wished Stafileo to show the pope that a refusal to grant his just request might lead to a diminution of the authority of the holy see.[173] That month, too, Wolsey ordered Casale to remind the pope of the danger of incurring the loss of Henry's friendship by refusing his request or by delaying his response to it.[174] In February 1528 Wolsey warned the pope that he feared that, if the pope did not rule in Henry's favour, then Henry would be driven by divine and human law to seek his rights from the whole of Christendom. Wolsey's own life was at stake.[175] Henry's agents, Stephen Gardiner and Edward Foxe, were then told to say that if the king could not obtain justice from the pope he would be compelled to seek it elsewhere and live outside the laws of the holy church. However reluctantly, he would be driven to this for the quiet of his conscience. The king was resolved to move forward, whether the pope acceded to his wishes or not.[176] Wolsey expressed his fears to Cardinal St Quatuor that, despairing of obtaining what he sought from the pope, the king would seek those remedies which divine and human law suggested elsewhere, so very likely diminishing the authority of the holy see.[177] Gardiner warned the pope of Henry's attitude, 'not doubting but that his Majesty would use domestica remedio apud suos' (sic) (a remedy within his realm among his own people) rather than allowing his case to be tried among those whose hearts were already prejudiced.[178] A little later Gardiner warned that refusal would provoke a 'marvellous opinion' against the pope, the papal courts and the authority of the papal see. According to their instructions, Gardiner, Foxe and Casale together warned the pope on the eve of Palm Sunday that 'the king's highness would do it without him'.[179] In May Wolsey urged Campeggio to begin his journey to England at once if he wished the authority of the church to be undiminished: it could not be delayed longer without irreparable harm.[180]

During the summer and early autumn there are no recorded threats —but it was precisely in this period that Henry hoped that the imminent arrival of Cardinal Campeggio would lead to a speedy resolution of the matter. On his arrival in England in October, Campeggio urged Wolsey to join him in persuading the king to give up the divorce.

But Campeggio had no more success, he lamented, than if he had spoken to a rock. Instead Wolsey reminded him that if the king's desires were not met, what would follow would be the rapid and total ruin of Wolsey himself, and of the church's influence in the kingdom: in short, the total ruin of the kingdom. Wolsey repeated many times to Campeggio that he should beware lest, just as the greater part of Germany had become estranged from the holy see and from the faith, the same should happen with England. Wolsey often impressed upon Campeggio that if the divorce was not granted, papal authority in England would be annihilated.[181] At the beginning of the next month Wolsey, lamenting that Campeggio would not entrust him with the decretal commission that he had brought with him, and that he was taking an entirely different direction, trying to dissuade the king from pursuing the divorce, wrote how the king's honour had been gravely affected. If Campeggio persisted, Wolsey saw 'ruin, infamy and subversion of the whole dignity and estimation of the See Apostolic'. Wolsey feared that the sparks of opposition to the pope which had so far been extinguished in England with such care and vigilance would then blaze forth. Casale should therefore request the pope to send suitable commissions.[182] In November 1528 two royal agents newly sent to Rome, Francis Bryan and Peter Vannes, were urged to threaten the pope with the withdrawal of English obedience and devotion to the holy see: their instructions were signed at the beginning and end by the king.[183] Wolsey and Campeggio wrote jointly to Clement emphasising the risks that the pope was running.[184]

Threats against the papacy continued in early 1529. Du Bellay reported in January how Gardiner had been instructed to tell the pope that if he did not order Campeggio to hurry the divorce, the king of England would throw off his allegiance.[185] Inigo de Mendoza, the imperial ambassador, noted on 4 February that the king was 'so hot upon it' that there was nothing he would not promise to gain his end.[186] In April 1529 Campeggio reported how Henry had questioned the justice of the church holding temporal wealth, and remarked how the Lutherans were critical of the sins of churchmen in Rome: the implication was surely menacing.[187] In April the imperial ambassador at Rome reported that the English ambassadors there were threatening to take up with Luther and his sect.[188] In his instructions to Gardiner, Bryan and Casale in April, Wolsey declared that if the king were refused the grace and lawful favour of the church, the pope would lose both England and France.[189] In April 1529 Gardiner, then at Rome, referred in a letter to the king to 'that which your Highness showed me in your gallery at Hampton Court'—

that is, before Gardiner had left for Rome, 'concerning the sollicitation of the princes of Almayn [Germany]'—which, besides 'all other means used to the Pope's holiness for attaining and achieving your highness's purpose and intent', he had shown to the pope, 'and such other matter as should and ought to fear the Pope's said holiness', adding reasons to make him ally with Henry and Francis, 'and so to take the more courage to accomplish your Highness's desires'.[190] Henry was evidently prepared to use overtures that the German princes made to him as early as 1528 as a diplomatic threat against the pope. He was clearly aware of the potential advantages of a German alliance right from the start of his campaign for a divorce.

But in the spring it was becoming abundantly clear that Cardinal Campeggio would not settle the king's matter in England, and in particular would not allow the legatine trial which opened in May to pronounce in the king's favour. Moreover, it was increasingly likely that the next stage would be the advocation—or transfer—of the case to Rome. That prospect was anathema to Henry. In May Wolsey instructed Gardiner, Bryan and Vannes to take special care to prevent the advocation of the cause.[191] In late June and July Henry's servants did all they could to make it plain to the pope what the consequences would be. On 22 June 1529 Wolsey wrote to Vannes and Casale that 'ye may constantly affirm unto his holiness that if he should at any person's pursuit grant the said advocation he should not only thereby lose the king and devotion of the Realm from him and the see apostolic but also utterly destroy me for ever'.[192] Of course, this could be taken as mere bluster: but it is worth pausing to note that the destruction of Wolsey and, ultimately, the break with Rome did indeed ensue after the advocation. On 23 June the king sent instructions to William Benet (whom he had just sent to the court of Rome), Casale and Vannes, urging them specially to take care that the pope did not advoke the case. They were not to forget, in their lobbying, to insist on what was presented as the prerogative and jurisdiction royal of the crown of England.[193] A few days later Wolsey warned Casale that the advocation of the case would cause his ruin: it would risk losing the king, and depriving Wolsey of his authority, reputation and, indeed, his very life.[194] On 25 June Stephen Gardiner, back in England, wrote to Vannes on similar lines:

This advocation of the cause is greatly pondered and considered here, not only with the King's Grace, but also with all other nobles of the realm: for in case the Pope, as God forbid, should advocate the said cause, not only thereby the King's Grace and all his nobles should

decline from the Pope and See Apostolique, but also the same should
redound to my Lord Cardinal's—our common master's—utter
undoing.[195]

On 9 July Benet and Casale, in Rome, reported to Wolsey how they had
shown the pope 'the immense and manifest scandal and irreparable ruin'
which the advocation would cause.[196] On the same day Benet, writing
alone, gave Wolsey a longer account of how he had implored Clement
'to believe these undoubtedly to follow'. If he advoked the case 'he
should not only offend the king's highness which hitherto hath been a
stay a help and a defence of the see apostolic but also by reason of this
injury without remedy shall alienate his majesty and realm with other
from the devotion and obedience of the see apostolic'. Moreover, if he
advoked the case, Benet feared 'by that act the church of England utterly
to be destroyed and likewise your [Wolsey's] person'. Benet concluded
his appeal to the pope by saying how Wolsey 'with weeping tears most
lamentably' instructed him to tell Clement all this.[197] Once more the
pope was being warned that the advocation would lead to the alienation of the king and his kingdom from Rome, and to the destruction
of the church of England and of Wolsey's person. And the picture of a
lachrymose Wolsey reinforces the claim that these were substantial, not
empty, threats, not least since they succinctly state what was in fact to
happen.

A few days later Benet, Casale and Vannes reported that they had left
nothing undone to warn the pope of the dangers that any advocation
would provoke.[198] Wolsey repeated his warnings when writing to the
three men on 27 July. The king was resigned to the advocation. But
rather than be kept in suspense waiting for it to happen, Henry had
thought it best 'to study and excogitate some other ways and means
here for remedy' of his case: 'better it shall be to begin betimes to the
experimenting and actual execution of the said other ways and means'.
As for any advocation, which would involve the citation of the king to
the court of Rome, under pain of interdiction and excommunication,
'the dignity and prerogative royal of the King's crown, whereunto all
the nobles and subjects of this Realm will adhere and stick to the death,
may not tolerate nor suffer that the same be obeyed'. If the king ever
came to the court of Rome, 'he would do the same with such a main
and army royal, as should be formidable to the Pope and all Italy'. To
summon the king to the court of Rome was 'no more tolerable than the
whole amission [loss] of his said estate and dignity royal, and that may
ye well assure the Pope'. If the pope could not satisfy the king, and
quickly, 'surely ye see not but it will be a mean to alienate this Realm

from the obedience of that See'.[199] It is important to note here the principled refusal to accept the validity of papal excommunications. Wolsey's warning that Henry might break with Rome and seek other means of gaining his divorce could hardly be more plainly expressed.[200] And that Wolsey might himself prove to be a victim of such alternative methods was confirmed by Catherine of Aragon who, according to Mendoza, had written that the king's disappointment and passion at not being able to carry out his purpose were such that the cardinal would inevitably be the victim of his rage.[201]

All this shows that Henry was losing confidence in the ability of Wolsey to secure his divorce, and that he was losing it well before the adjournment of the legatine trial at the end of July. Wolsey from an early stage saw himself as a likely victim of the king's anger at the pope's unwillingness or inability to grant Henry the divorce. Moreover, it is abundantly clear that long before the fall of Wolsey the possibility of a break with Rome and of a domestic divorce was being used as a threat against the pope.

It was Henry who sent Charles Brandon, duke of Suffolk, to make a public statement at the legatine court. According to Hall, when reports that Campeggio had declared that the court would adjourn at the end of July until October reached the king, Henry complained to the dukes of Norfolk and Suffolk that he 'should then have no end', and ordered them at the next session to require the legates to bring matters to a conclusion, saying he would accept any judgment they gave. Accordingly,

> the noble men desired them to make an end . . . but they answered that they could sit no more till October which answer sore displeased the noble men, *which the king had sent thither* [my italics] in so much that Charles Duke of Suffolk, seeing the delay, gave a great clap on the Table with his hand and said 'by the Mass, now I see that the old said saw is true, that there was never Legate nor Cardinal, that did good in England'.[202]

It is important to note that Suffolk was not speaking on his own account: Cavendish describes how, when Campeggio announced the adjournment, 'with that stepped forth the Duke of Suffolk from the king. And *by his commandment* [my italics] spoke these words with a straight and hault [high] countenance'.[203] Cavendish and Hall both clearly present Suffolk as acting on royal instructions, not independently.[204] By late July it was clear to the king that Campeggio would not agree to find for him, not least given the vigorous and public opposition of Catherine of Aragon. The adjournment of the court was to be expected—and indeed was foreseen by Wolsey, who treated it as a standard practice.[205] Henry could not have imagined that Campeggio would be intimidated by his presence, or by the declaration of Suffolk, into passing judgment for him. But what took place before the legates was a strikingly theatrical and polemical declaration of the king's purposes. It was a carefully stage-managed royal threat against papal authority in England.[206] Henry's anger at the cardinals was specific and tactical. Before long he was again urging the pope to make Jerome Ghinucci, bishop of Worcester and one of the king's agents in Rome, a cardinal, just as he had in December 1528, and he was still pressing that suit as late as November 1532.[207] And Campeggio, who was recalled by the pope and took his leave of Henry in September,[208] does not seem to have borne any grudges against the dukes: in June 1536 he counted Suffolk and Norfolk among his friends in England in whom he chiefly trusted.[209]

The fall of Wolsey in autumn 1529 must then be seen as an anti-papal act: Wolsey was after all the pope's legate. Chapuys reported speculation in September 1529 that one of the matters to be discussed in the imminent parliament would be that there should be no more legates in England.[210] What is especially significant is that, although a long list of miscellaneous misdemeanours allegedly committed by Wolsey was drawn up by Lord Darcy and other councillors—'every man of the king's council began to lay to him such offences, as they knew by him'[211]—and was seemingly endorsed in parliament, what Wolsey was in fact prosecuted for in King's Bench, to which he pleaded guilty, were offences against the fourteenth-century statute of *praemunire* (16 Richard II), specifically by securing bulls from Rome creating him legate and publishing them at Westminster.[212] This implied that 'all his work as legate, his preferments, his judgments, his building, were thereby damned'.[213] Wolsey's conviction for *praemunire* was a reassertion of the challenge to papal authority and of the claim of royal supremacy implicit in the original statute.

The humiliation of Cardinal Wolsey, papal legate, by the king was a pointed attack on the pope and on papal powers, however much Wolsey's original elevation to those dignities had been at the king's desire. And Henry regularly attacked the pope and asserted his own supremacy at this time. No sooner was his case revoked to Rome than he insisted that he was forbidden by law to appear there.[214] The act of pluralities of autumn 1529 forbade anyone to 'procure and obtain at the Court of Rome or else where, any licence or licences, union, toleration, dispensation to receive and take any more benefices with cure than is above limited', a precise restriction of papal powers in England.[215] In December 1529 Henry told Chapuys that if the pope did not accept the opinions of the universities which he was currently await-ing and annul his marriage accordingly, he would declare the pope an heretic and marry where he pleased.[216] Chapuys feared there would be no more obedience shown to the pope in England than in Germany.[217] Catherine of Aragon reported Henry's threat to disregard papal deci-sions and his intention to warn the archbishop of Canterbury that if the pope did not consent to the king's new marriage, papal and clerical authority in England would be at an end.[218] In July 1530 the duke of Norfolk, one of the king's closest counsellors, told Chapuys that there were enough people in England who could understand the matter and that the English bishops could settle this divorce just as well as they did thousands of others—Norfolk exaggerated—which were settled in England without recourse to Rome.[219]

There was more than just rhetoric in this anti-papalism. In July 1530 Henry assembled the nobility of the realm, as well as bishops and abbots, and invited them to sign a letter written in a remarkably fine italic script to Pope Clement pointing out the evils which arose from the delays over the king's divorce.[220] That was a striking and public warning to the pope. Clement evidently felt threatened by the letter, referring in his reply 'to their menace that unless the request is granted, they will be left to take care of themselves into their own hands, and seek the remedy elsewhere'.[221]

At some point in late summer 1530 Henry instructed his agents at Rome, Edward Carne, Benet and Ghinucci, the Italian bishop of Worces-ter, to assert the custom of England that no one should be compelled to attend a court outside the kingdom. But they held back from voicing such claims—which provoked the king to bolder assertions. Why should a pope thus treat a king who acknowledged no superior on earth? Why should Henry be compelled to have a case tried at Rome which con-cerned not only his own conscience but also the succession to the kingdom? The king who was supreme in his own kingdom could deny to all inferior to him the right to appeal elsewhere.[222] Benet replied on 27 October that they had now pressed the arguments that the pope could not with reason or justice hear the case at Rome because of the customs and privileges of the realm, and that the king would not suffer the violation of those prerogatives he was sworn to maintain. Pope Clement later replied that he would prove his own jurisdiction better than the king could prove his custom.[223] Scarisbrick saw this as 'a deci-sive change':

now . . . Henry not only challenged the pope's authority but threatened withdrawal from it; and, to do so, began to advance a new
authority of his own over and against the papal. This explicit assertion may have been an obvious conclusion to a previous, implicit
denial. It was none the less momentous . . . now he enunciated a new
theory of English monarchy. . . . The late summer of 1530 . . . was
probably the crucial moment in the story of Henry's jurisdictional
struggle with universal papalism.[224]

Graham Nicholson saw this as marking 'a new direction', 'a change of
approach'.[225]

But, as we have seen, such defiant rejection of the principle of exterior jurisdiction had characterised the king's approach ever since 1527,
above all the whole scheme of having the divorce settled by Wolsey and
Campeggio in England without any possibility of appeal to Rome, the
object of policy in 1528–29. The particular elaboration in summer 1530
was prompted by the likelihood that Catherine's appeal would be held
by the Rota in June 1530. Henry, for obvious reasons, wished to prevent
that. In September Chapuys reported that the king had begun to abuse
the pope and then more generally the Roman court. The king had
recently informed Clement of privileges granted by several earlier
popes—whose greater sanctity made their grants more efficacious than
those of modern popes—declaring that no cause begun in England could
be determined outside the realm. If the pope did not accede to his just
request he would know with whom he was dealing.[226] That month
Henry issued a proclamation. Fearing that various parliamentary
statutes for the reformation of clerical abuses might be hindered by
'ways and means' sought from the court of Rome, Henry commanded
that no one 'do pursue or attempt to purchase from the court of Rome
or elsewhere, nor use, put into execution, divulge, or publish, anything
. . . containing matter prejudicial to the high authority, jurisdiction, and
prerogative royal of this his said realm'.[227] Chapuys saw this edict as
intended to spite and in some measure to intimidate the pope.[228] A little
later Chapuys recorded the opinion of the papal nuncio that it had been
published to prevent him from taking any measures on behalf of the
queen.[229] An alternative interpretation of this proclamation may be
gleaned from the letters of the Milanese and Venetian ambassadors.
They suggested that three bishops—John Fisher of Rochester, John
Clerk of Bath and Wells, and Nicholas West of Ely—had appealed to
Rome against the anticlerical legislation of 1529, particularly the act
concerning pluralities. In reply Henry had issued this proclamation and

arrested these bishops, possibly on account of their appeal, possibly because they were supporters of the queen, charging them with *praemunire* offences.[230] Whether Henry acted to prevent some bishops from appealing to the pope to halt royal measures against the church or to deny the validity of Catherine of Aragon's legal actions against him at Rome, the fundamentally anti-papal character of Henry's proclamation is abundantly clear. Elton is misleading in his claim that it was 'well in line with the fourteenth-century legislation and nothing novel'; 'the proclamation was expressly intended only for the protection of the recent reform legislation against papal interference, but since it tilted at a shadow there is little significance in the action'.[231] On similar lines, a draft bill from early 1531 would, if enacted, have made it treason to publish within the realm any writing from foreign parts to the king's dishonour or that was 'to the damage or diminishing of his crown and majesty or jurisdiction royal'.[232]

In September Henry wrote to Pope Clement blaming not him but his ignorant and fearful counsellors for making him act so inconstantly and deceitfully. He reasserted his claim, supported by the advice, he insisted, of every learned man, that the pope had no right to dispense from what God had clearly forbidden. If Henry were to obey the pope, he would offend God. But Henry insisted, despite the plainness of his language, that he had no intention of impugning the pope's authority—unless, he went on, he were compelled to.[233] Twice in October Chapuys reported anti-papal complaints by Henry's counsellors. The duke of Suffolk and the earl of Wiltshire, respectively Henry's brother-in-law and Anne Boleyn's father, began to tell him that they cared not for popes in this kingdom, not even if St Peter should come to life again, because the king was emperor and pope absolutely in his kingdom. Pope Clement, they said, was doing all he possibly could to lose the affection of a kingdom which had done so much for him.[234] A little later Wiltshire had begun slandering the pope and cardinals so much that, horrified by his words, Chapuys had left immediately.[235] In mid-October, after greatly reproving the pope for his conduct in this affair, Henry went on to warn the papal nuncio that if Clement would not in future show him more consideration than he did at present, he would take up his pen and let the world know that the pope possessed no greater authority than that held by Moses, which was only grounded on the declaration and interpretation of scripture, everything beyond that being mere usurpation and tyranny. Should he be driven to take that step, the damage would be irreparable.[236] In mid-November he told the papal nuncio that the flooding of the river Tiber (according to Hall, almost twelve thousand drowned in and around Rome) showed God's displeasure with the pope.[237] At the end of November Wolsey was arrested, which was at least in part an anti-papal act: but for his death on the journey to London, he would very likely have faced a show trial. In December Henry wrote to Clement in a threatening tone. Appeals to Rome in the king's cause should not be accepted by the pope but rather referred back to England. The pope should not think that the king or the nobility would allow the settled laws of the kingdom to be set aside. The king would not brook denial.[238] Archbishop Warham appealed to a new council of the church, and issued a protestation, as legate of England, that the cause of the king's divorce belonged to him by the privilege of the kingdom, and should neither have been committed to the two legates, Wolsey and Campeggio, nor revoked to Rome.[239] It is little wonder that Chapuys should report that the king did not give a straw for the pope's authority and interpret the 'strange' reception given to the auditor of the Rota as a sign that offensive measures were about to be taken against the pope.[240]

Throughout 1530, then, Henry repeatedly attacked papal powers. Again and again he asserted that his great matter could be settled only in England, not at Rome. Again and again he denied the validity of papal jurisdiction over him. Again and again he, and his closest counsellors, made threats against the pope that were less and less veiled. Again and again he took specific measures that restricted papal power. His agents travelled through France and Italy in search of academic support for his divorce.

From the very start, in 1527, Henry had raised the possibility that he might achieve his aims unilaterally, without papal involvement or blessing: Pope Clement was repeatedly threatened, as we have seen, that the king was prepared to act alone. The advocation of the case to Rome in summer 1529 greatly reduced the chances that Henry would obtain what he sought from the pope. And consequently there are increasing indications from then on that Henry was exploring means of securing his divorce in other ways.

There are several reports by ambassadors, not least reporting Catherine of Aragon's fears, that Henry was thinking of using parliament to settle the matter and to deal with the church.[241] A parliament met in autumn 1529 and was repeatedly prorogued in 1530.[242] The very fact of prorogation suggests that parliament was being kept in readiness for a definite purpose. Our sources are, however, tantalisingly vague on precisely how parliament might be used by the king to secure his aims. In September 1530, for example, Chapuys reported how Henry told him that if the pope refused his requests, he would wait only for the reply of his agent at Rome and would according to that 'fere la determination en ses estatz'—secure a verdict in his parliament—which would soon be assembled, in part for this business.[243] Most historians, notably Elton, have interpreted such vagueness as evidence that Henry was at a loss as to what to do. But that might be an unwise inference. In October 1530, seeing that the pope would not accede to his wishes, Henry, Chapuys informs us, called together the clergy and lawyers of the country to ask them whether in view of the privileges of the kingdom, parliament could enact that the divorce could be settled by the archbishop of Canterbury, even if the pope prohibited it. Clergy and lawyers studied and discussed the proposal and answered that it could not be done (Chapuys does not say on what grounds). Henry was very angry and prorogued parliament until February in the hope of winning over lawyers and members of parliament.[244] There are many reports in the following months of an imminent parliament at which action would be taken.[245]

That Henry was thinking of using parliament to empower the archbishops to pronounce on his marriage is further suggested by a draft bill. It declared that 'diverse & sundry notable & holy universities and also many grave sage virtuous & well disposed persons' had clearly resolved that a marriage between a man and his deceased brother's childless widow was against divine law and not open to papal dispensation. The king wanted a final decision on the matter 'according to the laws of Almighty God and the holy canons of the church and also agreeable to the liberties immunities jurisdictions & prerogatives of the Imperial estate of his crown'. Unfortunately, the pope was following his predecessors who desired nothing 'but to aspire to the most supreme honour & authorities of the world and to usurp upon the jurisdictions & prerogatives of all christian princes' for lucre and ambition, disregarding the king's 'good purpose and godly intent'. The pope had deliberately delayed resolving the matter. Moreover, the truth could not be so conveniently determined 'in outward parts' as it could 'by the prelates & clergy of this realm . . . men of an excellent learning study & knowledge of the laws of almighty God' who knew the 'ancient customs' of the realm. It was therefore enacted—with the assent of the king, the spiritual and temporal lords and the commons in parliament—that all the evidence concerning the marriage that had been gathered at the legatine trial should be delivered 'in to the hands of the Archbishops metropolitans of this realm or to any one of them'. 'The said metropolitans, or one of them', after calling on the assistance of such churchmen as they thought discreet and sage, should 'maturely & gravely' examine the depositions, and then declare 'with all possible speed' their answers to various key questions about the marriage. After that the metropolitans, or one of them, should summon 'to them or him' the bishops, or most of them, with 'full power & authority finally & summarily to determine' whether the marriage 'stood with the laws of almighty God & holy church and the good & honourable customs of the church of England or not'. Any decree so made should be 'constant & perpetual . . . without any let provocation appellation or any impediment what so ever'. And it was further enacted that 'if the pope's holiness will attempt to do any thing to the derogation of the execution of this act by any manner of process of personal citations or interdicts or excommunications or any other means', then any such process whatsoever 'shall not be obeyed allowed accepted admitted nor executed within this realm nor in any the kings dominions'. The king and his subjects should continue lawfully to 'have use & enjoy full ministration & execution of all the sacraments of the church and all other holy things belonging to christian people according to the laudable usage & customs of the realm'. Anyone attempting to derogate the execution of this act or the decisions of the archbishops would run the risk of the penalties imposed by the statute of provisions.[246]

It is unfortunately impossible to date this draft bill with any certainty. The reference to the two legates puts it at the earliest in autumn 1529 and it had clearly been overtaken by events by late 1532/early 1533. The repeated mentions of the metropolitans, 'or one of them', may offer a clue. Archbishop Wolsey of York died in November 1530 and was not succeeded by Edward Lee until November 1531. Perhaps Henry hoped that Archbishop Warham would be prepared to preside alone over a church court in England that would grant him his divorce. Or perhaps, uncertain as to Warham's likely response, Henry hoped either to persuade Wolsey or, after Wolsey's death, to secure the appointment of a pliant new archbishop of York to pronounce Henry unmarried whatever Warham did. On 31 December 1530 Chapuys wrote how Henry 'a aussi de nouveau represente larchevesche dijorck a celluy dont ay dernieremant escrit a vostre majestie luy usant plusieurs propoz tant doulz que aspres mays yl ne le encoures peu convertyr' (also again offered the archbishopric of York to the man of whom I lately wrote to your majesty, using many words, both tender and tough, but he had not yet been able to persuade him). Was Henry personally searching for a tame archbishop of York to do his bidding and pronounce on the divorce? Was Reginald Pole, younger son of Margaret, countess of Salisbury, the man in question here?[247]

There was nothing half-hearted about this draft bill: it is quite clear that 'to enact this would have meant a breach with Rome'.[248] That answers Elton's claims that the king's repeated prorogations of parliament revealed 'disarray in his counsels' and that they 'certainly indicate that if there was a way in which parliament could help him Henry had not yet thought of it'.[249] Henry clearly had thought of a way. It is also significant that the remedy for Henry's troubles is suggested in *A Glass of the Truth*, a tract in defence of the king's claims, in the form of a dialogue between a lawyer and a divine. The lawyer thought 'that the way might be found well enough, if the whole head and body of the parliament would set their wits and good wills unto it'. The divine elaborated: 'methinketh the king's highness and his parliament should earnestly press the metropolitans of this realm (their unjust oath made to the pope notwithstanding) to set an end shortly in this'.[250]

Of course, no such bill was actually introduced into parliament. Did Henry and his counsellors hesitate because they feared it would not win sufficient support? The bill neatly illustrates the challenge that Henry faced in securing his divorce without papal blessing. He would have to find senior churchmen prepared to pronounce in his favour on the canon law of his marriage. But that would not be the end of the matter. The pope would not accept such a judgment and would seek to reverse it by excommunicating the king. A schismatic king would risk internal rebellion and external invasion. More immediately, he would encounter practical difficulties: for example, without papal sanction, no bishops could be appointed, and the pope might even inhibit priests generally from saying mass. The draft bill defiantly declares that, should the realm be placed under an interdict, everything should continue as before. If, however, such bold defiance were to succeed, Henry would need the support, or at least the acquiescence, of a broad section of the church.

Threats against the Church

How would Henry set about securing that support, or at least acquiescence? The church in England was very much a monarchical church, closely linked to the crown. Although the form of episcopal appointments was papal, in practice bishops were chosen by the king, often from among his close counsellors, and frequently they remained leading ministers despite their episcopal dignities and responsibilities. Thomas Wolsey is only the most striking example. Thus in the years in which he sought his divorce, Henry appointed to bishoprics, as vacancies occurred, several of those who had been intimately involved in the elaboration of his case in canon law (as Catherine of Aragon feared).[251]

John Stokesley was appointed bishop of London in July 1530 (on the transfer of Cuthbert Tunstal to the bishopric of Durham).[252] Stephen Gardiner was nominated as bishop of Winchester and Edward Lee was nominated as archbishop of York in September 1531.[253] Most remarkably of all, because he was promoted from relative scholarly obscurity directly to the leading place within the English church, Thomas Cranmer succeeded Warham as archbishop of Canterbury. The effect was to establish, within the church hierarchy, a nucleus of committed Henricians. But while such appointments were undoubtedly of crucial importance, they depended on the incidence of episcopal deaths: for Henry, considering his position in late 1529 and 1530, such a use of patronage would not have seemed a speedy remedy. Moreover, new appointments would not in themselves have dealt with the potential problem of those existing bishops and senior churchmen who, if he defied the pope and was excommunicated, would not support the king.

Despite its 'monarchical' character, the church in principle enjoyed extensive privileges and was part of a larger international body. Did Henry see that as an obstacle to the realisation of his plans? We lack any detailed statement from the king about what he was really thinking, planning and fearing in these years. Consequently, we have to infer what was in his mind from what he did, or did not do. Elton, in his earlier writings, saw Henry as floundering, full of bluster and boasts, but lacking any clear sense of direction in the years to 1532. Elton's first graduate student, Scarisbrick, presented evidence showing rather that these years saw a concerted onslaught on the privileges and independence of the church, though he at first rather played down the significance of what he had found.

Those pressures against the church, especially leading churchmen, in the years after the fall of Wolsey deserve closer scrutiny. Of course, no sharp distinction can be made between measures against the church and measures against the pope: there was an obvious connection. But it is worth looking carefully at the intimidation of leading churchmen, intimidation intended to put them in a position from which opposition to the king would be impossible. Later, we shall return to these events and consider them from the perspective of those who were appalled and tried to oppose what was happening as best they could. But here we are concerned with the king's aims and methods.

Henry had brought Wolsey down in autumn 1529 for alleged offences against *praemunire*. Of course, these legal proceedings were, morally, a sham: what Wolsey had done had been done with the king's approval, while those other bishops and churchmen with whom Wolsey had made 'compositions' had had little option but to make administrative and financial arrangements with him. And that strongly suggests that the *praemunire* charges against Wolsey, and the subsequent *praemunire* manoeuvres against others, were not pursued for their own sakes—i.e. because serious offences had been committed and because the offenders had to be punished both to stop them reoffending and as an example to others tempted to follow them—they were rather a weapon in a larger, more political, struggle. The significant point was that Wolsey accepted his guilt on *praemunire*: and since he had had dealings with every bishop, all churchmen were theoretically now in jeopardy. The arrest and conviction of Wolsey was effectively a suspended attack on the church as a whole. Chapuys noted that whoever had treated or negotiated with Wolsey as papal legate would be subjected to the same penalty as him.[254]

In autumn 1530 that suspended threat became reality. Fifteen of the higher clergy were accused of offences against the *praemunire* statute: a move that served admirably at once to challenge the authority of both pope and church and to assert the supremacy of the king. The court of King's Bench was informed that the clerics named had made an agreement with Wolsey whereby he received a portion of their annual income from casualties (that is, miscellaneous and irregular revenues), so supporting that legatine authority which Wolsey had admitted as illegal in October 1529.[255] Only those named were specifically affected. But many more could have been charged if making compositions with Wolsey were to be seen as an offence. Not surprisingly, observers saw these *praemunire* manoeuvres as an attack on the church as a whole. Chapuys said that the clergy were being fined for acknowledging Wolsey's legation: all priests who tacitly or expressly recognised Wolsey's legatine powers were liable.[256] Edward Hall wrote that 'the whole clergy of England ever supported and maintained the power legatine of the Cardinal wherefore the king's council learned [the king's legal advisers] said plainly that they all were in the Premunire'. Later, according to Hall, Bishop Stokesley explained that 'by frailty and lack of wisdom we have misdemeaned our self toward the king . . . all we of the Clergy were in the Premunire', to which a London priest robustly retorted: 'we never offended in the Premunire, for we meddled never with the Cardinal's faculties.'[257] The first bill, introduced into parliament in the Lords and apparently lost in the Commons, pardoned the church for offences arising from the abetting of Wolsey's legatine authority.[258]

But the concerns of the church went beyond the specific charges concerning the clergy's relationship with Wolsey. In a draft petition the clergy of Canterbury asked the king to grant to all and singular the prelates and clergy of the province of Canterbury and to all the Registers and Scribes of whatsoever prelates which were ministers in the exercising of spiritual jurisdiction within the province of Canterbury his general and gracious pardon of all their trespasses of penal laws and statutes of this Realm.[259]

In a later petition the clergy asked for confirmation of their ancient privileges and a precise definition of *praemunire* offences and the illegal exercise of spiritual jurisdiction.[260] The statute finally passed pardoned churchmen

> which have exercised practised or executed in spiritual courts & other spiritual Jurisdictions within the said Province, have fallen & incurred with diverse dangers of his laws by things done perpetrated & committed contrary to the order of his laws, especially contrary to the forme of the statutes of Provisors Provisions & Premunire . . . [and] all other which within the said province of the Archbishopric of Canterbury at any time heretofore have administered exercised practised or executed in any jurisdictions within the said province as officers or ministers of the said courts; or have been ministers or executors to the exercise or administration of the same & all persons vicars curates chantry priests stipendiaries.[261]

At first sight it appears that the clergy were initially attacked for their association with Wolsey, yet were ultimately pardoned for the illegal exercise of spiritual jurisdiction. But there is less confusion and shifting of purpose here than has been supposed. The pardon did mention offences against *praemunire* and provisions. On the other hand, the original charges involved more than guilt by association with Wolsey. As John Guy has shown, the accusation, along with the clerics, of the layman Anthony Hussye, notary public, proctor of the court of arches and subdelegate in the court of admiralty, is highly significant:

> it has to be seen as an implied attack on the independent jurisdiction of church courts as enshrined in chapter one of Magna Carta. Even if only one lay proctor was accused, the whole Canterbury province, when it reassembled, was potentially committed to securing a pardon for its advocates, registrars, scribes and other officials—exactly what happened.[262]

It may be that Guy is also right to suggest that the precise form of the pardon was determined by the need 'to locate a charge which would ease the new bill safely through the commons' after the first had failed, because they had feared that they would be dangerously vulnerable to charges of complicity in Wolsey's legatine authority.[263] But Guy has failed fully to grasp the significance of what he has shown to be a much more consistent attack on churchmen and the church for exercising an allegedly illegal ecclesiastical jurisdiction contrary to the authority which the king claimed over the church. This is also an essential context for the proper understanding of the argument over the royal supremacy clauses put forward in February 1531.

Guy is mistaken in supposing that 'Henry VIII had no intention in January 1531 of using the subsidy prologue to announce a novel grant of royal supremacy by the clergy':[264] what Henry really wanted, Guy claims, was money, and it was only because he demanded too much too soon that the clergy were provoked into seeking clarification over *praemunire*, which in turn provoked the king to raise large constitutional issues. But that is fanciful.[265] Guy fails to explain why the king, if his principal purpose was financial, did not simply accept the grant and issue a pardon in the form first requested by the clergy.

It is much more likely that the king saw the *praemunire* manoeuvres, which had begun with the attack against Wolsey in autumn 1529, as intimately connected with his efforts to secure his divorce. Chapuys assessed matters in this light as soon as news of the *praemunire* charges against churchmen was known in summer 1530: the king threatened churchmen with prosecution and the loss of their goods and offices in order to make them agree to favour and take part in his marriage.[266] On 30 December 1530 Chapuys wrote that 'jay este aduerty de la grande instance que le roy faysoit envers les prelatz de ce royaume de se determiner de juger en sa faueur les menassant que autrement il les destruira'.[267] That directly links Henry's attack against leading churchmen to his desire to secure from them a favourable judgment on his divorce: he threatened the bishops that if they did not determine in his favour, he would destroy them.

From persuading and intimidating the bishops to accept that they had been guilty of *praemunire* offences for which he now pardoned them, Henry moved on to demanding a still more explicit recognition of his authority over the church. No sooner had the bishops acknowledged their collective guilt and petitioned the king for relief than he sent them a demand, on 7 February 1531, that the churchmen recognise him as their supreme head. Such a conviction underlies much of what Henry had been saying and doing in the years since he had first sought an annulment of his marriage. In that sense it was not at all novel. But what was unprecedented was for the king to ask the clergy explicitly to recognise *his* authority over them.

The demand for an explicit acknowledgment by the church of the royal supremacy can also be linked back to the colourful exposition of notions of imperial power by the duke of Norfolk in January, that is, well before the leaders of the church had supposedly provoked the king by their tactlessness.[268] In January the duke of Norfolk sent for Chapuys to inform him of a statute prohibiting anyone from executing mandates from Rome to the detriment of the honour and authority of the king. It was then that Norfolk launched on his elaboration of imperial ideas that Chapuys found so comical but that should be borne in mind in any assessment of the quarrel over royal supremacy in the following month. Kings existed before popes; the king of England was absolute master in his own kingdom and acknowledged no superior; an Englishman, Brennus, had once reduced Rome to his obedience; the inscription on the tomb of Arthur read 'Patricius Arcturus Britannie Gallie Germaniae Dacie Imperator'—to which Chapuys countered that he was sorry that he was not also titled Emperor of Asia. A little later Norfolk told the papal nuncio that he was surprised to find that the pope had made, or was about to make, provisions and mandates highly detrimental to the supreme authority of the king and kingdom.[269] The papal nuncio was sufficiently concerned to visit Archbishop Warham on 13 January in order to exhort him to have due regard to the authority of the pope[270] and to go to the assembled bishops to urge them to uphold the honour, immunity and authority of the church.[271]

Henry did not wholly get his way. The churchmen meeting in convocation were divided and there was much unease. In the end the church agreed to recognise the king as their head *quantum per christi legem licet*—so far as the law of Christ allows. It is not clear whether that qualification was inserted by bishops as a destructive amendment, or whether it was a compromise proposal made by the king. In practice, Henry regarded the agreement as having given him what he wanted. Chapuys reported how under the threat of *praemunire* the English clergy had been induced and compelled to declare and accept the king as chief and principal head of the whole English church, which amounted, said Chapuys, almost to making him pope in England. The clergy had added a clause—that this was to be understood to be the case as far as it was compatible with divine law—but Chapuys thought that for the king himself the restriction was null and void.[272] A week later he quoted the wording of the recognition, commenting that it would affect the queen's interest and the pope's authority. The king was assuming sovereignty over the church in England; the papal nuncio had broached this 'nouvelle papalite'—new papacy—with the king, who denied it was anything of the sort. Clearly the nuncio had interpreted events differently. By going on to say that it was not intended against the authority of the pope provided that the pope paid due regard to him, and that otherwise he knew well what he would have to do, Henry was plainly using what had happened as a threat.[273] And he exploited his recognition by the church when putting pressure on Catherine of Aragon. In June 1531 Catherine was told by a deputation of councillors how displeasing the king found it to be summoned to appear personally at Rome—as her appeal to Rome would require—since that could lead to great disorder within his realm. Moreover, the king was entirely sovereign chief in his kingdom, in regard to both the temporality and the spirituality of his subjects, as had been lately recognised and approved by the parliament and clergy in England. Catherine was therefore asked for the quietness of the king's conscience to refer the matter to four bishops and four lords rather than abide by her appeal.[274] In other words, Catherine's appeal to Rome was invalid; and, implicitly, the king thought his courts could settle the matter in England.[275]

Vigorous efforts were made to set out the king's case. On the question of his marriage, by early 1531 Henry and his agents had secured a defensible series of university opinions in his favour. As we have seen, the universities offering them were largely in France and northern Italy, by no means representing the whole of Christendom. But there were enough for the purposes of propaganda. Thomas More, the lord chancellor, was asked to present the opinions to the House of Commons in March.[276] An enhanced version of the materials that had been compiled in support of the king's divorce was printed in Latin as *Censurae academiarum* in 1530 (or 1531) and—more significantly, considered as propaganda aimed at the English political nation—translated by Thomas Cranmer as the *Determination of the Universities* in 1531.[277]

Henry's claim that he could not be cited before the papal courts in Rome was vindicated by the *Collectanea satis copiosa*.[278] This compilation from the Bible, the fathers and various commentators, assembled in justification of the king's cause—with some forty-six brief marginal notes in Henry's hand—defended the king's right to have final authority in matters temporal and spiritual. Old Testament kings, Roman emperors and earlier English kings were invoked in support of Henry's claims. Some historians have wished to see the compilers of this document as the true makers of royal policy. But it is more convincing to see the *Collectanea* as an exercise in propaganda or, given that it was not itself printed, as a resource for those producing defences of the king's cause, rather than as an exercise in policy-making. The threats made against the pope in 1527 and 1528 show that Henry had never had any doubt as to where ultimate authority lay. What he needed in 1530 and 1531, however, were detailed precedents so that he and his ministers could make the best public case for his claims. And that—in, it must be said, somewhat tedious and repetitious detail—the *Collectanea* offered.

Henry had made some headway, by fair means and foul, in pressing the church to accept his theoretical supremacy—an acceptance that might protect him against any papal retaliation should he later face papal excommunication. He had made renewed efforts to vindicate his claims, both on his marriage and on the proper legal procedures by which the matter ought to be resolved. He had made potentially helpful episcopal appointments. If he had not yet got what he wanted, it was not for lack of trying or for lack of ideas. Elton and other historians have made a good deal of the delays—if the king knew what he wanted and how he could get it, why did it take so long?[279] But that underestimates the difficulty of the king's position. He knew, in 1527, that one way of resolving his problem was to act unilaterally and defy the pope. But he also recognised that such a course of action would carry great risks unless he could win the support of the church in England, and the politics of 1529–32 are in many ways the politics of securing the acquiescence of leading churchmen in the king's designs.

What he was pursuing was a desperately challenging aim, and it is not surprising that he was cautious. Elton argues that Henry compromised his position in these years by, on the one hand, claiming autonomy but, on the other, still trying to get the pope to grant his divorce, an implicit acknowledgment of papal authority. But the king was not engaged in the implementation of a theoretical position, nor was he in the business of making consistent philosophical statements about sovereignty: he wanted a divorce, and he wanted to persuade the pope to grant him his divorce, one way or another, because that would be the best resolution of his particular problem. But that does not mean that Henry failed to understand the possibility and implications of autonomy. That he understood them well emerges clearly from the assertions of royal authority and from the pressures and threats against the papacy and churchmen in these years.

1532

The events of the first months of 1532—the passage of the act of annates, the Supplication against the Ordinaries, the submission of the clergy—have long been regarded as crucial in any account of the break with Rome and they have provoked much controversy. But what all previous approaches lack is a clear understanding of the position of Henry VIII. Since he was very much in command of the making of policy—though by no means always and immediately able to get his way—it is only by looking at events through his eyes that any sense can be made of them.

At the beginning of 1532 Henry's aim was, as it had long been, to secure his divorce. He was keenest to do so by persuading the pope, if not to resolve the matter in his own favour, then at least to allow the case to be heard in neutral territory, away from Rome. But Henry was also anxious to stop the pope from taking action against him, to delay any final trial of the case in Rome itself. Once Catherine's appeal had been advoked to Rome, what Henry saw as his own great matter was likely to be determined in courts and through procedures largely outside his control. Therefore much effort was expended, with some success, to delay the hearings at Rome, and find some procedures by which the case could be brought back to England, or at least to some neutral ground, with judges approved by the king. Between March and September 1530 Henry had largely succeeded; and further postponements were secured that autumn. Pope Clement was unable and increasingly unwilling to oblige him over the divorce itself; but, perhaps mindful of the seriousness of the threats that the king was voicing against papal powers, he was very obliging in granting adjournments and delays. That Clement was anxious that Henry would act unilaterally appears from the decision in consistory in December 1530 inhibiting him from marrying until the case was settled in Rome and prohibiting the archbishop of Canterbury or any other judges from taking cognisance of the suit.[280] Charles V's agent at Rome reported rumours in May 1531 that the English affair was deliberately to be delayed, so as not to drive Henry to despair.[281] In April 1531 Henry ordered Benet to use all means available to get the trial deferred till Michaelmas at least—suggesting, as a ploy, that he might agree to a neutral place and to impartial judges. Benet was to 'abuse them as they have abused us, for they have been to us always like the willow tree, showing fair buds and leaves without any fruit'.[282] The more immediate question in 1531 and early 1532 was whether Sir Edward Carne should be admitted as Henry VIII's 'excusator' or representative in the papal courts even if—because the king flatly refused to recognise the jurisdiction of the court over him— Henry would not give him a mandate to speak in his name. Henry's agents cleverly exploited this nicely tricky legal issue.[283] In June 1531 the king obtained determinations from several universities, including Orléans and Paris, that he could not be compelled to appear in Rome.[284] And at the end of July it was reported that Pope Clement would observe the holidays.[285] Not till late November was it resolved to hear the excusator no further,[286] though Henry's agents pressed the pope again, successfully asking for more time to bring lawyers to Rome, though this was granted only till the end of the Christmas vacation.[287] Not surprisingly, Henry again urged Benet to do all he could to secure further delays.[288] After much wrangling it was concluded on 13 February 1532 that the excusator should not be admitted unless formally mandated by the king; yet after further debate it was agreed on 23 March that the matter should be resolved not in consistory but in special congregations before the pope.[289] Efforts to delay a papal decision against Henry in the divorce continued throughout these months and form a backcloth against which the more immediately striking matters of annates and the supplication must be seen. Henry's anxiety was that ultimately his arguments would be rejected and that he would be pronounced contumacious for his refusal to accept the authority of the court: then the pope might pass judgment against him. Henry wished to prevent that—or at the least to delay it as long as possible.

What Henry was seeking to achieve was to delay any final hearing of the divorce, since it seemed likely that that would go against him. In that context what he wished was to prevent the pope from taking any punitive measures against him, particularly excommunication. All these aims were well served by putting pressure on the pope—by diplomatic negotiations with the French, and by threats to withhold payment of annates to Rome.

But Henry was also keen to put himself in a position in which he could, if necessary, act independently of the pope if he continued to receive no joy from Rome. Here his difficulty was, as we have seen, to persuade the church in England to accept the royal supremacy, to agree to act in his favour even against a prohibition issued by the pope. That was not an easy task. Efforts to assert the royal supremacy over the church appear to have failed to secure assent in February and March 1532. It took a good deal of pressure to cajole the English church. These twofold objectives—pressure on the pope, pressure on the English church—and the various tactical weapons that we shall shortly consider—a threat to withhold annates, a bill to remove the legislative independence of the church, charges that churchmen had broken the laws of *praemunire* and *quo warranto*, the supplication against the ordinaries—were subordinate to the overall aim of securing the divorce, and, while largely distinct, they did in part overlap, since (for example) the consequences of withholding annates could affect the church in England, and the subordination of the clergy following the supplication against the ordinaries did affect the role of the papacy in England. This was no 'master plan' but rather a set of responses to the challenges posed by the king's desire for a divorce. It was an intrinsic and vital part of policy that options be kept open. At any moment a favourable resolution of the divorce might emerge. (Suppose Catherine of Aragon had died in early 1532 instead of four years later.) This was not hesitancy for lack of knowledge of what to do, nor bumbling confusion. And Henry VIII played a leading part in events, as careful examination of his actions in 1532 reveals.

Henry continued to complain regularly about papal actions.[290] At the beginning of 1532 he personally complained to the papal nuncio that the pope had criticised him in public in full consistory for treating Catherine badly.[291] A little later Henry insulted an auditor of the Rota then making his way to Scotland.[292] When in March a preacher was accused of heresy for, among other things, denying that the pope was head of the Christian church, Henry retorted that that claim should not be listed among the charges, since it was certain and true. And the king also warned the papal nuncio that he would sort out his cause, whatever the pope did, adding that he cared nothing for the pope's excommunications, invoking God's words: 'follow me and not others.' The duke of Norfolk later echoed these sentiments: if the pope issued ten thousand excommunications, he would not care a straw for them.[293]

In these weeks the impression is of a busy, active king. He saw the papal nuncio himself. About this time he also saw Chapuys and gave him a detailed account of his attitude to the Turks and to German affairs. In letters to Gardiner, and to Ghinucci, Benet and Casale in Rome, he gave further evidence of his interest in relations between the German princes and the emperor, and in the nature and extent of the Turkish threat to Hungary.[294] A little later it was the king himself who wanted Sir Thomas Eliot, returning from an embassy to the emperor, to remain in Brussels in order to apprehend the exiled heretic William Tyndale: Eliot had wanted to return home, Norfolk had spoken to the king on his behalf, but Henry had wanted him to stay.[295] Moreover, the king had been actively involved in preparations for a meeting of parliament which began on 15 January. Henry told Chapuys 'que toute son occupation estoit destudier ou entendre aux afferes de son parlement' (he was wholly occupied in dealing with parliamentary business).[296]

The most important measure that Henry put before parliament in early 1532 was a proposal to abolish the payment of annates to the pope. Annates were fees amounting to one or two years' income paid by bishops to Rome when provided to their sees. They averaged £4,500 p.a., but that scarcely made them the 'great and inestimable sums of money . . . daily conveyed out of this Realm' to its impoverishment.[297] Chapuys saw this measure as squarely the king's doing. 'Ce roy a faict mectre en auant au parlement de abbatre les annates' (this king has placed before parliament the abolition of annates).[298] In late 1529 Henry had told Chapuys that he was about to 'undertake the annates', so the idea of using the annates against the pope had been in his mind for some time.[299] That Henry was fully involved emerges even more obviously from his actions. In mid-March the king went in person three times to the parliament and, according to Chapuys, played his part so that the bill passed.[300] Chapuys repeatedly noted opposition: from all the bishops,[301] from two abbots, from the earl of Arundel,[302] and from a large minority of members of the House of Commons.[303] Much pressure was applied on the latter. They were told that the king would do nothing against the pope for a year. Finally, seeing that such arguments were fruitless, Henry 'fust aduise' that 'pour cognoystre ceulx que vouloint consentir au vray et bien du royaulme, lon les deust faire passer dune part et les contrarians de lautre, lors plusieurs pour crainte de lindignation du roy masserent de son couste, et pour ce moyen obtint quelques voix davantage' (he was advised that to know those who would agree to the truth and the good of the realm they should come on one side and those who did not agree on the other; so several out of fear of the king's anger gathered on his side, and by this means the king obtained a majority of a few votes). It must have been an extraordinary occasion. In order to secure the bill the king had had to resort to such doubtful practices. He had also had to make some concessions. Chapuys noted that the bill was agreed to but 'vng peu plus modestement quil navoit este propouse au commancement' (a little more moderately than it had originally been put forward).[304] Some support for this comes from contradictions in the text of the act. It boldly asserts the cessation of payments of annates 'hence forth utterly' but also provides for discussions between the king and the pope and for payment of 5 per cent of what had previously been due, a figure also cited by Chapuys. Perhaps it was because of these blatant contradictions that the king refused to give the papal nuncio a copy of the act.[305] Possibly the survival of a draft bill without concessions reinforces this.[306] So does the short draft in Cromwell's handwriting of one section of the bill. It reads as a first, but unsuccessful, attempt at a compromise between crown and critics. While recording the concession that the act would not come into effect at once, it is nonetheless more forcefully worded than the final act and less conciliatory towards the pope. The final version insists that king and parliament 'neither have nor do intend to use in this or any other cause, any manner of extremity or violence before gentle courteous and friendly ways and means first approved and attempted, and without a very great urgent cause and occasion given to the contrary'.[307] That there was some opposition, and in part effective opposition, to the bill of annates seems very likely, even though Chapuys is our only, if explicit, source and even though Edward Hall, MP, is silent on the matter.

What the king hoped to achieve was clear: to use annates as a bargaining tool with the pope. Henry told the papal nuncio that 'si sa sanctite voulait fere quelque chose pour luy, quil luy remedirast bien a tout et si feroit merueilles pour la reshistance des turcqs; et synon quil ne feroit riens pour sa sanctete' (if his holiness wanted to do something for him he would repay him and would do marvels for the defence against the Turks; if not, he would not do anything for his holiness).[308] Immediately after the passage of the act the king sent the duke of Norfolk to threaten the papal nuncio by pointing out how the people were angry at the payment of annates: the nuncio responded by alluding to the parliamentary manoeuvres which the king and his men had used.[309] Then the king spoke to the nuncio himself 'pour luy donner entendre et faire escripre que sa este grande benefice pour sa sanctete pourueu que luy soit ouctroye ce quil demande' (to let him know and write that this would be greatly to the pope's advantage provided the king received what he sought).[310] And the king separately sent two messengers to Rome 'pour mettre en craincte le pape a cause de ces annatez' (to put the pope in fear over the annates).[311] He instructed Ghinucci, Benet and Casale, his men at Rome, to tell the cardinals and the pope that this statute would be to their advantage if they showed themselves deserving of it.[312] As Pommeraye, the French ambassador, observed:

toutes ses choses viennent au desauantage grandement du St Siege Apostolique, mais il [Henry] a vse de grand astuce, car ayant consenti en cest affaire les Gentilshommes et le peuple, a faict que tout est remis a son vouloir, afin que le Pape entende que s'il ne faict riens pour luy, il a dequoi le chastier [all these things came greatly to the disadvantage of the holy see, but Henry had used great skill, for having secured the consent in this matter of the lords and commons, everything had been entrusted to the king's will, so that the pope understood that if he did nothing for the king, the king had that with which to beat him].[313]

For all the compromises and contradictions within it, the act of annates went a long way towards repudiating papal authority. It was a unilateral act passed with no attempt to resolve the alleged difficulties by negotiation beforehand. It implies a royal supremacy. It is interesting that Chapuys presented Henry's claims in that way: 'les annates que le pape prende des benefices vaccans lesquelles il vouloit luy estre appliquees comme au souerain des ecclesiastiques en son royaulme' (the king wanted the annates that the pope took from vacant benefices to be paid to him as the sovereign of churchmen in his realm).[314] The king was described as bound by 'the duty of a good Christian Prince for the conservation and preservation of the good estate and common wealth of this his Realme'.[315] More pointedly still, if, as a result of the cessation of the payment of annates, bishops did not receive the necessary bulls from the pope, then, it was asserted, they should be consecrated within the realm by the metropolitan archbishops (the archbishops were to be consecrated by two bishops named by the king).[316] If the pope resorted to excommunication or interdiction, then the king and his heirs were empowered to have all the sacraments and ceremonies of the church ministered and celebrated throughout the realm, disregarding any papal prohibitions. No excommunications were to be published by the clergy. These were very striking and explicit repudiations of papal authority.[317] It is worth pausing to note, however, that the draft bill for the archbishops to determine the divorce contained very similar provisions.

It may have been the resistance to the bill of annates that deterred any sustained effort to push another measure through parliament, namely a more direct attack on the legislative independence of the church. A draft bill survives that appears to set out just such a measure. It declared that the king was 'alone supreme imperial head and sovereign, of whom all laws compulsory be to be made ordained executed within this realm taking their vigour solely next god only of his highness and of none other'; the king was

the true minister and vicar of god according to his laws and precepts which authority and jurisdiction royal is so united and knit by the high providence of god to the imperial crown of this realm so that the same is not under the obedience or appellation of any worldly foreign prince.

And so that that royal authority should in no way be usurped, it provided that no ordinances could be made in any convocation that went against the laws and customs of the realm. Moreover, if any bishops made or implemented any laws 'except the same be confirmed by act of parliament', then they should incur the penalties set out in the statute of *praemunire*. Without royal assent, no law made in any future convocation could in any way trouble any of the king's subjects.[318] That would amount to a striking limitation of the powers of the church.

Unfortunately, this draft bill cannot be precisely dated, and any suggestions for its timing must be speculative. But a case can be made for seeing the ideas that it reflects as in the air in the early months of 1532. The thrust of its arguments was similar to what must have been the reasoning underlying the *quo warranto* indictments laid before the court of King's Bench by Christopher Hales, attorney-general, on 8 February against sixteen churchmen—including Warham, Bishop Skeffington of Bangor, Richard Pace, dean of St Paul's, seven heads of religious houses, the warden of All Souls College, Oxford, and the president of Queens' College, Cambridge—and six laymen for misusing ecclesiastical jurisdiction: such accusations questioned their (long-practised) rights to hold the view of frankpledge and assige of bread and ale, to return writs and appoint coroners, and so on.[319]

The draft bill also corresponds neatly with the arguments put forward in February by the duke of Norfolk when, after failing to persuade Archbishop Warham, he assembled a group of great men and claimed that the pope was treating the king badly, against the privileges of the kingdom; matrimonial cases were secular, and 'au Roy qu'est empereur en ce Royaulme appertenoit la jurisdiction, sans que le pape ait a sen mesler' (to the king who is emperor in this kingdom belongs jurisdiction, without the pope having to be involved with it).[320] It is implausible that Norfolk was here acting on his own initiative. Later that month he wrote to the king about his meeting with the Venetian ambassador,[321] and saw the papal nuncio.[322] He was surely playing the role of the king's spokesman on each of these occasions: he concluded a letter reporting his activities and a recent visit by Chapuys, 'if your highness would I should any further wade with him therein, it may please your grace to advertise me of your pleasure therein'.[323] On 24 February Archbishop Warham protested against any parliamentary statutes in derogation of the apostolic see or the power and prerogatives of the church and liberties of the province of Canterbury.[324] Obviously he was defending the pope and the church against the annates bill, but the terms that Warham used would also cover rather more, including the arguments put forward by Norfolk and the thrust of the draft bill. Interestingly, Chapuys wrote on 6 March that 'lon traicte en ce parlement de abroger lauctorite que les archeuesques ont sur les autres prelatz et lappliquer au roy leur souerain chef' (in this parliament measures were being proposed to abrogate the authority that the archbishops had over the other bishops and to transfer it to the king their sovereign head). According to Chapuys, Wiltshire, Anne Boleyn's father, was one of the principal supporters of such a proposal and had boldly declared that no pope or prelate had power to exercise jurisdiction or make any law or constitution in England.[325] Again it seems implausible that Wiltshire would have pushed this independently of the king. What was happening was made crystal clear by the French ambassador in two letters in late March. On 20 March he wrote how 'ce prince a grand enuie de chastier les Prestres de ce pays et ne leur laisser iouir de si grans preuilleges quils ont accoustume, dont en est cause le tort quon luy faict a Rome' (this prince has a great desire to punish the priests of this realm and not to allow them to enjoy such great privileges as they have been accustomed to have—and the cause of this is the harm done to the king at Rome).[326] On 23 March he reported the abolition of all, or almost all, of the annates, adding 'les gens d'eglise n'ont riens consenti remettant premier en sauoir l'opposition de leur chef nostre S. Pere, mais a cela l'on ne s'arrestera puis que les autres deux parts sont d'accord: il y a parmi plusieurs autres franchises et libertez qui leur oste' (the churchmen did not agree to anything, emphasising the opposition of their head, the pope; but that did not stop the measures, because the other two parts [i.e. the secular peers and the Commons] agreed to them: there are several other franchises and liberties which are under threat).[327] The French ambassador linked the annates, the royal supremacy, ecclesiastical liberties and privileges—and the king. All were part of the king's campaign. Yet while Henry secured the passage of the act of annates, no bill removing the liberties of the church or limiting the power of convocation to make law emerged from parliament at this point.

What did emerge was that collection of grievances against the church, especially the procedures of the church courts, known as the Supplication against the Ordinaries (churchmen exercising jurisdiction in ecclesiastical courts). Controversy has raged over its precise significance. Geoffrey Elton constructed a complex model on the basis of a highly technical interpretation of the sequence of and relationships between different drafts in which Thomas Cromwell allegedly took up grievances against the church which had been expressed in the House of Commons in 1529 and revived them to put pressure on the English church through parliament in 1532. 'The hand of Thomas Cromwell is as manifest in these proceedings as the hand of Henry VIII is absent.'[328] J.P. Cooper countered that the evidence that these grievances had been voiced earlier was unconvincing and argued instead that they were spontaneously raised by the Commons in 1532 rather than being the work of Cromwell.[329] John Guy has put forward an even more complex version of Elton's model, in which Cromwell made the Commons believe that the king wanted them to attack the church while at the same time using that anticlericalism, and the clericalist self-defence which it provoked, to encourage the king to take more radical measures against the church and against his supposed factional political rivals, notably Thomas More.[330]

Was it then a 'government' measure? Did the king sponsor it? Did Cromwell deploy it, with or without the king's knowledge? Or was it a spontaneous reflection of the concerns of the Commons which the king and/or Cromwell took up to further their own ends? The root concern of the Supplication was the 'unreasonable and extreme rigour indiscrete and uncharitable behaviour' of churchmen who investigated cases of heresy. It was alleged that they subjected those accused 'to such subtle interrogatories concerning the high mysteries of our faith as are able quickly to trap a simple unlearned or yet a well witted layman without learning' and so quickly bring them 'by such sinister introduction' to 'confusion'. In consequence, individuals inadvertently confessed to heresy, 'yet never committed nor thought in deed': but they were nonetheless punished. The Supplication asked that the people might be informed how they might avoid being charged with heresy.[331] Hall, who should have been well informed about attitudes in the Commons, said that the latter 'sore complained' of the cruelty of the ordinaries for calling men before them ex officio, accusing them of heresy and giving them the choice of abjuration or burning.[332] That broadly rings true. There *had* been more cases of heresy in recent years, including a handful of burnings. In turn, that makes it difficult to see the Supplication as government-sponsored, or the work of Cromwell, since it went against the thrust of current policy, which was severity against heretics. There would therefore have been politically neater ways to begin anticlerical measures than this, for example by concentrating much more on the inadequacies and costs of the church's legal procedures in less sensitive areas than that of heresy, in which critics ran the risk, as their self-defence showed, of being accused of sympathy with heretics.

Moreover, the Supplication is a remarkable *miscellany* of grievances: an official measure, or even a Cromwellian measure, would have been tighter, with fewer loose ends, concentrating on the principal aim of depriving the clergy of their independent law-making jurisdiction.[333] It is interesting that one of the bills passed in this session was the citations act: bishops were not to cite laymen out of their own diocese except in exceptional circumstances.[334] It is likely that this is the act referred to by churchmen in their later answer to the Supplication as 'passed by the assent of the lords temporal and the commons', a pointed reference to the refusal of the clergy to agree: 'the spiritual prelates of the clergy consented not to the said act'.[335] That fits well with Hall's emphasis on the Commons' concern with the legal procedures of the church. There was also a bill tightening up on benefit of clergy.[336] When Norfolk wrote to Benet, Henry's agent at Rome, on 28 February about 'the infinite clamours of the temporality here, in Parliament, against the misusing of the spiritual jurisdiction', that would most appropriately describe the kind of grievances that were to find expression in the Supplication, however much the emphasis was tactical, to increase the pressure on the pope by stressing that the king would protect the church from such clamours—provided that the pope assisted the king.[337]

That some of the corrections in some of the drafts of the Supplication (A, B, C1, C2, but not D or E) were in Cromwell's hand is less revealing of authorship and motivation than Elton has claimed. Little *necessarily* follows from such undatable evidence; and it would place unbearable weight upon it to claim (as Elton does) that some drafts *must* date from 1529. Edward Hall, MP and chronicler, makes no effort to link the demands of 1532 with the grievances of 1529. Moreover, if Cromwell had a master plan ready made in 1532, it is curious that he did not set about implementing it earlier. Why did he not prepare a complete text wholly in his own writing? That all the surviving evidence of Cromwell's involvement lies in corrections to texts written by others does rather suggest that he was reacting to matters which others had raised. The corrections are not obviously concessions (as are those made to the bill of annates) that a minister would make in order to secure the passage of a controversial governmental measure. Interestingly, Hall says that the Commons decided that their grievances should be put in writing and delivered to the king, which 'by great advice' was done.[338] Does that not adequately explain the part that Cromwell and the speaker of the Commons, Thomas Audley, played? Their corrections have been seen as watering down the violence of the language, insisting on the horrors of heresy, but making the wrongs of the procedures quite plain.[339] But to see this as Cromwell's machinations directed against More and intended to bounce the king lacks plausibility.[340] It suggests that Cromwell held a degree of control over the Commons on this issue that he evidently lacked over the annates or over taxation (on which there was effective reluctance in the Commons in 1532). If Cromwell could manipulate the Commons on this matter, then why was he less successful over other matters of controversy in this session?

Moreover, this line of reasoning has Cromwell encouraging the Commons to support the Supplication in the belief (which Cromwell fostered even though it was not true) that the king wanted it.[341] But were the Commons so pliantly royalist? The resistance to the bill of annates and difficulties over taxation hardly support that. And Hall's account stresses the spontaneity of the Commons' Supplication. Furthermore, Elton's and Guy's arguments do rather rest on the Supplication being taken up by Cromwell halfway through the session, which depends on their interpretation of Cromwell's letter to Gardiner noting about the bill of annates 'to what end or effect it will succeed surely I know not'.[342] They treat this not as a straightforward factual report but as evidence for a change in direction, from measures dealing with annates to the Supplication against the Ordinaries. Yet the claim that nothing had been done in parliament by the end of February—a crucial point in Elton's argument is that it was then that Cromwell came to the rescue—rests on a misreading of Chapuys's letter of 28 February. Chapuys wrote that 'yl nont riens icy conclut en leur parlement' ('nothing has been settled in their Parliament). He did not write that nothing had been raised or attempted. His words cannot be used to reject the impression that Hall leaves of the Commons raising the issue of the church courts as soon as business began in January.[343]

Cromwell was less prominent and important a figure in these months than Elton and Guy claim. He was administering Wolsey's college lands (appointed to those responsibilities by the king, who described him as his 'trusty and well beloved councillor');[344] sorting out disputes between landowners;[345] acting as recipient for apologies for absence from parliament;[346] corresponding with Stephen Vaughan, the government's agent in Bruges;[347] sorting out payments due to the king;[348] handling patronage;[349] dealing with a request for a licence to destroy rooks, choughs, crows and buzzards with handguns.[350] A list of instructions 'given by the king's highness unto his trusty councillor Thomas Cromwell to be declared on his behalf to his learned council' does not show that Cromwell was initiating or influencing policy.[351] Only that letter to Gardiner reporting that the bill of annates had that day been read in the Upper House but that Cromwell did not know 'to what end or effect it will succeed', and that Henry described Gardiner's absence as 'the lack of my right hand', suggests any closer involvement. Yet even that falls short of the making and presentation of policy, and Henry's regret at Gardiner's absence, 'for I am so much pestered with business and have no body to rid nor despatch the same', shows that Cromwell had not yet become the king's factotum.[352] By contrast, the duke of Norfolk regularly spoke to Chapuys, the imperial ambassador,[353] the French ambassador (explicitly on Henry's instructions),[354] the Venetian ambassador,[355] and the papal nuncio.[356] It was Norfolk who assembled a group of lords in February in the hope of persuading them to accept that the divorce should be dealt with in England. It was Norfolk who, with Wiltshire, pressed Archbishop Warham.[357] It was Norfolk who went to Dover in March to consider the need to make a harbour there,[358] and it was Norfolk and More who went to the Commons in April to make the case for taxation to pay for it and for fortifications on the Scottish border.[359] Norfolk emerges as the leading minister in these months—though it would be more appropriate to see both him and Cromwell as essentially royal servants, in different ways executing their master's will.

The royal purpose was more settled than those historians allow who stress the unwillingness and unpreparedness of the king to attack the church.[360] It is true that Hall suggests that Henry was less than enthusiastic about the Supplication, insisting on the need to consult the wronged party, and telling the speaker and deputation of MPs that 'the christian men are your spiritual brethren'.[361] But all that could, of course, like so many set-piece stories from Hall, have been no more than play-acting on Henry's part, intended partly to make tactical points against the Commons, who had by no means given him all he had sought, especially over annates and uses, and partly to emphasise to churchmen his role as their prospective protector against lay anticlericalism if they played his game. Here Henry posed as a potential champion of the church: but the weight of evidence is against such a characterisation of his attitudes in these months.

Pace Elton and Guy, Henry was fully prepared and willing to attack the church in various ways in these months. He had roundly criticised Francis I for being too easily led by bishops. In saying that, Henry was making clear that he would not tolerate any refusal of his bishops to go along with whatever means he chose to persuade the pope.[362] The Venetian ambassador reported on 21 March that the king had used foul language against Archbishop Warham.[363] Henry's anticlericalism is further documented by the French ambassador's reports, already cited, written immediately after the presentation of the Supplication—and for the French ambassador there was no doubt that Henry wanted to punish the churchmen.[364] Elton and Guy adduce Stephen Gardiner's evident surprise when Henry took a tough line at the end of April in support of their argument that Henry's 'pose . . . as an impartial adjudicator carried conviction even among his councillors'.[365] If Henry was clearly hostile to the church, then, Elton and Guy claim, Gardiner, as the king's secretary, would have toed the line, instead of exposing himself to a royal rebuke. Yet that does not necessarily follow. Henry's councillors did not always agree with him, as the example of Thomas More shows. Here a broad argument in support of factional manipulation of the king seems to want a royal minister to have obsequiously followed Henry's wishes. That Gardiner was simply wrongfooted is only one way in which the evidence may be read, and not the most plausible.[366] Gardiner may instead have thought that Henry would hold back from attacking the church; or perhaps he was, like some other churchmen, prepared to defy the king, suspicious that those behind the Supplication against the Ordinaries were dishonest in their proclaimed denunciation of heresy.[367] In a letter written in mid-May, Gardiner expressed regret that illness made it impossible for him to come in person and lamented that the king thought less well of him. But he reaffirmed his conviction that in writing the church's response to the Supplication, what he had declared was precisely true; and in support he cited Henry's book against Luther, the book written in defence of the king's case for his annulment and the verdict of the Council of Constance condemning Wyclif. 'If it be God's authority to us allotted . . . we cannot give it away', he roundly declared.[368] After all, none of the bishops, including, presumably, Gardiner himself, had supported the king over the bill of annates, and their opposition had compelled the king to offer some concessions. None of the bishops had supported the citations bill. Archbishop Warham was prepared to make a statement of defiance. Moreover, Henry would show no charity to the churchmen after they responded to the Supplication. Did he swiftly grasp the opportunities offered by the Commons' anti-clericalism? Did he need here to be persuaded by Cromwell or anyone else? Would it not have been fully within the evolving logic of policy for the emergence of the Supplication to lead to the shelving of plans for radical parliamentary action against clerical legislative independence in favour of more direct pressure on the church to submit 'voluntarily' to such a royal supremacy?

In that continuing struggle in the spring, Henry played a very large part. But he faced quite widespread opposition and there was nothing very certain about his ultimate success. Indeed, his hopes that parliament would grant him taxation and agree to tighter control of uses, the legal device by which landowners sought to avoid heavy financial burdens on their patrimony after their death, were dashed. But Henry did manage to subdue the church. On 12 April convocation began discussing the Supplication,[369] and on 27 April Henry received their firm and unyielding response. On 30 April he sent for the speaker of the Commons, Thomas Audley, and informed the Commons of his view of it: 'we think their answer will smally please you, for it seemeth to us very slender.'[370] Meanwhile, when the Commons had been asked for a grant of taxation to defend the Scottish borders, two members said that if the king were to take back his wife there would be no risk of invasion and consequently no need for taxation. Henry referred to this on 30 April, marvelling that 'one of the parliament house called Temse had spoken openly how the queen was no longer ever with the king, and moved the Commons to sue to the king to take the queen again into his company'—exactly what Pope Clement was, through his nuncio in England, calling on the king to do.[371] Henry responded firmly to Temse's request: 'which matter was not to be determined there for he said it touched his soul'. It was, he said, the doctors of the universities who had determined the marriage to be void and detestable before God. He denied it was any foolish or wanton appetite that caused him to abstain from Catherine's company,[372] and made 'vne meruelliesemant grand arengue' (a wonderfully great harangue) in justification of his divorce. What is intriguing here is that, according to Chapuys, Henry went on graciously to offer, not openly, but, Chapuys says, by letting it be understood, to protect the laity against the churchmen and 'de remedier a la rigueur de linquisition quilz ont yci quest a ce que lon me dit plus aspre que en espaigne' (to remedy the rigour of the inquisition which, according to what I have been told, is harsher here than in Spain). We are here getting glimpses of some complex bargaining: if the Commons would support the king over the divorce, Henry would take action to meet their concerns that the church was pursuing heretics in improper and threatening ways.[373] It is entirely credible that the king should subordinate his dislike of heresy to his more immediate need for support over the divorce.

Royal pressures on churchmen markedly increased in early May. On 10 May the king sent Edward Foxe with an ultimatum, containing certain articles 'quibus rex omnes subscribere voluit' (to which the king wanted them all to agree): no laws were to be agreed or put into execution without the king's assent, and all existing church law was to be reviewed by a commission of sixteen laymen and sixteen churchmen, all of whom were to be nominated by the king.[374] On 11 May the king elaborated to the speaker and a dozen of the Commons and eight members of the Lords:

> we thought that the clergy of our realm had been our subjects wholly, but now we have well perceived that they be but half our subjects, yea, and scarce our subjects: for all the prelates at their consecration make an oath to the Pope, clear contrary to the oath that they make us, so they seem to be his subjects, and not ours.[375]

Quite likely Henry's words were prompted by the bishops' recent declaration to the king, reported by the Venetian ambassador, that they could not assent to the divorce without the pope's consent, because, when created, they had sworn not to oppose the pope's wishes.[376]

It is possible that in parallel with royal pressures on churchmen, there were further debates in parliament on similar lines. Chapuys reported on 13 May that in parliament 'il se traicte . . . de reuocquer casser et anuller toutes les constitutions tant sinodales que autres quont este faictes par cy devant de tout la clergie de angleterre' (it is being proposed . . . to revoke, break and annul all the constitutions, synodal and others, which have been made up to now by the clergy of England). In future the clergy would not be able to meet without explicit royal authority, relegating them, Chapuys noted, below cobblers, who were able to meet and make their own statutes. The king, he said, also wished to restrict the powers of the clergy in cases of heresy. Chapuys's habitual imprecision is especially frustrating here. His location of this discussion in parliament may be evidence for further pressures on convocation in parallel with the direct demands made by the king's agents.[377] However that may be, it was not in parliament that the issue was resolved. Presumably there would not have been a majority for such a measure there then.[378] In another letter written on the same day, Chapuys noted that all the bishops were resisting these measures but that their opposition was making the the king very angry.[379] But if there were a simultaneous threat in parliament to the church's independence, that might have made at least some churchmen sense that resistance against the clear determination of the king would no longer avail, and that their best bet was to make a submission to the king, with the most satisfactory compromise they could get, before any parliamentary statute did it for them. Maybe that explains the compromise offered by the upper house of convocation on 13 May: convocation would refrain from legislating without the specific licence of the king, and it agreed to moderate or annul existing canons as the king saw fit. But it added a clause saving the immunities, liberties and provincial constitutions which stood with the laws of God and the realm and which the clergy implored Henry to confirm. The lower house restricted the offer to the king's lifetime only, and allowed the interim exercise of episcopal jurisdiction until existing canons had been reviewed: these changes were added.[380] Overall, the church was conceding a great deal; but the various qualifications meant that these concessions fell short in crucial respects. Henry was not yet satisfied.

A new version of royal demands claimed that 'convocation is, always hath been, and must be assembled only by your [the king's] high commandment or writ'.[381] The king also sent a writ proroguing convocation to November. The duke of Norfolk, the marquess of Exeter, the earl of Oxford, Lord Sandys, and the Boleyns *père et fils* then went to convocation—'an unprecedented congregation of laymen in a Canterbury synod'. Apparently they quickly left, and then returned again with some modified articles. Then Warham asked the prelates to agree to a submission, promising—now without any qualifications whatsoever—not to execute any new canons or provincial constitutions without the royal assent and authority.[382] And to this, convocation (though with several bishops absent, and others expressing reservations) formally agreed.[383]

The purpose of the whole business was made plain by Chapuys on 31 May. 'Tout cecy fait il pour faire tenir le pape a sa volente ou en deffault de ce que leglise anglicane ne le ose contredire a son mariage' (all this he did in order to hold the pope to his will, or failing that in order that the English church did not dare contradict him over his marriage).[384] Henry was attacking the church to persuade the pope to grant him his divorce and, failing that, to make sure that the English church would not dare defy him over his marriage. Now that the church had surrendered its independent legislative powers, now that, more generally, church leaders had been bullied into accepting royal demands, now that the church had seen its protestations against lay criticism cast aside, Henry would be in an even stronger position to get his way.

One further event was important: the death of Archbishop Warham in August 1532. We shall later return to consider how far Warham had assisted Henry's cause and how far, at times, he had seemed to be on the verge of open opposition. As we have just seen, he was personally involved in the pardon of the clergy in 1531 and the submission of the clergy in 1532. Henry can have had little reason to doubt his essential loyalty. And yet there were hints, at times, of disquiet at the course of events; and Henry evidently never asked Warham to pronounce on his marriage. His death opened the way to the appointment of an archbishop who would grant Henry the annulment he sought. Thomas Cranmer, Henry's chosen archbishop, had been involved in the making of the king's case and had, as we have seen, contributed much, arguing that the mere betrothal of Arthur and Catherine constituted an obstacle to Henry's marriage from which no pope could dispense.

And the tempo quickened in the summer of 1532. Henry created Anne Boleyn marquess of Pembroke on 1 September 1532.[385] That month Francis welcomed Henry and Anne at a meeting just inside the French king's territories south of Calais:[386] Francis's show of diplomatic support was invaluable for Henry. A year later, Anne gave birth to a daughter, Elizabeth, implying—if Henry is accepted as her father—that Henry and Anne, after years of restraint, slept together from no later than January 1533. It was in that month, on 25 January, that Henry and Anne were secretly married.[387] At Easter the preachers at court prayed for Anne as queen,[388] and shortly afterwards Henry ordered Catherine and her servants to stop using that title.[389] In April 1533 the upper house of convocation voted by 197 to 19 that the pope did not have the power to issue a dispensation allowing a man to marry his deceased brother's widow; and the canon lawyers, forty-four of whom were present, agreed, with five or six dissenting, that consummation had been sufficiently proved.[390] A parallel discussion took place in the northern convocation at York, with similar decisions.[391] Archbishop Cranmer held a special session of his court to pronounce on the king's first marriage, having first sought and obtained permission from the king to determine the matter.[392] Catherine was cited to appear before the court but refused to attend.[393] The trial began at Dunstable on 10 May. Since Catherine did not appear, she was declared contumacious.[394] Cranmer set a date for a final verdict: he was nervous that Catherine, after hearing rumours of the proceedings, might yet be stirred to come in person, which would delay things.[395] But on 23 May Cranmer was able to give sentence: the pope could not license such marriages.[396]

The chronology of these events, and in particular the fact that Anne's conception preceded the official hearing into the king's first marriage by three months, may suggest that the secret marriage took place once Anne knew she was pregnant or, perhaps even more plausibly, once Henry and Anne began full sexual relations. If, as legend has it, Anne had been determined to hold out until Henry made her his lawful wife, she evidently yielded just a few months before a formal marriage, presumably now confident, with Cranmer's appointment, that her position would very soon be certain. If, however, as has been argued above, it had been not Anne but Henry who had held back, it was Henry who was now sure, as he had not been as recently as a few months earlier, that he would get his way very soon. It had been a long haul, but at last Henry had succeeded. On Whit Sunday, 1 June 1533, Anne Boleyn was crowned queen of England.[397]

The Reformation Statutes

On this reading the famous statutes that followed—the act of appeals, the act of succession, the act of supremacy and more—were from our perspective an anti-climax. The royal supremacy they proclaimed and defended, the anti-papalism with which they were imbued, were by 1533–35 in no sense enunciating anything new. These statutes set out, elaborated and justified the ideas that from the very beginning of Henry's quest for a divorce had underpinned his action. That is not to say that in 1527 Henry formulated a master plan which he then implemented. Not least, what had happened by the beginning of 1535 was not what would have been Henry's preferred outcome in 1527. At that date he expected that the pope would readily, and relatively speedily, annul his first marriage and grant him the dispensation needed to wed Anne Boleyn. The longer the period in which that did not happen, the more likely it was, however, that the threats that Henry and his counsellors had voiced from the start would have lasting effects, whatever the eventual outcome of the king's divorce and, indeed, would ultimately be implemented. As early as 1527 Henry threatened to go it alone; from 1533 that is what he did. Throughout, he had sought advice and assistance. Wolsey worked indefatigably from 1527 to his fall in 1529, making unavailing efforts to obtain his master's desire. Stephen Gardiner, Edward Foxe, Richard Wakefield, John Stokesley, Nicholas de Burgo and Thomas Cranmer toiled on the rebarbative compilations of canon law that justified the king's stand on his marriage and his refusal to accept the advocation of the case to Rome. The duke of Norfolk frequently acted as the king's public spokesman. The hands of Thomas Cromwell and Thomas Audley are found on much draft legislation. But Henry's leading role is visible throughout.

The purpose of the reformation statutes was sixfold. The first was directly practical, to give Henry what he wanted and needed. The act of appeals—more exactly 'an act that the appeals in such cases as have been used to be pursued to the see of Rome shall not be from henceforth had nor used but within this realm'—enacted what Henry had claimed from the moment that Catherine's appeal had been advoked to

Rome in 1529, namely that no cases involving Englishmen were to be determined outside England. Almighty God had furnished the king 'with plenary whole and entire power pre-eminence authority prerogative and jurisdiction to render and yield justice and *final* determination [italics added]' to all within his realm in all matters occurring within it, 'without restraint or provocation to any foreign princes or potentates of the world'. But 'diverse and sundry inconveniences and dangers . . . have risen and sprung by reason of appeals sued out of this realm to the see of Rome', with 'causes of matrimony and divorces' included in the list. That had led to great costs and delays. In matters relating to 'the law divine' the English church was declared sufficient, without external meddling, to resolve any such doubts. And all such matters, 'already commenced' or occurring later, were to be 'finally and definitively adjudged and determined' within the king's jurisdiction 'and not else-where'. In future appeals that might have gone to Rome should be settled by the ecclesiastical courts within the realm. Once a matter was determined by the archbishop, that was to be definitive: in matters concerning the king appeal might be made to the upper house of convocation.[398]

The act of appeals dealt directly with the king's divorce. The act of succession dealt with the consequences of the king's divorce at his death, declaring the king's issue by Anne his lawful children and heirs.[399] Another act declared that Catherine of Aragon should be called Lady Catherine, Princess Dowager, and assigned lands for her maintenance.[400] Other statutes were practical measures dealing with the consequences and implications of the repudiation of papal authority. An act for the punishment of heresy included a paragraph stating that speaking against 'the bishop of Rome called the pope' was not to be regarded as heresy.[401] The second act of annates elaborated on the practical arrangements for the election and consecration of bishops now that bulls were no longer to be obtained from the pope.[402] Another act deprived the Italian bishops of Salisbury and Worcester, Campeggio and Jerome Ghinucci, of their sees: no longer would prominent Italian officials at the papal court in Rome be acceptable as absentee bishops of English dioceses.[403] An act 'for the exoneration from exactions paid to the see of Rome' set out all manner of revised arrangements for securing dispensations and licences.[404] The act for the submission of the clergy set out what the church had conceded in May 1532.[405]

The second purpose of these acts was to prevent effective retaliation against Henry. Importantly, the act of appeals, having prohibited appeals to Rome, went on to reject any papal measures taken against the king and realm. The statute should apply, notwithstanding 'Any foreign inhibitions appeals sentences summons citations suspensions interdictions excommunications restraints judgements . . . from the see of Rome or any other foreign courts', and notwithstanding any excommunications that might be fulminated [declared] against this act. All priests should administer the sacraments and hold divine service, notwithstanding any interdictions.[406]

The third purpose of these acts was propaganda: to assert, to justify, to explain. 'Diverse sundry old authentic histories and chronicles' were said by the act of appeals to declare that 'this realm of England is an empire . . . governed by one supreme head and king having the dignity and royal estate of the imperial crown of the same.' Previous kings— Edward I, Edward III, Richard II, Henry IV—and parliaments had made laws to preserve the realm 'from the annoyance as well of the see of Rome as from the authority of other foreign potentates'.[407] The attainder of Elizabeth Barton, the Nun of Kent, rehearsed the king's case over the divorce. The act dealing with dispensations roundly asserted that 'this your grace's realm, recognising no superior under God but only your grace, hath been and is free from subjection to any man's laws but only to such as have been devised made and ordained within this realm for the wealth of the same'.[408] The act of succession reiterated the king's case for his divorce, both in detail and in asserting the principle that 'no man of what estate degree or condition so ever he be hath power to dispense with God's laws'.[409] The act of supremacy 'for corroboration and confirmation' declared the king was 'the only supreme head in earth of the church of England'.[410] It was in the same spirit that the legislation of 1534 referred to the pope as the 'bishop of Rome', a phrase encapsulating the rejection of papal pretensions.[411] The reformation statutes should in this sense be seen together with the more overt works of propaganda printed in these years in defence of the king's case on the divorce and of his royal supremacy: A Glass of the Truth (printed 1532), Articles Devised by the Whole Consent of the King's Most Honourable Council (1533) and A Little Treatise against the Muttering of Some Papists in Corners (1534).[412]

The fourth purpose was to flush out potential opposition. The act 'for the more sure establishment of the succession' laid down that all the king's adult subjects should 'make a corporal oath . . . that they shall truly firmly and constantly without fraud and guile observe fulfil maintain defend and keep to their cunning wit and uttermost of their powers the whole effects and contents of this present act'. To refuse would incur the penalty of misprision of treason.[413] This act did not include the wording of the oath. A further act remedied that: 'Ye shall swear to bear faith truth and obedience only to the king's majesty and to his heirs of his body of his most dear and entirely beloved lawful wife Queen Anne begotten and to be begotten'; and to the heirs of the king according to the statute of succession; and to repute any oath to others as vain; and to maintain and defend the act of succession; and 'in no wise do or attempt, nor to your power suffer to be done or attempted, directly or indirectly, any thing or things privily or appartly to the let hindrance damage or derogation thereof'.[414]

The fifth purpose was to allow the king to claim that his policies had been freely endorsed by the political nation. In a circular letter to JPs on 25 June 1535, Henry insisted that papal authority had been abolished

> both upon most just and virtuous foundations grounded upon the laws of almighty god and holy scripture and also by the deliberate advice consultation consent and agreement as well of the bishops and clergy as by the nobles and commons temporal of this our realm assembled in our high court of parliament and by authority of the same.[415]

The sixth purpose was to make it possible to punish those who did not conform. The act of appeals declared that to the king, the supreme head, people were bound and owed 'next to God a natural and humble obedience'. Any priest who in the event of a papal interdict refused to minister the sacraments and hold divine service was to be imprisoned for a year and fined at the king's pleasure. Anyone having recourse to the papal courts from within the realm would face the penalties of the statute of *praemunire* of 16 Richard II. c. 5.[416] The act of succession laid down that any who 'by writing or imprinting or by any exterior act or deed' did anything to the peril of the king, and in particular any who 'by writing print deed or act' did anything 'to the prejudice slander disturbance or derogation' of the lawful matrimony between Henry and Anne, or of their heirs, would risk being declared guilty of treason. Those who without writing or any exterior deed nonetheless 'maliciously and obstinately publish divulge or utter any thing or things to the peril' of the king, or to the slander of the marriage between Henry and Anne, or to their heirs, should be declared guilty of misprision of treason and be liable to imprisonment at the king's will and loss of their goods and lands.[417] A new treason act protected the king and queen: if any do maliciously wish will or desire by words or writing, or by crafty imagine invent practise or attempt any bodily harm to be done or committed to the king's most royal person, the queen's, or their heirs apparent . . . or slanderously and maliciously publish and pronounce by express writing or words, that the king our sovereign lord should be heretic schismatic tyrant infidel or usurper of the crown,

or rebelliously withhold from the king any of his castles or ships, they should be adjudged traitors and denied the benefit of sanctuary.[418] Most pointedly and directly of all, the act of succession provided that anyone who refused to swear the oath required would incur the penalty of misprision of treason.[419]

*   *   *

And so the king had secured his divorce and imposed the break with Rome. Henry had been more resourceful and decisive than is often allowed: there is an essential continuity between the threats of 1527 and the logic and philosophy underlying the parliamentary statutes of 1533–35. The king had found loyal, shrewd and learned advisers to assist him; he had cajoled and bullied the church into granting him what he needed; and he had secured the acquiescence of the political nation. What we must now do is to look more closely at those who were uneasy to the point of opposition and refusal, and to consider how close they came to stopping Henry and how far they can be seen as an effective opposition. In so doing, we shall be shedding damaging light on the methods and pressures that Henry and his counsellors employed in order to achieve their ends.

2

Opposition

Catherine of Aragon

Was Catherine of Aragon the first to oppose Henry VIII? In a fundamental sense, of course, Catherine opposed the royal will simply by
refusing to agree that her marriage to Henry was invalid. By holding
firm to the conviction that she was Henry's lawful wife, she stood as a
great obstacle to the realisation of his plans. Moreover, knowledge of
her stand may well have influenced the attitude of others, most especially that of her daughter, Mary. But did Catherine, after refusing to
agree to the annulment, limit her opposition to arguing directly with the
king? Beyond that, did she trust that she would, before long, be vindicated by the pope, while largely accepting, if sometimes fearfully, what
fate had in store? Or did she play an openly political role in opposition,
stirring up criticism of the king, recruiting supporters and stiffening their
resistance? Was Froude right to say that 'she became the nucleus of a
powerful political party'?[1] Are modern historians justified in writing of
an 'Aragonese faction'?

Immediately her marriage was questioned in 1527, Catherine took it
'displeasantly', bursting into tears.[2] When the king showed her his book
outlining his case in canon law, Catherine was unconvinced and declared
that she would rather accept the judgment of the church.[3] On hearing
that Henry wanted a formal inquiry into the marriage, she demanded
proper legal assistance.[4] She refused to be persuaded by Cardinals
Campeggio and Wolsey (who saw her on 24 October 1528) that she
should enter a monastery if the judgment went against her (following
the example of Jeanne de Valois, sometime wife of Louis XII): instead
she declared her determination to live in the state of matrimony to which
God had called her.[5]

Catherine's refusal was not simply passive. She played a tactical game. She threatened to produce papal bulls from Spain removing all impediments to the marriage. She revealed the second dispensation for Henry to marry her—the so-called Spanish brief—in the autumn of 1528, though she had most probably obtained it by April that year.[6] Catherine was being legally awkward in defence of her position.

At the legatine trial Catherine challenged the authority of the court, and the competence of Campeggio and Wolsey as judges.[7] Bishop Fisher, her principal advocate, could hardly have made so dramatic and fundamentalist a defence of her position as he did without the queen's approval.

Catherine's most striking act of defiance, however, was her appeal to Rome: calling for the case to be heard in the highest papal court. In itself that was by no means an unreasonable or indeed an unusual course of action for anyone involved in a legal dispute in the ecclesiastical courts. But, manifestly, in Henry's great matter, asking for the advocation of the case to Rome had a special resonance. For Henry it meant the certainty of delays and the likelihood that he would lose any guiding influence over the proceedings, which would now be controlled by the pope and resident cardinals. Much energy was expended by Wolsey and by Gardiner, as we have seen, in efforts to prevent the advocation. And undoubtedly Henry saw Catherine's request as a hostile act. At the legatine trial, Catherine publicly asked for her case to be advoked; she had privately done so as early as February, illustrating again that she was playing her cards tactically.[8]

After the legatine trial, Catherine continued to try to persuade the king. She argued with him, complaining that he would neither dine with her nor visit her, and telling him to his face that he knew perfectly well that there was no case for a divorce since she had come to him a virgin. It was at this time that she offered to accept as truth whatever the king would swear on oath on the matter: Henry, significantly, refused.[9] On 12 June 1530 she urged him to be a good prince and husband again and to leave the evil life he was leading. They argued over the recent papal brief executed in Flanders that urged restraint on the king.[10] Nonetheless, Henry was still prepared to send her some cloth and to ask her to have it made into shirts for him,[11] and continued to see her from time to time: they kept Christmas together in 1530.[12]

In summer 1531 Henry sent several noblemen—the dukes of Norfolk and Suffolk, the marquess of Dorset, the earls of Shrewsbury, Northumberland and Wiltshire, and churchmen—John Longland, bishop of Lincoln, John Stokesley, bishop of London, Dr Edward Lee, the king's almoner, Dr Richard Sampson, dean of the chapel royal, and Dr Stephen Gardiner, the king's secretary—to see Catherine. They came armed with the opinions of the universities in the king's favour on the divorce. Catherine refused once more to yield. She insisted that all the scholars consulted at her father's request had long ago endorsed her marriage and the pope had then ratified it. In consequence she prayed God to send the king 'a quiet conscience', and to assuage the scruples he said he felt. Defiantly Catherine added, 'I say I am his lawful wife and to him lawfully married', reasserting that she had come to Henry a virgin, a matter on which she knew the truth better than anybody in the world.

Norfolk explained that they had been sent by the king to show her his displeasure that she was responsible for his being cited to appear at Rome. They urged Catherine to abandon that action—not least since Henry was supreme chief and sovereign in his kingdom both temporally and spiritually, as the clergy had recognised—and instead to agree that the dispute be resolved elsewhere. Catherine defended herself vigorously. The pope, she claimed, had shown Henry greater favour than he had to her. She would serve and obey the king as her sovereign; but in spiritual matters, it was not pleasing that he had such intentions, since the pope was the only true sovereign and vicar of God, with the power to judge in spiritual matters including marriage. She would insist on the validity of her marriage 'till the court of Rome which was privy to the beginning have made thereof a determination and final ending'. One by one the churchmen argued against her, but she always concluded by urging them to make their case at Rome. The king was very sorry to hear of her 'wilful opinion' and 'in especial that she more trusted in the Pope's law, then in keeping the precepts of God'.[13] For good measure Catherine complained at the way so many had come to argue with her when she was alone—and on the point of retiring for the night—and lacked counsel.[14]

In July Henry lost his temper with her after she regretted that he had not given her a chance to see him before he left for his summer progress. She had, Henry complained, caused him annoyance and sorrow in a thousand ways—especially by attempting to disgrace and humiliate him by having him summoned to appear personally at Rome. The king suggested they stop their practice of sending each other messages every third day.[15] He then left her; and never saw her again.

In October 1531 a group of councillors—Edward Lee (by then archbishop-elect of York) the earl of Sussex, Sir William Fitzwilliam and Dr Sampson—were ordered by the king to warn her what would follow if she persisted. Catherine responded that, as she knew that Henry was moved not by scruples of conscience but by passion pure and simple, she would be ill advised to agree to the supposed compromise procedures proposed by the king. Everybody in the realm, Catherine added, because threatened or corrupted, would say that white was black and black was white. The councillors fell on their knees, pleading with her to agree to the case being determined in England; she in turn threw herself on her knees, praying them to persuade the king to return to her, whom she knew to be his true and lawful wife.[16]

Catherine, then, refused to accept Henry's opinion of the invalidity of their marriage, and refused to surrender her right to be heard at Rome. Those continued to be her guiding principles in the years that followed. In May 1533, as we have seen, she refused to appear before Archbishop Cranmer at Dunstable when the king's matter was finally determined.[17] A month earlier, when Henry sent Norfolk and Suffolk to tell her about the passage of the act of appeals, and specifically to ask her to give up her appeal to Rome, she had maintained her determination not to yield. They then told her that the king had married. After they left, William Blount, Lord Mountjoy, her chamberlain, came to instruct her that she was no longer to call herself queen, but rather 'the old widow princess', and that the king would reduce the sums he was making available for her household. She replied that as long as she lived she would call herself queen, and that became a further issue on which she would never yield.[18] On 3 July 1533 Mountjoy saw her again on the matter. She refused once more to accept the title 'princess dowager', and struck it out with pen and ink wherever she found it. She insisted that she was the king's true wife and that her children were legitimate. The case was the pope's to judge.[19] That Catherine held out successfully on this point is shown by the king's reproaches to Mountjoy in October 1533 that several of Catherine's servants had never stopped calling her queen; Mountjoy explained that he could not stop her chaplains and her gentlewomen, and offered to resign his office.[20]

In December 1533 Suffolk and other councillors were sent to the queen and used much sharp language, Chapuys reported, to persuade her to accept the divorce. Once again she refused, declaring herself queen; she would suffer a thousand deaths rather than consent. She also refused to move from Buckden to Somersham—described by Chapuys as the most unhealthy and pestilential house in England.[21] 'We find here', Suffolk wrote, 'the most obstinate woman that may be': there was no other remedy 'but by force to convey her from hence to Somersham'. They had had 'no small travail' to persuade the servants to take the new oath to serve Catherine as princess dowager; but many of them had now done so.[22] Chapuys reported that Suffolk had dismissed many of her household—including her chamberlain, chancellor, almoner and master of the horse[23]—and imprisoned others, including her chaplain, Thomas Abel.[24] Catherine was upset: not leaving her room except to hear mass, and refusing to eat or drink what her new servants provided.[25]

In 1534 Catherine refused the new oaths that were imposed on everyone in support of the act of succession. One of Cromwell's memoranda in April 1534 noted: 'to send the copy of the act of the king's succession to the princess Dowager and the lady Mary, with special commandment that it may be read in their presence and their answer taken'.[26] In May 1534 Catherine refused to swear the oath.[27] The same month a group of bishops—Archbishop Lee, Tunstal and Foxe—were sent by the king to threaten Catherine with trial followed by execution, but she still refused to swear the oath.[28] That was in a sense passive resistance: she simply refused to do what the king wanted. But she also asserted her conviction that the marriage was valid. She denied, once again, that Arthur had consummated his marriage; called Cranmer a shadow and declared that she was not bound to stand by the divorce, since the pope had now decided in her favour; insisted that she would never give up the title of queen; denounced Henry's marriage with Anne as invalid; claimed that as the king's wife she was not bound to the acts of parliament; and insisted that she would always hold herself as the king's lawful wife.[29] If there was anyone who had come to execute her, let him come forward, she said.[30]

Catherine, then, consistently refused to yield to the pressure put upon her to accept the king's claim that their marriage had never been valid. Whenever councillors, noblemen or bishops came to persuade her, she would not agree and always insisted that she was the king's rightful queen, a virgin when the king married her. She refused to accept that she should no longer be styled queen, since to concede that would be to admit that the king had been right from the start.

Catherine did not limit herself to voicing her refusals only when she was put under pressure by groups of visiting councillors. She was undoubtedly concerned that her case in canon law should be fully set out. It is likely that she encouraged Bishop Fisher to speak forcefully on her behalf at the legatine trial in 1529. She wanted canon lawyers at Spanish universities to write in her defence. It is likely that her chaplain, Thomas Abel, who wrote and preached in her defence, did so with her encouragement.[31] Two foreign Observant Franciscans, sent to England by William Peto, who had gone into exile after preaching in defence of Catherine on Easter Sunday 1532, were with her in October 1533, which hints at links and contacts.[32] And yet, even at this level, there were limits to Catherine's activity: it is striking that there was so little written in support of her in English and aimed at a wider public in the realm. Later, Catherine would react against particular measures taken against her. In 1534 she was not allowed to hold her maundy to the poor according to custom, since she was not the queen.[33] The following year she let it be known that she intended to keep a maundy in the old way, despite royal orders the previous year. Henry responded that he was prepared to allow it if she did it as princess dowager but not if she did it as queen. What Catherine did is not known.[34]

If refusing to agree to the king's wishes turns a queen into an opponent, then Catherine clearly was one. But did her refusals amount to more than merely personal statements? Was she in any meaningful sense the leader of a political opposition? Did she encourage others to speak out in her favour?

Undoubtedly she won the sympathies of some noblewomen who served in her household and in that of her daughter. Anne Hussey, wife of John, first Lord Hussey, served in Mary's household and was compelled to make an abject submission after she was interrogated for calling Mary by the title of princess.[35] Lord Hussey, as we shall see later, in 1534 spoke to Chapuys about the prospects of a rebellion against royal policies.[36]

Margaret, countess of Salisbury, daughter of Edward IV's brother George, duke of Clarence, was sympathetic to Catherine, in whose household she had long served, and Princess Mary, whose lady governess she was.[37] In 1533 she refused to deliver jewels and plate when required to by Lord Hussey, Mary's chamberlain (who was here acting on royal orders).[38] Margaret was soon afterwards dismissed when Mary's household was dissolved and Mary was placed with Princess Elizabeth.[39] Margaret offered to serve her at her own expense, but that was unacceptable to the king.[40] In February 1535 Chapuys protested to Henry at the poor treatment of Princess Mary, who was ill, and asked that the king put her under the care of her former governess, Margaret, whom she regarded as her second mother. Henry railed against her, telling Chapuys that the countess was a fool, of no experience, and that if Mary had been under her care during her current illness, she would have died, for the countess would not have known what to do.[41]

All that might be seen as essentially personal rather than political. But there was possibly—or potentially—a little more to it than that. Margaret's younger son, Reginald Pole, was singled out by Chapuys in

September 1533 as a possible pretender to the kingdom and as a prospective husband for Princess Mary. He and his brothers—Henry, Lord Montagu, and Sir Geoffrey Pole—had, Chapuys added, many kinsmen and allies whose services his master, the emperor, could use and gain the greater part of the realm.[42] Over a year later, in November 1534, Chapuys reminded Charles V how he had praised Reginald Pole as of good race and for his grace of person and singular virtues: Queen Catherine, Chapuys significantly added, knew no one to whom she would rather marry her daughter. That suggests that Catherine was indulging in dynastic dreaming. How much further did Catherine go? We shall return to consider Reginald Pole, who had gone into exile in Italy rather than remain in England and support Henry over his divorce, and evaluate the nature of his dissent. Here we need only note that Chapuys went on to explore the possibilities of a dynastic coup against the king. Chapuys emphasised Reginald Pole's family's connections. Many, Chapuys noted, held that the family of the duke of Clarence had the true title to the kingdom. Chapuys cited the Poles' close ties to George Nevile, Lord Bergavenny, father-in-law of Lord Montagu, and a great and powerful lord, who was displeased with Henry because he had been detained long in prison when the duke of Buckingham fell in 1521 and because a great part of his revenue had been withheld by the king. Citing discontent in Wales, Cheshire, Lancashire and Ireland— places with which he had no first-hand acquaintance—Chapuys was confident that if the emperor came with an army, everyone would declare for him, especially if Reginald Pole was there. But Chapuys's enthusiasm for his cause was running away with him. Reginald Pole was in exile—and not, as we shall see, actively opposing Henry in these years. Reginald's younger brother, Sir Geoffrey, was, however, often with Chapuys, and would have visited him more often still had Chapuys not dissuaded him from taking such risks. Sir Geoffrey unceasingly urged Chapuys to tell the emperor how easily the kingdom might be conquered.[43] Chapuys's communications weave a vivid impression of deep disaffection and incipient noble rebellion and imperial usurpation, but a closer reading reveals only the urgings of Sir Geoffrey. There was little substance beyond the words. And there is scanty evidence for any contacts between Catherine and Mary on the one hand and the Poles on the other. One exception was the message that Sir Geoffrey Pole brought to Catherine from his elder brother, Lord Montagu, present at Henry's meeting with Francis I in September 1532, 'to show her that nothing was done at that meeting touching the marriage with the Lady Anne, and that the king had done the best he could but the French king

would not assent thereunto'.[44] Such a message reveals the Poles' sympathies, and hints at a close relationship between them and Catherine.
But what the Poles did here was to inform Catherine of how things
stood: Catherine was not leading or co-ordinating their actions.

From such evidence, some historians have been tempted to build up
a picture of a potentially powerful conservative conspiracy. But that is
to read far too much into what are essentially expressions of sorrow
and regret, rather than politically directed anger. Even Lord Hussey
attempted dutifully to carry out the king's wishes, trying—unsuccessfully—to secure Mary's jewels and plate on Henry's orders in autumn
1533.[45] Discontented though he may have been, Hussey does seem to
have tried to enforce royal policy by imposing the required oath on her
servants the following year. Chapuys exaggerated the likelihood and
immediacy of disagreement with the king's government over the position of Catherine and Mary. Read carefully, the evidence for Hussey's
wife and for Margaret, countess of Salisbury points to disquiet, not to
any large-scale conspiracy. More importantly still, there is little in
the sources to suggest, whatever noblemen or their wives did, that
Catherine was encouraging, let alone recruiting, them in her cause. And
Catherine, interestingly, would have nothing to do with the prophecies
of Elizabeth Barton that we shall shortly be considering, even though
Barton tried several times to talk to her.[46] She was distressed by the executions of Thomas More and Bishop Fisher, but there is no evidence of
any substantial contacts between her and them. Letters in an unknown
hand to the queen were found in Fisher's study: but Fisher said he had
never addressed the queen in private after the time that the king had
commanded him to give her his counsel in her matter.[47] There is one
intriguing, possibly contrary, detail. Among Fisher's papers was found
a list of articles sent from Catherine, including reference to a chaplain
of the bishop of Bath who had told her almoner that Thomas More and
the bishops of Bath, Exeter and Chichester would favour her cause as
much as she could desire.[48] But it is hard to make much of this, as we
shall see: the bishops of Bath, Chichester and Exeter, whatever their
private sentiments, did not stand by Catherine very vigorously; and
Thomas More's attitude to Catherine's plight was more equivocal than
is often realised.

Moreover, a major obstacle to any argument that claims the existence
of an effective 'Aragonese' faction is that Catherine was increasingly
placed under pressure by the king, was less and less a free agent and
more and more a prisoner under house arrest, in (relatively) remote
regions. Contact between queen and noblemen was theoretically possi-

ble, but none dared visit her, as far as we know, delegations sent by the king apart. No doubt Chapuys exaggerated the awfulness of the conditions in which the queen was now compelled to live, but she was moved away from court, and then, often against her wishes, from house to house, first to the More, near St Albans,[49] then, in May 1532, in response to a papal brief, to Bishop's Hatfield, then in July 1533 to Buckden[50] (successfully resisting a move to Somersham in the following winter), and then in May 1534 to Kimbolton.[51]

Catherine's daughter, Mary, who, like her mother, refused to accept the reduction in her status and to swear the oath to the succession demanded of her, was under greater pressure. In January 1534 Henry came to see her to persuade her to renounce the title of princess of Wales.[52] In August 1534 she was humiliatingly required to accompany Princess Elizabeth, Anne Boleyn's child: it made her ill.[53] In November 1534 Chapuys reported that the efforts of Anne Boleyn's aunt to persuade Mary to renounce her title of princess had made her ill again.[54] In January 1535 Chapuys reported that Mary had been threatened with being sent to the Tower if she called herself princess or refused to swear the oath.[55]

Did Catherine, however, appeal to her nephew Charles V to use force on her behalf? The evidence turns on a number of requests that Catherine made to Charles over the years: none of them unambiguously called for him to use armed force against Henry. Instead, what she repeatedly asked Charles to do was to put pressure on the pope to determine her case speedily. In November 1531 Catherine bemoaned her daily tribulations to her nephew: what she hoped from him was simply that he should say how much he felt her troubles, and how surprised he was at the way Henry was treating her—that would encourage those in England who wished her well, and show them that there was someone who grieved at her troubles.[56] Those were not the words of a rebel. In December 1531 Catherine begged Charles to urge the pope to do justice, dispelling his fears: Catherine prayed that God would enlighten the king (in other words, make him realise that he was wrong in seeking his annulment).[57] In February 1532 Chapuys reported that Catherine had begged Charles to ask the pope to make a final decision on the case, for, Chapuys wrote, she has suffered as much as she can bear.[58] In May 1532 Monsieur de Montfalcolnet, Charles's maître d'hotel, visited Catherine. She asked him to beg the emperor to hasten the pope to deliver his judgment in her case: everyone, she claimed, was displeased with the pope for not yet having done so. She still showed great love for the king. She said that if she could speak to him, all that had happened would be nothing, as he was so good, and that he would treat her better than ever—but she was not allowed to see him. And she thought that it was a mistake to suppose that if the papal sentence was given against the king, he would not obey.[59] In September 1532 Catherine importuned Charles again, somewhat awkwardly suggesting that the aggressions of the Turks and what was happening to her were perhaps equal in the offence they caused God. God would give the victory, she said, to those who served him with good works—and one of the best good works would be to get her cause settled. And Catherine warned him that books were being published in England full of falsehoods and filth touching the faith.[60] In November 1532 Catherine, congratulating Charles on his victory over the Turks in Hungary, expressed her certain hope that the pope would now slay the second Turk—by which she meant her matter. And again she railed at the pope's delay in pronouncing on it.[61] Catherine's references to the Turks, and the language of victory and slaying, might be taken as an implicit request to Charles to use armed force against Henry. But that is not certain. She may simply have been emphasising to Charles that her own matter was just as important in God's eyes as the emperor's resistance against the Turks, rather than encouraging Charles to fight Henry VIII. Again, in February 1533, Catherine, on hearing of yet further procedural twists in her case at Rome, begged Charles to urge the resolution of the matter.[62] In June 1533 she hoped that if Charles saw her household greatly reduced he would apply an—unspecified—remedy.[63] In February 1534 Catherine urged that the remedy was for the pope to determine the case; she begged the emperor to take action, but without saying what form it should take.[64]

By contrast with Catherine, Chapuys increasingly and explicitly advocated the use of force against Henry VIII. It might be that he was writing what Catherine felt but dared not say openly. But more probably Catherine did not want the use of force. In June 1533 Chapuys told the council on her behalf that she would neither build castles and fortresses, nor raise armies against Henry.[65] For the love she bore her husband, Chapuys asserted in October 1533, she dared not speak of any remedy but law and justice.[66] In January 1534 he wrote that the queen daily charged him to beg the emperor not to think of making war on her behalf as she would rather die.[67] In February 1534 Catherine agreed with Charles V on his reasons for not sending 'a power' to England—presumably meaning 'not using armed force against England'—in a letter that implies that someone (Chapuys?) had raised the question.[68] In May 1534 Chapuys wrote that the queen now knew that it would be necessary to proceed by other remedies which she did not dare propose herself for fear her letters should be intercepted and so as not to contradict what she had previously written. An immediate remedy was necessary.[69] That again might be read as a request for the use of force. Nothing much more was heard of this, in however veiled a form, for some time. Of course, Catherine may simply have refrained from asking for force because she knew that Charles was heavily committed on other fronts. But anyone wishing to present Catherine as an advocate of an imperial invasion of England is compelled to dramatise what are at best vaguely ambiguous urgings.

More than a year later, with not only the king's marriage to Anne Boleyn a *fait accompli*, but the royal supremacy receiving the acquiescence of the nation, and the final papal judgment against Henry not having resolved the matter as Catherine would have wished, Catherine may have toyed with something more forceful. The recurring illness—probably psychosomatic—of her daughter, Mary, must have added to her anxieties. In August 1535 she informed Mary of Hungary that she was compelled to implore those who could help to remedy what she described as 'the offence here given to God'.[70] Then in October 1535 Catherine sent anguished letters to Charles V, expressing her hope that since he had won a great victory (against the Turks), he would now put an end to her troubles and devise some remedy with the pope for the things attempted against the church. If it were delayed and God in his mercy did not help, they would do to her and her daughter what they had done to many holy martyrs.[71] In December 1535 Catherine herself wrote to the emperor about the necessity of remedying what she coyly called the affairs of the king her lord, herself and her daughter, which would be affected by what she was told was being done in parliament. She implored Charles for the remedy, since it could be had only with the aid of God and of the pope and the emperor.[72] What precisely did she intend by that? In a letter to Dr Pedro Ortiz, Charles V's representative at the papal court in Rome, she declared that what the pope did and would do was the true remedy for the evils suffered by her and her daughter. Ortiz ought to use all diligence in urging that something be done quickly.[73] But still Catherine did not explicitly say what she wanted. Her daughter was even more insistent, but still tantalisingly vague. In November 1535 Mary implored Chapuys that, more than ever, his services were urgently required: she trusted that the emperor would apply a prompt remedy, especially once he understood the nature, weight, importance and dangerous position of affairs in this country, to which end she urged Chapuys to send to Charles one of his men, rather than relying on letters in cipher. Beg him, she urged, to take the matter in hand: the work would be highly acceptable in the eyes of God and no less glory would be gained by it than by the conquest of Tunis or even Africa.[74] It is possible that at this point Mary considered flight abroad: a later letter by Chapuys, written just after Catherine's death, alludes to this.[75] But fate intervened. Catherine's sufferings came to an end. By late December she was unwell, so much so that Chapuys rushed to see her at Kimbolton on 2 January 1536. She died on 7 January.

How far Catherine wished for a forceful resolution of her situation remains unclear. When her daughter compared the glory that Charles would win by remedying matters in England to that which he had won by the conquest of Tunis, she may have been urging a military crusade against England; or she may simply have been, once again, emphasising that what was happening in England deserved the same attention as the emperor's Mediterranean affairs. None of these letters and reports convincingly establishes that Catherine or Mary were advocates of war. Rather than putting forward practical policies, Catherine's increasingly desperate pleas to Charles read more as if she felt that he had in his hands a magic wand that could, if only he would wave it, solve her problems. Chapuys, from an early stage, urged force on the emperor, only to be rebuffed time and again: his sincere sympathy for Catherine and Mary's plight is not, however, evidence that Catherine and Mary agreed with him, nor even that they had much discussed the matter with him. In one letter, Catherine explicitly denied any bellicosity: 'I do not ask his Holiness to go to war, because that is a thing I would rather die than provoke.'[76] What she most wanted was a definitive resolution in her favour.

There is a much better way of explaining Catherine's reaction to her situation. Above all she trusted in God, and in successive popes, God's instruments on earth, to achieve what she wanted. Sceptical modern historians might think she would have been more successful as the leader of a political cabal. But that her trust in God proved unavailing should not lead us to disregard the intensity of her religious commitment. No less than Henry, Catherine was convinced that her cause was just and that God would vindicate her. What she hoped and expected over the long years from 1527 was that Henry would come to his senses and return to her as her husband. In July 1533, when told that Henry would never take her back, she replied that she had perfect confidence that he who in a moment converted St Paul, and turned him from persecutor to preacher, would inspire the king's conscience and not permit such a virtuous prince long to continue in error.[77] In trusting in God, Catherine pinned her hopes on his vicar in this world, the pope. She trusted in a swift—or, as time went by, in an eventual and belated—papal declaration in her favour, and believed that Henry would then see the error of his ways, and restore her to what she saw as her rightful place as queen. Such thinking proved a cruel delusion, and arguably it was self-delusion from the start. But it would be wrong to suppose that it was not sincere. It explains why Catherine felt so hurt by the repeated delays. In the early stages, she had expected that the pope would at once declare the king to be in the wrong and order him to dismiss Anne Boleyn from court. But by February 1531, she lamented, it seemed as if the pope had no great desire to settle the question. What she hoped for, as an interim measure, was what Clement finally issued in January 1532 and what his nuncio presented to the king in May: namely, a letter remonstrating with Henry as a loving father for removing Catherine from his court and for cohabiting with Anne, observing that the king would not have approved but would instead have punished any of his subjects who did what he himself was said to have done, and expressing the hope that he would put Anne away and take Catherine back again.[78] But if the king was momentarily astonished and troubled by the letter, as Chapuys noted, the admonition did not help Catherine a jot.[79]

What Catherine wanted above all, of course, was for a final papal pronouncement on the validity of her marriage, ordering Henry to take her back as his lawful wife. In August 1533 Clement issued a bull commanding Henry to restore Catherine and put away Anne within ten days on pain of excommunication, and calling on Charles V and all other Christian princes to assist in the execution of the bull by force of arms if Henry disobeyed.[80] Chapuys in September 1533 duly urged Cromwell to do his utmost to induce the king to take back the queen.[81] On 24 March 1534—finally—Catherine secured the papal verdict that she had wanted: but Henry simply defied it. Catherine a year earlier had supposed that there would be no difficulty in Henry's obeying any papal decision against him; and if he did not he would, she believed, be forced to obey it by his subjects.[82] Whenever there were hopeful signs—for example in January 1533 when she heard that the king regretted having sent her so far away—she was quick to think that God had inspired Henry to recognise his error.[83] When it turned out that she had been too optimistic, Catherine took consolation in the inscrutable workings of divine providence. In April 1535 she wrote to Charles that she had hoped that the pope's definitive sentence would have led to some good,

but she perceived that God for their sins had permitted otherwise. Providentialism did not mean resignation: she knew God would not desert
her in so just a cause, and that she should offend him gravely if she did
not use the help of those who could apply a remedy. She warned Charles
about Mary's illness: I am as Job, waiting for the day when I must go
sue for alms for the love of God, she wrote.[84] If the pope would not do
what was necessary—she wrote to Dr Ortiz at Rome—all she could do
was to pray to God to remedy the evil.[85]

It is possible too that Catherine felt that her misfortunes were the fruit
of her sins and the sins of those responsible for her. Reginald Pole in
1549 claimed that she had thought that a great part of her troubles
emanated from God: she was being punished for the sin of her father,
King Ferdinand, who, when negotiating her marriage to Prince Arthur,
saw some disturbances at the time which he imagined were caused by
the favour borne by the people to the earl of Warwick (Pole's uncle),
son of the duke of Clarence, and incited Henry VII to have Warwick
executed.[86] Much less likely is the insinuation in the interrogatories for
Bishop Fisher that Catherine despaired of the mercy of God because in
swearing on the sacraments that she had never been carnally known by
Prince Arthur she knew that she was committing perjury.[87]

Catherine remained unshakable in her conviction that she was
Henry's true lawful wife. She died praying that God would pardon the
king for the wrong he had done her.[88] Only God and direction from
God's vicar on earth could rightly change the king's mind. Catherine
could herself seek to dissuade the king, as she did in the early stages of
the divorce, she could secure the support of canon lawyers, and she
could—though at greater cost—appeal to the pope. But for Catherine
to have espoused other means—whether by attempting to build up a
party in England with the intention of stirring rebellion, or whether by
urging the emperor to launch an invasion against the schismatic king—
would have been fatally to undermine her moral stand as Henry's true
lawful wife. No true lawful wife could contemplate making war against
her husband, however much he wronged her. Nor could she have readily
caballed and protested against the policies, against the pope and against
the church, on which Henry had now embarked. It is hard to see how
she could have issued a declaration inviting the king's subjects to force
Henry back to the marital bed, even harder to see how she could have
asked the king's subjects to depose the man whose lawful true wife she
claimed to be. And so Catherine could do no more than pray to God,
and urge Charles V to hurry the pope and in some unspecified way to
resolve the situation. Perhaps she was misguided; perhaps she should

have come to terms from the start with the irretrievable breakdown of her marriage. She would, however, have recognised no such concept. And if she had, she would still not have felt able to accept it, not least since to accept that her marriage had been legally null and void from the start, as Henry claimed, would have been to deprive her daughter, Mary, of her legitimacy and her dynastic future. But when she failed to persuade Henry, and when Henry defied the papal judgment in her favour, then Catherine's position was hopeless; and the papal church in England would unavoidably share in her misfortunes.

Catherine's death left her daughter weakened. Mary continued to appeal to Charles for unspecified help. In February 1536 she wished him to give his full attention to the means necessary for the general and total extirpation of the evil: it would be a most meritorious work in the eyes of God and the means of saving souls now on the verge of perdition.[89] But the imperatives of international power politics were driving Charles into an accommodation with Henry VIII, and the months after Catherine's death were marked by a remarkable thawing of Anglo-imperial relations, vividly and publicly symbolised by Chapuys's recognition of Anne Boleyn, previously reviled by him as the 'concubine', in April. And that in turn made Mary's position no less hopeless than her mother's had been. In June, following threats in what still reads as a remarkably unpleasant letter by Thomas Cromwell, Mary, whom Cromwell had called 'the most obstinate woman that ever was', the most 'ungrate, unnatural and most obstinate person living', yielded and accepted that her mother's marriage had been incestuous and unlawful (and thus implicitly that she was a bastard) and that her father was supreme head of the church in England under Christ. A little later she even assured Cromwell that, as to her opinion touching pilgrimages, purgatory and relics, she had none but such as she should receive from the king.[90] Of course, Mary's true feelings were very different, but her acquiescence in the king's new order had been secured. She remained a potential threat, a potential focus of opposition, but she had been intimidated and humiliated into an abject and compromising submission.

Elizabeth Barton, the Nun of Kent

Elizabeth Barton, the Nun of Kent, dismissed by Elton as 'that deluded prophetess',[91] was the most extraordinary and most awkward critic of Henry VIII's search for a divorce. In the late 1520s a popular cult developed in east Kent after Barton, a servant of Thomas Cobb, one of the archbishop of Canterbury's tenants at Aldington, fell ill, experienced trances, delivered speeches and was, we learn, miraculously cured at her local chapel, Court at Street. Barton then became a nun at St Sepulchre's, Canterbury, continued to have visions, often returned to Court at Street, and was said to have performed miracles. The story of her life and deeds was recorded in at least one book,[92] which survives today only in the extracts printed much later by William Lambard in his *A Perambulation of Kent: conteining the description . . . of that shyre* (1576). All this happened *before* Henry VIII sought an annulment of his first marriage: it could not therefore have been in any way inspired by or intended as a reaction against the king's matrimonial trials.[93] In these years Barton took her place in a long succession of medieval holy women: her life would not have seemed out of place in much earlier centuries.[94]

Barton's activity was officially sanctioned by Archbishop Warham and she was placed under the tutelage of a monk of Christ Church, Canterbury, Dr Edward Bocking. That looks like an effort on the part of the church to channel the enthusiasms of popular piety. Much the same could be said of the compilation of the book of the miracles she wrought. Of course, a sceptical age will doubt that Barton really experienced visions or performed miracles, but that does not dispose of her. She may conceivably have invented everything in search of worldly glory or social aggrandisement ('perceiving her self to be much made of, to be magnified and much set by' because of her speeches, as was held against her),[95] though it is not at all clear that that is what she in fact achieved for herself. Clerical manipulation remains, of course, a possibility, for example with the motive of building up Court at Street as a centre of pilgrimage. But if Barton continued to visit that chapel, it was the nunnery of St Sepulchre's in Canterbury that she joined. She was certainly at times unwell (whether afflicted by epilepsy or by hysteria); steeped in the piety of her time, and tutored in the worlds of St Bridget and St Catherine of Siena, she interpreted the world as she experienced it within their terms,[96] and genuinely thought she had seen visions. However that may be, what is significant is that (as far as we know) Barton's holiness was questioned by no one in these early years. We could, of course, with our superior wisdom, read our sources as meaning the opposite of what they appear to say, and suppose that all involved in the emergence of this cult, from the nun to the archbishop to the crowds that gathered to witness her cure, were actors in a charade, doing and saying what they knew was expected of them, but well aware that it was all imposture. Such a reading might, however, be thought to reflect not our superior wisdom but rather the 'condescension of posterity'. And this matters in light of what was to happen next: if Elizabeth Barton was widely and sincerely regarded as a holy maid, specially privileged by God, then the criticisms she would voice of Henry VIII not only carry weight but, relevantly here, need not be read in terms of political manoeuvring.

Barton began to have visions relating to Henry VIII's quest for a divorce. An angel told her to go to the king and command him to amend his life. If he married Anne Boleyn, the vengeance of God would plague him. He was not to take away any of the pope's rights, but should destroy all those holding to the new—i.e. heretical—learning. A little later the same angel told Barton to tell the king that she had seen him, Anne Boleyn and Anne's father devising how to bring the matter to pass: a devil stood next to Anne and insinuated that Anne should send her father to the emperor to win him over with money.[97] Barton saw by revelation that 'God was highly displeased' with the king: if he persisted and married again, 'then within one month after such marriage he should no longer be king of this realm, and in the reputation of almighty God should not be a king one day nor one hour'; moreover, 'he should die a villain's death'.[98] Worse still, Barton had seen the particular spot and place prepared for the king in hell.[99] God also commanded Barton to say to Archbishops Wolsey and Warham 'that if they married or furthered the king's grace to be married' to Anne 'they both should be utterly destroyed'.[100] When Henry—with Anne Boleyn—passed through Canterbury in summer 1532, Barton said that 'the king was so abominable in sight of God that he was not worthy to tread of no hallowed ground'.[101] In September 1532 Henry and Anne crossed the Channel to meet Francis I. When the king heard mass at Calais, God was so displeased with him, Barton said, that an angel took the holy sacrament—the holy bread—away from the priest so that the king did not see it, and instead it was ministered there to Barton, present but invisible.[102] Barton also claimed that she had thwarted the king's intention of marrying while overseas.[103] She did not, of course, prevent Henry and Anne from marrying in January 1533. And when Henry and Anne survived their first month of marriage, apparently confounding her prophecy, the nun allegedly reinterpreted her revelation, saying that the king, though not destroyed, was no longer king in the eyes of God.[104]

Barton did not keep these visions to herself or to a group of associates. Archbishop Warham had been involved with her earliest non-political visions, and she saw him several times, warning him of his destruction if he married Henry to Anne.[105] Before she informed Warham of her latest visions, she asked him to write to Wolsey to get

him to agree to see her.[106] Barton warned Wolsey similarly.[107] The angel
whom Barton saw in her visions had told her to tell the king to his
face—and Barton did so, seeing him at least twice.[108] Those must have
been astonishing encounters: sadly we have no eyewitness accounts of
them.

Barton told others, too, notably various priests and monks, including
Henry Gold, priest of Aldermary, London,[109] young novice monks at
Christ Church, Canterbury,[110] several Observant Franciscans at Canterbury (notably Hugh Rich), Greenwich and Richmond, Henry Man at
the Charterhouse of Sheen,[111] and the Bridgettine nuns of Syon and the
priests there. Several of these monks and friars spread the word, according to the official sermon denouncing the nun, to all they knew 'to
grudge and not to favour' the king's intended marriage to Anne
Boleyn.[112] Barton also informed the pope that God would be displeased
with him if he found against Catherine and would send him plagues,
communicating her revelations to the pope's representatives in England,
Silvester Darius and John Pulleon.[113] Among the laity who met the nun
was the marchioness of Exeter. On one occasion the marchioness rode
from Kew to Canterbury with her servant Constance Boyntayn, each
disguised as the other.[114] On another occasion it was Barton, then
staying at Syon Abbey, who was encouraged by the abbess to visit the
marchioness at her house at Horseley, Surrey, meeting both the marchioness and the marquess.[115] Barton also met John Fisher, bishop of
Rochester, who wept for joy on hearing her revelations,[116] and Thomas
More, who, however, would not listen to her political prophecies and
warned her of the risks she was running, as we shall see later. Interestingly, Catherine of Aragon always refused to see the nun, even though,
according to notes made by the French ambassador, she and Princess
Mary were 'seduites' (captivated) by her.[117]

How large and how widespread was Barton's audience? According to
the sermon denouncing her, 'many of the spirituality' put their trust in
her revelations, and 'infected a great number of the king's grace's people
with like grudge of mind';[118] according to the statute of attainder which
condemned her, 'by such her false and feigned hypocrisy with dissimuled
sanctity was brought in a great bruit and fame of the people in sundry
parts of this Realm'; 'a great number and multitude of . . . the king's
subjects . . . by their great negligences and follies inclined to newfang-
ledness . . . have had relation and knowledge to theme given' of Barton's
revelations.[119] Ethan Shagan has described the lists of those to whom
Barton's associates showed her revelations as 'staggering',[120] but that is
an exaggeration. Hugh Rich, for example, listed some fifty people,

which is impressive at one level but small in relation to the political and religious nation as a whole.[121] Moreover, not all those listed by Rich necessarily welcomed the news, as Thomas More's reaction shows. If Barton's prophecies struck a chord with those who were deeply unhappy over the king's divorce, they did not attract—or perhaps did not yet attract—a larger audience. Cranmer was perhaps trying to excuse the convent of his cathedral church, but it is worth noting his claim, in December 1533, that 'few in comparison of their great number appear to be knowing or consenting to the said false revelations or illusions; and almost only such as were Doctor Bocking's novices, men of young years, and of less knowledge and experience'; Thomas Goldwell, the prior, 'a man of great simplicity and void of malice', had told only his superior, Archbishop Warham, but no one else.[122] Some, indeed, reacted firmly against the nun: the countess of Rutland condemned the nun's prophecies as 'one of the most abominablest matters that ever I heard of in my life'.[123]

How did Henry respond? It is revealing of his caution that he did not act against her immediately after she had shown him her prophecies, and of his cynicism that—if Barton is to be believed—he attempted to buy her off by offering to make her an abbess, which she refused, to his great displeasure.[124] Barton's first political visions dated back to a time when Wolsey was still in office, but it would not be till summer 1533 that the king began to take action against her. Did Henry feel it prudent to wait until one of the nun's prophecies—that if he married Anne, he should not be king a month after—had disproved itself before he struck? Was Henry at first wary, fearing that any move against Barton might simply provoke her to voice more damaging prophecies, and that she might inhibit churchmen whose support, or at least acquiescence, he needed from declaring themselves for the king over the divorce? Archbishop Cranmer, no less, thought that 'she did marvellously stop the going forward of the king's marriage by the reason of her visions'. She had seen both Wolsey and Warham in the matter, 'and [in] mine opinion, with her feigned visions and godly threatenings, she stayed them very much in the matter'.[125] According to the sermon denouncing the nun, Wolsey had been

as well minded and bent to go forth in the king's grace said cause of matrimony and divorce as any man living, according to the law of god and the law of nature, till he was perverted by this nun—and induced to believe that if he proceeded in the same God would sore strike him.[126]

According to the attainder denouncing the nun, she had revealed her visions to Warham who 'was allured brought and seduced to a credit therein'.[127] In short, as the sermon put it, 'under this manner, by false visions and revelations of the nun, hath grown the great sticking, staying and delaying' of the king's marriage: 'the malice of certain persons devised and found out a way and mean to stop it by false miracles, false visions and revelations'.[128] There is little further in support of these accusations against Barton—or tributes to her influence over the most powerful churchmen of her age—and it was useful for the government to present her as a political threat, but it is interesting that Henry should have been willing to hear public reference to the reticence of both Wolsey and Warham over his divorce: maybe there was indeed something in it.

But by the summer of 1533, Cranmer had succeeded Warham as archbishop of Canterbury, Henry had married Anne Boleyn, a child was on the way—and the nun's political prophecies had come to naught. The king was thus in a stronger position to act. But perhaps Barton's revised prophecies were more threatening still. Once the king had survived the first month of his new marriage, the nun had reinterpreted her revelation as meaning that the king was not king in the sight of God.[129] That approached treason, and could be seen as justifying any attempts to depose Henry, since if he were not king in God's eyes, then his subjects would be absolved from their duty of obedience and would be entitled to overthrow him. Once under interrogation, several monks and priests—Henry Gold, Hugh Rich, Richard Risby, John Dering, Richard Master—would admit that if she had sent them word that it was God's pleasure, then they would have preached to the people that the king was no king before God. It seems, however, that the nun had not—or not yet—given them any such instructions.[130] But that would not have been an unreasonable fear for the king to have. Moreover, Barton might have been expected to go on to voice further, and more defiant, prophecies.

And so in July 1533 Henry ordered Cromwell to press Cranmer to inquire into the demeanour of the hypocritical nun.[131] Barton then privately confessed 'many mad follies' to Cranmer.[132] In September Cromwell sent Christopher Hales, attorney-general, to investigate further, a sign of the seriousness with which the government was treating the matter. Hales had apprehended Dr Bocking, the nun's mentor, together with Mr Hadley, one of the penitentiaries of Christ Church (who had been sent with Bocking to Barton in the beginning—but nothing incriminating was found in his chamber).[133] Bocking was sent to the Tower at the king's command—he was more worthy of punish-

ment than others who were destitute of learning, according to Hales[134]—
and his rooms searched for incriminating writings: letters from Henry
Man of the Charterhouse at Sheen praising the nun were evidently
found. Richard Master, parson of Aldington, in whose parish the chapel
of Court at Street stood, would also shortly be arrested.[135] An anchorite
in Canterbury was interrogated.[136] Cromwell's remembrances—notes he
regularly made of things to do—show how rapidly matters were now
moving. 'The monk Dering to be sent for'; 'The other monks of
Christchurch to be sent for also with diligence, and to know the king's
pleasure'; 'The monk of St Augustine's to be sent for who wrote the
letter that was imagined to come from heaven', Cromwell noted in reference to the letter Barton supposedly received from Mary Magadalene
but which was allegedly written by a monk named Hawkhurst. 'To
move the king touching Thwaytes' (the editor of the book of the nun's
miracles); 'To make the allegations which Mr Solicitor hath showed me
touching the nun's book, and what are the opinions of the judges
therein'; 'To know the king's pleasure whether all which have been privy
to the nun's book shall be sent for.'[137] A little later Cromwell noted
down: 'to declare the names of all the offenders accused with the nun';
'The king's pleasure for sending the nun to Canterbury, and whether she
shall return.'[138] Under interrogation, Friar Risby confessed (though we
do not know exactly what).[139]

In mid-November the government was ready to take decisive action.
On 12 November Chapuys reported the arrest of Barton and several
friars and others associated with her.[140] A week later, Chapuys reported
how Henry called a meeting of not just his ordinary council but also
the principal judges of the kingdom, a good many bishops and a large
number of the nobility, who met from morning to evening for three days
running to advise on the crimes—or, Chapuys corrected himself,
the foolish superstition—of the nun and her adherents.[141] On 23
November she was placed on the high scaffold before St Paul's Cathedral, together with the Observant Franciscans Hugh Rich and Richard
Risby, the Canterbury monks Edward Bocking and John Dering,
Richard Master, the parson of Aldington, and Henry Gold, the parson
of Aldermary, London, Gold's brother Thomas, and John Laurence of
Canterbury, the archdeacon's scribe who had copied out Bocking's book
of the nun's miracles. A fierce sermon of denunciation was preached by
John Salcot (or Capon), abbot of Hyde, bishop-elect of Bangor,[142] and
the text was repeated by Nicholas Heath (later archbishop of York) at
Canterbury on 7 December.[143] Barton and the others did open
penance.[144]

What was remarkable in all this is that Barton apparently admitted that everything she had done had been feigned. An extant slip of paper appears to constitute a form of confession in which Barton acknowledges herself as 'the original' (the cause) of all this 'mischief', and that by 'my falsehood' she had deceived all those persons then present with her (most probably at the reading of the sermon denouncing her) and many more.[145] Put under pressure, Barton said that all that had been alleged against her was true, that she had committed treason against God and the king[146] and, eventually, that her visions were feigned. Cranmer reported her admission 'that she never had vision in all her life, but all that ever she said was feigned of her own imagination, only to satisfy the minds of them the which resorted unto her, and to obtain worldly praise'.[147] Such also was the drift of the scaffold speech that Edward Hall put into her mouth. Acknowledging that she was 'the only cause' of her death, yet, she continued, she was not so much to be blamed, considering that the learned men who were to be executed with her knew that she was 'a poor wench without learning', and that it was

> because the things which I feigned was profitable unto them, therefore they much praised me and bare me in hand that it was the holy ghost and not I that did therein, and then I being puffed up with their praises fell into a certain pride and foolish fantasy with my self and thought I might feign what I would.[148]

In the sermon Barton was denounced as a fraud. Barton had recovered her health *before* her supposedly miraculous cure at Court at Street. She had knelt before the image of Our Lady of Court at Street 'and said then she was made perfectly whole'. But, the sermon insisted, 'she was perfectly whole *before* she came thither'. The clinching point came next: 'as she hath plainly and openly confessed before divers of the king's grace council, and before the most part of the lords of this realm, by her confession subscribed with her own hand'.[149] Moreover, 'that all her revelations contained in the said great book [of her miracles] be falsely imagined, feigned and contrived without any ground of truth', the sermon declaimed, 'ye shall understand that she her self, examined by divers of the king's grace council, without fear or compulsion, hath confessed that she had never in her whole life any revelation from God, but that they were of her own feigning'.[150] That confession then allowed the government to present the whole business as a 'false, forged and feigned matter'.[151] Examples were offered. The sermon claimed that she used 'a paper full of brimstone, arcefetida, and other stinking gums and powders', found in the bedstraw of her cell at St Sepulchre's, with which she was 'wont to make great stinking smokes . . . that savoured griev-ously through out all the dorter [dormitory] at such times as she feigned the devil to have been with her in her cell', once inviting one of her 'simple sisters' into her cell, showing her the rising smoke and saying that the devil would soon appear.[152] That Barton had feigned that Mary Magdalene had written a letter in heaven in Barton's name was demon-strated by the confession by a monk of St Augustine's, Canterbury, that he had written it.[153] In short, the government could present Barton's works as a conspiracy contrived to endanger the king and to damage his reputation in time to come, 'as though his grace had been the most wicked and detestable prince that ever reigned in this world hitherto' and had put the realm in 'continual strife, dissension war and mutual effusion of blood'.[154] It is striking that the government should have found it so important to insist that all the nun had done had, by her own admission, been a fraud: that testifies to the seriousness with which a holy maid's visions were still treated.

But did Barton willingly confess? Clearly, she and her friends were under a good deal of pressure. When she admitted that all her visions had been feigned, she was saying what the government wanted her to say. But that she did not mean it is suggested by a rather awkward passage in the sermon denouncing her. Having made much of the nun's deceit, towards the end the preacher highlighted 'what corrupted mind the said nun continued after the making of her said confession, notwith-standing her great semblance ['pretence' was inserted above the line] of repentance and penance . . . a right crafty point of this false nun'.[155] Further, after she had confessed to the king's council that 'she never had revelation from God', she fortuned to speak with Thomas Gold and showed him that she had confessed 'by reason of a vision and revela-tion, which she feigned her self to have had in the Tower, in which God willed her by his heavenly messenger that she should say that she never had revelation from God'. And now, the preacher continued, Barton 'hath confessed this last revelation to be counterfeited by her own subtle and false imagination'.[156] The attainder echoed the sermon: though at one point she told Thomas Gold that God had willed her in a revela-tion to say that she had never had any divine revelation,[157] she then admitted that that revelation was feigned too. And Gold 'by his message hath comforted diverse others to stand stiffly by her revelations that they were of God, notwithstanding that she had confessed all her said falsehood before divers of the king's counsellors, and that they were manifestly proved found and tried most false and untrue'.[158] Here we enter into a world of infinite regression. What is plain is that Barton's confession should not be taken at face value: it would be wrong to think that she voluntarily and genuinely repudiated her visions and prophecies. At one point she said 'how the angel of God that commanded her to say that all are but illusions, for the time is not come that God will put forth the work'.[159]

In her confession, Barton had claimed that Dr Edward Bocking had influenced her. The government, of course, suspected a conspiracy. It was Bocking, it was claimed, who had suggested to Barton that she should petition God whether he was displeased with Henry for proceeding in the divorce, telling her that he and many other notable learned men, as well as many of the common people, firmly believed that the divorce was against God's laws.[160] According to the sermon, Bocking had asked Barton to petition God after she had heard him 'rail and gesture like a frantic person' against the king's intended marriage.[161] It was Bocking who had counselled the nun to reinterpret her revelation that the king was not king in the eyes of God.[162] Barton allegedly confessed that Bocking daily told her details from St Bridget's and St Catherine of Siena's revelations to help her 'make up her fantasies and counterfeit visions', and berated her whenever she did not show him anything new.[163] It is obviously possible that Bocking was manipulating Barton all the time. But it need not have been so one-sided a relationship. Bocking may have 'counselled and steered' Barton.[164] But, despite Barton's self-presentation at her execution as (if Hall is to be believed) 'a poor wench without learning',[165] nothing that Barton said was so complex or so sophisticated that she could not have thought of it for herself. In the attainder, Bocking's steering of Barton is attributed to the 'procurement and secret conspiracy of diverse persons unknown' who criticised the king's divorce,[166] which is suggestive of a government bent on denouncing a plot for which it had little hard evidence. And the government's belief in Bocking's instigations is perhaps further discredited by claims in the sermon that Bocking and Barton enjoyed a sexual relationship. The preacher insinuated that 'she came with the said Bocking's servants to Canterbury in an evening; and Doctor Bocking brought her to the said priory of Saint Sepulchres in the morning'.[167] By feigning that she was so often vexed by the devil, she frightened her sisters from stirring at night, with the result that she might go out without being seen— 'without controllment of any of them'—which she did two or three hours a week: 'and it is supposed that then she went not about the saying of her Pater Noster', the preacher added.[168] The attainder developed the charge: Barton had become a nun in the priory of St Sepulchre's, where Bocking 'had commonly his resort, not without probable, vehement and violent suspicion of incontinency'; Bocking moreover urged her to say 'that she was much provoked and tempted as well to the sin of the flesh as otherwise by her ghostly enemy the Devil, at diverse and sundry times and in diverse and sundry ways and fashions, and yet nevertheless that she by the grace of God was preserved and steadfastly resisted such temptations'; 'her stealing forth of the dortor [dormitory] in the night (which was once or twice weekly) was not for spiritual business nor to receive revelations of God, but rather for bodily communication and pleasure with her friends, which could not have so good leisure and opportunity with her by day'.[169] It was when 'subtly and craftily conceiving the opinion and mind of the said Edward [Bocking]' that the nun, 'willing to please him', revealed that she knew by divine revelation that God was displeased with the king over the divorce.[170] Again, all this is not outside the bounds of possibility; but given the extent of public interest in Barton, it would have been highly risky. Once she was under suspicion, if she had really been behaving like this, it might have been expected that someone would have been found to denounce and testify against her in detail. The charge therefore remains implausible.

Nonetheless, by mid-December Henry might have felt that he had publicly discredited the nun, denouncing her as a fraud with her apparent acquiescence. But that was not sufficient for the king. He saw her behaviour as treason. Earlier Chapuys had reported how vehemently the king had insisted 'a plus non pouvoir' that the accomplices of the nun be declared heretics for having believed her and that they were guilty of high treason for not having revealed what concerned the king. Yet so far, Chapuys noted, the judges refused to agree, since there was no proof, or even appearance, of complicity, for more than a year ago the nun had told the king to his face.[171] A little later Chapuys reported that Henry had still not succeeded in his attempt to make the judges declare those who had any dealings with the nun guilty of high treason. The most learned and impartial judges had declared that they would die rather than deal with the accused in that way. Yet Chapuys feared that if the king came to argue the case in person no one would dare contradict him—unless he wished to be treated as mad or as disloyal.[172]

But evidently the king did not get his way. Unable to take action through the law courts, the government instead staged the dramatic public condemnation of the nun and her accomplices in the sermon preached at Paul's Cross and in Canterbury. But clearly there was

hesitation over what should be done next. Cromwell's memoranda calendared under January 1534 include a note 'to know what the king will
have done with the nun and her accomplices'.[173] What *was* done next
was to employ the procedure of parliamentary attainder against them
in the session that began in mid-January. That act declared that Barton
and her named accomplices were guilty of treason—and by doing so
avoided the complexities of a trial conducted according to common law,
in which it is not at all sure that they would have been found guilty.
Barton and those closely associated with her—Edward Bocking, John
Dering, Richard Master, Henry Gold, Hugh Rich and Richard Risby—
were attainted of treason. On 20 April 1534 Barton and all the others
except Master were drawn on a hurdle from the Tower to Tyburn and
there hanged and beheaded, and their heads set on London Bridge or
gates of the city.[174] Interestingly, Master was granted a stay of execution and pardoned, with restitution of his goods and possessions.[175]
Richard Rex speculates, from the fact that the executions coincided with
the swearing of the citizens of London to the oath of succession in April
1534, and from a garbled later account by an exiled Franciscan, that
Rich and Risby were offered a similar deal, that Master may have saved
his life by swearing the oath, and that in a sense some, at least, of those
executed died less owing to the act of attainder than to their refusal of
the oath.[176] It is hard, nonetheless, not to see the king as bent on
vengeance against the nun whose prophecies had embarrassed him; but
clearly one of the aims of these procedures was to secure the compliance and acquiescence in the king's policies of those who, in large ways
and small, had been caught up with her. That was especially the case
with those who were attainted of misprision of treason—the lesser
offence, punishable by imprisonment at the king's will and by confiscation of goods, committed by those who concealed the offences of the
nun and her friends. Thomas Gold, Thomas Lawrence and Edward
Thwaites (who had been involved in the compilation of the original
book of the nun's miracles) were duly so attainted. Thwaites was pardoned on payment of 1,000 marks.[177] Henry Gold wrote an abject letter
asking for compassion for his brother Thomas.[178] Evidently there was
official consideration of whether William Hawkhurst, the Canterbury
monk who confessed to writing a letter that the nun had claimed to be
written by Mary Magdalene, should be included.[179] More interestingly
still, Thomas Abel, the staunch defender of Catherine of Aragon in
several books, was attainted of misprision of treason and placed in the
Tower. And—as we shall consider further later—the government wanted
to have both Bishop Fisher (together with his chaplain Adison) and Sir

Thomas More declared guilty of misprision of treason for their contacts
with the nun: Fisher and his chaplain were duly attainted, but More
succeeded in convincing the king that he had not shown Barton any
support, and was discharged.[180]

Was Henry right to take such drastic action against the nun and
against those involved with her? How far was she an opponent of the
king and a threat to his divorce and then his break with Rome? What
is crucial is to determine the frame of mind in which she received her
revelations and in which those who were willing to hear them listened.
The act of attainder condemning her began by reciting the circumstances
of the king's 'divorce and separation lawfully had and done'. The statute
aimed to punish those who, 'maliciously and maligning against the
same', traitorously attempted 'many notable acts', with the intention of
disturbing the peace and tranquillity of the realm. 'Divers and sundry
wilful and inobedient' people, 'being maliciously fixed in a contrary
opinion against the pure judgement of the king's own conscience, and
also the determinations of the said sundry universities and well learned
men' over the king's divorce, saw clearly that 'they being but a few in
number' could not prevent it 'by any lawful means'—one wonders what
those might have been—and therefore 'by false feigned hypocrisy dis-
simulated sanctity and cloaked holiness' let many know that they had
'knowledge by revelation from Almighty God and holy saints that God
should be displeased with our said Sovereign Lord, for his said proceedings in the said divorce and separation of the said detested and
unlawful marriage'.[181] On such an account, Barton was the instrument
of those who refused to accept the king's divorce. Ethan Shagan has
echoed such sentiments, transposing the propaganda of Henry VIII's
government into the language of present-day politicking.[182] Rightly
noting that Barton's reputation for holiness was already well established
and 'wholly apolitical', he goes on to say that she 'found herself in a
unique position' to challenge Henry's authority. She claimed 'to speak
for a higher power' and 'she also had in position a network of well-
placed supporters already experienced in publicising her miracles both
in print and by word-of-mouth'. Religious conservatives, 'by hitching
themselves to Barton's immaculate reputation for holiness, and by defin-
ing their positions around a commonly circulating pool of Barton
prophecies . . . could begin to construct a rationale for legitimate
dissent'.[183] But that is to take too instrumental a view. In these pages
Barton has emerged not as a tool of manipulative politicians leading an
active and organised opposition to the king, but rather as a woman
whose devotions and revelations struck a chord in her locality. Her

prophecy that if he married Anne Boleyn, Henry would not be king a month later, which she told the king to his face, was a warning set in the tradition of frank counsel to monarchs, rather than (as the attainder claimed) a clarion call to political conspiracy and then to rebellion and deposition. Describing her actions as 'a story . . . of resistance to the Reformation'[184] risks slipping into exaggeration and anachronism, and offers too monochrome and simple an account of her life: it is to swallow whole Henry VIII's propaganda.[185] The nun's actions and contacts were striking, but they were too haphazard, too intermittent and too limited to serve as evidence of extensive and planned political campaigning, of 'a network of well-placed supporters'. What she offered to those who heard her revelations was not 'a rationale for legitimate dissent', but rather consolation that they were not alone in their dismay at the king's actions, and the hope that, through the mysterious workings of God's providence, things would yet turn out for the best. Friar Risby,[186] the warden of the Canterbury Observants, told the prior of Canterbury Cathedral that she was a person much in the favour of God and that what she said gave him 'great comfort'.[187] This amounts to spiritual consolation for the powerless. But it was no platform for political action. Henry, then, brutally overreacted in as much as he treated the nun and her friends as if they were rebels actively engaged in treason against him, as if they were so dangerously and immediately threatening that any methods, such as the use of parliamentary attainder, however doubtful in law, were reasonable in the circumstances. And yet the nun's prophecies, uttered with the authority of one who was the centre of a new and flourishing popular cult of healing, had the potential to turn into something more. A holy maid who had had revelations that the king was not king in the eyes of God could not but be seen by Henry as unsettling and troubling. That he went to such lengths to discredit and to destroy her—not least by his demand that all books and scrolls relating to her were to be handed in within forty days, a measure intended to obliterate her memory[188]—suggests the depth of his concern.

A further detail hints at the king's fears. A denunciation of Bocking and the nun, too briefly summarised in *Letters and Papers*, and therefore overlooked by scholars, offers variant versions of the charges to be found in the sermon and in the act of attainder. But one point did not appear there, perhaps because it was too disquieting for the king. The nun had allegedly petitioned God to know 'what fearful war should come whether men should take my lady Mary's part or no'. Repeating that was to venture into dangerous territory. What God in revelation allegedly told her was that 'no man should fear but she should have succour and help enough that no man should put her from her right that she was born unto'. Very understandably this provoked the comment: 'to what other intent was this devised and written but to set the king's grace people against him and the queen, and to comfort my lady Mary and her friends to rebel or make battle against the king's grace upon trust of good success according to the said revelation?' That was to turn a prophecy into a call for rebellion.[189]

Bishop John Fisher

Of all the bishops of the English church, only John Fisher (1469–1535), bishop of Rochester, firmly refused to go along with the divorce and with the ensuing break with Rome. Little in his life before the late 1520s would have suggested a dissident in the making. A son of a Beverley merchant, he had enjoyed a remarkable academic career at the university of Cambridge: fellow of Michaelhouse from 1491, master of Michaelhouse 1496/7 to 1498, chancellor of the university in 1504 (and again for life from 1514), and (an admittedly not very active) president of Queens' College from 1505 to 1509. The crucial event in his life was when he became a chaplain and confessor to Lady Margaret Beaufort, mother of Henry VII, in about 1498 (though, as usual, we know little about the circumstances, and certainly not from precisely contemporary sources). His commitment to Cambridge and to Lady Margaret fused in his considerable involvement in the refoundation of Christ's College and St John's College, both largely endowed by Lady Margaret 'by his procurement and solicitation'.[190] He also persuaded Lady Margaret to found lectures in divinity both in Cambridge and in Oxford.[191] Royal favour was reflected in his appointment as bishop of Rochester in 1504: the king 'of his own mere motion, inspired by the holy Ghost' named Fisher, whom he greatly revered on account of 'the pure devotion, perfect sanctity and great learning he saw in him', so his biographer claimed.[192] Just how close he was to both king and queen mother is shown by his appointment to preach the sermons at their funerals— which came within weeks of each other in 1509. So far, then, so conventional, if successful beyond the norm: a career rooted in academic ability and royal patronage.

In two ways, however, Fisher was unusual. First, unlike many a career bishop, he maintained his scholarly, not just his university, interests. In 1517 he set out to learn Greek; he also dabbled in Hebrew, probably receiving lessons from his protégé Robert Wakefield between 1515 and

1519.[193] He encouraged Erasmus in his labours in translating the Bible, and drew on Erasmus's Greek text in his polemical writings.

Secondly, this scholar–bishop refused greater preferment (to Lincoln in 1514 or 1521, and to Ely in 1515)[194] and became instead a model diocesan bishop. Ascetic, deeply committed to his pastoral duties, he ordained priests in person—though he was no reformer and did not demonstrate the administrative dynamism of a bishop such as Sherburne of Chichester.[195]

Fisher never became a prominent royal counsellor: he was no Wolsey, no Richard Foxe. In Henry VII's reign, he continued to attend Lady Margaret as confessor and chaplain; in Henry VIII's, he took part in various state occasions (for example, the Field of Cloth of Gold in 1520) and offered hospitality in his diocese to important visitors to the realm such as Cardinal Campeggio in 1518 or Emperor Charles V (in company with Henry VIII) in 1522, but he never became involved daily in the minutiae of government business, either in the later years of Henry VII's reign or in the reign of Henry VIII. 'When did he frequent the courts and houses of princes and noble men to the intent (as the old proverb says) to see and be seen?' as his early biographer rhetorically asked.[196] In synod in 1519 Fisher attacked the distractions such service entailed:[197]

> For sundry times when I have settled and fully bent my self to the care of my flock committed unto me, to visit my diocese, to govern my church and to answer the enemies of Christ, straight ways, hath come a messenger for one cause or other sent from higher authority by whom I have been called to other business and so left of my former purpose. And thus by tossing and going this way and that way, time hath passed and in the mean while nothing done but attending after triumphs, receiving of ambassadors, haunting of princes' courts and such like.

But in one respect he did play a national, public role, and that was in preaching against Luther. In sermons at Paul's Cross in 1521 and 1526 he unsparingly denounced Luther's heresies. His sermons were afterwards put in print; and he also wrote polemical treatises against the new heretics.[198] Fisher, then, was a man of firm theological convictions, prepared to be combative; personally ascetic, unworldly and devout; a bishop who owed his preferment not to Henry VIII but to the king's father and grandmother, twenty years earlier. Not surprisingly Henry VIII sought his support as soon as he called his marriage to Catherine of Aragon into question. The endorsement of a churchman of Fisher's stature would lend weight to the king's cause.

How did Fisher respond? Maybe he did at first accept the force of the king's scruples. That, at least, is the impression that Wolsey, who went to see him at Rochester in early July 1527, gave in his report to Henry of their conversation. Of course, at this point even Wolsey may have taken the king's concern at face value; and Fisher may understandably have thought that what the king sought was balm for a conscience troubled by the growing realisation that he had made an improper marriage. If Fisher expected that the matter would be readily resolved by a fresh dispensation, then he might well have thought that Catherine was simply indulging in flights of fancy when she said she feared that the king would divorce her.[199]

That is also the impression left by the account given by Fisher's early biographer, though not easily datable. Henry summoned Fisher, walked with him in the Long Gallery at Westminster, flattered him, 'upon special confidence in his great learning, he had now made choice of him to use his advice above all others'. Then the king told him about how 'his conscience was tormented' and asked him freely to declare his opinion. Fisher fell on his knees; the king lifted him up with his own hands. And in response, Fisher offered to take on his own conscience all the danger that the king might be in by continuing his marriage.[200] That, of course, was not quite what the king wanted to hear.

But before long—and perhaps even at the time of this encounter—Fisher concluded that Henry's conscience had no cause to be uneasy and that his case for an annulment did not hold water. After some reflection, on finding the authorities differing greatly among themselves, Fisher decided that the issue turned on the fullness of the authority given by Christ to the popes as his successors, not least their power to resolve ambiguous passages of scripture, very much the point at issue here. He could not see any sound reason to show that it was prohibited by divine law for a man to marry the widow of his brother who had died without children. He now firmly declared that the dispensation that had permitted the king's marriage had been fully within the pope's power to grant.[201] Soon Fisher was moving on from disagreement on the fine points of the canon law of marriage to at least implicit criticism of Henry:[202]

for kings usually think that they are permitted to do whatever pleases them, because of the magnitude of their power. Therefore it is good for these kings, in my opinion, to submit themselves to the decrees of the church, and this is beyond doubt to be praised in them, lest otherwise they kick over the traces and do what they please, as long as they can weave together some appearance and colour of right.

Had Fisher discovered, to his dismay, that what the king sought was not reassurance that his marriage was allowed by God, but rather an annulment so that he could marry someone else? Was Fisher's reaction the more vehement because he felt that he had, at first, been misled as to the king's true intentions?

Did Fisher have contacts with Catherine? At the very beginning, he admitted to Wolsey that he had received a message from her by word of mouth: she had asked his counsel; he had replied he would do nothing without the king's commandment. Nonetheless, that hints at some prior understanding and relationship.[203] Fisher soon became Catherine's staunchest advocate. That he was seen as having a special relationship with the queen was vividly demonstrated in autumn 1528. One plan then afoot was for Catherine to enter a nunnery, thus relieving Henry from his marital vows. On arriving in England, Cardinal Campeggio explored this possible solution to the king's great matter. Significantly, it was with Fisher that Campeggio had a long interview, trying to get him to help persuade the queen to agree.[204]

But not only did Fisher now refuse to assist the king, he began to write refuting the king's arguments. Presumably it was at this time that he wrote the book on the divorce which Robert Wakefield answered.[205] Fisher was becoming known as a critic of the king's position: Giovanni Stafileo, a French scholar who had written on the impediment of public honesty, and whom Wolsey had invited to England, went to argue with the bishop at Rochester.[206] In November 1528 the French ambassador noted Fisher as of the queen's opinion.[207]

It was at the legatine trial in June 1529 that Fisher made his rejection of the king's case dramatically public. Since the king was pursuing his case in the ecclesiastical courts, due procedure demanded that the queen's interests be protected, yet Fisher's position as counsel for Catherine did not have to turn into open opposition to the king. But it did.

Fisher declared that 'hoc matrimonium regis et reginae nulla potestate humana vel divina potest dissolvi, pro qua sententia asseruit etiam se animam positurum' (no power, human or divine, could dissolve this marriage, an opinion for which he would lay down his life) adding that the Baptist in olden times regarded it as impossible to die more glor-

iously than in the cause of marriage. In support of this claim he produced a book, the fruit of two years' most diligent study of the matter.[208]
Did later accounts perhaps dramatise his stand, and present it as more
hostile to the king and more unexpected than it really was? If so,
Campeggio, one of the joint legates, was nonetheless surprised by the
force of Fisher's objection.[209] According to Cavendish, when Archbishop
Warham acknowledged that, as the king declared, all the bishops had
signed and sealed the licence requiring testing of the king's matter, Fisher
interjected: 'No, my lord, not so; under your favour, all the bishops were
not so far agreed, for to that instrument you have neither my hand nor
seal.' When Warham maintained that Fisher's seal was indeed attached
to it, the bishop countered that

> indeed you were often in hand with me for my hand and my seal, as
> other of my lords have done; but then I ever said to you, I would in
> no wise consent to any such act, for it was much against my con-
> science to have this matter so much as once called into question; and
> therefore my hand and seal should never be put to any such instru-
> ment, God willing.

'Indeed,' Warham replied, 'true it is that such words you had with me;
but after our talk ended, you were at last resolved and content that I
should subscribe your name and put to your seal, and you would allow
the same as if it had been done by your self.' Fisher, stung by 'seeing
himself so unjustly charged', retorted, 'No, no, my lord, by your favour
and licence, all this you have said of me is untrue', and wanted to say
more. But Henry stopped him, saying, 'We will not stand with you in
argument about this business, for *you are but one man among the rest,*
if the worst fall.'[210]

Fisher, as the queen's counsel, 'stood stiff in her cause';[211] though if
Catherine frequently sent a servant to him,[212] she also complained, in
June 1531, that he had done no more than to tell her to keep up her
courage.[213] Fisher returned to his studies of the canon law, and over the
next few years wrote and published several books—in 1535 he would
admit to having written seven or eight—in defence of the queen's marriage.[214] The matter was so serious, he said, that he devoted more attention to examining the truth of it than to anything else in his life.[215] He
was clearly busily writing in 1530[216] and in 1531 when he responded
to what was described as the book printed by the king, possibly *A Glass
of the Truth* or the *Determination of the Universities.*[217] He used
Chapuys, the imperial ambassador, to send his texts to the emperor to

arrange for them to be put in print.[218] One book was first drafted by him and then sent to two Spaniards in England who redrafted it: it was printed in Antwerp in August 1533.[219] He may have shown them to Queen Catherine.[220] He sent a copy of one of his books to John Fewterer, confessor-general, and Richard Reynolds, one of the monks, at Syon Abbey (and also showed them copies of a letter he had written to the king, and the king's answer).[221] He corresponded with Archbishop Warham and Bishops Clerk and Sherburne over the divorce.[222] How effective were his books? Were they, as Elton claimed, simply repetitious? But did that matter, even if true? Fisher no doubt continued to hope that the king would come to his senses and Henry was therefore an intended reader. Fisher also wrote to stiffen the pope and the officials of the papal curia in upholding Queen Catherine's marriage. Yet Fisher denied writing in order to persuade Archbishop Warham—he wrote to show the depth of his own conviction: 'I did not so write in order to change his opinion but that he might refrain from urging me to assent to anything against my conscience.'[223]

In December 1530 Archbishop Warham summoned him to his house, and there, with Bishop Stokesley of London and two of the king's principal advisers on the divorce, Edward Lee and Edward Foxe, both future bishops, pleaded with him to retract his writings on behalf of the queen and to take the king's side, calling him self-willed and obstinate.[224] Fisher later denied having sent his books, or having agreed to their despatch, abroad: but that denial is unconvincing.[225]

Fisher's opposition was not confined to the king's divorce. In autumn 1529 he spoke out in parliament against anticlerical legislation. How he behaved then foreshadows his later actions. He was determined, but also extravagant in his language and analogies; he was quick to attribute evil motives, making little attempt to win over waverers or to conciliate. Such political tactlessness itself calls into question claims such as those of Dickens that he was a 'devoted organiser of opposition'.[226]

It was a bill on the probate of wills that especially irked him. 'You see daily what bills come hither from the common house and all is to the destruction of the church': the church 'shall now . . . be brought into servile thralldom', he openly declared in the House of Lords.[227] He went on to make a provocative comparison with the mood in the Commons and the Hussite heretics in Bohemia: 'Now with the Commons is nothing but down with the church, and all this me seemeth is for lack of faith only';[228] 'For God's sake see what a realm the kingdom of

Bohemia was, and when the church went down, then fell the glory of the kingdom,' he warned. And he implied that the Commons were driven by greed for the wealth of the church: 'They . . . hunger and thirst after the riches and possessions of the clergy.'[229] Not surprisingly, the Commons hit back, sending a 'grievous complaint' through their speaker, Sir Thomas Audley. Henry was 'not well contented' with Fisher, and called on senior bishops, including Fisher, to see him. Here the sources diverge. Fisher's early biographer has Fisher holding his ground. 'Being in council he spoke his mind in defence and right of the church, whom he saw daily injured and oppressed among the common people, whose office was not to deal with her, and therefore said that he thought himself in conscience bound to defend her, all that he might.' Henry 'willed him nevertheless to use his words temperately . . . and so the matter ended much to the discontentation of Mr Audley and diverse others of the Common House'.[230] But Hall offers a less flattering portrait. On his account, the bishop claimed that when he spoke of things done for lack of faith, what he had in mind was the doings of the Bohemians, not those of the Commons, a somewhat weaselly 'blind excuse', that, Hall tells us, did not please the Commons.[231] Was Fisher a principled opponent of the king, ready and able to face him down? Or was he easily cowed by a storm of protest from the Commons into trying to talk his way out of trouble by a mealy-mouthed self-justification, rather than making a stand?

Possibly Fisher did succeed in 1529 in defeating a proposal to dissolve the smaller abbeys, those worth under £200 a year, and to use the revenues to meet the king's great charges over the divorce. It was a measure 'hardly urged' by many counsellors, 'with all the terrible show that might be of the king's displeasure, if it were not granted according to his request and demand'. Some members of convocation, fearing the king's indignation and cruelty and thinking that if they yielded on this point they would save the rest, wanted to agree, but Fisher 'openly resisted it with all the force he could'. He convinced them that the king would then demand the greater abbeys as well by retelling Phaedra's fable. An axe that lacked a handle came to a wood, and sighed to the tall trees that, since he lacked a handle, he had to sit idle; and he asked them to grant him some young sapling to make himself a handle; they granted him a young small tree, he shaped himself a handle, and made himself a perfect axe—and then fell to work, with the result that neither great nor small tree was left standing.[232] But there is no contemporary evidence that would corroborate any of this[233]—there is no other evidence that any such bill was proposed—though Wolsey was reproached in parliament in 1529 for having suppressed thirty smaller monasteries.

In the following year, Fisher, together with two other bishops, John Clerk of Bath and Wells and Richard West of Ely, may have gone on to appeal to the pope against the anticlerical legislation passed in 1529, complaining particularly against the act of pluralities, and it is possible that they were all briefly arrested.[234] In early 1532 Fisher sent word to Chapuys that, if they were to meet in public, the imperial ambassador should on no account talk to him and should not be offended if Fisher similarly ignored him: clearly he felt under pressure.[235] A little later he would ask Chapuys to make sure that anything he wrote to the emperor about him be put in cipher.[236]

Intensifying his campaign against the pope and the church, Henry, as we have seen, brought spurious charges of offences under the *praemunire* statute against fifteen churchmen and church officials in July 1530. Those named included Fisher. In January 1531 Fisher was active in resisting consequential royal demands that the church recognise the king as supreme head and pay £100,000 as a fine for its supposed offences in infringing the statute of *praemunire*. He urged that it was not the churchmen's fault that the king needed money, nor was there any just cause for which he should have spent a single penny.[237] The 'Early Life of Fisher', mistaken in supposing that it was the bishop's resistance to royal financial demands that led to charges of *praemunire* which in fact came before convocation met,[238] tells how Fisher then resisted the demand that the clergy acknowledge the king to be their supreme head, pressed by the king's orators, notably Audley, 'sometime by faire words and sometime by hard and cruel threatenings'.[239] In particular, seeing how ready some of the churchmen were to help forward the king's purpose, he 'opened before the bishops such and such and so many inconveniences by granting to this demand, that in conclusion all was rejected and the king's intent clean overthrown for that time'.[240] In response, Henry made threats; but also offered a promise 'in the word of a king' that if they acknowledged him as supreme head of the church, he would never assume any greater jurisdiction over them than any of his predecessors had done, nor would he take it upon himself to make any spiritual laws or to meddle in any spiritual business.[241] Once again it was Fisher who held out, never sparing 'to open and declare his mind freely in defence of the church, which many others durst not so frankly do for fear of the king's displeasure'. Henry's counsellors came again, accusing the churchmen of lacking trust in the king. That 'subtle and false persuasion' made the clergy 'somewhat to shrink and for the most part to yield to the king's request, saving this holy bishop who utterly refused to condescend thereunto', warning of the damage that would be done to the whole church 'by this unreasonable and unseemly grant, made to a temporal prince', never before demanded. The counsellors countered that it should be understood that the king 'can have no further power or authority by it then quantum per legem dei licet [than is allowed by the law of God]'. Moved by Fisher's arguments, however, the bishops did not consent; the counsellors left saying that whoever would not agree was not worthy of being counted a true and loving subject of the king.[242]

Yet knowing Henry 'to be all cruelly bent against the clergy', the bishops finally agreed to his demand. Fisher, seeing this hasty grant, 'only made for fear', 'stood up again all angry and rebuked them for their pusillanimity in being so lightly changed and easily persuaded'. Accordingly he seized on the king's promise. Henry 'by his own mouth' and in several speeches by his spokesmen had solemnly sworn that he required no more than what was permitted by the law of God, and that he had no intention to interfere in ecclesiastical jurisdiction and government any more than his predecessors had done. In that case, argued Fisher, if the bishops, against his wishes, were determined to grant the king what he was demanding, then they should at least include the conditional words 'quantum per legem dei licet'. The king's counsellors 'cried upon them with open and continual clamour' to have the grant pass absolutely, but could not prevail; the clergy insisted on the additional phrase, and the king, seeing no remedy, accepted it.[243] The early biographer's account is a unique source for these discussions. It reads very plausibly as an account of the dynamics of a committee under unpleasant pressures from a powerful external force, with Fisher emerging as a crucial opponent of the king, with the skill and authority to rally his fellow bishops, to seize the maximum polemical advantage from tactical concessions by Henry's counsellors.[244]

Chapuys offers a less triumphant account, and in his subsequent despatches treated the outcome of these discussions as a heavy defeat for the church. He reported how Fisher had opposed as much as he could, but after being threatened that he and his friends would be thrown in the river, he had been forced to agree to the king's will. Anne Boleyn's father had told him afterwards that he could prove by the authority of scripture that when Jesus left this world he left no successor or vicar—which, Chapuys said, had made Fisher quite ill.[245]

Was Fisher the target of intimidation? There were two curious incidents around this time. In February 1531 one of Fisher's household gentlemen and a poor woman who had come for alms died after eating porridge; many others were taken seriously ill. Fisher, however, did not touch the porridge and was unharmed. His cook, Richard Roose, admitted that, for a joke, he had put laxatives in the food. Was his action more sinister than that? Had someone persuaded him to put poison into it? Or did a stranger who visited him put the poison in while Roose went out briefly into the buttery? And if it was more than a prank that went disastrously wrong, was Fisher its intended victim? Accounts also differ as to how the bishop escaped. On one account, he simply was not hungry that day and delayed eating his meal; on another, he was saved by his charitable practice, since he 'never dined before the pore people were serv[ed]': on that occasion they played the fatal role of food tasters. In response, an act was passed by parliament, at the king's instigation, making murder by poison treason and the punishment boiling alive: Richard Roose, declared guilty in the act, was duly boiled alive at Smithfield. Yet just what happened and why remains unclear. An accident devoid of any malicious purposes remains thinkable. So does the possibility that this was a deliberate attempt, perhaps by the king, perhaps by Anne Boleyn's father, the earl of Wiltshire, or brother, to murder—or perhaps to frighten into silence—the defiant bishop of Rochester, as Chapuys mused.[246] The king's extraordinary reaction—making murder by poison treason punishable by boiling alive, employing an act of attainder that simply declared Roose guilty without recourse to the law courts—reflects not so much a royal concern to restrict benefit of clergy,[247] since boiling alive was a penalty wholly out of proportion to any such jurisdictional reforms, but rather hints at an uneasy conscience and an anxiety to deflect responsibility.

At much the same time, the early biographer tells us, without warning gunshot was fired through the top of Fisher's house not far from the study in which he was accustomed to sit, making a horrible noise and bruising the tiles and rafters. It came from the earl of Wiltshire's house on the opposite side of the Thames. Fisher, we are told, 'then . . . perceived that great malice was meant towards him' and resolved to leave London for Rochester.[248] The 'Early Life', once more, is a unique source. It is not at all unthinkable that the earl of Wiltshire or one of his servants should have wished to intimidate Fisher at this time. Interestingly, Fisher's early biographer suggests that the king may have been indirectly responsible. 'Sure it is that the king at that time ought him his hearty displeasure, and spoke such and so many dangerous words of him, both at his table and elsewhere, that others, hearing the same, were the more emboldened to use violence and injury towards him.' That is how terror spreads: an angry king, ranting, in effect encourages his servants to think that they will be rewarded if they turn his 'dangerous words' into intimidatory, even fatal, acts.[249]

In the period between spring 1529 and early 1531, Fisher had publicly opposed the king over the divorce, defended the interests of the church against parliamentary criticism and rallied churchmen to resist, up to a point, the demand Henry and his counsellors were making that the church recognise the king as its supreme head. Fisher had, in consequence, faced pressures from his fellow bishops (especially Archbishop Warham), legal proceedings and, possibly, poisoning and shooting. Yet it is important to note that Fisher's actions had been essentially reactive. He would not agree to the king's divorce, and wrote and had printed books explaining why. He spoke out in parliament and in convocation when measures he feared would damage the church were proposed. But that did not make him a politician or campaigner in a larger sense. He never seems to have taken a political initiative that might have drawn in large numbers of supporters. His tracts against the king's divorce were all written in Latin. He may have sent an appeal to the pope over anticlerical legislation but he did not publicise it. He made no attempt to turn his opposition to a royal supremacy into a cry of 'the church in danger'. Perhaps he felt any such action would be ineffective—because he feared that influential laymen were hostile to the church—or counterproductive. Perhaps he was too fearful of what he saw as popular heresy—Lollardy—to risk trying to rouse the laity. Or perhaps he was deterred because he knew that too few of his fellow bishops would join him in outright protest. More probably, however, his sense of loyalty to the crown and his sense of what was fitting were too strong for him to consider any kind of independent campaigning, such as writing tracts in English in defence of the church.

And he may have felt intimidated. The 'Early Life' insists that Fisher, though 'he stood in continual danger of his life . . . yet considering the quarrel he had taken in hand, he never seemed to be one whit dismayed thereat, neither yet to be moved for any worldly trouble that could happen unto him'.[250] Maybe things were more complicated than that. Fisher's opposition was in essence a series of outbursts, made when sorely provoked, rather than sustained resistance; at times he defiantly disregarded attempts at intimidation, but at others he seems quiescent if not submissive.

Efforts were made to dissuade him from coming up to parliament. These might be tactfully veiled, as in October 1531 when Anne Boleyn, supposedly fearing him more than anyone else, sent him a message not to come to London and parliament, ostensibly to protect him from catching fever, in fact because of his defence of Catherine of Aragon's cause. But Fisher, the imperial ambassador reported, was determined to come and to speak in the queen's favour.[251] In early 1532, strikingly, the bishop did not receive a summons to parliament, implying that the king was trying to exclude a feared critic. But Fisher was resolved not to be absent, and came up to court with the intention, so Chapuys reported, of telling the king 'la pure verite'—the plain truth—about the divorce. Henry let him know that he was pleased that he had come and that he had several things to say to him. Fisher feared that the king wanted to persuade him not to speak on the divorce. To defy so personal and direct a royal request would have raised all manner of dilemmas in Fisher's mind; consequently he tried to avoid paying his respects to the king before mass in order to forestall any such conversation. To no avail: Henry welcomed him in a friendlier manner than previously and sug- gested a discussion after mass. Fisher then slipped away before the end of the service to prevent their further meeting. His reported initial resolve to speak his mind had evaporated.[252] Perhaps Fisher did a little later summon up the courage to speak out to the king—to which Henry responded vigorously. The bishop, writing to Henry some years on, would recall 'your much fearful words that your Grace had unto me for showing unto you my mind and opinion in the same matter [the divorce], notwithstanding that your Highness had so often before and so straightly commanded me to search for the same before'.[253] Thomas Cromwell referred to Fisher's charge that the king 'hath unkindly entreated you with grievous words and terrible letters for showing his grace truth in this great matter', i.e. the divorce.[254] Those sentences strongly suggest that Fisher had spoken frankly to the king—and that Henry had rebuked him sharply. We can only wonder what the king's 'fearful' and 'grievous' words and 'terrible letters' expressed—and just how intimidated Fisher felt.

Was the intimidation effective? Presumably Fisher was among the bishops who unanimously refused to agree to the bill for the conditional restraint of annates in March 1532, but there is nothing in our sources to show that he spoke out. Would Chapuys have failed to report it if he had? It may be that illness had compelled him to be absent.[255] What Fisher did in May 1532 when the clergy submitted to the king is largely unknown. Some other bishops do appear to have gone to see him to receive his advice—an interesting glimpse of his standing in their eyes—but that suggests that he was not present at convocation, and if he urged them to resist the king (for which there is no evidence), he failed.[256] And the absence of evidence for any public opposition is striking.

Fisher does seem, however, to have written a brief vindication of the rights and dignity of the clergy, defending the legislative independence of the church, based on scripture, the witness of saints, the usage of general councils and a sort of anthropological argument that in every society a group of men is entrusted with the oversight of religious worship.[257] And in mid-June Fisher, in a surge of courage, preached openly and firmly in favour of Catherine of Aragon, Chapuys reported, shutting the mouths of those who spoke in the king's favour, and risking imprisonment.[258] Interesting, too, is the printing on 28 June 1532 of Fisher's sermons, including that on the Field of Cloth of Gold,[259] just as Henry and Francis were planning a further meeting. The sermon included praise of Queen Catherine—'the noble Queen our mistress, the very exemplar of virtue and nobleness to all women'[260]—utterly conventional sentiments in 1520–21, less so in summer 1532. Another of the reprinted sermons included a warning against succumbing to carnal temptations. That was conventional enough, of course; but just possibly in the summer of 1532, as Henry was preparing to take Anne Boleyn on his visit to Francis I, it was intended to have a more pointed meaning:

> Thou man seest peradventure a fair woman, and thou hast a carnal liking of her, and a pleasure to behold her so that thy body is stirred and moved with an unclean desire to have her at thy will. If thy soul do not assent unto this stirring and motion of thy body, yet art thou safe from any certain sin except thy negligence to repel this thought from thee, and the sufferance of it to abide in thy mind without any resistance. . . . But if thee will once assent to this desire of thy flesh, though thee never go any further, or though thou never come to the actual deed, thou dost offend and sin deadly by this only consent of thy self. Nevertheless, if thou revoke this consent betimes, it is much less offence, and more pardonable, than if thou performed thy desire with the actual deed.

This was like Adam's folly, 'that he would prefer the pleasure of his life before the pleasure of God'. 'Oh wretched sinners, Oh most stinking lechers', Fisher lamented, 'that live thus sinfully against the laws and commandments of our saviour Jesu that so waste your bodies and destroy your souls in the foul sin of lechery.'[261] When he first wrote those wholly conventional sentiments, Fisher cannot possibly have had Henry's infatuation with Anne Boleyn in mind; but it is just thinkable that when those words were put into print in summer 1532, Fisher, or his printer, did. But even so, this was at most an oblique criticism of the king. It was well short of an organised campaign.

A similar pattern of absence, outburst and intimidation is to be found in 1533. In early 1533 Fisher was absent from the House of Lords (according to the attendance lists in the *Lords Journals*), possibly excluded deliberately by the king, along with two other bishops.[262] Convocation was then asked to pronounce on Henry's divorce. So strongly were the churchmen pressed, Chapuys reported, that they had scarcely time to eat or drink. No one dared open his mouth to oppose—except the bishop of Rochester. He was alone—and now despaired.[263] Chapuys's account is confirmed by Cromwell's later reproach: 'men report that at the last convocation ye spoke many things which ye could not well defend.'[264] Fisher duly voted against the king on the validity of papal powers of dispensation and on the issue of whether Catherine's first marriage had been consummated.[265] As a result the king had Fisher placed under house arrest under the eye of Bishop Gardiner 'pour ce quil a si virilement deffendu, et soubsetenu la querelle du pape, et de la royne' (because he had so vigorously defended and supported the cause of the pope and the queen).[266] He was released immediately after the coronation of Anne Boleyn: was it feared that he might otherwise make some public protest?[267] Once again, Fisher had shown courage in speaking out and in publicly dissenting from royal demands. He had paid a price in intimidation. And, once again, his protests were essentially reactions to demands for his acquiescence, not independent initiatives of his own. Fisher does not appear to have made the slightest attempt to campaign or to recruit followers.

Fisher's dealings with Sir George Throckmorton, a Warwickshire gentleman and knight of the shire, are thin evidence for any political conspiracy. In 1537 Throckmorton, interrogated under suspicion of treason, made a lengthy confession. He admitted that on several occasions he had gone to see Fisher and had much conversation with him about the acts of appeals, annates and supremacy, and over the authority given by Jesus to St Peter. The last time Throckmorton saw him, Fisher gave him a book of his own devising on the matter (this is our only evidence that Fisher wrote a book on this subject) which Throckmorton said he gave to Cromwell.[268] It was Throckmorton who took the initiative, going to visit those he believed would be sympathetic, but after he had begun to oppose in the Commons. Fisher advised him to see the theologian Dr Nicholas Wilson, which Throckmorton did. Throckmorton also went to see Richard Reynolds at Syon. Interestingly, he received very different counsel. Throckmorton should stick to his opinion to death, and should not hold his peace in parliament, even if he thought his speaking could not prevail, said Reynolds. But Fisher (and Wilson) had offered very different advice, allowing restraint; Fisher advised him not to persist if he felt that he could not prevail. If this was a conspiracy, as it has often been taken to be, the conspirators were giving contradictory advice.[269] The contacts revealed by Throckmorton's confession read more like a search for consolation by those who know they are losing because they are powerless, rather than proof of an organised political campaign.

But in autumn 1533 Fisher made an appeal to the holy Roman emperor, Charles V, Catherine of Aragon's nephew. What he wanted is not, however, crystal clear. Chapuys twice referred to it. On 27 September he wrote how Fisher had said: 'que les armes du pape pour ceulx cy que sont obstinez sont plus fresles que de plomb et que convient que vostre majeste y mecte la main et que en ce elle fera oeuvre tant agreeable a dieu que daller contre le turcq' (that the weapons the pope has at his disposal against those who are obstinate are more frail than lead (the material with which papal bulls, including excommunications, were sealed) and that it would be fitting for Charles V to put his hand to it. In so doing, he would be performing a service as agreeable to God as going against the Turk).[270] A fortnight later Chapuys wrote how Fisher (not named but described as 'le bon et saincte euesque' (the good and holy bishop)) 'vouldroit bien que quant a quant vostre majeste y mit la main ainsy quescripuiz dernierement a vostre maieste laquelle chose ma encoires naguerez enuoye dire': Fisher wanted Charles V to put his hand to it by and by, as Chapuys had lately informed the emperor and as Fisher had again sent to him to tell the emperor.[271]

The challenge here is to decide just what Fisher had in mind. Was he asking Charles V to launch a military invasion of England? Did he envisage a trade embargo? Or was he leaving the methods to the emperor, while desperately but vaguely appealing for help? However that may be, this would certainly have been regarded as a treasonable appeal by the king: presumably he never knew of it. Historians have judged it in varying ways. J.-P. Moreau saw it as vague but treasonable, though he stressed that it was only in these conversations, and thus only briefly, that Fisher crossed the threshold of illegality.[272] Maria Dowling hinted that Fisher did not seriously expect Charles to answer his call.[273] Sir Geoffrey Elton dismissed Fisher's behaviour as irresponsible, like a child crying for help. Eamon Duffy countered by insisting that Fisher here shrewdly grasped that Christendom was imperilled and that it was time that its secular head, the emperor, should put things right. A more plausible reading of Fisher's appeal is that it reflected plain despair on his part, just after the birth of Elizabeth, rather than a considered and sustained position. Fisher was no diplomat, much less a soldier: he had never been a councillor–bishop in the mould of Wolsey, used to thinking strategically about international power politics. Nothing more is heard of the appeal: perhaps historians have paid it too much attention.

In autumn 1533 Elizabeth Barton, the Nun of Kent, who had voiced prophecies warning the king against marrying Anne Boleyn, was denounced as an impostor, as we have seen; in early 1534 she was attainted for treason. Fisher was caught up in her fate. In autumn 1533 he came under suspicion owing to his involvement with her. 'Whether the king will have my lord of Rochester sent for', reads one of Cromwell's notes, made most probably in autumn 1533.[274] Under arrest, one of those involved with Barton recalled that she had shown her revelations to Fisher and that he had wept for joy on hearing them, saying he gave them the more credence because she had been with the king several times and reproved him for his sins.[275] Chapuys, noting Queen Catherine's relief that she had never had anything to do with the nun, added pointedly and by implied contrast that Fisher had been on very intimate terms with her.[276] And among Cromwell's remembrances is the note 'the bishop of Rochester's saying to Resby', hinting at some contact between Fisher and Friar Risby, who spread the nun's revelations.[277]

The government was determined to use Fisher's involvement against him. Cromwell rebuked him in a frighteningly unpleasant letter replying to Fisher's response to an earlier letter from Cromwell. Where Fisher had pleaded that he had not deserved the 'heavy words or terrible threats' that Cromwell had sent, Cromwell denied having sent them, but thought Fisher's excuses quite insufficient and regretted that he had not simply admitted his guilt and sought the king's pardon. Fisher had heard, believed and concealed the nun's revelations. He had not adequately tested her honesty. He should have examined not just one or two but a good number of witnesses; 'likewise ye should have tried by what craft and persuasion she was made a religious woman', spoken with her confessors, looked at her book of revelations. 'For if credence should be given to every such lewd person as would affirm him self to have revelations from God, what readier way were there to subvert all commonwealths and good orders in the world.' Devastatingly, Cromwell concluded that it was not Barton's reputation or the testimony of her confessor that made him give credence to her, 'but only the very matter whereupon she made her false prophecies, to which matter ye were so affected'—and here Cromwell added a sideswipe, 'as ye be noted to be on all matters which ye enter once into'—'that no thing could come amiss that made for that purpose'. Suppose, Cromwell went on, she had shown as many revelations that confirmed the king's marriage, would Fisher have believed her? Moreover, Fisher had sent to her to know more of her revelations. The bishop had been 'in great default', 'believing and concealing such things as tended to the destruction of the prince', which it had just been proved by a great assembly of noblemen that they were. How did Fisher know that the nun had told the king? Should he not have told the king himself? If the matter came to trial, 'your own confession in these letters, besides the witnesses which are against you, will be sufficient to condemn you'.[278]

Fisher then wrote directly to Henry, protesting against the act of attainder which condemned him without any further legal process for not informing the king of the words that Barton had spoken about the king. Fisher admitted seeing her three times. She had come to his house, unsent for, and said she had been with Henry and shown him a revelation from God that, if he went on with his purpose, he should not be king seven months later. Fisher now wrote to Henry that he did not think any malice was intended by any mortal by that, since these were 'the threats of God', as she did affirm. Fisher did not know, he said, that her words were invented, nor had he advised her to invent them. If she had told him this and not also told him that she had already told the king, he would indeed have been to blame for not disclosing it. But since she had assured him that she had plainly told the king, he feared that if he had mentioned it to him, Henry would have thought that he did it 'to renew her tale again unto you, rather for the confirming of my opinion, than for any other cause'. 'To my no little heaviness', Henry's 'grievous letters . . . sticketh yet . . . in my heart'. He had been reluctant, bearing in mind the 'fearful words' that Henry had earlier spoken to him when he had declared his opinion on the divorce (as we have seen), to go to him with such a tale, dreading that he would have provoked the king's further displeasure. In any case Archbishop Warham had told him that Barton had been with the king, so confirming that there was nothing secret about it; and Warham had told him more about what she was prophesying than she had told him herself. He was unwell and his body was much weakened with many diseases and infirmities; 'and my soul is much inquieted by this trouble that my heart is more withdrawn from god, and from the devotion of prayer than I wold. and verily I think that my life may not long continue.' He appealed to be allowed 'to prepare my soul to god and to make it ready against the coming of death, and no more to come abroad in the world'.[279] Did Fisher expect the king to agree with him that the nun had intended no malice by her revelations? His insistence that he knew that the king already knew them was a stronger point to make. His letter certainly gives a sense of a man intimidated, though there were obviously tactical reasons why he should do this.

Fisher also drafted an appeal to the Lords in parliament (though it may never have been heard by them). Again he denied having asked Barton to call on him. He had believed that she was honest and virtuous. People where she lived called her the holy maid. After seeing visions, she had entered a nunnery. And her confessor and other priests testified to her holiness, which had been confirmed by the archbishop of Canterbury. Fisher was bound, he insisted, to believe the best of every person until the contrary was proved. He knew no evil intended by her against the king: her prophecies referred not to any temporal power but to the power of God.[280]

All Fisher's appeals were to no avail. He was convicted of treason for not revealing what the nun told him: at first he was imprisoned, then the penalty was reduced to a year's revenue from his bishopric.[281] Chapuys thought that all this happened because he had supported Catherine.[282] Fisher's early biographer noted in this context that the king 'thirsted after his life' since 'he bare so great a sway in the convocation house'.[283] Yet it is not necessary to suppose that Henry was pursuing a vendetta against Fisher: Fisher's involvement with the Nun of Kent was quite provocative in itself. That would still be so if Fisher, once more, far from seeking Barton out, or encouraging her, was simply reacting to what others were doing and saying. That he should have wept on hearing the nun's revelations seems typical of the man: heartfelt emotional responses characterise him, not Machiavellian scheming. This was no political leader.

In April 1534 Fisher refused to swear the oath demanded to the act of succession. Sent to the Tower, after a few days in the custody of the abbot of Westminster, he was soon reported as offering to compromise. Bishop Rowland Lee reported that he was 'ready to make his oaths for the succession and to swear never to mell [meddle] more in disputation of the validity of the matrimony or invalidity with the lady deeger [dowager] but that utterly to refuse'. That was apparently a significant concession if sincerely meant, given his prolific writing. But as for 'the prohibition levitical' (the king's case for an annulment of his marriage to Catherine), Fisher's conscience 'is so knit that he cannot rent it'. He nonetheless fervently expressed his allegiance to the king.[284] In December Fisher assured Cromwell that he had been willing to swear the part of the oath concerning the succession, since he accepted that the prince of any realm might with the assent of his nobles and commons make arrangements for that, but that he had refused to swear some other parts because his conscience would not let him do so.[285]

Archbishop Cranmer speculated that what made Fisher refuse to swear was 'either the diminution of the authority of the Bishop of Rome, or else the reprobation of the king's first pretended matrimony'. Cranmer urged that Fisher—and also More, who was offering a comparable compromise—should be given what they wanted. If Fisher was willing to swear to the succession, that should be welcomed. Fisher's (and More's) oaths 'might not a little avail' in achieving the consent of all the realm 'with one accord'.[286] As so often, it was Henry who was most uncompromising against those who crossed him. He refused to allow any partial oaths. In his view that would be implicitly to agree to the bishop of Rome's authority and to deny the validity of the second marriage.[287]

An act of attainder was passed in late 1534 declaring how Fisher and others, 'contrary to their duties of allegiance intending to sow and make sedition murmur and grudge within this realm', had since 1 May obstinately and maliciously refused to take the oaths made by a statute 'made for the surety establishment and continuance of the king our sovereign lord and his heirs in the succession of the imperial crown of this his realm'. Fisher and the others were thus declared convicted of misprision of treason. In consequence Fisher was deprived of his bishopric on 2 January 1535.[288]

Beyond that, Fisher was inexcusably badly treated. He was old and unwell when first imprisoned. Rowland Lee reported how 'truly the man is nigh gone and doubtless cannot stand unless the king and his council be merciful to him for the body ca[n] not bear the clothes on his back'.[289] Just before Christmas Fisher appealed to Cromwell, 'for I have neither shirt nor sheet nor yet other clothes that are necessary for me to wear but that be ragged and rent too shamefully'. He would easily put up with that, however, if they 'would keep my body warm'. He complained that 'my diet also god knoweth how slender it is at many times' and that if he did not have the few things his digestion could handle, then it made him ill. 'I beseech you', he pleaded, 'to have some pity upon me and let me have such things as are necessary for me at my age and specially for my health.' And he implored Cromwell (to whom he wished 'our lord send you a merry christmas') 'by your high wisdom' to persuade the king to show him favour again and to end his 'cold and painful imprisonment'.[290]

Why exactly did Fisher refuse to swear the oath in the form demanded by the king? He was understandably nervous about saying. He feared that in explaining his refusal to swear he would incriminate himself: 'I dread me that I can not be so circumspect in my writing but that some word shall escape me wherewith his grace shall be moved to some further displeasure against me.'[291] A few weeks before his imprisonment he begged not to be compelled to answer letters that Cromwell had sent him. In particular, concerning the king's great matter, Fisher declined being obliged to offend the king: 'I should not be straited to offend his grace in that behalf for then I most needs declare my conscience.'[292]

In spring 1535 Henry increased the pressure. Chapuys reported that he gave Fisher (and More) six weeks to take the oaths, threatening them with the fate of the Charterhouse monks, recently executed, if they refused.[293] Fisher was subjected to a series of interrogations by various councillors and bishops. We lack full or contemporary accounts and depend instead on depositions made at or for Fisher's trial, and on material in later lives of Fisher. On 7 May (or possibly a week earlier), Cromwell and other councillors came saying they had been sent by the king to examine Fisher. After Cromwell had read the act of supremacy, Fisher, according to his servant Richard Wilson, said that 'he could not consent nor find in his heart to take the king to be supreme head of the church of England according to the said statute'.[294] According to the later indictment against him, on 7 May Fisher declared that the king was not supreme head on earth of the church of England.[295] If he said it as starkly as that, then he was surely technically guilty of treason, given the new laws,[296] and the government would at once have had sufficient evidence to move against him. But most probably Fisher did not go that far, saying rather that he could not consent, and that it was not proved to be right, rather than roundly denying it. That would explain why Henry did not act against him there and then, but made renewed attempts to persuade him to agree—or to get him to speak his mind more fully and more definitely, with a view to using his words against him.

No doubt Henry was incensed by the news that on 20 May the pope had made Fisher a cardinal.[297] According to the early biographer, Henry said to Cromwell, 'though he have a hat, I trust so to order the matter before it come at him, he shall never have a head to set it upon'.[298] Henry angrily declared that he would give him another hat, and send the head afterwards to Rome for the cardinal's hat.[299] But how far what Henry undoubtedly saw as a provocation—not least since it challenged Cranmer's position as leader of the church—led to increased pressure on Fisher depends in part on when the news reached the king.[300] There is no doubt that the pressures were intensifying.

On 3 June Audley, Suffolk and Wiltshire were sent to interrogate Fisher. He refused to answer directly:

> I will not meddle with that matter, for the statute [of supremacy] is like a two-edged sword; and if I should answer one way, I should offend my conscience, and if I should answer the other way I should put my life in jeopardy; wherefore I will make no answer to that matter.[301]

The 'Early Life' amplified that. If Fisher were to admit that the king was supreme head of the church, something which 'both his knowledge and his conscience taught him to be clean false and untrue', then he would manifestly incur the displeasure of God and endanger his soul. But if 'I answer you directly with denial of the king's supremacy, then am I sure of death'.[302] Not surprisingly, the councillors said that the king would not like this response.[303]

Fisher's response raised the question of his dealings with Thomas More: both men used much the same formulation on 3 June. Letters between them showed that More had used the metaphor of the two-edged sword on 12 May. That was seen as evidence of conspiracy. But perhaps the metaphor was more commonplace than that allows. Fisher had used it in a much earlier sermon—'If there be deadly sin in us, it must take punishment by the two edged sword, the which of that one side slayeth the body, and of that other, the soul, and both at one stroke'[304]—and since it so precisely described the predicament of both men, it is not so surprising that it was used by both. Both men spoke in similar terms about conscience. More, as we shall see, famously told Rich that 'your conscience will save you and my conscience will save me'. Intriguingly, Fisher had defended himself in much the same way to Cromwell in January 1534: 'Not that I condemn any other man's conscience', Fisher wrote; 'their conscience may save them and mine must save me.'[305] That shows how warily historians must treat arguments for collaboration between Fisher and More that rest on similarities of phraseology. In passing, it must be noted that Fisher was not a modern liberal defender of human rights *avant la lettre*: he was standing for what he in his conscience knew to be right. But when he insisted that he would not pass judgment on other men's consciences, far from allowing that they were entitled to their opinions or that they might be right, he was implying that they were in fact jeopardising their souls. Attacking heresy in 1526, Fisher had written that 'if every man should have liberty to say what he would, we should have a marvellous world'; 'many must be compelled according as the gospel saith'.[306]

According to the 'Early Life', six or seven bishops came to see Fisher, presumably to reason with him, much as Bishops Tunstal and Gardiner and others had been 'set on' by the king to persuade him 'not to show himself obstinate, but to go as far as he might, quantum cum verbo Dei'.[307] Instead—according to his biographer—he lectured them. They ought to be sticking together to defend the church against the 'violent and unlawful intrusions and injuries, daily offered to our common mother the holy church of Christ', and 'to seek by all means the temporal destruction of these ravening wolves that daily go about worrying and devouring everlastingly the flock that Christ hath committed to our charge and the flock that himself died for'. 'The fort is betrayed even of them that should have defended it', he lamented; what was happening was 'so faintly resisted' by them.[308] It would be misleading to suppose that Fisher was here inciting opposition: he certainly made no attempt to moderate his convictions, but he voiced them forcefully only in response to the bishops' attempts to persuade him otherwise.

On 12 June Fisher was interrogated about conversations with his brother, and his letters to and from Thomas More.[309] On 14 June Fisher was interrogated further. In response to the question whether he would obey the king as supreme head on earth under Christ of the church of England, he stood by his previous answer—presumably that made on 7 May—which he offered to elaborate with his own hand at more length. In response to a question whether he would approve the king's marriage to Anne Boleyn as good and lawful and the king's previous marriage to Catherine as naught, he would obey the act of succession, 'saving always his conscience', but he desired to be excused from answering this question yes or no, 'lest he should fall thereby into the dangers of the statutes'.[310]

At this point it is far from clear that the king had what he needed to convict him in a court of law, namely a fully explicit declaration by

Fisher that the king's divorce and his royal supremacy were unlawful. Should a problematic source, the fragments of Rastell's *Life of More*, be given credence here? This tells how the king, still not having enough to act against Fisher, 'began now a new way how to entrap him by a policy'. Henry sent Richard Rich, his solicitor-general, to speak with Fisher, and at his trial Rich was to claim that Fisher had said that he 'believed in his conscience and by his learning knew that the king neither was nor by any right could be supreme head in earth of the church of England'.[311] That went beyond what Fisher is shown in other sources as having said on other occasions. How did he come to say it? Rich pressed him, saying that he alone of the bishops refused to consent. He then set the trap. Henry, he said, 'for the better satisfaction of his own conscience', had sent Rich 'to know my [Fisher's] full opinion in the matter, for the great affiance he had in me, more than in any other'. Having thus passed on Henry's flattery, Fisher recounted that Rich went on that 'if I would herein frankly and freely advertise his majesty of my knowledge herein that upon certificate of my misliking he was very like to retract much of his former doings and make recompense for the same, in case I should so advise him'. Not surprisingly, Fisher countered by reminding Rich of the act of parliament[312] which might endanger him very much if he said anything against the law. To that Rich said:

the king willed him to assure me on his honour and in the word of a king, that whatsoever I should say unto him, I should abide no danger nor peril for it, neither that any advantage should be taken against me for the same; no, although my words were never so directly against the statute, seeing it was but a declaration of my mind secretly to him as to his own person. And for the messenger himself he gave me his faithful promise that he would never utter any words in this matter to any man living, but to the king alone.

And so Fisher fell into the trap, declaring his opinion to Rich.

According to the Rastell fragments, this was then held against him at his trial. Fisher protested against an outrageous breach of faith.

What a monstrous matter is this: to lay now to my charge as treason the thing which I spake not until besides this man's oath, I had as full and as sure a promise from the king, by this his trusty and sure messenger, as the king could make me by word of mouth, that I should never be impeached nor hurt by mine answer that I should send unto him by this his messenger, which I would never have spoken, had it not been in trust of my princes promise, and of my true and loving heart towards him, my natural liege lord, in satisfying him with declaration of mine opinion and conscience in this matter, as he earnestly required me by this messenger to signify plainly unto him.

According to the Rastell fragments, the facts were not denied, but the king's promise was held invalid as a discharge: kings may exempt from punishment but not from conviction. Fisher insisted that this would be against all equity, and insisted above all that what he had said had not been spoken maliciously, and therefore he had committed no treason. But some of the judges, 'utterly devoid of worldly shame', answered, carrying with them the rest, that 'the word maliciously in the statute was of none effect, for that none could speak against the king's supremacy by any manner of means but that the speaking against it was treason'; and also that no message or promise from the king could discharge him. By declaring his opinion against the king's supremacy, he had committed treason. Only the king's pardon could spare him from the penalty of death provided for in the statute. No doubt this was correct in law. If the jury then convicted Fisher, they did so, according to the Rastell fragments, 'by the persuasion and threats of some of his judges and of the king's learned counsel', yet 'the most part of the xii men did this sore against their own conscience', fearing after they had been 'sore menaced' that their lives would have been in danger had they acquitted him.[313]

How much credence can be placed in this account? Elton simply swept it aside. All that is in the indictment is the statement that Fisher denied the supremacy on 7 May. And Chapuys, in his report of Fisher's trial, did not tell of any such outrage. But maybe that is too hasty. Indictments are brief: more could have been alleged in the course of the trial. Chapuys's account of Fisher's conviction is remarkably short: he may simply not have known what happened. Arguments from silence are not always conclusive. An Eltonian test of plausibility weighs in favour of the Rastell fragments. After all (as we shall soon see in detail), Richard Rich was undoubtedly sent to entrap Thomas More (if with no promise of immunity), and what Rich claimed that More said—denied by More—was somewhat doubtfully used against him. It is not impossible that Rich was sent to ensnare Fisher in much the same spirit. And Fisher, fundamentally loyal to the king, trusting in the king's word, not familiar with the fine points of common law, and maybe in the end far from unwilling to declare his opinion, not least in the hope that he might yet call Henry to his senses, spoke out against the royal supremacy. He denied that he had done so maliciously. Elsewhere Fisher anchored his defence on the need for malice to be proved before a successful prosecution could be brought. It is thus far from implausible that Fisher was deviously led to say what it was no longer lawful to say.[314] And that sealed his fate. He was convicted and executed.

Fisher had been imprisoned for refusing to swear the oath required in spring 1534, not for any overtly political activity. His prolific writings on the divorce were, of course, a series of acts of defiance. But those books were not explicitly concerned with the break with Rome or the royal supremacy. He tried hard to avoid having to express an opinion on the king's supremacy, and may only have done so when promised—falsely—immunity if he did. On the supremacy, he kept his convictions to himself and did not attempt to organise any campaign of opposition. What distinguishes him from the dissidents of Eastern Europe in the 1980s is that if he obeyed the call of his own conscience, he did not issue a general clarion call for the rights of anyone to follow his conscience, and he remained fundamentally loyal to, indeed reverentially in awe of, the king. According to his early biographer, though he would not please the king by swearing the oath, he would, however, spend the remnant of his days in praying to God for him. At his execution he told the people to be loving and obedient to the king, who was good by nature but had been deceived in this matter.[315] 'For as I will answer before god I would not in any manner of point offend his grace my duty saved unto god whom I must in every thing prefer.'[316]

Thomas More

Among the laity who opposed the break with Rome, Thomas More has pride of place. More disagreed with Henry over it, and ultimately paid with his life, at the same time as Bishop Fisher. But the questions of what he did and what exactly he believed demand more sensitive analysis than they have usually received. In particular, claims that More led an 'opposition', that he should be placed 'firmly with one of the political groups of the time that organized to oppose the king's Great Matter and to support the cause of Catherine and Rome',[317] are quite misleading.

Elton saw More, and Bishop Fisher, as 'at the heart of this conspiracy' largely on the basis of a letter that Thomas Cromwell sent Gregory Casale, Henry VIII's long-serving agent in Rome, in September 1535, some weeks after More and Fisher had been executed. Cromwell accused them of having alone opposed laws passed in parliament that were beneficial to the whole realm. They 'debated in private among themselves' about these bills; they then 'chose out persons on whose courage, readiness and devotion to themselves they could depend' and 'fed them with the poison they had conceived'. They pretended that they were entirely given up to the contemplation of divine things but attempted to refute and to evade those laws by fallacious arguments which they sought to impose on the common people. They had continued to oppose while in prison, writing letters using chalk and coal when ink was not to be had.[318] That was seen as especially heinous. Bishop Edward Foxe was instructed to tell the German protestant princes with whom he was negotiating that, even when they were in prison, More and Fisher had planned an insurrection within the realm.[319] Cromwell's letter to Casale echoed the circular letter sent by the king to JPs, dated 25 June 1535—after Fisher's conviction but before that of More. In it Henry denounced their treasons: 'by diverse secret practises' they wished to spread 'a most mischievous and seditious opinion' among the king's subjects.[320] Elton reworked what he saw as the lessons of such evidence: 'what Cromwell called a conspiracy we may more properly call an organized opposition outside parliament but able to obtain information from within it, sufficiently coherent to prepare counter-efforts to the king's propaganda, and able to arrange for its members to speak publicly against the king's proceedings.'[321]

Moreover, Elton makes a good deal of Sir George Throckmorton's confession, made around 1537. Throckmorton, a Warwickshire gentleman, had been arrested after he had been denounced, a year after the events, for showing a sympathetic interest in the Pilgrimage of Grace.[322] In an abject and detailed confession, Sir George, who had been a knight of the shire in the reformation parliament, admitted that some years earlier Thomas More had sent for him after he had spoken out against the king's policies. More had urged him, Throckmorton recalled, to continue as he had begun, unafraid to 'say his conscience'—he would thus, More promised, 'deserve great reward of God'.[323] Which bill was at issue here? From the circumstantial detail, it appears to be the act of appeals in 1533, yet More was by then out of office. Still, the story should not be dismissed entirely. If true, at some point—though on a single occasion—Throckmorton had been summoned and encouraged by More to continue his public criticism of royal policy. That Throckmorton also met others critical of the government who, he recalled, offered rather more cautious advice, may lend greater credibility to his portrayal of a More who was keen for him to continue outspoken. At the same time his testimony makes it hard to see More as part of an organised group of opponents, precisely because their advice to Throckmorton was so varied. And on Throckmorton's account, More had not incited him: Throckmorton came to see him only *after* he had begun to oppose.

Throckmorton apart, it is not easy to find further evidence to support Elton's view of More as conspirator or faction leader. Quite a few relatives and servants of More sat in the 1529 parliament: his sons-in-law William Dauntsey, Giles Heron (for Thetford, a Duchy of Lancaster borough) and William Roper (for Bramber), and his brothers-in-law John Dynham and John Rastell. But none of them can be identified as having opposed any measure put forward by the king. Of course, it is impossible to prove a negative: More may have had contacts with members of the Commons critical of Henry's policies about which we know nothing, members of his 'circle' may have made speeches that were not recorded. But it is hard to build on such speculations—not least since, as we shall see, there was only limited parliamentary opposition to the break with Rome.[324]

Until the matter of the king's divorce, More had enjoyed a brilliantly successful career as lawyer, scholar and royal servant and adviser. Some episodes in his career might conceivably lend support to a view of him as a conspirator. According to Roper, in 1504, More, as a burgess of parliament, successfully opposed Henry VII's demand for a grant of taxation on the occasion of the marriage of the king's eldest daughter; More's father was allegedly punished by being kept in the Tower till £100 was paid.[325] More's plea for members of the Commons to enjoy freedom of speech in the parliament of 1523 has been read as a critique of royal power: he asked that it might please the king to give to all his Commons 'your most gracious license and pardon, freely, without doubt of your dreadful displeasure, every man to discharge his conscience, and boldly in every thing incident among us to declare his advice'.[326] But this should be read with due allowance for conventions and context. What Henry VIII and Wolsey sought above all from that parliament was a grant of taxation, and they succeeded in securing parliamentary acquiescence in an unprecedented sum. More was rewarded after parliament was prorogued, suggesting that the king and Wolsey saw him as having played a constructive role.[327]

A clearer insight into More's career is offered by his long and intimate service to Henry. Roper described how More's 'wise and discreet dealing . . . coming to the king's understanding . . . provoked his highness to cause Cardinal Wolsey (then Lord Chancellor) to procure him to his service',[328] with More becoming master of requests and one of the king's counsellors. In those years the king would 'in matters of Astronomy, Geometry, Divinity and such other Faculties and sometimes of his worldly affairs . . . sit and confer with him'; More was often invited to sup with Henry and Queen Catherine.[329] As Henry's secretary, More was regularly in king's presence and frequently reported to Wolsey on the king's reactions to news, especially of military and diplomatic developments abroad. All that is not the natural background of a political conspirator plotting against the king.

Did he agree with Henry's conviction that his first marriage had never been valid? Our sources are his own later recollection in a letter to Cromwell on 5 March 1534, and Roper's and Harpsfield's lives, which, of course, very likely draw on what More had said. It is unlikely that More in 1534 would have told Cromwell anything that was demonstrably untrue, especially anything that the king would have known was false. More's account then deserves credence. What it shows is that he was unpersuaded by the king's reasons for thinking his marriage to Catherine null and void. On a number of occasions, not always precisely datable, Henry asked More's opinion and, when More failed at once to offer his support, urged him to read and to reflect on materials that had been gathered in support of the king's cause, and to discuss them with those involved in preparing his case. On every such occasion More had demurred—both before he was appointed lord chancellor and afterwards.

On his own account, More had been aware of the technical objections to the papal bull of dispensation that had permitted the marriage, but it was on returning from abroad and going to see Henry at Hampton Court (this can be dated to October 1527) that the king himself

> suddenly . . . walking in the gallery, broke with me of his great matter, and showed me that it was now perceived that his marriage was not only against the positive laws of the church and the written law of God, but also in such wise against the law of nature, that it could in no wise by the church be dispensable.

Moreover, Henry had attempted to convince More directly: he 'laid the Bible open before me and there me showed the words that moved his highness and diverse other erudite persons so to think'. When the king asked him his opinion, More gave it—but unfortunately in his account he does not say what that was or elaborate on his reasons. But manifestly what More did not say was that he was convinced by the king. If he had, then Henry would not have told him to discuss the matter further with Edward Foxe and 'to read a book with him that then was in the making for that matter'. Having done that, More again gave Henry his opinion, but in his recollections he did not go into details.[330] In Roper's account More read what the king asked him to, and then 'as one that had never professed their study of divinity, himself excused to be unmeet many ways to meddle with such matters'. The king, 'not satisfied with this answer, so sore still pressed upon him therefore, that in conclusion he condescended to his grace's motion'. It was then that More was sent to consult with Cuthbert Tunstal and John Clerk. According to Roper, More also read in the scriptures and patristical writers. He then told the king plainly that neither Tunstal nor Clerk nor himself was a fit counsellor on this matter. 'If your grace mind to understand the truth,' More continued, 'such councillors may you have devised, as neither for respect of their own worldly commodity, nor for fear of your princely authority, will be inclined to deceive you', naming St Jerome, St Augustine and other church fathers, 'and moreover showed him what authorities he had gathered out of them'. Not surprisingly, Henry did not, Roper tells us, like this very well, but took More's response in 'good parte', and 'oft times had thereof conference with him again'. Roper goes on to show More being encouraged to consult with John Stokesley, recently appointed bishop of London. 'But for all his conference with him', Roper concludes, More 'saw nothing of such force as could induce him to change his opinion therein'.[331]

Is Roper's account credible? More himself, after telling Cromwell that he had informed the king of his opinion, though without elaborating, went on to give a somewhat coolly detached account of the meeting of learned men at Hampton Court. They had agreed on a book containing 'good and reasonable causes' that made the king 'conceive in his mind a scruple against his marriage'; he had then acted virtuously in having that doubt resolved by the judgment of the church. More added that he took no part at that point: the legates—Campeggio and Wolsey—were sitting, 'during all which time I never meddled therein, nor was a man meet to do, for the matter was in hand by an ordinary process of the spiritual law, whereof I could little skill'.[332]

More's own account of his attitudes before he became lord chancellor is thus studiedly noncommittal. Evidently he had not gone along with the king, and he took no part in the making of the king's case for a divorce. But had he mumbled and demurred, saying he was ignorant and unskilled in the matter—or had he spoken out more boldly in defence of Queen Catherine and against what Henry was seeking? Roper's *Life* suggests that he had indeed spoken out, pointing out that the king's counsellors from fear and self-interest took Henry's side but that the church fathers did not support him. If More had really said that, then it would have been rather provocative—to say the least—to have denied any meddling in the matter, on the grounds of his ignorance, when he made his account to Cromwell in 1534. Henry would not have been taken in for a second. Much more probable than Roper's account is the impression that More himself gave in 1534. It is not impossible that in the years 1527–29 More felt somewhat uncomfortable about what the king was doing, but simply hoped the problem would go away, perhaps by being resolved by the cardinal legates or, indeed, the pope on some technicality. At the same time, he might, very understandably, have been reluctant to speak out vigorously against the king. Roper cites John Stokesley as reporting to Henry after his discussions with More that he was 'in his graces cause very toward and desirous to find some good matter wherewith he might truly serve his grace to his contentation'.[333]

In autumn 1529, on the enforced resignation of Wolsey, More was appointed lord chancellor, both a signal mark of royal favour and testimony to More's willing service to the king. In the light of later events, it is intriguing that More accepted this post. But maybe he did not have the choice that we might suppose he had: it would not have been straightforward for a royal servant of long standing to refuse what would have appeared as a request for further, and more important, service. But More did not simply slip unostentatiously into his new post. Publicly and blisteringly, doubtless at the king's behest, he attacked Wolsey, 'the great wether which is of late fallen', in the first session of parliament in autumn 1529. Should More have grasped that the humbling of Wolsey was part of Henry's campaign for his divorce? If that would have been to expect too much foresight, perhaps More should have been struck by the fact that, in appointing a layman as lord chancellor, the king had broken with precedent and this might have been a warning of difficulties ahead for the church. What More thought of the anticlerical legislation of autumn 1529 we cannot know.

Soon after he was made lord chancellor—he recalled to Cromwell in 1534—Henry asked him 'to look and consider his great matter, and well and indifferently to ponder such things as I should find therein'; 'if it so were that thereupon it should hap me to see such things as should persuade me to that part, he would gladly use me among other of his councillors in that matter.' But nevertheless the king 'graciously' told More—as More now claimed—

> that he would in no wise that I should other thing do or say therein, than upon that that I should perceive mine own conscience should serve me, and that I should first look unto God and after God unto him, which most gracious words was the first lesson also that ever his Grace gave me at my first coming into his noble service.

Accordingly Henry asked More to consult with Thomas Cranmer, Edward Lee, Dr Foxe and Nicholas de Burgo, the Italian friar. More 'not only sought and read, and farforth as my poor wit and learning served me, well weighed and considered every such thing as I could find my self, or read in any other man's labour that I could get, which any thing had written therein' but also had 'diligent conference' with those advising the king. He was sure that none of these counsellors ever found him obstinate but rather 'a mind as toward and as conformable as reason could in a matter disputable require'. That last phrase—'a matter disputable'—hints that More remained unpersuaded, even though 'to have been able and meet to do him service I would as I then showed his Highness have been more glad than of all such worldly commodities as I either then had or ever should come to'. More recalled that

> his highness graciously taking . . . my good mind in that behalf used of his blessed disposition in the prosecuting of his great matter only those (of whom his Grace had good number) whose conscience his Grace perceived well and fully persuaded upon that part, and as well my self as any other to whom his Highness thought the thing to seem other wise, he used in his other business, abiding (of his abundant goodness) never the less gracious lord to any man, nor never was willing to put any man in ruffle or trouble of his conscience.[334]

Does that ring true? Roper's account has Henry giving More greater freedom of action than More himself recalled: Roper's king tells More that 'if he could not therein with his conscience serve him, he was content to accept his service otherwise' while using other counsellors whose consciences did agree with the matter; and promised not only that he would 'nevertheless continue his gracious favour towards him' but also that he would 'never with that matter molest his conscience after'.[335] Was Roper turning More's somewhat neutral, though not wholly accurate, and essentially tactical, description of how Henry had not required his involvement in his divorce, and had not troubled any man's conscience, into an explicit promise by the king? That would have been polemically useful, since it made Henry appear as a king—or tyrant—who had gone on to break his word. Again, in Roper's version, More's opposition to the divorce is heightened. It was in order to persuade More to agree, Roper says, that Henry made him lord chancellor. That is implausible. If More had already made his outright opposition plain, it is hardly likely that Henry would have risked appointing More to such an important post. Much more likely is that, as he himself later described, More had been uneasy, noncommittal, but unwilling openly to oppose, while anxious to continue serving the king. Once more, Roper dramatises More's reluctance to support Henry, presenting More as falling on his knees and reminding the king of what he had said to him when he had first entered royal service, 'willing him first to look unto god and after god to him'.[336]

In the light of later events, it is tempting to present More as fundamentally and outspokenly hostile to the king's great matter. But the evidence does not support so clear-cut a reading. On Roper's account, as we have seen, More did on one occasion invoke church fathers against the king. But, and not least on More's own later testimony, he was not as openly critical as that might at first suggest.

According to Chapuys, More was very much Queen Catherine's friend. Chapuys claimed in September 1530 that More was speaking so much in the queen's favour that he had narrowly avoided being dismissed,[337] and a month later reported that More was still in danger of dismissal, solely because he hesitated to sign as others had done the king's letters to the pope—the petition in June.[338] Chapuys believed that More was horrified by the pardon of the clergy in early 1531 and that he wanted nothing more than to leave his post.[339] In March 1531 Chapuys wrote that More conducted himself most virtuously in the matter of the queen, and had always been very attentive to her.[340]

But did he attempt to block the king's divorce? More vehemently denied it. He did nothing, wrote nothing, encouraged no one else to write against the king. Following Henry's effort to persuade him, soon after he had been appointed lord chancellor, More claimed that he took no further part in any discussion of the king's great matter. He had, he said, 'gladly read afterward diverse books that were made on his part', but he refused to read books made by Thomas Abel or others on the other side, 'nor never gave ear to the Pope's proceedings in the matter'. When he found a book by John Clerk in his study, prepared on

Catherine's behalf for the legatine trial of 1529, he offered to return it, and then burnt it when Clerk told him he had long since changed his mind on the matter. More further insisted that 'beside this diverse other ways have I so used my self that if I rehearsed them all, it should well appear that I never have had against his grace's marriage any manner [of] demeanour whereby his highness might have any manner or cause or occasion of displeasure toward me'. More insisted: 'I am not he which either can, or whom it could become, to take upon him the determination or decision of such a weighty matter, nor boldly to affirm this thing or that therein, whereof diverse points a great way pass my learning.'[341] He reiterated the point to Nicholas Wilson in 1534. He had told the king his 'poor opinion' and, seeing that he could not serve the king further in the matter, 'I determined utterly with my self to discharge my mind of any further studying or musing of the matter', and sent away or burnt any books he had on it. As far as faults found in the original papal dispensation, he had never meddled, 'for I neither understand the doctors of the law nor well can turn their books'. Many further aspects had since arisen on which he was neither sufficiently learned in the law nor fully informed on the facts: 'therefore I am not he that either murmur or grudge, make assertions, hold opinions or keep dispicions [disputations] in the matter'.[342]

Despite Chapuys's assertions of More's devotion to the queen, it is not at all sure that Henry's marriage to Catherine was such a sticking point for More. In his self-justification to Cromwell in 1534, and referring to Henry's marriage to Anne Boleyn, More insisted that 'his Highness being in possession of his marriage and this noble woman really anointed Queen' he would

> neither murmur at it, nor dispute upon it, nor never did nor will, but with out any other manner meddling of the matter . . . faithfully pray to God for his Grace and hers both, long to live and well and their noble issue too, in such wise as may be to the pleasure of God, honour and surety to themself, rest, peace, wealth and profit unto this noble realm.

In saying that, More was treating the king's marriages as matters beyond dispute and argument: remarkably, he said he was praying for the king and for Anne Boleyn and their issue.[343] He said much the same to Nicholas Wilson: he prayed for the preservation of the king, the queen, their issue and the realm.[344] In his fateful conversation with Richard Rich on 12 June 1535, when Rich asked him whether, if an act of parliament were passed requiring that all the realm should take him for king, More would do so too, More replied that he would, explaining that a king could be made or deposed by parliament.[345] And in spring 1534, when first imprisoned for refusing to swear the oath to the act of supremacy, More did offer to swear to the succession itself, an offer that Cranmer would have accepted, but that the king adamantly refused. When on 14 June 1535 More claimed that he never spoke against the king's marriage with Queen Anne[346] he was not lying.

That all this was not simply tactical is confirmed by More's public behaviour in his years as lord chancellor. Whatever his private reservations may have been, however forcefully he may have spoken to Henry to his face, whatever impressions Chapuys may have formed, what More publicly did in March 1531 was to present university opinions in favour of the divorce to parliament, thus associating himself with the king's cause. In his speech, he went so far as to deny that the king was pursuing the divorce out of love for some lady rather than out of a scruple of conscience—at a moment when the role of Anne Boleyn cannot have been any secret for him. When the bill enacting the pardon of the clergy was then read, two bishops spoke in favour of the king; others denied that the time and place were appropriate. When More was asked his opinion, he said he had many times declared it (but had he?) to the king, and said no more. After the bill was read in the Commons, More added that the king wished them to be informed about this matter so that when they returned to their houses they might in turn tell their neighbours the truth 'that the king hath not attempted this matter of will or pleasure, as some strangers report, but only for the discharge of his conscience & surety of the succession of his realm'.[347]

All that has been seen by later commentators as More dissembling, formally endorsing the king's line but leaving no doubt about his true feelings;[348] but it would have required an act of remarkable perspicuity on the part of his audience to have suspected that at the time. It is hard to think that anyone seeing and hearing More's speech can have supposed that More himself was violently hostile to the king's great matter. More's biographer was clearly embarrassed by it. In his account, More was now so anxious that he might be required further to compromise himself that he sought to resign his office, invoking the assistance of the duke of Norfolk and succeeding before long. Such an account drastically telescopes the chronology: More did not resign till over a year later. And it may well offer a distorted impression of what More's deepest concerns really were. If he were truly a passionate advocate of Queen

Catherine's cause, then it is hard to see how he could have gone along with the reading of the university opinions in parliament.

But was More a Machiavellian politician, playing an essentially tactical game, disguising his true feelings while vigorously involved during the years 1530 to 1532 in a factional struggle with Thomas Cromwell for influence with the king? Is it true that 'down to April 1532 he had actively opposed the king's policy'?[349] That is the merest surmise. Guy and Elton have offered no evidence for such an interpretation, but rather narratives that take faction as a given that needs no proof: the concept of faction becomes an organising principle. In so doing, they have seriously underestimated the driving role of the king. In these years Henry was increasing his threats against churchmen and his pressures against the church, an essential course of action if he were ultimately to be able to get his way on his great matter against the pope. And it is in that context—Henry's determination to subordinate the church to his royal authority—that More's position may properly be understood. In May 1532 threats and pressures had culminated in the submission of the clergy. It was then that More left the king's service. He presented this as a resignation, but it might be preferable to treat it as an enforced resignation, if not an actual dismissal.

It is at this point that for a time More did embark on what can be read as a kind of political opposition to royal policies. He still did not openly oppose the king's divorce. Perhaps his absence from Anne's coronation might be seen as veiled opposition. If Roper is to be believed, More, declining an invitation from several bishops to come, warned them that first they would be expected to attend the coronation, then to preach, and finally to write books, in defence of it.[350] That may be fanciful. But More should not be presented as he was by his earliest biographer and, surprisingly, by Elton, as 'now resolved to spend the remainder of his life away from great affairs and in contemplation of "the immortality of the life to come"'.[351] What he did vigorously engage in was debate over the rights and powers of the church. In polemic against the lawyer Christopher St German, he defended the church.[352] It is hard to read More without seeing him as rerunning the arguments over the submission of the clergy. Here More may be seen as a politician, in some measure. What he was essentially doing was asserting the continuing validity of the independent jurisdiction and law-making powers of the church. Implicitly this was to reject the king's royal supremacy, but More did not say that explicitly.[353] So in a qualified sense here More was indeed opposing the king, not in the conspiratorial political machinations alleged by Elton, but, rather, more subtly and more quietly.

It is striking that More did not, however, directly respond to official works such as the *Book of Articles Lately Put Forth by the King's Council*, insisting to Cromwell in February 1534 that it raised matters about which he knew neither the law nor the exact facts, and so he would not presume to answer it. Furthermore, no one had had any books of his to print since the *Book of Articles* had appeared; his most recent work was directed against an unknown heretic who had attacked the mass, and it had, More said, been made and printed before Christmas, despite the printer's dating it to 1534.[354]

Intriguing too are More's reactions to the Nun of Kent. He might have been expected to have been one of her boldest admirers. Indeed, he did praise her devotion, but he would have no truck with her prophecies about Henry's marriage to Anne Boleyn and vigorously urged her not to meddle in political matters. More insisted that all his dealings with the nun were innocent of what we would call political intentions.[355] He offered a lengthy account. Eight or nine years ago Archbishop Warham sent a roll to the king giving details of what she had said in her trances, which the king showed him, asking his opinion. More thought there was nothing that 'a right simple woman' might not 'speak of her own wit' but, given the talk of a miracle, he would not dare to be bold in judging the matter. The king, he believed, at that time 'esteemed the matter as light as it after proved lewd'. More presents his reaction as cool. Since the king would have known at once if More was not telling the truth, it is highly likely that he was. Some time later, when two Observant Franciscan friars had on separate occasions attempted to tell him about her revelations concerning the king, he had, he said, refused to listen. When about Christmas 1532 Richard Risby, an Observant friar from Canterbury, lodged with More, he greatly praised the nun—'giving her high commendation of holiness'—and enlarged on what she had said to Wolsey and the king, including about the king's marriage, adding that Wolsey's soul had been saved by the nun's mediation. More had, however, refused to listen to reports about the king's matters—saying that 'I doubt not but the goodness of God should direct his highness with his grace and wisdom that the thing should take such end, as God should be pleased with, to the king's honour and surety of the realm'—and never saw Risby again till he was denounced at Paul's Cross.

About Shrovetide 1533, Father Hugh Rich, an Observant friar from Richmond, came to More and asked him about the nun. But once again

More refused, he said, to listen to her revelations. She had told the king, so there was no need to tell him or anyone else. Rich had told More only about her revelations concerning mean folk, not the king. If Rich had told him that the nun herself had told him the tale of Mary Magadalene and the king's mass at Calais, then, More claimed, he would have thought the worse of both of them. That tale was 'too marvellous to be true'; it was very likely that someone to whom she had described a dream had then talked of it as if it were a divine revelation. More had no doubt that some of the tales told about the nun were false, but since these were never reported as actually spoken by her, he thought that many of the tales might be true, and that she was indeed a virtuous woman, just as some lies were written about saints in heaven who worked miracles. But More claimed he had warned Rich to be cautious in believing 'these strange tales' which were 'no part of our creed'.[356] On More's account, he did not warm to the nun's political prophecies and warned Rich against them. Rich or Risby—it is not clear which—in testifying offered a different picture. If at first More had not thought much of the nun's prophecies, later he allegedly rejoiced to hear them.[357] But that may have been false testimony.

According to More, when he was at Syon, the fathers told him that they disliked some things about the nun. They wished that they had met when she was there because they would have liked to have seen what he made of her. Accordingly, when More heard she was at Syon again, he came to see her. They met alone in a little chapel. More said that he saw her not because of what God had revealed to her—the political prophecies—but because she was reported as very virtuous: he asked her to remember him in her prayers. She replied that she already did. More told her how one Helen, from Tottenham, 'of whose trances and revelations there hath been much talking', had been with him of late. Helen had told him that she had seen the nun, but that the latter had told her that her visions were not revelations but 'plain illusions of the devil'. Her evident modesty and piety impressed More: 'of truth I had a great good opinion of her'. But he insisted that they had not talked about the king. And he never saw her again.[358]

But on learning that many people came to see her, he wrote her a letter. He reminded her that he had told her that 'I was not only not desirous to hear of, but also would not hear of . . . any matter of princes or of the realm', supposing that God had revealed anything to her in such matters. To include in a letter to the nun such a recapitulation of their conversation suggests that he wanted to have supporting evidence in case he came under suspicion. More then reminded her of the downfall of Edward Stafford, third duke of Buckingham, 'who moved with the fame of one that was reported for an holy monk and had such talking with him as after was a great part of his destruction and disinheriting of his blood and great slander and infamy of religion'. He admonished her:

> I nothing doubt your wisdom and the spirit of God shall keep you from talking with any persons specially with lay persons, of any such manner things as pertain to princes' affairs or the state of the realm, but only to common and talk with any person high and low of such manner things as may to the soul be profitable for you to show and for them to know.

He addressed her as 'my good Lady and dearly beloved sister in our Lord', he asked for himself and his family to be recommended in her prayers, but he did not hear, let alone welcome or rejoice in, her prophecies.[359] Chapuys reported, in connection with this letter, that More could not have been more prudent.[360] And, writing to Cromwell, when under suspicion of involvement with the nun, More congratulated him on doing a very meritorious deed in bringing to light such 'detestable hypocrisy'.[361] 'And that in the matter of that wicked woman there never was on my part any other mind than good', More insisted.[362] More used similar language when he sent word to the proctor of the Charterhouse that 'she was undoubtedly proved a false deceiving hypocrite'.[363] After he was detained for refusing to take the oath in April 1534 he reiterated to Cromwell that he had had no part in the Nun of Kent's affair.[364] To Henry himself, More insisted that his conscience was clear on the matter.[365]

Of course, it is possible that More, looking back, was minimising his involvement in order to save his skin. Yet the fact that he was not convicted in 1534—by the end of March he had been discharged[366]—does suggest rather that the king, however reluctantly, accepted More's account of what he had (or had not) done.[367] And once again this reinforces the sense that More was not implacably opposed to the king's search for an annulment or to his new marriage, and above all that he was not engaged in any political campaign of opposition to it.

What kind of an opposition leader is this? On 5 March 1534 More defended himself at length to Cromwell on his behaviour over the divorce and over the Nun of Kent, as we have seen. But, significantly, he also expressed himself at length on the primacy of the pope. 'I no thing meddle in the matter', he insisted.

More made—surely teasingly—a debating point, claiming that he had not thought it 'should be begun by the institution of God' until he read what the king had written in 'his most famous book against the heresies of Martin Luther', the *Assertio Septem Sacramentorum*, printed in 1521. Even more playfully, he described how he had 'moved the King's Highness either to leave out that point, or else to touch it more slenderly', for the very good reason that things might later 'hap to fall in question between his highness and some pope as between princes and popes diverse times have done'. On More's account, Henry brushed such concerns aside. And More had since found all the holy doctors 'so consonant and agreeing in that point, and the thing by such general councils so confirmed also', but nothing of any consequence on the other side of the argument, and so he had come to think that he would be 'in right great peril' if he denied that the papal primacy was instituted by God.

It was by reference to the general opinion of Christendom that More justified his conviction. 'That primacy is at the least wise instituted by the corps of christendom and for a great urgent cause in avoiding of schisms and corroborate by continual succession more than the space of a thousand year at the least.' How attached More was to Christendom he made plain in his assertion 'therefore sith all christendom is one corps, I can not perceive how any member thereof may without the common assent of the body depart from the common head'.

More located ultimate authority in the general councils of the church. Whatever they declared ought to be taken as of unquestioned authority: 'or else were there in no thing no certainty, but through all christendom upon every man's affectionate reason, all thing might be brought from day to day to continual ruffle and confusion'.

More made the tactical point that, having appealed to a general council, which might depose the pope, Henry should not now do anything—whether making laws or producing books—that might be seen as denigrating the authority of the pope or of the general council. Finally, More denied that he had written anything in English that extolled the position of the pope. 'I never intended any thing to meddle in that matter against the king's gracious pleasure, what so ever mine own opinion were therein.'[368]

More here revealed his unease at what the king was doing, his devotion not so much to the papacy but to Christendom. Once again he insisted that he had been careful not to work against the king. He had given his opinion because he had been asked for it, but he had been careful not to persist in any public expression of his views, suppressing five lines on the authority of St Peter in one of his recent books after Henry had broken with Rome. Of course, this can be read as tactical, and consequently as showing a More who is concealing his true feelings. But it need not be tactical, given that what More said does readily fit in with what he had been saying and doing—or rather not saying and not doing—in these years. More's expression of loyalty to the king rings true: he had, after all, as we have seen, long been the king's servant. And nothing in his self-defence hints that he is about to become a political leader. Indeed, these letters would at once have damned him if he had gone on to do anything remotely suspicious.

What, however, is intriguing in More's defence is that while on the divorce he does no more than to insist on his lack of expertise and to suggest that he had not been persuaded rather than that he was opposed, and say that he had not listened to the political prophecies of the Nun of Kent, when it came to the breach with the pope, More did not evade the issue, or say it was beyond his comprehension or interest. He did not, significantly, defend the papal primacy as such. Indeed, he made a clever debating point of the king's book in 1521. But he did boldly defend the idea of Christendom and the authority of lawful general councils of the church.

In spring 1534 More refused to swear the oath of succession and after four days in the custody of the abbot of Westminster was sent to the Tower, where he remained until he was tried and executed in July 1535. Why exactly did More die? In a series of letters to his daughter Margaret Roper, and in what he said at and after his trial, amplified by his biographers, More explained and justified his position.

The king, More wrote in June 1535, 'thought that by my demeanour I had been occasion of much grudge and harm in the realm, and that I was an obstinate mind and an evil toward him'.[369] But at his trial More denied encouraging any slander, tumult or sedition against his prince.[370] He denied speaking or writing any word against any statutes passed by parliament. 'I never wrote, nor so much as spoke in any company any word of reproach in any thing the parliament had passed'; 'I take not upon me neither to define nor dispute in these matters.'[371] Referring particularly to the act of succession, he insisted that 'neither hath there at any time any word or deed maliciously scaped or proceeded from me against your statute'.[372] He vigorously denied that he had spoken out against the oath that he had refused to swear. More denied having disclosed or opened his conscience to anyone.[373] To his daughter in April 1534, More had insisted that he was 'not blaming any other man that had sworn'.[374]

More denied that he had recruited anyone to join him in refusing the oath, denied that he had encouraged anyone already resisting to continue in refusing the oath: 'I give no man occasion to hold any point one or other, nor never gave any man advice or counsel therein one way or other.'[375] 'I meddled not with the conscience of any other man, that either thinketh or saith he thinketh contrary unto mine.'[376] Repeatedly, he emphasised that he made no criticisms of anyone who did swear the oath. 'I damn none other man's conscience.'[377] 'I meddle not with the conscience of them that think otherwise . . . I am no man's judge.'[378] 'As touching the whole oath, I never withdrew any man from it, nor never advised any to refuse it, nor never put, nor will, any scruple in any man's head, but leave every man to his own conscience.'[379]

Obviously, that denial can be read tactically: to have expressed open criticisms would have been dangerous, while by doing nothing more than refusing the oath, he was implicitly questioning the behaviour of those who did. That was what Cromwell reproached him with in May 1535: 'my demeanour in that matter was of a thing that of likelihood made now other men so stiff therein as they be'.[380] On any index of open political engagement, however, More's refusal would not score highly. Pregnant with implication More's stand may have been, but in politics implications are not always speedily drawn. It is not at all clear that anyone was influenced directly by More's refusal to swear in 1534–35, however much he has become a symbol of dissent in the present.

More, however, was not quite as silent or noncommittal as he presented himself. He nit-picked, pointing out that the oath and statute did not correspond: tellingly, since the statute was modified.[381]

He *was* prepared to swear in part. He told his daughter that 'I would not deny to swear to the succession', though he could not swear the oath he was offered.[382] He told Fisher's servant that he had not refused to swear to the succession—confirming the impression we have already noted, that, whatever his hesitations, the king's divorce and marriage to Anne Boleyn were not a sticking point for him.

According to Harpsfield, after he had been convicted, More declared to the king that 'it was not for this supremacy so much that ye seek my blood, as for that I would not condescend to the marriage'.[383] How much credence may we place upon this? Is Harpsfield here stressing More's opposition to the marriage precisely because he had not been so fully opposed to it as events had unfolded?

However that may be, if Roper is to be believed, More was privately outspoken about the king and his councillors, saying to his daughter that 'surely, daughter, it is great pity that any christian prince should by a flexible council ready to follow his affections, and by a weak clergy lacking grace constantly to stand to their learning, with flattery be so shamefully abused.'[384]

And More *did* comment to his daughter on his attitudes towards the oath taken by others. According to Margaret, writing to Alice Alington, More had explained to her why most had sworn:

> some may do for favour, and some may do for fear. . . . And some may peradventure think that they will repent and be shriven thereof, and that so God shall remit it them. And some may be peradventure of that mind, that if they say one thing and think the while the contrary, God more regardeth their heart than their tongue, and that therefore their oath goeth upon that they think, and not upon that they say.

More added the lapidary comment: 'I can use no such ways in so great a matter.'[385] He also commented on those who had taken the oath but previously espoused contrary views:

> it is well known that of them that have sworn it, some of the best learned before the oath given them, said and plain affirmed the contrary, of some such things as they have now sworn in the oath, and that upon their truth and their learning then, and that not in haste nor suddenly, but often and after great diligence done to seek and find out the truth.

More would not 'misjudge any other man's conscience, which lieth in their own heart far out of my sight'. What he would say is that he never heard any explanation for their change of mind.

And More apparently went on, not uncynically, that some men might swear against their convictions or 'frame their conscience afresh to think other wise than they thought'. What might weigh with them were 'the keeping of the prince's pleasure, and the avoiding of his indignation, the fear of the losing of their worldly substance'. But, he said, he would not believe that men had changed their mind for such reasons. After all, if such things swayed them, then why had they not swayed him, 'for in good faith I knew few so faint hearted as my self'. He would think no worse of others for having sworn: 'but as I know well in mine only conscience causeth me to refuse the oath, so will I trust in God, that according to their conscience they have received it and sworn'.

Yet for all More's reluctance openly to criticise, he did suggest that 'it were . . . well possible that some men in this realm too think not so clear the contrary, as by the oath received they have sworn to say'[386]— which at the very least casts doubt on their integrity.

But if More felt deeply critical of those who swore, there is little to suggest that he expressed his distaste beyond his family circle. Christopher Chaitor, Bishop Tunstal's servant, much later recalled that More asked one Burton, another of Tunstal's servants, whether his master would be joining Fisher and himself—but More then said 'if he live he may do more good than to die with us'.[387] It is impossible to be confident that such a rueful remark was intended to mean the opposite of what it said. More said he had wished Dr Nicholas Wilson, who he had heard intended to swear the oath, good luck. It was always possible that More hoped that his remark would change Wilson's mind.[388] Elton thought More stiffened the resolution of the martyrs Richard Reynolds of Syon and John Houghton, prior of the London Charterhouse, but offers no specific evidence, except that their executions coincided with the timing of 'belated' attempts to bring More round.[389]

Did More and Fisher conspire together in the Tower? They never met there. But they were evidently able to send servants with letters and messages to each other, though the sum of their contacts remains small. Each was anxious to know what the other had said under interrogation. But that hardly amounts to a conspiracy. Conceivably each drew strength and comfort from the knowledge that he was not alone. Understandably the government took this seriously. Bishop Fisher's servants and John Wood, More's servant, were interrogated about More's contacts with Fisher in the Tower. Fisher himself was interrogated on 12 June. Very little of significance emerged. The indictment against More accuses him of maliciously upholding Fisher's attitude: aware that Fisher had expressly denied the royal supremacy, More wrote to him 'continuando maliciam suam predictam' (continuing in his habitual ill-will) on 12 May 1534.[390] Whether this is true is unclear. Fisher's own testimony has More asking him what answer he had given to the council[391] and More as fearful that, given that their answers would be similar, the council would suppose that one had 'taken light' of the other.[392] Fisher also claimed that a year later More again took the initiative in asking him what he had said when questioned.[393] The testimony of George Gold, servant to the lieutenant of the Tower—the nearest we have to a neutral witness—further casts doubt on any notion of a conspiracy. Gold recalled that soon after Fisher and More were imprisoned, Fisher had sent him to find out More's answer, and learnt how More had refused to dispute the king's title but would devote himself to his beads. Soon after More had sent a letter, Gold said, advising Fisher not to make the same answer, lest the council became suspicious.[394] Both More and Fisher would use the metaphor of the double-edged sword to describe their predicament. More had allegedly informed Fisher that he had been silent on the statute since 'the act of parliament is like a sword with two edges, for if a man answer one way it will confound his soul, and if he answer the other way it will confound his body'.[395] But despite the councillors' suspicions, that does not have to be evidence of any prior agreement or current plotting. As we have seen, Fisher's and More's positions were not exactly the same—as More put it, Fisher was content to have sworn 'either somewhat more, or in some other manner than ever I minded to do'[396]—but they had both been put in the Tower for refusing to swear the oath, and it did not necessarily follow that they had plotted together for them to have responded to their interrogators in broadly similar terms. Neither man was responsible for the refusal to swear of the other; each, however, was no doubt cheered by the other's stand. As More put it, as they were both in one prison, and for one cause, he was glad to send to him, and to hear from him again.[397] More admitted receiving letters from and sending letters to Fisher but claimed that these were for the most part nothing but comforting words and thanks for meat and drink[398]—nothing 'but certain familiar talk and recommendations, such as was seemly and agreeable to our long and old acquaintance'.[399] One letter was an exception. Fisher wrote to More saying that since the statute used the word 'maliciously', anyone who spoke nothing of malice did not offend the statute: More agreed, but feared that it would not be interpreted in that way.[400] He was correct: his refusal to give a direct answer was seen as malicious perseverance.[401]

It is hard, then, to see More as a political conspirator, and his execution in July 1535 is difficult to interpret as a reaction to any outright opposition or plotting on his part. For a year he had been in the Tower, declining to swear the oaths demanded of him, and declining to give his reasons for his refusal. He had apparently offered to set down in writing the causes that moved him, so long as he was licensed by the king to do so without harm; but he was unwilling to declare his reasons if these put him in jeopardy.[402] Denied that licence—and, as we have seen in the case of Fisher, it would not have availed—More maintained his silence, except to use the metaphor of a two-edged sword. That image, however, implied that if he swore as was demanded of him, it would endanger his soul. Not surprisingly, Henry did not find that attitude acceptable. And in spring 1535, the king evidently took the decision to force the issue. On several occasions, Henry sent his councillors to order More to declare plainly whether he thought the statute lawful or not.[403]

This was a trap. Any explicit criticism of the royal supremacy could be seen as treason. It is not surprising, then, that More should have refused to be drawn when he was told that the king's pleasure was that Cromwell and several councillors should demand his opinion whether the king and his heirs were, ever rightly have been and perpetually should be supreme head of the church of England under Christ. More refused to give his opinion. He was sure that the king would never have ordered any such question to be asked of him, since he had 'ever from the beginning' declared his mind 'well and truly from time to time' to the king, and more recently to Cromwell. In saying this More was not dissembling: he had, as we have seen, made his views forcefully clear to Cromwell in March 1534, before they had been rendered illegal by the act of supremacy.

It was at this point that More famously declared: 'now I have in good faith discharged my mind of all such matters, and neither will dispute Kings' titles nor popes'. He insisted upon his fundamental loyalty to the king: 'the king's true faithful subject I am and will be, and daily I pray for him and all his, and for you all that are of his honourable council and for all the realm, and otherwise than thus I never intend to meddle'. He insisted that 'I do nobody harm, I say none harm, I think none harm, but wish every body good. And if this be not enough to keep a man alive in good faith I long not to live.'[404] In response to Cromwell, who warned that the king 'would exact a more full answer', More insisted that 'I would never meddle in the world again. . . . I had fully determined with my self, neither to study nor meddle with any matter of this world, but that my whole study should be, upon the passion of Christ and mine own passage out of this world.'[405]

He was given six weeks to swear. Henry demanded that More give his opinion on the royal supremacy. He would not allow him to remain silent. He was not going to allow the possibility of private thought— private dissent—behind a public neutrality or silence. The king, as we have seen in Fisher's case, would not treat silence as anything other than malicious. On 3 June Audley, Cranmer, Suffolk, Wiltshire and Cromwell came to press More to give the king his answer to the question whether the statute of supremacy was lawful or not. More would not be drawn, though he did once again liken the statute to a two-edged sword:

the law and statute whereby the King is made supreme head . . . be like a sword with two edges; for if a man say that the same laws be good, then it is dangerous to the soul; And if he say contrary to the said statute, then it is death to the body. Wherefore I will make thereunto none other answer because I will not be occasion of the shortting of my life.[406]

More lamented that it was 'somewhat hard' that he should be compelled to give his opinion on the statutes:

> for if it so were that my conscience gave me against the statutes (wherein how my mind giveth me I make no declaration) than I nothing doing nor nothing saying against the statute it were a very hard thing to compel me to say either precisely with it against my conscience to the loss of my soul, or precisely against it to the destruction of my body.

This formulation, as we have seen, came close to saying that the statute would damn the soul of anyone who agreed to it.[407]

On 12 June Richard Rich, the king's solicitor-general, entangled More in what proved a fateful discussion. Suppose, said Rich, that parliament enacted that Rich were king and that it would be treason to deny it, would More accept him as king? Yes, replied More; but he immediately countered, suppose parliament enacted that God should not be God, and opposing the act should be treason, would Rich say that God was not God? No, replied Rich, 'sith no parliament may make any such law'. At that point the accounts of their interview diverge. According to the indictment, Rich countered, what if the king were declared supreme head on earth of the English church? To that, according to the indictment, More replied traitorously. The cases were not the same, More declared. A king could be made or deposed by parliament, to which everyone in parliament may give his assent; but the question of the royal supremacy was not a matter to which anyone could assent in parliament: most foreign countries did not accept it. In this way More had, it was alleged against him, maliciously deprived the king of his title.[408] In Roper's account, all that is telescoped: when Rich says that no parliament might make any such law that God was not God, ' "no more", said Sir Thomas More, as master Rich reported of him, "could the parliament make the king supreme head of the church" '.

Whether More actually said this remains a matter of uncertainty. Another important source for More's trial, known to scholars as *X, does not mention the conversation at all.[409] More vigorously denied saying any such words: would he have 'in so weighty a cause, so unadvisedly overshot my self as to trust master Rich', a man he had always reputed as 'of so little truth', and 'say to him the secrets of my conscience touching the king's supremacy . . . a thing which I never did, nor never would, after the statute thereof made, reveal either to the king's highness himself, or to any of his honourable councillors'? And More added that even if he had said it, it could not be taken to be malicious.[410]

More was tried by a commission of oyer et terminer on 1 July. According to *X and (presumably following *X) Harpsfield, he began by denying the charge (which is not in the indictment) that he had maliciously opposed the king's marriage to Anne Boleyn. He had never spoken maliciously about it, but only according to his very mind, opinion and conscience—and he had suffered as a result.[411] He insisted that he had been silent on the act of supremacy ('a man dead and mortified toward the world, and to the thinking upon any other matters than upon the passion of Christ and passing out of the world'); insisted that 'for this my taciturnity and silence, neither your law nor any law in the world is able justly and rightly to punish me, unless you may besides lay to my charge either some word or some fact in deed'. Even if silence were construed as an action, the presumption that silence gives consent precluded the charge against him: ' "Qui tacet, consentire videtur" . . . this my silence implieth and importeth rather a ratification and confirmation then any condemnation of your statute.'[412] He defended himself against charges of conspiring with Bishop Fisher, by this time a convicted traitor. He declared that his letters to Fisher—burnt by Fisher—were nothing 'but certain familiar talk and recommendations, such as was seemly and agreeable to our long and old acquaintance'.[413] He insisted that his reference to a double-edged sword was conditional; if Fisher's answer corresponded with his own, that happened because of the correspondence of their studies. More insisted that 'neither hath there at any time any word or deed maliciously scaped or proceeded from me against your statute'.[414] And then he rebutted the supposedly treasonable conversation he had had with Rich (in both Roper and Harpsfield, but not in *X). That conversation proved the crux, and on the strength of it More was convicted of treason. The crown lawyers evidently accepted More's argument that the first three counts against him showed no offence; but the words Rich claimed he had spoken were seen as damning.[415]

For what, precisely, did More die? If he was not a conspirator or a leader of opposition, was it for conscience? More repeatedly invoked his conscience. What he meant by that has—as several historians have pointed out—been grievously misunderstood. When, in that fateful conversation with Richard Rich on 12 June 1535, he told him, 'your conscience will save you and my conscience will save me',[416] his words must be read ironically. He was *not* upholding Rich's right to believe whatever his conscience might prompt him to believe while at the same asserting his own right to believe whatever his conscience compelled him to believe. He was rather defying Rich—and implying that Rich's conscience, far from saving him, would lead him to hell. More was not dying for the right of men and women to *choose* their faith and their church. Rather, he was appealing to conscience to justify a stand he was taking because it and it alone was right. This was not, as Moreau rightly observes, an absolute stand on conscience. 'If I were alone on my side . . . I should be terrified to rest on my sole opinion,' he wrote from prison.[417] The importance More attaches to the number of those who shared his opinion saves his position from deserving the label 'fanatical'.

What gave More confidence that his own understanding was just and worth giving his life for was that the opinion of Christendom, in his lifetime, and over the centuries of Christian history, concurred with it. Essentially More's stand was a defence of Christendom. He insisted that on his side of the matter he had the general counsel of Christendom, meaning by that the majority, in Christendom, of learned and virtuous men, including those now dead. He restated his position to his daughter Margaret Roper in August 1534. If it were possible to do what might content the king without offending God, he would gladly do it. But according to his conscience, he could not do it. He thought that 'in Christendom about, of those well learned men and virtuous that are alive, they be not the fewer part that are of my mind'; and of the dead 'I am sure that it is not the fewer part of them that all the time while they lived, thought in some of the things, the way I think now'.[418] If, he had earlier informed his daughter, there were many of his opinion, 'I am not than bounden to change my conscience, and conform it to the council of one realm, against the general council of christendom'.[419] If in any particular part of Christendom a new law were made which some thought against the law of God, but others not, whoever thought it against God's law was not bound to change his conscience. Unless a general council decreed it or unless it was a general belief that had spread by the working of God universally through all Christian nations, then 'I can see none that lawfully may command and compel any man to change his own opinion'.

The implication was that Henry was unlawfully ordering his subjects to obey a new law not sanctioned by any general council or generally accepted throughout Christendom. Pressed by Cromwell to explain why, for all his appeal to conscience, he had been hard on heretics, More insisted that if

> a man would in a matter take away by him self upon his own mind alone, or with some few, or with never so many, against an evident truth appearing by the common faith of christendom, this conscience is very damnable . . . a very good occasion to move him, and yet not to compel him, to confirm his mind and conscience unto theirs.[420]

'The common faith of christendom': that was More's guiding light. It was, of course, a less steady guide than he perhaps realised: inherent in this position was the possibility that, if opinion within Christendom shifted, then so must his: truth was a matter of Christian consensus, not an absolute. It is far from sure that More grasped such an implication. Christendom was a given from which Henry (temporarily?) had strayed. More, in conscience, could not follow the master he had served so loyally for so many years along a road so perilous to his soul and to those of all Christians.

After he was convicted, More spoke out more boldly and directly, emphasising once more the centrality of Christendom in his thought. In Roper's account, More attacked the indictment against him as grounded on an act of parliament 'directly repugnant to the laws of God and his whole church'. He directly rejected the royal supremacy and defended the authority of the pope. No temporal prince might presume to take upon him the supreme government of the church. That rightfully belonged to the see of Rome, 'a spiritual pre-eminence by the mouth of our Saviour himself, personally present upon the earth, [only] to St Peter and his successors, bishops of the same see, by special prerogative granted'. And then More insisted on the role of Christendom. This realm, being but one member and a small part of the church, could not make 'a particular law disagreable with the general law of Christ's universal catholic church', any more than the city of London could make a law against an act of parliament to bind the whole realm. 'No more might this realm of England refuse obedience to the See of Rome then might the child refuse obedience to his natural father.'[421] When told by the lord chancellor that all the bishops, universities and best learned men had agreed to the act of supremacy, and that 'it was much mar-velled that he alone against them all would so stiffly stick [thereat], and so vehemently argue there against',[422] More replied, according to *X and Harpsfield, that he had studied the matter for seven years and found no doctor or ancient writer to support the supremacy.[423] According to Roper, More declared that in Christendom most well-learned bishops were of his mind; 'the far greater part' of dead bishops, many of them saints in heaven, thought as he does now; 'therefore am I not bounden, my Lord, to conform my conscience to the council of one realm against the general council of Christendom'.[424] According to *X and Harpsfield, More pointedly added: 'For of the foresaid holy bishops, I have, for every Bishop of yours, above one hundred; and for one Council or Parliament of yours (God knoweth what manner of one), I have all the Councils made these thousand years. And for this kingdom, I have all other christian realms'; 'pour ung vostre parlement, Dieu scait quel, j'ay tous les concilles generaulx depuis mille ans; et pour ung royaulme, j'ay la France et tous les autres royaulmes de la chrestiente'.[425]

If More died for any single thing, it was not so much for the papacy[426] but for Christendom. On the scaffold he 'desired all the people thereabout to pray for him and to bear witness with him that he should now there suffer death in and for the faith of the holy catholic church'.[427] According to the Paris newsletter (an account in French of More's trial and execution that was circulated soon after his death), More—in words that have become famous—died 'the king's good servant, but God's first'.[428] It seriously misleads, then, to present More as an opponent of the king, as a political leader. Guy 'suspects that More himself wanted to be remembered not for *Utopia* or his achievements as Lord Chancellor, but for his stand against Henry VIII':[429] but More had not so much stood *against* the king as *for* Christendom. It was Henry who with increasing passion saw More as a political enemy and threat and resolved that, if he did not submit, he would be destroyed. How far the king was justified in this is open to debate. Elton saw More's fate as reflecting 'the behaviour of a government forced by political circumstances into a thoroughly unhappy and bad decision', but Elton went on to describe that behaviour as 'scrupulous rather than tyrannical. Cromwell, for one, does not seem to have wanted More's death at all'. Elton was at pains to pin the blame on the king: Cromwell, for Elton, acted against More 'when Henry finally demanded his death'.[430] 'Cromwell did what he thought he had to do; the hatred and vindictiveness belonged to the king.'[431] 'The king's outburst of ungovernable fury closed the road of wisdom and compassion, and though More may have died for the papacy he died because of Henry VIII.'[432] Henry may well have sincerely feared that More was—or might become—a source of political infection, though in reality his exemplary influence was limited. Of greater importance was More's position as symbol of dissent: his mute presence in the Tower silently but constantly reproached the king. *Raison d'état* in such terms justified Henry's destruction of More; and no modern historian can be sure that, in a range of hypothetical circumstances, More might not have offered more active opposition to the king. But from the evidence of what he said and did—and did not say and did not do—it is very hard to see him as an active and threatening political opponent of the king. Compelled to swear an oath he could not swallow, what More did was to bear witness to his profound conviction of the moral authority of Christendom.

Observant Franciscans

Open and public defiance of the king's desire for a divorce came first from within the Observant Franciscans. This was a strict order of friars with six English houses, at Greenwich, Canterbury, Richmond, Newark, Newcastle and Southampton. They were among the most rigorous of monastic orders in early Tudor England. Their European origins lay in a split within the Franciscan order in the late fourteenth century, centred on the extent to which friars should be allowed to accumulate material possessions: the Observants urged greater austerity. Within England their flowering was largely the work of royal patronage. When Edward IV was enlarging his palace at Greenwich, he was encouraged by his sister Margaret of York (who had married Charles the Bold, duke of Burgundy) to invite the vicar-general of the Observant Franciscans to set up a house there in 1481–82. Henry VII renewed their charter in 1485. By the early 1490s their church was complete. The proximity of the Observant Franciscans to what was a much-used royal palace gave them an influence and a prominence far beyond what might have been expected. In 1498 three houses of the old Conventual Franciscans, in Canterbury, Newcastle and Southampton, were transferred to the Observants. When Henry VII rebuilt his palace at Richmond (formerly called Sheen) between 1498 and 1501, it was an Observant Franciscan friary that he established there, physically linked to the palace.[433] The Observant Franciscan friary at Newark was established by men formerly connected to the late William, Lord Hastings, who were among Henry VII's most trusted supporters.[434] Their Tudor connections were reflected in displays of arms, especially the Tudor rose, the Beaufort portcullis and the Richmond greyhound.[435] The Observant Franciscan houses provided kings and queens with spiritual advisers, confessors and preachers; they reflected the crown's fashionable piety and its awareness of the highest and best practices within the church. Henry VII had his son Henry, the future king, baptised in the Greenwich friary church in 1491.[436] That must have been a deliberate decision since his elder son, Arthur, had been baptised at Winchester in 1486.[437] In his will he requested huge numbers of masses from the Observant Franciscans and sought to leave them large sums.[438] Henry VIII had his children christened in the friars' churches: his son at Richmond in January 1511, Mary at Greenwich in February 1516 and, intriguingly in the light of events, Elizabeth at Greenwich in September 1533.[439]

That background must have made what happened seem specially insulting and threatening to the king. On Easter Day 1532, William Peto, who had been warden of Richmond, and who in March 1532 had been elected for a three-year tour of duty as provincial minister of the Observant Franciscans—that is to say, the leader of the English province—preached at their convent church at Greenwich before the king. According to Harpsfield, Peto compared Henry to King Ahab, who gave ear to false prophets but would not listen to God's prophet Mychaeus (Micaiah), whom he imprisoned and starved: 'Sir I am the Mychaeus that you deadly hate for prophesying and telling you the truth.' And what Peto as Mychaeus told Henry was that he should not divorce. He warned him that if he followed Ahab he would incur the same unhappy fate: dogs would lick his blood.[440] When Henry spoke to him after his sermon, Peto told him in no uncertain terms that, in pursuing his divorce, he was putting his throne in jeopardy: both the great and the common people were muttering. Later Peto recalled how he had told the king that in his conscience he could never have another wife while Catherine lived, unless he could prove carnal knowledge between Prince Arthur and Catherine. And that could never be proved, Peto added, since Catherine, who was in the best position to know the truth, had received the sacrament to the contrary. She was so virtuous, Peto declared, that her oath should be given credence. Peto also said that he had told the king to his face that it was said that he had meddled both with Anne Boleyn's sister, Mary Boleyn, and their mother.[441]

Henry's reactions to Peto's public sermon and private warning can only be wondered at. Given Catherine's refusal to accept his wishes, he must have expected that at some point there would be open criticism of his search for a divorce. Harpsfield's account, with Peto declaring that Henry hated him for telling the truth, hints that this was not the first time he had raised the matter. Nonetheless, even if that were so, Peto's sermon must have come as a shock. So public a declaration was extraordinary. That Peto did it on Easter Sunday, the central holy day in the Christian calendar, when Henry would be present to hear his sermon, strongly suggests that this was no sudden outburst but rather carefully premeditated. We learn from later evidence that Peto had been preparing a book in defence of Catherine of Aragon, probably a reply to the king's own *Glass of the Truth*, printed in Lüneburg in 1533.[442] And yet Peto's sermon makes more sense as a personal rebuke to the king, comparable to that from a confessor calling for personal repentance, rather than as an overtly political manoeuvre or as the beginning of a preaching campaign.

Intriguingly, the king allowed Peto to go abroad to attend the general chapter of the Observant friars which was to be held at Pentecost in Toulouse. Presumably he did not realise that Peto's additional purpose in going was to have his book printed. As soon as Henry knew that Peto had left, he ordered one of his chaplains, Dr Richard Curwen, to preach in the friars' church, against all custom, and against the wishes of the warden, Henry Elston. When, at the end of his sermon, Curwen claimed—quite falsely—that all the universities were in favour of the divorce, Elston, in the presence of the king, declared that this was not so. Henry, very angry, ordered all the bishops to tell Peto, on his return, to deprive Elston of his office and to make him confess his mistake. Peto refused. Henry had both Peto and Elston arrested. They were still under arrest at Lambeth in May. The king sent to Rome for a commission to enable Dr George Browne, provincial of the Austin friars, to try them, but nothing came of it.[443] Elston did appear several times before the bishops and once before convocation: he was sent by the king to the Greyfriars at Bedford.[444] It was while in prison in Lambeth Tower that Peto told Throckmorton about his sermon, and advised him that if he were in parliament he should stick to that matter—meaning that he should continue to oppose the government's bills—if his soul were to be saved.[445]

Eventually Peto and Elston were released and sent into exile, to Antwerp, from where they intrigued continually. In June 1533 Cromwell learned that they and other friars from Greenwich, Richmond and Canterbury were at Antwerp, writing books against the king's great matter.[446] They arranged the importing into England of a book printed there that had first been drafted by Bishop Fisher. Peto 'laboureth busier than a bee in the setting forth of this book'. Every week a friar came from England to meet him. Cromwell's informant Stephen Vaughan remarked that 'the king never had in his realm traitors like his friars'. Thomas More had sent them copies of his books against Tyndale and Frith.[447] Vaughan called Peto an hypocrite knave, as the more part of his brethren be, a wolf, a tiger clad in a sheep's skin; it is a perilous knave, a raiser of sedition, an evil reporter of the king's highness, a prophesier of mischief, a fellow that I would wish to be in the King's hands, and to be shamefully punished.[448]

The vehemence of the language eloquently conveys both fear and irritation. Peto, then, had spoken out boldly; he had held firm to his beliefs when imprisoned; he had accepted exile but had used it as a platform for printing books and sending them to England, using Observant friars as carriers. Perhaps more was considered: in April 1534 Elston was reported as saying that the Spanish were preparing an invasion of England.[449]

How far did Peto and Elston reflect the mood of the friars generally? In 1532 another Observant, John Forest, preached what was described as an 'indiscreet' sermon at Paul's Cross. We do not know precisely what he said. He may have been threatened by the king.[450] Thomas Pearson, a young preacher at Greenwich, said to be most favoured by Forest, was reported to be as much against the king's cause as he dared, and to have recently reproved another preacher for speaking against Queen Catherine.[451] King Henry tried in vain to secure the deprivation of John Robinson, deputy warden at Richmond, and another friar there, Curson.[452]

Some of the Newark friars also spoke out. One was reported to Sir John Markham, a local landowner, as having preached seditious sermons in 1533 (and the friar admitted nearly all that he was accused of, though details do not survive): Markham warned of the inconvenience if such men were allowed to preach and stir men in their confessions.[453] Two Newark friars, Hugh Payne and Thomas Hayfield, went on a preaching tour in the West Country, an intriguing choice of location: Bristol in June 1534, then through Somerset, Devon and Cornwall, before being captured in Cardiff, where they were caught bargaining with the master of a Breton ship to take them to Brittany. Wherever they went they urged people to hold to the bishop of Rome, calling him pope, saying they would die in his cause. They said that the water that Princess Elizabeth was christened in was not hot enough. They denounced Hugh Latimer, who had vigorously defended the break with Rome and called for further reforms, as a heretic, along with those who followed him.[454] Payne had earlier been in touch with Peto in Antwerp.[455] Yet on their capture Payne and Hayfield abjectly submitted to the king, remarkably denying they had ever spoken against him or upheld the pope: they had prayed for him by name after the old custom only until they heard the contrary.[456] Characterising the house at Newark as 'something of a hotbed of conservative resistance'[457] colour-fully exaggerates, but clearly for a time several friars were prepared to speak out—until repressed.

Other Observant Franciscan friars, as we have seen, became closely involved with Elizabeth Barton, the Nun of Kent. Two from Canter-bury, Hugh Rich, the warden of the convent, and Richard Risby, had paid with their lives in spring 1534. Rich in particular had been active in spreading the nun's revelations: he had gone 'to sundry places of this realm and made secret relation' of them to Princess Mary, the countess of Salisbury, Lord and Lady Hussey, the marchioness of Exeter, Bishop John Fisher, the countess of Derby, Sir Thomas More, Thomas Abel (Catherine of Aragon's chaplain), three London merchants, several of the nuns at Syon and monks at Sheen, several priests including Henry Gold, and several gentlemen including Sir Thomas Arundell.[458] Risby, the warden of the Canterbury Observants, confessed his part; he told the prior of the cathedral at Canterbury that she was a person much in the favour of God and that what she would say would give him great comfort.[459] In spreading news of the nun's revelations, Rich and Risby had obviously played a significant part. And yet it is far from sure that their actions should be seen in terms of a modern political campaign. What Risby promised Prior Gold that the nun would give him was, it should be noted, 'great comfort'. Her revelations offered those who were dismayed by what the king was doing hope that all would yet be well. And the activities of Rich and Risby should not then be seen in terms of intrigue but rather as bringing to the politically powerless a measure of spiritual consolation.

Several Observant Franciscans, then (and these not the least signif-icant members of the order) were among the most active of those who declined to follow the king on the divorce. Peto and Elston were clearly defiant and organised, prepared to go into exile and arrange the printing of works in defence of Catherine of Aragon's marriage. Forest (presumably), Robinson and other friars, notably two from Newark, preached on the same lines. Rich and Risby had welcomed and spread the prophecies of the Nun of Kent. Several nameless friars were involved in importing books from Antwerp. For the king, such defiance from one of the most influential religious orders with a high reputation for moral integrity must have been painful. In a sense the Observant Franciscan houses had become a standing reproach to the king.

Not everyone in the order was opposed. John Lawrence, a friar, and Richard Lyst, a lay brother, did what they could, encouraged by Thomas Cromwell, to promote the king's cause, but succeeded largely in making themselves unpopular.[460] Their behaviour shows, however, that all was not sweetness, light and concord in the Observant Franciscan convents, and that the Observants did not put up a wholly united fight against the king over his divorce. Manifestly, those sympathetic to the king's cause remained in a minority. Nevertheless, some such there were. And, more generally, there were limits to what the friars could and did do. They did not—they could not—attempt to mobilise the political nation or the realm as a whole. Peto's sermon was a warning to the king, a bold gesture of defiance, but its wider impact was small. If a few other friars spoke out, there was nothing that could be called an organised preaching campaign involving most of the friars. Rich spread the Nun of Kent's prophecies to some fifty people—but they were mostly already sympathetic, and welcomed the consolation that the prophecies offered. It would be wrong to belittle the courage that the various friars showed in their varied acts of dissent; but it would still be misleading to present them as leading an active and organised opposition to the king's plans. To write that, in the early 1530s, 'the friars played a major role in the opposition which gathered around the queen, aiding ... in co-ordinating the parliamentary opposition and arranging the publication of bishop Fisher's works against the king's divorce proposals' is to sys-tematise and to dramatise their actions.[461] 'Co-ordinating the parlia-mentary opposition' is an exaggerated description of Peto's encouragement of Throckmorton to speak out against the king's bills in parliament. Peto and Elston were indeed involved in the printing of one of Fisher's books, and Peto published a riposte to *A Glass of the Truth* in 1533, but he did not venture a short and succinct work in English. 'The opposition which gathered around the queen' again suggests some-thing organised and substantial. Many of the Observant Franciscans in England did not accept the king's case for his divorce, and some of them, not least heads of convents, in various ways and at various times made their sentiments known. There may well have been more friars preaching sermons against the divorce than we know from surviving records. But their dissent must be finely calibrated.

Henry was undoubtedly irritated and uneasy at the presence, close to the heart of his power, of highly regarded religious houses, many of whose members were unsympathetic to his plans and actions and some of whom at times spoke out against them. The oath imposed on the Observant Franciscans in 1534 was designed to resolve that situation. Every adult in the realm had to swear; but a special form of oath was devised for the Observants, no doubt to heighten the pressure. George Browne, prior of the Austin friars, and John Hilsey, prior provincial of the Blackfriars, were sent to visit the Observants, in itself a somewhat provocative gesture, since the very emergence of the Observants had been, and remained, a critique of the existing orders of friars.

On their arrival, all the Observants were to assemble in their chapter house, where they were to be examined separately about their faith and obedience to Henry VIII. They were asked to swear an oath of allegiance to the king, to Anne Boleyn as queen and to her present and future children. They were also asked to swear an oath that they would preach and persuade the people of this at every opportunity. They were asked to acknowledge the king as supreme head of the church. They were to make a new profession to observe their rule in obedience to the king rather than to the pope. They were required to agree that the bishop of Rome had no greater authority than other bishops. They were not to refer to him as pope, publicly or privately.[462] If the friars swore allegiance to the king's new marriage and to the break with Rome, Henry would have publicly secured the support of those who had so far begrudged it. If, on the other hand, the friars refused, then the king would have succeeded in forcing them into a public declaration of their opposition, rather than simply the rumbling disaffection and intermittent outbursts that had marked the previous two years, and that refusal could then be punished as treason according to the king's new law.

But at Canterbury only two refused: the rest did swear.[463] Elsewhere, the most important Observant to take the oath was Friar Forest, who had briefly dissented in 1532. There are some letters in which he assured Catherine of Aragon that he was ready to die for Christ: he hoped, he said, that he would not be found inconstant at the age of sixty-four. He had learned, and taught others, to despise worldly things.[464] But these letters (which are to be found in a printed book of 1583) may not be genuine: if they are, and if they date from 1534, then Forest must have succumbed to Henry.[465] There is no doubt that in 1534 Forest swore the oath required. He was recorded as being in prison, and he may well have sworn under great pressure.[466] Later he would declare that 'he took his oath with his outward man, but his inward man never consented thereunto',[467] and in 1538 he would be executed for treason (as we shall see).

But many of the Observants refused to swear. At Richmond there was general reluctance. Rowland Lee and Thomas Bedell, the king's men, went there in May and in June. The prior was willing enough. Lee and Bedell had several meetings with the friars, 'and have all this time been in despair of their reconciliation till this morning', but now at last hoped to bring them to conformity. The Carthusians of Sheen had urged them to follow their example and take the oath.[468] But in June, Lee and Bedell found that, despite 'all the means and policies' they could devise, the Richmond friars refused to consent to the articles which their provincial had earlier delivered. Both the warden and the convent showed themselves 'very untoward'. Lee and Bedell were thus compelled to move the convent to put the matter to the arbitration of their four seniors or 'discretes', giving them full authority to consent or dissent for them all, when they came to Greenwich.[469]

At Greenwich, Lee and Bedell again tried to have the matter entrusted to the seniors, thinking that if they refused to consent, it would be better 'to strain a few then a multitude'. But at Greenwich the convent 'stiffly' insisted that 'where the matter concerned particularly every one of their souls, they would answer particularly, every man for him self'. After 'much reasoning and debating', Lee and Bedell asked each of them individually, and found them 'in one mind of contradiction and dissent from the said articles'. They were especially opposed to the article that the bishop of Rome had no more authority than any other bishop in his diocese. They said that this was 'clearly' against their profession and the rules of St Francis. Lee and Bedell told them that the archbishops, the bishops of London, Winchester, Durham and Bath and other prelates and heads and 'all the famous clerks of the realm' had subscribed to the conclusion that the Roman pontiff did not have any greater jurisdiction in the realm of England than other bishops. But, Lee and Bedell admitted, all their reasoning 'could but sink into their obstinate heads'. The Observants insisted that 'they had professed saint Francis' religion and in the observance thereof they would live and die'.[470]

It looked at first as if Gabriel Pecock, the warden of the house at Southampton, would not comply. He preached at Winchester on the theme of a heretic who refused to execute a command from his prince contrary to God's law but preferred to suffer martyrdom rather than to resist his prince by force. Pecock went on to justify the primacy of the pope, and urged the people to live and die as he did. Cromwell ordered his arrest and the mayor of Southampton duly sent him up to Cromwell, though noting that he was 'of a very good behaviour'[471] and that there was 'no obstinacy' in him.[472] That seems to have ended Pecock's outspoken opposition. The tone of a letter he wrote to Cromwell a few months later, anxious about the constitutional niceties of a subsequent visitation, suggests that, whatever he may have preached earlier, Pecock was now, fearful of the king's displeasure, fully co-operating with the government.[473]

The government dealt briskly and harshly with those friars who refused to swear the oath. In June two carts full of friars were taken to the Tower.[474] The imperial ambassador wrote in early August that five of the houses had been emptied of friars, and that those in the other two houses also expected to be expelled;[475] and in late August that all of the Observants had been driven out of their monasteries and sent to other houses where they were locked up in chains and treated worse than if they were in prison.[476] A document listed as many as thirty-two Observants who had died (presumably while under arrest, though the circumstances are unclear), thirty-six (including some lay brethren) who were deemed exempt, which presumably means that they had sworn the oath required, thirty who had gone into exile (nineteen of them to Scotland), and forty-five who had been dispersed around the country.[477] Some of those who went into Scotland later preached that Henry was schismatic.[478] But there is little sign of any public protest in England. The Observants were not given time; the pressures against them were brisk and harsh; there was little tradition of co-operation or co-ordination between religious houses.

Exactly what became of each of the convents is by no means clear. Catherine of Aragon, who died in January 1536, wished to be buried in a church of the Observants;[479] but, as Cromwell pointed out, this was not possible, for there remained no Observant convents in England.[480] Very pointedly, the house at Greenwich was transferred to the Conventual Greyfriars in 1536–37; those at Newark, Richmond and Southampton to the Austin friars. In Canterbury, where most had sworn the oath, the remaining friars may have lingered on.[481] Some individual Observants continued their opposition when circumstances allowed, especially in the time of the northern rebellions in 1536, as we shall see.

The Observant Franciscans, then, steadily refused to accept the king's divorce and the break with Rome. Most of them could not accept Henry's policies and refused to comply. Occasionally some of the friars, notably Peto, denounced them in public, but it was difficult freely to do this for long. Peto and Elston went into exile in Antwerp after Peto's bold sermon of Easter 1532, and intrigued by writing or sending over books for a time. Rich and Risby spread the revelations of the Nun of Kent in 1533 and 1534 and paid with their lives. Of those Observant Franciscans who remained in England, none in 1534 and 1537 attempted to write any kind of manifesto, and none of them joined with those in other religious orders in any concerted attempt to restrain royal policy. Later, a handful of Observant Franciscans would be involved in the

Pilgrimage of Grace. Striking the balance is essential. Undoubtedly there is something noble in the refusal of many Observants to go along with royal policy; and the visibility of Peto's protest and the very widespread refusal of the oaths in 1534 and 1535 are both striking and remarkable. But if there is something noble, there is also something forlorn about the Observants' dissent. They failed. The king was never deflected from his course. That owed much to the overall strength of his position, and there was little that the Observants could have done about it. When Peto or other preachers spoke out, they were silenced by exile or by imprisonment. But perhaps they might have written and published more, not least in English, and organised more of a preaching campaign; perhaps they might have attempted to make links with other religious houses, rather than responding in almost complete isolation; they might also have done more to attract support from the bishops and from noblemen. However that may be, Henry VIII clearly saw the Observants as actual or potential traitors: when many of them refused the oaths that he proposed as tests of loyalty in 1534, he effectively abolished the order in England.

Charterhouses

The monks of the Charterhouses were also reluctant to accept the break with Rome, though their refusals occurred later than those of the Observants—and even less than the Observants can their refusals be seen in terms of political intrigue. There were just nine houses with some 170 monks in England: Witham (founded 1178–79), Hinton/Henton (1222–27), Beauvale (1343), Hull (1377), Coventry (1381), Axholme (1397–98), London (1371), Mount Grace (1397–98) and Sheen (1413–15). But they were more influential than their number and size might suggest. Carthusian monks followed a remarkably austere rule. They wore simple clothes, slept on straw beds and ate basic diets. They vowed to live in silence. Each monk had a small set of rooms in which he spent his days and nights in solitude, except for services and chapter meetings. Some Charterhouses were royal foundations, such as Sheen, founded by Henry V from 1413. Sheen was closely associated with the Bridgettine house at Syon, itself founded by Henry in 1415. It remained closely connected to the monarchy: it is probable that Henry VII and Henry VIII attended services there while staying at Richmond.[482]

Like the Observant Franciscans, the Carthusians had been aware of the Nun of Kent. Hugh Rich, the Observant Franciscan, had told the prior and officers of the Charterhouse at Sheen about her revelation.[483]

Henry Gold, the priest of Aldermary, London, had told Fathers Michael and Henry Man, and Brother William Howe of Sheen.[484] Father Man had also heard about it from Dr Bocking, cellarer at Canterbury.[485] But there is little sign that these Carthusians did anything more than listen to the news. Once again, it is clear that what the Nun of Kent offered was spiritual consolation. Unlike the Observant Franciscans', the Carthusians' mission did not include preaching outside their houses (as Thomas Salter, a London Carthusian monk who took the king's side, complained).[486] And while many of the Carthusians may be presumed to have been opposed to the king's policies, there is little to suggest that they did anything at all deliberate or active to resist them.

In spring 1534, at the time that the Observants had refused to swear the oath to the act of succession, the Charterhouse monks had complied, after some uncertainty when John Houghton, prior of the London Charterhouse, and Humphrey Middlemore, one of the monks there, had refused and been briefly held in the Tower, where Edward Lee, archbishop of York, persuaded them to take the oath so far as it might be lawful. Houghton had begun, on 4 May 1534, by telling the royal commissioners that the actions of the king did not concern him: was he in effect declining to take the oath?[487] Two of the Charterhouse monks were taken to the Tower on 4 May 1534;[488] and Prior Houghton was reported to be in the Tower in mid-May.[489] Three visits, the last intriguingly with men-at-arms hinting at continuing reluctance, were needed for all (or most) of the monks to swear. Forty-eight signed, including Houghton and Middlemore, but did so conditionally, in so far as it was legal.[490] Clearly things had not gone altogether smoothly for the king. One Carthusian monk, Thomas Salter, had given unspecified information to Cromwell and was then kept by the prior in something like solitary confinement for his pains. If his trouble may have reflected one monk's increasing discontent with the monastic rule rather than anything directly connected to government policy, it is nevertheless interesting that Salter was in touch with Cromwell, once more showing how the government was seeking to exploit divisions within religious houses.[491] And Cromwell's agent Thomas Bedell, hinting at dissent from the royal supremacy, referred in August to some of the Charterhouse 'which be minded to offer them self in sacrifice to the great idol of Rome'.[492]

At Sheen, efforts to secure oaths succeeded—and the prior and monks even urged the Observant Franciscans of Richmond to do the same.[493] At Henton there may have been momentary difficulties. The prior had 'a marvellous vision'. He had seen on a stage all the noblemen of the realm: by 'one consent' they then drew up Anne Boleyn to join them. Suddenly the prior repented his folly that he had done so much against the law of God and holy church—meaning the oath which he had sworn—and, striking himself on the breast with his fist, he cried, 'God defend that ever I should consent to so unjust and unlawful a deed.'[494] The prior was duly sent up to Cromwell. Judging from his later letter to the king declaring that he had subscribed and sealed a certain profession as Henry had commanded and begging the king on his knees to accept it, with a promise to defend the truth against all that oppose it, he must have been placed under great pressure to deny his vision.[495]

On the face of it, the Charterhouse monks—unlike the Observant Franciscans—had complied with the king's will. But Henry was not satisfied. 'What the king will have done at the Charterhouse of London and Richmond', read one of Cromwell's remembrances in March 1535.[496] Perhaps it was the condition—as far as it was lawful—that the London Charterhouse monks had succeeded in adding to their oaths that irritated Henry. However that may be, fresh oaths were imposed. And in April 1535 John Houghton, prior of the Charterhouse of London, Robert Lawrence, prior of the Charterhouse of Beauvale, Nottinghamshire, and Augustine Webster, prior of the Charterhouse of Axholme, Lincolnshire, refused to swear further oaths recognising the royal supremacy.[497]

On 20 April Lawrence and Webster were interrogated by Cromwell.[498] Would they be content to obey the king as supreme head on earth under Christ of the church of England? Both answered that they could neither agree nor believe that he was supreme head.[499] In addition, Lawrence asserted that there was one catholic church, of which the bishop of Rome was the head.[500] Houghton, interrogated later, declared that he could not take the king to be supreme head of the church of England,[501] and questioned Cromwell how far a layman could be head of the church:[502] he pressed the king's almoner on whether a layman could be the successor of St Peter.[503]

John Whalley, Cromwell's agent, reported from the London Charterhouse that the monks were exceedingly superstitious, ceremonious and pharisaical, and wonderfully addicted to their 'old mumsimus'. He suggested a plan for their conversion. Various churchmen of the popish sort, and several bishops (and he named those who were conservative in their theology but who had gone along with the break with Rome) were to preach to them.[504] But the king preferred more brutal methods.

Royal action was swift. Ten Charterhouse monks were sent to Newgate on 20 April 1535.[505] Houghton, Webster and Lawrence were tried and convicted and executed for high treason for denying the king's supremacy over the church.[506] Cromwell was reported to have had much ado with the judges and sergeants about them.[507] According to a foreign reporter, the hangman cut out their hearts and bowels and burned them while they were still alive; they were then beheaded and quartered.[508] That such vindictiveness was the king's is shown by Cranmer's unavailing suggestion to Cromwell that it would be better to convert their consciences by sincere doctrine.[509]

Three more Carthusian monks—Sebastian Newdigate, William Exmew and Humphrey Middlemore—were indicted, convicted and executed in June.[510] They had refused to comply; on 25 May they had each said that they could not agree to obey the king and to take him to be supreme head on earth of the church of England under Christ.[511] Thomas Bedell, the king's agent, tried to persuade them, bringing them several books, annotated by himself and by others, about the bishop of Rome and St Peter, and holding 'long communication more than one hour and a half' with them. But they would not be persuaded.[512]

Further pressure was then placed on the rest of the monks.[513] Cromwell intruded two of his servants, John Whalley and Jasper Fyloll, to intimidate them.[514] The monks' diet was to be restricted. Fyloll sent a list of names of the whole household—with a 'g' for good and a 'b' for bad by every man's name.[515] The monks were deprived of their books, their worship was disrupted and divisions within the monastery encouraged. Some were sent away from London to the other Charter-houses. One, John Darlay, had a vision in which a recently deceased monk, Father Raby, appeared to him on St John Baptist's day (24 June) and asked him why he did not follow Prior Houghton, a martyr in heaven next to angels. He reappeared the next day, lamenting that he had not lived until he became a martyr.[516]

In September 1536 the king took further and final action. The Char-terhouse in London was not ordered as he would have it. 'I commanded . . . my Lord Privy Seal a great while ago to put the monks out of the House and now he wrote . . . that they be reconciled; but seeing that they have been so long obstinate, I will not now . . . admit their obedience.'[517] Some eventually accepted the royal supremacy: twenty, including William Trafford, who had become prior, and Edmund Sterne, vicar, signed an acknowledgment of the king's supremacy on 18 May 1537.[518] A little later they were persuaded by Bedell to surrender their priory to the king, in recognition of their offences which had provoked his indignation against them. Bedell praised Trafford for his labours in persuading his brethren.[519]

Ten remained who in May 1537 still refused to swear: Thomas Johnson,[520] Richard Bere, Thomas Green, professed monks; John Davy, renderer; Robert Salt, William Greenwood, Thomas Redyng, Thomas Scriven, Walter Pierson and William Horn, conversi.[521] John Hussee reported that 'the monks of the Charterhouse shall the same way [as those condemned for treason]: they will not take the king for supreme head'.[522] They were transferred to Newgate, where they were chained. By 14 June Greenwood, Davy, Salt, Pierson and Green were dead; Scriven and Redyng were on the point of death; Johnson and Horn were sick; only Bere was healthy. Bedell reported how the monks, 'which were committed to Newgate for their traitorous behaviour long time continued against the king's grace, be almost despatched by the hand of God . . . whereof, considering their behaviour and the whole matter, I am not sorry'.[523] By the end of June eight had died, according to Hussee.[524] All but one had died by September 1537: the survivor, William Horn, was moved, and then executed at Tyburn in August 1540. Later accounts suggest the king decided to starve them to death, rather than putting them publicly on trial; but, Elton maintains, that was not the usual policy of the government, since what was intended was their submission and compliance, not their death—an argument that could justify any tyranny. Yet even Elton concedes that 'the government behaved abominably'.[525]

We know little about what happened at the Charterhouses of Beauvale and Axholme, the priors of which were executed with Houghton. From Beauvale, William Trafford—who we have seen as very much the government's man in the London Charterhouse in 1537—had earlier as procurator been sent up to London after asserting the royal supremacy. Arriving three days after the execution of Prior Lawrence, he seems to have wavered in his determination. Sent first to Sheen before being made prior of the London Charterhouse, he then notably conformed.[526] Yet in August 1537 two Beauvale Carthusians were sent to Syon for instruction, which hints at lingering dissent there.[527]

At Sheen, the most significant of the Charterhouses after London, given its proximity to the royal palace at Richmond, the monks were divided. The prior, John Michael, and the procurator, Henry Man,[528] evidently accepted the royal supremacy, as did many of the monks.[529] But others disagreed. Henry Ball, the vicar, noted that they thought it better to suffer than to give in, even though they could not resist the king's power.[530] In June 1535, a year later, one of the monks, Henry Marshall, informed Cromwell that the royal supremacy was not being declared there every Sunday and holy day, hinting at some continued disaffection.[531] Since the Sheen monks do not appear to have suffered as did those of the London Charterhouse, it has always been deduced that in the end they outwardly complied.[532] Indeed, Henry Man, the last prior, would be awarded the huge pension of £133 6s. 8d. on the suppression of the house, and then became dean of Chester in 1541 and bishop of Sodor and Man in 1546, evidently conforming to the Henrician reformation. Yet—perhaps revealingly—in his will of October 1556 he left all his books to the refounded Sheen, thereby hinting that he had not altogether willingly or sincerely conformed to the way things had gone.[533]

The monks of Hull Charterhouse conformed in July 1535.[534] In March 1537, just after the Pilgrimage of Grace, one of the monks there, John Rochester, who had been transferred from London, found himself in trouble. He provocatively appealed to the duke of Norfolk, the king's lieutenant in the north, whom he described as ordained and chosen by God to be his minister, to use his influence with the king. Rochester, espousing the sort of interpretation of Henry's policy that has since warmed the hearts of factional historians, offered to prove that the king

hath been deluded and defamed by them that have provoked and enticed his grace to take upon him the authority of supreme head and confessed his grace to be of right the only supreme head of the church of England next and immediately under god and to have care and charge both of body and soul.[535]

Another Charterhouse monk, Walworth, was also involved. Norfolk reported that he would sit personally when the two Charterhouse monks who denied the king's supremacy were tried, 'unless they do openly recant from their false opinion which I think they will not do':[536] they were executed at York in May 1537.[537] Norfolk sent the king the letter that Rochester had written him, no little marvelling that Rochester, 'one of the most arrant traitors of all others that I have heard of', had been sent there rather than being executed in London, considering that he had made no secret of his opinions.[538] 'Two more wilful religious men in manner unlearned I think never suffered', Norfolk added.[539] Unfortunately we know nothing of what Rochester and Walworth may have done in the years leading up to the Pilgrimage of Grace.

At Mount Grace two monks, Thomas Leighton and Jeffrey Hodeson, refused the oath in 1534.[540] Another, Richard Marshall, and a lay brother, James Newey, refused to be sworn, ran away to Scotland, but were eventually caught.[541] In 1540 the prior, looking back, would recall the difficulty he had had in persuading the brethren of the illegality of the pope's supremacy.[542] But in 1535 the earl of Northumberland found the prior and most of the monks quite conformable to the things passed in parliament.[543] That month the prior urged Archbishop Lee to send Dr Horde, prior of Hinton Charterhouse, to all the houses to instruct the monks: in every house there were some weak simple men of small learning and little discretion. That does at least hint at continuing reluctance, even if such dissent is portrayed as ignorant and shallow.[544] During the rebellions, Sir Francis Bigod got the impression that the prior saw most of his brethren as traitors.[545] At much the same time a monk of Jervaulx was reported as emboldened in his treason in defending the pope by monks of Mount Grace.[546]

Many Carthusians, not least the leaders of the order, did, then, refuse to accept the royal supremacy in 1535 and beyond, and some of them paid for it, at once, or over time, with their lives. They were undoubtedly dissenters and they were obviously seen by the king as opponents. Historians sympathetic to catholicism have, however, tended to be embarrassed by those Carthusians who would not die for the cause. Knowles, after describing the fate of the London Charterhouse, went on to deem that 'the conduct of the other Carthusian priories was less heroic than might perhaps have been expected from a body living such a strict life'.[547] Of those at Sheen who conformed, Beckett wrote that they 'did not have the strength of character' to follow the example of Lawrence, Webster and Houghton,[548] while admitting that 'no more after than before could any opposition at Sheen have halted the royal programme'.[549] That doubtless explains why the sufferings of the Carthusians are, perhaps, not as well known as they should be. But it would be equally misleading to build up a picture of the Carthusians as active political opponents of Henry VIII. They were not, as we have seen, wholly united. In some houses the priors dissented to the point of death, though not all their monks agreed; in others, priors conformed but several of their monks murmured and dissembled. Above all, those who became martyrs suffered not for anything they had done but rather for what they had not done. They had been required to swear a series of oaths committing them to the royal supremacy, and in the end many of them found themselves unable to do so. There is little, however, to suggest that the Carthusian monks did much to oppose the king, or that they would have done anything at all if left alone. Intriguingly, as we have seen, that was the thrust of the advice given to Cromwell by John Pyzaunt, one of the monks at Sheen. Having noted that many would accept the king as supreme head, but that others would rather die than give way, he went on to say that however inveterate their opinions, many things come to pass in time. And he urged that those who declined to take the oath might nonetheless be suffered and borne with: they will not, he insisted, do or say anything that shall sound contrary to the king's prerogative.[550] The king, as we have seen, preferred a more ruthlessly direct approach.

Syon

At the Bridgettine nunnery at Syon, Middlesex, there was also dissent. Another strict order, maintaining high standards, it had been founded for sixty nuns, and for twenty-five monks who served as the nuns' spiritual directors. It was valued at £1,731 p.a. in the *Valor ecclesiasticus*, making it the wealthiest nunnery and tenth richest house in the country. For the chronicler Charles Wriothesley it was 'the most virtuous house of religion in all England'.[551] Its unique system of testing vocations—a probationary year spent away from the monastery—made profession a more deliberate act than usual.

Elizabeth Barton, the Nun of Kent, stayed there. According to Thomas More, who met her at Syon, several of the priests there told him that she had been with them, though, on his account, some had misliked 'diverse things', which he did not specify, in her.[552] Bishop John Fisher of Rochester had contacts with Syon: he sent copies of one of his books in defence of the king's first marriage, and lent copies of secret correspondence he had had with the king.[553]

Some of the monks at Syon refused the oaths demanded by the king. It may well be that the Bridgettine nuns did take the oath in 1534,[554] but matters came to a head the following year.

Richard Reynolds, a Syon monk who never held any office there but who had been a fellow of Corpus Christi, Cambridge, and who possessed a varied and up-to-date library, declared in April 1535 that he could not accept the king as supreme head of the church nor deny that the pope was head of the universal church. He meant no malice to the king but he would spend his blood that 'he is head of the church who has been so these 300 years'. Twelve months earlier he had also allegedly said that Catherine was the true queen.[555] Interrogated by the lord chancellor, he defiantly asserted that the larger part of the kingdom was with him—however much outwardly, partly from fear (presumably of punishment) and partly from hope (presumably of rewards), it went with the king. And so, he claimed, were all the general councils and the holy doctors of the church. He was much grieved that the king was in such error.[556] Convicted of treason, he was executed on 4 May 1535, alongside the Carthusian priors Houghton, Lawrence and Webster.[557]

How far should Reynolds be regarded as a leader of opposition? Clearly he had some years earlier acquired a reputation as someone unsympathetic to the king's break with Rome. The Warwickshire gentleman and JP, Sir George Throckmorton, who had spoken out in parliament, had been to see him at Syon: Reynolds advised him to stick to his beliefs to the death, since if he did not he would surely be damned. He should not keep quiet, he advised, even if he thought it would be of no avail.[558] That shows Reynolds as a martyr-in-the-making and also that he was known as a dissident outside the monastery. And his advice to Throckmorton was unambiguous. When interrogated, Reynolds was pressed on why he had maliciously counselled many not to agree with the king. Reynolds responded that he had only declared his opinion if it was asked of him in confession, when he could not refuse to give it. It was because he was so sorry that the king was so much in the wrong that he had, he said, never voiced his opinion in public.[559] Since Reynolds was on trial for his life, his testimony cannot be accepted without some hesitation; but it does ring true. He had not (as far as we know) spoken out in public; and if, when hearing confession, he had advised more boldly, nonetheless the extent of his influence cannot have been very large.

Despite the bloody example of the executions of Reynolds and the Carthusian priors, there were continuing difficulties at Syon in 1535. The nuns and monks had to be sworn. The king regularly sent bishops and counsellors, not least Cromwell, to Syon, to bribe and threaten the nuns and monks there.[560] At times this appeared to work. In May Bishop Rowland Lee and a lawyer who served the king and Cromwell as a general factotum, Thomas Bedell, reported that they hoped to have the king's pleasure concerning the oath obeyed.[561] But in August Bedell was sorry to see 'the foolishness and obstinacy of diverse religious men, so addict to the Bishop of Rome and his usurped power', and lamented 'diverse of the Friars at Sion, which be minded to offer them self in sacrifice to the great idol of Rome'.[562] A month earlier Bedell and Bishop Stokesley had found the abbess and sisters conformable, but two men who had laboured busily to infect their fellows against the king's title of supreme head, 'vauntperlers, and heads of their faction', needed weeding out.[563]

Richard Whitford was the more significant of this pair. Under suspicion since he had preached without mentioning the king's title of supreme head,[564] he was one of the leading scholars of his age, the author of some fifteen books, including devotional works for nuns and for the laity, notably the *Werke for Housholders*. That did not stop Bedell from saying of him that 'this man hath but small learning but is a great railer'.[565]

The other monk was Richard Leche, who had advised John Hale, the vicar of the neighbouring parish of Isleworth (who was himself executed, as we shall see later), not to appear before the commissioners when they came to take the oaths. He was duly sent for a brief sojourn in the Tower on Cromwell's orders.[566] Another brother, one Ricot, did duly preach the king's title on 24 August, but added 'that he, which commanded him so to preach, should discharge his conscience', implying that he did not believe what he was saying. As soon as he began to declare the king's title, nine of the brothers had walked out, including Leche.[567]

The seesaw of opinion continued. In September Bedell had found the abbess and all her religious sisters 'well contented' with the king's title and ready to declare their consent.[568] But in December, when a monk called Bishop—who in August had walked out during Ricot's sermon[569]—preached and declared the king's title, he was called a false knave, and the lay brethren accused him of various sexual misdemeanours.[570] Bedell reported that he and Layton had had much business after Cromwell had left. The brethren remained obstinate. Two of the monks, Leche and John Coppinger, who had also walked out of that sermon in August, had been sent up to the bishop of London. Dr William Butts, the king's physician, and John Skip, Queen Anne Boleyn's almoner, had come to persuade Whitford and a monk called Litell (another of those who had walked out of the August sermon). Four royal chaplains had been sent by the king to reinforce Butts and Skip, but to no avail. Bedell reported how he had handled Whitford in the garden with fair words and foul, and warned him that he would be held up to shame for his irreligious life and for using bawdy words to ladies at confession. But 'he is a brazen forehead which shameth at nothing'. Another monk called Turnington (who had also walked out of the August sermon) was very strongly against the king's title. Bedell had stopped Whitford and Litell from hearing the ladies' confessions—in which, presumably, they had counselled the nuns not to swear the oaths required. Bishop Stokesley had been there and, together with the confessor-general, John Fewterer, had taken it upon his conscience and peril of his soul that the ladies ought to consent to the king's title, something that gave them much comfort. Bedell asked those nuns who consented to sit still, those who would not consent to leave: none got up. That was a procedure that was frankly intimidating. And one of the nuns, Agnes Smith, went on to urge her sisters not to agree. But Bedell remained hopeful.[571]

Perhaps he had been encouraged by the support of John Fewterer, the confessor-general. Fewterer, who, as we have seen, had been informed of the Nun of Kent's revelations, had translated *The Mirror of Christ's Passion*, which defends communion in one kind, the sacrament of penance, the value of good works in salvation and the unity of the church, dedicating the work to Lord Hussey, in 1534. That leaves little room for doubt about his opinion of the royal supremacy. Yet he conformed. By July 1535 he was sharing his 'wisdom' with Bedell. Fewterer was willing secretly to reveal that Bishop Fisher, who had just been executed, had lied when he had claimed that he had shown no one but the king certain letters: Fisher, he revealed, had sent Reynolds, him and another, now-deceased brother a copy of one of his letters and the king's answer. Fisher had also sent them, he added, a book he had written in defence of his first marriage.[572] In August Fewterer was described as well contented with the king's title.[573] What was the explanation for not just his acquiescence but also his willingness to offer information and, in December, to join Bedell in putting pressure on his fellow monks and nuns? Was he frightened? Or did he think that acquiescence might protect his brothers?[574]

But if the conformity of Fewterer encouraged Bedell, his optimism was not yet fully justified. In January 1536 Bishop Stokesley received letters with subscriptions by the abbess and sisters of Syon—but with conditions attached.[575] John Mores explained to Bedell that, after communing with their confessors, the ladies of Syon had been brought into such scrupulosity that they would no longer agree to subscribe, nor would they accept a revised version that Stokesley had devised.[576] So renewed efforts were made to win over one of the monks, John Coppinger, in January 1536. What concerned him most, Stokesley believed, was the continuance of good religion in Syon, which he saw as impaired by two monks, including Bishop, who had preached in December. Stokesley thought it worth trusting Coppinger. If those two monks were expelled, and if the monks and nuns were allowed to keep their rule and ceremonies as before, Stokesley thought he would be conformable. And he thought that Richard Leche, whom he described as rude in comparison, would follow Coppinger's lead.[577]

And Coppinger and Leche were eventually persuaded to conform by Stokesley.[578] Together they wrote a letter to the surviving monks of the London Charterhouse in January, with an endorsement by John Fewterer, confessor-general. They admitted having earlier shared their opinions and been in trouble and in danger for them. But they denied they had changed their minds for fear of bodily pain, penury, death, worldly shame, or for honour or preferment. What had convinced them, once they had been fully informed about the matter, was charity alone. They had much laboured concerning the authority of the prince over the church of England. In both the Old and New Testaments they had found great truths for the king and nothing for the bishop of Rome. The Old Testament showed how David, Joshua, Jehosaphat and Ezechias, who were of the most perfect kings, set orders and ordinances among priests. Christ, in the New Testament, did not diminish the power of kings, but warned his apostles that they should not look for such dominion or authority.[579]

Coppinger and Leche had moved a long way from the moment the previous August when they had walked out of that sermon in defence of the royal supremacy. It is hard to judge, but the suspicion must be that, in the end, they had been intimidated into supporting the king, not least given the apparent hopelessness of any further resistance. Whatever they might have done, they were most unlikely to have changed the king's mind; they followed the advice they offered the Carthusians, not to die for the cause, but to save themselves and their house by submitting to Henry.[580] Not everyone conformed. Thomas Bownell, a lay brother and also one of those who walked out of the sermon in August 1535, would die in prison in Newgate in October 1537.[581] But in September 1536—a month before the outbreak of the Pilgrimage of Grace—John Coppinger would offer Thomas Cromwell their perpetual prayers for Cromwell's great charity towards them which they could not recompense. And Coppinger was working to overcome the scruples of the Carthusian monks who had been sent to Syon—for Coppinger to win over to the royal supremacy.[582] Two Beauvale Carthusians would be sent to Syon for the same purpose in August 1537.[583]

Intimidation and persuasion had neutralised what seemed like principled opposition from Syon. Reynolds had been ruthlessly tried and executed. Whitford refused—but retired from Syon. Fewterer, it seems, acquiesced at once; Coppinger, Leche and others who held out for a time eventually complied. The abbess and nuns, whose part in all this remains frustratingly shadowy, apparently complied, though possibly with some reservations. Syon's monks were already known for their reservations over the divorce. It is obviously significant that the Nun of Kent should have stayed there. Sir George Throckmorton turned to John Reynolds for guidance—and Reynolds practised the unyielding actions that he counselled to Throckmorton. Syon symbolised concern over the king's policies. Yet to call it a centre of resistance is to go too far. For Henry, it was enough that the monks and nuns of Syon should have failed at once to accept his supremacy: hence the ruthlessness with which Reynolds was despatched, the repeated subsequent pressures, the exploitation of divisions within Syon. There were indeed hints of contacts with others uneasy about the tide of events (Bishop Fisher sent the monks his books) but this shows more that those concerned were reinforcing and confirming each other's concerns, offering each other spiritual consolation, than that there was some kind of organised and active political opposition.

Bishop Fisher's Episcopal Colleagues

If there was to be effective opposition to Henry VIII's divorce and break with Rome, the Observant Franciscans, the Charterhouse monks and the Bridgettine nuns and their confessor-monks could hardly have been expected to provide it alone. John Houghton, Robert Lawrence, Augustine Webster, John Reynolds and several others were prepared to die rather than to acquiesce in the royal supremacy; William Peto went into exile after speaking out over the divorce. They displayed a magnificent and heroic courage in defence of their convictions. But they were not political leaders in any sense, and it is hard to see how they could have taken on such a role.

It was rather the bishops, the shepherds of the church, who might have been expected to resist with effect. And, indeed, we have already seen how Bishop John Fisher, the most spiritual prelate of his generation, paid with his life for his refusal to accept the king's stand. But however much he must have struck Henry as a determined and troubling opponent, Fisher never aspired to be the leader of anything that might become a political movement. More remarkably still, it was Fisher alone of the bishops who stood firm to the end. Why did none of his episcopal colleagues join him?

Here the general position of bishops in a monarchical church is highly relevant. Bishops had for centuries been the king's men. Often they had earlier in their careers served their royal masters in administration and diplomacy: appointment to a bishopric was frequently a reward for secular service. Ties of loyalty and respect to the king who had advanced them would make personal opposition very hard to consider. It is perhaps significant that Bishop Fisher was very much Henry VII and Lady Margaret Beaufort's protégé, not Henry VIII's. Churchmen promoted by Henry VIII would find it much harder to refuse his wishes. Thomas Wolsey, memorably characterised by Peter Gwyn as 'the king's cardinal', might well have put a brake on Henry's divorce had he firmly rejected it in 1527, and threatened to resign and to excommunicate the king if he did not comply. But such actions would have been almost inconceivable to a man who had not only risen in the king's service but was personally very close to him. Despite being told less than the truth by Henry in the early stages, Wolsey quickly came to press the king's case for a divorce with determination and skill. That made effective dissent, much less opposition, from within the church far more difficult and dangerous: the church leaders would not be speaking with one voice.

Wolsey committed himself wholly to the king's cause; the irony was that by 1529 Henry came to blame him for what he saw as the unconscionable delay in resolving the matter. Wolsey's fall in autumn 1529 was, as we have seen, orchestrated by the king in order to put pressure on the pope and on the church in England. There is little to suggest that Wolsey reacted to his dismissal by in any way intriguing against the king. It would not have been altogether surprising if once out of office Wolsey had found his voice as an opponent, if he had then spoken out against the divorce. But he had been genuinely committed to the king's cause, and he was not going to change the loyalties of a lifetime, however shabbily he had been treated by Henry. Wolsey signed the general appeal to the pope in July 1530.[584] How he would have responded if he had lived to face trial in late 1530, or if he had been required by Henry to pronounce his first marriage invalid in defiance of papal authority, we cannot tell.

William Warham, archbishop of Canterbury since 1502, had no special personal ties of loyalty to Henry VIII, who (most probably) had encouraged him to resign as lord chancellor in 1515. In many ways he would have been the obvious churchman to have defied Henry. At times, indeed, he seems to have been on the verge of doing just that. After Catherine expressed doubts about his loyalty to her in August 1530, he responded, on sight of the papal inhibition of discussion of the case, that he would obey the pope's demands.[585]

But he was an old man, which possibly explains the inconsistencies in his behaviour. Warham frequently appears as one of the advocates of the king's cause, even pressing those unenthusiastic to support Henry. The chronicler Edward Hall tells us that in the winter of 1528–29 Warham sent for 'the famous doctors of both the universities to Lambeth, and there were every day disputations, and commonings of this matter'.[586] In spring 1530 Warham as chancellor had written firmly to the convocation of the university of Oxford and to the commissary and doctors and bachelors of divinity there urging them to declare their minds on the divorce 'to the accomplishment of the king's grace's desire'; it was to be greatly marvelled that they made any difficulty as Paris and Cambridge had already declared their resolute minds in the matter.[587] This shows that he publicly supported the divorce and wished to assist Henry by gathering together so strong a body of academic support that the pope would grant Henry what he sought. In July 1530 he signed the appeal to the pope.[588]

In December 1530 he appealed to a general council of the church and issued a protestation, as legate of England, that the cause of the king's divorce belonged to him by the privilege of the kingdom, and should neither have been committed to the two legates, Wolsey and Campeggio, without his consent, nor revoked to Rome. Chapuys glossed this by pointing out that Warham had moved away from the queen; he was naturally timid and old age had somewhat abated his constancy.[589] Might Warham have been contemplating resolving the divorce by his own authority? One possible reading of the undated draft bill (discussed in an earlier chapter) empowering the archbishops—and significantly 'any one of them'—to hear and determine the case is that the bill was intended to reinforce Warham's position and allow him to pronounce Henry unmarried.[590] A year elapsed between Wolsey's death in November 1530 and the appointment of a successor, and it is plausible that the drafters of the bill were expecting that Warham might be able to act alone. Warham's protestation matches closely the tenor of the draft bill.

With three other bishops Warham summoned the dissident Bishop Fisher to his house and tried to persuade him to retract what he had written in favour of the queen and to take the king's side.[591] A little later Chapuys, describing Warham as the man on whom much depended for good or ill, reported how the king had just visited him in his private dwelling to try to win him over to his cause. Warham told the papal nuncio, who—perhaps alarmed by what he had heard of all this—had gone to see him in January, that he had told the king that he would not act against the pope's prohibition and his own conscience.[592]

Warham acted rather differently in convocation in January–February 1531. That assembly of the church had to respond to the charges made against fifteen churchmen under the *praemunire* statute, and to the king's demand that the church recognise him as its supreme head on earth. Whatever he had told the papal nuncio, in this convocation Warham generally acted as the king's spokesman, or at most as a mediator between king and church. It was Warham who presented the articles demanded by the king to convocation on 7 February.[593] On 11 February Warham formally proposed the king's title including the words 'quantum per Christi licet'.[594] The contrast between Warham's part and that of Bishop Fisher, who, if his first biographer is to be believed, pressed his fellow bishops not to yield, is striking. Had Archbishop Warham simply said no in early 1531, he would probably have carried most of the bishops with him. But he did not. And in June 1531 Catherine of Aragon would complain that when she asked Warham's advice, he said he would not meddle in these affairs, repeating frequently the words 'ira principis mors est' (the anger of the prince is death).[595] In July 1531 Henry vigorously urged his agents in Rome to put Warham forward to the pope as the man to whom judgment of his great matter should be referred: in doing so, Henry must have been confident that Warham would, if entrusted with the responsibility, find in his favour.[596] It is vital not to antedate the self-consciously Becket-like stand he was to take in 1532. In late 1530 and early 1531 Henry's hopes of enlisting Warham to grant his divorce were not unrealistic.

What apparently changed Warham's mind? Warham's successor as archbishop, Thomas Cranmer, believed that Elizabeth Barton, the Nun of Kent, 'did marvellously stop the going forward of the king's marriage by the reason of her visions'. She had seen both Wolsey and Warham, 'and [in] mine opinion, with her feigned visions and godly threatenings, she stayed them very much in the matter'.[597] According to the attainder denouncing Barton, she had revealed her visions to Warham 'who by false and untrue surmises tales and lies . . . was allured brought and induced to a credit therein, and made no diligent searches for trial of their said falsehoods and confederations'.[598] The chronology is awkward and there is less supporting evidence than one would wish. But manifestly in 1531 Archbishop Warham did not pronounce the king's first marriage invalid nor marry him to Anne Boleyn. No bill permitting him to do so, on the lines of the draft discussed above, was enacted. Archbishop Warham did not accompany Bishops Longland and Stokesley when they, together with noblemen led by the dukes of Norfolk and Suffolk, went to persuade Queen Catherine in June 1531.[599] But to go on to assert that Warham blocked the divorce is to run well ahead of the evidence. And it might rather be that in 1531 Henry did not yet feel sufficiently confident of carrying the political nation with him to risk having done then what would be done two years later: on that reading, Warham did not have to oppose because Henry did not ask him to do anything he did not wish to.

Warham's subsequent protest in 1532 might simply reflect his reaction to the increased tempo of royal threats against the church: enough was enough. He was of course himself under considerable pressure. In February 1532 Chapuys reported that the duke of Norfolk and earl of Wiltshire never ceased to work to suborn the archbishop of Canterbury, but they had not succeeded.[600] The king's bill for the restriction of the payments of annates was introduced in parliament and had a rough passage (as we have seen). And a draft bill removing the legislative independence of the church may well (as we have seen above) have been proposed at this time.

On 24 February 1532 Warham issued a formal protest against all enactments in parliament in derogation of the pope's authority or the ecclesiastical prerogatives of his province. That was a remarkable step, indeed 'a step of great courage and exasperated anguish'.[601] Charges of offences against the *praemunire* statute were brought against him: these were on the grounds that he had consecrated Henry Standish as bishop of St Asaph before Standish had agreed with the king over his temporalities. As usual, such charges were 'absurd',[602] if not monstrous. Warham prepared a striking defence, revealing the depth of his concern. On the particular issue he pointed out that it was not a normal part of an archbishop's examination of a bishop-elect to check the arrangements that had been made with the king:[603] this charge was unprecedented.[604] Obedience to the pope should not, he declared, lead to penalties.[605] More generally, the principles that the charge implied were troubling. It made the archbishop dependent on the temporal power of the prince. If applied to the papacy, it would make the pope dependent on the emperor—'there should be no pope but at the emperor's pleasure', a condition of 'perpetual bondage'.[606] More broadly, Warham warned Henry VIII of what had happened to other princes who had acted against the church and incurred divine punishment: he cited the deaths of Henry II, Edward III and Richard II, and Henry IV's leprosy.[607] He compared his position to that of Becket resisting what Henry II demanded from him at Clarendon: Becket became a martyr, 'the best death that can be'.[608] Warham's personal devotion to Becket is apparent from the fact that he had chosen to be buried in Becket's chapel in Canterbury Cathedral.[609] If noblemen were encouraged to draw their swords and hew him into small pieces, 'yet I think it were better for me to suffer the same than against my conscience to confess this Article to be a premunire for which saint Thomas died'.[610] He hinted that he might excommunicate the king.[611] 'Who soever lay violent hands upon a bishop in taking him and after imprisoning him is accursed.'[612] He recommended his cause and that of the church to God and St Thomas.[613] Warham's sentiments were magnificently expressed; but it is not clear how widely they were known. Warham was never tried, so these words were never uttered in court. Perhaps he sent Henry his defence. And what he truly felt remains unknowable. An intriguing hint appears in the line 'rex tanquam tyrannus opprimit populum suum' (the king like a tyrant oppresses his people) that Warham's sometime secretary, Thomas Baschurche, wrote some years later: in writing those words, was the secretary fairly reflecting his master's opinions as well as his own?[614]

And how far did Warham's actions match his passionate language? According to the Venetian ambassador, he spoke against the king when parliament discussed the affair of the divorce on 15 March: the king, indignant, used foul language against him, saying that, but for Warham's age, he would make him repent of saying what he did against his majesty.[615]

Yet, as before, Warham's outspokenness did not last. In May, churchmen were subjected to renewed royal demands that they acknowledge the king as supreme head of the church and that they agree not to introduce any new laws without the king's assent and authority. Archbishop Warham was one of just three bishops (the others were West of Ely and Veysey of Exeter) who unequivocally accepted what was being demanded. And it was Warham who (with Longland of Lincoln, Standish of St Asaph and possibly Clerk of Bath and Wells) presented the articles to the king.[616] Why did Warham agree when only a short while before he had prepared a vigorous defence of the church? He was a very old man (he would die in August) and it is doubtless unreasonable to have expected more from him. But clearly if he had spoken out, if he had preached or gone into print on the lines of his defence against the *praemunire* charges, if he had actively striven to lead the episcopal bench in defence of the liberties of the church and against royal supremacist pretensions, that would have presented a formidable difficulty for Henry. Perhaps it was the threat of further *praemunire* action that deterred Warham[617]—though, given his earlier stand, that is not entirely convincing. Perhaps he thought that defiant resistance would be useless. The bishops' response to the supplication against the ordinaries, devised largely by Gardiner, had, after all, succeeded only in inflaming the king. Perhaps Warham believed that the apparent submission of the clergy in May 1532 would be neutralised by the work of the thirty-two-man commission then established to review the canon law. Perhaps he believed that the war against heresy, exemplified by his citation of Hugh Latimer in March for his preaching on purgatory,[618] was more important than the constitutional relationship of church and monarch. However that may be, the fact remains that Archbishop Warham, in the late spring of 1532, no longer took the stand he had seemed to be taking in February and March, and in effect once more became an instrument of the king's will.

Edward Lee, appointed archbishop of York in December 1531, was not likely to oppose where Archbishop Warham did not. He was, of course, very much Henry's nominee, at a time when it would have been very obvious to the king that supportive bishops would be immensely valuable. And Lee had since the late 1520s been heavily involved with the team of scholars preparing and defending the king's cause. He was among the deputation of churchmen-scholars despatched to persuade Queen Catherine in June 1531.[619] But perhaps Lee had his doubts about acting unilaterally in the king's cause. Somewhat later, Chapuys alluded to his having changed his opinions after he had been raised to the archbishopric.[620] There is no supporting evidence; but again the provisions of the draft bill empowering the archbishops or, significantly here, one of them, to determine the king's divorce might offer some circumstantial support. It is important to emphasise that the most that Lee's actions amounted to was a reluctance to go ahead—illegally, in terms of the laws of the church—rather than open defiance to settled royal policy. Even less was this a sign of an incipient leader of an opposition to the king. Perhaps Henry had yet to find an archbishop willing to pronounce his first marriage invalid—but he had not elevated an open critic.

If all the bishops opposed the bill in restraint of annates in February 1532, as Chapuys reported, then Lee was among them.[621] But thereafter there are few signs of anything but acquiescence, however reluctant, in the measures of the early 1530s. He was one of four bishops who in April 1534 John Hussee, Lord Lisle's agent, thought might be sent to the Tower.[622] It may well be that it was in response to such a threat that Lee agreed to swear the oath then demanded. In May 1534 Chapuys was summoned to meet councillors and churchmen. Archbishop Lee was among them. He took his turn to speak, using (if Chapuys is to be trusted) a single argument against the validity of the first marriage that was so feeble that it was disposed of in two words. Chapuys suspected that Lee was very glad that what he had said had been so well confuted.[623] True, in July 1535 Lee jailed a priest who denied the royal supremacy.[624] But a little earlier Lee was forced to defend himself against the charge that he had been less than enthusiastic in teaching the royal supremacy in his diocese. He had, he insisted, implemented the king's commandment that every preacher should before Easter declare the just causes that had led the king to repudiate the jurisdiction of the bishop of Rome and justify Henry's divorce from Catherine of Aragon and subsequent marriage with Anne Boleyn. Lee had himself preached before the mayor of York. He had arranged for services to end at such time as would allow everyone to be present at the sermon. He had specially required the mayor and aldermen to be present, and there and then in front of a 'great multitude', including men from the county as well as the city, he explained 'the injuries done' to the king by the bishop of Rome. Intriguingly, he continued that he had not touched on the title of supreme head, 'forsomuch as no order was given then, but only to make mention thereof in the prayers'; but as was well known to all who had heard him preach in the diocese, in order to speed the proceedings he had never included prayers in his sermon. He had had copies made and sent a whole book to every preacher and curate. They had followed his orders: 'I have not yet heard but that every one of the said curates followeth their books in every point and specially pray for your highness as chief head of the church.' For Good Friday, 1535, he had ordered the treasurer to leave out the collect for the pope and the deacon to omit the pope in the hymn 'Exultet angelica'. The tone of Lee's defence suggests, however, that while he had not opposed royal policy, he had done as little as he could get away with.[625]

In July 1535 he sent Cromwell two books, possibly written by himself, the first containing articles which all clergy and preachers were to declare to their flocks, the second a brief declaration of the king's supreme headship and rejection of the authority of the bishop of Rome. Yet he accompanied them with a ringing denunciation of the ignorance of the clergy and the impossibility of getting them all to preach the royal supremacy. He emphasised that, however willing he was to preach himself every Sunday and feast day, he could not put learning and cunning to preach in the heads of those who did not have them already. Was Lee here excusing himself in advance for a less than vigorous enforcement of the royal supremacy in his diocese?[626]

By early 1536, further concerns had evidently been raised, judging from the tone of a reply Lee sent to the king when challenged. He flatly denied the rumour that he had told John Fewterer, the confessor-general at Syon, that he would stand against the royal supremacy if he thought he might prevail. On the contrary, Lee insisted that when the Carthusians at Richmond, Coventry, Hull and Mount Grace had sought his counsel, he had always told them to do what he and many others, including great learned and good men, had done.[627] He had, he emphasised, persuaded the priors of Hull and Mount Grace, who had been determined to die rather than to yield, to change their opinions. He had told them that men might consent with a safe conscience. He had often declared that these were not causes to die for. He had marvelled that Bishop Fisher had been so stiff as to die for them. Moreover, he insisted that whenever he preached the king's title he had not just lightly touched it, but rather presented it as supported by scripture and by other good reasons. He had published some books on the matter even though he had not expressly been commanded by the king to do so, proof of his good will and his firm opinion on the matter. He had sent a book to all his archdeacons so that they could have these arguments set out in every parish.[628]

Was Lee being disingenuous? A lack of enthusiasm for royal policy may, perhaps, be read into the tone of his self-exculpation. He may well not have cared very much for the drift of policy. He may have temporised, doing what he was told to the letter but no more (though he claimed that he had gone beyond the call of duty). But none of that amounts in any sense to opposition. Whatever his private doubts, what Lee did in public was to uphold Henry's policies.

Cuthbert Tunstal, promoted from bishop of London to bishop of Durham in 1530, and in Chapuys's words one of the wisest, most learned and virtuous prelates of the kingdom,[629] offers a more complex series of attitudes. At some point he wrote in defence of Catherine.[630] In May 1531 he protested against the title granted by convocation to the king—'supremum caput'—and urged that the words 'in temporalibus post Christum' (in temporal matters after Christ) be added, since the king could not be head 'in spiritualis' (in spiritual matters).[631] Tunstal's letter does not survive) the offending passages have been torn out from his episcopal register.[632] Henry responded vigorously. He insisted that the words to which Tunstal objected had been agreed by convocation in the presence of many learned men, including several other bishops, such as Fisher and Standish. Why, he asked, did Tunstal not 'conform your conscience to the conscience and opinion of the great number'?[633] A little later the northern convocation protested strongly over the king's title: one can only wonder whether Tunstal encouraged such defiance.[634] Little came of this, however, and there is nothing to show what Tunstal felt about the submission of the clergy in May 1532. He was not summoned—presumably deliberately—to parliament that year.[635] At some point, possibly in that connection, Tunstal appointed Bishops Clerk and West as his proxies in the House of Lords, instructing them 'never in my name to consent to any such thing proposed, either harmful or prejudicial to the marriage, but expressly to dissent unto the same', and to declare this openly if necessary.[636]

The following year Tunstal was clearly unhappy at the way in which Henry's marriage to Catherine was annulled. When the king sent Rowland Lee, one of the canon lawyers who had been involved in the elaboration of the king's case, north in May 1533 to secure the assent of the northern clergy to the divorce, and twice told Tunstal the king's pleasure and what had been done by Cranmer in the southern province, Tunstal had demurred. Since he had been on the queen's council from the beginning, he would not reveal his thoughts publicly at convocation, but would rather stay away and send his opinion according to his conscience directly to the king. In no wise, he said, would he subscribe. But he did not expect others to follow him: 'would God we were of one mind, but the diversities of minds in ourselves shall hurt us'. Presumably Lee succeeded in persuading—or ordering—him to attend; presumably (though we cannot be sure) Tunstal was one of the four who voted against the divorce. According to Chapuys, in the debate Tunstal opposed 'virilement' (manfully) though Chapuys's citing the bishop of London, who was not present, as his source raises doubts about that.[637] If the bishop of Durham did indeed publicly refuse to support the king over the divorce, that was a remarkable act of defiance. But it was also bound to be futile, since Tunstal was in a tiny minority, and since the southern convocation had already overwhelmingly ratified Cranmer's actions in pronouncing the king's marriage to Catherine null and void. And once again, here is no political leader organising a campaign of opposition, but rather an individual—albeit a prominent churchman—refusing, when pressed, in conscience to accept what he thought wrong. Tunstal emerges less as an opponent than as a dissident bearing witness.

Tunstal sent a letter to Henry voicing his objections to the pamphlet *Articles Devised by the Whole Consent of the King's Council*, issued in December 1533. He feared schism. He feared invasion. He rejected the claim that a national church could unilaterally diverge from what had been agreed at church councils. He reminded Henry of the expedition against the would-be schismatic Louis XII in 1512. Tunstal's letter was a striking act of defiance. Henry responded point by point. It was a matter of choosing Christ and abandoning the pope and his church; or of following the pope and his church—and abandoning Christ. There was no schism in adhering to the word of God. No Christian princes would abandon them for following Christ. No church can be bound by any interpretation of scripture which is forbidden by God. The papacy would shortly vanish if it were not reformed.[638] Shortly afterwards, the king moved to have the abolition of papal authority formally enacted.

Tunstal had set off for parliament in early 1534 but received a letter from the king ordering him to stay at home, which he obeyed.[639] Once parliament and convocation had duly ratified the king's demands, Tunstal was summoned south to take the oath.[640] John Hussee reported rumours that he would be committed to the Tower.[641] Tunstal was subjected to special pressure. His house was searched. In May 1534, according to royal letters and instructions that the king had signed with his own hand, the earls of Westmorland and Cumberland and Sir Thomas Clifford had gone secretly to the bishop's residence at Bishop Auckland, and taken the keys of his lodgings and studies and of his officials' chambers. In one they found a copy of Edward Foxe's *De vera differentia regiae et ecclesiasticae potestatis*[642] containing hostile marginal comments by one of Tunstal's officials, Dr Robert Ridley, together with a book of Ridley's against those who would take away the possessions of the church. But they found nothing incriminating against Tunstal. Only four letters had been found in Tunstal's chamber, and almost no writings of his own. A letter from Ridley's nephew, warning him and the bishop that they would be sent for by the king, may explain why: they had had time to make all clean.[643]

Tunstal was clearly being put under pressure. He had been summoned south; his residences had been searched, his worldly goods placed in custody. He would have known that Fisher and More had just been sent to the Tower for refusing the oath of succession. This was the moment of decision for him. Chapuys noted that he had hitherto upheld Queen Catherine's cause. But he did not wish, Chapuys added, to be a martyr or to lose his benefice. And so he had been compelled to swear the oath demanded. Chapuys noted that Tunstal had sworn with certain— unspecified—reservations, by which he thought, Chapuys drily noted, to satisfy his conscience.[644]

But almost at once Tunstal was evidently compelled to compromise himself further. Chapuys was invited to Westminster, where he was met by several councillors and churchmen, including Archbishop Lee (as we have already seen) and Tunstal. Tunstal would have heard Dr Edward Foxe, one of the king's closest advisers in the divorce, set out the reasons why Henry had made a statute declaring the succession, and how, if Catherine and Mary continued to refuse to acquiesce, he would be compelled to proceed against them. After Chapuys had replied, it was Tunstal who spoke next. They had for some days studied their parts, Chapuys commented. Tunstal declared that the statute had been very well considered for the tranquillity of the realm. He justified Henry's divorce, citing the opinions of the universities and the brief that the pope had sent at the beginning of the king's suit. Chapuys responded—and added that Tunstal (and Archbishop Lee) seemed very glad that his arguments had been well confuted, since, as Chapuys insisted, they were compelled to go against the truth. One of the purposes of the interview had been to make it clear to Chapuys that Tunstal (and Lee) had turned their coats. And having been compelled to justify the divorce to Chapuys, both were next being sent to Queen Catherine to tell her of their change of opinion to her face.[645] Tunstal and Lee reported back to Henry. Archbishop Lee had stated the king's position on the divorce; Catherine had replied angrily. Tunstal had then told her that where she claimed that he had always shown her that her matter was just and good, that had related only to the validity of the papal bull and brief in question. Several other questions had arisen since which had been debated in the universities. 'By then [it had been] concluded that after the decease of the brother, who had carnal knowledge with his wife, the brother living might not marry the said wife, by any dispensation of the pope, because it was forbidden by the law of God.' The pope had indicated that he would give sentence for Henry against Catherine 'because that he knew that your [i.e. the king's] cause was good and just'; and in a decretal letter brought by Cardinal Campeggio, he had pronounced that 'if marriage and carnal knowledge were had betwixt Prince Arthur and her, the Legates should pronounce for the divorce'. The pope's sentence against Henry, Tunstal had added, was not valid because it pronounced the dispensation, which he had no power to grant, to be good. 'Therefore I had now changed my former opinion', Tunstal said that he had told Catherine, urging her to do the same, and 'to forbear to usurp any more the name of a Queen'.[646] In his account Chapuys added that the bishops and others sent to Catherine had used rude and harsh words against her and threatened her with the penalties in the statute, including death.[647]

It is worth pausing to imagine the appalling dilemmas and struggles of conscience faced by Tunstal in early/mid-1534. He had to decide what was right: and to judge what it was possible for him to achieve. That Tunstal had previously refused but now acquiesced is testimony to the pressures he was under. Fear readily explains why a bishop who opposed vigorously in 1532 should yield in 1534. His earlier opposition makes explanations such as loyalty to the king, ingrained habits of obedience, a reluctance to ask searching questions, hopes that the quarrel with the papacy would prove short-lived, let alone opportunism, less than persuasive: such considerations would have applied even more strongly in 1532. The choice that Tunstal faced in spring 1534 was either to comply, with all that would involve, not least when he was sent to tell Queen Catherine that he no longer believed that she was in the right over her marriage, or to refuse, and consequently to join Bishop Fisher in the Tower. The ransacking of his episcopal palace—for letters or books that might incriminate him—must have reinforced his awareness that there would be no quiet or comfortable way out. Some years later, one Cray asked Tunstal's servant Christopher Chaitour why Tunstal had not had a 'like conscience' as More and Fisher: Chaitour responded that Tunstal was indeed of the same judgment as them and had prepared a protestation on both the divorce and the royal supremacy, in which he was determined to have stood. His servant Burton was asked by Thomas More whether he would come to Bishop Fisher and him, and be as they were; Burton did not know; and More, intriguingly, said that if Tunstal lived he might do more good than by dying with them. And then when Tunstal came to London, the king and the council persuaded him rather to join with Henry.[648] Moreau believes that Tunstal's conversion was sincere and genuine: but that strains credulity. There is little to suggest that Tunstal had been changing his mind as a result of his own studies. And judging from the arguments he was then to voice to Catherine, what the king and council told him was nothing new. If Tunstal was now for the first time intellectually convinced by the merits of the king's case, it is rather surprising that he had not found it convincing before. It is far more likely that Tunstal, placed under extreme pressure and pragmatically calculating the costs of continued dissent and refusal, now agreed to yield. We can only speculate about the personal dynamics of such discussions. It is important to note that Tunstal had addressed his earlier protests directly to the king; it may be that he responded in May 1534 to a very personal appeal from Henry. As early as 1531, Catherine of Aragon had complained that, when she sought his advice, he had replied that he dared not give it, for he was the king's subject and vassal, a formulation that hints at his devotion and subservience to Henry.[649] If indeed More had advised him not to resist further, that might have prompted him to yield, or reinforced his growing inclination that he had done as much as was possible, short of martyrdom. And one of Tunstal's calculations—though hard to document—may have been a hope that his acquiescence in the king's royal supremacy might at least contribute to deterring Henry from throwing his lot in with the Lutherans.

But, having changed his mind, having sworn the oath, having told Queen Catherine that he had previously got it wrong, Tunstal was compromised. His earlier dissent meant that he would never fully be trusted by Henry, and would from time to time be required to prove his loyalty by sermons denouncing the papacy.[650] In January 1536 Thomas Legh praised Tunstal's preaching against the pope and in setting forth the royal supremacy: 'marvellous discreetly and clerkly him self preached and set forth the primacy and the king's high authority of supreme head in diverse and sundry parts of his diocese with substantial learning vehement reasons', and so persuaded the people. Legh and Richard Layton urged Cromwell to send for Tunstal 'and familiarly common with him and to hear but his advice and mind for the utter extirpation' of papal power 'and how other princes might be persuaded to the same'. If Tunstal would write a book on it, 'he wold so handle it that all the kings christian [i.e. kings in Christendom] would shortly after follow the steps of our master: his judgement is such and so known that all the great learned men of Europe would harken to it'.[651] Yet he would also be open to jibes from those who remained loyal to Catherine and defended the papal primacy. Writing to Reginald Pole in 1536, Tunstal declared that 'where ye do find fault with me, that I fainted in my heart, and would not die for the bishop of Rome authority; when this matter was first purposed unto me, surely it was no fainting that made me agreeable thereunto'.[652] Tunstal would no longer be a credible opponent of Henry's break with Rome and royal supremacy. From time to time he would argue forcefully, and even debate with the king, over points of doctrine and liturgy, but he would never now oppose on the fundamentals. It is not surprising that he should have gone to ground during the Pilgrimage of Grace: the Tunstal of 1532 and 1533 would surely have much sympathised with the aims of the pilgrims.

John Clerk, bishop of Bath and Wells, 'the complete politician-bishop',[653] probably sympathised with Catherine of Aragon, but he did not turn into an opponent of the king. He wrote a book in defence of Catherine in 1529.[654] He wrote Fisher a letter on how to interpret the Levitical law banning marriage to a brother's wife: Clerk suggested this meant only the brother of a husband who was alive. The government suspected that this might have influenced Fisher.[655] Clerk (and Standish) spoke out when Bishops Stokesley and Longland attempted to use the presentation of the opinions of the universities in the Lords to push the matter forward: this was not the place and there was not enough time.[656] That was a minor tactical success. With Fisher (and West of Ely), Clerk may have protested to the pope in 1530 against the anticlerical legislation passed by parliament the previous year. He was one of the bishops accused of offences under the *praemunire* statute in 1530. Of the bishops present in convocation in May 1532 only Clerk roundly opposed the submission of the clergy (though he joined Warham, Longland and Standish in presenting it the next day, inconstancy that is not easy to explain).[657] In April 1533 he voted against the king over his marriage.[658] One of the questions in the interrogatories put to Bishop Fisher asked him about articles that Queen Catherine had sent him: they included an account that one of Clerk's chaplains had told her almoner that Clerk (and More and the bishops of Exeter and Chichester) would favour the cause as much as she could desire.[659] We are not very fully informed about any of this. Clerk had not consistently dissented: in May 1531 Henry could include his name in a list of bishops who had earlier that year accepted him as supreme head as far as the law of Christ allowed.[660] In September 1532 Clerk accompanied Henry and Anne to Calais to meet Francis I.[661] And if he did not agree to the divorce in April 1533, subsequently—whatever he might have assured the queen's almoner—he seems to have become a loyal Henrician. He attended Anne's coronation as queen.[662] He swore the oath of succession in July 1534,[663] and renounced the jurisdiction of the see of Rome and all allegiance to any foreign potentate on 10 February 1535.[664] When Thomas More found his book on the divorce and spoke to Clerk about it, Clerk said he had discharged his mind about it and burnt his own copy, and advised More to do the same.[665] If Clerk had been a quite outspoken critic in the years to 1533, from then onwards he followed the king. We may do no more than speculate as to why. According to a list of men fined by the king—most of them churchmen—Clerk was made to pay the sum of £700 for the escape of seven prisoners: he had paid £300 by February 1532; £133 6s. 8d. was recorded as due from him in March 1533, £400 in February 1535.[666] Just what all this amounted to is not clear. Was it a means of persuading him to conform?[667] But it does not explain his continued dissent over the divorce in April 1533. It remains hard to reconcile Clerk the critic and Clerk the loyal exponent of the royal supremacy.

Another of Catherine's early defenders was Henry Standish (d. 1535), bishop of St Asaph. One of the bishops accused of *praemunire* offences in 1530, in March 1531 (with Clerk) he protested in the Lords when Longland and Stokesley attempted to exploit tactically the absence of three other bishops sympathetic to Catherine[668] (though, as Scarisbrick notes, this is the only evidence for his attitudes).[669] He was accused under *quo warranto* in 1531 and vigorously and successfully defended himself in autumn 1532. *Praemunire* charges were brought against him (together with his vicar-general Robert ap Rice) in 1533,[670] to which he pleaded guilty in February and was pardoned in April 1534.[671] In June 1533 he attended the coronation of Queen Anne.[672] Was he intimidated into submission?

Of the senior bishops long in post, Bishop Longland of Lincoln was perhaps the most significant. He had (as we have seen above) been involved in the making of the divorce from the start. In March 1531, sensing a tactical advantage in the absence of three principal defenders of the queen, Bishop Longland (with Stokesley) attempted to use the presentation of the opinions of the universities in the Lords, and spoke in the king's favour.[673] He was among the churchmen who visited Queen Catherine to persuade her in July 1530. In May 1532 he went along with the submission of the clergy, though he wanted the existing body of canons to remain valid until reviewed and found wanting. He accompanied Henry and Anne to Calais in September 1532.[674] He attended the coronation of Queen Anne in 1533.

Was he in private more hesitant than this suggests? In January 1534 Chapuys reported that Longland, at the beginning one of the promoters of the divorce, had said several times since Christmas that he would rather be the poorest man in the world than ever have been the king's councillor and confessor. That is a vivid illustration of the pressures that the bishops were under. There is, however, no sign that he ever expressed any such distaste in public: certainly no open opposition to the statute of supremacy.[675] It is possible that he was intimidated. A note in Cromwell's remembrances—to remember my lord of Lincoln for his *praemunire*—hints at the pressures he may have been under.[676] However that may be, he swore the oath of succession as required on 26 February 1535.[677]

In June 1535 he set forth the king's title of supreme head throughout his diocese and had two thousand copies of Cromwell's letter printed.[678] And, as we shall see, in October 1536 he was very much regarded as one of those responsible for the religious changes against which the commons of Lincolnshire rebelled. In 1538 he would denounce the bishop of Rome's arrogant and money-grabbing ways.[679] If Longland ever regretted having gone along with the king's wishes—as Chapuys once claimed—there is little to suggest that it affected what he did. In no sense can Longland be seen as an opponent of the king.

Richard Nix, bishop of Norwich, one of the bishops accused under *praemunire* in 1530, was, in Michaelmas 1531, accused under *quo warranto*, but forcefully and successfully defended his position in autumn 1532.[680] He was again indicted in early 1534 for offences under the *praemunire* statute. One involved the bishop's alleged infringement of the customs of Thetford. Another arose from his having condemned a heretic two years earlier (i.e. in early 1532) before receiving the king's approval, though this did arrive before the execution. 'To make an end for the bishop of Norwich' reads one of Cromwell's remembrances.[681] He defended himself at first but then pleaded guilty and was convicted. He was briefly imprisoned until, pardoned, he agreed to pay £10,000. Chapuys supposed that Nix, who was nearly ninety and blind, was been pursued for having taken the queen's part and for having burnt the heretic.[682] An act of parliament set out the terms of his royal pardon.[683] In February 1535 he was summoned to appear before the council in star chamber but declined owing to ill health.[684]

Charles Booth, bishop of Hereford, was accused of offences under the *praemunire* statute in 1531: royal instructions to Cromwell stated that the king's attorney was 'to make process, and to prosecute against Charles, Bishop of Hereford, according to the laws, with all speed, if he do not agree'.[685] He swore the oath of succession in March 1535, having in his will first disowned anything he might do 'ex debilitate cerebri aut infirmitate vel ex instigatione diaboli . . . aut errore ductus' (from debility of mind or infirmity, or by the instigation of the devil or being led into error) not in conformity with his true belief.[686]

John Veysey, bishop of Exeter, expressed reservations over the submission of the clergy in 1532. One of the questions in the interrogatories put to Bishop Fisher asked him about articles that Queen Catherine had sent him: as we have seen, they included an account of one of Clerk's chaplains telling her almoner that the bishop of Exeter, the bishop of Chichester, the bishop of Bath and Wells and Thomas More would favour the cause as much as she could desire.[687] There is nothing to support this view of Veysey. He renounced papal jurisdiction in March 1535[688] and nothing would suggest any greater activity: he was, it must be remembered, an old man.

Nicholas West, bishop of Ely, wrote two non-extant books in defence of Catherine and spoke in defence of the marriage.[689] With Fisher and Clerk, he appealed to the pope in October 1530 against the anticlerical legislation of 1529 against pluralism.[690] He was one of the bishops accused of *praemunire* offences in 1530. He accompanied Henry and Anne Boleyn to Calais in August 1532.[691] He died in spring 1533, shortly after writing warmly to Thomas Cromwell.[692]

Robert Sherburne, bishop of Chichester, was apparently mentioned, as we have noted, by one of Bishop Clerk's chaplains, along with More, Clerk and Veysey, as someone who would favour the cause as much as Queen Catherine could desire; but there is nothing to support such gossip.[693] He was one of the bishops accused of offences under the *praemunire* statutes in 1530. Sherburne swore the oath required in 1534, and in June 1535 preached denouncing the authority of the bishop of Rome.[694] In 1536 he resigned: there is little to suggest why.

Maybe the panel paintings by Lambert Barnard in the south transept of Chichester Cathedral, *The Saxon King Caedwalla Granting the See of Selsey to St Wilfrid* and *Henry VIII Confirming to Sherburne the Royal Protection of Chichester Cathedral*, offer a clue. Dated by George Vertue (1684–1756) to *c.* 1519 but more recently to *c.* 1535–36 or 1533–34,[695] they make no acknowledgment of papal authority, and as such it may well be that 'these are propaganda pieces such as Henry VIII himself commissioned from Holbein and others to illustrate the claims and strengths of the Tudor monarchy'.[696] In the panels Sherburne petitions Henry, 'most sacred king, on God's account [to] confirm your church at Chichester, now the cathedral, as did Caedwalla, king of the South Saxons, with the church at Selsey, once the cathedral'. A matching painting shows Caedwalla doing just that: Henry bears a book in which the words 'For the love of Christ I grant your petition' can be seen. Perhaps these paintings, if they are from the mid-1530s, do simply illustrate what the royal supremacy meant. But just possibly they were intended more provocatively than that. In 1535 Henry forcefully asserted his royal supremacy, including his jurisdiction over bishops.[697] These panels might be a qualified commentary, saying in effect that the king did indeed possess supremacy, but that in his wisdom he readily delegated his powers to the cathedral. But it would be unwise to erect too complex an edifice of reasoning on so tantalising a source.

John Stokesley was involved from an early stage in the making of the king's case for an annulment in canon law, and he was one of many who were rewarded for their work by appointment to a bishopric. Stokesley was appointed bishop of London in 1530. He was fully behind the king's campaign for a divorce. In March 1531 (as we have seen), sensing a moment of opportunity, given the absence of three principal defenders of the queen, Stokesley (and Longland) attempted to make use of the presentation of the opinions of the universities to the Lords, and spoke in the king's favour.[698] In June 1531 Stokesley was one of a delegation of bishops and councillors sent by the king to persuade

Catherine, but Chapuys does not report that he spoke.[699] When the
lower clergy in convocation were reluctant to agree to contribute to the
fine their superiors had agreed to pay the king in February 1531 in
exchange for the pardon of the clergy for offences under *praemunire*,
Stokesley called together all the priests of London at St Paul's in
September. He intended to see them in groups of six or eight and so
persuade them. But there were six hundred priests, together with many
laymen, and they would not let the bishop see them in small numbers.
The laymen encouraged the priests, so much so that they entered the
chapter house by force. Stokesley explained how through their frailty
and lack of wisdom they had 'misdemeaned' themselves towards the
king and his laws over *praemunire*, but that the king had mercifully
accepted just £100,000 over five years. The clergy urged their poverty;
and denied that they offended in the *praemunire*, since they never
meddled in the cardinal's faculties. Let the bishops and abbots pay, they
said. 'Diverse temporal men which were present comforted the priests
and bade them agree to no payment.' Several of the bishops' servants
were 'buffeted'. Later fifteen priests and five laymen were arrested and
sent to the Tower, the Fleet and other prisons, where they remained long
after.[700] A bill was filed in the Chapter House by Christopher Hales, the
attorney-general, against nearly a score of priests for conspiring to
murder the bishop and evade the subsidy; they had assembled riotously,
assaulted the bishop's palace at St Paul's for an hour and a half, and
then, returning to the chapter house, made a new assault on the bishop
and his officers, putting them in fear of their lives.[701] In 1532 Stokesley
was among the bishops who accompanied Henry and Anne Boleyn to
Calais.[702] In the following year he evidently accepted the king's case for
an annulment of his first marriage: he attended the coronation of Anne
Boleyn,[703] and officiated at the christening of Elizabeth.[704] Stokesley evidently swore the oaths required of him without fuss—though one of
Lord Lisle's correspondents heard gossip in March that he might be
accused of *praemunire* offences[705]—and swore to renounce papal
authority on 11 February 1534.[706]

Stokesley's part in the making of the divorce and his steady support
for the king are clear. But if he was entirely persuaded about the merits
of the king's case, he may have been less committed to the royal
supremacy. In May 1532 Stokesley agreed to the submission of the
clergy, though with the reservation that he did so in so far as the
articles were not against divine law or general councils.[707] When in
summer 1535 all the bishops were ordered to preach publicly in support
of the king's supremacy,[708] Stokesley may have been less enthusiastic.

According to Chapuys, he had never preached in his life, on account of his stammering and bad speaking. But that was not his greatest problem. He was ordered by the king to preach in his cathedral on 11 July, and Cromwell was present to hear him denounce the king's first marriage, and the authority of the pope and those who upheld it. Cromwell wanted Stokesley to write out his sermon and turn it into a book. He told Chapuys that he would have paid £1,000 for the emperor to have heard a sermon preached by Stokesley on the invalidity of the first marriage and the usurped authority of the pope. He would send it to him in writing, begging him to forward it to Charles V.[709]

Stokesley, squirming, told Bedell, Cromwell's agent, that while he was glad that the king was pleased with his sermon to the people, he was unable to write it out as he had delivered it, since he had had so much to say that he could not remember what he had said and what he had omitted. He had never had the gift of sure memory and could not remember an hour's communication. He had not written out a word of the sermon, except a few things he had read before, but which, when he woke in the morning, seemed so undigested that he was uncertain where to begin and what would follow. If he were to write out his sermons, he could not deliver them as they were written, for much would come to him that was better than what was premeditated.

Taking a different tack, Stokesley said that, moreover, much of what he said was in the king's book that Edward Foxe, Dr Nicholas de Burgo and he had made, many years earlier, before going abroad on embassy, and which had later been translated, with additions by Cranmer. That was more sufficient to prove the invalidity of the marriage than twenty sermons. It would be superfluous to print his. He offered instead to collect the pith of his sermon and preach it every Sunday during the next parliament.[710] Cromwell was unimpressed, as a note in his remembrances suggests—'I have commanded the bishop of London to write his sermon that he hath preached and to make a book against the authority of the bishop of Rome'—though we shall soon consider the exact wording of this note again.[711]

If Andrew Chibi is correct in his deduction that a text that he has edited is this sermon, then Stokesley may have incurred Cromwell's displeasure because he had not done what was expected of him. In this text Stokesley insists that God's commandments must be straightly observed. Some precepts are merely ceremonial; others are moral. It was as great an offence against God to violate his commandments 'as [for] a man carnally to know . . . his brother's wife carnally known before of his other brother'. He referred to the determination of the universities, to scripture, to church councils, and dealt with objections. Interestingly, all this concerns the canon law of the divorce. Nothing here touches the royal supremacy at all. If Stokesley had answered the call to preach by expounding on the merits of the case for an annulment of Henry's first marriage, while remaining totally silent on the supremacy, that might well account for his embarrassment at being asked for a full verbatim text.[712] Cromwell's remembrance that we have just quoted—'I have commanded the bishop of London to write his sermon that he hath preached and to make a book against the authority of the bishop of Rome'—might be more pointed than it at first seems.[713] Or, of course, it may be that Chibi's text is not the sermon that Stokesley preached then, or only part of it.

If Stokesley was indeed holding back in July 1535, his reward was to be put under greater pressure. Within a few months he was to be found cajoling the nuns and monks of Syon to accept the royal supremacy. 'At Syon my lord of London declared admirably the reasons for the king's title of supreme head and against the bishop of Rome's jurisdiction', so Thomas Bedell reported.[714] His difficulty was that nothing would ever quite satisfy the king. Stokesley protested against calumnies that he was not well affected to the king's cause: on the contrary, he had saved it when it slipped through the ambassadors' fingers and was despaired of, he protested, referring presumably to events around 1529. At St Paul's—at the legatine trial—he almost alone supported it.[715]

Perhaps Stokesley, and other bishops who felt as he did, went along with events partly because he hoped at least to stem the flow of protestant ideas into his diocese. But if so, once again the pressures were too great. Sir Geoffrey Pole later said that Stokesley had told him that he was but a cipher for first Cromwell, then Hilsey, bishop of Rochester: far from controlling the pulpit, despite some early success,[716] Stokesley found himself powerless as Cromwell and Hilsey appointed men whom he regarded as heretics to preach at Paul's Cross.[717]

Maybe some bishops may have had more personal reasons for compliance. Stokesley, it was insinuated, had a mistress, the abbess of Wherwell. She was interrogated: was she not too familiar with the bishop when she was a nun; had not the late Bishop Foxe of Winchester prohibited him from entering her monastery and from her company in order to avoid suspicion; had not the abbess, after she had a baby, come from her house to the bishop's palace at Fulham to be merry with the bishop; was she not lodged in his chamber?[718] Did Stokesley conform in part because of the risk that otherwise his behaviour might be used to discredit him?

Stokesley, then, was no opponent, no critic: on the contrary, he was an early proponent of the divorce. If he had doubts about the royal supremacy, he was effectively bullied into compromising himself by publicly denouncing the pope.

Stephen Gardiner, bishop of Winchester, was the lost hero of any resistance to Henry VIII's break with Rome. In April 1532 he did stand up for the rights of the church, in the famous *Answer to the Supplication of the Ordinaries*, but in vain. Thereafter, however, he readily conformed. He had, of course, been heavily involved in the king's divorce campaign, bullying the pope in Rome in 1528–29, and there were obvious personal ties of loyalty between Gardiner and Henry VIII. He may well have felt intimidated by the force of royal disapproval when he defended church courts in spring 1532, and he would have been reminded of the cost of royal displeasure when he was in effect dismissed as the king's secretary (Cromwell succeeded him) in April 1534.[719] In April 1535 Henry voiced doubts about Gardiner's commitment to the cause.[720] He would have been under no illusions about the price of continued dissent. Given what we know of his actions in the reigns of Edward VI and Queen Mary, he might have been expected to have stood with Fisher, and more boldly, and to have acted in the manner of a Machiavellian politician. Moreau has consequently deduced from his willingness to defend the church in 1532 and his preparedness to suffer imprisonment under Edward VI that his acceptance of Henry's royal supremacy must have been sincere.[721] But more plausible is Armstrong's argument that Gardiner remained crypto-papist throughout and never truly accepted Henry's royal supremacy.[722]

Moreover, accepting as he did the king's case over the divorce, and consequently believing that the pope had wronged him, Gardiner was able to construct a somewhat inconsistent but serviceable framework in which the tyrannies of the current pope amply justified the king's actions. In *De vera obedientia* he could denounce papal power in terms of permanent principle but, crucially, leave the way open for an eventual compromise.[723] Gardiner would have illicit contacts with the papal nuncio in France in 1536; he would advise Henry to compromise with the northern rebels in early 1537.[724] And such a position, however illogical, served admirably to relieve him from any immediate need openly and defiantly to oppose the king. He could continue to serve, to preach obedience, to avoid any direct criticisms, indeed even agreeing that the primacy of the bishop of Rome was begun by the policy of man,[725] while pinning his hopes on, and no doubt directing his prayers to, a royal change of heart, and all the time doing his best to exploit such political and diplomatic opportunities for reconciliation and reunion that turned up.[726] Such a position was light years distant from that of Fisher, and explains how Gardiner could write so vigorously attacking him.[727]

Any consideration of Fisher's episcopal colleagues might profitably include a glance at his potentially episcopal colleagues—the pool of senior church court officials and archdeacons from which bishops were usually chosen. Here there was some unease in 1531–32. The southern convocation protested against the recognition of the king's supremacy embodied in the pardon of the clergy of early 1531.[728] In the lower house of convocation there was some opposition and obstruction from the ranks of the churchmen who held national or provincial office below that of bishop.[729]

A protest in the name of Peter Ligham, dean of Arches, survives, emphasising the inviolability of things spiritual. It acknowledged the king as 'singularem et clementissimum protectorem' (only and merciful protector)—but no more—and went on to protest (in Scarisbrick's translation) 'that he intends that nothing he has done or said in convocation or will say or do in a future convocation should endanger ecclesiastical constitutions or whittle away obedience to the holy see'. This protest was also signed by Robert Shorton (Catherine's almoner, archdeacon of Bath), Adam Travers (archdeacon of Exeter), Richard Featherstone (schoolmaster to Princess Mary), Richard Harrison (archdeacon of St Asaph), Thomas Pelles (chancellor of the bishop of Norwich), John Quarre (archdeacon of Llandaff) and Rowland Phillips (vicar of Croydon). It was not an official statement by the lower house of convocation, but clearly it had attracted the support of several important churchmen.[730] A second protest referred to the title granted to the king, declaring that 'it should in no way impugn the roman primacy'. This was signed by Nicholas Metcalf (archdeacon of Rochester), Robert Johnson and John Willor (Rochester), and Robert Ridley (London).[731]

Was it in response to that opposition that several (but not all) of the signatories were accused of offences under the *praemunire* statute? A surviving set of royal instructions to Cromwell commands that the king's attorney was to proceed against Adam Travers, Robert Cliff (chancellor of Bishop West of Ely), Thomas Pelles, John Parker and Rowland Phillips, 'which already have confessed before his Justice their offence in the Premunire'; and against Peter Ligham, dean of Arches, 'which Peter as yet hath not confessed, but standeth in terms of defence'.[732] In November 1531 Travers, Cliff, Pelles and Phillips were granted a protection despite an adverse judgment: they had been convicted, but any sentence would be suspended.[733] Adam Travers would nonetheless vote against the king over the divorce in April 1533.[734] Phillips evidently continued to oppose. Cromwell's remembrances in October 1533 and January 1534 noted 'of the taking of the vicar of Croydon', Rowland Phillips.[735] Phillips would then abjectly appeal to Cromwell for pity: ill, in need of surgeons, deprived of the diet he needed, and entirely ignorant of the unspecified great rumour and of the unspecified deed of the late archbishop of Canterbury for which he had been imprisoned, he pleaded to be freed to go to his benefice.[736] Evidently he was, since in early 1534 he was licensed by the king to dispute with Hugh Latimer, under suspicion for heresy.[737] In April 1534 there were rumours that he had been sent to the Tower.[738] But according to Thomas More, he was sworn to the act of succession.[739] And in July 1536 Bishop Stokesley emphasised to Thomas Bedell how zealously Phillips had in the summer of 1535 laboured in Stokesley's presence to bring the Carthusians to accept the king as head of the church.[740]

Ligham refused to accept that he had offended under *praemunire* but was convicted in Trinity term 1532.[741] A list of fines included Ligham at £133 6s. 8d. for offences against the statutes of provisors and *praemunire*.[742] A list of bills and obligations in Cromwell's papers includes a note of £100 in part payment of a fine of £133 6s. 8d. made by Peter Ligham for his pardon.[743] A later account had Ligham owing £66 13s. 4d.[744] In October 1532 Ligham, thanking Bishop Fisher for his venison, informed him how the king had vetoed his appointment as vicar-general by the prior of Christ Church, Canterbury: he had heard that Ligham was a good priest but he wanted more experience of whether he was *plene conversus* (fully turned around) before he should hold any such position. He had not heard from Catherine for many days: he was very desirous to know how she did.[745] Ligham did in the end secure an appointment as commissary-general of Canterbury.[746] Among Cromwell's remembrances, alongside the note 'copies of pardons', Ligham's name is listed.[747] Interestingly, Ligham became a visitor of the religious houses of Canterbury and secured the monks' signatures and seals to the repudiation of the pope.[748] In his will, dated 23 August 1538, he left a basin to Christopher Hales, the attorney who acted against him in 1531, and his best horse to his wife.[749] Ligham's contacts in the early 1530s with Catherine and Bishop Fisher are obviously intriguing. Among the interrogatories to Fisher were questions about letters Ligham wrote containing the words

I beseech our lord Jesus to give us grace and spiritual strength to show the truth, putting all fear apart; for by all conjecture that I see there be many solicitors corrupt intending to make division and schism in taking away the pope's authority, but would God they were cut off and separated which trouble the king.[750]

Bold words, though perhaps fearful—and in his own case prescient— that they would not have the courage to continue showing the truth. What Ligham's true feelings were can only be wondered at: was he intimidated, was he won over by preferment, was he intellectually convinced? All one can confidently say is that from 1532 he was no longer a dissident.

*   *   *

Bishop Fisher's episcopal colleagues joined him neither in refusing to support Henry's divorce nor in then refusing to accept the royal supremacy. Some may have hesitated before accepting the king's divorce. Archbishop Warham was never asked to pronounce Henry's marriage invalid and that might be significant. Archbishop Lee may have been promoted by the king with that role in mind, but if so he declined. Tunstal of Durham dissented more publicly in 1533. Clerk of Bath and Wells wrote against it. And yet all this amounted to little by way of effective and lasting opposition. As episcopal vacancies occurred, Henry filled them by appointing those who had been actively engaged in elaborating his case in canon law and in pressing it through diplomacy: Stephen Gardiner was appointed to Winchester in 1529, John Stokesley to London in 1530, Edward Lee to York in November 1530. And the pattern would continue with the appointment of Cranmer (in 1532), Rowland Lee and Edward Foxe.[751] Bishop Fisher resolutely opposed the king's divorce, but many other churchmen either did not think the king was wrong, or if they did so privately, nonetheless did not see it as an issue of principle. Royal marriages, for churchmen, were usually seen as second-order and technical issues, on which a range of compromises was possible; to insist on one reading of canon law in what was clearly an arguable and complex matter was foolish in the context of the position of the church as a whole. In 1533 (as we have seen elsewhere), under Archbishop Cranmer's lead, the church overwhelmingly supported the king.

Perhaps Fisher's episcopal colleagues did not realise the implications of what Henry was doing, and in particular the likelihood that the king's arguments for his divorce would ineluctably lead to an outright confrontation with the pope: more of them might have sided with Fisher if they had. But perhaps it was precisely because they did realise those dangers that they supported the king. Wolsey, in summer 1529, set out the risks to the church and the papal authority in England if the king's matter was not resolved in terms that are often dismissed as extravagant, but that are rather to be seen as prescient.

Or perhaps bishops and churchmen felt increasingly under pressure. The fall of Wolsey, the *praemunire* manoeuvres and the machinations that led to the pardon and the submission of the clergy in 1531 and 1532 made the king's determination unmistakably clear. Resistance, however justifiable (and opinions on the merits of the king's case were divided), would evidently be punished, and might well be futile anyway. Even Fisher, as we have seen, understandably hesitated in the face of threats and pressures and appeals to loyalty. It is not surprising that the church, in 1531 and 1532, should have found it hard to resist effectively. It is astonishing, and discreditable, to see just how many senior churchmen were threatened with plainly malicious accusations under *praemunire* or with *quo warranto* writs in these years.

Perhaps, if they did not follow him over the king's divorce, Fisher's episcopal colleagues should have followed him on those more direct royal attacks on the church. But no bishop made any gesture in defence of Wolsey or against the king's use of *praemunire* against him in 1529. Only Fisher spoke out (but not very tactfully) against the anticlerical legislation that autumn. Faced by renewed royal pressures in late 1530 and early 1531, churchmen yielded to the king, despite Fisher's efforts to stiffen their resistance. In 1532 there was greater defiance for a time. The annates and citations bills were opposed by all the bishops. Bishop Gardiner drew up a spirited defence of the independence of ecclesiastical jurisdiction. Even Archbishop Warham was prepared to compare himself to Becket. But, in circumstances that remain somewhat mysterious, the royal will prevailed and the church submitted in May 1532. Intimidation played a large part. And no doubt then, as at other times, bishops who accepted that which they would have preferred to reject did so in the hope that what was being lost would in more favourable times be recovered.[752]

When Henry formally broke with Rome and called on bishops to swear to the succession and to the royal supremacy, only Fisher refused. If several bishops had done so, that would undoubtedly have had a dramatic political effect. But by 1533–34 there were several recently appointed bishops, notably Cranmer, who fully supported Henry over the divorce. Others—Tunstal, Gardiner, Stokesley, Clerk—may have had reservations about the royal supremacy but they did not join Fisher in the Tower. Partly, no doubt, fears and pressures explain his isolation: it took courage to accept martyrdom. Partly, no doubt, those bishops who had earlier accepted the king's view of his marriage accepted the measures that he had subsesequently felt impelled to take to vindicate it. Perhaps they hoped that what was essentially a dispute over jurisdiction might yet be resolved by compromise. Perhaps too they were anxious about what would happen if they stood with Fisher: would that force Henry into abandoning his policies, or might it drive him into the arms of the protestant princes of Germany or the radical preachers of Switzerland? It is not, however, as easy as is sometimes claimed to document the suggestion that bishops such as Gardiner, Tunstal, Longland and Stokesley accepted the divorce and the royal supremacy because they feared heresy, much less because there was a bargain—unspoken more than spoken—between themselves and Henry, by which, in return for their support for his divorce and the royal supremacy, Henry would support their efforts to halt the spread of heresy.[753]

What makes most sense of what bishops did—and did not—do in the early 1530s is a series of accounts of their individual responses, and that in itself is significant. What they did not effectively do was to stand as one man in rebuke of, or in opposition to, Henry VIII. It would, I suggest, have made a real impact if they had. If his fellow bishops had refused to endorse Wolsey's admission of offences under the *praemunire* statute in 1529, if all the bishops had flatly rejected royal demands over *praemunire* in 1531, if all the bishops had refused to subscribe to the submission of the clergy in 1532, if all the bishops had declined the oath of succession in 1534 . . . But (unlike their successors in 1558–59, after a generation of religious strife) Fisher's episcopal colleagues were neither intellectually nor emotionally ready for such acts of collective defiance. Nothing in their careers would have prepared them for any dramatic and united public defiance of the king. Even Fisher's dissent is hard to turn into outright resistance: he was never a leader of anything that could be termed a campaign. It was Henry's political skills and his utterly ruthless methods that in good measure explain why the bishops never acted together. The oaths of 1534–35 compelled bishops to declare themselves for the king—or to risk their lives. The king's insistence that they preach the royal supremacy, and indeed write books on the theme, as several did, further compromised them and bound them, whatever their inner feelings, irremediably to the king's cause.

If senior churchmen did not resist effectively, it would have been very difficult for individual parish priests to have done so. Some clergy did speak out against the king's divorce and marriage to Anne Boleyn. Ralph

Wendon allegedly called Anne Boleyn a whore and a harlot.[754] James Harrison, parson of Leigh, Lancashire, declared that he would have none for queen but Queen Catherine: 'who the devil', he declaimed, 'made Ann Bullen, that whore, queen?'[755] Edward Powell preached in Bristol and in Salisbury, referring to the adultery of King David.[756] Some voiced their opposition to the break with Rome and royal supremacy. Several priests in Southampton spoke much for maintaining the pope's power.[757] 'It is said there is no pope,' declared Christopher Michell, parish priest of Winestead, Yorkshire, 'but I say there is a pope.'[758] Richard Crowley, curate of Broughton, Oxfordshire, called the bishop of Rome pope, and declared that Fisher, Reynolds and More had died for the true faith.[759] Gilbert Rouse, parson of Rouslynch, Worcestershire, had said that the monks and others who had been put to death were martyrs before God and saints in heaven.[760] There were several more, but it is not to belittle the courage that must have been required to speak out to note that the overall number of dissident clergy known to us was low. Overwhelmingly, priests conformed, however reluctantly, evidently swearing the oath of succession required in 1534. Since, as we have seen, all the bishops except Fisher complied, and since Fisher did not attempt a public preaching campaign, that is not surprising. Speaking out was a highly public act. Priests who did so risked detection— by other clergy, or by parish constables and JPs, who had been ordered to report any dissent—and punishment. Edward Powell was held in Dorchester gaol and complained of the severity of his treatment: he was lying in sticks, with gyves (shackles) on his legs.[761] Moreover, few, if any, of those priests who did speak out did so collectively, as part of a group.[762] None of that should be taken as showing that most clergy welcomed or were indifferent to what was happening. We shall see, when we consider the Pilgrimage of Grace, what priests might do in more propitious circumstances.

Nobility, Parliament and People

Effective opposition to the break with Rome did not, as we have seen, come from the bishops. 'A real threat to the regime could only come,' as Penry Williams has noted, 'from local or regional concentrations of power under effective magnate leadership'.[763] How did the nobility react?

The most prominent nobleman, Thomas Howard, third duke of Norfolk, may well have had some private doubts, but for all practical purposes he took the king's side. In the years after Wolsey's fall in 1529, he emerges as the king's leading minister, frequently acting as the king's spokesman in negotiations with Chapuys. The imperial ambassador may have claimed that Norfolk would not agree to the renunciation of papal authority,[764] but Norfolk did nothing whatever to block it. There is no hint of contacts with More or Fisher or any who had dissented from the tide of events. In 1536–37, as we shall see, he played a decisive part in defeating the Pilgrimage of Grace. And clearly if the premier duke stood with the king, that in itself meant that any nobleman who did oppose Henry could not do so in the name of the nobility as a whole.

Charles Brandon, duke of Suffolk, was a first-generation duke, elevated by Henry VIII in 1515, and very much the king's friend and the king's man. Whatever his private thoughts—and there are some hints that he was not altogether enthusiastic—there is nothing to suggest that he would go against Henry.[765]

Most greater noblemen—those of ancient lineage and regional patrimonies—seem largely to have followed the king's lead. Occasionally there are hints of some unease. Almost all our knowledge of this comes from Chapuys. Some of his reports inform us of words spoken in a range of *ad hoc* meetings, for example in gatherings of noblemen for consultations on the divorce, or in deputations to Queen Catherine. More often Chapuys attributes words of discontent to individual noblemen, though it is usually far from clear that such words were spoken directly to Chapuys himself, who in any case could not speak English. Since Chapuys's reports are rarely confirmed by other evidence, much less matched by actions, it is essential to strike a balance between dismissing them out of hand and giving them full credence.

In March 1531 Chapuys wrote how George Talbot, fourth earl of Shrewsbury, had the responsibility (as Lord High Steward) of keeping the crown of the queen of England: he would take care, Chapuys believed, not to allow it to be put on any other head.[766] And indeed Shrewsbury was not present at the coronation of Anne Boleyn in June 1533. But since his son and heir, Francis Talbot, was, that makes the significance of the remarks reported by Chapuys hard to evaluate. True, when in June 1531 a deputation of bishops and noblemen was sent to Catherine to persuade her to withdraw her appeal to Rome, it was Shrewsbury who voiced restraint. Those present were almost all the nobility of the kingdom, he told them, and it was their role to act in accordance with their name, that is to say, nobly. They should not for any prince in the world speak any villainous words or agree to any perversion of justice: if they did what was right then they would not wrong anyone. But for Shrewsbury—so Chapuys was informed—they would have used stronger language to the queen than they did: two or three times Shrewsbury successfully restrained them.[767] The depth of his concern and opposition to what the king was doing is striking. But what Shrewsbury openly objected to was excessive pressure on the queen. When a little earlier, in March 1531, he had been asked in the House of Lords about the king's matter, Shrewsbury said it was not for him to give an opinion on the subject: he would defer to those to whom knowledge and judgment belonged. That was an entirely proper response; it may have been prudential and tactical, but it shows further how Shrewsbury wished to avoid public confrontation.[768] Shrewsbury, like most Tudor noblemen, would not lightly abandon his fundamental loyalty to the crown. There is nothing whatever to suggest that he spoke any further words, much less took any action, against the drift of royal policy: he must have sworn the oaths required in 1534; and in 1536 he would instinctively and immediately set his face against the Pilgrims of Grace.

William Fitzalan, earl of Arundel, was reported by Chapuys as opposing—alone of the noblemen—the annates bill in the Lords in March 1532.[769] That would be remarkable, not least because the king (as we have seen) had gone to parliament in person three times: to oppose was to oppose Henry personally, not just to stand on abstract principle. But the rest of the lay peers did not join Arundel, and there is nothing to suggest any further opposition.

William Blount, Lord Mountjoy, who served Catherine of Aragon as chamberlain, reluctantly informed her, as we have seen, that the king had sent orders that she should no longer call herself queen.[770] In October 1533 Henry would reproach him that several of the queen's servants had never stopped calling her queen; ruing the 'high displeasure' he had incurred, Mountjoy explained that he could not stop her chaplains and her gentlewomen—'the further I do wade herein the more shall be my business yet it shall not lie in me to accomplish the king's pleasure herein which hath caused me to absent my self from the princess's house by a good space'—and offered to resign his office.[771] Perhaps Mountjoy had colluded with Catherine more than this account suggests: his withdrawal from her house was hardly the most effective way of persuading her. Yet it was the queen's intractability and his consequent powerlessness that most upset him: however distasteful he might have found what the king wanted from him, there is nothing to suggest that this was turning into anything resembling active opposition.

A few noblewomen close to Catherine were clearly upset by events, as we have already seen: Gertrude, marchioness of Exeter, Margaret, countess of Salisbury, and Lady Hussey.

But whenever it mattered, in public the nobility went along with all that the king did. In July 1530 several noblemen subscribed to the threatening letter to the pope: Chapuys claimed that they had been persuaded one by one.[772] We do not have *Lords Journals* for the years between 1529 and 1533, but in early 1534 the dukes of Norfolk and Suffolk, the marquess of Exeter, and the earls of Arundel, Oxford, Northumberland, Westmorland, Shrewsbury, Derby, Rutland, Cumberland, Sussex and Huntingdon were all present and evidently assented, in the king's presence, to the act of succession imposing an oath of obedience to the king.[773]

Within a few years, however, Lord Darcy and Lord Hussey (neither present in 1534) would be executed for their part in the Pilgrimage of Grace, and Lord Montagu and the marquess of Exeter for treason. What must be emphasised here is that the opposition of these noblemen to Henry's policies was more private, less concerted and more restrained than a casual reading of their fate might suggest. Henry's ruthlessness should not be taken as in itself evidence of organised and sustained political conspiracy. There is quite plentiful, and colourful, evidence from Chapuys about Darcy and Hussey in particular, and it makes an intriguing portrait. But Darcy's and Hussey's unease demands a nuanced appreciation.

Thomas, Lord Darcy, was a first-generation peer, ennobled for his service to Henry VII, and now an old man resident on his estates in the West Riding of Yorkshire. In February 1532 Darcy voiced his disquiet over the king's divorce at an assembly of great men in which the duke of Norfolk—obviously acting as the king's spokesman—claimed that the pope was treating the king badly by infringing the privileges of the kingdom. Matrimonial cases were secular, and 'au Roy qu'est empereur en ce Royaulme appertenoit la jurisdiction, sans que le pape ait a sen mesler' (to the king who is emperor in this kingdom belongs the jurisdiction, without the pope having to interfere in it). Darcy responded by declaring that, although his goods and person were at the king's disposal, he had heard and read that matrimonial causes were spiritual and under ecclesiastical jurisdiction. Most of those present agreed with Darcy's answer, Chapuys tells us.[774] In saying that, Darcy was roundly confronting the king's position. Moreover, at some other point in these years Darcy 'had in the parliament chamber declared before the lords his whole mind, touching any matter there to be argued, touching their faith', or so he would claim during the rebellion of 1536.[775]

In 1534 Darcy reappears as a critic, once again in the correspondence of Chapuys, together with John, Lord Hussey—like Darcy a courtier-administrator who had been ennobled by Henry VII, but who now lived mostly on his estates centred on Sleaford in Lincolnshire. On 30 September 1534 Chapuys reported that Hussey had had a secret interview with him. Hussey had emphasised how dismayed he and honest men were that Charles V did nothing to remedy matters in England. Almost everybody, he told Chapuys, was expecting that Charles V would assist them, naming Darcy especially. And Hussey added that Charles ought—though from here the wording is opaque—to begin by stimulating an insurrection of the people which would be joined immediately by the nobility and clergy. Clearly, Hussey was bitterly dissatisfied with the tide of events, and contemplating treason. But what is most striking is that he was looking to Charles V to put things right, rather than taking any initiatives himself.

Darcy, then approached by Chapuys, declared that he considered himself as one of the most loyal vassals the king had in matters which did not injure his conscience and honour, but the things being done in England were such an outrage against God and reason that he could not take himself for an honest man or a good Christian if he consented to them, especially in matters concerning the faith. That again was a notable declaration of dissent. In the north, Darcy added, there were sixteen (not 1,600, as *Letters and Papers* mistakenly says) earls and other great gentlemen who were of his opinion. After the defeat of the Pilgrimage of Grace, Robert Aske, the leader of the rebellion, recalled how Darcy had told him that 'there was diverse great men and Lords which before the time of this late insurrection had promised together to do their best to suppress heresies /and its maintainers . . ./ in this realm': they numbered fifteen.[776] But whether Darcy was correct that there were fifteen or sixteen noblemen who sympathised with him is more than debatable. In his message to Chapuys, he immediately qualified his claim by adding that he had talked about these matters with one or two only. He had not even given any indication of his views to his own sons, Sir George and Sir Arthur, the younger of whom had just been made captain of Jersey. Of course, Darcy may conceivably have been right that those with whom he had not spoken agreed with him; but another way of reading this is that Darcy had not dared to broach the matter with others because he doubted that they would, in fact, agree with him.

Darcy intended, Chapuys noted, to seek the king's permission to leave court and return home. He would then do his best to stir the people against what he saw as imminent parliamentary legislation aimed at introducing Lutheranism. With the assistance of Charles V he would raise the banner of the crucifix together with the emperor's, and among his first actions would be to seize noblemen who favoured these follies. Once again, it is the hesitations and doubts that demand attention. A moment earlier, there were many noblemen who favoured Darcy's cause: now there turn out to be noblemen who were happy with Henry's policies and who would have to be dealt with by force. Darcy called on the emperor to plan a simultaneous invasion of England with the king of Scotland. Charles V should send a small force to the mouth of the Thames, and some soldiers armed with arquebuses and money to the north to deter poor gentlemen from joining the king. Again it is striking that Darcy thought there were northern gentlemen who would support the king. Darcy offered to put eight thousand of his own men in the field. Possibly it is Chapuys, not Darcy, who exaggerates here: but Darcy would have done very well to raise a tenth of that number.[777] On 1 January 1535 Darcy had sent Chapuys a handsome sword as a new year's present, which Chapuys interpreted symbolically: Darcy was itching to take up arms. But for all his bluster, Darcy had not yet been able to get leave to retire to the country.[778] On 28 January Chapuys confirmed that Darcy stood firm and constant, adding, extravagantly, that Darcy had the greatest following in the kingdom, and there was no doubt that, with a little money, ten thousand men could be mustered.[779] At the beginning of May, Chapuys reported that Darcy had sent word that he was going home immediately and would lose no time for the advancement of the business.[780] A little later Darcy sent an old relative to Chapuys to say that he had resolved to go to Charles V to tell him the urgent necessity of remedying matters.[781] In July he urged that Charles should obtain a licence from the pope to deal with the schismatic king of England.

All that, on the face of it, leaves little doubt that Darcy was profoundly opposed to royal policies. But we are heavily dependent here on a single witness, Chapuys, who was himself keen to persuade his master, the emperor, to launch an invasion of England. Darcy was telling Chapuys what he wanted to hear; or perhaps Chapuys was somewhat embellishing the messages Darcy was sending him. But even if we accept Chapuys's reports as entirely accurate, problems remain. Darcy's fine words were not, in these years, matched by much action. Not only did he not attempt to raise rebellion, he did not even dare return to his house in Yorkshire without the king's permission. Presumably he swore the oath of succession without qualification. And considerable scepticism must be applied to Darcy's claims that large numbers of other noblemen were of his mind.

Hussey, as we have seen, once spoke with Chapuys. That he was indeed of Darcy's persuasion is strongly suggested by his wife's service in Queen Catherine's household. But there is no more evidence in these years of Hussey's opposition. Chapuys sometimes named other noblemen. He had heard from his physician that Henry Percy, sixth earl of Northumberland, was not too well pleased with the king or his ministers. Northumberland had supposedly said that the whole realm was so indignant at the oppressions and enormities now being practised that if the emperor would make the smallest effort the king would be ruined.[782] Again, however, there is little to suggest that Northumberland was more than privately uneasy, if indeed that. Interestingly, Chapuys noted that Darcy had warned him of the lightness of Northumberland, implying that he was not to be depended upon.[783] Chapuys informed the emperor that he was certain that there were innumerable lords who, if they dared, would say as much as Darcy did. He named two whom he described as among the most powerful in the kingdom, Edward Stanley, third earl of Derby, and Thomas, Lord Dacre, adding that Dacre had little reason to be satisfied with the king.[784] Chapuys was no doubt correct that Dacre was not pleased to have been accused of treasonous dealing with the Scots in 1534 when he had been doing no more than wardens had generally done to preserve his own lands.[785] Chapuys claimed that Anne Boleyn had used her influence against Dacre since he had always maintained the cause of Catherine and Mary:[786] but there is no evidence of how that maintenance had been done. And, crucially, neither in Dacre's case nor Derby's is there anything to suggest open opposition to the king's religious policies. That, it may be noted here, also seems to be true of the rising in Ireland involving Gerald Fitzgerald, ninth earl of Kildare, and his son Thomas, in 1534: if their political disaffection had fused with religious opposition, then Henry could well have faced a serious challenge, and the history of the 1530s would have to be written in a British context. But no such fusion occurred.[787] In January 1535 Chapuys claimed that Darcy was allied with Lord Sandys, the lord chamberlain, the best captain in the kingdom: Sandys, Chapuys claimed, was disaffected and was staying at his house pretending to be ill.[788] On 4 March 1535 Chapuys reported a prophecy that there would be a mutiny against the rulers of the realm, a prophecy sought on behalf of Lord Bray.[789] On 25 April 1535 Chapuys reported that Bray had assured him that a score of the principal lords and more than a hundred knights were quite ready to employ their persons, goods, friends and dependants if they had the smallest assistance from Charles V, at a time when popular dissatisfaction with taxation was great.[790] Once more, a degree of scepticism is in order. This was not a period of heavy taxation. And everything, again, would depend on the emperor taking the first step.

When rebellion broke out in autumn 1536, Chapuys, reporting how Henry summoned the duke of Norfolk to deal with the rebels, presented Norfolk as secretly pleased by the rebellion because it would discredit Thomas Cromwell, and halt the demolition of the churches and religious change in general, which was not to his liking—or so Chapuys declared. Norfolk had previously incurred the displeasure of the king because he had to some extent spoken his mind on these matters. He was one of those whom Darcy counted as willing, when occasion required, to defend the cause of the church—though Chapuys at once added that he did not rely much upon him, considering his inconstancy.[791] Nothing supports Chapuys here. Norfolk may well have been privately uneasy at the pace of religious change, but, as we have seen, he conformed. And, as we shall see, he was to take an aggressively and cynically hostile stand against the Pilgrims of Grace.

Virtually all these indications of noble dissent from royal religious policies are known to us from Chapuys alone; and from one or two mentions at that. Only Darcy is referred to repeatedly over time. What should we make of this? In a later chapter, we shall turn to the Pilgrimage of Grace in autumn 1536 and there consider the role of noblemen, not least Hussey and Darcy. But it is important to note here that, whatever they did or did not do in autumn 1536, it is very hard to show that Darcy or Hussey or any other nobleman significantly, consistently and actively opposed royal policies before then. Doubtless many noblemen accepted that Henry's divorce was in a sense a personal and private matter, and that the king was entitled to seek an annulment, though some, for example Shrewsbury, may well have sympathised with Catherine, as did noblewomen in the queen's household. What noblemen felt about the break with Rome and royal supremacy can only be guessed at, Darcy apart. One obvious difficulty, as Darcy pointed out, was that 'the custom of that house among the lords before that time, had been that such matters should always, touching spiritual authority, be referred unto the convocation house & not in the parliament house',[792] and, given the (enforced) acquiescence of the bishops and senior clergy, it was doubly awkward for lay lords to raise these issues. On what grounds could a lay nobleman—especially if not openly supported by many others—question what the bishops had agreed to, however unwill-ingly? Chapuys, as we have seen, recorded how Hussey had urged Charles V to put things right, how Darcy called on him to invade England, how Bray urged that he send them assistance. Such appeals and urgings were obviously treasonable in themselves. Yet they are weak evidence that these noblemen were actually contemplating rebellion themselves. It was of course entirely realistic for them to think that only with the active intervention of Charles V could anything be achieved. For Darcy or Hussey to have tried to launch a rebellion alone would have been suicidal. But that limits the practical significance of their dissent as voiced to Chapuys: it was little more than the expression of deeply felt disquiet. It may well be that Darcy and Chapuys were correct to suppose that many noblemen would have welcomed an imperial inva-sion, and would have joined it enthusiastically if it had prospered. But no such invasion ever came, and anyone reviewing matters in the late summer of 1536 would have concluded that the English nobility, however much some of them may have grumbled to each other, or to Chapuys, had nonetheless, whenever it mattered, conformed to the royal will.[793] Some, indeed, had at times been active on the king's side. In May 1534 the earls of Westmorland and Cumberland (together with Sir Thomas Clifford) had intimidatingly searched Bishop Tunstal's house for incriminating writings.[794] There is just one further exception to be considered, Reginald Pole; but before we discuss him it is necessary to consider how far the wider political nation reacted to events. How much dissent was there in the parliaments of the early and mid-1530s among the knights and burgesses in the Commons, and how far was this stim-ulated, and furthered, by noblemen?

From time to time dissent and criticism were expressed in parliament. In December 1530 Chapuys wrote how three or four members had been to see him to ask whether he had some papal provision on which they could ground their opposition.[795] In early 1531 the Commons wanted to be granted an exemption from *praemunire*, the offence allegedly com-mitted by churchmen. After great murmuring in the Commons against the financial oppressions imposed by the king, Henry yielded and granted the exemption.[796] When Thomas More, the lord chancellor, read out university opinions on the king's divorce in March 1531, the Commons were reported by Chapuys to have shown displeasure and regret,[797] though Hall does not offer any comment that might confirm that. In early 1532, the bill for the restraint of annates had a difficult passage in the Lords, as we have seen. According to Chapuys—who is our only source—it was not until the king came in person to the

Commons, and asked those who agreed with him to stay on his side of the house, and those who did not to go to the other side of the house, that he gained a majority for the bill. Some passed to his side for fear of his indignation, Chapuys commented.[798] All that does hint at considerable unease at the king's anti-papal measure. Moreover, it is quite likely, as we have seen, that the Commons did force the king to make significant concessions, notably delaying the implementation of the bill for a year and allowing a small payment to the pope. But unfortunately we lack detailed information about individual MPs that would allow a more nuanced understanding.

A little later the king, asking for taxation in order to strengthen border fortifications against the Scots, was opposed, Chapuys tells us, by two worthy MPs, who claimed that the best fortification was to do justice and maintain friendship with the emperor: the king should therefore take back his wife and treat her well, or risk ruin. Herbert of Cherbury names one of the MPs, Temse—of whom we know nothing more—and says that he urged the Commons to petition the king to take Catherine back again.[799] According to Chapuys, these words were well taken by all present, except two or three, and no taxation was granted. The king responded by sending for the majority of the members and making a long speech in justification of his conduct in the divorce, as a result of which the Commons agreed to grant a fifteenth.[800] On Herbert of Cherbury's account, it was the speaker, Sir Thomas Audley, who was summoned to hear the king marvel that any of them should meddle in business that could not properly be determined there.[801] No dissent is recorded by Hall: according to him, the Commons lovingly granted a fifteenth, but the grant was not enacted owing to a sudden outbreak of plague, which led to the prorogation of parliament.[802]

We know tantalisingly little about the detailed events in the Commons in 1532. There are abundant signs of unease among the knights and burgesses, together with hints of rather more significant opposition. Temse's attempt to link the granting of taxation to the king's marriage is a striking example of the Commons seeking to link redress of grievance with the granting of supply. It is frustrating that we can say little more than that about it. Slightly earlier, Henry evidently had to use his personal charm and authority in order to secure the passage of the bill of annates. But in the end he did. And in other ways, notably in presenting to the king the supplication against the ordinaries, the Commons and the king were of one mind. There may well have been unease over the king's divorce and over the implications of anti-papal policies, but the Commons were no defenders of the liberties and privileges of the church.

According to Chapuys, in early 1533 there was opposition in parliament to the bill of appeals to such an extent that it was delayed. The ground of opposition was practical: fear of economic retaliation by the emperor against the wool trade.[803] One MP suggested offering £200,000 if the king would agree to refer the divorce to a general council of the church.[804] Once more this points to unease at the king's anti-papal policies, though whether that concern was simply at the possible diplomatic and trading consequences, rather than on principle, it is impossible to say with confidence. It was obviously safer, and tactically shrewder, to concentrate on trade. There is one further piece of evidence, the later confession of the Warwickshire MP, Sir George Throckmorton, that 'I have spoken some thing in the act of appeals'—but beyond the fact that this displeased Henry, Throckmorton does not reveal what he said. That Throckmorton consulted Thomas More, Bishop Fisher and John Reynolds about his future course of action does, however, make it clear that his concern was principled and religious.[805]

In early 1534 further measures were enacted by parliament, notably the act of succession, which imposed an oath on all the king's subjects. Chapuys reported in March that some who had not dared openly to oppose the divorce did now oppose the measures against the pope as much as they could,[806] but these acts were passed as a result of the threats of the king.[807]

There was also some opposition to the succession bill, discussed in March 1534.[808] According to Bishop Fisher's brother Robert, member for Rochester, there was 'much sticking' in the Commons at a bill that made speaking against the king treason. Fisher's brother thought it would not pass unless it were made clear that such words would have to have been spoken *maliciously*.[809] Elton points out, however, that the word 'maliciously' was always in the drafts of the bill: it was not added at the insistence of the Commons. Perhaps, then, the 'sticking' was that the word should remain, or at just how it should be defined.[810]

Whatever the extent of such opposition in parliament, any review of the legislation of the early 1530s would suggest that the king essentially got his way. Some compromise on detail there may at times have been, but essentially parliament rubber-stamped the king's will.

How far this was the result of intimidation is an intriguing question. Thomas More, after his conviction, declared 'pour vn vostre parlement, *et Dieu scait quel* [my italics], j'ay tous les saints Conciles generaux depuis mille ans' (for one parliament of yours, *and God knows of what kind* [my italics], I have all the holy General Councils for a thousand years)[811]—elaborated by Harpsfield as 'for one Council or

Parliament of yours (*God knoweth what manner of one*), I have all the Councils made these thousand years. And for this kingdom, I have all other christian realms'.[812] In speaking thus, was he pointedly emphasising the levels of fear? When the Pilgrims of Grace would call for a *free* parliament to be held at York, were they too implying that MPs had been subject to excessive pressure during the Reformation Parliament? On 8 January 1537 Robert Aske, who had spent Christmastide with the king, wrote to Lord Darcy how the king intended to hold his parliament and have his queen crowned at York, and had, revealingly, granted 'free election of knights and burgesses and like liberty to the spirituality to declare their learning with out his displeasure'.[813] Sir George Throckmorton confessed how he had spoken out on the bill of Appeals, adding 'whereupon the king's grace did send for me and spoke with me in diverse matters'. That the king should send for an MP who had, presumably, criticised what became the Act of Appeals is itself interesting and revealing. Throckmorton emphasised in his statement to the king especially 'how good and gracious lord ye were to me at Grafton to pardon and forgive me all things past concerning the parliament': that the king should pardon and forgive an MP things concerning the parliament is again an interesting indication of the limits of freedom of speech in parliaments.[814] Throckmorton recalled how he fell in communication with Sir Thomas Dingley about parliamentary matters, Dingley 'marvelling greatly that such acts as the appeals and other should passe so lightly as they did'. Throckmorton retorted that 'it were now marvel for that the common house was much advertised'—an intriguing word to use—'by my lord privy seal [Thomas Cromwell] and that few men there would displease him'.[815] Chapuys regularly reported that the king would get or had got his way by intimidation: in March 1534 he wrote that anti-papal legislation was passed as a result of threats by the king.[816] As early as August 1530 he wrote that two members well disposed towards Catherine had told him how much they feared that they would be induced and compelled to obey the will of the king, especially if they were taken one by one.[817]

How far did those opposed to the divorce or the break with Rome work together? Can one speak not just of opposition in parliament but of a parliamentary opposition? It is very tempting. Clearly men saw each other at parliaments and that made possible at the very least the exchange of information and opinions. Later Sir Geoffrey Pole testified that at various parliaments the earl of Huntingdon and Lord Montagu told each other that those who agreed to what the king wanted were just knaves and heretics, and those who agreed did so from fear while continuing to murmur and grudge.[818] But evidence of more organised groups is thin. A damaged list of some thirty-five MPs, datable (by reference to by-elections and by the timing of conferral of knighthoods) to early 1533, includes several names of men otherwise known to have been critical of the divorce and of the break with Rome. It has often been taken as a list of those opposed to the act of appeals passed in March and April. And Sir George Throckmorton's name heads the list. But it is tricky to press this document too hard as evidence for disaffection on clearly religious grounds. Many of the MPs listed cannot be shown ever to have expressed any conservative religious views, and they may have opposed the bill for fear of economic reprisals against the cloth trade, in which several of those named were engaged. The list remains suggestive but inconclusive.[819] Another list of some fifty names of MPs, drawn up by Cromwell in late 1534, possibly to sit on a committee reviewing the treasons bill, is hard to take as a list of possible or actual opponents of royal policy.[820]

In his later confession, Sir George Throckmorton described how he and four other county burgesses, Sir William Barrantine (knight for Oxfordshire), Sir William Essex (Berkshire), Sir Marmaduke Constable (Yorkshire) and Sir John Giffard (Staffordshire), were in the habit of meeting at the Queen's Head Tavern, Fleet Street, over dinner and supper to discuss parliamentary matters.[821] To elevate a gathering of like-minded friends enjoying a gossip and, no doubt, consoling each other on the tide of events into the 'Queen's Head faction' is to run ahead of the evidence. That they sent their servants out of earshot confirms that they spoke critically of what was happening, but as Throckmorton pointed out, had these men been engaged in a serious conspiracy, they would hardly have chosen such a location in which to plot.

Throckmorton boasted to his friends that he had spoken defiantly to the king—but it is unlikely that he had actually done so. He said he had told Dingley that he thought the king's conscience was troubled because God was not pleased with his marriage.

And I said to him [Dingley] that I told your grace [Henry VIII], I feared if ye did marry queen Anne, your conscience would be more troubled at length, for that it is thought ye have meddled both with the mother and the sister. And his grace said never with the mother. And my Lord Privy Seal standing by said: nor never with the sister neither, and therefore put that out of your mind. And this is all I said

to him or he to me or words much like to the same effect to my
remembrance, as god shall judge me at my most need.

But Throckmorton never spoke these words (that the king had meddled
both with Anne's sister and with her mother) to Henry: he *pretended* to
have done so 'upon a proud and vainglorious mind', so that those to
whom he told this tale 'should note me to be a man that durst speak
for the commonwealth, and never for untruth in thought word or deed'.
Throckmorton wanted to show his friends that Henry had not intimidated him; but he had.[822] In mid-November 1536 he would meet with
Sir William Essex at the Queen's Head for supper; they talked about the
northern rebels, and Throckmorton lent Essex a copy of their articles.
Presumably Throckmorton had some sympathy with the rebels. But that
had not stopped him raising three hundred men and bringing them to
Ampthill to serve in the king's force against them.[823]

Clearly our sources are meagre, but even so it is hard to turn Throckmorton and his friends into a significant political force. Throckmorton
had contact, as we have seen, with Sir Thomas More, Bishop Fisher and
John Reynolds, but there is little to suggest links between Throckmorton and noblemen. Once more, protests against some of the king's
measures are best seen as just that: expressions of dissent, shared for
consolation between friends. Once again, it is hard to say just what more
Throckmorton could or should have done. If there had been fifty or a
hundred knights of the shire like him, things might have turned out
differently; but there were not, at least as far as we know.

And if noblemen and MPs did not oppose the king effectively, it is
not likely that the common people would have been able to do so. That
is not to say that they were uninformed or indifferent. Edward Hall,
against the thrust of his account that is largely favourable towards
Henry VIII, shows that there was much popular sympathy for the plight
of Catherine of Aragon: women especially were critical of the king.
Once Henry stopped seeing Catherine from July 1531, 'the common
people daily murmured and spoke their foolish fantasies'.[824] Chapuys
repeatedly wrote of popular hostility. In July 1532 he reported how
Henry had turned back when intending to hunt because, in two or
three places that he passed through, the people urged him to take back
the queen, and the women insulted Anne Boleyn.[825] But Chapuys's
despatches presented popular disenchantment in very general and menacing terms: on 29 May 1533 he reported that he was told the multitude's indignation increased daily;[826] in January 1535 he insisted on the
alienation of the people from the king;[827] in July 1535 he wrote of the

great grief of the whole people at the executions.[828] But because Chapuys's reports were so general, and because he was so obviously trying to persuade the Emperor Charles V to mount an invasion of England, they must be treated warily by the historian. In these years several individuals were reported to Cromwell for speaking out. In April 1534 Henry Kylbie of Henley reported that one John Snappe of Horsingdune had said openly at dinner that if he had £2,000 he would spend it defending Mary's title against any issue that came from Anne.[829] Margaret Cowpland called the king an extortioner, knave and traitor, and Queen Anne a strong harlot, on various occasions.[830] In February 1534 Margaret Chancellor, of Bradfield St Clare, Suffolk, called the queen a naughty whore, 'a goggyll yed hoore' (a goggle-eyed whore); she continued, 'God save queen Catherine', the rightful queen, whom she trusted to see as her queen again. Margaret's excuse was that she was drunk.[831] But the number of such colourful examples is small, and there is little hint of contacts between those detected. None of this is to deny that there was popular disquiet at the course of events. When we turn to consider the Pilgrimage of Grace, strong convictions will appear very clearly. It was rather that, as Hall put it, 'the affairs of Princes be not ordered by the common people'.[832]

Reginald Pole

Yet one man of noble blood did, however, turn into one of the fiercest critics of Henry VIII. Reginald Pole, a younger son born *c*. 1500 of Sir Richard Pole and Lady Margaret Plantagenet, only daughter of George, duke of Clarence, and thus a cousin of Henry VIII, studied at Oxford in the 1510s, and then at Padua from 1521 to 1526, financially supported by the king. Dean of Wimborne Minster in 1518, he was made dean of Exeter Cathedral in 1527. In October 1529 he was granted royal permission and an exhibition of £100 to study in Paris; a further payment of £70 to Mr Pole, the king's scholar, is recorded in April 1530.[833] It was at this time that he became caught up in the politics and theology of Henry's divorce; indeed, it was with that in mind that the king had sent him to Paris.[834] And at this point there is nothing to suggest that Pole was anything but a committed royal servant. In summer 1530 he was involved in the solicitation of opinions on the king's cause from the university faculties in Paris. On 1 May Henry formally requested the faculty of theology to consider his case, and to listen to 'lord Reginald Pole our dearest relative'.[835] On 13 May Pole reported assurances that Francis I had sent letters to the faculty 'as effectually written as could be desired for your grace's purpose'.[836] He reported on 7 July that the faculty had concluded in the king's favour, but warned that the adverse party were using every means to undermine their decision, despite all 'soliciting of our part that were your agents here which never ceased to labour all that lay in us for the expedition of it both with the premier president and with all such as we thought might in any part further or aid us therein'.[837] How actively Pole was involved emerges from an unsigned letter written to him at the duke of Norfolk's command: Pole should be 'heartily congratulated' for acting so stoutly on the king's behalf without being asked or ordered to by the king.[838] Pole himself took credit for the decision to send Edward Foxe to lobby in Paris.[839] Not surprisingly, rather later Pole would play down his role in Paris in 1530;[840] what matters here is that, however vigorous and uncompromising an opponent of the king Pole was to become, in 1530 he was Henry's active agent.

Recalled to England by the king in July, Pole tried to retire to the Charterhouse at Sheen, and there is no recorded evidence of his activities in the rest of that year. That hints that, for all his active involvement in the king's great matter, Pole was increasingly uneasy at the direction of royal policy. But it would not be possible for him to retreat into monastic life untroubled by political events. Soon after Wolsey's death on 29 November 1530, he was offered the vacant see of York by the king. In any other circumstances, that would have been an honour as well as an obligation. The drawback was that he would obviously have to support Henry over his divorce.

What the king had in mind may well have been much more than just mere acquiescence. As we have seen, from an early stage in his efforts to secure his divorce, Henry had considered settling the matter in England by getting parliament to pass a bill enabling the archbishops of the English church—or, intriguingly, one of them—to hear his case, and to determine it without any subsequent papal interference. Wolsey's death in November 1530 offered him the opportunity to secure the appointment to the archbishopric of York of a churchman sympathetic to his cause and, maybe, willing to act on his own to grant his divorce. And it was Reginald Pole that Henry first had in mind.

On 31 December Chapuys wrote how Henry had again offered the archbishopric of York, so far unavailingly, using both tough and tender words.[841] That the unnamed target of Henry's persuasion was indeed Pole is made clear by Pole's later recollections. Writing to the lords of the council in February 1537, Pole called particularly on the duke of Norfolk to confirm it: 'Here now my good lord of Norfolk I take testimony of your conscience if [I wou]ld [have] agreed to that matter of divorce wherein [my sen]tence was so often asked when the archbishopric of York was void, your lordship can tell whether I might have had that honour or no.' Interestingly, Pole went on to say that he considered accepting that offer—and the conditions attached, realising just how committed the king was to his divorce—'I saw the king so set in that cause that no man's sentence nor reason could bring him therefrom'. He discussed his dilemma with his friends. 'When I saw and my friends saw the same, that there was but one gate open to enter in to the king's favour at that time which was by favouring the matter of divorce', the upshot of their deliberations was the conclusion that 'albeit my conscience could never perfectly agree' to the king's divorce, nevertheless since this was an opportunity 'to advance my self in all honour to the great furtherance of all my friends', he should agree to do so. Pole remembered: 'I said then to doctor [Edward Fo]x[e] which had been with me for the king's matter, that I trust I had found a way to satisfy his grace and that same also I showed to my lord my brother which both showed the same to the king.' Henry then summoned Pole and, remarkably, 'his grace was the first that showed him self at the door which I entered to speak with him'. At that point he experienced, he recalled, something of a conversion, or rather a reversion to his previous convictions. 'I had no sooner cast my eyes to look upon him but I testify god my mind was so changed from that I had purposed afore as though I had never thought it.' What follows is somewhat obscure: 'And instead of that, my mind next to my duty to god ran upon nothing else but how I could find in my heart . . . to go about to confirm in that opinion which not only was dishonour but extreme peril' in the world to come and to 'his honour and wealth in this life'. Instead of coming to the king with a new willingness to join in his cause, as Dr Foxe and Pole's brother Lord Montagu had reported, he had evidently on the spur of the moment refused to support Henry.[842] That must have angered the king. Chapuys would some years later recall how Henry had offered Reginald the archbishopric of Canterbury (Chapuys meant to say York) provided he would take his part, 'using such persuasions as might have sufficed to convert one of the most obstinate Jews', and threatening the most terrible things in the case of refusal; but he could not make him waver.[843]

Pole, upset by Henry's anger, and obviously feeling the need to justify his behaviour, sent a letter—or perhaps a book 'much contrary to the king his purpose', which does not survive but which was summarised by Cranmer in a letter to the earl of Wiltshire, Anne Boleyn's father, on

13 June 1531. In it Pole warned against the troubles that would be likely to arise in the realm from a disputed succession, recalling the 'misery and trouble' of the time of Lancaster and York. The people within this realm 'think surely that they have an heir lawful already, with whom they all be well content': it would be hard to persuade them to take any other, and to abandon Princess Mary. He dismissed the king's attempt to justify his case by divine law—the opposite could just as well be justified by scripture. And he warned of the dangers of an imperial economic blockade. The emperor, 'a man of so great power', 'without drawing of any sword, but only by forbidding the course of merchandise into Flanders and Spain', might cause England 'great damage and ruin'. And what if Charles V drew his sword? When weaker than he was now, he had subdued the French and the pope. The French would be unreliable and self-interested allies. Henry's proposals were putting the succession, and thus the political stability of the realm, into jeopardy. Moreover, to accept the king's case in canon law would be to accuse him of living for more than twenty years 'in a matrimony so shameful, so abominable, so bestial and against nature' that ignorance could be no excuse: Pole could not bring himself, he said, to accuse the king in that way. Preaching would not persuade the people to accept the king's case: it would rather discredit learned men and the name of learning. As for the authority of the universities, 'many times they be led by affections'. 'With how great difficulty' they were brought to take the king's side, Pole declared, doubtless recalling his own part. There were precedents against the king: the emperor and the duke of Savoy had married sisters of the king of Portugal. Cranmer praised the book, written 'with such wit' that Pole 'might be for his wisdom' one of the king's councillors: moreover, the book was 'of such eloquence that if it were set forth and known to the common people, I suppose it were not possible to persuade them to the contrary'.[844] Thomas F. Mayer believes that Cranmer was exaggerating: Pole was here, Mayer says, presenting 'far from principled opposition', but rather emphasising the diplomatic hazards of the course on which the king had embarked.[845] But if Pole drew attention vividly to the internal and external risks that the king was running, nonetheless his stand was indeed uncompromising and based upon principle. The duke of Norfolk—surely acting as Henry's spokesman—complained about Pole's book to Lord Montagu, his brother; but Montagu had a surprisingly amicable discussion about the matter with the king. Pole then (possibly in May/June 1531) asked the king's permission to return to his studies abroad. In January 1532 Henry gave him that permission. Chapuys claimed that Pole had in fact threat-

ened the king. He had told Henry that if he remained in England he must attend parliament (as dean of Exeter he sat in convocation) and if the divorce came up, he must speak according to his conscience. In response Henry licensed him to go to study abroad while continuing to draw an income from his English benefices.[846] Mayer does not trust Chapuys's account, on the grounds that Pole had not spoken out in 1531 in the lower house of convocation, but that does not prove that he would not have been prepared to say what he thought privately to the king.[847] Pole's biographer, William Schenk, criticised him for 'shirking the worldly duties that happened to come his way': by retreating into the shelter of continental universities, he was avoiding the responsibility of opposing the king more openly. He had refused to sully his hands by supporting the king—but he was not prepared to defy him in public.[848] Diarmaid MacCulloch has remarked on his 'uncomfortable lack of heroic suffering'.[849] What is most relevant in any consideration of the effectiveness and extent of opposition is that, by going into exile and by keeping his counsel, he clearly made matters easier for Henry and gave little comfort to those who were uneasy at the course of events. Thanks to Cranmer, we know what Pole wrote to the king; but there is no sign whatever that he disclosed his thoughts to anyone else.

Once in northern Italy Pole devoted himself to his studies: 'there was never gentleman out of England more regarded for his learning and wisdom than is master Powell in these parts', Lord Lisle was informed.[850] But there is little to suggest in these early years in exile—1532, 1533, 1534, early 1535, the years in which Henry accomplished his divorce, married Anne Boleyn and proclaimed his royal supremacy—that he did or said anything that Henry would have deplored.

True, Catherine of Aragon, if Chapuys's report of September 1533 is to be believed, saw him as a fitting husband for Princess Mary. Chapuys, noting Pole's descent from the duke of Clarence, somewhat extravagantly added the phrase, 'to whom, in the opinion of many, the kingdom belonged'. That was awkward, since Pole was a younger son, and his elder brother, Henry, Lord Montagu, would clearly come before him in any claim to the succession. And Chapuys's further remark that Pole and his brothers had many kinsmen and allies was evidently meant to hint at the possibility of a noble rebellion against Henry VIII.[851] No more was heard of this till November 1534, when Chapuys hoped that Pole's background might incline the queen to a marriage alliance between him and Princess Mary and perhaps to more.[852] Nothing, however, suggests that in 1533 and 1534 the exiled Pole was in any way encouraging such speculations. Mayer cites Martin de Cornoca, the Spanish consul in

Venice, who in August 1534 stressed to Charles V how militarily powerful Pole's English and Welsh connections were. Cornoca went on to admit that he did not know what Pole himself thought about all this—though he believed he would wish to deliver his country from tyranny.[853] Mayer, arguing against what Cornoca actually said, claims that his knowledge must have come from Pole, and that when Pole claimed that Cornoca approached Charles V without his knowledge, he was lying. Yet if Cornoca wished to persuade Charles V to take military action against Henry VIII, and knew that Pole was keen on it, why should his case have been strengthened by saying that he did not know what Pole's opinion was? It is far more probable that Cornoca, like Chapuys, was urging militancy on the emperor, but without any encouragement from Pole.[854] It is of course conceivable that in these years Pole was plotting against the king in various ways that have left no trace, but it seems very improbable, especially since he would confront Henry quite directly in 1536.

What led to that? In April 1535 Pole had received letters concerning 'the king's most noble request and pleasure, which was in few words clearly and plainly without colour or cloak of dissimulation, to show your sentence in his lately defined causes'. Henry, 'somewhat marvelling that you should take so much pleasure in your quiet and scholastical studies', desired him, according to his duty to the king and his country, 'to set apart all such scholastical respects, to the declaration of your learned judgement'; there were hints of promotion too.[855] Henry's politician's contempt for disinterested scholarship could hardly be more explicit: the function of men of learning was to lend their support to the king's cause.

Henry had just questioned his chaplain, Thomas Starkey, who, like Pole, had been studying in Padua between 1532 and 1534, but who early in 1535 had returned to serve in the king's court, about Pole's wellbeing, about his studies—and about his opinion on the king's marriage and royal supremacy. Starkey noted his 'prudent silence' on the king's marriage and the authority of the pope. Nonetheless, Starkey hinted, somewhat opaquely, that Pole would 'stretch and extend' his knowledge and learning 'to the maintaining of such things as his grace wisdom by court of parliament therein had decreed'. Henry was not satisfied by that, and wanted to know his opinions more plainly. He ordered Starkey to write to him asking him to declare his opinion, not in a great book, but briefly and plainly setting out his reasons.[856]

In May, and later, Starkey accordingly further urged Pole to declare his opinion. To assist him, Starkey offered his own arguments against papal supremacy, in defence of the king's position on the divorce and new marriage, and in justification of the executions of the Carthusians.[857] At some point in these months Pole was sent several books attacking the papal primacy—including Stephen Gardiner's *Of True Obedience* and Richard Sampson's *Oratio de dignitate et potestate regis*.

The king's purpose in all this was surely not, as Chapuys supposed, to have a pretext for injuring Pole.[858] All Englishmen living in England had recently been required to swear oaths in support of the royal supremacy: here Henry was in effect seeking to extend his authority to a prominent Englishman in exile. If Pole would lend his support, that would be an undoubted advantage in the king's campaign to secure general compliance at home and recognition abroad. Moreover, Henry was so self-righteously convinced of the validity of his arguments that he expected that everyone would be persuaded by them. As Starkey put it to Pole, 'for sorry his highness would be to see you not to reach unto so manifest a truth'.[859] Later Henry (our source is Sir Geoffrey Pole recalling what the French ambassador had told him) would say what a pity it was that such a man 'should be blinded so that he could not see the truth'.[860]

Perhaps Starkey, on his return from Italy, unwittingly misled the king about Pole's likely agreement: 'truth this is, that I never thought him to be of so corrupt a judgement and sentence in this matter of the primacy', he explained to Cromwell, 'and thereof I put you in hope and expectation, and so I did the king also'; though he vigorously denied that consulting Pole was his idea.[861] In 1535 and through the winter of 1535–36, Starkey, and another royal agent in Italy, Edmond Harvel (who had earlier helped Henry to secure judgments on the divorce from the university of Padua), at first had the impression that Pole would indeed support the king.[862] By December 1535 he was 'in vehement study of writing' to satisfy the king.[863] As late as April Harvel was reporting in a hopeful tone the imminent completion of the book.[864] That he would support Henry was a deception that Pole successfully maintained well into spring 1536. But now not only did he break his silence, but he roundly rejected the king's claims.

Possibly Pole had come to feel the need to speak out in response to events in England, notably the executions of More, Fisher and the Charterhouse monks in spring 1535. His opinions had changed, Thomas Starkey later claimed, after More and Fisher 'defended the cause with the shedding of their blood'.[865] It is possible too that, as Pole would later inform Tunstal, the timing of his book was partly prompted by the fall of Anne Boleyn in May 1536: 'I had trusted that woman that hath been cause of all these dishonours had taken away all dishonour with her, specially hearing what a good lady the king hath now taken.' [866] But most probably Pole had been provoked into declaring what he thought by Henry himself, and by the books in support of the royal supremacy that Henry sent. In letters to Gasparo Contarini, Pole declared himself irked by the king's insistence that he give his opinions and by Gardiner's work *Of True Obedience*.[867] Henry's request had galvanised him into vigorous study.[868]

On completing his book, *De unitate*, Pole sent it to the king on 27 May 1536. He insisted his only purpose in writing it was 'the manifestation of the truth in that matter'. He took Cromwell's letters as 'a commandment to show my sentence'. And Pole claimed that 'otherwise I think I had never set pen to book in so little hope of persuasion and in such a matter as the time was so likely not to be all the best accepted'— given his previous silence, that may well be true.[869] The king might have done better to have allowed him to remain abroad in silence. Once Pole had worked out his ideas, however, he clearly did not feel any need to pull his punches against the king.

In *De unitate*, he criticised Sampson's defence of the royal supremacy, arguing that no prince could ever be supreme head of the church in his realm. St Peter's words, cited by Sampson—'honour the king'—were an inadequate foundation for the royal supremacy. Pole taunted Sampson as a Judas for accepting money from the bishop of Norwich and the promise of succeeding him. The royal supremacy was thus presented as the intellectual construct of a corrupt would-be prelate. He attacked the executions of Fisher, More, and the Carthusians and Bridgettines, especially of Prior Reynolds, and the Observants. He thus associated himself with those who had openly defied Henry to the death. He compared Henry to Nero and Domitian, and warned him of the fate of Richard III, so identifying the king with past tyrants and a recent ruler generally and officially also regarded as a tyrant. He warned Henry that he could not expect his subjects to keep faith with him when he had broken it so shamefully with them, an opinion that implicitly endorsed rebellion. Colourful language marked the whole book—Henry was a wild beast, incestuous, a robber, a murderer, a greater enemy to Christianity than the Turk.[870]

What was Pole's exact purpose in writing and sending Henry such a book? The instructions that he gave the bearer who brought *De unitate* to the king illuminate his intentions. In the books sent to him defending the royal supremacy Pole saw 'the truth marvellously suppressed and cloaked all colours that could be invented'. Unless the truth was set out purely, the king might be undone. Pole offered the king a way out. Henry had been 'by perverse persuasion brought from those opinions which were for his honour most to maintain'. And then Pole invoked the examples of David and Solomon, both of whom had been 'recovered by the mercy of God again', and compared himself to the prophet who showed David the truth. If Henry maintained his schism 'many sore dangers' might follow. Experience showed that the king's subjects 'cannot be quieted with these innovations touching opinions in religion'—not a bad prophecy to have voiced in summer 1536. Dangers would also come from other princes who would defend the laws of the church. Pole admitted that these were 'vehemently set forth' in his book. But he denied that he was 'the greatest adversary of his grace's honour that ever any hitherto hath been'. Anyone who read the whole book would know that Pole's purpose was to save the king from 'great dishonour and peril both in this world and that to come'. If Henry would accept 'this warning to return to the unity of his church', then 'it shall be taken for one of the greatest miracles that hath been showed this many ages'.[871]

Pole meant his book only for the king's eyes, together with those of the wise councillors whom he suggested that the king might consult. He insisted that he had intended that the book should remain secret until Henry had seen it, and regretted that his intentions had been frustrated when two quires of the book went astray, though they were soon found.[872] Although the pope had repeatedly asked to see the manuscript while it was being drafted, Pole, as he later insisted, 'kept it as close from him as it were in the king's chamber'.[873] In early 1537 he assured the lords of the council that he was not intending to put it in print.

> You may soon think if I had the boldness to send the book so written into the king's hands that same boldness might better serve me here both to print it and set it forth that every man might see it. The which thing that I have not done *hitherto*. What thing doth hold me but that I tender the king's honour more then I think few other would in like case.[874]

Here there are hints of a threat, but the emphasis is on Pole's restraint. Eventually the work was indeed set up in type and printed in 1538 but not, it seems, widely distributed. In 1549 Pole would apologise in a letter to Edward VI that his book had been published without his authority or knowledge.[875]

If, then, Pole had not written his book with the intention of presenting it to a European public, what was his aim? In his letter to the lords
of the council in February 1537, he presented himself in the role of the
king's confessor—'a sharp ghostly father', as Tunstal put it[876]—urging
him to turn dishonour into honour. 'There was never confessor desired
to be so secret as I desired to be in that book, having none other purpose
but that only the confessor hath [towards a] delinquent, to make him
understand well his offences.' [877] What Pole saw himself as doing—
however unlikely his chances of success, which he fully recognised—was
acting as a confessor and an Old Testament prophet calling upon the
king to repent.[878]

Henry must have been very angry.[879] But he skilfully informed Pole
that he was not displeased; since their opinions differed, however, he
wanted him to return to England to discuss them. There were several
passages in Pole's book that would be best dealt with by conferring,
rather than in writing. Both Pope Paul III and Cardinal Contarini
warned the author not to return to England.[880] Chapuys feared that he
would be executed if he returned.[881] Pole responded that he would be
insane to put himself in Henry's hands.[882] Replying at great length on
15 July to the king's letters of 14 June (which do not survive), he
declared that there was nothing that he desired more in his life than to
obey and 'have this one great pleasure to be interpreter of my own
writing'. But he could not come except 'temerariously'. Only the king
stopped his coming. 'Every man is made a traitor that will not agree to
give you title to make you head of the church in your realm': those who
do not agree were 'with such extremity executed'. A law had been put
into effect

> against the best men of your realm both in virtue and learning put to
> execution of death for the same, and suffering the pain of traitors
> which in heart and mind as all their deeds showed from the begin-
> ning of their life to the latter days had ever been your most faithful
> servants.

Since that law was still in force, the king could see that it was a sufficient impediment against Pole's return to England.

Pole insisted that 'my whole desire is was and ever shall be that your
grace might reign long in honour in wealth in surety in love and estimation of all men', but, 'remaining those innovations your grace hath
made of late in the church', his desire could not take effect, but rather
the contrary. He then defended his purpose in writing, referring to the

king's command that he should show his opinion on the royal supremacy. Henry had grounded his case on scripture, as several books written justifying the king's cause had shown. The first of these that Pole had seen was Sampson's: confident in his own learning and reasoning, he roundly told the king that 'I doubt not but who so ever read my book shall clearly perceive all his reasons and arguments as nothing concluding that he purposes'. Pole pointed out that the justice of a belief is to be assessed not only through argument but by its fruits: and he referred bitingly to what had followed Henry's royal supremacy, meaning the execution of More and Fisher and the monks and friars. If any spark of that 'generosity of nature' that Pole believed to be in Henry had remained, then he could never have done or allowed to be done deeds that brought not only 'great dishonour to your grace' but also 'manifest jeopardy and peril'. The remedy, he insisted, 'standeth only in returning to the ordinances of the church'. Henry's faults were spelt out more boldly still. Solomon, considered the wisest of princes, made diverse great errors, 'being blinded by the same that took also knowledge from your grace which was but inordinate affect he bare to women'. Who, Pole continued, would point out such failings in a king? 'But now here is all the difficulty in a prince, who is he that will tell him his fault . . . who is he that will not rather maintain by words and say it is well when it is amiss, fearing if he should do other he should displease his prince.' If there was anyone who would tell the truth, 'yet where is the prince that will hear him?'

But in Henry's case, God's providence intervened. God 'first provided to put one of your faithful servants in such place that he might at liberty speak, and afterward putting in your mind to ask his sentence gave him occasion withal to say, and occasion with that to be heard better by writing then by present communication'. Pole had then seized the opportunity. He compared Henry's reply to that of an injured patient, greatly in need of a surgeon to cut off dead and superfluous flesh, who cried out against him as soon as he saw him and would not allow him to use his craft. Pole insisted his aim was 'to make you see the truth in all these matters'.[883]

Meanwhile, by 13 July Cuthbert Tunstal had read his book and letter and sent his response, 'heavy in heart': 'in all your book there is not one quire without bitterness'. Tunstal roundly asserted that the royal supremacy did not separate England from the catholic church, as Pole had claimed, but rather ended her captivity to a foreign power. The king's purpose was to see God's laws purely preached and Christ's faith observed without blot: he did not wish to break away from the unity

of Christ's catholic church, but rather to remove England from subjection to foreign powers. The people were not offended, as Pole had
claimed, but welcomed the fact that money that used to go Rome—
'which was no small some but great and excessive'—was now kept
within the realm. If Henry were to attempt to restore the authority of
the bishop of Rome, he would have much greater difficulty in securing
assent in parliament than with anything he had previously put
forward.[884] Thomas Starkey too wrote to Pole to protest against 'your
bloody book': 'you must leave Rome if you love England, you must
forsake the bishop thereof if you will win the king'. [885]

   But Pole was unyielding. On 1 August he responded to Tunstal, whose
letter he had received on 27 July. 'I think you have not thoroughly read
my book, albeit you write you have perused it through', he lamented.
He insisted that the king had indeed separated from the church in refusing to offer obedience as all his ancestors and Henry himself in the best
part of his reign had done. Teaching the king 'softly and gently', as
Tunstal suggested, had not worked. The king 'thinketh not he hath done
any offence to God but rather that he hath done so that no prince can
do better'. Pole denied that his book was written 'against the king'. He
devoted several wordy pages to the defence of the papal primacy, and
he once more lamented Fisher, More and the other 'holy learned men
that died for this cause'.[886]

   And he redoubled his epistolary efforts to win over the king. On 1
January 1537,[887] he sent to London letters written with his own hand,
altogether and openly denying the royal supremacy. To the lords of the
king's council he wrote defiantly on 16 February. He wished to know
whether in a matter of such weight he could have refused to give his
opinion when commanded to do so by the king. He wished to know
whether he should have written 'according as my learning and conscience did give me' or whether 'setting these apart' it was rather for
him to 'direct all my discourse of writing to please'. He wished to know
whether, if a loving subject had fears that royal policy was leading to
dishonour and danger, he should 'keep them close and speak never word
of such dishonour such peril that might come to his prince hereof or
with all wit and learning to set them afore his eyes'. He had no purpose,
he insisted, 'but to make this plain whereof the ignorance might be the
undoing both of the king and the realm'.[888] What Pole hoped for was
that the king would see the error of his ways. By the summer of 1536,
that was as far as he went. In due course we shall reflect on Pole's later,
more active attempts to persuade Henry.

3

Authority and Reform

The Defence of the Royal Supremacy—Reforming Rhetoric

Henry VIII's break with Rome, and the quality of the opposition to it
that we have seen, called for repeated and extended defence and justification. These it received in the mid-1530s. At one level, Henry's break
with Rome might have been thought to be simply a jurisdictional quarrel
with the pope that could potentially be resolved by further negotiation,
especially after the passage of time, or the deaths of those most involved.
What is remarkable, however, is that Henry remained insistent on his
royal supremacy for the rest of his reign. In January 1536 Catherine of
Aragon died, but that made no difference to the vigour with which
Henry continued to assert that he had been right over the invalidity of
his marriage. Nor did the fall of Anne Boleyn on charges of adultery in
May 1536 lead to any reconciliation with the pope or any lessening of
the force with which Henry claimed that he was supreme head of the
church. The principle of the royal supremacy remained inviolable for
the rest of Henry's reign.

But there is more to be said about the way in which the king justified his royal supremacy. His defence was not couched just in terms
of jurisdiction. He did indeed assert that the pope had no lawful
authority over him. But Henry's profound originality was that he har-
nessed the rhetoric of Erasmian humanists[1] (but pushing it in directions
that most of them would not have intended) and the rhetoric of protestant reformers (but not, as we shall see, their theology) to this task.
References abound to 'the laws of God and Holy Scripture', to 'the word
of God', to preaching 'the gospel of Christ', to the 'opening of God's
truth'.[2] When Bishop Tunstal of Durham objected to the *Articles
Devised by the Whole Consent of the King's Council* in December 1533
(a tract defending the break with Rome), Henry responded point by

point, but above all insisted that it was a matter either of choosing Christ and abandoning the pope and his church, or of following the pope and his church and abandoning Christ.[3]

The king's instructions to William Paget, who was sent on a mission to the German protestant princes, stressed how Henry saw them as zealous in advancing the sincere truth and right understanding of God's word and the justice of his laws. He himself, he said, sought the extirpation of old corrupt errors, customs and abuses by which Christ's people had long been seduced and kept bound under the yoke of the bishop of Rome. Paget was to praise Henry's contribution to the reformation of abuses, the maintenance of God's word, the faith of Christ and the wealth of Christendom, properly fitting the office of a Christian prince.[4] An appeal to a general council (placed in April 1534 by the editors of *Letters and Papers*) insisted that in scripture the bishop of Rome was accorded no greater jurisdiction than any other bishop, yet because people had been willing to put up with it, and because princes had been blind, they had done themselves 'too great injury' by allowing papal authority to continue. Now it was vital to denounce the bishop of Rome to the people, 'to the intent they no longer honour him as an idol, being but a man', adding a personal innuendo: 'and what manner a man, a man neither in life, nor learning, christ's disciple'.[5]

A year later the king's instructions to Edward Foxe, bishop of Hereford, sent to negotiate with German protestant princes, noted how Henry and a good number of the German princes had worked 'to advance and set forth the glory of God, and the plain perfect and most certain truth of his world'. The king bore special love to the (Lutheran) duke of Saxony since he continued 'to set forth maintain and defend the sincere teaching of the gospel and the perfect true understanding of the word of God'. Henry himself was 'also illuminated with the same spirit of truth and wholly addicted and dedicated to the advancement thereof', and had gone to 'great pain labour and travail' to bring the word of God to the knowledge of his subjects. 'By good consultation' he intended to go further 'to the augmentation of the glory of God and the true knowledge of his word'.[6]

Bishop Tunstal, defending the king's position to Reginald Pole in 1536, declared that Henry's

full purpose and intent is to see the laws of Almighty God purely and sincerely preached and taught, and Christ's faith without blot kept and observed in his realm; . . . and to reduce his church of England out of all captivity of foreign powers, heretofore usurped therein, into the pristine state that all churches of all realms were in at the beginning.[7]

An act of parliament exempting the universities and the colleges of Eton and Winchester from paying taxation imposed on the church referred to 'the fervent zeal which his Majesty hath conceived and beareth as well principally to the advancement of the sincere and pure doctrine of God's word and Holy Testament'.[8] In a circular letter to all JPs on 25 June 1535 Henry described the great benefit if bishops and clergy 'should sincerely, truly and faithfully set forth, declare and preach unto our said subjects the very true word of God, and without all manner colour, dissimulation, hypocrisy, manifest, publish and declare the great and innumerable enormities and abuses' of the bishop of Rome. Just how Henry equated the word of God with his royal supremacy is shown by the way in which he went on to express his confidence that the recipient of his letter would be 'of such singular zeal and affection towards the glory of Almighty God, and of so faithful and loving heart towards us' that he would do all that was 'to the preferment and setting forward of God's word' and 'the defence of the king's rights and title'.[9]

Once more the rhetoric of the reformation was used in justification when in 1536 an act was passed by parliament abolishing papal authority. The bishop of Rome had 'obfuscate[d] and wrest[ed] God's holy word and testament a long season from the spiritual and true meaning thereof'. The act roundly attacked the pope's 'worldly and carnal affections, as pomp, glory, avarice, ambition and tyranny'. He had used 'politic diverse traditions and inventions set forth to promote and stablish his only dominion, both upon the souls and also the bodies and goods of all christian people, excluding Christ out of his kingdom and rule of man his soul'. By 'dreams vanities and fantasies' the pope had seduced many of the king's subjects into 'superstitious and erroneous opinions'.[10] The association of the pope with superstitions and erroneous opinions would prove highly significant. At Michaelmas 1535, Henry sent for his bishops to come to Winchester and commanded them 'by mouth' to preach against the bishop of Rome's false and unjust usurpation.[11] On his return to Canterbury, Cranmer preached that the pope was not God's vicar on earth—but also that Rome was a centre of covetousness, unchaste living and the maintenance of all vices.[12]

Henry's supremacy was being justified on grounds more radical than the proper extent of jurisdiction. The rhetoric of such denunciations of the papacy and defences of the royal supremacy was, as has been insufficiently noticed, quasi-protestant. But precision is required.

Henry VIII's Religion

To understand Henry's attitudes in the 1530s, it is essential to explore the piety of the king in the years before the dramatic events of the break with Rome. That shows Henry as devout in his attachment to the mass and surprisingly competent as a polemicising theologian, but somewhat detached from many features of traditional religion, especially pilgrimages and monasteries. Influenced by Erasmus, Henry believed that the church was in need of purifying reform. The king's encouragement of Cardinal Wolsey's direction and reform of the church should be seen in that light.

Henry VIII was never much committed to monasteries. In this he was in good company. Concern over the condition of monasteries was not new. Criticism had been aired amid the religious debates of the age of Wyclif. Henry V had been involved in reform of the Benedictines. The flourishing of newer and stricter orders, often under royal patronage, such as the Observant Franciscan friars and the Carthusian monks in the fifteenth century implicitly criticised the lukewarm religion of too many of the rest. Of course, monasteries, like gardens, were organic entities; all that grows decays; gardening, including weeding and cutting out dead wood, was always necessary and always attempted. Clearly such routine reformation must be distinguished from deeper disquiets.

Yet there is little doubt that many bishops, in the early Tudor period, saw monasteries as greatly in need of reform. Wolsey stands out here. In June 1519 the pope appointed Wolsey and Campeggio as legates for the reformation of monasteries, to which end Wolsey summoned abbots and priors to a conference at Westminster.[13] That authority was renewed in 1521, and amplified in 1524.[14] Wolsey, it should be emphasised, was not alone in his concern. Bishop Richard Foxe of Winchester was worried about the Benedictine abbey of Hyde and the Augustinian abbey at Bristol. Bishop John Longland of Lincoln was concerned at the condition of monasteries in his diocese, especially Peterborough, and worked closely with Wolsey to deal with difficulties at the exempt Cistercian house at Thame, Oxfordshire.[15] Indeed, concern over monasteries was the hallmark of the reforming bishop in early sixteenth-century Europe.

Erasmus articulated those disquiets. He believed it would be useful if monks were brought more completely under the authority of the bishops.[16] That was just what Wolsey attempted to achieve. What such tighter episcopal supervision meant was the extension of episcopal oversight to houses legally exempt from such control, regular and more frequent visitations, and a renewed emphasis on observance of each house's rule. Many Augustinian and Benedictine houses were exempt from episcopal oversight, as were all Cistercian houses and the Dominican and Franciscan friars. Under the powers Wolsey acquired in 1519, that would change. For example, Wolsey appointed the bishop of Salisbury as his deputy to visit the nunneries in his diocese and take action against those that were not well run or in which the nuns were guilty of slanderous living: in such cases nuns should be transferred to other houses.[17] That visitation led to the suppression of Bromehall nunnery for unspecified enormities.[18] It was not an easy task. Bishop Foxe lamented to Wolsey in 1521 his difficulties in doing within his diocese what Wolsey had attempted in the whole country. He had found—what he did not at first expect—the monks so depraved, so licentious and so corrupt that he despaired of any perfect reformation.[19] Foxe later attempted to forbid nuns in his diocese from leaving their monasteries, which aroused controversy.[20] Advised by the abbess of Wherwell and the prioress of Whitney that a basic weakness was that the nuns insufficiently understood their rule, since it was in Latin, Foxe translated the rule of St Benedict into 'common, plain, round English, easy and ready to be understood by . . . devout religious women', adding a running commentary to the text.[21]

Wolsey's concerns were well illustrated by the letter he sent in 1518 to the chapter of regular Augustinian canons at Leicester. Learning, Wolsey maintained, was the greatest prerogative of the catholic faith, the great distinction between men and brutes. For that reason he regretted that so few monks went on to study, and he was determined to establish a college for the order, exclusively for learning. In response the chapter appointed him a brother and submitted itself entirely to his authority as a reformer. But it was afraid of carrying out measures against monks who broke the rules for fear of being sued under the *praemunire* statutes; this made the discipline of the order ineffective.[22] In March 1520 Wolsey issued orders and statutes for Augustinian canons. They were to hold a general meeting every three years. Unsuitable persons and women were not to be admitted within the cloisters. Monks were not to go out of the monastery. They were not to go hunting and hawking. They were not to wear furs and shoes worn by the laity. They were to keep the canonical hours. They were allowed the use of the organ, but they were to confine themselves to plainsong, not prick-song.[23] Should Wolsey thus be seen as a 'tough disciplinarian' who 'looked to more rigorous application of the founder's rule, an enforced retreat from worldliness, reform through discipline'?[24] Pope Clement VII would in July 1524 urge him to use gentleness and tact, rather than severity, in admonishing the Observant Franciscans.[25]

That Wolsey may have been justified in his concern emerges from the responses of the Benedictines in 1520 to his proposed reforms. Many of the rules ought to be followed by all good monks, they agreed, but others were too austere for the times in which they lived. The number of monks and monasteries in England was too great, they damagingly admitted, to allow them to be enforced without provoking murmurs and a rebellious spirit. They begged Wolsey to modify the reformation of their order, so as not to drive the weak into flight, apostasy or rebellion, or to deter those who intended to enter the order. Without doubt, if the reformation were conducted with too much austerity, there would not, they said, be sufficient monks. But 'those who desire a life of austerity and of regular observance are few, and indeed most rare'. Only the Carthusians, Bridgettines and Observant Franciscans could succeed in such aspirations.[26]

The most striking expression of episcopal concern over the condition of the monasteries was the widespread conviction that it would be for the best if smaller and decayed monastic houses were suppressed, and if their revenues, instead of supporting monks and nuns who prayed in buildings set apart from the world, were diverted to more relevant purposes—namely the education, in grammar schools and at new colleges at the universities, of men who would serve not in enclosed orders but as parish priests. That belief in the superiority of parish service marks the early Tudor episcopate.[27] Warham justified this approach to the inhabitants of Tonbridge, Kent. Wolsey and he thought it would be better for them and their descendants to have forty children of that country brought up in learning and afterwards sent to the university of Oxford than for there to be six or seven canons locally. Several bishops adopted similar beliefs. So convinced were they by the cause that they did not scruple over much about methods. Bishop Alcock of Ely made the questionable claim that the convent of St Radegund, Cambridge, was in the patronage of the bishops of Ely and, in 1496, secured the king's licence to expel the two nuns, and turn the buildings into what became Jesus College.[28] Several other bishops were similarly engaged: John Fisher, on behalf of Lady Margaret Beaufort, at Cambridge; Richard Foxe, bishop of Winchester, at Corpus Christi College, Oxford.

It was, however, Wolsey who did the most along such lines. His reforms in this context have been given their deserved importance by Peter Gwyn. Wolsey dissolved some twenty-nine houses in order to found Cardinal College, Oxford, and a grammar school in Ipswich.[29] His ambitions went still further.[30] In May 1529 Wolsey was granted executive powers to proceed, converting abbacies into bishoprics, creating new dioceses, suppressing houses worth six thousand ducats, and uniting monasteries unable to support twelve members.[31] On 12 November 1528 a bull allowed the uniting of monasteries with fewer than twelve inmates (a number symbolising the twelve apostles), a measure that especially threatened the many small houses of Augustinian canons.[32] In justification, it was maintained that religion could not be properly observed except in communities with sufficient monks or nuns. Individuals scattered in small monasteries brought nothing but discredit on religion. If Wolsey and Cardinal Campeggio might have powers to unite at their discretion those monasteries which could not support twelve religious observants from their fruits, that would be to make one perfect out of several imperfect.[33] These bulls hint at the imminence of fundamental reform—'a wholesale reform of the church in which the suppression and unification of religious houses or their conversion into seats of bishoprics formed an integral part'.[34]

Of course, such measures could be seen as personal aggrandisement by Wolsey. Many—mostly protestant—historians have dismissed any reforming impulse, and have seen Wolsey's aims as purely personal and financial, entirely lacking a spiritual dimension. That fails to convince. Many other bishops, as we have seen, were, on a smaller scale, doing the same. That such measures were sexist—nunneries were being dissolved in order to fund an all-male college at Oxford—is a criticism that a modern feminist might make, but that does not make them any the less reforming in thrust. And that was not a sentiment that was expressed in early Tudor England. What is remarkable rather is the localist defence of monastic houses facing suppression. At Tonbridge in 1525 all but three of a delegation said they wished the canons restored and the priory to continue.[35] Such local attachment to monasteries, however small and corrupt, is striking. When, in autumn 1529, it was open season for attacks on Wolsey, Lord Darcy hoped that in future no abbeys would be pulled down 'by untrue surmises', and attacked the 'abomination, ruin, and seditious and erroneous violations used at the pulling down of the abbeys by his commissioners and servants at his commandments, and the great robberies and spoilings', comparable, in his view, to the worst act of Luther.[36] Such a characterisation of what he was doing was mistaken, but its vehemence testifies to the substantial nature of Wolsey's monastic reforms.

And what is vital to grasp here is that Henry was fully behind Wolsey in such efforts. In 1525 Bishop John Longland wrote to Wolsey that he had told the king how glad Wolsey was that Henry rejoiced in Wolsey's establishment of Cardinal College, Oxford; he had also spoken of the good that it would do by bringing youth up to virtue, and by promoting the faith and the king's honour. The king said more good would come of it than any man could imagine—as no doubt he would tell Wolsey himself when he next came to him. A little later Henry had invited Longland to tell the queen about the learning and the learned men at Wolsey's college at Oxford; Longland praised Wolsey's project, saying that literature would be so encouraged that men would come to England from all parts of Christendom for learning and virtue.[37] Such glimpses suggest that Henry shared Wolsey's concern at the condition of the monasteries and supported his efforts to use his legatine powers to visit and reform them, and to reallocate funds from decayed monasteries in support of colleges at the universities. In 1525 Wolsey planned to visit the London Greyfriars himself, accompanied by Henry—strong evidence both of Wolsey's personal commitment and of Henry's support for such reform. But the planned visitation coincided with the arrival of the news of the battle of Pavia and was consequently postponed so that Wolsey and the king could attend to more urgent diplomatic concerns. Neither took part in the eventual visitation.[38]

Not only did Henry share contemporary episcopal reservations about the quality of the monasteries, he seems to have had little time for features of late medieval piety associated with them, particularly pilgrimages to shrines. Henry VIII's accounts contain several payments to religious institutions. It is immediately obvious, however, that his expenditure on building and gambling was far greater. There was a routine character to many, if not most, of the offerings the king made. Regular annual payments were made to a priest at Walsingham, for the king's candle there, for the king's candle at Doncaster, for an offering at Canterbury on St Thomas's Day, to the Lenten preachers, or at Easter. When the king travelled, and came to a town or city with a shrine, an appropriate offering was duly made. For example, during the military campaign of 1513 he made offerings—6s. 8d. on each occasion—at the high altar at Canterbury, at the shrine of St Thomas Becket, at the high altar of St Augustine's and at St Augustine's shrine on 21 June; at the high altar again on 24 June; at St Augustine's on 26 June; at Dover on 28 June; at Calais on 3 July; at St Mary's Church on 7 July; at the Resurrection and high altar on 31 July; at the Staple Hall on Relic

Sunday at receiving the sacrament and at the offertory; in the field beside Thérouanne on 6 August, St Lawrence's Day, 21 August, St Bartholomew's Day and 28 August; in the camp beside Tournai on St Matthew's Day; in three places within Tournai on 23 September. On the king's coming to Windsor in July 1510, offerings were made at Eton College and at the tomb of Henry VI in St George's Chapel, Windsor. On the king's coming to Reading, Romsey and Southampton in August 1510, and to Salisbury in September 1510, offerings are duly recorded. A year later offerings are recorded to the rood of the wall and our lady of grace at Northampton, to the rood at the Whitefriars, Nottingham, to our Lady at the tower at Coventry, and at Merivale Abbey. In September 1514 offerings were made when the king came to the rood of grace at Boxley, at St Augustine's, Canterbury, and at St Thomas Becket's shrine in the cathedral. In June 1519 offerings were made at the tomb of 'good king' Henry VI on Henry VIII's coming to Windsor.[39] The characteristic feature is that these payments were made on the king's coming to a place; it was rarely the case that the shrine was itself the purpose of the journey. This was not devotional travel, undertaken in the spirit of pilgrimage to a particular shrine, making a special journey, going out of one's way.[40] Only once can Henry VIII reasonably confidently be presumed to have gone deliberately and out of his way on pilgrimage, namely to Walsingham in January 1510 on the birth of his short-lived son. It is very striking that he did not go there again. And it is revealing that Hugh Rich, the Observant Franciscan condemned for his association with the Nun of Kent, should have remarked of Henry that all the time the king was at Canterbury—presumably in 1532—he visited neither the cathedral nor St Augustine's.[41]

Many people went on pilgrimage or vowed to do so when they were ill. Henry was undoubtedly very frightened when sweating sickness swept the country between 1516 and 1518 and again in 1528. In 1517 Cardinal Wolsey was moved to go on pilgrimage to Walsingham. But as far as we know Henry did not go, nor made any vows, nor asked anyone to go on his behalf. Indeed, his approach was determinedly sceptical. When in October 1517 a Spanish friar, called by his fellows a saint, arrived at court, alleging that he worked miracles in the late tempest at sea, which ceased at his bidding, he had an hour's interview with the king; afterwards Pace, the king's secretary, commented that the king esteemed him more a friar than a saint.[42] In 1528, when Henry gave Wolsey advice on how to escape sweating sickness, his approach was entirely secular:[43]

His highness willed me to write unto your grace, most heartily desiring the same, above all other things, to keep your grace out of all air, where any of that infection is, and that if, in one place any one fall sick thereof, that Your Grace incontinently do remove to a clean place; and so, in like case, from that place to an other, and with a small and clean company; saying, that that is the thing, whereby His Highness hath purged his house, having the same now, thanked be God, clean. And over that, His Highness desireth your grace to use small suppers, and to drink little wine, namely that is big, and once in the week to use the pills of Rasis; and if it come in any wise, to sweat moderately the full time, without suffering it to run in; which, by Your Grace's physicians, with a possetale, having certain herbs clarified in it, shall facilely, if need be, be provoked and continued; with more good wholesome counsel by his highness in most tender and loving manner given to your grace, then my simple wit can suffice to rehearse.

Henry VIII, then, was a rare pilgrim and does not appear to have been much involved in the intercessory practices and beliefs of what Eamon Duffy has characterised as traditional religion. Payments by the king did include some miscellaneous payments for religious buildings or ornamentation, but these were relatively few. In June 1511 £20 and in November 1512 £23 11s. 4d. were offered towards the costs of glazing Our Lady's Chapel at Walsingham. In October 1515 the Observant Franciscans were given £6 13s. 4d. towards the building of their church. In November 1518 two Londoners were paid for mending the organs at Woodstock parish church. In January 1519 £40 was given towards building the parish church within the Tower of London, and £100 for the roof of the chapel in the Tower. In July 1531 the hermit of Deptford was given £3 6s. 8d. towards the repair of his chapel.[44] None of this amounts to very much, and some of it was for essential maintenance. Even more striking is Henry VIII's artistic patronage in general. It is striking that where the Tudor volume of Howard Colvin's *History of the King's Works* contains a substantial chapter on Henry VII's 'works of piety'—the completion of King's College Chapel, Cambridge, the foundation of the Observant Franciscan house at Richmond (including the erection of the building at the king's expense), the establishment of the Savoy hospital next to Charing Cross as a nightly hostel for a hundred poor folks, Henry VII's almshouses, Westminster, and what we now call Henry VII's Chapel at Westminster Abbey, intended as a shrine for King Henry VI—no such chapter can be compiled for Henry VIII. There is absolutely nothing comparable, even though Henry VIII was one of the greatest builders in the history of the monarchy. What is astonishing, as Colvin has pointed out, is how *exclusively secular* his works were.[45] This is highly significant. Henry VII's works of piety show how immersed he was in conventional piety and reveal an almost desperate search for intercession for his soul in purgatory. To be fair, it is true that most of Henry VII's projects (though not the foundation of the Observant Franciscans at Greenwich) were begun or planned near the end of his life; and it must be noted that Henry VIII did contribute to the costs of the completion of religious projects which he inherited: particularly to St George's Chapel at Windsor and to the embellishment of King's College Chapel at Cambridge. King's College Chapel was funded by Henry VII's executors, and structurally complete by 1515; an undated petition to Henry VIII asked him to order executors to provide funds for paving, stalling and glazing; and glazing was carried out after 1515 apparently at the king's expense, according to later testimony of John Caius and the author of a sixteenth-century catalogue of the fellows of King's.[46] Between 1533 and 1536 (as the inclusion of the initials of Henry and Anne Boleyn shows) the rood loft, organ screen and associated stalls were constructed, and a warrant of 1538 confirms that Henry met the costs. But Colvin points out that significant intended embellishments were not carried out: the gilding and painting of the great vault, the glazing of the great west window; and some forty-eight niches, plus two on either side of the west door, were not filled.[47] This was not an involved commitment, even though the costs were significant. (There is no direct evidence of Henry VIII's involvement in completion of the Savoy hospital, except payments to the king's glazier, Barnard Flower.)[48]

Henry VIII *began* nothing of the kind himself. And the building works with which he is most obviously associated—Eltham, Bridewell, New Hall, Whitehall, St James's, Hampton Court, Nonsuch—were essentially secular palaces. True, they did include chapels for religious services. A list of sixteen works to be done at Eltham includes 'item to take down our old chapel and a new to be set up and made of timber work set upon a vault with a foundation of stone . . . the same chapel to be set xii foot near the hall than the old chapel doth'.[49] A warrant was issued for the payment of £200 for the gilding and painting of the Chapel Royal at Greenwich, though that sum also included the costs of making two lodgings there.[50] At Hampton Court the chapel built by Wolsey was remodelled from 1535, with the insertion of an elaborate timber vault.[51] The ceiling of the Chapel Royal, St James's Palace, was painted in 1540.[52] But there was nothing remarkable about such works—they were functional, decorative, but not demonstrative in any religious or pious sense. Indeed, the construction of Nonsuch palace involved the destruction of the parish church at Cuddington.[53] Henry VIII commissioned no primarily religious works.[54] Even the tomb he ordered Pietro Torrigiano to make—a tomb of white marble and black touchstone for himself and Queen Catherine, one-fourth larger than the one he had already made for Henry VII—does not invalidate that generalisation.[55] At Nonsuch palace, built from 1538, the inner courtyard was decorated by an extraordinary series of stucco panels—some twenty-eight or thirty-one caesars, mythological arts and virtues. Their origins, meaning and purpose are obscure, but what is immediately obvious is the absence of any explicitly Christian references, certainly no saints, no medieval piety.[56] This example, of course, dates from well after the break with Rome, but it does fit well with what went before.

In many ways some of the attitudes discussed can be seen as Erasmian, particularly the critical attitudes to the monasteries and the lack of enthusiasm for certain features of late medieval piety. How far can Henry be seen more broadly as Erasmian?[57] That is all the more intriguing as a question given that many of the measures taken in the mid-1530s (to be considered later), notably the dismantling of the shrines in 1538, make sense only if they are seen as an attempt at reform of the church, cleansing it of superstition and idolatry. Erasmus's correspondence with Henry certainly reveals a good deal of mutual admiration. Erasmus repeatedly praised Henry's learning and commitment, and much more so than the demands of patronage might lead one to expect. Henry's attitude is harder to gauge. But there is one revealing letter, of 1527/28 (not yet re-edited in the *Collected Letters*), which deserves to be taken at something approaching face value. Henry was grieved to hear from the archbishop of Canterbury that Erasmus thought he was in danger. He wrote to Erasmus how 'we have followed the incomparable endowments of your mind with both the highest admiration and benevolent goodwill'. Henry declared:

In the tender years of our youth when we knew you, our zeal for you was not slight; and that caused us diligently to study the books you have written, in which you make honourable mention of us. . . . Now you strenuously excel . . . in propagating and illustrating the christian faith . . . we desire . . . to succour and to provide aid for your very pious and holy endeavours. . . . For we have felt for several years, and now feel, that very thing: our breast, incited without doubt by the Holy Spirit, is kindled and inflamed with passion that we should

restore the faith and religion of Christ to its pristine dignity . . . so
that, the profligate and impious impotence of the heretics having been
shattered, the word of God should run freely and purely.

Inviting Erasmus to England, where he had spoken of seeking refuge in
his old age, Henry declared roundly that 'once you come, we shall, by
our joint efforts and pooled resources, spread the gospel of Christ better
and further'. Henry manifestly understood what Erasmus was seeking
to achieve, and he here firmly associated himself with Erasmus's
aspirations.[58]

Of course, what Henry VIII understood as the gospel of Christ and
as the word of God would not command universal assent. But this does
strongly suggest that Henry's religion cannot be characterised as simply
catholicism without the pope, or as essentially conservative, but was
rather in significant respects reformist; and Erasmian is by no means an
unhelpful description of that reforming thrust.

Of course, neither Erasmus, nor all or many of those English bishops
and scholars who were most closely associated with Erasmus, would
approve of Henry's policies: in particular, they would not follow him in
breaking from Christendom. But that does not mean that the impetus
behind Henry's attitudes to traditional religion was not Erasmian.
Events intervened; Henry went further, more ruthlessly, more destruc-
tively, than Erasmus and many of his English followers would have
allowed. That has confused modern scholars, especially those sympathetic to Erasmus and More, and involved in the great projects of publishing editions of their works. They have been reluctant to admit Henry
as a humanist-Erasmian. Yet that makes best sense of his actions. His
sympathy towards Erasmian criticisms of the church gives the lie to
characterisations of Henrician religion post-break with Rome as catholicism without the pope.

To see Henry as hostile to some characteristic features of late medieval
piety is not, of course, to deny that Henry was a Christian. Nor does
Henry's sceptical attitude to monasteries and pilgrimages and works of
piety make him a Lutheran. In one respect he was singularly devout,
and that was his attendance at mass, in the chapels in his palaces on
feast and holy days, in his privy closet on other days.[59] There are
many references showing that Henry heard mass several times daily.
Giustinian, the Venetian ambassador, reported how Henry VIII heard
three masses a day when he hunted, sometimes five on other days, and
attended the daily office in the queen's chamber (vespers and com-
pline).[60] Pace referred to Henry's second mass time on 16 April 1521,

as did Clerk on 1 March 1528.[61] In June 1528—perhaps in reaction to the epidemic of sweating sickness—Henry heard three masses.[62] It is interesting that at his manor at Ampthill, Bedfordshire, a closet was made in the chapel in 1540 'for the kinges grace to hear mass in'.[63] And in his will Henry would make provision for perpetual masses for his soul.[64]

With respect to the mass, Henry was conventionally devout. That ties in with his vigorous defence of it in his polemic against Luther in 1521, the *Assertio Septem Sacramentorum*.[65] Luther, as Henry presented it, claimed that the bread and wine remained after consecration. Henry countered that what Jesus gave *seemed* to be bread and wine but was in fact his body and blood; the forms of bread and wine remaining, the substance changed into his body and blood. Henry went on to consider the meanings of key words and to cite patristic authorities. He insisted that transubstantiation was not an invention of three hundred years ago. The sense of transubstantiation predated the word itself, a perceptive and subtle suggestion. He cited Augustine in support—we honour invisible things, that is to say, the flesh and blood in the visible form of the bread and wine. No one would trouble Luther to believe in transubstantiation, Henry went on, as long as he believes that the bread is changed into the flesh and the wine into the blood. Henry then criticised Luther's view of the mass as a testament, as a promise of Christ, and therefore not a good work. Did not Christ do a good work when he consecrated the bread and wine at the Last Supper, Henry asked, and do not priests similarly do a good work in the mass? Henry agreed that every man's faith profited him and that no one should think the mass of any priest could save men. Yet the mass of every priest, he insisted, helps those to salvation who by their faith have deserved to be partakers of the greatest good communicated in the mass.[66] That was a sensitive presentation. Overall, Henry seems to me to be using logic, linguistic analysis and his reading of the scriptures and the fathers in a clever, if somewhat first-principle way: it does not seem ineffective or naive.[67] What is interesting is that Henry would consistently hold to his view of the mass in the 1530s and beyond. However much idolatry and superstition were then assailed, nonetheless Henry continued to insist on the traditional understanding of the mass, as we shall see later, issuing a proclamation emphasising that the sacrament of the altar was 'the very body and blood of our Lord Jesus Christ, our only Saviour and Redeemer', and taking an active part in the show trial of John Lambert, a former Cambridge don, Henry even confuting him by scripture at York Place.

Henry's concept of the mass, as demonstrated in the *Assertio*, was fundamentally opposed to that of Luther; and on a related point of doctrine Henry would reject the central tenet of Lutheranism. In criticising Luther in 1521, Henry insisted that the masses sung by every priest helped those who by their faith deserved salvation. But faith alone was insufficient. When a few years later Erasmus was under pressure, not least from Henry VIII,[68] to differentiate his views from those of Luther, it is very interesting that, in responding to the call, the theme Erasmus chose to emphasise was that of free will. And it is striking that Henry VIII much approved of what Erasmus wrote. In November 1524 a copy of the book was presented to the king, who read a few pages, seemed pleased and said that he would read it through. He pointed out to the Spanish scholar, Ludovico Vives, a passage where Erasmus deterred men from immodest curiosity as to divine mysteries, which he said delighted him much.[69] A few days later Vives reported that the king was highly satisfied, especially when Erasmus warned men about searching too narrowly into the secrets of omnipotence.[70] Here Henry seems to anticipate the attitudes of later rulers—Elizabeth, James I and Charles I—to the reformation debates over predestination. A few months earlier he had written to Dukes John and George of Saxony how Luther boasted of the grace of God so as to destroy free will, extolled faith so as to give licence to sin and placed the inevitable cause of evils in the only good God.[71] In 1525 he wrote to Luther arguing against his doctrines concerning salvation by faith, and free will.[72] Once more there are interesting continuities here.

In the 1530s Henry always refused to declare himself a Lutheran, and he consistently refused to accept Lutheran doctrines of justification by faith alone, even when, in the course of the 1530s, it might have been useful in cementing international alliances with German protestant princes. Henry was never prepared to accept, as it stood, the Augsburg Confession and Apology, the statements drawn up largely by Philip Melanchthon in 1530 justifying the German protestant princes' position. In late 1534 negotiations with the Germans foundered over Lutheran views of the mass and justification by faith alone: so much so that the Germans came to doubt Henry's good faith.[73] When in December 1535 Duke John Frederick of Saxony and Philip Landgrave of Hesse appealed to him to accept the Augsburg Confession, he refused. Henry declared that he had long wished to set forth true and sincere doctrine. He would be willing to confer with learned men sent by them. He was willing to join them in all general councils for the defence of true doctrine, but ceremonies, he asserted, might differ and were to be

ordered by the governors of every individual dominion.[74] In March 1536
Henry made the need for compromise quite clear. He very much wished
'that his bishops and learned men might agree with theirs'. But that
could not be 'unless certain things in their confession and apology' were
mitigated by them in discussion. Henry accordingly urged them to send
some learned men to negotiate. Meanwhile he insisted that 'it should
not be sure nor honourable for his majesty before they shall be with his
grace agreed upon a certain concord of doctrine' to take on the title of
protector of the Schmalkaldic League.[75] Henry's absolute refusal to
espouse full-blown Lutheranism would endure, as we shall see, throughout the 1530s and beyond.

Because Henry's religion was neither straightforwardly traditional
catholic nor Lutheran-Zwinglian, it has consequently been dismissed by
many. Henry is seen as incapable of clear religious thought at all, and
his religion as 'a ragbag of emotional prejudices'.[76] That is usually linked
to a view of Henry as weak and dominated by factions.

Too often, religious policy in the 1530s and 1540s has thus been presented as fluctuating and inconsistent. Henry was supposedly influenced
on religious matters first by one group of courtiers and counsellors and
then by another, a view memorably expounded by the martyrologist
John Foxe. 'Even as the king was ruled and gave ear sometimes to one,
sometimes to another, so one while it went forward, at another season
as much backward again, and sometimes clean altered and changed for
a season, according as they could prevail, who were about the king.'
That explained 'the variable changes and mutations of religion in King
Henry's days' and why Henry did not consistently support reform.[77]
Such a scenario enabled Foxe, with his own convictions and aspirations
for the early Elizabethan church, to emphasise what he saw as the positive features of the reign, notably the moves towards what he regarded
as true reformed religion. On such a factional view of religious politics,
reform reflected the influence of Henry's queen, Anne Boleyn, or
his principal minister Thomas Cromwell or his archbishop Thomas
Cranmer; reaction the work of Stephen Gardiner, bishop of Winchester,
or Thomas Howard, third duke of Norfolk; and the king was simply
'the prisoner of his own advisers'. And in consequence religious policy
was inconsistent, lurching from reform to reaction according to the swirl
of faction. It is extraordinary how many historians have adopted some
such version of events in the 1530s: a collage of quotations shows this
clearly. For A.G. Dickens, 'during the revolutionary years 1532–40 two
pressure-groups contended for the ear of the King', one of which was
'the radical group, headed by Cromwell and Cranmer'.[78] E.W. Ives

explains how 'when in the 1530s the country moves towards religious reform, it means that Henry is trusting Cromwell and Cranmer; when the government becomes anxious about anabaptist heresy it means that Henry is listening to the duke of Norfolk and the conservative bishops'.[79] Susan Brigden opines that 'faction struggles in Court and Council produced shifting policies towards reform: first advancing it, then repressing it'.[80] C.S.L. Davies urged that 'in 1535 . . . there began a more definite move towards protestantism. This was largely due to the balance of power at court . . . For a few years . . . Cranmer and . . . Cromwell were able to use the situation to undermine catholic beliefs, in spite of Henry's own conservative theological views.'[81] Two detailed studies of the 1530s are based on such ideas. For Joseph Block,

> two factions surfaced in the 1530s to contest for power and place in England. Both drew energy and coherence from religious ideology. . . . For a decade and more, conservatives and reformers fought bitter and often fatal political battles to determine which factional ideology would drive the mainspring of royal government and administration.[82]

For Rory McEntegart,

> just as there were evangelicals encouraging the king to go further with reform, so there were religious conservatives—men like Stephen Gardiner and Bishop Cuthbert Tunstal of Durham—seeking to persuade him to retrench. This contest for the king's ear began during the middle years of the decade to develop into what may properly be called faction politics: small elite groups within the inner governmental ring, competing for influence over the king; and made up of the key politicians, their servants and their immediate associates.[83]

But Henry was far more actively involved than such a reading of factional battles and influences would suggest. There is overwhelming evidence for the king's close involvement in religious matters. We have just seen Henry's participation in anti-Lutheran polemic. Earlier his very personal involvement in the search for a divorce was quite plain. In following chapters we shall see further evidence for Henry's leading role: in debates over the nature of true religion, in copious annotations in his own hand on various statements of faith, in his letters arguing with leading churchmen.

What then was Henry's religion in the years following the break with Rome? Historians who allow that it was more than conservatism intermittently provoked into action nonetheless tend to dismiss it as theologically incoherent. But if Henry's personal theology would not altogether pass muster in a faculty of theology, if close analysis would find it logically unsound, that does not mean that it could not, in many respects, be made to work in practice, and that it did not have a kind of coherence.

Henry, as we have seen, vigorously justified his royal supremacy. He did so in quasi-protestant terms. The act confirming the king's royal supremacy in 1534 claimed to do so 'for increase of virtue in Christ's Religion within this realm of England, and *to repress & extirpate all errors heresies and other enormities & abuses* heretofore used in the same'; the king and his successors were fully empowered

> from time to time to visit repress redress reform order correct restrain and amend all such errors heresies abuses offences contempts and enormities what so ever they be, which by any manner spiritual authority or jurisdiction ought or may lawfully be reformed repressed ordered redressed corrected restrained or amended, most to the pleasure of Almighty God *the increase of virtue in Christ's Religion* and for the conservation of the peace unity and tranquillity of this Realm.[84]

These were large claims and responsibilities. The assertion of authority and the desire for reform were the two most immediate characteristics of Henry's religious policy after the break with Rome. Henry fully meant both. He was wholly committed to his royal supremacy and determined to assert it. He was also—but this has been insufficiently recognised—committed to purifying reform. The break with Rome and its consequences placed the responsibility for the extirpation of abuses and for the 'increase of virtue in Christ's religion' squarely upon his shoulders. His experiences at the hands of the papacy simply intensified his Erasmian and righteous conviction that the church was in need of purifying reform. An early target was papal pardons and indulgences 'corruptly and deceitfully obtained of the bishop of Rome', attacked in a proclamation on 1 January 1536. Henry presented himself as a king who

> daily studieth to extinct vice and exalt and increase virtue in this his realm, to the glory of God and quietness of his people. . . . By occasion of such corrupt and deceitful indulgences many of his loving subjects have been encouraged to commit sin and to withdraw their faith, hope, and devotion from God.

'Divers and sundry light persons' went about declaring them, and spent the money on ribaldry and carnal vices. No more pardons and indulgences, the king ordered, were to be published.[85] At much the same time, the act 'extinguishing the authority of the Bishop of Rome' accused the pope of having 'deceived the king's loving and obedient subjects, persuading them, by his laws, bulls, and other deceivable means, such dreams, vanities and fantasies as by the same many of them were seduced and conveyed unto *superstitious and erroneous opinions* [my italics]'.[86] The reforming supreme head of the church of England was not just ending the jurisdiction of the pope; he was assailing the pope for his encouragement of errors and superstitions. Here Henry was attacking papal pardons and indulgences. But it is the monasteries that offer the most substantial demonstration of the combination of the assertion of authority and the drive for reform that characterised Henry's policies, and so it is to the monasteries that we must now turn.

Monasteries: Visitation and Supremacy

It was from some monasteries that (as we have seen) forceful opposition to Henry VIII's divorce and the break with Rome had been expressed, especially in the years 1532–35: the Nun of Kent, some Observant Franciscans, the Charterhouse monks and the priests at the Bridgettine house at Syon. Of course, those involved were only a small number of the monks, nuns and friars in England, and it would be quite wrong to suggest that there was any general active opposition to Henry VIII from English monasticism. Nonetheless, the religious orders involved in criticism and opposition were those which contemporary critics and reformers regarded as the best exemplars of the monastic ideal. How troubling this was for the king is best illustrated by his ruthless responses. The Nun of Kent and the monks and priests who had assisted her were executed for treason. The Observant Franciscan house at Greenwich was in effect closed down and the friars sent to the Tower. Three Charterhouse priors who refused to swear further oaths recognising the royal supremacy were tried and executed for treason in May 1535, and three Charterhouse monks were executed for the same reason in June: further pressures were put on the remaining monks to comply. Henry VIII could not risk the development within his realm of groups disaffected and unwilling to accept his royal supremacy. Ruthless pressure was the only way he felt he could deal with determined monks, friars and nuns, many of whom owed legal allegiance to superiors outside the realm, rather than to English bishops.

It is not surprising that the imposition of oaths of allegiance in 1534–35 should have been directed especially against monks, friars and nuns. A set of instructions on how the friars should be handled survives. They were to be assembled in their chapter houses and examined separately concerning their faith and obedience to Henry VIII. They were to swear an oath of allegiance to the king, to Queen Anne and her present and future issue. They were to be bound under oath to preach the legitimacy of this to the people at every opportunity. They were to acknowledge the king as supreme head of the church and that the bishop of Rome had no more authority than other bishops. They were not to call the bishop of Rome pope, either in public or in private, or to pray for him as pope. Preachers were to be warned to commend to God and the prayers of the people first the king, as head of the church of England, then Queen Anne with her child, and then Archbishop Cranmer, with the other orders of the clergy.[87] It is very likely that similar instructions were issued for all monastic houses. In the spring and summer a great many religious houses subscribed to such a declaration: most likely every house was asked to swear.[88]

Under such pressure, and with the example of the fate of the Carthusian monks before them, overwhelmingly the religious conformed. How far did they more actively follow royal instructions? How far did they remain attached to the papacy? It is hard to grasp their innermost thoughts. Can we, nonetheless, infer them from their actions, or rather their inaction? They were supposed to remove the word pope from all their service books. But Richard Beerly, a monk of Pershore, informed Cromwell:

> now I will Instruct your grace somewhat of religious men, and how the king's grace commandment is kept in putting forth of books the bishop of Rome's usurped power. . . . abbots, monks, priest, do little or nothing to put out of books the bishop of Rome's name, for I my self do know in diverse books where his name and his usurped power upon us is.[89]

It would, of course, be unwise to trust Beerly's testimony entirely, since he may simply have been trying to ingratiate himself with the government. But if he was saying what the king and Cromwell expected, or feared, to hear, then that is in itself revealing.

It is in that light that the famous monastic visitations of 1535–36 must be seen, in particular those carried out by Richard Layton, Thomas Legh, John ap Rice and John Tregonwell, the royal visitors, in the second half of 1535 and early 1536. These visitations may best be understood by being placed firmly in their immediate context. The act of first fruits and tenths, passed in autumn 1534, had used the opportunity created by the abolition of annates, the fees paid by newly appointed bishops to the pope, to reform clerical taxation, including the taxation of monasteries. In consequence, commissioners had been appointed on 30 January 1535 to survey all the monasteries in the realm, producing a record of the numbers of the religious communities and details of the lands and rental incomes of each house. The *Valor ecclesiasticus* was largely complete by autumn 1535. Often this exercise is viewed as simply a prelude to the seizure of monastic wealth, but it would be more fitting to see it as a necessary consequence of the changes in clerical taxation, and moreover 'not [a] major innovation ... but merely yet another in a succession of almost annual revaluations of benefices and reassessments of clerical incomes which had been almost commonplace since c. 1522'.[90] It did not necessarily presage a greater revolution: we should be wary of drawing on hindsight here.

Why then did further sets of commissioners visit the monasteries in the autumn of 1535 if it was not to prepare the way for their humiliation and dissolution? The explanation once again is best sought in the general context of the break with Rome and the royal supremacy. New procedures for discipline had been introduced. Many monasteries had been accustomed to episcopal visitations—but quite a few, notably the Cistercians, Observants, Gilbertines, Premonstratensians and Cluniacs, had been exempt; now all would be subject to periodic inspection by visitors acting on the authority of the king's vicegerent in spirituals. On 20 March 1534 parliament declared that the matter of the visitation of exempt religious houses—those not previously subjected to episcopal visitation—pertained solely to the king; on 17 November 1534 Henry was given the right to conduct visitations of all religious houses; and on 21 January 1535 Thomas Cromwell was appointed vicegerent in spirituals, not for all ecclesiastical matters, but 'for the sole purpose of undertaking a general ecclesiastical visitation'.[91] At some point in such circumstances any vicegerent could be expected to exercise his newly conferred visitorial authority: it is not surprising that this took place immediately after the completion of the survey of monastic wealth. It was important simply to assert and demonstrate that new authority—ultimately the royal supremacy—over the monasteries. In visiting, the commissioners tested what they found against a set of guidelines which, as we shall see, were based on a strict and somewhat ascetic reading of monastic rules. But the wish to exert authority was crucial. This is neatly shown by the way that Thomas Legh justified giving orders that neither abbots nor monks should set foot outside their monasteries without a licence granted by the king or his vicegerent. In applying to the king or to Cromwell for exemptions they might more fully grasp the king's supreme ecclesiastical power.[92] There are many letters to Cromwell from abbots and priors asking for licences to go out, all implicitly recognising his authority as the king's vicegerent.[93] Interestingly, some monasteries objected to the visitation on principle: at Bruton the abbot said that if Legh visited them again it would be the very undoing of all abbots and monasteries.[94]

The defence of the royal supremacy was fundamental. It is striking and revealing that the injunctions issued by the king's commissioners to all monasteries in 1535 began with a resounding declaration of the royal supremacy and an assertion of its practical powers. Abbots, priors and monks were to instruct their juniors that 'the king's power is by the laws of God most excellent of all under God in earth, and that we ought to obey him before all other powers', that the usurped authority of the bishop of Rome was by no means founded on holy scripture but

> partly by the craft and deceit of the same bishop of Rome, and by his evil and ambitious canons and decretals, and partly by the toleration and permission of princes, by little and little hath grown up, and therefore now of most right and equity is taken away and clean expelled out of this realm.

Heads of houses were informed that by the king's supreme power and authority they were absolved from all obedience and from any oaths sworn to the bishop of Rome. If the rules of their monastic house appeared to commit them to obeying the bishop of Rome, or any other foreign power, they were to be declared void and were to be struck out from the books in which they were to be found. The visitors were empowered to search monastic charters and 'to dispose all such papistical escripts as shall there be found'. More directly, monks were required to endorse the new order: 'every brother of this house that is a priest shall every day in his mass pray for the happy and prosperous estate of our sovereign lord the king and his most noble and lawful wife queen Ann'. The adjective 'lawful' was crucial here.[95] All this once more confirms the importance of political fears of monastic opposition or obstruction. No doubt the stipulation that

> if either the master or any brother of this house do infringe any of the said injunctions, any of them shall denounce the same, or procure

to be denounced as soon as may be to the king's majesty or to his
visitor general, or his deputy; and the abbot or master shall minister
spending money and other necessaries for the way to him that shall
so denounce

was in large part intended to meet such political concerns. The visitors
were alert to the threat of treason, and in a few places they claimed to
have found it, for example at Lewes, where the subprior, Anthony
Bolney, confessed, and accused the prior, Robert Croham, of complicity.[96] Prior More of Worcester resigned, 'possibly under pressure', after
Legh and John ap Rice had found quarrels between monks, especially
John Musarde and Richard Clive, in the course of which Clive was
accused of treason by Musarde for railing against the king and Queen
Anne, for upholding the authority of Queen Catherine and the pope,
and for declaring that it was as lawful to appeal to the weathercock as
to the chancery, 'a denunciation of one aspect of the royal supremacy'.[97]
Prior More's direct involvement seems unlikely, but presumably he was
blamed for disorders and came under suspicion.

Reform

Verifying and securing loyalty, dealing with suspected treason, declaring and obtaining explicit acquiescence in the royal supremacy, asserting that supremacy through detailed instructions: all these were indeed
fundamentally important in the evolution of policy in 1534–36. But
there was also a strong reforming impulse.

To argue that Henry's government sought to reform the monasteries
is to fly in the face of a powerful historiographical tradition that sees
the ultimate dissolution of the monasteries as an essentially financial
measure. On such a reading, the king (or his adviser Cromwell), aware
of the constraints on royal finances, consciously plotted the fall of the
monasteries, picking off first the smaller, and then the larger, houses.
Here, however, it will be argued that financial considerations were not
the most significant factor, that there was no plot: instead a coherent
set of explanations will be offered without invoking avarice and
plunder.

Beyond verifying the loyalty of the monks to the royal supremacy,
were the visitors seeking to reform—or merely to discredit—the monasteries they inspected? An important clue is offered by the fact that the
four principal visitors of the religious houses were also involved in
visitations of the universities of Oxford and Cambridge: Layton and
Tregonwell at Oxford, Legh and ap Rice at Cambridge. What the

visitors did at Oxford and Cambridge strengthens the case that they were generally engaged in a process of reform.[98] Their actions are worth summarising before their visitations of the monasteries are discussed. They have been seen as the first intrusion of the power of the state into the internal affairs of English universities: all statutes of the university or college repugnant to the articles the visitors brought with them were held to be void, and heads of colleges were to be sworn to these articles.

The universities were compelled to accept royal supremacy over the church, once again demonstrating its central importance. Surviving injunctions to the university of Cambridge laid down that heads and fellows of colleges should swear to the succession, to obey the laws made, or to be made, for the extirpation of papal usurpation, and to conform to the king's jurisdiction. A declaration by the president and fellows of Corpus Christi College, Oxford, that they would in future refuse obedience to any foreign prince and that they would never agree to negotiate for the re-establishment of papal supremacy, but would rather inform the king of any letters the pope or his nuncio might send them, was probably made by the heads and fellows of other colleges too, and it vividly testifies to the anxieties of the government about what the pope and the universities might attempt against the royal supremacy.[99]

The visitors did also inquire into sexual misconduct—in this respect the universities were not, as has been suggested, treated differently from monasteries.[100] Thomas Legh urged Cromwell on 3 September 1535: 'praying you heartily that ye well consider whom ye send to the universities of Oxford and Cambridge, where either will be found all virtue and goodness or else the fountain of all vice and mischief'.[101]

But after securing acquiescence in the royal supremacy, the visitors' most important task was to reform the university curriculum, a task to which they devoted much energy. Sweeping changes were envisaged. Several colleges were to found daily public lectures in Greek and Latin. The principal medieval theological textbook, Peter Lombard's *Sentences*, was to be abandoned, and with it the tradition of systematic, speculative theology. Students should read Aristotle, and humanist commentators alive to philology and interested in ancient history and classical writers; they should abandon the frivolous questions and obscure glosses of Duns Scotus and Walter Burley, 'more concerned with argument than with truth: their endless hair-splitting, it was felt, was the enemy of true knowledge'. All students were by contrast to be permitted to read the scriptures privately and to attend lectures on them.

Lectures were no longer to be given in canon law. Ceremonies, constitutions and observances which hindered polite learning should be
abolished.[102] Richard Layton, writing from Oxford on 12 September,
duly informed Cromwell how they had set up lectures in Greek and
Latin. Those in canon law had been replaced. 'We have set Dunce in
Bocardo [the gaol in Oxford], and have utterly banished him Oxford
for ever, with all his blind glosses, and is now made a common servant
to every man, fast nailed up upon posts in all common houses of ease-
ment.' On their second visit to New College 'we found all the great
quadrant court full of the leaves of Dunce, the wind blowing them into
every corner'; they were gathered by Mr Greenfield, a gentleman of
Buckinghamshire, to make himself 'sewelles gross or blawnsherres gross
to keep the deer within the wood, thereby to have the better cry
with his hounds'.[103] In practice, the changes were not quite as wholesale as that: canon law remained in use pending the making of a
new collection of laws, which was never achieved, while Lombard's
Sentences became optional, with study of his work still permitted.[104]
But the visitation of Oxford and Cambridge reveals very clearly that
the government's policy towards the universities embraced a quite
radical vision of reform. If it is recognised that the government did
have serious reforming intentions here, that makes it harder to dismiss
the possibility that it also had equally serious reforming plans for the
monasteries—which once again reinforces doubts that there was
any master plan intended to lead to a total dissolution of the
monasteries.

What the government's vision of monastic reform was may be teased
out from the eighty-six questions that the commissioners were to ask at
those monasteries previously exempt from episcopal visitation. They are
deeply revealing of the government's underlying attitudes. The very first
question, 'whether divine service be solemnly sung said observed and
kept', implies an acceptance of the fundamental purposes of the monasteries, and the qualification, 'accordingly to the number and the
abilities thereof', implies a recognition of realities. Some questions were
straightforward requests for information: how many monks or nuns
there were, how great the landed income of the house was, and how its
lands had been acquired. But when the visitors were to ask whether the
number of monks or nuns matched the founder's will or the statutes or
laudable custom of the house, then one can catch a hint of a view of
monasteries as requiring a proper complement of monks or nuns to
function effectively, of doubts whether houses small in size could be
fulfilling their obligations.

Questions about abbots reveal concerns about the quality of leadership they provided. How had the master of the house been chosen? Did he make his accounts, as he ought to do, once a year before his brethren? Did the master ensure that the monastic church, its buildings and its lands were kept in good repair? Did he give corrodies (pensions), annuities or offices to his kinsfolk and friends for long periods, to the impoverishment of the house? Had the master, in admitting any novice, received any money; did he take any pension when exercising patronage? Did he use his brethren charitably, without partiality, malice, envy, grudge or displeasure? Did he use his disciplines, corrections and punishments upon his brethren with mercy, pity and charity, without cruelty, rigorousness and enormous hurt, no more favouring one than another? Was he charitable when brethren were sick? Did the novices have a preceptor to teach them grammar and good letters, and had a senior been deputed to instruct them in their rules? There was much concern about financial mismanagement and worse. Did any religious persons hold more than one office? Did the officers make their accounts without taking anything for their own use? Was there an inventory of the movable goods? Were the muniments and evidences of lands, rents and revenues safely kept free from vermin and damp? Were the revenues employed according to the founder's intentions? Were any of the lands rented out, especially for small sums, or less than they were wont to be, in order to raise ready money? Had any plate or jewels been laid to pledge? Were there any debts?

Questions put to the monks and nuns reflect concern over the sincerity of their vocation. Had any monks taken upon themselves the habit and profession of their religion chiefly from the ambition of becoming master of their house? Had any sisters been professed in any way under the compulsion of friends and kinsfolk? The visitors were to ask what the rule followed by the house was. Did the monks know the rule they professed and did they keep it? Did they, in particular, keep the three substantial and principal vows, namely poverty, chastity and obedience? Did the brethren have money or plate in their chambers? Did monks and nuns keep silence, fasting and abstinence, as specified in their rule? Was the clothing they wore not too excessive, not too exquisite? Did they wear their religious habits continually? Were brethren able for no good reason to move on to other houses, or had they been admitted from other houses without special licence? Had any, since they made their profession, gone out of their house to friends, and if so, how often, for how long? Did they shave weekly? Was their hair too long?

They were also asked questions that suggest doubts over their chastity. Was the master, or any brother of the house, suspected of incontinency, or defamed for being 'much conversant' with women? Did women often come into the monastery by back ways, and were they lodged within the precincts? Did the master or any brother have any boys or young men lying with him? Did the brothers sleep all together in the dormitory under one roof or not, did they all have separate beds, or did any of them lie with another? Did any of them write or receive any letters of love or lascivious fashion? Did anyone secretly come to and go from them with tokens or gifts from any secular persons? Did they speak with anyone through grates or back windows? A section in the interrogatories dealing with nuns asked whether any sister had familiarity with religious men, secular priests or laymen, not being of near kin, and whether any strangers had communication with the sisters of the house.[105] From these questions a sceptical standpoint may be inferred: there were evidently doubts about the way monasteries had been run, and doubts about the extent of obedience to the rule, especially on poverty, enclosure and chastity. Underlying these questions was the conviction that the rule should be followed more strictly.

That was even more obvious in the injunctions or instructions for conduct in the future which were issued after the visitation. Monastic enclosure was to be strictly enforced. No monk was to go out of the precincts. Women were to be utterly excluded from entering, unless they first obtained licence from the king or the visitor of the house. Monasteries were to have a single entrance only, diligently watched by a porter, who 'shall repel all manner of women from entrance into the said monastery'. Monks were to sleep in the dormitory, but every one by himself in his own bed; no monk was to have any child or boy lying with him, nor was any boy to be alone with him in private, except to help him with mass. The brethren were to take their meals together in the misericorde when they ate meat, and otherwise in the refectory. They were not to demand any particular cut of meat but to be content with what was set before them. The abbot's table, both for himself and for his guests, was to be furnished with common dishes. The almoner was to gather the leavings and distribute them to poor folk but not to idle beggars and vagabonds. Abbots were to find wood and fuel for a fire in the refectory from All Hallows' Evening or Eve to Good Friday. Sick brethren were to be kept in the infirmary. Abbots were to make a full and true reckoning to their brethren of their receipts and expenses; they were not to waste woods, nor to lease out any farms or reversions, without the consent of the convent. All such transactions were to be recorded in a register. No one was to profess religion until they were twenty-four years old. Strict orders were given 'that they entice nor allure no man with persuasions and blandishments to take the religion upon him'. No fairs or markets were to be held within the limits of religious houses.

More revealing of reforming impulses was the gloss on the instruction that abbots were to keep one or two of their brethren at university. Again this was nothing new in itself, but it was now required since these 'brethren after they be learned in good and holy letters when they return home may instruct and teach their brethren and diligently preach the word of God'. Moreover, every day for an hour a lesson of holy scripture was to be held attended by all except those singing long hours. At every meal some chapter of the Old or New Testament was to be read by the brethren to the others who were to keep silence and listen.

Monks were also given guidance on the observance of their rules, but the way in which those rules were to be followed further demonstrates the reforms the government sought. 'All and every brethren of this house shall observe the rule, statutes and laudable customs of this religion, as far as they do agree with holy Scripture and the word of God.' That was a striking qualification, implying that some monastic rules went against the word of God and holy scripture. The abbot or prior was to expound to the brethren in English a certain part of the rule:

> he shall teach them that the said rule and other their principles of religion (so far as they be laudable) be taken out of holy scripture, and he shall show them the places from whence they were derived; and that their ceremonies and other observances of religion be none other things than as the first letters or principles and certain introductions to true christianity, or to observe an order in the church.

The injunctions made it plain that these monastic ceremonies and observances 'were instituted and begun, that they being first exercised . . . , in process of time might ascend . . . as by certain steps . . . to say to the chief point and end of religion'. Monks should therefore be diligently exhorted

> that they do not continually stick and surcease in such ceremonies and observances, as though they had perfectly fulfilled the chief and uttermost of the whole true religion, but that, when they have once past such things, they endeavour themselves to higher things, and convert their minds from such external matters to more inward and deeper

considerations, as the law of God and the christian religion doth teach and show.

What this might mean in practice was shown by the more specific instruction 'that they shall not show no relics or feigned miracles for increase of lucre, but that they exhort pilgrims and strangers to give that to the poor that they thought to offer to their images or relics'. In short:

> true religion is not contained in apparell, manner of going, shaven heads, and such other marks, nor in silence, fasting, uprising in the night, singing, and such other kind of ceremonies, but in cleanness of mind, pureness of living, Christ's faith not feigned, and brotherly charity, and true honouring of God in spirit and verity.[106]

That was the essence of the government's monastic reform. In so far as the government was insisting on stricter observance of the rule, it was simply repeating what many a monastic reformer had demanded in the past, echoing many sets of episcopal injunctions, though perhaps with a new sharpness of tone, and more uncompromisingly. (It is surprisingly hard to compare these questions with previous episcopal visitations of monasteries: the interrogatories do not seem to have survived.) But in asserting the word of God and holy scripture as the criteria by which a monastic rule should itself be judged, the government was undermining the authority of that rule. More fundamentally still, in questioning the intrinsic value of monastic observances and ceremonies, here defended for their contribution to spiritual edification, not as sufficient in themselves, the government was in effect putting in doubt the basic function of monasteries: prayer to God. The criticisms of relics struck at the heart of the traditional religious practice of pilgrimage and at the ways in which monasteries had been funded.

Here a letter that Richard Layton wrote in June 1535 is revealing.[107] Knowing that Cromwell was about to set up a visitation of monasteries, he asked that Legh and he might be appointed his commissaries for the north country. In support of his request he declared that they had acquaintances within ten or twelve miles of every monastery 'so that no knavery can be hid from us in that country', implying that knavery was a common feature of monasteries. They saw monasteries as potential centres of disaffection and rebellion: 'We know and have experience both of the fashion of the country and the rudeness of the people, our friends and kinsfolks be dispersed in those parts in every place ready to assist us if any stubborn or sturdy carle might perchance to found a rebellion.' Apart from those overriding concerns about the political loyalties of monasteries, Layton expressed concern about embezzlement and, crucially, about superstition. Referring to a book of articles he had compiled some time ago, he asked Cromwell to note the questions listed there.

> Doubtless there is matter sufficient to detect and open all coloured sanctity, all superstitious rules of pretensed religion, and other abuses detestable of all sorts, hitherto cloaked and coloured by the reformitors (so named of every religion which ever, by friendship, till this day hath found crafty means to be their own visitors, thereby no reformation intending neither good religion (if any be) to increase, but only to keep secret all matters of mischief, with much privy murmuring among themselves, selling their jewels and plate to take half the value for ready money, with great ruin and decay of their houses, which must needs yet continue and endure daily more and more with increase, unless ye now set to your helping hand.

Monasteries were seen as wasting their resources. More importantly still, the remarks about 'good religion (if any be)' and about 'superstitious rules of pretensed religion' are revealing of a large, and potentially fundamental, hostility to monasteries: the implication was that there was no good religion, in the sense of the proper following of a monastic rule, but only superstition.

It is interesting that, in the reports of their visitation, Legh and Layton would note pilgrimage shrines and relics in monasteries alongside the marginal category 'superstitio'. Their tone was sceptical, even mocking. At St Mary's, Derby, the nuns had part of the shirt of St Thomas of Canterbury which was revered among pregnant women. At Grace Dieu, Leicestershire, they held in reverence the girdle and part of the tunic of St Francis which were *supposed* to help lying-in women. At Selby they had the belt, as it was *pretended*, of St Mary. At Kirkham—the commissioners did not comment on the duplication—they had, *as was pretended*, the belt of the Blessed Mary, good for lying-in women. At Wetherall they *thought* they had part of holy cross and of the milk of St Mary. At Haltemprice there was a pilgrimage to Thomas Wake for fever; they revered the arm of St George, a part of the holy cross and the girdle of St Mary, *thought* to be helpful in childbirth. At Nunkeeling they had a part of the holy cross. At Bridlington, St John of Bridlington and three 'lamina' (*sic*) of the wood of the holy cross were worshipped. And there are many, many more examples.[108]

The visitors in the diocese of Norfolk noted much superstition in feigned relics and miracles at Walsingham.[109] A fragment in the same hand of a similar record survives, listing relics at an unnamed monastery:[110] St Etheldreda's wimple, through which they drew knotted strings or silken threads, which women thought good for sore throats; St Audrey's wimple for sore breasts, and comb for headaches; Aaron's rod for children troubled with worms, St Etheldred's ring for lying-in women to put on their fingers. At Bury St Edmund's there were vain and fictitious relics: St Edmund's shirt, the blood of Christ, some parts of the holy cross, the stone with which St Stephen was stoned, the coals with which St Lawrence was roasted, parings of the nails and of the hair of St Edmund in a pyx, some skulls including that of St Petronilla, which simple folk put on their heads, hoping thereby to be delivered from fever. They had also St Thomas of Canterbury's boots and St Edmund's sword. It was the custom whenever rain was wanted to carry in procession the shrine containing St Botolph's bones. Some were in the habit of lighting wax candles at one end of a field while wheat was being sown in the hope that as a result neither tares nor weeds would grow among the wheat.[111]

What is striking here is the assumption that the veneration of relics— often described as worship—was intrinsically superstitious and fit only for ridicule. Such relics were of questionable authenticity and doubtful efficacy. Yet to pour scorn on such devotion was to strike at central features of monastic practice. Of course, bishops had long sought to control and regulate the exuberance of popular piety. Here, however, the implications for reform were very different. Superstition on this evidence was not an isolated abuse or excess but so widespread that its eradication was going to be problematic.

Whether the government had come to such a conclusion yet is, however, unlikely. Henry VIII, Cromwell and the visitors saw monasteries as places involved in the sort of religion Erasmus had satirised— lax, wasteful of scarce resources, steeped in superstition—and thus in need of thorough reformation. The visitation and the accompanying injunctions were intended to bring about just such a reformation. The awkwardness was that reform along such lines implicitly denied much that was central in monasticism, and the mocking tone in which abuses were described and denounced came over more strongly than the aim of reform. The reformation that was sought went so much against the spirit of late medieval monasticism that in practice change on these lines would be very difficult, if not impossible. It was not just the many practical problems at once raised by abbots. For example, did the prohibition on profession below twenty-four years apply to those just a few weeks short of that age?[112] How could abbots manage their monasteries' estates if they and office-holding monks could not leave the precincts of their house? It was not just that monks who had become used to a relaxed and worldly style of life could not easily be reformed, as the abbot of Wardon would complain (the brethren blamed him for enclosing them, few or none of the monks came to the newly arranged daily divinity lecture, one of them subverted the purposes of the injunctions by reading out carefully chosen carnal passages from the Bible, and they continued to spend evenings in an alehouse—five of the monks were, the abbot claimed, common drunkards—and to have sexual relations with boys or women).[113] It was even more that so many of the injunctions not only demanded a very high standard of obedience to the rule, but also in effect called into question the traditional basis of the monastic life: the relics, the pilgrimage shrines, the sequence of prayers. But if Henry VIII, Cromwell and perhaps the visitors as well did not yet grasp the full implications of what they had embarked upon, what should not be doubted at this stage is the seriousness of their concern and the depth of their reforming aspirations.

Abbots do seem to have made some effort to implement the injunctions. Outsiders were brought in to read and teach the scriptures, for example the friar Robert Legate came to Furness Abbey.[114] This offers a truer perspective from which to assess the reports the visitors made of the condition of the monasteries in 1535, especially their catalogue of the sexual misconduct of monks and nuns. It suggests strongly that the purpose of the visitation was not deliberately to create humiliating and demoralising conditions in which monasteries would collapse or could readily be suppressed. The interrogatories were certainly thorough: if there were abuses, abbots and monks would have to lie, or admit them; and there was plenty of scope for monks to denounce others. But it would be rash to deduce from this that the questions were deliberately designed to find fault in order to damn the monasteries. The very first question, after all, asked about the observance of divine service.

Whether or not the commissioners were deliberately sent out to find material with which to damn the monasteries, what they reported was highly damaging, so much so that those later commentators who wish to defend monasticism are compelled to attempt to discredit the commissioners in turn. 'The chief motive of the visitation and the special desire of the visitors was to discover evil,' wrote Gasquet.[115] 'Their principal task was to gather material for a campaign designed to bring celibacy and relics into disrepute, and the religious orders with them', asserted Woodward.[116] Others treat the presentation of monks as immoral largely as propaganda designed to justify a dissolution sought above all on financial grounds.[117] For Hoyle, 'this was not a careful, studied investigation of either the state of monasticism or of individual houses: it was undertaken largely for effect and to gather damaging evidence of the state of monasticism'.[118] A good deal of what the commissioners reported may, of course, simply have been gossip, malicious rumours or suspicions. Were the visitors of 1535 inventing, dramatically exaggerating or repeating the remarks of those who were inventing or exaggerating?

What was so damning in the commissioners' reports? Not the reports of financial mismanagement, as at Vale Crucis,[119] but of sexual misconduct. Monks and nuns were supposed to be chaste, renouncing the pleasures of the flesh in the service of God. According to the commissioners, many failed that test.

At Chertsey Thomas Legh criticised an earlier report by Stephen Gardiner, bishop of Winchester, and Sir William Fitzwilliam, treasurer of the household, that all was well. Instead, he submitted a report pointing to sexual misdemeanours committed by the monks.[120] Richard Layton in particular sent colourful accounts of sexual misconduct. The prior of Maiden Bradley had six children and a licence from the pope to keep a whore.[121] At Shulbrede the prior had seven women, his monks four or five each: the bishop of Chichester had intended to suppress the house a decade ago.[122] At West Langdon, Kent, Layton got no reply at the abbot's lodging, so he picked up a short poleaxe and smashed the door to pieces, eventually capturing the abbot's whore. The abbot was worse than all the rest, 'the drunkenest knave living'; he had made his chaplain go to bed with a woman. The house was in utter decay: Cromwell, he urged, should depose the abbot at once.[123] The prior of Dover was as bad as the others: he and his monks had no lack of women. At Folkestone the house was in utter decay and the prior monk was 'maximus sodomita'—Layton suggested that the prior's be deposed and that the priory should be turned into a parsonage with himself as its vicar.[124] Was Layton recording the truth or inventing fantastic tales? Thomas Bedell, Henry Polstead and John Anthony would later report that the honest inhabitants of Dover were now sorry for the prior and that the prior of Folkestone was a good husband beloved by his neighbours.[125] The prior of Dover defended himself: he had been prior for three years, had reduced the debt, had repaired the church, bakehouse and dormitory.[126] Was Layton too hasty in his condemnation? But that priors were well liked locally and that they had managed their monasteries well are not necessarily rebuttals of charges of sexual misconduct.

Legh and Layton joined forces at Lichfield around Christmas time. Layton described their subsequent journey. At Chicksand and Harrold, Bedfordshire, Layton found sexually active nuns; at St Andrew's, Northampton, debt; at Leicester Abbey an honest abbot, but obstinate and factious canons, against whom Layton intended to object buggery and adultery;[127] at Fountains, an abbot, William Thirsk, who kept six whores.[128] Layton reported finding great corruption among religious persons, worse than in the south, including examples of the practice of *coitus interruptus* and the use of contraceptive potions.[129]

In a substantial document, the *Compendium Compertorum* of the visitation by Layton and Legh of the dioceses of York, Coventry and Lichfield, drawn up by John ap Rice for the king, are listed the names of monks and nuns who were guilty of sexual misconduct.[130] *Letters and Papers* misleads somewhat since it simply gives the numbers of offenders; in the documents themselves the categories 'sodom', or 'sodomite', and 'incontinentia' are given in the margins, names of offenders are then bracketed alongside, together with further brief descriptions of the offence. At first sight, and not least because of the way the information is set out in *Letters and Papers*, there were apparently a good many 'sodomites'. But the categories into which 'sodomites' were divided presents problems, and points to the need for precision in setting out just what breach of the vow of chastity those monks admitted. There were sodomites with boys—'cum puero', 'cum pueris', 'cum diuersis pueris', or with a specified number of boys. But there were just thirteen such cases. There was only one monk alongside whose name is the phrase 'passus sodomitica' (presumably meaning a person who has submitted sodomitically). All the rest, overwhelmingly the most common category, some 170, are bracketed together monastery by monastery as 'sodomites' in the margin, but alongside their names is the phrase 'per voluntarias polluciones'.[131] In several monasteries this was the only category of 'sodomy' given. It is puzzling that masturbation, which must be what 'per voluntarias polluciones' means, should be seen as a sub-category of sodomy,[132] though it might obviously be confessed as a breach of the vow of chastity. Could the lumping of masturbation alongside the much more rarely found category of sodomy have been a propaganda ploy, designed to make the monks' sexual offences seem worse than they were? Would John ap Rice, the writer of the compendium, have done that in order to persuade the king—or did he do it at the king's request in order to persuade the Lords and Commons in parliament? Yet the incidence of sexual offences as a proportion of the total numbers of monks is smaller in the monasteries covered by the northern compendium than in those in Chertsey and the diocese of Norwich, which makes it hard to present the visitors as deliberately piling up as many and as serious cases of sexual misconduct as possible. However that may be, the *Compendium Compertorum* carefully read—and if in particular masturbation is distinguished from sodomy—offers very little in support of any substantial association of monks and homosexuality.

The *comperta* also named many monks guilty of 'incontinentia' with women, numbering their partners and often specifying whether the women in question were single or married. Some 113 monks were so recorded. The *comperta* recorded that seventeen nuns had borne children and a further eleven were incontinent.

A similar list survives from the diocese of Norwich. But there the categories of sexual misconduct were somewhat differently handled. Here 'per voluntarias polluciones' was recorded alongside the marginal category 'incontinentia', that is, together with sexual relations with women, not sodomy. There were some seventy-six monks recorded. There were two sodomites: one at Westacre 'cum duabus feminis et fatetur se passum esse sodomiticum' (with two women and allowed himself to be sodomised), and one at Binham 'passus sodomiticum'. The nature of the incontinence of the others is not always specified. But some twelve were recorded as incontinent with women, and some thirty-eight as incontinent 'per voluntarias polluciones'. There were two pregnant nuns at Shouldham, and five at Marham (including one by the prior of Pentney).[133]

From what may have been a document drawn up at an earlier stage of the proceedings, since it is much more discursive, some further details about East Anglia monasteries may be drawn.[134] Once again the most common category is that of 'voluntarias polluciones': some sixteen monks confessed this. Eight monks confessed to relations with women, one to sodomy. Four nuns, including the prioress of Crabhouse, confessed to having children. Two monks at West Dereham said that there was not a single monk or priest who either 'utatur femineo congressu' or 'masculo concubitu aut pollucionibus voluntariis vel aliis id genus nephandis abusibus' (by congress with women or lying with men or by voluntary pollutions or other wicked abuses): for that reason they all sought leave to marry.

Should we believe all this? Could, to raise an obvious objection, the visitors have invented these details? It is perhaps damaging that Layton wrote in advance that he expected to find much evil disposition in the abbot and convent at St Mary's, York.[135] Troubling, too, is his remark that he could not find any sexual misconduct at Bruton and Glastonbury only because the brethren were kept so straight that they could not offend—they would if they could.[136] On the other hand, even if that points to excessive suspicion on Layton's part, he did nonetheless report the lack of misconduct, rather than invent some. And there are other instances where he found no sexual misconduct, only debt: St Andrew's, Northampton; the college of Newark, Leicester; and Witham.[137] Nor did his fellow visitors find fault everywhere. Legh and ap Rice found nothing wrong at Lacock, and only one unsatisfactory novice at Edington.[138] No sexual misconduct was recorded at several of the monasteries treated in the northern *Comperta*. The reports of the visitors of the mid-1530s were not uniform: in particular, they found considerable differences in the quality of heads of houses. Some, such as those of Brewerne and Chacombe, were learned in holy scripture; some, such as those of Canons Ashby and Wroxton, were unlearned. Some, such as those of Eynsham and Bruern, kept their houses in good repair; others, such as those of Clattercott, did not.[139] The prior of Boxgrove was a great husband and kept great hospitality.[140] On the other hand, the abbot of Fountains, William Thirsk, had allegedly greatly dilapidated his house and wasted the woods,[141] and the abbot of Shrewsbury could supply no inventory and kept no accounts: there was no infirmary, and when it rained the monks sat wet in the choir of the church.[142] Contrasting judgments such as these, supported by details, suggest a genuine attempt to discover what was happening, and to discriminate. The visitors' reports, while overall very damaging to the monastic cause, do not come across as consistent and co-ordinated black propaganda.

It is usually impossible to test such evidence against other sources. But it has often been suggested that generally episcopal visitations found far fewer sexual lapses than did the royal visitors of 1535. The archbishop's visitation of St Mary's, York, in November 1534, found no sexual offences; but we are told by Woodward that the royal visitors in January 1536 'were able to report that no fewer than seven of the brethren were practising homosexuals'.[143] In fact, what the commissioners actually recorded against the names of seven monks was the phrase 'per voluntarias polluciones': only by one of them were the additional words 'cum puero'.[144]

The reports made by the commissioners subsequently appointed to implement the dissolution enacted by parliament were often more favourable than the earlier *comperta*. 'On the whole, the commissioners' reports in most areas are quite favourable to the religious.'[145] The Black Canons of Ulvescroft, in a wilderness in Charnwood Forest, Leicestershire, were particularly praised: the house refreshed many poor people and wayfaring people; the prior was wise and discreet; the six canons were good, virtuous, religious and of good qualities as writers, embroiderers and painters.[146] Two direct comparisons are possible. At Garendon, where the visitors had named five monks in the category 'sodomites'—one with ten boys, one 'passus sodomitica', and three 'per voluntarias polluciones'—the commissioners found fourteen monks, including the abbot, of good conversation, with God's service well maintained, and all desiring to continue their religion or be assigned to some other house. At Grace Dieu, where the visitors found two nuns who had given birth, the dissolution commissioners found fifteen nuns of good and virtuous conversation, all desirous to continue their religion.[147] The overall impression from the commissioners' reports is that many monks and nuns were of 'good conversation and living' and wished to continue or to be transferred.[148]

But perhaps the significance of these differences can be overplayed. The dissolution commissioners were implementing the new act of dissolution, which gave monks and nuns the choice of transfer to another monastery or of release from their houses together with a capacity, that is, a licence to serve as a secular priest. These commissioners were not carrying out a full visitation. Their instructions and the certificates they drew up were above all concerned with the wealth and income of the religious houses they were surveying. Only one question concerned the monks or nuns themselves, and that asked their number, their 'conversations', and how many wished to remain in religion and how many sought capacities. This was in no way comparable to the searching and detailed set of questions relating to the observance of the rule of the house that the visitors had been asked to put, and it is not surprising that the commissioners consequently recorded few offences.

Whether the far greater incidence of sexual misconduct reported by the visitors reflects more precisely targeted questions, superior efficiency, an over-eager recording of gossip or deliberate fabrication[149] is impossible to determine with certainty. There are obvious problems with the evidence. One point, however, deserves emphasis. When Henry VIII, responding to the Lincolnshire rising in autumn 1536, declared that the dissolution of the smaller monasteries had not diminished the service of God, 'for there be none houses suppressed where God was well served but where most vice or mischief and abomination of living was used', he added the words, 'and that doth well appear by their own

confessions subscribed with their own hands in the time of our visitations'.[150] Richard Morison, in a response to criticism of his attack on
the Lincolnshire rebels in 1536, would also refer to those who 'with
their own mouths had given sentence against themselves, and by writing
testified that both by God's laws and man's laws they deserved to die':
'I was loth that men should think abbeys were put down for saying of
de profundis, for rising at midnight, for giving alms to the lame, poor
and blind.'[151] Should we accept that the sexual misconduct found by the
visitors was in each case admitted by the monks and nuns concerned?[152]
Confronted by visitors who asked searching questions about their sexual
conduct, monks and nuns had little choice. Nuns who had become pregnant would presumably have found concealment difficult: confession
might well have seemed prudentially as well as morally the best option.
Cynical reprobates might well have thought little of adding lies to their
tally of sins and consequently have denied everything. But if monks, and
especially frequently abbots and priors, had quite openly had relationships with women, then their fellow monks, when pressed, could be
expected to give evidence against them. In some houses, such as Furness,
the abbot may have succeeded in persuading the monks to keep quiet.
Interesting here is the later testimony of Robert Legate, a friar intruded
into Furness Abbey to teach the monks scripture. He described how the
abbot, before the visitors came, commanded the brethren 'by virtue of
their obedience' to 'tell them nothing at all'. Some of the monks subsequently told Legate that they did 'sigh every day in their heart because
they took so much upon their conscience, saying that if every one of
them had truly expressed such things as they were bound to do by their
oath, they should have been a sorry house'.[153] That reveals interesting
states of mind. Chastity, however much disregarded in practice, was evidently not rejected as an ideal, and its infringement could still provoke
feelings of guilt, compounded when that guilt was denied or kept concealed. If monks did feel such guilt, and if they knew that at visitations
they owed it to God to confess their failings, then it is perhaps not to
be wondered at that many monks and nuns did admit and enumerate
their sexual indiscretions. If the phrase 'per voluntarias polluciones'
does indeed mean masturbation, then that in particular must have been
admitted by monks who felt such guilt since it would have been almost
impossible to prove against them otherwise. Does this line of argument
place too much weight on the fact that monks and nuns confessed their
misconduct? Certainly they were put under pressure. Layton roundly
declared, as we have seen, how he intended to object buggery and adultery against divers canons at Newark, knowledge of which offences he

had from others; what he would find, he could not tell.[154] The Pilgrims of Grace would later complain at the rough methods used by Layton and Legh.[155] But if monks and nuns were reluctantly intimidated into admitting their sexual indiscretions, that does not necessarily mean that their admissions were false. The variations in detail between monasteries suggest that the visitors had no predetermined plan that every religious house should condemn itself for sexual misconduct. The pressures which the visitors could apply, while real, were nonetheless not so great as to result in confessions from more than a small proportion of monks and nuns. Most monks and nuns were not recorded as guilty of sexual offences. And masturbation, above all, could surely have remained concealed and unrevealed if monks had not admitted it.

Perhaps a judgment made in the spirit of the beginning of the twenty-first century might rather be that what the commissioners reported, and what monks and nuns admitted, was indeed very largely true, but that that sexual misbehaviour was not as wildly promiscuous and publicly scandalous and ubiquitous as some of the commissioners or later writers implied. In a few houses all or most of the monks had broken their vows of chastity, but more generally the visitors numbered offenders in ones, twos or threes: chastity was not defunct. In most of the houses visited, the majority of monks and nuns evidently did not confess to any sexual misdemeanours. For example, at Repton, where four monks confessed to masturbation, there were fifteen monks in total; at Garendon, where one monk confessed to sodomy with ten boys, another to sodomy 'passus sodomitica' and three to masturbation, there were fourteen monks in total; at Westacre, where one monk was incontinent with various women and eight confessed to masturbation, there were seventeen monks in all.

Total numbers cannot be found for every monastery. There are some forty-eight religious houses in the northern *comperta* for which Knowles and Hadcock give numbers. In this sample, some seventy-four monks confessed to incontinence with women, four to sodomy with boys and 114 to masturbation, out of a total of 674 monks. Some 28 per cent admitted breaking their vow of chastity. Less than 1 per cent, however, did that by sodomy with boys. Some 9 per cent were incontinent with women, and some 17 per cent admitted masturbation. Over 70 per cent of the monks in these houses did not admit breaking their vows of chastity, and nearly 90 per cent did not admit any sexual relations with others. Such figures are obviously rough and ready. If the monasteries at which no sexual misconduct was recorded were added to the calculations, then obviously the chastity index would rise, but since it has been speculated that the absence of names for sexual misconduct is simply evidence that commissioners did not visit the monastery,[156] or reflected orchestrated concealment, that has not been attempted here. In houses where some monks admitted offences, it is hard to see that any others, especially those who had had sexual relations with women, would have been able to avoid confessing.

On the basis of such an interpretation of the northern *comperta*, a case could be made for the continuing vitality of the ideal of chastity, even though there were clearly lapses. Just how complete an observance is it reasonable to expect? Many monks and nuns had, after all, entered their houses when very young, well below the age of mature commitment. John London in July 1539 would remark that many nuns were wonderfully glad of the act of parliament allowing those who had been professed when younger than twenty-one years to marry: many of them had been professed when ten or twelve years old, and had afterwards lived in imperfect chastity.[157] Moreover, the monks and nuns who admitted their sins to the visitors must have expected that they would be individually subjected to appropriate penance. They were no doubt astonished and shocked to see their behaviour collectively labelled as an 'abomination' and used to justify the dissolution of the smaller monasteries.

What happened in monasteries as an immediate consequence of the visitation in 1535? In a few instances, when the visitors were especially critical, they in effect closed the monastery. At Langden, Folkestone and Dover the abbots and convents were required to surrender under the seals of the convents, in response to the king's commission; inventories were duly taken.[158] Weaker monasteries simply gave up. A handful of houses seem to have been dissolved in effect by royal fiat or by local landowners acting with royal approval. The duke of Norfolk had secured possession of the priory of nuns at Bungay 'whereunto his highness and ye were privy', he wrote to Cromwell, and the priory at Woodbridge.[159] Marton, Yorkshire, surrendered on 9 February 1536, Hornby, Lancashire, on 23 February, St Mary Bilsington, Kent, on 28 February, Tilty, Essex, on 28 February.[160]

An important consequent concern, addressed in the eventual legislation, was to confirm the legality of such surrenders to the king.[161] But that affected only a handful of monasteries.

Beyond that, what the commissioners' reports did was to confirm and amplify long-held convictions, that monasteries were generally in need of reform. It is not unthinkable that the visitors and the government were somewhat shocked by what was apparently found. Even if they had long held Erasmian doubts about the quality of monastic life in general, no doubt the specific details reported by the visitors made it seem much worse: more concrete, more widespread, more hypocritical, more abominable. The non-judgemental historian of the early twenty-first century is neither shocked nor surprised by confessions of incontinence, sodomy and masturbation. It is no doubt revealing of contemporary assumptions that what surprises is the apparent extent to which chastity was honoured, both as an ideal and in practice, if the argument from the silence of the overwhelming majority of monks holds. But for the visitors, and not least for the king, what was noticed, in an age not strong on a sense of statistical proportion, was the extent of misconduct by named individuals, glaringly revealed, vividly confirming their worst fears of what was wrong with monasticism. That was no doubt how the stereotypical association of monasticism and sodomy emerged.[162]

There was, as we have seen, by now a long tradition of reforming by suppressing supposedly weak and decayed monastic houses. In the light especially of Wolsey's dissolutions in the 1520s, it would make sense for the government to respond to further and greater evidence of the need for reform by dissolving more of those weaker, smaller houses. Was the distinction between small and abominable and large and honourable monasteries that was to be made in the act actually supported by the evidence from the visitations, as is usually assumed? It is striking, as has been recently observed, that the large Benedictine houses came through the visitation 'as in a much better condition than the houses of the other orders'. Layton could find no fault at Durham or at Glastonbury, though there he suspected the abbot had concerted the responses of his brethren.[163] Ap Rice also found little wrong at Bury and St Albans but suspected a conspiracy of silence. At Worcester, Legh found only one example of incontinence. Tregonwell praised the nuns of Godstow; Bedell found Ramsey in good order.[164] By no means all small houses were full of abuses, but most of those houses that received the sharpest criticisms were indeed small and poor. And governments find it more straightforward to adopt seemingly objective criteria by which policy decisions can be made and implemented, rather than to make a host of particular value judgements. Thus, it may well be that it was in response to the visitors' reports, seemingly confirming the reasons for earlier reforms, that the government embarked on the parliamentary dissolution of the smaller monasteries. In one of his remembrances, Cromwell noted 'the abomination of religious persons throughout the realm, and a reformation to be devised therein'.[165] Richard Morison, as we have

seen, would insist, against the Lincolnshire rebels, that the monks and
nuns of the dissolved monasteries had condemned themselves by their
admission of sexual misconduct: that was why the abbeys had been put
down.[166]

There may have been a debate within the government whether the
best means of reform would be general exhortation, closures of individual houses or a general dissolution of all the weak monasteries. The
preamble of a draft bill said how the king had sent commissioners

> to see and search out heresy, idolatry, superstition, hypocrisy, buggery,
> adultery, and other kinds of incontinency with other diverse crimes
> enormities and excesses which have sprung of the fountain and origi-
> nal of all misery and abomination the usurped power of the bishop
> of Rome, and by report craftily have been cloaked under colour of
> sanctimony and pretence of religion, and so have privily crept in
> among such religious persons, and infect a great number of them.

The commissioners had searched diligently, and in several places found
'the crimes and excesses aforesaid diversely to have insurged and of long
time hitherto continued'. The king would be prepared to forgive the
monks and nuns their offences but order them not to err again. In a
passage that was more critical of monastic values, the preamble went
on that each monk should execute his vocation and office

> as he may best discharge his conscience, profit him self and also the
> commonwealth, and help them that lack such qualities as God hath
> endowed him withal, and not only to profit him self, but also by his
> industry diligence and labour to help other, and not to addict him self
> to any private or common place where in ease and idleness he may
> lead his life and like a drone bee eat such alms and sustentation as
> should be given to poor impotent and miserable persons.

That was to challenge the validity of monastic prayer and intercession.
The body of the bill went on to ban monks from alluring or seducing
anyone into coming on pilgrimage, from giving 'any peculiar office to
any saint', and from setting forth any images or relics for lucre. That
struck at the heart of the relationship between the laity and monasteries.[167] But all this remained in draft: no legislation directly reflecting such
sentiments emerged.

The Pilgrims of Grace would blame certain bishops, notably Hilsey
of Rochester and Barlow of St David's: 'by reason of their information,

rather religion was not favoured, and the statute of suppression take rather thereby place, for they preached as it was said against the benefit of habits in religion and such like, and against the common orders and rules before used in the universal church', suggesting that campaigning by more radically minded churchmen, hostile to monasticism as such, had led on to the act of dissolution.[168] But however much such an opinion may have represented 'the common voice of all men' in the northern rebellion, it is hard to find any evidence for a substantial campaign of reformist preaching and, whatever prejudices were vented in the preamble of the draft bill we have just considered, the act actually passed in 1536 did not, as we shall see, attack monasteries—their rules and observances, in liturgy and in dress—in principle at all.

An early seventeenth-century account—a doubtful source—suggests that Cromwell, reminding fellow councillors of the disquiet provoked by Wolsey's dissolutions, proposed that 'it should be done by little and little not suddenly by parliament'. Given how 'horrible' and 'odious' this kind of religion was, monks might easily be persuaded to give up and grant their possessions to the king. On related lines was a legal opinion in early 1538 stating that if monasteries had willingly fallen short in numbers or failed to observe divine service enjoined by their founders, then their lands should escheat to the king.[169] According to the seventeenth-century source, most councillors thought fears of popular fury against dissolution overdone and urged that it should be done by act of parliament. Audley and Rich accordingly prepared legislation.[170] That Cromwell may have had some tactical reservations about a large-scale dissolution is suggested by Chapuys's report on 1 April that, although at first Cromwell had promoted what Chapuys referred to as the demolition of the churches, nevertheless, having reflected on the risks, Cromwell was now anxious to prevent dissolution. For that, Chapuys reported, the king had been somewhat angry with Cromwell, which sheds a revealing light on the king's convictions—here it is Henry, not Cromwell, who is pressing for the dissolution.[171]

But what was in fact done was to secure a bill in parliament dissolving the smaller monasteries. The bill was introduced in the Lords on about 6 March.[172] It is likely—though there seems to be no direct evidence—that the 'abominations' revealed by the visitation were reported to parliament in justification of the dissolution,[173] since the statute states that the king thought it good that 'a plain declaration should be made' to the Lords and Commons.[174] An account of the dissolution written in Charles I's reign, and seeing Cromwell as responsible for everything, noted that 'the black book . . . dividing all the religious persons in England into three parts—two of these parts at the least were sodomites and this appeared in writing with the names of the parties and their facts . . . was showed in parliament and the villains made known and abhorred'.[175] That such a 'black book' was indeed prepared is suggested by John ap Rice's later petitioning of Henry for monastic lands worth £50, and listing among his past services that he wrote for the king the abridgements of the *comperta* of the late visitation.[176] It is possible, as we have already noted, that the lumping of masturbation into the category of sodomy was a propaganda ploy, designed to make the monks' sexual offences seem worse than they were. Would John ap Rice, the writer of the compendium, have done that to persuade the king—or, more likely, at the king's request, in order to persuade the Lords and Commons in parliament?

The preamble of the act emphasised the 'manifest sin, vicious, carnal and abominable living . . . daily used and committed' among 'the little and small' monasteries of fewer than twelve members, whose governors and convents 'spoil destroy consume and utterly waste' their monasteries, lands and goods, 'to the high displeasure of almighty God, slander of good religion and to the great infamy of the king's highness and the realm if redress should not be had thereof'. Their possessions were 'now being spent spoiled & wasted for increase and maintenance of sin'. 'Vicious living', it was claimed, 'shamelessly increaseth'. 'By a cursed custom so rooted & infested', it was asserted, a great multitude of the religious persons in such small houses do rather choose to rove abroad in apostasy than to conform them to the observation of good religion' despite many visitations over the past two hundred years and more. The king knew that these charges were true 'as well by the compertes of his late visitations as by sundry credible informations'. The only remedy was the suppression of such small houses and the commitment of the religious persons in them to 'great and honourable monasteries of religion', 'great solemn monasteries of this realm wherein, thanks be to God, religion is right well kept & observed', though they were 'destitute of such full numbers of religious persons as they ought and may keep'. The chief governors and convents of such great monasteries were ordered to accept from time to time such persons as were transferred by the king, and 'keep them religiously during their lives'. Interestingly, a section allowed the king at his pleasure by his letters patent to permit some religious houses which should have been suppressed to continue.[177]

Was there any opposition? Had the statute been modified at all? So important a measure might have been expected to arouse considerable interest. But there is no direct evidence of opposition. Hall offers a brief account of the passage of the bill:[178]

> In this time was given unto the king by the consent of the great and fat abbots all religious houses that were of the value of ccc marks [£200] and under, in hope that their great monasteries should have continued still. But even at that time one said in the parliament house that these were as thorns, but the great abbots were putrified old oaks and they must needs follow: and so will others do in Christendom, quod Doctor Stokesley, bishop of London, before many years be passed.

That, written with hindsight, long after all the monasteries had gone, suggests that the abbots of the larger monasteries in effect agreed to the dissolution of the smaller in the hope that their houses would be spared. But someone evidently criticised the larger houses as well, and Bishop Stokesley suspected that all the houses would soon go. Should this be taken as evidence of a manipulating government, preparing the way for ultimate dissolution? If the abbots in the House of Lords put up little resistance, does that suggest that the measure was generally acceptable? Latimer preached a Lent sermon at Paul's Cross attacking covetous abbots, and in 1549 would claim that when the enormities of abbeys were read before parliament, 'there was nothing [said] but "down with them"'.[179] A later account by Sir John Spelman tells how 'the bill . . . stuck long in the commons, and would not pass till the king sent for the commons and told them he would have the bill pass or have some of their heads'. Apart from the much later date of this early seventeenth-century source, it is also not certain which bill he is describing. Chapuys, reporting the passage of the legislation, immediately added that the king had also determined to prohibit most monks from hearing confessions: instead this was to be done only by the curates, who were to be ordered not to absolve anyone who did not take the pope for antichrist and the king as head of the church. Does this, as has been suggested by Andrew Chibi, hint at a bargain struck between bishops and government and explain the relative lack of opposition by the higher secular clergy to the dissolution?[180] Once more the argument, though not implausible, is speculative.

More interesting is the tension between the preamble and the sub-stance of the act, often a clue to a bill's controversial passage through parliament. The preamble damned monasteries with twelve or fewer monks or nuns (the normal number held necessary in the high Middle Ages for the proper worship of God); the act itself dissolved those monasteries worth less than £200 p.a. The earliest report of the bill was that of one of Lord Lisle's correspondents, Sir Richard Wetthill, who wrote on 3 March 1536 that abbeys and priories 'under iij marks by year and having not xij in convent shall down'.[181] It is interesting that he mentions both criteria. Does that simply mean that he had not read the fine detail of the bill? Or could it be that the ultimate absence of the numerical qualification as a criterion was a concession to opposition?

Again, it is interesting that the act allowed the king to exempt individual monasteries from dissolution. There may well have been important reasons for this, as we shall see, but it is worth raising the possibility that it was offered in response to criticism. Against that, however, is the absence of any strong and direct evidence of opposition. Indeed, the emphasis that the rebels in the autumn would place on the holding of a freely elected parliament at York suggests that they felt that the parliament that dissolved the monasteries had been intimidated into acquiescence.

Was the bill dissolving the smaller monasteries intended as a first step towards total dissolution, as is often assumed? The income of the smaller monasteries was some £18,000 p.a., from which any provision for pensions or transfers of monks would have to be deducted: what was left for the crown would not have been a very large sum. If the dissolution was intended as an essentially financial measure—'that financial considerations were uppermost in the crown's decision to close houses of less than £200 net annual income hardly needs to be said'[182]— then what happened in 1536 makes sense only if it was already intended to dissolve all the monasteries, including the wealthiest. But there are serious difficulties in treating the act of 1536 as simply a preconceived stepping stone towards total dissolution. The act explicitly praised the 'great and honourable monasteries of religion in this realm wherein, thanks be to God, religion is right well kept & observed', and saw their only weakness as a shortfall in numbers.[183] That would be remedied by allowing those monks and nuns who wished to remain in religion to transfer to them from the smaller monasteries which were being dissolved.

Transfers did take place. Woodward identified seven surviving Yorkshire 'certificates'- reports made by the commissions appointed to dissolve the smaller monasteries—originally drawn up in 1536, but significantly enhanced in 1539 by the addition of sixteen names. And comparing the numbers recorded in 1536 at fourteen of the fifteen exempted houses (117 nuns and fifteen monks) with the lists drawn up in 1539 of pensions payable to monks and nuns now leaving the cloister, he found an additional thirty-six religious by 1539. Possibly some were new recruits, although the climate in those years was hardly propitious. Most surely represent transfers from suppressed smaller monasteries, even though Woodward could only definitely trace six back to their former houses.[184] It is hard to see the provision for transfers as anything but a commitment to the continuation of monasticism. That is also how the policy of granting pensions automatically only to heads of houses should be read. Transfers of abbots would obviously be awkward and conflicts of authority could destabilise monasteries receiving former abbots: it was better that abbots of dissolved monasteries should in effect retire. But by failing to offer the rest of the monks pensions, the act gave them a great incentive to ask for transfers to other houses, since otherwise they would lose their livelihood. A government bent on total dissolution would have offered pensions to all monks straight away.

Moreover, despite the rhetoric, the smaller monasteries were not in practice condemned *en bloc*. As we have seen, the king was granted discretion to issue exemptions at his pleasure. Was that simply a paper concession, a sop to opposition? That it was rather intended seriously is suggested by the considerable numbers of monasteries that did secure exemptions. Only some 243 smaller houses out of the 419 worth less than £200 p.a. were actually dissolved following the passage of the bill in 1536.[185]

What explained such exemptions? Many houses and their supporters lobbied Cromwell, as vicegerent in spirituals, and the king, for their continuation. Some heads of houses lobbied that their houses should not be suppressed. The prioress of Legbourne trusted that Cromwell would ensure that her priory would be preserved (was Cromwell the steward?).[186] The abbot of Rewley appealed to Cromwell—offering £100 if it was allowed to remain, though perhaps transformed into a college.[187] Richard Price, abbot of Conway, lobbied for the continuation of his house, offering Cromwell a pension.[188] William, abbot of Waverley, petitioned Cromwell for the continuation of his house.[189] The prior and convent of St Wolston's petitioned the king for their continuation, and asked Cromwell to support them: the king had agreed to suppress their monastery and give it to John Alen, master of the rolls.[190] The priory of Carmarthen claimed that it was actually worth £209 and had been presented as worth less than £200 by the fault of the commissioners: the prior petitioned Henry VIII accordingly.[191]

Archbishop Lee of York urged, in vain, that St Oswald's, a free chapel, and Hexham should stand. Hexham had once been a bishop's see, and many holy men, sometime bishops, were buried in that church: what comfort the monastery was, especially during war, was well known.[192] Bishop Rowland Lee wrote in favour of the house of Aconbury by Hereford where the gentlemen of those parts had commonly had their women and children brought up in virtue and learning.[193] John Dakyn, rector of Kirkby Ravensworth, and archdeacon of Richmond, later testified how 'sith the suppression of abbeys I have heard diverse lament the estate of the church as religious persons and such as have had livings by their houses and desire that the king's highness might have pity of them'. He himself had at Easter belaboured an acquaintance who was one of Queen Anne's servants and also a servant of a servant of Cromwell for Nunmonkton nunnery to stand.[194] The earl of Derby asked that the church at Burscough might stand even if the priory were suppressed, and offered to fund a priest there at his own cost to do divine service for the souls of his ancestors and for the ease and wealth of his neighbours.[195] Friends of St Faith's, Norfolk and Cockesford successfully lobbied (or bribed) Cromwell for the continuation of their house; Cromwell asked the abbot of Cockesford to lend him £40 'and for your payment ye shall receive a bill of my hand wherein is set no sum but look how much as ye deliver so much to write in and this done I shall be ready to keep you out of danger'.[196] Even the commissioners for the dissolution sometimes spoke up in favour of the monasteries they were suppressing. The Hampshire commissioners recommended some exemptions: at St Mary's, Winchester, where there were good sisters of very clean, virtuous, honest and charitable conversation,[197] at Netley and Quarr, for their relief to poor people and travellers by sea.[198] Sir Ralph Ellerker, Marmaduke Constable, Leonard Beckwith and Hugh Fuller petitioned that the monastery of the Hull Charterhouse should continue: the abbot and brethren were ready to accomplish the king's articles, and were well favoured and commended by the honest men of Hull and others for their good living and great hospitality.[199] The commissioners for Northamptonshire wrote in favour of Catesby, Wolstrop and Polesworth.[200]

But, as Woodward has persuasively argued, drawing on close analysis of the smaller monasteries in Yorkshire, lobbying and favours alone do not explain the incidence of exemptions. 'In many cases of exemption there is no evidence of any "influence" being brought to bear or any fine being offered.' Rather, exemptions were determined by the need to house those monks and nuns who, according to the terms of the act of 1536, wished to continue or transfer. Where suitable accommodation was available locally, in a house of the same order, this was straightforward. But where, for example in Yorkshire, a large number of nuns wished to continue, there had to be correspondingly large numbers of exemptions, simply because there were not enough larger nunneries to take them. In Yorkshire (not including the archdeaconry of Richmond) there were fifty religious houses, thirty-three of them worth less than £200 p.a. One (Marton) surrendered before the passage of the 1536 bill. Three were Gilbertine monasteries, an order wholly exempted from the provisions of the legislation. But only fourteen of the remaining twenty-nine were suppressed. Seven eventually received letters patent of exemption, and in 1539 would surrender 'voluntarily' in the same way as the larger monasteries. The rest did not obtain letters patent and were ultimately dissolved under the act of 1536 simply by the withdrawal of the king's pleasure.[201]

What is interesting is that thirteen of the twenty nunneries were allowed to continue, but only two of the nine men's houses. Does this differential throw light on the reasons for the granting of exemptions? No nunnery in Yorkshire was worth over £200 p.a. (indeed, only nineteen in the whole country were), and most were worth well below that figure—they were small and poor. But only three out of 105 nuns at fourteen Yorkshire houses for which records survive sought capacities (licences to leave)—the rest wished to continue or to transfer.[202] Presumably nuns at the unrecorded Yorkshire nunneries opted similarly. Woodward suggests, convincingly, that the putative need to rehouse at least 102, and probably as many as 153, nuns explains why only seven of twenty nunneries in this district were suppressed: there were obvious physical limitations on the number of extra nuns that could be accommodated in the other nunneries, especially given that there were no large and rich nunneries in Yorkshire.[203] By contrast, it was easier to deal with the smaller men's houses. There were only nine of them, as compared with twenty women's houses; and there were no fewer than fifteen surviving larger houses that could take in monks from the smaller houses who wished to continue. Evidence survives for the preferences of only two of the men's houses, but it hints that fewer of the monks affected wished to continue. All at Grosmont wanted capacities. The Hull Charterhouse is the exception that proves the rule. All nine monks wished to continue; there was no obvious larger house to which to transfer the Carthusian monks, not least given the Carthusian requirement of individual cells; that difficulty, and the payment of 400 marks, secured their exemption.[204]

Woodward concludes that the provision for exemptions shows that

the government of the day had good reason to believe that there was
sufficient contentment within the cloister to make it impossible for
them to sweep away even the smaller abbeys without getting into difficulties over finding room elsewhere for those of the dispossessed who
did not want to abandon their accustomed way of life.[205]

On that reading, the government allowed exemptions because it recognised the risk of serious problems if it compelled contented monks and
nuns to give up. But another way of reading the provision for exemptions is that the bill of 1536 was straightforwardly reforming in thrust.
If one of the reasons why monasteries needed reform was that many
were simply too small for the religious offices to be performed properly,
then transfers would be a very sensible means of rationalisation and
consolidation. The policy does not have to be read as a stage on the
road to total dissolution. Exemptions and transfers were not the tools
of a government already intending to bring monasticism to an end.

But the king was determined that the suppression should not be
affected by local vested interests, and he reacted vigorously if he suspected that they were impeding reform. When the commissioners in
Northamptonshire, Edmond Knightly, John Lane, George Gifford and
Robert Burgoyne, defended Catesby priory, the king responded firmly.
They had described it as in very perfect order, with a wise, discreet and
very religious prioress, and devout and religious nuns. It offered much
relief for poor people. 'Wherefore if it should please the king's highness
to have any remorse that any such religious house shall stand, we think
his grace cannot appoint any house more meet to show his most gracious charity and pity . . . than . . . the said house of Catesby.'[206] Criticised for their defence by the king, to whom the chancellor of the
augmentations had shown their letter, 'where the king's highness was
displeased, as he said to my servant Thomas Harper, saying that it was
like that we had received rewards which caused us to write as we did',
Gifford nonetheless went on to defend Wolstrop. This had eight religious persons

being priests of right good conversation and living religiously, having
such qualities of virtue as we have not found the like in no place; for
there is not one religious person there but that he can and doth use
either inbrotheryng [embroidering], writing books with very fair
hand, making their own garments, carving, painting, or graffyng

[engraving]. The house without any slander or evil fame [keeping hospitality, relieving the poor inhabitants] . . . God be even my judge, as I do write unto you the truth, and non other wise to my knowledge, which very pity alone causithe me to write the premisses whereof considered, in most humble wise I beseech you to be a mean unto the king's majesty for the standing of the said Wolstrop

by which his grace would do 'a much gracious and a meritorious act for the relief of his poor subjects there, and ye shall be sure not only to have the continual prayer of those religious persons there, butt also the hearty prayer of all the inhabitants within iiii or v mile about that house'.[207]

It is interesting to note the role of Henry in this. The king was displeased, accusing the commissioners of responding to bribes. When Gifford later petitioned Cromwell 'to be a mean unto the king's majesty for the standing' of Wolstrop, he clearly saw the policy and the determination to see it through as Henry's,[208] as he did when he and other commissioners wrote in favour of the nunnery of Polesworth, asking Cromwell to be a mediator with the king for the house to stand, 'for . . . ye shall not speak in the preferment of a better nunnery nor of better women'.[209] The importance of the king's decision is shown by the pleasure that Joyce, the prioress of Catesby, took at the intercession of the queen (Jane Seymour? Anne Boleyn if *Letters and Papers*' implied dating is correct) with the king on their behalf, offering 2,000 marks, but without yet receiving a perfect answer. The prioress asked Cromwell to arrange for the 2,000 marks to be paid in yearly instalments and offered him 100 marks together with her prayers. She trusted that he would second the queen's efforts, and hoped that he had not forgotten the report the commissioners had sent of her and her sisters.[210] Again the king is seen as central, with Cromwell and the queen being in a position to lobby him, but without certain success. All the lobbying in this case was in vain, for on 27 June Gifford reported how, by order of the chancellor and attorney of the court of augmentations, the commissioners had returned to Catesby to begin their suppression.[211] The king was determined on the implementation of the policy: exemptions would be dictated by the needs of reform in general, and the incidence of transfers in particular, not by lobbying by commissioners or at court in favour of this or that house.

What the commissioners for the dissolution felt as they carried out their instructions can only be wondered at. Gifford and his fellow commissioners had tried to save Catesby, Wolstrop and Polesworth, and they also wrote in favour of St James's, Northampton, where 'a discreet abbot did great good to the poor'.[212] Gifford was no opposition figure: he had been nominated by Cromwell as a burgess for Buckingham in the parliament summoned in May 1536.[213] And he was not prepared to make a stand, loyally implementing the final decision on Catesby.[214] He was also quite prepared to profit from the spoils of dissolution. On 14 July he begged Cromwell and the chancellor of the augmentations to be named the farmer of St James's, Northampton, whose abbot had just died, leaving the house in, as he supposed, irrecoverable debt.[215] He also made suit for Erbury, thanking Cromwell for the pains he took, though the lord chancellor seemed to be opposed.[216] On 23 August he moved Cromwell for a grant to his poor brother John, the bearer of his letter, of the late priory of Delapre near Northampton: Cromwell had already given it away, but promised to be Gifford's good lord for something else. There was in Leicestershire a house not yet (in December) surrendered, Olescroft, which might bring his brother some little profit: he asked accordingly that the priory of Olescroft might be in the next commission of surrender.[217] And yet Gifford had lobbied for the continuation of several houses. Was the government stretching the loyalties of the county magistrates to the limit? That gentry like Gifford put in bids for monastic lands, and that many were successful, does not of itself undermine the reforming intentions of the government, nor does it necessarily reveal more than grudging acquiescence in royal policy.

The dissolution of the smaller monasteries is thus best seen as the most immediate and practical demonstration of Henry's right and duty to reform and to purify the church. To seek to reform implies a vision of how things should be. And in places, in the questions to be put to abbots and monks, in the subsequent injunctions, in the act of suppression and in various letters, there were implicit and sometimes explicit statements on what true religion was. The monastic order of worship had been questioned: ceremonies and observances were not to be seen as 'the chief and uttermost of the whole true religion'. Relics, miracles and pilgrimages had also been questioned. That amounted to a profound change. We must now turn to Henry's first efforts to pronounce on doctrine and liturgy: why these were necessary and what they were.

The Ten Articles of 1536

Henry's twin impulses—the assertion of his royal supremacy and the purification of the church—also characterised the first definition of doc-

trine and first elaboration of liturgy under the royal supremacy, in the
Ten Articles and the Injunctions of 1536.

In order fully to understand these and later codifications of religion,
we must begin by remarking how central to the king's purpose was his
wish to maintain, or rather to re-establish, religious concord. That his
subjects should believe and worship as one was the king's heartfelt
desire. Perhaps the most striking illustration of this royal ambition
would be the title of the statute (to be discussed later) that we know as
the act of Six Articles (1539), but the contemporary heading of which
was 'An act abolishing diversity in religion'. In 1536 the preface to the
Ten Articles declared that, among the responsibilities of the king's office,

> we have always esteemed and thought . . . that it most chiefly
> belongeth unto our said charge diligently and foresee and cause, that
> not only the most holy word and commandments of God should most
> sincerely be believed, and most reverently be observed and kept of our
> subjects, but also that unity and concord in opinion, namely in such
> things as doth concern our religion, may increase and go forthward,
> and all occasion of dissent and discord touching the same be repressed
> and utterly extinguished.[218]

Such aspirations have totalitarian overtones, yet were plainly unrealistic. That does not mean that Henry did not intend them firmly and
sincerely.

Why should Henry have been so eager to establish 'unity and concord'
in religion? The explanation is that his break with Rome, and his drive
for a purifying reformation of the church, coincided with religious
ferment in Europe. In large parts of Germany, Switzerland and the
kingdom of Denmark not only had papal authority been repudiated but
varying forms of religious reformation had been introduced since
Martin Luther's first challenge to the church in 1517. Luther, the Swiss
reformer Ulrich Zwingli and many other theologians were developing
and expounding revised understandings of Christian religion: by the
early 1530s what we know as the protestant reformation was well under
way. Henry VIII's England was not immune. As we have already seen,
Henry reacted vigorously against Luther's works, and published his own
refutation of Luther in 1521. But neither that nor public bonfires of
heretical books, in 1521 and 1526, could prevent scholars and students
at the universities of Cambridge and Oxford from reading and discussing the writings of the continental reformers. The number of committed English followers of Luther or Zwingli in the 1520s was small,
and there is little to suggest that they were a threat to the church.

There were a few important figures among them. William Tyndale, an Oxford graduate (but before Luther wrote), and then a priest and tutor in the household of Sir John Walsh of Little Sodbury, Gloucestershire, translated Erasmus's *Enchiridion militis christiani* (1501). In 1524, frustrated in his ambition to join the household of Cuthbert Tunstal, bishop of London, who was notably sympathetic to humanist learning, Tyndale went abroad, to Luther's Wittenberg, to Cologne, to Worms, and later to Antwerp. By 1526 Tyndale had completed his translation into English of the New Testament: revisions and a series of polemical attacks on the church and of expositions of Lutheran theology would follow, especially *The Parable of the Wicked Mammon* (1528: *RSTC* 24454), *The Obedience of a Christian Man* (1528: *RSTC* 24446), *The Practice of Prelates* (1530: *RSTC* 24465). Tyndale's New Testament in English, with marginal notes much influenced by Luther, and in some editions with a Lutheran prologue and epilogue, alarmed Henry: it was among the heretical books burnt in 1526.[219] Thomas Bilney, Cambridge graduate and fellow, embarked on a preaching tour in 1527 that quickly got him into trouble. The letters he then wrote to Bishop Tunstal show that he had espoused the central Lutheran doctrine of justification by faith alone. Allowed to make a qualified abjuration, Bilney was increasingly distressed at the compromises that he had had to make (including an oath denouncing Luther), and by 1530 felt impelled to bear public witness to his real faith. He preached again, and distributed copies of Tyndale's New Testament, a course of action that led to his arrest, trial and burning at Norwich in 1531.[220] Simon Fish, Oxford graduate and lawyer, published *A Supplication for the Beggars* in late 1528/early 1529. This tract attacked the financial exactions of the church, and its thrust is more anticlerical than doctrinal, but in places it does approach Luther's justification by faith alone. John Frith, Cambridge graduate and one of the young scholars whom Wolsey recruited to Cardinal College, Oxford, avoided arrest on suspicion of heresy by going to Antwerp, where he assisted Tyndale in his translation of the Old Testament. He translated works of theology by Luther and Melanchthon; his *Disputacion of Purgatory* (1531) showed that he had been influenced by Zwingli. When he returned to England, he was captured, tried and burnt for heresy.[221] There were a few other notable early protestants: George Joye, fellow of Peterhouse, who went abroad and published biblical translations and expositions of doctrine; Richard Bayfield, monk of Bury St Edmunds, who bought and distributed forbidden books, notably Tyndale's New Testament; James Bainham, son of a Gloucestershire gentleman, who married Simon Fish's widow, possessed books by Tyndale and Frith, and upheld the doctrine of justification by faith alone. But this list cannot be greatly lengthened. That exile and martyrdom were their common fate shows that the authorities were largely on top of what they saw as a serious heretical challenge.

But in two ways matters were not so clear-cut. First, the influence of books, especially Tyndale's New Testament in English, and of ideas, especially Luther's justification by faith alone and all that flowed from it, could not so easily be cut off. Henry VIII, as we have seen (and we shall see again later), was firmly opposed to the central teachings of Luther and Zwingli. But by the early 1530s many scholars and priests, especially those who had studied in the 1520s, as well as some merchants, including those who had trading contacts with continental towns affected by the reformation, had encountered them—and some of them had been intrigued, or even converted. They were not very many, but neither were they negligible. Open advocacy of Luther's or Zwingli's doctrines remained highly risky; but a few priests in the early 1530s, notably Hugh Latimer, the future bishop, tested the limits of what was permissible, preaching doctrines that sailed close to the wind.

Secondly, and more importantly, Henry VIII, as we have seen, broke with Rome, asserted his royal supremacy and sought to purify the church. Loyalty to the king and fear of the ruthless pressure that Henry was prepared to exert on those who refused to comply largely secured outward acquiescence. But the king demanded more than mere acquiescence: he wanted enthusiastic endorsement of his policies. A series of tracts justified the royal stand on the divorce and vindicated the break with Rome. But Henry also wanted bishops and parish priests to assert the royal supremacy. And in his continuing campaign, he would obviously find more willing adherents among those who were finding the protestant message attractive.[222] On such a matter evidence is problematic. But the record of Henry's promotions to bishoprics is revealing. It is striking how many of the new bishops of the years from 1529 had been involved in the making of the king's case in canon law for his divorce. And it is striking that several, though not all, of the bishops appointed from 1532 would, in various ways, show sympathy towards the continental reformation. Henry's choice of Thomas Cranmer as archbishop of Canterbury in late 1532 is intriguing in this context. Of course, Cranmer had already proved invaluable in his contribution to the king's great cause. And it is not easy to be sure just how far Cranmer had, by 1532, moved towards Lutheranism (though it is likely that that was the year of his conversion). Moreover, as we shall see, Cranmer would throughout the reign keep his convictions to himself, except when the king explicitly asked him (and other bishops) for their opinions. Then Cranmer (and several other bishops) consistently, though not uniformly, took theological and liturgical positions that revealed an affinity (and sometimes rather more) with the continental reformation. Emblematic of Henry's search for committed support is the experience of Robert Barnes, an Augustinian friar at Cambridge from 1511 to 1512, and later in Louvain before returning to Cambridge as prior, who (according to John Foxe) had been converted by Bilney. In 1525 he had preached a sermon highly critical of the temporal wealth of the bishops and questioned characteristic practices of the church, notably holy days, indulgences and crosses. He abjured and was placed, in effect, under house arrest with the Austin friars in London, where he evidently acquired a copy of Tyndale's New Testament. Later he escaped to Antwerp and then to Wittenberg. By the early 1530s he had become a committed Lutheran. Strikingly, now that Henry had broken with Rome and was looking to the princes of Lutheran Germany for alliance, he turned also to Barnes, who would be allowed to return home from exile—but who would ultimately, as we shall see, fall foul of the king's wrath.[223]

All these influences contributed to a ferment of religious debate. As Foxe put it, 'after the abolishing of the pope, certain tumults began to rise about religion'.[224] Perhaps the king's fears of discord undermining legitimate authority were exaggerated; but the sheer novelty of pulpit debates such as that between Hugh Latimer and William Hubberdyne in Bristol in 1533[225] may have made what strike the modern historian as isolated disputes appear far more threatening to Henry. As Cranmer put it, at Easter 1534,

> divers persons at this present time, under the pretence of preaching to the people the word of God, which is the word of charity, unity and concord, do minister unto their audience matter of contention, slander, debate, and murmur, as well concerning the true catholic doctrine of Christ's church, as also other public matters, nothing meet ne convenient for their audience.

Accordingly, Cranmer required would-be preachers, including curates authorised to preach in their own parish churches, to secure new episcopal licences. They were not to touch on anything that might bring into doubt 'the catholic and received doctrine of Christ's church' or the prince's laws and succession, 'considering that thereupon can ensue no edification in the people, but rather occasion of talking and rumour to their great hurt and damage, and the danger and perils of their bodies and souls'.[226] Henry feared that 'there swarmeth abroad a number of indiscreet persons which although they be furnished neither with wisdom learning ne yet good judgement are nevertheless authorised to preach and permitted to blow abroad their folly whereby among our subjects is only engendered great contentions and variety of opinions'.[227]

What the king attempted was a delicate balancing act: he wanted the pope denounced and his own royal supremacy asserted; he wanted those measures that he was taking to purify the church to be defended; but he wanted no Lutheran or Zwinglian reformation. Henry therefore needed to control and to limit the zeal of those converted. And that he sought to do by securing from his leading churchmen, and then by imposing on all his subjects, statements of true doctrine from which dissent would be heresy and treason.

Thus it was the king who assembled the bishops and some leading scholars together in spring 1536 and put pressure on them to agree. Recognising his duty, as supreme head, of providing unity, concord and agreement among his subjects in religion, he had (he declared in a circular letter to the bishops on 12 July 1536), for the profit and setting forth of the truth of God's word, for the suppression of errors and for reducing of such controversies to one good and catholic conformity— stated aims that clearly reveal his intentions—caused the bishops and clergy in solemn convocation to agree to 'certain articles most catholic conceived', minding only 'the unity that God's holy word doth require', to the intent that 'all diversity in the manner of teaching and preaching may be avoided and eschewed as a thing most offending our people, and that conformity ensue in the lieu thereof'.[228] 'We were constrained to put our own pen to the book', Henry later declared, and 'conceive certain articles agreed by the bishops as catholic and meet'.[229] It was then 'with his majesty's advice and partly with his grace's help in putting thereunto his own pen' that the bishops set forth three of the sacraments 'most necessary to be known and to be for our salvation believed' and added 'sundry other things in matters touching certain rites ceremonies customs'.[230] Archbishop Lee would emphasise the pains the king had taken to set forth articles subscribed by all the bishops and clergy.[231] William Barlow, bishop of St David's, declared how the king 'for the ardent zeal that his highness beareth towards the advancement of God's word, most graciously tendering the quiet unity of his subjects, late assembled the prelates of this realm'.[232] They had 'long and mature deliberation and disputations'.[233] It appears that pressure from the king was crucial: Henry, as we have seen, *caused* the bishops and clergy to agree.[234] Thomas Starkey stressed the king's involvement.[235] The preamble of the Ten Articles declared how 'we [Henry VIII] have . . . in our own person at many times taken great pains, study, labours and travails' for 'an honest policy and decent order'.[236] All that strongly suggests that the Ten Articles reflect the king's concerns.

What were they? The king sought to set out a middle way in religion between Rome and Wittenberg, Rome and Zurich. As Thomas Starkey, scholar and would-be counsellor to the king put it in July 1536, Henry and his counsellors were studying to set forth a tempered doctrine: doctrine was now purged of the old abuses, and defended from the errors of this time and from false religion.[237] Henry would not accept central Lutheran or Zwinglian doctrines, and the Ten Articles reflect that. Some of the king's bishops, however, especially those more recently appointed, chosen no doubt because of the vigour with which they defended the king's supremacy and denounced the pope, were rather more sympathetic towards continental ideas. And the Ten Articles consequently reflect the challenge of combining their views with those of more conservative bishops—and with the preferences of the king. There is much that is ambiguous, even contradictory, in the Ten Articles—in the treatment of justification by faith alone, of purgatory, of the mass, of the sacraments generally. But the way in which such themes were treated was neither Lutheran nor—crucially—should it be seen as a step on the Lutheran road.[238] The Ten Articles are brief.[239] The creeds were to be taken as necessary for salvation. There was an explanation of the sacraments of baptism, penance and the altar, followed by an account of justification and short statements on images, saints, prayers to saints, rites and ceremonies, and purgatory. What is crucial to a proper understanding here is to consider how central themes are treated.

The treatment of justification by faith alone appeared, in places, to endorse that central Lutheran doctrine, only then to qualify it by presenting works of charity as necessary to salvation. The article on baptism declared (quoting St Paul) that 'God hath not saved us for the works of justice which we have done but of his mercy by baptism, and renovation of the Holy Ghost',[240] and the article on penance declared that a penitent

must conceive certain hope and faith that God will forgive him his sins, and repute him justified, and of the number of his elect children, not for the worthiness of any merit or work done by the penitent, but only for the merits of the blood and passion of our saviour Jesu Christ.[241]

Those statements would appear to endorse a Lutheran position of justification by faith alone. But the article on penance also declared that this 'certain faith and hope is gotten, and also confirmed, and made more strong by the applying of Christ's words and promises of His grace and favour, contained in his gospel, and the sacraments instituted by him in the New Testament', and that confession to a priest was necessary to attain that certain faith, undermining the thrust of the previous section. The article on penance then offered a whole series of retreats from the bold principle of justification by faith alone that had—apparently—been enunciated previously.

Although Christ and his death be the sufficient oblation, sacrifice, satisfaction and recompense, for the which God the Father forgiveth and remitteth to all sinners not only their sin but also eternal pain due for the same; yet all men truly penitent, contrite, and confessed, must needs also bring forth the fruits of penance, that is to say, prayer, fasting, alms, deeds ... [restitution to neighbours,] all other good works of mercy and charity ... or else they shall never be saved.[242] ... These precepts and works of charity be necessary works to our salvation; by penance and such good works ... we shall not only obtain everlasting life, but also we shall deserve remission or mitigation of these present pains and afflictions in this world.[243]

The article dealing directly with justification declared that it was attained 'by contrition and faith joined with charity'. As if the writers were aware of the tension between those words and the principle stated earlier, they quickly continued:

not as though our contrition, or faith, or any works proceeding thereof, can worthily merit or deserve to attain the said justification; for the only mercy and grace of the Father, promised freely unto us for His Sons sake, Jesu Christ, and the merits of his blood and passion be the only and sufficient causes thereof.

Still, however, the articles do not endorse full-blown justification by faith, but instead insist on the necessity of good works: God requires

us that 'after we be justified we *must* also have good works of charity';
'for although acceptation to everlasting life be conjoined with justification, yet our good works be *necessarily* required to the attaining of
everlasting life'; 'it is our *necessary* duty to do good works'.[244] The
ambiguities are neatly illustrated by the statement in the article dealing
with praying to saints that 'grace, remission of sin, and salvation, cannot
be obtained but of God only by the mediation of our saviour Jesus
Christ, which is only sufficient mediator for our sins', which is immediately qualified by the proviso 'yet it is very laudable to pray to saints
in heaven everlastingly living, whose charity is ever permanent, to be
intercessors'.[245]

In short, some of these articles seem to endorse justification by faith
alone, but others sharply qualify that by insisting on the necessity and
the effectiveness of good works. The sentences that appeared to endorse
justification by faith alone no doubt came from those of Henry's bishops
more committed to Lutheranism, especially Cranmer and Latimer. Archbishop Cranmer had in autumn 1535 preached two sermons declaring
that 'our sins be remitted by the death of our Saviour Christ Jesus', and
that it were injury to Christ to impute the remission of our sins to any
laws or ceremonies, demonstrating his understanding of the issue and
his (apparent) commitment to a Lutheran formulation.[246] Doubtless
Cranmer, on being asked for his views in spring 1536, responded on
similar lines. Undoubtedly other bishops would have differed. How
would such disagreement be resolved? Henry, as we have seen, later
described how 'we were constrained to put our own pen to the book',
and 'conceive certain articles agreed by the bishops as catholic and
meet'.[247] Given what we have already seen of Henry's consistent unwillingness to endorse justification by faith alone, the crucial qualifications
and the insistence on good works as the necessary accompaniment to
faith in the sections dealing with justification very probably reflected
royal preoccupations. Most likely Henry would have preferred a clearer
statement on the subject, making it plain that Lutheran theology was not
acceptable. But in the circumstances of spring 1536, Henry was willing
to settle for an ambiguous and contradictory formulation. He had called
on his bishops to give their opinions on a range of issues—and justification by faith alone was among the most contentious. He could not
simply tell them what to say, nor could he expect churchmen too readily
to repudiate their convictions. He could cajole and guide them, but no
such committee was likely to formulate crystal-clear and consistent statements. But in some ways, the ambiguities and contradictions of the Ten
Articles on this vexed question did go a long way to meeting the king's

wishes. His own concern—that good works were necessary—was not just included within the text but forcefully stated. It would be possible to object against any preacher setting out pure Lutheran doctrine that the articles of faith significantly qualified it. And the king might hope that the Ten Articles—which were not a full statement of doctrine but simply dealt with some contentious issues—would serve as the basis for further articles that would meet his wishes more exactly.

Again, the article dealing with the sacrament of the altar, while avoiding the word 'transubstantiation' and open to sympathetically creative interpretation by those of a Lutheran persuasion, largely endorsed the traditional view of the mass.[248]

> Under the form and figure of bread and wine, which we there presently do see and perceive by outward senses, is verily, substantially, and really contained and comprehended the very selfsame body and blood of our Saviour Jesus Christ . . . and that under the same form and figure of bread and wine the very selfsame body and blood of Christ is corporally, really, and in the very substance exhibited, distributed, and received unto and of all them which receive the said sacrament.[249]

Significant here are the words 'substantially' and 'very substance', as Haigh has noted.[250] And the implicit rejection of Zwinglian teaching that treated the sacrament of the altar as a remembrance is scarcely veiled. As Elton pointed out, the bishops 'effectively endorsed the doctrine of transubstantiation without saying so explicitly'.[251] Context is vital here. It is striking that, at much the same time that the Ten Articles were being settled, the king should have publicly declared his commitment to the mass by taking part (with Jane Seymour) in the Corpus Christi procession on 15 June.[252]

A similar analysis makes sense of the treatment of purgatory. The article dealing with purgatory in many ways reflected Henry's views. It rejected 'popish purgatory' with a further blast against papal pretensions. It insisted upon the need to put abuses away, characteristic of Henry's commitment to purifying reform. It rejected the mechanical aspects of purgatorial practice—that masses might deliver souls to heaven—so reflecting Erasmian critiques. In short, it did not offer an exposition of traditional teaching on the subject. But, in what almost seems a response to advocates of a more radically dismissive position, it nonetheless declared that prayers and masses for the departed were beneficial: it was meet and expedient to pray for their souls. This was a middle way with a vengeance—a marked departure from, yet a long way from the complete rejection of, current practice.

William Barlow, the new bishop of St David's, sympathetic to reform, gave an account of the prelates' discussions of purgatory—a question 'seriously reasoned upon and earnestly debated by such places of authentic scriptures as in times past were thought to have made for that purpose', citing Matthew 5:25–6 and Corinthians 3:11–15. They could not find anything in support of purgatory. They then studied the apocryphal books, and found a relevant passage in 2 Maccabees (12:40–5) 'that seemed to allow praying suffrages and sacrifices to be done for them that be departed'. They diligently perused the ancient doctors of the church but found 'no little contrariety among the most part of them all' and even 'often contradiction in themselves'. They had no intention of reviving what they called 'a popish purgatory': the belief that obtaining pardons, or lighting candles or saying paternosters before some specified altar released souls from purgatory and sent them straight to heaven. But 'notwithstanding, because diverse of them have so taught custom of long continuance approving the same, we agree that it was meet and expedient to pray for the souls departed without determination of any special place or expressed affection of any name . . . referring it to God'.[253] They accepted—Thomas Starkey recorded— that 'such a place there is wherein souls departed remaining may be relieved by the prayer and alms deed of their posterity'.[254] But they declined to be specific: 'forasmuch as the place where they be, the name thereof, and kind of pains there, also be to us uncertain by scripture'. Nonetheless, they agreed that, 'as due order of charity requireth, and the Book of Maccabees, and divers ancient doctors plainly show', it was 'a very good and charitable deed' to pray for souls departed, and to ask others to pray for them in masses and exequies. The churchmen came to that conclusion not because they had found any scriptural justification for the practice, but because the views of some of the church fathers were corroborated by 'custom of long continuance'. No one, they insisted, should be grieved by the continuation of such prayers.

> It standeth with the very due order of charity, a christian man to pray for souls departed, and to commit them in our prayers to God's mercy, and also to cause other to pray for them in masses and exequies, and to give alms to other to pray for them, whereby they may be relieved and holpen of some part of their pain.

Yet, at the same time, article ten emphasised that

it is much necessary that such abuses be clearly put away which under the name of purgatory hath been advanced, as to make men believe that through the bishop of Rome's pardons souls might clearly be delivered out of purgatory, and all the pains of it, or that masses said at scala coeli, or otherwise, in any place, or before any image, might likewise deliver them from all their pain and send them straight to heaven.[255]

What all this meant in practice was mixed. Not surprisingly, contemporary observers were misled: it was rumoured—wrongly—that 'many in sundry parts of this realm affirm the popish purgatory to be found again'.[256] On the one hand, Henry subsequently (12 July) required bishops to order parish priests to pray 'for the souls that be departed, abiding the mercy of almighty God, that it may please him the rather, at the contemplation of our prayers, to grant them the fruition of his presence',[257] and in return for exempting the universities and colleges of Oxford and Cambridge from new general clerical taxation, required them to hold twice-yearly masses in perpetuity for himself and his family.[258] On the other hand, the summer months also saw the implementation of the act suppressing the smaller monasteries. That measure may well have been intended, as we have argued, in a reforming rather than a destructive spirit; but Thomas Starkey's remarks are pertinent:

> this is certain, that many there be which are moved to judge plainly this act of suppression of certain abbeys both to be against the order of charity, and injurious to them which be dead because the founders thereof and the souls departed seem thereby to be defrauded of the benefit of prayer and alms deed there appointed to be done for their relief by their last will and testament.[259]

Starkey went on to present the suppression as a justifiable attempt to restrict the level of resources devoted to such intercession:

> for though it be so that prayer and alms deed be much to the comfort of them wych be departed, and though God delight much in our charitable minds clearly declared, yet to convert over much possession to that end and purpose and to appoint over many persons to such office and exercise cannot be without great detriment and hurt to the christian commonwealth, good order, and true policy.[260]

To limit the extent of intercession, and especially to stop it altogether in those houses that were suppressed, was to go in a different direction from that indicated in the king's instructions to bishops. As Latimer put it, 'the founding of monasteries argued purgatory to be; so the pulling of them down argueth it not to be. What uncharitableness and cruelness seemeth it to be to destroy monasteries if purgatory be.'[261] Chapuys perceptively spotted the ambiguities and tensions in the king's search for a middle way. In April he recorded how Henry would admit purgatory, or at least some third place that was neither paradise nor hell, and accepted that prayers assisted the dead, yet he was willing to suppress monasteries and take over foundations established precisely for the redemption of the dead.[262] Modern commentators have understandably offered a variety of views.[263] Perhaps the shrewdest is Elton's comment that the article on purgatory

> struck a delicate balance, again with a slight bias toward the reform—prayers for the dead 'a very good and charitable deed', but the place where souls departed dwell 'be to us uncertain by scripture'. This then is the via media at its inception, rather mechanically constructed by infusing tradition with a dissolving dose of the new teaching.[264]

Several sections of the Ten Articles deal with laudable ceremonies. Once again the middle position they adopt reflects the king's attitudes, and in particular his determination to purify religion. No Zwinglian scythe was wielded to cut down the profusion of images and ceremonies. Ceremonies were defended as good in principle, yet many abuses that characterised current practice were condemned. Images were defended. They were 'representers of virtue and good example . . . the kindlers and stirrers of men's minds, and make men oft to remember and lament their sins and offences, especially the images of Christ and our lady; and therefore it is meet that they should stand in the churches'. But they were 'none otherwise to be esteemed'. So that 'the rude people should not from henceforth take such superstition' and idolatry might be avoided, bishops and preachers were diligently to teach them.

> And as for censing of them, and kneeling and offering unto them, with like other worshippings, although the same hath entered by devotion, and fallen to custom; yet the people ought to be diligently taught that they in nowise do it, nor think it meet to be done to the same images, but only to be done to God and in his honour.

Saints could be honoured as they were known to be the elect persons of Christ; they could be prayed to as intercessors, so long as it was done 'without any vain superstition, as to think that any saint is more merciful, or will hear us sooner than Christ, or that any saint doth serve for one thing more than another, or is patron of the same'. A reference to Old Testament images 'for the great abuses of them sometime destroyed and put down' hinted at the possibility of active measures against superstitious images. But the same sentence continued by noting that 'in the New Testament they have been also allowed, as good authors do declare'.[265] A large number of ceremonies were listed and explicitly defended: the use of vestments; the sprinkling of holy water to remind us of baptism and of the blood of Christ on the cross; the giving of holy bread to remind us of the sacrament of the altar and the mystical body of Christ of which all Christians are part; the bearing of candles on Candlemas day, in memory of Christ the spiritual light; the giving of ashes on Ash Wednesday; the carrying of palms on Palm Sunday; creeping to the cross on Good Friday; setting up the sepulchre of Christ. 'All other like laudable customs, rites, and ceremonies,' the article declared, 'be not to be contemned and cast away, but to be used and continued as things good and laudable, to put us in remembrance of those spiritual things that they do signify, . . . renewing them in our memories from time to time'. But it was insisted that 'none of these ceremonies have power to remit sin, but only to stir and lift up our minds unto God, by whom only our sins can be forgiven.'[266] As a later draft preface, referring back to the Ten Articles, would put it, ceremonies 'were first instituted for good considerations . . . as they may be used to the honour of god, and ought not to be contemned, so they may be abused, and the abuse of them is not to be suffered'.[267]

This middle position was open to different interpretations. Those seeking to dispense with ceremonies altogether would highlight obvious abuses and excesses. They would see the attack on them in this article as the thin end of a wedge that would in due course open the way to their complete abolition. Those seeking to retain ceremonies, however, would readily go along with attacks on abuses that few late medieval churchmen would have openly defended and that could be seen as a sop to more radical critics;[268] but their purposes were rather different. The rhetoric of abuses offered polemical tools to both reformers and conservatives. The article dealing with images might then reflect an uneasy compromise, on the meaning of which reformers and conservatives disagreed.[269] But it is more likely that it reflected Henry's preferences. It is interesting that it was Latimer who was chosen (by the king?) to preach at the opening of convocation. He vigorously attacked the abuse of images and ceremonies, and fraudulent pilgrimages,[270] and provoked

Gardiner into a response (which does not survive).[271] As Duffy points out, the choice of Latimer 'can only have been intended as a deliberate official endorsement of the radical preaching which was causing so much disquiet',[272] though the endorsement was less wide-ranging than that allows.

Moreover, it is striking that, as Duffy has noted, the veneration of images and the use of ceremonies were given 'a didactic and symbolic explanation, rather than the apotropaic [sacramental] significance which was often explicit in the liturgical texts, and which was certainly a dominant part of popular understanding of the ceremonies': the emphasis was on remembrance and devotion, rather than on actively curing, or expelling demons; they were good 'in so far as they symbolise and remind men of spiritual things', but not if used sacramentally.[273] Holy water, candles at Candlemas, ashes on Ash Wednesday, palms on Palm Sunday, and the veneration of the crucifix and the consecrated host were all intended 'to put us in remembrance of those spiritual things that they do signify'.[274] There was nothing essentially unorthodox about such justifications; late medieval churchmen would have endorsed them.[275] Conservatives in the mid-1530s could use such arguments to preserve ceremonies from abolition.[276] Yet such formulations, however conventional, fail to tell the whole story: they do not convey the emotional tone of late medieval piety. Here, as elsewhere, if the Ten Articles were neither Lutheran nor Zwinglian, in significant respects they cut across a good deal of late medieval practice.

There was a similar ambiguity in the presentation of just three of the sacraments as commanded expressly by God and necessary to salvation: baptism, penance and the sacrament of the altar. That could be seen as at least a step on the way to more full-blooded protestant reform. More plausibly, it should be seen as the adoption of the 'adiaphoristic' approach: the position that says that while certain beliefs are essential, other beliefs and practices may be useful but they are not essential to salvation, which makes their precise details 'things indifferent'.[277] The three sacraments were presented, it must be noted, in a largely orthodox way, and the other four sacraments were not explicitly rejected.[278] As Rex and Haigh point out, all this did not necessarily have to be interpreted as radical. 'The omissions do not mean that Henry (much less the more traditionalist bishops) had surrendered four sacraments.'[279] A draft of a later statement of doctrine, which reinstated all the sacraments, explained what had happened. The king had assembled his prelates and asked them 'to set forth plainly sincerely and purely as many of the said sacraments as the time that they might then conveniently tarry together would give them leave substantially to entreat of'.

They accordingly set forth 'three of the said sacraments most necessary to be known and to be for our salvation believed'. Some 'contentious or rather seditious' persons 'did straight way blow abroad that because there were but three sacraments expressed being they the most necessary to be first spoken of . . . the other four sacraments were clearly abolished and forsaken'. But they had not been abolished, and the Ten Articles were not a deliberate step on the path to full-blooded Lutheran or Zwinglian reform either here or elsewhere. The official explanation of the omission of the other four sacraments was time. It was because 'the time not suffering them for sundry necessary causes to tarry any longer together' that the prelates had concentrated on the three most necessary sacraments. It was to counter seditious talk that the king would assemble his prelates again and have the other four sacraments added.[280]

All this strongly suggests that the Ten Articles reflect the king's concerns. It was nonetheless a position easily misinterpreted, or hijacked by those with more conservative or radical purposes. And the rhetoric of abuses offered polemical opportunities both to conservatives who swallowed criticisms of abuses in the hope of retaining duly purified ceremonies themselves, and to radicals who welcomed criticisms of abuses in the hope that they would point the way to their total abolition. That, incidentally, makes it vital to read with great sensitivity the sermons of those who criticised abuses: they might be conservatives, radicals or exponents of the king's middle way.[281] Yet whatever the true characterisation of the Ten Articles judged as theology (to repeat, that is not the principal concern here), no less important than the reality were the perceptions of the general direction of religious policy, however inaccurate these might be, however much they were a misreading of the king's intentions. It is not difficult to grasp why religious policy was loosely seen as 'heretical', since 'traditional' religion was not being straightforwardly endorsed.

Much the same can be said of the injunctions to clergy issued in August 1536. These were essentially an elaboration of the Ten Articles (and not, as is often claimed, a Cromwellian extension and radicalisation of them). As Elton pointed out, the Ten Articles required enforcement, and that is what the injunctions aimed to do.[282] It is worth noting that they do repeatedly refer to 'certain articles . . . lately devised and put forth by the King's Authority' (that is, the Ten Articles).[283] They required the clergy to expound the Ten Articles in sermons: 'their observance was made compulsory by Cromwell's injunctions'.[284] That the injunctions forbade sermons about images, relics and miracles reflects the royal concern that preaching on controversial topics would lead to disorder.

The injunctions echoed the scepticism of the Ten Articles over the invocation of saints.

> To the intent that all superstition and hypocrisy crept into diverse men's hearts may vanish away, they shall not set forth or extol any images relics or miracles for any superstition or lucre nor allure the people by any enticements to the pilgrimage of any saint (otherwise than is permitted in the articles . . .) as though it were proper or peculiar to that saint to give this commodity or that sithens all goodness, health and grace ought to be both asked and looked for only of God, as of the very author of the same.

Instead, parishioners were to be urged to apply themselves 'to the keeping of God's commandments and fulfilling of his works of charity'. The clergy were to 'persuade them that it doth conduce more toward their souls' health if they do give that to the poor and needy that they thought to bestow upon the said images or relics'.[285] Between the issuing of the Ten Articles and the issuing of the injunctions, Henry had published a proclamation as supreme head that the feast of the saint to whom a church was dedicated should in future be kept on the first Sunday in October, and not on the traditional saint's day.[286] The injunctions set out the practical implications of such abrogation. In proscribing holy days and in discouraging pilgrimages, the injunctions were working out the practical implications of the Ten Articles rather than going radically beyond them. All that was not, however, Lutheran in inspiration. Bishop Tunstal in London, as long ago as 1523, had declared that all dedication feasts were to be celebrated on 3 October.[287] The injunctions were not, in the king's mind, the forerunners of greater theological and liturgical reform: none is anticipated in them. But if the injunctions were once again an assertion of royal supremacy aimed at a purification of pious practices without moving to the extremes of Wittenberg or Zurich, in the context of the dissolution of the smaller monasteries in the summer and autumn of 1536 such measures undoubtedly appeared provocatively radical to many.[288] Holy days and pilgrimages were part of the life of all English men and women: more than anything discussed in this book so far, these measures would affect everyone quite directly.[289]

4

4

4

Rebellion and Conspiracy

Religion and the Lincolnshire Rebellion

Up to the autumn of 1536, resistance to—or refusal to acquiesce in—the religious measures of the 1530s had been largely individual and isolated. We have seen Bishop John Fisher, Thomas More and several monks and friars refuse to accept the royal supremacy. But such refusals had not been part of an organised 'opposition', and there had been no rebellion. The religious changes that followed on the break with Rome—notably the dissolution of the monasteries and the reforms announced in the spring and summer of 1536—were seemingly introduced without striking dissent. But then, in autumn 1536, a series of risings took place in northern England. At their height, at the beginning of December, some thirty thousand men were in the field. Those risings, it will be argued here, were essentially popular risings that became a general rebellion against the king's reformation, directed in particular against the dissolution of the monasteries.

If my case is valid, then it would be reasonable at once to go on to cite the rebellions as a further, larger and deeper illustration of refusal and opposition, and to explore how Henry VIII overcame them, and what the consequences of unsuccessful rebellion were. But these rebellions have been the subject of much controversy. A surprising number of their historians have sought to play down, to dilute, if not to eliminate, the place of religious grievances in the commotions. Moreover, few have adequately recognised that the defence of the monasteries was central to the rebellion and grasped how central the rebellion was in the subsequent suppression of all the monasteries.

Even those historians who have taken the religious dimension seriously have not always done full justice to the nature, extent and forcefulness of the religious concerns expressed by the rebels. C.S.L. Davies, for all the sensitivity of his pioneering analysis, puts forward a view of the role of religion that is open to question. 'The Pilgrims needed an ideology: in certain circumstances this could have been northern patriotism. . . . But it was, in fact, religion.' Religion 'provided the necessary slogans which gave coherence to the movement'; it 'served to give the movement cohesion, to bind together different classes with widely different interests, providing slogans and scapegoats, in the last resort legitimating resistance to the king.'[1]

Such remarks reflect too instrumental a view of religious attachment. They imply a pre-existing movement, the participants in which were on the lookout for some means of legitimation, for some unifying ideology, which just happened to be religion, but which could, on this analysis, just as readily have been something else, and may have been religious largely because of the role of the clergy in stirring up and manipulating the commons: 'in a society in which clergy, however crude and unlearned, were by-and-large the most articulate members, it is hardly surprising that the programme should give priority to ecclesiastical grievances, or that the rebels should sum up their programme in ecclesiastical slogans'.[2] Davies furthermore offers a very restrictive definition of 'religion', which he sees as 'ecclesiastical matters', declining 'to pass judgment on the extent to which the rebels' motives were, in any sense, "spiritual"'.[3] On the face of it this is not unreasonable, since matters ecclesiastical—the rights and procedures of the church—offer the historian tangible facts to assess. But such a way of proceeding risks prejudging the inquiry. If the rebels' motives were essentially materialistic, then little would be lost by leaving 'spiritual' factors alone, as outside the purview of the historian. But if the rebels' motives were indeed 'spiritual', and if such spiritual motivations were central to the risings, as will be argued here, then to ignore that dimension risks significant distortion. To be fair to Davies, he was writing in the mid-1960s when quasi-Marxist materialistic interpretations were at the height of their influence, and to have given religion even as much of a place as he then did was in itself boldly iconoclastic.[4]

In spring 1536, as we have seen, parliament had agreed to the dissolution of the smaller monasteries, the implementation of which was proceeding in the summer and autumn of that year. In summer 1536 two declarations on religious practice were issued: the Ten Articles in June 1536 and the injunctions to the clergy in August 1536. Significant changes were undoubtedly being made, the reduction in the number of holy days being that with the most striking impact on religious observance in every parish church.[5] These changes led to speculation and rumours that further changes were intended. After the rebellion one deponent recalled how 'there was a common voice in Richmondshire that master doctor Layton and master doctor Lee should come down as visitors unto the country and would pull down all chapels dependent and many parish churches and that they would leave but in every ten miles one parish church' and 'take away all the chalices through the country of silver and leave chalices of tin . . . as much that it was openly spoken that they were come to the town of Topcliffe'.[6] Dr Richard Layton and Dr Thomas Legh, two of the visitors inquiring into the state of the monasteries, were indeed at work in the later part of 1535 and early 1536. Layton and Legh's commission did not extend to parish churches and chapels, nor to liturgical equipment used in churches, but evidently it seemed to some observers a logical next step. That rumour, obviously stimulated by their visitation, must have arisen after they had finished their work and left the north in early 1536. But it was roughly in the month or two before the outbreak of rebellion in Lincolnshire, at the beginning of October, that—according to some dozen later depositions—such rumours became widespread.

Two themes predominate in these remembered rumours. The first was the threat to parish churches. The abbot of Barlings had heard that 'ii or iii parish churches should [be] put in one'.[7] William Morland had heard that 'there should be but one parish church within vi or vii miles compass'.[8] The other fear that recurred in the rumours was, as Philip Trotter recalled, that 'all the jewels of the church, that is to say crosses, chalices and censers, should be taken away from the churches and chalices, crosses and censers of tin put in their places'.[9] Talk that the men of Hull had sold the crosses and jewels of their church in order to thwart the king's commissioners provoked the rising in Louth, according to the vicar there, Thomas Kendal.[10] A glimpse of the passions that such talk could arouse is offered by the recollections of Thomas Mawre, a monk of Bardney. He recalled how, when a suspected servant of Thomas Cromwell boasted that the silver dish they were using in procession 'was more meeter for the king than for them', the people began to murmur, and one of them made as if to draw his dagger, saying that the people of Louth 'should make the king and his master such a breakfast as he never had'.[11]

But wild talk and angry gestures are not in themselves uncommon. If one man was responsible for turning these rumours that church crosses would be confiscated into action, it was Thomas Foster, yeoman and a 'singing man' in the choir of Louth church, driven to act, he later recalled, by the rumours. 'Going in procession with his surplice upon his back within the church', on Sunday 1 October, Foster said to one of those with him, Robert Jonson, a smith, 'go we to follow the crosses for and if they be taken from us, *we be like to follow them no more*'.[12] Foster's forebodings struck a chord. At mass time it was agreed to take the keys from the churchwardens so that none of the jewels of the crosses could be taken by the king's commissioners and the bishop of Lincoln's chancellor who were due in Louth the next day.[13] And 'a great number of people' gathered after evensong, took the keys, checked the jewels and rang the common bell.[14] The following morning they prevented John Heneage, the bishop's commissioner, from carrying out his duties, and rapidly the protests grew into an armed rising that spread across most of central and northern Lincolnshire.

Of course, the rumours that provoked these demonstrations were indeed false in the sense that the government in autumn 1536 had no intention of closing parish churches or seizing church goods (though possibly a draft bill for the amalgamation of churches placed under 1539 in *Letters and Papers* might be of 1536),[15] but that is clearer to the modern historian than it would have been at the time. There is little reason to doubt that clergy and commons who spread such rumours feared that they were true. There was enough in recent events to convince them that the future was bleak. Hoyle, in a brief examination of northern religion, deduces from the lack of reformed preaching in the north that the rebels' opposition to reform 'was to something of which they had heard at second hand, but of which they almost certainly had no experience'.[16] But that is to take too narrow a definition of reform. People feared that something was afoot. The most revealing evidence comes from William Stapleton, who described how 'there was a common bruit in Yorkshire that div[erse] parish churches in that country should be put down and the g[oods] thereof to be taken to the kings use, so that several parishes should be but one'.[17] It was not just a vague rumour: specific parishes were named. At that time one of the king's commissioners sitting at Tadcaster ordered the churchwardens to bring an inventory of the goods of the church, which made people say that the rumour that chalices made of copper would be used in future was true.

John Hallom, examined on 24 January 1537, and describing the outbreak of rebellion in the East Riding, the first area to which the risings spread from Lincolnshire, explained why the rumours were believed. On the Sunday (8 October) before St Wilfrid's day (12 October) the priest in bidding the beads at Watton did not announce the imminent saint's day as a holy day; asked why not, he replied that all feasts were put down by the king's authority and by the consent of the whole clergy in convocation. As soon as mass was over, 'the whole parish was in a rumour for that matter and said they would have their holy days bid and kept as they had before and so they had ever since'. And John Hallom memorably highlighted the special significance of the dissolution: 'because the people saw many abbeys pulled down in deed, they believed all the rest to be true'.[18] To believe rumours that churches would be closed and church treasures confiscated was not irrational: it was an entirely reasonable extrapolation from what was already happening.[19]

Overwhelmingly these rumours reflected fears of further religious change. Two issues recurred. The first was the fear that parish churches would be closed, leaving just one every five or, in some sources, every seven miles. It is not clear how that would have worked, but it is not hard to grasp that closures of churches on such a large scale would have provoked anger. Attachment to parish churches emerges very boldly here.

The second feature of these religious rumours was the fear that the jewels of churches, and in particular crosses used in processions and chalices used in masses, would be confiscated and used for the king's pleasure. That there would be no more processions following the cross was the first rallying cry in the disturbances. Once more the rumour testifies to the depth of attachment to parish churches. But, more than that, it illustrates the character of religious observance and religious life in the parishes. Chalices show the centrality of the mass. Crosses show the importance of liturgical processions (a splendid example of a processional cross is displayed as exhibit eleven in the 'British 1500–1900' galleries in the Victoria and Albert Museum). It is hard not to see the substance of these rumours as bearing witness to the vitality of parochial religious life.

Whether the king's government was really threatening to close down parish churches and confiscate crosses and chalices or not, the fact that parishioners were prepared to defend them vividly testifies to the depth of their faith and its prominent place in their daily lives.

It will not do to see these rumours as revealing essentially material/secular concerns. The commons obviously objected to the material dimensions of royal actions or feared royal actions, and, clearly, there was concern at the persistence and scale of royal exactions and their consequent impact on the commons in the north. The subsidy commissioners sworn by the rebels near Caistor reported that the commons objected that they 'should be put of new to enhancements and other importunate charges which they were not able to bear by reason of extreme poverty'.[20] Michael Bush consequently sees the revolt at Caistor as beginning as 'a tax revolt'.[21] Henry's first responses, in which he denied any plans to take away the goods of parish churches or to demand extra taxation, certainly leave the impression that the commons' protests were essentially material, and that the king judged that the best way of defusing tensions would be to show that he had no such oppressive intentions. But when he pointed out that fewer than one in ten who were engaged in what he saw as a rebellion were affected by the parliamentary taxation granted in 1534, Henry was unwittingly undermining his supposition that this was an essentially fiscal protest. If so few were liable to pay that tax, is it really plausible that so many who were not affected by it would have gathered together to protest so forcefully? Henry was mistaken about the concerns of the rebels; historians should be wary about repeating his error. Possibly the subsidy commissioners misled him: it would have been natural for them to think that protests in which they were compelled by the commons to swear an oath must have been essentially concerned with the taxation that they were currently raising.[22]

The commons undoubtedly saw the king and his government as oppressive, but it is a little misleading to suppose that 'the church issue was the focus of the general fear of spoliation by the government' or to say that 'the pockets of the poor, and community investment, community pride seemed to be under attack simultaneously by a rapacious king misled by a scheming minister'.[23] True, the concern over crosses and chalices may be seen as material—fear of seizure of material goods held for the local community; true, concern over further taxation was aired at the same time.

And in one sense concern over religion is itself material, or at least self-interested, in so far as people are concerned with their salvation and life after death. But it would be crassly insufficient to see the alarm at the confiscation of crosses and chalices as merely material. Such concerns should not be dismissed on the grounds that 'it is difficult to see much religious fervour in these doubts and fears'.[24] Only on an austerely Calvinist definition of 'religious fervour' would church buildings and church plate be denied their place in any such 'fervour'. For clergy such concerns may well have reflected in part concern for their livelihoods: but it would be harsh not to allow them at least a measure of spiritual concern as well. And it would be misleading to suppose that the commons' reaction to the feared removal of church treasures was only or simply or even mainly of a material kind. The thrust of the

complaints of the Lincolnshire commons was not royal fiscal oppression. The commons were defending their parish churches and the liturgical equipment within them. If they saw their church and its liturgical
treasures as in this sense their own, that would alone point to a striking attachment to the church. This is not to be dismissed as 'a few rash
men [who] wished to demonstrate their pride in the achievements of
their fathers'.[25] In writing of 'the defence of the parish church; the
embodiment of the village community, the centre of its pride', or in referring to 'the investment, emotional and monetary, in the parish church
and its furnishings',[26] Davies is more moderately pointing in the same
direction. So too is Andy Wood: 'Religious reformation represented an
assault upon the material culture of medieval christendom in which
parishioners had invested so much money and meaning.'[27] Doubtless the
men of Louth were proud of their new church spire, partially paid for
from parishioners' contributions from 1501–02 to 1515.[28] But 'pride in
the achievements of their fathers' was not what they were about. Their
concern went far beyond any proprietorial or ancestral or civic or
parochial pride. They would not have been assuaged if, for example,
the king had responded by removing the crosses and chalices from
parish churches but allowed the parishes to keep their value in money.
The commons were not objecting to the confiscation of crosses and
chalices and to the closure of parish churches on the grounds that these
would impoverish them materially. Exactions of church jewels were of
a different order from conventional fiscal demands. Davies recognises
that it was not 'only a money matter'.[29] So it is a little misleading to say
that 'there was a strong feeling that the plate was the parishioners' own,
and its confiscation, therefore, a direct attack on parishioners by the
king'.[30] Wood, ever class-conscious, sees the parishioners' anger as
directed at the 'rich men' benefiting from the spoliation, 'a vague class
of "rich oppressors"'.[31] Such remarks are out of focus. What the rebels
feared was the religious and liturgical consequences of confiscation:
services improperly conducted, the lack of crosses to follow. And it is
hard to see that concern at the closure of parish churches can be treated
as no more than a materialistic protest at seizure of buildings and
property; and even the formulation that the parish church was 'the
symbol, too, of the belief that there might be more to life than an unend-
ing and precarious fight for subsistence', 'its splendours, however
meagre, some alleviation of the austerity and utilitarianism of everyday
life',[32] or was the symbol of their 'cultural identity',[33] does not quite do
these concerns justice: it was the threat to the spiritual services that
churches offered that was the protesters' concern.[34] And if their

grievances were in this sense religious, that suggests that they saw the government as pursuing religious, and not simply materially oppressive, policies, which they did not approve. Thomas Foster's outburst in Louth must be weighed carefully here. Foster did not denounce the king's exactions and declare how greatly the commons would be materially impoverished by them. What he rather warned was that processions following the cross were under grave threat, with damaging liturgical and spiritual consequences if they were ended. And it is vital to note that the issue over which the anger generated by rumours boiled over into disturbances and then rebellion was that of church treasures and their place in the liturgy. It was the fear that the crosses used in processions would before long be used for the last time that drove Foster and others into action in Louth on the evening of Sunday, 1 October, and then led to the assemblies the next day. The spark of revolt was the defence of the liturgy in their parish church—and that makes it very hard indeed to minimise the place of religion in the rebellion.

Here we must pause and address what was once a much-vaunted explanation of the rising, namely that it was really the work of the nobility, notably Lord Hussey, and the Lincolnshire gentry, pressing their griefs under the cover of a popular rebellion. Were that the case, it would not dispose of the emphasis here on religion, and if, on such an account, the commons followed the lead of the nobility and gentry on religious matters, that would in itself, unless the commons were to be seen as totally subservient, be significant. But this view of the rising as an upper-class conspiracy is seriously flawed. On this account, John, first Lord Hussey, long sympathetic to Catherine of Aragon, had been not just uneasy about but, along with others, especially Lord Darcy, whom we shall encounter shortly, actively hostile to the break with Rome. Earlier in 1536, the argument follows, Hussey had hoped that the overthrow of Anne Boleyn by a conservative faction at court would put matters to rights, but when Thomas Cromwell trumped it, he and those who felt as he did then had no alternative but to stir up rebellion in the country. The evidence for such a claim is largely drawn from the letters of Chapuys in 1534: as we have seen, Lord Hussey had personally told Chapuys that there ought to be an insurrection of the people which would be joined immediately by the nobility and the clergy, a proposal superficially not very far removed from what happened in 1536.[35] Yet in 1536 Chapuys seemed surprised by events and his letters that autumn offer no sense that he understood what was going on, much less that he was in any way co-ordinating it or knew anyone who was: he did not report the risings as the implementation of what had been talked about two years earlier. Moreover, Hussey's behaviour strongly suggests that he was taken by surprise by the rising and by its size and extent. Hussey was a first-generation peer, a sometime courtier and administrator in the last years of Henry VII's reign, who, after that king's death, never regained the influence he had previously enjoyed. By the mid-1530s he was an old man, living on his estates at Sleaford, in the south of Lincolnshire. For M.E. James he was the central figure in the rebellion; for Sir Geoffrey Elton he helped it spread.[36] Both those views may be mistaken. Hussey made efforts to resist the rising, planning for a general rendezvous of loyalists, but such plans were overtaken by events. Possibly he failed to grasp the strength of the rebellion at first, but he was simply not powerful enough—measured by the number of men that he could raise—to be able to do much to stop it. He informed Cromwell that the 'most parte' of his 'countrymen' said 'they will be glad to defend me' but warned Cromwell that 'I shall not trust them to fight against the said rebellious'.[37] That should not be read as self-exculpatory, or disingenuous: it echoes what the wholly loyal courtier-nobleman Charles Brandon, duke of Suffolk, heard his tenants tell him eleven years earlier, during the disturbances in and around Lavenham over the financial demand known as the Amicable Grant.[38] And Hussey's difficulties in raising troops and deterring rebels were matched by those confronting the unequivocally loyal Lincolnshire gentleman, John Harrington, showing that the initiative in the rebellion came from below. Quite probably Hussey sympathised with the demands of the rebels; quite possibly he hoped to act as a mediator between them and the king, perhaps by serving as a link between the rebels and a great nobleman such as the earl of Shrewsbury. But that does not amount to starting or furthering the rebellion. If Hussey had wished to launch a rebellion, why did not more happen in south Lincolnshire, near his residence at Sleaford? Louth, Caistor and Horncastle were a very long way from Hussey's estates. Hussey maintained his innocence of treason to the end. Appealing, after he had been convicted, to the king to pay off his debts, he pleaded 'now in the honour of Christ's passion, have pity of my sinful soul and forgive all my defaults and negligence but treasons—and for that I will ask no pardon, for as I be saved I never offended his grace in treason'; he never offended the king 'in will, deed or thought'.[39] The case against Hussey rested largely on a somewhat prejudiced reading of his contacts with the rebels, all of which, taken at face value, show him doing what he could to restrain them. A good illustration is the way that the commons' pressures on him were later noted by the government.

It appeareth that the commons of Sleaford diverse times came to the Lord Hussey upon the Thursday next following to take such part as he would and saying they would live and die with him. And he called them busy knaves and made answer that if he lust to go he would go and if he would not than he will tarry.

The comment that followed—'whereby should appear that he favoured the traitors'—is in no way warranted by the details previously given. Similarly, if 'the Lady Hussey gave a cart of victuals to the rebels', it did not necessarily follow that 'it is to be supposed that she knew her husbands mind therein'.[40] That was to dismiss out of hand any possibility that Hussey and his wife were under real pressure, threatened with violence by the commons.

The reality of popular violence is also the most damaging objection to any interpretation of the Lincolnshire rising that sees it as planned and directed, secretly at first, openly later, by the Lincolnshire gentry. That was the argument excitingly, but in the end unpersuasively, urged by James.[41] To a large extent he was deceived by the editors of the *Letters and Papers*, who too tersely summarised many of the depositions made by the Lincolnshire commons, and in particular omitted or moderated their many references to force and to threats. Close reading of these depositions—for example the account of Sir William Sandon, forced off his horse and compelled, highly provocatively for a gentleman, to walk three-quarters of a mile by the commons[42]—strongly suggests that the passions that swelled into revolt came from below. The gentry of Lincolnshire were thus reluctant rebels, forced by the commons to take their part. Like Hussey, they doubtless shared the concerns of the commons, however much they deplored the means by which the commons raised them, and as the rising developed, they formulated articles of grievances and were prominently involved in day-to-day tactical decisions. But it had not been their revolt at first.

So far we have concentrated on the rumours that sparked off the risings in Lincolnshire. Rumours reflecting fears of future destruction and confiscation angered men and drove them into revolt. But that does not mean that the rebellion was only about the particular issues—parish churches and church treasures, charges they were too poor to bear—highlighted in the rumours; they were not 'the extent of the complaint'.[43] Nor does it mean that the rebellion can somehow be dismissed as a mistake or as based on a misunderstanding if these particular rumours can be shown to have been unfounded. The vitally important point is that what the clergy and the commons were opposed to was much more than just those concerns prominent in the rumours. Rumours, after all, are by definition about what is unknown. They reflect fears about what the future—the fairly immediate future—holds. In addition, rumours may be concerned with aspects of the present, or even the immediate past, that are neither open nor public. But they do not deal with anything that has already, and visibly, happened. Of course, rebellions are not only sparked off by rumours. It is entirely possible for some definite government policy—such as the demand for an 'amicable grant' in 1525—to provoke rebellion. In Lincolnshire in 1536, however, it does seem very likely that it was these rumours that were the trigger of revolt. They provoked widespread anger and desperation. By contrast, a specific action, such as the dissolution of a single smaller monastery, was perhaps less likely to lead to focused and general and active opposition. Once accomplished, the dissolution of a monastery would be a fact that might be lamented, even bitterly resented locally, but such sentiments would usually lead to resignation rather than to political action. Rumours of future seizures and closures of parish churches were rather different. It was not just that what happened to parish churches affected the lives of the laity more directly: it was more the threat of losing control over the immediate future—combined with the hope that it was not yet too late to act to prevent the rumoured calamities—that made concerted protest appear the only remedy. Rumours, then, may well illuminate the timing and the geographical location of the earliest outbreaks of rebellion, and that certainly makes sense in the Lincolnshire and East Riding disturbances in autumn 1536.

Such a conclusion is in direct contradiction of a recent and inadequate treatment of the Lincolnshire rumours.[44] Shagan claims that rumours were first and foremost a medium through which ideas were moulded and transmitted:

> the protean character of rumours allowed individuals to express their opinions about church and state by either changing a rumour's wording or surrounding the core content of a rumour with their own gloss; every person in the chain of a rumour's transmission thus participated to some degree in the creation of a popular political discourse.

Since 'the purveyors of rumours were in constant dialogue with their consumers', these rumours were 'allowing people a new and legitimised way of saying things already in their minds'.[45] That is a mixture of the obvious and the preposterous. Shagan thinks it significant that there were many different versions of these rumours. But their central content—the confiscation of church treasures, the closure of churches, the fear of financial exactions—was remarkably stable: it was the detail of over what area churches were to be closed that varied. There was in that sense no 'discourse' or 'dialogue'. There were simply persistent and very similar (but not identical) rumours about events that were about to take place in the future—in the immediate future. And there was sufficient circumstantial evidence to lend support to the rumours. People believed them because they thought they were true. It was simply not the case that the 'claim to legitimacy' of a rumour 'depends more on the resonance of its content than upon the reliability of its source'.[46] People in Lincolnshire did not want the rumours to be true: they believed them because they were convinced that they were true. What was rumoured as about to happen did indeed alarm many people, but they gave credence to the rumours not because they were about things that mattered greatly to them, but because they had good reason to think them true. That is not the same as Shagan's somewhat portentous characterisation of rumours as 'allowing people a new and legitimised way of saying things already in their minds'.[47] Legitimacy hardly comes into it. No one seems to have had any inhibition in repeating the rumours (if neighbours were uneasy, it was not out of constitutional propriety but out of fear of government reprisals). Shagan seems to be suggesting that the commons of Lincolnshire were spoiling for a rising, for some unexplained reason, and latching on to any rumours that might be thought to give one legitimacy. To write that 'when it was rumoured in the autumn of 1536 that the king intended to tear down parish churches . . . it confirmed people's worst fears about the government's greed and sacrilege'[48] is to turn matters the wrong way about. It was because people feared—on the evidence of the continuing suppression of the monasteries—that the government was embarking on radical religious change that they believed the rumours about the suppression of parish churches. Shagan is on much safer ground in suggesting that these rumours were evidence of a massive undercurrent of antipathy towards the government—though he seems curiously reluctant to go along with that conclusion.[49]

How rumours worked is revealed in greater detail in an account from Buckinghamshire some months later. In February 1537 'there was a rumour at Buckingham for the pulling down of the churches'. There was 'great multitude of people by reason of the fair where this matter was hotly talked of'. A more specific rumour was reported by the barber's boy of Aylesbury: 'the jewels of Aylesbury church should be fetched away'. It had been necessary for the wife of the clerk of the church there to declare that her husband knew nothing of it before people were satisfied.[50] Henry Robbins of Buckingham, servant of Edward Billing, baker, said he had heard 'diverse and many reports that Buckingham church should go down . . . it is a common tale [about] all the country there . . . he heard it first about christmas and more often since'.[51] Robbins explained how he carried bread daily from Buckingham to some thirteen townships round about: as he was delivering his bread, he was frequently asked whether Buckingham church would go down. A servant of a baker that he knew had spoken of how a local gentle-man would be urged 'that he should raise the country viii miles about Buckingham to the intent to come to Buckingham with an hour's warning to take part with Buckingham to resist the pulling down of the church'.

Fired by rumours of threats to their parish churches and crosses, the commons disrupted the work of royal commissioners and servants. At the very beginning, they forcefully insisted on the swearing of an oath: that was to be repeated everywhere in these risings. As Kendal, the vicar of Louth, testified, those who gathered there on the morning of Monday, 2 October

> watched of the coming of the commissioners to the intent they would swear them to take their part and the first that came was Mr John Henege and they took him very rigorously and swore him to them in the church. . . . Immediately after that came Sir William Skipwith and they rang the common bell to gather the company together and took him *very rigorously* [these words are not in *LP*] and swore him to take their parts.

That Monday, moreover, they 'did threaten the rich men of Louth [with hanging] at their own doors unless they would take their parts'; in response, most were sworn.[52] Demanding that the bishop's steward and the gentry swear an oath was the commons' first demand: and not only was it made on the very first day, but it evidently had been planned in advance. It is worth emphasising just how quickly an oath was devised and imposed: almost as soon as the disturbances broke out, oaths were sworn.

The wording and content of the oaths imposed on the bishop's steward, on the rich men of Louth, and then on the Lincolnshire gentry are thus likely to be revealing. Cobbler Melton, describing John Heneage's fate, told how 'they swore him to be true to god the king and the commonalty'.[53] The loyalists Sir Marmaduke Constable and Sir Robert Tyrwhit reported the oath sworn by 'an honest priest' from Louth at the command of the Horncastle commons: 'ye shall swear to be true to almighty god *to christ's catholic church* to our sovereign lord the king and unto the commons of this realm so help you god and holy dam and by this book'. The sequence is intriguing: God, church, king and commons in that order; there is no reference to councillors, noblemen or bishops.[54] Sir Edward Maddison, examined before the king's council, described how he had been compelled to swear 'to be true to God and the king'.[55] Robert Sotheby would later recall how Sir Edward Dymock, the sheriff, and the gentlemen with him at Scrivelsby near Horncastle were sworn 'that they should be true to God, the king and the commons and the faith of the church'.[56] When Sheriff Dymock sent out orders for 'all the true king's subjects' to gather near Lincoln, he included instructions that every man should swear to be true to God, the king and common wealth.[57] Anthony Irby, a JP of Holland,[58] reported how the gentlemen of Holland had been compelled by some commons at Boston to swear 'to be true to god and the king the commons and the common wealth'. 'Naked' [i.e. unarmed] men clad in bands of leather had said that 'they will die in god's quarrel and the king's'. George Huddeswell's later deposition confirmed the loyalists' account: he gave Sir William Askew 'an oath upon a book in manner and form following, that is to say to be true to god the king and to the commons'; John Porman, gentleman, now one of their captains, gave Sir Robert Tyrwhit and Thomas Portington 'an oath to be true to god the king the commons and to holy church'.[59] It was about that time Huddeswell compelled Robert Aske, a Yorkshire lawyer on his way to London for the beginning of the new legal term, to swear the oath or die: Aske swore 'to be true to god and the king and the commonwealth'.[60]

The barely veiled implication in these oaths was that the policies of the government were *not* true to God, the catholic church, the king and the commons. These oaths are profoundly religious in their concerns; they are not bothered by fiscal oppression or constitutional improprieties, rather they focus on God, on Christ's catholic church. In proclaiming their attachment to God and their grievances as 'God's quarrel',[61] the Lincolnshire rebels were speaking the language of religious crusade, not of tax revolt. It is quite misleading to see the Lincolnshire oath as 'only a bland and generalised assertion of solidarity with the commons' or to talk of 'the vacuity of the common's [*sic*] oath', and to see it as 'simply defending the status quo', as 'essentially meaningless, almost something out of the playground'.[62]

Symbols are also revealing. The first banner that one witness saw carried in the field had a picture of the Trinity.[63] In Lincoln a new banner was painted 'with the five wounds a chalice with an host a plough a horn with certain scripture'.[64] Philip Trotter, mercer of Horncastle,[65] offered a gloss:[66] if the horn represented Horncastle and the plough was to encourage the husbandmen, 'the meaning of the chalice was to the jewels of the church should be taken away, the meaning of the v wounds was to the encouraging of the people to fight in christ's cause'. The banners reinforce the impression of the centrality of religion in the minds of the commons who were up.

They quickly went further than the fears for parish churches and church treasures voiced in the widespread rumours. Sir Marmaduke Constable and Sir Robert Tyrwhit soon informed Cromwell that what the commons petitioned and wished the king to offer was first a pardon, and then 'that they may keep their holydays fair day and offering day according to their old customs and that all religious houses being suppressed may stand and that his grace shall ask no more money of them and also that they would fain have you'. That done, 'they will live and die with the king's grace and in his service give him all that they have'.[67] The commons were objecting to the abolition of holy and fair days, the dissolution of the monasteries, and to any further taxation: they wanted Cromwell as a scapegoat. Already, and more strikingly still, the commons of Louth who had interrupted the work of the bishop's commissioners had taken Dr Frankish's books and writings and burnt them at Corn Hill. And not only did they burn administrative documents, they also seized 'as many English books of the new testament and other new books as they could gather by proclamation of which Master Gray brought one called Frith his book and others Thomas Spencer and Robert Walley's books with many other more which made a great fire'.[68] Religious concerns—an informed awareness of religious concerns—predominate here. The commons doubtless had not read John Frith's works, but they knew what Frith, what the English New Testament, represented, and they detested it. We may surmise that the commons were acting under the guidance of the priests gathered in Louth—but that is not what our source says and, in any case, even if they were, the significant point would still be how strongly the commons felt about heresy. A few days later, Irby, whose wording of the oath has already been quoted, reported that[69] they will that the church of England shall have all such privileges as they have had by old custom without any exaction. And other is that all the houses of religion that are suppressed to be restored again except which houses as the king hath suppressed for his pleasure and only the iii^de is to have the bishop of Canterbury the bishop of Rochester bishop Latimer the bishop of Lincoln the bishop of Ely and diverse others and also my Lord Privy Seal the master of the Rolls Mr chancellor of the augmentation to be delivered unto them or else banished the realm for ever And the iiii th is that the king shall not now nor at no time hereafter take nor demand no money of his subjects but only for the defence of the realm in time of war with diverse others wilful and rebellious opinions that is not worth.

This amounts to a remarkably full programme.[70] What lay at its heart? There was indeed a rejection of taxation except in time of war. But the heart of the demands lay in religion. The privileges of the church should be restored—a scarcely veiled rejection of much of the parliamentary legislation since 1529, and of the myriad pressures against churchmen, especially on the matter of *praemunire*, in those years. Suppressed monasteries should be restored (except for those in which the king had a special personal interest)[71]—a defiant rejection of the dissolution just enacted in 1536. Certain bishops and councillors not named but identifiably listed by their office should be handed over or banished— and the selective listing of bishops and office-holders shows that the commons were not simply blaming the king's councillors in general, but singling out those they saw as particularly responsible for the policies to which they objected. What linked these bishops and councillors—Cranmer, Hilsey, Latimer, Longland, Goodrich, Cromwell, Audley, Rich—was their involvement not in taxation or in agrarian matters but rather in the making of the divorce and the subsequent or consequent religious policies of recent years. And that once more points to the wider religious significance of the rebellion. It also conclusively shows that the rising was already, in its first days in Lincolnshire, a rebellion against 'the king and the Cromwellian ascendancy'.[72]

The articles of grievances which the rebels had quickly begun to compile were more a wide-ranging critique of government policy and a call for reform than simply a reflection of the content of the rumours which had sparked off the rising. But that does not mean that the rebellion had been hijacked away from its original purposes, rather that the rumours in themselves only inadequately convey the full concerns of those who protested. Hoyle is wrong to say that the Lincoln articles 'tell us little or nothing about why the revolt began only a week previously', and misleadingly argues that 'it is simply methodologically illegitimate to employ statements of aims created at the end [*sic*] of the revolt to illuminate the causes of the rising'.[73] Hoyle's caution is reasonable, but he goes wrong when he supposes that the revolts are only about the precipitants which provoked people to come together in the first place.[74] What is becoming clear is that in broader terms, the commons were not just fearful of confiscations of church treasures or closures of parish churches but were opposed to the whole thrust of royal religious policy in the 1530s.

Who actually compiled the various articles, and what inferences are acceptable? Clearly, literate men did the writing; clearly, some of the details were highly sophisticated; and, clearly, some of the grievances, notoriously that relating to the act of uses, were socially restricted. But all this must be treated carefully. Famously, Robert Ledes 'says that George Staines went about the field [the assembly of the Lincolnshire commons at Langworth field] and the sheriff with him declaring to the people the foresaid articles [which Thomas Dighton declared had been devised by him, Thomas Dymock and the sheriff the night before] and many more demanding of the people how they liked them'.[75] Yet it is scarcely plausible that the sheriff of Lincolnshire would have attempted to impose on the commons a set of articles wholly different from their concerns (however much there might have been scope for intruding further detailed specific grievances). Hoyle believes that the Lincolnshire gentry did all they could to weaken the demands. He contrasts the demands reported by Irby—'radical indeed'—with the articles now read to the commons at Langworth, describing them as 'a considerable watering down'.[76] But that, too, is open to the objection that the commons would hardly have found any 'watering down' acceptable. Moreover, it is not at all clear that these articles were in any sense a watering down of the earlier demands. On Hoyle's account (following Robert Ledes's deposition), the latest articles included a denunciation of Cromwell and the bishops, and demands that abbeys should stand, the subsidy be remitted and the statute of uses repealed.[77] These articles were then further discussed and modified and rewritten at Lincoln on Saturday and Sunday. According to Thomas Bradley, subprior of Barlings, George Staines read a proclamation to the assembled rebel host at Lincoln on Sunday, 8 October, saying in his first article 'that he should be messenger to the king's highness in the name of them all'. The king would be asked that he should ask no money of them for taxes and taleings and that no more monasteries nor churches should be suppressed or pulled down and that his highness should take noble men to his council and remove from him the Lord Cromwell and the chancellor of the augmentations and certain heretic bishops as the bishop of Lincoln the archbishop of Canterbury the bishop of saint Davids and other which proclamation was made in diverse places that day.[78]

In such a list there is little sign of any dilution of the commons' demands. Moreover, openly to call Cranmer, Longland, Barlow and others 'heretic bishops' was to challenge not any supposed royal or ministerial avarice but rather the government's religious policies, and to attack them not as financially motivated but rather as motivated by heresy. For the commons saw the government's policy not only as oppressive: they also, and far more importantly, saw the king as led astray by the advice of councillors and bishops who were heretics. It would be hard to conceive of any more damning criticism of a Christian monarch.

A final set of articles was then taken to the king by George Staines on Monday. Once again Hoyle sees these as further watered down from a series of demands into a series of complaints: 'the gentry were shaping the common's [sic] fears into more conventional political terms', as a device to delay the commons, 'that were swinging the rank and file away from their gut fears towards a more general programme'; these articles 'tried quite hard to be anodyne'.[79] But the moderation in tone and form and the absence of violent language should not be mistaken for a retreat from, or a gentry subversion of, the original demands of the commons. The points made were not minor. Material matters were raised in the articles. They called for the repeal of the act of uses. They protested at the imminent fifteenth and tenth. If the king had reversed his policy on uses, and if he had pledged not to ask for taxation, that would have had some significance in the conduct of fiscal and financial matters, but it would not have been that dramatic or wide-ranging a change: it is not clear that the government was actually demanding further taxation, and the statute of uses, while significantly affecting the transmission of lands by the upper classes, was nonetheless a technical and restricted matter. By contrast, the religious issues raised were much more substantial and significant. The articles lamented 'the suppression of so many religious houses whereby the service of God is not well performed but also the poverty of your realm be unrelieved . . . a great hurt to the commonwealth'—emphasising what we should see as the devotional and charitable functions of monasteries. They accused 'persons as be of low birth and small reputation' whom 'your grace takes of your council' (note the attribution of responsibility to the king) to have 'procured the profits' of the dissolution of the monasteries, naming Cromwell and Sir Richard Rich. And, as 'your true subjects', they were 'grieved' that the king had promoted bishops who had—the manuscript is torn but the word is presumably 'not'—'the faith of Christ', listing the bishops of Canterbury, Rochester, Worcester, Salisbury, St David's, Dublin and especially Lincoln, who were seen as the 'beginnings of all the trouble . . . and vexation'. Hoyle makes much of the absence of specific demands that the suppressed monasteries be re-established and that Cromwell and the bishops be handed over to the rebels, and of the fact that nothing was said about the feared confiscation of church goods. Bush sees the concerns of this petition as 'preponderantly secular'.[80] But, read more sensitively, the text is a thunderous denunciation of religious policy in the 1530s: it is hard to see how any concessions to it could have amounted to anything other than a fundamental reversal of all that Henry and his councillors had been doing since 1529.[81]

To speak against the royal supremacy was treason, so little should be made of the absence of specific reference to it in the rebels' more formal demands.[82] The rebels have indeed sometimes been presented as accepting the break with Rome, accepting official denunciation of the pope, and accepting Henry VIII's royal supremacy.[83] John Porman, according to Huddeswell, declared to the subsidy commissioners that they would take the king to be supreme head of the church. But before that is seen as an expression of a spirit of compromise, attention should be paid to the full thrust of the commons' demands, not least as Porman then voiced them. This was rather to call the king's supremacy into question. Porman might say that the commons would take the king to be the supreme head of the church. But according to him the commons demanded that Henry suppress no more monasteries. It would be a milk-and-water supremacy were the king to accept that. The commons' further demand, reported by Porman, that 'the commons will have the bishop of Canterbury the lord chancellor the bishop of Lincoln the bishop of Rochester the bishop of Ely the bishop of Worcester the bishop of Dublin to the intent to murder them', amounted to a total negation of the supremacy—indeed, of the king's traditional right in effect to appoint bishops.[84] Guy is nearer the mark when he says that the rebels 'swore an oath that contradicted the crown's oath of supremacy'.[85] An interesting vignette is offered by Simon Maltby, parson of Farforth. After a frustrating time on the Saturday before the insurrection before Dr Raynes, the bishop's chancellor, at the consistory court at Bolingbroke, Maltby returned home determined, he said, to strike down the chancellor if he sat there again. Then he 'did bid the beads the next Sunday after this insurrection and prayed for the pope of Rome with the College of Cardinals'.[86] Such a man was unlikely to accept the royal supremacy if ever he had a chance to reject it.

Thus the implications of the rebels' criticisms of government policy were far-reaching. Thomas Kendal, vicar of Louth, showed this very clearly in his later deposition.

> Truly the people grudged very sore that the king's grace should be the supreme head and the bishop of Rome put down And after the putting down of holy days . . . and putting down of monasteries namely . . . of the sacrament. . . . The people also murmured sore against the . . . calling them . . . saying that the world would never be good before that [they were] put down. All these I think in my conscience were the things that caused the insurrection to be proposed for half a year before the insurrection began.

So much disquiet was there that (in Kendal's opinion) 'if any o[ne would ri]se all would rise . . . it lacketh but a be[ginning]'.[87] Kendal also admitted that 'all men with [w]hom he had any communication did grudge and murmur at the new erroneous opinions touching Our Lady and Purgatory and himself also did grudge at the same'.[88]

The immediate cause of the rising was, as Kendal insisted, the rumours about the confiscation of church jewels (and closure of churches): but the grievances of the commons of Lincolnshire were far more wide-ranging, and encompassed all the religious measures the government had taken since the early 1530s, including the break with Rome, the dissolution of the smaller monasteries, and heretical new teaching. As Kendal put it himself, 'My desire was never other but for the establishment of our faith and putting down the schismatic english books wherein the unlearned persons taketh many errors'.[89]

If government policy in the 1530s amounted to a religious revolution, then what the Lincolnshire commons were demanding was nothing less than a religious counter-revolution. By gathering in such large numbers, they demonstrated the force of their convictions. But the implementation of any counter-revolution did not lie within their powers. For religious policy to be reversed, the king, his councillors and his bishops, not the commons, would have to act. What the commons could do was to set out their concerns in petitions and demands. They could also, as we have seen, disrupt the work of royal and episcopal commissioners with the intention of preventing rumoured further damage, as they saw it, to religious life in their parishes. But in one practical matter on the ground they were able to do more, namely the dissolution of the smaller monasteries. This demands renewed attention since it illustrates so vividly the commons' concerns.

We have seen the repeated references to the fate of the monasteries whenever the commons articulated their grievances. On 5 October the loyalists Sir Marmaduke Constable and Sir Robert Tyrwhit reported the petition of the Lincolnshire rebels, including the demand 'that all religious houses being suppressed may stand'.[90] Anthony Irby listed four grievances voiced by the (Horncastle) commons, three of them religious, including the demand that suppressed houses of religion should be restored.[91] Chapuys evidently heard much the same, reporting on 7 October that the rising in Lincolnshire was directed against the king's commissioners who levied taxes and put down the abbeys.[92] The articles agreed by Lincolnshire commons and gentlemen on 8–9 October included the declaration that 'by the suppression of so many religious houses whereby the service of God is not well performed but also the poverty of your realm be unrelieved . . . [is done] a great hurt to the commonwealth'.[93]

The importance of the dissolution is further shown in the depositions made by men questioned about the troubles when they were over. As we have seen, Thomas Kendal, vicar of Louth, where the troubles first flared up, stressed as the immediate cause of the commotions the rumours that in Hull men had sold the crosses and jewels of their church to thwart the king's commissioners. He added, however, that the commons had long grudged the royal supremacy, at the putting down of holidays—and at the suppression of monasteries.[94] According to George Huddeswell's later confession, on the day that the commons of Louth joined those of Caistor, Sir William Askew and other gentlemen asked the causes; John Porman, gentleman, duly listed them, concluding that the king 'shall suppress no more abbeys'.[95] Robert Aske later set out the articles of Lincolnshire: 'first to have redress of the abbeys suppressed'.[96] George Staines read a proclamation to the assembled rebel host at Lincoln on Sunday, 8 October: including the article that 'no more monasteries nor churches should be suppressed or pulled down'.[97] Nicholas Leche, parson of Birchford, deposed that gentlemen of Lincolnshire at length brought forth 'certain articles touching diverse of their griefs whereof one was that the king's highness should remit the subsidy and one other article was that his grace should let the abbeys stand'.[98] The significance of the monasteries is further shown in the rumours of further dissolutions. The abbot of Barlings, Matthew Mackerell, examined in March 1537, said that when the commissioners had almost completed their survey of the monasteries to be suppressed in Lincolnshire, a common rumour was reported, by Thomas Eskridge among others, that the surveyors and their servants were saying that after Michaelmas they would return and dissolve the greater monasteries, and Barlings should be one of the first.[99] Robert Ledes said 'he heard it commonly spoken among the people that many abbeys were put down and more should be put down and said it was a common report that many abbeys were put down and more should be'.[100] Philip Trotter said that 'about one month before the insurrection it was commonly bruited in all places that all the abbeys of England should be suppressed save only the monastery of Westminster'.[101] He also reported John Benson of Horncastle saying 'diverse and sundry times' that 'surely these abbeys shall be put down and the jewels of the church shall be taken away. Rather then it so should be I will spend xx nobles ere it be Christmas day next'.[102]

We must also note how frequently those looking back saw the dissolution as a central cause in the rebellion. John Hallom, yeoman of Calkeld, told William Horsekey, yeoman of Watton, that at the first insurrection 'all Lincolnshire and Beverley were up for throwing down of the abbeys', the tenths 'and pulling down of the abbeys' and 'such other matters as they rose first for'.[103] Robert Sutton of Little Walsingham would testify in June 1537 that two or three Lincolnshire men who came on pilgrimage to Walsingham just before Christmas said that the rising was for abbeys and the maintaining of God's service.[104] And John Hallom, as we have seen, memorably highlighted the special significance of the dissolution: 'and because the people saw that the abbeys were thrown down in deed they believe all these tales the rather to be true'. That is to say, seeing the smaller monasteries suppressed, they consequently believed the rumours that parish churches would be stripped and many closed. Hallom reiterated the point: 'because the people saw many abbeys pulled down in deed, they believed all the rest to be true'.[105]

The suppression of the smaller monasteries was thus central to the Lincolnshire revolt. But two misconceptions must be addressed here. First, to say this is not to claim that monks or ex-monks were leaders of the rebellion, though one former monk was certainly prominent. William Morland (also known as Burreby, Boreby or Borrowby), from the suppressed house of Louth Park,[106] 'an out rider to move and stir the people forward',[107] was asked by the Louth commons to read the books seized from John Heneage on the first day of the rising,[108] and was among the ringleaders at Caistor, according to Sir Edward Maddison and a later indictment.[109] He may have devised the articles of grievances[110] which he brought to the commissioners,[111] and he was accused of having read at Louth Cross a letter declaring that the king would have parish churches six miles apart.[112] William Langley, a priest, deposed that Morland had gone to Ovingham (Alvingham?) and forced the abbot there to give him a gelding, and then returned to the rebels until they dispersed.[113] In his statement on 9 February, Morland presented himself as initially a largely passive spectator of events, and then, once caught up in them, doing what he could to restrain the commons. He admitted that he did bring the articles devised by the men of Horncastle to Louth, that he was appointed one of four spiritual men to go with the commons at Caistor, and that he was one of five hundred sent in vain by Sir William Skipwith to fetch Lord Hussey. But he emphasised his more helpful actions. He intervened to prevent the burning of the book of the registrar of the bishop of Lincoln at Louth. Later he went to help the servant of Lord Borough who had been struck down by the commons, securing surgeons for his assistance and confessing him. The next day he tried unsuccessfully to stop the Louth commons from ringing the common bell. He then made great efforts to save one Wolsey, captured by the commons, from hanging. He managed to stay the commons from murdering the prisoners from Legbourne: that is, the dissolution commissioners.[114] Later he added that, after coming into Yorkshire, he had gone to Meaux Abbey in Holderness, and then to Byland and Rievaulx, but 'he never counselled exhorted or provoked any man living to stir or to continue the insurrection'.[115] If any credence is given to this, he becomes a monk anxious to contain rather than to spread the rising; but a more sceptical reading would present him as stirring and co-ordinating. However that may be, Morland was not typical, for no other Lincolnshire monks or ex-monks are to be found so prominently involved.

Secondly, the experience in the Lincolnshire rebellion of the larger monasteries has been misunderstood as showing that the commons were indifferent or even hostile to the fate of the monasteries, or that the larger monasteries were unsympathetic to the rising. But an examination of what happened to one of the largest monasteries in Lincolnshire, Barlings, during the commotions will rather reinforce the importance of the monasteries in the concerns of the commons, not least since its experiences were matched by those at the two other substantial religious houses in the county, Kirkstead and Bardney.

Once up in arms, the commons looked for support—food and drink, men in harness, and the presence in their host of abbots and monks— from the larger monasteries that were not affected by the dissolution. Neither in Barlings nor in Kirkstead nor in Bardney is it at all certain that the abbots and monks wholeheartedly embraced the cause. Abbot Mackerell of Barlings claimed that he had told the rebels that 'their cause is nought and directly against the law of god and men and surely god must of justice take vengeance of them' and one of his monks testified that Abbot Mackerell had said that 'it was against the laws of God and man that any religious person should go to any battle and specially against their prince': so overwrought was the abbot that for a long time after the rebels had visited his house he wept so much that he could not say divine service.[116] What the commons who came to their houses demanded was practical support. Significantly they added—revealing the depth of their religious commitment—'that on the Friday an host might eat flesh for lack of other victuals': they were appealing to the abbot to spare the rebel host from the blasphemy of being compelled to eat meat on a Friday.[117] But the commons wanted more than such practical aid. They wanted the abbots and monks—and not only their lay servants—to join them in their rising. Why? Because that would give legitimacy and authority to their action—as the abbot of Barlings recognised when he claimed to have refused to sanction it. That the commons wanted the participation of abbots and monks shows how important the monasteries were to them: they would not have troubled to involve abbots and monks if they had been unconcerned about the dissolution and engaged in no more than a fiscal or agrarian revolt. They threatened abbots and monks with force, if the abbots' and monks' testimonies are believed. Abbot Mackerell of Barlings gave a lively account of how he had been threatened by well-armed commons on horseback and feared that his monastery would be spoiled, and how he gave the large number of commons that came to Barlings that night meat and drink in response to their threats. But all that does not mean that they were hostile to monasticism: on the contrary, they were rather acting in what they saw as these larger monasteries' own best interests, and it was doubtless their sense of frustration at what they saw as the timidity of those whom they had risen to protect that prompted their threatening language and behaviour. Once with the rebel host, Abbot Mackerell asked that his contribution should be widely publicised in order to halt the threats of force against his monastery. He also asked that his monks should be allowed to return home and serve God, but was told that tall men could not be spared. Bargaining took place: the abbot was asked to bring first sixteen, then ten, and then six men the following day. And the abbot tried to obtain a passport licensing him to leave—but was inhibited from fleeing by news that neighbouring areas had risen and so did not offer any haven.[118] And, of course, whatever Abbot Mackerell's reservations, his and his monks' presence in the rebel host at Lincoln looked bad. William Longbotham could testify that he saw the canons 'riding in the field [in] their spiritual apparel'.[119] If we believe the abbot, he had been treated by the rebels in much the same way as the noblemen and gentlemen claimed to have been: threatened with force and 'persuaded' to join in the rebellion. It is not obvious that he had much choice. His reluctance may well have reflected calculation of the risks rather than any deep-rooted conviction of the wickedness of rebellion. But no doubt he sympathised with the commons' cause. And he was already doubtful about the long-term future of the monastery. On hearing rumours that the commissioners dissolving the monasteries would return and dissolve the larger monasteries, with Barlings as one of the first, he had called his monks together and urged them to sell some of their plate and vestments so that they would have at least something when dissolution came. That was not, as was insinuated against him, evidence that he expected a rising[120] but rather that he was an abbot hostile to the dissolution but resigned to its likelihood and making preparations in anticipation of the closure of his house.

And yet there are some hints, in the conflicting depositions, that abbots and monks, while not always endorsing the commons' methods and, in the case of abbots especially, wary of the costs of a failed rebellion, were not altogether unhappy at the train of events. One Fletcher testified that Abbot Mackerell, when bringing sheep to the rebel host, had said, 'Masters I have brought you her[e] certain victuals and go forward and stick to this matter'. Brought face to face with his accuser, Mackerell roundly denied it.[121] The abbot deserves the benefit of the doubt: he may well have been a most reluctant participant in the rebellion, however much he sympathised with its aims. But what matters as much is how his role was perceived by the king. And there is little doubt that the abbot—'Holy Doctor Mackrel'—was seen as one of 'the great doers of this matter', as Thomas Wriothesley described him.[122] He was in ward by 22 October,[123] listed as a traitor,[124] possibly saved by the earl of Shrewsbury from execution in November for aiding the commons with money and victual,[125] sent up to the Tower where he spent three months,[126] indicted on 5 March 1537, found guilty by a special commission on 28 March of riotous assembly and of compassing and imagining the death of the king, and executed on 29 March.[127] Four of his monks had already been condemned and executed on 6 March.[128]

Most revealing of all in any analysis of the place of monasteries in the Lincolnshire revolt is what happened at the beginning of the commotion. We have seen how at Louth the commons took possession of the parish church so that its treasures could not be confiscated, and then disrupted the work of the commissioners Frankish and Heneage on Monday 2 October. But even more significant was what the commons of Louth did next that afternoon.[129] After disrupting the work of Heneage and Frankish, and then swearing the principal men of the town, what the Louth commons did—their first external action—was to go to Legbourne nunnery, just one and a half miles away. A few weeks earlier, despite an appeal from the prioress and convent to Cromwell that they should be preserved,[130] the nunnery had been formally suppressed, and Cromwell had been appointed its farmer. Either on the way to Legbourne or at the nunnery itself, the commons met and captured one of Cromwell's servants there, John Bellow, 'all the country crying to kill the said Bellowe'.[131] They also took John Millisent (Cromwell's receiver in July)[132] 'with great violence' and 'carried them [Millisent and Bellow] to the said town of Louth and when they came to the said town they imprisoned the said Millisent in the stocks with the said Bellow'.[133] There were wilder tales: 'and Millisent your servant they have hanged or baited Bellow to death with dogs with a bullskin upon his back'.[134] But both survived their imprisonment at Louth.[135] Bellow and Millisent were working as administrators following the surrender of the nunnery: subjecting them to such public and humiliating punishment was an unmistakable and bold criticism of the dissolution itself.

Moreover, if the loyalist earl of Shrewsbury was correctly informed, the commons also seized the king's surveyors of dissolved monasteries at the neighbouring priory at Louth Park, just south of the town, dissolved the previous month, 'and did burn their books before their faces', a further remarkably defiant action, eloquent testimony of the commons' loyalty to the priory.[136]

The loyalist Christopher Askew's report to Cromwell on 6 October hints that the commons had not only disrupted the work of Cromwell's servants, but that they had restored nuns and monks to these dissolved houses: 'they have made a nowe [nowne? nun? anew?] in your abbey Legborne and an abbot in Louthpark'.[137] Since there is no definite evidence of the restoration of monasteries in Lincolnshire,[138] we must be cautious (Askew may have been misinformed), but it would have been an obvious step to take after seizing Cromwell's servants. All that makes Guy Kyme of Louth's response to the question later put to him by the commons at Beverley—what they did in Lincolnshire with the suppressed monasteries—'that they meddled with none' somewhat disingenuous, or at best incomplete.[139]

But the Lincolnshire rebels did bring the process of dissolution in that county to a halt. And the immediacy with which they went to Legbourne and the violence with which they handled Bellow and Millisent vividly illustrate the passions that the suppression of the smaller monasteries was provoking. The Lincolnshire rising was essentially a defence of religion as the commons had understood it—and the one way in which their actions could make an immediate and real impact was to disrupt the suppression. Given that chalices had not been confiscated and parish churches had not been closed down, whereas several smaller monasteries had been or were about to be suppressed, halting and reversing the dissolution was the most specific way in which the church was, in the eyes of the Lincolnshire commons, to be preserved as they wished. The dissolution was not the unique grievance in Lincolnshire, but it was without doubt a very important concern. The action of the commons in stopping the post-dissolution commissioners from going about their work at Legbourne and Louth Park vividly illustrates what the rebellion was about.

The Lincolnshire rising, in the end, lasted just a fortnight. Fearing an imminent assault by the loyalist earl of Shrewsbury, the commons agreed to disperse. That should not be seen, as it sometimes is, as evidence of lack of commitment to their cause: the experience of the south-western rebels in 1549, ultimately smashed by Lord Russell's forces, with thousands killed, hints at what they might have risked. Maybe they were aware of fresh risings further north, especially in the neighbouring East Riding of Yorkshire, but presumably at the time when they went home they had no sense of just how large and widespread these were becoming.

Religion and the Pilgrimage of Grace

The rumours that sparked off, and the concerns that underlay, the commotions in Lincolnshire were not unique to that county. They were current elsewhere. In Cornwall in September 1536 it was rumoured that Dr John Tregonwell was coming to take away crosses, chalices and other idols of the churches. That Tregonwell used such language—referring to sculptures in churches as idols—hints at how misunderstanding was possible. And Tregonwell had been fearful, nearly turning back at his first entry into Somerset. In fact, he had found general obedience to the king's instructions and orders. But his letter illustrates just how widespread fears of confiscations were and just how much the government was mistrusted. A summoner near Bridgwater had begun the rumours. Nothing significant—certainly no rising—grew from these rumours in Cornwall, Devon and Somerset. But considering how much resistance there would be in the south-west to religious change in 1549, and considering how rumours could, as we have seen, in certain circumstances spark off a rising, perhaps Henry was fortunate not to be facing rebellion in the south-west as well as in the north.[140]

More intriguing still are the rumours and disturbances in Dent, Sedbergh and Wensleydale that were reported on 6 October by Lord Darcy. Those 'countries' and their neighbours 'are sworn altogether to certain unlawful articles', exactly what the Lincolnshire commons had been. 'Great bruits and murmur' had consequently been spread all over Yorkshire.[141] And in a set of instructions for his son Sir Arthur, Darcy summarised the substance of the oaths:

> they will suffer no spoils nor suppressions of abbeys, parish churches nor of . . . jewels and ornaments. Nor also more money they will not pay for commissioners nor others. For they be sure as they say that such acts against God the king and his common's wealth is not his grace's pleasure.

Such concerns were astonishingly close to those of the Lincolnshire commons.[142] Indeed, so similar are the concerns of Dent to the concerns voiced in Lincolnshire, and rumoured also, as we have seen, in Cornwall, that—given the unlikelihood of direct links between the three regions—it hardly seems unreasonable to postulate that in the late summer and early autumn 1536 fears for parish churches and church treasures, opposition to the dissolution of monasteries and resentment at financial exactions were countrywide.[143] As intriguing is the timing of events in Dent. In his later account William Breyar, a petty criminal on the run, reported hearing news of the swearing of Dent and four other parishes on a Monday. Since Breyar then went on to report how several days later he heard that there was an insurrection in Lincolnshire, the assemblies in Dent may well have occurred on 25 September, a week before the outbreak in Louth.[144] For lack of greater information, not least about what precisely happened next at Dent, all this must remain tantalising.

What is abundantly clear, nonetheless, is that in early October risings spread through the East Riding of Yorkshire. The dynamics of revolt were, however, rather different from those in Lincolnshire. Disturbances were not sparked off directly by rumours of confiscations of church treasures and closures of churches: rumours—or rather, not so much rumours as hard news—of what was going on in Lincolnshire acted as a catalyst of revolt. What men of the East Riding learned, then, was that there was an armed uprising in Lincolnshire, quickly emulated in Beverley, directed against government religious policy. They heard the articles of grievances compiled in Lincolnshire. Knowing that the commons of Lincolnshire were up, several men in adjacent areas of the East Riding evidently encouraged their fellows to rise as well—though obviously in their later depositions (we lack contemporary reports from loyalists)—they tried to deflect responsibility. Edward Lee, archbishop of York, tried in vain to halt the spread of rebellion by ordering that news of the earl of Shrewsbury's advance against the rebels should be widely declared.[145]

The commons' actions in Yorkshire were similar to those of the commons in Lincolnshire. As we shall see, they swore oaths and they protested against, and attempted to reverse, the suppression of the monasteries. Just as in Lincolnshire, they mobilised in large numbers and made for the county capital. York yielded to them; a few days later so did Pontefract Castle, in which Lord Darcy, the archbishop of York and several noblemen had sheltered. This was now a full-blown regional rebellion. In meetings at Doncaster at the end of October, and again at the beginning of December, the king's lieutenants, the earl of Shrewsbury and the duke of Norfolk, would have no choice but to compromise with the rebels.

No more than the rising in Lincolnshire were the risings further north the work of noblemen and gentry. R.B. Smith, followed by Sir Geoffrey Elton, argued that what happened in Yorkshire was Lord Darcy's work.[146] As with Lord Hussey in Lincolnshire, the case depends heavily on Darcy's conversations with Chapuys in 1534. Chapuys reported that Darcy had said to one of Chapuys's servants that the things treated here were so outrageous against God and reason that he could not consent. In the north he knew that there were sixteen earls and other great gentlemen who were of his opinion. With the assistance of Charles V, Darcy would raise the banner of the crucifix and put eight thousand men in the field.[147] In May 1535 Chapuys reported that the 'good old lord' of whom he wrote was going home and would lose no time in advancing the business. In July 1535 the same good old lord sent to Chapuys that the emperor should obtain executorials.[148] Such correspondence is certainly treasonable and, if accurate, it shows that Darcy, as much as Hussey, was willing to contemplate rebellion, but, as with Hussey, any links between the grumblings of 1534 and the risings of 1536 are hard to find. Darcy seemed surprised by what happened in autumn 1536. On hearing of the rebellion in Lincolnshire, he reportedly (according to the loyalist Sir Henry Savile) said, 'Ah, they are up in Lincolnshire. God speed them well. I would they had done this three years past for the world should have been better than it is.'[149] For Savile such sympathy with the rebels was damning; but inadvertently Savile revealed that Darcy, far from planning the rising, was taken by surprise by events. That Darcy was regarded by Henry and Cromwell as responsible for the rebellion and would eventually be executed does not necessarily prove that he instigated the troubles. It would obviously be useful if the government could make the rebellion look the work of a handful of partisan and treasonous malcontents, rather than the expression of resentments widely held among the northern nobility, gentry and common people. Perhaps that is too cynical: maybe the king sincerely believed that his loyal and loving subjects could not possibly have risen up as they did unless led into it by ringleaders among their social betters; perhaps such assumptions made it impossible for the king dispassionately to review the evidence concerning Darcy's role. However that may be, it is legitimate to ask how far modern historians who have seen Darcy and Hussey as instigators of the revolt have fallen for the government's propaganda (if the king was tactically emphasising the role of ringleaders) or the government's justification (if the king genuinely believed it).

Darcy did not, on hearing of unlawful assemblies of commons, immediately mobilise men in the way that George Talbot, fourth earl of Shrewsbury, did in October 1536. At an early stage Shrewsbury asked Darcy's son Sir Arthur how many men his father might raise, and received the answer five thousand—with the qualification, if abbeys might stand. When Darcy sent out a letter prohibiting all assemblies except meetings of gentlemen and household servants, that could be construed as impeding loyalists who wished to serve the king. There is a mysterious and arguably suspicious letter charging 'cousin' to come to him at once to discuss certain 'urgent and weighty causes'.[150] A list of Yorkshire gentlemen and the numbers of men they could raise, dated 1 October, prompts questions about his intentions. He quickly withdrew to Pontefract Castle, of which he was constable, and that may have been tactically unwise: he yielded to the rebels without a fight. Perhaps, like Hussey, he appealed to Shrewsbury in the hope that the involvement of a greater nobleman would shield him from criticism. And he subsequently, while always protesting his loyalty to the king, apparently furthered the Pilgrims' cause. Shrewsbury and Henry VIII evidently thought that he could and should have stopped the rising.[151]

But none of that is as damning as it might at first glance seem. Darcy was not an especially powerful nobleman. Another first-generation peer (ennobled in 1505), from Yorkshire gentry stock, he exercised authority in the West Riding of Yorkshire largely because he held several royal offices, especially stewardships on Duchy of Lancaster lands, including the post of constable of Pontefract Castle. He lacked independent and long-established personal influence. It is therefore quite plausible that he could not have done much more than he did to stop the rebellion. That list of gentlemen and the numbers of soldiers that they could make has been misdated: the word 'in' has been misread as '1'. A list of gentry compiled 'in October', rather than on the first day of that month, can reasonably be seen as a response to rebellion rather than preparation for one.[152] The rebellion in Yorkshire did not begin in the West Riding, the area in which Darcy's lands and offices were concentrated: it seems rather to have spread from Lincolnshire, across the Humber, and flared up in the East Riding, notably at Beverley, before moving westwards. In saying that he could make five thousand men to withstand the rebels *if abbeys might stand*, Darcy was simply highlighting the attachment of the commons to the monasteries, not laying down any condition of his own devising. It is highly credible that, as Darcy complained, Pontefract Castle was bereft of ordnance: reports by definite loyalists from the castles at Nottingham, Huntingdon and Stamford similarly lamented the lack of ordnance. Darcy's son's children were threatened by the rebels. Darcy may well have felt much more under pressure than some modern historians have been prepared to recognise.[153] The earl of Cumberland, a more powerful magnate, nonetheless was besieged by the rebels in his castle at Skipton, and if he was able to hold out, it was partly because that castle was intrinsically more defensible, and partly because, since it was in use as a residence, there were adequate supplies.

Of course, Darcy did not react as firmly against the rebellion as Shrewsbury did. 'What he did not do was declare himself unilaterally against the rebels.'[154] In part, that was because it would simply have been too dangerous, though he probably could have fled from Pontefract or defected later on.[155] But Darcy clearly sympathised with the rebels (as Hoyle does not fully recognise). John Markham, a servant of Archbishop Cranmer, joined Darcy at Pontefract. That suggests that he saw Darcy as a loyalist intent on repressing the rebels. But when 'by communication had with the said lord Darcy [he] had perceived that there was no towardness of fidelity in him, he withdrew himself out of the said castle, to his great jeopardy and loss of all his goods, which at that time were specially spoiled, because he was so unobedient to their minds' which shows the very real threats to life and property.[156] There are hints revealing Darcy's attitudes. On 6 October Darcy, while warning against entering into hasty follies, expressed hopes of receiving 'comfortable answers from the king touching his true subjects' reasonable griefs that they grudge with'.[157] Nowhere did Shrewsbury, for example, express such sentiments; though, equally, this letter suggests a Darcy who is reacting to, rather than creating, events; if anything, holding back.

After the first Doncaster truce, Darcy was asked (not least to dispel suspicions at court that he had deliberately surrendered Pontefract Castle to the rebels) by Norfolk and Hussey (the letter was carried by Percival Cresswell, Hussey's servant and legal adviser) to take Robert Aske dead or alive, preferably alive so that he could be sent up for trial and punishment.[158] According to Cresswell, Darcy asked his credence, implying that Cresswell, Hussey's servant, carried some secret message, and refused to break his promise to Aske and send him up.

> I cannot do it in no wise for I have made promise to the contrary. And my coat hitherto was never stained with any such blot. And my lord's grace your master knoweth well enough what a nobleman's promise is. And therefore I think that this thing cometh not of his grace's device nor of none other nobleman's. And if I might have ii dukedoms for my labour I would not consent to have such a spot in my coat.

Similarly, writing to Norfolk, Darcy protested:[159]

> alas m[y good lord] that ever ye being a man of so [much honour] and great [experience] should advise or choose me a man to be of any such sort or fashion to betray or dissaw any living man French man Scot yea or a Turk. Of my faith to get and win to me and mine heirs four of the best duke's lands in France I wold not do it to no living person but what I [may or] can do that becomes a true knight and

subject to do for his sovereign lord shall be ready as his grace shall command me.

In mid-November Thomas Treheyes, Somerset Herald, engaged Darcy in conversation. If we can trust his account, Darcy, although again emphasising the pressures he had been under to yield Pontefract Castle, refused to take Robert Aske and send him to the king, saying he had promised to be true to him. 'Think you my lord that it were an unlawful act to take or kill him and send him to the king if he be a rebellion as some do take him?', Somerset Herald asked. 'Peradventure it were lawful for you and not for me', Darcy replied, explaining: 'for he that promisseth to be true to one and deceiveth him may be called a traitor which shall never be said in me for what is a man but his promise'. Intriguingly, Darcy did not regard a promise that he had made and an oath that he had sworn under duress as invalid: that would have been a very reasonable way out for him. He took the moral high ground: he did not, for example, say that he would be ready to take Aske prisoner but lacked the practical power to do so, which was almost certainly the case.[160] Pressed by Somerset Herald whether the exclusion of the bishop of Rome's authority was 'against our faith', Darcy declared 'by my truth I think that is not against our faith and what I spake therein to Cromwell he know himself well enough'. (We shall return to Darcy's view of the royal supremacy.) But in insisting that

> for all lawful things which is not against *our faith* he is not living that shall be more ready to do his grace commandment than I for if his highness would command me to go with you his herald to defy the great turk by the faith that I owe to God and him I should do it with a good will as old as I am

Darcy was setting up 'our faith' as his touchstone against which whatever the king commanded would be judged. Only if the king commanded what was not against 'our faith' was he to be obeyed. In saying this, Darcy did not see himself as a traitor: 'for it shall never be said that old Thomas shall have one traitor's tooth in his head but the king nor no other alive shall make me do any unlawful act as to strike off your head and to send it him in a sack'. But he had been too mistrustful of the king's intentions towards him to flee from the rebels at Doncaster. He had spoken words against Cromwell, which he now regretted:

I know I spake foolishly words of him [Cromwell] myself at Doncaster the which now I am sorry for, for to say truth every man had
a beginning and he that the king will have honoured we must all
honour, and God forbid that any subject should go about to rule the
king in his own realm or be against his pleasure in any lawful thing.

Darcy privately asked Percival Cresswell that if he saw the king he
should ask him to 'be contented', if Darcy or anyone else had spoken
'somewhat largely' against Cromwell: 'for that should please the people
best', he added, apparently excusing himself for his language by implying that he had said it to calm the commons. Even after he had yielded
Pontefract to the Pilgrims, he still did not see himself as behaving as a
rebel, striving instead to moderate the fury of the commons by acting
as their spokesman and voicing their grievances in an orderly fashion.
He did not see himself as disloyal; rather, he repeatedly proclaimed his
loyalty to the king, and insisted that he was doing the king good service:
'how that as for his parte if ever he served the king's grace or his father
afore that truly he did and intended the same at this time as much as
in him was'.[161] What he expected, one may surmise, was that Henry
would see the force of the commons' complaints, recognise the validity
of their fears that false counsel had led him dangerously astray, and
adjust his policies accordingly: like a model counsellor, Darcy was being
loyal to the king's best interests.

The revolt was not, then, a noble-inspired rebellion; but Lord Darcy
nonetheless sympathised with the rebels' aims. We must now explore
just precisely what these were.

It was in Yorkshire that the rebellion first came to be described as a
pilgrimage or, possibly slightly later, as a 'pilgrimage for grace'. The title
that the rebellion acquired, whether 'Pilgrimage', or 'a Pilgrimage for
Grace', the more frequent contemporary phrasing, or 'the Pilgrimage of
Grace', in its modern rendering, was a profoundly religious nomencla-
ture. Pilgrimage was a widespread and flourishing form of religious
observance and devotion. Recent measures—the suppression of monasteries, some of which housed shrines that were the objects of pilgrimage, the abolition of saints' days, the unenthusiastic language in which
pilgrimages had been described in the Injunctions to parish clergy issued
in summer 1536—had implicitly put the practice of pilgrimage under
threat. For the rebels to see and to present themselves as pilgrims was
in itself a very pointed commentary on government policy. Guy Kyme
testified how on the Friday (13 October) he met with Aske *et al.* near
Beverley: 'saying they were pilgrims and had a pilgrimage gate to go'.[162]

Lancelot Collins, treasurer of York, described how Aske led the Pilgrims to evensong at York on Monday, 16 October:

> Captain Aske accompanied with iiii or v thousand men as it was reported came to York and at evensong time this examinate and the whole quire of the cathedral church then received him at the church door and so brought him with upon the Monday then next following procession to the high altar where he made his oblation.

Shagan jauntily suggests that 'this was a carefully staged performance mimicking the final stages of a real pilgrimage': maybe 'mimicking' is not the best description.[163] When Aske first came into the chamber at Pontefract Castle, he declared that they were 'entered in to that holy prergrimage [pilgrimage]':[164] Archbishop Lee would later note that 'they called their journey the holy peregrimaige [pilgrimage]' and contrasted what they were doing with a rather different conception of pilgrimage as a lifelong path from the font to the heavenly city of Jerusalem.[165] Lancaster Herald reported how, when he had been sent to Pontefract on 21 October, Aske told him that one of his articles was that he and his company should go to London on pilgrimage to the king.[166] Towards the end of October the earl of Derby's servants were informed by one Atkinson that 'they had a pilgrimage to do for the commonwealth which they would accomplish or iepode [jeopardise] their lives to die in that quarrel'; 'they would not fight with the said earl, but if he interrupted them of their pilgrimage'.[167] More strikingly still, William Collins, bailiff of Kendal, declared that the vicar of Clapham, as well as being the common swearer and counsellor in all that business, persuaded people that they should go to heaven if they died in that quarrel.[168]

Hoyle argues that in adopting the title of 'Pilgrimage of Grace', the Pilgrims 'stole the spiritual high ground', and this 'distinguished the East Riding rebellion from the failed Lincolnshire movement . . . it gave it a powerful brand-name and a collective identity'. But that is misleading. The Lincolnshire rebels, as we have seen, had made very bold religious claims: of them too it could be said that they declared themselves 'arbiters of the true church'[169] or, more precisely, capable of judging whether Henry VIII's reformed church was a true church, not least when they attacked Cranmer and Longland as heretic bishops. And if Aske was using the term 'pilgrimage' on Friday, 13 October, that was before the Lincolnshire rebellion had collapsed, and well before Monday, 16 October, the first point at which he could have known about its collapse.[170] Thus the term 'pilgrimage' could not have been adopted deliberately as a way of distancing the East Riding risings from those in Lincolnshire.

As in Lincolnshire (and in Dent, Sedbergh and Wensleydale,[171] as in the north-west), the swearing of an oath was central to the rebellion and not least to its spreading. At Giggleswick, Sir Stephen Hammerton reported how a bill had been set on the church door and that later a group of commons had come to him and asked him 'whether he would be sworn to be true to god to the king and for the maintaining of the faith'.[172] Robert Aske would later say that 'he used no means to rise up the people but by sending the oath abroad'.[173] Aske reworded the oath, but, it will be argued here, he did not change its essence. Drawing on Aske's rewording, Hoyle has claimed that Aske was 'a fanatic'[174] who transformed the rebellion from a rising concerned with material and essentially secular grievances into a religious crusade. That the Lincolnshire rising was about material matters has already been repeatedly questioned: the oaths sworn in Lincolnshire have been presented as powerful declarations of religious commitment. What needs to be done next is to show that the wording of the revised oath used in Yorkshire does not support the interpretation that Hoyle would place upon it.

What Robert Aske was to do in Yorkshire was to elaborate, not redirect, the Lincolnshire oath. As he himself would explain, one of his reasons was 'that part of the commons petitions might appear in the same':[175] he was making the oath fuller, but not adding anything new. In particular, he did not, as is often suggested, inject religious concerns into the rising, nor did he intensify them, nor should the Yorkshire oath be seen as now giving preference to religious over material—economic, fiscal and agrarian—grievances. Hoyle characterises Aske's approach thus: 'shifting the weight of the articles away from commonwealth grievances towards the defence of the church and the cleansing of the council'.[176] Davies similarly presented Aske as 'disclaiming . . . any "Commonwealth" motivation'.[177] But the contrast with Lincolnshire misleads since (as we have seen) it would be wrong to suppose that the Lincolnshire rebels were not fundamentally concerned with religion.

And more importantly, the Pilgrims' Oath must be read with greater care. Here the editor of *Letters and Papers* has been unhelpful in quoting just the words 'ye shall not enter to this our pilgrimage of Grace for the common wealth but only', then breaking off at that point and adding, in indirect speech, the words, for the maintenance of God's faith and church militant. That gives the misleading impression that those being addressed will not join in the rising 'for the commonwealth' but only for religious reasons. Such is the interpretation preferred by Hoyle.

Hoyle separates 'You shall not enter to this our Pilgrimage of Grace' from 'for the commonwealth', and assumes that 'for the common-wealth' is an *adverbial* phrase that qualifies the verb 'enter to': the sentence could be reordered 'You shall not, for the commonwealth, enter to this our Pilgrimage of Grace', or 'You shall not enter for the commonwealth to this our Pilgrimage of Grace'. In other words, if your concern is for the commonwealth, you will not join the rebellion. And Hoyle further assumes that in this context 'commonwealth' means 'for economic and material reasons',[178] and in particular fiscal and agrarian grievances. Aske, says Hoyle, had from the start denied that the movement was about taxation. That denial was carried over, Hoyle continues, into his reworded oath; Hoyle then quotes the words 'You shall not enter into this our Pilgrimage of Grace for the commonwealth' in support.[179] In a footnote Hoyle amplifies his claim, rhetorically and approvingly asking of this clause, 'is it saying that the oath-taker does not enter the Pilgrimage to advance the interests of the commonwealth but for the higher purposes then listed?'[180] Thus for Hoyle, Aske 'reshaped the ideology of the Yorkshire movement, omitting the commonwealth concerns of the Lincolnshire manifesto from his oath'.[181] Since the oath then goes on to assert 'but only for the maintenance of God's faith and church militant', Hoyle continues that the only justification given for joining the rebellion was religious. And since in turn that differs—Hoyle claims—from what had been sought by the Lincolnshire rebels, that shows that Robert Aske, in writing this oath, had rebalanced the rising in favour of religious grievances.

In part, all this reasoning rests on an excessively narrow understanding of the term 'commonwealth', and the anachronistic assumption that material and spiritual concerns can be neatly divided. This is similar to Bush's attempts sharply to divide concern for the spoliation of the church from 'the issue of faith', implying, for example, that concern over the dissolution of the monasteries was somehow separate from the defence of the commonwealth, a question to which we shall return.[182] But in Tudor England the spiritual and the material overlapped: the defence of the church was also the defence of the commonwealth.

And above all, Hoyle has misunderstood the wording of the oath. The words 'for the commonwealth' are not, as his reading demands, an adverbial phrase qualifying the verb 'enter to' but rather an *adjectival* phrase describing 'our Pilgrimage of Grace'—a Pilgrimage of Grace for the commonwealth. This sentence could thus be repunctuated: 'You shall not enter to this our-Pilgrimage-of-Grace-for-the-commonwealth.' 'Commonwealth' is an integral part of the pilgrimage and has not been

discarded at all. What the religious concerns—'but only for the maintenance of God's faith and Church militant'—are being contrasted with
is not the commonwealth but rather the later instruction (which Hoyle
fails to quote) 'not to enter into our pilgrimage for private profit or displeasure to any private person, but by counsel of the commonwealth'.
Aske most certainly did not omit the commonwealth concerns of the
Lincolnshire manifesto from his oath.

The full text of the oath, not printed in *Letters and Papers*, makes
the sense quite clear.[183] Here is a transcription of the original spelling,
followed by a translation into modern spelling:

> The othe of all men sworne unto theym. Ye shall not entre to this our
> pilgramage of grace for the commine welthe but oonly for the love ye
> bere to goddes faithe and church mylitant and the mayntenaunce
> therof, the preseruacyon of the kinges person his issue and the puri-
> fying of the nobilitie and to expulse all vilaynes bloode and eveill
> councesailours against the comen welth of the same. And that ye shall
> not entre into our said pylgremaige for no peculyar profet to yor selves
> ne to do no dyspleasure to no private personne but by counsaile of
> the commen welthe nor sle [i.e. slay] nor murdre for no envye but in
> yor hertes to put away all feare for the commen welthe And to take
> before you the crosse of cryste and yor hertes faithe [not in *LP*] to
> the restitucyon of his church and to the suppressyon of heretykes opy-
> nyons by the holy contentes of thys boke.

> The oath of all men sworn unto them. Ye shall not enter into this our
> Pilgrimage of Grace for the common wealth but only for the love ye
> bear to God's faith and church militant and the maintenance thereof,
> the preservation of the king's person, his issue, and the purifying of
> the nobility and to expulse all villein blood and evil councillors against
> the common wealth of the same. And that ye shall not enter into our
> said pilgrimage for no peculiar profit to yourselves nor to do no dis-
> pleasure to no private person but by counsel of the common wealth
> nor slay nor murder for no envy but in your hearts to put away all
> fear for the common wealth. And to take before you the cross of
> Christ and your heart's faith to the restitution of his church and to
> the suppression of heretics' opinions by the holy contents of this book.

It is only for love of the church, and not for any private profit, that individuals are to join this Pilgrimage of Grace for the commonwealth; and
it is only by the counsel of the commonwealth that any displeasure may
be done against any private person.[184]

A damaged later version of the oath required the swearer to pledge to 'nor slay nor murder for no envy nor malice old' and 'to put away all fear for the promise of the common wealth'. The swearer was moreover 'to take before you [in yo]ur hearts his faith to the restitution of his church and the suppression . . . and subverters of the just laws of god'. The rejection of the pursuit of enrichment or old quarrels, the positive reference to the commonwealth, and the fundamental emphasis on the restitution of the church amplify what we have already seen in earlier oaths.[185]

It would, of course, be absurd to think that anyone in Henrician England—least of all the king—would have openly claimed to be acting against the interests of the commonwealth, or to have said that there were some 'higher purposes' than the 'interests of the commonwealth'.[186] Many other uses of the word 'commonwealth' confirm that the pilgrims saw themselves as striving for the commonwealth.

In a proclamation—Hoyle suggests it is a letter sent to the city of York, but it is addressed, as he says, to lords, knights, masters, kinsmen and friends[187]—in mid-October to which we shall shortly return, Aske wrote of the rebels as 'us that intendeth the commonwealth of this realm and nothing else'.[188] At much the same time, a letter from the commons of Yorkshire, Richmondshire and the bishopric of Durham was sent to the commons of Westmorland and Cumberland commanding them to assemble and to take an oath 'to be true to God, to the faith of the church [not just 'the Church' as *Letters and Papers* puts it], to our sovereign lord the king and to the common weale of this realm', and threatening them that 'otherwise doing they must accept and take them as enemies to the christian faith and to the commonwealth'.[189] That version shows clearly that for the rebels the faith of the church and the common weal of the realm were in no sense in conflict. Thomas Miller, Lancaster Herald, reported on 21 October how companies of common people he met near Pontefract told him they were up 'for the commonwealth and said if they did not so, the commonalty and the church should be destroyed',[190] showing yet again how church and commonalty were seen as bound together in the commonwealth. A recipient in Lancashire wrote of orders from 'our captain in this our pilgrimage of grace for the commonwealth'.[191] A proclamation in Lancashire came 'by the whole consent of the herdmen in this our pilgrimage for grace to the common wealth'.[192] In mid-November the loyalist Sir Brian Hastings sent a brief summary of the rebel demands in mid-November: 'The oath is to be true to the king, his issue and the commonwealth of the realm', once more stressing the commitment of the rebels to the commonwealth.[193]

Another illustration is offered by Aske's remark, when asked about royal councillors criticised as heretical, that 'there was diverse of the council the which the commons never blamed, but took them for honourable and good catholic men and willers of the commonwealth'.[194]

What, then, did the Pilgrims want? We have already received a fair impression from oaths and from the ways in which men were raised by the commons: now we must consider the more formal statements of grievances that the Pilgrims devised. In a proclamation in mid-October, probably intended for those whom Lord Darcy had gathered together in Pontefract Castle before it had yielded to the commons, Aske set out to refute the charge that the rebellion was because the king had had 'many impositions' from them—had made many material demands on them, as we should say.[195] The proclamation went on to set out 'the cause of this our assembly and pilgrimage'. It leaves little doubt about the essentially religious character of the rising: it denounces the 'many and sundry new inventions, which be contrary to the faith of God ... the commonwealth of this realm'; their fears that evilly disposed persons were working to destroy the church of England; and insists that they were making a pilgrimage 'for the preservation of Christ's Church of this realm of England'. The first of the summary articles listed was the suppression of monasteries, the last was the new bishops. And once more it is worth noting the continuities with the demands expressed in the Lincolnshire rising.[196]

Our next source is Archbishop Lee's later account of how Robert Aske told the lords gathered in Pontefract before the castle was surrendered to the rebels that the assembly was 'for reformation of many things that were amiss'. Archbishop Lee, perhaps suffering from selective amnesia, said that 'surely I do not remember what things they were', but went on to recall that Aske had gone on to say that 'therefore they were entered in to that holy peregrimage [pilgrimage]', which once again strongly suggests that Aske was presenting the cause as a religious crusade. Bush (once again) sees this as 'essentially a secular' message about the exactions of the government.[197] According to Lee, Aske, when pressed, said that they had no articles, which led Lee—he claimed—to tease Aske that the commons had made so great a business but could not say why. Lee was here distancing himself from the rebellion and demonstrating his loyalty to the king, since he then went on to say how he had refused Aske's request to draw up articles for them. It would be most unwise to deduce from Lee's testimony that Aske and the Pilgrims did not know what they were about. What, of course, they wanted was the archbishop's open support for their cause. And Archbishop Lee knew more than he was here letting on of what they were about.[198] Later he informed the king that the rebels at the beginning of the rebellion required him to deliver his opinion in some points of religion. Accordingly he went to them, and showed them the king's book of articles—the Ten Articles. They took it ill, Lee recalled, that mention was made but of three sacraments, and no purgatory.[199]

On 21 October Lancaster Herald came to Pontefract Castle to read a proclamation to the rebels: his report offers a summary of the Pilgrims' concerns. They intended to go 'to London of pilgrimage to the kings highness and there to have all vile blood of his council set from him and all noble blood set up again'. That echoes what Archbishop Lee remembered Aske as saying. But, revealingly, Lancaster Herald went on to report that the Pilgrims also wanted 'the faith of Christ and his laws to be kept and full restitution of christ's church of all wrongs done unto it and the commons to be used as they should be'. When Lancaster Herald requested all this in writing, Aske said that their articles were included in their oath, and gave him a copy.[200]

Towards the end of October, as the rebels approached Doncaster, they were confronted first by the earl of Shrewsbury and then the duke of Norfolk. There were brief skirmishes—in which one of the rebels killed another. Consequently there was a cry for all men to wear a badge both before and behind so that identities could not be mistaken in this way. What is striking is that this cry was for badges of the five wounds of Christ, a crusading emblem and a motif of religious devotion highly popular in the later middle ages, or of Jesus, again referring to a popular late medieval devotion. It was the badge of the five wounds of Christ that was chosen, possibly for pragmatic reasons because Darcy had a store of them, but nonetheless the badge remains vividly revealing about the purposes and nature of the rebellion. Men engaged in a fiscal or agrarian or social revolt would not have worn such a badge. Cromwell's later questions to Lord Darcy about why these badges were distributed sees them as designed to make the rebels think that they were engaged in a religious crusade. Was it not to make the soldiers believe they fought in defence of the faith of Christ, so that they should not fear to die in that cause? Were those who wore these badges not told that they were Christ's soldiers? Despite the reluctance of the government to admit the sincerity of the Pilgrims' religious convictions, these questions in fact further illustrate their depth.[201]

At Doncaster in late October the leaders of the rebellion and the duke of Norfolk and the earl of Shrewsbury agreed that two representatives of the Pilgrims, Sir Ralph Ellerker and Robert Bowes, should take a copy of their articles—which they then set down in writing—to the king.

The surviving copy is damaged, but it leaves no doubt about the central place of religious grievances. The first article is 'for the maint[ena]nce of the faith of christ. For the maintenance of the church and the [liber]ties of the s[ame].' That leaves little room for discussion or compromise. Nor does the third article: that '[s]uch as hath been the subverters of God's laws and the laws of the realm may be corrected . . . according to their demerits as the Lord Cromwell the archbishop of Cant[erbury the] bishop of Worcester And diverse other the maintainers of the same sect'. The rebels also called for the common laws of the realm to be used as at the beginning of the reign, when 'his nobles did order under his highness', and for a pardon to be enacted in parliament for any offences which they may have committed by insurrection.[202] The loyalist Sir Brian Hastings sent on a brief summary of the rebels' demands in mid-November and noted that they called for 'abbeys to be restored again'.[203]

In early November, while Bowes and Ellerker were at court,[204] John Pickering, a Dominican friar of York,[205] who would be regarded by Henry VIII as among the worst offenders in the rebellion,[206] and who was then at Bridlington Priory, wrote a ballad 'to encourage the commons [in their] rebellion', beginning 'O faithful people'.[207] Not only did Pickering share it with the prior, William Wood, who praised him saying that 'it was well don', and with the rest of the brethren, but he also showed it to several townsmen. Archbishop Lee, who was at Pontefract Castle, sent for Pickering to join him; he said that he had heard that many copies of the ballad were 'spread abroad' and that it was 'almost in every man's mouth thereabout'.[208]

For Pickering the 'faithful people' of the 'boryalle region'—the north—had been chosen by God's divine providence to make reformation of 'great mischieves and horrible offence', and to overthrow the 'southern heretics devoid of all virtue', 'this southern turk' who was 'perverting our law'. These heretics included bishops and above all Cromwell, who was compared to Aman: Cromwell was persecuting the commons in the north just as Aman did the Jews (Aman was the leading councillor of King Asseurus, or Artaxerxes of Persia, who bore a grudge against the Jews because of a private quarrel). They should, he urged, be ready to die if necessary in battle. 'Now God in whose cause we take upon hand/not against our prince/. . . but faith to maintain and right of this land.' Pickering's call appears to hint intriguingly at a northern self-perception and identity, but his notion of northerners as God's instrument for religious reform shows that religious considerations were uppermost in his mind, and the contrasting references are not to southerners as a whole, but rather to 'southern heretics'.

Interrogated later, Pickering amplified his verses. He called the rebels 'faithful people' because he thought 'that they went about to amend them that were against the faith of Christ'. By heretics he meant 'the bishop of Canterbury, Worcester and Salisbury and that they were void of all virtue and their faith untrue'. When he urged the faithful people 'tyranny restrain', he meant by tyranny 'the violent setting forth of their heresies'.[209] Pickering explained how 'At the first beginning of the said insurrection I and divers other had hope of the mutation and reformation of diverse laws lately made within this realm': it is hard not to think that it was the religious legislation of the reformation parliament that he had in mind.[210]

Henry's responses further show the centrality of religion in the rebellion. Lancaster Herald, sent with a proclamation to read to the rebels, was to insist to them that rebellion was against God's will. After denying the rumours about the church, he was to add that the king had done nothing but what the clergy of the province of York, as well as the clergy of the province of Canterbury, had agreed was in accordance with God's holy word.

> And how can the simple people then say the contrary? or what madness and presumption is it for them to take the knowledge of God's law upon them, whereof they be, of their own knowledge, ignorant, and not to believe them, that have knowledge thereof, as of duty they ought to do?

In accusing the commons of 'taking the knowledge of God's law upon them', and in insisting that nothing had been done in religion but what the convocations of the church had accepted, the king was admitting that religious concerns were at the heart of the rebellion.[211] This he did in the instructions issued to Norfolk and Fitzwilliam, whom in late November Henry decided to send with his answer to the rebels' petitions.[212] Norfolk and Fitzwilliam were to emphasise the mercy that the king was showing to subjects who had attempted rebellion and who were continuing to make unlawful assemblies. What is interesting is that in his response to the Pilgrims, Henry began with religion: 'for first their pretence was to maintain the faith', to which he countered that nothing was more contrary to God's commandment than rebellion. And rising like madmen against their prince, leaving lands untilled and corn

unsown, was not, the king observed, the behaviour of a proper commonwealth.[213] That sort of reproachful and unyielding response stimulated the rebels, disappointed not to have received more, into
preparations for new negotiations. What Henry still hoped was that a
show of authority and firm rejection of rebellion would cow the Pilgrims into giving up Aske and a number of ringleaders and into abjectly
suing for pardon. Attempts were to be made to divide the rebels, offering Darcy special treatment if he came on board. Norfolk was then to
act as the king's lieutenant and pacify the north.[214] That proved wholly
illusory.

The Pilgrims agreed to call a meeting at York for 21 November (possibly it had always been intended to meet when Ellerker and Bowes
returned from the king).[215] There the nobles and commons agreed that
representatives should meet the duke of Norfolk for further negotiations
on St Nicholas's Eve at Doncaster. They resolved on a further prepara-
tory meeting at Pontefract to elaborate their petitions.

As part of these preparations it was agreed at York, as Aske recalled,
'that the clergy should declare their learning touching the maintenance
of the faith'.[216] Robert Pullan, the captain from Penrith, amplified this,
noting how Aske ordered that 'the clergy should show their minds and
their opinions in their conscience of the oppressions of abbeys; of the
supreme head of the church with many other'; but the clergy would not
do so and rather 'referred their minds to the archbishop of York with
such learned council as they heard say would be at Pumfrett [Ponte-
fract]'.[217] All that again shows the centrality of religion in the rebellion:
the fact that clergy learned in divinity were being asked to produce articles and opinions is itself interesting. No group of estate officials or
lawyers was being called together to draw up detailed articles on land
law, the statute of uses, or rents and agrarian customs.

Archbishop Lee, however, was clearly uneasy about the whole business, securing permission to stay at home, provided that he sent in his
opinion.[218] There was no need to draw up articles concerning the faith,
as Aske had demanded, 'seeing what pains the king's highness hath
taken in setting forth articles subscribed by all the bishops and the clergy
for the contentation and quieting of all his people'.[219] In his Advent
Sunday sermon in the parish church in Pontefract, Lee would reiterate
the point, expounding the king's book of articles, in particular (according to John Pickering) those touching baptism, penance and the sacrament of the altar.[220] He was in effect saying that there was nothing to
complain about. Moreover, he told his audience that they had no
authority to draw their sword or to give battle.[221] Lee's testimony—

however much it may underplay his own role[222]—emphasises once again just how important it was to the Pilgrims that he and other learned clergy should 'conceive articles concerning the faith'.

If Archbishop Lee was reluctant, sufficient senior clergy met and drew up 'The opinion of the clergy of the north parts'. This was boldly counter-revolutionary. They began—doubtless in response to the Ten Articles and Injunctions issued in the summer—by declaring that 'preaching against purgatory, worshipping of saints, pilgrimage, images, and all books set forth against the same or sacraments or sacramentalies of the church be worthy to be reproved and condemned by convocation', and called for those guilty of such preaching and writing to be punished according to the statutes against heresy introduced in Henry IV's reign. They urged that the 'new statutes whereby heresies now lately have been greatly nourished' should be annulled: in particular they wanted holidays and the practice of bidding of bedes to be observed according to old and laudable customs.

On the break with Rome, they thought that 'by the laws of the church general councils interptrys [interpretations] of approved doctors and the consent of christian people the pope of Rome hath ben taken for the head of the church and vicar of christ and so ought to be taken'. They denied the validity of the royal supremacy: 'the king's highness nor any temporal man may not be supreme head of the church by the laws of God to have or exercise any jurisdictions or power spiritual in the same'. They wanted all acts of parliament made to the contrary to be revoked. Archbishop Lee emphasised how he 'did stick long with them and told them that he [the pope] neither had primacy nor jurisdiction here by the law of God'.[223] But they urged that churchmen who had been imprisoned or had fled abroad for resisting the king's supremacy should be freed or allowed to return without danger. Books treating the papal primacy should be freely available. They wanted offences under the statute of *praemunire* to be specified in acts of parliament so that no one could be unwittingly caught out by them. They thought 'dispensations upon just causes lawfully granted by the pope of Rome to be good and to be accepted'—implicitly questioning the king's justification for his divorce—and declared that pardons had been sanctioned by past church councils. They stood up in defence of church liberties: no clerk should be put to death without degradation by the laws of the church, no man should be taken from sanctuary except when permitted by the laws of the church. No temporal man had any authority to claim tenths and first fruits from the church: all sums paid so far should be reimbursed. They added that the northern clergy had never granted or consented to the introduction of these new taxes. They denied that lands given to God, the church or to monasteries could be taken away and put to profane uses. They attacked the recent revision of university syllabuses. It would be hard to reconcile such sharply antagonistic views with the king's reformation: they represent the authentic voice of counter-revolution.[224]

Historians who wish to play down the place of religion in the Pilgrimage of Grace attempt, however, to minimise their significance. Dickens claimed that the clergy who drew up these articles were a self-selected and unrepresentative group of bold spirits, goaded on by the Pilgrims. 'Three or four enthusiasts backed by the pressure of the lay rebels seem to have overborne the lukewarm and undecided majority.' It is hard, nonetheless, to see on what grounds their representativeness is to be doubted, and if they were 'bold spirits', that would seem to concede that they openly and loudly voiced what clergy generally were more quietly thinking.[225] Indeed, Hoyle calls their gathering a 'pseudo-convocation' and Shagan a 'quasi-convocation', adding that its members 'were mostly the same abbots, chancellors and archdeacons who would have sat in a proper convocation'.[226] Of course, afterwards they would gloss what they had done as best they could, and no doubt some of them had been present under duress. John Dakyn, archdeacon of Richmond, would claim that 'every one of us then being at Pontefract [had] come thither for fear',[227] but the forceful tone of the opinion hints rather at deep commitment.

The Pontefract Articles, drawn up in late November 1536 for submission to the duke of Norfolk as the king's lieutenant, and influenced by the discussions of the northern clergy, show clearly the central place of religious grievances.[228] Hoyle's ingenious analysis suggests that the first eight articles, together with the request for a parliament at York or Nottingham, were the core articles: the rest, together with some additions to the first eight, were pressed by a variety of lobbyists. Only articles 1–2, 4–8, 15 and 20 use the formula 'to have'; and in his later examination, Aske would refer to the 'nine articles'.[229] These nine articles are overwhelmingly religious in concern: they attack heresies, they qualify the royal supremacy, they seek to have the suppressed abbeys and the Observant friars restored, they want heretic bishops and laymen to be punished, especially Cromwell, Audley and Rich. They want Lady Mary to be legitimised. They want the ending of heavy clerical taxation.

The very first article was religious, denouncing heresy:

The first touching our faith to have the heresies of Luther, Wyclif, Hus, Melanchthon, Oecalampadius, Bucer's confessio Germanie, Apologia Malantons [Melanchthon's Apology], the works of Tyndale, of Barnes, of Marshall, Raskell, Saint German and such other heresies of Anibaptist[230] clearly within this realm to be annulled and destroyed.

Later articles called for 'the heretics, bishops and temporal, and their sect, to have condign punishment by fire . . . or else to try the quarrel with us and our partakers in battle', and for Cromwell, Audley, the lord chancellor, and Sir Richard Rich 'to have condign punishment as the subverters of the good laws of this realm and maintainers of the false sect of these heretics and the first inventors and bringers in of them'. The absence of the names of heretical bishops may have been a tactical retreat, as Hoyle suggests,[231] or naming them may simply have seemed unnecessary. On heretical bishops, Aske said that he, like 'all the commons for the most part' took the bishops of Canterbury, Worcester, Rochester and St David's—Cranmer, Latimer, Hilsey and Barlow—to be heretics and maintainers of Luther's and Tyndale's opinions.[232]

They were seen[233]

to be maintainers of the new learning & preachers of the same, & that by reason of their information, rather religion was not favoured, & the statute of suppression take rather thereby place, for they preached as it was said against the benefit of habits in religion and such like, and against the common orders & rules before used in the universal church this was the common voice of all men.

Aske added that all the rebels greatly blamed them 'for division in preaching & the variance in the church of England in opinions, & though[t] that much of this insurrection rose by them'. They also blamed several of the king's council for the statute dissolving the smaller monasteries which 'the north parts thought was not for the common wealth of the realm'.[234] All that was entirely coherent as a grievance.[235]

The second article urged a return to papal obedience touching the cure of souls: 'to have the supreme head of the church touching cura animarum [the cure of souls] to be reserved unto the see of Rome as before it was accustomed to be'. What exactly did that mean? This article gave rise to discussion—and since denying the royal supremacy

was treason, it is not surprising that afterwards Robert Aske and Archbishop Lee both played down their involvement in its drafting. But there
is little doubt that serious consideration was given to the practical implications of a return to papal obedience. The right to consecrate bishops
would be restored to the pope. The next clause stated that no first fruits
or pension should be paid to the pope, the clause after that allowed 'a
pension reasonable for the outward defence' of what was revealingly
described as 'our faith'. Such details would have been irrelevant unless
it was intended to renounce the royal supremacy over the church. And,
indeed, Aske admitted that, 'as touching the supremacy, they would
have annulled the whole statute, as he thinks'. All men, he continued,
'much murmured at the same, and said it could not stand with God's
law'. He delivered to Archbishop Lee 'a whole sheet of paper or more'
in Latin and another in English containing 'diverse reasons thereof
made'. 'But the great bruit in all men's mouths then', Aske insisted, 'was
that never king of England, sith the faith come in within the said realm,
claimed any such authority.' Accordingly, in their negotiations with the
duke of Norfolk they demanded the summoning of a convocation in
which 'men might with out fear and by the king's favour declare their
learning without his grace's displeasure'.[236] Elsewhere Aske played down
his involvement in the debate on the royal supremacy, saying that as far
as he could remember he knew nothing of the learned clergy's articles
until they were delivered to him in the archbishop's chamber. And then
when Aske required the archbishop's opinion touching the supreme
head, Lee declared, according to Aske, that 'touching *cura animarum* it
belonged not to the king as king but punishment of offences of sin and
such other as the head of his people that therein he was supreme head
and other such like reasons'. Aske said this was the first time he had
heard such a distinction made touching the supremacy.[237] Quite likely
Lee's response determined the final shape of the article: Aske said that
'he himself put in touching *curam animarum*, which should belong to
the bishop of Rome'.[238] But the Pilgrims were more hostile to the royal
supremacy than this wording suggests. Aske, indeed, may have been
more active in support of the papal supremacy than his recollections
reveal. According to the friar, John Pickering, in the council house
among the learned clergy Aske said[239]

> that if they lacked books as touching an answer to be made to certain
> of the articles he had in store one book of my lord of Rochester's
> making the which would help . . . saying also that except the bishop
> of Rome were head of the church in England and his laws to go

1 Hans Holbein, *Desiderius Erasmus*, *c.* 1523.

2 Hans Holbein, *William Warham, Archbishop of Canterbury,* 1527.

3 *Thomas, Cardinal Wolsey*, artist unknown.

4 *Catherine of Aragon*, *c.* 1530, artist unknown.

5 Hans Holbein, *John Fisher, bishop of Rochester*.

6 Hans Holbein, *Thomas More*, 1527.

7 *Anne Boleyn*, artist unknown.

10 Hans Holbein, *Anne of Cleves*.

11 Frontispiece of the Great Bible, 1539.

12 Girolamo da Treviso, *Four Evangelists Stoning the Pope*, c. 1542.

forward as they have done heretofore he would surely die in that quarrel.

And Aske admitted that Darcy, Sir Robert Constable and he had surely talked of the supremacy, and thought it 'doubtful by the law of God to belong to the king', though they never greatly argued about it—presumably because they were largely in agreement. Aske could remember Darcy's telling him how he had urged the Lords in parliament that this was a spiritual matter which should be referred to convocation.[240] Shagan makes much of Darcy's response to Somerset Herald who asked him whether the exclusion of the bishop of Rome's authority was 'against our faith': Darcy declared, 'by my truth I think that is not against our faith and what I spake therein to Cromwell, he knew him self well enough'. But it would be misleading to read this as Darcy agreeing with the royal supremacy. He had, after all, sworn the oath to the succession in 1534. To have openly asserted to the king's messenger that the repudiation of papal authority was against the faith would have been to commit treason, as the law stood. Darcy was much more likely a crypto-papist in sentiment: and much more in agreement with Aske than Shagan allows.[241]

Interestingly, the later interrogatories to Aske pressed him on the supremacy—no doubt because it might lay him open to charges of treason. It is not surprising that when Aske, Darcy and others were tried, it was with conspiring to deprive the king of his title of supreme head of the English church that they were charged.[242] Why did you note bishops of the new learning to be heretics and schismatics—was it not because they spoke against the bishop of Rome? Did you not account them schismatics because they maintained the king was supreme head of the church of England? Did you favour the insurrections in order that those bishops might be punished? Do you think those who consent to the king's title of supreme head are heretics?[243] And, questioned what acts of parliament they resented, Aske said 'that they grudged chiefly at the acts of suppression of abbeys and the supremacy of the church, because it was thought it should be a division from the church'.[244] He agreed that one reason why they thought several bishops schismatics was that they spoke against the bishop of Rome and his power. They wanted them deprived 'because they were supposed to be occasion of the breach of the unity of the church'.[245] Questioned about the treason act, Aske said 'they grudged against the statutes of treason for words, of the supreme head, and thought it very straight that a man might not declare his conscience in such a great case, but the same to be made treason', implicitly referring to Fisher and More.[246] Questioned about their attitude to Lady Mary's illegitimacy—the articles request that 'the lady Mary may be made legitimate'—Aske said that Mary was 'marvellously beloved for her virtue in the hearts of the people', and that he

> and all the wise men of those parts then much grudged she should so be made by the laws of this realm, seeing she on the mother side was comen of the greatest blood and par[ent] age of christendom . . . whose aunsitores [ancestors] was always, or of long time have been, great friends & favourers of the commonwealth of this realm.

More pointedly still, Aske added that 'then it was thought, that the divorce made by the bishop of Canterbury, hanging that appeal, was not lawful, yea, and then men doubted the authority of his consecration, having not his pall as his predecessors had'.[247] By implication this rejected the king's grounds for an annulment of his first marriage, and implicitly made the break with Rome unnecessary.

Not only did the Pontefract Articles accuse several bishops of heresy and call into question the king's supreme headship over the church, they also raised further religious demands. They wished 'to have the abbeys suppressed to be restored unto the houses land and goods'. That was to call for the repeal of the act dissolving the smaller monasteries. The associated demand 'to have the friars observants restored unto their houses again' was remarkable, not least since the Observants had included the earliest and most persistent principled critics of the divorce and the break with Rome. The king's northern commissioners, Dr Legh and Dr Layton, were to have condign punishment for their extortion of bribes when visiting the northern monasteries.[248] And there was also a demand for an act of parliament confirming the privileges and rights of the church, and for the repeal of recent restrictions on benefit of clergy and sanctuaries. There were also wholly secular demands, but the religious articles were by far the most contentious and those that most amounted to a revolutionary or, more exactly, counter-revolutionary programme. If anything like these articles had been accepted and acted upon by the king, the break with Rome would have been over and the religious changes that had followed would have been reversed.[249]

Criticising the royal supremacy was, as we have already noted, treasonable, so understandably its expression was often muted. Nonetheless, there are further suggestive signs that it was indeed called into question in the Pilgrimage of Grace. It is interesting that Sir Arthur Darcy, a notable loyalist, should later have referred to 'the papist errors and their kindlings' disclosed by the late commotion.[250] It is similarly revealing that the duke of Norfolk should remark at the end of March 1537 that 'the opinion of the people in these parts is clearly turned from the old belief of the bishop of Rome'.[251] A note in Cromwell's remembrances—referring to 'the apprehension of Doctor Waldby and of the conventicle in sending to the Emperor and the bishop of Rome for aid in the time of the rebellion and how that Doctor Marmaduke should have been the messenger'[252]—shows that the rebels eventually came round to sending to Charles V and the pope. Waldby confessed that he had been involved in plans to appeal to Mary of Hungary, Charles V's sister, in Flanders for money, two thousand arquebusiers and two thousand horsemen. She was also to send word to the pope that they should have absolution for all offences—which might have meant their raising rebellion, but also for all their past acquiescence in Henry's break with Rome and the royal supremacy. Waldby admitted being asked by Lord Darcy, Sir Robert Constable and Robert Aske to go as messenger; but once he got to Hull, Darcy ordered him to wait, and in the event he never left England.[253] What matters in this discussion is what it reveals about the convictions of the leaders of the rebellion. This would have been an appeal to a catholic power for military assistance against their own king. And the implications of seeking absolution from the pope are huge.

Several later incidents are also relevant in gauging the place of the royal supremacy in the Pilgrimage, and in particular in showing that it was not just a concern of Darcy and Aske. John Dakyn, archdeacon of Richmond, testified that after Christmas he told the parishioners of Richmond, where he had been parson four years previously, 'that their belief in the bishop of Rome authority was *nihil ad salutem*' (of no use for salvation). For this, 'lewd fellows of the town would have pulled me out of the church at mass time', had not some 'honest men' persuaded them not to.[254] In Kendal there was trouble at much the same time after Christmas. 'Certain lewd persons of Kendal town' who had been 'the most busy' in the rebellion 'stirred up suddenly at beads bidding and would have had the priest bid the beads the old way and pray for the pope'. William Collins, bailiff of Kendal, tried, he said, to persuade them to be still; they cried, 'down false carle, thou art false to the commons.' Eventually James Layburne, the priest, managed to persuade them for the time being to let the beads be bid in the new way. But a month later, Walter Brown, the second curate there, 'upon a tumult by divers lewd persons, said commons I will bid the beads as ye will have me, and so did and prayed for the pope and cardinals'.[255] Parson Layburne essentially confirmed that account: three hundred men and women in Kendal church threatened that the priest 'should proclaim the pope to be head of [the] church, or else they would cast him unto the water'.[256] Similarly, Robert Thompson, vicar of Brough under Stainmoor, claimed that 'it was the parishioners' commandment that I should pray for the pope for they said all places there about that they did so. . . . and so for fear of my life I durst do no other but pray for the bishop of Rome when I bade the bedes'.[257] At much the same time a bill was nailed on the door of Arncliff church, Littondale, asking Master Deyn, the vicar of Arncliff and rural dean of Craven, to bid the beads and to pray for the pope, the head of our mother church.[258] At Watton Priory, involved in Hallom-Bigod's rising, William Horsekey had heard the subprior, the nuns' confessor, the vicar and one of the canons say several times since Christmas that it would never be well as long as the king was supreme head of the church.[259] These incidents occurred between late December and early February. Did the 'lewd persons' responsible acquire their devotion to the pope and cardinals only then? Or would it be more reasonable to suppose that fear of offending against the act of treason had previously inhibited any public expression of such sentiments, which were much more widely shared?

All that was a formidably counter-revolutionary programme, a fundamental rejection of the Henrician reformation. But in order to grasp fully the nature of the Pilgrimage of Grace, we must focus more sharply on the place of the monasteries in the rebellion.

The suppression of the monasteries was clearly a vital issue north of the Humber from the start. Soon after their rising, the commons of Beverley asked a deputation from Lincolnshire on 11 October what they did with the suppressed abbeys.[260] And the fate of the monasteries recurs, as we have seen, whenever the Pilgrims stated their grievances. But what we must examine next are the actions of the Pilgrims during the rebellion: actions testify still more dramatically than words to the central purposes of the rebellion.

Against whom did the Pilgrims use force? The Yorkshire rebels attacked the houses of the local officers of the court of augmentations, the administrative department handling the suppressed monasteries. Leonard Beckwith, receiver of the augmentations in Yorkshire, complained that his house at South Cave had been spoiled; William Acclom of Moreby, Yorkshire, described how the commons seized two 'trussing bedsteads'.[261] William Blithman's house in the country was spoiled: his best bed, 'a coat of plate' and many books and writings were taken.[262] Early beneficiaries of the suppression suffered too. William Maunsell, agent to Sir Arthur Darcy (and brother of Thomas, vicar of Brayton), had acquired a large part of the estate of Holy Trinity, York and Sawley, and was farmer of the site and demesne of St Clement's, York: he was now spoiled of goods worth, he claimed, 100 marks.[263] Robert Asporner of Cotescue, Middleham, was spoiled of all his goods by the commoners: he had been in the king's service at Coverham when the insurrection broke out.[264] Such actions hint at the depth of feeling aroused by the dissolution.

Not only did the commons vent their frustrations, they also restored several of the monasteries that had recently been suppressed. A servant of Robert Hotham, receiver of the earl of Westmorland, reported early on that the Beverley and Howdenshire rebels 'would put in religious persons in their houses again and live and die in the right of God's faith and the church'.[265] Of course, given that the suppression of the smaller monasteries in Yorkshire, including the dismantling of roofs and sale of livestock, had essentially been completed in the summer, restoring monasteries would be challenging: but hardly 'a foolhardy and empty gesture'.[266] It would, after all, be perfectly possible to make good in time what had been lost; and the very act of reoccupation was highly symbolic. These restorations have of course been noticed by historians, but the evidence is scattered and often circumstantial, with the consequence that the extent of what was done has only sometimes been fully grasped, notably by Haigh. The reality, it will be suggested here, was subtle and complex. It would be easier for the historian looking back if the Pilgrims had first published and then put into practice an explicit programme. But rebellions are not like that. Inevitably they are more haphazard, more opportunistic, with much depending on local circumstances and personalities. What the Pilgrims did for the northern monasteries deserves close re-examination: from that the crucial importance of the monasteries will emerge.

It seems highly likely that the suppressed smaller monastery of North Ferriby in the East Riding was restored. At the request of the men of Swanland in the parish of Ferriby, 'seeing other houses was stayed or restraunte [?restrained]'—a remark tantalising for the modern historian— William Stapleton asked them to put two brothers in the house of North Ferriby so that nothing would be taken or destroyed, and to stay there till the fate of all the monasteries was settled. This was a measure directed against Sir William Fairfax, the farmer of the priory, thought to be intending shortly to take away the goods of the house. The commons objected to him because he would provide neither hospitality nor employment.[267] The implication of Robert Aske's later remarks in midwinter[268] is that another suppressed house in the East Riding, Haltemprice, was restored by the rebels.[269]

Several monasteries were restored in the North Riding. About Healaugh, we know from William Stapleton's testimony alone that its prior was reinstated by the commons.[270] Marmaduke Nevill would later testify how Ralph Gower and Charles Johnston, captains of the commons of Richmond, restored the canons of Coverham and put the king's commissioner to flight.[271] Marmaduke Nevill said that Gower and Johnston reinstated the canons of St Agatha's beside Richmond, also known as Easby Abbey.[272] At York, 'those knaves which be now up in Yorkshire' restored the suppressed Benedictine nunnery of St Clement's (Clementhorpe by York)[273] and Holy Trinity:[274] they seemingly remained undisbanded until October 1538.[275]

In the north-west of Yorkshire, the abbey of Sawley was restored. It had—oddly—been deemed suppressed even though it was not a small monastery by the definition of 1536; and Sir Arthur Darcy, son of Lord Darcy, had been granted its estates. The following year Sir Arthur was suspected of deception, of having said that the abbey was worth 700 marks whereas the king had since been informed that it was worth over 900 marks.[276] Sir Arthur defended himself by claiming that he did not know what Sawley was worth till he had been granted it, and that the complex exchanges of lands, of which the grant of Sawley was part, had been fairly agreed.[277] Whatever the exact rights and wrongs and values, so exceptional a procedure could hardly fail to have created a great deal of resentment. In his later examination, George Shuttleworth, servant to the abbot of Sawley, would describe how on Innocents' Day (28 December) he went to Richmond, where he was asked where he came from. When he said Sawley, 'then the men of the town . . . said fye on them that dwell nigh about that house that ever they would suffer the monks to be put out of it and that was the first house that was put down in this country'.[278] If feelings ran so strongly in neighbouring Richmondshire, it is not surprising that Sawley should have been restored in the Pilgrimage of Grace.

We first know this from the petition that the monks sent Robert Aske in late October, saying that they had 'entered unto the house by certain of the said commons the xii day of this present month'—the word 'entered' replacing the original word 'put'.[279] Bush claims that 'although the monks presented the restoration as the work of the commons and the abbot even claimed that it happened against his will, in reality the monks were artful accomplices', but that cannot be proved by the document he cites, a petition by the monastery to Aske, since, as we have just seen, it of course implies the opposite.[280] When later captured by Sir Arthur Darcy, the abbot would lay all the blame on the commons, who, he said, had put him in against his will, though obviously he was trying to present his behaviour in the best possible light.[281] Not surprisingly, Sir Arthur Darcy, deprived of his grant, complained that the religious persons 'stirred this pestilent sedition' and would have readily revived it.[282] The government very quickly condemned the monks, regarding them as to blame for the insurrection. As early as 20 October the king ordered the earl of Derby to arrest the abbot and monks of Sawley and 'without any manner of delay, in their monks apparel, cause them to be hanged up as most errant traitors and movers of insurrection and sedition', a procedure that manifestly bypassed any kind of trial.[283] It proved impractical, however, for the earl of Derby to implement the order.

Once back in possession, the abbot and monks of Sawley were dangerously active. What they did next does not necessarily show that they had instigated the reoccupation of their house, but it does reveal their determination to continue. The difficulty they faced was that their house had been suppressed several months before, and Sir Arthur Darcy had already taken steps to secure his revenues. That left the newly reinstalled abbot and monks without material support. They appealed for help accordingly. Their petition to Aske in mid-October concerned the very specific but vital matter of the tithe corn due to the monastery from St Mary's, Tadcaster, now withheld by Sir Arthur Darcy.[284] Did Aske send them in return an oath suitable for swearing, but with a tailor-made reference requiring their tenants to pay the abbot and convent—and not Sir Arthur Darcy—all such sums due?[285] Very likely Aske's intervention succeeded: Sir Arthur would complain in February that the rebels had taken his half-year's rents.[286] The abbot and convent would later also petition Sir Thomas Percy, younger brother of the earl of Northumberland and Sir Stephen Hammerton for help.[287]

More revealing about the attitudes of the monastery than such requests for material support was the ballad 'Christ Crucified', written by a Sawley monk (Skeltonic in form and language). The second verse is a scarcely veiled lament for the dissolution:

Gret Godes fame	Great God's fame
Doith Church proclame	Doth church proclaim
Now to be lame	Now to be lame
And fast in boundes	And fast in bounds
Robbyd, spoled and shorne	Robbed, spoiled and shorn

From catell and corne	From cattle and corn
And clene furth borne	And clean forth borne
Of housez and landes	Of houses and lands

The next verse began by asserting 'Which things is clear/Against God's lere'.[288]

In the north-west two smaller houses that had duly been suppressed were also involved in the rebellion. Conishead had been suppressed by mid-September 1536. By 16 October the monks were back in the house. We do not know whether they were reinstated by the commons or by their own initiative.[289] The monks certainly appealed for assistance. On the Monday before St Luke's day (18 October, so this must be 16 October) the prior and convent of Conishead sent William Collins, bailiff of Kendal, and others, a letter asking them to come the next day—or else, they feared, all they had should be taken from them.[290] The government, Haigh argues (because of the way it was referred to in subsequent interrogatories), thought that the rebellion in Lancashire was begun by this letter.[291] But did the government know that Conishead had been restored before the revolt collapsed?[292] A list of those to be tried for their part in the rebellion included 'the whole convent of Conishead' and William Collins of Kendal, but both were crossed out,[293] and none of the Conishead canons was tried. They were rather allowed to leave their monastery in peace.

Cartmel was also restored. At its suppression, eight monks had expressed a wish to go to other houses, but they were all issued with capacities instead: 'it is hardly surprising that they were all later indicted for helping the rebels'.[294] The exact circumstances in which the monks returned are not known. The prior, however, was put back by the commons of Cartmel against his will, according to the earl of Derby on 1 November. The prior then stole away to the earl at Preston before news came of the truce that had been agreed in Yorkshire.[295] Renewed efforts would be made, as we shall see, to get the prior to return to his house in December. On the face of it, this monastery was restored at the initiative of the commons.

Just as in Lincolnshire, larger monasteries in Yorkshire and in the north-west, not falling within the provisions of the act dissolving the smaller monasteries, were called upon for material support, and abbots and monks were threatened if they did not agree. Once more, this should not be read as evidence of the commons' hostility or indifference to monasteries: such pressures were aimed at those who would not help the cause, and no doubt, if challenged, the Pilgrims would have claimed they acted for the monasteries' greater good. According to George Lumley, Lord Lumley's son and heir, Sir Nicholas Fairfax declared 'that the same matter that they rose for was a matter for the defence of the faith and a spiritual matter'—itself a significant comment—'wherefore he thought meet that the priors and abbots and other men of the church should not only send aid unto them but also go forth in their own persons'. For that reason he had gone to the houses of St Mary's, York, Newburgh, Byland, Rievaulx, Whitby, Malton and Kirkham, and sent servants to Mount Grace, Bridlington and Gisburn, to persuade the abbots or priors, together with two brethren from each house, to come forward with their best crosses.[296] What the rebels sought, in addition to food, drink and money, was the presence of abbots and monks, not to fight, but to show their commitment to the cause. Some abbots were, they said, reluctant to go in person or allow their brethren to do so, but they generally sent financial and material assistance. Some claimed to have been intimidated and to have acquiesced under threats—but their pleas would not be believed by the government. According to Fairfax, they all said they could not come in person but would send aid. In fact, reactions were more complex than that, and not always easy to discern, since we must usually rely on later depositions. If the experiences and the extent of involvement of different monasteries varied, it is clear that several were intimately caught up in the rebellion; throughout, the commons manifestly saw the fate of monasteries as important, as the restoration of several suppressed houses shows.

That is suggested even more strongly by the negotiations between the duke of Norfolk and the earl of Shrewsbury on behalf of the king and the Pilgrim leaders at Doncaster in December. The fate of the monasteries was central. Norfolk, Shrewsbury, Fitzwilliam and Russell were forced to compromise with the Pilgrims: they failed to divide the rebels, and they were too weak to contemplate a military solution. The terms of the compromise are instructive.

Norfolk granted a free general pardon to the rebels, without excepting any ringleaders as the king had originally and passionately demanded before giving way to the advice of his council.[297] What the Pilgrims were granted on the substance of their demands was a promise by Norfolk that he would be a suitor to the king that a parliament should be held at York. In the articles brought from Yorkshire in early November by Sir Ralph Ellerker and Robert Bowes, the Pilgrims had called for a pardon of any offences they might have committed to be granted by the authority of parliament. Consequently they had called for a parliament to be held.[298] In early December Henry referred back to these demands: 'of likelihood the rebels will then show themselves very stiff and wilful touching the two points before specified of the free pardon and the parliament'.[299] That the holding of a parliament had become accepted as a likely outcome of the rebellion is clear. Sir Anthony Wingfield reported on 26 November that the Pilgrims would have parliament kept where they might safely come and go. The Pilgrims' Pontefract Articles included the request 'to have the parliament in a convenient place at Nottingham or York and the same shortly summoned'.[300] Darcy had emphasised the importance of parliament in a letter to Norfolk on 11 November, in which he asserted that the best way of staying the people would be for the king's answer to their articles to be declared to the lords and gentlemen at a meeting at York, 'and most specially, if it may stand with the king's pleasure that there may be a parliament appointed therein, which is the thing that they most desire and rest upon'.[301] The reason for the rebels' desire for a free and general pardon is obvious enough, but their demand for a parliament is more intriguing. Why did they want a parliament?

In the articles agreed after the first Doncaster meeting, the holding of parliament was directly linked to the rebels' desire that the pardon should be granted by the authority of parliament.[302] But by the second Doncaster agreement, the rebels intended rather more. The implication of the summoning of a parliament in such circumstances was that the legislation of the most recent parliaments of which the rebels disapproved would be reversed. That might well have included the royal supremacy and taxation. It would undoubtedly have included the repeal of the act for the dissolution of the smaller monasteries.

John Dakyn, archdeacon of Richmond, admitted that the Pilgrims sought 'by the means of a parliament to compass the alteration of some things from their present estate'; from the tone of the questions to which Dakyn was responding, the government believed that too. But Dakyn insisted—somewhat disingenuously—that he had been content with laws recently made, arguing that if many learned divines said that a government measure was not against God's law, and if it were commanded by the king through an act of parliament, then it could safely be obeyed.[303] But anonymous advice drawn up for the rebels before these negotiations countered precisely that argument, specifically rejecting royal claims that the dissolution of monasteries was valid because legislation had been passed by parliament.[304]

Where it is alleged that the king hath authority granted him by parliament to suppress these abbeys, I think that these parliaments was of none authority nor virtue, for if these should be truly named, they should be called councils of the king's appointment, and not parliaments, for parliaments ought to have the knights of shire and burgesses of the towns at their own election that could reason for the wealth of the shire or town, that he . . . not such men as the king will appoint for his priva[te] lucre.

The implication was that a new parliament—not manipulated by the king—might be expected to work differently, and to reverse the detested laws.

The king and Cromwell may well have seen the concession of a parliament as no more than a formal guarantee of the grant of a free pardon—a meeting of parliament was 'not comprised in their articles but named only for the surety of their pardon', the king insisted.[305] Gardiner and Wallop, the king's ambassadors in France, were similarly informed that the rebels' first condition was a pardon, and that the chief article after their pardon was for a parliament to confirm it.[306] The government tried to weasel its way out, denying that the Pilgrims had actually been granted a parliament. Indeed, it was agreed, they had petitioned to obtain certain articles, but[307]

in the end they went from all and remitted all to the king's highness pleasure only in most humble and reverent sort desiring their pardon with the great repentance that could be devised in so much as in their chief articles which next their pardon was for a parliament for that they might have their pardon confirmed they remitted the appointment of the same wholly to the king's majesty without the naming of time place or any other thing touching that matter.

But that was not how the Pilgrims saw it by the time of the second Doncaster agreement. As Aske later explained, 'upon communication had between them and my lord of Norfolk at Doncaster, the said examinate [Aske], lords, gentlemen, and commons concluded at Pontefract for a reformation to be had of the said statutes by parliament'.[308]

An intriguing undated document, 'Devises for the appeasing and quieting of the commons in the north parts', has been seen by Bush as the work of Darcy.[309] In it the suggestion was made that the king should summon a parliament and declare that if anyone could prove any act of parliament or order of council passed in his reign contrary to the laws of God or the commonwealth, then he would see it reformed. The implications are far-reaching.

However that may be, at Doncaster in December Norfolk did not simply agree to a free pardon and a parliament, which is what he judged to be the minimum necessary to appease the rebels.[310] He also agreed that until that parliament met at York, abbeys should stand and religious persons should have 'victum and vestitum' of their monasteries (we shall return to that) till further direction was taken. No formal record of the second Doncaster agreement survives; indeed, none may ever have been made.[311] But its terms may readily be inferred from the king's immediate response to Fitzwilliam and Russell,[312] and his later instructions to the duke of Norfolk and the earl of Sussex.[313] To Fitzwilliam and Russell Henry expressed his dismay[314] that they had not managed to achieve

> that thing which we do most desire . . . the reservation of some persons to have punishment for the example of others, nor to appease the fury of the commons unless we should condescend to the standing of such abbeys as in those parts be to be suppressed by virtue of the act of parliament passed for that purpose.

This shows both how central the abbeys were to the rebellion and how determined Henry was on the suppression. The king clearly understood what Norfolk had conceded at Doncaster as a substantial reverse, not some technicality.[315] His somewhat truculent querying whether concessions on the abbeys were really necessary to calm the fury of the commons makes this clear:[316]

> We cannot a little marvel at the contents of the same [letters] being written in such a desperate sort as though it were neither possible to finish that matter with the accomplishment of any part of that thing which we do most desire that is with the reservation of some persons to sore punishment for the example of others nor to appease the fury of the commons unless we should condescend to the standing of such abbeys as in those partes be to be suppressed by virtue of the act of parliament passed for that purpose

That bears out other evidence for their importance in the Doncaster compromise.

According to Aske's later testimony, in the negotiations at Doncaster 'the commons there appointed reasoned much for abbeys and specially for the possession thereof to the parliament time of the king's farmers'.[317] Hoyle rightly wonders whether Aske meant this: what he

presumably accepted was that the king's farmers should have possession till the parliament met.[318] When the proposed terms of the agreement had first been reported back to the commons, Lord Lumley at once
sent a letter saying 'how the said commons would not be contented
except they saw the king's most merciful pardon under seal and'—
significantly—'that the abbots new put in of [restored to] houses
suppresse[d] should not avoid their possession to the parliament time'
and that the parliament should be held at York, or else they would burn
beacons and raise the whole country.[319] And the explicit commitment
made at Doncaster that abbeys should stand with their monks having
'victum and vestitum'—which was no doubt understood by the Pilgrims
as much more than a temporary expedient—was the only one of
their grievances to be dealt with specifically, vividly illustrating its
fundamental importance in the rising. It was the fate of the abbeys, and
the particular procedures by which that fate should be resolved, rather
than other religious issues, rather than taxation, rather than the
king's councillors, that was the most detailed sticking point for the
commons.

Norfolk had no authority to call a parliament himself (though
the king had already, if reluctantly, willed him to condescend to a
parliament to be held at such place as the king would appoint next
Michaelmas),[320] so technically he could agree to no more than going as
a suitor to the king. Earlier, the king, commenting on any promises
Norfolk might make to stay the rebels until his forces came, had trusted
that 'in all your proceedings you will have such a temperance as our
honour specially shall remain untouched and yours rather increased
than by the certain grant of that you cannot certainly promise appear
in the mouths of the worst men any thing defaced'.[321] But manifestly the
Pilgrims, believing that Norfolk was negotiating in good faith, took it
that, whatever the technicalities, the king would, without further question, agree to what the duke sought on their behalf. They did not think
that all they had done was humbly to accept a gracious royal pardon.
When Norfolk agreed that there should be a parliament at York and
that meanwhile abbeys would stand, they must have thought that the
outcome of their rebellion was victory.[322] A little later, in referring to
'the articles now concluded upon at Doncaster', Aske showed his conviction that the Pilgrims had secured a mechanism by which their grievances would be remedied.[323] Although Aske knelt when making his
obeisance before Norfolk, it was in a spirit of triumph, not submission,
that he and the others pulled off their badges and crosses with the five
wounds of Christ, and the commons dispersed.[324]

Hoyle's claim that at Doncaster the gentry leaders of the Pilgrimage together with the duke of Norfolk 'wound up the Pilgrimage of Grace in return for a pardon, a number of ill-defined promises to assuage the commons, and the promise of a parliament' is misleading. Hoyle argues that the leaders of the Pilgrimage who put together the articles at Pontefract did so as a 'gesture' intended to impress the commons. But his reasoning—'they never made for practical politics' because the king would never agree to them—does not persuade. And he goes on to present the Doncaster agreement as a successful operation by both the duke of Norfolk and the leaders of the Pilgrimage to secure the disbanding of the commons—'a cynical exercise to disperse the Pilgrims'. Undoubtedly that is what Norfolk sought; and he made concessions that the king thought excessive in order to bring it about. But that is not what Aske and Darcy and the leaders of the Pilgrimage were seeking. Of course, they wanted a return to normality: noblemen and gentlemen did not want to see large and protracted assemblies of the commons. But there is little doubt that they were committed to the articles of grievances prepared at Pontefract, and that they fully expected that what irked them would shortly be reformed. They believed that the king would take wiser counsels and that a parliament to be held shortly in the north would reform what was amiss. Hoyle's puzzlement that no celebratory ballads were written is misplaced: since there seemed to be no further need to mobilise large numbers of people, such ballads were no longer necessary. More generally, there is a contradiction between Hoyle's splendid emphasis on the coercion of the gentry by the commons at the beginning of the rebellion, and what on his account was the gentry's sudden acquisition of the power to weaken, neutralise and disperse the commons in December.[325]

On 18 December Darcy sent Archbishop Lee

> a letter signed by the king which was, as my lords at Doncaster did affirm, sent to my lord of Canterbury and others, wherein all true catholics may joy and ye, and others clerks take comfort to utter and set forth the truth and true learning with his grace's favour.

It is hard to read that other than as a hint that Henry was preparing to make religious concessions, and that Darcy, seeing himself as a 'true catholic', welcomed them.[326]

Archbishop Lee, himself no rebel (if not without some sympathy for the rebels' desires), wrote to Cromwell on 9 December that he was very glad that the king had condescended to the pardon and—a significant further point—to the requests of the northern men: there was now some hope of quiet again. Lee did not specify those requests, though he went on to blame the commotions on the collection of clerical taxation and warned against resuming it. But his letter makes it quite plain that the Pilgrims had not simply accepted a pardon.[327] 'The requests of the northern men' amounted to much more than a promise that a parliament would be held.[328] And later he recalled having said to Aske, just before the latter set off for the Doncaster meeting, 'that for monasteries, if it were true that was spoken, that the king's highness would be content to take some order for them, that I thought ways might be devised that his highness should lose no thing although they stood'.[329]

Marmaduke Nevile, Lord Latimer's brother, boldly declared how 'all abbeys in England be beholden to us, for we have set up all the abbeys again in our country, and though it were never so late they sang mattins the same night'.[330] John Dakyn, vicar-general of the archdeaconry of Richmond, said that 'at my departing from Pontefract it was parlayed as I heard say and also at York when I came there it was voiced in every man's mouth that the abbeys should stand in such manner as they were put in unto the next parliament'.[331] On the second Sunday of Advent (10 December), signing himself as vicar-general, he wrote from York to the priors of Cartmel and Conishead how[332]

order is taken that all religious persons by the king's highness consent shall enter their suppressed houses again and there remain until a further direction be taken by parliament as the gentlemen and other your neighbours can show you. I exhorte you so to do without any further delay, and doubt you not but such order shall be taken as I trust you shall there remain and your monasteries stand for ever.

It is quite plain that he was not making up that order but acting on what he believed had been agreed at Doncaster. Under interrogation, Dakyn later said he had not kept a copy, but as he remembered he had written to this effect:[333]

That for so much as all religious persons in the north parts had entered their houses by putting in of the commons, and as I am informed you meaning the prior of Cartmel being required so to enter do withdraw your self. I think you may safely enter and do as other do keeping your self quiet for the season, and to pray for the king. And at the next parliament than to do as shall be determined. And I have no doubt but so doing you may continue in the same with the grace of god who keep you.

He later, while regretting his 'simplicity', insisted that his letter was written 'at another man's instant desire', 'grounded upon the communication at Doncaster, as it was then and there openly voiced and parlayed'. He excused himself further by affirming that by saying that he referred his trust and confidence to the order of the parliament 'which can not be but indifferent', and by advising the prior of Cartmel to pray for the king, he showed clearly that he was not intending any commotion or insurrection or other sedition against Henry.[334] When he added that 'to say truly my affection and desire was ever that if God and the king's highness were pleased (and by those terms I expressed my mind and none otherwise) that no abbey should have been suppressed',[335] he showed, as he had in his letter when he said he trusted that their monasteries should stand for ever,[336] that he could distinguish between what he understood had already been agreed—an immediate return of monks to dissolved houses—and what he trusted would ensue—the abandonment of the policy of suppression.[337]

Dakyn, the duke of Norfolk later testified, had been a loyalist, even though he had written out the rebels' articles concerning the spirituality:[338] 'at the first insurrection no priest in these parts stuck more firmly to the king's part than he'—he was 'diverse times in danger of his life therefore, and was once fain to give money out of his purse to save his life and yet was diverse times spoiled'.[339] Dakyn's testimony was that of someone loyal to the king but sympathetic to the cause of the rebels. And his letter demonstrates how, after their deal with Norfolk, the Pilgrims must have thought that they had won.

Similarly at Newcastle, the Observant friars re-entered their house in December, after Norfolk's departure south. The mayor reported how to his chagrin he had had to suffer the friars—'our ungodly and dissembling knaves'—to enter their house, since Sir Thomas Hilton and others supported them and would have quarrelled with those who resisted it: allowing them in was against the mayor's will, but by permitting it he hoped to preserve the town without strife, and so keep a good part of the country quiet.[340] Evidently in Newcastle Sir Thomas Hilton believed that the Doncaster agreement implied that religious houses would be safe.

What the general principle that abbeys should stand till the next parliament obviously did not clarify, however, was what should happen to individual houses that had been reoccupied by monks during the rebellion. What was the position of their 'farmers'—those laymen who had taken leases of the sites and lands of such monasteries? Were they to be reinstated, at least for the time being, until the future of the monasteries was permanently settled? That is implied by Cromwell's later letter regretting that the gentlemen had not performed their promises lately made to Norfolk concerning the delivery of the possession of the suppressed houses of religion to those whom the king had appointed as their farmers.[341] Norfolk could refer to 'the promise, made at all our last being at Doncaster, that the nobles should put the king's farmers in possession of the religious houses to be suppressed', though noting at the same time that none of the northern nobility and gentry had dared to act on that promise.[342] Once again the fate of the abbeys appears an integral part of the Doncaster compromise.

But the potential for friction was considerable and there was trouble in several places. William Collins, bailiff of Kendal, later testified how because 'certain farmers of priories ... showing him how diverse brethren took away their corn from them and therefore like to have been murder between them about the same', Clarencieux Herald

> gave commandment openly in the king's name upon pain of high treason that commanded in king's name that no man should disturb any man about the possession of lands tithes or farms, but that they should be in like case as they were at the last meeting at Doncaster and to continue till the duke of Norfolk come again to the country.

It is interesting that a royal herald should announce a delay in the implementation of what Norfolk thought had been agreed at Doncaster. Two of the brethren of Cartmel arrived and asked him to write the order out for them 'that they might show it to their neighbours'—the herald asked Collins to do so, which he did.

> Neighbours of Cartmel, so it is that the king's herald hath made a proclamation here that every man, on pain of high treason, should suffer every thing as farms, tithes and such other to be in like stay and order concerning possessions as they were in time of the last meeting at Doncaster except ye will of your charity help the brethren somewhat toward their board till my lord of Norfolk come again and take further order therein.

Collins then delivered the letter.[343]

It seems as if a sort of legal fiction was staged in some places, with monks formally accepting the dissolution of their houses but at once re-entering them until the next parliament—not by their own wills or by the pressure of the commons, but ostensibly by royal authority.[344] Aske and Sir Thomas Percy both advised the abbot of Sawley at Christmas that he should not resist anyone who came in the king's name to put them out of possession.[345] Aske was clearly anxious to observe the letter of what had been agreed at Doncaster strictly, to avoid any misunderstanding. Indeed, he may have been more directly involved in these procedures since he later described how he had gone to Sir Robert Constable's house to meet Sir Ralph Ellerker 'for the putting in of the king's farmers into the abbeys of Haltomprice and Ferriby'.[346] But in no way does this imply that Aske now knew that the king would not let monasteries stand.[347]

In the weeks that followed, some monasteries were involved in further troubles. Sir Henry Savile informed Cromwell on 29 January how religious houses 'kept nothing their injunctions but uses still their old fashions and says the commons caused them to break them'. The abbot of Kirkstall (who had been among the 'learned clergy' at Pontefract immediately before the Doncaster agreement)[348] had 'made a fray' since the pardon against Sir Christopher Danby's servants: several on both sides, including a monk or two, had been hurt. He suggested that the abbot be deposed.[349] It is quite clear that the defence of the monasteries remained a central concern after the Doncaster agreement. George Shuttleworth, a servant of the abbot of Sawley, was told at Richmond on 29 December: 'rather than our house of Saint Agatha [Easby] should go down, we shall all die; and if any insurrection should happen here again, where there was but one in the same before, now there would be three'.[350] Darcy's servant Parker reported after Christmas that 'all the north country is in a readiness if any man will put out the monks of Sawley'.[351] Darcy reported on 19 January 1537 how the commons wanted no abbeys pulled down nor any taxes paid till after the parliament.[352] Sir William Fairfax informed Cromwell on 22 January how 'the houses of religion not suppressed be most apt to make friends and wag the poor to stick hard in this opinion'; and how the former monks from suppressed houses now lived in the villages around their houses and daily laboured to 'wag' the people to put them in again. There would never be peace, he claimed, so long as the spiritual men had so much temporal power.[353]

Nothing as widespread as the commotions of the autumn occurred in January or February, though there were potentially serious outbreaks of discontent. What these well show is the continuing importance of the fate of the monasteries.

In January there was a rising in the East Riding of Yorkshire, involving Sir Francis Bigod and John Hallom. It foundered when John Hallom's attempt to take Hull was successfully resisted by the mayor and aldermen on 16 January, especially John Eland and William Knowles, who, like Hallom, were seriously injured in the skirmishes.[354] Between 16 and 18 January Bigod raised some commons, initially intending to take Scarborough, but then moving south in the hope of rectifying the failure at Hull, though with lamentable confusion: the attempted rebellion barely happened.[355] What underlay all this was the general fear that the king would not honour the Doncaster agreement, which, as we have seen, singled out the monasteries. A surviving undated manifesto, which most probably reflects Bigod's and Hallom's grievances, gives a prominent place to the fate of the monasteries. Its first article declared how the suppressed abbeys had been restored by the commons, not by the agreement at Doncaster. Another article attacked farmers of suppressed monasteries who had taken possession, sold their goods and then left the region.[356] Watton Priory was involved in the abortive rising. Bigod and Hallam met there on 10 January:[357] three canons would later be arrested for their part in events.[358]

Further north, there were rumblings in the North Riding of Yorkshire, especially in Massamshire. Asked what was the cause, Ninian Staveley described how two monks of Jervaulx Abbey, Roger Hartlepool (who later fled to Scotland) and John Stainton (who would be executed), had between Christmas and Candlemas urged Edward Middleton (who also fled to Scotland) and Staveley himself to raise men against the duke of Norfolk, with the intention of destroying him, claiming 'that if he were destroyed, their abbey should stand as it did and so should holy church in such state, as it was in king Henry the viith days'. If the duke came into the country and remained there—a phrase such as 'without challenge' is implied—'their abbey should be put down and they should go a begging'. By Sunday, 28 January, Hartlepool and Stainton had won over Staveley and Middleton. Together they prepared bills to be set on church doors throughout Richmondshire, calling on all men aged between sixteen and sixty to appear in harness at Middleham Moor on 30 January 'under the pain of death'. Then Hartlepool and Stainton asked first the monks, then the abbot, for money: 'all that they went about was for their wealth and preservation of their house,' they insisted. The abbot referred them to the quondam abbot of Fountains, William Thirsk, resident in retirement at Jervaulx, who gave them two angels and promised them more once that was spent.[359] Staveley and Middleton[360] claimed that they 'were in full mind to meddle no further with the said insurrection'. But the monks came at midnight to Staveley's house in harness and carrying battleaxes, and forced him to rise from his bed, threatening that, if he would not go forward with them, they would all be destroyed. Staveley and Middleton and their friends, ten strong, then went to Jervaulx Abbey. The abbot asked them to leave his brethren at home, promising that they would all come the next day. He gave them meat and drink. Thirsk was there, and asked Staveley and Middleton

> that in case there should be any new insurrection, they would help to put him into his room at Fountains again promising them xx nobles if they so did. And he showed them that they might do it with good conscience, seeing he was put out of his abbey by the visitors without just cause.

The abbot of Jervaulx and Thirsk had earlier urged Staveley and others to persuade Sir Thomas Percy to come forward with such company as he could make and 'they wold mete with him with such as they could make'. Another muster took place at Richmond. It was agreed that all bailiffs and constables of Richmondshire, the bishopric (of Durham), Cleveland and Westmorland should be ordered to send two men from every parish to assemble at Richmond the day after Candlemas to determine how they would meet the duke of Norfolk. The gathering evidently took place. But because so many gentlemen had already gone to meet Norfolk, no decisions were taken.

Why was there such concern in Richmondshire? Staveley recalled how it had been agreed that the abbot of Jervaulx would send his servant Simon Jackson to Lincolnshire, on pretence of gathering rents, but really to stay near Newark, and then 'to bring word after whether the duke came in harness or forth of harness with a great company or with a small'. The word that Jackson then brought was that the Lincolnshire men were 'busily hanged and that their charter stood them in no stead'. He 'showed that the duke wold deal with these of the north parts as the Lincolnshire men were handled'. Not surprisingly, Jackson's report, together with the urgings of Hartlepool and Stainton, the former monks 'were the special causes and occasions of the last insurrection in Richmondshire'.[361] In particular, that news of repression in Lincolnshire should have sown the seeds of doubt in Yorkshire seems eminently plausible.

Much of this was confirmed by William Thirsk. About the beginning of Lent he had been in his chamber at Jervaulx Abbey. First he had reluctantly acceded to demands for money, giving Middleton an angel noble, and then another when they said it was cracked. Staveley, he claimed, had said, 'ye churlish monks, ye have too much, and we have nothing, and neither of these thou gettest again'; Thirsk had insisted, 'if ye be true men ye will not take my money away'. But when a week later Staveley and Middleton returned in harness and urged him and the abbot of Jervaulx (Thirsk was in the abbot's chamber) 'on pain of death, and all their brethren and servants to go with them to Middelham More forthwith', both were reluctant. 'It was not mete that religious men should go about any such business'. they claimed, and, as for himself, Thirsk asked to be let alone, since he was old and feeble. But they agreed to go nonetheless. 'Many other of the commons were in the hall and about the house.' The quondam abbot denied, however, that he had ever encouraged Staveley and Middleton, if there was a new insurrection, to reinstate him as abbot of Fountains, or that he was privy to the sending to Sir Thomas Percy, as they alleged. He had been in London during the first insurrection and could say nothing about it.[362]

The abbot of Jervaulx offered a less incriminating account: he had lost thirty sheep, and had asked Middleton ('because he was a hunter') to make inquiries; Middleton had no luck, but since he had taken trouble, the abbot gave him 2s. or 3s. 4d. for his labour. Four or five days later Middleton returned with Staveley and many more; Staveley complaining that the abbot had deceived them. They wanted him to come together with several of his monks. The abbot refused, but against his will Staveley and Middleton took some of his servants with them. Realising that they were meeting in great numbers at Richmond, he went instead to the safety of Bolton Castle and Lord Scrope, waiting there till news came that the commons had dispersed.[363]

A bill circulating at Richmond on 19 January called for the commons to rise and to make the lords and gentlemen swear on the mass book to four articles. The quasi-religious ceremony is itself striking. The first article was 'to maintain the profit of holy church', which was 'the upholding of the christian faith'. The third article called on them to put down Cromwell, 'that heretic and all his sect the which made the king put down praying and fasting'. The other two articles reflected distrust of lords and gentlemen, declaring that none should go to London or take anything from their tenants except their rents.[364] But when the commons from Wensleydale, Dent, Sedbergh and Mashamshire attempted to meet at Richmond on 5 February, Norfolk succeeded in preventing them,[365] by sending 'such sharp messages' to Richmondshire and Middleham that he thought they would be afraid to meet.[366] Bush notes the absence of lords and gentlemen,[367] but the point is as much that the commons did not gather in sufficient strength and for sufficient time to put pressure on lords and gentlemen in the way that they had in October.

The other substantial rising in early 1537 culminated in an attempt by the commons to besiege Carlisle in early February. We are relatively less well informed on this than on other incidents in the rebellion, which no doubt accounts for its relative neglect in the historiography until its treatment by Bush and Bownes.[368] But it proved something of a turning point. The duke of Norfolk, sent northwards, but with only his own household servants, not an army, to deal with what the king saw as the aftermath of the revolt, found himself facing a renewed military threat. Had that succeeded, matters would have been very serious indeed for Henry VIII's government. On 12 January the earl of Cumberland had warned the king and Cromwell that the people in Cumberland, Westmorland and adjoining parts of Yorkshire were so wild that there was danger of further rebellion: 'albeit in case the commons in these quarters break again then I fear me your grace's town and castle of Carlisle shall be in great jeopardy both of the commons and of the Scots.' The walls of both town and castle were much decayed and could not stand a siege without aid.[369] On 21 January Sir Thomas Curwen reported that the west of Cumberland was more rebellious than ever both in words and deeds: he had been in danger of his life after the commons had taken him to Cockermouth on suspicion that he had letters from the king. There were rumours that the commons were assembling to attack Carlisle.[370] On 29 January Sir Henry Savile reported that from Sawley abbey northwards 'they are somewhat wild'.[371] On 2 February Norfolk noted that the gentry of Cumberland and Westmorland were not yet able to rule their counties;[372] and on 4 February that Westmorland and Cockermouth were 'in great disobedience'.[373]

On 14 February Norfolk reported troubles at Kirkby Stephen two days earlier, when attempts were made by Thomas Clifford, bastard son of the earl of Cumberland, to arrest two men, Nicholas Musgrave and Thomas Tibbey, who controlled the steeple. Clifford's horsemen spoiled the town; the inhabitants defended their goods; one or two were killed in skirmishes; and Clifford retired to Brougham Castle.[374] That led to a rising of some four or five thousand, provoked, Norfolk thought, by the mishandling of the enterprise.[375] If Thomas Clifford had not brought with him border thieves, and if they had not spoiled the town, this rising would not have happened, Norfolk insisted on 16 February. A day earlier he had been informed that the commons were moving towards Carlisle.[376]

What then did these commons seek? Clearly immediate events and fears had precipitated their actions. The commons did not issue any manifesto, so far as we know, or specify their demands: everything happened too quickly for that. But that what they were doing once again very much concerned the defence of the monasteries may be seen from the remarks of the abbot of Holme Cultram. As the commons began the siege of Carlisle, the abbot allegedly called upon Almighty God, 'prosper them, for if they speed not, this abbot is lost'. He commanded Cuthbert Musgrave and his tenants to ride to the commons the day before they laid siege to Carlisle. And one of charges later laid against the abbot claimed that all the insurrection there was owing to him. It is remarkable that the commons should have responded so vigorously to the abbot's fears. Since this rebellion happened after the royal pardon granted in December, the abbot was vulnerable to charges of treason, though there is no record of any execution. But his role and his remarks are sufficient to call into question Bush's dismissal of the enterprise against Carlisle that 'it merely revealed Cumberland society behaving in its normal manner'.[377]

On 15 February, Norfolk, learning how the commons were preparing to assault Carlisle, urged and pleaded with Sir Christopher Dacre (to whom he had already written the day before) to do what would deserve the king's favour. He would not instruct him on what to do, for he would know that better than Norfolk. But Norfolk did not hesitate to urge Sir Christopher,

> spare not frankly to slay plenty of these false rebels. And make true mine old sayings that Sir Christopher is a true knight to his sovereign lord, an hardy knight, and a man of war. Pinch now no courtesy to shed blood of false traitors. Finally Sir Christopher, now or never: your loving cousin if ye do well now, or else enemy for ever.[378]

Sir John Lowther, Thomas Clifford and John Barnfield commanded Sir Christopher Dacre to come to join them in Carlisle Castle with as many men as he could trust.[379] Norfolk would later reveal the extent of the threat: there was no lord or gentleman of Westmorland and Cumberland whose servants and tenants had not joined in this new rebellion;[380] when the rising was over, no fewer than six thousand submitted.[381] On 16 February Norfolk wrote anxiously to Cromwell from Richmond, having 'with me the best parte of the nobles and gentlemen of this shire with a good band of chosen men, not daring to assemble the people of the country, for I know not how they be established in their hearts notwithstanding that their words can be no better'. That Norfolk should have felt unable to raise the commons shows how difficult his position was. He assured Cromwell,

> doubt not my Lord that I will adventure any thing without good likelihood. I know too well what danger it should be to the [w]hole realm if we were overthrow. . . . If my Lord Dacre's company come to mine aid, we shall beat them with ease and without great loss.

If not, then Norfolk intended to keep them in play with his horsemen, avoiding any losses.[382] In fact, William, Lord Dacre, was at Doncaster on 19 February when he heard that the rebels of Cumberland and Westmorland threatened Carlisle; he took horse, but got to Carlisle on Tuesday, 20 February, after the rebels had already been dispersed.[383] Meanwhile Norfolk was expecting to have to fight. What saved him from that, and what may have contributed greatly to stabilising Henry VIII's throne, was neither 'the work of Norfolk',[384] nor Norfolk's success at raising a force of four thousand led by nobles and gentry by 17 February,[385] but the bold action of Sir Christopher Dacre in response to the commons' onslaught. 'When they gave the assault to Carlisle and being put back, like a good knight [he] set upon them and hath taken as they that were there say above vii or viii c.' Sir Thomas Clifford, captain of Berwick, 'hath made a bloody chase'. That gave the duke of Norfolk the opportunity to hasten there and 'do such execution that others shall have cause to be afraid'.[386] Dacre's instinctive, bold and ruthless charge against the commons outside Carlisle was the first, and the last, violent encounter in the rebellion. The emergency (and the situation at Carlisle in mid-February was a true emergency) was suddenly over. The consequences of the failure of the commons were profound.[387] But the depth of the failure should not make it seem in any way inevitable: it is easy to envisage a very different scenario, in which the commons—some six thousand strong according to Norfolk[388]—captured Carlisle, perhaps if its garrison had yielded after some botched attempt at relief. And that would have had a devastating effect. Conversely, one might look back to the Yorkshire rebels' occupation of York in October: suppose that York had resisted their advance—as Exeter would resist the rebels in 1549—and suppose a Yorkshire equivalent of Dacre had then ridden out against the commons and dispersed them in the way that Sir

Christopher had. Norfolk would reveal his gratitude in later letters in support of those who had won the day. He praised Roger Middlewood as 'the first man that issued out of the town and slew one [of the rebels] with his own hands'.[389] Three months later he would endorse Robert Graham's petition for freedom from rent: he was the first man, even though he only had two men with him, who 'began with the commons afore the assault to Carlisle', and the first 'that ever broke spear' upon any of the commons after they gave the assault to Carlisle; he continued crying and shouting at them for more than an hour before he received support. He helped put the rebels to flight and captured seven score.[390] And the smashing of the commons outside Carlisle proved to be the end of the northern risings.

Throughout this study, emphasis has been placed upon religion, and especially the place of the monasteries. At this point two misleading interpretations that minimise the significance of the dissolution must be dealt with directly. M.L. Bush offers an extraordinarily perverse reading of the place of monasteries in events.[391] 'By now,' he writes of the period after the Doncaster compromise, 'the restored religious houses were a pawn in the power struggle between the crown and the pilgrims.' That implies that the dispute between king and rebels was over power, and that the monasteries, far from being a central issue, were no more than a bargaining counter. 'It was of vital strategic importance to the rebels', says Bush, 'that the religious remained in occupation until the matter' (Bush does not say what that consisted of)

> had been determined by the York parliament, because, arguably, if the restored religious abandoned their houses beforehand, the rebels' bargaining position would be seriously weakened. Hence the rebels' determination that 'the abbeys should stand until the next parliament'. The evidence of December 1536 and February 1537 therefore offers inadequate proof of what the commons actually did to restore the two houses in October and how they felt at the time about their suppression.

That is astonishingly contrary. There is nothing whatever to suggest that the religious were unclear about their position, except for some of the abbots and priors who, while sympathetic to the commons, were understandably nervous of committing treason. The continuation of the religious houses was not a 'bargaining position'; it was a fundamental demand. Curiously, at one point Bush, contradicting himself, half-recognises this by saying that 'on the other hand, for the region the general issue of dissolution was undoubtedly a matter of concern and a cause for revolt'.[392]

Another tack taken by some historians is to draw large conclusions from the fact that only some of the northern monasteries already suppressed were restored during the rebellion. Scott Harrison notes that, of the nine smaller monasteries in Westmorland and Cumberland, one had already been exempted, and only three of the remaining eight, Conishead, Cartmel and (on the strength of a reference in a letter from the king alone) Lanercost, were involved in the commotions: Armathwaite, Seaton, Wetheral, St Bees and Calder were, as far as we know, unaffected.[393] For Harrison, the involvement of Conishead and Cartmel, and the sympathy of the larger monasteries of Furness, Holme Cultram and Carlisle, shows, very fairly, that 'the men of Westmorland and north Lancashire ... seem to have wanted the monasteries to survive'. But Harrison fails to convince in his further deduction that 'generally speaking ... the religious zeal of the inhabitants of the Lake Counties was not directed towards the defence of the monasteries'. That the abbot of Holm Cultram failed to persuade his 'followers' (presumably Harrison means tenants) to join in the renewed rebellion at Carlisle in February, allowing, for the sake of argument, the veracity of a detail for which Harrison gives no evidence, might be accounted for by greater (if misguided) trust in the Doncaster agreement. Nor should the willingness of people subsequently to testify against the abbey of Furness be taken to show that 'Furness was too isolated to expect mass support'. It may well be that the witnesses were, under pressure, telling what they saw as the truth about what the abbot and monks had done, rather than expressing any views about their commitment to the abbey. Harrison's conclusion is unconvincing.

> With the exception of the men of Kendal and the southwest of the region the rebels of the Lake Counties were lacking in sympathy with the monasteries. . . . The fact that the monasteries of the Lake Counties were sparsely spread across the region and distant from the chief centres of rebellion made them irrelevant to the rebels, and while help from the brethren was no doubt gladly accepted, their preservation was not high on the list of rebel priorities. . . . With the exception of the southwest of the region the rebels had little sympathy with the monasteries, but these institutions were not common in the Lake Counties, and those which did exist had a severely tainted reputation.[394]

For such deductions there is simply insufficient evidence. We simply do not have evidence that the smaller monasteries that (as far as we know) were not involved in rebellion accepted their fate willingly, and that the commons did not care to save them. Moreover, the prominent place in the rebels' demands that the monasteries held and the considerable, if not universal, actions of the rebels in restoring and defending monasteries might be thought to weigh far more strongly in any balance than the silence of some of the smallest houses.

It is worth noting here later references to the 'commotions' of 1536 and the implied or explicit place of the monasteries as an issue in provoking them. When on 26 December 1537 William Saunders reported to Cromwell that one James Maycock of Buckby (Northamptonshire) said that 'abbeys be now made granges', which he said was 'long of men of law, and if the northern men had come they would have been first had by the head', that (however cryptic the wording) was directly relating rebellion to the suppression: lawyers who had gained monastic lands would have been the rebels' first victims.[395] A preacher in trouble claimed that what caused the rising 'was but for to maintain superstition hypocrisy and abominable living that is and was used amongst monks canons friars and nuns'.[396] Anthony Budgegood, a former servant of Thomas Cromwell who defected to Rome, claimed that 'the promotion of heretic bishops and the suppression of monasteries was the chief cause of the great rebellion that was in England made by the northern men'.[397] A list of objections of high treason against Lord Montagu in autumn 1538 included the admission by the priest John Collins that 'the Lord M[ontagu] and he coming by the augmentation house said this house is the cause of the commotion', by which he must have meant the Pilgrimage of Grace; the very next point refers to the 'pacifying of the insurrection'.[398]

The abbot of Colchester (one of the few abbots who was to prove unwilling to surrender his house to the king in 1538/39), after praising Fisher, More and monks of the Charterhouse who 'died holy martyrs', went on to say (according to his servant Edmund Troman) that the northern men were 'good men, mokyll in the mothe [?], great cracars [boasters?] and nothing worth in their deeds'. At the time of the insurrection he had said, 'I would to Christ the rebels in the north country had the bishop of Canterbury, the lord chancellor and the lord privy seal amongst them and I trust we should have a merry world again.'[399] Thomas Nuthake, physician and mercer, testified that the abbot of Colchester said[400] that those which had made the king's majesty supreme head of the church be false heretics and all that consented to the same were accursed of god's own mouth; asking a vengeance of the archbishop of Canterbury the Lord Chancellor and of other the king's majesty's most honourable council saying that they were arch heretics and do go about to destroy the church and the law of God rehearsing these words . . . meaning that God should take vengeance of such as destroyed abbeys.

Nuthake described how the abbot told him:

> I send for you to tell unto you news which I have in writing for a truth the northern men be up in a great number and will in no wise that abbeys shall be put down, nor holy days to be taken away and rather then they will suffer the new laws which now in hand go forward they will die xl ml [40,000] men.

Afterwards, when the king's commissioners 'were in suppressing the abbey of Louth and other abbeys the heads whereof were offenders', the abbot, talking to Nuthake in an orchard, lamented: 'What a world is this I hear say that all abbeys shall go down these tyrants and bloodsuckers doth thrust out of their houses these good religious fathers against all right and law but let them hang and draw as fast as they will I shall keep one.'

Robert Rouse, mercer of Colchester, testified how the abbot said

> that the king's highness had evil counsel that moved him to take on hand to be chief head of the church of England and to pull down these houses of religion which were founded by his grace's progenitors and many noblemen for the service and honour of God the commonwealth and relief of poor folks and that the same was both against God's law and man's law.

Immediately after the abbot heard of the insurrection in the north, he sent for Rouse and said 'the northern lads be up and they . . . say plainly that they will have no more abbeys suppressed in their country'.[401]

But some historians would cast doubt on just how much the monasteries meant to the rebels. By questioning the place of monasteries in the religious and spiritual life of the north, they once again, in effect, minimise the part that the defence of the monasteries played in the rebellions. But just what did the monasteries mean for the laity of the north?

That is, of course, an exceptionally difficult question to which to offer a firm answer. If the monasteries were not the dens of sexual iniquity that government propaganda claimed, then it is easier to understand that they could continue to hold the affections of many. The most substantial contemporary discussion is in Robert Aske's apologia and responses to later interrogations. Aske offered a detailed account of events and his part in them.

During his Christmastide stay at court (to which we shall return), Aske was in no doubt about the importance of the monasteries in the risings. He claimed that 'in all partes of the realm men's hearts much grudge with the suppression of abbeys and the first fruits by reason the same would be the destruction of the whole religion in England'.[402] Bush attempts to play this down, noting how, 'when explaining the causes of complaint prior to the truce [at the end of October], he singled out first fruits as well as the suppression of abbeys for special mention'.[403] That is misleading.

In April 1537, now under arrest, Aske was questioned in detail. Were not, it was put to him in April, the false rumours that church goods would be taken away and only one church left every seven miles one of the greatest causes of the insurrection in the north? Aske's reply neatly emphasises the place of the suppression, rejecting the suggestion put to him that it was simply the spreading of rumours—false rumours—that had provoked the rebellion. Aske grasped the point at once but was quite firm. 'He thinks those bruits were one of the greatest causes, but the suppression of abbeys was the greatest cause of the said insurrection, which the hearts of the commons most grudged at, as he saith.'[404] Did he think that there would have been any general insurrection if those rumours had been extinguished at the beginning? Aske insisted that 'he thinks that only the suppression of the abbeys /and division of preachers/ [inserted above line] had caused an insurrection, though the said bruits had not been spoken of at all'.[405] What acts of parliament had been complained against? Here Aske produced a comprehensive indictment of the legislation of the 1530s. 'He saith that they grudged chiefly at the acts of suppression of abbeys and the supremacy of the church', the act allowing the king to bequeath the crown by will, the illegitimation of Princess Mary, the statute of uses, the first fruits and the act that words should be treason. There were many grievances, but the dissolution was prominent once again, and Aske listed it first.[406]

Aske was then invited to give his own opinions on these acts. He began with the suppression, and it was here that he made his well-known declaration about the monasteries. He admitted that 'to the statute of suppressions, he did grudge against the same & so did all the whole country'. He explained why.[407]

> Because the abbeys in the north partes gave great alms to poor men and laudably served God; in which parts of late days they had but small comfort by ghostly teaching. And by occasion of the said suppression the divine service of almighty God is much minished [diminished], great number of masses unsaid and the blessed consecration of the sacrament not now used and showed in those places, to the distress of the faith and spiritual comfort to man's soul, the temple of God ruffed and pulled down, the ornaments and relics of the church of God unreverent used, tombs and sepulchres of honourable and noble men pulled down and sold, none hospitality now in those places kept, but the farmers for the most part lets & taverns [?lease] out the farms of the same houses to other farmers, for lucre and advantage to themselves. And the profits of these abbeys yearly goeth out of the country to the king's highness, so that in short space little money, by occasion of the said yearly rents, tenths and first fruits, should be left in the said country. . . . Also diverse and many of the said abbeys were in the mountains and desert places, where the people be rude of conditions and not well taught the law of God, and when the abbeys stood the said people not only had worldly refreshing in their bodies but spiritual refuge, both by ghostly living of them and by spiritual information, and preaching.

The emphasis on the spiritual is striking. Aske went on to describe the part the abbeys played in more worldly matters. They looked after their tenants and servants:

> none was in these partes denied, neither horsemeat nor man's meat, so that the people was greatly refreshed by the said abbeys, where now they have no such succour; & wherefore the said statute of suppression was greatly to the decay of the commonwealth of that country, and all those parts of all degrees greatly grudged against the same & yet doth, their duty of allegiance always saved. Also the abbeys was one of the beauties of this realm to all men and strangers passing through the same; also all gentlemen much succoured in their needs with money, their young sons there succoured; and in nunneries their daughters brought up in virtue; & also their evidences & money left to the uses of infants in abbeys' hands, always sure there;

& such abbeys as were near the danger of sea banks, great maintainers of sea walls & dykes, maintainers & builders of bridges & hedge-ways, such other things for the commonwealth.

Aske then went on to explain the rebels' attitudes to the statute declaring Mary illegitimate, the act of first fruits, the statute of uses, the statute allowing the king to declare the succession of the crown by will, the act of supremacy and the treason act. The suppression was not Aske's unique concern. But it was clearly highly important.

Some historians, of whom Bush and Hoyle are the most recent, have presented Aske's defence of the monasteries as essentially a social and economic document. Bush again and again stresses the rebels' material objections to the dissolution—notably its impact on employment, charity and hospitality.[408] Hoyle similarly emphasises the material. 'Apart from the loss of divine service, the reduced number of masses, and Aske's evident distaste for the sacrilegious treatment of church ornaments and fabric'—a pretty large exclusion—'this is an apologia for monasteries couched in utilitarian social and economic terms'.[409] Davies sees opposition to the dissolution as reflecting fears of local impoverishment, as rents would be paid to the king and not spent locally, and of a general attack on local institutions.[410] Shagan says that Aske 'listed practical reasons why they should be preserved', although Shagan himself then refers to prayers for the dead as well as almsgiving, hospitality and education.[411]

The problem with such an approach is that it implicitly redefines religious matters so as to exclude the charitable, hospitable and educational role intrinsic to late medieval monasteries. Monks and nuns would hardly have seen themselves and their functions as somehow distinct from 'the commonwealth'. In their petition to Sir Thomas Percy in December, the monks of Sawley referred to themselves as 'special brethren of this our pilgrimage of grace for the commonwealth':[412] if monks used this phraseology, it hardly suggests that they regarded their house and monasteries in general as anything but a full part of 'the commonwealth'. Moreover, it would be a gross distortion to read Aske's defence of the monasteries as in any sense unmindful of their first responsibility, the divine service of almighty God. Aske was rather emphasising how much the monasteries did in the north, and what damaging effects the suppression was having on the local economy. In stressing their broader activities, he may also have been attempting to persuade a king and ministers who, as he would have grasped by now, were not committed to the traditional religious functions of monasteries. It is notable that Aske does not here refer to monasteries as centres of pilgrimage or as shrines housing relics, and in a sense the very notion of a Pilgrimage of Grace with no specific destination in view was a subtle reworking of the medieval tradition of pilgrimage. But any suggestion that Aske's defence of the monasteries lacked a significant spiritual dimension would be a travesty. He had after all earlier expressed dismay that the bishops 'had not done their duty in that they had not been plain with the king's highness', over among other things, 'the ornaments of the churches and abbeys suppressed and the violating of relics by the suppressors with the unreverent demeanour of the doers thereof'.[413] Hoyle's scepticism—'he may have been genuinely committed to monasticism, but overall one senses that he was a man in search of a movement, more of an opportunity to fulfil a destiny', seeking 'to secure his political ambitions', in short an 'opportunist' who 'perhaps saw himself as supplanting Cromwell'[414]—is unwarranted. And it would seem to contradict Hoyle's surmise that 'whilst there was a degree of local support for dissolved houses, it seems most likely that the opposition to the dissolution which forms a strand of the Pilgrimage was largely the result of Aske's own preoccupations'.[415] Nor is it fair to reproach Aske, as Hoyle does,[416] for not openly challenging the king's right to dissolve the monasteries.

There is a pervasive tendency in recent historiography to assume that revolts must have had many causes and to dismiss any historian insisting that a revolt had a dominant cause (such as religion in this case) as naively monocausal in approach. 'The strong evidence of social conflict in the 1536–7 insurrections acts as a warning against monocausal interpretations of popular politics', opines Andy Wood.[417] Yet this warning is issued in flagrant defiance of the evidence that he cites. Wood describes the northern commons marching behind banners of the five wounds of Christ, presenting themselves as pilgrims, seeking to maintain what he terms 'established religion'[418]—but, rather than seeing the revolt as essentially religious, he goes on to describe the commons' complaints as 'defined by a common concern over taxation, religion and social change'.[419] Wood's evidence for social conflict is based on Sir Christopher Dacre's assault on the besiegers of Carlisle, quarrels over rents and dues, the commons' suspicions of the loyalty of gentry during the risings, and the commons' emphasis on the commonwealth.[420] But all that misses the point. There was indeed a perennial undertow of social resentment, but such a constant cannot explain the outbreak of the particular risings in 1536 and 1537, nor can it account for the form they took. And most importantly, the hostility towards gentlemen that was expressed in those risings was above all, and selectively, directed against those who would not support the cause, which, it has been shown here, was religious.

What must now be considered are the reactions of Henry VIII, since these explain why the rebels ultimately failed. The ferocity of his response was remarkable. From the start he saw the insurrection as treason to be dealt with firmly. He quickly perceived the suppression as a central issue in the rebellion. And the intensification of his hostility had great consequences for the future of the monasteries.

If the king's earliest replies to the JPs in Lincolnshire and to Lord Darcy do not mention monasteries, but rather deny rumours that the goods of parish churches and new taxes would be taken,[421] by 9 October Henry had added 'the suppression of abbeys' to the first two grievances.[422] On 19 October he would reply firmly[423] to the traitors and rebels of Lincolnshire that the suppression of religious houses was granted to the king by parliament and was not a policy 'set forth by any councillor or councillors upon their mere will and fantasy as ye full falsely would persuade our realm to believe'. That shows that the king saw the dissolution as a central feature of the rebellion and as a non-negotiable plank in his own policies. He picked out that demand, together with the criticisms of his choice of councillors, as the first issues to answer, 'because upon them dependeth much of the rest'. Compelled by Norfolk and Shrewsbury's truce with the rebels at Doncaster in late October to agree to consider a pardon, the government drew up a proclamation on 2 November. Interestingly, a draft included the instruction that those accepting the pardon should assist the king's commissioners in re-entering dissolved monasteries that had been restored by the rebels—revealing a determination to proceed with the dissolution—but this section was omitted from the final text.[424] In early November, Lancaster Herald, sent to proclaim the pardon and to defend the king's policies to the rebels, was given detailed instructions. He was to declare that the suppression of abbeys and the new clerical taxes 'appertaineth nothing at all to the commonalty'. The more the prince had 'of his own', the less the necessity for taxes and the greater his ability to preserve his subjects in peace and tranquillity from foreign enemies. Lancaster Herald was to find out which monks and nuns had been restored by the rebels and 'of what inclination the people is for their continuance'.[425] To Norfolk and Fitzwilliam, Henry in mid-November insisted,

what is more contrary to God's commandments then for subjects to attempt a rebellion against their prince and sovereign lord who by

God's holy word and scripture they be bound in all things in such reverent sort to obey that though their king did them injustice they ought in no wise to redouble their injuries with violence.[426]

Henry firmly demonstrated his commitment to the dissolution as early as 9 October when he instructed Darcy to arrest as seditious all persons who spoke critically of the suppression of abbeys.[427] A little later (19 October) the king wrote a bloodthirsty letter to the earl of Derby.[428] Having heard of an insurrection and assembly 'in the borders of Lancashire specially about the Abbey of Sawley and other parts thereabout, so much as the abbot and monks be again by the traitors of that assembly restored to the possession of their said abbey', Henry commanded him 'immediately upon the sight hereof' to

> proceed . . . to the repression of the said assembly. . . . to travail to the uttermost of your power to apprehend the captains and chief doers of the same and either incontinent to cause them like traitors to be there executed or else to send them up hither unto us in sure and safe custody. . . . and if ye shall find the late abbot and monks thereof remaining there in the possession of the house having required again at the hands of such traitors and rebels, we will that you shall take the said abbot and monks with their assistants forth with violence and without any manner of delay in their monks apparell cause them to be hanged up as right arrant traitors and movers of insurrection and sedition accordingly.

That was uncompromising language. There was no mention of any trial or due process of law. Derby reported to Henry on 24 October that he and gentlemen of the shire had finally concluded to set forward towards Sawley 'where the late abbot and monks . . . yet remain', on Saturday next (i.e. on 28 October).[429] Henry thanked Derby for the news that he had advanced towards Sawley against the rebels, and instructed him what their fate should be:[430]

> In case you shall at your coming to Sawley find the abbot and monks or canons thereof in the same restored again unto the house by the mean of such rebellion, whereby it must needs follow that they were either authors or at the least favourers and abetters of the same, you shall then without further delay cause the said abbot and certain of the chief of the monks to be hanged upon long pieces of timber or otherwise out of the steeple and the rest to be put to execution in such

sundry places as you shall think meet for the example of others, and in semblable manner to use all such persons as were notable captains or doers with them putting the rest of the people that were assembled with the same in no manner of doubt or fear of our mercy.

The bloodthirsty details are remarkable.[431]

On hearing about the disturbances at Norton—the abbot gathered two to three hundred men, and the commissioners were compelled to shelter in a tower[432]—Henry responded directly. He had seen Sir Piers Dutton's letter to Audley showing the 'traitorous demeanour' of the late abbot and canons. The king's 'pleasure and commandment' was that Dutton and Sir William Brereton should at once 'without any manner further circumstances of our law or delay cause them to be hanged as most arrant traitors in such sundry places as ye shall think requisite for the terrible example of all others hereafter'.[433] Once again Henry's hostility is absolute and terrifying: legal processes are no more than a conduit to punishment.[434] Sir Thomas Boteler pleaded for two of the canons, John Penketh and Henry Barnes, imprisoned (together with the late abbot) in the king's gaol at Chester: the 'common fame of the country', they said, imputed 'no fault at all' to them. He recommended 'indifferent [i.e. impartial] examination', and he urged Cromwell to intervene, as it was said that Sir Piers Dutton would have put them to execution 'without any manner examination at all'.[435] That appeal seems to have been unavailing. On 30 November Dutton acknowledged receipt of the king's letters; they had, he said, appointed a day for the execution of the abbot and canons, but before that day came, they had received letters from the earl of Derby, informing them of the gist of a letter from the earls of Shrewsbury, Rutland and Huntingdon, and asking Dutton to dismiss his company. Dutton accordingly deferred the execution of the king's command, meanwhile keeping the offenders in Chester Castle. But Sir William Brereton, joined in commission with Dutton, was less willing to follow royal orders.[436] Later Lord Chancellor Audley would note that Brereton had saved the abbot of Norton.[437] Brereton's hesitations emphasise the contrary determination of the king to punish the supposedly rebellious abbot and canons as finally as possible. Evidently the abbot and canons got off, as the dispensation the abbot obtained in December 1537 shows.[438] But that the king was not easily able to transform hostility into destruction on the ground should not leave any doubts about the strength of that hostility.

At the meeting between Norfolk, Shrewsbury and the rebels in December, the king's lieutenants agreed, as we have seen, that a parliament should be held at York and that abbeys should stand till then. But Henry was fundamentally opposed to any concession on monasteries. He wrote to Sir William Fitzwilliam and Sir John Russell[439]

> to ascertain you plainly of our mind in that point touching the abbeys, we shall never consent to their desires therein by any such mean but adhere to our right therein to the uttermost being as justly entitled thereunto as to the imperial crown of this our realm, and resolved with the force of the one to maintain and defend the other as a member so united and knit thereunto that whiles it shall please god we shall enjoy the one we purpose not with any violence to depart with one piece of the other.

That absolute royal refusal did not prevent Henry from giving Robert Aske and others involved in or sympathetic to the rebellion a very different impression. The king would dissemble his true feelings towards Aske. After the first Doncaster agreement at the end of October, Henry wanted to exclude 'a very small number of the notable villains that have begun this insurrection'.[440] Among them was Aske. Norfolk, writing from Windsor on 6 November (clearly at the king's command after he had briefed him on the first Doncaster agreement), advised Lord Darcy to take that 'most arrant traitor' Aske alive or dead, but alive if possible.[441] In instructions to Norfolk and Fitzwilliam, Henry referred to the rebels' leader as 'a traitorous villain'.[442] In a letter to Suffolk in late November that does not survive, Henry had evidently again called for the apprehension of Aske, something Suffolk resisted as 'a very doubtful thing to accomplish' unless it was certain that he would not find out in advance.[443] Henry showed his hostility to Aske clearly in his letter to Sir Ralph Ellerker and Robert Bowes on 27 November 1536. The king thought it no little shame to all the noblemen to have suffered such a villain as Aske, a man who lacked wit and experience, to sign the letters sent to the duke of Norfolk as if he were their ruler.

> Where is your nobility become to suffer such a villain to be privy to any of your affairs, who was never esteemed in any of our courts but as a common pedlar in the law? It is only his filed tongue and false surmises that have brought him in this unfitting estimation among you.[444]

In a letter from the king to Norfolk, Aske was again 'that villain Aske'; 'there is no gentleman or other man of any honesty in our realm that we repute so little, as to put him in pledge for such a vile villain';[445] in a letter to Derby, Aske was 'the traitor Aske'.[446] Responding to Fitzwilliam and Russell's reporting of the outlines of the Doncaster compromise in early December, Henry, as we have seen, was not pleased that they had not been able to reserve ringleaders for exemplary punishment and that they had had to make concessions over monasteries.[447] The king evidently did not feel bound by the general pardon he had granted. After the first Doncaster agreement at the end October, Henry had clearly been intending to win time and hoped eventually to defeat the rebels by stealth; both shires (Lincolnshire and Yorkshire) were, he then informed Bishop Gardiner and Sir John Wallop at the French court, at the king's mercy, 'neither having our pardon nor any certain promise of the same'.[448] But by 2 December Henry was, perforce, prepared to extend his pardon to include Aske, or so he informed Shrewsbury, who, with Russell, was to 'practise' with him and with Darcy.[449] He was persuaded by his councillors, and no doubt by the hard facts of the situation, that he would have to grant a pardon without any exceptions. Although he believed that the granting of a free pardon would not be honourable for him but rather an encouragement for the rebels, 'yet giving place to the advice of our council therein' he had sent Norfolk a free and general pardon—though he was not to grant it 'unless very extremity shall enforce the same'.[450] And then Henry had to accept the bitter pill that at Doncaster, as we have seen, Norfolk and Fitzwilliam had promised the rebels a general free pardon and a meeting of parliament in the north.

So it was that, on 15 December, Henry wrote to 'trusty and well-beloved' Aske. Informed, he said, that 'notwithstanding your offences committed against us in the late rebellion attempted in those parts, you be now in heart repentant for the same' and that Aske was determined to be a faithful subject, the king went on that 'we have co[nceived] a great desire to speak with you and to hear of your mouth the whole circumstance and beginning of that matter'. He therefore ordered Aske as his true and faithful subject—'for so we do now repute you'—to come to court, but without letting anyone know, and to 'use such plainness and frankness in all things that we shall demand of you that we may besides have cause to reward you further'.[451] Henry attached a credence that 'he should safe come and safe go', and return before the twelfth day of Christmas.[452] Aske was thus invited to spend Christmastide at the royal court. It was then that he was encouraged to make a lengthy declaration of all that he had done.[453] Was it then that Aske also received a royal gift to which he would later refer: 'a jacket of crimson satin that the king's grace gave me'?[454] Whatever the case, Henry clearly misled Aske at this time. Aske would indicate his sense of betrayal immediately before his execution, declaring that he was aggrieved since 'at one time he had a token from the king's majesty of pardon for confessing the truth'—a royal pledge, which, it was unnecessary to add, had now been broken.[455] Nonetheless, it was not that Aske went up to court wide-eyed. Darcy and Aske agreed that Aske should lay post horses between Darcy's house and London so that if Aske were imprisoned or other-wise badly treated, Darcy would hear about it, and promised—so Thomas Estoft claimed—that 'he would again raise the people for his deliverance'.[456]

Aske was the victim of royal deception. Not only did Henry evidently convince him of his personal affection towards him, he also evidently led him to believe that he now accepted the justice of the commons' crit-icisms of his government. Alongside Aske's account of his actions during the rebellion is a brief in the same hand, recommending that in order to obtain (we should say to win) the hearts of his subjects in the north, the king should 'direct with Aske a proclamation' that he agree that his subjects there 'shall have free election' of the knights of the shire and burgesses, and that a 'like liberty' will be granted to churchmen so that 'with out his grace's displeasure they shall and may speak and show their learning and free mind in the convocation'. The king would be content 'to *all* persons there to confirm his gracious and liberal pardon'. Norfolk would declare to them the time and place of the parliament. In recognition of the fact that, despite the large size of Yorkshire, of its towns only Scarborough sent burgesses to parliament, the king's pleas-ure was that burgesses should in future be returned in Beverley, Ripon, Richmond, Pontefract, Wakefield, Skipton and Kendal.[457] Had the king encouraged Aske not only to tell him what had happened during the rising but also to submit a draft of what should be done next? Did Aske feel that he was being involved in the making of policy?

Aske left London 'with most haste' on 5 January.[458] On 8 January he wrote to Darcy how 'the king's grace is good and gracious sovereign lord to me'. Henry had 'affirmed his most liberal pardon to all the north parts by his own mouth'. The king intended to hold his parliament and have his queen crowned at York, and had granted 'free election of knights and burgesses and like liberty to the spirituality to declare their learning with out his displeasure'. Aske added his own gloss, assuring Darcy that 'his grace in heart tendrith the commonwealth of his sub-jects and extendith his mercy of his own benignity plentuously to his people from the heart'. He trusted that he had done my duty as well to the king's grace under his favour as to my country and played my part truly; the king esteemed the commonwealth of the realm and the love of his subjects more than any other earthly riches and would send the duke of Norfolk to minister justice.[459]

Aske issued a manifesto to his neighbours on much the same lines. The king 'by his own mouth plainly hath declared unto me that his grace will that the general pardon granted at Doncaster [should extend] to all his subjects of the north parts', and that 'your reasonable petitions shall be ordered by parliament'. The king, 'for the great lief [love] he beareth unto [this] country, intendith surely to keep his parliament at York and to have the queen's grace crowned there'.[460] A little earlier, on 5 January, Archbishop Lee wrote to Darcy that he had word from London that Aske had had 'good words and countenance at London' and that the parliament and coronation should be at York at Michaelmas.[461] At some point on returning home, Aske went to Darcy at Templehurst and showed him 'how the king's grace had done with him'. Aske[462]

had opened unto his grace the griefs of the country and his highness gave him very comfortable answers concerning the reformation of them and how my lord of Norfolk should forthwith come down and afterward the king's highness would come himself and have the queen's grace crowned at York and a parliament shortly kept there wherein all things that were reasonable should be reformed; and entertained this examinate very graciously and benignly and desired of this examinate nothing else but to declare the truth of this examinate's first taking and of his progress and proceeding in all things afterwards.

It was not just Aske who was given such an impression of the king's intentions. John Hussee, Lord Lisle's London agent, reported on 31 December 1536 that he had been told there should be a parliament at York and the queen should be crowned there.[463] Sir Oswald Wilstrop reported how 'the king's highness hath declared *by his own mouth*' to him 'that we shall have our parliament at York frankly and freely for the ordering and reformation of all causes for the commonwealth of this realm, and also his frank and free convocation for the good stay and ordering of our faith and of all spiritual causes'. That declaration would be sent down under the great seal by the duke of Norfolk. Parliament, convocation and the coronation of the queen would take place at Whit-suntide.[464] If the king spoke those words, presumably interpreted by Darcy as meaning a *free* parliament, that was seemingly a highly significant admission. For Henry to declare that the commons should have their parliament and convocation freely and frankly was implicitly to admit that previous meetings of parliament and convocation—those in which the dissolution of the smaller monasteries and the royal supremacy had been enacted—had been less than free and frank. No wonder Pilgrims such as Wilstrop continued to trust the king: Sir Oswald assured Darcy that both of them were in the king's favour.[465] Dramatic royal gestures such as that recorded by Gregory Conyers in a letter to Sir John Bulmer on 28 January 1537 must have strengthened that sense of trust:[466]

> I assure you sir the king himself on Sunday after twelfth tide which was the same Sunday was a fortnight openly in the presence of all the noblemen and worshipful men of the country and many other he laid his hand off [*sic*: on] his breast and swore by the faith that he did bear to God and Saint George he had not only forgiven and pardoned all his subjects of the north by his writing under seal, but also freely in his heart; he ordered that men should wear crosses of St George so that the king may know those who have thankfully accepted his free pardon and mean to be as loyal as before the insurrection.

Many people of the town of Hull were soon after reported as wearing red crosses,[467] as were the commons of Scarborough.[468]

Just how much Aske trusted the king is most vividly revealed in the letter he wrote to Henry on his return to Yorkshire on 12 January. He informed him of the commons' doubts that he would not fulfil the Doncaster agreement—'they do think that they shall not have the parliament in convenient time', and their sense that Cromwell, 'against whom they most specially do complain', was in as great favour with the king as ever. Aske warned Henry of the consequent dangers of further popular risings.[469] To write in that way, not least in reporting the commons' continuing hostility to Thomas Cromwell, Aske must have been utterly convinced that the king was himself wholly committed to the fulfilment of the Doncaster agreement and anxious to put it speedily into operation to avoid the risk of further disturbances. As popular fears of betrayal were swelling into what is known as Bigod's rising in the East Riding of Yorkshire, Aske informed Sir Robert Constable of the king's actions, and encouraged him to calm the commons.

Constable accordingly declared on 16 January—in what was clearly a widely circulated letter: there are no fewer than five copies in the Public Record Office—how the king 'hath declared by his own mouth' to Aske that 'we shall have our parliament at York frankly and freely for the ordering and reformation of all causes for the commonwealth of this realm and also his frank and free convocation for the good stay and ordering of the faith'; both parliament and convocation would be held at Whitsuntide, together with the queen's coronation.[470] Constable attributed the new insurrections to 'lack of knowledge of reformation to be had by parliament and convocation upon their petitions'; that he described Bigod's and Hallom's actions as 'folly' shows that he still confidently expected that reformation.[471] On 18 January Sir Robert Constable marvelled to Sir Francis Bigod that he assembled the commons,

> seeing the king's grace by his own mouth declared to Robert Aske how he intended to keep his parliament at York and the coronation also of the Queen; and how there should be free and frank parliament and convocation for the commonwealth. . . . And if the commons any thing doubt of their pardon or the parliament the said Aske will with all haste to do his best to bring knowledge [thereof under] his seal which he affirmeth the duke of Norfolk bringeth.[472]

On 18 January Aske referred to Constable's circular letter which he sent on to the king, and described his own efforts to stay the people, who feared betrayal. The commons, Aske said, 'as I brought no writing' from the king, 'begin to suspect me'; so 'I declared your grace's mind', much after the tenor of Constable's letter, or they would not have been stayed. Aske advised the king to hasten the arrival of Norfolk.[473]

Aske clearly still had every confidence in Henry and in Norfolk. That is shown by his response to the king's recent letters inviting Darcy[474] and Sir Robert Constable to come up to court. Aske explained to the king how 'by my simple advice for the danger that I saw towards I desired my lord Darcy and Sir Robert Constable to remain' and stay the country; 'if they had repaired up to your grace upon your grace's letter all the country had been up before now again'. To have acted in this way—ordering Darcy and Constable to disobey a royal command—and to have openly told the king about it, strongly suggests that Aske fully trusted the king and was confident that he would support his assessment of the local situation.[475] The king himself countermanded the order to Constable (and, one may assume, that to Darcy on 16 January), giving as his reason that he had that day sent Norfolk northwards.[476]

Aske himself issued an appeal to the commons who were making assemblies in late January, reiterating that 'his grace by his own mouth declared to me' that he intended to hold a parliament at York and to have the queen crowned there.[477] On 20 January Aske in a letter to the commons declared that 'Bigod intendeth to destroy the effect of our petitions and commonwealth'.[478] On Tuesday he met the commons at Beverley and told them that the king was 'good and gracious lord' to the commons and that 'he hath granted us all our desires and petitions', citing the parliament to be held 'shortly' at York and, as evidence of the king's favour and goodwill towards the north, his intention of having the queen crowned there.[479]

Darcy—no doubt influenced by Aske's optimism—was just as confident as Aske was of the king's intentions. The general pardon to him issued on 18 January and freeing him from any penalties would have reinforced that confidence.[480] On 17 January he urged that the people show restraint and wait for the coming of the duke of Norfolk: Darcy believed that Norfolk would bring 'gracious answers of the parliament and petitions'.[481] A day later he wrote how he heard that Norfolk would bring 'both great authority and comfortable answers for all happy and good men . . . of the king's liberal and gracious mind and pleasure'.[482] On 19 January he assured the mayor and inhabitants of Pontefract that Aske, Sir Ralph Ellerker, Sir Oswald Wilstrop and Sir Robert Bowes had all come from the king, reporting that he was 'favourable and gracious to all the north parts'. He added that 'I have and shall keep a clean true part to god to the king and ever to further and be a true petitioner for all good commons' wealth'.[483] On the same day he assured William Babthorpe of 'the king's liberal pardon and gracious words to Mr Aske and others affirming the same good'.[484] On 20 January he wrote to Sir William Fitzwilliam, one of the architects of the Doncaster agreement. Nowhere does Darcy voice any doubt that that compromise was still valid. The gentlemen had come home, he noted, 'in good time'. Darcy's point here was that the renewed commotions of the commons, far from needing to be repressed by military might, would be quickly calmed by the public declaration by the duke of Norfolk and other gentlemen of the agreement that Norfolk and Fitzwilliam had reached with him at Doncaster in December: 'the duke at his coming down which shall be hastily will affirm the same and more of the king's pleasure will in my conceit stay more then by force xl thousand men should do.'[485] The next day Darcy sent a circular letter to his deputies and friends saying how 'my friends from above in the court'—presumably Sir Oswald Wilstrop was one—

hath written unto me specially this week, and also as my lords cousins and friends that came thence of these parts hath showed that they heard the king's majesty like our most natural gracious sovereign lord of his own mouth by the word of a king declare and affirm his pardon to be wholly good and beneficial to all his subjects of the north.

Norfolk was to come down straight 'to minister justice and to affirm the same'.

And a free parliament to be, and liberty for spiritual and temporal to utter their learnings truly there as they may justify and more that any of his subjects shall may [sic] at the same with his gracious favour show their griefs and complaints accordingly and rich and poor to have justice against all that was named in the bill of the commons at Doncaster ... and such as shall be tried offenders to have condign punishment. More no true honest and good men can desire.

That condign punishment could only have been intended for those held responsible for the policies against which the Pilgrims had been protesting. Darcy went on to refer to those who assembled with Bigod near Scarborough, adding 'whereof I am heartily sore'; even they now were sorry, 'and cursed their captains that with lies stirred them'. Darcy insisted that 'neither God the king nor the common's wealth can be served' by such men.[486]

Was all this simply tactical manoeuvring intended to bounce the king back into accepting the concessions that Norfolk and Fitzwilliam had made at Doncaster in December? Were Aske, Darcy and the others trying skilfully to stir up just enough trouble to intimidate Henry but not so much as to incriminate themselves? Was John Folbery, interrogated on 19 February, right to say that the consequence of the letters in which Sir Robert Constable and Aske had written that 'no man should stir' was that 'when these that be true men would have had their neighbours and tenants to have served the king against Bigod, they made them answer that they would not stir, for Sir Robert Constable and Aske had given them commandment in any wise to sit still and to stir for no man'?[487]

Was Darcy mistrustful of the king, as his response to Henry's summons to him on 6 January to come up to court is often interpreted as showing? It does not have to be read in this way: apologies are not always only excuses. He was indeed a very old and sick man. The king's summons explicitly asked him to come up 'with all diligence that you may use with the preservation of your health', and that qualification, which Darcy quoted back to the king, should not be disregarded. His insistence on his loyalty and his denial of the gossip that he had heard had been reported to the king that he had freely joined in the rebellion also deserves to be taken at face value; it is reminiscent of similar gossip against Norfolk. And in any case that does not suggest that he thought the Doncaster agreement was in jeopardy.[488]

Or were Aske, Darcy and Constable using such tactics for a different purpose? Had they engineered the Doncaster agreement not because it reflected their own concerns, but because they saw it as the minimum necessary to persuade the Pilgrims to disperse? Sir Robert Constable would, after he was convicted of treason, insist that the yielding of Pontefract 'was for lack of furniture and for fear of our lives', and then assert that 'and yet as it proved we did his grace good service at Doncaster in staying of the fury of the commons whereby his grace hath his pleasure of them without battles'. But that should be read as a bitterly ironic reflection as Constable looked back in May on what had happened, including his own arrest and conviction: it is much less reliable evidence for his sentiments in December 1536 than his behaviour in January 1537, which shows confident expectation of a parliament at York that would address grievances.[489]

Had Aske, as the Dodds puzzlingly supposed, realised when at court that Henry had absolutely no intention of conceding on the monasteries, and were Aske's actions merely intended to calm popular fears while preparing for an unavoidable submission to the royal will? The Dodds based that surmise on an exchange of letters between Aske and his sister Dorothy Green and her husband. Dorothy Green wrote to her brother after Christmas that it was reported that 'the king will not be so good to him as his grace promised to be to them in as concerning the church and the abbeys and other articles';[490] Aske was later interrogated on the point 'that he sent a letter to her husband the contents whereof appeareth not by her letter but she wrote to Aske that diverse persons report and say that the king will not be as good to them as he promised to be as concerning the church abbeys and other articles'.[491]

But there is no reason to credit the Dodds's speculation that Aske had earlier written this news to Dorothy's husband. If he had, she would not then have needed to inform him that this was being said by several persons. All that speculation seems highly unlikely. Throughout January, Aske showed complete confidence in the king; others who had seen and heard Henry commit himself were just as certain. Darcy, who had not been to court, plainly believed them. Darcy, it may be noticed, continued to expect justice on all that was in their bill of articles, in other words a substantial reversal of policy by the king:[492]

> Surely the said gentlemen's coming home in post was in good time and verily the sooner all the lords and Sir Richard Tempest and vyrs [others] be sent home into their countries with good comfortable words of the parliament free for the spiritual and temporal and of the king's free and mere pardon of his own benign grace granted and that then true justice shall have place against all that was in their bill of articles and vyrs what so ever they be that of right they can complain of less or more therein as shall stand with his majesty's pleasure.

Aske, Darcy and Constable were taking real risks here, since, as we have seen, there was by mid-January widespread popular mistrust of the government. Aske and Darcy were in danger of becoming victims of that popular anxiety. At Christmas 1536 Ralph Swenson, one of the monks of Lenton Abbey, Nottinghamshire, told the subprior and other monks that the king 'will not keep no promise with God him self but pulls down his churches' and 'will not keep promise with them'; Swenson was sure that 'if he can overcome them he will do so'. Many of the monks then spoke ill of the king, queen and lord privy seal.[493] Aske and Darcy, as we have seen, insisted that any such mistrust was misplaced, since the king had committed himself personally. Was Aske in particular naive, outwitted by the king? Was his trust in part the instinctive trust of a one-eyed man?[494] Later, one of the reproaches against Lord Montagu (who was executed for treason) would be that when, after the insurrection, it was said that the king had promised to hold a parliament at York for satisfaction of the northern men's articles, and when it became clear that the king would not go to the north for that purpose, Montagu had said, the time had been when nothing was more sure to reckon upon than the promise of a prince, but now they account 'it no promise but a policy to blind the people', and added that 'after the people should arise again they would trust no promise'. That eloquently mirrors the hopes that the commons had placed in the Doncaster agreement and their profound sense of betrayal.[495]

And yet, and yet. Aske had not grasped the deceit of the king. He should have done. Perhaps it would have been too much to have expected him to reflect as Bigod did, 'having so good cause to doubt that the duke of Norfolk shall be sent rather to bring us here in to semblable captivity than they of Lincolnshire be in then to keep touch of fulfilling our petitions'.[496] Aske ought to have been troubled that when he left court on 5 January 'all things are kept secret', as John Hussee reported, rather than being publicly declared.[497] He ought to have noticed what the historian with the advantage of hindsight will have noticed straight away, namely that in all that Henry said when jollying Aske and the others along there was absolutely nothing directly relating to the monasteries, a most significant omission. For the king had not the slightest intention of yielding on that matter. We have already seen plentiful evidence of Henry's hostility to monasteries; now we may amply document his duplicity.

On 25 October the duke of Norfolk had asked the king[498]

> to take in good part what so ever promise I shall make unto the rebels (if any such I shall by the advice of others make) for surely I shall observe no part thereof for any respect of that other might call mine honour distained longer than I and my company with my lord marquess may be assembled together, thinking and repeating that none oath nor promise made for policy to serve you mine only master and sovereign can destain me who shall rather be torn in a million of pieces then to show one point of cowardice or untruth to your majesty.

Henry endorsed his approach,[499] though he would have preferred a more forceful response, reproaching Norfolk on 2 December, 'then wrote you from Welbe[c]k [not Newark as *Letters and Papers* has it] all desperately and yet in the end is said you would esteem no promise that you should make to the rebels nor think your honour touched in the breach and violation of the same'.[500]

Responding to Fitzwilliam and Russell's report of the Doncaster compromise, Henry maintained that the rebels could not be reduced to obedience unless they submitted without insisting on conditions repugnant to the laws.[501]

> And rather then we will permit their malices to enforce us to such extremity, we shall we doubt not as God so provide for their repression that those shall first repent it that be the greatest fautors maintainers and abettors of them in their mischief and therewithal cut away all those corrupt members that with wholesome medicines will not be recovered and brought to perfect health.

That was not the spirit of compromise. If the Pilgrims had known that such was the king's attitude, they would not have disbanded. Sir Robert

Constable, for example, could not have known how the duke of Norfolk, while still at Kenninghall in January, would react to his circular letter. Norfolk said that Constable had 'written things as I think might have be forborne for he hath said more then I can perform and it might be taken his large sayings therein not true might be due to a scant good purpose as well concerning the coronation and parliament as other things'.[502] Norfolk referred to him not as a colleague exuberantly and rashly going too far but as someone committed 'to a scant good purpose'.

Damningly revealing light on the king's intentions is shed by the instructions that he sent out early in the new year to Norfolk, sent as the king's lieutenant in the north, and to the earls of Sussex and Derby, jointly serving as the king's lieutenants in Lancashire. Drafts of two very similar letters survive, and their details are conflated here.[503]

Henry sent Norfolk as his lieutenant 'for the indifferent administration of justice' and 'for the more certain appeasing of the people and the perfect establishment of the country in quiet unity and due obedience'. Those are not the terms used by a conciliatory ruler. Norfolk was not being sent north to confirm the Doncaster agreement and the assurances that Henry had himself given Aske and other northern gentry that there would be a parliament at York.

Norfolk and Sussex were required to administer, in stages, an oath to the 'notable leaders' and gentlemen of Yorkshire and Lancashire. In swearing the gentry, they were to 'declare at length unto the people as well the great clemency of the king's highness which hath thus taken them to mercy that so wretchedly unkindly and unnaturally have offended him and his whole realm'. They were to declare the damage caused by insurrections as well as the great offence committed against God by any who rebelled. Sussex and his fellow councillors were to

> travail to the uttermost of their power in all places as they shall pass secretly to ensearch and know the very grounds and causes of the said late insurrection who were the first and chief setters forth of it and who devised every of the articles that were put in at the last assembly at Doncaster.

These were the instructions of a king who continued to see the rebellion as a personal slight and who, far from accepting the deal struck by his lieutenants at Doncaster, sought revenge against those responsible.

That appears clearly in Norfolk's instructions over the administration of the oath. Anyone refusing it was to be treated for that reason alone as a rebel against the king and as exempted from the king's pardon, which was conditional on submission to Henry. He was to be apprehended, and judged by law to suffer execution. If proceeding to such a punishment proved dangerous, the earls should pretend to make light of such 'wilful fools', and await a better opportunity.[504]

Just what this meant depends on what exactly was in the oath that the Yorkshire gentry were being asked to swear. Our difficulty is that several versions survive, and it is impossible to know which was used.

Anyone swearing to what appears to be the strongest versions of the oath[505] was in effect apologising to the king for offending him ('ye shall swear that ye be heartily sorry that ye have offended the king's highness in this rebellion'). He committed himself never again to make any unlawful assembly, and promised to inform against anyone who 'shall utter and declare unto you privily or appertly [openly] any contentious or seditious matters move you to any insurrection and such unlawful assembly or speak any unfitting or slanderous words of the king's highness his grace or successors or of any of his or their chief and notable councillors'. He accepted the king again as supreme head of the church ('from henceforth ye shall be a true and faithful subject unto the king our sovereign lord Henry the viii king of England and of France defender of the faith lord of Ireland and in earth supreme head of the church of England'). He acquiesced in all acts of parliament made during the king's reign ('you shall from henceforth support approve obey and allow all laws orderings and statutes not being repealed made in any of the sessions of the parliaments sithens the beginning of his most gracious reign, or in the time of any his most royal progenitors'). Moreover, not only did the oath require acceptance of all the laws that had been made, but also their maintenance against any who would break them 'yea to the effusion of your blood'. Just in case there was any doubt that those laws included the statute dissolving the smaller monasteries, the oath further committed all who swore that 'to the best of your power ye shall assist all such commissioners as the king's highness shall appoint for the taking of possession in any of the monasteries being within the act of suppression'. No one who thought the December agreement a victory for the rebels could possibly have taken this oath with conviction.

Another version of the oath[506] is close to those just discussed, but with a more abject declaration of submission: the jurors here 'being repentant and sorry do most humbly and vppon your knees aske the king's highness mercy and forgiveness'. They swore to maintain all statutes made since the beginning of the realm, but there was no explicit mention of assisting the commissioners in dissolving the smaller monasteries.

There is a less abject version of the oath.[507] In this, the jurors acknowledge having made oaths contrary to their allegiance 'and to the great offence of God', utterly renounce them, and swear to be the king's true and faithful subjects, and 'specially' commit themselves to obey and indeed 'to spend their blood' in maintaining all parliamentary statutes made since the king's accession and to assist any of the king's commissioners in their duties. It was hardly necessary to spell out that this included the dissolution of the smaller monasteries.

Another text of the oath[508] is apparently milder still. Again the king is not described as supreme head of the church and the monasteries are not mentioned. The juror does not admit any personal wrongdoing or offence to the king or to God; any oaths sworn during the commotion are simply renounced; and parliamentary statutes are not explicitly referred to. The juror simply swears[509] to 'be obedient unto our said sovereign lord and his lieutenant in all his laws and precepts as a true liegeman ought to be to the uttermost of [his] power cunning and wit'. All the same, swearing to this commits the juror to obeying the laws of the realm, which implicitly include all the laws made in the reformation parliament, and to obeying the precepts of the king's commissioners. It is certainly less explicit in what it commits the juror to than the first versions we considered, but, even so, it is hardly in keeping with the spirit of the Doncaster agreement or with what Henry had evidently been saying to Aske, Wilstrop and others. The juror was accepting that what had happened was wrong, and that he would in future obey the king's laws and his lieutenant's orders. There was no place here for a parliament in York in which all could speak freely and frankly about the ills of the realm and in which the laws of the realm might be revised.

Bush has argued that both the instructions to the commissioners and the oath were originally drawn up to be used in Lincolnshire; that the oath was modified for use in Yorkshire in early December before the second Doncaster agreement; and that a further version of the oath was prepared and then used in February. He believes that the bolder denunciations of rebellion and reassertions of the king's supremacy were drawn up first, and that the more conciliatory versions were drawn up in early 1537, having been tempered by reality. But since none of the versions can be dated, there is a danger of circularity of reasoning here.

The harsher versions of the oaths are, it must be said, rather more in keeping with the details and the tone of the instructions to Norfolk and Sussex than is the mildest version. That does not, of course, mean that these were the oaths that were used: it might still be that the mildest was in the event preferred as less risky. Nonetheless, even that version implicitly repudiated the Doncaster compromise. And if Bush's arguments are mistaken and it was not the mild version of the oath but rather the strongest oath with which we began this discussion that was employed in February, then those being sworn were being required to confess their own wrongdoing and to welcome the king's mercy, to accept Henry as supreme head of the church, and much more explicitly to accept all the laws made since the beginning of the reign, and to assist commissioners in taking possession of monasteries according to the act of suppression.

What is significant here is the intention of the government—that is, what the instructions to Norfolk and Sussex, and the policy of swearing oaths, reveal about the king's attitude to the December Doncaster agreement. Bush believes that the king was then quite prepared to go along with the concessions made. My reading is that Henry had disguised his true sentiments to Aske and that he was always determined that he would prevail. He insisted on the evil of rebellion. He insisted that the gentry should make submission and receive the king's mercy. He was imposing an oath that would compel the northern gentry openly to renounce the rebellion. He wanted the instigators of the rebellion and the devisers of its articles to be searched out—even though he had pardoned them for any offences they had committed.

Above all, Henry railed against the monasteries. The one specific and immediate concession that Norfolk had made in December was that monasteries should stand until parliament met. As we have seen, the Pilgrims interpreted this as a substantial retreat, implying that the suppression of monasteries would be reversed in the forthcoming parliament. That manifestly was not the king's attitude, as we have seen in his letter to Norfolk and Fitzwilliam, bemoaning the concession they had made. Now, in January, in his instructions to Norfolk and Sussex, the king denounced the monasteries.

The instructions to the royal lieutenants went into passionate detail on the question of the monasteries.[510]

Diverse monks, nuns and canons have, in the time of the rebellion, entered again into certain monasteries being within the act of suppression, and others of the same sort not yet suppressed have kept their houses with an unseemly force as men that would manifest thereby their naughty minds towards the king's majesty so trusting to have had the said rebellion continue till they might have enforced his grace to relinquish his right in such monasteries where unto by law he is justly entitled.

Norfolk, after he had secured oaths from the Yorkshire gentry, and the earls of Sussex and Derby after their areas of responsibility were quiet, were to restore the farmers of the houses already suppressed, and to try to recover the goods of those houses. They were also to assist any commissioners sent to dissolve any other houses. They were to arrange for monks in houses dissolved to transfer to other houses, or to accept licences to leave (capacities); failing that, they were to punish them as vagabonds and 'enemies to the commonwealth'. In short, Henry wanted Norfolk, Sussex and Derby to implement the act dissolving the smaller monasteries.[511]

What this shows plainly is that anyone who did not accept the dissolution of the smaller monasteries was to be considered a traitor as soon as this became possible. Was not such action against the Doncaster agreement that abbeys should stand until a parliament was held at York? In his instructions for Norfolk, Sussex and Derby, the king simply rewrote the Doncaster agreement.[512] 'If it shall be alleged that the duke of Norfolk and the Lord Admiral [Fitzwilliam] at their being at Doncaster made promise that the monks canons and nuns of the said houses suppressed should have victum and vestitum of their revenues of their monasteries till further direction[513] should be taken',[514] the earls should answer 'that no such promise was made, but that the said duke of Norfolk and lord Admiral did only promise to be suitors therein to the king's majesty'.

They were instead to criticise the monks. Norfolk was to make a speech to all who appeared 'so much affectionate' towards the monks in which he was to 'dilate how far they vary from good religious men, from them that will be wilfully poor, yea from their subjects that would direct their prince and sovereign lord that will not live but as they list themselves'. He was then further to declare how the king 'is by his laws rightfully entitled to those monasteries', and to insist that those who would try to 'direct' the king over that issue were not to be taken as the king's true subjects but rather to be punished as traitors and rebels.

Another version was more emotive still.[515] They were to 'dilate' to the people how far monks who would not accept transfer to other monasteries were at variance with their vows 'which consist in their principal points in wilful poverty, chastity and obedience'. How could they call themselves 'wilfully poor' if they would not live except as they themselves wished? 'What obedience', Norfolk was to ask, 'is in him that will direct his prince and sovereign lord to whom by God's commandment he ought in all things to obey and give place?' Such 'obstinate persons' should rather be regarded 'as sturdy and idle vagabonds' than as men who have forsaken the world as they claimed. If the people looked well at the way in which monks lived, they would see that as far as 'wilful poverty' went, they had amassed possessions and put themselves outside the law. They were 'richer than a prince', yet they were more certain to be able to enjoy their wealth than a prince who had to attend to the welfare of his subjects.

Henry undoubtedly saw the dissolution as a central issue in the Pilgrimage of Grace; he was determined that the rebellion should not derail that policy, to which he was firmly committed. It is striking how roundly the monks are condemned and how the gap between their vows and their practice is mocked. It is striking how the king is in effect appealing to the people to join him in alliance against the monks, an alliance that will be to their material advantage. All these instructions were being prepared *before* the renewed, if limited, outbreak of rebellion known as Bigod's rising in mid-January; what is quite plain is the king's determination to enforce the dissolution of smaller monasteries, despite the— apparent—concessions made by Norfolk and Fitzwilliam in December, and despite the king's humouring of Robert Aske, Sir Robert Constable and others. Governments often make promises that they do not intend to keep, but it is rare to be able to document their duplicity so clearly. Bush and Bownes, remarkably, suggest that the 'instructions . . . provide compelling proof that the government intended to fulfil its part of the Doncaster agreement'.[516] Reginald Pole, in exile, was more astute when he noted on 17 February that, by asking for the people's petitions, and then pretending to approve them and promising to accept them, the king had perhaps sought to escape their fury, with the intention of ignoring his promises once he was out of danger, and then getting rid of the authors of the sedition on one pretext or another.[517]

The king had at some point in December or January asked Norfolk 'in the gallery concerning mine opinion of causes of religion'. What had it been about? Norfolk referred to that conversation with the king after Cromwell had written these words to him in February: 'if your grace can frame your self to satisfy the king's majesty touching the suppression of the abbeys and the acceptation of the traitors being in the same as they be worthy'. Dealing with the monasteries had evidently been uppermost in Henry's mind. Norfolk knew that his own commitment to the king's wishes was being questioned—and he now responded by assuring Cromwell, 'doubt ye not I shall do my best therein and of such sort that I trust no default shall be found in me'. He then reminded him of 'what I hath answered and promised to do' when the king examined him. 'If true report be made of what I have openly said since my coming hither I am sure it shall be well known to his majesty that I have performed my promise unto this time and so will continue.' What exactly had the king wanted and what had Norfolk promised? Cromwell's remark about satisfying the king 'touching the suppression of the abbeys and the acceptation of the traitors being in the same as they be worthy' offers a clue that the monasteries were a central concern. So does Norfolk's assurance that he would continue 'of such sort that neither in these partes I am now nor shall be hereafter reputed papist nor favourer of naughty religious persons'—incidentally a form of words once again showing what sort of rebellion Norfolk and the king thought it had been, one fomented by papists and naughty monks. Moreover, Norfolk added that what he had said there had prompted several gentlemen to warn him to take care what he ate or drank in monasteries: he had evidently spoken out so critically against the monasteries that he was thought to be at risk of being poisoned by monks. It is highly likely that Henry had denounced the monasteries involved in the Pilgrimage, berated Norfolk for having made the concession that suppressed monasteries should stand until the next parliament, cast doubt in consequence on his loyalty, and then got him to promise to deal with them.[518] Henry's berating of Norfolk may well have been the more wounding, given that earlier—we may infer from Norfolk's responses—the king had already criticised his handling of the rebels.[519] That is why Norfolk again defended himself on that score. He may have written 'desperately', but he protested that he had a 'good record'. No one with him at the time of greatest danger had found any fault in his conduct. Nonetheless, Norfolk implored the king to pardon his 'unwise proceedings' and asked him 'to consider that my years do require rather to pray withe my book and beades then to meddle in such great affairs as your highness doth put me unto', sentiments echoed in his letter to the council; 'but to be plain with you', he added, 'there is none so much to blame as his highness and you of his council to put such weighty causes in the hands of an old forgetful fool more meet to sit in a chair by the fire to keep me warm then to main [sic] such great affairs'.[520]

All that doubtless explains the haughtily defensive tone of many of Norfolk's letters from the north after he had returned there in late

January/early February. He declared to Cromwell that almost all the gentlemen and substantial yeomen of the shire would bear witness that he was neither a papist nor a favourer of traitors or rebels.[521] When still anxious about the siege of Carlisle in mid-February, Norfolk wrote to Cromwell, 'now shall appear whether for favour of these country men I forbear to fight with them at Doncaster as ye know the king's highness showed me it was thought by some I did'.[522] On 24 February he wrote to Cromwell again following a long letter to Henry, begging him to be informed as he would inform his friend if the king took exception to any of his proceedings.[523] Norfolk would again complain later to Cromwell and the king that[524]

> some false malicious men should noise that at such time as I declared to the people mine opinions against the bishop of Rome and other religious men with other things to impress your royal authority given by almighty god in the peoples hearts here . . . I should have done the same with so heavy cheer and countenance that it might appear I spoke not as I thought whereunto for answer to your majesty God doth know I do not remember my countenance but well I am sure all that were present will bear me record that I spoke the same with no little vehemence and frankly as ever they herd man speak. And of such sort that as they all of your council here say unto me they wold not have believed without hearing that I could have handled it so well And that they think my words did more good then the sermons of any vi bishops of your realms should have done. Alas sir it is pity that a true man remaining so entirely true as I did should have be so falsely reported and spoken of as I am. . . . And I think no man of truth will bear record with any of those surmises And almighty god from whom nothing is hid doth know that I spoke nothing but that I thought And will adventure my poor body in defence of . . . the same where such false caitifs wold be loath to show their faces.

Where might such charges have come from? In Thomas Master's notes prepared for Lord Herbert of Cherbury a century later, there is a remark that Darcy, during his imprisonment, had accused Norfolk of favouring the rebels' articles when they first met at Doncaster; Norfolk denied it, offering a duel, and saying that Darcy had borne him ill will ever since Norfolk had urged him to deliver up Aske into his hands.[525] Aske would evidently claim before his death that Norfolk had expressed some sympathy with the Pilgrims.[526] Had Norfolk given the impression that he was more sympathetic than he was? However that may be, in his actions in early 1537 he showed not the slightest hesitation in dealing firmly with those involved in the rebellion. And in May Henry responded by reassuring him that his service was 'most acceptable' and that he had a 'good opinion' of his 'true and faithful heart': he denied that he had ever heard any malicious reports against him.[527] Norfolk responded with effusive gratitude:[528] 'Sir if I had a thousand bodies and as many good wills in every of them as is in this little poor carcase that I have, all were not able to recompense your great kindness at all times showed to me.' All that shows, however, that when Norfolk returned to the north in January he did so under pressure to deliver to his royal master not just a pacified region but also the reversal of the concessions he had made at Doncaster on the monasteries.

Norfolk certainly took an immediate interest in monastic affairs on his return to the north. From Lincoln he suggested that three monks of Watton who had just been captured should, if they were found to be implicated in any new rebellion, be sent to York to be executed: it would be the best place, and the sooner the better. Interestingly highlighting the king's determination on sanguinary revenge, Norfolk asked Henry, 'if it shall chance me to cause to be apprehended xx xl lx or a c or moo which hath gone about to make new rebellion how many your pleasure shall be I shall put to execution'.[529] On arriving in Yorkshire, he lamented that the noblemen and gentlemen 'be well afraid' and had yet to put—or dare to put—the king's farmers in possession of the religious houses due to be suppressed, as Norfolk understood the agreement he had made at Doncaster required.[530] That encouraged the king to explore specious excuses that might serve as loopholes to escape from those Doncaster concessions. When the earl of Sussex showed Norfolk's letters to the king, Henry noted that, despite the promise made at Doncaster, the gentlemen had not taken possession of any of the religious houses for the king's use, because, as Norfolk wrote, they did not dare. The king remarked that if the gentlemen had broken their promise with him, he might break his with them.[531] By 7 February Norfolk was swearing Yorkshiremen, as the king had ordered, 'not finding any man making any manner of ill countenance against the same', though he pointed out to Henry that 'force must be meddled here with pleasant words as the case shall require. . . . Quod differtur non aufetur' (to postpone is not to abandon).[532] While at York he kept sessions at which some people were condemned for treason.[533]

That done, Norfolk's actions centred on dealing with those monasteries involved in the rebellion. He began with Sawley. Sir Arthur Darcy (who had been granted Sawley in March 1536) reported Norfolk as bent on expelling the monks whom he saw as rebels.[534] Then on 13 February Norfolk sent up a list of those captured and awaiting execution, including some monks: two canons of Warter (one formerly subprior), to be hanged in chains at York (there is no earlier evidence of their involvement in rebellion); and the subprior of Watton, to be hanged in chains at Watton.[535] Norfolk moved on to Fountains, writing directly to Henry VIII on 14 February.[536]

There was then an interruption, as news came of the renewed insurrection in the north-west, and the commons' siege of Carlisle, which, as we have seen, Norfolk saw as a test of his loyalty and determination. He managed to persuade Yorkshire gentry to agree to raise forces (some two to three hundred light horsemen[537]) but, maybe fortunately for Norfolk's reputation, news soon came of Sir Christopher Dacre's rout of the commons. Norfolk rushed to Carlisle and exploited his new-found military advantage to impose martial law in the north-west. The smashing defeat of the commons made that as unnecessary, in military terms, as it was now practical politically. Norfolk explained that, if he had proceeded by common law, 'many great offenders' would be acquitted on the excuse that they had acted under compulsion against their will.[538] So while the banners were displayed, seventy-four men, selected on the advice of the gentlemen of those parts, were condemned.[539] Norfolk was now supported by the northern gentry; but the involvement of, notably, Robert Bowes and Sir Ralph Ellerker—who had taken the Pilgrims' petitions to the king in November—in the meting out of punishments under martial law does not in itself show that 'the rebellions of October/November 1536 and January/February 1537 were mutually opposed movements, rather than complementary parts of the same revolt'.[540] What it points to is the changed balance of forces at the end of February. All that remained possible by way of continued protest was the action of the widows of those seventy-four men who were executed in the north-west: at night their dead bodies were taken down from the various places in which they had been set up as an example, and buried in churchyards. This was a last gesture of defiance, hard for Norfolk to counter,[541] but it was no political threat. And no doubt news of the commons' defeat outside Carlisle, and the harsh punishments subsequently meted out, served as a warning and helps explain the subsequent quiescence of the north.

The defeat of the commons outside Carlisle allowed Norfolk to press on with the final suppression of Sawley. He sent a letter to the abbot and convent and compelled them to surrender possession. Sir Arthur Darcy, who, as we have seen, had been granted the monastery, went to

Sawley, and his men then captured the abbot. One of his tenants blamed monks for stirring up the rebellion and said that they 'would have eft-soons quickened and revived the same'.[542] But this time there was no resistance. Clear evidence that the government was determined on the dissolution of the smaller houses in the north appears in Norfolk's acknowledgment on 21 February of receipt of a commission and a letter from the council of augmentations 'for suppressing of the houses in the north partes'.[543] Henry's hostility to the monasteries again leaps from the page of his letter to Norfolk on 22 February, responding to Norfolk's reports, but clearly enlarging upon them. He attacked monks as hypo-crites. Since 'all these troubles have ensued by the solicitation and traitorous conspiracies of the monks and canons of those parties', Henry gave Norfolk further instructions. On coming to Sawley, Hexham, Newminster, Lanercost, Easby and all other places that 'have made any manner of resistance, or in any wise conspired, or kept their houses with any force' since the Doncaster agreement, 'you shall without pity or circumstance, now that our banner is displayed, cause all the monks and canons, that be in any wise faulty to be tied up, without further delay or ceremony, to the terrible example of others; wherein we think you shall do unto us high service'.[544] Henry was bent on pitiless pun-ishment of those monks and nuns who had been involved in the rebel-lion. Simply to have 'kept their houses with any force' since the Doncaster agreement was taken as a heinous offence. More than that, the king accused monks of hypocrisy and superstition, terms that, as we shall see, might imply a wider and more general condemnation of monasticism.

Norfolk had already begun to deal with Sawley. He now informed Cromwell that he had been sent incriminating evidence: a letter from the abbot to Sir Thomas Percy which 'I think will touch the said abbot very [sore]'.[545] He wrote to Henry from Carlisle on 24 February about the unwillingness of local men to act as farmers and receivers of suppressed monasteries.[546] He dissolved the monastery at Hexham on 26 February.[547] By 7 March 1537 Norfolk could report to the council that he had suppressed all the religious houses within his commission.[548]

Henry continued to send Norfolk fierce instructions. Norfolk was to proceed against the abbot of Jervaulx and the quondam abbot of Foun-tains William Thirsk ('for whose apprehension we give unto you our right hearty thanks'); 'and semblably we will ye shall proceed vppon the abbot of Sawley if you may perceive matier in him worthy the same, as we doubt not but you shall, wherein you may remember the letter by him sent to Sir Thomas Percy'. Henry was also angry at the behaviour of the Observant Franciscans, presumably of Newcastle: from Tunstal's declaration and other evidence, he wrote, 'we perceive and see the same [the Friars Observants] be disciples of the bishop of Rome and sowers of sedition among the people'; he ordered Tunstal to make a search and to detain any captured friars in other friaries, 'to abide there as captives without liberty to speak to any man till we shall further determine our pleasure upon them'. The abbot of Jervaulx was duly arrested by 17 March.[549] Norfolk expelled the Observant Franciscans from the Greyfriars at Newcastle.[550] They had re-entered their house in December, after the Doncaster agreement, against his will, the mayor claimed.[551] On 27 March Norfolk received further advice from Richard Bowier, a lay church lawyer, that he should discover 'how such an army as was assembled at the first rebellion was so shortly gathered and thorough whose aid', and that he should begin by questioning 'abbots priors and spiritual men', comments that are revealing as to perceptions of the origins of the commotions, though Bowier was very likely trying to deflect responsibility from himself.[552]

Meanwhile, even as Norfolk was dealing with the aftermath of the rebellion, the dissolution of the smaller monasteries was resuming. Given the terms of the Doncaster agreement, that is in itself very revealing. By early December a new audit of abbeys suppressed in Lincolnshire was taking place.[553] Evidence of activity survives from several counties. Commissioners were at work in Bedfordshire and Norfolk by January, in Suffolk by February, and in Hertfordshire, Staffordshire and Sussex by March.[554] The commissioners in Norfolk, Sir Roger Townshend, Richard Southwell, Sir William Paston and Thomas Mildmay, acted vigorously, visiting eighteen monasteries between 10 January and 18 February.[555] There is not the slightest indication that the government was waiting for any resolution by a parliament to be held in York. Further evidence of Henry's hostility to the monasteries may be seen in his blaming the deputy and council of Ireland severely in February 1537 for not having proceeded to the suppression of the monasteries there.[556]

The way in which Aske and Sir Thomas and Sir Ingram Percy were further tricked confirms that the government had no intention of honouring the Doncaster agreement. Sir Thomas and Sir Ingram came to the duke of Norfolk at Doncaster on 2 February. The latter intended to send them up to London, but to encourage them he would write a letter to the council in their favour and show it to them: 'whom with good words I shall send unto you with haste and to encourage them the more to haste up I shall write a letter to you in their favour which I will show them, not doubting you will weigh the cause of my so writing.'[557] He duly signed such a letter, saying that he thought that Sir Thomas and Sir Ingram would be found of better sort than the council had been informed by their brother the earl of Northumberland, 'whom I think you shall not find so ill, but of better sort then you have ben informed by my lord their brother, heartily beseeching you therefore to be good lords unto them according to their deserts'.[558] By 6 February Sir Thomas Percy was in the Tower.[559]

Norfolk tricked Aske in the same way at the end of March.

> I have caused Aske to ride with me all this journey that I have had northwards, thinking him to be better with me then at home, the man is marvellous glorious, often time boasting to me that he hath such sure espial that nothing can be done nor imagined against the king's highness, but he will shortly give me warning thereof. I can not perceive he hath any such favour amongst gentlemen, nor honest persons, for as many as doth talk with me of him doth marvellously abhor him, every man imputing the hole beginning of this mischief to be by him. If he have any such credit or knowledge I am sure the same is of very light persons. I have by policy brought him to desire me to give him licence to ride to London,

he informed Cromwell on 22 March, 'and have promised to write a letter to your good lordship for him', adding, cold-bloodedly, 'which letter I pray you take of like sort as you did the other I wrote for Sir Thomas Percy'.

> If neither of them both come never in this country again, I think neither true nor honest men will be sorry thereof, nor in likewise for my Lord Darcy nor Sir Robert Constable. Hemlock is no worse in a good salad then I think the remaining of any of them in these parts should be ill to the common wealth.

Norfolk thought that 'surely if the king's majesty would secretly common [talk] with the said Aske, and wade with him with fair words, as though he had great trust in him, he should make him cough out as much as he knoweth concerning my lord Darcy and Sir Robert Constable'; and if the king would not, then Cromwell should 'be in hand with him'. As a postscript Norfolk added that Aske 'desired me to write a letter to the king in his favour which I have done, nothing doubting but ye will see the same may be weighed accordingly'.[560] On

22 March Norfolk signed a letter to the king, beseeching him 'to be good and gracious lord' to the bearer, Robert Aske, 'who hath ridden with me all this progress and can right well advertise your highness of your affairs in these partes', and who 'hath desired me to be content that he might at this time come up to London',[561] and a similar letter to Cromwell, asking him 'for my sake to be good lord unto Robert Aske the bearer in such his pursuits as at this time he shall declare unto you who hath desired licence of me to come up to London at this time'.[562]

Governments are doubtless entitled to protect themselves against those they regard as traitors. What is important for the argument here is that Henry VIII, Cromwell and Norfolk clearly had not the slightest intention of yielding to the Pilgrims' demands, whatever might have been agreed at Doncaster, whatever the king had himself said to Aske and others.[563]

The interrogations of Aske and Darcy after they were committed to the Tower on 7 April on suspicion of treason[564] show that their stand on monasteries was especially held against them. The official line was that it was for their offences since the pardon granted in December that they were being interrogated and punished. The king insisted that Darcy, Aske and Sir Robert Constable were held in captivity for combining to attempt new treasons against him: his subjects in the north should 'conceive not, that any thing is done for their former offences done from before the pardon, which his grace will in no wise remember or speak of, but for those treasons which they have committed again sithens, in such detestable sort'. Writing to Sir Thomas Wyatt at the court of Francis I in June, Cromwell instructed him to affirm that if they had not offended since their pardon, the king would never have remembered their previous offences.[565]

But the questions that Darcy and Aske faced clearly treated any continuing expression of support for a parliament at York to reform certain articles of grievances as itself treasonable. Where Darcy had sent out a circular letter on 21 January that the duke of Norfolk would arrive soon and declare 'a free parliament to be kept and also free liberty to the spirituality and temporality to utter their learning truly as they may justify and also that any of the king's subjects shall and may at the same parliament show their griefs and complaints against all offenders according to the bill of the commons at Doncaster', that was taken to show that Darcy 'continueth in his traitorous heart' since 'he rejoyseth of the parliament trusting then to have his unlawful desires reformed which is well known to be high treason'.[566] Where Darcy had reassured the mayor and commons of Pontefract on 19 January that 'he hath and shall keep a clean true heart to God and to the king and that he will ever more further and be a true petitioner for all good common's wealth', signing the letter 'yours faithfully T Darcy', that was also taken to show that Darcy 'changed not his traitor's heart and opinions'.[567] After he had returned from the king, Aske had written to the commons referring to their 'reasonable petitions' and 'parliament'—the document is so faded that even under ultraviolet light more cannot be read— 'whereby yet appeareth that if there be not a parliament and a convocation and a general pardon according to their pleasure and unreasonable requests then they [Darcy, Aske, and Constable] will revive their traitors' hearts'.[568]

The indictment against Darcy, Aske, Constable and many others accused them of conspiring to deprive the king of his title of supreme head of the church; seeking to compel him to hold a parliament and convocation; levying war against the king; continuing to conspire for the first two purposes after the pardon granted on 10 December; seeking the annulment of 'divers wholesome laws made for the common weal'; and wishing to depose the king.[569] In other words the government did not regard the promises it made at Doncaster as binding—upholding them was treason. More specifically, it was held against Darcy that one of his servants had written to him after Christmas that all the north was ready should any one put out the monks of Sawley. That was interpreted as revealing Darcy's 'traitorous heart'.[570] 'How many acts of the king's parliament they have grudged at, and what be the special acts where against they grudged', Darcy, Aske and Constable were asked in further interrogatories.[571]

The indictment against Lord Hussey and several others in Lincolnshire (including William Burrowby, Thomas Moigne, George Huddeswell and Philip Trotter) held that they had conspired in October 1536 to deprive Henry of his title of supreme head, to subvert and annul 'divers salutary laws' that had been made in the king's reign, and to depose him by force.[572] They were unprotected by any pardon, and so technically guilty. What is interesting here is that once more simply wishing to annul laws was seen as treasonable.

Aske, 'the grand traitor and worker of that insurrection' (as Henry would describe him to Sir William Parr on 24 June 1537), was sent to be hanged in chains at York, 'where he was in his greatest and most frantic glory'.[573] Robert Wall, servant of Aske, 'brought up with Aske as a child', died six or seven days after Aske was moved to the Tower, 'for sorrow, and in his death bed cried and said the king's commissioners would hang him draw him and quarter him'.[574] According

to Richard Curwen, Aske, when he was laid on the hurdle, openly confessed that

> he had grievously offended God, the king and the world. God he had
> offended in breaking of his commandments many ways, the king's
> majesty he said he had greatly offended in breaking his laws, where
> unto every true subject is bounden by the commandment of god as
> he did openly affirm, and the world he offended for so much as he
> was the occasion that many had lost their lives lands and goods.

After that, he 'declared openly that the king's highness was so gracious
lord unto all his subjects on these parts that no man should be troubled
for offences comprised within the compass of his gracious pardon'. As
he was drawn through the most notable places in the city, he desired
the people to pray for him. He repeated his confession when he was
taken off the hurdle, and again when he ascended up into the tower
where the gallows were prepared, 'asking diverse times the king's highness forgiveness, my Lord Chancellor, my Lord of Norfolk, my Lord
Privy Seal, my Lord of Sussex and all the world'. So far, so conventional.
But Curwen, who reported his confession, noted that Aske said he was
aggrieved that Cromwell 'spoke a sore word and affirmed it with a
stomach, swearing that all the northern men war but traitors whereat
he was somewhat offended'. Moreover, he told Curwen that Cromwell
'sundry times promised him a pardon of his life, and that at one time
he had a token from the king's majesty of pardon for confessing the
truth': Curwen added that Aske had shown these only to him.[575] Had
Cromwell and the king tricked Aske into giving his versions of events?

Lord Darcy was convicted of treason by his peers on 15 May[576]—
possibly despite Cromwell's promise to the lords at Darcy's arraignment
to do his best to spare his life and goods (if Lord Delaware, reported
by George Crofts, may be believed[577])—and was executed at Tower Hill
on 30 June.[578]

Sir Robert Constable, 'a principal traitor against us', was condemned,
despite imploring his son Sir Marmaduke to entreat the earl of Rutland
and Sir Edward Seymour, Lord Beauchamp, the queen's brother, to get
the queen to sue to the king for his life:

> to entreat my lord of Rutland to be mean unto the queen her grace
> of pity to sue unto the king's majesty to pardon me my life with as
> poor a living as may be to the intent that I may all my life time lament

mine offences and quietly serve God and pray for the king's majesty and her grace and die a natural death.

And more insistently:

> My son Marmaduke to labour unto my lord Bewchamp and his lordship to be mean for me unto the queen her grace for my life and to labour by all the ways and mean he can according unto his natural duty if he can get my lord of Rutland and him both to labour unto her grace than I doubt not but all shall be well.

He insisted that he had been loyal, and made a declaration of his actions to his son that reads as a defiant assertion of his innocence: 'item the king's letters were that I should stay the country unto the duke of Norfolk's coming and so I did as is well known and right taken I did the king good service'. He added the bitter reflection that 'death is a very small reward of service I made way for other men's thanks'.[579]

Constable was convicted on 16 May.[580] Pressed further as to whether his written confession was all he knew, he admitted knowing 'sundry naughty words and high cracks that Darcy had blown out', and voiced a doubt as to whether he had offended God in receiving the sacrament while keeping this to himself.[581] He was sent up to Hull,[582] to be hanged in chains there,[583] where Norfolk reported he 'doth hang above the highest gate of the town, so trimmed in chains . . . that I think his bones will hang there this hundredth year'.[584] But he died defiant: he would not declare openly that he had committed treason since the pardon.[585]

Technically, Darcy, Aske, Constable and the others had been executed for their offences since the pardon granted in December. Morally, they were executed for what they had said and done earlier, as the tone of the interrogatories makes plain. And with these executions the rebellion was well and truly over, and the concessions that Norfolk had made at Doncaster in December shown to be of no value. No parliament would be held at York and no statutes would be repealed. The dissolution of the monasteries would resume.

Yet what is most striking, and most surprising, is not that the risings failed, but rather that they ever took place, and that for much of October, November, December and January it appeared that the Pilgrims held the whip hand and would succeed in extracting substantial concessions from Henry VIII. Those concessions, it has been argued here, were above all on matters concerning religion, especially the fate of the monasteries. The Pilgrimage of Grace, more than is currently fashionable to recognise, even more than was once believed, was a critique of the Henrician reformation revealing the depth and breadth of concern over Henry VIII's religious policies; for a time it seemed to have achieved the Pilgrims' dreams. But it was not to be; and especially in intensifying Henry's deep-rooted animosity towards the monasteries, the Pilgrimage of Grace had immensely lasting consequences.

Reginald Pole's Legation

If, from one perspective, the Pilgrimage of Grace lasted for a remarkable space of time, from another it did not last long enough. We have earlier seen how Reginald Pole's opposition to the king had developed over the years. Unwilling to support the king's divorce, but reluctant to oppose it in public, he had chosen the relative calm of academic exile. In 1535, however, shocked by the executions of More, Fisher and the Carthusian monks, he was approached by the king for support for his break with Rome. Provoked beyond measure, he wrote at length and defiantly. In *De unitate*, which he sent Henry in spring 1536, he denounced the king's actions. Up to this point, his approach was, however, essentially personal; that of a counsellor, or a confessor, warning against misguided, even wicked policies and actions, and calling on the king to repent and reform.

How would Pole react to the Pilgrimage of Grace? Judging from his correspondence, he had little detailed knowledge or understanding of it, and never referred to its leaders or actions.[586] But the mere fact of rebellion in England appeared to offer opportunities. It may well be that, as was often the case for him, an important turning point in his life depended upon the decisions of others. Not only was he reacting to a rebellion that he had had no part in making, but it was at this time that Pope Paul III appointed him a cardinal and legate.[587] Pole denied any personal ambition: he told Michael Throckmorton, his servant, that if the king gave up his title of supreme head, then he would give up his dignities, become a hermit and burn his book.[588] All the while he saw his purpose as reclaiming the king for Christendom.

But now Pole went far beyond personal appeals to the king. In February 1537 the pope sent him to Flanders, where he was to negotiate with any representative that Henry sent there.[589] No doubt he also tried strenuously to persuade Francis I and Charles V to take forceful action against the schismatic Henry. It is hard to see that he could have responded to the Pilgrimage more quickly, but, as things turned out, it proved to be too late, as Charles V realised.[590] Henry, as we have seen, was deviously and ruthlessly riding out the storm and by April 1537 was able to arrest those whom he blamed. Had rebellion continued, and in particular had there been an armed confrontation between rebels and royal forces, foreign powers might have been tempted to intervene and even to invade. Pole's legation might have made a dramatic impact in such circumstances.[591]

In the context of Norfolk's pacification of the north, how great a threat to Henry did Pole now pose? Were his actions not 'the comic-opera machinations of a slightly befuddled, if saintly, scholar wholly unequipped to deal with the rigors of European diplomacy' but rather 'a real challenge' to the king, as Mayer has claimed?[592] Clearly Pope Paul III, in his bull appointing Pole as legate a latere, hoped that the rebels would rise again. He feared that Henry would not be brought to reason except by the force of arms, but thought it better that the king and his adherents should perish than that he should be the cause of perdition to so many.[593] That was threatening indeed. Henry countered angrily. He asked Francis I for 'the deliverance of our rebel Reynold Pole'. The French king responded that Pole had been given a safe conduct and that it would be dishonourable for him to deliver him to Henry, but nonetheless he promised to expel him within ten days. He did so, allowing him to travel to Cambrai, under the jurisdiction of Charles V.[594] First, however, Francis gave Reginald an audience in April.[595] Henry ordered Stephen Gardiner, bishop of Winchester (since 1535 his ambassador at the French court) and Francis Bryan, his trusted courtier whom he had sent to join Gardiner, to protest at 'the solemn and pompous receiving of Pole in Paris'. Henry had thought 'the manner of proceeding then to be very strange'. According to previous treaties, Henry asserted, Pole should have been apprehended, the more so since Francis had warned him of 'the traitorous purpose of the said Pole'.[596] According to the papal nuncio at the French court, 'this ribald Winchester [Gardiner] has done against the legate those offices which one can expect from devils and not men', and had put Francis in fear of losing Henry's support.[597] Henry also urged Mary of Hungary, the regent of Flanders, to forbid Pole to enter the emperor's dominions,[598] and then, when he reached Cambrai, to expel him.[599]

More pointedly still, Henry urged Gardiner and Bryan that 'we wold be very glad to have the said Pole by some mean trussed up and conveyed to Calais'. Gardiner and Bryan, if they thought it feasible, were to find trustworthy kidnappers whose expenses Henry undertook to meet.[600] The papal nuncio at the French court reported that Bryan had been sent there to seize Pole: having failed, he was desperate and very discontented with the French, and boasted that if he found Pole, he would kill him with his own hands. As the nuncio noted, this clearly showed Henry's mind.[601] Pole apparently got wind of Henry's intentions,[602] and by mid-May the king was not minded to advance more money to pursue his capture. If, nevertheless, the deed was done, then Henry would not fail to reward it; but he was now pessimistic.[603] All that sounds somewhat shambolic. Yet Pole might have been captured. And that Henry should have been so keen on such an outcome highlights his fears of the potential threat that Pole's activities posed—as Pole himself pointed out.[604]

Intriguingly, efforts were also made to win Pole back. He had a gentleman servant, Michael Throckmorton, whom he sent to England with letters to several friends.[605] To Cromwell, in August, Throckmorton protested his loyalty to the king, and suggested that Pole might be won over for the king by Dr Nicholas Wilson. Cromwell regarded this as a pretence of loyalty, but nonetheless Wilson and Nicholas Heath, both royal chaplains, were duly ordered to see Pole, taking with them a sermon by Archbishop Lee, an oration by Stephen Gardiner and a copy of the most recent formulation of faith, the Bishops' Book. They were to stress the great probability that the king would yet be merciful if Pole returned home and acknowledged his fault.[606] It does not seem that they ever went. Soon Cromwell was berating Throckmorton as a traitor and lamenting Pole's obstinacy. 'Pit[y it] is that the folly of one brainsick Poole or to say [manuscript torn] better of one witless fool should be the ruin of so gre[at] a family.' Few would disagree that he deserved a shameful death, he reflected. Ways enough might be found in Italy 'to rid a traitorous subject'. And Throckmorton was himself warned either to come to Henry's allegiance or to face dying a shameful death.[607] It was in that context that Throckmorton's brother Sir George was interrogated in October about his opposition to the king's divorce in parliament and his contacts with Fisher, More and others.[608]

Pole refused to change his tune. But the Pilgrimage of Grace was now over, and by 18 May Reginald informed the pope that the cause seemed hopeless, since the popular rising had been appeased and the leaders were in the king's hands.[609] Francis would not allow him to stay in France, nor would Charles V allow him to remain in the Low Countries. He noted percipiently that if the present generation transmitted their opinions to their children, England would for ever be lost to the church.[610] He dawdled, but was summoned again by Paul III at the end of June and expressed his obedience on 21 July,[611] returning to Rome by October.[612] In retaliation, Henry VIII had him declared a traitor. He was deprived of his benefices, including the deanery of Wimborne Minster.[613] And that, seemingly, was that. Pole remained a latent threat. If Charles V and Francis I one day made peace with one another and attacked the schismatic Henry, he might yet be useful. Understandably Henry VIII was wary. But there is little to suggest that Pole was doing or plotting anything in the later months of 1537, or in 1538.

The Poles and the Marquess of Exeter

Reginald Pole's actions throughout the 1530s were the more significant because he was not just a learned scholar, but a man of noble blood and royal ancestry, the younger son of Lady Margaret Plantagenet, countess of Salisbury, only daughter of George, duke of Clarence (executed in 1478), brother of Edward IV. Towards the end of 1538, Reginald's mother, his elder brother, Henry, Lord Montagu, his younger brother, Sir Geoffrey Pole, and their kinsman Henry Courtenay, marquess of Exeter, were arrested on suspicion of treason. How far were they in opposition to Henry VIII?

Henry, Lord Montagu had been one of the signatories of the petition to the pope in July 1530.[614] At that point Reginald Pole, as we have seen, was actively engaged in securing university opinions for the king. But after he went abroad, their paths diverged. Montagu accompanied Henry and Anne to meet Francis I at Calais in September 1532.[615] He was carver for the queen at Anne's coronation in 1533.[616] When Thomas More and the prior of the London Charterhouse were tried in 1535 for refusing the oath of succession, Montagu was on the Middlesex commission of oyer et terminer.[617] In 1536 he raised men to serve against the Pilgrims of Grace. On the face of it, Montagu was loyally supporting the break with Rome: inwardly and privately, he may have felt rather differently, but outwardly he conformed.

Pole's younger brother, Sir Geoffrey, was more outspoken. He often saw Chapuys in these years, and would have seen him more often still had Chapuys not dissuaded him, on account of the risk. Sir Geoffrey unceasingly urged Chapuys to write to Charles of the ease with which the kingdom might be conquered, in effect calling on the emperor to invade and depose the king. Chapuys urged him to warn Reginald not to return lest he meet the same treatment as Fisher or worse: Sir Geoffrey did so several times and made his mother write also.[618] Evidently Henry VIII was ignorant of all this, and it did not surface in the investigations several years later. It leaves no doubt of his disquiet at the

course of events. But there is little to suggest that Sir Geoffrey did anything more: outwardly, he too conformed in these years. In February
1537 Thomas Starkey wrote to him about Reginald's elevation by the
pope in a tone that suggested that he was sure that Sir Geoffrey felt as
angry as he did.[619]

Pole's mother Margaret was evidently sympathetic to Catherine and
Mary. She was Princess Mary's lady governess.[620] In 1533 she refused
to deliver up jewels and plate to Lord Hussey, Mary's chamberlain,
when required to do so by Lord Hussey who was doubtless acting on
royal orders.[621] Margaret was soon afterwards dismissed when Mary's
household was dissolved and Mary was placed with Princess
Elizabeth.[622] Margaret offered to serve her at her own expense, but that
was unacceptable to the king.[623] Catherine of Aragon asked her daughter to pray Margaret to have a good heart, 'for we never come to the
king of heaven but by troubles'.[624] Hugh Rich, the Observant
Franciscan, had shown her the Nun of Kent's revelations.[625] In February
1535 Chapuys protested to Henry at the poor treatment of Princess
Mary, who was ill, asking that he put her under the care of her former
governess, whom she regarded as her second mother. Henry railed
against Margaret, telling Chapuys that the countess was a fool, of no
experience, and that if Mary had been under her care during her current
illness, she would have died.[626] All that might have been seen as essentially personal rather than political. But the Poles were more than just
friends of Catherine and Mary. As we have seen, Chapuys in September
1533 wrote about Reginald as a possible pretender to the kingdom and
as a prospective husband for Princess Mary.[627]

When Reginald Pole in *De unitate* denounced what the king had done,
Henry called upon his mother and his brother, Lord Montagu, to rebuke
him, speaking personally to Montagu about the issue. 'Alas', Margaret
lamented in a letter she then wrote to Reginald, 'that ever you should
be the cause that I bearing toward you so motherly and tender heart (as
I have done) should for your folly receive from my sovereign lord such
message as I have late done by your brother.' She sent him God's blessing and hers, 'more of my charity then of your deserving'. She had hoped
to have comfort of him: instead it had turned to sorrow.[628] She reminded
him how the king had showed her 'such mercy and pity', which she
could never have deserved by her service, 'trusting that my children
should by their service do some parte of my bounden duty for me'. To
see him now in the king's 'high indignation' was devastating. 'Unless
God show his power upon me I am not able to bear it. Trust me Reginald
there went never the death of thy father or of any child so nigh my

heart as this hath done.' Accordingly she called on him to serve their
master, 'as thy bounden duty is to do unless thou will be the confusion
of thy mother'. Where he had written of a promise he had made to God,
his mother responded, 'Son that was to serve God *and* thy prince, whom
if thou do not serve with all thy will with all thy power I know thou
can not please god'. The king, she reminded him, had brought him up
and supported his studies. If Reginald would not use his learning in the
king's service, 'trust never in me'. She would pray daily to God to give
him grace and make him the king's servant 'or else take you to his
mercy'.

Reginald's brother Henry, Lord Montagu wrote to him on 13 September, responding to his letter of 15 July. He described how the king
'declared a great part of your book so to me at length [incidentally
showing how closely the king had read it], that it made my poor heart
so to lament that if I had lost mother, wife and children it could no more
have done'. He reminded Reginald that next to God he had received
everything from the king, who had shown his charity and mercy in
setting up their family when it was 'clean trodden under foot'. Henry
had patiently borne Reginald's slanders and was content that his friends
should instruct him. Montagu declared his own lack of learning, but
'could never by any reason conceive that laws made by man were of
such strength but that they might be undone again by man . . . for that
which seemeth politic at one time by abusion at another time proveth
the contrary'. 'Gentle Reginald,' Montagu implored, 'let no scrupulosity so embrace your stomach'; instead let them join together to serve the
king as their duty required. 'And for that,' Montagu insisted, 'what
soever part you take, shall I spend the best blood in my body (God
willing).' He warned Reginald: 'learning you may well have, but doubtless no prudence nor pity, but showeth yourself to run from one mischief to another'. In particular he warned him not to join the pope in
Rome. If he did, 'then farewell all my hope', and 'farewell all bonds of
nature'; instead of Montagu's blessing he would have his curse. Yet he
could not imagine that 'superstition should so reign in you'.[629]

How willingly did Margaret and Montagu write? They certainly
emphasised their obligation to Henry in fulsome terms: a mother and a
brother dismayed by behaviour they deplored by someone they loved.
However much they may have disagreed with the king's policies, they
here objected far more to Reginald's protests against them, both on
moral grounds—it was simply wrong for him to disobey—and prudential grounds—his disobedience would taint his family. Interestingly,
there are no such letters of reproof from Sir Geoffrey Pole, who in the

early 1530s had been regularly in touch with Chapuys. But since there is little to suggest that Margaret and Montagu were in any active sense opponents of the king, it is possible that they were indeed dismayed by Reginald's act of defiance. No doubt Margaret and Montagu had been instructed to write rebuking him, and very likely their letters were vetted by Henry or Cromwell. But the letters contain no defence of royal policy, no response to the claims in *De unitate*: their reasoning is personal.

Pole was moved deeply, he said, by the letters from his mother and brother; but less so by the threats in Cromwell's letters.[630] Not much later, he directly and openly challenged the king as legate. How far did his family in England now support him? And did Henry VIII respond to his hostility abroad by working to destroy his family at home, as has so often been supposed? Hollger, for example, claims that the true reason for Montagu's later arrest and execution was Henry's decision to have the Poles exterminated;[631] moreover (though this is a rather different reason) 'someone had to suffer for the annoyance caused to the king by the rebellious cardinal'.[632] In November 1538, after the arrests, Castillon, the French ambassador, would write that 'il y a bien longtemps que ce roy m'avoit dict qu'il vouloit exterminer ceste maison de Montagu, qui est encore de la Rose Blanche' (it is a long time since this king told me that he wanted to destroy this house of Montagu, which is also of the white rose), though his failure to mention this supposed royal wish earlier reduces the interpretative weight that it can be given— by this time it was in no sense a prediction.[633] More interestingly, Sir Geoffrey Pole would testify—the manuscript is torn—how Montagu said that 'the king's grace told him . . . of Scots which killed not only . . . [p]oisoned the queen of Scots but also all her . . . blood that were not guilty therein. And so, quod he, the king to be revenged of Reynold [Reginald], I fear, will kill us all.'[634]

But that Henry was bent on the destruction of the Poles is easier to claim than to substantiate. There is nothing to suggest any co-ordinated action against the family—nothing in the details in the sources, nothing that can be safely inferred from the circumstances of their downfall. There is not even convincing evidence that there were royal spies in the Pole households.[635] And there is correspondingly little to suggest that they were engaged in any kind of active conspiracy against the king. When the Poles fell, and with them Henry Courtenay, marquess of Exeter and Sir Edward Nevill, the bulk of the evidence that damned them in the king's eyes came from Sir Geoffrey. Richard Morison, author of *An Invective against the Great and Detestable Vice, Treason*,[636] claimed that when 'Sir Geoffrey Pole was committed to the tower, neither the king's highness, nor any of the council suspect[ed] either the Marques, either the lord Montacute [Montagu] his brother, or sir Edward Nevill, . . . of *any* of all these things, that they were found guilty of'.[637] That makes sense, since if the king and council had suspected them earlier, they would surely not have left them at liberty for so long. Of course, it might be (as we shall see) that the king had had some inkling that they were generally disaffected, but had simply sent them warnings—until it became clearer just how disaffected they were. And Sir Geoffrey's evidence remains crucial to the arrests and trials. What then needs to be explained is how and why Sir Geoffrey came to be committed. It was at the end of August 1538 that he was sent to the Tower for corresponding with his brother, Cardinal Pole, without showing the king their letters.[638]

What is striking is how accidental it all was, owing everything to tensions within the household of Margaret, countess of Salisbury. Richard Ayer, a surgeon involved in a hospital founded by the countess, was sympathetic to the thrust of government religious policy, and consequently found himself threatened with dismissal. He voiced his concerns to one of his patients in the hospital, Gervase Tyndale, a sometime schoolmaster at Grantham, similarly sympathetic to the 'new learning'. Ayer had 'said there were a company of priests [in] my lady's house which did her much harm and kept her [from] the true knowledge of God's word'. He also claimed that '[My Lad]y off Salsborys [Salisbury's] council shall command openly in [the king's name] that no mane so hardy which be her tenants shall occupy [books of] the new testament in English or any other new [books] which the king's highness hath privileged'. Ayer told Tyndale that he and the others must leave the countess's service since she was 'credibly informed' that they were all 'of the new learning'. He gossiped about Hugh Holland, one of Sir Geoffrey Pole's servants, accusing him in effect of treasonable communication with Reginald Pole, calling him 'the marchany [merchant] man and the broker' because he carried letters from the countess and from Sir Geoffrey Pole to him. On hearing this, Sir Geoffrey took Holland and Ayer to see Cromwell, presumably to demonstrate his innocence. At first Cromwell sent them away, seemingly not taking it all that seriously.[639] Maybe Henry's attitude to the Poles was (as was later stated in instructions to the king's ambassadors at the court of Francis I) like that of Caesar: he would 'conquer their cankerdness' with clemency.[640] Or maybe Henry was just biding his time. On progress, and at Portsmouth on 11 August, he did not visit the countess or Montagu. There are two suggestive details. On 27 August Sir John Wallop reported that

Cromwell had left court to go to Lewes.[641] Miscellaneous royal payments for September 1538 record the payment by Wriothesley of 40*s.* to two servants of the bishop of Thetford for bringing Gervase Tyndale and 22*s.* 6*d.* to the said Geoffrey ('Gervase' was obviously intended) for his costs in coming and returning, and tarrying at Lewes two or three days.[642] Did the king send Cromwell to Lewes to speak with Tyndale again? Or did Tyndale so importune Cromwell that Cromwell felt he had to see him? And did Tyndale present so convincing a case this time that something had to be done? However that may be, Hugh Holland was then arrested, though not without a 'ruffle'.[643] He would not have had to say very much to confirm the accusations of Ayer and Tyndale. Soon afterwards Sir Geoffrey Pole was arrested. In short, there was no obvious drive by the king, and no long-term factional conspiracy spearheaded by Cromwell, to bring down the Poles. It was only 'of late' that the king had been informed of the matter.[644] And the crucial part that disaffected servants played in the downfall of noblemen is once more highlighted.

For two months Sir Geoffrey was kept in the Tower, without, it seems, saying anything incriminating. But then his spirit broke, and he unsuccessfully attempted suicide.[645] John Hussee reported on 28 October that after he was examined by Sir William Fitzwilliam he was 'so in despair that he would have murdered him self and hath . . . hurt him self sore'.[646] Perhaps it had been his interrogation on 26 October (his first recorded interrogation) that precipitated his attempted suicide. Richard Morison suggested that Sir Geoffrey was impaled on the horns of a dilemma. If he told the truth, he would have to admit that he, his brother Montagu, and his cousins the marquess of Exeter and Sir Edward Nevill were guilty of treason. If he lied, and denied everything, then he would jeopardise his soul. It did not occur to him to justify lying by the greater good of the cause. Instead he often thought of committing suicide. That would have several advantages: preserving the life of his brother and the honour of his family.[647] Once his attempt at suicide had failed (the knife was too blunt) Sir Geoffrey, fearful of divine anger, 'saw before him the loss of his soul, and thought it much better, they lost their heads'. Morison insisted that he had not been tortured. More probable, and entirely credible, as an explanation of Sir Geoffrey's desperation is the cumulative effect of weeks of intense psychological pressure while imprisoned in the Tower.

The marquess of Exeter responded by charging Sir Geoffrey 'with frensy, with folly, and madness'. Here he was perhaps unknowingly echoing Lord Montagu's remarks to Sir Geoffrey's wife that 'he heard say that this examinate was mad and in a frensy'.[648] Sir Geoffrey retorted that it was rather when 'I fell with them in conference to be a traitor, disobedient to god, false to my prince and enemy to my native country' that he was 'out of my wit, and in a great frenzy'. It was when he chose to kill himself rather than charge his brother and cousins with treasons which he knew would cost them their lives that he was 'out of my wit, and stricken with a sore kind of madness'.[649]

On 26 October, after making the first of his declarations, Sir Geoffrey 'most humbly beseeched the king's highness that he may have good keeping and cherishing', saying that 'he then wold truly and fully open all that he did know or may remember whom so ever it touch whether it be mother brother uncle or any other'.[650] And in a total of nine interrogations he gave damning accounts of conversations and letters. Although he had admitted his own guilt, Sir Geoffrey would be pardoned on 2 January 1539.[651] Chapuys reported on 9 January that his life had been spared, but that he was to remain in perpetual prison. He had just tried to suffocate himself with a cushion, hinting at a continually troubled mind.[652] By 18 June Sir Geoffrey was evidently free, though not calm in spirit—'I am fatherless, motherless and friendless'.[653] His emotional turmoil in these months can only be wondered at. In September 1540, Sir Geoffrey would send for John Gunter, a Sussex JP, provoke a quarrel with him for having revealed what they had 'communed of together in secret' before Sir Geoffrey's arrest (Gunter had at first appeared to shield Sir Geoffrey by committing to prison a local gossip against him[654]) and then 'sore hurt and wound' him in the head. Wriothesley, who reported the incident to the king, declared that he was in some doubt what to do. He had not committed Sir Geoffrey to prison as he deserved, considering 'the ill and frantic furious nature of the unhappy man' and 'fearing lest the same should reduce him into his frenzy or some other inconvenience'; nor had he taken sureties, since he knew that no man would stand surety for him. Wriothesley wanted to know whether the king would have him treated according to the laws and committed to prison, or whether he would extend his 'accustomed clemency' towards him, 'as in times past ye have done most largely. . . . and that he discovered to your grace of so great moment and necessary to be known for the safeguard of your most royal person'.[655] We do not know the outcome, other than that there is no record of action against him. If he did continue to enjoy royal favour, the personal cost to Sir Geoffrey of his revelations was nonetheless evidently devastating.[656]

It was Sir Geoffrey's evidence that brought down his brother Lord Montagu and his cousins the marquess of Exeter and Sir Edward Nevill. It was corroborated by depositions by his former servant Hugh Holland, by George Crofts, chancellor of Chichester Cathedral, and by John Collins, Lord Montagu's chaplain. It is important to emphasise how dependent the government was on these further depositions for the detail of the charges brought against those convicted of treason.

Just what had Sir Geoffrey Pole, his brother Henry, Lord Montagu, the marquess of Exeter and the others been saying and doing? Have we here found the nucleus of an organised and effective opposition to the government of Henry VIII? Were these traitors 'destructive anachronisms',[657] standing dangerously in the path of modernisation, enlightenment and progress, and by implication were they justly condemned? Or were they destroyed for no more than private grumbles? The bulk of our evidence comes from Sir Geoffrey Pole, supported in places by the testimonies of priests and servants. What is striking above all is that Sir Geoffrey, Lord Montagu, the marquess of Exeter and several of their servants clearly felt considerable unease at the drift of religious policy. They voiced their discontents to each other. Asked what they meant when they talked of wishing for a change, Sir Geoffrey said that 'they desired this world of plucking down abbeys images and pilgrimages and this manner of preaching to be changed'.[658] They complained about those close to the king. Montagu had declared, Sir Geoffrey recalled, that 'they were flatterers that followed the court [and] that none served the king butt knaves'.[659] He had said that 'this world will turn up so down, and I fear me wee shall have no lack but of honest men'. Vaguely menacing though that was, it was hardly devastating evidence.[660] It is not surprising that Sir Geoffrey was pressed for more. On 7 November he came up with further general denunciations: 'Neither the lord Montacute neither the lord marques ever liked any doing of the king.'[661] He also offered rather more damning remarks by Montagu. The latter had once told him that 'knaves rule about the king',[662] and, 'shaking his fist, said, I trust to give them a buffet one day'.[663] Montagu had another time told Sir Geoffrey that 'I dreamed that the king is dead'; two days later[664] he said that the king was not dead but that he 'will one day dye suddenly—his leg will kill him—and then we shall have jolly stirring'.[665]

According to the indictment on 1 (or 14) April 1537 Montagu said to Sir Geoffrey that 'the king said to the lords that he should goo from them one day', adding, 'if he will serve us so we shall be happily rid. I never loved him from childhood'.[666] In a mutilated statement by Sir Geoffrey in his own hand is a list of what his brother Lord Montagu had said and done over the years. He had comprehensively criticised the king's religious policies in the 1530s. It was because the pope would not

allow what Montagu called his divorce that the king forsook his authority. Before the king had been caught 'in the snare of unlawful love with
the lady Anne, the king could bide well enough the authority of the pope
though he misliked his abuses': in effect, this was to accuse the king of
hypocrisy. Montagu had helped his brother Reginald go into exile so
that he was not involved in 'the king's ill purpose in the forsaking off
his wife'. Montagu had claimed that wise and virtuous men were against
both the divorce and the repudiation of papal authority: those who
assisted the king in both these 'unlawful enterprises' were 'knaves and
heretics'. Montagu had compared the king adversely to the Turk—
though unfortunately this section of the manuscript is so damaged that
the precise details cannot be read. Although 'the king gloried with the
title to be supreme head next god', yet, Montagu had observed, 'he had
a sore lege that no pore man wold be glad of and. . . . he should not live
long for all his authority next God'. Montagu's resentments, although
also against 'knaves and heretics', were manifestly directed against the
king himself. According to Sir Geoffrey, he said 'that yet we should do
more, and here when the time should come what with power and friendship, nor it is not the plucking down of these knaves that will help the
matter; we must pluck down the head'. Montagu had told Sir Geoffrey
that he was 'but a fool to think otherwise'.[667] Sir Geoffrey also testified
that he had many times heard Sir Edward Nevill 'deprave' the king,
saying that his highness was 'a beast and worse than a beast'[668] and that
'the king keepeth a sort of knaves here, that wee dare neither look nor
speak And if I war able to live, I would rather live any life in the world,
than tarry in the privy chamber'.

   In this series of interrogations Sir Geoffrey had thus, step by step,
revealed the words of malcontents who had sharply criticised the king's
religious policy while hoping for a change. That he gave an essentially
truthful picture of what they had been saying is confirmed by the testimony of others. George Crofts, chancellor of Chichester Cathedral, testified how Sir Geoffrey had told him that it was permissible to have
copies of Sir Thomas More's books, and gave him part of More's
Richard III to read—the latter was of course a study in tyranny.[669]
Crofts hinted that Sir Geoffrey was not wholly loyal in spirit during the
Pilgrimage of Grace. As he was taking a muster of men to go with him
northwards, Sir Geoffrey had allegedly told him: 'I must go northwards
but I will shift for one ['me' in the indictment] well enough, if they come
to fighting I will save one.'[670] Sir Geoffrey was not prepared to die for
the king's cause and he was open about this to Crofts. Crofts later heard
him 'lament the pulling down of Bisham [Abbey] because his kin and

ancestors lay there'.[671] Crofts also testified that Sir Geoffrey had been willing to go into exile overseas to save his life.[672]

Most damagingly of all, Montagu and Sir Geoffrey had maintained contact with their brother abroad. They had warned their brother that Henry VIII was seeking to assassinate him. There were more cryptic letters which have been seen as evidence of some wider conspiracy. According to Sir Geoffrey, Montagu had often wished that they were both overseas. The indictment accused him of saying 'I like well the doings of my brother the cardinal and I wold we were both over the see for this world will one day com to stripes.'[673] One of Montagu's servants was instructed to go overseas and kill anyone who killed Cardinal Pole.[674] Hugh Holland, one of Sir Geoffrey's servants, recalled how, on hearing that Holland was going to Flanders, Sir Geoffrey asked him to go to see Reginald and

> show him I would [that] I were with him, and will come to him if he will have me, for to show him the world in England waxeth all crooked, Goddess law is turned up so down, abbeys and churches overthrown, and he is taken for a traitor and I think they will cast down parish churches and all at the last.[675]

Holland was also to warn Reginald that men were daily sent from England to destroy him, 'and that much money wold be given for his head'. The day before Holland sailed, Sir Geoffrey asked him, what if I go with you? Holland said that the ship was full.[676] Elizabeth Darell, daughter of Sir Edward Darell, examined on 6 November, said that she had heard that the king had sent Peter Mewtas to France to kill Cardinal Pole with a hand gun. 'Sir Geoffrey said at the same time, by God's blood and if he speaking of the said Peter Meotes had slain him, I would have thrust my dagger in him though had been at the king's heels.'[677] Sir Geoffrey admitted that he had warned Reginald that he was at risk of assassination and that he had offered to join him abroad, in effect associating himself with Reginald's treason.[678]

Sir Geoffrey's testimony touched his brother Lord Montagu most directly. It is not then at all surprising that Montagu was committed. On 7 November he was examined.[679] He said he had lived 'in prison these vi years', an eloquent characterisation of his disquiet over royal policy from late 1532.[680]

Montagu's servants were examined and, unsurprisingly, both confirmed Sir Geoffrey's testimony and offered further details illustrating their master's disaffection with religious policy. Jerome Ragland[681] amplified many of Sir Geoffrey's charges. He confirmed that Montagu praised Reginald (regarded by the king as a traitor) as 'ordained of God to do good';[682] and he revealed that Montagu showed him copies of letters from Reginald Pole to Bishop Tunstal, so hinting at regular communication between the brothers. He confirmed that Montagu regretted the king's divorce, the break with Rome and subsequent religious changes. He had heard Montagu

> many times lament grudge and murmur at the estate off this world liking not the king's proceedings and trusted once it should be better and feared that it would else come to further inconveniences and mischief and that such as ruled about the king and they take [here the paper is torn] would mar all.

Montagu had deplored

> that such acts as the king had caused to be made in his parliament were very cruelly made as the act of treason and other acts and if he were of the council notwithstanding these acts he would give his advice to be charitable in punishment so that men should not die therefore.

In particular Ragland had heard Montagu 'lament the pulling down of abbeys and specially Bisham and that he trusted one day to see Bisham abbey in as good state as ever it was'.[683]

Ragland's recollection that Montagu complained that Henry had broken his promise after the Pilgrimage of Grace was especially significant. At the second Doncaster agreement in December 1536, the Pilgrims, as we have seen, were promised a general pardon, the holding of a parliament at York and the suspension of the dissolution of the monasteries until parliament met. No such parliament (which would surely have been expected to repeal much of the religious legislation of the previous years) was ever held. Henry, as we have seen, broke his promise. That Montagu should have regretted that is highly eloquent evidence of his beliefs and hopes.[684] Ragland confirmed Montagu's contempt for the king's counsellors and courtiers; Montagu, he said, complained 'that knaves rule about the king saying also if he live to see the change of the world that then they shall have ... punishment for their offences without cruelty';[685] that 'the king hath a sort of knaves in the privy chamber'; that 'the king never made man but he destroyed him again other with displeasure or with the sword'.[686] And Ragland also confirmed his master's hopes of the king's imminent demise: Montagu had said that 'the king is full of flesh and unwieldy and that he can not long continue with his sore leg',[687] and that 'his leg will kill him'.[688]

John Collins, Lord Montagu's chaplain and parson of Rushale, Southampton, examined (for the third time—we have no record of the first two occasions) on 14 November, said that he had heard Montagu much praise his brother Reginald's learning.[689] At the time that abbeys were first 'plucked down', Montagu declared 'that both the king and the lord privy seal [Cromwell] would hang in hell for that mater one day'; he had said 'that he trusted to see the abbeys up again one day';[690] and he had once remarked, as the abbeys were being suppressed, 'I fear that within a while they will pull down the parish churches also.'[691]

In response to Sir Geoffrey Pole's evidence, the marquess and marchioness of Exeter were committed to the Tower. In his nine surviving interrogations Sir Geoffrey had had much less to say about Exeter than about Montagu. He did complain how the marchioness of Exeter 'once bore him good mind but after it was perceived the king favoured this examinate they said he would tell all and therefore trusted him no longer'.[692] That may have been sufficient to trigger the examination on 6 November of the marchioness.[693] (Henry may also at this point have recalled the interest that the marchioness had shown in the prophecies of Elizabeth Barton, the Nun of Kent, for which she had afterwards made an abject submission to the king.)[694] In Sir Geoffrey's surviving depositions, the most that emerges is his claim that Exeter 'at the beginning was of the same mind'; if Sir Geoffrey had not spoken with him for almost two years, he knew, he insisted, by communication with his brother, Montagu, that he and Exeter 'were of one opinion'. But in what is clearly a set of extracts from depositions against Exeter appears this note: 'Geoffrey Pole saith that the lord marquess said I trust once to have a fair day upon these knaves which rule about the king and I trust to see a m[erry] world one day.'[695] Those words appear also in a badly damaged list of charges against the marquess.[696] When Exeter was indicted these alleged remarks were central to the charges: they were dated to 20 August 1537 (Lord Montagu) and 24 July 1537 (Sir Geoffrey Pole).[697] Exeter was also charged with saying (on 24 July 1536, 25 August 1536, 1 and 20 September 1537) that 'knaves rule about the king' but, extending his clenched fist, 'I trust to give them a buffet one day'.[698] What is somewhat troubling is that these opinions are remarkably similar to those allegedly voiced by Montagu and Sir Geoffrey. Sir Geoffrey recalled how Montagu told him that 'knaves rule about the king, and shaking his fist, said, I trust to give them a buffet one day'.[699] While Montagu and Exeter may well have shared such sentiments, it is implausible that they independently formulated them in such similar terms. Exeter was also indicted for holding divers treasonable conferences with Montagu, knowing him to be a false traitor, and (here echoing the words of the indictments of both Montagu and Sir Geoffrey) for saying that he liked well the proceedings of Cardinal Pole and that 'I like not the proceedings of this realm and I trust to see a change of this world.'[700] All three men were supposed to have said that.

Perhaps the most important reason why Exeter was charged did not appear in the indictments. In a miscellaneous list of offences committed by the marquess of Exeter against the king's most royal person—most of them easily recognisable extracts from the depositions—there is a brief note of what 'diverse of the tenants of the lord marques [Henry Grey, third marquess of Dorset] lord Mountjoy [Charles Blount, Lord Mountjoy] and the abbott of Bukland [John Tucker, abbot of Buckland, Devon] said in the house of John Assheley in Bereregys [Bere Regis]': 'but yet no fear for the king hath but a little season to come and then the lord marques shall be king and then all shall be cured'.[701] According to Joan, wife of Thomas Saye, one John Davy, clothier, said that 'the date of the king was almost out and that there was but iiii or v years to come and then my lord Marquess would be king and they lords';[702] Kendal said, 'my lord will be king after the death of this [torn MS.]'; various servants spoke of how the marquess 'should wear the garland'.[703] That the marquess of Exeter's servants, tenants and neighbours should have spoken of him as prospective king (perhaps after the birth of Prince Edward in autumn 1537) must have been deeply unsettling, especially if there was any suspicion that Exeter himself had encouraged such gossip. It is interesting that, on 9 January, Chapuys reported that, according to what the king and Cromwell had said to the French ambassador (who evidently passed on the information to Chapuys), the guilt of Exeter and his two accomplices (presumably Montagu and Sir Edward Nevill) had been fully proved, since their death, by copies in the hand of the marchioness of Exeter of letters between him and Cardinal Pole—found in a coffer of the marchioness, along with some letters of the late queen and the princess. Exeter and his wife had used their influence to suborn Princess Mary, encouraging her to persist in her obstinacy against her father and refuse to swear to the statutes. Cromwell had added that it was clear that the marquess had planned to usurp the kingdom by marrying his son to Princess Mary and destroying Prince Edward.[704] That charge was repeated by the king to Sir Thomas Wyatt on 13 February, informing him how

> by the counsel of the cardinal, his brother Montagu and the marquess of Exeter with their adherents, had conspired not only diverse seditions within this our realm, but also imagined the way to destroy us and our dearest son the prince with the Lady Mary and the Lady Elizabeth our daughters for to take vppon them the whole rule. Whereunto the said Marquess had fixed his mind and sought his opportune occasion these ten years and practised to have conduced that mischief to his intent (had not God favoured us and we been wary in all things of such practices and taken heed thereunto, all these things have been disclosed by Sir Geoffrey Pole, Montagu's own brother and openly proved before their faces and by the law convicted thereof).[705]

Sir Nicholas Carew, arrested on 31 December after an incriminating letter had been found in a coffer of the marchioness of Exeter, had, in the hope of receiving a pardon, revealed that the marquess was very melancholy when Queen Jane was delivered of a son—and so, we are left to infer, removed his hopes of succeeding Henry on the throne.[706]

Margaret, countess of Salisbury, also fell under suspicion. She was interrogated on 12 and 13 November, and then placed 'in hold', under the supervision of Thomas Wriothesley, at his house at Cowdray.[707] She denied that, before going abroad, Reginald had told her what he thought about any statutes or actions of the king. When Sir Geoffrey had told her that the king intended to have Reginald slain, 'she prayed God heartily to change the king's mind'. When both Montagu and Geoffrey told her Reginald had escaped that danger, 'for motherly pity she could not but rejoice'. She denied that she and her sons ever had any conversation much commending Reginald's doings, especially trusting that he should be pope one day and come to England again: 'she hath wished oft times her self to see him once again in England with the king's favour though he were but a poor parish priest'. She utterly denied having conversations lamenting the king's proceedings and wishing for a change; but agreed that she had regretted the dissolution of the monasteries, particularly those houses where her ancestors lay. She denied burning any letters concerning the king, or receiving any messages or letters from the marquess of Exeter or his wife prejudicial to the king or his realm. She denied she had ever heard her son wish for Henry's death. Repeatedly and vehemently she denied having heard various alleged sayings. She had treated her son Reginald as a traitor, as we have seen. Montagu had counselled her to declare him a traitor to their servants, in order that 'they might so report him when they came in to their countries': accordingly Margaret told them 'that she toke her said son for a traitor and for no son and that she wold never take him otherwise'.[708]

The countess's interrogations had been vigorous, but unavailing. Wriothesley and Thomas Goodrich, bishop of Ely, reported on 14 November how the previous day

> we travailed with the Lady of Salisbury all day both before and after none till almost night. Albeit for all that we could do though we used her diversely she wold utter and confess little or no thing more than the first day she did but still stood and persisted in the denial of all togethers.

Wriothesley and Goodrich had returned to the task, 'sometime with doulx and mild words, now roughly and asperly by traitoring her and her sons to the ixth degree', but she denied everything. Wriothesley and Goodrich were impressed.[709] On 16 November they reported how they had been 'travailing sundry times and after sonde sorts with her' and now believed they had secured 'somewhat else of new' which 'wee deem material'. They had dealt, they assured Cromwell, 'with such a one as men have not dealt to fore us. Wee may call her rather a strong constant man than a woman': she was 'so earnest vehement and precise that more could not be'.

A letter from the countess to her son Montagu had been found in a gentlewoman's chest and they had interrogated her about it.[710] But once more it did not prove incriminating. She sent Montagu God's blessing and her own. 'This is the greatest gift that I can send you for to desire god of his help which I perceive is great need to pray for.' Her advice to Montagu was 'to refer you to god principally, and upon that ground so to order you both in word and deed to serve your prince, not disobeying God's commandment'.[711] The countess's advice to Montagu matches that she had given Sir Geoffrey, as testified by Oliver Franklin on 20 November. When Franklin had 'admonished' the countess 'of Sir Geoffrey Pole, bidding her beware of him and saying I pray god madam he do you no hurt one day': 'only because his stomach gave him he knoweth not wherefore', she had replied, 'I trowe he is not so unhappy that he will hurt his mother and yet I care neither for him not for any other for I am true to my prince'. This exchange took place 'since that the said Sir Geoffrey hurt him self in the Tower'. The countess was determinedly emphasising her loyalty to the king.[712] It is interesting that nothing in Sir Geoffrey's depositions incriminated his mother.[713] More-over, even after the execution of her son Montagu, Margaret responded to Wriothesley's description of Reginald as 'that arrant whoreson traitor' who 'went abouts from prince to prince to work such trouble' to the king, by replying

> with a wonderful sorrowful countenance that albeit he were most unhappy and an ill man to behave himself so unkindly and traiterously unto his sovereign lord and master who hath ever ben so good and gracious lord to him and his friends yet was he no whoreson for she said she took god to record she was both a good woman and a true woman.

She wished her 'wretched son' were in heaven or here in the king's presence. But she trusted the king 'would not impute his heinous offence unto her innocency'.[714]

All that is consistent with the countess's earlier attitudes, as we have seen. She had, together with Montagu, written to Reginald on hearing rumours that he would become a cardinal, urging him not to accept.[715] She had reproved him for his folly, and reminded him how the king had showed her undeserved mercy.[716] And Reginald's extraordinarily chilling remark to Hugh Holland that 'if mother, brother or any other of his kin were of that opinion the king and others of the realm war, he defied them and wold tread upon them with his foot' does seem to confirm that Margaret had indeed written reprovingly to him.[717]

The countess, if charges made by Ayer and Tyndale are believed, had refused to allow the 'new learning' in her household, provoking dismissed servants to reveal what they knew about Hugh Holland. That Margaret disapproved of the religious changes in the 1530s is scarcely to be doubted. She had commissioned a magnificent new chantry chapel in Christchurch Priory. But according to her own account she had resolutely refused to support her son Reginald's treachery to the king and she had upbraided him in no uncertain terms—and nothing that was found or said disproved her account, though efforts were made to discover such material. On 16 December Wriothesley reported how he had gone to the countess and demanded to see her testaments, and found both an old one drawn up ten years earlier and one drawn up as recently as September. But once again, nothing incriminating emerged.[718] She was angry at her treatment: 'The Lady Salisbury maketh great moan for that she wante the necessary apparel both for to change and also to keep her warm', Thomas Phillips, the keeper of the Tower, reported.[719] Early in

1539 Robert Southwell, one of the commissioners overseeing, the dissolution of the monasteries and reporting the surrender of Christchurch Priory, went on to emphasise how they had defaced the monument 'curiously made' of Caen stone by the countess for her burial.[720] Margaret was attainted in parliament in May 1539 along with the others. At that point the government suddenly found evidence that was thought incriminating. John Worth, a servant of Lord Lisle, reported how a coat of armour had been discovered in the countess's coffer: on one side were the king's arms, and about them were pansies for Pole, and marigolds for Lady Mary. The implication was that Pole intended to marry Princess Mary 'and betwixt them both should again arise the old doctrine of Christ. . . . This was the intent the coat was made.'[721] After her attainder in May 1539 Margaret was committed to the Tower. At last the suspicions that the countess had been arousing since at least mid-November, and possibly earlier if the king's failure to visit her in July/August was deliberate, had been vindicated from the government's point of view.

Lord Delaware also fell under suspicion. On 26 October Sir Geoffrey included him among those with whom he had conferred about a 'change of this world'—though his name was subsequently struck out in the manuscript.[722] He claimed that Delaware 'about xii months was of that opinion, howbeit of late at such times the king's highness was in Sussex he sayeth the Lord Delaware declared him self to be indifferent in such conferences' as Sir Geoffrey had had with him, 'not so much affectionate to that part' as before.[723] Indeed, according to Crofts, Delaware had attempted to persuade him to accept the royal supremacy. Crofts testified that he had told Delaware of his hostility to preaching that called into question pilgrimages, the honouring of images and praying to saints, but what Delaware's reaction was he does not say. Crofts had advised Delaware to dismiss from his service a keeper and another servant named Thatcher (a skinner) because they were of 'these new opinions and also of a light living otherwise', and this Delaware had done.[724] Sir Henry Owen testified that he had many times heard Lord Delaware 'openly say that he liked not this world of plucking down abbeys' and 'that he hath openly spoken against sundry acts and statutes which have passed by authority of parliament and that a time wold come and then God wold punish for this plucking down of abbeys and the reading of these new English books and such other heresies'. He knew of 'much familiarity' between Delaware and Exeter[725] and spoke of 'great confederacy' between Exeter, Montagu and Delaware.[726] Crofts testified that Delaware had 'grudged much at' the act of uses.[727] It was Owen's evidence that was most damaging to Delaware: the other witnesses seemed rather to present him as working for conformity with the king. Crofts recalled that 'he heard the Lord Delaware lament the said insurrection [the Pilgrimage of Grace] and rejoice when the same was ended'.[728]

And the councillors were evidently persuaded of his loyalty. On 1 December, presenting themselves as the king's 'most humble subjects and obedient servants', they wrote deferentially but pointedly to Henry VIII, 'your most excellent majesty', a letter that throws much light on the relationship between king and councillors.[729] They had that day used 'all our most diligence, industry and activity' to discover all that Lord Delaware had done that offended the king. But 'as yet we can find no sufficient ground to commit him to prison into your grace's Tower'. They had instructed him to make a further full statement. But then

> beseeching your most noble and benign grace that seen upon consideration that we find as yet no sufficient matter against him and that having respect as well to your merciful clemency as also to your grace's honour that would not have him upon a weak ground (whereof he might clear him self afterward) to be extremely handled we have respited his imprisonment. It may please your highness not to be offended therewith but to pardon us as we trust your highness of your most gracious disposition will.

It would have been an irrecoverable rebuke to his reputation had he been committed to the Tower. 'Again most humbly prostrate at your majesty's feet', the councillors implored the king to pardon them for their presumption. This letter was signed by Thomas Audley, the dukes of Norfolk and Suffolk, Thomas Cromwell, and the earls of Sussex, Hertford and Southampton.

But Delaware *was* imprisoned the very next day.[730] It is possible that he had been sent to the Tower for nothing more than his refusal to serve as foreman of the jury trying Lord Montagu (rumours to that effect were reported on 15 December).[731] But, whatever the reason, the fact of Delaware's imprisonment vividly illustrates the reality of the king's authority over that of his prostrate councillors. Henry evidently felt that there was enough to justify his commitment, and that overrode his councillors' pleas. It may be that the councillors were right to think Delaware essentially innocent, since on 21 December John Hussee could report that he had been discharged from the Tower,[732] though the recognisance that Delaware agreed to the next day—binding him, the dukes of

Norfolk and Suffolk, the earl of Sussex, Sir John Dudley, Sir Owen West, Sir William Goring, George Blunt and John Guildford to the king in £3,000 to appear in person before the king and council whenever called upon—suggests that he had come close to being prosecuted.[733]

Meanwhile, trials had taken place. Commissions had been issued on 23 November;[734] Montagu and Exeter were arraigned on 30 November;[735] Montagu was tried and convicted on 2 December,[736] Exeter was tried and convicted on 3 December,[737] and Sir Geoffrey Pole, George Crofts, John Collins, Hugh Holland and Sir Edward Nevill were convicted on 4 December. Morison would write of Exeter's 'sturdy denial': he 'was stiff at the barre, and stood fast in denial of most things laid to his charge, yet in some he foiled and staggered, in such sort, that all men might see his countenance, to avouch that his tongue could not without much faltering deny';[738] Sir Edward Nevill also pleaded not guilty, and while he put himself at God's and the king's mercy, he insisted 'that I never did nor said the thing that should be contrary to my allegiance nor heard no other as God shall judge me at my death but that I have rehearsed, which clears my own conscience'.[739] Executions followed on 9 January: Montagu, Exeter and Nevill were beheaded at Tower Hill; Crofts, Collins and Holland were drawn to Tyburn and there hanged and quartered.[740] According to Morison, Exeter now weighed the dishonour of having committed treason less, or came to think confessing treason was less dishonourable than doing treason, and joined Montagu and Nevill in acknowledging their offences to the king—though Morison may be being misleading in suggesting that Nevill admitted them.[741] Sir Geoffrey Pole escaped their fate, as we have seen. The marchioness of Exeter and Exeter's son, Henry, continued to be detained in the Tower. Margaret, countess of Salisbury remained 'in hold' at Cowdray, where she was still in March,[742] but by 20 May had already been in the Tower for some time.[743] In the parliament begun on 28 April 1539 the countess was attainted,[744] as was the marchioness of Exeter. Undated remembrances drawn up for Cromwell include entries 'for the diets of young Courteney [the marquess of Exeter's son] and Pole and also of the countess of Sarum [Salisbury] and to know the king's pleasure therein';[745] and 'what the king will have done with the lady of Sares [Salisbury]'.[746] These notes are further eloquent testimony to the dominant role of the king.

There was a further casualty of these events, as we have noted in passing. On 31 December 1538 Nicholas Carew, a prominent courtier, was arrested. This was prompted by the discovery of a letter in the marchioness of Exeter's coffer, in which, the imperial ambassador reported,

Carew had informed her of some conversations held in the king's privy chamber. That was obviously a shocking breach of trust, and it must have looked very damaging now that Exeter had been condemned as a traitor. Carew was, Chapuys said, required to testify further against Exeter. In the hope of a pardon, he incriminated himself and revealed several things against Exeter—including the report that Exeter had been very melancholy when Queen Jane was delivered of a son.[747] Henry would inform Sir Thomas Wyatt on 13 February that after the execution of Exeter and Montagu it was found, by their letters, 'that Sir Nicholas Carew was one of the chief of and principal of that faction'.[748] In his indictment on 14 February, Carew was accused of falsely abetting Exeter on 20 August 1538 and of having conversations with him on 24 August 1538 about the 'change of the world'. He had allegedly written letters to him on 4 September and at other times; and then, on 29 November, knowing Exeter was indicted, he had traitorously said, 'I marvel greatly that the indictment against the said lord marquis was so secretly handled and for what purpose, for the like was never seen'.[749] Carew was duly beheaded at Tower Hill on 3 March. According to Edward Hall, Carew confessed both 'his folly and superstitious faith' on the scaffold. While imprisoned in the Tower he had undergone a religious conversion. There 'he first savoured the life and sweetness of God's most holy word meaning the Bible in English', which the keeper of the prison, Thomas Phillips, let him read.[750] Perhaps the king did not know this; perhaps he thought it insincere and too obvious a ploy to warrant a royal pardon. Taken at face value, it reinforces the argument that the dissent of the Poles, Exeter, Nevill and Carew had been essentially religious. Moreover, if Carew had indeed been in close contact with the marquess of Exeter, and revealed to the marchioness the secrets of the king's chamber, then the depth of his guilt in the king's eyes can hardly have been in doubt. Once again Henry must have felt, above all, the ingratitude of a close servant whom he had richly rewarded.

*   *   *

What then did all this amount to? Was Robert Warner justified in writing to Lord Fitzwalter that Montagu, Exeter, Sir Geoffrey Pole and Sir Edward Nevill 'would a made a foul work in England as ever was heard of'?[751] There is very little in all of this that could be used in support of any notion of a political and military conspiracy against

Henry VIII. There were clearly contacts between Reginald Pole and his brothers Henry, Lord Montagu and Sir Geoffrey Pole. The initiative seems to have come from Sir Geoffrey, but these contacts were haphazard, unplanned, unsystematic. Reginald was told of the danger of assassination, but he had already been warned by sympathisers in Francis's court. Sir Geoffrey was at times tempted to join him abroad, but George Crofts discouraged him, and his brother Montagu settled debts that might have been a more pressing reason for him to go overseas than religious principle. Reginald in any case told his brothers to stay in England and to wait on his yea or nay. Despite the petering out of his efforts in early 1537, he was clearly hoping that he would be the spiritual spearhead of a political and military assault by Charles V and Francis I against the schismatic Henry VIII, and he did not want his brothers to become involved in any premature and unsupported action. Yet it is hard to see Sir Geoffrey Pole or Lord Montagu as laying the ground for an internal rebellion in support of an external invasion. Both brothers were clearly deeply unhappy at the king's divorce, the break with Rome, the royal supremacy, the dissolution of the monasteries, the dismantling of images and the discouragement of pilgrimages. They thought the king's councillors and courtiers no better than knaves, but they were in no doubt that it was the king who was responsible for the policies they deplored. When they met they voiced their discontents, grumbling at the turn of events. In their minds and in their private conversations, they were dissenters. Outwardly they did little. Their grumbles amounted to no more than the consolations of the powerless. Maybe they hoped against hope for a reversal of policy. They held a somewhat providential view of life; interestingly, given the association of providentialism and protestantism. When (according to the indictment) Montagu lamented that knaves ruled about the king, he added, 'I trust the world will amend and that we shall have a day upon these knaves and this world will com to stripes one day';[752] 'this world will one day com to stripes. A time will come. I fear me we shall not tarry the time. . . . It must needs come to this passe one day'.[753] Did they have the character for anything more active? The Dodds were hard on Sir Geoffrey: 'stupid and extravagant, timid and untrustworthy'.[754] Lord Stafford warned Sir Geoffrey that Montagu 'dare speak so largely'.[755] However tempting it is to speak of them as the 'White Rose party', or as 'the Carewe-Exeter "faction" ',[756] 'the only properly political faction until the late years of Henry VIII's reign',[757] they were very much individuals. Montagu and Sir Geoffrey were not always in agreement.

Exeter and Montagu objected to Sir Geoffrey's pursuit of advancement at court in 1536 and 1537: Sir Geoffrey disagreed, until he found that Henry would not let him come into the court on the day of Prince Edward's christening.[758] Nor were Exeter and Montagu that close.

Mayer has tried to construct an impression of scores of contacts—'Pole had foot soldiers and clergy in some numbers to call on'—but he only names Pole's servant Michael Throckmorton, John Walker, Morgan Wells, Hugh Holland, John Helyard, John Collins and George Crofts: they hardly amount to an army.[759] That notwithstanding, Mayer claims that 'Pole's friends outnumbered his enemies in places of power'. In support, he builds up an improbable network, citing Stephen Gardiner, Sir William Paulet, Sir Anthony Windsor, Sir William Fitzwilliam, Richard Sampson, Cuthbert Tunstal, the duke of Norfolk, the earl of Shrewsbury, the duke of Suffolk, Sir John Russell, Lord Delaware, Lord Dacre of the South and Francis Hastings—before conceding that 'some of this treatment of Pole's likely supporters has been unavoidably impressionistic'.[760]

More significant is that the Poles themselves and the marquess of Exeter did not join the Pilgrimage of Grace in autumn 1536. Indeed, the marquess raised forces to resist the rebels, and reported to the king on how faithfully, diligently and loyally his captains had endeavoured to serve him against the rebels in Lincolnshire;[761] Sir Geoffrey Pole prepared to do the same; Montagu was instructed to 'have a vigilant eye to the preservation of the quiet of the country thereabout you' and to put his friends, servants and tenants in a readiness to be able to serve at a day's warning, and presumably did so.[762] The Pilgrimage of Grace was a popular rebellion, and most of the northern nobility, gentry and abbots who swore had been coerced to do so by the commons; in the south, Montagu and Exeter's country, there was no popular rising and no popular threats against them. Exeter was in the city of Exeter at the time of the rebellion and 'took direction' that all commissioners of the subsidy should stay their work for a time.[763] Noble-led risings against royal religious policy simply did not happen. Montagu later wished the Pilgrims had succeeded, and blamed Lord Darcy for not striking against the king: Darcy 'played the fool he went about to pluck a way the counsel he should first have begun with the head, but I beshrewe him for leaving of[f] so soon'.[764] But at the time Montagu had done nothing himself. As far as actions rather than words went, they dismissed—as the countess of Salisbury did—servants and chaplains who took to the new learning. In that lay the seeds of their downfall, as former servants sought their revenge by gossiping and, in the end, by informing the government of what their past masters and mistresses had been saying. No doubt Exeter, Montagu and Sir Geoffrey Pole thought that their conversations were private. But, as Sir Geoffrey admitted, 'Collyns and Jeram Ragland were diverse times present when the lord Montague and he talked secretly of the proceedings of the king and of the not liking of this world'.[765] No doubt great men assumed that their servants and chaplains did not, or would not, hear them, or at any rate would never tell. But that left the possibility that one day disaffected servants could wreak vengeance by revealing what they had heard, and that loyal servants would then under interrogation confirm the gist of what had been said.

Were then Montagu, Exeter, the countess of Salisbury and the others martyrs? They were convicted and lost their lives because of their dissent from the king's religious policies and because of their contacts with Cardinal Pole, whose exile and denunciation of Henry were entirely provoked by religious concerns. But only Cardinal Pole had been active in defence of the church. That Montagu, Sir Geoffrey and their mother maintained contacts with him was obviously troubling for the government but not in itself evidence of active conspiracy. Exeter, Montagu and Sir Geoffrey had voiced criticisms of government religious policy in private; the countess of Salisbury had tried to dismiss servants too sympathetic to the new learning. The centrality of religious grievances in their dissent is vividly shown by Carew's conversion once he had been put in the Tower and condemned to death. But they had not openly and boldly stood up for their faith. They must have sworn the oaths of supremacy and succession in 1534–35. The marquess of Exeter agreed reluctantly to a royal exchange in which he received former monastic lands.[766] The countess of Salisbury on the face of it disowned her son the cardinal and disapproved of his actions. In many ways, all that is a reflection of the times in which they lived. They did not fully grasp, or they did not wish fully to grasp, the purposefulness, the depth and the likely irreversibility of many of the religious changes of the 1530s— the break with Rome, the dissolution of the monasteries, the dismantling of pilgrimage shrines. (The marquess of Exeter, pressed by Lord Montagu about his acceptance of former monastic lands, had said, 'good enough for a time; they must have all again one day', showing his disbelief that what was happening would last.)[767] They shared the contemporary conviction that obedience to the king was obedience to God and, Cardinal Pole apart, they had not faced up to the possibility that these were contradictory principles: not surprisingly, since the consequences of concluding that obedience to God meant disobedience to the king were immense and incalculable. Moreover, nothing particular happened to trigger any more open dissent—no rebellion in the south, no appeals from other noblemen, no call from Cardinal Pole. Nor did the king offer them any opportunity to exploit any political weakness— the king did not call a parliament in the wake of the Pilgrimage of Grace, he did not get himself into military-cum-fiscal difficulties, the sorts of situation in which earlier and later kings might, in their weakness, open themselves to political pressures. The step-by-step nature of the religious changes in the 1530s meant that Exeter and Montagu had in effect acquiesced in parliamentary legislation breaking with Rome and dis- solving the smaller monasteries, and thereby undermined any subse- quent objections they might make. The defeat of the Pilgrimage of Grace removed any chance of exploiting popular discontent. From late 1537 (as we shall soon be considering in depth) the dissolution proceeded apace, with larger monasteries surrendering to the crown: however involuntary and enforced those surrenders were, the fact that they were being made, with next to no resistance by abbots and monks, under- mined any efforts by laymen to co-ordinate resistance. Changes in doc- trine and liturgy had been agreed by bishops and churchmen in the Ten Articles of 1536 and (as we shall see) the Bishops' Book of 1537: it was again at best awkward for largely untutored laymen to express dissent. Exile was an option already taken by Reginald Pole, but he had been a younger son and a scholar, and he had first gone abroad with the king's blessing and financial support. For landowners to flee abroad without royal permission (and merely seeking it would have been dangerously disloyal) raised all sorts of risks; and Cardinal Pole in any case dissuaded Sir Geoffrey from joining him. And of course there was a host of social pressures and promptings of self-interest making for caution. A gener- ation later it would be different, not least since the issues and divisions would become clearer, and men and women would have grown up with them. In the mid- to late 1530s it is not surprising that Montagu, Sir Geoffrey Pole, Exeter and the countess of Salisbury should have lamented and prayed, but done no more.

From Henry VIII's perspective, what they had said and done was damning. In the international circumstances of 1538 he may well have been more fearful than objective realities warranted, but that would nonetheless have been very understandable. 'It was impossible that they could be dangerous to Henry',[768] the Dodds have written. But Henry was far from being paranoid in taking a less relaxed approach, though the punishments inflicted may be thought excessive (Henry VII would have imposed potentially crippling conditional fines). And he may well have sought to maintain the initiative, to surprise those who did not support his aims. Any talk among the Poles of military strength—Montagu allegedly said he 'had lever dwell in the west parts than at Warblington for in the west parts the lord Marquess of Exeter is strong' and regretted that Lord Bergavenny had died, since 'if he were alive he were able to make ten thousand men'[769]—raised suspicions about the possibility of rebellion in a region reasonably accessible from the continent. Any contacts at all with Reginald Pole—even of a purely familial and personal kind—raised doubts about loyalties. Perhaps on first hearing of Hugh Holland's trips abroad, the king was prepared to be restrained in his response, in the belief that these were not primarily political contacts, but, presumably in response to further accusations by informers about the extent of disaffection, in late August 1538 Sir Geoffrey Pole was arrested. His attempts at suicide cast a disquieting shadow over Henry's government. It may well be, as Richard Morison says, that he was not physically tortured in any way, but the psychological pressures must have been unbearable. When he cracked and began to talk, what Henry learned in detail about the family's private dissent from his policies must have struck him not just as treasonable but also as ungrateful. Morison's *Invective* makes a great deal of the king's past favours to Margaret, countess of Salisbury, to the marquess of Exeter and to Sir Geoffrey Pole, and roundly condemns them for their ingratitude.[770] Instructing Sir Thomas Wyatt, his ambassador to the emperor, on 13 February 1539, Henry declared how he had 'made his house and [w]hole family of nought and enhanced them to so high degree nobility and honour', had 'specially favoured and gave honest exhibition out of our own coffers to the said Pole and maintained him to the study', and insisted that Pole had proved himself 'so lewd and so extremely ingrate' that no prince should listen to him. In his discussions with the emperor, Wyatt should 'ever inculcate the ingratitude of the Poles, the benignity we ever used towards them'.[771] Henry could not tolerate dissent over the break with Rome or over his religious policies—the dissolution of the monasteries and the dismantling of images—which he believed were the will of God. No less than the countess of Salisbury (as she wrote to Cardinal Pole), Henry believed that obedience to the prince and obedience to God were one and the same. Sir Geoffrey Pole not only gave evidence against his brother but he underwent a conversion, recanting his past errors and professing abject loyalty to the king: although he was convicted, his life could be spared, because he had bent so abasedly to the king's will. But for Henry there could be no mercy shown to Exeter or Montagu; and the countess of Salisbury would remain confined in the Tower until what Elton calls her 'belated' execution in 1541.[772]

5

The Final Suppression of the Monasteries

Attainders and Surrenders

From the king's hostility to the monasteries, which we saw intensifying during the Pilgrimage of Grace, emerged in spring 1537 the method by which the larger monasteries would, within the next three years, all be dissolved: the 'voluntary' surrender of the houses by their abbots.

The starting point was to hold that the treason of an abbot justified the seizure by the crown of the monastery. As Knowles explained, 'the Crown lawyers had apparently developed the doctrine that not only was a community, as a corporation, subject to the feudal law and so the law of escheat, but that the treason of the head of the corporation, the abbot, constituted valid grounds for seizure'.[1] A list of 'acts necessary to be made at this parliament', most probably prepared in late autumn 1533, included the proposal that any bishop, dean or abbot convicted of high treason should forfeit the lands held in right of their corporations.[2] That intention was achieved in the treason act of November 1534. By adding the word 'successors' to 'heirs', it made possible, as Elton pointed out, the confiscation of the property of a monastery whose head had been executed for treason: Elton thinks this was quite deliberate. Christopher Levyns shortly afterwards voiced the opinion to Cromwell that the goods of a monastery were forfeit if the abbot were proved to be a papist: the king 'is justly entitled by his laws thereunto, upon this offence done, to have the whole moveable goods of the house'.[3] Nothing much, however, occurred as an immediate consequence.[4]

But in March 1537, after the rebellions, the crown confiscated the lands, properties and goods of three monasteries, Whalley, Barlings and Kirkstead, the heads of which were attainted of treason. Abbot Paslew of Whalley Abbey was tried for treason committed during the rebellion, together with two Whalley monks, William Haydock and John Estgate, and two monks of Sawley, Richard Estgate and Henry Banaster (the last of whom was not captured).[5] John Estgate was acquitted, the others were 'attainted'—that is, convicted.[6] The abbot was executed at Lancaster on 10 March, Haydock at Whalley, and Richard Estgate by 17 March. The earl of Sussex, serving as the king's lieutenant in Lancashire jointly with the earl of Derby, thought 'the bringing to passe of which mater of Whalley' was 'the ordinance of almighty god', given the abbot's connections with local gentlemen—'for particular cheer as at all times he was accustomed to make them in keeping of a great house'— which Sussex evidently feared would have deterred them from finding him guilty. But now, Sussex noted with satisfaction, 'it shall be such a spectacle and terror to all other corrupt minds hereafter'.[7]

What would happen next with the monastery and the remaining monks? Sussex, on the execution of the abbot, had 'taken order for the good direction of the house and the safe keeping of the goods without embezzlement' until the king sent further instructions: Henry much approved his 'good foresight'. Since Whalley 'hath been so sore corrupt' and there were very few monks there who were fit to continue as such, Henry thought it 'meet' that 'we should take the whole house in to our hands as by our laws we be justly by the attainder of the said late abbot entitled unto it' (even though at one point he wanted Sussex to 'devise for such a new establishment . . . as shall be thought meet for the honour of God our surety and the benefit of the country'). Accordingly Sussex was ordered to see whether the monks would accept transfer to other houses or whether they would rather 'take capacities and so receive secular habit', though Henry's preference was for transfers, since 'we think it cannot be wholesome for our commonwealth to permit them to wander abroad'. It is interesting that at this stage the king should have thought the transfer of monks to other religious houses a safer option than sending them out into the secular world. Sussex duly dealt with the monks, and the monastery was taken into the king's hands, with an inventory of the goods of the monastery being made on 24 March 1537.[8]

Much the same was done at Kirkstead and Barlings in Lincolnshire following the trials and executions of their abbots in Lincoln and London in March.[9] That their monasteries were confiscated by the crown may be inferred from the king's instructions, delivered by Richard Pollard on 18 March, that the lead of 'the late attainted monasteries of Kirkstead and Barlings' which 'be not as yet plucked down nor melted to his grace's use' should be 'plucked down, melted and cast in fodders';[10] and also from the instructions the council sent Sir William Parr, who was already preparing inventories, declaring a 'new way and direction' to be taken with the goods, monks and canons of the two monasteries (even though the surveys at Barlings were running a little ahead of events since the abbot was yet to be convicted[11]). By late April the king was issuing orders for the repair of the dykes of Kirkstead and Barlings.[12]

It is possible that the same procedure—confiscation through the conviction of the head of the monastery for treason—also occurred at Lenton Abbey, Nottinghamshire. Nicholas Heath, the prior, seven monks and one secular priest were tried for treason: three were executed.[13] The prior had allegedly said,

> I hear say the king is now married and to one of the same generation as evil as the other queen was before. The devil is in him, for he is past grace; he will never amend in this world. I warrant him [to] have as shameful a death as ever king had in England. A vengeance on him!

He was also accused of concealing Ralph Swenson's treason.[14] That links him to the Pilgrimage of Grace, for Swenson, one of the monks of Lenton, had voiced doubts that the king would not keep his promise (the Doncaster agreement of December 1536) but would overcome the commons if he could. Swenson added that anyone who hanged a man in this world for speaking words would himself be hanged in another world.[15]

At Whalley, Kirkstead and Barlings the abbots had been convicted of treason and executed. But it was not necessary to prove treason outright for the crown to acquire a monastery: it was sufficient to threaten an abbot with charges of treason. That is what happened at Furness. Noting that 'it appeareth that the abbot of Furness and diverse of his monks have not been of that truth towards us that to their duties appertained', Henry instructed the earl of Sussex to discover exactly what they had been doing, and with whom, during the rebellion, 'for we think verily that you shall find thereby such matier as shall show the light of many things yet unknown'. Meanwhile, Sussex should detain the abbot and any of his monks whom he suspected until the king decided otherwise.[16]

What evidence did Sussex find against the monastery? Alexander Richardson, bailiff of Dalton, testified on 14 March 1537 that, a fortnight before, a monk, Henry Salley (presumably from Furness), had said that 'it was never a good world with us since that secular men and knaves had rule upon us and the king is head of the church', and insisted that 'no secular knave should be head of the church'.[17] In this the abbot of Furness was at fault since, despite knowing of such treasonable remarks, he had not reported them to the king or council.[18] Earlier still, Sussex had said that the monks of Furness 'have been as of evil hearts and minds as any other'.[19] But evidently he did not think that sufficiently incriminating, nor did he believe that he would discover anything more. So he took a different course.

> I the said earl devising with my self if one way would not serve how and by what other mean the said monks might be rid from the said abbey and consequently how the same might be at your gracious pleasure, caused the said abbot to be sent for to Whalley and thereupon after we had examined him and in deed could not perceive that it was possible, for us to have any other matter, I the same earl as afore by advice of other of your council determined to assay him as of my self whither he would be contented to surrender give and grant unto your highness your heirs and assigns the said monastery which thing so opened to the abbot surely we found him of a very facile and ready mind to follow mine advice in that behalf.

The abbot, Sussex continued, believed that Sussex and he together could easily obtain the consent of the convent. Then, after the judge, Sir Anthony Fitzherbert, arrived, Sussex showed him what he had done. Fitzherbert 'liked the same very well, saying that he thought it was the most convenient way that could be to conduce that monastery to your grace's hands'. Fitzherbert had then drawn up an enrolled deed, a copy of which Sussex sent to the king.

> With which our doings in this point proceeding of me the earl of Sussex, I beseech your highness not to think any presumption in me but to pardon me in case any thing be otherwise than well as we trust all that your majesty will take the same in good part according to our true intents being further minded to proceed as we have begun with all diligence possible to consummate and make perfect the said matter.

They intended to discover as much as they could about the corruption of the monks.[20] Sussex's ploy worked. On 5 April 1537 Abbot Roger of Furness wrote that

> knowing the misorder and evil life both unto God and our prince of the brethren of the said monastery, in discharging of my conscience do freely and wholly surrender, [I] give and grant unto the king's high-

ness and to his heirs and assigns for evermore, all such interest and title as I have had, have, or may have, of and in the said monastery of Furness.

This action came 'freely of my self and without any enforcement, in consideration of the evil disposition of the brethren of the said monastery'. His statement was written in the presence of Sussex, Fitzherbert and several others.[21] On 9 April a further document of surrender of the monastery with its lands for the profit of the realm and for the defence and good rule of 'this far portion' [these distant parts] was signed by Sussex, Fitzherbert, several gentlemen and twenty-eight monks.[22] Henry duly thanked Sussex for his 'discreet, prudent and politique proceedings in the conducing of the house into the king's hands', and asked for an inventory.[23] It is no doubt fitting that, when the king granted Sussex the dissolved monastery of Cleeve, Somerset, in January 1538, it was done in consideration of his services against the rebels in the north.[24] Sir Anthony Fitzherbert emphasised and praised Sussex's role, telling Cromwell[25] that 'I have not seen any nobleman more circumspect and diligent and more earnest to set forwards the king's causes' than Sussex, who had shown himself 'a man of high wisdom':

and doubtless as touching the bringing of the possessions and goods of the monasteries of Whalley and Furness to the king's grace's hands after the manner as they be now came and was first invented and found by my lord of Sussex and brake hit to me and by his policy and wisdoms brought the same to this good effect that hit is come unto now which could not in my poor opinion be brought to passe to the king's honour by any other means conveniently to the king's hands. And therefor therein my lord of Sussex hath done as high service to the king's grace as may be done in that point.

It is interesting to note here that Sussex was instructed to persuade as many of the monks of Furness as he could to transfer to other monasteries.[26] In fact, the monks of Furness did not readily go along with what their abbot had done. When Robert Southwell arrived there on 23 June 1537, expecting to find the monks ready to disperse on receiving their capacities and 20s. reward, the monks as one denied that they had agreed to any specific sum, only that Sussex had promised to act as intermediary between them and the king to improve the terms they were being offered. In support, the monks gave Southwell a signed bill, confirmed by those commissioners who had been with Sussex in April.

When Southwell heard the monks began to murmur that the 'gift' of the monastery had been compulsory, he devised an instrument in parchment which he had read in the hall: all signed and sealed it. Southwell then refused them capacities, saying that the king wished them sent to other religious houses unless they were unfit to continue in religion. Southwell was scathing about those monks—'such gentle companions'—who were willing to be taken as infirm and granted capacities, but unwilling for their infirmity to be declared publicly. What the monks wanted was 20s. wages due at Michaelmas as well as the promised reward of 20s. So Southwell gave them 40s. as the reward, instead of 20s., the least he thought he could give, since the 'traitors' of Whalley had had no less. For a moment, while this bargaining was under way, Sussex feared a fresh rising. A bill was set upon the door of the monastery at Shap, not far from Furness, declaring that if the people would rise and come to Lancashire again, they would find a captain with money ready to receive them. Sussex accordingly alerted local men of worship. And the monks of Furness were reminded of 'the goodly experiments that hangeth on each side of York, some in rochetts, some in cowls': in other words, of those executed for their part in the rebellions. One way and another, at the expense of much time, but without provoking any disturbances, Sussex managed to despatch the monks, their servants and twelve poor men. He sold their cattle, melted their lead and surveyed their lands in Lancashire.[27]

While Sussex was dealing with Furness, the duke of Norfolk turned his attention to Bridlington, in the East Riding, advising Cromwell in March to question the friar, Dr Pickering, about the prior of Bridlington, William Wood, 'with whom he is great'. Later notes referred to 'much traitorous conference' between Pickering and Wood.[28] The prior was accused of being 'a principal procurer doer and setter forth' of the first insurrection and 'a great procurer and mover' in the second;[29] he was also suspected of knowing of Bigod's rising.[30] A little later Norfolk suggested that the prior of Bridlington (as well as two gentlemen under suspicion for their part in the risings, Sir Stephen Hammerton and Nicholas Tempest, both of whom were to be executed at Tyburn)[31] would willingly go up to court if summoned under the privy seal: they were in no fear.[32]

Norfolk's request to the king linked the fate of Bridlington to that of Jervaulx, in the West Riding of Yorkshire, both suspected of involvement in further commotions after the Doncaster agreement: 'if your highness pleasure be to have the houses of Bridlington and Herves [Jervaulx] to be suppressed, upon your pleasure known therein I shall with diligence ride thither and accomplish your commandment'. In that event, Norfolk thought that he should be present at the suppressions, 'as well because the countries about them be populous, and the houses greatly beloved with the people'. He would make arrangements to survey the lands. Jervaulx was well covered with lead; Bridlington had a barn covered in lead—the longest, widest and deepest roof that Norfolk had ever seen, with lead worth £3,000–4,000. It is worth remarking in passing that it was Norfolk who was asking the king for instructions, repeatedly entreating 'if I may know your pleasure'.[33] Henry replied that he did wish them suppressed—they 'shall come to our hands by the attainder of the governors of the same'—and that Norfolk should go in person, and arrange for the taking of inventories of goods and survey of lands.[34] Henry had anticipated the dissolution of Jervaulx when writing to the earl of Sussex about Whalley: 'the house of Gervayse [Jervaulx] is in some danger of suppression, by like offence as hath been committed [at] Whalley'.[35] Norfolk duly set off for Bridlington on 16 May and intended, a week later, to go to Jervaulx.[36] By 18 May he had had the goods of Bridlington viewed.[37] Cromwell on 22 May conveyed the king's thanks for the order Norfolk had taken.[38] The abbot of Jervaulx and the prior of Bridlington were condemned on 16 May,[39] drawn to Tyburn and executed on 25 May.[40] Bridlington was duly dissolved by 23 May; Jervaulx on 24 May.[41] Thus the abbeys of Jervaulx and Bridlington were now in the king's hands.

Here the abbots had been convicted of treason. But it was what had happened at Furness, where the abbot had surrendered without being formally convicted of any offence, that was to point the way in future action. A few weeks later saw the end, through the same means, of the London Charterhouse, previously such a thorn in Henry's side, but, by mid-1537, housing only those monks who had, eventually, accepted the royal supremacy. Twenty, including William Trafford, the new prior, and Edmund Sterne, vicar, had signed an acknowledgment of the king's supremacy on 18 May 1537; though three monks, the renderer and six *conversi* declined.[42] The timing (this coincided with the trials of Aske, Darcy, Hussey and others, not least on charges of having sought to deprive the king of his title of supreme head) may not be a coincidence.[43] Robert Holdsworth would follow his account of Darcy and others in the Tower with the news that eight or nine monks of the London Charterhouse were being brought to Newgate,[44] where they died.[45] Significantly, a little later, the remaining monks were persuaded by Cromwell's servant Thomas Bedell to surrender their priory to the king, in recognition of their offences which had provoked the king's indignation against them, rather than abiding the extremity of the king's laws.[46]

It would be a combination of such threats, pressures and inducements as were used at Furness Abbey that would, from later that year, be used to achieve the 'voluntary' surrender of all the monasteries in the realm. No 'smoking gun' has been found that would enable the historian to indicate a precise date or to see this as a policy for which particular individuals were responsible. In the absence of clinching evidence, a plausible explanation is that the shock of the Pilgrimage of Grace, in which the defence of monasteries was a prominent concern, greatly intensified Henry VIII's reservations about monasticism. Where abbots had been convicted of treason and monasteries had surrendered, involvement in rebellion was evidently the principal factor.

If the experience of the Pilgrimage of Grace had not been enough, there was a further reminder for the government of the potential links between monasteries and sedition further south.[47] In April 1537, at Walsingham (home of the most famous pilgrimage shrine in the country), George Gisborough, a yeoman and lay chorister at the priory, and a member of the Walsingham guild of the annunciation of St Mary the Virgin,[48] said

> he thought it very evil done for the suppressing of so many religious houses where as God was well served, and many other good deeds of charity done. And said if men were willing to make insurrection and go wholly together he thought it was never better time to have their purpose then now.[49]

He also testified how Ralph Rogerson, a yeoman farmer also employed as a lay chorister at Walsingham priory[50] (referring to the speedy work of the commissioners for the suppression of smaller monasteries), said, 'you see how these abbeys go down and our living goeth away with them; for within a while Binham shall be put down and also Walsingham and all other abbeys in that country'. Rogerson drew the threatening conclusion: 'When these men shall come to put down the abbeys some men must step to and resist them and I will assay to get company for that purpose' and then 'come up to the king to complain'.[51] But one of those they appealed to, John Galant of Letheringsett, a servant of Sir John Heydon, informed his master of 'a great disturbance and insurrection like to be among the king's subjects about Walsingham'; and Heydon in turn informed Richard Gresham in London and through him Thomas Cromwell.[52] Galant revealed that George Gisborough had told him of his plan with several others to 'make an insurrection'. 'Their purpose is to take the head constables of all the hundreds and compel them to cause the under-constables of every hundred to raise the people'; their intention was to 'go forth in to the north country to aid and help the northern men'.[53] The JPs arrested Gisborough and others at once.[54] Sir Richard Southwell reported, on 29 April, Sir John Heydon's assessment that 'the whole sort conspirators pass not in number as far as he yet knoweth xii persons or thereabouts and they all very beggars' and how 'the parts where the said conspirators were in an as good quiet obedience as ever it was'.[55] Sir Roger Townshend and Southwell reported on 3 May 1537 that, by the confession of one Watton, it appeared that Nicholas Mileham, the subprior of Walsingham, was 'infected', 'a man of lewd inclination'. It was rumoured that a game of shooting at Binham was intended only to assemble the conspirators and their adherents.[56] They were ordered to execute, without exception, all offenders.[57] Sir Richard Southwell on 29 May reported the attainting of the late rebels in these parts, how they had confessed their crime and had been executed.[58]

If the conspiracy at Walsingham has an insubstantial feel, it might nonetheless have turned out otherwise, and it was justifiably treated as much more serious by the government.[59] Just before the executions the JPs heard a confession from John Turner of Old Buckenham that before Easter John Lock, servant to Mr Gray the priest, said he had been offered (by Hugh Wilkinson of Buckenham St Andrew and John Browne of Old Buckenham) an angel noble to kill the king's visitors (the commissioners for the suppression of abbeys, including Townshend and Southwell) in their beds that night at Buckenham Abbey.[60] And, a little earlier, the duke of Suffolk had reported to Cromwell on 16 May talk that the people would have risen at Walsingham but for the actions of one man: Robert Seyman confessed that one false knave revealed the intended rising.[61] Those involved were not, as Sir Richard Southwell claimed, of low degree.[62] The charges against the accused were that they had conspired to make an insurrection 'as well for staying of abbeys putting down as for reformation of gentlemen for taking of farms'. Elton attempts to play down 'defence of abbeys and fears of the king's doings', which, he says, 'weighed much less in the scale' than 'hatred of the exploiting landlords of the shire' which 'stood paramount'; 'agrarian grievances, exacerbated by fears about the fate of abbeys, had been behind it all: just the ingredients that had made their appeal in Yorkshire the previous year'; 'but on both occasions the real troubles had little enough to do with religion'.[63] Obviously there were important social grievances here too, but the attachment to monasteries, in part economic, was nonetheless real.

From the king's perspective, monasteries were once again associated with sedition. As we have already seen, time and again Henry had been provoked by what he saw as monastic treachery into vigorous denunciation of monks. Anthony Budgegood, a defector to Rome, neatly made the connection: seeing the suppression of the monasteries (and the promotion of heretic bishops) as the chief cause of the great rebellion by the northern men, he revealingly commented, 'so that I suppose there will be very few or none standing', but all in the king's hands.[64] Such very obvious practical political considerations—were abbots and monks disloyal? was their disloyalty likely to lead to rebellion?—clearly provoked the king. But that meshed with Henry's increasingly hostile attitude to monasticism as such, a hostility that was as much principled as it was pragmatic. The instructions that Henry would give Sir Ralph Sadler, sent to the Scottish court in January 1540, are informative too. What the king criticised about monks was their beastly living and, significantly, their *untruth*; that would justify the Scottish king's taking such of their houses as might best be spared, and converting the rest to better uses as Henry had done. But, Sadler was to warn James V, he should keep any such plans secret, for if the clergy got wind of it, they would thwart him by provoking war or rebellion, a revealing insight into the king's conviction that the dissolution of the monasteries had provoked the risings in 1536–37.[65]

By the spring of 1537, it has been argued here, Henry had doubts about the political loyalties of the monasteries and reservations about their spiritual contribution, doubts and reservations that were turning into something more like anger. And whether through careful thought or accidental stumbling, a procedure had evolved by which monasteries could be taken over by the crown.

Refoundations?

It has, however, been interestingly argued that, as late as 1537, Henry VIII had yet to commit himself fundamentally against monasticism but was rather still refounding monasteries. These refoundations, says Hallam Smith, 'suggest that no overall suppression was contemplated in 1536–7'; 'the notion of retaining a number of religious houses, whether through expediency, sheer conservatism or religious scruple, was adhered to probably until the middle of 1538'.[66]

This claim rests on two case studies. The first is Stanfield, Lincolnshire. A small nunnery, it would have been dissolved under the act of 1536 had it not been granted a royal licence to continue. Yet on finding that 'much inconvenience' would ensue from its preservation, Henry afterwards instructed commissioners to suppress it entirely. According to an earlier decision, all the monks of the Cistercian monastery of Stixwold, Lincolnshire, were to be put out: now the nuns of Stanfield were to take their place; 900 marks (£600) would be taken in fine from the revenues of Stixwold, with lands worth £34 10s. 7d. a year reserved for the king's use.[67] On 8 January 1537 the convent of Stixwold (presumably the new Stixwold, now housing the nuns who had come from Stanfield) complained, and asked for the remission of the annual payment to the king, otherwise they would have to surrender the house to the crown, since they were only eighteen nuns, fifty people in all, and their stock and cattle (their chief living) had already been given up to the king.[68] It was this petition that presumably led to the 'refoundation' of Stixwold by the king in July 1537, with a much-reduced annual payment of £15 5s. 1d., described as the 'true tenth', and with the nuns required to pray for the good estate of the king and queen.[69]

None of this is evidence of the king's commitment to monasticism in summer 1537. Quite simply, it was no more than the resolution of a technical problem arising from the dissolution of the smaller houses. For reasons unknown to us, it was thought preferable to close the nunnery of Stanfield down, and to transfer the nuns to another house. But, instead of moving them to other continuing houses of religion, what was done in this case was wholly to empty another house, Stixwold, of its existing inmates, and move the Stanfield nuns there. The financial arrangements proved too burdensome, however, and they were shortly afterwards reviewed. Technically this revision constituted a 'refoundation', but it makes much more sense to see it as a minor adjustment, with no broader significance. Since the old Stixwold had surrendered to the king, the buildings and lands were now legally Henry's, and any new arrangements necessitated a royal grant of those buildings and lands. But this was not a work of piety by Henry: it reflected no spiritual impulses. It was just another exemption from dissolution, though one involving an unusually complex procedure. Exemptions in general were intrinsic to what the government sought and obtained at the time the act of dissolution was passed in March 1536. The granting of exemptions was essentially a technical and practical matter. The granting of an exemption, and the working out of the practical arrangements at Stixwold, should not be seen as evidence that the king was still broadly in favour of monasteries. The new Stixwold enjoyed no special protection later; it would ultimately surrender in September 1539.[70]

The second example of supposed 'refoundation' is that of Bisham. In July 1537 the abbot of Chertsey surrendered Chertsey on condition that its Benedictine community should be refounded at Bisham.[71] Chertsey was a larger monastery, not affected by the 1536 act dissolving the smaller monasteries.[72] Why the king should have wished to acquire it is unclear, though such wishes were entirely consistent with Henry's actions elsewhere when he took a fancy to a house or an estate held by a nobleman or a bishop. What attracted Henry to Chertsey was quite possibly the prospect of using Chobham Park, long the possession of Chertsey Abbey, as a residence: it had been viewed on the king's behalf in 1533, and work was in progress on the kitchen in 1534.[73] If the king were to take over Chertsey, that obviously posed the problem of what to do with the monks of a large monastery with Lancastrian associations (Henry VI had originally been buried there). Offering them the site of another monastery already dissolved was an obvious solution. Bisham had been granted to the king by William Barlow, the commendatory prior, in a charter dated 5 July 1536.[74] In itself, exchanging Chertsey for Bisham would not be a good bargain for the abbot and convent of Chertsey, so adding a substantial endowment reflecting the value of Chertsey (lands worth £600) would make sense. All that would require formal legal documentation and might technically be described as a 'refoundation'. What the story reflects, however, is not any special commitment to monasticism but rather Henry's desire to possess Chertsey.

That the refounding of Stixwold took place, and that of Bisham was begun in July 1537, has been seen as connected to the pregnancy of Jane Seymour: 'these new foundations may . . . have been intended to please her at a time when the birth of a son to Henry was vitally important'. Perhaps they also reflect 'some kind of religious scruples in the king himself'.[75] That is an interesting speculation. The nuns of Stanfield, newly installed at Stixwold, were indeed required to pray for the good estate of the king and queen;[76] the monks of Chertsey, now installed at Bisham, were required to pray for the good estate of the king and—as Jane Seymour had died after giving birth to Edward—for the soul of the late Queen Jane.[77] Yet since the fundamental purpose of monasteries was intercession for their founders, these provisions were entirely conventional, showing the king's continuing commitment to the practice of intercession (though, it should be noted, to Almighty God and to the Blessed Virgin, not to individual saints). For technical and legal reasons, two monasteries, one small and one large, had in effect been refounded on different sites. Appropriate charters were required, and they were set out in standard form.

There is a further example of 'a serious refoundation by the king', the supposed 'refoundation' of Observant Franciscan friaries. That is a very misleading way of describing what was in effect a humiliating subjection of the Observants to the Conventual Franciscans, a very pointed act and in no sense whatsoever an encouragement to the Observants. At one point Hallam Smith recognises that 'this could of course have been prompted as much by a spirit of revenge against the Observants'.[78] Moreover, the precise dating of these 'refoundations' is hard to pin down. A royal warrant of March 1537 (cited by Hallam Smith) referring to an annuity backdated to the previous Michaelmas 1536 is not really compelling evidence of the date of refoundation. It may all have happened much earlier: Stow suggests August 1534,[79] soon after the Observants refused the oaths of supremacy. Furthermore, later descriptions of Newark (1543–44) and Southampton (1538) describe them as houses of Austin friars, implying an Austin takeover, rather than any 'refoundation'.[80] The Observants had been suppressed because of their opposition to the royal supremacy; the remaining houses of friars were not affected by the act dissolving the smaller monasteries, but they would be very vigorously dealt with in 1538. What was done to the Observants was more a vindictive act than a reprieve.

But if Henry was not suppressing all the monasteries in the course of 1537, that does not disprove the argument above, namely that Henry was angrily voicing increasingly fundamental denunciations of monasticism. Instead of considering the cases of Stanfield/Stixwold and Chertsey/Bisham in isolation, it is more illuminating to set them in the context of the hostility to monasteries so strongly present in the king's reaction to the Pilgrimage of Grace and beyond. What was done at Stanfield/Stixwold and Chertsey/Bisham in no sense contradicts that hostility. No supposed continuing commitment to monasticism ('the king remained committed in principle and in practice to the monastic ideal'),[81] no religious scruple, let alone any special religious fervour, need be invoked to account for what happened there: technical factors are an entirely sufficient explanation.

The Generalisation of the Policy of Voluntary Surrenders

In the summer of 1537, then, the dissolution of the smaller monasteries had resumed and gathered pace; a number of larger monasteries which had been involved one way or another in the Pilgrimage of Grace had been surrendered to the crown for the treason of their abbots and monks; and Henry VIII had voiced deep-rooted hostility to monks, reflecting his fear of and anger at their potential for treason, but also a more fundamental hostility to monasticism as such, criticised as wasteful, unproductive, selfish, superstitious and hypocritical. The impact of the rebellions of 1536–37 (in which the defence of monasteries played a great part) was to emphasise their bad qualities in the king's eyes even more.

From time to time there were further isolated expressions of opposition to the dissolution. In August 1537, Sir William Parr had a man nailed to the pillory in Northampton by his ear for saying that he trusted to see those who were of counsel for plucking down of abbeys hanged before he died.[82] One Nicholas Came on 7 October 1537 was asked when the melters of lead should come to the abbey church in Norwich—and got into trouble for replying that the church would stand, and that Rome was taken up again and purgatory was found, dangerously linking the criticism of the dissolution with allegiance to Rome.[83] Wriothesley's *Chronicle* remarked, 'Again it was pity the great lamentation that the poor people made for them, for there was great hospitality kept among them, and, as it was reported, ten thousand persons had lost their living by the putting down of them, which was great pity.'[84] George Crofts, resident clerk at Chichester Cathedral, while he 'always in my conscience thought the life of religious men such that God of his justice would send them no less punishment', went on to praise the conserving of the walls of Titchfield Abbey church: 'it was a good deed to save the walls of the church there standing to a use and a piteous sight to see them thrown down where they might stand to a use'. Crofts's concern went beyond the architectural: 'it was a good deed to take the great possessions from religious men and that it had been as good a deed to suffer them to remain in their houses with a poor living if they would be glad so to do and keep their religion'.[85] At a higher political level, as we have seen, Lord Montagu's laments for the pulling down of abbeys, especially Bisham, his ancestral mausoleum, would later be held against him,[86] as were Sir Geoffrey Pole's remarks that God's law was turned upside down, abbeys and churches overthrown.[87] The equation of monasteries and popery, monasteries and rebellion, was never far away.

In summer 1537 the bishops and other churchmen were involved in compiling the Bishops' Book, a statement of true doctrine, to which we shall later turn. Interestingly, there was nothing in it directly on the monasteries, though the way in which the place of images was reduced implicitly affected the monasteries as centres of pilgrimage, and the treatment of purgatory raised questions over intercessory prayer. Not a single abbot subscribed to the published version of the Bishops' Book, though twenty-one bishops, eight archdeacons and seventeen professors of theology and law, ecclesiastical and civil, did.[88] That suggests that in the king's eyes monasteries were marginal. It is interesting that among the many 'position papers' was a set of fifteen questions on theology, including a question on the validity of certain canons of the council of Chalcedon against monasteries once consecrated being made residences for laymen, evidently exploring the theological implications of grants of former monastic lands to noblemen and courtiers.[89] No abbot was placed on the newly reordered council in the north.[90] In fairness, it might be noted that abbots were prominent in the obsequies for Jane Seymour in October (the abbots of St Albans, Waltham, Reading, Stratford, Westminster, Ramsey and Tower Hill were among those saying mass on successive days, and five of them assisted the bishops at the funeral).[91]

Were all the monasteries already doomed? Would the king's marked hostility to monks voiced in the aftermath of the rebellion lead to more drastic measures? Some gossiped along those lines. At Whitsun 1537 Robert Jons of Thame predicted that the king would suppress all abbeys.[92] In September 1537 one William Barnard of Barrow-upon-Soar, Leicestershire, was in trouble for reporting that the king would suppress all the houses of religion beyond the Trent but one.[93]

At some point in the autumn of 1537 something like a decision to persuade monasteries to surrender must have been taken. Very probably that reflected a wish to bring English monasticism to an end. Announcing it as a policy may well have been thought risky, in light of the protests against the parliamentary legislation of 1536. It would be much safer simply to 'persuade' individual monasteries to surrender their buildings and lands to the crown, the procedure first employed at Furness in spring 1537. The outcome of such an approach would then depend on how much resistance and reluctance there was in the face of such 'persuasion'. There would be plenty of opportunities for public opinion to be won over by the publicising of such abuses as the king's visitors uncovered, particularly when these were admitted by abbots and monks themselves.

Unfortunately such an explanation of events can be no more than a historian's surmise. There is no statement of policy, no report of conversations or gossip, that would clinch the claim, or allow it to be attributed to the cautious determination of the king. But that important developments began in late 1537 appears incontrovertible. Early clues lie in the surrenders of a handful of larger monasteries that were neither affected by the act of dissolution of 1536 nor implicated in rebellion.

The first sign of something significant was the surrender by the prior and convent of St Pancras, Lewes, together with its cell priory of Castle Acre, Norfolk, on 16 November 1537; the priory of Castle Acre, Norfolk, also surrendered separately on 22 November.[94] Negotiations on the terms were clearly under way a little earlier.[95] The monks were to be given a reward of £2 and quarterly pensions.[96] That was a novelty. This was the first occasion on which pensions were to be paid to all the monks of a dissolved monastery; previously only heads of houses had been accorded them, while monks had either been transferred to other houses or given 'capacities', that is, licences to serve as secular priests. The introduction of general pensions strongly points to a new policy.

There are some tantalising hints of how it was first put into practice in this case. A little earlier, the duke of Norfolk informed Cromwell of his conversation with the king the previous day. After consoling Henry on the loss of Queen Jane, Norfolk thanked him for being content to give him Lewes 'if we might conclude the bargain': 'we' were Norfolk and Cromwell. And Norfolk went on to give an account of Cromwell's service to the king in justification of the grant, saying that Cromwell was content that they should divide up the properties between them so that Norfolk should have two parts and he one. Henry responded—as Cromwell had already told Norfolk—that he thought it well bestowed.[97] The duke of Norfolk and Cromwell evidently shared the proceeds of these surrenders between them, interesting not least in light of the tenacious assumption that the two men were bitter factional rivals. A memorandum of 1 December 1537 dealing with the partition of lands noted that Norfolk granted Cromwell Lewes.[98] One of Cromwell's remembrances at this time noted 'to know the true value of the goods of Castellacre for my part thereof'.[99] A royal grant of Castle Acre to Norfolk came on 22 December.[100]

At much the same time there is evidence of similar practices over Titchfield Abbey. In the quinzaine of St Martin—St Martin's day is 11 November—John, Bishop of Thetford, abbot of Titchfield, granted the king various manors in the possession of the abbey.[101] By the beginning of December, total surrender was under discussion. But there was uncertainty over the precise legal procedures to be used. Cromwell sent Audley, the lord chancellor, a letter (which he acknowledged on 1

December) empowering Mr Shelley, a judge, to record a fine and recovery by the abbot and convent of Titchfield to the king's use. Audley duly 'sent with speed to Mr Croke for the course thereof'. That appears to have been the legal procedure by which Lewes and Castle Acre surrendered: the king was plaintiff, the priors deforciants (accused of keeping the king wrongfully out of the possession of the estate), and fines were levied. But Audley went on to suggest that if the abbot and convent were content to give their monastery, a deed of gift might be drawn up covering the monastery and all its lands, acknowledged before Mr Shelley the judge, and so enrolled. A fine and recovery could not be executed till the next law term, and if the house were dissolved before such execution, it would be as if a man had died before executing a deed. Audley intended to examine precedents with Croke, expected that morning.[102] The next day Audley informed Cromwell that a deed of gift by the abbot and convent to the king, sealed and acknowledged before a judge of record, would be sufficient; but if Cromwell would have a fine or recovery, he explained how it might be taken.[103] The significance for our purposes of such technical details is that they reveal a government bent on dissolution but nonetheless still very much feeling its way on the precise details of the procedures to be followed. By 22 December John Crayford and Roland Latham had carried out a careful investigation into grants made by the convent, and drawn up an inventory of vestments, kitchen equipment and livestock. The abbot expected to receive a pension of 100 marks, eight priests £6 13s. 4d. and three novices £5.[104] Titchfield duly surrendered on 28 December 1537.[105] And on 30 December Audley received a grant of Titchfield Abbey.[106]

Another monastery that surrendered at this time was the abbey of Wardon, Bedfordshire, on 4 December.[107] By 10 December Sir Francis Bryan was writing to Cromwell in favour of one Mr Birch to have part of it.[108] Westacre Priory surrendered on 15 January 1538. The prior declared that as early as 9 December 1537 they had been informed by Charles Wingfield that it was the king's pleasure that they should sell their house to him and his heirs; the goods of the priory were sequestered by 16 December. Richard Layton, Sir Robert Southwell and Sir Thomas Lestrange reported how the monastery had made a variety of sales and leases which made it difficult to sort out its affairs; Southwell had made an instrument of the offences committed by the religious against the king. Richard Layton lamented to Cromwell 'what untruth and dissimulation we find in the prior, what falsehood in false knaves among the convent, what bribery, spoil and ravin [robbery] with crafty colours of bargains contrived by the inhabitants, it were too long to write'.[109]

What was going on? The ever-shrewd John Hussee reported on 14 December 1537 that the abbey of Wardon was suppressed, and that others were named to go down, including Peterborough, Ramsey, Sawtry and St Albans. It was thought that most would go down by the consent of their abbots and priors, Hussee added, correctly anticipating the general thrust of what was to happen and how it would happen (if not entirely accurate in details). Hussee trusted that something would fall to his master, Lord Lisle.[110] He informed Lady Lisle on the same day that several abbeys were to be suppressed, and it was thought that most would be in due course.[111] Hussee's reports were characteristically terse. But he had realised that a new policy was under way. That something on a large scale was happening was also noticed by others. On 8 January 1538 John Uvedale was persuaded that the holy word of God would in brief time hunt all manner of religious persons out of their monasteries and cloisters (and he asked Cromwell for the farm of the house of Marrick nunnery when that happened).[112]

There can be little doubt, in light of these letters, and the facts of the surrenders of Lewes, Titchfield and Wardon, that at some point in the autumn of 1537 (probably in October) Henry had determined on a more general dissolution of the monasteries. This was more than a response to the importunity of his councillors and courtiers seeking one or two monastic properties. There was clearly something more organised afoot.

That a campaign was beginning is further suggested by the report of Thomas Legh that on 3 January 1538 he had begun his visitation according to Cromwell's instructions. Legh, of course, had been one of the visitors in 1535 and his involvement in 1538 is revealing. The first monastery he visited was Muchelney, Somerset. His methods are interesting. He evidently inquired how far the head and his brethren were living up to the instructions laid down two years earlier. He found the abbot very ignorant and accused of sexual misconduct, and ten monks, all also very ignorant. After they had been examined, they all subscribed to the instrument of surrender, sealed it with their common seal, and delivered it in the presence of knights and gentlemen. Inventories were then taken, and bells, lead and gold removed. On 5 January the abbot, with a letter of attorney from his brethren, came before the lord chief justice and acknowledged the instrument they had sealed as their voluntary deed, asking for it to be enrolled in Chancery.[113] Such surrenders were to become the pattern for the dissolution of the larger monasteries. The government was evidently embarking on a new visitation of the monasteries: on this occasion, however, the commissioners were to encourage abbots and monks to surrender their houses.

Clearly the government was appointing groups of commissioners to carry out its policy. John Tregonwell, Nicholas Poyntz, John Poyntz, John Freeman and Edward Gostwick were named as commissioners appointed for the dissolution of Kingswood Abbey on the surrender of that house dated 1 February.[114] Sir Giles Capell and John Wentworth were commissioned by the king's writ for the surrender of Coggeshall Abbey, which took place on 5 February.[115] There is a surviving draft commission (though it is undated and might be later): the recipient was to take the surrender and receive the possession of the monastery of N. which the king understands is not now used for the honour of God or the benefit of the commonwealth.[116] A policy had been worked out and was being implemented.

Among those who noticed the trend of events were abbots and monks themselves. Many evidently judged that they would shortly face dissolution and accordingly attempted to raise as much money as they could, presumably to provide for their livelihood in an uncertain future. Such actions are for us, in the absence of more concrete evidence, a very suggestive indication of what the government's ultimate intentions by early 1538 were thought to be. Richard Layton (one of the visitors in 1535, in early January 1537 sent into East Anglia) reported that as soon as he arrived at Barnwell it was rumoured that the priory would be suppressed, that Ely and Bury St Edmunds would be next, and that the king was determined to suppress all monasteries for which purpose he had sent Layton and Robert Southwell (formerly solicitor, now attorney, of the court of augmentations) to Norfolk. In order to stop the rumours, Layton went in person to monastic houses, assembled 'honest men' living nearby, and ordered abbots and priors not to alienate any property. 'Babblers', who alleged that the king would suppress all the monasteries, slandered their natural sovereign: abbots and priors were to put such knaves into the stocks. Layton feared that if he had not done that, abbots and priors would have spread rumours, and continued to make sales and leases.[117] But Layton ordered the public punishment of those who spread rumours that the king intended to dissolve all the monasteries not because they were false but because they were true, and because abbots and priors might act on them, wasting their assets and so damaging the king's interests. It would be foolish to take this letter at face value as showing that the king had not yet developed a policy of total suppression: it more plausibly confirms the belief that he had indeed determined to do just that.

The government continued to deny that there was any policy of general surrender. Cromwell outlined government policy on 21 March 1538 (possibly, as *Letters and Papers* suggests, to the abbot of

Glastonbury). The king had not long before signified 'that using your-selves like his good and faithful subjects', he 'would not in any wise interrupt you in your state and kind of living': 'no man's words nor any voluntary surrender made by any governor and company of any religious house ... shall put you in any doubt or fear of suppression or change of your kind of life and policy'. The king had now commanded Cromwell to write that 'unless there had been overtures made by the said houses that have resigned, his grace would never have received the same'. He did not intend in any way 'to trouble you or to devise for the suppression of any religious house that standeth, except they shall either desire of themselves with one consent to resist and forsake the same, or else misuse themselves contrary to their allegiance'.[118] Should we believe this? Was it not exactly the defence that a government embarked on a policy of total suppression through voluntary surrender would make, denying that that was its intention, and insisting on the voluntary actions of those that had surrendered?

The Attack on Shrines and Friars

A further very significant pointer occurred with the surrender of Boxley Priory, Kent, on 29 January 1538.[119] Boxley was of national importance. The rood of Boxley was one of the most significant pilgrimage shrines in the country. The surrender of Boxley thus marked a new stage in the dissolution of the monasteries. From the beginning of the break with Rome, concern had been expressed that the monasteries were tarnished by superstition. The interrogations of the visitation of 1535 and the pre-amble of the act dissolving the smaller monasteries in 1536 had associ-ated monasteries and superstition.[120] Legh and Layton listed pilgrimage shrines and relics under the heading 'superstition', in a sceptical, even mocking, tone, as we have seen. This was to strike at the heart of monas-ticism.[121] Any dissolution of a monastery necessarily involved the dis-mantling of any shrines there: for example, Richard Southwell reported how he now had in his possession the cross of Bromholm.[122] When in the spring of 1537 the duke of Norfolk dissolved Bridlington Priory, a larger monastery condemned because of the involvement of its prior in the Pilgrimage of Grace, he was ordered to dismantle the shrine.[123] But the scale of such dismantling as a result of the 1536 act may well have been small, since few of the smaller monasteries were large pilgrimage centres.

With the surrender of Boxley, the destruction of 'superstition' would become more prominent. The Rood of Grace would be examined, dismantled and denounced as a fraud on market day at Maidstone.[124] Other monastic images to which pilgrimages were made that were similarly dismantled and denounced included the shrine at Bury St Edmunds (January/February), the rood at Bermondsey Abbey (May), the images of Our Lady from Ipswich and from Walsingham (July), the image of Our Lady at Caversham (September); and the blood of Hailes (October), which was revealed as duck's blood or wax or gum.[125] The most important pilgrimage shrines were housed in monasteries: to dismantle them was to take aim at one of the most fundamental features of the monastic life, not least when 'abuses' were so publicly displayed. To suggest, however, that 'the driving force' behind the condemnation of superstition was 'the determination of the regime, and in particular of Thomas Cromwell, to use the disclosures to justify the king's proceedings', that is to say, the royal supremacy, is to take too instrumental an approach.[126] From the actions of the commissioners in 1538 and 1539, it appears that the aim of government policy was to secure the surrender of every monastery. All monasteries were affected: there was no deliberate 'targeting' of those monasteries known to be centres of pilgrimage and housing important shrines. What happened was that 'superstitious' images were uncovered and shrines dismantled from time to time as individual monasteries surrendered. Even in the case of Hailes, there was a striking gap between Bishop Hilsey's denunciation in February 1538, itself provoked by the surrender of Boxley Priory and the dismantling of the Rood of Grace there, and the inquiry into the blood of Hailes in the autumn. Beyond that, there was no national campaign of preaching against monastic pilgrimage shrines. Yet where 'superstition' was found, it was denounced because superstition was wrong in itself, not for some ulterior purpose such as the broader defence of the break with Rome. But in the king's mind, the association between papal power and superstition was well established.

On 5 February, Richard Ingworth, bishop of Dover, Cranmer's suffragan,[127] was commissioned by the king to visit all houses of friars in England, with power to examine and correct abuses,[128] and later given authority to put the goods of houses visited into safe custody.[129] What is striking is that Ingworth's visitation resulted not in the correction of abuses but in the surrenders of houses of friars. He was given no general commission of dissolution. Rather, he was expected to conduct his visitation in such a way that would leave the friaries with little choice but to surrender 'voluntarily' to the crown. He tended to emphasise the poverty of the friars—donations were drying up—and to present friaries as economically unviable.

Here he may well have been correct. Modern calculations of the percentages of testators leaving bequests to friars show a fall from 23 per cent (in the 1520s) to 21 per cent (between 1530 and 1534) and then to 9 per cent (between 1535 and 1539) in Devon and Cornwall, from 43 per cent to 33 per cent and then to nil in London.[130] Lord Wentworth noted the poverty of the Greyfriars of Ipswich owing to the diversion of local charitable giving to the poor and impotent.[131] In May 1538 Ingworth reported how by the end of the year few of the houses would be able to survive. Friars everywhere were making shift by selling jewels and leasing: he put a stop to that by making inventories and sequestering common seals, and in so doing removed the expedients that could provide at least temporary relief.[132] He amplified that claim in July: there were not two in ten houses able to continue.[133]

What then happened is exemplified by the Greyfriars and Austin friars in Stafford. The bishop told them that he had no commission to put them out. He had been sent to make sure that good order was kept. If they agreed to reform and to observe the instructions he would give them, and if they were financially viable, then he was content that they should continue. But if they could not, and if 'of their own minds and wills' they would give their houses to the king, then he was bound to agree. Heads and brethren unanimously gave him their houses for the king's use, 'without any counsel or coaction'.[134] Much the same happened at Shrewsbury, where the Greyfriars similarly unanimously surrendered,[135] at Bridgnorth where the Greyfriars said that they were financially unviable: the charity of the people was so small that in three years they had not received 10s. a year, but survived only through fees in the chapel on the bridge.[136] The Lichfield Greyfriars surrendered for very poverty.[137] So did the friars of Chester.[138]

But the government wanted the bishop of Dover to do more than just accept the surrenders of friaries fallen on hard times. He was expected to persuade where there was resistance. There was some dissent: he reported from Staffordshire, Shropshire and North Wales that the friars in these parts had many supporters who were working hard so that they might continue.[139] At Bristol, the Blackfriars were ready to give up, but the others were obstinate—the Greyfriars because the warden, Robert Sanderson, was also warden of the Greyfriars of Richmond, and in favour (with whom? asks Elton) the bishop reported.[140] Reporting on Worcester, Bridgnorth, Atherstone and Lichfield, Ingworth said that several friars were very reluctant to leave their houses, yet they were not able to support themselves.[141]

That the bishop of Dover was expected to contrive the end of the friaries may be further inferred from the reaction when he temporarily reprieved one. At one point he was forced to defend himself, in a pained response to Cromwell, who thought him too sympathetic to the friars and who had insinuated, he said, 'that though I have changed my habit, I have not changed my friar's heart'. God would be his judge, he protested, 'my friar's heart was gone ii years before my habit'. What he had conceded was simply 'to bring all things with the most quiet to passe', since 'off truth their hearts be clean from the religion the more parte'. Rather than showing them favour, where he found them faulty 'I declare their faults after such fashion that they rather will give up the houses, than I should declare their demeanours'.[142] At Shrewsbury he had left one friary—the Blackfriars—standing, because, he said, he had no commission to suppress any house, except such as were no longer financially viable. He made a virtue of this necessity: 'it shall declare that I do not suppress the houses, but such as give up, seeing that some stand, and not all put down'.[143] That was disingenuous and should not be read, out of context, as a fair description of his or the government's policy. Later, the bishop revealed his true feelings, urging that the Shrewsbury Blackfriars should not be allowed to continue, 'for the standing of that maketh me to have more business in diverse places than I should have'. He also hoped the pleas of the prior of the Austin friars, Shrewsbury, that his house should stand, would be resisted.[144] And, shortly afterwards, both 'these two naughty friars houses' duly surrendered. Interestingly, a later reference described them as suppressed by the bishop of Dover.[145]

Government Policy 1538–39

By early 1538, then, the government was not only committed to, but actually practising a policy of dissolution by 'voluntary' surrender, leading to the total dissolution of the monasteries, including friaries; this policy also involved the dismantling, and often the ridiculing and destroying, of pilgrimage shrines. This was, by any standards, a fundamental break in the religious history of England. From early 1538 a steady stream of surrenders is recorded in *Letters and Papers*. The abbeys go down as fast as they may be, and are, surrendered to the king, George Rolle informed Lord Lisle on 8 February.[146] Readily identifiable groups of commissioners were touring the country throughout 1538 and 1539, 'persuading' the abbots and priors to give up their houses.

There was a brief interlude in the spring of 1539. That was when the government secured an act that declared that the surrender of abbeys by their abbots and convents was legal—something that might have seemed highly dubious—and that all leases made by abbots should be treated as continuing in force. It is important to note that the act did not itself dissolve any monastery; all the larger monasteries, and all the smaller monasteries that had been exempted from the act of 1536, were dealt with by the visiting commissioners. Why did parliament agree to such a measure? Was there no voice of resistance to the surrenders? Did no MP think that issues of constitutional principle were raised by the practices of commissioners going from monastery to monastery? Of course, the meeting of parliament took place at a time of national emergency, soon after the national musters held at the end of March, and in London on 8 May, directed against 'the cankered and venomous serpent Paul, bishop of Rome' who had stirred the great princes of Christendom to invade England, many noblemen and gentry had been ordered to have men ready to serve on the sea against 'the most pestilent idol' the bishop of Rome, 'enemy of all truth and usurpator of princes'.[147] That was not a climate in which dissent could flourish.

Moreover, many noblemen and gentlemen had already acquired monastic lands, and no doubt others expected to do so. Often that is presented as a leading motivation for the dissolution, indeed as an astute means by which the king secured general acquiescence in the break with Rome. But it is much more reasonably seen as a reaction to what was taking place. It is important, however, to note the mixture of motivations. In 1536 Sir Simon Harcourt wrote for Routon, Staffordshire, a little house of canons, built and endowed by his ancestors. He asked Cromwell to be a mediator to the king that the house might continue, offering them £100 each. But if the king was determined to dissolve it, Harcourt desired to have it, as it adjoined such small lands as he had in that country.[148] An important factor was landowners' fears of the consequences for the local balance of power if a neighbour acquired monastic land. Such defensive anticipations of, or reactions to, changes in the pattern of local influence are perhaps more important than greed, in understanding the concern of noblemen and gentry to secure the lands of dissolved monasteries.

The abbots who sat in the House of Lords do not appear to have made a fuss about the bill in 1539. The sheer fact of surrender would have made opposition problematic. It is hard to stand up for the rights of those who are not standing up for those rights themselves. However involuntary the 'voluntary' surrenders really were, on the face of it, and publicly, they appeared voluntary.[149]

Moreover, to some extent what had happened could still be presented as a work of reform, especially when related to the reform of bishoprics based on the redeployment of monastic wealth, as Marillac, the French ambassador, reported.[150] Some of the monasteries were being 'altered', to use the term employed by the government, meaning that they were being converted into non-monastic religious foundations. That was most visibly and directly the case at the monastic cathedrals, where priors became deans and many monks prebendaries. The priory of the cathedral of Holy Trinity, Norwich, was transformed into a deanery and chapter, with the prior made a dean and the monks prebendaries in May 1538.[151] There were also some monasteries whose churches were considered for conversion into cathedrals as part of a reform of bishoprics that took up unfinished business left over from Wolsey's last years. The 1539 act allowed the use of the lands of some houses as endowments of new bishoprics. There is also a very interesting draft bill,[152] significantly in the king's hand, with alterations and corrections, criticising the

> slothful and ungodly life which hath been used amongst all those sort which have borne the name of religious folk, and to the intent that henceforth many of them might be turned to better use . . . whereby God's word might the better be set forth, children brought up in learning, clerks nourished in the universities, old servants decayed to have livings, almshouses for poor folk to be sustained in, readers of Greek, Hebrew and Latin to have good stipend, daily alms to be ministered, mending of highways, exhibition for ministers of the church, it is thought therefore unto the king's highness most expedient and necessary that more bishoprics, collegial and cathedral churches, should be established instead of these foresaid religious houses, within the foundation whereof other titles afore rehearsed shall be established.

Henry VIII here once again appears as a Christian reformer, espousing a grand and idealistic vision.[153] There then followed a list of new bishoprics by county, in the king's hand.[154] There were two further categories: 'places to be altered according to our device which have sees in them'—Christchurch in Canterbury, Saint Swithun's, Ely, Durham, Rochester (with a part of Lydd), Worcester; 'and all others having the same'—and 'places to be altered into colleges and schools only': Burton-upon-Trent.[155]

The scheme of bishoprics included provisions for readers of humanity in Greek, divinity in Hebrew, divinity and humanity in Latin.[156] Henry evidently consulted Cromwell, one of whose remembrances notes 'first for mine opinion touching the bishoprics; item, touching the monasteries of Launceston, and others in Cornwall; item, touching the monastery of Leicester which is already suppressed; item touching Newenham and Elstow, already suppressed; item, touching Fountains and the archdeaconry of Richmond'.[157] That only six bishoprics (Bristol, Chester, Gloucester, Oxford, Peterborough and Westminster), and two colleges (Thornton and possibly Burton-upon-Trent), eventually emerged from these proposals does not, as Scarisbrick conceded, necessarily show that they were insincere; indeed, that as many as six bishoprics were erected might be seen as a substantial reform.[158] This was an ambitious package. It immediately raised real practical and per-sonal difficulties. One of the plans was for Richard Sampson, bishop of Chichester, to take the intended new bishopric of Westminster: Sampson, in a remembrance to the king, expressed his willingness, but begged Henry to consider his first fruits and grant him some little house in the country for his health.[159] In a remembrance that hints at other problems, Cromwell noted 'what the king will have further done with the late abbot of Westminster'.[160]

That the suppression could be seen as being carried out in the name of reform further emerges in the way the visitors made a good deal of any abuses they uncovered—ranging from failure to observe the stricter rules introduced by the Injunctions of 1535, to mismanagement and debt—and engaged in face-to-face argument and persuasion. At St Albans, Thomas Legh and William Petre found grounds for the depri-vation of the abbot, Richard Boreman,[161] 'not only for breaking of the king's injunctions, but also for manifest dilapidation, making of shifts, negligent administration, and sundry other causes'.[162]

The bishop of Dover, visiting the friars, had similarly made use of the abuses he encountered to persuade friars to surrender. Three houses had surrendered to avoid having them made public: 'some sticking fast in windows naked going to drabs, so that the pillar was fain to be sawed to have him out; some being plucked from under drabs' beds'.[163]

The commissioners exploited any past misdemeanours or suspicions of anything less than total loyalty. At Woburn, Robert Hobbes, the abbot, surrendered his house in order to dispel accusations of treason made against him and his convent. These arose from the regrets that he had voiced that he had not suffered with the 'good men', meaning Fisher and More. He admitted that he had failed to declare the king supreme head when preaching: he had rather stiffly maintained the bishop of Rome's part. He believed Cranmer's consecration of bishops unlawful, as was Cranmer's granting of dispensations to monks to marry and capacities to leave the cloister. He had marvelled that Henry could not be content with his true wife, Catherine of Aragon. He had said that it was wonderful that the king was not content with what parliament had given him but broke down the holy monasteries his ancestors had founded. He urged his monks not to agree to any surrender of their house. He had the bulls of the monastery copied before they were given over, in the hope that if in the future the king and the bishop of Rome came to an agreement, they might be confirmed again. To put down the houses of God and to expel the monks was unmerciful. He had defended the intercession of saints and criticised the English translation of the Bible for its misleading interpretations.[164] The monks now surrendered 'upon our knees'.[165] The abbot blamed the monks and urged them to repent and to pray. The 'great affliction' came from 'their own sin and shameful living', like the children of Israel sent to Babylon for their wicked living, and was not to be thought to have been invented by the king or council.[166] Woburn was treated as an attainted monastery.[167]

It is striking that very often[168] abbots, monks and friars who surrendered their houses did not just make them over to the king. They also signed denunciations of their past way of life. Such self-criticism went beyond the acknowledgment of specific instances on which particular monks or monasteries had fallen short of the ideals of their rule. It was, rather, a far more fundamental renunciation of monasticism. Similarities of wording hint that monks and friars were asked to endorse an official pre-existing statement.

Abbot Richard Green and the convent of Bittlesden Abbey admitted that 'the manner and trade of living' which they and others of 'our pretensed religion' had long practised principally consisted in 'certain dome [dumb] ceremonies'. They had always obtained papal exemptions from diocesan visitations, but neither the bishop of Rome nor the abbot of Cîteaux ever came to reform the 'disorder of living and abuses' that were now found to have been prevalent among them. Therefore they acknowledged that it was most expedient for them to be ordered by their supreme head under God, namely the king.[169]

The prior and convent of St Andrew's, Northampton, professed, at great length, their contrition for the enormities of their past way of life 'under the pretence and shadow of perfect religion', and for the 'crafty deception and subtle seduction of the pure and simple minds of the good christian people' with 'vain superstitions and other unprofitable ceremonies the very means and plain inductions to the abominable sin of idolatry'. Since they were unable to live as they ought, they begged the king to accept their free gift, and to be charitable towards them. Their revenues had not been employed, as their founders intended, either in the pure observance of the Benedictine rule or in charity, in the relief of poor people and the provision of hospitality. Instead they led lives of 'idle quietness', not in humility but 'in a stately estimation'. They had 'devoured' their annual revenues to feed their 'voluptuous and carnal appetites'. 'For damnable lucre' they led the people to dead images and counterfeit relics: that was 'hypocrisy cloaked with feigned sanctity'. Now they daily sorrowfully pondered and saw the bottomless gulf of everlasting fire that would devour them if they persisted in their way of life. They begged the king's pardon for their offences, omissions and negligences. They acknowledged that as supreme head of his church immediately after Christ, Henry was the 'general and only reformator' of all monks, friars and nuns, with full authority to correct or to dissolve all monastic houses at his pleasure. The king had 'of long time past' just cause to take them back into his hands, but he had put it off in the hope that they would amend themselves. Now, so that no one would be 'abused with such feigned devotion and devilish persuasions under the pretext or habit of religion by us', and so that their goods should no longer be squandered, they humbly pleaded with the king to accept their free gift of all the possessions of the monastery and to discharge them. They insisted that this was done voluntarily and 'without any compulsion or inducement other than of our own proper conscience'.[170]

The declarations by the Aylesbury and Stamford Greyfriars were very similar. The Aylesbury Greyfriars declared that perfect Christian living was not 'in dome [dumb] ceremonies, wearing of a grey coat, disguising ourself after strange fashions, docking and becking, in girding ourselves with a girdle full of knots, and other like papistical ceremonies', but in following Christ and conforming to the will and pleasure of the supreme head on earth under Christ, the king, rather than 'the superstitious traditions of any potentate or power'.[171]

Such language condemned the vocations of monks and friars alike. It left no room whatsoever for improvement through reform. The Reading Greyfriars added general disaffection to the reasons for which they surrendered: 'as well the high estate of this realm as the common people do note in wise and daily doth lay unto our charge the detestable crimes of hypocrisy dissimulation and superstition and therefore withdraweth their benevolence and supportation'.[172]

Clearly it was of concern to the government that the surrenders of monasteries should beyond dispute be seen as voluntary. That no doubt explains why the prior and convent of St Andrew's, Northampton, in order to prove that their surrender was their mere and voluntary act, declared that they had published it openly before Sir William Parr, Dr

Richard Layton and Sir Robert Southwell, the king's commissioners,[173] and why so much emphasis was placed on the fact that (as was declared at Stafford) all the brethren with one assent, without any counsel or coaction, gave their houses to the visitor for the king's use.[174] When the Aylesbury Greyfriars surrendered, they declared that 'withe mutual assent and consent [they] do surrender and yield up' their house, lands and tenements to the king; they concluded by declaring that 'we all faithfully shall pray unto almighty god long to preserve his most noble grace withe increase of much felicity and honour'.[175]

When the king, Cromwell and government agents acted more privately, however, then they left a very different impression. The prior of Canterbury, writing in August 1538 of rumours that 'religious men shall leave or forsake their habit and go as secular priests do', felt impelled to remind Cromwell that 'ye have sent me word before this time that I and my brethren should not be constrained so to do'. Religious men had been in his church for nine hundred years and more.[176] William Blithman, writing to Cromwell from York on 24 August 1538, had secured letters from him ordering three northern priors to come up to court: he had done so because he had found them less willing to surrender than he had expected.[177] Thomas Thacker reported that he had laboured for three months to persuade the abbot of Darley to surrender his house to the king—so giving the lie to any suggestion that surrenders only happened if the monasteries themselves took the initiative.[178] Cromwell informed Thomas Legh and William Cavendish in November 1538 that 'the king's grace's pleasure is that with convenient speed ye repairing to the monasteries of Saint Oses [St Osyth] and Colchester shall for certain reformation and other considerations which his grace intendeth as well there as in other places, dissolve and take the same to his use', assigning annual pensions 'by your discretions': there was no pretence here about voluntary surrender (though the abbot of Colchester may, as we shall see, have refused).[179] Dr Tregonwell, Dr Petre and John Smyth reported how they could not bring the prioress of Amesbury to any conformity in March 1539.[180] Anyone with influence might seek to persuade monks to surrender: Cranmer informed Cromwell in March 1538 that since 'I am about, through the help of such friends as I have in these parts, to procure that the said prior shall willingly resign the same in to the king's hands', there was no need for Cromwell to depose the prior of the Charterhouse of Axholme, accused by three monks of taking goods out of the monastery and going about to 'undo the house'.[181] At Evesham the commissioners apparently brought divine service to an abrupt end: according to a note in an English Bible (the property of Evesham Abbey shortly before dissolution), the monastery was suppressed by Henry VIII 'the xxx day of January at evensong time the convent being in their quire at this verse deposuit potentes and [the commissioners?] would not suffer them to make an end'.[182]

By summer 1539 the government was becoming more direct. On 28 August 1539 Henry VIII wrote to Rowland Lee, the bishop of Coventry and Lichfield and president of the council in the marches, and Sir William Sulyard about the abbey of Haughmond, Shropshire, 'which remaineth at this present in such state as the observance of the same neither redoundeth to the honour of God nor to the benefit of our common weal'. The king continued that 'therefore being minded to take the same into our own hands for a better purpose, like as we doubt not but the abbot and convent of the same will be content to make their surrender accordingly.' So much for any independent decisions by the monastery.[183] On 27 September 1539 Sir John Neville informed Cromwell that the king had commanded him to remind Cromwell about the suppression of Guisborough: he asked Cromwell for a commission for the suppression.[184] Audley sent for the abbot of St Osyth's before the dissolution and 'induced him to yield the house to the king's majesty with his good will, and that he should exhort his convent to conform them to the same, who by my advise and exhortation conformed them selves as humble subjects without rumours or grudge'.[185] As such instances show, the government was prepared to go beyond mere persuasion.

Before long what was happening was so obvious that many monasteries were clearly keen to get it over with. John Freeman told Cromwell in October 1538 that everyone was ready to surrender.[186] Even when an abbot was unhappy, his monks might be ready to give up. Robert Hamlyn, abbot of Athelney, was apparently reluctant to resign his house—it would be destroyed, the country round about undone—but when the monks were spoken to, all said they would be glad to surrender.[187] John Marshall in Nottinghamshire in June 1539 noted that the abbots and priors of the religious houses still standing had sold everything in the expectation that the king's commissioners would soon come.[188]

Compliance, Reluctance and Resistance

How much reluctance and resistance was there? How did the government's agents deal with those who would not surrender?

Some monks and friars positively welcomed the developments. The abbot of Hailes thanked almighty God 'that ever I was born to live to this time of light and knowledge of his true honour, which is now so purely and sincerely set forward by the king's most gracious goodness and your most faithful travail and diligence'. He urged Cromwell to investigate the blood of Hailes, since 'I have a conscience putting me in dread lest idolatry be committed therein giving the very honour of the blood of christ to that thing'. Once the shrine was dismantled, he urged Cromwell to license him to pull down every stick and stone of the case in which the feigned relic had stood (though he seems to have hoped that his house would continue).[189] The warden of the London Greyfriars assured Cromwell that God had moved the heart of the prince to take away their papistical apparel.[190] Some observers thought the monks had brought the developments upon themselves. As we have seen, George Crofts, resident clerk of Chichester Cathedral, claimed, 'I have always in mine conscience thought the life of religious men such that God of his justice could send them no less punishment.'[191] Humphrey Reynolds, king's yeoman of Coventry, proposed a scheme for utilising the lands of the abbeys and declared that 'their ile [ill] living and conversation was partly the cause of the pulling down of the abbeys; and few or none of theme do live after their profession that they be bound unto'.[192] The abbot of Woburn told his monks that it was for their own shameful living that they were afflicted: when they had repented, God would put in the king's mind to set up these monasteries as fast as they had been put down.[193] John Marshall, writing from Nottinghamshire, at Cranmer's instigation, perhaps looking back to the days of the Pilgrimage of Grace, assured Cromwell that the abbeys 'were now nothing pitied'; the commons saw more 'common wealth' to grow from their suppression, though with the qualification that they had lost the monks' prayers.[194]

Some accepted that the status quo was no longer an option, but sought reincarnation as religious foundations of another kind. John Draper, the last prior of Christchurch, Dorset, and king's chaplain, petitioned Henry against the suppression of the monastery. Their church served as the parish church, offering worship for 1,500 people, their house daily relieved the poor and offered education to local children.[195] Audley, the lord chancellor, on hearing rumours of the imminent dissolution of St John's, Colchester, and St Osyth's, reminded Cromwell of his former plea that these houses should continue, not as abbeys but as colleges: he made his plea because many poor people depended on St John's for relief, and, without St Osyth's, there would be little hospitality in that part of the shire.[196] The prior of St Oswald's asked Cromwell to intercede with the king so that the house might be established as a college for the 'nourishment of youth in virtue and learning, to the increase and advancement of the lively word of God'.[197] The university of Cambridge hoped that the monasteries formerly given over to superstition might be made into colleges to promote 'good letters and the true doctrine of Christ'.[198] Humphrey Reynolds proposed a reform in which abbots and monks would receive salaries but would no longer deal with temporalities.[199] Bishop Latimer evidently hoped that the monasteries would not simply be confiscated by the king. In December 1538 he endorsed the suit of the prior of Great Malvern, who, fearing the suppression of his house, beseeched Cromwell and the king

> for the upstanding of his forsaid house, and continuance of the same to many good purpose, not in monkery, he meanneth not so, God forbid, but any other way as should be thought and seem good to the king's majesty, as to maintain teaching, preaching, study with praying, and (to the which he is much given) good housekeeping.

'Alas, my good lord, shall we not see ii or iii in every shire changed to such remedy.'[200] The abbot and convent of Evesham appealed to Cromwell that, since the king intended to change the monasteries of the realm 'for the true and sincere preaching and teaching of the word of God unto his poor loving subjects', 'for the education and bringing up of youth in virtue and true knowledge of the same', and 'for the relieving and succouring of the pore needy lame and impotent persons', their house should be reserved for such purposes. It 'is and hath ben always reputed a house of keeping of good hospitality and hath good provision for the same. . . . There is no such monastery to all ententes within the compass of xii miles of the same. . . . The few inns in the town cannot lodge all the noble men who repair there.'[201] The mayor and aldermen of Coventry wanted the friary churches of the grey- and whitefriars left standing. They justified their request by the impact that dissolution would have in time of plague when sick people were anxious to hear divine service in church. There were just two parish churches in Coventry; if those who were used to going to the friary churches in future went to the parish churches, they would infect the whole city.[202] When Dr London, one of the commissioners, arrived and defaced the church of the greyfriars and started to do the same at the whitefriars, they persuaded him to wait while they appealed once more to Cromwell to intercede with the king so that they might be granted the churches. Dr London expressed some qualified support, suggesting that they be given the Whitefriars church and churchyard away from the heart of the city. But he sharply criticised the local custom of collecting corpses in time of plague and leaving them at the great door of the cathedral until mass was said in the parish church.[203] Having failed to prevent the suppression of the friaries, the mayor and aldermen then lobbied to prevent the suppression of the cathedral church. Rowland Lee, bishop of Coventry and Lichfield, strongly supported them, and suggested—in vain—that the cathedral be turned into a college church as at Lichfield.[204] Cromwell may have been sympathetic to such plans: we learn that he had laboured, unsuccessfully, for the conversion of the former priory at Walsingham into a college.[205]

Some houses attempted to bribe their way to survival. The abbess and convent of Shaftesbury were at first attracted by the king's liberality to all who surrendered; but in December 1538 they declared their wish to continue, offering 500 marks to Henry and £100 to Cromwell. They appealed to Sir Thomas Arundell: despite 'the long and earnest practising of the said Mr Doctor [Tregonwell] for their surrenders', they would not willingly agree, claiming that they enjoyed the king's favour. They asked Arundell to write to Cromwell to persuade the king 'that they may remain here by some other name and apparel, his highness poor and true bedeswomen'.[206] The abbot of Peterborough wanted his monastery to continue; he offered a year's rent (2,500 marks) and £300 to Cromwell for his house to stand.[207] The abbot of Pipwell told Sir William Parr in July 1538 that he feared for the dissolution of his house and offered Cromwell £200 that it might stand.[208]

Some reluctance was also voiced, privately, by noblemen and gentlemen. We have already heard Lord Delaware and the Poles. Silence need not mean consent either. Christopher Chaitour, Bishop Tunstal's servant, was asked by one Cray: 'is there none that grudgeth with such pulling down of abbeys in your country?' 'No', replied Chaitour, 'for if there be any such, they keep it secret, for there hath been so sore punishment'.[209]

Some made a fuss against the procedures. Katherine Bulkeley, abbess of Godstow, appealed to Cromwell in November 1538 against her rough handling by Dr John London. London had opposed her promotion, which Cromwell had furthered with the king. Now London had arrived suddenly, 'withe a great rout with him', and threatened her and her sisters, saying that he had the king's commission to suppress the house 'spite of my teeth'. She refused to surrender to him, her enemy. The abbess insisted that she would only surrender if commanded to do so by the king or Cromwell.[210] Cromwell evidently supported

Bulkeley, who thanked him for staying Dr London 'which was here ready to suppress this poor house against my will and all my sisters and had done it in deed if you had not so speedily sent contrary commandment'. In return she offered Cromwell her prayers, and assured him that

> there is neither pope, nor purgatory, image, nor pilgrimage, nor praying to dead saints used or regarded amongst us but all superstitious ceremonies set apart, the very honour of God and the truth of his holy words as far as the frail nature of women may attain unto it most tenderly followed and regarded with us not doubting but this garment and fashion of life doth nothing prevail toward our justifying before God by whom for his sweet son Jhesus sake we only trust to be justified and saved.[211]

The abbess had conceded a great deal: what would be the point of monasticism on such terms?

There are several examples of heads of houses who were far from keen on surrender and who did what they could, short of outright defiance of the royal will. Florence Bonnewe, prioress of Amesbury, refused in March 1539 to follow the example of Shaftesbury and Wilton and surrender her house: 'she said that if the king commanded her to leave the house she would gladly go though she begged her bread, and she cared for no pension, and prayed them to trouble her no further'.[212] But after she received letters from the king and from Cromwell in August, and was pressed by the commissioners John Incent and Thomas Legh, she resigned and the house surrendered.[213] This was clearly a principled, not a materialist, stand by Florence.

The reluctant abbot of Vale Royal took a similar line. Defiantly he informed Cromwell: 'the truth is, I nor my said brethren have never consented to surrender our monastery, nor yet do, nor never will do by our good wills, unless it shall please the king's grace to give to us commandment so to do'.[214] But shortly after he seemed to make a deal, perhaps on being threatened with interrogatories asking about his financial interest in the monastery. Allegedly, the abbot had asked Thomas Holcroft, one of the king's commissioners, hastily to despatch the monks, 'for they were but knaves'.[215]

John Wilson, prior of Mount Grace for twenty years, was one of the last to surrender his house, on 18 December 1539.[216] A servant of Dr Legh had gone to the prior and advised him to meet Mr Henley, the chief commissioner for the suppression, two miles from the monastery, and, if he wanted a good pension, to offer him a horse worth five marks. The prior responded that he would not leave the cloister to meet Mr Henley 'nor give him the least hair of my horse's tail to be good to me for that purpose'. Dr Hilliard, one of Tunstal's chaplains, thought that the prior and three or four of the monks had determined never to surrender—but in fact they did.[217] The prior was interrogated after a brief imprisonment at York Castle: he declared his reluctance to surrender his house, 'if it might have stood with the king's pleasure that he might have kept it', but he thought it best to obey the king. Earlier he had been convinced by Tunstal and Archbishop Lee of the illegality of the papal supremacy. He had to imprison four of his monks for three months before he could persuade them.[218]

The prior of Hinton Charterhouse, Edmund Horde, was content to obey, if the king would take his house, but his conscience would not allow him willingly to give it up.[219] It was not theirs to give, but God's. They had been offered no reasons why they should be put down: they had observed the service of God, religious conversation, hospitality and almsgiving as well as any house in this realm or in France. But since he had heard of the king's and Cromwell's displeasure, he would try to get his brethren to conform so that neither Henry nor Cromwell would be displeased.[220] Eventually the prior succeeded, though one of his monks, Nicholas Balande, continued to deny the royal supremacy, affirming the bishop of Rome to be the supreme head of the church: the prior said he was a lunatic.[221]

The canons of Bruton and the monks at Montacute were unwilling to surrender their houses. The abbot of Bruton and the prior of Montacute were obstinate, Sir Hugh Pollard and William Petre reported, suspecting collusion: to judge by the prior's answers, there had been some privy conference between them. Repeated visits, persuasion and threats were needed before the surrender of Montacute on 20 March and Bruton on 1 April 1539.[222]

Richard, abbot of Winchcombe, trusted, in August 1539, that he had not done anything against the laws of God and the king to merit the suppression of the monastery,[223] though Richard Tracy reported that some thought the convent was minded to surrender.[224]

Glastonbury, Colchester and Reading

All discussed so far, however reluctant, acquiesced in the end, without punishment. But three abbots were executed. Hugh Cooke, abbot of Reading, was executed on 14 November; Richard Whiting, abbot of

Glastonbury, on 15 November; and Thomas Beche (or Marshall), abbot of Colchester, on 1 December.

Glastonbury was 'the goodliest house of that sort that ever we have seen . . . a house meet for the king's majesty, and for no man else', according to the commissioners' initial findings in September 1539.[225] By then the government simply wanted Glastonbury to surrender. Cromwell marvelled that Richard Layton, who had been a visitor in 1535, had then praised the abbot, who now, according to Cromwell, appeared 'to have no part of a Christian man'. Layton protested that he was a man who might err and that he could not know the inward thoughts of a monk, outwardly conformable, inwardly cankered.[226] What offended Cromwell? Simply the abbot's refusal to surrender? Or suspicions about his past loyalties? However that may be, Layton and the other commissioners examined the abbot. When he did not tell them what they wanted to hear, they pressed him, and then searched his study for letters and books, finding 'secretly laid' both a 'book of arguments' against the king's divorce, and several pardons, copies of papal bulls and 'the counterfeit life of Thomas Bequet [Becket] in print', but no incriminating letters. Under examination, however, the abbot revealed further 'his cankered and traitorous heart and mind against the king's majesty and his succession'. And the commissioners found a gold chalice and much other plate which the abbot had hidden from earlier commissioners. They sent him—a very weak and sickly man—to the Tower.[227] A few days later they reported that they had each day found money and plate hidden by the abbot and by the monks in walls, vaults and secret places. This was 'so arrant and manifest robbery' that they put the two treasurers and two lay clerks in gaol. Their suspicions had been aroused when they first went into the treasury and vestry and found insufficient jewels, plate and ornaments to serve a parish church. The abbot and monks had stolen enough plate to have begun a new abbey, the commissioners complained.[228] On 2 October they reported that they had now found out 'diverse and sundry' treasons committed by the abbot of Glastonbury, sending details in a book.[229] Even with all this, the abbot would not admit to any more than he had earlier confessed, and refused to implicate anyone apart from himself. He asked God and the king to show him mercy for his great offences.[230] On 14 November he was duly arraigned, condemned by a jury of local men, and the next day executed on Glastonbury Tor with two of his monks, for robbing the church. He was quartered and his head was struck off: quarters were displayed at Wells, Bath, Ilchester and Bridgwater.[231] In short, the abbot had been destroyed because of the evidence of his opposition to the divorce, the royal supremacy, and because of his embezzling of the money and plate of the abbey. It is possible, though the evidence is not conclusive, that he had refused to surrender and that it was that refusal that had led to searches and then to prosecution when incriminating evidence was found.[232] If the abbot had agreed to surrender, he might have kept his life.

The abbot of Reading may well have struck the government as uncooperative. In September 1538 he was reported by John London as saying—as they all did—that he was at the king's command, but London noted how reluctant he was to agree to any voluntary surrender.[233] The abbot showed London the relics of the abbey, including two pieces of the holy cross, St James's hand, St Philip's stole and bones from many saints, this at a time when such shrines and relics were generally being pulled down and suppressed.[234] A little later, perhaps maliciously, the abbot reported rumours of the death of the king.[235] In summer 1539, Sir William Penizon warned Cromwell that, preparing for the dissolution, he was selling sheep, corn and woodland to the disadvantage of the king.[236] Thomas Moyle, one of the dissolution commissioners, and Thomas Vachell, a local man, were to be found checking furniture and fittings in September 1539, presumably looking for evidence of embezzlement and political disloyalty.[237] They found one priest-monk who was clearly hostile to the regime. John Rugg, priest, was interrogated as to how he came to have a book that he knew to be written against the king's supremacy and his divorce in his chamber in Reading Abbey, why he had asked Thomas Vachell to place it so that it would not be found, and how he had a relic, St Anastasius's hand, at Reading, knowing that the king had sent visitors to the abbey to put down such idolatry.[238]

What did they find against the abbot himself? According to the indictment,[239] he was accused of saying, 'The king is not supreme head of the Church of England.' He had added that he trusted shortly to see the pope bear as great rule in England as he had ever done, and that he would say mass once every week for him. 'I will say that there is a pope as long as I live,' he declared defiantly. A somewhat colourful discourse against treason attacked him for political disloyalty and echoed some of these charges. It claimed that when he was sworn to the king's supremacy, 'he added, in his own conscience, of the temporal church . . . but not of the spiritual church'. On the day of his death, the abbot of Reading, according to this hostile witness, confessed before a great crowd of people that he blamed four traitors for his fall, three bishops and the vicar of Croydon. One was the former bishop of London, John

Stokesley, pardoned by the king for offences under the statute of *prae-munire*; the other bishops were Archbishop Warham and Henry Standish, and the other churchman was Rowand Phillips—four names that would have linked him with supposed conservatives in religion.[240] In short, what did for the abbot of Reading was his continuing papalism and chafing against the royal supremacy. What is not exactly clear is how and why he came to be investigated at just this time. Once he was, and evidence of his sympathy for the pope came to light, he found himself in deep trouble. Despite pleading not guilty, he was convicted of treason and executed.[241]

For the government the abbots of Glastonbury and Reading were traitors. As John Butler reported to Bullinger on 24 February 1540, the two abbots had been condemned for treason and quartered; each of them was now rotting on a gibbet near his abbey gate—a worthy recompense for their imposture.[242] Cromwell's remembrances include a note 'for the indictment against the abbot of and other [*sic*], a commission of oyer et determiner into Berkshire for his indictment and trial'. It continues, 'certain persons to be sent to the Tower for the further examination of the abbot of Glaston', which is fair enough, but then follows the notorious entry: 'The abbot Redyng to be sent down to be tryed and executed at Reding with his complyces. Item the abbott of Glaston to be tryed at Glaston and also executyd their with his complycys' (the abbot of Reading to be sent down to be tried and executed at Reading with his accomplices. Item the abbot of Glastonbury to be tried at Glastonbury and also executed there with his accomplices).[243] Elton comments that, 'so far from regarding the trials as a formality', Cromwell 'was concerned that his own assurance of the accused persons' guilt should be properly transmitted to the jury', citing the subsequent sentences to the effect that councillors were to give evidence against the abbot of Glastonbury and that they were to see that the evidence was well sorted and indictments well drawn.[244] But there are other, less flattering, ways of reading this note, namely that the guilt of the abbots was presumed to be certain in advance of the trials, seen here as merely an administrative formality prior to their executions.

A third abbot, of Colchester, was executed a month later. His case is striking because he is a rare case of an abbot who—at least at times—expressed his hostility to the dissolution of the monasteries. God should take vengeance, he allegedly said, on those who destroyed abbeys, naming Cranmer and Audley.[245] He had informed Robert Rouse, mercer of Colchester, about the Pilgrimage of Grace—about which he had not previously heard—saying the northern lads were up and that no more abbeys would be suppressed.[246] After the commotion was over, and commissioners were suppressing those monastic houses whose heads had been caught up in the rebellion, he said that these tyrants and blood-suckers thrust out the good religious fathers against all right.[247] He saw greed as the motive behind the suppression. A servant had heard the abbot say that 'two or three of the king's council hath brought his grace in such a covetous mind that if all the water in temsse [Thames] did flow gold and silver it were not able to quench his grace's thirst'. More specifically the abbot had, allegedly, declared his determination not to surrender his abbey to the king. There was no law that could compel him to do so, since the king could not lawfully suppress any house with an annual income of over £200. When he discussed the likely surren-der by the abbot of St Osyth with Sir John St Clair, the abbot of Colch-ester declared that 'the king shall never have my house but again my will and again my heart, for I know by my learning that he cannot take it by right and law wherein in my conscience I cannot be content nor he shall never have it with my heart and will'. St Clair had heard the abbot say several times in the last year that the king could not lawfully suppress any house of religion above the yearly value of £200; that 'he would never surrender up his house and lands to the king's hands', and 'that he had as well die as to forsake his living'; and he wished that every abbot was of his mind.[248] St Clair warned him not to stick with what he had learned at Oxford when he was young: if he did so he would be hanged.[249] It is possible that the abbot refused a specific invi-tation to surrender his house. In November 1538 Cromwell ordered Dr Legh and William Cavendish to dissolve the monasteries of St Osyth and Colchester in November 1538, but while St Osyth surrendered, Colchester did not.[250]

Such reluctance to surrender was obviously an obstacle for the gov-ernment. But the abbot had allegedly also expressed opinions on the royal supremacy that the government saw as treason and that offered a renewed opportunity. St Clair, informing Cromwell, said he feared the abbot had a cankered heart—he had been accused of voicing traitorous words, but there were no witnesses.[251] Robert Rouse would later testify that he had left the abbot's company two years earlier because he rea-soned against the king's supremacy and acts of parliament for extin-guishing the authority of the bishop of Rome. He inveighed against the tyranny of executing the monks of Syon, and Fisher and More.[252] Thomas Nuthake, physician of Colchester, who used to go to the abbey, said that he had heard the abbot say that the reason the king forsook the bishop of Rome was so that he might be divorced from the lady dowager and wed Queen Anne. He had declared that the bishop of Rome was the only supreme head of the church by the laws of God, next under Christ. He had lamented the deaths of Fisher and More, who died martyrs in his conscience for holding with our holy father the pope for the right of all holy church.[253]

All that was not as conclusively damning as it might appear. The testimony of the abbot's servant Edmund Troman suggests that the abbot went to some lengths to temper his feelings. Troman said he had never heard the abbot say anything about the supremacy of the bishop of Rome. He had never heard him say the bishop of Rome was the immediate successor to St Peter. But he had heard him say that Fisher, More and the monks of the Charterhouse 'died holy martyrs'; soon after their executions, he said that they 'dyed like good men & that it was pity of their deaths for they were great learned men & wise men'. The abbot had said that the northern men were 'good men, mokyll [large?] in the mothe [mouth?], great cracars [boasters] and nothing worthy in their deeds'; at the time of the insurrection he had said, 'I would to Christ the rebels in the north country had the bishop of Canterbury, the lord chancellor and the lord privy seal amongst them and I trust wee should have a merry world again.' 'Well this world will boil no water at length.'[254] The abbot's sentiments are palpable; but there was very little here that could directly be used against him.

Similarly, when confronted with accusations of treason, the abbot denied that he had criticised the royal supremacy. The indictment accused the abbot of saying that by the laws of God the bishop of Rome was the only supreme head of the church 'next immediately unto Christ and none other'; that those who had styled the king supreme head of the church were false heretics; that all who agreed to the royal supremacy were accursed; that the king had usurped the dignity of the pope and of God; and that those who were responsible for the deaths of Fisher and More were 'wretched tyrants and bloodsuckers'.

The abbot denied most of this. He thought the king had good right to be supreme head, being elected by the free consent of his whole realm. He had said that More and Fisher were great learned men and with the grace of God they might have contrition for their offences, and that with the grace of God the northern men would be vanquished. He denied the remark that all the water in the Thames would not slake the king's covetousness. He said that if the suppression was the will of God, it was well done; if not, God would punish it at length. As to his own house, if the visitors had come to suppress it, he would have given it up rather than incur the king's displeasure, 'but I thought somewhat to stand in it, for that I would my pension should be the more'.[255]

He was nonetheless prosecuted. One of Cromwell's remembrances notes 'of the abbot of Colchester to be sent down in the latter end of this term'.[256] The abbot was a prisoner in the Tower by 20 November 1539,[257] indicted on 1 December for treason, convicted and executed.[258] According to Sir Christopher Jenny, the abbot, after judgement, asked the king's forgiveness, acknowledged himself in substance to be guilty, and showed himself penitent, 'saving that he stood somewhat in his own conviction that the suppression of abbeys should not stand with the law of God', which continuing defiance made Jenny think him an evil man.[259]

Elton, accepting the evidence of Nuthake and Rouse, argues that 'it is not really possible to doubt that [the abbot] was guilty of those treasons': attacking the royal supremacy, defending the pope and sympathising with the Pilgrims of Grace.[260] But Elton himself, while noting that 'Formally he died for treason committed in denying the royal supremacy', and insisting that 'he had committed that treason', goes on to say that 'In inner reality he died for his absolute conviction that the king had no right to take his abbey from him', and that he was 'the only martyr . . . for the monastic institution as such that the Dissolution threw up'. But when he suggests that

> almost certainly this was also the reason for the vigour with which he was persecuted. . . . he had made it very plain that he would not surrender his abbey, and when means were sought to put pressure on him the search turned up such plain and rank treasons that there could be only one end to the story[261]

it once again makes the destruction of an abbot for treason appear as the means whereby a government now determined on the suppression of all the monastic houses dealt with the handful of unco-operative abbots. The charges were not wholly fanciful, of course, as Elton points out. But they were by no means as clear-cut and as damning as the government might have wished.

What is most striking in the end about the fate of Glastonbury, Reading and Colchester is not any heroic resistance but the determination of the government to winkle out evidence of what it saw as treason—denial of the royal supremacy—and of any corruption, and to use that to destroy the monastery. Striking, too, is how readily virtually all the abbots and priors responded to the invitations of the commissioners in

1538–39 to surrender their houses. There was almost no co-ordinated resistance, or even much discussion. Ultimately the monasteries were vulnerable to the withdrawal of royal support. Resistance through rebellion, whether directly or by the commons on their behalf, had failed in 1536–37 to preserve them. In the absence of renewed rebellion, or some effective foreign intervention by, say, Reginald Pole and imperial forces, there was little—indeed nothing—that monasteries could do. The executions of the monks and friars who had refused to accept the royal supremacy in 1534–35 and of those abbots and monks who had been caught up in the rebellions of 1536–37 made the price that those who resisted would have to pay all too plain. The way in which, in the years after 1537, pressures were brought to bear by travelling royal commissioners on individual houses, on individual abbots and priors, was especially hard to resist. That is, after all, how tyrannies operate. Moreover, the way in which the surrenders were presented as the correction of admitted abuses further undermined the *raison d'être* of monasteries, in much the same way as the dismantling of pilgrimage shrines undermined their devotional purpose and to some extent their economic base. It is not surprising that by early 1540 not a single monastery—the special case of the monastic cathedrals apart[262]—remained in the realm.

6

The Making of Religious Policy

The Bishops' Book: The Search for Unity

The Pilgrimage of Grace was a great shock to Henry. Reginald Pole's subsequent legation had raised fears of international action against him and accounts for his ruthless concern on learning of the disaffection of the Poles and the marquess of Exeter. That the Pilgrimage had been in large part a rising in defence of the monasteries had turned Henry's scepticism towards the monasteries into something like monachophobia: the final suppression of the monasteries had followed. All that increased the perceived need to declare what true religion was, to set out agreed doctrine and agreed forms of worship. Henry, as we saw earlier, had begun to meet that challenge in spring 1536, with the making of the Ten Articles. Then, the extent to which the Ten Articles would have been understandably felt as sanctioning a radical shift in religious policy was emphasised. But now the king's religious policy will be considered more on its own terms, and what will be shown is that there was greater coherence and consistency in royal policy than the fashionable notion of factional rivalry for the king's ear allows. What the king sought was concord based on his own religious convictions, best characterised as a search for a middle way between Rome and Wittenberg, between Rome and Zurich.

In 1537 Henry maintained, rather than (as is often said) changed, his course. (Still less did he have it changed for him.) He saw ignorance and contention as root causes of sedition and rebellion, and so, in the aftermath of the Pilgrimage of Grace, once again sought to secure from leading churchmen a statement of true religion; this time, however, much more thorough and comprehensive than the Ten Articles of 1536, which had dealt only with the most important matters. Henry's first concern was unity: it was disagreements, he held, that had provoked rebellion. 'Forasmuch . . . as great trouble, unquietness, and tumult might arise among the multitude in case there were no certain rules, ordinances, and ceremonies prescribed unto them, bishops and priests should make certain rules and canons', following 'the saying of St Paul, "look that all things be done in the church seemly and in a decent order" '.[1] With such intentions, the king ordered the bishops and leading theologians to meet and to set out the rudiments of Christian doctrine, and a catechism for instructing the young.[2] The bishops echoed Henry's instructions; they aimed to produce a plain and sincere doctrine to the 'perfect establishing of your said subjects in good unity, and concord, and perfect quietness'.[3] When work on the Bishops' Book was completed, the king reiterated these themes. 'We will that all preachers agree', he demanded. 'We will no wresting of things, no glosses that take away the text.' He wanted no more contentions which set people against each other.[4] Henry's demand for unity is remarkable, given the manifest divisions over doctrine and liturgy in the Bishops' Book itself.

The bishops' discussions were protracted. By 18 February 1537 most of the bishops had met.[5] From then till late July there were lengthy debates. On 30 April they were waiting for a conclusion;[6] on 12 May they were 'at a point yet unknown';[7] on 20 July they were agreed.[8] According to the bishops' preface to the resulting document, they had 'long and mature consultation'.[9] Gardiner—who was not present— asserted that the book 'resembled a common storehouse, where every man laid up in store such ware as he liked, and could tell where to find to serve his purpose'. On his return from France, where he was serving as ambassador,

> it was showed me that Bishop Stokesley . . . after he had stiffly with-stood many things, and much stoutness had been between him and the Bishop of Hereford . . . then Bishop Stokesley would somewhat relent in the form, as Bishop Foxe did the like. And then, as it were in a mean, each part, by placing some words by special marks, with a certain understanding protested, the article went forth; and so to a new article, and so from one to another. There is sometime as evident contradiction as if it had been saved by a proviso.[10]

Latimer found the whole business of debate distasteful:

> verily, for my part, I hade lever be poor parson of poor Kington again, then to continue thus Bishop of Worcester; not for any thing, that I

have hade to do therein, or can do, but yet, forsooth, it is a troublous thing to agree upon a doctrine, in things of such controversy, with judgements of such diversity, every man (I trust) meaning well, and yet not all meaning one way. But I doubt not, but now, in the end, we shall agree both one with another, and all with the truth, though some will then marvel.

He hoped that the king would expunge anything that was rotten, or at least indicate that it was only because of the frailty and grossness of his subjects that he would still tolerate it for a time.[11]

The bishops divided into reformers and conservatives, but not identically on every issue, and those inclined to reform or to conservatism differed in the degree of vehemence with which they argued their views. According to the bishop of Chichester Richard Sampson's testimony (when accused of treason in 1540), he, Tunstal and Stokesley were working together to defend 'the old usages and traditions of the church'. Tunstal, Sampson maintained, had 'an old book in greek' in which were 'divers things of the old usages and traditions of the old church'. He had 'divers times' brought it with him to Lambeth, 'and as I went with him in his barge he will tell me of divers places there written for that purpose and off divers things than used and ordained by the greek church'. In the same book, or another, there was a form of mass. Stokesley also brought books in Greek 'to set forth the old usages and traditions of the church' because 'they were thought of authority'. 'Divers times at Lambeth', both in the gallery and when they left Cranmer, Stokesley 'would be very earnest' with Sampson 'for those old usages of the church'. Tunstal and Stokesley 'were fully bent to maintain as many of the old usages and traditions as they might', especially praying for souls so that they might be delivered from pain.[12] If Sampson, Stokesley and Tunstal, together with Clerk, Longland and Lee of York, tended to conservatism, Cranmer, Latimer, Shaxton, Foxe and Goodrich tended to reform. How the proceedings were arranged is hinted at by a surviving set of statements on the sacrament of confirmation: bishops and churchmen individually stated their views.[13] Fragments survive on other subjects; presumably each churchman submitted similar statements on all the matters under consideration.

Latimer's comments point to the central role of the king. But it is vital to grasp the context in which Henry was operating. As in 1536, he had called churchmen together to pronounce on doctrine and liturgy. This time, he kept them assembled for much longer, and expected them to produce a comprehensive statement of Christian belief, dealing with a greater range of matters than had the Ten Articles the previous year. Henry had definite views, but he could not just impose them upon his bishops. They were, after all, highly educated churchmen with carefully worked-out convictions on contentious matters. He could, however, cajole and argue with them; he could exploit the many divisions between them; and he could put pressure on them to agree, not least since all were committed in principle to unity and concord. What made his action something of a balancing act was that on some points he agreed with the reformers, on others he was with the conservatives, but often in complex ways.

What specific guidance did the king give the churchmen in their task? He wanted unity—but that aspiration could not in itself offer much assistance. His wish was

> to have a sure and certain kind of doctrine, not as made by men, but by them searched out of the holy scripture. And such things chiefly elected and chosen as were both best to be known, and also meetest to be observed, of men that profess Christ and his religion.[14]

Again, while that appeared to offer both method and criteria, clearly it would not resolve divisions. More revealing of the king's intentions is a draft preface which explains how it was in response to seditious tales that the four sacraments not expounded in the Ten Articles the previous year had been abolished that 'his highness minding to testify to the [w]hole world his most catholic mind and disposition with his great zeal both to the advancement of the pure will and testament of god and to the continuance of all honest laudable and virtuous rites ceremonies and customs' had 'for the satisfaction of all partes called his said prelates and clergy together'.[15] Henry sought both 'the advancement of the pure will and testament of god' (seemingly endorsing the aspiration of those sympathetic to Luther and continental reformers) and 'the continuance of all honest laudable and virtuous rites ceremonies and customs' (seemingly endorsing the traditional religion). Henry wanted a middle way. He sympathised both with Latimer and Cranmer over purifying reform, and with Tunstal and Stokesley over ceremonies—but with neither wholly or exclusively.

That makes the fashionable view that Thomas Cromwell, as vicegerent in spirituals, and Thomas Cranmer, archbishop of Canterbury, were responsible for the assembly of churchmen, supposedly gathered in a strikingly new council, and that they determined the outcome, highly misleading.[16] The gathering was much more of an ad hoc body. It was not formally constituted with a defined membership or procedures, and no provisions were made for regular future meetings. Those historians who see Cromwell and Cranmer as responsible for it also tend to see them as pursuing a radical agenda. Yet, even on its own terms, such an analysis seems misconceived. Suppose, for the sake of argument, that Cromwell and Cranmer were indeed actively trying to push the church in more protestant directions. It seems most unlikely that they would have supposed that they could persuade conservative bishops to go with them, especially in the immediate aftermath of the Pilgrimage of Grace. An assembly including Stokesley, Tunstal and Sampson was an unpromising venue for radical reform. It is much more probable that it was Henry who had decided upon the meeting. The instructions to the pursuivant of Berwick, on a mission in April 1537 to the regents of Scotland, laid down that 'if asked for news, he was to say none, that the kingdom was never quieter, for the king had assembled great part of the prelates and learned men to establish matters touching religion like a catholic prince'.[17] The preface of the Bishops' Book says that 'your highness commanded us now of late to assemble ourselves together'.[18] Cromwell, in his introductory speech, emphasised the king's anxiety to settle controversies in church; he hoped that they would conclude all things without brawling or scolding. The king would not allow scripture to be wrested or defaced by any glosses or papistical laws.[19] That sounds like a reflection of the king's concern for unity.[20] More striking is the testimony of the draft preface, which tells of the involvement of the king. 'Joining himself with them in the mature and deliberate advise debatement and perfect examination of the said things . . . [he] hath also caused the other four sacraments to be inserted and joined to the other discourse of the three sacraments and other things before mentioned.'[21] It is interesting, too, that when Cranmer in July asked Cromwell to be intercessor to the king for them so that they might all have his licence to depart, given the virulence of plague in London, the authority sought was the king's.[22]

How far did the Bishops' Book reflect the king's views? How far did Henry succeed in obtaining its endorsement for his religious middle way? It is clear that, while approving much, he had reservations about some sections. When the book was completed, Bishop Foxe asked Cromwell to know the king's pleasure about possible prefaces and whether the book should be published in the king's name, as he had earlier suggested, or in the name of the bishops.[23] Cromwell responded by asking Foxe to write a preface. Foxe replied—very revealingly for any assessment of Henry's role—that he must first know the king's pleasure as to what its argument should be, and whether the book would go forth in the king's name or in that of the bishops.[24] Henry responded by saying that he had not had time to look over the work but that he would allow it to be printed. Scarisbrick suggests that Henry was too lazy to do more 'than flip over a few of its pages' in summer 1537, not least with Jane Seymour pregnant, and that is why it was issued without a full royal approval.[25] But Henry's remark may well have been disingenuous. As Sampson would put it, the king was content that the book should be taught and obeyed—'till that his majesty shall otherwise order some things with a more mature and deliberous counsel: in the mean time no person ought to reprove that book'.[26] In other words, Henry was satisfied with much of the Bishops' Book, but intended in due course, following further discussion, to make some changes. The king's letter, prefixed to the book, deserves careful attention. Henry does indeed admit 'that hitherto we have had no time convenient to overlook your great pains taken in the long search and diligent debating of this your book . . . much less time to ponder and weigh such things as you therein have written', yet nevertheless in response to their petition he had agreed to its printing and distribution to all parts of his realm, without doubting that they had achieved their common aim, namely that of having 'a sure and certain kind of doctrine'. 'We nothing mislike your judgements', the king proclaimed. 'Notwithstanding that we are otherwise occupied, [we] have taken as it were a taste of this your book, and have found therein nothing but that is both mete to come from you, and also worthy our praise and commendations.'[27] That was a broad but not a wholly enthusiastic endorsement.

Yet the Bishops' Book seems too important and too central for the king to have done no more than insouciantly glance at it. Much more likely is that Henry was cautiously distancing himself, preparing to correct sections he disliked. What he sought was the unanimous agreement of the churchmen in his own religious middle way. That was a tall order. In large part, however, he had succeeded. Most of the matters on which his own convictions were strongest were indeed reflected within the Bishops' Book. In places, however, there were formulations and wordings not altogether to his liking, even if, often, balanced elsewhere by more congenial statements. Henry evidently calculated that he had drawn from the churchmen an agreed statement of doctrine that was as close to what he wanted as he could reasonably expect to get by asking them to deliberate and to agree. Now he would seek less formal ways to improve the text.

That the Bishops' Book would be reformed—'as it had need in many points'—was noted in October 1537 by Thomas Wriothesley, writing to Thomas Wyatt.[28] At some point shortly afterwards[29] Henry engaged in a remarkable dialogue with Cranmer in the margins of his copy, 'a monument to his theological enthusiasm'.[30] The king offered no fewer than 250 emendations.[31] He also consulted George Day, master of St John's College, Cambridge, Nicholas Heath, archdeacon of Stafford, and the future bishops Thomas Thirlby and John Skip on theological points.[32]

Cranmer set all other business aside to respond to the king,[33] producing twenty-nine pages of commentary. To Cromwell he trusted that the king would pardon his presumption. He had been 'so scrupulous' and 'a picker of quarrels', 'making a great matter of every light fault, or rather where no fault is at all', he admitted, defending himself on the ground that 'because the book now shall be set forth by his grace's censure and judgement, I would have nothing therein that Momus could reprehend'. Yet Cranmer referred all his annotations 'again to his graces most exact judgment'.[34] Henry then prepared a final version—a printed copy with neat insertions of his corrections, together with additional folios of more radically revised pages.[35]

What concerned the king? For Cranmer it was plain (writing in October 1537) that the Bishops' Book endorsed the doctrine of justification by faith alone: under the heading 'things requisite to our salvation', he included 'our justification by Christ's passion only'.[36] And it was over justification by faith alone that the principal differences between Henry and his archbishop arose. Despite Cranmer's assertion, the Bishops' Book was in many respects ambiguous, or even contradictory, in thrust on the matter. Much of its language seemed to endorse a Lutheran doctrine of justification by faith alone: the utter inability of man to observe by himself the commandments of God; the passion of Christ that made a sufficient satisfaction to God; the freedom from anxiety about a man's ultimate passage to heaven. Yet it was still the case that at Doomsday men would be judged according to their deeds and works done while living in the world: there would be no mercy for those who had not deserved it in their lifetime. Faith and hope could only be obtained through confession to a priest, followed by priestly absolution and prayers, fasting and alms. That was a remarkable mixture of theological stances.[37] Selective quotation could make it seem consistently Lutheran; rounded consideration suggests that it was far less certain in thrust. It served Henry's purpose to have secured the agreement of Cranmer to such a text; it would serve his purpose even better if the text might be modified further, removing key phrases or neutralising their force by shrewd emendations. At this point Henry faced Cranmer's objections. It is worth emphasising, however, that it was not Cranmer, supposedly acting as a politician, who was trying to manoeuvre Henry into radical positions. Henry had required the bishops to state their opinions, and they had done so; he was now trying to finesse their agreed, but often uncertain, ambiguous and contradictory text, building on those passages with which he was in sympathy, and revising, skilfully, those he liked less, while carrying Cranmer with him.

For example, Henry brilliantly added two words—here in italics— that completely transformed the sense of the following passage:

> the penitent must conceive certain hope and faith that God will forgive him his sins and repute him justified, and of the number of his elect children, not *only* for the worthiness of any merit or work done by the penitent but *chiefly* for the only merits of the blood and passion of our saviour Christ.

Henry's addition of 'only' and 'chiefly' neatly reversed the meaning: Cranmer replied that 'these two words may not be put in this place in anywise'.

> They signify that our election and justification cometh partly of our merits, though chiefly it cometh of the goodness of God. But certain it is, that our election cometh only and wholly of the benefit and grace of God, for the merits of Christ's passion, and for no part of our merits and good works.[38]

Henry deleted the strongly protestant statement that the anointing, in the sacrament of extreme unction, was 'an assured promise' that the sick man should be restored and his sins forgiven.[39] To the declaration 'I believe . . . that he is my very God, my Lord, and my father, and that I am his servant and his own son by adoption and grace, and the right inheritor of his kingdom', Henry had added 'as long as I persevere in his precepts and laws' before 'the right inheritor of his kingdom'. Elsewhere, after similar declarations of faith in salvation, Henry had added: 'I being christian, and in will to follow his precepts';[40] 'I being in will to follow God's precepts'; 'rejecting in my will and heart the devil and his works';[41] 'I doing my duty' (after 'I believe that by this passion and death of Our Saviour Jesu Christ' and before 'not only my corporal death is so destroyed that it shall never have power to hurt me . . . but also that my sins, and the sins also of all them that do believe in him and follow him, be mortified and dead', which Cranmer disliked since 'no man doth do all his duty';[42] 'I willing to return to God'; 'if I continue not in sin'; 'continuing a christian's life';[43] 'if I follow Christ's precepts';[44] 'we living well';[45] 'we living as we ought to do';[46] 'if we order and conform our will in this world to his precepts'.[47] Such amendments placed a responsibility on the believer to follow God's law and to live a Christian life: they thereby limited the place of God's grace alone, and made salvation conditional on good behaviour.[48] To them Cranmer retorted that the unamended Bishops' Book spoke 'of the pure christian faith unfeigned': whoever had this 'trusteth assuredly that for Christ's sake he [God] will and doth remit his sin'. By contrast, for Cranmer the king's idea was 'a most certain proposition, which also the devils believe most certainly', but 'because they lack the very christian faith, not trusting to the goodness and mercy of God for their offences', they would not have their sins forgiven.[49] Instead Cranmer insisted that 'the right christian faith' was 'that their own sins by Christ's redemption be pardoned and forgiven'. He conceded that many pretended to have the Christian faith but had it not: 'examine every man, if he trust in God and love God above all things; and in words he will answer, yea; but examine every man's acts and deeds, and surely in a great number their acts and deeds condemn their words', since they followed their own wills and pleasures, not God's commandments. 'Our own flesh and carnal mind is contrary to the Spirit and motion of God.' St Paul said that those who followed the works of the flesh would not inherit the kingdom of God; 'very notable and fearful sentences', commented Cranmer.[50] Moreover,

> no man can surely have the right faith and sure trust of God's favour towards him . . . except he . . . have a willing and glad mind, and a delight to do all things that may please God, and a very great repentance and sorrow that ever he did any thing that should offend and displease so loving a Father, whose goodness he can never account.

Faith must lead to 'a good will and mind to help every man and to do good unto them'. Such was 'the very right, pure, perfect, lively, christian, hearty and justifying' faith. Thus, since true faith was linked with actions, it was unnecessary for the king to add all sorts of conditional clauses whenever faith was mentioned: 'for without these conditions is no right faith'.[51] But here Cranmer was being disingenuous as he struggled with the reformers' challenge of explaining why men should do good works if these in themselves contributed nothing to their salvation. And Henry's insertions were very much to the point, blunting or removing any hint that justification could rest on faith alone. By penance, the king wrote, we 'shall be made meet and apt and assured to receive the virtue of Christ's passion': Cranmer objected that good works were not the cause.[52] Where justification was said to be attained 'by contrition and faith, joined with charity', Henry substituted 'that the chief and first mean' was 'only by the great zeal and love which that Christ bare and beareth to us'.[53] Where the Bishops' Book said that adversity should be attributed to 'thy godly will', Henry replaced that with 'to our desert'.[54] That provoked Cranmer: 'all punishments, tribulations, and persecution, be of the sending of God'.[55] Where the Bishops' Book spoke of Christ who 'made due satisfaction and propitiation' to God, Henry preferred 'became and made himself our redeemer, saviour, and intercessor'.[56] Cranmer objected that it was essential to emphasise that it was Christ who made due satisfaction

> to take away the root, ground, and fountain of all the chief errors, whereby the bishop of Rome corrupted the pure foundation of christian faith and doctrine. For upon this satisfaction did he build his sticks, hay, and straw, satisfactory masses, trentals, scala coeli, foundations of chantries, monasteries, pardons, and a thousand other abuses, to satisfy the covetousness of him and his.[57]

Henry knew what he was doing. That his beliefs were a highly idiosyncratic mixture of old and new[58] or 'a unique jumble of theological notions'[59] does not mean he was stupid or being manipulated. 'Many of Henry's interventions were designed to undermine the assertion that justification was through faith and by the merits of Christ.'[60] 'He insisted that grace was conditional on works.'[61] 'Throughout Henry's revision of the Bishops' Book runs a strand of "law-and-order" moralism, of emphasis upon human effort and individual accountability.'[62]

The treatment of ceremonies and images in the Bishops' Book largely followed Henry's wish to combine the elimination of superstitious abuses with the maintenance of valuable traditions. Ceremonies were presented as 'a certain necessary introduction or learning expedient to induce and teach the people reverently to use themselves in their outward worshipping of God, and be also . . . certain painted histories, the often sight and contemplation whereof causeth the people the better to remember the things signified and represented in the same'.[63] That was far from outright conservatism, since the ceremonies were not being valued in themselves, but for their didactic and pastoral value. Nonetheless ceremonies were firmly retained, rather than being abolished and replaced by alternative—Lutheran—forms of worship.

The treatment of images was still more complex, and elicited royal modifications. The emphasis in 1537 was on the *dangers* of images. The Bishops' Book, in a somewhat confused passage, said that 'although all images, be they engraven, painted, or wrought in arras, or in any otherwise made, be so prohibited that they may neither be bowed down unto nor worshipped', but went on to assert:[64]

yet they be not so prohibited but that they may be had and set up in churches, so it be for none other purpose but only to the intent that we (in beholding and looking upon them, as in certain books, and seeing represented in them the manifold examples of virtues, which were in the saints, represented by the said images) may the rather be provoked, kindled, and stirred to yield thanks to our Lord and to praise him in his said saints, and to remember and lament our sins and offences and to pray God that we may have grace to follow their goodness and holy living.

The example of

the image of our Saviour . . . hangeth on the cross in the rood, or is painted in cloths, walls, or windows, to the intent that beside the examples of virtues which we may learn at Christ we may be also many ways provoked to remember his painful and cruel passion, and also to consider ourselves, when we behold the said image, and to condemn and abhor our sin.

Similarly, the lives of the holy saints could be represented by their images.

Therefore the said images may well be set up in churches, to be as books for unlearned people, to learn therein examples of humility, charity, patience, temperance, contempt of the world, the flesh, and the devil, and to learn example of all other virtues. . . . For which causes only images to be set in the churches, and not for any honour to be done to them. For although we use to cense the said images, and to kneel before them, and to offer unto them, and to kiss their

feet . . . yet we must know and understand that such things be not nor
ought to be done to the images self, but only to God, and in his
honour, or in the honour of the holy saint or saints which be represented by the said images.

Characteristically, strong emphases are here tempered by firm qualifications. Both Lutherans and traditionalists could find matter to support
their positions; and Latimer's and Gardiner's descriptions of how the
Bishops' Book was made ring very true here. The second commandment
was reworded: 'thou shalt not make to thyself any graven thing, nor
any similitude of any thing that is in heaven above, or in earth beneath,
nor in the water under the earth. Thou shalt not bow down to them,
nor worship them.'[65] The commentary says: 'by these words we be
utterly forbidden to make or to have any similitude or image, to the
intent to bow down to it, or to worship it'.[66] The matter was glossed
further. The fathers of the church, considering the dullness of man's wit,
had allowed the picture of the father of heaven to be set up in churches,
to put us in remembrance that there is a father in heaven. There followed a sentence that went much further in questioning the value of
images: 'nevertheless if the common people would duly conceive of the
heavenly father without any bodily representation, it were more seemly
for christian people to be without all such images of the Father, than to
have any of them.' Not surprisingly, this was a sentence that Henry
struck out; not surprisingly, Cranmer marvelled that he did.[67] Henry
also reworded and added phrases to the prohibition of graven things.
The clear free-standing commandment, 'Thou shalt not bow down to
them, nor worship them', was rewritten and linked instead to the previous sentence. As reworded, it prohibited the making of graven images
'to the intent thou shalt bow down to them, or honour them as God or
Gods'.[68] That significantly redirected the thrust of the commandment,
now aimed at the makers of such images, while in effect removing the
direct prohibition against bowing before and worshipping images. That
provoked Cranmer into a lengthy explanation of how the purpose of
images was to stir us to remember Christ's passion. Moreover, Henry
added clauses on praying, kissing and kneeling before images, allowing
such practices.[69] Once again, much of what was said about images was
acceptable to the king; but he did not endorse any fundamental objection to images in principle.

The treatment of the mass in the Bishops' Book largely reflected
Henry's beliefs. Many historians have misunderstood this. Scarisbrick
misleads in writing that Henry 'allowed the almost complete silence of

the Bishops' Book about the central event in the spiritual life of a catholic' to pass unrepaired,[70] as does Hughes, who complains that just one page out of 180 was allotted to it.[71] Yet the text declares that

> the form and figure of bread and wine . . . is verily, substantially, and really contained and comprehended the very selfsame body and blood of our Saviour Jesu Christ . . . under the same form and figure of bread and wine the very selfsame body and blood of Christ is corporally, really, and in the very same substance exhibited, distributed, and received.[72]

The thrust of such wording is to uphold traditional expositions of the mass. The king's continuing attachment to ceremonies was demonstrated in the scale—several thousand masses for her soul—and the style—mass and dirige, censing with holy water, procession with priests following with crosses—of the obsequies he ordered after the death of Queen Jane in October 1537.[73]

The Bishops' Book was intended as a comprehensive declaration of doctrine. The four sacraments passed over in silence by the makers of the Ten Articles were here included. Conservatives presented this as a restoration—for example, Archbishop Lee reported that 'those four sacraments that were omitted be found again anew': they would be restored.[74] But that, as we have seen, is not wholly fair. Lee, Longland, Clerk, Sampson, Stokesley, Repps and (probably) Tunstal[75] backed the seven sacraments; Cranmer, Latimer, Shaxton, Foxe and Goodrich disagreed.[76] Gardiner, in France, was not consulted, it seems.[77] And it appears that it was Henry whose influence was decisive in insisting on the inclusion of all seven.[78] But the sacraments were ranked, and the three that had been included in 1536 were given greater weight now. Baptism, the eucharist and penance had been instituted by Christ and conveyed grace to remit sins; matrimony, confirmation, holy orders and extreme unction had been recognised by the church and conveyed spiritual benefits.[79] The expositions of the four minor sacraments were especially contradictory. This appears particularly in the discussion of extreme unction. Its traditional sacramental operation is minimised, its symbolic dimension emphasised. 'It is a visible sign of an invisible grace.' The oil was 'a very convenient thing to signify and figure the great mercy and grace of God', and 'the grace conferred in this sacrament is the relief and recovery of the disease and sickness wherewith the sick person is then diseased and troubled, and also the remission of his sins, if he be then in sin'.[80] But the Bishops' Book rejected the idea that this sacrament was the extreme or the last unction, to be administered only on the point of death: it should be administered during any dangerous sickness.[81]

The Bishops' Book, then, offered the king a good deal of what he wanted. In places its ambiguities and contradictions offered both those more radical and those more traditionalist than he was the opportunity to latch on to particular passages as endorsements of their positions. This has been echoed by modern historians who in turn find the Bishops' Book 'a godly book of religion'[82] or, conversely and more commonly, 'a reaction from the policy of the Ten Articles'.[83] But it is misleading to present the Bishops' Book as the arena for a struggle between conservatives and reformers for the king's ear, to say that 'Cromwell and Cranmer had failed to browbeat the traditionalists into acquiescence in a Lutheran formulary'.[84] It was rather the churchmen, of all persuasions, who were being manipulated, cajoled and bullied by the king into putting their signatures to a document with which none of them could have felt wholly at ease, conservatives because of its reformist rhetoric, reformers because it defended so much of traditional practices. But for the king's purposes it served tolerably well, and left open the possibility that it might yet, through a series of emendations, be tailored more tightly to suit the king's convictions. The Bishops' Book cannot be seen as an essentially traditional formulary. But nor was it a step towards Lutheran or Zwinglian reformation. The purifying reforms it endorsed, the abuses of traditional religion that it pruned, were those that Henry had personally assailed. The Bishops' Book largely reflected the king's search for a middle way: conservative when measured against Luther's Germany or reformed Switzerland, radical when measured against the counter-revolutionary aspirations of the Pilgrimage of Grace.

And any just evaluation of the Bishops' Book must be set in a broader context. Too often, discussions of religious policy, while rightly focused on the elaboration of points of doctrine, are nonetheless pursued in isolation. Yet no consideration of the Bishops' Book, drawn up between February and July 1537, can ignore the events of those months. It was then, as we have seen, that the Pilgrimage of Grace was finally defeated by the king's trickery: Darcy, Hussey, Constable, Aske and many others were exemplarily executed. Monasteries implicated in rebellion were suppressed, and the suppression of smaller monasteries resumed. All that also reflected royal religious policy.

Before we turn to the next statements on doctrine, it is vital to go back to events already discussed above, the 'voluntary' surrenders of the larger monasteries that began in early 1538. In a sense, there is a missing exposition of royal religious policy here. If, as was argued above, at some point in late 1537 the king resolved to secure the surrender of every monastery, we must imagine the parliamentary statute, including its explanatory preamble denouncing monasticism, that would have been required had Henry proceeded by legislative means, and we must then read the statements of doctrine and royal proclamations of these years in that light. The suppression of the monasteries does not feature much in the statements we shall be considering: in order to understand them properly, we must fill that gap by bearing in mind throughout that in 1538, in 1539 and in early 1540 one by one all the monasteries in England and Wales surrendered to the king. As they did so, monks, nuns and friars condemned, on religious grounds, their former way of life. Moreover, the surrenders of the larger abbeys in particular had a dramatic effect on religious life. As we have seen, as religious houses surrendered, so commissioners dismantled shrines and pulled down images, and in so doing effectively brought to an end the deeply rooted practice of pilgrimage. In the case of the image of Darvel Gadarn, a statue of a giant to which pilgrimage was made at Llandderfel, North Wales, it was brought to London—despite the protests of the parson and parishioners, who offered Cromwell's agent £40 to allow it to remain there—and ceremonially burnt at Smithfield on 22 May, along with the Observant Fransciscan friar John Forest, condemned and burnt for heresy, in his case for his continued recognition of papal authority in general and papal pardons in particular.[85] It was in late 1538 that Henry ordered the destruction of the shrine of St Thomas Becket at Canterbury Cathedral: efforts were also made to rewrite the history of the saint's death. Becket was seen as 'stubbornly' withstanding 'the wholesome laws' that Henry II, the king's 'most noble progenitor', had established 'against the enormities' of the clergy.[86] In an official justification of the king's reformation written a little later, Becket was presented as defending 'the detestable and unlawful liberties of the church nothing concerning the common weal but only the part of the clergy'. His death was his own fault: 'the causes why he died was upon a wilful rescue and a fray by him made and begun at Canterbury' when he 'gave opprobrious words' to certain gentlemen who advised him to leave his stubbornness. Becket took one of them, Tracy, 'by the bosom and violently shook and plucked him in such manner that he almost over threw him to the pavement of the church'. One of the other gentlemen, seeing the fight, struck Becket, 'and so in the throng Becket was slain'. In short, his death was an accident provoked by his own violent response to those who had come to negotiate and to mediate. He was subsequently made a saint by the bishop of Rome only 'because he had been a champion to maintain his usurped authority and a bearer of the iniquities of the clergy'.[87] Now Henry VIII, by the advice of his council, thought it appropriate to declare to his subjects that, despite Becket's canonisation, nothing in his life, nothing that he had said, justified his being called a saint rather than a rebel and traitor to his prince. Henry commanded that Becket should be referred to as just Bishop Becket in future, and not as a saint. Moreover, he ordered that all images and pictures of Becket throughout the realm should be taken down and removed from all churches and chapels, that Becket's feast day should no longer be observed, and that the services in his name should be razed from all service books.[88] Here we see the royal supremacy boldly in action: sainthood is determined by king and council, not by the pope or churchmen, and king and council could pronounce on whether or not Becket died as a martyr. The king, moreover, could order the removal of images and the amendment of liturgies.

All that is an indispensable context in which the king's actions and aims must be read.

The Proclamation of 16 November 1538

Following the appearance of the Bishops' Book, the next substantial public declarations and explanations of religious policy came in autumn 1538. In his proclamation of 16 November 1538, Henry asserted his attachment to a unity based upon the middle way. There the king criticised those who

arrogantly attempt of their own sensual appetites and froward rash wills to contemn, break, and violate divers and many laudable ceremonies and rites heretofore used and accustomed in the church of England, and yet not abrogated by the King's Highness' authority; whereby daily riseth much difference, strife, and contention among divers and sundry his loving subjects, as for and concerning the ceremonies of holy bread, holy water, procession, kneeling and creeping on Good Friday to the Cross, and Easter Day, setting up of lights before the Christi, bearing of candles upon the day of the Purification of Our Lady, ceremonies used at the purification of women delivered of child, and offering of their chrisoms, keeping of the four offering days, payment of tithes according to the old customs of the realm, and all other such like laudable ceremonies heretofore used in the church of England, which as yet be not abolished nor taken away by the king's highness.

The king wanted to avoid such contentions. His subjects were accordingly charged to observe them 'so as they shall use the same without superstition, and esteem them for good and laudable ceremonies, tokens, and signs to put us in remembrance of things of higher perfection, and none otherwise, and not to repose any trust of salvation in them', but to treat them as 'good instructions' until such time as the king might change or abolish any of them.[89] But Henry also referred to

the great and manifold superstitions and abuses which have crept into the hearts and stomachs of many of his true, simple, and unlearned loving subjects for lack of the sincere and true explication, and the declaring of the true meaning and understanding of Holy Scripture, sacramentals, rites and ceremonies, and also the sundry strifes and contentions which have and may grow among many of his said loving subjects for lack of the very perfect knowledge of the true intent and meaning of the same.

For that reason he ordered the clergy

to set forth first the glory of God and truth of his most blessed word, and after, the true meaning and end of the said sacramentals and ceremonies, to the intent that, all superstitious abuses and idolatries being avoided, the same sacramentals, rites and ceremonies might be quietly used for such only intent and consideration as they were first instituted and meant.[90]

Some historians have been confused by this proclamation. 'How those disparate pieces ever came to be joined together is a mystery, though one may conjecture disputes in the council ending in a compromise', opines Elton;[91] 'how such disparate orders ever came together remains mysterious: maybe the conservatives on the Council were willing to compromise with the reformers, but why should the king?' echoes Brigden.[92] But such bewilderment is unnecessary: there was nothing confused about the king's position, although it was neither conservative nor Lutheran. Henry wanted an end to rancorous dissension. He wanted lawful ceremonies upheld. He wanted superstition extirpated. These were not impossibly incompatible aims—though, as before, those who agreed with him over lawful ceremonies might be less keen on the

extirpation of superstition, and those who agreed with him on superstition might be less keen on those ceremonies regarded as lawful.

Nor was the proclamation of 16 November 1538 a retreat into conservatism, as is often supposed. It is quite wrong to argue that 'November [1538] altogether brought signs that the Reformation was beginning
to run into difficulties'[93] or that 'in general . . . Henry was giving a warning that change had gone far enough'[94] or that the proclamation should
be seen as 'marking a retreat from a reformed position'.[95] Even less is
it true that 'on 16 November 1538 Henry VIII stopped the Reformation dead'.[96] What such comments overlook is the continuity between
the stand taken in this proclamation and the treatment of ceremonies
and images in the Bishops' Book of 1537 and the Ten Articles of 1536.

John Lambert

Historians who see autumn 1538 as some sort of conservative turning
point cite here the case of John Lambert, a former Cambridge don, who
was subjected to a show trial in November 1538.[97] Henry was present
at the hearing in the King's Hall at York Place in London, together with
most of the nobility, bishops, theologians, judges, as well as the mayor
and aldermen of London. When Lambert stuck to his opinions on the
sacrament of the altar, expressed in his *Treatise upon the Sacrament*,
and in an argument with Dr John Taylor, the king reasoned with him
in person, on several occasions, we are told, confuting him by scripture.
Lambert denied that the sacrament of the altar was the body and blood
of Christ, except spiritually: the king responded by citing Christ's words:
hoc est corpus meum.[98] The king's intervention was intended to make
it public that seeing the presence of Christ in the sacraments as figura-
tive was unacceptable doctrine.[99] Henry, as we have repeatedly seen,
remained attached to the traditional understanding of the mass, and he
could not have made it more plain here.

The royal proclamation of 16 November 1538 denounced the 'wicked
and abominable errors and opinions' of the anabaptists and sacramentaries.[100] It asserted that 'the most blessed and holy sacrament of the
altar is the very body and blood of our Lord Jesus Christ, our only
Saviour and Redeemer, and so hath and ought to be taken and believed
by the whole congregation of Christian men, upon the peril of damnation'.[101] Again, in his proclamation Henry ordered any strangers—for-
eigners resident in England—who held contrary views to leave the realm,
whether they had recanted or not, and declared that no one holding
such erroneous opinions and heresies should enter his realm. In addi-

tion, the king 'straightly chargeth and commandeth that none of his own loving and natural subjects be so hardy to hold, keep, or teach any errors or heresies contrary to God and his Holy Scriptures'. All bishops, noblemen, JPs, mayors, sheriffs, bailiffs, constables and, indeed, all other ministers and the king's loving subjects were to apprehend anyone they knew or heard to hold or teach such heresies.[102]

The language of the proclamation was firm and uncompromising. But none of this amounted to anything new. It simply upheld what had always been taught. Those historians who see it, or the trial of Lambert, as some sort of turning point are greatly mistaken. There was absolutely nothing new in Henry's policy in November 1538. Ever since radical—Zwinglian—notions on the mass had come to influence some within England, Henry had reacted firmly and boldly. This was not something that only came late in the 1530s, when he supposedly woke up to what Cromwell and Cranmer had been doing in his name but without his knowledge. It was there from the start. As early as March 1535 a proclamation[103] fiercely denounced strangers who had presumptuously rebaptised themselves and who denied that the blessed and most holy sacrament of the altar was really the body of Christ.[104] If there was a novelty in autumn 1538, it was the perception that such heresies were spreading through the realm and that heretics with a high profile, such as Lambert, needed to be dealt with publicly so that others might learn from their unhappy example. Duffy is correct in saying that Henry 'was ferociously opposed to any deviation from traditional teaching on the mass',[105] as is Davies in saying that 'the catholic doctrine of the mass, which protestants regarded as blasphemy, remained the official doctrine of the English church as long as Henry lived'.[106] But to conclude that 'primarily it was a signal to Henry's catholic subjects that he was, after all, one of them'[107] is to fail to set Henry's position on this particular issue, the mass, in a larger context. No 'catholic' aware of the 'voluntary' surrenders of the monasteries and the dismantling of pilgrimage shrines can have believed that Henry was 'one of them'. That also undermines any attempt to read the proclamation of 16 November 1538 and the trial of Lambert as essentially political, an effort to present the king's policy as conservative and traditional at the moment when the Emperor Charles V and Francis I, king of France, were making peace and might conceivably jointly attack the schismatic king of England.[108] Orthodox Henry may have proclaimed himself to be on the mass; but the dissolution of the monasteries and the assault on pilgrimage shrines, to repeat, told a different story, as did the arrest and condemnation of the marquess of Exeter and Lord Montagu. While Henry was certainly wary of an international alliance against him, he remained utterly unyielding on the question of the authority of the pope: consequently his actions against Lambert and the sacramentarians can hardly be seen as an attempt to deflect international opposition. Indeed, the fortifications built along the south coast in 1538–39 testify to his determination to resist anything done against him, rather than to any willingness to compromise. Henry surely blasted against sacramentarians for the straightforward reason that he sincerely believed them to be wicked.

The Injunctions of 1538 and
the Proclamation of 26 February 1539

A few weeks later on 26 February 1539 the king, referring back to his earlier proclamation, clarified the meaning of a range of ceremonies, the use of holy bread, the bearing of candles on Candlemas, the giving of ashes on Ash Wednesday, the carrying of palms on Palm Sunday, creeping to the cross on Good Friday. The exact meaning of such practices was spelt out, in terms that echoed the Ten Articles of 1536. Holy water was sprinkled 'to put us in remembrance of our baptism, and of the blood of Christ sprinkled for our redemption upon the cross'; holy bread was 'to put us in remembrance of unity, that all christian men be one mystical body of Christ, as the bread is made of many grains'; the bearing of candles on Candlemas day was done 'in the memory of Christ, the spiritual light'; ashes on Ash Wednesday were given to every christian man 'in remembrance of penance at the beginning of Lent, and that he is but earth and ashes'; the bearing of palms on Palm Sunday 'reneweth the memory of the receiving of Christ in like manner into Jerusalem before his death'; on Good Friday creeping to the cross 'signifieth an humbling of ourself to Christ before the Cross, and the kissing of it a memory of our redemption made upon the Cross'. The proclamation commented further that none of these practices was to be seen as 'the workers or works of our salvation', but only as outward tokens by which we were reminded of Christ's passion 'from whence all good christian men receive salvation'. Once again the purpose was to follow a middle way. No one was 'neither by deed, word, nor behaviour [to] despise these ceremonies . . . nor superstitiously [to] abuse them'. Instead, the king wished 'that the said ceremonies should be observed and used in their right use (all ignorance and superstition clearly taken away)'.[109]

In similar vein the injunctions that Cromwell, as the king's vicegerent in spirituals, issued to the clergy in 1538, insisted that images served no purpose except 'but as to be books of unlearned men, that can no letters [cannot read], whereby they might otherwise be admonished of the lives and conversation of them that the said images do represent'. The people were to be encouraged to works of charity, mercy and faith specially prescribed and commanded in scripture,

> and not to repose their trust or affiance in any other works devised by mens fantasies besides Scripture; as in wandering to pilgrimages, offering of money, candles or tapers to images or relics, or kissing or licking the same, saying over a number of beads, not understanded nor minded on, or in suchlike superstition.[110]

Any clergy who had previously extolled to their parishioners pilgrimage, relics or images or any such superstition should 'now openly afore the same recant and reprove the same', saying that they had been 'led and seduced by a common error and abuse crept into the church through the sufferance and avarice of such as felt profit by the same'.[111] The clergy were henceforth to allow

> no candles, tapers, or images of wax to be set afore any image or picture, but only the light that commonly goeth across the church by the rood loft, the light afore the sacrament of the altar, and the light about the sepulchre; which for the adorning of the church and divine service ye shall suffer to remain . . . as to be books of unlearned men that can no letters.[112]

The clergy were to take down 'such [feigned] images as ye know of in any of your cures to be so abused with pilgrimages or offerings of anything made thereunto' in order to avoid 'that most detestable offence of idolatry'.[113]

Some historians have seen these injunctions as an intensification of protestant reform, the peak of Cromwell's influence. For Duffy 'the Injunctions of 1538 are far starker [than those of 1536] . . . designed not to moderate but to discredit the traditional cultus'. 'In one fell swoop', Duffy goes on, 'these Injunctions outlawed not merely pilgrimage, but virtually the entire external manifestation of the cult of saints', by forbidding the burning of candles before images (except the rood), the sacrament of the altar and the light about the sepulchre. 'In short, the saints were squeezed out of the litany'.[114] For Aston

> the second set of Injunctions . . . differed markedly from the first. In 1536 the value of images was still granted, and venerating them,

pilgrimaging to them, adorning, and offering to them were all activities that were allowed, even though they were not on the same plane
as charitable works. . . . Now, however, scriptural works of mercy
were held to exclude other acts of devotion

—including pilgrimages, offering money or candles to images or relics,
or kissing them—which were seen as superstitions and errors.[115]

Yet it would be fairer to see, with Haigh, the injunctions of 1538 as
'in the main extensions of the 1536 orders', with 'some [that] went much
further'.[116] 'In every way they continued the policy of the First Injunctions', judged Elton.[117] The injunctions do not present the king's policy
as a sudden and radical new departure, but rather as a continuing
attempt at necessary reform: 'the king's highness, graciously tendering
the weal of his subject's souls, hath in part already, and more will hereafter, travail for the abolishing of such images as might be occasion of
so great an offence to God, and so great danger to the souls of his loving
subjects.'[118] A covering letter from Cromwell to Cranmer dated 30 September 1538 explains that this second set of injunctions was intended
for the enforcement of the first.[119] Much had already been said in criticism of images and relics in 1536 and in 1537, and much more about
images was being uncovered in the course of the dissolution of the
monasteries in these years. Henry's middle way did not mean traditional
catholic religion—but nor did the dismantling of the shrines mean the
introduction of Lutheranism. And, once again, the impetus behind the
assault on images should be seen as the king's, rather than being
presented as some Cromwellian manipulation, 'the fulfilment of
Cromwell's evangelical ambition'.[120]

Just as it is mistaken to see the injunctions of 1538 as newly radical,
so it is mistaken to see the royal proclamation of February 1539, as so
many historians do, as marking a brief counter-attack by reformers. In
late February 1539 'the reforming party was well in the saddle again';[121]
'the proponents of reform seemed to have won a victory', Duffy con-
tends, with a new proclamation on ceremonies which stressed their
didactic and symbolic value only and a pardon for sacramentaries and
anabaptists.[122]

Of course, the king's line on images was based in part on wishful
thinking. As Aston pointed out, the 1538 ruling on imagery proved
hopelessly ambiguous:[123]

the attempt to redress abuses by removing some images while retaining others, on the basis of a distinction between false worship and

proper use, was confusing, and ultimately unworkable. . . . If lights were superstitious before some images were they not intrinsically superstitious? If statues of saints induced idolatry, should not images of Christ also be done away with?

Aston shrewdly characterises the tensions within Henry's thinking: the king was not building on the surest of ground.

For Henry the unity and quiet that he sought would be achieved by continuing to try to set a middle way between the papists on the one hand and the sacramentaries and anabaptists on the other, a dichotomy neatly set out in a draft proclamation of April 1539. In this the papists were characterised as

> some of them minding craftily by their preaching and teaching to restore into this realm the old devotion to the usurped power of the bishop of Rome, the hypocrite religion, superstitious pilgrimages, idolatry and other evil and naughty ceremonies and dreams justly and lawfully abolished and taken away by authority of God's word.

The sacramentaries and anabaptists were seen as

> some other, taking and gathering divers Holy Scriptures to contrary senses and understanding, [who] do wrest and interpret and so untruly allege the same to subvert and overturn as well the sacraments of Holy Church as the power and authority of princes and magistrates, and in effect generally, all laws and common justice, and the good and laudable ordinances and ceremonies necessary and convenient to be used and continued in this realm, which were ordained for the increase and edifying of virtue and good christian living.[124]

An official defence of the Henrician reformation compiled about this time detested the heresies of sacramentaries and anabaptists while emphasising the need to reform the abuses of religion and to refer to the Bible rather than 'old fabulous and fantastical books'.[125]

The Act of Six Articles

Many historians characterise the period 1538–40 as one of intense factional struggle in which the conservatives got the upper hand and released the king's innate conservatism, halting the reformation and ultimately destroying Cromwell, seen on such a view as the leader of the reformers. That is highly questionable in the light of what has been argued so far. What had been done up to 1539 largely reflected the king's views. What happened next was broadly consistent with what had been done earlier, and continued to reflect the king's somewhat idio-syncratic but entirely coherent policies, certainly not protestant, but not conservative either, rooted in a desire for unity and presented as a middle way.

The act of Six Articles of 1539 has been especially bedevilled by such factional misinterpretations. Yet the act quite simply reflected royal beliefs and aspirations. Henry VIII sought unity and concord. Of course, that very search is itself evidence of religious divisions, but that in no way calls into question the king's purpose, however unrealistic or total-itarian this was. That purpose was strikingly asserted in the very title of the act—'an act abolishing diversity in opinions'. And the preamble of the statute elaborated such aspirations. Lehmberg, reluctant to think that the king might have taken the initiative, supposed that 'whoever did the drafting was obviously eager to flatter Henry'.[126] It is far more likely that the drafting was done in close consultation with the king and that it reflected royal policy. The preamble declared that the king 'intending the conservation of the . . . church and congregation of England in a true, sincere and uniform doctrine of Christ's religion', and remembering both 'the great and quiet assurance, prosperous increase and other innumerable commodities which have ever ensued, come and followed of concord, agreement and unity in opinions' as well as 'the manifold perils, dangers and inconveniences which have heretofore in many places and regions grown . . . of the diversities of minds and opin-ions, especially of matters of christian religion', accordingly desired that such a unity might be established on all these matters to the honour of God, 'the very author and fountain of all true unity and sincere concord'. For that reason the king had summoned his parliament and convocation. He was 'in a full hope and trust that a full and perfect resolution of the said articles should make a perfect concord and unity generally amongst all his loving and obedient subjects', and therefore had got his archbishops, bishops and other learned men to debate the articles, and then

most graciously vouchsafed in his own princely person to descend and come into his said high court of parliament and council and there like a prince of most high prudence and no less learning opened and declared many things of high learning and great knowledge touching the said articles . . . for an unity to be had in the same.[127]

That Henry should have attended parliament in person, and that he should have 'declared many things of high learning and great knowledge touching the said articles', further demonstrates that what was enacted very much reflected his own wishes. So does the survival of a text of the act with corrections in the king's own hand.[128] Intriguing too are Cranmer's much later remarks, in his reply to the south-western rebels of 1549: the act of Six Articles was so much 'against the truth, and common judgments both of divines and lawyers, that if the king's majesty himself had not come personally into the parliament house, those laws had never passed'. No doubt in 1549 Cranmer was wishing to distance himself from the doctrines expounded in an act that he had not opposed: but his emphasis on the king's personal role is striking.[129]

The language of manipulation, to which so many historians have had recourse in their accounts of the Six Articles, thus appears more and more inappropriate. That Henry appointed a parliamentary committee to consider religious matters is taken as evidence that 'the king, urged towards protestantism by Cranmer and Cromwell, towards orthodoxy by Gardiner and Norfolk, had not yet made up his mind'.[130] Elton endorses Froude's view that 'it seems, indeed, very probable that the king did not know himself' which way he was inclining: 'he may well', Elton speculates, 'have been trying to discover where majority opinion lay and what would be most acceptable all round'.[131] And when, shortly afterwards, the duke of Norfolk, responding to the divisions of opinion on the committee, proposed six articles of religion to the whole parliament, factional historians have taken that as evidence that Norfolk and Stephen Gardiner, bishop of Winchester, 'managed to swing the king to their way of thinking, with which in any case he was in sympathy', as Elton deduces, in a confused and somewhat contradictory analysis.[132] The passage of the Six Articles is generally presented as the triumph of conservatives over radicals, presaging the fall of Thomas Cromwell the following year. For Elton, 'throughout the session [of parliament in 1539] . . . Norfolk was to outmanoeuvre Cromwell, obviously because Henry was drawing away from the vicegerent's radical policies and backing the conservatives on the council'.[133] Such formulations are fundamentally mistaken in two senses. First, as we have already seen and will see again, they belittle the role of the king: Henry was far more directly and purposefully involved in the making of the act than such interpretations allow. Second, they rest on a flawed interpretation of what the act was about. It is a mistake to see the Six Articles of 1539 as in any important sense a reversal of royal policy. It is mistaken to suppose that 'it seemed a public and final rejection of the Reformation',[134] or that it 'reaffirmed the English position of maintaining essential catholic doctrine despite the break with Rome'.[135]

What is wrong about such assertions is their assumption that 'progress towards protestantism' had been the previous direction of policy. It manifestly had not been, as we have seen. Nor did the Six Articles make it any clearer than it had long been that there would be no full-blooded Lutheran reformation in Henrician England—that had always been quite plain. Nothing in the Six Articles contradicted Henry's previous aims. Above all, it is essential to grasp that the act was not a comprehensive statement, let alone a revision, of doctrine: it was in no sense a replacement or revision of the Bishops' Book. Its purpose was what the preamble said it was: to pronounce on key matters of doctrine and practice that were coming into dispute, with the aim of halting damaging current controversies. An examination of the articles will show that the act as a whole should not be seen as reactionary.

The Six Articles did not modify, let alone reverse, any of the king's earlier, or current, reforms. It is vitally important to bear in mind that the dissolution of the monasteries had been continuing unabated, with many abbots and convents surrendering their houses, right up to the assembly of parliament. If there was then a pause—no houses surrendered in May or June 1539, while parliament was meeting,[136] although the king did take the lands of the Order of St John in May after the death of their lord[137]—in July the surrenders of monastic houses resumed: and so fierce was the tide that by spring 1540 not a single monastic house remained. The fate of the monasteries is an essential context for the proper understanding of the Six Articles. Moreover, antipapal measures continued.

> Even amid the show of catholicism, the rejection of the pope continued to be emphasised. Half a dozen maintainers of papal supremacy were executed in London a matter of days before the Six Articles came into effect; and, shortly after the obsequies of the empress, a mock naval battle was staged on the Thames in which a royal ship trounced the pope and a boatload of cardinals.[138]

More detailed analysis of the constituent parts of the act will make its purpose quite plain. The first article concerned the sacrament of the altar. The central question was whether the substance of bread and wine remained or not. The response followed Henry's preferences. The king's personal involvement in the debate is striking. Lord Sandys noted that it had pleased the king to resort 'in his graces own person'—sundry times, noted John Hussee—to the bishops 'to determine and discuss such arguments and doubts as were in controversy concerning the blessed sacrament of the altar'.[139] There was much discussion and division: in Hussee's words, 'there was great hold among the bishops for the establishment of the blessed sacrament of the altar; the lords had sat daily in council on the matter'.[140] According to Marillac, the French ambassador, the bishops had great altercation about the sacrament: some were for abolishing it, others for making it anew, the majority for retaining the ancient custom and celebration, which, Marillac said, was the king's position. Indeed, 'ce roy comme chef en ceste partye en a faict telle declaration qu'il estiot convenable, c'est que l'on eust a croire, adorer et reverer ledit Sainct-Sacrement avec les ceremonies accoustumes ainsi que l'Eglise de si long temps l'a inviolablement observe' (the king as chief of the party in favour of retaining the mass has declared that it is fitting to worship and revere the holy sacrament with the traditional ceremonies as the church has so long without fail observed).[141] It was finally agreed that

> in the most blessed sacrament of the altar, by the strength and efficacy of Christ's mighty word, it being spoken by the priest, is present really the natural body and blood of our saviour Jesu Christ . . . under forme of bread and wine and that after the consecration there remaineth *none other substances but the substance off his foresaid natural body*.

That last passage was added by the king himself. Instead of 'neither the substance of bread nor of wine', he wrote the words given in italics here. And, justifying the retention of communion in one kind only, he wrote 'that it is to be believed and not doubted of but that in the flesh under form of bread is the very blood and in the blood under form of wine is the very flesh as well apparent as though they were both together'.[142]

It is important to gauge the overall thrust of these formulations, rather than getting caught up on the presence or absence of particular words. There is no explicit mention of the word 'transubstantiation' here.[143] It is possible (as Rex surmises from the fact that the word was originally included in the questions put to the churchmen, but was evidently later deleted)[144] that Archbishop Cranmer had succeeded in removing it. Yet the thrust of the formulation was so orthodox that any such deletion was of little significance. And here, as in the article on the sacrament of the altar more generally, what was stated was nothing new. The term 'transubstantiation' did not appear in the Bishops' Book either—yet there, as in the Six Articles, the treatment of the mass was essentially orthodox. That is to say, the first article of the act changed nothing: in no sense did it alter doctrine, let alone alter doctrine from radicalism to conservatism. A priest was reported to have declared that transubstantiation had been declared an article of faith,[145] but such gossip should not be read as implying that it had previously not been. What the act did do was to make quite plain what the true nature of the sacrament of the altar was: that encouraged conservatives such as John Hussee to hope that people would not be 'so busy' in future:[146] in other words, he saw the act as a restraint on would-be reformers. Hussee's reports are evidence not of reaction, or of a change in direction, but of a royal resolution to halt controversy over the issue, and to remove any prospect of a move to a radical position. Even the report that those who denied the real presence would suffer as traitors and heretics did not indicate a new policy—as John Lambert's death some months earlier testified. Trueman is mistaken in saying that 'the Six Articles in 1539 . . . enforced the belief in the Real Presence and made deviation on this point a capital offence': it already was, as Lambert had found. And consequently Trueman is also mistaken in deducing from this that 'England in 1539 was thus somewhat less disposed towards reform than it had been in 1536'.[147] Brigden misleads in saying that 'by this draconian act the automatic and intransmutable penalty for those guilty of sacramentarianism was death'—as if it had not been a capital offence earlier, or as if prosecution had not earlier been possible.[148] Hussee's wording testifies to the continuity of policy: 'the fate of traitors and heretics awaited any who reasoned and spoke about the sacrament of the altar after the consecration, *otherwise than hath been in time past* [my italics]; that is, the very body of God to be there in flesh and blood, realiter et essentialiter.'[149]

The second article raised the question of the necessity of communion in both kinds, but declared it 'not necessary ad salutem by the law of god since there was blood in the bread and flesh in the wine as though they were both together'. Again, this was in no sense a reaction or a change, but a clear restatement of existing practice. It was an explicit rejection of radical change. We know some of the churchmen's opinions on this point. Cranmer and Barlow (or possibly Hilsey) thought it necessary in both; Abbot Boston (of Westminster) thought it was first ministered by Christ in both kinds, but he wanted to study further before giving a 'resolute' answer; Lee and the others, a clear majority, thought it unnecessary.[150]

The third article declared that priests might not marry. Once again, that simply restated the existing position, and rejected the new Lutheran reformed model. The churchmen disagreed over clerical marriage (Cranmer, Shaxton, Latimer, Hilsey, Barlow and the abbots of West-minster and St Albans approving, Goodrich undecided, the rest—a clear majority?—against).[151] Cranmer would not have agreed on priestly celibacy without Cromwell's persuasion, according to Barlow.[152] Cranmer (himself secretly married) implored the king 'how not only men of the new learning (as they be called) but also the very papistical authors do allow that by the word of god, priests be not forbidden to marry, although they were not ignorant that many expounders of scrip-ture were of the contrary judgement'. He pleaded for a suspension of sentence: 'wherefore . . . it may please your highness to suspend your judgement for a time and not to determine the marriage of priests to be against scripture but rather to put both parts to silence' on the subject; or failing that the king should 'grant that the articles of priests' mar-riage may be openly disputed in both universities under indifferent judges'.[153] But clerical celibacy was reasserted. Christopher Mont explained that the king was concerned because the clergy 'must preach the word of God and that it is thought that the common people as yet weak in the knowledge of the word and of other things might thereby conceive an opinion of concupiscence in them, and by reason thereof contemn their preachings and the word of God'. Henry, he added, 'did nothing without good cause and reason, and with great considera-tion'.[154] Of course, a plausible implication here was that the king might yet move further when the people were stronger in the knowledge of the word, but in no sense was that a bankable promise.[155]

The fourth article held that vows of chastity made by men and women were binding. Again that changed nothing: what it did was to disap-point those who saw the dissolution of the monasteries as synonymous with the rejection of monastic celibacy. An act of 1539 that allowed former religious to purchase lands, and to sue and to be sued in the courts, ended by declaring that all religious persons put at their liberties by reason of the surrender or dissolution of their monasteries were not to marry (even if they had taken their vows of celibacy when under twenty-one but could not show that they had done so under coercion).[156]

The fifth article dealt with the question of private masses. It was agreed that 'it is meet and necessary that private masses be continued and admitted . . . whereby good christian people (ordering them self accordingly) do receive both godly and goodly consolation and benefits and it is agreeable also to God's law'. All churchmen agreed that private masses might stand with the word of God.[157] Once again this marked no significant change from the position set out in the Bishops' Book.

The final article dealt with auricular confession, declaring that it 'is necessarily to be retained and continued used and frequented in the church of god'. It is worth noting the way in which this doctrine is set out in the Six Articles. As one witness expressed it, none would now dare say 'that it is not necessary to have auricular confession', a formulation that carefully avoids declaring that it was a divine necessity.[158] To that extent the formulation should not be seen as conservative or reactionary. A dozen churchmen—Cranmer, Goodrich, Salcot, Shaxton, Latimer, Hilsey, Repps, Barlow, Worton and Holgate, and the abbots of Westminster and Gloucester—'can find not expressly by the word of God that auricular confession is necessary by the same but they do say and affirm that it is very requisite and expedient to be observed and used'; Archbishop Lee and all the other bishops and abbots said that it was necessary and required by the law of God.[159] That division of opinion was confirmed by the king's response to Tunstal, which further illustrates the inadequacy of characterisations of the Six Articles as a conservative reaction. After matters had been agreed by a majority in the House of Lords, Tunstal wrote a detailed memorandum to the king expressing his disquiet and calling for a more conservative statement, namely that auricular confession was positively required by God.[160] Henry gave Tunstal what Scarisbrick called a 'stinging riposte'.

> Since me thought (my lord of Durham) that both the bishops of York Winchester and your reasons and texts were so fully answered this other day in our house as to my seeming and supposal the most of the house was satisfied I marvel not a little why eftsons you have sent to me this your writing being in a manner few other texts or reasons then there were declared both by the bishop of Canterbury and me to make smally or nothing to your intended purpose but other I esteemed that you do it to prove my simple judgement alone . . . and so by mine ignorant answer seem to win the field or else that you be too much blinded in your own fancy and judgement to think that a truth which by learning you have not yet proved nor I fear me cannot by scripture nor any other directors provable ground.

Henry told Tunstal 'that your own author in places by you alleged maketh plain against your opinion'; that 'you gather a wrong sense upon his words'.

All your labour is to prove that auricular confession were by God commanded and both your authorities of Bede and Paul showeth nothing but that they did confess their sins and yet do not they affirm that it was by commandment wherefore they make for mine argument and not for yours. . . . This is matter so apparent that none can but perceive except he will not see.

Again, Tunstal had conceded that the church had on several occasions changed the details of whom confession should be made to and when 'if it were by god's commandment they might not do this'. For Henry it was quite plain that auricular confession was not required by God's law: nothing in scripture, in reason or in good authorities would prove that it was. It was simply expedient, but no more: it was not a divine command.[161] This article dealing with auricular confession was the only one of the Six Articles to raise matters not dealt with before—and its treatment was somewhat ambiguous, as Tunstal's conservative dissatisfaction shows.

The king's vigorous involvement over auricular confession reinforces further the overwhelming case that the Six Articles reflected royal convictions—and the king's convictions were not, as the debate over auricular confession shows, to be characterised as straightforwardly conservative. The conventional treatment of the act as an instrument in supposed factional strife has thus obscured what it actually was: a restatement, supported by all the force of law and punishment, of the doctrines of the church of England in order to curb what the king saw as dangerous diversity. It was neither a conservative reaction nor was it the work of some conservative political faction. It was never Henry's intention to set up and to run an inquisition: the Six Articles did not produce a wave of persecution.

The account given thus far of the king's religious policies after the break with Rome has emphasised the king's leading role, and has characterised these policies as significantly reforming without being Lutheran, and as being consistently, and effectively, pursued. Such claims are, it must be admitted, highly controversial, and challenge much that has been written on the subject. What we must do next, then, is to reflect more closely on the current orthodoxy, and to show how it is misleading. On such conventional views, Henry was always being influenced, with varying degrees of success, by those more committed to religious reform than he was himself. So we must examine the religious convictions, and political actions, of those who supposedly manipulated, or sought to manipulate, the king.

Cranmer's Religion

Thomas Cranmer, archbishop of Canterbury since 1533, would be an obvious contender for such a role. It was over Henry's divorce that he came to prominence, as we have seen, and it was no doubt for his unshakeable and creative commitment to the king's great matter that he was elevated to Canterbury. Most of what he subsequently said and did was entirely consistent with Henry's policies as presented in this book, and does not constitute evidence of any intended manipulation of the king.

Cranmer was a committed reformer from an early stage, it might be objected. But Cranmer's religion is more complex than might at first appear, especially if it is simply assumed that he already held in the 1520s the radical convictions that would flower in Edward VI's reign. There is little to suggest that Cranmer had any interest in or sympathy towards protestantism before the early 1530s.[162] He undoubtedly came to assail papal authority after the break with Rome. In sermons that he preached in autumn 1535 (as he recalled them in August 1536), he said that for 'many years' he had daily prayed to God that he might see the power of Rome destroyed, and that they might be separated from that see, since he saw it 'work so many things contrary to God's honour and the wealth of this realm'—but we may doubt how far back those 'many years' actually stretched.[163] He put the anti-papal case nicely to Lord Lisle, deputy of Calais. 'It is not the person of the bishop of Rome, which usurpeth the name of the pope that is so much to be detested, but the very papacy and see of Rome, which hath by their laws suppressed Christ, and set up the bishop of that see as a God of this world.' Since 'the word of God' was against 'his authority, pomp, covetousness, idolatry, and superstitious doctrine', the pope had become its enemy, 'suppressing it by policy, bye-laws and doctrines contrary to the word of God'. The see of Rome had intolerably impoverished all Christian realms.[164] Cranmer's eloquence is clear: but it would be hard to distinguish his denunciation of the pope in its objection to papal jurisdictional imperialism, and in its association of the papacy with idolatry and superstition, from that of the king.

In spring 1536 the church of England was manifestly neither a Lutheran nor a Zwinglian church. And yet Cranmer praised it as reformed. On Anne Boleyn's fall, he declared that he loved Anne 'not a little for the love which I judged her to bear towards God and his gospel'. He trusted that Henry 'will bear no less entire favour unto the truth of the gospel than you did before; forasmuch as your grace's favour to the gospel was not led by affection unto her, but by zeal unto the truth'. In writing these words, Cranmer was identifying the king with his own beliefs; and in presenting Henry as bearing favour to 'the truth of the gospel', he was in effect endorsing the religious policy that Henry was following. Here Cranmer seems to be echoing Henry in using reformist rhetoric, yet without presiding over a reformed church. How much more than rejection of the papacy did 'favouring the truth of the gospel' mean for Cranmer at this point?[165] When he regretted that Bishop William Repps, elected bishop of Norwich from May 1536, 'doth approve none to preach in his diocese that be of right judgment', was he simply regretting the lack of vigorous anti-papal preaching there?[166]

Cranmer followed the king's policy in ordering silence over matters in controversy. In 1534 he issued an injunction restraining curates from preaching or teaching anything that might slander or bring in doubt 'the catholic and received doctrine of Christ's church'.[167] In Lent 1535 he asked the king to allow Hugh Latimer to preach before him on the Wednesdays of Lent, defending him as 'a man of singular learning, virtuous example of living, and sincere preaching the word of God', against the 'great obloquy' he had recently suffered: Cranmer had himself been criticised, he said, for licensing Latimer to preach, but insisted that he intended 'the furtherance of the truth and the pure dispensation of the word of God'.[168] Revealingly, Cranmer then admonished Latimer to ignore, in the sermons he was to preach before the king, matters recently in controversy, avoiding criticism of any named man's acts or sayings, though no offence or superstition should go unreprehended. Latimer should not speak for more than an hour, or an hour and a half at the outside, lest the king and queen waxed weary.[169] Cranmer tended eirenically to defend those he saw as unfairly accused of radicalism. In response to complaints by the inhabitants of Hadleigh in 1534 against their curate Thomas Rose, he replied that he was credibly informed that Rose had not said that 'a man's goods spent for his soul after his death prevaileth him not' but rather 'that a man's goods, given out of charity, and so the child of damnation, spent after his death shall not prevail his soul' by which he meant a man who 'died out of charity and was buried in hell'.[170]

Cranmer moreover defended something like the king's middle way. On returning from an assembly of bishops before the king at Winchester in autumn 1535, he preached at Canterbury Cathedral. He spoke of ceremonies which, he argued, should be neither rejected nor despised, nor yet to be observed with this opinion, that they of themselves make men holy, or that they remit sin. For seeing that our sins be remitted by the death of our Saviour Christ Jesus, I said it was too much injury to Christ to impute the remission of our sins to any laws or ceremonies of man's making.

Just as the common laws of the realm were not made to remit sin, but 'for a common commodity, and for a good order and quietness to be observed among your subjects', so 'were the laws and ceremonies first instituted in the church for a good order, and remembrances of many good things [later he repeated that phrase and added 'or a disposition unto goodness'], but not for remission of our sins'. But it was not good to observe them in the belief that they remitted sin, or that their bare observance was a holiness before God. 'The people ought to observe them, as they do the laws of your grace's realm, and with no more opinion of holiness, or remission of sin, than the other common laws of your grace's realm.' In taking up this position, Cranmer was rejecting traditional attitudes to ceremonies which saw them as possessing quasi-sacramental, apotropaic powers. But it is worth stressing that he fully accepted them as remembrances, and insisted on their observance for good order and quietness. This is an Erastian position, far removed from any wish to destroy all ceremonies as idolatrous.[171] Given that Cranmer expressed these views in a letter to the king summarising the sermon he had preached, it is very likely that these were (or Cranmer thought they were) the views of the king; and they are close to the position taken in the Ten Articles of 1536 and the Bishops' Book of 1537. Cranmer's remarks on purgatory were similarly in line with royal thinking. In August 1536 Cranmer referred to the belief that the pope had authority in purgatory as one of several false things taught in times past as articles of faith: but he did not here seem to be impugning purgatory itself.[172] The first time Cranmer expressed any criticism of monasteries and friars was *after* the dissolution. In October 1536 he referred to the 'urgent and godly considerations' that had prompted Cromwell to suppress divers friars' houses, and trusted that 'the irreligious religion' at Canterbury would be extinguished—and put in a plea that Thomas Cobham, Lord Cobham's brother, should have the greyfriars there.[173]

Cranmer took a firm stand against religious radicals, showing that he agreed with Henry on the nature of the mass. In June 1533 he reported having tried unsuccessfully to win over John Frith, who 'thought it not necessary to be believed as an article of our faith that there is the very corporal presence of Christ within the host and sacrament of the altar, and holdeth of this point most after the opinion of Oecolampadius': 'he looketh every day to go unto the fire'.[174] In 1537, on receipt of a treatise dedicated to the king, Cranmer wrote to Wolfgang Capito: while the king had liked much of this, he could not approve some parts—those, Cranmer suspected, concerning the mass.[175] Cranmer wrote more vigorously to Joachim Vadian, who had attempted to disprove the real presence in the sacrament of the altar. Cranmer had, he wrote, seen almost everything written by Oecolampadius and Zwingli. As far as they had endeavoured to point out, confute and correct papistical and sophistical errors and abuses, he commended and approved them. But he wished that they had not trodden down the wheat with the tares. Cranmer would, he said, never be convinced that the ancient doctors of the church were on their side. If it were an error, it had been handed down by the fathers themselves. What godly man could believe that? Our gracious Lord would never have left his beloved spouse in such lamentable blindness for so long. The catholic faith respecting the real presence had been declared to the church by such evident and manifest passages of scripture and commended by the first ecclesiastical writers. This was a doctrine well grounded and supported: had it not been firmly founded on a rock, it would long since have fallen with the crash of a mighty ruin. The controversy had impeded the full course of the gospel. Cranmer appealed to Vadian instead to agree and unite with him so that they might extend as widely as possible one sound, pure, evangelical doctrine, conformable to the discipline of the primitive church.[176] In 1537 Cranmer manifestly rejected radical doctrines about the eucharist and was clearly in line with Henry's insistence on the real presence. In June 1538 he could write to Cromwell how 'that error of the sacrament of the altar was so greatly spread abroad in this realm and daily increasing more and more' and so 'for the suppressing thereof' it was necessary for one Atkinson who had been convicted of it to do his penance at Paul's Cross, and not just his parish church, so that as many people as possible would see him being punished and be wary of committing a like offence.[177]

There is one confusing piece of evidence that might point in a different direction. A little later, in conversation with Adam Damplip, who had been accused of preaching in Calais that the body and blood of Christ were not present in the sacrament of the altar, Cranmer had learnt that Damplip denied that charge, but said that the controversy arose because 'he confuted the opinion of the transubstantiation, and therein'—Cranmer added—'I think he taught but the truth'.[178] That could mean that Cranmer had adopted the Lutheran doctrine of consubstantation—but it need mean no more than that Cranmer was fully in accord with Henry's belief in the true presence.[179] What is clear, however, is that at this point Cranmer had not yet reached his convictions of the late 1540s.

Further light on Cranmer's religious beliefs is shed by an exchange he had with the Kentish gentleman Sir Thomas Cheyney in autumn 1537. Cranmer was trying to persuade Cheyney 'to favour the word of God' and by setting a good example so encourage the king's subjects in Cranmer's diocese to obey royal ordinances extirpating superstition and the bishop of Rome's 'erroneous doctrine'. Cheyney, Cranmer alleged, could not stand any reformation or alteration of abuses in the church; for him, everything set forth contrary to the late custom used by the authority of Rome seemed 'new learning' and erroneous. Cheyney's servants had wrongly claimed that the Bishops' Book had silenced 'all the knaves of the new learning' and had restored to their old use ceremonies, pilgrimages and purgatory. Cranmer was surprised that Cheyney should so misrepresent the king's 'godly intent in the reformation of doctrine'. It was not true, Cranmer insisted, that ceremonies, purgatory and pilgrimages were restored, as Cheyney seems to have believed. It was, however, true that 'old good usages', those of the primitive church, were restored, but not 'the fantasy of ceremonies, pilgrimages, purgatory, saints, images, works and such like, as had these three or four hundred years been corruptly taught'. Purgatory, pilgrimages, praying to saints, images, holy bread, holy water, holy days, merits and works had been set 'in their right use and estimation'. Cheyney should therefore tell the people how they 'are bound to give God eternal thanks' that in their lifetime he had been pleased to reveal the error, superstition and blindness into which they had been led, and that God had sent so good and virtuous a prince to cause these things to be opened.[180] Whether Cheyney had actually upheld the beliefs that Cranmer attributed to him or not—and Cheyney denied what had been said against him, roundly declaring that he was no papist, and set no more store by the bishop of Rome, or his traditions or usurpations, than he thought the bishop of Rome set by Cranmer; Cranmer had too lightly given credence to all that[181]—what is interesting is the incidental light cast on Cranmer's religious convictions and on his understanding of what religious policy was in 1537. Henry, as a virtuous prince, had revealed the extent of superstition, but 'old good usages' were maintained. That balance was defended by Cranmer here.

But in one respect this exchange reveals Cranmer moving beyond what Henry permitted. Where Cheyney claimed that he loved God and his most blessed word, Cranmer retorted that he did not doubt that, but doubted rather whether Cheyney's fervent zeal was 'according to knowledge or no'. In the quarter sessions Cheyney had not been so diligent, Cranmer alleged, in spelling out 'things requisite of necessity to our salvation' as he had been when setting out 'mere voluntary things', not grounded in scripture. What Cranmer meant by 'things requisite of necessity to our salvation' was

> our justification by Christ's passion only, the difference between faith and works, works of mercy to be done before voluntary works, the obedience towards our prince by the authority of the word of God, and such other concerning the stiff opinion of the people in alteration of ordinances and laws in the church, as holidays, fasting days etc.[182]

Cheyney retorted that matters requisite for our salvation were more pertinent to the office of a standing preacher in a pulpit than to that of a sitting justiciar in a temporal session of peace. He did not know what Cranmer meant by 'voluntary things' (Cranmer had been vague on this, not listing any ceremonies and practices) and asked him to explain in detail.[183] For our purposes, however, what this heated exchange reveals about Cranmer's convictions is interesting, in particular his declaration of 'our justification by Christ's passion only', and his playing down of 'voluntary' things. In this Cranmer went beyond Henry VIII's theology, a disagreement that was also reflected in the marginal dialogue between king and archbishop over the Bishops' Book.[184] But for all that, there were limits to Cranmer's espousal of the predestinarian implications of belief in justification by faith alone. Thomas Baschurche, sometime secretary to Archbishop Warham, fell into despair in April 1533, and 'saith he is assured that he shall be perpetually damned'. Cranmer's chaplains and other learned men had reasoned with him, 'but no man can bring him in other opinion, but that he, like unto Esau, was created unto damnation': he had several times tried to kill himself. Cranmer was a long way from the double predestinarian convictions of later Tudor divines.[185]

What we find, then, in the Cranmer of the 1530s is a churchman aware of continental European debates, and, in his espousal of the doctrine of justification by faith alone, significantly at odds with the king. But in most other respects—in his anti-papalism, in his abhorrence of contentious preaching, in his approach to ceremonies and the sacrament of the altar—he appears as very much the king's archbishop. And there is little to suggest that Cranmer attempted to manipulate the king. From

time to time, as we have seen, Henry asked his churchmen for their opinions on matters of faith, and then Cranmer candidly expressed his views
on justification. He did not campaign on this point, as we shall see
further later. Invited to comment on the Bishops' Book, Cranmer did so
in detail: yet, as he explained, 'I refer all mine annotations again to his
grace's most exact judgement'.[186] Asked for his views on the sacraments,
on the authority of bishops, on whether a learned Christian prince
(accompanied only by temporal learned men) who conquered dominions of infidels might preach and teach the word of God there, and on
whether, if all the bishops and priests of a region were dead, the king
should make bishops and priests, Cranmer set out his convictions, but
added 'this is mine opinion and sentence at this present which I do not
temerariously define but do remit the judgement thereof wholly
unto your majesty'.[187] It may well be—though hindsight is treacherous—
that Cranmer was praying for the king's conversion. Meanwhile, he was
biding his time in the 1530s, waiting for Henry to change his
mind. Cranmer's remarks on the downfall of Anne Boleyn offer a clue
to his mind. God had sent it as a test, he told the king, 'to try your
grace's constancy', to see 'whether your highness can be content to take
of God's hand as well things displeasant as pleasant'.[188] Cranmer, like
so many, believed in providence, that God's will determined all that happened; that all that happened was God's will. Bad things were sent as
a test. One day God would change the king's mind. Rather than an ecclesiastical politician scheming and manipulating a weak king, Cranmer
was waiting, praying, hoping, seizing the opportunity to put forward
his views whenever asked (for example, in discussions leading to
the formulation of religious articles), but never independently or
gratuitously.

Cromwell's Religion

More frequently it is Thomas Cromwell, successively the king's secretary and lord privy seal, as well as the king's vicegerent in spirituals,
and manifestly his leading counsellor in the mid- to late 1530s, who has
been seen by historians as manipulating Henry and attempting to steer
him into more evangelical, reforming or protestant waters. Whether
Cromwell's relationship with Henry should not rather be seen as that
of a loyal servant assiduously undertaking the manifold tasks assigned
to him by an imperious master is a matter I have considered elsewhere.
Sir Geoffrey Elton assumed, rather than demonstrated, that Cromwell's
intelligence was behind everything, that 'whatever of lasting value was

done in England under Henry VIII was done while Cromwell was in power'. But an analysis of the language that Cromwell used in his many 'remembrances'—often Cromwell made a note 'to know whether the king will . . .', or 'to know the king's pleasure' or 'what the king will have done with'—strongly suggests rather that the minister did not dare act without knowing what the king wanted.[189]

And that prompts reconsideration of the fashionable view that Cromwell, allegedly more radical in religion than the king, seized every opportunity to push a supposedly conservative monarch into further reformation, but ultimately went too far, provoking Henry into dismissing him for being a religious radical in 1540. It was the martyrologist John Foxe who influentially portrayed Cromwell as 'this valiant soldier and captain of Christ' who showed 'a flagrant zeal to set forward the truth of the gospel' and sought 'all means and ways to beat down false religion and to advance the true'.[190] Modern historians have been confident in categorising Cromwell. Dickens, calling him a 'crypto-protestant', saw his 'obvious (and ultimately fatal) leanings towards Lutheranism': 'throughout his ministry he stood deeply involved with the radical group, which was protestant, or turning protestant as fast as it dared'.[191] For Davies, Cromwell (and Cranmer) were 'convinced, if cautious, Protestants'. If both were discreet and dissembled their opinions, nonetheless 'Cromwell *had* protected heretics, he *had* influenced national policy to his own ends. There is no question about his protestantism and his use of office to further protestantism.'[192] For Block, 'Cromwell unveiled an ideologically inspired policy for the church'.[193] Brigden has no doubt that 'Cromwell was a convinced evangelical, and one of the first'; 'his protection of them suggests his support for their cause'.[194] 'Cromwell', she notes, 'insistently led the king towards reform in religion more radical than the king could countenance.'[195] But his 'protection of his friends among the brethren made him vulnerable'.[196] For Walker, 'at heart, however keen he was to fulfil his master's wishes, Cromwell would have liked to limit Henry's religious options to one— the furtherance of godly reformation—whilst the king was unprepared to undertake such a commitment wholeheartedly'.[197] 'It is hard to deny', Elton claimed, 'that Cromwell throughout tried (and until 1539 with some success) to push on with the reform of religion much faster and further than Henry approved.'[198] Elton tended, however, somewhat inconsistently to see Cromwell's faith as an essentially secular vision designed to produce a better commonwealth in this world. Cromwell 'had become convinced that only a form of protestantism could serve the polity he was building, but his faith was not hot enough to override his awareness of the political possibilities'. 'To Cromwell, the reformed church was to serve the purposes of the reformed commonweal'—'the creation of a better life here and now'—though Elton at once admits that this was 'in preparation for the life to come'.[199] But that still left Cromwell, in Elton's eyes, as objectively a promoter of protestant reform.

This is a formidable consensus of historians.[200] Yet widespread as such an interpretation is, it rests on surprisingly thin evidence. As early as 1536 Cromwell was seen as a heretic by the Pilgrims of Grace. But if many denounced Cromwell as a heretic,[201] that may not be as revealing of his *independent* religious convictions as it at first seems. After all, in his defence of the royal supremacy, in his organisation of the visitation and suppression of the monasteries, in his involvement in the destruction of (abused) images, in his sponsorship of the Bible, in his promulgation of the injunctions of 1536 and 1538 with their criticisms of pilgrimages and intercession to saints, Cromwell could easily be seen as heretical by those who deplored and feared such changes, and who might not grasp either the limits of his radicalism or, importantly, the extent to which what he was doing was energetically to implement what have here been presented as essentially the king's policies. After all, he was the king's vicegerent in spirituals, and that task was defined (in the act for placing lords in parliament in 1539) as 'for good & true ministration of Justice to be had in all causes and cases touching the ecclesiastical jurisdiction and for the godly reformation and redress of all errors heresies and abuses in the said church'.[202] Perhaps it was his vigorous energy that made it appear that the responsibility for policies and measures was his own: but we should take care not to be deceived.

Not surprisingly, there is very little in sources more contemporary than Foxe directly bearing on the question of Cromwell's religion. One of the few definite statements that Cromwell made emphasises just how much he saw himself as the king's spokesman. In January 1540 Cromwell told Franz Burchard, vice-chancellor of Saxony, and Ludwig von Baumbach, envoys of the German Lutheran princes, that 'er siehe unser maynunge den glauben betreffen aber wie die weldt iczt stehet wesz sich sin her der konnig halte desz wolle er sich auch halten' (he sees our opinions in matters of the faith, but the world standing now as it does, whatever his lord the king holds, so too will he hold), glossed by Elton as 'On the whole he was of their persuasion but would "as the world stood, believe even as his master the king believed" '.[203] What did Cromwell's hints to the German envoys that he agreed with them mean? It is possible that they show that in his heart Cromwell was a committed Lutheran. But it is also possible that he was saying no more than a royal councillor engaged in delicate diplomatic negotiations would say in the hope of winning over the envoys, smoothing over differences and making a deal. If Cromwell gave the vague impression that he sympathised with their religious opinions, what he left them with was the firm declaration that he would believe what the king believed.[204]

The case that Cromwell was a committed reformer cannot fairly rest on the charges made against him in the act of attainder in 1540. Too often historians have implicitly reinterpreted the accusations of religious radicalism made against Cromwell on his fall as evidence of what they see as his underlying evangelical commitment. The attainder was firm: Cromwell, 'being a detestable heretic, and being in himself utterly disposed to set and sow common sedition and variance among your true and loving subjects', had secretly set forth a great number of erroneous books declaring 'manifest matters to induce and lead your subjects to diffidence and refusal of the true and sincere faith and belief which christian religion bindeth all christian people to have in the most holy and blessed sacrament of the altar'.[205] In addition, he 'hath openly and obstinately holden opinion and said that it was as lawful for every christian man to be a minister of the said sacrament as well as a priest'.[206] In addition, Cromwell

> by his crafty and subtle means and inventions, hath not only defended the same heretics from punishment and reformation; but being a fautor, maintainer, and supporter of heretics, divers times hath terribly rebuked divers of the said credible persons being their accusers, and some others of them hath persecuted and vexed by imprisonment.[207]

If all that were true, then he was unquestionably a religious radical. But the attainder should not be accepted as an unimpeachable source. Elton rightly points out how 'very vague and unsupported' the charges against Cromwell were: his enemies 'had no case against him that would have stood up to a moment's judicial scrutiny'.[208] We shall later consider whether, as was alleged, Cromwell had on 31 March 1540 defended the radical preacher Robert Barnes and others. But what must at once seem highly implausible is that he did not simply look for ways of protecting them, but openly declared, 'if the king would turn from it, yet I would not turn; and if the king did turn and all his people I would fight in the field in my own person with my sword in my hand against him and all other', and that he should have held up his dagger, saying, 'or else this dagger thrust me to the heart if I would not die in that quarrel against them all; and I trust if I live one year or two it shall not lie in the king's power to resist or let it if he would'.[209] It would be much safer to reach a view on Cromwell's religion uninfluenced by the accusations in his attainder.

Cromwell's religion, closely scrutinised, seems to have contained many orthodox elements. In 1529 he drew up (and no later than 1536 revised in detail, but not in essentials) a conventional will, beseeching the intercession of Our Lady and the holy company of heaven, and asking for 'an honest person' to sing for his soul for seven (extended in 1536 from three) years, and prayers from the five orders of friars in London.[210] His attitude to the saints presumably changed: they were invoked in his will of 1529, but he did not appeal to them on the scaffold in 1540.[211] The imponderable is how far that change reflected a personal conversion, and how far Cromwell loyally followed the evolution of royal policy.

In 1530 he lamented the existence of Luther: 'the fame is that Luther is departed this life. I would he had never been borne.'[212] In the same year he informed Wolsey that he had recently discovered some who favoured Luther's sect: books confiscated included John Frith's *Revelation of Antichrist* and Simon Fish's *Supplication for the Beggars*, described by Cromwell as 'pestiferous books' which 'if they be scattered among the common people so destroy the whole obedience and policy of this realm'. Cromwell exhorted Wolsey to stop this doctrine.[213]

Cromwell's dealings with the exiled William Tyndale are inconclusive. Elton's account of efforts to recruit Tyndale in 1530–31 place the initiative squarely with Stephen Vaughan, not Cromwell.

> Vaughan brought the matter into the open on 26 January 1531 when he wrote to Henry about his attempts to find Tyndale and persuade him to return . . . the covering note to Cromwell—'I pray you, let me know how the King taketh my letters'—shows clearly that this was to be the first that Henry had heard of the business.[214]

But as Elton notes, in May Henry saw Tyndale's *Practice of Prelates* and exploded with rage. Soon afterwards 'Cromwell hastened to stop Vaughan's activities in a letter in which he hurriedly accepted the whole of the king's opinion of Tyndale—a man "replete with venomous envy, rancour and malice"'.[215] Vaughan did not immediately obey, as Elton notes.[216] What the episode shows is not Cromwell's involvement in religious reform but his subservience to the king's wishes.

It is just possible that Cromwell tried to save Tyndale in 1535–36 but there is nothing very definite to prove this, only Hall's somewhat cryptic account: 'true it is, that after he had been in prison more than a year & almost forgotten, he was laboured for by letters written by the lord Cromwell, & then in all haste because he would recant no part of his doings, was burned'. That hints at a personal intervention, rather than outright sympathy with Tyndale's views. Cromwell sent Vaughan two letters for Tyndale in September 1535.[217] Cromwell's memorandum 'To know the king's pleasure for Tyndalle, and whether I should write or not'[218] could just possibly hint at his own sympathies, but what it most importantly shows, once more, is that the king, and not Cromwell, was in charge.

What exactly Cromwell's personal views were on the matters of controversy in the 1530s it is impossible to establish. Cromwell wrote no works of theology nor was he consulted in the way that the bishops were on articles of faith. It is possible that his views were reflected in the writings of others, such as Thomas Starkey and Robert Barnes, but in the absence of clear links the risks of circular argument are plain. More helpful are Cromwell's actions. It is worth noting how enthusiastically he took part in the trial of John Lambert in November 1538, even ordering his imprisonment (according to Lambert),[219] and his robust repudiation of sacramentarian heresy in Calais. (Some historians think Cromwell protected such heretics, as we shall see; nonetheless what he actually said against such doctrine was quite clearly critical.) Cromwell evidently held traditional views of the mass. An inventory of his household goods includes a 'tabernacle of the nativity of our lord', a 'table of the passion of our lord', a 'table of the pity of our lady' and 'tables of the salutation of our lady', hinting at an orthodox piety.[220]

Cromwell's speech on the scaffold offers tantalisingly inconclusive evidence. He asserted that 'I die in the catholic faith, not doubting in any article of my faith, no nor doubting in any sacrament of the church'. In his prayer he placed his trust in Jesus, but his formulation, 'I have no merits nor good works which I may allege before thee', is ambiguous. It can be read as an endorsement of Lutheran justification by faith alone; but it can also be seen as an expression of modesty that does not deny the possibility that someone else in his position might have such efficacious merits or good works. Unlike in his earlier will, Cromwell did not invoke the Virgin or saints nor ask for prayers on his behalf: in that he was following his own injunctions rather than asserting anything new.[221]

Cromwell's voluminous correspondence reveals surprisingly little interest in theology.[222] In his papers, there is little that touches on doctrine. More common are jottings referring to the views of others. 'Remembrances to be remembered to the king's highness . . . item, the determination of Mr Day, Heath, Thirlby, and Skip upon the x commandments, justification and purgatory.'[223] Here Cromwell was gathering views from churchmen of differing persuasions for the king's benefit: it is hard to read into this any opinions of his own.

Cromwell's household might appear to offer evidence of his religious convictions. A former royal chaplain (Elton suggests John Oliver),[224] evidently accused of being a papist, defended himself by referring to 'divers dinners and suppers' he had had at Cromwell's house

> which were the very cause of the beginning of my conversion. For me thought it were a stony heart and a blockish wit that could carry nothing away of such colloquy as was at your honourable board. And that made me to note them well, And when I came home to meet them withe mine english Bible. And I found always the conclusions which you maintained at your board to be consonant with the holy word of God.

He then compared the English translation of the Bible with the Vulgate and with Erasmus's translation, and then learnt Greek (being taught by Robert Wakefield). All that hints at an evangelical piety, but just what Cromwell was arguing in his household is left frustratingly vague. Elton suggests that 'as early as 1531 or 1532, therefore, Cromwell was thinking along reformed lines and lines of evangelical theology, and dinner-time in his household was an occasion for learned discourse',[225] but it remains tantalisingly unclear just what doctrine Cromwell was purveying and his guest imbibing. It may simply have been the king's divorce justified by reference to scripture.[226]

For many who got into difficulties when they preached reform, Cromwell appeared as a protector. Modern historians have been quick to build on this. 'It is certain that the reformers saw in him their patron', Elton has asserted.[227] 'More probably,' says Rex,

> Cromwell was playing a complicated game, passing off to Henry as loyal preachers of the supremacy ('God's word') those whom he knew in fact to be heretically inclined. The promotion of heretical preachers without the king's knowledge and against the king's will was to be one of the main charges brought against him in his attainder in 1540.[228]

On such a view 'the prophets of reform naturally flocked to him. Humanists, Protestants and economic thinkers, ardent men and self-seekers and cranks, genuine idealists and men disgruntled by failure or envy, all presented themselves, wrote letters, sent tracts or memorials or bad encomical poems.'[229] Brigden has put together an article on 'Thomas Cromwell and the "brethren"' based on such materials.

But there are difficulties with this approach. If Cromwell was hailed as a reformer by early protestants, so after all was Henry. Since in many respects government policy was reformist in nature, it was not unreasonable of reformers to acclaim them. As Brigden notes, Cromwell by no means always helped those evangelicals who sought his aid. Thomas Somer died in the Tower in 1532, despite a friend's supplication to Cromwell.[230] Cromwell could be firm with reformers, as his treatment of Bishop Shaxton shows.[231] Shaxton had wanted a monk of Reading to be silenced; but Cromwell, he complained, was allowing the monk to continue to preach that scripture was not absolutely sufficient of itself for a Christian to live by, that faith justified no man before God without his own works, and that a man might deserve grace, justification and a higher place in heaven by his own works. Shaxton undoubtedly thought Cromwell would support him, as his pained response when Cromwell did not do so shows: 'is this your encouraging of men to do their duty?'[232]

All this shows how much Cromwell's relations with known reformers need careful and nuanced reading. For it is striking, too, how many conservatives and conformists appealed to him to restrain radicals, and even to reverse policy. Thomas Abel, Catherine of Aragon's defender (author of *Invicta Veritas*, and long imprisoned for his pains) of all people, appealed to Cromwell 'to be so good lord unto him as to move the king to go to church and say mass'. This came when Abel said that he had been in prison for three years and a quarter.[233]

> Your lordship knoweth very well that there was never man [in this] realm that ever was so unjustly condemned as I am for I was never since I came hither asked nor examined of any offense that should be laid onto my charge. . . . And all that was put in my condemnation is untrue, as I have written onto your lordship largely once before this time, and I judge and suppose in your lordship so . . . natural pity and so much charitable compassion, that your lordship would of your own mere goodness have moved and besought the king's grace to have been so gracious lord unto me as to have granted me the liberty which I now desire, though that I had been culpable after so long time of punishment and being in prison as I have been. Wherefore I doubt not

but rather trust that your lordship will so do now for me seeing that your lordship doth know that I am innocent and have so great wrong and therefore I do not rehearse.

This is a context for pleas such as that of Thomas Wylley, vicar of Yoxford, that 'the Lord make you the instrument of my help, Lord Cromwell, that I may have the liberty to preach the truth . . . aid me for Christ's sake that I may preach Christ'. What had provoked Wylley's fellow priests in Suffolk was a play he had made against the pope's counsellors, namely error, 'cool clogger of conscience', and incredulity. He was also making a play about purgatory.[234]

Bishop Longland asked him to repress one Swynnerton, who was preaching on matters prohibited, thanking Cromwell 'for all your goodness to me always showed'.[235] Sir William Godolphin in April 1537 begged him to move the king that the people might hold the day of their head saint at St Keverne, Cornwall.[236] If Godolphin's concern was tactical—anxious not to provoke another rising—clearly he did not see Cromwell as a militant evangelical. Katherine Bulkeley, abbess of Godstow, appealed to Cromwell against Dr John London in November 1538: Cromwell had preferred her, against Dr London's wishes, and now London was threatening her and her sisters that he had the king's commission to suppress the house—she refused to allow him to do so without the king's or Cromwell's commandment and complained at London's treatment.[237] Thomas Goldwell, prior of Canterbury Cathedral, had been better treated by the chancellor of the augmentations and other royal commissioners as a result of Cromwell's letters.[238] In August 1539 Bishop Longland asked Cromwell to deal with the former chancellor of the bishop of Worcester who openly ate buttered chickens at Islip on the eve of the Assumption.[239]

What these solicitations reveal is how a royal councillor, who was also the king's vicegerent in spirituals, was the natural focus of appeals from all those involved in local difficulties. The letters that Cromwell, received must be studied with care. In particular the effusive praise of Cromwell couched in evangelical language in some of them, should not too readily be taken as evidence that Cromwell himself shared the convictions of his correspondents.

In May 1540 Cromwell spoke in parliament on matters of religion, saying that[240]

there was nothing which the King so much desired as a firm union among all his subjects. . . . He knew there were many incendiaries, and much cockle grew up with the wheat. The rashness and licentiousness of some, and the inveterate superstition and stiffness of others in the ancient corruptions, had raised great dissensions to the regret of all christians. Some were called papists, others heretics; which bitterness of spirit seemed the more strange, since now the Holy Scriptures, by the King's great care of his people, were in all their hands, in a language which they understood. But these were grossly perverted by both sides, who studied rather to justify their passions out of them, than to direct their belief by them. The king leaned neither to the right nor to the left hand, neither to the one nor the other party [Elton: 'favours nor one side nor the other but, as becometh a christian prince, professes the true christian faith'] but set the pure and sincere doctrine of the Christian faith only before his eyes; and therefore was now resolved to have this set forth to his subjects without any corrupt mixtures; and to have such decent ceremonies continued and the true use of them taught, by which all abuses might be cut off and disputes about the exposition of the scriptures cease, and so all his subjects might be well instructed in their faith and directed in the reverent worship of God; and resolved to punish severely all transgressors, of what sort or side soever they were.

That is an elegant exposition of the royal middle way. If Cromwell sincerely believed it, then he was less evangelical than some modern historians have claimed, and his religious convictions were much the same as the king's. If he did not believe it, but was mouthing what he knew would please the king, then Henry was clearly more dominant than the historians of faction would allow, and Cromwell, whatever his private thoughts, was evidently ready to subordinate his convictions to the demands of royal service.

Cromwell and the Bible

Cromwell undoubtedly took a considerable interest in the promotion of the Bible in English. John Foxe presented his life as nothing 'but a constant care and travail to advance and further the right knowledge of the gospel'.[241] Among modern historians Elton had no doubt that, in pressing for the Bible to be made available in English, Cromwell ran ahead of the king. 'The story of the English Bible in the 1530s provides very clear proof that, notwithstanding his careful professions of subservience, the vicegerent was quite capable of pushing on reforms not altogether pleasing to the supreme head and of doing this by disguising the truth of events from his master.'[242] 'It was he [Cromwell], not the King, who promoted the vernacular Bible, going so far as to use versions derived from the translation of Tyndale whom Henry abominated.'[243] How persuasive is this?

There is indeed a good deal of evidence to show that Cromwell was greatly involved in the production of an English Bible, and that in 1537–38 he was seen as persuading the king to allow it to go ahead. On 4 August 1537 Cranmer sent Cromwell a Bible in English. It had been prepared by John Rogers, under the pseudonym Thomas Matthew, but in fact mostly followed Tyndale's translation of the New Testament.[244] In an introductory epistle, which Cranmer thought well done and commended to Cromwell, it was dedicated to the king. Cranmer liked what he had so far read of the translation better than any he had seen before. He urged Cromwell to show it to the king, and obtain from him, if he could, a licence that it might be sold and read by everyone—until the bishops produced a better translation, which he thought would not happen till a day after Doomsday.[245] It is worth pausing to note that the initiative here is very much Cranmer's, though he clearly expected that Cromwell would be receptive.[246] On the face of it, Cromwell, responding to Cranmer's urgings, then succeeded in persuading the king. Cranmer reiterated his thanks on 28 August: 'these shall be to give you most hearty thanks that any heart can think, and that in the name of them all which favoureth God's word, for your diligence at this time in procuring the king's highness to set forth the said God's word and his gospel by his grace's authority'.[247] A little later Cromwell asked Richard Grafton, printer, to send him six Bibles, which Grafton sent as a gift 'for those most godly pains for which the heavenly father is bound even of his justice to reward you with the everlasting kingdom of God'. Grafton's remarks, it might be noted in passing, fall some way short of an endorsement of justification by faith alone: for Grafton, heaven would be Cromwell's reward for promulgating the English Bible. Grafton eulogised Cromwell:

> for your lordship moving our most gracious prince to the allowance and licensing of such a work hath wrought such an act worthy of praise as never was mentioned in any chronicle in this realm. And as my lord of Canterbury said, the tidings thereof did him more good then the gift of ten thousand pound.[248]

Cromwell was undoubtedly seen as instrumental in persuading the king. Thereafter his role seems largely technical, receiving appeals for various forms of practical assistance from Grafton, though he may have given £400 of his own money towards the costs of printing.[249]

But Cromwell's undoubted zeal for the Bible in English must be carefully glossed. We should note just how necessary it was for Henry to be persuaded. We should also note just how remarkable a feat persuading the king was seen to be—suggesting that the king was not known to be easily persuaded.[250] That in turn raises questions about the king's attitude to the Bible. As early as 1530 a royal proclamation had envisaged the possibility of a translation of the Bible made generally available one day. Now, the king had then declared, it was 'more convenient' that the people had the holy scripture expounded to them by preachers in their sermons as had long been the custom.

> All be it if it shall hereafter appear to the king's highness that his said people do utterly abandon and forsake all perverse erroneous and seditious opinions, with the new Testament and the old corruptly translated into the English tongue; now being in print; And that the same books and all other books of heresy as swell in the French tongue as in the Dutch tongue be clearly exterminate and exiled out of this Realm of England for ever: his highness intendeth to provide that the holy scripture shall be by great learned and catholic persons translated into the english tongue if it shall then seem to his grace convenient so to be.[251]

In short, Henry was prepared in 1530 to contemplate an official translation of the Bible in English: and this was not just tactical rhetoric. Hall says that the conference of bishops had been called because of complaints of the people against More's imprisoning and the punishing of a great number of people for possessing English translations of the New Testament. Henry, 'considering what good might come of reading of the new Testament with reverence and following the same, and what evil might come of the reading of the same if it were evil translated, and not followed', accordingly consulted with his council and prelates in Star Chamber on 25 May 1530. After lengthy discussions, the king banned all the Bible translations by Tyndale and Joye: they were untrue and they contained prefaces and prologues that approached heresy. Instead, Henry commanded the bishops to call the best learned men of the universities together and to order a new translation to be made, 'so that the people should not be ignorant in the law of God'.[252] Scarisbrick wondered whether Henry had called this conference of bishops in May 1530 with the intention of launching, or preparing to launch, a translation of the New Testament, but had then recoiled in the face of opposition from the bishops.[253] However that may be, Henry's bishops do seem to have been assigned sections of the Bible to translate. In 1537 Grafton referred to it being seven years since the bishops promised to translate the Bible.[254] By June 1535 Stephen Gardiner, bishop of Winchester, reported that he had finished the translation of St Luke and St John 'wherein I have spent a great labour'.[255] Progress was evidently slow, and possibly obstructed by more conservative bishops. Stokesley of London refused to look at the portion he had been assigned.[256] Cranmer, as we have seen, thought they would not finish it by Doomsday.[257] All that nonetheless shows that Henry was not opposed to an English Bible in principle and, indeed, that he was prepared to take measures to bring it about in due course. It is remarkable to think that during the momentous events of the 1530s most of the bishops were also busy translating sections of the Bible into English.

Against that background, what Cromwell did in 1537 appears less startlingly novel. What Henry permitted in August 1537 was the diffusion of the Bible as prepared by Matthew/Tyndale. But that was not the first Bible in English that the king had authorised. Cromwell's injunctions of 1536 required every parson to provide a book of the whole Bible, both in Latin and *in English*, and lay the same in the choir, 'for every man that will to look and read thereon'; they were not to discourage any man from reading any part of it but rather to exhort every man to read it as the very word of God.[258] It is not altogether clear that all versions of the injunctions contained this instruction. Some diocesan injunctions in 1536–37, for example those for Worcester and Lichfield and Coventry, do require the provision of Bibles, while others do not. Bishops would hardly have acted without royal instructions on this point, and perhaps there was some confusion.[259] However that may be, the translated Bible then available was that which Miles Coverdale, an exiled Augustinian friar, had completed while drawing heavily on Tyndale's translation of the New Testament. In that context, the subsequent decision in mid-1537 to license the Matthew/Tyndale Bible was not quite as revolutionary as it has sometimes been made to appear.

Why should Henry have been prepared to change his mind, at least to the extent of now going along with a revised version of a translation he had up till now banned? It may be that the continuing failure of the bishops to produce a translation made him realise that he must look elsewhere. More important, in 1537, was the legacy of the Pilgrimage of Grace. That rebellion was seen as the result of ignorance:[260] 'the lack of this word of the almighty god is the cause of all blindness and superstition'.[261] The dispelling of such dangerous ignorance, the cause of tumults,[262] became even more imperative. It was asserted that through 'the education of your people in the knowledge of Christ's true religion'—'a plain and sincere doctrine concerning the holy sum of all those things which appertain unto the profession of a christian man' and comprising the rudiments of Christianity—'that by the same all errors, doubts, superstitions and abuses might be suppressed, removed and utterly taken away' to the perfect establishment of good unity and concord.[263] The duke of Norfolk and the earl of Sussex, repressing the Pilgrimage of Grace, were informed that, in the belief that those enormities were the result of ignorance, the king had determined to send certain grave, discreet and learned persons to preach the truth, to teach the word of God sincerely.[264] Norfolk, praising one of them, Mr Addison, said that if three or four such preachers had been continually in these parts instructing the unlearned, no such follies would have been attempted.[265] It is in that light that the royal sanctioning of the diffusion of the Matthew/Tyndale translation of the Bible in August 1537 should be seen. No doubt the conviction that the contention in the realm—'some calling them of the old and some of the new'—should be ended 'should we all follow one God, one book and one learning', as Grafton hoped, was naive, but it was understandable.[266] Thus Cromwell's persuasion of the king was more a tactical matter of timing than a triumph of radical principle.

The Matthew/Tyndale Bible was not, however, regarded as a definitive text. Very soon afterwards, Cromwell asked Coverdale to revise it, and the Great Bible was then printed in Paris in the latter part of 1538 and early 1539. It appeared in April 1539; a new edition with a preface by Cranmer followed in 1540. Coverdale's text was more eirenic. Where the traditional Latin Vulgate had included anything not to be found in the Hebrew or Greek texts from which the translations were made, the details were added in small type in brackets. Luther's prefaces and notes were omitted. Tyndale's original translation, with its overtly Lutheran terminology and marginal notes, was in effect amended in order to make the translated Bible a suitable part of the Henrician middle way.[267]

Here it is worth emphasising that a vernacular Bible was not necessarily an evangelical or protestant matter. Dispelling ignorance was as much a humanist as a protestant aim. An interesting illustration of the essentially humanist character of interest in biblical translation is provided by Sir Francis Bryan. In 1538 the highly conservative abbot of Woburn testified how he had seen one of the newly translated Bibles in Bryan's bedchamber. The abbot judged it not well interpreted in many places; Bryan turned to the words in Luke on the consecration of the most blessed body and blood of Christ, read them to the abbot, and asked him how he liked them. Interpreters, he said, must sometimes follow the letter, and sometimes the sense. The abbot accepted that that passage was 'very well and justly set out'. Bryan is presented by his most recent student as a religious conservative, under suspicion of having close contacts with supporters of Princess Mary, and of being prepared to warn Cardinal Pole, the previous year, of the threat of assassination or capture. When the abbot of Woburn talked treasonable talk, Bryan, high steward of Woburn Abbey, listened to him. Yet here we find Bryan reading the newly translated Bible and evidently approving it.[268]

It is also important to note that from the beginning the Bible was issued to the laity in the vernacular on condition that it be read without contention but with the deference due to informed authority. Cromwell fully endorsed such an approach: that was not just the king's later reaction. In Cromwell's injunctions of 1536 the clergy were instructed to exhort every man to read the Bible, but

> ever gently and charitably exhorting them that using a sober and a modest behaviour in the reading and inquisition of the true sense of the same, they do in no wise stiffly or eagerly contend or strive with one another about the same but refer the declaration of those places that be in controversy to the judgment of them that be better learned.[269]

The injunctions of 1538 required the clergy not to discourage the laity from reading or listening to the Bible, but they were to admonish them 'to avoid all contention and altercation therein, but to use an honest sobriety in the inquisition of the true sense of the same, and to refer the explication of obscure places to men of higher judgement in scripture'.[270] Cromwell ordered parish priests to warn their parishioners not to argue about doubtful passages of the Bible in taverns and alehouses—'not giving too much to your own minds fantasies and opinions nor having thereof any open reasoning in your open taverns or alehouses'—but rather to resort to 'such learned men' as were authorised to preach and to pronounce on such matters, 'so . . . avoiding all contentions and disputations in such alehouses and other places unmeet for such conferences'.[271] All that is very much in line with the attitude represented by the proclamation of 16 November 1538 (with corrections in the king's hand) on the Bible,[272] and the proclamation (possibly only a draft, but also corrected by the king) in April 1539,[273] which may be taken as evidence of Henry's attitude to rival interpreters of the Bible.

Each of them dispute so /earnestly/ [struck out] /arrogantly/ [added] against the other of their opinions as well in churches, alehouses, taverns, and other places and congregations, that there is begun and sprung among themselves slander and railing at each other as well by word as writing, one part of them calling the other papist, the other parte calling the other heretic; whereby is like to follow /sedition/ [struck out] /dissention/ [added] and tumult not only to their own confusions that teach and use the same, but also to the disturbance and likelihood to destruction of all the rest of the king's true and well beloved subjects.

If any readers found any doubtful passages, they should 'be wary and take heed of their own presumptions and arrogant expositions', and humbly seek instruction from those learned in holy scripture. King and minister were thus well agreed on the proper way that the translated Bible should be used.

The frontispiece of the Great Bible printed in 1539 shows Henry presenting it to Cranmer and Cromwell, his archbishop and his vicegerent in spirituals. This was not 'a plea from the evangelical promoters of the Word for royal support', but rather a vigorous assertion both of royal dominance and of the king's commitment to evangelising.[274] And that means that Cromwell's undoubted and energetic involvement in the production of the vernacular Bible must nonetheless fail to clinch the case for him as more of a religious reformer than was the king.

Calais

It is necessary here to deal with what has become an orthodoxy but is in fact a red herring: namely the claim that Cromwell (and Cranmer) foisted religious radicals on to the Calais authorities and defended them against the complaints and intrigues of Lord Lisle, the king's deputy there, and supposed factional rivals, especially the duke of Norfolk. All that is then presented as a significant factor in Cromwell's downfall in 1540, since his supposed conservative enemies allegedly poisoned the king against him by citing what was happening in Calais as evidence of his dangerous religious radicalism. 'Nowhere is there more evidence to justify the charges [brought against Cromwell in 1540] of supporting heretics and favouring heretical opinions than in the Calais story.'[275]

Such an interpretation is deeply improbable. After all, Calais was a frontier post, a garrison town, always exposed to the possibility of a surprise French attack. It was not somewhere remote and unimportant where religious experiments could be carried out without anyone noticing. Why would it have been such a good place for Cromwell and Cranmer to have urged on evangelical reform? Would it not have provoked damagingly public quarrels? And how exactly would it have helped them foster religious change in England?

Not only is such a reading implausible, above all it is not supported by a close examination of the evidence. This makes it plain that what Henry VIII (who must not, as is so often done, be omitted from the political history of his reign) and his servants Cromwell and Cranmer were concerned to achieve in Calais, as elsewhere in the realm, was quite straightforwardly the imposition of the king's royal supremacy, the break with Rome, the dissolution of the monasteries and the dismantling of the shrines.[276] That led them to an often awkward balancing act: excusing fiery preachers who were very effective denouncers of Rome but who strayed dangerously close to heresy in doctrine. Yet, to repeat, that was no independent and underhand pursuit by Cromwell or Cranmer of some evangelical strategy: the policy that they were implementing was not their own, but the king's.

Obviously Calais was an especially sensitive and dangerous place in which to enforce the policies of the 1530s. Accordingly, the king was particularly keen to have the royal supremacy effectively preached there. The ecclesiastical standing of Calais was anomalous: located in the diocese of Thérouanne, it was in practice appended to the diocese of Canterbury and administered by a commissary appointed by the archbishop. It contained several plump benefices held by absentee Englishmen; was peopled by French and Flemish speakers; and was open to all manner of foreign influences.

Arthur Plantagenet, Lord Lisle, had been appointed lord deputy in Calais. Not a man of the highest competence and by no means sympathetic to religious reform, he was wholly loyal to Henry's break with Rome, yet from time to time aroused royal misgivings that he was not. As such he faced an awkward combination of challenges. He did not get on well with John Butler, the commissary appointed by Cranmer. But the tensions and difficulties have been misinterpreted in terms of political and religious faction.

What concerned Henry, Cromwell and Cranmer throughout was the effective enforcement of the royal supremacy. In July 1537 Cromwell sent Lisle and the council of Calais a stinging rebuke. Henry had heard that two priests of doubtful loyalty were there: 'His grace cannot a little marvel to hear of the papistical faction that is maintained in that town and by you chiefly that be of his grace's council.'[277] Interestingly,

Cromwell followed this up a few days later with a personal letter to Lisle, referring back to his having written 'somewhat sharply' by the king's command, warning 'some of the said council which lean much to their superstitious old observations and rites'. But he assured Lisle that

> I remain still your perfect and sincere friend, and that by such sharpness ye are none otherwise touched to thereby than to take an occasion to be concurrent with me to alter such evil instructed and inclined hearts to leave their old ceremonies and observations and exhort them to know and follow the truth declared unto them.[278]

What is intriguing is that Cromwell is here attempting to soften the force of the royal rebuke sent to Lisle, suggesting that relations between Lisle and Cromwell were not as hostile as many historians have claimed. The problem was that Lisle's less than competent handling of matters left him open to suspicion. Both in early 1539 and in early 1540 Henry sent special commissioners—Edward Seymour, earl of Hertford in 1539, the duke of Norfolk in 1540—to investigate and report on the situation in Calais. In May 1540 Lisle was imprisoned in the Tower after one of his chaplains, Gregory Botolf, defected to Rome, raising understandable questions about Lisle's underlying sympathies, though, in fact, as far as we can see, Lisle appears loyally to have enforced the royal supremacy throughout.

But it is through the prism of royal wariness and determination over the supremacy that events in Calais must be seen. In 1538 there was much noise over the arrival of Adam Damplip and his engagement by John Butler, the commissary, to preach against the pope, and to denounce the shrine of the resurrection (which had been condemned as superstitious). Damplip may have gone too far: he may, although the evidence is uncertain, have gone so far as to question the real presence in the mass, the heresy for which John Lambert paid with his life in October 1538. But it is quite wrong to think, as so many historians have done, that Cromwell protected Damplip against Lord Lisle's complaints. On the contrary, on hearing of the charges against Damplip, Cromwell ordered him to be sent to London, and Cranmer then interrogated him, before Damplip managed to flee.

What concerned Cromwell was that Damplip was being maliciously and falsely accused of religious radicalism by men such as Prior Dove of the Calais Whitefriars, who were, he feared, unreconciled to the royal supremacy and unsympathetic to the dismantling of shrines. It is in that context that on 14 August 1538 Cromwell sent Lisle 'a sharp letter' taxing him 'for persecuting those who favour and set forth God's word and for favouring those who impugn it'.[279] Confronted by similar problems the following year, Cromwell remarked in February 1539 that Lisle should 'wax grave' and not give credit to every 'light tale', and not to be too hasty in writing,[280] that 'it is sore to note any man for a sacramentary, unless the reporter knows well what a sacramentary is' and, with Damplip or possibly another priest accused of radical preaching in mind, he added simply that he and others might perhaps have been more circumspect in some things.[281]

In June 1539, a year after Damplip had been summoned to London on suspicion of heresy, Cromwell was 'much to marvel' that the schedule just submitted by Lisle and the council of Calais of certain articles preached by Damplip had not been presented against him when he was accused over transubstantiation.[282] Did this reflect Cromwell's disingenuousness? Must he have been fully informed about all this in 1538, and must he consequently have been lying through his teeth in denying all knowledge of it till the following year? So argues Byrne, followed by others.[283] But Byrne damages her claims when she speculates that the council of Calais had compiled the list of articles in 1538 but, fearing that they were dynamite, had not sent them.[284] In that case Cromwell's profession of ignorance and his manifest irritation later would be fully justified. Certainly in June 1539 Cromwell made no bones about what was and what was not acceptable. He had perused the articles outlining Damplip's views and found them very 'pestilent': if he taught such things, then he taught 'most detestable and cankered heresy'. If John Butler taught them, Cromwell added, then he was unfit to serve as commissary and deserved severe punishment.[285] He that neither fears God nor esteems the king's injunctions is 'no meet herb to grow in his majesty's most catholic and virtuous garden', Cromwell continued. But rather than seeing that as essentially disingenuous, rather than marvelling at Cromwell's 'sheer nerve' and 'effrontery', as Byrne does,[286] we should rather see Cromwell as suspicious that Lisle's conservatism might have made him exaggerate the extent of heresy and consequently accuse of being sacramentaries those who were simply enforcing the king's policies. Cromwell could also reasonably have felt annoyed with Lisle that he had not dealt more circumspectly with these problems. Seymour had just reported back on the religious divisions in Calais, which were real enough. Cromwell, understandably, was irritated that he had not been informed earlier about what was an undeniable problem, that 'the town of Calais should be in some misorder by certain sacramentaries alleged to be in the same'.[287] Criticised, Lisle and his council, in turn, in an effort to defend themselves against perceptions of incompetence, claimed that they had reported the problems before. All this dramatised the divisions and exaggerated the extent of radicalism.[288] And it is worth adding that blaming Lisle for not detecting heretics earlier (whether with good reason or not) would not have been an obviously effective way of protecting radicals, which reinforces the claim that that is not what Cromwell was doing. In many ways the reproachful orders sent to Lisle sound much more like the reaction of Henry VIII, typically, and unfairly, blaming his servant for problems in the execution of near-impossible or contradictory policies.

That Cromwell and Cranmer saw themselves not as leaders of a faction but as royal servants implementing royal policy and concerned above all to maintain order and to minimise division, is seen by their treatment of Prior Dove. In summer 1538, Cranmer severely criticised Dove for hindering the word of God and maintaining superstition,[289] and kept him in custody till Cromwell returned, not doubting that enough would be found to justify Dove's deprivation of office.[290] The questions put to him show that he was suspected of intriguing with the bishops of London, Chichester and Durham, presumably against that spring's policy of dismantling shrines.[291] But, interestingly, Cromwell and Cranmer did not destroy Dove, which, on a factional view, they might have sought to do. Instead, by a mixture of threats and promises, they won him over. By October he was reported as returning to Calais 'to recant things by him misspoken': for so doing Cranmer and Cromwell promised him favour.[292] In November he was reported to be on the point of surrendering the priory to the king.[293] But this reinforces the point that what Cromwell and Cranmer were pursuing was the enforcement of the government's policies, the outward acquiesence of those seemingly opposed and the maintenance of order, not the private encouragement of some evangelical agenda independent of royal policies.

That there were serious religious divisions in Calais was made dramatically visible at this time by the protests in parliament against the Six Articles by Thomas Brook, one of the two burgesses for Calais, who argued for communion in both kinds and condemned transubstantiation.[294] Meanwhile, Thomas Boyes, the other burgess for Calais, presented information against religious radicals to the king. It would hardly have been possible to ignore the religious divisions in Calais. Henry was clearly annoyed by the dissension in the town. He told William

Feilding: 'I have more ado with you Calais men than with all my realm after.'[295]

In the course of summer 1539 a full inquiry took place. John Butler, the commissary, and William Smith, the parish priest of Calais, were sent up at the king's pleasure.[296] Together with Ralph Hare, a soldier in the garrison, and Jacob, a Fleming who was a barber in Marke, they were heard by the lords of the council, including the duke of Suffolk, the bishop of Durham and the earl of Oxford.[297] What is striking is just how thoroughly the accusations of religious radicalism were dealt with. Not all those examined were to be punished, and not all those punished were punished severely, but that again shows that efforts were made to determine the truth of the charges, rather than that Cromwell or Cranmer or anyone else was shielding radicals. Those investigated differed widely in the range of their religious beliefs, further casting doubt on the notion that Cromwell and Cranmer were protectors of a coherent religious faction. That influential people in Calais were, in somewhat different ways, seeking religious reform beyond what Henry VIII's reformation allowed is clear. It is much harder to show that Cromwell or Cranmer were instigating and co-ordinating their actions, or even protecting them. What characterised Cromwell's approach best were his words of advice, sent to Lisle and the Calais councillors on 23 July 1539, ordering them to sort out a quarrel that had arisen between two members of the Calais garrison. They were to work towards 'a gentle and indifferent order':

ye shall nourish and bring a very union and concord between all them there and conduce them to such a knot as there shall be perfect union amongst them without strife which is one of the strongest fortresses that can be in any such town of war as the same is.[298]

There is thus little to suggest that the behaviour of Damplip in 1538 or the revelations of religious radicalism in Calais in 1539 harmed or embarrassed Cromwell's standing with the king or influenced the making of religious policy. Instead, these events demonstrate the challenges that royal policy faced. What happened in Calais in 1538–39 also fails as an explanation for the fall of Cromwell in 1540: if all this had tarred Cromwell with the brush of religious radicalism, it is not easy to explain why he did not fall in summer 1539. It was then that matters were brought into the open and underwent close scrutiny. In September 1539 Lisle crossed to England and saw the king.[299] A committee of bishops heard further charges against a number of Calais men in

November, debating the extent and reliability of the evidence brought forward against them.[300] That suggests that the problems of religious division were real and enduring: but no historian has so far suggested that these particular matters had political significance.

Cromwell and Diplomacy: German Alliances

Throughout the 1530s Cromwell was much engaged in negotiations with the protestant princes of the German Schmalkaldic League. Should such contacts be seen as Cromwell 'pursuing, independently of the king, a clandestine religious agenda',[301] in the hope that Henry would be swept along with the tide of reformed doctrine?[302] In his recent study, Rory McEntegart has taken Cromwell's advocacy of an alliance with the German protestant princes as strong evidence for his evangelical religious convictions.[303] These are important claims and therefore demand careful scrutiny here.

What is McEntegart's evidence? First, the diplomatic contacts with German princes in late 1533 and early 1534. Cromwell dominates, we are told, the correspondence with Christopher Mont and Stephen Vaughan, sent as ambassadors to Germany in 1533.[304] Yet the fact that the king's secretary wrote (or dictated) letters to them does not prove that he was in charge and pursuing a policy independent of the king. McEntegart, following Elton, sees the corrections in Cromwell's hand on the record of a council meeting of 2 December 1533 as showing that what was proposed was 'substantially the work of Cromwell. He controlled the agenda and discussions of the particular meeting from which it came and his pen was prominent in correcting and amending the succession of drafts which preceded the final memorandum.'[305] McEntegart does concede that Cromwell, and possibly other councillors, went to see Henry to discuss these proposals,[306] but he fails to draw out the significance of this visit.

What were these proposals? Point fourteen stated: 'certain discreet and grave persons to be appointed to repair into the parties of Germany to practise and conclude [some league or amity] with the princes and potentates of Germany [and also to inserche of what inclination the said princes and potentates be of]...towards the King and this realm'. Nothing in this formulation allows the deduction that Cromwell had originated the policy. In the margin alongside it are written the words that the matter stood by 'the king's arbitrement'. That would rather suggest that Henry was fully and decisively involved. Point fifteen dealt with an approach to the cities of Lübeck, Danzig, Hamburg and others: in the margin are written the words 'to know when of the king'. Three further notes state how 'the king's highness hath appointed' various matters.[307] Nothing here shows that Cromwell, rather than the king, was in charge of the making of diplomatic policy towards the German princes in 1533.[308]

McEntegart goes on to claim that 'just as Cromwell had been the dominant influence in proposing, discussing with the king and instructing the embassy to Germany, so he took charge of all other aspects of its despatch'.[309] This rests on a letter that Cromwell wrote to Cranmer, asking him to send to Henry one Nicholas Heath, whom 'the king's highness intendeth to send into the parts of Germany in Ambassade to treat there with the princes of Germany'. The reference to the king's intentions seems rather to point to the king's role, as does Cromwell when he writes that the king has ordered him to desire Cranmer to send Heath; and when he says that the king intends to practise certain things in Germany concerning the bishop of Rome.[310] It is even more curious that a note in Cromwell's list of remembrances 'to know what diets the king will give Dr Lee Mr Heath and Paget' should be read as evidence for Cromwell's authorship of the policy of sending them as ambassadors to Germany: if the king had to be consulted on the routine matter of their travelling expenses, it is unlikely that he was ignorant of or had to be pushed into the decision to send them.[311]

McEntegart's case would be more plausible if such approaches to the Germans in 1533–34 had been wholly new. But they were not. In April 1529 Stephen Gardiner, then at Rome, referred in a letter to the king to 'that which your Highness showed me in your gallery at Hampton Court' (that is, before Gardiner had left for Rome) 'concerning the solicitation of the princes of Almayn', which, after 'all other means used to the Popes holiness for attaining and achieving your Highness's purpose and intent', he had shown to the pope, 'and such other matter as should and ought to fear the Pope's said holiness', adding reasons to make him ally with Henry and Francis, 'and so to take the more courage to accomplish your Highness desires'.[312] Henry was evidently prepared to use the overtures that the German princes made to him, as early as 1528, as a diplomatic threat against the pope. He was clearly aware of the potential advantages of a German alliance right from the start of his campaign for a divorce. In October 1529 Chapuys reported that there was a young man sent by the duke of Saxony who had much business with the king and bishop of London.[313] The following year Henry sought Duke George's support over the divorce; the king's awareness of the possibilities of German support are more important here than the duke's apparent attempt to assuage the king's scruples.[314] In 1531 Henry had approached German princes and theologians in detail over the divorce: Bucer, Melanchthon, Luther and many others were asked to express opinions, though, as it turned out, they did not support the king. Chapuys surmised that that lay behind the despatch of Cranmer to Germany in January 1532.[315] Henry had, with Francis I, been encouraging the German princes to cause trouble for Charles V, for example, by urging them to press for a council of the church[316] or by deterring them from making a deal with Charles V[317] (as a means of distracting him from Henry's determination to secure a divorce from his aunt). And German princes had themselves appealed to Henry for support in 1531. It is by no means the case, then, that the pursuit of a German alliance began when Cromwell became the king's chief minister. The attractions of a German alliance were obvious: both Henry VIII and the German princes had common enemies: Charles V and the pope. Efforts were made to cement such an alliance at various points in the 1530s. Immediate military fears or concern over papal actions at times added a degree of urgency to these endeavours. Habsburg–Valois rapprochement in 1538 created a sense of emergency in England. But it does not follow that 'the search for allies in Germany was part of Cromwell's response, though it proved disastrous in his relations with his master'.[318] The search for German allies was a perfectly obvious response that any ruler or minister would have considered. And it continued beyond clear moments of crisis.

The principal purpose of the search for German allies in 1533–34 was to secure support for the king's break with Rome. That search cannot therefore be treated as evidence that those who were behind it wished to push England in the direction of a protestant reformation. It was the king's great matter, especially the injuries done by Henry to the pope in refusing to grant the divorce, on which the king and his diplomats concentrated in their efforts to persuade the Germans to support the king: for example, when asking them to defend Henry's cause at a general council.[319] The princes to be visited included catholics as well as protestants: the king of Poland, the dukes of Bavaria, the bishops of Mainz, Trier and Cologne. This further demonstrates that the approaches of 1533–34 cannot be seen as evidence of protestant commitment. As usual, the rhetoric of the reformation was used—'The king has sent to them out of old friendship and for the zeal which they bear to God's word and the extirpation of errors by which Christ's people have been kept under the yoke of the bishop of Rome'[320]—but Henry's purpose was essentially political and diplomatic. Chapuys noted how the king was trying to stir up trouble for the emperor in Germany and so prevent him from attacking England: Henry wanted the Lutheran princes to invade Italy and make war on the pope.[321] Thus the diplomatic overtures in Germany in 1533–34 in no way support the claim that Cromwell was pushing an evangelical foreign policy on an unwilling king.

McEntegart makes similar claims about Anglo-German contacts in 1535. 'Once again Thomas Cromwell was at the forefront of the planning process.'[322] But his evidence lies in two of Cromwell's remembrances: one of which reads 'what the king mindeth for sending into Germany',[323] and the other 'to remember the sending into Almayn and Dr Barnes'.[324] The first once again appears to present the initiative as the king's. Yet McEntegart declares that 'Cromwell remained the dominant influence over the despatch of the embassies',[325] based on another remembrance in which Cromwell wrote: 'what I shall give to doctor Barnes at his going for Melanchthon. Item how I have spoken with doctor Barnes'.[326] Curiously Cromwell mistakenly called the Schmalkaldic League 'the league Swebyk' [i.e. the Swabian League], by then defunct: was Cromwell that well informed about Germany? In suggesting, when describing Foxe's despatch, that 'as usual, Cromwell took charge of the arrangements for the embassy's despatch',[327] McEntegart relies on Cromwell's remembrance headed 'first, for the despatch of my lord of Hereford [i.e. Foxe]', followed by a list which reads like a list of tasks—letters to get written and sealed, sums of money to prepare, commissions to arrange. Significantly, the one item in the list involving a new decision (rather than simply the implementation of what had already been determined) reads: 'Item to know whether he shall have any other commission to the residue of the princes of germany.'[328] Cromwell was an important link in the chain of the implementation of policy. But policy very clearly originated from the king.

In a similar fashion, McEntegart misses the significance of a letter Sir William Fitzwilliam sent Cromwell in 1537[329]—reading it as evidence that Cromwell had persuaded the king to send an ambassador to Germany.[330] What it actually says is:

> this afternoon the king's highness riding to Hanworth showed me by the way that he had forgotten to commune with you in one thing, which is that in the instructions to bee given to him that shall go into Germany his majesty thinks it good that there will be an article put

to know what the states there will do for his grace in case the emperor, the french king and the bishop of Rome do join and conclude upon a general council and do at the same anything which should be contrary to the laws of God, his purpose and theirs.

This strongly suggests a king in control of policy, discussing it in detail with Cromwell, but adding further details on his own initiative.

McEntegart claims that, on a number of occasions, Cromwell, Cranmer and other evangelicals went beyond royal policy, and encouraged the German princes to encourage Henry to adopt evangelical reforms. For the years 1533–34, that seems wholly speculative. For the embassy of 1535 such a claim turns on a supposed new extension of Barnes's instructions: he was not just to meet German princes and seek out Melanchthon, but also to announce a future embassy that would discuss the possibility of Henry's joining the Schmalkaldic League. But for this there is no evidence, simply surmise that Cromwell 'proposed and gained the king's blessing to go further than the Rochford-Norfolk letter'.[331] Here McEntegart is making a good deal of a letter that the duke of Norfolk and Lord Rochford wrote to Cromwell on 19 July 1535. It does not, however, support his contention that Cromwell extended Barnes's instructions. The letter conveyed detailed orders from Henry to Cromwell: Henry did not ask for advice. It ended by saying that Barnes and Haynes are not to wait for any further instructions from Archbishop Cranmer or anyone else: Henry will send them by his almoner, Edward Foxe, and Heath. In other words, Henry was already planning to send on more detailed instructions.[332] So it would be more reasonable to deduce that any further instructions would come from the king, not from Cromwell.

Moreover, there is nothing to show that Henry would not have endorsed the proposals that Barnes actually made to Duke John Frederick of Saxony in autumn 1535.[333] There is little reason to doubt that the instructions given to Foxe reflect the king's preferences: they are drawn up in the king's name, and are in Wriothesley's hand. As Henry explained to Bishop Gardiner, the embassy to the German princes was 'to know their estate in religion, to thintent that upon communication and deliberation of the truth an unity in christ's religion might be established, wherein the king's highness will by all ways and means employ all his labour, study, travail and diligence'.[334] The instructions to Foxe reek of evangelical rhetoric. The king noted how Duke John Frederick and other German princes 'have employed their labours travails and studies to advance and set forth the glory of god, and the plain perfect and most certain truth of his word'; the king bore special love to the duke of Saxony since he continued

> to set forth maintain and defend the sincere teaching of the gospel and the perfect true understanding of the word of God, in which matier the king's highness also illuminated with the same spirit of truth and holly addict and dedicate to the advancement thereof hath employed great pain labour and travail to bring the same to the knowledge of his people and subjects.

The king added—simply tactically, to encourage the German princes, or sincerely?—that he was 'intending also so further and further to proceed therein as his grace by good consultation shall perceive may tend and pertain to the augmentation of the glory of god and the true knowledge of his word'.[335] If these proposals are indeed the king's, Henry was using evangelical rhetoric by 1535. Such language cannot then alone serve as evidence of differences between king and minister over policy.

McEntegart very fairly emphasises the genuine interest that Henry was showing in theology here, not playing a diplomatic game but 'pursuing a serious interest in the new religious ideas which the events of the early 1530s had awakened in him'.[336] Yet Henry was always quite clear that he would not accept the Lutheran position en bloc. That was so right from the start. In May 1531 he informed the German princes that he rejoiced to know of their orthodoxy and zeal for the reformation of the church: but he warned them against restless men who only looked for change in religion and put themselves on a level with princes.[337] The instructions he gave Foxe in 1535 showed that he sought first a high-powered delegation from the Germans and then detailed consideration and negotiation of the religious articles.[338] In March 1536 Henry much desired that his bishops and learned men might agree with theirs, 'but seen that it cannot be unless certain things in their confession and Apologie should by their familiar conferences be mitigate', he wanted them to be sent to confer.[339] He said much the same to the German ambassadors in June 1538. He noted that 'some articles of the confession [of Augsburg] require explanation and discussion, and that some are widely contended. . . . And each side must concede to the other, so that one may well achieve complete unity for the promotion of the holy truth and all christendom.'[340] He had not changed his mind in 1540 when he told the German ambassadors that 'he holds his view to be justified, and desires that he or his be written to on these and other essential articles and our reasoning be demonstrated'.[341] McEntegart recognises Henry's consistent refusal to accept a Lutheran confession of faith; but when he puts forward his factional model of politics, he sees Henry as open to persuasion on this issue. 'Henry was uncertain as to how far he wanted theological change to go'. McEntegart writes;[342] 'it was Henry's desire to establish an independent English faith—while not declaring (or even knowing) what the shape of that faith should be—which effectively inaugurated the factional contest over the religion of the realm';[343] but Henry was rather, as McEntegart elsewhere recognises, all too certain that he did not want a Lutheran reformation in England.

McEntegart then makes a good deal of Cromwell and Cranmer sending Thomas Theabold, godson of the earl of Wiltshire, with a secret message to the German princes. What was their supposed purpose? To persuade the Germans to send Henry a sufficiently high-powered delegation, including the leading theologian Philip Melanchthon, in the hope, as McEntegart sees it, of persuading the king to adopt more evangelical policies. What is odd here is the assumption that it was Cromwell, Cranmer and their evangelical friends who wanted Melanchthon to come to England. Throughout it was Henry who was very keen on such a visit. As early as July 1535 he wanted Melanchthon to come.[344] Melanchthon did not come, but sent a book, *Loci communes*, dedicated to the king.[345] When despatching Christopher Mont to Germany in 1538, Henry particularly asked that Melanchthon should come, 'especially for that his highness hath conceived a very good opinion of his virtue, learning, temperance and gravity, and wold gladly confer with him at his coming in sundry of the points of religion'. When the German ambassadors met Henry in June 1538, he told them he regretted the failure to send Melanchthon. Some of the articles of the confession of Augsburg were 'widely contended'; 'he would gladly talk with Master Philip [Melanchthon]' about them.[346] In letters to Duke John Frederick of Saxony and Landgrave Philip of Hesse in October 1538, as the German ambassadors departed, Henry declared his continuing interest in consulting with Melanchthon on doctrine.[347] That was what Henry always wanted: it was not some secret manipulative ploy by covert evangelical ministers. The precise evidence in support of the claim that Theabold was engaged in such secret activity is limited: apart from a letter that Theabold appears to have taken from Cranmer to Bucer, it rests on surmise based on Bucer's report to Grynaeus, which McEntegart sees as reproducing what Theabold told him orally.[348]

McEntegart also makes a good deal of Bishop Foxe's recommending to the Germans that they send an embassy to England and adding that his name must not be mentioned—'so that he does not come into any danger with the lord his king'. But that was a familiar trope in diplomatic negotiations: it in no way shows that Foxe was acting on his own initiative or that of some supposed evangelical group. Rather, he was conveying royal annoyance at the low status of the previous diplomatic contacts, through a Hamburg sailor, and voicing what had been consistent royal demands, not something new.[349]

And McEntegart makes a great deal of diplomatic correspondence in the late 1530s, in which German ambassadors reported Cromwell's encouragement and enthusiasm. Such reports, McEntegart insists, show Cromwell's true convictions, and also show how Cromwell was trying to use the negotiations as a means of pushing Henry into more radical courses. The difficulty with such reasoning is that it makes what are brief remarks made in the context of vigorous negotiation bear a great deal of interpretative weight. Ministers engaged in bargaining with foreign rulers and their ambassadors often expressed themselves in sympathy with them and blamed others, not least the king, for obstacles to a formal agreement.

Cromwell sent a letter of his own to Landgrave Philip of Hesse on 20 January 1538, expressing his firm hope and trust that friendship between Henry, John Frederick and Philip would be useful, and promising not to 'neglect any occasion, nor such offices as I possess, with which to strengthen and establish such friendship daily with a strong bond'. McEntegart suggests that 'Cromwell was revealing quite a lot here' and takes his promise as evidence of 'the unofficial religious agenda that truly defined the man'.[350] Perhaps, however, it was no more than standard negotiating practice, with the king's leading minister writing a seemingly private letter reinforcing his master's diplomacy. Soon after their arrival in England in May 1538, Duke John Frederick's ambassadors, Burchard and Myconius, met Cromwell, and described him to their master as 'the highest counsellor in England, who is most favourably inclined and affectionate towards the affairs of the christian religion and the German nation'.[351] Burchard further reported how Cromwell had told him that 'the king's majesty is agreed with almost all the articles of the christian religion of the League; only in one or two articles does the king's majesty still have reservations, but with time he should also be moved on these'.[352] A little later Burchard reported Cromwell as saying that Henry would unite completely with the Christian faith of John Frederick and the League.[353] It is indeed possible that Cromwell sincerely hoped that some such religious alliance between the king and the German Lutherans would be reached. Yet such a deduction might be mistaken. All these words were spoken in the course of difficult diplomatic and theological negotiations that quickly appeared to be foundering and did not succeed. In September 1538, at a delicate moment, Cromwell assured the German ambassadors that 'the king is agreed throughout with the substance of the confession' and that on remaining matters of disagreement 'it is very much to be hoped that he will allow himself to be led by the holy writ'.[354] Cromwell's assurance can on the face of it be read as evidence of his own religious beliefs and of his hopes of converting the king. But there are problems with that reading. In autumn 1538 Henry was increasingly anxious that the growing rapprochement between Charles V and Francis I might lead them to launch an invasion against him as a schismatic king. A military and diplomatic alliance with the German princes was more than ever a vital insurance. Yet Henry was fundamentally unwilling to accept that the price of such an alliance would be the introduction of the Lutheran reformation in England. To have made that plain from the start would, however, have risked undermining hopes of a political alliance. What better way for Henry to keep negotiations going, and to give Charles and Francis the impression that an Anglo-German alliance was seriously in the making, than for the king's leading councillor to encourage the German ambassadors to think that the king already largely agreed with them, and that he would soon do so fully? That was the deceptive message that Cromwell repeatedly gave them.

Such diplomatic reassurance was even more necessary in the autumn of 1539. The Six Articles had by then made it clear that Henry would not join the Lutheran reformation. Yet in September Cromwell told the ambassadors of the duke of Cleves how 'the thing was introduced by some bishops during his illness' but that 'up to now no execution has taken place, and he believes very strongly that because it has not at this time that the execution of the act will not proceed'. The king, Cromwell asserted, 'is not inclined with great grace to those who caused the legislation'.[355] Once more, such remarks have been taken as evidence of Cromwell's own religious convictions and of his disapproval of the legislation. But if the point of the act had been to declare the truth on contentious matters, and especially on those in contention between the king and the German ambassadors, as was argued above, then Cromwell's remarks can be read rather differently. Henry was anxious that the duke of Cleves should not see him as a persecutor of evangelicals, and for the Six Articles to be presented as the work of some bishops, rather than his own responsibility, would smooth the way for an alliance between them. Cromwell, as ever, was the king's messenger. When, a little later, Cromwell suggested that a political and military alliance should come first, to be followed by the working out of the religious differences, he was setting out the framework that Henry had consistently been working within in these years, a framework that would give Henry political and military support right away, while allowing him to delay, maybe indefinitely, over religion.[356]

If, instead, Henry had indeed, as Cromwell at times said he would, adopted the Lutheran confession of Augsburg, then Cromwell would no doubt have accepted it. Perhaps he would have done so with conviction; perhaps Cromwell's inner religious beliefs by the late 1530s were, like Cranmer's, more Lutheran than those of the king. Yet that is much harder to document in his case than has generally been supposed.

Cromwell and Anne of Cleves

In early 1540 Henry married again. His new bride was Anne, daughter of the duke of Cleves. But the marriage, as we shall see, was a disaster. What is at issue here is how far Henry's marriage was the work of Cromwell, and how far Cromwell's fall in June 1540 was the consequence of its failure. Factional historians see that failure as giving conservatives additional and powerful material to use against Cromwell; other historians tend to see Cromwell's fall as, in effect, his punishment for his role in persuading the king to marry Anne.

Neither view is at all persuasive. The Cleves match needs to be set in a broader perspective. As we have already seen, a German alliance was contemplated by Henry as early as 1528, as soon as Henry had decided to repudiate his marriage to Catherine of Aragon, and repeatedly explored during the 1530s. As early as 3 May 1530 Herman Ryngk, a Hanseatic merchant, wrote the king a memorandum suggesting a matrimonial alliance with the house of Cleves in particular.[357] In the context of the striking rapprochement between Charles V and Francis I in 1538 which created a sense of emergency at Henry VIII's court, it is not in the least surprising that Henry should have intensified his efforts to make some sort of German alliance. It does not, however, follow that 'the search for allies in Germany was part of *Cromwell's* [my emphasis] response, though it proved disastrous in his relations with his master'.[358] A renewed search for German allies was a perfectly obvious response that would have readily occurred to any king or diplomat. Henry himself later testified how he had welcomed the invitation that he should marry Anne of Cleves, 'trusting to have some assured friend by it; I much doubting that time both the emperor and France, and the bishop of Rome'.[359]

That phrasing shows that it is a mistake to see the Cleves marriage in terms of a protestant or evangelical alliance allegedly fostered by Cromwell.[360] The principal purpose of the earlier search for German allies had been to secure support for the king's break with Rome, not least political and military support against any action that Charles V and Francis I might take against him. That remained the case in 1538–40: it was above all his royal supremacy that Henry was defending. An alliance with Cleves had many attractions for Henry. As Herman Ryngk had pointed out, with perhaps a little exaggeration, the duke of Cleves possessed three powerful duchies, Cleves, Julich and Berg, and two earldoms, March and Ravensburg, which were so populous that, if England were in danger, he alone could raise an army to defend it. And the duke of Cleves had powerful connections. His eldest daughter, Maria, was married to John Frederick, son of Duke John of Saxony; and he was allied in various ways to the rulers of Hesse, Pomerania, Mecklenburg, Lüneburg, Prussia, Denmark and the Hanse towns. His younger sister was betrothed to the son of Duke Anthony of Lorraine, heir of the duke of Gueldres.[361]

Henry had always been quite clear throughout the 1530s that he would not accept the Lutheran confession of Augsburg: as we have seen, he was instead keen to receive a theological as well as a diplomatic embassy from Germany, since with regal confidence he hoped that he could persuade the Germans to modify their religious articles. In many ways the Cleves marriage alliance in 1539–40 should be seen in the context of Henry's continuing pursuit of his religious middle way. It is important here to note that the dukes of Cleves were neither Lutheran nor popish: 'they stood betwixt and between the new and the old, strongly under the influence of Erasmus, rather as did Henry himself', as Scarisbrick has put it.[362] This was not an 'alliance with a Lutheran state';[363] nor was it 'a fail-safe device to bring England and the League together if the Anglo-Schmalkaldic discussions ran into further difficulties'.[364] Duke John's church ordinance of 1533 had introduced in Cleves what James McConica called 'a completely Erasmian reform': reforms were introduced in consultation with Erasmus, but the writings of Luther were prohibited as heretical. Duke William, who succeeded his father, continued the reformist but anti-Lutheran line.[365] Henry, the French ambassador reported, 'par intercession du duc de Cleves et la sienne . . . espere faire adoulcir beaucoup de choses qu'on a innove en

Alemaigne, qui sont trop aigres et aspres pour trouver quelque honneste mediocrite de composer tant de troubles et differents' (through the duke of Cleves's and his own intercessions, he hopes to soften many of the new initiatives in Germany, which are too bitter and sharp, with the intention of finding some honourable middle way to resolve so many quarrels and differences).[366] True, the duke of Cleves's sister was married to the duke of Saxony, but that did not make the duke of Cleves himself a Lutheran; it rather offered scope for an oblique approach to an alliance with the German Lutheran princes.

It is worth pausing further to remark that at the same time there was a complementary scheme to marry Princess Mary to the catholic Duke Philip of Bavaria. Duke Philip visited Henry's court, arriving in December 1539:[367] he was reported to have kissed Mary and an agreement was expected by the French ambassador.[368] Cromwell was fully involved in these negotiations: a meeting took place in his house.[369] This was Henry's attempt to maintain a middle way in foreign relations, making alliances with both protestant and catholic rulers hostile to Charles V.[370]

That the Cleves alliance was not, as it is so often presented, an evangelical alliance emerges, interestingly, from the fact that it was not fully supported by some whom modern historians wish to claim as pursuing an evangelical strategy. Cranmer, if Thomas Wakefield's testimony given in July (and recorded only in Thomas Master's notes made for Lord Herbert of Cherbury) is accurate, may well have been unenthusiastic about it, saying 'that I thought it most expedient the king to marry where that he had his fantasy and love for that would be most comfort for his grace'. When Cromwell responded that there was none meet for him within his realm, Cranmer countered 'that it wold be very strange to be married with her that he could not talk withall'.[371]

If the Cleves alliance should be seen as essentially political and military, and if in so far as it had a religious dimension (for religion was not mentioned in the marriage treaty)[372] that involved the king's Erasmian middle way rather than any commitment to Lutheran reform, then, if Cromwell were its author, that would once again undermine the case for seeing him as a religious reformer pursuing an agenda more radical than the king's.

But is it so clear that the marriage was Cromwell's doing? The correspondence does not show that the Cleves alliance was Cromwell's idea. As early as June 1538 Chapuys reported that the king—he did not say Cromwell—had sent a painter to make portraits of members of the Cleves ruling family: the duke's son was supposed to be destined for

Princess Mary and a kinswoman for the king.[373] In July 1538 Castillon, the French ambassador, reported that the duke was making overtures for his son to marry Princess Mary.[374] In August 1538 Chapuys discussed the affairs of Cleves with Cromwell.[375] In November 1538 the king instructed Sir Thomas Wyatt, then with the emperor, to tell him, among other things, that Henry had considered marrying Mary to the young duke of Cleves.[376] In January 1539 Christopher Mont was instructed by the king to test the inclination of the dukes of Cleves, father and son, to the bishop of Rome, whether they were still of the old popish fashion, and whether they would be prepared to alter their opinions. Such instructions interestingly hint at Henry's religious preferences.[377]

Cromwell gave the diplomats further instructions. Mont was, when talking with Burchard, the duke of Saxony's vice-chancellor, to remind him of a conversation Cromwell had had with him when he was in England about a marriage between Princess Mary and the young duke of Cleves. Cromwell said that, on hearing that the duke of Saxony was keen to take the matter further, he had now suggested it to the king, who appeared, by the way he looked, to approve it. But Mont was to avoid having a picture of Mary sent, since that would be undignified, and Burchard had in any case seen her in England. Mont was further to enquire diligently about the beauty and qualities of the eldest of the two daughters of the duke of Cleves—her shape, stature and complexion—and if such reports were favourable, Mont was to tell Burchard that Cromwell would be glad to induce the king to join with them and make a cross marriage between the young duke of Cleves and Princess Mary. Cromwell's allusion to his powers of persuasion over the king should not be taken too literally: these were diplomatic negotiations, and in delicate matters such as marriages it was good for the dignity of the monarch if the initial overtures, which could easily be rebuffed or go wrong, came from a minister as if on his own initiative, rather than from the king, when they would appear as official policy: they could the more easily be repudiated or denied if circumstances changed.[378]

In March 1539 Edward Carne, Nicholas Wotton and Richard Berde were sent to the duke of Cleves to remind him of the old friendship between them, to offer him any suitable marriage in England and to hint that Henry might be prepared to marry within the duke's dominions. They were to have sight of the duke's eldest daughter, and hint strongly that if the conditions were reasonable and the king liked her, Henry would be glad to honour his house and family with matrimony.[379]

In the same month Cromwell reported to the king on letters received from Christopher Mont and Thomas Paynel (Peynell). The duke of Saxony had promised to advance the affair. A picture by Cranach was promised: the lady's beauty was greatly praised.[380] In May Wotton and Berde reported their discussions with the duke about the possibility of Henry's marrying Anne; they would be given portraits of both of the duke's younger sisters which had been made six months before by Holbein.[381] A little later instructions were prepared for William Petre, sent to Cleves to negotiate further, showing again just how seriously Henry was considering marrying one of the daughters of the duke.[382]

All this was in train in spring 1539 and continued after the passage of the Six Articles, often, but, as we have noted, wrongly, seen as representing a reversal of direction. In August Holbein's portraits were received. 'An excellent painter' that the king had sent to Germany to bring back 'un portraict au vif' (a lifelike portrait) of the duke of Cleves's sister had just returned to court, Marillac reported on 1 September.[383] Then the duke's ambassadors arrived to negotiate; the treaty was agreed in October 1539;[384] Anne would arrive in January 1540.

There is nothing to show that the match was anything but welcomed by Henry; he was fully involved in the negotiations, informing Marillac, the French ambassador, himself of their outcome in October 1539, affirming that Anne was the right age, healthy, elegant in stature and endowed with other natural graces.[385] And thus there is no reason to present the match as Cromwell's policy, rather than the king's.[386]

So much for the negotiations and preliminaries. Did, however, Cromwell force Henry to go through with the marriage itself, and did Henry then blame him, and ultimately destroy him for it? Is it the case that Henry proceeded 'against his will'? And is it fair to deduce

> after all theories about Cromwell's fall have been exhausted—faction, diplomacy and changing religious dynamics—[that] the central reason remains this story-book misjudgment of his king's 'fantasy'. . . . The Cleves embarrassment was the real reason . . . why Henry had listened to the farrago of half-truths and irrelevancies which made up the conservative charges against Cromwell.[387]

That is among the most recent renditions of what has often been claimed. But there is virtually no evidence to support it.

It is worth examining the circumstances of the marriage more closely. In June Henry wrote in his own hand a series of questions that were to be put to Cromwell. Cromwell was asked to confirm that the king's immediate reaction, as soon as he had seen Anne of Cleves, was one of repulsion, that he had hesitated to go through with the marriage and that matters were worse still once he had. Cromwell, testifying from prison in June, after he had been placed under arrest, not surprisingly confirmed all that the king asked him to.

What had happened? When Cromwell had asked Henry's opinion after the king had returned from Rochester where he had seen Anne for the first time, Henry lamented that she was 'nothing so well as she was spoken of', and that if he 'had known so much before, she should not have come hither'. A few days later he had said, 'say what they will, she is nothing fair', though allowing her to be 'well and seemly'—'but nothing else'. After the wedding, Cromwell asked the king if he liked her any better. Henry replied, 'nay, my lord, much worse', for 'by her breasts and belly she should be no maid; which when I felt them struck me so to the hart that I had neither will nor courage to prove the rest'. After that Henry had several times said to Cromwell 'how that his nature hath abhorred her ever sithens so far that if his grace would (which he never minded nor thinketh to do) go about to have a do with her, his highness verily thinketh that his nature would not consent thereto'.[388] Here Henry was seeking testimony from Cromwell to support his case that Anne and he were incompatible and that the marriage had not been consummated.

In a formal statement, Henry himself, writing in his own hand, declared that he had been glad of the match, having heard of Anne's 'excellent beauty and virtuous conditions'. But on first seeing her, 'I liked her so ill, and so far contrary to what she was praised, that I was woe that ever she came into England'. Above all, Henry asserted that he never consented to marry Anne for love, nor, 'if she brought maidenhead with her, had he taken it from her by carnal copulation'.[389]

A number of witnesses confirmed the king's reactions. The Fitzwilliam earl of Southampton said how sorry he had been to see the king, on sight of her, 'so to mislike the personage of the queen', and to see him 'so coldly to proceed to the execution of the solemnisation of the marriage according to the treaty'. He added that Cromwell had told him eight days after the marriage that the queen was 'than a maid for the king's highness, and that the king's highness had no affection to her, and misliked her body'; and that a little before Easter the king himself 'brake his mind frankly' and told him directly that he 'had not yet carnally known the queen' nor, given 'the disposition of her body', could he be 'provoked thereunto'. And the king had since shown him more.[390] Sir

Thomas Heneage deposed that 'as so often as his grace went to bed' to Anne, the 'looseness of her breasts' made him doubt her virginity. The king had, in Heneage's judgment, never consummated the marriage.[391] Sir Anthony Denny said much the same: Henry had told him, probably before Lent, that the queen 'had her breasts so slack, and other parts of body in such sort, that his highness somewhat suspected her virginity, and concluded that her body was of such indisposition to his, that he could never in her company be provoked and stirred to know her carnally'.[392] Dr Chamber testified how Henry said that he 'found her body in such sort disordered and indisposed to excite and provoke any lust in him; yea, rather ministering matter of loathsomeness unto the same, that his Majesty could not in any wise overcome that loathsomeness, ne in her company be provoked or stirred to that act'.[393] Dr Butts, the king's doctor, testified how Henry had told him the morning after the first night that he had not known the queen carnally; the second night he did not sleep with her; the third and fourth he did, but again confessed that he could not know her—and so it had been to the present day. Meanwhile, the king had had 'duas pollutiones nocturnas' (two wet dreams), he confessed to his doctor.[394] Dr Chamber testified that he did not think Henry had carnally known the queen. The king had told him as much after the first night, and on several other occasions. He had sought Dr Chamber's advice: Chamber had 'counselled his Majesty not to enforce himself, for eschewing such inconveniences as by debility ensuing in that case were to be feared'.[395] Sir Anthony Browne said he himself had never been more dismayed in all his life than when he looked upon Anne of Cleves. He noted how immediate the king's revulsion was, how the king said no more than twenty words to her, how he put off sending her the prepared presents but only sent them next day with a cold message,[396] and how sad and pensive he became: 'I see nothing in this woman as men report of her, and I marvel that wise men would make such report as they have done'—a remark that made Browne fear for his brother the earl of Southampton, who had written praising her. Browne's wife told him that 'she saw in the queen such fashion and manner of bringing up so gross and far discrepant from the king's highness's appetite, that in her judgment the king would never heartily love her'. On the evening before the marriage Browne heard the king say that 'he had a great yoke to enter into'; on the next morning he prepared himself 'so slackly' to go to the chapel to solemnise the marriage that he showed 'in his countenance, fashion and behaviour' that he was doing something to which he was not moved 'by his entire and hearty consent'.[397] The duke of Suffolk testified how, from the king's 'countenance, fashion and behaviour', he thought that he 'liked not the queen's person', and that he would have been glad not to have had to go ahead with the marriage.[398]

Whether Anne of Cleves was in fact attractive is hardly relevant. Warnicke tries to dismiss the evidence that Henry found Anne physically repellent. 'It does seem odd . . . that the king instantly found a lady so repugnant whom men from different social ranks had claimed was attractive.'[399] Hall, she points out, presented Anne as of 'so goodly a stature and so womanly a countenance'.[400] Marillac, the French ambassador, had, Warnicke says, on first seeing her, noted her 'beaulte moyenne'—her average beauty—not, perhaps, as ringing an endorsement as Warnicke supposes.[401] And Marillac went on to cite the judgment of several who saw her close up that she was neither as young nor of as great beauty as everyone had claimed; all that could be said was that her height, confident demeanour and vivacity 'supplye le surplus de beaulte qu'on pourroit desirer' (made up for the wished-for beauty).[402] Yet even if Anne had indeed been a great beauty, such are the vagaries of human desire that it remains entirely believable that Henry could not respond physically to her charms. It may well be that the king was unfair in thinking that Anne's slack breasts were proof that she was no virgin. The reports by the queen's ladies that Anne was sexually innocent do not tally with his assumption. Eleanor, countess of Rutland, Jane Lady Rochford and Catherine Edgcombe testified to Anne's sexual naivety: she said the 'king kissed her, and took her by the hand, and said goodnight, sweetheart, at night; and in the morning kissed her and bade her farewell, darling'. Is this not enough? she asked her ladies. Lady Rutland retorted, 'madam, there must be more than this, or it will be long before we have a duke of York, which all this realm most desireth'.[403] Warnicke thinks this all *ben trovato* as no interpreter is mentioned—words put in her mouth;[404] but since it reveals Anne as an inexperienced virgin, contrary to Henry's claims, it is hard to see it as a government-inspired invention. There is no reason why Anne should not have been both sexually innocent and, in Henry's eyes at least, physically unattractive.

Given that revulsion, why did Henry go through with the marriage? 'What remedy now [?]' he asked Cromwell, lamenting his predicament.[405] He did try to avoid it. He 'deliberated with [himself] that if it were possible to find means to break off, [he] would never enter yoke with her'. Southampton and Browne could confirm this. Cromwell could say what Henry then said to him.[406] Henry postponed the espousals by two days, and ordered Cromwell to call together Cranmer, Audley, Norfolk, Suffolk, Southampton and Tunstal to discuss the marriage with the duke of Cleves's ambassadors, and in particular to study the contracts of marriage previously made between the duke of Lorraine's son and Anne of Cleves, clearly in the hope of finding some legal impediment that might reasonably allow the postponement, and eventually the abandonment, of the marriage. But the duke's ambassadors could say no more than that these contracts had been made when they were minors, that they had never taken effect and that they had been revoked: and they promised to send secure confirmation that would put all out of doubt.[407]

If Henry was looking for an immediate technical excuse for not going ahead with the marriage, none could readily be found. 'Then is there no remedy, quod his majesty, but [that I must needs against my will] put my neck in the yoke.'[408] So, again, why did Henry proceed? Later Southampton would insinuate that Cromwell influenced the king: 'the ending of which controversies'—over the precontract—'the earl of Essex [Cromwell] repairing secretly unto the king, did procure; but what he said to the king' he 'cannot tell'. But since Southampton was here anxious to deflect responsibility from himself (he had much praised the queen in his letters from Calais) his testimony, in any case speculative, not eyewitness, should be treated with caution.[409] More credible is Cromwell's account, responding to Henry's questions—written in the king's own hand, revealing who was behind all this[410]—and therefore unlikely to be saying anything that the king would have known at once to be untrue. Cromwell echoed how Henry had explained:

If it were not that she is come so far into England [and that great preparations had been made] and for fear of making a ruffle in the world and driving her brother into the Emperor and the French king's hands, now being together, I would never have her, but now it is too far gone, wherefore I am sorry.[411]

More significantly still, Cromwell further recollected how Henry lamented that 'if it were not to satisfy the world and my realm, I would not do that I must do this day for none earthly thing'.[412] If Henry had negotiated the marriage alliance in the first place, and if he now went ahead with it, and had done, he claimed, as much to move the consent of his heart and mind as ever man did, it was quite simply because the marriage made, and continued to make, excellent diplomatic sense, and not because Cromwell—or any other of his councillors—was in any way manipulating him. Henry felt he had to go through with the marriage because of the diplomatic risks if he did not. As Sir Anthony Browne judged from the king's behaviour, 'if outward respects had not enforced him to that act' he would never have married her.[413] The timing is significant. January 1540 was a month of considerable anxiety for the English: Charles V and Francis were meeting together in France. That was not a moment at which Henry could afford to alienate the duke of Cleves and his friends, the German protestant princes. He knew that very well; he did not need Cromwell or anyone else to tell him.[414]

Did Henry blame Cromwell for his plight? There is no evidence that he did. In so far as he blamed anyone, it was those who had told him how attractive Anne of Cleves was—that is to say, those whom he had sent to Germany as diplomats. Thomas Heneage had heard the king say, both before and since the wedding, 'how that his Highness had been evil served of them that his grace had put in trust'.[415] Lord Russell testified how the king felt deceived by the praise she had received: 'Alas, whom should men trust? I promise you, saith he, I see no such thing in her as hath been showed me of her, and am ashamed, that men have so praised her as they have done, and I like her not.'[416] Sir Anthony Browne feared that his brother Southampton might be criticised for having written in her praise, as we have seen.[417] Southampton testified that Cromwell had berated him ('laid sore to his charge'), as soon it seems as he had brought Anne to court—for praising Anne so much in his letters from Calais: which, interestingly, does not suggest that Cromwell was set at all costs on the marriage. Southampton saw this rebuke as Cromwell 'declaring thereby his malicious purpose, how he intended to take occasion to do displeasure to the said earl, and to turn all the king's miscontentment upon the shoulders of the said earl of Southampton', which does hint at some rivalries, but suggests the tensions characteristic of the fearful servants of an angry despot, rather than factions competing to influence and manipulate the king. If Cromwell feared that the king might be angry with him, that does not prove that he was responsible for the Cleves marriage, only that he suspected that the king would look for a scapegoat to cloak his own responsibility. And Southampton had, in turn, every reason to present Cromwell in a bad light as a man of malice. But all this needs careful reading. It is just as possible that Cromwell was sincerely irritated that Southampton had not reported the truth about Anne of Cleves. But this illustrates the nature of Henry's rule: close servants did what they believed the king would commend them for having done, and told him what they believed he wanted to hear. If Southampton told him how attractive Anne of Cleves was, not how plain, that was not because Southampton was pushing for a German alliance: it was simply because he wanted to please his master. He readily admitted that he 'did by his letters much praise her': but he did that 'considering it was then no time to dispraise her' given that 'so many had by reports and paintings so much extolled' her. And by the time Southampton made his statement, Cromwell was in the Tower and could readily be accused of malice.[418]

On several later occasions, Henry lamented his fate to Cromwell: after Candlemas and before Shrovetide; after Easter and in Whitsun week, in his chamber at Greenwich; and many times since Whitsuntide. But there is nothing in Cromwell's declarations that shows that Henry was in any way blaming Cromwell for his predicament: far from that, he was clearly still willing to reveal his deepest emotions to him, 'many other times also since Whitsuntide'. If Henry had come to think that Cromwell had duped him or had manoeuvred him into an impossible situation, he would not have continued to see Cromwell as a trusty counsellor.[419] That the king did frequently talk to Cromwell about it all—as he himself wrote in his own hand, referring to his lack of will and power to consummate the marriage—does suggest that he did not hold him personally responsible for the débâcle.[420] But Cromwell was not the exclusive recipient of the king's secrets. Henry declared that he had expressed his doubts to Suffolk, Russell and Sir Anthony Browne at the beginning, as well as to Cromwell; and a little before Easter the king, Cromwell said, told Southampton that the marriage had not been consummated.[421]

Was Henry angry with Cromwell for having told Southampton eight days after the wedding that he had not consummated the marriage, as Southampton now revealed? Can Cromwell's fall be attributed to the king's blaming him for revealing his secrets, after Southampton informed against Cromwell? Was Southampton responding to Cromwell's attempt to deflect responsibility for the marriage away from himself? And did Henry turn so fiercely against his long-serving minister in consequence? It is an intriguing scenario.[422] But there is nothing to substantiate it—and Cromwell was under arrest well before Southampton's revelation in his deposition made on 7 July.[423] Southampton does not give the impression of believing that what he said was of any special importance, much less that it was damning to Cromwell. And his testimony that eight days after the marriage, Cromwell had told him that the queen was a maid would have been welcome corroboration for the king, not something unwelcome. Moreover, on 30 June, Cromwell wrote to the king from the Tower that Southampton could show him what Cromwell had said to him after Henry came from Rochester—presumably the king's remark that Anne was nothing so well as she was spoken of by those who had praised her, including, of course, Southampton.[424] If Cromwell was by then thinking that Southampton was not a friend, he would not have invoked his testimony.

A misleading variant of this interpretation is that offered by Warnicke: Cromwell's 'downfall was almost certainly the result of misunder-standings about his reaction to Henry's inability to consummate the marriage with Anne and of royal suspicions about the reasons for his violation of the privy chamber ordinance of secrecy'. For Warnicke, it was Cromwell's revelations to the earl of Rutland, the queen's cham-berlain, that the queen needed to order herself more pleasantly, that brought him down: 'it was his unauthorized discussion with Rutland about Henry's domestic crisis in late May that was the immediate cause of his downfall'.[425] But it is far from certain that it was in late May, rather than very much earlier, soon after the marriage, that Cromwell spoke to Rutland about the need for Anne to be more pleasant; and in any case it is only from Cromwell's self-defence that we know that he told Rutland.[426]

In that self-defence Cromwell responded to the accusation that he had revealed 'a matter of great secrecy'—most likely, the king's decision to divorce Anne—shown him by Henry within fourteen days of 12 June. But he was also accused of treason and of retaining. It is hard to see that the charge of revealing a great secret was in itself either an impor-tant charge, in the context of the others, or the trigger for Cromwell's arrest. Cromwell declared that the only person to whom he had shown the matter, and then, Cromwell insisted, 'by your grace's commandment' 'on Sunday last in the morning', was 'my lord Admiral'—Southampton. And Cromwell went on to recall how Henry 'had opened the matter first to me in your chamber and declared your lamentable fate declaring the things which your highness mislikes in the queen'. Here Cromwell was extending the 'matter' under consideration from Henry's decision (at the end of May or beginning of June) to end his marriage to cover his instant revulsion from Anne at their first meeting. Cromwell recalled that then (and from the king's testimony of what he had told Cromwell, that must have been as early as January) the king had urged Cromwell to speak to Anne of Cleves. Lacking the opportunity to do that, Cromwell said that he had spoken instead to her chamberlain, the earl of Rutland, 'desiring him . . . to find some mean that the queen might be induced to order your grace pleasantly in her behaviour towards you thinking thereby for [to] have had some faults amended to your majesty's comfort'. For having spoken to Rutland, Cromwell asked the king's mercy. But he insisted again that he had done this *before* the king told him about his 'secret matter'. Clearly, if Henry believed that

Cromwell had been discussing with Rutland how Anne might behave more pleasantly to him *after* he had told Cromwell that he was going to end the marriage, he would have had every reason to suspect the loyalty of his minister. Cromwell evidently feared that Henry was under such a misapprehension.[427] And that hints at a possible explanation of the timing of Cromwell's arrest. At the end of May or beginning of June Henry reached the decision (to which we shall return) that he would end his marriage to Anne of Cleves. He told Cromwell this. Within a few days, Henry came to suspect that Cromwell was still trying to save the marriage. That suspicion was almost certainly a misunderstanding. But, just as Henry had come to doubt Wolsey's commitment to his search for an annulment of his marriage to Catherine of Aragon in 1529, so in late spring 1540 he came to doubt a loyal servant to whom, right up to this point, he had confided his most intimate secrets.

But that is not to say that the king's suspicions were in any respect valid. Did Cromwell fall because he could not or would not free Henry from Anne? Can we agree that 'the minister was, of course, reluctant to find the king a convenient exit from his marriage'?[428] Was Elton correct to say that Cromwell 'could not get Henry clear of Anne of Cleves—and he could not do so because he would have handed power and influence to the Howards, his enemies . . . what destroyed him in 1540 was Catherine Howard rather than Henry Tudor'?[429]

It is difficult to find evidence that would support such a reading. There is nothing in the record to show that Henry was already seeking to marry Catherine Howard, though it is, of course, by no means impossible. However that may be, there is nothing to suggest that Cromwell was blocking a divorce. In response to the accusations against him, he wrote that he had spoken about the king's 'matter of great secrecy'— Henry's decision to repudiate Anne—only to Southampton, as Henry had commanded him: he found Southampton was

> as willing and glad to seek remedy for your comfort and consolation and saw by him that he did as much lament your highness state as ever did man and was wonderfully grieved to see your highness so troubled wishing greatly your comfort for the attaining whereof he said your honour saved he would spend the best blood in his body.

Cromwell added that 'if I would not do the like ye and willingly die for your comfort I would I were in hell and I would I should receive a thousand deaths'. Obviously Cromwell was defending himself here, and, unsurprisingly, he protested his loyalty to the king. But the extraordinary fulsomeness of his protestations rings true: it is all of a piece with his tireless service to his master.[430]

Thomas Wriothesley, Henry's principal secretary, testified to two conversations that he had with Cromwell on 6 or 7 June. Cromwell told Wriothesley that 'one thing resteth in my head, which troubleth me': 'the king, quoth he, liketh not the Queen, nor did ever like her from the beginning. Insomuch as I think assuredly she be yet as good a maid for him as she was when she came to England'. Wriothesley responded by urging Cromwell, 'for God's sake devise how his Grace may be relieved by one way or other'. But Cromwell had no answer: 'yea, how? quoth he'. The next day Wriothesley insisted: 'for God's sake devise for the relief of the King; for if he remain in this grief and trouble, we shall all one day smart for it. If his Grace be quiet, we shall have our parts with him'. And Wriothesley recorded Cromwell's response in his account: 'It is true, quoth he, but I tell you, it is a great matter.'[431] Wriothesley clearly thought—or hoped—that Cromwell might find some way out: yet it is worth noting how it would be the king's reactions that would be crucial in their own futures. Wriothesley was not, however, accusing Cromwell of somehow obstructing a resolution of the matter: he was rather warning him of the strength of the king's feelings. Nothing here would support any view of a Cromwell reluctant to bow to the king's wishes.[432] Nor can Wriothesley's *Chronicle* be believed when it says that Cromwell had kept Anne's precontract with the eldest son of the duke of Lorraine secret from the king, since that had been checked in January and earlier.[433] The notes by Thomas Master—'Item, that the earl of Essex (who made this mater) was sent [to] the tower because he would not consent to the divorce'—do not count as contemporary evidence that Cromwell had indeed opposed the divorce. There is, once again, nothing to support such an assertion. These manuscript notes continue, 'Item my Lord of Winchester procureth this divorce', endorsing an interpretation of Gardiner's role that we shall shortly question.[434]

Thus there is no reason to suppose, and no convincing evidence to show, that Cromwell was such an obstacle to Henry's divorce from Anne that his fall became an indispensable preliminary. It would not be legally difficult for the king to secure a divorce if, as he insisted, he had not consummated the marriage,[435] and if the queen agreed, as Anne would.[436] But that offers an explanation for Cromwell's inability to give Wriothesley an answer. Clearly it would not have been easy for a servant such as Cromwell to suggest to the king that he should make so humiliating an admission—that he had been unable to consummate his marriage—in public. Cromwell was embarrassed and uncertain; he was not opposed to the divorce.[437]

Nor does it persuade to see Cromwell as blocking the divorce because he feared that it would wreck the German alliance. As we have seen, he had not been the author of such a policy. More relevantly, Henry was very careful to preserve what he could of that alliance. He was anxious to get Anne's brother's approval lest 'all shall remain uncertain upon a woman's promise, that she will be no woman; the accomplishment whereof, on her behalf, is as difficile in the refraining of a woman's will, upon occasion, as in changing of her womanish nature, which is impossible':[438] Anne duly gave it on 21 July.[439] Anne of Cleves continued to live in England, saying that the king treated her 'as a most kind loving and friendly brother' would. She was assigned an annual income of 8,000 nobles and two manors, Bletchingley and Richmond.[440] She continued 'not in lamentation thought or pensiveness but with a good cheer and manner, devising daily the politique order of the estate she now hath and enjoyeth'.[441] Marillac later reported with distaste how 'she showed that she was as joyful now as she was then, wearing different clothes every day'—out of either prudence, or great simplicity.[442] Not only, then, did Anne not take offence, but the Cleves alliance in general continued after Cromwell's fall. Henry instructed Wallop, his ambassador in France, to insist to Francis I that 'we never minded upon the chance of the matter between us and the duke of Cleves sister, to abandon the said duke's friendship unless the cause thereof should rise in his side and party'; Henry would be 'right glad' to continue 'such a firm friendship'.[443] Draft speeches survive which were to be delivered to the duke of Cleves and his advisers offering friendship and treaties.[444]

The Fall of Thomas Cromwell

We must now, however, focus more closely on the fall of Thomas Cromwell in June 1540, which has long been among the most puzzling conundrums in Tudor political history. For several years the chief and dominant minister of Henry VIII, Cromwell reached the apparent apogee of his power when promoted to the earldom of Essex in April 1540. Just a few weeks later, in June, he was arrested and condemned for treason. Thus far, we have rejected suggestions that Cromwell was pursuing a radical religious policy independent of the king and expressed doubt that Cromwell fell because he was blamed for the failure of the Cleves marriage which he had allegedly masterminded. Why then did he fall, apparently so suddenly and spectacularly?

Here it will be argued that Cromwell fell because Henry wanted him to. We have just seen that Henry quite suddenly came to suspect Cromwell's loyalty, angrily supposing, quite mistakenly, that Cromwell was trying to maintain the marriage once the king had decided to repudiate it. But the king's actions had much deeper purposes. Henry brought him down, it will be shown, because the destruction of Cromwell, on the grounds of Cromwell's alleged religious radicalism, strengthened the king's negotiating position in diplomatic bargaining with the emperor and the king of France, and dramatically emphasised the precise nature of royal religious policy within his realm.

To offer such an explanation is, however, to fly in the face of a generation of historical consensus that Cromwell was a victim of competing cliques at court, who exploited his supposed sympathies for evangelical religion to undermine his standing with the allegedly conservative king. Many historians have adopted such an interpretative framework. 'No one has doubted'. Sir Geoffrey Elton claimed, 'that the machinations of Cromwell's enemies, with Norfolk and Gardiner at their head, were decisive in turning the king against his minister', by bringing false charges against him.[445]

A factional explanation of the fall of Cromwell is at once called into question by an examination of Norfolk's relations with him. Despite their alleged rivalry, the duke of Norfolk's relationship with Cromwell appears in the sources to have been remarkably warm. In August 1536 Norfolk made his will and left one part with Cromwell as his principal executor, at a time when Cromwell's son was hunting vigorously at the duke's residence at Kenninghall.[446] In September 1536 he offered Cromwell 'a million of thanks for your pains in my affairs'.[447] When serving in the north in the aftermath of the Pilgrimage of Grace, he placed his affairs under Cromwell's protection,[448] entrusting him with his will, sealed in a box, and asking him, should he die, to see it performed.[449] He could not, he said, recompense fully Cromwell's kindness in his absence. He would be his friend for life, 'groinge qui vouldray' (grudge who will).[450] Later that year he wrote to Cromwell of his fears that he had 'back' friends who wished him out of the world,[451] scarcely a remark that would be made to a factional rival. And Norfolk clearly valued Cromwell's intercession with the king—his letters show that if he feared anything in these years, it was not Cromwell's displeasure, but the king's. In November 1537 the two supposed factional rivals shared the proceeds of the surrenders of the monastery of Lewes and its dependent cell, Castle Acre, the first of the large houses to surrender.[452] So thin is the evidence of enmity between Norfolk and Cromwell that even Elton is compelled to write of the period 1534 to mid-1539 as one of '*ostensibly* [my italics] friendly relations', and refer to the '*pretended* [my italics] friendship' of the two men, a significant concession: the relationship was really, he implies, much more hostile than the evidence shows. That is a dangerously convenient way of arguing.[453] Moreover, Norfolk's high favour and the trust the king had in his diplomatic skills were dramatically illustrated when he was sent in February 1540 on a special mission to Francis I.[454] Norfolk had been entrusted with a task of the greatest importance and delicacy. There is nothing to suggest that Cromwell was marginalising the duke. There is little evidence, then, of any hostility between Norfolk and Cromwell, and little to suggest that Norfolk would have had any particular motivation for wishing to see Cromwell overthrown in 1540. Nor is there any clear evidence that Stephen Gardiner, bishop of Winchester, was an active enemy of Cromwell and an author of his fall, and even less that Norfolk and Gardiner were working together. Indeed, Norfolk was as critical of Gardiner's work as ambassador in France as of that of Gardiner's successor, Edmund Bonner, bishop of London. When in February 1540 he urged Henry to recall Bishop Bonner from France, he added that 'Bishops be no meet men for ambassadors here, for the bishop of Winchester [Gardiner] is little better favoured here than the other'.[455]

A factional interpretation of events rests on the claim that the 1530s saw bitter and continuing political rivalries, leading to increasing difficulties for Cromwell and culminating in his enemies' persuasion of the king that he was a dangerous radical who should be dismissed. The chronology of events rather undermines that view. There is simply very little evidence that Cromwell was in trouble until the moment of his arrest. That makes it tricky to argue that a series of mishaps combined to create the conditions in which he could be toppled. On this sort of account of politics, it would have been very neat if the move towards reform supposedly embodied by Cromwell had come to a halt in late 1538/early 1539 with the supposedly reactionary Six Articles, and if Cromwell had shortly afterwards lost his influence. Alternatively, it would have been almost as neat if Cromwell had been destroyed as soon as the king's marriage to Anne of Cleves (which he supposedly masterminded) turned out to be a great mistake. But Cromwell did not fall in the spring of 1539 or the winter of 1539–40: he was arrested in June 1540.

In addition, there is a good deal of evidence of Cromwell's continuing royal favour in 1539–40. Factional historians are thus forced into contortions, as they see Cromwell making comebacks from supposed declines, and contradiction, as they present Cromwell as simultaneously both weakened and as strong as ever. Selective reading of the despatches of Marillac, the French ambassador, can be used to develop the view that factional struggles were intensifying. But against Marillac there is plenty of evidence of Cromwell's continued unequivocal prominence and favour. Interestingly, in early April, Henry, in a postscript to a letter to his ambassador in France, Sir John Wallop, wrote that since the matters to be dealt with were overtures,

> we have not opened the hole of the same to all our council and therefore will that you shall either direct your answer to ourself, or to our right trusty and wellbeloved councillor the Lord Privy Seal; not participating the same to any others, till you shall know further of our pleasure

– showing unequivocally that Cromwell was still trusted by the king in early April and given an exclusive role among councillors.[456] Cromwell was still despatching business.[457] 'Cromwell's influence was as strong as ever two months before his fall', as even Elton recognises.[458] On 18 April 1540 Cromwell was created earl of Essex, an 'astonishing promotion'[459] and appointed great chamberlain.[460] On 10 April he had been granted St Osyth's priory, Essex.[461] On 24 April Marillac reported Cromwell's elevation to an earldom and that he was in as much credit with his master as ever he had been (though Marillac did qualify this striking formulation by saying also that he was near being shaken).[462] There is a typical list of memoranda, seemingly dating from April.[463] On 9 May Henry wrote to Cromwell asking him at once to come to him to treat great and weighty matters 'as whereupon doth consist the surety of our person, the preservation of our honour, and the tranquillity and quietness of you, and all other our loving and faithful subjects'.[464] In May 1540 Cromwell spoke in defence of the king's middle way in parliament: 'the fact that he made the speech indicates how far he was as yet from disgrace'.[465] There are surprisingly few surviving routine letters by Cromwell in these months, but there is one dated 4 June to Sir George Lawson about buildings at Berwick.[466] Cromwell was evidently involved in the interrogation of the arrested Bishop Sampson, sending William Petre, a councillor, and Dr Anthony Bellasis, his servant, to see him on 7 June.[467] Within fourteen days before 12 June (that is, on or after 30

May) the king, as we have seen, committed to Cromwell 'a matter of great secrecy', presumably his decision to repudiate the marriage.[468] Once again that shows how great Henry's trust in Cromwell still was.

But in late May/early June, Henry VIII, it is contended here, turned against his minister, and brought Cromwell down. Why? And why then? First, we have to consider the potential diplomatic advantages of Cromwell's fall. This must be set in the context of international relations in the immediately preceding years. The overriding diplomatic event that gave Henry great cause for concern was the rapprochement between the Emperor Charles V and Francis I, king of France. Henry could not, as we have seen, confidently dismiss the possibility that the two rulers would combine to attack him, not least with the pope's blessing for what could be presented as a crusade against an excommunicated schismatic king. Such international action could conceivably arouse sympathies within England. Thus Henry's chief concern was to reduce any such threats. An obvious stratagem was to seek diplomatic alliances elsewhere. That largely explains Henry's marriage to Anne of Cleves in early 1540. But it would be wrong, as we have seen, to regard Cromwell as the author of that marriage, and then to read the failure of that marriage as the primary cause of his downfall: it did not take the supposed genius of Cromwell to discover the merits of a German alliance, and Henry was fully involved and enthusiastic about the negotiations. But in one vital respect the failure of the Cleves marriage *was* crucial to the fall of Cromwell—and its timing. Henry VIII had gone through with the marriage because, as we have seen, of the diplomatic risks of not doing so. In January 1540 the Franco-imperial rapprochement still seemed menacing. But by June 1540 it looked less and less of a threat. The repudiation of Anne was unthinkable in January but plausible by June. And the fact of the repudiation of Anne, and the consequent possible loss of the German alliance, would create new diplomatic circumstances in which Henry would urgently need to strengthen his bargaining position.

When the Cleves match was in the making, Henry was very anxious about the Franco-Habsburg entente. In November 1539 Charles left Burgos to travel through France to the Low Countries,[469] news of which was given to Henry jointly by Marillac and the imperial ambassador: the king's councillors seemed especially astonished and anxious, though Henry himself struck Marillac as more confident and at ease.[470] Henry's ministers told Marillac that the meeting of Francis and the emperor raised fears that they were intending to agree upon war against the king;[471] in February Sir Ralph Sadler, in Scotland, spoke of recent rumours that the emperor, French king and bishop of Rome would invade England, and that James V was reported to have said that 'he would do against Henry VIII as the emperor or French king did';[472] in December and January, just when Anne of Cleves arrived in England and was married to Henry, Charles had travelled through France.[473] It all seemed rather threatening. Marillac noted how much the English feared the complete and sincere understanding between Francis and the emperor: nothing could be more troubling for them, for they assumed that it would work to their own disadvantage.[474] It appeared to them that Francis and Charles would take arms against them.[475] What the English most wanted, Marillac emphasised in March, was to survive the year without war and remain at peace with their neighbours.[476]

How would Henry meet these threats? First, by making preparations to resist any invasion of England. In January 1539 the king reviewed his navy; in March 1539 musters were held throughout the country. Most strikingly of all, Henry ordered an inspection of vulnerable points along the south coast and then embarked on a remarkably comprehensive programme of fortification. In March he visited Dover himself. Work was under way on forts in the Thames estuary, at East and West Cowes, in the Downs, at Sandgate, at Calshot, at Portland and at Weymouth. The fort at Pendennis, intended to protect Falmouth Haven, was begun in April 1540. And the king was directly involved, as references to men at East Cowes building 'according to the platt devised by the king' show.[477]

Secondly, he would meet any threat by strengthening his alliance with the duke of Cleves. The duke was in dispute with Charles V over Gelderland. What suited the English best was the continuation of a cold war between duke and emperor over that province. With that in mind, Marillac said, the English would offer financial support to the duke of Cleves in his dispute with Charles over Gelderland, in the hope of distracting him.[478] Armed conflict would risk involving them in costly additional subsidies to the duke and even in war with the emperor. But, as time went on, there were increasing suspicions—or increasingly suspicious interpretations—that the duke was going to make a deal with Charles V over Gelderland. As early as 12 March Marillac reported news that the duke greatly hoped to patch up his differences with the emperor, retaining Gelderland by marrying the duchess of Milan.[479] On 26 March Marillac reported how Cromwell had told him that an agreement between the emperor and the duke was assured.[480] On 24 April Marillac again reported an English demonstration of joy that the duke had resolved his differences with the emperor. That meant that the English would not need to give him financial support and so risk irritating the emperor.[481] Marillac confirmed reports of an agreement between the emperor and the duke of Cleves that the duke should marry the duchess of Milan, relieving English fears that their new ally might lead them into war.[482] But the joy and relief that Marillac reported must have been relative. Why should the English be joyous? Because of the danger that the Cleves alliance might have led them into a war with the emperor in support of Cleves's claims in Gelderland. But any understanding between Charles and the duke would, if too warm, deprive Henry of hopes of support should Charles turn against him. By early June Henry was becoming doubtful about the depth of the duke's commitment. He informed Wotton how when on 31 May he had given audience to the duke of Cleves's resident ambassador, thinking to have had explained to him the whole state of his master's affairs, he had found that the ambassador could not answer his concerns, especially over what was happening over Gelderland and the duke's marriage alliance with Milan. Did the fact that the ambassador was found to be rather ill-informed about his master's plans make Henry significantly question just how committed the duke of Cleves was to an English alliance? If the duke truly valued Henry's alliance, he would have ensured that his ambassador was fully briefed. Consequently Henry wanted Wotton to find out more.[483] (When Wotton did, Hoghestein and Olisleger, the duke's representatives, responded by saying that the duke rested at the same point as before on the overtures concerning Gelderland, but that his affection towards the duchess of Milan had cooled since she wanted Gelderland.) The increasing imperial sympathies of the duke appeared to mean that the benefits of continuing the Cleves marriage would be limited because the duke was likely to make a deal with Charles over Gelderland.

Thirdly, Henry would seek to win the promise of military support from the German protestant princes. Such hopes foundered, as they had before, on German insistence that any alliance had to be based on English acceptance of Lutheran doctrine. In mid-May the duke of Saxony sent Henry a printed pamphlet containing the articles which they had agreed upon in their assemblies and diets, asking him to adopt them. Not only was Henry most unlikely to agree to this, but it also provided evidence that his hopes for a military-defensive alliance, with no commitment on religion, were not realistic.[484]

Fourthly, Henry worked hard at maintaining his French alliance, not least by attempting to reinforce French doubts about the sincerity of

Habsburg promises. Henry made determined efforts to maintain friendship with Francis. In February the duke of Norfolk was sent by Henry on a special mission to Francis, 'his dearest brother and perpetual ally', to deal with a 'certain matter of very great weight and notable importance'. Henry wanted to open his heart to Francis frankly and to seek his advice and counsel. Henry thought that Emperor Charles would greatly benefit from his meeting with Francis, since it would deter the Turks from making a French alliance. Charles was also seeking to draw the Germans away from Francis. That would leave Francis with only Henry as an ally. And Charles was seeking to sow seeds of unkindness between these two, as shown in a conference Charles had recently had with Sir Thomas Wyatt.

This went back to Henry's meeting with Francis at Calais in 1532, when, in return for giving up the pension he received from the French, Henry was promised, if he joined in war in the Low Countries with the French king and if the war was successful, all the coastal towns of the Low Countries, and also of Brabant and Holland. Charles had now found out about this. Henry feared that one of Francis's counsellors had told him in order to win favour from Charles. And Henry feared that Charles had revealed his knowledge of it to Wyatt in order to stir up suspicion between Henry and Francis, as Henry would blame Francis for embarrassing him. Henry protested, however, that this attempt would fail. Charles was characteristically trying to win time. But when Wyatt had pressed him over Brancetour, an Englishman in the emperor's service suspected of treachery, Charles had said that he showed no ingratitude to Henry, since the superior could not show ingratitude to the inferior. Charles was, Henry deduced, seeking to bring Christendom into a single monarchy.

The instructions Henry gave Norfolk show how he was trying hard to sow seeds of suspicion between Francis and Charles, notably by raising doubts over Charles's intentions over Milan, and to show the French king that a renewed English alliance would be beneficial. If Francis continued 'in good mind and affection towards the King's Highness', then Norfolk was to suggest that if a new straight amity were made between Francis and Henry, Henry would be willing to remit half the debt that Francis owed him and half the pensions for the rest of Francis's life. Moreover, Norfolk should ask Francis to note the amity between Henry and the duke of Cleves, and 'a like in very great towardness' between Henry and Duke John Frederick, Landgrave Philip, the duke of Bavaria, the marquis of Brandenburg, the counts palatine, 'not in causa religionis, but for aid and defence the one of the other in case of invasion'; it would be expedient if Francis joined in. It would be hard for the emperor to break such an enmity. Norfolk was to sound out Francis and report accordingly.[485]

Norfolk duly did so, warning Francis against Charles's ambitions[486] and remarking (to Cromwell) that if the French intended to make war against England he, Norfolk, was the most abused man living.[487] Henry did his best to further any French suspicions of Charles, and instructed Norfolk to tell Francis that if he allied himself with Henry, that would compel Charles to offer Francis what he sought over Milan and probably Flanders too. Francis was to be urged to join Henry, the dukes of Cleves and Saxony, and the other German princes.[488] In early May the king told Marillac how doubtful he was that Charles would exchange Flanders for Milan. Henry's ministers then amplified his concerns. Cromwell stressed Henry's singular affection for Francis and admitted that in the past he and others had been more imperialist than French; but now that they had learned of the emperor's ambitions, despite all his fine words, to make himself monarch of all Christendom, their eyes had been opened. The next day the duke of Norfolk asked Marillac to test him to see that he was now as French as he had once been Burgundian. Suffolk and Southampton said the same. But it would be wrong to read this as a decisive pro-French shift in English policy. As Marillac noted, Suffolk and Southampton claimed that they were being practised upon—'ilz estoient practiquez'—to make a close league with the emperor but they were standing firm against it. The English wanted to give the French the impression that their overtures were born of diplomatic strength, not weakness. But their efforts were spoilt when Marillac learned from the imperial ambassador that the English had complained over the trivial point that Charles had not solemnly celebrated St George's day and worn the order of England: that hardly suggested to Marillac that the emperor was wooing the English.[489]

Whenever there were signs that the friendship between Francis and the emperor was cooling, the English were pleased. And in these months they had increasing grounds for optimism. Not surprisingly, when in late January Charles left France, Marillac reported much joy at the news of Charles's departure;[490] when in March Marillac noted reports that Francis's journey to Flanders to meet Charles was delayed, indeed half-abandoned, he commented that this led the English to think that matters at issue between the two rulers would not be settled as soon as had been suggested.[491] In March Marillac could also report that the English had stopped making preparations for war: confidence was growing, and trade between England and Flanders had revived.[492] In April Marillac reported how the English were marvelling at the deferring of Montmorency's journey to the emperor—he had insisted that the friendship between the emperor and Francis was as good as it could be.[493] On 24 April he reported rumours that relations between the king of France and the emperor had grown chilly again, so much so that war between them seemed more likely than continuation of their recent strong friendship.[494] Francis was at pains to deny this.[495]

The diplomatic context was changing. In January 1540 Henry felt highly vulnerable; Francis and Charles were together; a joint invasion was not beyond the bounds of possibility; the Cleves marriage was a most useful counterweight at that time. But by June 1540 the duke of Cleves was proving an elusive ally; the German protestants were demanding religious concessions as the price of support; and above all relations between Francis and Charles were cooling, with Francis seemingly well disposed towards Henry. In January Henry, as he himself recognised, had no choice but to go through with his marriage to Anne of Cleves.[496] By June it was thinkable that he might repudiate it. What would he lose? The friendship of the duke of Cleves and the loss of German support might be the price—but neither the duke nor the German princes had fulfilled English hopes, and in any case it was not impossible that the Cleves alliance might survive the divorce, as the needs of international power politics might yet persuade the duke of Cleves and the German princes to overlook the insult to a German princess. It was a risk that could be taken, since Francis and Charles were now not so warmly agreed, and it was thus unlikely that they would make common cause against Henry. By June their growing rift made it thinkable that he might even be able to strike a deal with one of them. It was imperative therefore to put himself in the best position to do so as opportunity served. And here the dismissal of Cromwell could, as we shall see, prove useful.

How would Cromwell's fall assist Henry's diplomacy? It might well encourage Francis to treat with Henry. What is intriguing is the possibility that when Norfolk came on embassy in February, Francis told him that the price of an Anglo-French alliance was the removal of Cromwell. Elton noticed this, though without taking it very far: 'it is probable that Norfolk received much encouragement and may even have brought back a promise of French amity if only Cromwell were removed'.[497] The evidence lies in Francis's later reaction to the fall of Cromwell, 'nouvelle qui m'a este non seullement aggreable . . . j'en ay loue et rendu graces a Dieu' (news that was not just agreeable to me . . . I praised and gave thanks to God). Francis, interestingly, had criticised Cromwell. On hearing of his arrest in June, he expressed his satisfaction to Wallop, the English ambassador, recalling his conversation about Cromwell with the duke of Norfolk earlier that year.[498] Francis instructed his ambassador to say how Henry had great cause to thank God for having let him know 'des faultes et malversations' of Cromwell, 'qui seul a este cause de tous les suspections et malveillances qu'il a concues non seullement contre ses amys, mais contre ses plus privez, loyaulx et meilleurs serviteurs' (the faults and offences of Cromwell who alone had been the cause of the suspicions and ill-feelings which he bore not only towards his friends but also against his most private, loyal and best servants). And Henry would learn, 'apres avoir oste d'aupres de luy ung si meschant et mal-heureux instrument, combien de repoz, paix et tranquillite il mettra en son royaulme, au comun bien de l'eglise, des princes, des nobles et generalement de tout le peuple d'angleterre' (after having put aside so naughty and ill-fated an instrument, how much rest, peace and tran-quillity he would bring in his kingdom, for the common weal of the church, the nobility and generally all the people of England).[499] Marillac, presenting to Henry Francis's letters about Cromwell on 22 June, spoke of the harm Cromwell had done, and the expediency of removing him before he had completed his unhappy designs.[500] Francis, so Henry's ambassador, Wallop, reported, was very glad that so high a treason had been discovered, a very miracle of God. Francis had had more hope of Henry in the past fifteen days than he had had in a long time. And Wallop confirmed that there was much rejoicing at the French court when he told them that Cromwell was as good as dead.[501] Francis clearly saw Cromwell as symbolising, or arguing for, the king's more radical policies and for an imperial preference. Francis was keen to see Cromwell go, because it would point to pro-French, conservative reli-gious policies.

Why did Francis see Cromwell as a personal enemy? What is reveal-ing is how aware Henry was of Francis's attitudes, and how he fed them. It is interesting to note how quickly Henry sent a gentleman courtier to Marillac—who was writing to his king an hour after Cromwell's arrest—to explain what had happened: he told Marillac how Cromwell had always resisted the king's desire to 'establir le faict de la religion' (consolidate the religious settlement) and favoured instead those doctors who preached the erroneous doctrines, implying that policy would be different in future—a conclusion that Marillac boldly drew.[502] The con-sequence of all this, Marillac suggested, was that 'ilz changent entire-ment de cours et mesmement touchant ce qui avoit este innove en la religion, dont ledit Cramwel avoit este le principal aucteur' (they are completely changing direction, even with regard to religious innovation, of which the said Cromwell had been the main author).[503] In short, Henry wished to present Cromwell as a religious extremist, attached to German Lutherans, prepared to lead the king to the new doctrines. It suited him to present Cromwell in this way to the French in order to strengthen his conservative credentials in their eyes. We should be wary about swallowing it whole, however, even if Francis, perhaps influenced by the reporting of his ambassador, appears to have done so. Since his arrival in England in 1538, Marillac had been somewhat colourfully presenting politics in factional terms. Francis's Cromwell may well have been a reflection of Marillac's gossip. And what Marillac wrote may well in turn have reflected what Henry, a king well versed in deflecting responsibility for potentially unpopular policies on to his ministers, wished him to think, even though it was far from the truth.

Just as Cromwell was, somewhat unfairly, seen as a religious extremist, so he was also seen by many as an imperialist. That perception went back to the period after the death of Catherine of Aragon in January 1536 freed Charles V from his responsibilities to her and allowed the possibility of a renewed Anglo-imperial alliance. It was Cromwell whom the king used as his principal negotiator with Charles's ambassador, Chapuys, and Cromwell's characteristic vigour then made it look as if he was pursuing a pro-imperial policy of his own, even though the truth is that here, as elsewhere, he was doing nothing that his master had not first sanctioned. In May 1540 Cromwell even tried to turn this reputation to advantage when bargaining with the French ambassador.[504] When Cromwell fell, Norfolk told Marillac that the imperial ambassador would no longer have Cromwell to support him in the follies he had formerly attempted.[505] Of course, Cromwell would not be publicly condemned for his supposed imperial preferences because Henry would wish to keep open his options for an imperial alliance: this would be something that could instead be said quietly to Marillac.[506] But bringing the supposedly pro-imperial Cromwell down at the same time as the repudiation of Anne of Cleves could be useful in making Francis realise that the end of the Cleves marriage, though in a sense it weakened an anti-imperial alliance, was not necessarily the precursor of a pro-imperial policy.

And it is worth stressing a paradox: if the fall of Cromwell made Francis more sympathetic to Henry, it was also intended to enhance Henry's standing with Charles. It is striking to read how Richard Pate, Henry's ambassador with Charles, justified the fall:

all the while Thomas Cromwell lived, there were such slanders and obloquies of our realm, as might be to a true Englishman hearing the same, a great grief, some pronouncing that the blessed sacrament of the altar was utterly abolished with us, some affirming that we neither observed holy days, nor regarded saints, as we had none of their images standing within our churches; and some said that we no more fasted then dogs, the lent abrogated, so that all piety and religion, having no place, was banished out of England.

Such was the reputation that Henry now wished to remove.[507] Such a justification hinted to the emperor that Henry would not make any firmer alliance with the German protestant princes and would not adopt the Lutheran reformation. Such a ruler was clearly not one to be denounced or assailed in war as a schismatic heretic.

For both Francis and Charles, Cromwell symbolised the religious radicalism of England in the 1530s; for Francis, Cromwell also represented the pro-imperial strand in English diplomacy. Of course, those perceptions were mistaken, as has been argued above, and consequently very unfair. What they show is how effectively Henry had his policies enforced by his minister, while avoiding taking direct responsibility for them himself. We have seen the depths of the king's hostility to the monasteries—but ever since it has been Cromwell who has been credited with the dissolution. Of course, it would have been perfectly possible for Henry to have kept Cromwell on in 1540, and beyond, while negotiating with Francis and Charles. Yet if Henry destroyed Cromwell on the grounds of religious radicalism, and made dramatic and public condemnations of it, he was creating significant new diplomatic opportunities for himself. Francis, who had seemingly taken against Cromwell, would undoubtedly be the more willing to make an alliance. Similarly, Charles would be the more prepared to ally with Henry if he were persuaded that Henry was rejecting religious radicalism. Henry did not destroy Cromwell in order to make an alliance with Francis—or with the emperor—but to improve his diplomatic bargaining position, an aim well in keeping with his habitual practice of keeping his diplomatic options open. As Marillac put it in September 1539, 'ce roy, pour establir la seurete de ses estatz, cherche faire amitye avec tous ceulx qu'il luy est possible' (this king, to establish the security of his realm, seeks friendship with all he can);[508] 'ce roy qui ne cherche pour l'heure que faire alliances la ou il peult pour establir la seurete de ses estatz' (this king at present is only seeking to make alliances wherever he can in order to establish the security of his realm).[509] The timing of the fall of Cromwell can thus be linked to the king's perceptions of the growing rift between Francis and Charles and of the limited utility of a Cleves alliance. It was a purely pragmatic calculation by the king of the diplomatic advantages of now dispensing with a servant too closely, though in many respects unfairly, identified with religious radicalism.

The Fall of Cromwell and the Defence of the Middle Way

The fall of Cromwell, denounced as a religious radical, in June 1540 served admirably to defend the king's religious middle way at home, following the dissolution of the monasteries—a huge administrative task that had just been completed in May. Cromwell's identification as a religious radical was unjust: whether he was even an evangelical is, as we have seen, questionable. In much the same way as Wolsey was seen as responsible for the heavy taxation of the early 1520s, which was manifestly required to finance the aggressive foreign policy of the king, so Cromwell as the king's vicegerent in spirituals was seen as the architect of religious change. Chief executive of the dissolution of the monasteries and dismantling of the shrines in the late 1530s, Cromwell was, as we have seen, vulnerable to the charge of being a heretic: as early as 1536 the Pilgrims of Grace had thus labelled him. Clearly from the point of view of a traditional catholic, religious policy in the 1530s was indeed radical; but seen from Zurich or even Wittenberg it would have seemed as still somewhat frustratingly conservative, and such a formulation understates the anger, even the disgust, that those committed to reform would have felt at a regime that justified its policies in the language of religious reformation without adopting it. Moreover, if, as I have argued, religious policy was in origin the king's, not Cromwell's, and if Cromwell acquired his reputation as a heretic (for fearful or hostile contemporaries) or as a religious radical (among more or less sympathetic modern historians) simply because he was the man who was vigorously implementing the king's policy, then he was unjustly labelled, since he was doing no more than following royal policy. That Cromwell was blamed by those who were opposed to the king's reformation reflected Henry's supreme skill as a political operator, standing aloof from the detailed implementation of a policy he himself devised, shrewdly maintaining his 'deniability', allowing his ministers to take, and to deflect from himself, any criticism and blame. In the 1520s the king's ministers would attempt to raise the Amicable Grant, a huge financial demand;

but Henry, when it went wrong, would claim never to have known of it, and Wolsey remained indelibly associated with it. Wolsey was very much the king's cardinal, in Peter Gwyn's phrase, using his extensive papal legatine powers in the king's interests and following the king's wishes; but the public perception was that he was acting in his own and the pope's interests, which offered superficial grounds for what were actually spurious and unjust charges under the *praemunire* statute. Cromwell was no more and no less guilty of heresy than Wolsey had been guilty of fiscal rapacity when attempting to raise money, or of *praemunire* when reforming the church with the king's support in the 1520s. Henry would skilfully remain, on the face of it, distanced from what was being done; at times deliberately projecting an image of his weakness and manipulability that has taken in many since. After Cromwell's fall, Henry appeared to express regret, and imply that the responsibility lay elsewhere. Marillac wrote how some told him that the king had all but reproached them for the death of Cromwell on false accusations, on which he had sent to his death 'le plus fidelle serviteur qu'il eust oncques' (the most faithful servant he ever had).[510] But we should not be deceived. Of course Henry would blame the fall of Cromwell on those he now claimed had persuaded him—this was a king skilled at deflecting responsibility.

In fact, it was Henry who brought Cromwell down. By doing so on the grounds that he was a dangerous religious radical, Henry would emphasise his own reputation as a moderate and balanced ruler. The fall of Cromwell would dramatically show once again that the king was not going to adopt a fully fledged Lutheran or evangelical reformation. But the timing was significant. The dissolution of the monasteries and dismantling of the shrines was now complete, a *fait accompli*. That had been a radical religious policy if ever there was one. It was not to be reversed. Yet in denouncing Cromwell as a religious radical and announcing the limits to religious reform, what had been revolutionary measures were in effect represented and ratified as essentially moderate and balanced reforms of abuses. Of course, it would have been entirely possible for Henry to have kept Cromwell, to get him to continue to defend the middle way, as he did in parliament in May 1540. But another option for the king, always there, however unfair, was to destroy him, blaming him for alleged radical excesses. What may have prompted Henry to move in that direction was the angry religious controversy sparked off by the reformer Robert Barnes. Barnes's defiance may well have helped push Henry to the view that the destruction of Cromwell was necessary if his middle way was to be maintained.[511]

Barnes was not an obscure preacher but rather a theologian who had regularly served Henry on diplomatic missions to the German protestant princes in the 1530s. In March 1540 he was involved in a bitter public quarrel with Stephen Gardiner, bishop of Winchester, responding fiercely to a sermon Gardiner preached, denouncing him personally and all but challenging him to a fight. That was an extraordinary, extravagant and unacceptable reaction. Henry responded angrily, ordering both Gardiner and Barnes to defend themselves before king and council.[512] After some days of debate, Barnes then recanted, saying that in writing and in preaching he had overshot himself. He agreed 'with my heart to advance and set forth the said [Six] Articles', which he acknowledged 'to be most catholic and proper and necessary to be received observed and followed of all good christian people'. He then declared that

> though it so be that Christ by the will of his father the only which hath suffered passion and death for redemption of all such as will and shall come unto him by perfect faith and baptism; and that also he hath taken upon him gratis the burden of all their sins which as afore will hath or shall come to him paying sufficient remission for all their sins and so is become their only redeemer and justifier (of the which number I trust and doubt not but that many of us nowadays be of)

nonetheless if we did not follow God's commandments and laws 'we do lose the benefits and fruition of the same'. He then confessed that God was in no wise author or causer of sin; that whenever he offended his neighbour, he had first to reconcile himself before getting remission of his sins; he confessed 'that good works limited by scripture and done by a penitent and true reconciled christian man be profitable and allowable unto him as allowed of God for his benefit and helping to his salvation'; that laws and ordinances made by Christian rulers ought to be obeyed by subjects not only from fear but from conscience 'for who so breakith them breakith God's commandments'.[513] What Barnes now acknowledged was essentially the king's position on justification: a rejection of full-blown Lutheranism, and concern that good works were essential. Barnes had made a remarkable climb-down, largely at the king's insistence.

Barnes was not the only radical theologian to cause controversy at this time. William Jerome preached at Paul's Cross on 7 March. He denied that magistrates had the power to make that which was indifferent not indifferent—Gardiner commented that this 'maketh obedience to princes an outward behaviour only'—and taught that justification was unconditional: 'the promise of justification is without condition, for he that putteth a condition unto it doth exclude gratis doth exclude freely. So when we fall from that grace again we obtain remission of sins without works also which he called the second birth.' Gardiner commented that this 'engendrith such an assured presumption and wantonness that we care not greatly whither we obey God or no'.[514] That the king was very much involved in responding to these events appears in several details: Henry had Jerome brought before him, heard him and forgave him. Jerome recanted and agreed to make a full and open refusal of these pestilent doctrines where and when the king commanded him.[515]

All would depend on how Barnes and Jerome now conducted themselves. Barnes declared his recantation in a sermon at St Mary's, Spital, crying out and asking Gardiner's forgiveness. Then 'after the prayer', Barnes 'plainly and directly preacheth the contrary of that he had recanted', so evidently that the mayor himself asked if he should detain him for his contemptuous behaviour. Barnes declared his belief in the sufficiency of the passion of Christ, the 'only redeemer and justifier'.[516] Such defiance at the very moment at which he had agreed publicly to demonstrate his adherence to the king's reformation was bound to provoke Henry: Barnes was sent to the Tower.[517] Convicted of heresy, at the stake he reiterated his beliefs on justification. Christ's 'death and passion was the sufficient ransom for the sin of all the world'; 'there is none other satisfaction unto the Father, but this his death and passion only'. He asserted that 'I trust in no good work that ever I did, but only in the death of Christ', though denying that he spoke against good works, 'for they are to be done' and those that did not do them 'shall never come into the kingdom of God. We must do them, because they are commanded us of God, to show and set forth our profession, not to deserve or merit; for that is only the death of Christ.'[518] Similarly, in his recantation, Jerome continued to uphold predestination. While much that he said would have been acceptable to the king, especially Jerome's acknowledgment of the necessity of penance, contrition, attrition and renovation in salvation, a traditionally orthodox formulation, he added at the very end the subversive admission

that he was compelled to deny himself, yet was he not the first that so had done; for to deny himself is no more, but when adversity shall come, as loss of goods, infamies, and other like troubles, then to deny his own will and call upon the lord saying fiat voluntas tua,

and compared himself with Abraham and Job, 'wishing that some men nowadays would learn to do the same'.[519] As a sympathiser noted, 'how gaily they had all handled the mater, both to satisfy the recantation and also in the same sermons to utter out the truth, that it might spread without let of the world', came to light. Not surprisingly, both Barnes and Jerome were apprehended and sent to the Tower by the privy council. At the stake Jerome would demand that 'all christians put no trust nor confidence in their works, but in the blood of Christ'.[520]

In what ways, if any, did the troubles of Barnes and Jerome contribute to the fall of Thomas Cromwell? What angered the king was first Barnes's provocative and publicity-seeking preaching, and then his apparent subversion of the recantation he had personally promised the king. Henry must have felt outraged that what he would have seen as his merciful intervention to pacify the quarrel between Barnes and Gardiner had been spurned and in effect mocked. Henry deplored Barnes's religious beliefs; he clearly feared that a battle of the pulpits would lead to trouble; but it was Barnes's implied personal challenge to royal authority, not his supposed involvement in any popular sedition, that made his arrest inevitable. And it is hard to see Barnes as acting as anyone's pawn, which sharply qualifies any factional interpretation of these events. He was not acting at Cromwell's instigation: Cromwell may well have been dismayed at what happened. True, when he fell, he was accused of approving Barnes's preaching and teaching of 'lewd learning against your highness', affirming it to be 'good',[521] and of having threatened to fight the king in the field over Barnes.[522] But we do not need to believe the act of attainder. Nor is it likely that Gardiner, as Foxe hints, deliberately provoked Barnes in the hope of getting him to discredit himself: so risky and unpredictable a strategy is hardly plausible. Barnes need not have responded at all—Gardiner could not have been sure in advance how he would react. Indeed, at first the king, while reprimanding Barnes, was prepared to be merciful, and if Barnes (followed by Jerome) had held to his recantation, Gardiner would not have achieved much. And this line of argument rather assumes that for Gardiner to attack Barnes was to attack Cromwell.

If then Barnes's quarrel did not directly lead to the fall of Cromwell, nonetheless there is a looser sense in which it contributed to a climate in which the destruction of Cromwell as a religious radical made ghastly political sense. Barnes's preaching, and especially his defiance, deepened the king's fears of religious radicalism. Consequently it became more and more important to reiterate Henry's commitment to a middle way. Destroying Cromwell—as a religious radical, a sacramentarian, and thus even more dangerous than Barnes and Jerome—would serve to make the point very firmly. The council's letter informing Wallop in France of the reasons for Cromwell's arrest is revealing:

> where the king's majesty hath of long season travailed, and yet most godly travaileth, to establish such an order in matters of religion, as, neither declining on the right hand nor on the left hand, God's glory might be advanced, and the temerity of such as wold either refuse or obscure the truth of His word refrained, stayed, and, in cases of their obstinacy, duly corrected and punished,

Cromwell had 'wrought clean contrary to this His Grace's most godly intent, secretly and indirectly advancing the one of the extremes, and leaving the mean indifferent true and virtuous way, which His Majesty sought and so entirely desired'.[523] But Henry knew well enough that Cromwell was no sacramentarian.[524] If such charges were invented to suit the king's political needs, then once more all this makes Henry seem a monster, an egotistical tyrant, ruthlessly playing with the life of someone who had spent himself in his service. But that this is horrible does not, alas, make it untrue. And in 1540 Cromwell was not the only man executed because it advanced the king's religious policies.

The remarkable parallel executions of three religious radicals and three papists was designed to make a dramatic, vivid, public point: namely, that official religious policy was the maintenance of the king's middle way. When Cromwell was executed at the end of July 1540, at much the same time Barnes, Jerome and Thomas Garrett were burnt as heretics and three conservatives, Richard Featherstone, sometime tutor to Princess Mary, Edward Powell and Thomas Abel, were hanged as traitors for having in the past spoken in favour of the pope. Powell had preached in Bristol in 1533 and then in Salisbury against the king's marriage to Anne Boleyn. He was put in Dorchester gaol in 1534 and complained of the severity of his treatment there. In June 1534 he was committed to the Tower.[525] Richard Featherstone, Mary's schoolmaster for eight years (c. 1525–c. 1532) at least, was still able to see the princess and Mary was able to pass on through him to Chapuys the king's threat that she would lose her life for refusing to subscribe to the act of succession. In December 1534 Featherstone was committed to the Tower for himself refusing to swear the oath.[526] Featherstone and Abel (and presumably Powell) refused to take the oath demanded in 1535 and remained in the Tower. Nicholas Wilson was imprisoned for refusing the royal supremacy but was released in 1537 after submitting. In spring 1536 Chapuys reported how the king, having gone back on what had seemed to be a decision to introduce radical religious change, nonetheless made it clear that he had not changed his anti-papal policy by ordering offensive sermons against the pope; it was also being rumoured that he had determined to execute three doctors, Featherstone, Abel and Wilson. Nothing came of it at that time, but the king's evident willingness to use their lives to lend substance to public perceptions of his religious policy is striking, foreshadows what was to happen in 1540 and offers an important clue in understanding events.[527] The destruction of Featherstone, Powell and Abel in 1540 makes it hard to see the fall of Cromwell as the work of some conservative faction, since conservatives were simultaneously in trouble. As Marillac put it, 'certainement le spectacle fut merveilleux de veoir mourir en mesme jour et heure ceulx qui adheroient aux deux partys contraires' (surely it was an extraordinary sight to see die on the same day and hour those who belonged to the two opposing parties).[528] As Foxe was to write, 'which spectacle so happening upon one day, in two so contrary parts or factions', confused the ignorant and simple people, 'seeing two contrary parts so to suffer, the one for popery, the other against popery, both at one time'.[529]

Influentially, Foxe saw this as reflecting 'a certain division and discord among the king's council, who were so divided among themselves in equal parts, that the one half seemed to hold with the one religion, the other half with the contrary'.[530] Modern historians have tended to follow Foxe's confusions, and so miss the true significance of these events. They suggest that the execution of the radicals would lend weight to the charges against Cromwell, and go on from that to speculate that the destruction of the conservatives was part of the conspiracy. 'Maybe the martyrdom of the three Catholic priests was also, somehow, part of the plot against Cromwell—an attempt to confuse the issue, to placate, to intimidate.'[531] This is endorsed by Elton: 'the catholics probably suffered to announce the Henrician loyalties of the triumphant faction who were anxious to avoid any hint of links with the defunct treasons organized by Chapuys'.[532] Brigden follows Foxe: 'rather than an exhibition of Henry's scrupulous equity, as a Tudor Justinian, their hanging, drawing, and quartering as traitors alongside the burning heretics was part of the coup against Cromwell; a cynical sacrifice, Winchester's device "to colour his own tyranny", to confuse the issue and silence the murmurings of the people'.[533] That does seem highly improbable—and it would be extraordinary if a catholic group sacrificed some of their own men for such a purpose.[534] It would not resolve the matter to postulate a division between papists and Henrician conservatives, since that would undermine the straightforward division between conservatives and reformers that usually serves as an organising principle of factional histories of politics in these years. And in any case the division between papists and conservatives was not so great. If the conservatives had genuinely triumphed in 1540, it is hard to see that they would have destroyed papists: indeed, the conservative Gardiner may well have been something of a crypto-papist himself. It is much more plausible that the parallel executions of papists and radicals rather show the leading role of the king and reflect his continuing determination to assert a middle way.

Nor was the fall of Cromwell marked by a fundamental and lasting shift in religious policy, which a newly dominant faction might have been expected to promote. Brigden has suggested that there was a wave of arrests of radicals at this time, but little came of it. As Redworth noted, 'once he [Henry] had made his point, he ordered, immediately after Barnes' execution, that the quest be halted'.[535] Brigden notes the royal command but sees it as the fruit of intercession with the king by Thomas Audley, the Lord Chancellor, or Dr Edward Crome, parish priest of St Aldermary, London:[536] but given—as she also notes—that it was halted the very day after the burning of Barnes, Garrett and Jerome, by royal command, the policy may well have been the king's, to frighten people into conformity. Brigden half hints that the persecution was halted because it was engendering social unrest, but she cites no evidence, and the short timescale of arrests (just July on her argument) makes it unlikely that there was much disturbance. Certainly there is nothing in the sources. It is much more likely, if there was a quest at this time, that it was intended by the king as a warning, as a shot across the bows. But there was no sustained attack on radicals: nothing, in short, to suggest that the events of summer 1540 should be read as the triumph of religious conservatives. And, Marillac's later account of how Henry would blame the death of Cromwell on false accusations shows how the king, apart from characteristically deflecting responsibility, was, by blaming religious conservatives, emphasising to them that the fall of Cromwell did not mark the beginnings of any kind of religious reaction.[537]

That Henry, rather than being the prisoner of religious conservatives, was actively seeking his own religious middle way is shown in

Cromwell's speech to parliament in May 1540, quoted above, endorsing just that: 'the king leaned neither to the right nor to the left hand, neither to the one nor the other party but set the pure and sincere doctrine of the Christian faith only before his eyes' on which all should agree. That is an eloquent exposition of the royal middle way.[538]

Once more Henry called upon his bishops to agree on a revised religious formulary. It was not an easy matter: there was 'grande contention' between the bishops over doctrine.[539] They had still not agreed by 21 May. The king was intervening. 'Ce roy leur tient de pres . . . voulant oyer [et] examiner raisons et fondement de leur oppinion en y adjoustant et determinant comme bon luy semble' (the king was wanting to hear and to scrutinise their reasons and their opinion, altering and determining as he saw fit). A book would be issued showing all that should be believed in religion, following neither the doctrines of the Germans nor of the pope, but conforming to the ancient councils of the church.[540] A striking development was (as we have already seen) the arrest of Bishop Sampson in late May, imprisoned 'by the king's own commandment'.[541] The most likely explanation is the king's wish to put pressure on him and on the other bishops to agree.[542] Marillac thought that Sampson and Wilson had been arrested for having taken the pope's part and for having, while the marquess of Exeter was alive, secretly written letters to Rome. Sampson was accused of papal sympathies—but his position as a conservative defender of ceremonies was equally important, as his efforts to incriminate Tunstal show. Tunstal evidently denied having urged Sampson to stick to the old usages and traditions of the church: Sampson reminded him of what he had said during discussions with the Germans and the making of the Bishops' Book.[543] Wilson's self-defence illuminates the charges against both of them: he denied that he, and those with whom he spoke, ever sought anything contrary to any of the king's affairs, or to diminish his title or dignity—in other words, the king's royal supremacy; and even concerning the monasteries he was content to submit to the common judgment.[544] The rest of the bishops were very anxious, partly lest they were found guilty of the same deed (for which they could expect a similar punishment), and partly because of their divisions over certain points of doctrine.[545] The bishops remained irreconcilably divided in early June, Marillac reported. Everything was to be concluded in parliament, he added, and 'l'on devoit . . . prendre un moyen chemyn qu'on debvoit ensuyvre' (a middle way was to be taken, which was to be followed), though Marillac was sceptical that there would simply be a sequence of parliaments, and feared that uncertainty would rather increase.[546] On 10–11 June, when Cromwell was arrested, Marillac reported that there was still no final resolution on religion or agreement on any article: the bishops were assembled every day to resolve them.[547] Later, he thought that parliament had transferred its authority to the king, whose sole opinion would be law; but perhaps the king's intentions were less dramatic than that. As the ensuing statute declared, the deliberations of divines should not be hurried but should be published from time to time as necessary.[548] Henry had not secured the doctrinal agreement he sought but he remained committed to the elusive middle way.

All that makes it much more likely that Cromwell fell because Henry had decided that he had served his turn, and the manner of his fall emphasised the king's determination to preserve a middle way in religion, shunning both the desire of conservatives to go back and the wish of religious radicals to embark on further reformation. For Henry, Cromwell had been immensely useful in handling the paperwork relating to the break with Rome, dealing with its consequences and dissolving the monasteries, but by 1540 he was becoming more of a liability. Cromwell's reputation as a religious reformer, however exaggerated, was nonetheless a reality, and it might suit the king to distance himself from him, not least at a moment when Charles V and Francis I seemed on the point of quarrelling once more, and there might be the possibility of an alliance with the French or the imperialists, and not least when religious divisions flared up in England in the pulpit at Paul's Cross. To dismiss Cromwell on grounds of his religious heterodoxy was an excellent way of strengthening the English bargaining position with both Francis and Charles V and of re-emphasising the king's determination to establish a middle way in religion. Henry feared that papal catholics at home and abroad might yet undermine him; he was determined to restrain the passions that the religious divisions between a Gardiner and a Barnes might inflame. He wanted to have his religious cake and eat it: he wanted his royal supremacy, he wanted the destruction of the monasteries and the shrines; but he also wanted to maintain orthodoxy and unity. At times, the tensions between these aims were too great; and Cromwell in 1540 paid the price. This makes Henry appear as a manipulating monster, as guilty of using means that were disproportionate to his ends, and that may repel. Yet it matches exactly his ruthless disposal of ministers (Wolsey, Norfolk), wives (Catherine of Aragon, Anne Boleyn, Anne of Cleves and Catherine Howard), and noblemen (Edward Stafford, third duke of Buckingham, Henry Howard, earl of Surrey) who for whatever reason no longer suited his purposes, or who crossed his will. A different king might simply have dismissed Cromwell, or promoted him to another set of responsibilities. But Henry had from the start been prepared to sacrifice the lives and happiness of other people, including those previously close to him. It thus fits well with what we know of the politics of his reign to conclude that the fall of Cromwell was not the work of supposed factional enemies but the calculated act of a tyrant.

Religious Policy from 1540

Contrary to what is so often supposed, royal religious policy was not changed by the fall of Cromwell in 1540. The king continued to assert the need for unity, to emphasise the dangers of dissension, and to set out a middle way that was neither Lutheran nor traditional catholic. The church continued to serve the king's purposes. In the drought of summer 1540, the king ordered every bishop to exhort the people to fall to prayer and to go in procession in every parish in the realm; there was a general procession in London on 17 September, preceded by a sermon in the choir of the cathedral, repeated thereafter every Friday.[549] On 22 May 1544 there was a sermon in St Paul's lauding God and praising the king, with a sung *Te Deum* and a general procession, on the victory against the Scots.[550] A *Te Deum* was sung in St Paul's on 3 October 1544 for the return of the king after capturing Boulogne.[551] A solemn general procession, with a sermon and the bishop of London singing the *Te Deum*, took place there on 24 September 1545, to give praise for the king's victory in Scotland and the departure of the French army from Boulogne.[552] On the proclamation of peace on 13 June 1546 a sermon was delivered, followed by a *Te Deum* and a solemn procession, with the crosses and banners of all the parish churches of London.[553]

That was, of course, largely traditional. Yet it is mistaken to suppose that the reformation was now over, as Haigh suggests: the conservative bishops 'had now [1543] undone almost all that Cromwell had achieved between 1536 and 1538. . . . By the spring of 1543 the Protestant elements of the first Reformation had been reversed; only the break with Rome and the suppression of the monasteries survived.'[554] Such a judgment is breathtaking in what it omits. Too much had been destroyed—monasteries, images and practices such as pilgrimages; too much had been put in doubt—prayers for the dead in particular; too many people, however few they were as a proportion of the population, had absorbed the new learning, and too many more (one may suspect from evidence of falling bequests) had had their confidence in traditional religion shaken. There was no general purge of reformers, however much it might have appeared likely after Cromwell's fall. The fall of Cromwell (just like the passage of the Six Articles the previous year) did not mark the beginning of any sustained conservative inquisition. 'The expected conservative triumph did not materialize.'[555] 'A major inquisition for heresy' began in London in July 1540, says Brigden,[556] but in her view it was halted in August.[557] Duffy is mistaken in seeing a shift in attitudes to images in these years, away from what he saw as greater condemnation in the late 1530s to a 'benignly reforming attitude towards traditional ceremonies and devotional practices' set out by Tunstal in 1540, which 'explicitly approved the setting up of images of Christ and the saints in churches, and explained the "reverent" use of them, while attacking vows or pilgrimage to particular images'.[558] There was in fact rather more continuity in official policy than Duffy allows. The king's attitude was less hostile in the late 1530s and more critical in the early 1540s than Duffy admits. Duffy is similarly mistaken in his evaluation of attitudes to ceremonies, which were also more consistent than he allows. He sees a formulation of 1540 as 'a systematic and detailed defence of traditional ceremonial' and as a 'decisive reaffirmation of the value of the traditional ceremonies which had been under such intense evangelical pressure',[559] but that ignores the fact that ceremonies had been justified in the same way in 1538 and earlier. And in discussing those similar earlier justifications of ceremonies Duffy stresses their radicalism, because they were being justified for their didactic and symbolic, not their apotropaic, qualities, which must qualify the extent to which such justifications can, in the early 1540s, be seen as conservative.

Where the king had encouraged reform of abuses in the late 1530s, he continued to do so after Cromwell's fall. Indeed, in the very month that Cromwell fell, commissions were issued for the dismantling and removal to the Tower of London of the shrine of St Hugh at Lincoln, together with 'divers feigned jewels and relics by which simple people are deceived and brought into superstition and idolatry'.[560] The thrust against abusive images continued in the early 1540s. 'The conservative reaction of the 1540s took remarkably few steps backward from the positions of the late 1530s, and nowhere was this more true than in official attitudes to popular religion.'[561] It is a striking comment on perceptions of religious policy that Richard Pate, archdeacon of Lincoln, and the king's ambassador to Charles V, defected to Rome rather than returning to England in late 1540 (the pope would confer the bishopric of Worcester on him after Ghinucci's death).[562]

In 1541 Henry issued a further proclamation against superstitions and abuses. Foxe presents him as remembering and missing Cromwell and suspecting Gardiner, and so as beginning a little to 'set his foot' in the cause of religion. But it reads much more like a continuation of the measures that he had taken earlier, especially in 1538.

> Perceiving sundry superstitions and abuses to be used and embraced by our people, whereby they grievously offended him and his Word, we did not only cause the images and bones of such as they resorted and offered unto, with the ornaments of the same, and all such writings and monuments of feigned miracles, wherewith they were illuded, to be taken away in all pieces of our realm; but also by our injunctions commanded, that no offering or setting up of lights or candles should be suffered in any church, but only to the blessed sacrament of the altar.

It had, however, come to the king's notice that 'the shrines, coverings of saints and monuments of those things do yet remain in sundry places of this realm . . . being means to allure our subjects to their former hypocrisy and superstition'.[563] 'While he [Henry] was in the city [of York] the privy council gave orders to the archbishop of York to take down all the shrines remaining in his province': St William of York was to be dismantled.[564] In July 1541 Henry issued a proclamation restoring the traditional celebration of the feasts of St Luke, St Mark and St Mary Magdalene, 'considering that the same saints have been often and many times mentioned in plain and manifest scripture', though without requiring abstinence from meat on St Mark's day. But his balanced approach was shown when he at the same time abrogated the feasts of the Invention of the Cross and the Exaltation of the Cross: the king's subjects were to work as on other days. St Lawrence's day should not be kept as a fasting day.

> Divers and many superstitious and childish observations have been used, and yet to this day are observed and kept in many and sundry parts of this realm, as upon St Nicholas, St Catherine, the Holy Innocents, and such like, children be strangely decked and apparelled to counterfeit priests, bishops, and women, and so be led with songs and

dances from house to house, blessing the people and gathering of money.[565]

In 1541 Henry withdrew royal support for the custom of lighting bonfires on Midsummer Eve in his great hall (it was associated with the feasts of saints; the implication was that flames possessed magical properties).[566] In the same year he also stopped the tradition of sermons preached by boy-bishops.[567] In October 1541 he reasserted his concern over the abuse of images. Although he had acted to suppress all images and bones to which offerings were made, nonetheless some shrines still remained, luring the king's subjects 'to their former hypocrisy and superstition'. Searches should therefore be undertaken in cathedrals, 'and if any shrine, covering of shrine, or other pilgrimage do there continue', it should be suppressed without trace. 'Henry's personal commitment to the attack on the cult of saints', as Rex puts it, is inescapable here.[568]

Henry's advice in April 1543 to the earl of Arran, governor of Scotland, given in instructions to his ambassador Sir Ralph Sadler, with some corrections in the king's own hand, reveals very cogently his position. Henry was pleased that Arran showed zeal

> to the advancement and setting forth of the word of God, with his desire to the extirpation of hypocrisy and superstition maintained in the state of monks and friars, and the reducing of the clergy to such good order and reformation as they may abandon the usurped authority of the Bishop of Rome, and knowledge such obedience to their prince as they ought by God's laws.

Here Henry was giving equal weight to his royal supremacy, the rejection of papal authority, the destruction of superstition equated with monks and friars, and the advancement of God's word, whose precise meaning was otherwise left somewhat vague. That sentence neatly encapsulates the king's reformation, and in so doing reveals the inadequacy of interpretations that see it as merely conservative. A further paragraph did attempt to say how the word of God should be set forth. The scriptures should be published to the people, but they were to receive it reverently and humbly, rather than framing themselves vain and evil opinions that led to the subversion of policy and the confusion of godly order in the church. All books printed in English abroad should be banned; other books 'containing a pure true doctrine, neither swerving to the left hand of iniquity, nor to the right hand with other

pretence of holiness than is agreeable to God's truth', again aspiring to
a middle way, might be set forth by public authority. Henry especially
denounced the 'hypocrisy and superstition' of monks and friars.[569]

Doctrinal formulations in the early 1540s continued to reflect the
king's eclectic views. The direction was clear and definite.[570] The king
remained involved in the formulation of doctrine. In 1540, after the
Bishops' Book expired, Henry commissioned a replacement. Marillac
reported the bishops' discussions,[571] and surviving questions and
answers by bishops on the sacraments are probably part of these
debates.[572]

What those deliberations ultimately led to was the King's Book in
1543.[573] It is a mistake to see the King's Book and associated legislation
as a 'catastrophic set-back for the cause of reform'.[574] Most historians,
it is true, do see it as a conservative revision. 'Ostensibly a straightforward revision of the Bishops' Book of 1537, it was in fact', says Duffy,
'in theological terms, effectively a new work, and in almost every respect
more traditionalist than its predecessor', especially on images and sacrament.[575] 'Traditionalists saw in the King's Book a vindication of their
position.'[576] For Aston, it was 'conspicuously more conservative in
nature'.[577] For Haigh, it was 'a much more conservative compilation
than the 1537 version'.[578] Tyacke can refer to 'the 1543 King's Book
produced at the height of the Henrician reaction'.[579]

But in the light of what has been argued earlier, to present the King's
Book as a conservative revision is excessive. Not least, a good deal of
it is based very closely on the Bishops' Book, especially the commen-
taries on the Ten Commandments. Many other passages, especially the
characteristically balanced discussion of images, neither endorsing the
old ways, nor approving of the wholesale iconoclasm of the new, recur
almost word for word.[580] Indeed, the compilers of the *Revised Short
Title Catalogue* list it as 'a revised and enlarged edition' of the Bishops'
Book. Such similarities in themselves undermine claims that the King's
Book represents a change of direction.

It begins not by applying the brakes but by stressing how necessary
reform had been. 'Like as in the time of darkness and ignorance, finding
our people seduced and drawn from the truth by hypocrisy and superstition, we by the help of God and his word have travailed to purge and
cleanse our realm from the apparent enormities of the same.' And such
travail had borne fruit: 'by opening of God's truth, with setting forth
and publishing of the scriptures, our labours (thanks be to God) have
not been void and frustrate'. The house had been purged and cleansed.
Hypocrisy and superstition had been put away. The present was conse-

quently a 'time of knowledge'.[581] All that was not the language of conservative reaction.

But what Henry now feared was the upsetting of the balance he had achieved. The devil had tried to return. 'We find entered into some of our people's hearts an inclination to sinister understanding of scripture, presumption, arrogancy, carnal liberty, and contention.' The king thus felt constrained 'for avoiding of such diversity of opinions' to set forth with the advice of the clergy a declaration of 'the true knowledge of God and his word, with the principal articles of our religion', so that 'all men may uniformly be led and taught the true understanding of that which is necessary for every christian man to know', 'a perfect and sufficient doctrine, grounded and established in holy scriptures'.

The reform of abuses, the avoidance of contention and the elaboration of a 'perfect and sufficient doctrine' are readily seen to be continuing characteristics of the king's religious policy. Much else can also be seen in detail as a continuation of Henry's earlier concerns: the presentation of the sacrament of the altar ('the mass, wherein after the consecration is really present the very blessed body and blood of Christ, is celebrate in the church for a perpetual memory of his death and passion'),[582] the inclusion of all the sacraments, the rejection of communion in both kinds ('for the benefit or hurt that cometh to a christian man by receiving of this sacrament, standeth not in the fashion or manner of receiving of it, under one or both kinds, but in the worthy or unworthy receiving of the same'; when people receive it in one kind, 'they lose no part of the profit and benefit promised by virtue of the said sacrament').[583]

Was there, nonetheless, a decisively anti-protestant line on free will, justification, good works, 'in contrast to the studiedly ambiguous phraseology of the Bishops' Book', as Rex has claimed?[584] As we have seen, Henry had rejected, in his debate with Cranmer, precisely those aspects of the Bishops' Book that had appeared to flirt with Lutheran doctrine. The King's Book elaborated and amplified what Henry had earlier urged.

It is indeed the case that Lutheran doctrine was refuted. One new article reasoned: in places in scripture it is said that men are justified by faith. But that meant 'faith neither only nor alone', but rather faith joined with the virtues of hope and charity, together with repentance.[585] There was nothing in scripture nor in the doctors of the church to support the belief that a man might know that he has been predestined to salvation and would persevere to the end in that state. On the contrary, since 'our own frailty and naughtiness' were always to be feared, 'it is therefore expedient for us to live in continual watch and continual fight with our enemies the Devil, the flesh and the world, and not to presume too much of our perseverance and continuance in the state of grace, which on our behalf is uncertain and unstable'. God's promises made in Christ were 'immutable' but conditional—'we may yet fail of the promise, because we keep not our promise'. If we think our felicity is grounded on God's promise and 'do not therewith remember that no man shall be crowned unless he lawfully fight, we shall triumph before the victory, and so look in vain for that which is not otherwise promised but under a condition'.[586] At the Last Judgment Christ would, 'according to every man's own works and deeds done by him in his lifetime', pronounce the final sentence of everlasting salvation 'upon all those persons which in their lifetime obeyed and conformed themselves unto the will of God, and exercised the works of right belief and charity, and so persevering in well-doing, sought in their hearts and deeds honour, glory and life immortal'; 'upon all those which in their lifetime were contentious, and did repugn against the will of God, and followed injustice and iniquity rather than truth and virtue', Christ would pronounce 'the sentence of everlasting punishment and damnation'.[587] This article was added to the rest so that no one should take salvation for granted and think that they could live without obeying God's commandments. Rather, everyone should remember that the day of judgment would come and should consequently fear to do anything against God's will for which he might deserve to be sentenced to everlasting damnation. At the day of judgment every man would be called to account and would be finally judged according to his works, good or bad, done in his lifetime.[588]

Separate articles dealt further with the question of free will, justification and good works.[589] It was pointed out that the biblical instruction to keep the commandments would be pointless unless there was left in man 'some faculty or power' by which, with God's help, he could first understand the commandments, next consent to them, and then go on to obey them—or to choose evil. That was what was called free will.[590] Because of Adam and Eve's disobedience, men could not avoid sin, except with the grace of God: consequently they should embrace God's grace.[591] God, being naturally good, wanted all men to be saved. But he righteously damned those whose vices corrupted them. If men abused God's grace, then it was they, and not God, who were the authors of sin and of their own damnation.[592] But the balance so characteristic of

Henrician religion was reasserted. Everyone, especially preachers, was warned that 'neither they so preach the grace of God, that they take away thereby freewill, nor on the other side so extol freewill, that injury be done to the grace of God'.[593]

Much the same balance—by no means sound in logic—was followed when the process by which men might be saved was set out in some detail. Men were born in original sin and with a desire for the things of this world. Accordingly, with the intention of delivering them from such a wretched state, God had sent his only son 'to work the mystery of our redemption'.[594] That appeared to be leading on to a Lutheran position on salvation. And the King's Book did indeed go on to declare, resoundingly, that Christ had offered himself on the cross as 'a sufficient redemption and satisfaction for the sins of the world': 'only by his worthy merit and deserving' was a way opened for all men to come to God. But these fine phrases were preceded by the word 'although'; and that led to the qualification that salvation would not be enjoyed except by those who did as Christ taught.[595] God's grace was essential if men were to do good. But when a man willingly received God's grace, then he became 'a worker' in attaining his own salvation, doing 'such works as be requisite to his justification'.[596] Men must show repentance for their sins; they must trust to be forgiven by the passion of Christ.[597] They must be 'sworn to be the servants of God, and to be soldiers under Christ, to fight against our enemies, the Devil, the world, and the flesh'. They must do good works and abstain from sin.[598] Good works meant not only 'outward corporal acts and deeds' but also 'inward spiritual works, motions and desires, as the love and fear of God, joy in God, godly meditations and thoughts, patience, humility'.[599] It was always possible to fall from salvation.[600] Human frailty being what it was, men should not feel assured of their salvation. They should not engage in 'fantastical imagination' or 'curious reasoning' over predestination, much less trust that they were predestined to salvation.[601]

Not only was faith required for salvation, but also the gifts of God's grace, above all the desire to do good works. In some places of scripture our justification was ascribed to faith alone without reference to anything else. But only faith that worked hand in hand with charity was sufficient for justification. And the good works that men did by faith and charity, once justified, led to 'increase and end of our justification and everlasting salvation'. In case, however, this now seemed to be moving too much in the direction of the late medieval church, the King's Book went on to assert that although we could never be saved without faith, repentance, charity and doing good works, nevertheless we were justified gratis, from the mercy of God, and not because we deserved it.[602] Similarly, whenever men sinned, they should do penance: but the remission of sins came freely from God.[603] Yet in case that were misinterpreted, the King's Book reiterated the theme that 'as we continue and persevere in good works, so more and more we go forward and proceed in our justification, and increasing the same'.[604] Drawing on St Paul's instruction that men 'should live in this present world soberly, justly, and devoutly',[605] the King's Book insisted that we should 'most diligently, with all labour and care' apply our will to these good works, 'that we may make our election stable and sure'.[606] All that was far removed from the certainty expressed in Luther's conviction that men were saved through faith in Christ alone. Yet, as we have seen, the teaching of the King's Book on justification was not traditional catholicism, for all its ultimate rejection of Lutheran doctrine: there were too many phrases on justification that echoed Lutheran teaching. The rhetorical technique was to endorse, then qualify and modify them so that the overall thrust appeared different.

On other issues the reformist emphasis of the King's Book was marked: for example, monasticism was dismissed as among 'the superstitious works of man's own invention', the sort in which 'many christian men, and specially of them that were lately called religious (as monks, friars, nuns and such other) have in times past put their great trust and confidence'.[607] Significant features of 'traditional religion' were condemned in the discussion of the first commandment, 'thou shalt have none other gods but me'. Anyone who 'for any superstitious intent' drank holy water or wore a charm around his or her neck, hoping to live long and to drive away sickness, was offending against the commandment.[608] Traditional teaching on purgatory was no more endorsed in the King's Book than it had been in the Bishops' Book: indeed, in its treatment of prayer for the dead it went rather further.[609] It stated that 'although the intercession and mediation by prayer of saints departed, and of such the members of the catholic church as be yet living on earth, be good, acceptable and profitable unto us, yet that is only by the mediation and intercession of Christ our Head': all prayers ought always to finish 'with a remembrance of our Saviour Jesu Christ'.[610] A separate section dealt with prayer for souls departed, 'a very good and charitable deed' required by 'due order of charity' which 'men ought to judge and think ... well and profitably done'.[611] But there was a vital clarification. 'It is not in the power or knowledge of any man to limit and dispense how much, and in what space of time, or to what person particularly the said masses, exequies, and suffrages do profit and avail'; so they should also be done 'for the universal congregation of christian people, quick and dead'.

> Furthermore, because the place where the souls remain, the name thereof, the state and condition which they be in, be to us uncertain, therefore these, with all other such things must also be left to Almighty God, . . . and not we to take upon us, neither in the one part nor yet in the other, to give any fond and temerarious judgment in so high things so far passing our knowledge.[612]

That was a striking critique of traditional religion. Moreover, it led on to a renewed assault against papal abuses.

> It is much necessary that all such abuses as heretofore have been brought in by supporters and maintainers of the papacy of Rome, and their accomplices, concerning this matter, be clearly put away; and that we therefore abstain from the name of purgatory, and no more dispute or reason thereof. Under colour of which have been advanced many fond and great abuses, to make men believe that through the bishop of Rome's pardons souls might clearly be delivered out of it, and released out of the bondage of sin; and that masses said at Scala coeli and other prescribed places, fantasised by men, did there in those places more profit the souls than in another; and that a prescribed number of prayers sooner than other (though as devoutly said) should further their petition sooner, yea specially if they were said before one image more than another which they fantasised. All these, and such like abuses, be necessary utterly to be abolished and extinguished.[613]

Such passages elaborated on the scepticism about the precise nature of purgatory already revealed in the mid-1530s: but it is worth noting that that scepticism was already present in the Bishops' Book. And the thrust of the discussion of purgatory is reformist. It is not Lutheran or Zwinglian. Intercessory prayers for the dead are allowed. But, nonetheless, traditional understanding of purgatory was rejected.

The King's Book, then, shows that royal policy in the 1540s did not shed its radical side, the radicalism that had dissolved the monasteries and shattered the intercessory economy of saints and pilgrimages. But it also very clearly shows that such radicalism was not synonymous with Lutheran doctrine on justification, however much Lutheran phraseology was appropriated and briefly endorsed before then being qualified.

Henry continued to present his policy as a middle way. He told parliament in 1545:

> I see and hear daily that you of the clergy preach one against another, teach one contrary to another, inveigh one against another, without charity or discretion. Some be too stiff in their old mumpsimus, others be too busy and curious in their new sumpsimus. Thus all men always be in variety and discord and few or none preach truly and sincerely the word of God, according as they ought to do.

'There is one thing to which I require you, and that is charity and concord.'[614] The essential continuity of his aims since the mid-1530s was plain.

Those aims included the king's long-standing essentially Erasmian conviction that the superstitions and idolatries that had gathered around the church like barnacles on a ship needed to be dealt with by purifying reform. That had continued after Cromwell's fall, as we have seen, with further measures against idolatrous shrines.

But, time and again, such measures are best understood not as harbingers of some full-blown Lutheran or Calvinist reformation, but as reflections of the king's middle way. The so-called English Litany of 1544 should not be mistaken for a portent that the king was about to introduce a full vernacular liturgy. It was, as Roger Bowers has shown, 'merely an addition to the historic observance, running parallel to it but forming no part of it', best characterised as 'mildly evangelical, primarily traditional'. Within the conventional form of a supplicatory procession, 'the king was creating a wholly new observance for performance in perpetuity' that was, significantly, conducted in English. But it did not replace the traditional liturgy: it replaced the liturgy used in processions on the three Rogation Days (Monday, Tuesday and Wednesday before Ascension Day) and on St Mark's day (25 April), as well as in times of emergency owing to plague, famine and the like. Henry had called upon the archbishops to require twice-weekly processions from 17 September to 7 October 1540 as a response to drought, in June 1542 (renewed in July 1543) in search of divine assistance for the defence of Hungary, in August 1543 for relief from a wet summer. He was concerned (as he explained to Cranmer on 11 June 1544) that the people 'have used to come very slackly to the procession': popular incomprehension of Latin was one of the causes. Hence Henry opted for a solemn homily and a litany in English. And the ritual was shortened (taking half an hour instead of two hours) and simplified: no introductory antiphons, no penitential psalms, no mass. Only the litany and suffrages were retained. No longer were individual saints invoked. 'Such suppressions were . . . in conformity . . . with the values expressed in the "King's Book"', Bowers has pointed out: they did not amount to a radical new departure. But the Litany did invoke the Virgin Mary, and the whole of the 'blessed company of heaven' was asked to 'pray for us'. Henry's intention may have been to turn the ritual from an occasional supplication in emergency into a more frequent observance, but no specific days were stipulated. Large numbers of copies were printed. It was implemented in places but in August 1545 (with the French fleet threatening) the council ordered the archbishops to take fresh measures for general processions in the English tongue, returning to the form used in 1543, in English and on specified days. In early autumn 1545 Henry asked Cranmer to devise an English text for use in parochial festive processions (some fifteen annually), this time as part of the liturgy. This was a limited commission, not a request for a comprehensive vernacular liturgy; and no more is heard of it. What Henry did do, on 15 October 1545, was to order the vernacular litany to be sung on the days accustomed for procession, on Wednesdays and Fridays, and Sundays and festival days. This did not, however, replace the Latin procession preceding Sunday and feast-day high mass. It was a free-standing additional observance, independent of any other service. And the historic liturgy remained fully in use. How long the optional addition was observed is moot, especially once peace was concluded in June 1546.[615] Interesting, too, in this context is the clear evidence that Henry continued to attend mass in the Chapel Royal on holy and feast days.[616]

Henry's purifying zeal appears further in his response in January 1546 to Cranmer and the bishops of Worcester (Heath) and Chichester (Day), whom he had asked to peruse certain service books. Cranmer and the bishops requested that the all-night vigil and ringing of bells on Allhallows day, the covering of images in church in Lent, with the lifting up of the veil covering the cross on Palm Sunday and the kneeling to the cross at the same time, should be abolished on account of the superstition and other enormities and abuses of the same. Henry said that all the vigils 'which in the beginning of the church were godly used' had been 'many years passed taken away throughout all christendom' on account of 'the manifold superstition and abuses which after did grow by means of the same'. The vigil on Allhallows should be abolished, since it was abused as other vigils were. Henry accepted the other recommendations as well. He added that they made no mention of creeping to the cross, 'which is a greater abuse than any of the other': that too should be abolished. Interestingly, Cranmer responded by suggesting the need, when such things be altered or taken away', to 'set forth some doctrine therewith, which should declare the cause of the abolishing or alteration'.[617]

But none of that should be seen as showing incipient full-blown protestantism. Nor should the chantries act of 1545 be misread as an anticipation of the total abolition of chantries that would be undertaken in the next reign. The act was, as it declared, intended to deal with those chantries that had already been dissolved by private initiative or that had recently been affected by irregularities, and in particular to insist that 'if the chantries and colleges were to be dissolved, or if their endowments were to be plundered, it must be done by the government for the benefit of the king and the whole realm, not by private subjects for private gain'. The king emphasised his reforming ambitions by promising to order those chantries, colleges and hospitals which came to the crown 'to the glory of God and the profit of the commonwealth'. As Kreider concluded: 'it seems highly improbable that Henry VIII had any coherent doctrinal rationale for dissolving the English intercessory institutions in December 1545.' Not a great deal happened as a result of this act.[618]

Nor do Henry's arrangements for the education of the young Prince Edward suggest that the king was moving towards protestantism, despite what is so often supposed. Richard Cox, graduate of King's College, Cambridge, headmaster of Eton, fellow of Wolsey's new foundation in Oxford and chaplain to Goodrich and Cranmer, was appointed almoner to Edward in 1538 and tutor in 1540; he was more a 'director of studies' than a daily tutor. John Cheke, graduate of St John's and regius professor of Greek in Cambridge, was appointed to supplement Cox in 1544. Roger Ascham, tutor to Princess Elizabeth, was also called upon to teach Edward to write. Cox, Cheke and Ascham were all to be convinced protestants in Edward VI's reign, and Cox and Cheke were to take the path of exile under Mary Tudor. But, says Loach, 'it would be unwise to argue from this that they were more than "reformed" catholics or erasmians in the 1540s'. They were appointed by the king because they were leading scholars. And, whatever their private thoughts about or aspirations for the church might have been, during Henry's lifetime they evidently conformed to the king's religious settlement.[619]

Still more unwise would it be to take John Foxe's later third-hand account of what Cranmer had heard from the French ambassador in summer 1546—that the kings of both realms would change the mass into a communion service—as a clear sign that Henry was about to embark upon a protestant reformation.[620] Even if what was recorded was actually spoken, it is far from sure that it was ever meant. The words are better understood in the context of diplomatic bargaining, reminiscent of Henry's praise of Luther to Chapuys in 1529, and Henry's soft-soaping of the German diplomats in 1540.

And the political intrigues of the mid-1540s, known to us from Foxe, need similarly to be read cautiously as evidence of the king's religious policies. Accusations of religious radicalism against Cranmer and Queen Catherine Parr, Henry's last wife, that the king first encouraged and then dismissed, have been variously interpreted; if they are to be believed at all—and perhaps we should be sceptical—what they point to is the king's determination to hold to the middle way.[621]

Many historians have surmised that the dramatic political events in the last weeks of Henry's life show that the king himself was at last preparing the way for a protestant reformation. On such an account Henry deliberately destroyed the duke of Norfolk and his son because they were religious conservatives. That Norfolk was anything but a conformist is, however, highly doubtful; and his son the earl of Surrey does not seem to have been a young nobleman of deep religious convictions. However that may be, it is hard to avoid the conclusion that Surrey destroyed himself by his reckless behaviour. The fall of the Howards was not some premeditated conspiracy masterminded by the king. More interesting is the composition of the regency council that the king laid down in the revision of his will on 30 December 1546. Stephen Gardiner, bishop of Winchester, and Thomas Thirlby were excluded. That has been taken as evidence that Henry was deliberately appointing a council of protestant sympathisers, who would take the work of religious reformation further after his death. But a rather different explanation is more plausible. Gardiner was embroiled in a quarrel with the king over the exchange of lands. His obstinacy may have reawakened Henry's doubts about his commitment to the royal supremacy: as Colin Armstrong has suggested, Gardiner may well have remained crypto-papist in sympathy throughout the years of the break with Rome. In Henry's lifetime he conformed and did nothing to undermine the royal supremacy. But the king may well have feared that, in the minority of his son, Gardiner's true sentiments would resurface. If Henry feared that he could not, in any minority, be trusted to uphold the royal supremacy, then that would sufficiently explain Gardiner's exclusion from the regency council. That was a further blow against the papacy, not a sign of any move towards protestantism. The defence and maintenance of the royal supremacy were the foundation of Henry's religious policy, as we have abundantly seen. No more than the fate of the Howards does Gardiner's exclusion show that Henry was planning for a protestant reformation in his son's reign. Henry's actions rather reflect the quarrels of the moment read in the context of the king's continuing and fundamental commitment to his royal supremacy, the linchpin of his reformation.[622]

What Henry's will, brilliantly explicated by Roger Bowers, demonstrates is his continuing attachment to the middle way that had most recently been set out in the King's Book. He wished his body to be buried in St George's Chapel, Windsor, in the tomb that was almost ready, midway between the stalls and the high altar. Lands yielding £600 p.a. net were to be granted to the dean and chapter: in return they would provide for two priests to say masses at the altar daily in perpetuity, arrange four obits annually (matins, vespers of the dead [placebo, dirige], mass for the dead), including a sermon, and provide a weekly sermon in the town of Windsor. Henry was also preparing to revive Edward III's provision of almshousing for poor knights. A recently discovered memorandum set out the arrangements in detail, suggesting that Henry was very much and actively committed to the provisions he was making: these were no oversight or residue of earlier plans. All this, it must be emphasised, was very far from any protestant or even evangelical notion of salvation through faith alone. The charitable bequest was a conventional good work. And the king's request for masses for his soul in perpetuity reveals his continuing belief that the souls of the departed could be assisted by the acts of the living. It is hard to read this will and suppose that Henry was on the point of introducing a protestant reformation, either himself or by deliberately appointing protestant sympathisers to the council of regency for his son. Yet Henry's provisions were in keeping with his reforming middle way, rather than evidence of traditional conservatism. In no sense did they contradict the cautiously sceptical treatment of purgatory in his religious formulations from the Ten Articles onwards. What had repeatedly been rejected were attempts precisely and mechanically to spell out the nature of purgatory and the benefits to be obtained from the specific intercession of named saints. What had always been allowed were prayers for the dead. Henry's provisions were in keeping with all of this. There were no bequests or requests to the Virgin Mary or to individual saints. Henry's will reflects his nuanced view of what should not, and of what could, be done for the souls of the dead.[623] It is a fitting testament to the king's reformation.

Conclusion

Henry VIII emerges from this study as the dominant force in the making of what is best called the king's reformation. In the campaign for the divorce, in the break with Rome, in the making of the codifications of religion, in the dissolution of the monasteries, and in the neutralisation and, sometimes, the destruction of opponents, Henry's role was full and decisive.

What the king sought, he largely achieved. Not that he was an absolute potentate, nor that he behaved as if he were. In his quarrel with Pope Clement VII, Henry found that he could not readily secure what he wanted. In Thomas More and Bishop John Fisher, Henry found men who would die rather than openly endorse the break with Rome and the royal supremacy. In the Pilgrimage of Grace, Henry faced substantial opposition that for a time appeared as if it would compel fundamental concessions. In his dealings with his bishops, Henry had to cajole and to persuade in order to secure their acquiescence in the religious formulations to which he himself adhered. Time and again Henry was cautious in pursuing his aims, not least over the break with Rome itself. But time and again he not only found highly able servants to carry out his wishes – Wolsey, Cromwell, Cranmer, Norfolk – but also managed to get them to take the responsibility and the blame for what was done. (This is why it is no argument to deduce, from the volume of opposition to a minister – for example, the way in which the Pilgrims of Grace assailed Cromwell – that policy must have been independently that minister's.) So successfully did Henry maintain his 'deniability' that many historians have been taken in, and have supposed that he was a weak king, the plaything of factions, and that Wolsey, or Cromwell, or Norfolk, or Gardiner, or other groups of counsellors, were the true wielders of power.[1] This book has demonstrated the opposite. Here religious policy has been shown to have been essentially the king's.

Henry saw himself as God's lieutenant whose divinely ordained mission it was to purify the church. His self-righteous convictions have emerged forcefully in this study. But when Henry used the language of reform, it was not mere rhetoric. At one time, I believed that it was Henry's achievement to harness the rhetoric of the Lutheran reformation in support of his break with Rome, a limited conflict over jurisdiction, while remaining essentially conservative in religion, as his continuing devotion to the mass shows. But the study and reflection that have produced this book have led to the conclusion that, far from being opportunistically engaged in 'cynical posturing',[2] Henry, in his ambitions for reform of the church, was entirely sincere, not least stimulated by his own readings of the Bible, especially contemplating the prophet kings of the Old Testament,[3] and that he pursued them consistently throughout his reign. Henry knew his own mind and knew what he wanted: it would be a mistake to suppose that he was open to influence because he was undecided about the direction of religious policy.[4]

Striking, in this context, is the remarkable tribute to the king from the hard-bitten diplomat Sir Robert Wingfield in February 1539. 'I beseech your majesty to take these my letters in good part'. he ended his letter, 'as from your most humble and bounden servant which hath written many letters to your majesty of right great importance though as me semeth there were never any of these of like importance to these' – the most important letter, in his opinion, he had ever written to the king. It is an intense and convoluted letter that deserves close reading. Wingfield begins by suggesting that Henry had been provided before the creation of the world to seek a reformation of the church, for which God the Father and Jesus Christ his son were to be praised.

> For sure, by their most high provision your majesty hath been provided by them before their creation of the world to be a principal minister under them to restore again the principal of all conscience which was in manner so clearly abolished by the sorceries and enchantments that have been set forth by such as long have continued the usurpation of God's authority and likewise of all temporal christian princes and under the cloak of hypocrisy have used all such detestable ways as include in them all vicious living, all which by the grace and provision of the lord planted in your majesty and open to the laud honour and glory principally of almighty God and next to your majesty.

Previous attempts at reform had failed. 'For right many of diverse sorts in long time past have made a show as it were of a summer game to desire a reformation of Christ's church but it always proved vanity for lack of pure mind to god ward well grounded in faith.' It was just those qualities – 'pure mind to god ward well grounded in faith' – which 'hath appeared and doth so sincere and perfect that ever since that your majesty began the holy enterprise there hath been nothing omitted on your majesty's part that hath appertained to bring forth perfection'. That was because, Wingfield continued, 'your majesty hath not failed to employ your own travail about the imagination to investigate the very truth' but had also 'experimented all manner of ways with exceeding expenses to convey your godly mind'. 'Blessed be our saviour', Wingfield went on,

> your majesty hath now provided by so sincere and direct ways that God's power doth lead your majesty to induce the very truth to the special comfort and reparation of God's word; which by your doing advanced only by God is now in so good a train that God shall be better known and more universally served with due worship than he hath been in long time past.

That would greatly cheer his subjects: 'the remembrance of which your most royal and christian act is and must needs be the most principal rejoice to all true christians' and (in case that were not praise enough) 'that ever came to men, both for the profit that they themselves shall take thereby, and for the everlasting fame which must needs light upon your majesty for your godly act'. Wingfield declared:

> I would not for all the good of the world that I should have died in the dark ignorance that I was in before the light of grace had enlumined by your most godly and gracious act proceding from God's power . . . as from the proper instrument chosen by god for the comfort and salvation of many.

This is panegyric rhetoric – yet it sounds heartfelt. It was not necessary, and it came from an apparently worldly-wise, experienced diplomat. Above all, it presents Henry as a convincing reformer of the church, abolishing the sorceries and enchantments and hypocrisies of the church.[5] That was how Henry saw himself and what he was doing.

The best way of characterising the purifying reforming ideals that Henry pursued is to relate them to the inspiration and the satires of Erasmus. In his youth Henry was influenced by Erasmus, and in 1528, as we have seen, urged him to return to England to help him in the task of purifying the church. Henry shared Erasmus's distaste for the superstitious and idolatrous features of the church in which he grew up, and that impulse, together with their association with rebellion, largely explains the dissolution of the monasteries and the dismantling of the pilgrimage shrines in the later 1530s. A church totally without monasteries and pilgrimages is, however, a very different church: the consequences were profound. That was not a 'moderate' reform, as it is sometimes said to have been.[6] That the impulse behind such measures was Erasmian is not invalidated by the objection that Erasmus, for all his biting satire, would not have approved of the wholesale destruction and iconoclasm that marked Henry's dissolution of the monasteries, or the dissipation of the proceeds on war. All revolutions, as Hugh Trevor-Roper has remarked, tend to go too far. No doubt it is the immediate political circumstances of the mid-1530s – Henry's reaction to the Pilgrimage of Grace, a rebellion in defence of the monasteries – that explain the vehemence of the denunciations of monasticism and the scale and speed of the suppression.

All that makes 'catholicism without the pope' an inadequate and misleading characterisation of the king's reformation. Of course, that was how the king and his diplomats presented it to the Emperor Charles V,[7] and Henry would insist that it was of the holy catholic church of England that next immediately under God he was the head.[8] And, up to a point, the king's reformation can be understood as essentially an exercise in what Wooding has called 'rethinking catholicism', a development and elaboration of reforming strands at the heart of the late medieval church. But that understates the extent to which this developed into something very different from 'traditional religion'. The Pilgrims of Grace, as has been shown here, saw the religious changes, implemented, announced and feared, as altogether more revolutionary than labels such as 'reformed catholic' would imply.[9]

Much has recently been made of the extent to which most of the king's subjects, and especially his bishops and the political nation, went along with the break with Rome and subsequent policies. But that acquiescence should not be misread. Since religious policy was the king's and since the king was determined to have his way, refusal and resistance were highly risky – and went against ingrained and instinctive habits of loyal and obedient service to the king. The pressures on those few who would not comply have been amply explored in this book. It is hardly surprising that many felt that they could do no more than accept what was being done. That compliance should not be misunderstood as consent or complicity.

It is misleading to think of what happened in the reign of Henry VIII in terms of the division of 'English catholics': 'the politics of the royal supremacy, with its firm, bipartite division of the realm into conformists and traitors, hopelessly splintered the English catholic majority'.[10] That is an anachronistic formulation. In 1529 virtually all English men and women are better described as 'Christians' rather than 'catholics': the term 'catholic' implies the existence of an alternative and rival faith. What changed in the subsequent years is that the king's government required them to acquiesce in a variety of changes, presented not only as essentially true to the Christian faith but as truer than the practices they were replacing. The king's subjects were not a 'catholic majority' who had clearly, firmly and over a long period rejected some alternative faith: no such alternative had been on offer. In 1558–59, a generation later, Queen Mary's bishops, almost to a man, would see themselves as 'catholics' who could not compromise their beliefs by accepting the Elizabethan religious settlement. But Henry VIII's bishops, in the years from 1529, did not see matters in such a way. Many of them agonised over their responses, encouraged to conform by a variety of threats and pressures, and by their own deep-rooted loyalty to the monarchy and to Henry personally. In that process, intimidation and fear, as we have seen, played a significant part.

A recent variant of such notions seeks to emphasise the extent to which Tudor people collaborated with the government, implementing policies such as the dismantling of the shrines and informing against those who remained loyal to the pope, while allegedly 'negotiating' the policies that the government sought, 'co-opting state power for their own purposes'.[11] It is true, especially among the ruling classes, that some people collaborated: most noblemen, JPs, clergy, churchwardens and constables – as far as we know, though our knowledge is ever patchier as we descend the social scale – conformed, obeying the instructions given them. Images were taken down, Bibles were purchased. But caution is required here. There were some who were enthusiastic supporters – and these may well constitute the bulk of our evidence. Moreover, the most significant acts – such as the work of dissolving the monasteries – were undertaken by a small number of committed royal servants. Beyond that the regime could draw upon a reservoir of loyalty to the monarch of a kind an irreverent modern age finds hard to grasp in a political context. No doubt there were fears of material disadvantage and hopes of material benefit. Local and personal quarrels played their part.

It is much harder, however, to show that there was much, let alone effective, bargaining or negotiation, however loosely those terms are defined, between the king and his government, on the one hand, and the ruling classes and the people, on the other, on the policies that constitute the king's reformation. What 'negotiation' took place – whether between royal government and local rulers, or between those local rulers and the commons, on the break with Rome, the royal supremacy, the dissolution of the monasteries, the dismantling of the pilgrimage shrines, the codification of doctrine, the continuing rejection of Lutheran ideas? Even the debates among the churchmen called on by the king to set out true doctrine were, as we have seen, orchestrated within a framework determined by the king. Noblemen and gentlemen might just, to some extent, seal their households off from unwanted innovations, as the countess of Salisbury attempted, but outwardly they were called upon to conform no less than their social inferiors. And as far as the commons are concerned, terms such as 'negotiation', 'bargaining' and 'choosing' are insensitively misleading when applied to the grossly unequal relations between rulers and governed. Of course, individuals tried to make the best of things, but that should not be dignified as the expression of a willing choice. When all adults were required to swear the oath to the succession in 1534, no 'negotiation' was possible (and the fate of Friar Forest was eloquent testimony to the risks run by anyone who admitted swearing with the outer but not the inner man). And the vigorous efforts of the Pilgrims of Grace to secure a reversal of religious policy came to naught: Henry was simply not prepared to negotiate. Very understandably, most people conformed – or rather, complied. Yet such conformity – or compliance – should not be confused with consent: and the term 'collaboration' is best reserved for a conformity that is both willing and active.

To the question 'how did Henry succeed in achieving his aims?' the response 'because his subjects largely conformed' is inadequate. At best that is a description, not an explanation; it is another way of putting the question. Nor is it anything like a complete description: the scale of the rebellions of 1536–37 must call into question any picture of general conformity. Moreover, the responses of Henry's subjects can only be properly understood when the king's aims and methods are themselves fully understood. That is why this book has attempted an exploration of Henry's purposes, a more complex and controversial matter than is often realised, since many scholars have denied that policy was the king's, or was consistent. And the response that this book offers to the question 'how did he succeed?' is that he did so because the 'opposition' he undoubtedly faced was more often a refusal to comply or a plea for the king to revise his policies than outright and effective political opposition, and because Henry was ruthless in dealing with those who opposed him.

This study has therefore concentrated on the king's policies and on the high politics of his reign. What the king did and the ways in which he did it had important consequences for the realm. The rebellions of 1536–37 have been closely considered since at that point it looked as if the course of high politics, and religious policy, might be profoundly affected by popular politics. But it was not to be; and, generally, in Henry's reign, the influence of the commons on the making of religious policy was slight indeed. Judging the impact of religious policy on the commons is not straightforward, above all because of a lack of detailed evidence. But the depositions made by those involved in the rebellions in 1536–37 have been given full weight: they are sufficient in themselves to show how deeply mistrustful the commons were of Henry's policies and how attached they were to their parish churches, religious processions and local monasteries. There was indeed a 'popular politics' in Tudor England, and the acquiescence of the commons could never be taken for granted. But, as the defeat of the rebellions showed, the power of a determined, devious and ruthless king and his counsellors was too great. That most English men and women were dismayed by the dissolution of the monasteries, and by the suppression of the practice of pilgrimage and of the intercession of saints, seems highly likely. Nonetheless, they had little option but to acquiesce and comply.

Perhaps that was the easier for them because, while aspects of the king's reformation were radical indeed, in other respects much remained unchanged. The liturgy of the parish church was largely unaffected, as Henry's continuing attachment to the mass meant that there was no change in the central act of Christian worship. And many of the subtleties of the theological codifications that we have been considering impinged little on the lives of the people.

The king's reformation, for all its radicalism over monasteries and pilgrimage shrines, was not a road towards protestantism. Henry would have no truck with Lutheran notions of justification by faith or Zwinglian doctrines of the eucharist: it is not convincing to present Henry as a protestant, an evangelical or even a half-protestant.[12] But that did not, to repeat, make him a conservative exponent of traditional religion: 'catholicism without the pope' is an insubstantial characterisation of the king's ideals. And to go on to characterise Henry's religious policies as a search for the middle way between Rome and Wittenberg, between Rome and Zurich, is not to suggest that they were insipid or limited.

The king's reformation is best seen as *sui generis*, as unique. It is tempting, in studying religious change in the second half of Henry's reign, to focus narrowly on particular aspects, and then to draw large conclusions about the thrust of policy from such individual themes. Of course, close analysis can be highly illuminating, but distortion threatens if a theme is considered in isolation. If, for example, the codifications of doctrine from 1536 are studied as a series of set texts, without reference to the dissolution of the monasteries and dismantling of pilgrimage shrines, then much of what was deeply radical about the king's reformation will be missed. If, by contrast, historians concentrate on specific aspects in which marked change did occur – for example, the doctrine of purgatory and the practice of invoking the intercession of named individual saints – that can give the misleading impression that the king's reformation was not only generally radical but also purposefully moving towards protestantism.

Hindsight adds to such misperceptions. That under Queen Mary many of those who had been heavily involved in the making of the Henrician reformation would readily join in the recatholicisation of England does not mean that her policies were essentially those of her father. That under Edward a more full-blooded protestant reformation was attempted does not mean that what Henry had been striving for was no more than a stage on a road to that protestant reformation, much less that Henry had wished it. It distorts, too, to focus, in studying Henry's reign, on those who in Edward's reign and beyond would be clearly protestant in their writings and sermons. In Henry's reign their freedom of religious expression was limited and their influence small: any study that fails to recognise that – for example, by focusing on a small number of individuals without much reference to the wider context – risks giving the misleading impression of a rising tide of protestantism. Undoubtedly there were those, especially in the universities and in the church itself, who were increasingly aware of, and tempted by, continental protestantism. While Henry lived, however, they could do little. Of course, individuals might seek to convert others, but given the risks in any public preaching, such influence cannot have affected large numbers of people. At the end of Henry's life there is very little sign of much in the way of clandestine protestant congregations, and little sign in the early years of Edward's reign of any such groups emerging into the open. Dickens and Fines tried to argue that there were significant numbers of protestants. Scholars counting the formulae in the preambles of wills initially seemed to have found tangible evidence of a protestant advance, but more reflective analysis has suggested that if, in line with the king's attitudes, the invocation of saints was much diminished, nonetheless the difficulty of determining the authorship of wills and consequently of judging whether the preambles express the convictions of the testator or of the scribe, makes them a problematic source. Moreover, in this study, the king's reformation has been presented as much more reforming than is implied by the label 'catholicism without the pope'. And that means that what may appear an evangelical or proto-protestant sermon may in fact be no more than a restatement of the king's position.[13]

Those who wish to emphasise trends towards protestantism are now forced to argue that it was not a matter of numbers: in a hierarchical society, some opinions counted for much more than others.[14] Nowhere was that more true than in the case of the king, a claim that underpins the attention paid to royal policy in this book. Much of the writing of those who can be described as England's earliest protestants was printed abroad; survives in private correspondence, again often to those abroad; or was printed in the reign of Edward VI or later. Cranmer, as we have seen, kept his counsel; Hugh Latimer's experience vividly illustrates the limitations on the expression of evangelical-cum-protestant ideas in the reign of Henry VIII. Undoubtedly there were those whose convictions may reasonably be termed protestant and who, if allowed the freedom to implement religious policy, would have worked to produce something that would seem recognisably protestant. But in Henry's lifetime, such men and women would have taken great risks if they had spoken and published freely; and, by and large, they did not. That in itself is highly significant. For the most, if not overwhelming, part, the protestant reformers of later reigns, notably Archbishop Cranmer, conformed to the king's reformation. In details, not least in wording, some, for example Cranmer again, doubtless influenced Henry's policy – but the essential qualification there is the phrase 'in details'. The substantial thrust of Henry's religious policy, it has been demonstrated in this study, owed nothing much to protestant influences. Henry's purposes were, as we have seen, in part political, the search for the jurisdictional autonomy that would deliver and validate his divorce, and the consequent imperative to deal with those who were opposed and to secure compliance from the remainder, and in part a reflection of his absorption in an intellectual and theological world best characterised as Erasmian, issuing in a deeply felt, and ultimately radically articulated, mistrust of certain integral features of traditional late medieval religion, notably monasteries and pilgrimages.

Was the king's reformation inherently unstable? Did its radical features make a greater impact and exert a longer-lasting influence than its more conservative aspects? A society without monks, nuns, friars, pilgrimages and shrines, and with a vernacular Bible, was in a sense protestant. By destroying so much, the king deflated the confidence of the church; and the Bible would prove its own stimulus. Yet none of that necessarily had to lead to a full-blown protestant reformation: it could as well have led to a wave of catholic reform under a monarch blessed with longer life than Queen Mary. Henry's religious beliefs were and are deeply problematic from a theological point of view. Combining and conflating positions that souls are saved either 'by the means of grace channelled through Holy Church led if not by the pope, by a council or some other visible body to administer discipline' or 'by the direct intervention of a sovereign God', the Henrician formularies risk the bewilderment of theologians.[15]

As Marillac, the French ambassador, put it in August 1540, 'il est bien difficile d'avoir ung peuple entierement aliene de nouvelles erreurs qui ne tienne avec l'ancienne autorite de l'eglise et pour le siege apostolique, ny au contraire hayant tant le pape qu'il ne participe en quelques opinions avec les Alemans. Et toutesfoys celux cy ne veulent ni l'ung ni l'autre, ains desirent qu'on garde ce qu'ilz ordonnent' (it was rather difficult to have a people entirely opposed to the new errors who did not uphold the former authority of the church and the Holy See, or, on the contrary, to have a people hating the pope so much without sharing some opinions with the Germans. Yet here they wanted neither the one nor the other, but insisted that the people obeyed what was commanded).[16] Henry's policy was potentially destabilising. He was unleashing a tiger but hoping to ride it down paths of his own choosing. Henry was 'like . . . one that would throw down a man headlong from the top of a high tower and bid him stay when he was half way down'.[17]

But in a world ruled by kings rather than theologians, logical contradictions may survive much longer than might be thought possible. It is the contention of this study that, in the second half of his reign, Henry secured a series of formulations of faith that reflected not the contingent outcomes of factional rivalries but, consistently and robustly, his own aspirations. To secure such codifications, however much the modern theologian might deplore their logical shortcomings, was itself an achievement. Moreover, Henry maintained to the end of his life what appears as a curious hybrid – a middle way between Rome and Wittenberg, or Rome and Zurich. Masses for the dead were encouraged but not masses seeking the intercession of individual saints. Monasteries were dissolved, but the doctrine of justification by faith was rejected. And so on. How far individuals believed as Henry wanted is, of course, unknowable, and no doubt there were more who would have preferred things to continue as they had been and somewhat fewer who would have wished for a full-blown protestant reformation. But, once the emergency of the rebellions of 1536–37 had passed, overwhelmingly the king's subjects conformed outwardly to the course he had set, with all its tensions and contradictions. The deep sense of loyalty of the political nation to the king played its part here too. Was Henry, however, the only Henrician? 'The question must be whether there were any Henricians other than the king himself.'[18] Here it has been argued that Thomas Cromwell, rather than pursuing a more radical religious agenda of his own, was one. Stephen Gardiner and Thomas Cranmer doubtless wished that royal policy was very different, though in opposite directions, but they conformed. In this study they have been presented more as royal servants than as political campaigners. No doubt in emphasising those aspects of the king's reformation that they found agreeable and minimising and ignoring those that they did not, they believed that they were doing what the king really wanted. Cranmer sincerely believed that Henry shared his wish for further reformation within a context of order, but was prepared, while offering suggestions, to bide his time and wait on God's providence: he did not manipulate the king or pursue policies independently or in defiance of him. Conservatives such as Gardiner, Stokesley and Lee offered embarrassed support for the royal supremacy but tried to restrain the excesses of reformist preachers, in the sincere belief that that was the wish of the king. But neither Gardiner's nor Cranmer's view of royal religious policy should be taken as a true or full reflection of it. The effect of their actions was to advance the *king's* reformation, rather than catholic reform or protestant reformation.

And if there were not many wholehearted Henricians, arguably there was, in vital respects, one more: Henry's daughter by Anne Boleyn, Queen Elizabeth, whose long reign would perpetuate and entrench significant features of her father's reformation. This is not the place to embark on what would undoubtedly be a controversial characterisation of the church of England under Elizabeth and beyond.[19] In important ways, the religious settlement of 1559 was different from the church of England between the mid-1530s and the end of Henry's reign, notably in its English prayer book and its rejection of the mass. Yet, that admitted, in many respects the legacies from Henry's reign were marked. That in doctrine and liturgy the church of England was, as it remains, what the modern jargon calls a 'contested site', with rival interpretations of central doctrines and liturgical practices, reflects, in many ways, the preferences, by no means always logical, of Henry VIII. That the church of England was a church with bishops, cathedrals and ecclesiastical courts but without monasteries and pilgrimages reflects Henry's beliefs. Just as Henry justified his church as a middle way, so later writers would too. Just as Henry was convinced of his royal supremacy – his royal authority – so also was Elizabeth, prepared to go so far as to suspend an archbishop who defied her will.

It is hard, then, to deny Henry the credit due to a skilful ruler who accomplished much of what he sought. And yet it would do little justice to the thrust of this book if we left the king on so positive a note. While Henry may have been measured in realising his aims, repeatedly he has appeared ruthless, even bloodthirsty, in dealing with those whom he saw as traitors, whether arguably justifiably in terms of realpolitik, as in the case of Robert Aske and the rebels of 1536–37, or whether with supreme ingratitude for all that they had done for him, as with Thomas Wolsey, Thomas More and Thomas Cromwell. The way in which he sought to secure compliance and deal with dissent and resistance – the pressures on churchmen to acquiesce in the early 1530s, the repeated recourse to threats of legal action under the statute of *praemunire*, the imposition of oaths that bound all that swore them to maintain the truth of royal policy – crossed contemporary boundaries between politic rule and tyranny.[20] The persuasions of monks to surrender their monasteries to the crown, together with denunciations of the religious life, make especially painful reading. Exemplary punishment intended to terrify was characteristic. Throughout, the king, while scrupulous in following legal procedures, nonetheless treated the law and the courts as mechanisms for enforcement and punishment, to be manipulated to secure the desired result, not as the arena where truth is established and justice done. All that is troubling, all too readily supporting T.B. Pugh's charge that 'Henry VIII was the most wicked man that ever misruled England'. Henry was a more active and a more dominating king than most professional historians have allowed. He was in significant respects a committed reformer of the church, however much that was (or is) seen as simply destructive by those attached to traditional religion, or as confused and misguided by those seeking a fuller protestant church. But that forcefulness and purposefulness proved a dangerous combination: a committed king certain of his rectitude, subordinating means to ends. And that points to a final image of Henry: more than the dominant figure of Holbein's portraits, the scourge of popes and superstition; ultimately a king who in the 1530s turned into a tyrant.

Notes

Abbreviations

'Aske's examination' Bateson, M., 'Aske's examination', *English Historical Review*, v (1890), pp. 550–73.

BL British Library

Cal. S.P. *Calendar of State Papers*

Cranmer, Writings and Letters J.E. Cox, ed., *Writings and Letters of Thomas Cranmer* (Parker Society, 1846).

Hall, *Chronicle* Hall, E., *Chronicle* (1809 edn)

'Early Life of Fisher' van Ortroy, F., ed., 'Vie du bienheureux martyr Jean Fisher, cardinal eveque de Rochester', Analecta Bollandianna, x (1891), pp. 121–365, xii (1893), pp. 97–283.

LP Brewer, J.S., J. Gairdner and R.H. Brodie, eds, *Letters and Papers, Foreign and Domestic, of the Reign of Henry VIII* (21 vols in 36, 1862–1932).

PRO Public Record Office

Roper, *Life of More* E.V. Hitchcock, *William Roper's Life of Sir Thomas More* (Early English Text Society, 1935).

RSTC *Revised Short-Title Catalogue* (see under Pollard, p. 703 below).

'The manner of the taking of Robert Aske' Bateson, M., 'The manner of the taking of Robert Aske', *English Historical Review*, V (1890), pp. 330–45.

Wriothesley, *Chronicle* W. Hamilton, ed., *Wriothesleys Chronicle*, (Camden Society, 2 vols, cxvi, 1875).

1: The Divorce

1 *Cal. S.P., Spanish*, IV ii 967 (p. 472); Hall, *Chronicle*, pp. 728, 753; *LP*, X 752.
2 Hall, *Chronicle*, pp. 755–6.
3 'Early Life of Fisher', x 150, 293.
4 *Cal. S.P., Spanish*, III ii 69 (p. 193).
5 D. Hay, ed., *The Anglica Historia of Polydore Vergil*, Camden Society, lxxiv (1950), p. 325.
6 Roper, *Life of More*, pp. 30–1.
7 J. Foxe, *Acts and Monuments*, ed. S.R. Cattley and G. Townsend, (8 vols, 1837–41), v 47.
8 Nicholas Harpsfield, *The Pretended Divorce between Henry VIII and Catherine of Aragon*, ed. N. Pocock, Camden Society, xxi (1878), pp. 175–6.
9 Hall, *Chronicle*, pp. 755–6.
10 E.V. Hitchcock and R.W. Chambers, eds, *Nicholas Harpsfield's Life and Death of Sir Thomas More*, Early English Text Society, clxxxvi (1932) p. 41.
11 *LP*, IV ii 3641; cf. IV ii 3767 (2).
12 PRO, SP1/52 fo. 109ᵛ (*LP*, IV iii 5156).
13 Note how much later, when finally pronouncing on the matter, Cranmer would excuse himself to the king: 'I would be right loth and also it shall not become me . . . to enterprise any part of my office in the said weighty [matter] . . . without your grace's favour and licence obtained' (PRO, SP1/75 fo. 78 [Cranmer, *Writings and Letters*, p. 237; *LP*, V 327]).
14 *LP*, IV iii 5774 (6): Deposition of Bishop Nicholas West of Ely; G. Mattingly, *Catherine of Aragon* (1942), p. 95; Hall, *Chronicle*, p. 507.
15 *LP*, III i 432.
16 R.B. Wernham, *Before the Armada* (1966); P. Gwyn, *The King's Cardinal* (1990).
17 Hall, *Chronicle*, p. 703.
18 A. Hoskins, 'Mary Boleyn's Carey children: offspring of Henry VIII', *Genealogists' Magazine* (March 1997) (I am grateful to Anthony Hoskins for sending me a draft of his paper); cf. *LP*, VIII 567, J.J. Scarisbrick, *Henry VIII* (1968), p. 148.
19 Scarisbrick, *Henry VIII*, pp. 149, 151–2.
20 D. MacCulloch, *Thomas Cranmer* (1995), p. 83. Cf. most recently remarks on Anne Boleyn's 'failure to accept the mere status [*sic*] of royal mistress' (F. Heal, *The Reformation in Britain and Ireland* [Oxford, 2003], p. 117) and 'Henry might be king, but he could command neither this woman nor her love' (D. Starkey, *Six Wives: the queens of Henry VIII* (2003), pp. 275–84 at 278).
21 J.G. Dwyer, ed., *Reginald Pole's Defense of the Unity of the Church* (Westminster, Maryland, 1965), pp. 185–6.
22 *LP*, IV ii 3325. (My italics.)
23 Ibid. ii 3990. (My italics.)
24 Ibid. ii 4383, 4403, 4410.
25 Ibid. ii 4894.
26 Ibid. ii 4597.
27 Ibid. ii 4742.
28 Vienna, Haus-, Hof- und Staatsarchiv, England, Karton 4, Berichte, 1529, fo. 246 (*Cal. S.P., Spanish*, IV i no. 224 p. 352).
29 *LP*, IV ii 4251.
30 Ibid. iii 5679; Le Grand, *Histoire du divorce de Henry VIII* (Paris, 1688, 3 vols), iii 325.

31 Hall, *Chronicle*, p. 759. I owe the equation of 'honest' and 'chaste' to a paper given by Peter Marshall at the university of Canterbury in April 1992: cf. his more cautious presentation in P. Marshall, *The Catholic Priesthood and the English Reformation* (Oxford, 1994), pp. 52–3.

32 PRO, SP1/46 fos 231–6 at 234–34ᵛ (N. Pocock, *Records of the Reformation* [Oxford, 2 vols, 1870], i 22ff.) for wording of second draft bull for Knight. (*LP*, IV ii 3686 [1, 2] offers too brief a summary).

33 PRO, SP1/44 fo. 41ᵛ (*State Papers*, i no. cxxxv p. 271; *LP*, IV ii 3400).

34 PRO, SP1/45 fos 229–30 (*State Papers*, vii no. clxvii p. 3 (*LP*, IV ii 3422); PRO, SP1/45 fos 231–6 (*LP*, IV ii 3686).

35 Scarisbrick, *Henry VIII*, p. 204.

36 PRO, SP1/45 fos 246–53 (*State Papers*, vii no. clxxxv pp. 29–35; *LP*, IV ii 3693).

37 *LP*, IV ii 3694.

38 Ibid. 4120; PRO, SP1/47 fos 177–89 (*LP*, IV ii 4617); *LP*, IV ii 4166.

39 *LP*, IV ii 4345; PRO, SP1/48 fo. 172 (*LP*, IV ii 4380); *LP*, IV ii 4897.

40 E.g. PRO, SP1/48 fo. 142 (*LP*, IV ii 4355); PRO, SP1/49 fo. 129ᵛ (*LP*, IV ii 4540).

41 PRO, SP1/82 fo. 22 (*LP*, VII 21).

42 *LP*, IV ii 4881; cf. IV 5604.

43 PRO, SP1/50 fo. 135 (*LP*, IV ii 4803); *LP*, IV ii 4857.

44 *LP*, IV ii 4875, 4880; iii 5179.

45 PRO, SP1/50 fos 219–31ᵛ (*State Papers*, vii no. ccxxiii pp. 102–15; *LP*, IV ii 4897).

46 *LP*, IV ii 4977, 4980.

47 Ibid. 4977; PRO, SP1/51 fos 39–65 (*LP*, IV ii 4978; *State Papers*, vii no. ccxxvi pp. 117–40); cf. PRO, SP1/52 fos 109–21 (*LP*, IV iii 5156) on reasons for its being a forgery; *LP*, IV iii 5180, 5181, 5211, 5375, 5376, 5401, 5440, 5441.

48 *LP*, IV iii 5447.

49 Ibid. 5474.

50 PRO, SP1/52 fo. 105 (*State Papers*, vii 143ff; *LP*, IV iii 5152).

51 PRO, SP1/52 fos 158–59ᵛ (*State Papers*, vii 148ff; *LP*, IV iii 5213).

52 PRO, SP1/53 fo. 123 (*State Papers*, i no. clxxi p. 329; *LP*, IV iii 5393).

53 *LP*, IV iii 5416.

54 PRO, SP1/53 fo. 210 (*State Papers*, vii no. ccxxxviii pp. 166–9 at 167; *LP*, IV iii 5481).

55 PRO, SP1/53 fo. 245 (*State Papers*, vii no. ccxxxix pp. 169ff; *LP*, IV iii 5519).

56 PRO, SP1/54 fos 54ᵛ–55 (*State Papers*, vii no. ccxliv pp. 183–4; *LP*, IV iii 5635).

57 28 May says Hall, *Chronicle*, p. 756.

58 *LP*, IV iii 5685; Hall, *Chronicle*, p. 757. (She had privately done so as early as February: *Cal. S.P., Spanish*, iii [ii] 652 [p. 928], 676–7 [pp. 990–1].)

59 R. Scheurer, ed., *La Correspondance du cardinal Jean du Bellay* (2 vols, Paris, 1969–73), p. 47 (*LP*, IV iii 5702); cf. Hall, *Chronicle*, p. 757: 'my mind and intent, which only is to have a final end, for the discharge of my conscience'.

60 *LP*, IV iii 5732: cf. Campeggio's letter of 29 June cited in 'Early Life of Fisher', x 313.

61 E.g. tone of PRO, SP1/55 fos 5–8ᵛ (*State Papers*, vii no. ccl pp. 193–5; *LP*, IV iii 5797).

62 E. Surtz and V. Murphy, eds, *The Divorce Tracts of Henry VIII* (Angers, 1988), p. iii.

63 Ibid.

64 PRO, SP1/63 fos 244–407ᵛ.

65 *LP*, IV ii 4120 for Casale/Gardiner/Foxe's report of this.
66 *Ibid.* 4597; and cf. Brian Tuke's referring to Henry coming to see him 'for devising with me upon his book' (*State Papers*, i no. cxlvii p. 300 [*LP*, IV ii 4409]).
67 Surtz and Murphy, *Divorce Tracts*, p. 144: *LP*, IV ii 3913, from Hatfield microfilm M 485/52: Hatfield MS 198 fo. 31ᵛ; 'Henricus octavus', SP1/63 fos 303–13ᵛ, 360–84ᵛ; *LP*, V 5 viii; IV iii 5729.
68 Surtz and Murphy, *Divorce Tracts*, pp. iii–viii.
69 *RSTC* 14826–7: BL, 228 c. 38 (1).
70 PRO, SP1/48 fos 6–6ᵛ (*LP*, IV ii 4246).
71 *LP*, IV iii 5945.
72 Ibid. 5996, 6026; PRO, SP1/56 fos 98–102 (*State Papers*, vii no. cclxiv pp. 219–24; *LP*, IV iii 6073).
73 *LP*, IV iii 6105, 6149, 6251.
74 Ibid. 6450.
75 Ibid. 6595.
76 Ibid. 6633.
77 Ibid. 6531, 6247.
78 R. Wakefield, *Kotser Codicis* (c. 1534) (*RSTC* 24943), sig. P iii (v) (*LP*, IV ii 3234).
79 M. Dowling, *Fisher of Men: a life of John Fisher, 1469–1535* (1999), p. 39.
80 Wakefield, *Kotser Codicis*, sig. P iv–ivᵛ (*LP*, IV ii 3234); R. Rex, 'The earliest use of Hebrew in books printed in England dating some works of Richard Pace and Robert Wingfield', *Cambridge Bibliographical Society*, ix (1990), p. 521.
81 Surtz and Murphy, *Divorce Tracts*, p. xix from Wakefield, *Kotser Codicis*, P2; p. 142.
82 J.P. Carley, ed., *The Libraries of Henry VIII* (2000), pp. xxxi–xxxii, xxxvi–xxxviii.
83 *LP*, VIII 1054.
84 Surtz and Murphy, *Divorce Tracts*, p. ix.
85 Ibid., p. xix.
86 *LP*, IV ii 4858.
87 Ibid. 5053.
88 E. Rogers, ed., *Correspondence of Thomas More* (Princeton, 1947), pp. 496–7.
89 *LP*, VIII 859 (39); Harpsfield, *Pretended Divorce*, p. 33.
90 V. Murphy, 'The debate over Henry VIII's first divorce: an analysis of the contemporary treatises', University of Cambridge Ph.D. thesis (1994), pp. 139, 149, 298.
91 V. Murphy, 'The literature and propaganda of Henry VIII's first divorce', in D. MacCulloch, ed., *The Reign of Henry VIII: politics, policy and piety* (1995), p. 139.
92 Cf. D.S. Katz, *The Jews in the History of England 1485–1850* (Oxford, 1994), pp. 21–2.
93 Cf. R. Rex, *The Theology of John Fisher* (Cambridge, 1991), pp. 177, 167, 178–9; J.J. Scarisbrick, 'The conservative episcopate in England 1529–1535', University of Cambridge Ph.D. thesis (1955), p. 75, from *LP*, VIII 859 (39, 40).
94 Cf. as Pace claimed: *Kotser Codicis*, sig. P iii–iiiᵛ.
95 For the next section see Katz, *The Jews in the History of England*, pp. 15–48.
96 *LP*, IV iii 6661.
97 Ibid. ii 3234.
98 *Cal. S.P., Spanish*, IV i no. 194 p. 294.
99 Hall, *Chronicle*, p. 755.
100 *LP*, IV ii 5636; 'Early Life of Fisher', x 303 n. 1.
101 *LP*, IV iii 5862.

102 Harpsfield, *Pretended Divorce*, pp. 210–11.
103 Cranmer, *Writings and Letters*, p. 230.
104 *Cal. S.P., Spanish*, IV i 241 (p. 387).
105 Ibid. 249.
106 G. Bedouelle and P. Le Gal, eds, *Le Divorce du roi Henry VIII* (Geneva, 1987), pp. 60–5; cf. Oxford's very similar opinion, ibid. pp. 66–72.
107 *LP*, IV ii 3234. I am grateful to Stuart Staples for this reference.
108 Hall, *Chronicle*, p. 757.
109 PRO, SP1/84 fos 59–60ᵛ (*State Papers*, i no. xxiii pp. 420–1; *LP*, VII 695).
110 *LP*, IV ii 4875.
111 H.A. Kelly, *The Matrimonial Trials of Henry VIII* (Stanford, 1976), pp. 139–40.
112 *LP*, XII ii 952.
113 Vienna, Haus-, Hof- und Staatsarchiv, England, Karton 4, Berichte, 1529, fo. 245ᵛ (*Cal. S.P., Spanish*, IV i no. 224 p. 352).
114 *LP*, V 361.
115 Vienna, Haus-, Hof- and Staatsarchiv, England, Karton 5, Berichte, 1533, fo. 57ᵛ (*LP*, VI 351).
116 *LP*, IV iii 5774 (1, 3, 13).
117 Hall, *Chronicle*, p. 757.
118 *LP*, IV iii 5774 (6).
119 Vienna, Haus-, Hof- und Staatsarchiv, England, Karton 5, Berichte, 1531, fo. 19 (*LP*, V 112).
120 *LP*, V 340.
121 Cf. Hall, *Chronicle*, p. 755.
122 *LP*, V 217; 355.
123 *LP*, V 401.
124 BL, Cotton MS, Cleopatra E v fos 110–10ᵛ.
125 Vienna, Haus-, Hof- und Staatsarchiv, England, Karton 5, Berichte, 1531, fo. 62 (*LP*, V 401; *Cal. S.P., Spanish*, IV ii 786).
126 *LP*, IV ii 3641.
127 PRO, SP1/42 fo. 147 (*State Papers*, i no. cix pp. 194–5; *LP*, IV ii 3217).
128 *LP*, IV ii 4251.
129 Scarisbrick, *Henry VIII*, pp. 194–7. Scarisbrick's exposition was influential: D.M. Loades wrote of 'Wolsey's hopeful and highly relevant suggestion' (*Mary Tudor* [1989], p. 52); G.R. Elton remarked that 'Henry ignored this ingenious solution. . . . most probably we have here only an example of the king's blind obstinacy' (*Reform and Reformation* [1977], pp. 106–7).
130 *LP*, IV iii 5377.
131 *Cal. S.P., Spanish*, IV i 275.
132 Cited by Kelly, *Matrimonial Trials*, pp. 117–18.
133 Hall, *Chronicle*, p. 758.
134 Kelly, *Matrimonial Trials*, pp. 139–40: but not in *LP*, IV iii 5994.
135 *The Tablet*, 25 Jan. 1986.
136 *LP*, IV ii 4858.
137 P. Gwyn, *The King's Cardinal: the rise and fall of Thomas Wolsey* (1990), pp. 530–48.
138 Cf. *LP*, IV ii 4681–4.
139 Ibid. 4391.
140 Cf. John Casale's report of 17 Dec. 1528 (*LP*, IV ii 5038).
141 *LP*, IV ii 5072.
142 Vienna, Haus-, Hof- und Staatsarchiv, England, Karton 4, Berichte, 1530, fo. 293 (*Cal. S.P., Spanish*, IV i no. 265 p. 465).
143 PRO, SP1/42 fos 48–48ᵛ (*LP*, IV ii 3148).

144 Murphy, 'Henry VIII's first divorce', p. 262.

145 Surtz and Murphy, *Divorce Tracts*, p. 158.

146 Murphy, 'Henry VIII's first divorce', p. 263.

147 Surtz and Murphy, *Divorce Tracts*, p. 141.

148 Bedouelle and Le Gal, *Le Divorce*.

149 G.R. Elton, *Reform and Reformation* (1977), pp. 136–8.

150 G.R. Elton, 'King or minister? The man behind the Henrician reformation', *History*, xxxix (1954), reprinted in G.R. Elton, *Studies in Tudor and Stuart Politics and Government* (Cambridge, 4 vols, 1974–92), i. 173–88.

151 For the former claim, see much of Elton's earlier writings: e.g. 'The king of hearts', *Historical Journal*, xii (1969), pp. 160–2; for the latter suggestion, see E.W. Ives, 'Henry VIII: the political perspective', in D. MacCulloch, ed., *The Reign of Henry VIII: politics, policy and piety* (Basingstoke, 1995), pp. 32, 26.

152 Elton, *Reform and Reformation*, p. 132.

153 Murphy, 'Literature and propaganda', p. 145, citing *LP*, IV ii 4942. *LP*, IV ii 3913 should be cited also. Cf. Scarisbrick, *Henry VIII*, p. 231.

154 *LP*, IV ii 4942.

155 Ibid.; Le Grand, *Histoire du divorce de Henri VIII*, iii 216–17.

156 Murphy, 'Literature and propaganda', p. 145; Gwyn, *King's Cardinal*, pp. 521–2.

157 Murphy, 'Literature and propaganda', p. 141.

158 Ibid., p. 146.

159 Ibid.

160 *State Papers*, i no. cv p. 189 (*LP*, IV ii 3147).

161 PRO, SP1/44 fo. 43 (*State Papers*, i no. cxxxv pp. 267–77 at 272–3; *LP*, IV ii 3400; but the *LP* version does not bring out the reasoning).

162 *LP*, IV ii 3913.

163 Ibid. 4881.

164 PRO, SP1/42 fo. 147 (*State Papers*, i no. cix pp. 194–5; *LP*, IV ii 3217).

165 *State Papers*, i no. cxxxv pp. 267–77 at 273 (*LP*, IV ii 3400).

166 PRO, SP1/42 fo. 147 (*State Papers*, i no. cix pp. 194–5; *LP*, IV ii 3217).

167 M. Nicholls, *A History of the Modern British Isles: 1529–1603* (1999), p. 24; Gwyn, *King's Cardinal*, pp. 511–30.

168 Here I differ from D.M. Loades on Henry in late 1529: 'in spite of occasional outbursts, [he] had not yet seriously thought of taking the law into his own hands' (*Mary Tudor*, p. 57), and G.R. Elton's assertion that 'Henry . . . at this time gave no sign that he even contemplated taking his realm into schism' (*Reform and Reformation*, p. 108), two representative examples of what is the orthodoxy on the subject.

169 *LP*, IV ii 3641.

170 PRO, SP1/45 fos 139ᵛ–40 (*State Papers*, vii no. clxxviii p. 20; *LP*, IV ii 3644).

171 *LP*, IV ii 3646.

172 PRO, SP1/45 fos 246–53 (*State Papers*, i no. clxxxv pp. 29–35; *LP*, IV ii 3693).

173 *LP*, IV ii 3767 (2).

174 PRO, SP1/46 fos 62–70 (*State Papers*, vii no. clxxxiii pp. 37–44; *LP*, IV ii 3770).

175 PRO, SP1/46 fo. 205 (*LP*, IV ii 3912).

176 *LP*, IV ii 3913: cf. Scarisbrick: 'words which they may only have been intended to play and to bully with, but which give us a glimpse of how brittle things were and how easily the divorce could get out of hand' (*Henry VIII*, p. 207).

177 *LP*, IV ii 3920.

178 Ibid. 4120 (J. Strype, *Ecclesiastical Memorials* [Oxford, 3 vols each in two parts, 1820–40], I ii no. 23).

179 PRO, SP1/47 fos 180–80ᵛ (*LP*, IV ii 4167); *LP*, IV ii 4251.
180 *LP*, IV ii 4288.
181 Ibid. 4881.
182 PRO, SP1/50 fos 221ᵛ–23 (*State Papers*, vii no. ccxxiii pp. 102–15 at 105–7 (*LP*, IV ii 4897).
183 *LP*, IV ii 4977.
184 Ibid. ii 4980. The editors of *LP* – for no very good reason – question whether this and other letters were actually sent to the pope, showing again how reluctant scholars have been to take these threats and warnings as serious evidence of Henry's intentions.
185 Ibid. iii 5210.
186 Ibid. 5255.
187 Ibid. 5416.
188 *Cal. S.P., Spanish*, II ii no. 661 p. 966 (*LP*, IV iii 5417).
189 *LP*, IV iii 5428.
190 PRO, SP1/53 fo. 200 (J.A. Muller, ed., *Letters of Stephen Gardiner* [Cambridge, 1933], p. 12; *LP*, IV iii 5476).
191 *LP*, IV iii 5523.
192 BL, Cotton MS, Vitellius B xi fo. 169 (*LP*, IV iii 5703).
193 *LP*, IV ii 5707.
194 PRO, SP1/54 fos 96–7 at 96ᵛ (*State Papers*, vii no. ccxlviii pp. 189–90 at 189; *LP*, IV iii 5711).
195 BL, Cotton MS, Vitellius B xi fo. 166 (*State Papers*, vii no. ccxlviii; *LP*, IV iii 5715).
196 BL, Cotton MS, Vitellius B xi fo. 194 (*LP*, IV III 5762).
197 BL, Cotton MS, Vitellius B xi fo. 192 (*LP*, IV iii 5761).
198 BL, Cotton MS, Vitellius B xi fo. 203 (*LP*, IV iii 5780).
199 PRO, SP1/55 fos 5–8 (in cipher) (*State Papers*, vii no. ccl pp. 193–7 at 194 and 197; *LP*, IV iii 5897); dating and authenticity discussed by Gwyn, *King's Cardinal*, pp. 527–8.
200 Cf. Harpsfield's comment that Wolsey 'most earnestly travelled to have the said divorce with all speed and celerity set forth, and to stay the advocation of the said cause that it should not devolve from himself and his colleague to the court of Rome, and that he made his full account that the said delay and advocation would turn to his utter undoing, as in short space after it did'. Elton remarked, 'Accurate as this forecast proved, it is hard to tell how deeply he believed lamentations clearly used to move Rome for the sake of saving himself' (*Reform and Reformation*, p. 108) – a somewhat shaky attempt to play down Wolsey's warnings.
201 *Cal. S.P., Spanish*, IV i no. 83 pp. 132–3.
202 Hall, *Chronicle*, p. 758.
203 G. Cavendish, *Life and Death of Cardinal Wolsey*, ed. R.S. Sylvester (Early English Text Society, 1959) p. 90; cf. G. Walker, 'Cardinal Wolsey and the satirists: the case of *Godly Queen Hester* re-opened', in S.J. Gunn and P.G. Lindley, eds, *Cardinal Wolsey: church, state and art* (Cambridge, 1991), p. 247.
204 Cf. Fisher's biographer: 'And he spake with such a spirit of vehemence and with so clamorous a noise, that all men about him marvelled what he meant, and wise men thought he durst not thus have said, but that he knew the king's mind aforehand' ('Early Life of Fisher', x 331).
205 *Pace* MacCulloch, *Cranmer*, p. 44, who sees it as a disastrous end, 'an act of deliberate procedural sabotage'.
206 *State Papers*, vii no. ccl pp. 193–97 (*LP*, IV iii 5797) for Wolsey and the adjournment; cf. Gwyn, *King's Cardinal*, pp. 529–30.

207 *LP*, IV ii 5025, 5050, iii 6292, 6387, 6705, 6757; V 28, 33, 1036, 1522.
208 Hall, *Chronicle*, p. 758.
209 *LP*, X 1077.
210 Vienna, Haus-, Hof- und Staatsarchiv, England, Karton 4, Berichte, 1529, fo. 210 (*Cal. S.P. Spanish*, IV i no. 160 p. 236), cf. IV i 168 (p. 257); J.A. Guy, *The Public Career of Thomas More* (Brighton, 1980), p. 206.
211 Hall, *Chronicle*, p. 759; cf. Guy, *Public Career of More*, p. 206.
212 Hall, *Chronicle*, p. 759; Scarisbrick, 'Conservative episcopate', pp. 110ff, from PRO, KB 29/161 fo. 27b.
213 Scarisbrick, 'Conservative episcopate', p. 111.
214 *Cal. S.P., Spanish.*, IV i no. 160 pp. 224–5.
215 *Statutes of the Realm*, iii 293 (21 Henry VIII c. 13 ix).
216 Vienna, Haus-, Hof- und Staatsarchiv, England, Karton 4, Berichte, 1529, fo. 245v (*Cal. S.P., Spanish*, IV i no. 224 pp. 351–2).
217 *Cal. S.P., Spanish*, IV i no. 232 p. 367.
218 Ibid. no. 241 p. 386 and cf. 392; no. 252 pp. 436–7 (*LP*, IV iii 6256).
219 Vienna, Haus-, Hof- und Staatsarchiv, England, Karton 4, Berichte, 1530, fo. 323^v (*Cal. S.P., Spanish*, IV i no. 373 p. 629; cf. *LP*, IV iii 6307).
220 PRO, E30/1012a (currently in folder marked E30/1025) (*LP*, IV iii 6513).
221 Herbert of Cherbury, *Life of Henry VIII* (1649), pp. 303–6; *LP*, IV iii 6638.
222 *LP*, IV iii 6667.
223 Ibid. 6705.
224 Scarisbrick, *Henry VIII*, pp. 260–1, 273.
225 G. Nicholson, 'The act of appeals and the English reformation', in C. Cross, D. Loades and J.J. Scarisbrick, eds, *Law and Government under the Tudors* (Cambridge, 1988), p. 19.
226 Vienna, Haus-, Hof- und Staatsarchiv, England, Karton 4, Berichte, 1530, fos 337–37^v (*Cal. S.P., Spanish*, IV i no. 433 p. 722; *Cal. S.P., Venetian*, iv 621 p. 259).
227 P.L. Hughes and J.F. Larkin, eds, *Tudor Royal Proclamations* (3 vols, 1964–69), i 197.
228 Vienna, Haus-, Hof- und Staatsarchiv, England, Karton 4, Berichte, 1530, fo. 339^v (*Cal. S.P., Spanish*, IV i no. 433 p. 726).
229 *Cal. S.P., Spanish*, IV i no. 445 p. 735.
230 *Cal. S.P., Milan*, 831 (pp. 526–7); *Cal. S.P., Venetian*, iv 629 (pp. 259, 262), 634 (p. 264); cf. Scarisbrick, 'Conservative episcopate', pp. 102–7.
231 Elton, *Reform and Reformation*, p. 133 n.; idem, *Policy and Police* (Cambridge, 1972), p. 218.
232 PRO, SP1/65 fo. 83 (*LP*, V 52).
233 *LP*, IV iii app. 260.
234 Vienna, Haus-, Hof- und Staatsarchiv, England, Karton 4, Berichte, 1530, fo. 340 (*Cal. S.P., Spanish*, IV i no. 445 p. 734).
235 Vienna, Haus-, Hof- und Staatsarchiv, England, Karton 4, Berichte, 1530, fo. 353 (*Cal. S.P., Spanish*, IV i no. 481 p. 790).
236 Vienna, Haus-, Hof- und Staatsarchiv, England, Karton 4, Berichte, 1530, fo. 343 (*Cal. S.P., Spanish*, IV i no. 460 p. 759).
237 Hall, *Chronicle*, p. 773; Vienna, Haus-, Hof- und Staatsarchiv, England, Karton 4, Berichte, 1530, fo. 346 (*Cal. S.P., Spanish*, IV i no. 492 p. 797).
238 *LP*, IV iii 6759; 6760.
239 PRO, PRO31/18/2/1 fo. 680^v (*Cal. S.P., Spanish*, IV i no. 547 p. 853).
240 Vienna, Haus-, Hof- und Staatsarchiv, England, Karton 4, Berichte, 1530, fo. 363 (*Cal. S.P., Spanish*, IV i no. 547 p. 853; IV i no. 555 p. 863).
241 *LP*, IV iii 5862; PRO, PRO31/18/2/1 fos 411, 420^v, 424, 483, 493^v, 542^v (*Cal.*

S.P., *Spanish*, IV i nos 160, 168, 182, 224, 228, 252 [pp. 235, 257, 274, 352–3, 361, 433]); *Cal. S.P.*, *Spanish*, IV i nos 232, 241 (pp. 370–1, 387); *LP*, IV iii 6307; *Cal. S.P., Venetian*, IV 576–7 (pp. 241–2).

242 *LP*. IV iii 6356, 6469, 6697, 6699, 6738; *Cal. S.P., Venetian*, IV 576 (p. 241); *Cal. S.P.*, *Spanish*, IV i nos 290, 425, 429, 460, 509 (pp. 512, 711–13, 729, 758-9, 817); *Cal. S.P.*, *Milan*, 831 (p. 527), 843 (p. 534).

243 Vienna, Haus-, Hof- und Staatsarchiv, England, Karton 4, Berichte, 1530, fo. 337ᵛ (*Cal. S.P.*, *Spanish*, IV i no. 433 pp. 722–3).

244 Vienna, Haus-, Hof- und Staatsarchiv, England, Karton 4, Berichte, 1530, fo. 343 (*Cal. S.P.*, *Spanish*, IV i no. 460 pp. 758–9).

245 *Cal. S.P., Spanish*, IV i no. 509 p. 818; *LP*, IV iii 6742; *Cal. S.P., Venetian*, IV 642; PRO, PRO 31/18/2/1 fos 679–79ᵛ (*Cal. S.P., Spanish*, IV i no. 547 p. 853); *Cal. S.P.*, *Spanish*, IV i no. 555 p. 863; *Cal. S.P.*, *Spanish*, IV ii no. 584 p. 3 (*LP*, V 24); *Cal. S.P.*, *Milan*, 843 (p. 534); *Cal. S.P.*, *Spanish*, IV ii no. 590 p. 16 (*LP*, V 40); 598 (p. 28) (*LP*, V 45).

246 PRO, SP2/N 155–60ᵛ.

247 Vienna, Haus-, Hof- und Staatsarchiv, England, Karton 4, Berichte, 1530, fo. 366.

248 J.P. Cooper, 'The Supplication against the Ordinaries reconsidered', *English Historical Review*, lxxii (1957), p. 635 n. 5.

249 Elton, *Reform and Reformation*, p. 131.

250 N. Pocock, *Records of the Reformation* (Oxford, 2 vols, 1870), ii 418–19; Oxford, Bodleian Library copy, sig. F iᵛ–ii.

251 *LP*, V 432.

252 Ibid., IV iii 6517.

253 Ibid., V 418–19.

254 Vienna, Haus-, Hof- und Staatsarchiv, England, Karton 4, Berichte, fo. 226 (*Cal. S.P.*, *Spanish*, IV i no. 211 pp. 325–6); cf. *LP*, IV ii 6058, 6418 (21), 6600 (17); Scarisbrick, 'Conservative episcopate', pp. 111–13; M.J. Kelly, 'Canterbury jurisdiction and influence during the episcopate of William Warham, 1503–1532', University of Cambridge Ph.D. thesis (1965), p. 210.

255 Scarisbrick, 'Conservative episcopate', p. 115; J. Guy, 'Henry VIII and the *praemunire* manoeuvres of 1530–31', *English Historical Review*, xcvii (1982), pp. 482–3.

256 Vienna, Haus-, Hof- und Staatsarchiv, England, Karton 5, Berichte, 1531, fo. 11 (*Cal. S.P.*, *Spanish*, IV ii no. 615 p. 38; *LP*, V 62).

257 Hall, *Chronicle*, pp. 775, 783–4.

258 Guy, '*Praemunire* manoeuvres', pp. 492–4, from Hall, *Chronicle*, pp. 774–5.

259 PRO, SP1/56 fos 86–86ᵛ (*LP*, IV 6047 [3]) (very brief summary).

260 J.J. Scarisbrick, 'The pardon of the clergy', *Cambridge Historical Journal*, xii (1956), p. 32, from BL, Cotton MS, Cleopatra F ii fo. 240; cf. Guy, '*Praemunire* manoeuvres', p. 494; cf. *Cal. S.P.*, *Spanish*, IV ii no. 636 (*LP*, V 105).

261 *Statutes of the Realm*, iii 334–8 (22 Henry VIII c. 15).

262 Guy, '*Praemunire* manoeuvres', p. 486.

263 Ibid., p. 500; Hall, *Chronicle*, pp. 774–5.

264 Guy, '*Praemunire* manoeuvres', p. 491.

265 For a detailed refutation see G.W. Bernard, 'The pardon of the clergy reconsidered', *Journal of Ecclesiastical History*, xxxvii (1986), pp. 258–87.

266 PRO, PRO 31/18/2/1 fo. 627 (*Cal. S.P.*, *Spanish*, IV i no. 396 p. 673).

267 Vienna, Haus-, Hof- und Staatsarchiv, England, Karton 4, Berichte, 1530, fo. 366. This letter, the last in the box for 1530, escaped the attention of the transcribers for the *Calendar of State Papers, Spanish*.

268 *Cal. S.P., Spanish*, IV ii no. 598 pp. 22–8 (*LP*, V 45).

269 Vienna, Haus-, Hof- und Staatsarchiv, England, Karton 5, Berichte, 1531, esp. fo. 9 (*Cal. S.P., Spanish*, IV ii no. 598 pp. 22–7 [*LP*, V 45]).

270 *Cal. S.P., Spanish*, IV ii no. 598 p. 27 (*LP*, V 45).

271 *Cal. S.P., Spanish*, IV ii no. 615 p. 39 (*LP*, V 62).

272 Vienna, Haus-, Hof- und Staatsarchiv, England, Karton 5, Berichte, 1531, fo. 17 [14 Feb. 1531].

273 Vienna, Haus-, Hof- und Staatsarchiv, England, Karton 5, Berichte, 1531, fo. 22 (*Cal. S.P., Spanish*, IV ii no. 64; *LP*, V 112).

274 Vienna, Haus-, Hof- und Staatsarchiv, England, Karton 5, Berichte, 1531, fo. 48 (*LP*, V 287); Hall, *Chronicle*, p. 781.

275 Cf. Nicholson, 'Act of appeals', p. 27.

276 *LP*, V 171.

277 *RSTC* 14826–7: BL, 228 c. 38 (1).

278 BL, Cotton MS, Cleopatra E vi fos 16–135.

279 Elton, 'King of hearts', p. 162.

280 *LP*, IV 6770, 6772; V 27.

281 Ibid., V 256.

282 *State Papers*, vii 297–9 at 298 (*LP*, V 206), deciphering of PRO, SP1/65 fos 223–23^v.

283 *LP*, V 75; cf. 92, 93, 102, 130, 144, 147, 148, 167, 239, 245, 252, 326, 421, 428, 484.

284 Ibid. 306, 327.

285 Ibid. 361.

286 Ibid. 545, 580.

287 Ibid. 565, 580, 594.

288 Ibid. 611.

289 Ibid. 835, 895; PRO, SP1/69 fos 145–49^v (*LP*, V 852), PRO, SP1/68 fos 160–64^v (*LP*, V 867); *LP*, V 696, 748, 800; PRO, SP1/69 fos 126–37 (*State Papers*, vii no. cccxviii pp. 352–60; *LP*, V 836); *LP*, V 892.

290 *LP*, V 287.

291 PRO, PRO31/18/2 fos 689^v–90 (*LP*, V 696).

292 *LP*, V 747; PRO, PRO31/18/2/1 fo. 704^v (*LP*, V 762).

293 *LP*, V 148. Date should be March 1532.

294 Ibid. 791; PRO, SP1/69 fos 88–94 (*LP*, V 792 [1]).

295 *LP*, V 869.

296 Vienna, Haus-, Hof- and Staatsarchiv, England, Karton 5, Berichte, 1532, fo. 14 (*Cal. S.P., Spanish*, IV ii no. 898 pp. 379–82).

297 *Statutes of the Realm*, iii 385; J.J. Scarisbrick, 'Clerical taxation in England, 1485–1547', *Journal of Ecclesiastical History*, xi (1960), pp. 41–54.

298 Vienna, Haus-, Hof- und Staatsarchiv, England, Karton 5, Berichte, 1532, fo. 17 (*Cal. S.P., Spanish*, IV ii no. 907 pp. 340–1).

299 Vienna, Haus-, Hof- und Staatsarchiv, England, Karton 4, Berichte, 1529, fo. 246 (*Cal. S.P., Spanish*, IV i no. 224 p. 353).

300 Vienna, Haus-, Hof- und Staatsarchiv, England, Karton 5, Berichte, 1532, fo. 21 (*Cal. S.P., Spanish*, IV ii no. 422 pp. 410–12; *LP*, V 879).

301 Vienna, Haus-, Hof- und Staatsarchiv, England, Karton 5, Berichte, 1532, fo. 17 (*Cal. S.P., Spanish*, IV ii no. 907 pp. 390–1; *LP*, V 832).

302 Vienna, Haus-, Hof- und Staatsarchiv, England, Karton 5, Berichte, 1532, fo. 21 (*Cal. S.P., Spanish*, IV ii no. 422 pp. 410–12; *LP*, V 879).

303 Vienna, Haus-, Hof- und Staatsarchiv, England, Karton 5, Berichte, 1532, fo. 23 (*Cal. S.P., Spanish*, IV ii no. 926 pp. 416–18; *LP*, V 898).

304 Vienna, Haus-, Hof- und Staatsarchiv, England, Karton 5, Berichte, 1532, fos 23–23^v (*Cal. S.P., Spanish*, IV ii no. 926 pp. 416–18; *LP*, V 898).

305 Vienna, Haus-, Hof- und Staatsarchiv, England, Karton 5, Berichte, 1532, fos 27–27ᵛ (*Cal. S.P., Spanish*, IV ii no. 934 pp. 424–9; *LP*, V 941).
306 *LP*, V 721 (5).
307 G.R. Elton, 'A note on the first act of annates', *Bulletin of the Institute of Historical Research*, xxiii (1950), pp. 203–4.
308 Vienna, Haus-, Hof- und Staatsarchiv, England, Karton 5, Berichte, 1532, fo. 17 (*Cal. S.P., Spanish*, IV ii no. 907 pp. 390–1; *LP*, V 832).
309 Vienna, Haus-, Hof- und Staatsarchiv, England, Karton 5, Berichte, 1532, fo. 23ᵛ (*Cal. S.P. Spanish*, IV ii no. 926 pp. 416–18; *LP*, V 898).
310 Vienna, Haus-, Hof- und Staatsarchiv, England, Karton 5, Berichte, 1532, fo. 27ᵛ (*Cal. S.P., Spanish*, IV ii no. 934 pp. 424–9; *LP*, V 941).
311 Vienna, Haus-, Hof- und Staatsarchiv, England, Karton 5, Berichte, 1532, fo. 21ᵛ (*Cal. S.P., Spanish*, IV ii no. 422 pp. 410–12; *LP*, V 879).
312 PRO, SP1/69 fo. 181ᵛ (*State Papers*, vii no. cccxix p. 362; *LP*, V 886).
313 N. Camusat, *Meslanges Historiques* (Troyes, 1619), fo. 82: 23 March 1532; *LP*, V 150 (misplaced under 1531 as reference to annates makes clear).
314 Vienna, Haus-, Hof- und Staatsarchiv, England, Karton 5, Berichte, 1532, fo. 17 (*Cal. S.P., Spanish*, IV ii no. 907 pp. 390–1; *LP*, V 832).
315 23 Henry VIII c. 20 (*Statutes of the Realm*, iii 386).
316 Cf. Vienna, Haus-, Hof- und Staatsarchiv, England, Karton 5, Berichte, 1532, fo. 23 (*Cal. S.P., Spanish*, IV ii no. 926 pp. 416–18; *LP*, V 898).
317 23 Henry VIII c. 20 (*Statutes of the Realm*, iii 386–8).
318 PRO, SP2/L fos 78–80 (*LP*, V 721 [1]); fair copy SP2/P fos 17–19 (*LP* VII 57 [2]); Scarisbrick, 'Conservative episcopate', pp. 232–3 thinks it might date from May rather than earlier, cf. Vienna, Haus-, Hof- und Staatsarchiv, England, Karton 5, Berichte, 1532, fos 56ᵛ–57 (*Cal., S.P., Spanish*, IV ii no. 951 pp. 444–6; *LP*, V 1013).
319 Four more abbots were indicted in Trinity term 1532, two more in 1533 and two more in 1534. Scarisbrick, 'Conservative episcopate', pp. 194–5, 213–14 n. 1.
320 Vienna, Haus-, Hof- und Staatsarchiv, England, Karton 5, Berichte, 1532, fo. 16 (*Cal. S.P., Spanish*, IV ii no. 899 pp. 382–4; *LP*, V 805).
321 PRO, SP1/69 fos 118–18ᵛ (*LP*, V 824).
322 PRO, SP1/69 fo. 121 (*State Papers*, vii no. cccxvi p. 349; *LP*, V 831).
323 PRO, SP1/69 fo. 118ᵛ (*LP*, V 824).
324 *LP*, V 818.
325 Vienna, Haus-, Hof- und Staatsarchiv, England, Karton 5, Berichte, 1532, fo. 19ᵛ (*Cal. S.P., Spanish*, IV ii no. 915 pp. 404–6; *LP*, V 850).
326 Camusat, *Meslanges Historiques*, fo. 79 (*LP*'s, V 893 – but *LP*'s 'this is the cause of the wrong done to him at Rome' is a mistranslation).
327 Camusat, *Meslanges historiques*, fo. 82 (*LP*, V 150, misplaced under 1531).
328 Elton, *Reform and Reformation*, p. 155; idem, 'The Commons' Supplication of 1532: parliamentary management in the reign of Henry VIII', *English Historical Review*, lxvi (1951), pp. 507–34.
329 J.P. Cooper, 'The Supplication against the Ordinaries reconsidered', *English Historical Review*, lxxii (1957), pp. 616–41.
330 Guy, *Public Career of Thomas More*, ch. 8.
331 The most accessible text is in R.B. Merriman, ed., *Life and Letters of Thomas Cromwell* (2 vols, 1904), i 104–11.
332 Hall, *Chronicle*, p. 784.
333 M.J. Kelly, 'The submission of the clergy', *Transactions of the Royal Historical Society*, 5th ser., xv (1965), p. 105.

334 23 Henry VIII c. 9 (*Statutes of the Realm*, iii 377–8).

335 H. Gee and W.J. Hardy, *Documents Illustrative of English Church History* (1896), pp. 154–76; cf. Scarisbrick, *Henry VIII*, 217–18, 301 n.; S.E. Lehmberg, *The Reformation Parliament 1529–1536* (Cambridge, 1970), p. 141 n. 2.

336 23 Henry VIII c. 1 (*Statutes of the Realm*, iii 362–3).

337 *State Papers*, vii no. cccxvi pp. 349–50 at 349 (*LP*, V 831).

338 Hall, *Chronicle*, p. 784.

339 Cooper, 'Supplication against the Ordinaries', pp. 625–7, 630.

340 Guy, *Public Career of Thomas More*, pp. 187–8; C. Haigh is cautiously ambiguous, doubting that Cromwell would have dared to deceive the king, 'but it may be that he had little choice': it 'may . . . have been a desperate tactical ploy by Cromwell' ('Anticlericalism and the English', *History*, lxviii [1983], pp. 397, 399); Elton claimed that 'Cromwell, by the use of the "Supplication against the Ordinaries", succeeded in destroying the conservative party on the council, drove out Gardiner and forced More's resignation' ('King of Hearts', p. 163).

341 Guy, *Public Career of Thomas More*, pp. 187–8.

342 PRO, SP1/69 fo. 40ᵛ (*LP*, V 723).

343 *LP*, V 833; Vienna, Haus-, Hof- und Staatsarchiv, England, Karton 5, Berichte, 1532, fo. 17ᵛ (*Cal. S.P., Spanish.*, IV ii no. 907 pp. 390–1; LP, V 832); cf. fo. 15ᵛ (*Cal. S.P. Spanish*, IV ii no. 899 pp. 382–4; *LP*, V 805); Cooper, 'Supplication against the Ordinaries', pp. 617–18 (Cooper failed to find the transcript of Chapuys's letter in the Public Record Office – it is PRO, PRO31/18/2/1 fo. 715 – but his reasoning was nonetheless shrewd).

344 PRO, SP1/69 fo. 9 (*LP*, V 701).

345 *LP*, V 688; PRO, SP1/69 fo. 65 (*LP*, V 740); PRO, SP1/69 fo. 14 (*LP*, V 716).

346 PRO, SP1/69 fo. 10 (*LP*, V 708); *LP*, V 709; PRO, SP1/69 fo. 11 (*LP*, V 710); PRO, SP1/69 fo. 53 (*LP*, V 728); PRO, SP1/69 fo. 64 (*LP*, V 734); PRO, SP1/69 fo. 66 (*LP*, V 741).

347 *LP*, V 739; PRO, SP1/69 fo. 75 (*LP*, V 753); PRO, SP1/69 fo. 87 (*LP*, V 789); *LP*, V 804, 808, 813, 843, 870.

348 PRO, SP1/69 fo. 80 (*LP*, V 769); PRO, SP1/69 fo. 111 (*LP*, V 802) for archbishop of York; *LP*, V 822, 825, 842; PRO, SP1/69 fo. 143 (*LP*, V 849); *LP*, V 878.

349 PRO, SP1/69 fo. 113 (*LP*, V 803); PRO, SP1/69 fos 154–54ᵛ (*LP*, V 857); PRO, SP1/69 fos 170–1 (*LP*, V 874); PRO, SP1/69 fo. 193 (*LP*, V 902); PRO, SP1/69 fo. 210 (*LP*, V 920); PRO, SP1/69 fo. 212 (*LP*, V 922); PRO, SP1/69 fo. 242 (*LP*, V 963).

350 PRO, SP1/69 fo. 114 (*LP*, V 812).

351 *State Papers*, i 380–3.

352 PRO, SP1/69 fos 40ᵛ–41 (*LP*, V 723).

353 *LP*, V 762, 805, 832, 879, 898.

354 Ibid. 807.

355 PRO, SP1/69 fo. 118 (*LP*, V 824).

356 PRO, SP1/69 fo. 121 (*LP*, V 831); *LP*, V 1013, 1046.

357 *LP*, V 805.

358 Ibid. 850.

359 Ibid. 941.

360 Cf. Elton, *Reform and Reformation*, p. 153.

361 Hall, *Chronicle*, pp. 784–5.

362 Vienna, Haus-, Hof- und Staatsarchiv, England, Karton 5, Berichte, 1532, fos 708ᵛ–709 (*Cal. S.P., Spanish*, IV ii no. 898, pp. 379–82; *LP*, V 773).

363 *Cal. S.P., Venetian*, IV 330 (p. 754).
364 Camusat, *Meslanges historiques*, fo. 79: 20 March 1532 (*LP*, V 893).
365 Elton, *Reform and Reformation*, p. 153.
366 *Pace* Elton, ibid.
367 Cf. Scarisbrick, 'Conservative episcopate', p. 229.
368 Gardiner, *Letters*, pp. 48–9 (*LP*, V 1019).
369 *LP*, VI 276.
370 Hall, *Chronicle*, p. 788.
371 Vienna, Haus-, Hof- und Staatsarchiv, England, Karton 5, Berichte, 1532, fo. 60 (*LP*, V 1046).
372 Hall, *Chronicle*, p. 788.
373 Vienna, Haus-, Hof- und Staatsarchiv, England, Karton 5, Berichte, 1532, fos 41–41ᵛ (*Cal. S.P., Spanish*, IV ii no. 948 pp. 440–1; *LP*, V 989).
374 *LP*, VI 276.
375 Hall, *Chronicle*, pp. 788–9.
376 *Cal. S.P., Venetian*, IV 761 pp. 332–3.
377 Vienna, Haus-, Hof- und Staatsarchiv, England, Karton 5, Berichte, 1532, fos 56ᵛ–57 (*Cal. S.P., Spanish*, IV ii no. 951 pp. 444–6; *LP*, V 1013).
378 Cf. Kelly, 'Episcopate of Warham', p. 265 n.
379 Vienna, Haus-, Hof- und Staatsarchiv, England, Karton 5, Berichte, 1532, fo. 62ᵛ (Chapuys to Mary of Hungary, 13 May 1532, not calendared in *Cal. S.P., Spanish* or in *LP*).
380 Kelly, 'Episcopate of Warham', pp. 265–6, from BL, Cotton MS, Cleopatra F i fos 101–3.
381 Kelly, 'Episcopate of Warham', p. 270.
382 PRO, SP1/70 fos 29–31ᵛ (*LP*, V 1023).
383 Kelly, 'Episcopate of Warham', pp. 270–6.
384 Vienna, Haus-, Hof- und Staatsarchiv, England, Karton 5, Berichte, 1532, fos 68–68ᵛ (*Cal. S.P., Spanish*, IV ii no. 954 pp. 450–1; *LP*, V 1058).
385 Hall, *Chronicle*, p. 790.
386 Ibid.
387 Ibid., p. 794; *LP*, VI 351, 465.
388 *LP*, VI 351, 391.
389 Ibid. 391.
390 Ibid. 311, 317, 661.
391 PRO, SP1/76 fo. 46 (*LP*, VI 486); PRO, SP1/76 fo. 49 (*LP*, VI 487); *LP*, VI 492.
392 PRO, SP1/75 fos 78–78ᵛ (*LP*, VI 327); *LP*, VI 332.
393 *LP*, VI 391, 465.
394 Ibid. 461; PRO, SP1/76 fo. 35 (*LP*, VI 470).
395 PRO, SP1/76 fo. 54 (*LP*, VI 495); *LP*, VI 496.
396 PRO, SP1/76 fo. 84 (*LP*, VI 528); *LP*, VI 661.
397 *LP*, VI 584, 601, 661.
398 24 Henry VIII c. 12 (*Statutes of the Realm*, iii 427–9).
399 25 Henry VIII c. 22 (*Statutes of the Realm*, iii 473).
400 25 Henry VIII c. 28 (*Statutes of the Realm*, iii 484–6).
401 25 Henry VIII c. 14 (*Statutes of the Realm*, iii 455).
402 25 Henry VIII c. 20 (*Statutes of the Realm*, iii 462–4).
403 25 Henry VIII c. 27 (*Statutes of the Realm*, iii 483–4).
404 25 Henry VIII c. 21 (*Statutes of the Realm*, iii 464–71).
405 25 Henry VIII c. 19 (*Statutes of the Realm*, iii 460).
406 24 Henry VIII c. 12 (*Statutes of the Realm*, iii 428).
407 24 Henry VIII c. 12 (*Statutes of the Realm*, iii 427).

408 25 Henry VIII c. 21 (*Statutes of the Realm*, iii 464).
409 25 Henry VIII c. 22 (*Statutes of the Realm*, iii 472).
410 26 Henry VIII c. 2 (*Statutes of the Realm*, iii 492).
411 Richard Rex asserts that the use of this new formulation from 1534 disproves Scarisbrick's position that 'the main ideas originated with the king as early as 1530' ('The crisis of obedience: God's word and Henry's reformation', *Historical Journal*, xxxix [1996], pp. 863–94 at 856, 878–81). But that is to adopt a misleadingly nominalist approach: as we have abundantly seen, Henry was amply capable of seeing himself as supreme head of the church in England long before the pope was renamed the bishop of Rome.
412 A useful survey of printing details is offered by Elton, *Policy and Police*, pp. 175–86.
413 25 Henry VIII c. 22 (*Statutes of the Realm*, iii 474).
414 26 Henry VIII c. 2 (*Statutes of the Realm*, iii 492–3).
415 BL, Cotton MS, Cleopatra E vi fo. 218 (*LP*, VIII 921).
416 24 Henry VIII c. 12 (*Statutes of the Realm*, iii 427–8).
417 25 Henry VIII c. 22 (*Statutes of the Realm*, iii 474).
418 26 Henry VIII c. 13 (*Statutes of the Realm*, iii 508–9).
419 25 Henry VIII c. 22 (*Statutes of the Realm*, iii 474).

2: Opposition

1 J.A. Froude, *History of England from the Fall of Wolsey to the Defeat of the Spanish Armada* (12 vols), i 336.
2 PRO, SP1/42 fo. 155ᵛ (*LP*, IV ii 3231); Scarisbrick, *Henry VIII*, p. 157.
3 *LP*, IV ii 4120.
4 Ibid. 4875.
5 Ibid. 4858, 4875; cf. 5072.
6 Ibid. 4685.
7 Ibid. iii 5685; Hall, *Chronicle*, p. 757.
8 *Cal. S.P., Spanish*, III ii nos 652, 676–7 pp. 928, 990–1.
9 Ibid., IV i no. 224 pp. 349–53.
10 Ibid. no. 354 pp. 598–9.
11 Ibid. p. 600.
12 Hall, *Chronicle*, p. 774.
13 Ibid., pp. 781–2.
14 Ibid.; *Cal. S.P., Spanish*, IV ii no. 739 pp. 169–78; *LP*, V 287.
15 *LP*, V 361; *Cal. S.P., Spanish*, IV ii no. 775 pp. 222–3.
16 *Cal. S.P., Spanish*, IV ii no. 808 pp. 263–5; *LP*, V 478.
17 *LP*, VI 391, 461, 465.
18 Ibid. 324, 351, 534.
19 Ibid. 760, 765, 805, 1554.
20 PRO, SP1/79 fos 158–58ᵛ (*LP*, VI 1252); *LP*, VI 1253.
21 PRO, PRO31/18/2/1 fos 1031ᵛ–33ᵛ (*Cal. S.P., Spanish*, IV ii no. 1164 pp. 889–95; *LP*, VI 1558).
22 *State Papers*, i. no. xxii pp. 418–19 (*LP*, VI 1542); cf. list in *LP*, VII 135.
23 *LP*, VI 1558.
24 Ibid., VI 1571, 1541–3, 1558; VII 83, 337.
25 Ibid., VII 83.
26 Ibid. 420.
27 Ibid. 662.
28 Ibid. 690, 726.

29 Ibid. 695.

30 Ibid. 726.

31 Ibid., VI 19.

32 Ibid., VII 1369.

33 Ibid. 469.

34 Ibid., VIII 428, 435.

35 Ibid., VII 1036.

36 Ibid. 1206.

37 Ibid., VI 1199.

38 PRO, SP1/78 fo. 141 (*LP*, VI 1009); PRO, SP1/78 fo. 169 (*LP*, VI 1041).

39 *Cal. S.P., Spanish*, IV ii no. 1161 p. 882.

40 *LP*, VI 1528.

41 Ibid., VIII 263.

42 Vienna, Haus-, Hof- und Staatsarchiv, England, Karton 5, Berichte, 1533, fo. 118 (*Cal. S.P., Spanish*, IV ii no. 1130 pp. 813ff; *LP*, VI 1164).

43 *Cal. S.P., Spanish*, V i no. 109 pp. 323–4; *LP*, VII 1368; cf. VI 1164; cf. VIII 750.

44 PRO, SP1/138 fo. 156 (*LP*, XIII ii 795); PRO, SP1/138 fo. 182^v (*LP*, XIII ii 804 [6]); PRO, SP1/139 fo. 34^v (*LP*, XIII ii 830 [i]).

45 *LP*, VI 1009, 1041.

46 PRO, PRO 31/18/2/1 fos 999^v–1000 (*Cal. S.P., Spanish*, IV ii no. 1149 pp. 854–7).

47 *LP*, VIII 859.

48 Ibid. 859 (32).

49 Ibid., V 512.

50 Ibid. 1046, VI 918.

51 Ibid., IX 48.

52 Ibid., VII 83.

53 Ibid., VI 1085, 1193, 1297.

54 Ibid., VII 1437.

55 Ibid., VIII 189.

56 Ibid., V 513.

57 Ibid. 582.

58 Vienna, Haus-, Hof- und Staatsarchiv, England, Karton 5, Berichte, 1532, fo. 17^v (*Cal. S.P., Spanish*, IV ii no. 907 pp. 390–1; *LP*, V 832).

59 *LP*, V 1059.

60 Ibid. 1311.

61 Ibid. 1520.

62 Ibid., VI 142.

63 Ibid. 653.

64 Ibid., VII 162.

65 Vienna, Haus-, Hof- und Staatsarchiv, England, Karton 5, Berichte, 1533, fo. 91^v (*Cal. S.P., Spanish*, IV ii no. 1091 pp. 718–25; *LP*, VI 720).

66 Vienna, Haus-, Hof- und Staatsarchiv, England, Karton 5, Berichte, 1533, fo. 122^v (*Cal. S.P., Spanish*, IV ii no. 1133 p. 821; *LP*, VI 1249).

67 *LP*, VII 14.

68 Ibid. 171.

69 Ibid. 662.

70 Ibid., IX 48.

71 Ibid. 587–8.

72 Ibid. 966.

73 Ibid. 967.

74 *Cal. S.P., Spanish*, V i no. 219 p. 560 (*LP* IX 596).

75 *LP*, X 199.
76 *Cal. S.P., Spanish*, IV ii no. 833 pp. 291–2, misdated 22 Nov. 1531: Mattingly, *Catherine of Aragon*, p. 261. Catherine writes from Buckden, so post-1534, and refers to nearly six years' waiting.
77 *LP*, VI 805; cf. 760, 765.
78 Ibid., V 750; cf. 846, 974; 1046 for presentation.
79 Ibid., VI 1046.
80 Ibid. 953, 974.
81 Ibid. 1164.
82 Ibid. 142.
83 Ibid. 19.
84 Ibid., VIII 514.
85 Ibid., V 938.
86 *Cal. S.P., Venetian*, V 575 (pp. 257–8).
87 *LP*, VIII 859 (30).
88 Ibid., X 141.
89 *Cal. S.P., Spanish*, V ii no. 21 p. 43.
90 *LP*, X 1110, 1129, 1136–7, 1186.
91 Elton, *Policy and Police*, p. 274.
92 But probably more: cf. 25 Henry VIII c. 12 (*Statutes of the Realm*, iii 446–51 at 448).
93 Cf. D. Watt, *Sectaries of God: women prophets in late medieval and early modern England* (1998), p. 56.
94 For a fuller discussion see G.W. Bernard, 'Vitality and vulnerability in the late medieval church: pilgrimage on the eve of the break with Rome', in J.L. Watts, ed., *The End of the Middle Ages? England in the fifteenth and sixteenth centuries* (Stroud, 1998), pp. 199–233.
95 PRO, SP1/82 fo. 73ᵛ (L.E. Whatmore, 'The sermon against the holy maid of Kent and her adherents, delivered at Paul's Cross, November the 23rd, 1533, and at Canterbury, December the 7th', *English Historical Review*, lviii (1943), pp. 463–75, at 465. Whatmore prints a modernised text of PRO, SP1/82 fos 73–80ᵛ (summary in *LP*, VII 72 [iii]). The text has not been bound in the correct sequence and the error is repeated in Whatmore's transcript: fos 78–78ᵛ should precede fos 77–77ᵛ.
96 Cf. Watt, *Sectaries of God*, pp. 63–5, 70–1; D. Watt, 'Reconstructing the word: the political prophecies of Elizabeth Barton (1506–1534)', *Renaissance Quarterly*, 1 (1997).
97 T. Wright, ed., *Letters Relating to the Suppression of the Monasteries*, Camden Society (1843), pp. 14–15 (*LP*, VI 1466).
98 25 Henry VIII c. 12 (*Statutes of the Realm*, iii 449, 446); PRO, SP1/82 fo. 74ᵛ ('Sermon', p. 467).
99 *Cal. S.P., Spanish*, IV ii no. 1149 p. 857; *LP*, VI 1419.
100 PRO, SP1/82 fo. 74ᵛ (Whatmore, 'Sermon', p. 467).
101 PRO, SP1/80 fo. 128 (*LP*, VI 1468 [5]).
102 25 Henry VIII c. 12 (*Statutes of the Realm*, iii 448).
103 PRO, SP1/80 fo. 128 (*LP*, VI 1468 [5]).
104 PRO, SP1/82 fo. 75 (Whatmore, 'Sermon', p. 468); 25 Henry VIII c. 12 (*Statutes of the Realm*, iii 446).
105 PRO, SP1/82 fo. 74ᵛ (Whatmore, 'Sermon', 467); cf. *LP*, VI 1466 (Wright, *Suppression*, p. 15).
106 PRO, SP1/50 fo. 137. Text printed in *Archaeologia Cantiana*, i (1858), p. 40 (dated 1 Oct., most probably 1528) (*LP*, IV ii 4806).
107 PRO, SP1/82 fo. 74ᵛ (Whatmore, 'Sermon', p. 467).

108 *LP*, VI 1470, 1466; *Cal. S.P., Spanish*, IV ii no. 1153 p. 863; *LP*, VI 1445.
109 *LP*, VII 532 (1).
110 Ibid., VI 1519.
111 Ibid. 1149 (2).
112 PRO, SP1/82 fo. 74ᵛ (Whatmore, 'Sermon', p. 467).
113 Ibid.; 25 Henry VIII c. 12 (*Statutes of the Realm*, iii 449–50).
114 PRO, SP1/138 fo. 174 (*LP*, XIII ii 802); *LP*, XIII ii 831 (v); PRO, SP1/139 fo. 14 (*LP*, XIII i 827 [2]).
115 PRO, SP1/138 fo. 174 (*LP*, XIII ii 802); *LP*, XIII ii 831 (v); PRO, SP1/80 fo. 130 (*LP*, VI 1468 [7]).
116 PRO, SP1/80 fo. 128 (*LP*, VI 1468 [5]).
117 *Cal. S.P., Spanish*, IV ii no. 1149 p. 857, no. 1153 p. 864; *LP*, VI 1372, 1419.
118 PRO, SP1/82 fo. 80 (Whatmore, 'Sermon', p. 475).
119 25 Henry VIII c. 12 (*Statutes of the Realm*, iii 449, 451).
120 E.H. Shagan, 'Print, orality and communications in the Maid of Kent affair', *Journal of Ecclesiastical History*, lii [2001], p. 31; E.H. Shagan, *Popular Politics and the English Reformation* (Cambridge, 2002), p. 78.
121 PRO, SP1/80 fos 112–12ᵛ (*LP*, VI 1468; printed in Shagan, 'Maid of Kent affair', pp. 31–2).
122 Cranmer, *Writings and Letters*, p. 271, printing BL, Harleian MS, 6148 fo. 3 (*LP*, VI 1519).
123 *LP*, VI 1438.
124 PRO, SP1/80 fo. 128 (*LP*, VI 1468 [5]).
125 Cranmer, *Writings and Letters*, p. 273 (*LP*, VI 1546).
126 PRO, SP1/82 fo. 74ᵛ (Whatmore, 'Sermon', p. 467).
127 25 Henry VIII c. 12 (*Statutes of the Realm*, iii 448) (cf. Wright, *Suppression*, p. 17 [*LP*, VI 1466]).
128 PRO, SP1/82 fo. 75 (Whatmore, 'Sermon', p. 468).
129 Ibid.; 25 Henry VIII c. 12 (*Statutes of the Realm*, iii 446).
130 *LP*, VII 72 (i); PRO, SP1/82 fo. 75ᵛ (Whatmore, 'Sermon', p. 468).
131 Ibid., VI 887; Cranmer, *Writings and Letters*, p. 252 (*LP*, VI 869), printing BL, Harleian MS 6143 fo. 23.
132 PRO, SP1/78 fo. 106 (*LP*, VI 967).
133 PRO, SP1/79 fo. 62 (*LP*, VI 1149).
134 PRO, SP1/79 fo. 80 (*LP*, VI 1169).
135 PRO, SP1/79 fos 61ᵛ–64 (*LP*, VI 1149).
136 PRO, SP1/80 fo. 20 (*LP*, VI 1336).
137 *LP*, VI 1381 (1).
138 Ibid. 1382.
139 PRO, SP1/80 fo. 94 (*LP*, VI 1417).
140 *Cal. S.P., Spanish*, IV ii no. 1149 p. 857.
141 Ibid. no. 1153 p. 861.
142 Cf. ibid. no. 1154 pp. 866–7 (*LP*, VI 1460).
143 Cranmer, *Writings and Letters*, p. 271, from BL, Harleian MS 6148 fo. 3. From internal evidence it is clear that the sermon was delivered in front of Barton, the parson of Aldington and Dr Bocking; the words 'in Canterbury' were twice changed to 'in this town', showing alterations made for the delivery of the sermon in Canterbury: Whatmore, 'Sermon', p. 464. The amendments are in PRO, SP1/82 fos 73 and 78.
144 *LP*, VII 72.
145 PRO, SP1/82 fo. 71 (*LP*, VII 72 [ii]).
146 *LP*, VI 1433. (Whatmore puzzlingly reads this as 'merely an intrepid admission of her activities against the divorce': 'Sermon', p. 469 n. 1.)

147 Cranmer, *Writings and Letters*, p. 274 (*LP*, VI 1546).
148 Hall, *Chronicle*, p. 812.
149 PRO, SP1/82 fo. 74 (Whatmore, 'Sermon', p. 466).
150 PRO, SP1/82 fo. 75ᵛ (Whatmore, 'Sermon', p. 469); cf. fo. 79 (Whatmore, 'Sermon', p. 473).
151 PRO, SP1/82 fo. 73 (Whatmore, 'Sermon', p. 464).
152 PRO, SP1/82 fo. 76 (Whatmore, 'Sermon', p. 469).
153 PRO, SP1/82 fo. 78 (Whatmore, 'Sermon', p. 471).
154 PRO, SP1/82 fo. 73 (Whatmore, 'Sermon', p. 464).
155 PRO, SP1/82 fo. 79 (Whatmore, 'Sermon', p. 473).
156 PRO, SP1/82 fo. 80 (Whatmore, 'Sermon', p. 474).
157 Wright, *Suppression*, p. 18 (*LP*, VI 1466).
158 25 Henry VIII c. 12 (*Statutes of the Realm*, iii 450).
159 Wright, *Suppression*, p. 18 (*LP*, VI 1466).
160 25 Henry VIII c. 12 (*Statutes of the Realm*, iii 449).
161 PRO, SP1/82 fo. 74 (Whatmore, 'Sermon', p. 467).
162 PRO, SP1/82 fo. 75 (Whatmore, 'Sermon', p. 468); 25 Henry VIII c. 12 (*Statutes of the Realm*, iii 446).
163 PRO, SP1/82 fo. 75ᵛ (Whatmore, 'Sermon', p. 469).
164 25 Henry VIII c. 12 (*Statutes of the Realm*, iii 449).
165 Hall, *Chronicle*, p. 812.
166 25 Henry VIII c. 12 (*Statutes of the Realm*, iii 449).
167 PRO, SP1/82 fo. 74 (Whatmore, 'Sermon', p. 466).
168 PRO, SP1/82 fo. 76 (Whatmore, 'Sermon', pp. 469–70).
169 25 Henry VIII c. 12 (*Statutes of the Realm*, iii 448).
170 25 Henry VIII c. 12 (*Statutes of the Realm*, iii 449).
171 Vienna, Haus-, Hof- und Staatsarchiv, England, Karton 5, Berichte, 1533, fo. 132ᵛ (*Cal. S.P., Spanish*, IV ii no. 1153 p. 863; *LP*, VI 1445).
172 Vienna, Haus-, Hof- und Staatsarchiv, England, Karton 5, Berichte, 1533, fo. 136ᵛ (*Cal. S.P., Spanish*, IV ii no. 1154 p. 867; *LP*, VI 1460).
173 *LP*, VII 52.
174 Ibid. 522; 70; Wriothesley, *Chronicle*, i 24.
175 PRO, SP1/82 fos 67ᵛ–68 (*LP*, VII 71); *LP*, VII 1026 (10); Elton, *Policy and Police*, p. 344.
176 R. Rex, 'The execution of the holy maid of Kent', *Historical Research*, cxiv (1991), p. 219; Christopher Hales, attorney-general, had in September written damningly about Bocking but praised Master as 'a man of good fame and honest' (*LP*, VI 1169).
177 *LP*, VII 386.
178 PRO, SP1/82 fo. 129 (*LP*, VII 138).
179 Whatmore, 'Sermon', p. 471; PRO, SP1/82 fo. 66 (*LP*, VII 70).
180 *LP*, VII 384.
181 25 Henry VIII c. 12 (*Statutes of the Realm*, iii 446).
182 Shagan, 'Maid of Kent affair', p. 33; idem, *Popular Politics and the English Reformation*, pp. 61–88.
183 Shagan, *Popular Politics and the English Reformation*, p. 74.
184 Shagan, 'Maid of Kent affair', p. 21.
185 Such too ready acceptance of the government's propaganda makes Shagan's most recent discussion of the Nun of Kent (*Popular Politics and the English Reformation*, pp. 61–88) unconvincing.
186 PRO, SP1/80 fo. 94 (*LP*, VI 1417).
187 *LP*, VI 1470.
188 25 Henry VIII c. 12 (*Statutes of the Realm*, iii 451).

189 PRO, SP1/82 fos 69–70ᵛ (*LP*, VII 72 [i]).
190 'Early Life of Fisher', 145.
191 Ibid. 147.
192 Ibid. 143–4, 211–12.
193 Dowling, *Fisher of Men*, pp. 37–8.
194 E.E. Reynolds, *Saint John Fisher* (1955), p. 83; 'Early Life of Fisher', x 214.
195 S. Thompson, 'The bishop in his diocese', in B. Bradshaw and E. Duffy, eds, *Humanism, Reform and the Reformation* (Cambridge, 1989), pp. 67–80.
196 'Early Life of Fisher', x 217.
197 Ibid. 258; cf. Dowling, *Fisher of Men*, p. 54.
198 R. Rex, *The Theology of John Fisher* (Cambridge, 1991).
199 'Early Life of Fisher', x 299 n. 1; *State Papers*, i no. cx pp. 196–204 at 199, 201 (*LP*, IV ii 3231).
200 'Early Life of Fisher', x 298–9.
201 *LP*, IV ii 3148; text in 'Early Life of Fisher', x 295; cf. *LP*, IV iii 3147.
202 *LP*, IV ii 3232; cf. Dowling, *Fisher of Men*, p. 137.
203 *LP*, IV ii 3231.
204 Ibid. 4875.
205 Rex, *Theology of Fisher*, p. 260 n. 2; *LP*, IV ii 3234, from Wakefield, *Kotser Codicis*.
206 Dowling, *Fisher of Men*, pp. 135–6; *LP*, IV ii 3820.
207 *LP*, IV ii 4899.
208 Ibid. iii 5732: cf. Campeggio's letter of 29 June cited in 'Early Life of Fisher', x 313; *LP*, IV, iii 5734; 5827; H.A. Kelly, *The Matrimonial Trials of Henry VIII* (Stanford, 1976), p. 92; Hall, *Chronicle*, p. 758; Dowling, *Fisher of Men*, p. 134; Cavendish, *Life and Death of Wolsey*, pp. 113–15; Rex, *Theology of Fisher*, p. 260.
209 *LP*, IV iii 5732, 5734; Kelly, *Matrimonial Trials*, p. 92.
210 Cavendish, *Life and Death of Wolsey*, pp. 82–5.
211 Hall, *Chronicle*, p. 758.
212 *LP*, XIV i 190.
213 Ibid., V 287.
214 Dowling believes it impossible to reckon accurately how many: *Fisher of Men*, p. 148.
215 *LP*, VIII 859 (8).
216 Ibid., IV iii 6199, 6596, 6738, 6757.
217 Ibid., V 207, 342, 378, 460, 461, 546, and in 1533 (*LP*, VI 934); *Cal. S.P., Spanish*, IV ii no. 241. See Rex, *Theology of Fisher*, for a full elaboration; Dowling, *Fisher of Men*, p. 145.
218 *LP*, IV iii 6199; 6738; 6757; V 460.
219 *State Papers*, vii no. ccclxxii p. 489; *LP*, VII 934.
220 *LP*, XIV i 190.
221 Ibid., VIII 1125.
222 Dowling, *Fisher of Men*, p. 147: *LP*, VIII 859 (1, 4, 40).
223 Quoted Dowling, *Fisher of Men*, p. 147 (*LP*, VIII 859 [1, 4]: [26, 27]).
224 *Cal. S.P., Spanish*, IV ii no. 547.
225 *LP*, VIII 859 (1, 4): (10), (33); VI 934.
226 Dowling, *Fisher of Men*, p. 5, for Fisher's lack of tact; Dickens, *English Reformation*, p. 146.
227 'Early Life of Fisher', x 338.
228 Hall, *Chronicle*, p. 766.
229 'Early Life of Fisher', x 339; Reynolds, *Fisher*, p. 174.

230 'Early Life of Fisher', x 341.
231 Hall, *Chronicle*, p. 766.
232 'Early Life of Fisher', x 342–4. Cf. 'the motion that was lately made for the small monasteries to be taken into the king's hands': ibid. 339.
233 *Pace* R.W. Hoyle, 'The origins of the dissolution of the monasteries', *Historical Journal*, xxxviii (1995), pp. 284–90.
234 *Cal. S.P., Milan*, pp. 526–7 no. 831; *Cal. S.P., Venetian*, IV 629 (p. 529), 629 (p. 262), 634 (p. 624).
235 Vienna, Haus-, Hof- und Staatsarchiv, England, Karton 5, Berichte, 1532, fo. 5ᵛ (*Cal. S.P., Spanish*, IV ii no. 883 pp. 356–60; *LP*, V 707).
236 Vienna, Haus-, Hof- und Staatsarchiv, England, Karton 5, Berichte, 1532, fo. 8ᵛ (*Cal. S.P., Spanish*, IV ii no. 888 pp. 366–9; *LP*, V 737).
237 'Early Life of Fisher', x 352.
238 Ibid. 352–3.
239 Ibid. 357–8.
240 Ibid. 358.
241 Ibid. 359.
242 Ibid. 362.
243 Ibid. 363–5.
244 Ibid. 359–65.
245 Vienna, Haus-, Hof- und Staatsarchiv, England, Karton 4, Berichte, 1531, fos 19ᵛ–20 (*Cal. S.P., Spanish*, IV ii no. 641; *LP*, V 112).
246 'Early Life of Fisher', x 151–2, 345–6; Hall, *Chronicle*, pp. 780–1; Vienna, Haus-, Hof- und Staatsarchiv, England, Karton 5, Berichte, 1531, fo. 24ᵛ (*Cal. S.P., Spanish*, IV ii no. 646; *LP*, V 120).
247 As suggested by K.J. Kesselring, 'A draft of the 1531 "Acte for Poysoning" ', *English Historical Review*, cxvi (2001), pp. 894–9.
248 'Early Life of Fisher', x 346.
249 Ibid. 346–7.
250 Ibid. 349.
251 *LP*, V 472.
252 Vienna, Haus-, Hof- und Staatsarchiv, England, Karton 5, Berichte, 1532, fo. 8 (*Cal. S.P., Spanish*, IV ii no. 888 pp. 366–9; *LP*, V 737).
253 *LP*, VII 239; J. Bruce, 'Observations on the circumstances which occasioned the death of Fisher, bishop of Rochester', *Archaeologia*, xxv (1834), p. 91.
254 Wright, *Letters*, p. 33 (*LP*, VII 238).
255 *LP*, V 832, 879.
256 Christ Church, Oxford, Wake MS 306 fo. 48.
257 Scarisbrick, 'Conservative episcopate', pp. 163–5, citing PRO, SP6/11 fos 38–40ᵛ; J.J. Scarisbrick, 'Fisher, Henry VIII and the reformation crisis', in B. Bradshaw and E. Duffy, eds, *Humanism, Reform and the Reformation: the career of Bishop John Fisher* (Cambridge, 1989), pp. 163–4.
258 Vienna, Haus-, Hof- und Staatsarchiv, England, Karton 5, Berichte, 1532, fo. 73ᵛ (*Cal. S.P., Spanish*, IV ii no. 962 pp. 462–6; *LP*, V 1109); *LP*, V 1200.
259 C.A. Hatt, *English Works of John Fisher, Bishop of Rochester* (Oxford, 2002), pp. 211–25, dated by Hatt to 1 Nov. 1521 (p. 217).
260 Ibid., p. 227.
261 Ibid., pp. 245–6, 248.
262 PRO, PRO31/18/2/1 fo. 810ᵛ (*LP*, VI 160).
263 Vienna, Haus-, Hof- und Staatsarchiv, Englans, Karton 5, Berichte, 1533, fo. 38 (*Cal. S.P., Spanish*, IV ii no. 1057 pp. 625–8; *LP*, VI 296).
264 Wright, *Suppression*, p. 34 (*LP*, VII 238).

265 *LP*, VI 311 (3).

266 PRO, PRO31/18/2/1 fo. 839 (*LP*, VI 324).

267 PRO, PRO31/18/2/1 fo. 904ᵛ (*LP*, VI 653).

268 No such book survives: Fisher may have written on the subject in 1533. Scaris-brick has suggested another possibility: that Fisher showed Throckmorton the text of his sermon denouncing Luther in 1521 ('Fisher, Henry VIII and the reformation crisis', p. 164).

269 PRO, SP1/125 fos 202–6ᵛ, 207–9ᵛ (*LP*, XII ii 952); Scarisbrick, 'Fisher, Henry VIII and the reformation crisis', p. 160.

270 Vienna, Haus- und Hof- und Staatsarchiv, England, Karton 5 Berichte, 1533, fos 117ᵛ–18 (*Cal. S.P., Spanish*, IV ii no. 1130 pp. 813ff; *LP*, VI 1164).

271 Vienna, Haus-, Hof- und Staatsarchiv, England, Karton 5, Berichte, 1533, fo. 122ᵛ (*Cal. S.P., Spanish*, IV ii no. 1133 p. 821; *LP*, VI 1294). 'Quant a quant' does not mean 'immediately', as *LP* suggests.

272 J.-P. Moreau, *Rome ou l'Angleterre? Les réactions politiques des catholiques anglais au moment du schisme (1529–1553)* (Paris, 1984), pp. 64, 92.

273 Dowling, *Fisher of Men*, p. 150.

274 *LP*, VI 1381.

275 PRO, SP1/80 fo. 128 (*LP*, VI 1468 [5]); Dowling, *Fisher of Men*, p. 151.

276 PRO, PRO31/18/2/1 fos 999ᵛ–1000 (*Cal. S.P., Spanish*, IV ii no. 1149 p. 857).

277 *LP*, VII 143.

278 Wright, *Suppression*, pp. 27–34 (*LP*, VII 238).

279 BL, Cotton MS, Cleopatra E vi fo 156–8 (*Archaeologia*, xxv [1834] pp. 90–2; *LP*, VII 239).

280 *LP*, VII 240.

281 Ibid. 373; Reynolds, *Fisher*, pp. 215, 200.

282 *LP*, V 296, 373.

283 'Early Life of Fisher', x 108.

284 BL, Cotton MS, Cleopatra E vi fo. 160 (*LP*, VII 498).

285 BL, Cotton MS, Cleopatra E vi fos 168–68ᵛ (*Archaeologia*, xxv [1834], p. 93; *LP*, VII 1563); cf. B. Bradshaw, 'Bishop John Fisher: the man and his work', in Bradshaw and Duffy, *Humanism, Reform and the Reformation*, p. 24 n. 76.

286 BL, Cotton MS, Cleopatra E vi fos 175–75ᵛ (*LP*, VII 499; Cox, *Writings and Letters*, p. 286). Dowling thinks this would have been 'a tremendous propaganda coup for the regime': *Fisher of Men*, p. 153.

287 *LP*, VII 500.

288 26 Henry VIII c. 22 (*Statutes of the Realm*, iii 527–8). Did Fisher pay a fine of £300? ('Early Life of Fisher', xii 108).

289 BL, Cotton MS, Cleopatra E vi fo. 160 (*LP*, VII 498); cf. 'Early Life of Fisher', xii 128.

290 BL, Cotton MS, Cleopatra E vi fos 168–68ᵛ (*Archaeologia*, xxv [1834], p. 93; *LP*, VII 1563).

291 Ibid.

292 BL, Cotton MS, Cleopatra E vi fos 155–55ᵛ (*LP*, VII 136).

293 PRO, PRO31/18/2/2 fos 94–95 (*LP*, VIII 666).

294 PRO, SP1/93 fo. 40b/158/52 (*LP*, VIII 856 [3]). A variant is offered by the 'Early Life': Fisher could not be persuaded to take the oath, saying, 'it was not nor could not be by the laws of God proved that any temporal prince could be head of the church' (x 153). Cf. *LP*, VIII 856 (22).

295 *LP*, VIII 886 (iii).

296 Cf. Dowling, *Fisher of Men*, p. 157.

297 *LP*, VIII 742. Dowling, *Fisher of Men*, pp. 160–3 argues that Fisher's elevation reflected the politics of the papal court – Pope Paul III had been much criticised for nepotistic promotions the previous year – and was not intended to provoke Henry VIII. Pope Paul expected Henry would feel bound to set a cardinal free. Unaware of Fisher's frail health, he wanted Fisher to attend any forthcoming general council.

298 'Early Life of Fisher', x 153, 167.

299 *LP*, VIII 876.

300 Elton argues for late May, and attributes the increased pressure on both Fisher and More to Henry's reaction to Fisher's elevation (*Policy and Police*, pp. 407–8).

301 *LP*, VIII 974 (vi).

302 BL, Arundel MS, 152, fos 61ᵛ–62 ('Early Life of Fisher', xii 148).

303 BL, Arundel MS, 152 fo. 62.

304 Hatt, *English Works of Fisher*, p. 249.

305 BL, Cotton MS, Cleopatra E vi fos 155–55ᵛ (*Archaeologia*, xxv [1834], p. 89; *LP*, VII 136).

306 Dowling, *Fisher of Men*, p. 91.

307 'Early Life of Fisher', x 198.

308 BL, Arundel MS, 152 fo. 65.

309 *LP*, VIII 858.

310 Ibid. 867 (1) (*State Papers*, i no. xxxi p. 432).

311 'Early Life of Fisher', x 173; Hitchcock and Chambers, eds, *Harpsfield's Life of More*, Rastell fragments, p. 234.

312 'Early Life of Fisher', xii 174.

313 Hitchcock and Chambers, eds, *Harpsfield's Life of More*, Rastell fragments, pp. 238–40.

314 For a different view, see Elton, *Policy and Police*, p. 408 n. 2.

315 *LP*, VIII 985.

316 BL, Cotton MS, Cleopatra E vi fos 168–68ᵛ (*Archaeologia*, xxv [1834], p. 93; *LP*, VII 1563).

317 G.R. Elton, 'Sir Thomas More and the opposition to Henry VIII', *Bulletin of the Institute of Historical Research*, xli (1968), p. 31.

318 *State Papers*, vii 633 (*LP*, IX 240).

319 *LP*, IX 213.

320 BL, Cotton MS, Cleopatra E vi fo. 219 (*LP*, VIII 921).

321 Elton, 'Sir Thomas More and the opposition', p. 28.

322 *LP*, XII ii 921, 951.

323 Ibid. 952.

324 These themes were explored in an unpublished paper by Jennifer Loach, which I wish to acknowledge here.

325 Roper, *Life of More*, pp. 7–8.

326 Roper, *Life of More*, p. 17.

327 Gwyn, *The King's Cardinal*, pp. 374–6; G.W. Bernard, *War, Taxation and Rebellion in Early Modern England* (1986), pp. 120–3.

328 Roper, *Life of More*, p. 9.

329 Ibid., p. 11.

330 E.F. Rogers, ed., *The Correspondence of Sir Thomas More* (Princeton, 1947), p. 497.

331 Roper, *Life of More*, pp. 33, 37–8.

332 Rogers, *Correspondence*, p. 497.

333 Roper, *Life of More*, p. 38.

334 Rogers, *Correspondence*, p. 497.

335 Roper, *Life of More*, p. 50.

336 Ibid., pp. 49–50.
337 Vienna, Haus-, Hof- und Staatsarchiv, England, Karton 4, Berichte, 1530, fo. 339ᵛ (*Cal. S.P., Spanish*, IV i no. 433 p. 727).
338 *Cal. S.P., Spanish*, IV i 460 (p. 762).
339 Vienna, Haus-, Hof- und Staatsarchiv, England, Karton 5, Berichte, 1531, fos 19ᵛ–20 (*Cal. S.P., Spanish*, IV ii no. 641; *LP*, V 112).
340 Vienna, Haus-, Hof- und Staatsarchiv, England, Karton 5, Berichte, 1531, fos 25–25ᵛ (*LP*, V 120).
341 Rogers, *Correspondence*, p. 497.
342 Ibid., p. 536 (*LP*, VII 1116).
343 Ibid., p. 497 (*LP*, VII 289).
344 Ibid., p. 536 (*LP*, VII 1116).
345 Roper, *Life of More*, p. 85, indictment p. 276; *LP*, VIII 974 (vi).
346 *LP*, VIII 867 (iv [2]).
347 Ibid., V 171; Hall, *Chronicle*, p. 775.
348 Moreau, *Rome ou l'Angleterre*, pp. 49–50, based on Roper's remark about More 'not showing of what mind himself was therein': *Life of More*, p. 50.
349 Elton, *Policy and Police*, p. 419; Guy, *Public Career of More*, ch. viii.
350 Roper, *Life of More*, pp. 57–8.
351 Elton, *English Historical Review*, xciii (1978), p. 401.
352 Christopher St German, *A Treatise concerning the Division* (?1532) (*RSTC* 21586–7); J.B. Trapp, ed., *The Complete Works of St Thomas More: ix. The Apology* (1979); J. Guy et al., eds, *The Complete Works of St Thomas More: x. The Debellation of Salem and Byzance* (1987); S.M. Foley and C.H. Miller, eds, *The Complete Works of St Thomas More: xi. Answer to a Poisoned Book* (1985).
353 *Pace* Moreau, *Rome ou l'Angleterre*, p. 127.
354 Rogers, *Correspondence*, pp. 466–9 at 468 (*LP*, VII 149).
355 *LP*, VII 265.
356 Rogers, *Correspondence*, pp. 481–7.
357 *LP*, VI 1468 (5).
358 Rogers, *Correspondence*, p. 484.
359 Ibid., pp. 464–6, from BL, Arundel MS 152 fo. 298, Royal 17 D xiv fo. 380. (My italics.)
360 *LP*, VII 296.
361 Ibid. 287.
362 Rogers, *Correspondence*, p. 489 (*LP*, VIII 289).
363 Rogers, *Correspondence*, pp. 481–8 (*LP*, VII 287).
364 *LP*, VII 575, 1118.
365 Ibid. 288.
366 Ibid., VIII 384.
367 Elton says Henry wanted to include More in the act of attainder as a misprisioner of the nun's treason, but was dissuaded by his council: he offers no references (*Policy and Police*, p. 401).
368 Rogers, *Correspondence*, p. 500 (*LP*, VIII 289).
369 Ibid., p. 556.
370 Harpsfield, *Pretended Divorce*, p. 186.
371 Rogers, *Correspondence*, p. 528 (*LP*, VII 1114).
372 J.D.M. Derrett, 'The trial of Sir Thomas More', *English Historical Review*, lxxix (1964), pp. 450–77; Hitchcock and Chambers, eds, *Harpsfield's Life of More*, pp. 187–8.
373 Harpsfield, *Life of More*, p. 186.
374 Rogers, *Correspondence*, p. 503.
375 Ibid., p. 553.
376 Ibid., p. 528.

377 Ibid.
378 Ibid., p. 559.
379 Ibid., p. 507; cf. p. 537 (*LP*, VII 1116).
380 Ibid., p. 553.
381 Elton, *Policy and Police*, pp. 223–4.
382 Rogers, *Correspondence*, p. 503 (*LP*, VII 575).
383 Hitchcock and Chambers, eds, *Harpsfield's Life of More*, p. 196; Derrett, 'Trial of More', p. 220.
384 Roper, *Life of More*, p. 78.
385 Ropers, *Correspondence*, p. 521.
386 Ibid., pp. 527–8.
387 *LP*, XIV ii 750.
388 Rogers, *Correspondence*, pp. 532–3; 537 (*LP*, VII 1116; 1115)
389 Elton, *Policy and Police*, p. 406.
390 Hitchcock and Chambers, eds, *Harpsfield's Life of More*, p. 271.
391 *LP*, VIII 858 (5).
392 Ibid. 858 (6).
393 Ibid.
394 Ibid. 856 (41), 974 (vi).
395 Hitchcock and Chambers, eds, *Harpsfield's Life of More*, p. 272; *LP*, VIII 814, 974 (vi).
396 Rogers, *Correspondence*, p. 521.
397 *LP*, VIII 867 (4).
398 Ibid. 867 (iii [2]).
399 Derrett, 'Trial of More', pp. 217–18; Hitchcock and Chambers, eds, *Harpsfield's Life of More*, pp. 186–7; nothing in Roper's *Life*. The letters between More and Fisher are in *LP*, VIII 856 (6, 7, 10, 16, 17, 20, 24, 25, 28, 32, 33, 34, 36, 41); 858 (5, 6).
400 *LP*, VIII 867 (iii [2]).
401 Rogers, *Correspondence* 974 (vi).
402 Rogers, *Correspondence*, pp. 504–5 (*LP*, VII 1118).
403 Rogers, *Correspondence*, p. 556.
404 Ibid., p. 553.
405 Ibid., p. 552; Hitchcock and Chambers, eds, *Harpsfield's Life of More*, p. 271; *LP*, VIII 974 (vi).
406 Harpsfield, *Life of More*, p. 274; *LP*, VIII 974 (vi).
407 *LP*, VIII 974 (vi), 814; Elton, *Policy and Police*, p. 416.
408 Harpsfield, *Life of More*, p. 276; *LP*, VIII 974 (vi).
409 Derrett, 'Trial of More', p. 212.
410 Roper, *Life of More*, p. 89.
411 Derrett, 'Trial of More', pp. 212, 215–16; Hitchcock and Chambers, eds, *Harpsfield's Life of More*, p. 184. There is nothing in Roper on this.
412 Derrett, 'Trial of More', pp. 215–17; Hitchcock and Chambers, eds, *Harpsfield's Life of More*, pp. 185–6; nothing in Roper on this. Harpsfield's version is slightly different: 'For as for that you said, that every good subject is obliged to answer and confess, ye must understand that, in things touching conscience, every true and good subject is more bound to have respect to his said conscience and to his soul then to any other thing in all the world beside; namely when his conscience is in such sort as mine is, that is to say, where the person giveth no occasion of slander, of tumult and sedition against his prince, as it is with me; for I assure you I have not hither to this hour disclosed and opened my conscience and mind to any person living in all the world' (*Harpsfield's Life of More*, p. 186).

413 Derrett, 'Trial of More', pp. 217–18; Hitchcock and Chambers, eds, *Harps-field's Life of More*, pp. 186–7; nothing in Roper on this.

414 Derrett, 'Trial of More', p. 218; Hitchcock and Chambers, eds, *Harpsfield's Life of More*, pp. 187–8.

415 Derrett, 'Trial of More', p. 214.

416 Harpsfield, *Life of More*, p. 274.

417 Cited by Moreau, *Rome ou l'Angleterre*, p. 220.

418 Rogers, *Correspondence*, p. 528 (*LP*, VII 1114).

419 Rogers, *Correspondence*, p. 506.

420 Ibid., p. 526.

421 Roper, *Life of More*, pp. 92–4.

422 Ibid., p. 94.

423 Derrett, 'Trial of More', p. 219–20, Hitchcock and Chambers, eds, *Harpsfield's Life of More*, p. 195.

424 Roper, *Life of More*, pp. 94–5.

425 Hitchcock and Chambers, eds, *Harpsfield's Life of More*, pp. 196, 263–4; Derrett, 'Trial of More', p. 220; *LP*, VIII 996.

426 *Pace* Elton, *Policy and Police*, p. 419.

427 Roper, *Life of More*, p. 103.

428 Hitchcock and Chambers, eds, *Harpsfield's Life of More*, p. 266.

429 J. Guy, *Thomas More* (2000), p. 21.

430 Elton, *Policy and Police*, p. 418.

431 Ibid., p. 420; cf. p. 403.

432 Ibid., p. 419.

433 H.M. Colvin, ed., *History of the King's Works*, iii. *1485–1660* (1975), pp. 196–7; N. Beckett, 'Sheen Charterhouse from its foundation to its dissolution', University of Oxford D. Phil. thesis (1992), p. 147.

434 K.D. Brown, 'The Franciscan Observants in England, 1482–1559', University of Oxford D. Phil. thesis (1986), ch. 1, esp. pp. 24–42.

435 Beckett, 'Sheen Charterhouse', p. 145.

436 Brown, 'Franciscan Observants', p. 76.

437 J. Greatrex, 'St Swithun's Priory in the late Middle Ages', in J. Crook, ed., *Winchester Cathedral: nine hundred years* (Chichester, 1993), p. 158.

438 Brown, 'Franciscan Observants', pp. 76–80.

439 Ibid., p. 81.

440 PRO, PRO31/18/2/1 fo. 726^v (*LP*, V 941; *Cal. S.P., Spanish*, IV ii no. 934 [pp. 427–8]); Harpsfield, *Pretended Divorce*, p. 203.

441 *LP*, XII ii 952.

442 Ibid., VI 901; Pocock, *Records*, ii 422–5; Elton, *Policy and Police*, p. 176; M.D. Knowles, *The Religious Orders in England: vol. iii The Tudor Age* (Cambridge, 1959), p. 208.

443 *LP*, V 989; *Cal. S.P., Spanish*, IV ii 948 (p. 441); Brown, 'Franciscan Observants', p. 143.

444 Ibid. 266: this should be under 1532 not 1531.

445 Ibid., XII ii 952.

446 Ibid., VI 726; cf. 705, 900, 917.

447 *State Papers*, vii no. ccclxxii pp. 489–490 (*LP*, VI 934); *LP*, VI 889.

448 *State Papers*, vii no. ccclxxxiii pp. 517–18 (*LP*, VI 1324).

449 *LP*, VII 440.

450 BL, Cotton MS, Cleopatra E iv fo. 32 (*LP*, V 1525); *LP*, V 1313, 1591, 1525, 1738; *LP*, VI 116, 168.

451 *LP*, VI 168.

452 Ibid., V 1142, 1259, 1358.

453 PRO, SP1/81 fo. 118 (*LP*, VI 1664).
454 *LP*, VII 939, 1020.
455 Ibid., VI 836, 1370; VII 143.
456 Ibid., VII 1652.
457 Brown, 'Franciscan Observants', p. 181.
458 *LP*, VI 1468 (1), printed by Shagan, 'Maid of Kent affair', pp. 31–2; *Statutes of the Realm*, iii 450.
459 *LP*, VI 1417; ibid. 1470.
460 Ibid., V 1142, 1143, 1208, 1259, 1260, 1312, 1369, 1371, 1525, 1591, 1738, 1739; VI 115, 116, 309, 334, 512; VII 139, 580.
461 Brown, 'Franciscan Observants', p. 97.
462 LP, VII 590.
463 Ibid. app. 27.
464 Ibid. 129, 130, 131, 132, 133, 134.
465 Cf. Brown, 'Franciscan Observants', p. 213.
466 *LP*, VII 1607.
467 Foxe, *Acts and Monuments*, v 180; cf. *LP*, XIII i 1043 (1).
468 PRO, SP1/83 fo. 228 (*LP*, VII 622).
469 BL, Cotton MS, Cleopatra E iv fo. 40 (*LP*, VII 841).
470 BL, Cotton MS, Cleopatra E iv fos 40–1 (*LP*, VII 841).
471 PRO, SP1/83 fo. 81 (*LP*, VII 472).
472 PRO, SP1/83 fo. 82 (*LP*, VII 473).
473 *LP*, VII 982; J.A. Muller, ed., *The Letters of Stephen Gardiner* (Cambridge, 1933), pp. 56–7; Pocock, *Records*, ii 536; Elton, *Policy and Police*, pp. 14–15.
474 *LP*, VII 856.
475 Ibid. 1057. There were in fact only six houses.
476 Ibid. 1097.
477 Ibid. 1607.
478 Ibid., VIII 48.
479 Ibid., X 40.
480 Ibid. 141 p. 50; 284.
481 Brown, 'Observant Franciscans', p. 201.
482 Beckett, 'Sheen Charterhouse', p. 147.
483 *LP*, VI 1468.
484 Ibid.
485 Ibid. 835, 1149 (2).
486 Ibid., VII 1047.
487 Moreau, *Rome ou l'Angleterre*, p. 186.
488 *LP*, VII 614.
489 Ibid. 674.
490 Ibid. 728; Knowles, *Tudor Age*, p. 230.
491 *LP*, VII 1046.
492 *State Papers*, i no. xxiv p. 422 (*LP*, VII 1090).
493 PRO, SP1/83 fo. 228 (*LP*, VII 622). John Hussee's report that the prior of Sheen was in the Tower is most likely wrong: *LP*, VII 674; V 1749: Beckett, 'Sheen Charterhouse', pp. 170–1.
494 PRO, SP1/76 fo. 68 (*LP*, VI 510): probably 1534.
495 *LP*, VII 1127.
496 Ibid., VIII 475.
497 Ibid. 565, 566.
498 Ibid. 565 (1).
499 Ibid.

500 Ibid. 566.
501 Ibid.
502 Wriothesley, *Chronicle*, i 26–7.
503 *LP*, VIII 661.
504 Ibid. 600.
505 Ibid. 568.
506 Ibid. 609, 666.
507 Ibid. 606.
508 Ibid. 661.
509 Ibid. 616.
510 Ibid., XII ii 181.
511 Ibid., VIII 886 iii, iv, viii.
512 BL, Cotton MS, Cleopatra E vi fos 259–59ᵛ (*LP*, VIII 675).
513 Cf. *LP*, VIII 524.
514 Fyloll was not, *pace* Elton, *Policy and Police*, p. 328, 'more of a caretaker'.
515 *LP*, IX 283; cf. 523.
516 Ibid., VIII 932.
517 *State Papers*, i no. xlvi p. 460 (*LP*, XI 501).
518 *LP*, XII i 1232.
519 Ibid. ii 27, 64, 91.
520 Could this be the one in Beverley, Oct. 1537 (*LP*, XII i 392)?
521 PRO, SP1/120 fo. 140 (*LP*, XII i 1233); T. Rymer, *Foedera* (1739–45), xiv 589.
522 PRO, SP1/120 fo. 177ᵛ.
523 Wright, *Suppression*, no. lxxx pp. 162–3 (*LP*, XII ii 91 [i] and [ii]).
524 *LP*, XII ii 166.
525 Elton, *Policy and Police*, p. 391 n. 1.
526 *LP*, VIII 585: is this 1536? Cf. Beckett, 'Sheen Charterhouse', pp. 171–2.
527 M.D. Tait, 'The Brigittine monastery of Syon (Middlesex), with special reference to its monastic usages', University of Oxford D. Phil. thesis (1975), p. 286.
528 Man had earlier expressed great spiritual joy over Elizabeth Barton: *LP*, VI 835, 1149, 1468.
529 Ibid., VII 1091.
530 Ibid., VIII 610; VII 1091.
531 Ibid. 959.
532 Beckett, 'Sheen Charterhouse', p. 173.
533 Ibid., pp. 179, 185.
534 *LP*, VIII 968.
535 PRO, SP1/117 fo. 175 (*LP*, XII i 778).
536 BL, Cotton MS, Caligula B i fo. 319 (*LP* XII i 1156).
537 *LP*, XII i 778, 1172 (3).
538 PRO, SP1/117 fo. 174 (*LP*, XII i 777).
539 PRO, SP1/120 fo. 26 (*LP*, XII i 1172).
540 *LP*, VII 932: is the date safe?
541 Ibid., VIII 1038, 1039, 1069.
542 Ibid., XV 125.
543 Ibid., VIII 1038.
544 Ibid. 1011.
545 Ibid. 1069.
546 Ibid. 1033.
547 Knowles, *Tudor Age*, p. 237.
548 Beckett, 'Sheen Charterhouse', p. 170.
549 Ibid., p. 177.

550 *LP*, VII 1091.
551 Wriothesley, *Chronicle*, i. 109; Tait, 'Brigittine monastery of Syon', pp. 67–9; *LP*, XV 840.
552 Ibid., VII 287.
553 Ibid., VIII 1125.
554 Rymer, *Foedera*, xiv 491.
555 *LP*, VIII 565, 566.
556 Ibid. 661.
557 Ibid. 661, 663.
558 Ibid., XII ii 952.
559 Ibid., VIII 661.
560 Tait, 'Brigittine monastery of Syon', p. 79.
561 PRO, SP1/83 fo. 228 (*LP*, VII 622): not 1534 *pace LP*.
562 *State Papers*, i no. xxiv p. 422; *LP*, VII 1090/IX 200.
563 *LP*, VIII 1125, VII 1090/IX 200.
564 Ibid. 565.
565 *State Papers*, i no. xxiv pp. 422–5: Sept. 1535?
566 *LP*, VII 756: probably Sept. 1535.
567 Coppinger, Litell, Bishop, Parker, Browne, Turlington (or Turnyngton), Androw and Bownell (*State Papers*, i no. xxiv pp. 422–5; Tait, 'Brigittine monastery of Syon', p. 77).
568 *State Papers*, i no. xxiv pp. 422–5 at 424.
569 Ibid. pp. 422–5.
570 *LP*, IX 954.
571 Ibid. 986.
572 Ibid., VIII 1125.
573 *State Papers*, i no. xxiv p. 424; *LP*, VII 1090/IX 200.
574 Tait, 'Brigittine monastery of Syon', pp. 282–4.
575 *LP*, VII 15: not 1534 *pace LP*/Tait, 'Brigittine monastery of Syon'; cf. PRO, SP1/132 fo. 204 (*LP*, XIII i 1096).
576 Ibid. 22: not 1534 *pace LP*/Tait, 'Brigittine monastery of Syon'.
577 Ibid., VIII 77: not 1535 but 1536.
578 Ibid. 78; 25: not 1535.
579 BL, Cotton MS, Cleopatra E vi fos 173–74ᵛ (*LP*, VIII 78).
580 *LP*, VII 78: recte 1536: Moreau, *Rome ou l'Angleterre* disagrees, pp. 153–4.
581 BL, Add MS, 22285 fo. 60ᵛ; Tait, 'Brigittine monastery of Syon', p. 80.
582 *LP*, XI 487.
583 Tait, 'Brigittine monastery of Syon', p. 286.
584 *LP*, IV iii 6513.
585 *Cal. S.P., Spanish*, IV i 411 (p. 690).
586 Hall, *Chronicle*, p. 755.
587 W.T. Mitchell, ed., *Epistolae academicae 1508–1596*, Oxford Historical Society, new ser. xxvi (1980 for 1977–78), nos 197a, 197b (pp. 274–8) (*LP*, IV iii app. 254).
588 PRO, E30/1012a (*LP*, IV iii 6513).
589 Vienna, Haus-, Hof- und Staatsarchiv, England, Karton 4, Berichte, 1530, fos 362ᵛ–63 (*Cal. S.P., Spanish*, IV i no. 547 p. 853).
590 PRO, SP2/N fos 155–60ᵛ.
591 Vienna, Haus-, Hof- und Staatsarchiv, England, Karton 4, Berichte, 1530, fo. 678 (*Cal. S.P., Spanish*, IV i no. 547 pp. 852–3).
592 Vienna, Haus-, Hof- und Staatsarchiv, England, Karton 5, Berichte, 1531, fo. 9ᵛ (*LP*, V 45).
593 Lehmberg, *Reformation Parliament*, pp. 109–16; J.A. Guy, 'Henry VIII and the *praemunire* manoeuvres of 1530–31', *Journal of Ecclesiastical History*,

xxxvii (1986), pp. 491–2 (from *Cal. S.P., Spanish*, IV ii nos 619 [p. 44], 635 [pp. 61–3]), pp. 494–5 (from BL, Cotton MS, Cleopatra F ii fo. 240); (*Cal. S.P., Spanish*, IV ii no. 598 p. 27; *LP*, V 45).

594 *LP*, V 928, from D. Wilkins, ed., *Concilia Magnae Britanniae et Hiberniae* (4 vols, 1737), iii 724.

595 *LP*, V 287.

596 Ibid. 327.

597 Cranmer, *Writings and Letters*, p. 273 (*LP*, VI 1546).

598 *Statutes of the Realm*, iii 448. Cf. Wright, *Suppression*, p. 17 (*LP*, VI 1466): 'of the old bishop of Canterbury, how he had promised to marry the king, and of the warnings by the angel of God'. MacCulloch suggests that Warham 'was swayed from his lifetime of automatic obedience to the monarch's wishes towards passive resistance to the annulment plans' (*Cranmer*, p. 103); cf. Scarisbrick, *Henry VIII*, p. 253.

599 *LP*, V 287.

600 Vienna, Haus-, Hof- und Staatsarchiv, England, Karton 5, Berichte, 1532, fo. 15ᵛ (*Cal. S.P., Spanish*, IV ii no. 899 pp. 382–4; *LP*, V 805).

601 Elton, *Reform and Reformation*, pp. 152–3; *LP*, V 818.

602 Elton, *Reform and Reformation*, pp. 152–3.

603 J. Moyes, 'Warham: an English primate on the eve of the reformation', *Dublin Review*, cxiv (1894), pp. 401–2 (*LP*, V 1247).

604 Moyes, 'Warham', pp. 401–2, 406.

605 Ibid., p. 406.

606 Ibid., pp. 405, 412.

607 Ibid., pp. 409–10.

608 Ibid., pp. 410–12.

609 Scarisbrick, *Henry VIII*, p. 256, citing will; cf. *LP*, IV ii 2623.

610 Moyes, 'Warham', p. 412.

611 Ibid., p. 411.

612 Ibid., pp. 413–14.

613 Ibid., p. 412.

614 *LP*, X 113.

615 *Cal. S.P., Venetian*, IV 754 (p. 330); though Chapuys on 20 March said the queen's affair had not yet been mentioned in parliament (*LP*, V 879).

616 Kelly, 'Episcopate of Warham', pp. 271–2; Christ Church, Oxford, Wake MS, 306; *LP*, V 757; cf. V 1023.

617 Kelly, 'Episcopate of Warham', pp. 270–6.

618 *LP*, V 859–60.

619 Ibid. 287.

620 Vienna, Haus-, Hof- und Staatsarchiv, England, Karton 5, Berichte, 1533, fo. 20 (*Cal. S.P., Spanish*, IV ii no. 1053 pp. 608–10; *LP*, VI 180).

621 *LP*, V 879.

622 Ibid., VII 522.

623 Ibid. 690.

624 Ibid., VIII 1011.

625 BL, Cotton MS, Cleopatra E vi fos 236–8 (*LP*, VIII 869).

626 *LP*, VIII 963.

627 BL, Cotton MS, Cleopatra E vi fo. 238ᵛ (*LP*, X 99).

628 *LP*, X 99, 93.

629 Ibid., VII 690.

630 Scarisbrick, 'Conservative episcopate', pp. 75–6, citing PRO, SP1/54 fo. 262 (*LP*, IV iii 5768 [2]).

631 *LP*, V 819; Wilkins, *Concilia*, iii 745.

632 Scarisbrick, 'Conservative episcopate', p. 176.

633 BL, Cotton MS, Cleopatra E vi fo. 220 (*LP*, V app. 9; Wilkins iii 762).

634 *LP*, V 251; XII i 786 (ii) 2; *Cal. S.P., Milan*, i 869.

635 *LP*, V 737.

636 Scarisbrick, 'Conservative episcopate', p. 293.

637 *LP*, VI 451; Scarisbrick, 'Conservative episcopate', pp. 296–302; cf. *LP*, VI 437; PRO, PRO31/18/2/1 fo. 904 (*LP*, VI, 653).

638 We know Tunstal's letter only from Henry's reply: Moreau, *Rome ou l'Angleterre*, pp. 94–5, Scarisbrick, 'Conservative espiscopate', pp. 305–7, from PRO, SP6/9 fos 223–35 (*LP*, V 820).

639 *LP*, VII 121, 690; Scarisbrick, 'Conservative episcopate', pp. 308–9.

640 Scarisbrick, 'Conservative episcopate', pp. 309–10; *LP*, VII 522.

641 LP, VII 522.

642 *RSTC* 11218–19.

643 *LP*, V 986–7; recte 1534 not 1532: cf. VII app. 18–19.

644 Ibid., VII 690.

645 Ibid.; VII 696 for their instructions.

646 *State Papers*, i part ii no. xxiii pp. 419–22; *LP*, VII 695.

647 *LP*, VII 726.

648 Ibid., XIV ii 750 (i), (2).

649 Ibid., V 287.

650 E.g. PRO, SP1/101 fos 193, 195 (*LP*, X 182, 183).

651 Ibid.; Wriothesley, *Chronicle*, i 34–5; cf. RSTC 24322 – Tunstal's 1539 sermon, Palm Sunday, Paul's Cross (BL: 1026 a.7): 'a noble, victorious and virtuous king, hardy as a lion, who will not suffer thee to be so devoured by such wild beasts' (Elton, *Policy and Police*, pp. 189–90).

652 *LP*, XI 772.

653 Scarisbrick, 'Conservative episcopate', p. 61.

654 Cf. *LP*, VIII 859 (1) (33).

655 Ibid. 859 (1) (39, 40); I follow Scarisbrick, 'Conservative episcopate', p. 75.

656 *LP*, V 171; *Cal. S.P., Venetian*, IV 664.

657 Christ Church, Oxford, Wake MS 306 fo. 49; Wilkins, *Concilia*, iii 749.

658 *LP*, VI 311 (3).

659 Ibid., VIII 859 (1) (32).

660 Ibid., V app. 9.

661 Ibid. 1256, 1411, app. 33; Moreau, *Rome ou l'Angleterre*, p. 83.

662 *LP*, VI 661.

663 Ibid., VII 1024 (6).

664 Ibid., VIII 190 (3).

665 Ibid., VII 289.

666 Ibid., VIII 169 2 (ii).

667 Ibid., V 657, 825, 1285; VI 228.

668 Ibid. 171.

669 Scarisbrick, 'Conservative episcopate', p. 76.

670 *LP*, VI 62, 157, 1379.

671 Scarisbrick, 'Conservative episcopate', pp. 276–82, 283–91.

672 *LP*, VI 661.

673 Ibid., V 171.

674 Ibid., VIII app. 33.

675 Ibid., VII 14.

676 Ibid., VIII 190; Scarisbrick, 'Conservative episcopate', p. 324.

677 *LP*, VIII 190.

678 Ibid. 922.

679 STC 16796 (BL: C. 53 k. 14): Elton, *Policy and Police*, p. 189.

680 Scarisbrick, 'Conservative episcopate', pp. 283–4, from PRO, KB 27/1085.
681 *LP*, VIII 49.
682 Ibid., VII 48, 49, 54 (6), 171, 158, 262 (18), 296, 270.
683 *Statutes of the Realm*, iii 486–7.
684 *LP*, VIII 159.
685 *State Papers*, i 380 (*LP*, V 394).
686 Scarisbrick, 'Conservative episcopate', p. 324.
687 *LP*, VIII 859 (1) (32): cf. Scarisbrick, 'Conservative episcopate', p. 73, citing PRO, SP1/93 fos 67, 71ᵛ.
688 *LP*, VIII 311 (2).
689 Scarisbrick, 'Conservative episcopate', p. 74, citing PRO, SP1/54 fo. 262 and BL, Cotton MS, Vitellius B xii fo. 123.
690 *Cal. S.P., Milan*, I 831; *Cal. S.P., Venetian*, IV 629, 634.
691 *LP*, V 1256.
692 Ibid., VI 167.
693 Ibid., VIII 859 (1) (32): cf. Scarisbrick, 'Conservative episcopate', p. 73, citing PRO, SP1/93 fos 67, 71ᵛ.
694 *LP*, VIII 941.
695 Edward Croft-Murray, 'Lambert Barnard: an English early renaissance painter', *Archaeological Journal*, cxiii (1956), pp. 108–25, suggests c. 1535–36, a date broadly confirmed from communar's accounts: 1533–34 shows payment to Lambert Barnard the painter (J. Fines, 'Cathedral and reformation', in M. Hobbs, ed., *Chichester Cathedral* [1994], p. 52). 'Much of Barnard's work in the Cathedral after 1536 was paid for from Sherburne's bequest' (T. Brighton, 'Art in the cathedral from the foundation to the civil war', in ibid., p. 80).
696 Brighton, 'Art in the cathedral from the foundation to the civil war', p. 80.
697 M. Bowker, 'The supremacy and the episcopate: the struggle for control', *Historical Journal*, xviii (1975), pp. 227–43.
698 *LP*, V 171.
699 Ibid. 287.
700 Hall, *Chronicle*, pp. 783–4.
701 *LP*, V 387.
702 Ibid. 1256, 1411.
703 Cox, *Writings and Letters*, p. 245, from BL, Harleian MS, 6148 fo. 23 (*LP*, VI 601).
704 *LP*, VI 1111–12.
705 Ibid., VII 270.
706 Ibid., VIII 190.
707 Christ Church, Oxford, Wake MS, 306 fo. 49; Wilkins, *Concilia*, iii 749.
708 *LP*, VIII 600.
709 PRO, PRO31/18/2/2 fo. 108 (*LP*, VIII 1105).
710 *LP*, VIII 1019, 1043, 1054; cf. 527.
711 BL, Cotton MS, Titus B i. fo. 425 (*LP*, VIII 527) (calendared 10 April, possibly in July, after Stokesley's sermon); cf. Elton, *Policy and Police*, p. 189 n. 1.
712 A.A. Chibi, 'Henry VIII and his marriage to his brother's wife: the sermon of Bishop John Stokesley of 11 July 1535', *Historical Research*, lxvii (1994), pp. 40–56.
713 See n. 711.
714 *LP*, VIII 1125; cf. IX 954, 986; VII 15, 22; VIII 77.
715 Ibid., VII 15: probably 1536.
716 Before Hilsey's elevation to the bishopric of Rochester he had inhibited him from preaching there: ibid., VII 1643.

717 Ibid., XIII ii 695.
718 Ibid., VII 906–7.
719 Ibid. 483.
720 Ibid. 592.
721 Moreau, *Rome ou l'Angleterre*, p. 133.
722 C.D.C. Armstrong, *Journal of Ecclesiastical History*, xliv (1993), p. 311; idem, 'English catholicism rethought?', *Journal of Ecclesiastical History*, liv (2003), pp. 717–26.
723 *Pace* Moreau, *Rome ou l'Angleterre*, p. 131, who sees the virulence of Gardiner's attacks as revealing personal bitterness. Cf. Armstrong, 'English catholicism rethought?', p. 724.
724 *LP*, XII i 445.
725 Ibid., VII 592.
726 This develops further the remarks by Armstrong, *Journal of Ecclesiastical History*, xliv (1993), pp. 311–12.
727 Elton, *Policy and Police*, p. 187: *Si sedes illa*. But Scarisbrick dates this to the legatine court in 1529: 'Conservative episcopate', p. 83.
728 Scarisbrick, 'Conservative episcopate', pp. 176–92.
729 The northern convocation also protested in May, according to Chapuys (letter of 22 May 1531: *LP*, V 251); *Cal. S.P., Milan*, I 869.
730 Scarisbrick, 'Conservative episcopate', pp. 177–80.
731 Ibid., pp. 180–3.
732 *LP*, V 394, from BL, Cotton MS, Titus B i 486; *State Papers*, i 380.
733 *LP*, V 559 (22).
734 Ibid., VI 311 (3); Pocock, *Records*, ii 449.
735 *LP*, VI 1370; VII 143 (ii).
736 Ibid., VI 1672.
737 Ibid., VII 441.
738 Ibid. 483.
739 Ibid. 575.
740 Ibid., XI 186. For full details, see Scarisbrick, 'Conservative episcopate', pp. 189–90.
741 *LP*, V 1139 (10); Scarisbrick, 'Conservative episcopate', pp. 187–9.
742 Ibid. 657.
743 Ibid., V 1285 ix.
744 Ibid., VI 228 ii.
745 Ibid., V 1411.
746 Ibid., VII 876, 1371.
747 Ibid. 923 (xiii).
748 Ibid. 876.
749 Scarisbrick, 'Conservative episcopate', pp. 177–92.
750 *LP*, VIII 859 (1) (34–6).
751 Cf. Scarisbrick, 'Conservative episcopate', pp. ii–iii.
752 Scarisbrick's view of the hierarchy as acting 'in growing unity and, until the last moment, with growing courage', reflecting 'a coalition without a dissentient', is open to doubt: 'Conservative episcopate', pp. 246–7.
753 Cf. L.E.C. Wooding's remark, 'the supremacy could in fact be seen as the best defence against innovation'; 'it stood as the guarantor of true doctrine': *Rethinking Catholicism in Reformation England* (Oxford, 2000), pp. 72–3. Wooding does not offer detail in support of these claims.
754 *LP*, VI 733.
755 Elton, *Policy and Police*, p. 278.
756 Foxe, *Acts and Monuments*, vii app. ix; *LP*, VI 433 (i–ii).

757 *LP*, VII 381.
758 Ibid., VIII 1020; Elton, *Policy and Police*, p. 237.
759 Ibid., IX 46.
760 Ibid. 84.
761 Ibid. 534.
762 Cf. Moreau, *Rome ou l'Angleterre*, p. 114.
763 P.H. Williams, *English Historical Review*, lxxxviii (1973), pp. 594–5.
764 *LP*, VII 296.
765 S. Gunn, *Charles Brandon, Duke of Suffolk 1484–1545* (Oxford, 1988), pp. 118–19.
766 Vienna, Haus-, Hof- und Staatsarchiv, England, Karton 5, Berichte, 1531, fo. 25 (*Cal. S.P., Spanish*, IV ii no. 646 p. 80; *LP*, V 120).
767 Vienna, Haus-, Hof- und Staatsarchiv, England, Karton 5, Berichte, 1531, fos 50ᵛ–51 (*LP*, V 287).
768 Vienna, Haus-, Hof- und Staatsarchiv, England, Karton 5, Berichte, 1532, fo. 34ᵛ (*LP*, V 171).
769 *LP*, V 879.
770 Ibid., VI 324, 351, 534.
771 PRO, SP1/79 fos 158–58ᵛ at 158ᵛ (*State Papers*, i no. xviii pp. 408–9 at 408; *LP*, VI 1252–3).
772 Vienna, Haus-, Hof- und Staatsarchiv, England, Karton 4, Berichte, 1530, fo. 319 (*Cal. S.P., Spanish*, IV i no. 366 p. 616).
773 *Lords Journals*, p. 82.
774 Vienna, Haus-, Hof- und Staatsarchiv, England, Karton 5, Berichte, 1532, fos 713–13ᵛ (*Cal. S.P., Spanish*, IV ii no. 899 pp. 382–4; *LP*, V 805).
775 M. Bateson, 'Aske's examination', *English Historical Review*, v (1890), p. 568.
776 *LP*, XII i 852.
777 Vienna, Haus-, Hof- und Staatsarchiv, England, Karton 5, Berichte, 1534, fos 64ᵛ–65ᵛ (*Cal. S.P., Spanish*, V i no. 257 pp. 608–11; *LP*, VII 1206).
778 PRO, PRO31/18/2/2, p. 1 (*LP*, VIII 1).
779 *LP*, VIII 121. Not 100,000.
780 PRO, PRO31/18/2/1 p. 79 (*LP*, VIII 666).
781 Vienna, Haus-, Hof- und Staasarchiv, England, Karton 5, Berichte, 1535, fo. 14 (*Cal. S.P., Spanish*, V i no. 165 pp. 470–1; *LP*, VIII 750).
782 *LP*, VIII 1.
783 Ibid. 121.
784 Vienna, Haus-, Hof und Staatsarchiv, England, Karton 5, Berichte, 1534, fo. 65ᵛ (*Cal. S.P., Spanish*, V i no. 257 pp. 608–11; *LP*, VII 1206).
785 S.G. Ellis, *Tudor Frontiers and Noble Power: the making of the British state* (Oxford, 1995), pp. 202–3.
786 *LP*, VII 1013.
787 Ellis, *Tudor Frontiers and Noble Power*, ch. vii (though Ellis does not quite draw out this point).
788 PRO, PRO31/18/2/2 p. 4 (*LP*, VIII 48).
789 PRO, PRO31/18/2/2 p. 43 (*LP*, VIII 327).
790 PRO, PRO31/18/2/2 pp. 71–2 (*LP*, VIII 590).
791 *LP*, XI 576.
792 'Aske's examination', p. 568.
793 Cf. R.W. Hoyle, *The Pilgrimage of Grace and the Politics of the 1530s* (Oxford 2001), p. 39.
794 *LP*, V 986–7: recte 1534: cf. VII app. 18–19.
795 Vienna, Haus-, Hof- und Staatsarchiv, England, Karton 4, Berichte, 1530, fo. 679ᵛ (*Cal. S.P., Spanish*, IV i no. 547 p. 853).

796 Vienna, Haus-, Hof- und Staatsarchiv, England, Karton 5, Berichte, 1531, fo. 34 (*LP*, V 171).

797 Vienna, Haus-, Hof- und Staatsarchiv, England, Karton 5, Berichte, 1531, fo. 35 (*LP*, V 171).

798 Vienna, Haus-, Hof- und Staatsarchiv, England, Karton 5, Berichte, 1532, fo. 17 (*Cal. S.P., Spanish*, IV ii no. 907 pp. 390–1; *LP*, V 832); fo. 21 (*Cal. S.P., Spanish*, IV ii no. 922 pp. 410–12; *LP*, V 879); fo. 23 (*Cal. S.P., Spanish*, IV ii no. 926 pp. 416–18; *LP*, V 898).

799 Herbert of Cherbury, *Life of Henry VIII*, p. 335.

800 Vienna, Haus-, Hof- und Staatsarchiv, England, Karton 5, Berichte, 1532, fos 41–41ᵛ (*Cal. S.P., Spanish*, IV ii no. 948 pp. 440–1; *LP*, V 989).

801 Herbert of Cherbury, *Life of Henry VIII*, p. 335.

802 Hall, *Chronicle*, p. 786.

803 Vienna, Haus-, Hof- und Staatsarchiv, England, Karton 5, Berichte, 1533, fos 38ᵛ–39 (*Cal. S.P., Spanish*, IV ii no. 1057 pp. 625–8; *LP*, VI 296).

804 Vienna, Haus-, Hof- und Staatsarchiv, England, Karton 5, Berichte, 1533, fo. 43 (*Cal. S.P., Spanish*, IV ii no. 1058 pp. 628–32; *LP*, VI 324).

805 *LP*, XII ii 952.

806 Ibid., VII 296.

807 Ibid. 373.

808 Ibid. 393.

809 Ibid., VIII 858; PRO, SP1/93 fo. 40ᵛ (*LP*, VIII 856 [2]).

810 Elton, *Policy and Police*, p. 283.

811 J. Le Labourer, ed., *Les Mémoires de Messire Michel de Castelnau* (Brussels, 3 vols, 1731), i 417 (*LP*, VIII 996).

812 E.V. Hitchcock, ed., *Harpsfield's Pretended Divorce*, Early English Text Society, clxxxvi (1932), p. 196; Derrett, 'Trial of More', p. 220 (*LP*, VIII 996).

813 PRO, SP1/114 fos 49, 50 (*LP*, XII [i] 43 [1, 2], 44); PRO E36/118 fo. 111 (*LP*, XII [i] 848 I [13]); cf. PRO SP1/114 fo. 18 (*LP*, XII i 20), PRO SP1/10 fo. 34 (*LP*, XII [i] 1175 [1]).

814 PRO, SP1/125 fos 202, 203, 207, 208 (*LP*, XII [ii] 952 [1] and [2]).

815 *LP*, XII ii 952.

816 Ibid., VII 121, 296, 373.

817 PRO, PRO31/18/2/1 fo. 620 (*Cal. S.P., Spanish*, IV i no. 396 p. 671).

818 *LP*, XIII ii 804.

819 S.T. Bindoff, ed., *History of Parliament: 1509–58* (3 vols, 1982), i pp. 10–11 (from PRO, SP1/99 p. 234), 490.

820 Ibid., i 12–13, from PRO, SP1/87 fo. 106ᵛ.

821 PRO, SP1/125 fos 203–03ᵛ (*LP*, XII ii 952).

822 PRO, SP1/125 fos 202–6 is the original confession (*LP*, XII ii 952 [1]); PRO, SP1/125 fos 207–09ᵛ is a fair copy (*LP*, XII ii 952 [2]).

823 *LP*, XI 1406.

824 Hall, *Chronicle*, pp. 754–5, 780–1.

825 *LP*, V 1202.

826 Ibid., VI 556.

827 Ibid., VIII 48.

828 Ibid. 1105.

829 PRO, SP1/83 fo. 87 (*LP*, VII 497); but cf. *LP*, VII 754.

830 *LP*, VII 1609.

831 Ibid., VIII 196.

832 Hall, *Chronicle*, pp. 781–2.

833 *LP*, IV iii 6003; V pp. 315, 749.

834 Cf. T.F. Mayer, 'A fate worse than death: Reginald Pole and the Paris theologians', *English Historical Review*, ciii (1988), pp. 870–91 at 890.

835 Ibid., p. 883.
836 PRO, SP1/57 fo. 99 (*LP*, IV iii 6383).
837 PRO, SP1/57 fo. 248 (*LP*, IV iii 6505).
838 *LP*, IV iii 6252.
839 PRO, SP1/57 fo. 248 (*LP*, IV iii 6505).
840 Mayer emphasises the tension between Pole's later accounts of this and what he did at the time. In *De unitate* – but not in the version sent to Henry VIII – he said of what he did in Paris that 'nothing ever in my life more bitter [had] befallen me', and played down his part, saying a senior colleague took charge. In a letter to the king's council on 16 Feb. 1537 he rather insisted that despite the fact that his conscience could not perfectly agree to the same, he allowed himself to be persuaded (PRO, SP1/116 fo. 571; Mayer, 'Pole and the Paris theologians', pp. 874–5). In a letter to Edward VI, Pole explained how he went to Paris to avoid having to make a definite commitment (Mayer, 'Pole and the Paris theologians', p. 875). 'Open disagreement took much longer to develop than Pole averred in *De unitate*: Pole's later accounts offer 'a remarkably adroit piece of equivocation', Mayer insists ('Pole and the Paris theologians', p. 890).
841 Vienna, Hof- Haus- und Staatsarchiv, England, Karton 4, Berichte, 1530, fo. 366.
842 PRO, SP1/116 fos 56–57ᵛ (*LP*, XII i 444).
843 *LP*, VII 1368.
844 Ibid., V app. 10: Cranmer, *Writings and Letters*, pp. 229–31, from BL, Lansdowne MS, 115 fo. 1; J. Strype, *Memorials of Cranmer* (Oxford, 2 vols, 1812), ii 675–9; Pocock, *Records*, ii 130–1.
845 T.F. Mayer, *Reginald Pole: Prince and Prophet* (Cambridge, 2000), pp. 57–8.
846 Vienna, Haus-, Hof- und Staatsarchiv, England, Karton 5, Berichte, fo. 8ᵛ (*Cal. S.P., Spanish*, IV ii no. 888 pp. 366–9; *LP*, V 737).
847 Mayer, *Reginald Pole*, p. 56.
848 W. Schenk, *Reginald Pole: Cardinal of England* (1950), chs 1–2. Cf. Mayer's remarks (in connection with Pole's failure to advance Contarini's ideas, with which he sympathised greatly, in Rome): 'Pole had political skills, but his passivity in the face of crisis constantly negated them. Instead of the confrontational behaviour a high noble should have displayed when encountering opposition, Pole withdrew' (Mayer, *Reginald Pole*, p. 105).
849 D. MacCulloch, *Journal of Ecclesiastical History*, lii (2001), p. 742.
850 *LP*, VII 233.
851 Vienna, Haus-, Hof- und Staatsarchiv, England, Karton 5, Berichte, 1533, fo. 118 (*Cal. S.P., Spanish*, IV ii no. 1130 pp. 813ff; *LP*, VI 1164).
852 *Cal. S.P., Spanish*, V i 109 pp. 323–4; *LP*, VII 1368 and VI 1164 and VIII 750.
853 *LP*, VII 1040 (*Cal. S.P., Spanish*, V i 109); T.D. Hardy, *Report upon the Documents in the Archives and Public Libraries of Vienna* (1886), p. 69.
854 Mayer, *Reginald Pole*, pp. 36–7; *Cal. S.P., Spanish*, IV ii no. 888.
855 BL, Cotton MS, Cleopatra E vi fo. 372 (*LP*, VIII 801).
856 BL, Harleian MS 283 fos 131–31ᵛ (*LP*, VIII 218).
857 *LP*, VIII 801, 1156.
858 Ibid., IX 988.
859 BL, Cotton MS, Cleopatra E vi fo. 372ᵛ (*LP*, VIII 801).
860 PRO, SP1/139 fo. 6ᵛ (*LP*, XIII ii 822); SP1/139 fos 21ᵛ–22 (*LP*, XIII ii 829 [II]); SP1/139 fo. 41ᵛ (*LP*, XIII ii 830 [1 (iii)]).
861 BL, Cotton MS, Cleopatra E vi fo. 384 (*LP*, XI 157); PRO, SP1/105 fo. 46 (*LP*, XI 73); BL, Cotton MS, Cleopatra E vi fos 372–72ᵛ (*LP*, VIII 801).
862 BL, Cotton MS, Nero B vii fo. 108 (*LP*, VIII 535); Nero B vii fo. 107 (*LP*, VIII 579); Nero B vii fo. 107ᵛ (*LP*, VIII 874).
863 BL, Cotton MS, Nero B vii fo. 106 (*LP*, IX 927); Nero B vii 100 (*LP*, X 124).

864 BL, Cotton MS, Nero B vii fo. 116 (*LP*, XII i 398); BL, Cotton MS, Vitelius B xiv fo. 299; BL, Cotton MS, Nero B vii fo. 115 (*LP*, XII i 659).

865 PRO, SP1/105 fo. 46 (*LP*, XI 73).

866 BL, Cotton MS, Cleopatra E vi fo. 361 (*LP*, XI 210).

867 *LP*, X 7, 217, 276.

868 Ibid., IX 432, 927, 1029; X 124, 276, 420.

869 BL, Cotton MS, Cleopatra E vi fo. 347 (*LP*, X 974).

870 *LP*, X 975. *De unitate* is of course revealing at different levels: it hints at Pole's remarkable sympathy with Augustinian notions of justification by faith alone, and its standpoint is not that of a papal imperialist (cf. Mayer, *Reginald Pole*, pp. 14–33), but that is not the central interest here, not least given that such subtleties would not have affected Henry VIII's reading of the tract.

871 BL, Cotton MS, Cleopatra E vi fos 347–49ᵛ (*LP*, X 974).

872 PRO, SP1/105 fo. 33ᵛ (*LP*, XI 72); BL, Cotton MS, Cleopatra, E vi fo. 354 (*LP*, XI 210).

873 PRO, SP1/116 fo. 56 (*LP*, XII i 444).

874 Ibid. (My italics.)

875 Mayer, *Reginald Pole*, p. 195.

876 PRO, SP1/105 fo. 40ᵛ (*LP*, XI 72).

877 PRO, SP1/116 fo. 56 (*LP*, XII i 444).

878 Cf. D. Fenlon, *Heresy and Obedience in Tridentine Italy: Cardinal Pole and the counter reformation* (Cambridge, 1972), p. 39; and cf. Mayer, *Reginald Pole*, pp. 19–20 for citations of prophets and prophecies of destruction in *De unitate*.

879 *Pace* Mayer, who appears to think that Henry never saw *De unitate* ('A Diet for Henry VIII: the failure of Reginald Pole's 1537 legation', *Journal of British Studies*, xxvi [1987], p. 305).

880 *LP*, XI 71.

881 Ibid. 148.

882 Ibid. 229.

883 BL, Cotton MS, Cleopatra E vi fos 341–46ᵛ (*LP*, XI 91).

884 PRO, SP1/105 fos 32–44 (*LP*, XI 72); draft in BL, Cotton MS, Cleopatra E vi fos 389–93ᵛ.

885 PRO, SP1/105 fos 49, 50 (*LP*, XI 74).

886 BL, Cotton MS, Cleopatra E vi fos 359–61ᵛ (*LP*, XI 210).

887 According to the indictment of Lord Montagu: *LP*, XIII ii 979.

888 PRO, SP1/116 fos 54–5 (*LP*, XII i 444).

3: Authority and Reform

1 Wooding, *Rethinking Catholicism in Reformation England*, esp. pp. 48–52.

2 C. Lloyd, *Formularies of Faith* (Oxford, 1856), p. 215 for last.

3 Moreau, *Rome ou l'Angleterre*, pp. 94–5, from PRO, SP6/9 fos 223–35.

4 *LP*, VII 148.

5 PRO, SP1/83 fos 78–9 (*LP*, VII 462).

6 PRO, SP1/96 fos 13–13ᵛ (*LP*, IX 213).

7 PRO, SP1/105 fos 32–44 (*LP*, XI 72); draft in BL, Cotton MS, Cleopatra E vi fos 389–93ᵛ).

8 27 Henry VIII c. 42 (*Statutes of the Realm*, iii 599).

9 BL, Cotton MS, Cleopatra E vi fo. 214 (Cranmer, *Writings and Letters*, pp. 369–71).

10 28 Henry VIII c. 10 (*Statutes of the Realm*, iii 663).

11 Cranmer, *Writings and Letters*, p. 326; *LP*, XI 361 (BL, Cotton MS, Cleopatra E vi fos 234–5); Cranmer, *Writings and Letters*, p. 314.
12 Cranmer, *Writings and Letters*, p. 326.
13 *LP*, III i 475, 693.
14 Ibid., III i 1124, 1216; IV i 585.
15 M. Bowker, *The Henrician Reformation: the diocese of Lincoln under John Longland 1521–1547* (Cambridge, 1981), pp. 7, 17–28, 108–9; *LP*, IV ii 2378, 2391, 3175, 4047, 4078, 4796; V 1175; IX 328.
16 *LP*, IV ii 4692.
17 Ibid., III ii 1690.
18 Ibid. 1863, 2080.
19 Ibid. i 1122.
20 Ibid., IV ii 3815. This anticipated the policy of the government in 1535 (*LP*, IX 139 etc.).
21 B. Collett, *Female Monastic Life in Tudor England: an edition of Richard Fox's translation of the Benedictine rule for women* (Aldershot, 2002).
22 *LP*, II ii app. 48; 4231.
23 Ibid., III i 693.
24 R.W. Hoyle, 'The origins of the dissolution of the monasteries', *Historical Journal* (1995), pp. 280–1.
25 *LP*, IV i 477–8.
26 Ibid. i 953; W.A. Pantin, ed., *Documents Illustrating the Activities of the General and Provincial Chapters of the English Black Monks, 1215–1549, vol. iii*, Camden Society, 3rd ser., liv (1937), no. 283 pp. 123–4, redated; Gwyn, *King's Cardinal*, p. 273.
27 Cf. C. Harper-Bill, *The Pre-Reformation Church in England 1400–1530* (1989), p. 36.
28 *Victoria County History, Cambridgeshire*, ed. L.F. Salzman, *et al.* (1948) ii 218–19.
29 Higham, Kent, suppressed 1522, Lesnes and Tonbridge, Kent, suppressed 1525 (*Victoria County History, Kent*, ii 113). Gwyn, *King's Cardinal*, pp. 464–80 and cf. pp. 53–5 and 350–3. On 14 May 1528 a papal bull was ratified empowering Wolsey to convert the priory of St Peter, Ipswich, into a college (*LP*, IV ii 4297; cf. 4424, 4435, 4441; cf. IV ii 4307).
30 Rymer, *Foedera*, xiv 273–4; *LP*, IV ii 4921.
31 Rymer, *Foedera*, xiv 291–4; *LP*, IV ii 4900, iii 5266, 5638–9.
32 *LP*, IV ii 4921 (2).
33 Ibid. iii 5607 (iii).
34 Hoyle, 'Origins of the dissolution', p. 282.
35 *LP*, IV i 1470, 1471.
36 PRO, SP1/54 fos 204ᵛ, 206 (*LP*, IV iii 5749).
37 BL, Cotton MS, Vitellius B v fo. 8 (*LP*, IV i 995).
38 Gwyn, *King's Cardinal*, pp. 276–7.
39 References are from *LP*, II ii pp. 1441–80.
40 That is just as true of Henry's offerings to Our Lady of the Rock at Dover, to Our Lady of Boulogne and to Our Lady in the Wall at Calais, made during his journey to meet Francis I in October 1532 (*LP*, V p. 761), *pace* R. Rex and C.D.C. Armstrong, 'Henry VIII's ecclesiastical and collegiate foundations', *Historical Research*, lxxv (2002), p. 392 n. 14.
41 PRO, SP1/80 fo. 129 (*LP*, VI 1468 [5]); cf. R.B. Dobson, 'The monks of Canterbury in the later Middle Ages, 1220–1540', in P. Collinson, N. Ramsay and M. Sparks, eds, *A History of Canterbury Cathedral* (Oxford, 1995), p. 150.
42 *LP*, II ii 3747.

43 *State Papers*, i no. cxlvii p. 296 (*LP*, IV ii 4409); cf. *LP*, IV ii 4891: Henry, duke of Richmond, thanked his father the king for the preservatives he had sent: Richmond had survived the sweating sickness.

44 *LP*, II ii pp. 1441–80; V 755.

45 H.M. Colvin, ed., *History of the King's Works, 1485–1660 (Part I)* (1975), iii 1 (last remark), 187–222 (Henry VII's works of piety). This perception has recently been endorsed by Rex and Armstrong, 'Henry VIII's ecclesiastical and collegiate foundations', pp. 390–407, esp. p. 391.

46 Colvin, *History of the King's Works (Part II)* (1982), iv 193.

47 Ibid., p. 194.

48 Ibid., pp. 205–6.

49 Ibid., pp. 80–1.

50 *LP*, III i 483.

51 Colvin, *History of the King's Works*, iv 134–50.

52 Ibid. 242.

53 Ibid. 179.

54 Ibid. 1.

55 *LP*, III i 7: Indenture 5 Jan. 1518.

56 M. Biddle, 'Archaeology, art history and propaganda: Henry VIII's Nonsuch', paper read at History Faculty Centre, University of Oxford, 25 May 1990.

57 The word 'Erasmianisch' was used by a Swiss reformer in the 1520s: H. Trapman ' "Erasmianism" in the early reformation in the Netherlands', in M.E.H.N. Mout, H. Smolinsky, *et al.*, eds, *Erasmianism: idea and reality* (Amsterdam, 1997), p. 172 (I owe this reference to Alastair Duke).

58 'Incomparabiles illas animi tui dotes vt summa semper cum admiratione, tum fauore beneuolentiaque sumus prosecuti.' 'Fuit quidem in teneris quibus te nouimus annis studium in te nostrum neutiquam vulgare. At illud in maius indies prouexit, quod nos immortalitati consecrare, editis a te libellis quibus honorificam admodum nostri mentionem facis, sedulo studisti.' 'Nunc autem postquam in summum quidem creuit pertinax ille et indefessus animi tui tenor, quem in propaganda et illustranda Christiana fide non aestimandis laboribus tuis, sed ingenti sane cum Christiani orbis fructu commodoque, strenue prestas.' 'Quin incredibili quoque alacritate gestimus, quum solus propemodum prouinciam hanc sustineas, tam piis sanctisque conatibus tuis pro virili suc-currere et preasidio esse. Sentimus enim et ipsi iam aliquot annos vehementer incalescere et flagrare pectus nostrum, Diuino haud dubie spiritu huc incita-tum, vt Christi fidem religionemque pristinae suae dignitati asseramus . . . vt discussis et profligatis impiis haereticorum imposturis sermo Dei pure ac libere curreret.' 'Postremo Christi euangelium mutua opera et coniunctis opibus nostris longe melius propugnabitur.' The text of this letter is edited in P.S. and H.M. Allen, eds, *Letters of Erasmus* (Oxford, 12 vols, 1906–58), vii 179–81. There is a rather free (though essentially correct) translation in *LP*, IV ii 3438. I am most grateful to Dr A.T. Thacker for his help in elucidating the Latin text. For the suggestion that Henry VIII only spoke of 'scripture' in the 1520s, but began to talk of the 'word of God' in the 1530s, see Rex, *Henry VIII and the English Reformation*, p. 125.

59 F. Kisby, ' "When the king goeth a procession": chapel ceremonies and serv-ices, the ritual year and religious reforms at the early Tudor court, 1485–1547', *Journal of British Studies*, xl (2001), pp. 44–75.

60 *LP*, III i 402.

61 Ibid., III i 1233; IV ii 3992.

62 Ibid., IV ii 4404.

63 Colvin, *History of the King's Works*, iv 41.

64 *LP*, XXI ii 634; Rymer, *Foedera*, xv 110–17.

65 For the case that this was essentially Henry's book see G.W. Bernard, 'The piety of Henry VIII', in N.S. Amos and H. Van Nicrop, eds, *The Education of a Christian Society* (Aldershot, 1999), pp. 79–84.

66 Henry VIII, *Assertio septem sacramentorum* (1521) (*RSTC* 13078); the most recent scholarly English translation is L. O'Donovan, ed., *Assertio septem sacramentorum* (New York, 1908).

67 This shows, moreover, the inadequacy of any reductionist reading of the *Assertio* as 'a diplomatic propaganda exercise, which showed identity with the Emperor and Rome in a period when conflict with France was becoming likely again' (F. Heal, *The Reformation in Britain and Ireland* [Oxford, 2003], p. 19).

68 *LP*, IV ii 618.

69 Ibid., IV i 828.

70 Ibid., IV i 1760.

71 Ibid., IV i 40.

72 Ibid., IV ii 2446.

73 Ibid., VII 1141, 1482, 1544; VIII 121.

74 Ibid., IX 1016 (3).

75 Ibid., X 457.

76 D. MacCulloch, 'Henry VIII and the reform of the church', in D. MacCulloch, ed., *The Reign of Henry VIII: politics, policy and piety* (Basingstoke, 1995), p. 178. Cf. MacCulloch's question 'how can we take seriously the religion of a man whose theological outlook came to resemble a magpie's nest?': 'The religion of Henry VIII', in D. Starkey, ed., *Henry VIII: a European court in England* (1991), p. 160.

77 Foxe, *Acts and Monuments*, v 258–60.

78 A.G. Dickens, *The English Reformation* (2nd edn, 1989), p. 192.

79 E.W. Ives, 'Henry VIII: the political perspective', in D. MacCulloch, ed., *The Reign of Henry VIII: politics, policy and piety* (Basingstoke, 1995), p. 31.

80 S. Brigden, *London and the Reformation* (Oxford, 1989), p. 299.

81 C.S.L. Davies, *Peace, Print and Protestantism 1450–1558* (1976), p. 198.

82 J.S. Block, *Factional Politics and the English Reformation 1520–1540* (Woodbridge, 1993), p. 33.

83 R. McEntegart, 'England and the Schmalkaldic League, 1531–1547: faction, foreign policy and the English Reformation', Univ. of London, Ph.D. thesis (1992)', pp. 131–2.

84 *Statutes of the Realm*, iii 492 (26 Henry VIII c. 1).

85 Proclamation 1 Jan. 1536: *Tudor Royal Proclamations*, i no. 161, pp. 235–7 at 237. Why should this be seen an 'afterthought' as it is by Elton (*Policy and Police*, p. 220 n. 1)?

86 28 Henry VIII c. 10 (*Statutes of the Realm*, iii 663).

87 *LP*, VII 590.

88 Ibid., VII 665 (1), (2), (3); 921, 1024, 1121, 1216, 1347, 1594; VIII 31.

89 Wright, *Suppression*, no. lx pp. 132–3 (*LP*, XI 1449).

90 *Ex. inf.* Robert Swanson, personal correspondence, 3 Aug. 1994.

91 F.D. Logan, 'Thomas Cromwell and the vicegerency in spirituals: a revisitation', *English Historical Review*, ciii (1988), pp. 658–67; idem, 'The first royal visitation of the English universities, 1535', ibid., cvi (1991), p. 861.

92 *LP*, IX 167.

93 Ibid. 215, 280, 296, 375, 455, 590, 685, 744, 763, 781, 784, 790, 1170.

94 Ibid. 167, 159.

95 Wilkins, *Concilia*, iii 789–91.

96 In response, Richard Layton, the visitor, commanded the prior to appear before Cromwell (*LP*, IX 632). According to Elton, the prior was still in post at the surrender of the house in November 1537 (*Policy and Police*, p. 85).

97 Elton, *Policy and Police*, pp. 124–30; *LP*, IX 51, 52; X 597 (8) (licence to elect successor).

98 Logan, 'Visitation', pp. 861–3.

99 *LP*, IX 306 (9 Sept. 1535).

100 *Pace* Hoyle, 'Origins of the dissolution', p. 295 n. 74.

101 Wright, *Suppression*, no. xxviii p. 66; Logan, 'Visitation', p. 864 (*LP*, IX 265).

102 Logan, 'Visitation', pp. 865–9.

103 *Wright, Suppression*, no. xxx pp. 70–2 (*LP*, IX 350).

104 Logan, 'Visitation', pp. 865–7, 878; though see *LP*, XI 1184: Dr Whyte lost the lecture of the canon chair; see John London's complaints *(LP*, XII ii 429: 3 Aug. 1537) that he was accused of being a great papist and hinderer of good learning for refusing to give up Aristotle.

105 Wilkins, *Concilia*, iii 786–9, from BL, Cotton MS, Cleopatra E iv fos 13–19ᵛ.

106 Wilkins, *Concilia*, iii 789–91, from BL, Cotton MS, Cleopatra E iv fos 21–3.

107 Wright, *Suppression*, no. lxxvi pp. 156–7 (*LP*, VIII 822).

108 *LP*, X 364 (1).

109 Ibid. 364 (2).

110 A. Shaw, 'The Compendium Compertorum', University of Warwick MA thesis (1998), p. 10, identifies it as Ely Cathedral.

111 PRO, SP1/102 fos 103–03ᵛ (*LP*, X 364 [3]).

112 *LP*, IX 1080.

113 Ibid. 1167.

114 PRO, SP1/118 fo. 4 (*LP*, XII i 841 [3]).

115 F.A. Gasquet, *Henry VIII and the English Monasteries* (7th ed., 1920), p. 115.

116 G.W.O. Woodward, *The Dissolution of the Monasteries* (1966), p. 33.

117 C. Haigh, *English Heritage Magazine* (March 1991), p. 13.

118 Hoyle, 'Origins of the dissolution', p. 72.

119 *LP*, IX 244.

120 Ibid. 472.

121 Ibid. 168.

122 Ibid. 533.

123 Wright, *Suppression*, no. xxxiii pp. 75–7 (*LP*, IX 668).

124 *LP*, IX 669.

125 Ibid., IX 829.

126 Ibid., IX 756.

127 Ibid., IX 1005.

128 Ibid., X 37.

129 Ibid. 92.

130 PRO, SP1/102 fos 85–100 (or 91–114) (*LP*, X 364 [1]); BL, Cotton MS, Cleopatra E iv fos 147–59 is a copy.

131 That is my and *LP*'s extension of the abbreviations in the document; Knowles suggested 'pollutio voluntaria': *Tudor Age*, p. 296. Cf. J. Gairdner, 'Preface', *LP*, X p. xliii.

132 John Bale's Sodomismus would confess that 'I was with onan not unacquainted/ When he on the ground his increase shed': John Bale, *A Comedye concernynge Thre Laws*, 15 (4) 8 sig. B vi/v.

133 PRO, SP1/102 fos 101–02ᵛ (*LP*, X 364 [2]).

134 PRO, SP1/102 fos 103–04ᵛ (*LP*, X 364 [3]).

135 *LP*, X 92.

136 Ibid., IX 168.

137 J.H. Bettey, *Suppression of the Monasteries in the West Country* (Gloucester, 1989), p. 48.

138 *LP*, IX 160.

139 Ibid., IX 457.

140 Ibid., IX 509.

141 Ibid., X 137.

142 Ibid. 165.

143 Woodward, *Dissolution*, p. 34.

144 *LP*, X 364.

145 S. Jack, 'The last days of the smaller monasteries in England', *Journal of Ecclesiastical History*, xxi (1970), p. 116.

146 *LP*, XI 1191 (1).

147 Ibid., X 1191 and 364.

148 Ibid., X 1191; G.W.O. Woodward, 'The exemption from suppression of certain Yorkshire priories', *English Historical Review*, lxxvi (1961), pp. 397–8.

149 Cf. Hoyle, 'Origins of the dissolution', p. 73: 'as the commissioners for the two circuits with surviving comperta were clearly enquiring after evidence of both masturbation and homosexual practices, their questions may be regarded as *ultra vires* and part of a determined effort to gather salacious and damning evidence which could be used to smear the whole monastic estate.'

150 PRO, E36/118 fo. 92ᵛ (*LP*, XI 780 [2]; Dodds, *Pilgrimage of Grace*, i 126–7).

151 PRO, SP6/13 fos 16–24 at 17ᵛ (*LP*, XI 1409); cf. Alan Stewart, *Close Readers: humanism and sodomy in early modern England* (Princeton, 1997).

152 No written confessions survive, as Gasquet pointed out (*Henry VIII and the Monasteries*, p. 121), but that is not surprising and therefore not conclusive disproof.

153 PRO, SP1/118 fo. 4 (*LP*, XII i 841 [3]).

154 Wright, *Suppression*, no. xlii pp. 92–3 (*LP*, XI 1005).

155 PRO, SP1/112 fo. 119ᵛ (*LP*, XI 1246 [1]); *LP*, XII i 1175 (1 ii) (2); *LP*, XII i 786 (ii).

156 Woodward, *Dissolution of the Monasteries*, p. 33: not a convincing argument.

157 *LP*, XIV i 1321.

158 Ibid., IX 816, 829, 756.

159 Ibid., X 599, 1236, 601; cf. PRO SP1/106 fo. 157 (*LP*, XI 434); Jack, 'Last days of the smaller monasteries', p. 102.

160 *LP*, IX 816. Was the house at St Andrew's Northampton – greatly in debt – surrendered to the king, as Layton recommended? (*LP*, IX 1005; Wright, *Suppression*, no. xlii pp. 91–4; no. lxxxv pp. 168–9).

161 27 Henry VIII c. 27 (*Statutes of the Realm*, iii 570).

162 To be developed by John Bale, in whose *A Comedye concernynge Thre Lawes* (15[4]8), *RSTC* 1287, one of the characters is Sodomismus: 'if monkish sects renew,/ And popish priests continue,/ Which are of my retinue,/ To live I shall be sure' (sig. B vii/v). Cf. 'that sodomitical swarm or brood of Antichrist that we call the spirituality' (fo. 4); 'the men in their prelacies, priesthoods, and innumerable kinds of Monkery, for want of women hath brent in their lusts, and done abominations without number' (fo. 8ᵛ); 'I think few wise men will believe this physic to be true, as that a monk's cowle were able to restrain those ii heats ['the fire of concupiscence the fire of hell'] Rather should it seem to procure them, else we never had so many lecherous luskes and prodigious sodomites among them as we read of' (fo. 55ᵛ); 'abominable and most stinking knaveries'; 'the world shall well know what sodomites and devils they are ... leading their lives in unspeakable fleshly filthiness' (fo. 75): John Bale, *The Actes of Englysshe Votaryes* (1546), *RSTC* 1270.

163 *LP*, XIV ii 185; Ellis, *Original Letters*, III iii 247.
164 There was more to criticise, especially sexual misconduct, at St Mary's, York, Bath, Eynsham, Chertsey, Boxgrove: P. Cunich, 'The dissolution', in D. Rees, ed., *Monks of England: the Benedictines in England from Augustine to the present day* (1997), pp. 154–5.
165 PRO, SP1/102 fos 5–9 (*LP*, X 254).
166 PRO, SP6/13 fos 17ᵛ (*LP*, XI 1409); cf. Stewart, *Close Readers*.
167 PRO, SP6/1/25 fos 249–50/117–18 (*LP*, X 246 (16)); Lehmberg, *Reformation Parliament*, p. 224 n. 1 suggests it is by Thomas Starkey.
168 *LP*, XII i 901 (1); Bateson, 'Aske's examination', p. 567.
169 PRO, SP1/101 fo. 248 (*LP*, X 242).
170 Text of c. 1603: 'A chronicle and defence of the English Reformation', in D.M. Loades, ed., *The Papers of George Wyatt*, Camden Society, 4th ser., v (1968), pp. 159–60.
171 *LP*, X 601.
172 Lehmberg, *Reformation Parliament*, p. 226.
173 Cf. Hoyle, 'Origins of the dissolution', p. 296.
174 I am grateful to Tony Shaw for this point.
175 PRO, SP1/141 fo. 78 (*LP*, XIII i 1206).
176 *LP*, XIII ii 1225.
177 27 Henry VIII c. 28 (*Statutes of the Realm*, iii 575–7).
178 Hall, *Chronicle*, pp. 818–19.
179 H. Latimer, *Sermons*, Parker Society (1844), p. 123.
180 *LP*, X 494.
181 PRO, SP3/8 fo. 56 (*LP*, X 406).
182 Rex and Armstrong, 'Henry VIII's ecclesiastical and collegiate foundations', p. 395.
183 Hoyle ('Origins of the dissolution', p. 297) quotes PRO, E36/116 fo. 50 presenting the dissolution of the smaller monasteries 'as a means also to cause the great houses to have more vigilant respect and regard to their professions than they have had of many years used and accustomed'.
184 Woodward, 'The exemption from suppression of certain Yorkshire priories', pp. 396–7.
185 Ibid.
186 *LP*, X 384.
187 Wright, *Suppression*, no. xxxi pp. 72–3 (*LP*, X 337).
188 *LP*, X 1046.
189 Ibid., X 1097.
190 Ibid., X 1211.
191 Ibid., X 1246.
192 Ibid., X 716.
193 Ibid., XI 1370.
194 PRO, SP1/117 fo. 198 (*LP*, XII i 786 [ii] [15]).
195 *LP*, XI 517.
196 PRO, SP1/106 fo. 190 (*LP*, XI 485).
197 S. Parkinson, 'The catholics of Winchester and their response to religious change, 1553–1603', University of Lancaster MA thesis (1999), p. 26.
198 Jack, 'Last days of the smaller monasteries', p. 116.
199 *LP*, X 980.
200 Wright, *Suppression*, nos lviii, lxii, lxiv pp. 129–30, 136–7, 139–40 (*LP*, X 858, 1166; XI 176).
201 Woodward, 'Exemption from suppression', pp. 387–92.
202 Ibid., pp. 397–8.

203 Ibid., p. 398.
204 Ibid., pp. 392–3, 399.
205 Ibid., p. 401.
206 Wright, *Suppression*, no. lviii pp. 129–30 (*LP*, X 858).
207 Wright, *Suppression*, no. lxii pp. 136–7 (*LP*, X 1166).
208 Wright, *Suppression*, no. lxii pp. 136–7.
209 Ibid., pp. 139–40 (*LP*, XI 176).
210 *LP*, X 383.
211 Ibid., X 1215.
212 Ibid., X 916, 917.
213 Ibid., X 916.
214 Ibid., X 1215.
215 Ibid., XI 87, 96.
216 PRO, SP1/106 fo. 42 (*LP*, XI 353).
217 PRO, SP1/112 fo. 164 (*LP*, XI 1278).
218 Lloyd, *Formularies of Faith*, p. xv.
219 C.R. Trueman, *Luther's Legacy: salvation and English reformers 1525–1556* (Oxford, 1994), esp. pp. 83–120 is the best recent guide; W.A. Clebsch, *England's Earliest Protestants 1520–1535* (New Haven 1964) remains very useful; D. Daniell, *William Tyndale: a biography* (New Haven 1994) is full of information but uncritically indulgent; D. Rollison, *The Local Origins of Modern Society: Gloucestershire 1500–1800* (1992) builds on chains of speculation. There is little to support the suggestion (from a much later source) that Anne Boleyn drew Henry VIII's attention to Tyndale's *Obedience of a Christian Man* and that Tyndale subsequently influenced Henry's policy (J.G. Nichols, *Narratives of the Days of the Reformation*, Camden Society, 1st ser., lxxvii (1859), pp. 52–6). As we have seen, Henry did not need Tyndale to know what he might do, and Tyndale's refusal to support Henry over the divorce and his uncompromising adherence to the Lutheran doctrine of justification by faith alone made him unacceptable to the king. Anne Boleyn is an improbable 'evangelical' (see G.W. Bernard, 'Anne Boleyn's religion', *Historical Journal*, xxxvi [1993], pp. 1–20) and her fall in May 1536 was neither caused by nor had any effect on royal religious policy (see G.W. Bernard, 'The fall of Anne Boleyn', *English Historical Review*, cvi [1991], pp. 584–610).
220 G. Walker, 'Saint or schemer?: the 1527 heresy trial of Thomas Bilney reconsidered', *Journal of Ecclesiastical History*, xl (1989), pp. 219–38, reprinted with revisions in G. Walker, *Persuasive Fictions* (Aldershot, 1996), pp. 143–77, is the best guide; Foxe, *Acts and Monuments*, v 415.
221 Clebsch, *England's Earliest Protestants*, esp. pp. 78–136; Trueman, *Luther's Legacy*, pp. 121–55.
222 The general point has been widely commented on: e.g. 'Henry found his most reliable allies in the battle against Rome among men of specifically protestant tendencies' (Davies, *Peace, Print and Protestantism*, p. 182; cf. Duffy, *Stripping of the Altars*, p. 379; Haigh, *English Reformations*, p. 125; Rex, *Henry VIII and the English Reformation*, p. 144; Brigden, *London and the Reformation*, pp. 255–6; G. Redworth, 'Whatever happened to the reformation?', *History Today* (Oct. 1987), p. 36; A. Kreider, *English Chantries: the road to dissolution* (Cambridge, Mass, 1979) p. 108.
223 Clebsch, *England's Earliest Protestants*, pp. 42–77; Trueman, *Luther's Legacy*, pp. 156–97.
224 Foxe, *Acts and Monuments*, v 379.
225 Elton, *Policy and Police*, pp. 112–17.

226 Cranmer, *Writings and Letters*, p. 283 (*LP*, VII 463). That the king was behind this is hinted at by Archbishop Lee of York's later reference to the *king's* prohibiting preaching on articles such as purgatory for a year (*LP*, IX 704; VIII 869).

227 PRO, SP1/101 fo. 28 (*LP*, X 45); cf. *LP*, VII 750 (misdated: cf. Elton, *Policy and Police*, p. 244 n. 2).

228 *LP*, XI 65.

229 Wilkins, *Concilia*, iii 825; *LP*, XI 1110.

230 PRO, SP6/13 fos 122–22ᵛ (bald summary in *LP*, XII ii 404).

231 *LP*, XII i 1022.

232 PRO, SP1/101 fo. 233 (*LP*, X 225).

233 Lloyd, *Formularies of Faith*, p. xvi.

234 *LP*, XI 65 (Kreider, *English Chantries*, p. 122 for difficulties resolved by royal intervention).

235 PRO, SP1/105 fos 123–23ᵛ (*LP*, XI 156).

236 Lloyd, *Formularies of Faith*, pp. xv–xvi.

237 *LP*, XI 157.

238 It is unlikely that the Ten Articles were directly and specifically influenced by the Wittenberg Articles hammered out in spring 1536, as MacCulloch suggested (*Cranmer*, pp. 161–6). The affinities between the two texts are, as MacCulloch concedes, close only in part. And, as McEntegart (R. McEntegart, *Henry VIII, the League of Schmalkalden and the English Reformation* (Woodbridge, 2002)), pp. 150–1) has pointed out, the Wittenberg Articles are essentially an elaboration of the Confession of Augsburg of 1529. In short, the issues in contention on which the Ten Articles pronounce had already been in dispute for several years: the making of the Wittenberg Articles simply emphasised the need for an authoritative statement of belief.

239 BL, Cotton MS, Cleopatra E v fos 64–72; and printed version *RSTC* 10333: former in Burnet, *History of the Reformation*, iv 272–90 and Lloyd, *Formularies of Faith*, pp. 3–17; latter in Lloyd, *Formularies of Faith*, pp. xv–xxxiii. Lloyd suggests the latter, printed by Bethelet, is that given to the world and the Cotton MS version is the Convocation draft – changed by the king, e.g. 'by the commandment of *us* the supreme head', Lloyd, *Formularies of Faith*, p. vii.

240 Lloyd, *Formularies of Faith*, p. xx.

241 Ibid., pp. xxi–xxii.

242 Ibid., pp. xxiii: followed in the Bishops' Book of 1537: ibid., p. 98.

243 Ibid., p. xxiv; cf. 1537: ibid., p. 99.

244 Ibid., pp. xxvi–xxvii. (My italics.)

245 Ibid., p. xxix.

246 Cranmer, *Writings and Letters*, pp. 326–7 from BL, Cotton MS, Cleopatra E vi fo. 232 (*LP*, XI 361).

247 Wilkins, *Concilia*, iii 825; *LP*, XI 1110.

248 Cf. Parker, *English Reformation*, p. 90.

249 Lloyd, *Formularies of Faith*, p. xxv.

250 Haigh, *English Reformations*, p. 128 (cf. Rex, *Henry VIII and the English Reformation*, p. 146).

251 Elton, *Policy and Police*, p. 247.

252 *LP*, X 1147; cf. Rex, *Henry VIII and the English Reformation*, p. 145.

253 PRO, SP1/101 fos 233–4 (*LP*, X 225); cf. Kreider, *English Chantries*, p. 118 and n. 96 on pp. 245–6; Lloyd, *Formularies of Faith*, pp. xxxi–xxxii, 16–17, (followed almost exactly in Bishops' Book, ibid., pp. 210–11 and King's Book, ibid., pp. 376–7).

254 PRO, SP1/105 fo. 126 (*LP*, XI 156).

255 Lloyd, *Formularies of Faith*, pp. xxxi–xxxii, 16–17 (followed almost exactly in Bishops' Book, ibid., pp. 210–1 and King's Book, ibid., pp. 376–7).

256 PRO, SP1/101 fo. 233; cf. *LP*, X 831, 1043.

257 Wilkins, *Concilia*, iii 807–8; *LP*, XI 65.

258 27 Henry VIII c. 42 (*Statutes of the Realm*, iii 599–601), cited in Rex and Armstrong, 'Henry VIII's foundations', p. 394.

259 PRO, SP 1/105 fo. 126 (*LP*, XI 156).

260 PRO, SP 1/105 fos 127ᵛ–28.

261 BL, Cotton MS, Cleopatra E v fo. 142 (*LP*, XII i 1312). Probably 1536 (cf. Kreider, *English Chantries*, p. 246).

262 *LP*, X 752.

263 Duffy accepts that 'the article on purgatory similarly modified traditional teaching', but stresses that it still retained 'the belief that the dead benefit from the prayers of the living'. 'The article fell very short of Latimer's wishes' (*Stripping of the Altars*, p. 393). Rex notes the 'tangible comfort for reformers' offered by this article but notes also that 'even there the word was retained together with the concept of an intermediate state after death' (*Henry VIII and the English Reformation*, p. 147). For Brigden, the key point was that 'they allowed that purgatory existed, but denied that the soul's passage thence to heaven might be purchased', which gives a reformist thrust (*London and the Reformation*, p. 258). For Block, 'purgatory disappeared as it lacked scriptural authority' (*Factional Politics*, p. 108). For P. Marshall, this article marked a 'decisive turning away from the priorities of traditional religion', though Marshall at once qualifies that with the gloss that it was 'not all evangelicals wanted' (*Beliefs and the Dead in Reformation England* [Oxford, 2002], pp. 73–5, esp. p. 75).

264 Elton, *Reform and Reformation*, p. 257.

265 Lloyd, *Formularies of Faith*, pp. xxviii–xxx.

266 Ibid. pp. xxviii–xxxi.

267 PRO, SP6/13 fo. 122ᵛ.

268 Cf. Haigh, *English Reformations*, p. 129.

269 Cf. MacCulloch, *Cranmer*, p. 176, comparing two drafts of articles 6, 7 and 8, one evangelical and grudging on images and saints, the other more positive, but corrected to emphasise the avoidance of superstition.

270 Latimer, *Sermons*, pp. 33–57; cf. Rex, *Henry VIII and the English Reformation*, p. 145; cf. Duffy, *Stripping of the Altars*, pp. 390–1.

271 *LP*, XII i 953; cf. M. Aston, *England's Iconoclasts: Laws against Images* (Oxford 1988), p. 222 n. 9; A.F. Chester, *Hugh Latimer: Apostle to the English* (Philadelphia, 1954), pp. 104, 114–16.

272 Duffy, *Stripping of the Altars*, p. 389.

273 Ibid., pp. 393–4; Hughes, *Reformation in England*, i 351–2.

274 Cf. Rex, *Henry VIII and the English Reformation*, p. 100.

275 Cf. Duffy, *Stripping of the Altars*, p. 393: comparison with *Dives et Pauper*.

276 *Pace* MacCulloch, 'to defend ceremonies by explaining their educational purpose was an evangelical strategy under Henry VIII': *Cranmer*, p. 281; cf. p. 155 n. 63; cf. Elton, *Policy and Police*, p. 258. That was not necessarily the case: the context is crucial for determining their significance.

277 Cf. J. McConica, *English Humanists and Reformation Politics* (Oxford, 1965), pp. 159–60.

278 Dickens, *English Reformation*, p. 200; Wooding, *Rethinking Catholicism*, p. 64.

279 Haigh, *English Reformations*, p. 128; Rex, *Henry VIII and the English Reformation*, p. 188.

280 PRO, SP6/13 fos 122–5 (bald summary in *LP*, XII ii 404).

281 *Pace* E.W. Ives, 'Anne Boleyn and the early reformation: the contemporary evidence', *Historical Journal*, xxxvii (1994), p. 395, who misleadingly implies that the closeness of Anne Boleyn's almoner John Skip's treatment of ceremonies in his sermon to that of the Ten Articles means that he was not a conservative. Cf. D. MacCulloch, 'Henry VIII and the reform of the church', in D. MacCulloch, ed., *The Reign of Henry VIII: politics, policy and piety* (1995), pp. 280–1 n. 29). But the point here is that conservatives in the mid-1530s could use such arguments to preserve ceremonies from abolition. The tone and context of Skip's sermon make it quite plain that he wished to halt reform: why else tell the tale from Demosthenes of the Locrenses who required members of their parliament to stand under a noose whenever they introduced new laws, a noose that could be tightened by members who disapproved. Cf. Bernard, 'Anne Boleyn's religion', pp. 1–20.

282 Elton, *Policy and Police*, p. 247.

283 *LP*, XI 377; Merriman, *Life and Letters of Cromwell*, ii 29.

284 Rex, *Henry VIII and the English Reformation*, p. 145; cf. Elton, *Policy and Police*, p. 249.

285 Merriman, *Life and Letters of Cromwell*, ii 28 (*LP*, XI 377).

286 Cf. *LP*, XI 271; cf. Duffy, *Stripping of the Altars*, p. 394: Wilkins, *Concilia*, iii 823–4; Foxe, *Acts and Monuments*, v 164–5.

287 Rex, *Henry VIII and the English Reformation*, p. 95; *LP*, III ii 3292.

288 Cf. Haigh, *English Reformations*, p. 130.

289 Cf. Duffy, *Stripping of the Altars*, pp. 395ff: 'The first overt attack by the Henrician regime . . . on the traditional pattern of religious observances in the parishes.'

4: Rebellion and Conspiracy

1 C.S.L. Davies, 'The Pilgrimage of Grace reconsidered', *Past and Present*, xli (1968), pp. 62, 72–4, reprinted in P. Slack, ed., *Popular Protest and the Social Order in Early Modern England* (Cambridge, 1984), pp. 24, 34–5.

2 Ibid., p. 73.

3 Ibid., p. 62.

4 And writing on the Pilgrimage of Grace in the early 1980s, Davies would insist that 'I am not suggesting that a commitment to traditionalist religion was somehow a "cover" for communal self-interest; quite the contrary, the sense of communal proprietorship strengthened the natural conservative commitment to familiar forms and was in fact an integral part of it': 'Popular Religion and the Pilgrimage of Grace', in A. Fletcher and J. Stevenson, eds, *Order and Disorder in Early Modern England* (Cambridge, 1985), pp. 58–91 at 84.

5 See above, p. 292.

6 PRO, SP1/118 fo. 254 (*LP*, XII i 1011).

7 PRO, E36/119 fo. 7 (*LP*, XII i 70 [v]). Cf. E36/119 fo. 14 (*LP*, XII i 70 [x]); E36/119 fo. 13 (*LP*, XII i 70 [ix]); SP1/109 fo. 14ᵛ (*LP* XI 828 [xiii]); E36/119 fo. 8ᵛ (*LP*, XII i 70 [vi]).

8 PRO, E36/119 fo. 46 (*LP*, XII i 380); cf. SP1/109 fo. 204 (*LP*, XI 879 [2] but omitted from *LP*).

9 PRO, E36/119 fo. 14 (*LP*, XII i 70 [x]). Cf. E36/119 fo. 15 (*LP*, XII i 70 [xi]); E36/119 fo. 8ᵛ (*LP*, XII i 70 [vi]); E36/119 fo. 5ᵛ (*LP*, XII i 70 [iii]); E36/119 fo. 46 (*LP*, XII i 380).

10 PRO, SP1/110 fos 142–7, esp. 143^v, 144 (*LP*, XI 970). Cf. E36/119 fos 3–3^v (*LP*, XII I 70 [i]); SP1/109 fo. 8^v (*LP*, XI 828 [vi]); E36/118 fo. 5 (*LP*, XI 975 fo. 4).

11 PRO, SP1/109 fo. 10 (*LP*, XI 828 [vii]).

12 PRO, SP1/109 fos 4–5^v (*LP*, XI, 828 [i] [1]). (My italics.)

13 PRO, SP1/110 fo. 133 (*LP*, XI 968). Cf. SP1/110 fos 142–7, esp. 143 (*LP*, XI 970); SP1/109 fo. 76^v (*LP*, XI 854).

14 PRO, SP1/109 fos 4–5^v at 4^v (*LP*, XI, 828 [i] [1]).

15 R.W. Hoyle, *The Pilgrimage of Grace and the politics of the 1530s* (Oxford, 2001), p. 91; *LP*, XIV i 868 (15).

16 Hoyle, *Pilgrimage of Grace*, p. 44.

17 PRO, E36/118 fo. 71 (*LP*, XII i 392 [i]); cf. Hoyle, *Pilgrimage of Grace*, p. 91.

18 PRO, E36/119 fos 26–7 (*LP*, XII i 201 [1] [iv] [p. 90]).

19 Davies, 'Popular religion and the Pilgrimage of Grace', p. 68; idem, *Peace, Print and Protestantism 1461–1558*, p. 201.

20 PRO, SP1/106 fo. 250 (*LP*, XI 534); SP1/106 fo. 248 (*LP*, XI 533); M.H. and R. Dodds, *The Pilgrimage of Grace 1536–7 and the Exeter Conspiracy 1538* (Cambridge, 2 vols, 1915), i 98–9.

21 M.L. Bush, ' "Up for the Commonweal": the significance of tax grievances in the English rebellions of 1536', *English Historical Review*, cvi (1991), pp. 302–3; idem, *The Pilgrimage of Grace: a study of the rebel armies of October 1536* (Manchester, 1996), p. 17.

22 PRO, SP1/106 fos 301–02^v (*LP*, XI 569); *LP*, XI 598.

23 Davies, 'Popular religion and the Pilgrimage of Grace', p. 71.

24 James, 'Obedience and dissent', p. 16.

25 Hoyle, *Pilgrimage of Grace*, p. 92.

26 Davies, 'Popular Religion and the Pilgrimage of Grace', p. 72; idem, *Peace, Print and Protestantism*, p. 206.

27 A. Wood, *Riot, Rebellion and Popular Politics in Early Modern England* (Basingstoke, 2002), p. 59.

28 R.C. Dudding, ed., *The First Churchwarden's Book of Louth 1500–1524* (Oxford, 1941).

29 Davies, 'Popular Religion and the Pilgrimage of Grace', p. 79.

30 Davies, 'Pilgrimage of Grace reconsidered', p. 70. Cf. Davies's remark that 'The church issue was the focus of the general fear of spoliation by the government' ('Popular religion and the Pilgrimage of Grace', p. 71).

31 Wood, *Riot, Rebellion and Popular Politics*, p. 59.

32 Davies, *Peace, Print and Protestantism*, p. 206; idem, 'Popular religion and the Pilgrimage of Grace', p. 79.

33 Wood, *Riot, Rebellion and Popular Politics*, p. 60.

34 To be fair, Wood does refer to 'spiritual salvation' (*Riot, Rebellion and Popular Politics*, p. 60); Davies notes images and church furnishings as representing 'the sense of the holy' ('Popular religion and the Pilgrimage of Grace', p. 79). But the thrust of their presentations lies elsewhere.

35 Vienna, Haus-, Hof- und Staatsarchiv, England, Karton 5, Berichte, 1535, fos 328–29^v (*Cal. S.P., Spanish*, V i no. 257 pp. 608–11; *LP*, VII 1206).

36 James, 'Obedience and dissent', pp. 52, 58–61; G.R. Elton, 'Politics and the Pilgrimage of Grace', in B. Malament, ed., *After the Reformation* (Pennsylvania, 1980), p. 36, reprinted in G.R. Elton, ed., *Studies in Tudor and Stuart Politics and Government* (Cambridge, 4 vols, 1974–92), iii 194.

37 PRO, SP1/106 fo. 260 (*LP* XI 547). Cf. SP1/119 fo. 86 (*LP*, XII i 1087); SP1/106 fo. 291 (*LP*, XI 567).

38 G.W. Bernard, *War, Taxation and Rebellion: Henry VIII, Wolsey and the Amicable Grant of 1525* (Brighton, 1986), p. 81.

39 PRO, SP1/121 fo. 2 (*LP*, XII ii 2).

40 PRO, SP1/119 fo. 86 (*LP*, XII i 1087).

41 M.E. James, 'Obedience and dissent in Henrician England: the Lincolnshire Rebellion 1536', *Past and Present*, lxviii (1970), pp. 3–78, reprinted in M.E. James, *Society, Politics and Culture* (Cambridge, 1976), pp. 188–269.

42 'They took and swore him whether he would or no, and harried him forth by the arms toward Horncastle till he was for heat and weariness almost overcome . . . one of the said rebellious . . . said he should go on foot as they did and so they carried him forth the space of half a mile': PRO, SP1/110 fo. 126 (*LP*, XI 967 [v]; cf. SP1/119 fos 2–3 (*LP*, XI 828 [1] [2]); SP1/110 fos 124–24ᵛ (*LP*, XI 967 [i]); SP1/110 fo. 125 (*LP*, XI 967 [iii]).

43 Bush, 'Up for the Commonweal', pp. 302–3; Bush, *Pilgrimage of Grace*, p. 17.

44 E.H. Shagan, 'Rumours and popular politics in the reign of Henry VIII', in T. Harris, ed., *The Politics of the Excluded, c. 1500–1850* (Basingstoke, 2001), pp. 30–66; and see a brief reprise in E.H. Shagan, *Popular Politics and the English Reformation* (Cambridge, 2002), p. 91.

45 Shagan, 'Rumours and popular politics', pp. 32–3, 35.

46 Ibid., p. 35.

47 Ibid.

48 Shagan, *Popular Politics and the English Reformation*, p. 91.

49 Shagan, 'Rumours and popular politics', p. 31.

50 PRO, SP1/116 fos 75–75ᵛ (*LP*, XII i 456 [i]).

51 PRO, SP1/116 fos 76–76ᵛ (*LP*, XII i 456 [ii]).

52 PRO, SP1/110 fo. 143.

53 Ibid. fo. 134 (*LP*, XI 968). A.J. Fletcher and D. MacCulloch mislead in presenting this as 'swear on oath to be true to them': *Tudor Rebellions* (4th ed., Harlow, 1997), pp. 22–3.

54 PRO, SP1/106 fo. 268 (*LP*, XI 552). (My italics.)

55 PRO, SP1/106 fo. 295 (*LP*, XI 568).

56 PRO, SP1/110 fo. 124 (*LP*, XI 967 [i]), discussed by Hoyle, *Pilgrimage of Grace*, p. 129.

57 PRO, SP1/107 fo. 2 (*LP*, XI 571).

58 Identified by Hoyle as the author of PRO, E36/121 fos 72–72ᵛ (*LP*, XI 585): *Pilgrimage of Grace*, p. 141.

59 PRO, E36/118 fo. 54 (*LP*, XI 853).

60 PRO, E36/118 fo. 24ᵛ (*LP* XII i 6); cf. *LP*, XII i 945.

61 PRO, E36/121 fo. 72ᵛ (*LP*, XI 585).

62 Hoyle, *Pilgrimage of Grace*, pp. 206, 442. N. Housley, 'Insurrection as religious war, 1400–1536', *Journal of Medieval History*, xxv (1999), pp. 141ff is stimulating but does not quite grasp how close this was to a crusade.

63 PRO, E36/119 fo. 5 (*LP*, XII i 70 [ii]).

64 PRO, SP1/109 fos 3–4 (*LP*, XI 828 ii).

65 PRO, SP1/119 fo. 2 (*LP*, XI 828 [i] [2]).

66 PRO, E36/119 fo. 19 (*LP*, XII i 70 [13]).

67 PRO, SP1/106 fo. 270 (*LP*, XI 553).

68 PRO, SP1/109 fos 5–5ᵛ (*LP*, XI 828 [i] [1]).

69 PRO, E36/121 fos 72–72ᵛ at fo. 72ᵛ (*LP*, XI 585).

70 Bush has speculated that it is a hearsay account of the articles drawn up at Horncastle that do not survive as such: *Pilgrimage of Grace*, p. 303 n. 4.

71 Shagan is wrong to think this exception made the demand 'highly equivocal', that it was presenting the reversal of dissolution as open to negotiation (*Popular Politics and the English Reformation*, p. 100). It was rather a conciliatory gesture, recognising that the king might have had personal and particular reasons for specific suppressions. The general principle was robustly asserted while quarrels over the details of specific cases were avoided.

72 *Pace* Hoyle, *Pilgrimage of Grace*, p. 413.

73 Ibid., p. 21.

74 Cf. ibid., p. 66; and see his puzzlement at Lord Darcy, who 'expresses his sympathy with the rebels' complaints, even though he doubtless knew that the rumours which had provoked them were untrue': ibid., p. 268.

75 PRO, E36/119 fos 17ᵛ–18 (*LP*, XII i 70 [xii]).

76 Hoyle, *Pilgrimage of Grace*, pp. 154, 156; cf. p. 21.

77 PRO, E36/119 fos 17ᵛ–18 (*LP*, XII i 70 [xii] [Ledes]).

78 PRO, SP1/109 fo. 8 (*LP*, XI 828 [v]).

79 Hoyle, *Pilgrimage of Grace*, pp. 156–7, 353.

80 Bush, *Pilgrimage of Grace*, pp. 10–11.

81 PRO, SP1/108 fo. 45 (*LP*, XI 705 [1]), printed in Hoyle, *Pilgrimage of Grace*, pp. 455–6; cf. pp. 155–6.

82 Or, for example, from the various proclamations and oaths devised by Aske in mid-October that we shall shortly consider: *pace* Bush, *Pilgrimage of Grace*, p. 103.

83 Davies noted that 'the Lincolnshire rebels mentioned the royal supremacy only once, and then to accept it': he did qualify this by adding, 'though, be it noted, grudgingly rather than gladly' ('Pilgrimage of Grace reconsidered', p. 63, following Dickens, *English Reformation* [1st ed., 1964], p. 125). 'Opinion was divided on the papal supremacy', he wrote elsewhere (*Peace, Print and Protestantism*, p. 203). But his later comment that 'acceptance of Henry as Supreme Head was very much a reluctant acquiescence in the apparently inevitable' seems nearer the mark ('Popular religion and the Pilgrimage of Grace', p. 69 n. 49).

84 PRO, E36/118 fo. 54–54ᵛ (*LP*, XI 853).

85 J.A Guy, *Tudor England*, p. 149; cf. A. Shaw, 'Papal loyalism in 1530s England', *Downside Review*, cxvii (1999), p. 28, who sees Porman's accepting only a temporal but not a spiritual headship; and doubts how representative Porman was.

86 PRO, E36/118 fo. 5 (*LP*, XI 975 fo. 4).

87 PRO, SP1/110 fos 142ᵛ–43ᵛ (*LP*, XI 970).

88 PRO, E36/119 fo. 3ᵛ (*LP*, XII I 70).

89 PRO, SP1/110 fo. 146 (*LP*, XI 970). It is revealing that it was to the Coventry Charterhouse – as we have seen the Carthusians had resisted the royal supremacy, some paying with their life – that Kendal would go in search of sanctuary in November (*LP*, XI 970; PRO, SP1/114 fo. 73ᵛ (*LP*, XII i 69)), claiming to be a priest from near Colchester who came from Oxford; PRO, SP1/114 fo. 17 (*LP*, XII i 19).

90 PRO, SP1/106 fo. 270 (*LP*, XI 553)).

91 PRO, E36/121 fos 72–72ᵛ at fo. 72ᵛ (*LP*, XI 585).

92 PRO, PRO31/18/2/1, fo. 207ᵛ (*LP*, XI 576; cf. 597).

93 PRO, SP1/108 fo. 45 (*LP*, XI 705 [1]).

94 PRO, SP1/110 fos 143–6 (*LP*, XI 970).

95 PRO, E36/118 fos 54–54ᵛ (*LP*, XI 853). Bush reads this as implying that dissolution was acceptable so long as it went no further (Bush, *Pilgrimage of Grace*, p. 19 n.70).

96 PRO, E36/118 fo. 26 (*LP*, XII i 6; 'The manner of the taking of Robert Aske', p. 334); 'Aske's examination', p. 558.
97 PRO, SP1/109 fo. 8 (*LP*, XI 828 [v]).
98 PRO, E36/119 fos 15ᵛ–16 (*LP* XII i 70 [xi]).
99 *LP*, XII i 702.
100 PRO, E36/119 fo. 17 (*LP*, XII i 70 [xii]).
101 PRO, E36/119 fo. 14 (*LP*, XII i 70 [x]).
102 PRO, E36/119 fo. 19 (*LP*, XII i 70 [xiv]).
103 PRO, E36/119 fos 20–35ᵛ at 20ᵛ–21 (*LP*, XII i 201 [i]); Bush, *Pilgrimage of Grace*, p. 43).
104 PRO, SP1/121 fo. 35 (*LP*, XII ii 21 [2]).
105 PRO, E36/119 fos 26ᵛ–27 (*LP*, XII i 201 [iv] p. 90).
106 PRO, E36/119 fo. 45 (*LP*, XII i 380).
107 PRO, E36/118 fo. 4 (*LP*, XI 975 fo. 3).
108 PRO, SP1/110 fo. 146ᵛ (*LP*, XI 970).
109 PRO, SP1/106 fo. 294 (*LP*, XI 568; *LP*, XII i 734 [3]).
110 PRO, SP1/110 fo. 144 (*LP*, XI 970).
111 PRO, SP1/110 fo. 154ᵛ (*LP*, XI 971).
112 PRO, SP1/110 fo. 70 (*LP*, XI 973).
113 PRO, SP1/110 fo. 173ᵛ (*LP*, XI 974).
114 PRO, E36/119 fos 45–62 (*LP*, XII i 380).
115 PRO, E36/119 fo. 68ᵛ (*LP*, XII i 481).
116 PRO, E36/119 fos 7ᵛ–8 (*LP*, XII i 70 [v]).
117 PRO, SP1/108 fos 209–09ᵛ.
118 PRO, SP1/109 fos 7ᵛ–8 (*LP*, XI 828 [v]).
119 PRO, SP1/109 fo. 4 (*LP*, XI 828 [ii]).
120 *LP*, XII i 702; cf. details in PRO, SP1/117 fo. 160 (*LP*, XII i 765); PRO, SP1/117 fos 32ᵛ–33 (*LP*, XII i 677).
121 PRO, E36/119 fos 10–12ᵛ (*LP*, XII i 70 [viii]).
122 PRO, SP1/109 fo. 26 (*LP*, XI 834).
123 *State Papers*, ii no. lii p. 471 (*LP*, XI 834).
124 *LP*, XI 842 (4).
125 PRO, SP1/111 fo. 225 (*LP*, XI 1155 5 [ii]).
126 *LP*, XII ii 181.
127 Ibid. i 734, 764; Wriothesley, *Chronicle*, p. 62.
128 *LP*, XII i 581.
129 *Pace* Hoyle, 'the afternoon appears to have passed more peacefully'; no more than 'a bit of small-town trouble': *Pilgrimage of Grace*, pp. 109, 5.
130 BL, Cotton MS, Cleopatra E iv fo. 329 (*LP*, X 384).
131 PRO, SP1/109 fo. 2 (*LP*, XI 828 [i] [1]): testimony of Nicholas Melton.
132 *LP*, XI 135.
133 PRO, SP1/109 fo. 77 (*LP*, XI 854).
134 PRO, SP1/106 fo. 291 (*LP*, XI 567).
135 *LP*, XI 789, 854, 959: Bellow returned to Legbourne (XI 959).
136 PRO, SP1/106 fo. 252 (*LP*, XI 536).
137 PRO, SP1/106 fo. 291 (*LP*, XI 567).
138 Cf. Bush, *Pilgrimage of Grace*, p. 19 n. 70; p. 23.
139 PRO, SP1/109 fo. 14 (*LP*, XI 828 [xii]).
140 PRO, SP1/106 fos 134–34ᵛ (*LP*, XI 405).
141 PRO, SP1/110 fo. 35 (*LP*, XI 564).
142 PRO, SP1/106 fo. 286 (*LP* XI 563 [2]).
143 PRO, SP1/109 fos 37–41ᵛ at 37ᵛ (*LP*, XI 841).

144 Cf. Bush, *Pilgrimage of Grace*, p. 249 n. 9 for date; Cf. D. MacCulloch, *Journal of Ecclesiastical History*, xlviii (1997), p. 572.
145 PRO, SP1/119 fos 1–1ᵛ (*LP*, XII i 1022).
146 R.B. Smith, *Land and Politics in the England of Henry VIII: the West Riding of Yorkshire* (Oxford, 1970); Elton, 'Politics and the Pilgrimage of Grace', pp. 25–56, 183–215.
147 Vienna, Haus-, Hof- und Staatsarchiv, England, Karton 5, Berichte, 1535, fos 328–29ᵛ (*Cal. S.P., Spanish*, i no. 257 pp. 608–11; *LP*, VII 1206; cf. VIII 355, 666, 750, 1018).
148 PRO, PRO31/18/2/2 p. 106 (*LP*, VIII 666).
149 PRO, SP1/119 fo. 80 (*LP*, XII i 1087 p. 497); *LP*, XII i 848 I (12); XII i 1200.
150 PRO, SP1/117 fo. 191 (*LP*, XII i 783); SP1/107 fos 85, 88 (*LP*, XI 605, 606).
151 PRO, SP1/110 fo. 40 (vi) (LP, XI 604); SP1/107 fo. 154 (LP, XI 662); SP1/110 fo. 47 (xxi) (LP, XI 675); G.W. Bernard, *The Power of Early Tudor Nobility* (Brighton, 1985), pp. 35–8.
152 PRO, SP1/106 fo. 234 (*LP*, XI 522). I am grateful to Richard Hoyle for sharing with me his convincing rereading.
153 Hoyle is a notable exception: *Pilgrimage of Grace*, p. 7.
154 Ibid., p. 268.
155 Cf. Ibid., p. 281.
156 Cranmer, *Writings and Letters*, p. 363.
157 PRO, SP1/110 fo. 48 (*LP*, XI 566).
158 PRO, E36/121 fos 9–9ᵛ (*LP* XI 995); SP1/111 fo. 9 (*LP*, XI 1007).
159 PRO, SP1/111 fo. 60 (*LP*, XI 1045).
160 Cf. Hoyle's musings on what exactly Darcy had promised: *Pilgrimage of Grace*, p. 321.
161 PRO, SP1/119 fos 124ᵛ–25 (*LP*, XI 1086); E36/119 fos 79ᵛ–80 (*LP*, XII i 1013); cf. SP1/111 fo. 61 (*LP*, XI 1045), *LP*, XI 929, XII i 84.
162 Badly damaged MS: PRO, SP1/109 fo. 14ᵛ (*LP*, XI 828 xii).
163 PRO, SP1/118 fo. 267ᵛ (*LP*, XII i 1018); Shagan, *Popular Politics and the English Reformation*, p. 92.
164 PRO, SP1/119 fo. 5.
165 Ibid. fo. 8 (*LP*, XII i 1022).
166 *State Papers*, i 485 (*LP*, XI 826).
167 PRO, SP1/110 fo. 88ᵛ (*LP*, XI 947 [2]), cited in Hoyle, *Pilgrimage of Grace*, p. 237.
168 PRO, SP1/118 fo. 142 (*LP*, XII i 914).
169 Hoyle, *Pilgrimage of Grace*, p. 206.
170 Cf. Ibid., p. 202, drawing on Stapleton's account (*LP*, XII i 392).
171 PRO, SP1/106 fos 286–87ᵛ (*LP*, XI 563 [2]).
172 PRO, E36/118 fo. 14 (*LP* XII i 1034).
173 'Aske's examination', p. 560 (*LP*, XII i 6).
174 Hoyle, *Pilgrimage of Grace*, p. 208.
175 'Aske's examination', p. 572 (*LP*, XII i 6).
176 Hoyle, *Pilgrimage of Grace*, pp. 414, 206, 442.
177 Davies, 'Popular religion and the Pilgrimage of Grace', p. 77 n. 88.
178 Bush offers 'for the material good of the realm': *Pilgrimage of Grace*, p. 11.
179 Hoyle, *Pilgrimage of Grace*, pp. 206, 209.
180 Ibid., p. 206 n. 83.
181 Ibid., p. 209.

182 Bush, *Pilgrimage of Grace*, pp. 46–7. Later, on pp. 145–6, from PRO, SP1/117 fo. 204b (*LP*, XII i 786 [ii]) and *LP*, XII i 1011, Bush cites the statement of grievances compiled on 14 Oct. that (i) condemned the dissolution of the smaller monasteries and (ii) proclaimed that the rebels' cause was the defence of the commonwealth, but does not reflect on how much this undermines his attempt to separate monasteries from the 'commonwealth'.

183 PRO, SP1/108 fo. 48 (*LP* XI 705 [4]).

184 Compare slightly different phrases in another version: 'the love that ye do bear unto almighty God, his faith and to holy church militant [and] the maintenance thereof'; 'to expulse all villain blood and evil councillors against the commonwealth from his grace and his privy council of the same'; 'but in your hearts put away all fear and dread, and take afore you the cross of Christ, and in your hearts his faith, the restitution of the church, the suppression of these heretics and their opinions, by all the whole contents of this book' (T.N. Toller, ed., *Correspondence of Edward, Third Earl of Derby, During the Years 24 to 31 Henry VIII*, Chetham Society, n.s., xxix [1890], pp. 50–1, reprinted in Hoyle, *Pilgrimage of Grace*, pp. 457–8).

185 PRO, SP1/109 fo. 247ᵛ (*LP*, XI 902 [2]); reprinted in Hoyle, *Pilgrimage of Grace*, pp. 458–9.

186 Hoyle, *Pilgrimage of Grace*, p. 206 n. 83.

187 Ibid., pp. 204–5.

188 PRO, E36/118 fo. 21 (*LP*, XI 705 [2]; *State Papers*, i no. xlix pp. 466–7).

189 PRO, SP1/117 fos 48–56 (*LP*, XI 687 [2]); cf. PRO, E36/119 fos 71–4, not in *LP*, as Hoyle notes (*Pilgrimage of Grace*, p. 242 n. 95).

190 PRO, E36/118 fo. 90 (*LP*, XI 826).

191 PRO, SP1/108 fo. 205 (*LP*, XI 804 omits 'for the common welthe').

192 *LP*, XI 892 (2): n.b. this is the second item listed as (2): apparently the manuscript is missing from the PRO.

193 PRO, SP1/111 fo. 88 (*LP*, XI 1059 [ii]).

194 'Aske's examination', p. 571.

195 PRO, E36/118 fos 21–21ᵛ (*LP*, XI 705 [2]; *State Papers*, i no. xlix pp. 466–7).

196 PRO, E36/118 fo. 21 (*LP*, XI 705 [2]; *State Papers*, i no. xlix pp. 466–7).

197 Bush, *Pilgrimage of Grace*, p. 94.

198 PRO, SP1/119 fos 7–7ᵛ (*LP*, XII i 1022).

199 R.W. Hoyle, ed., 'Thomas Master's narrative of the Pilgrimage of Grace', *Northern History*, xxi (1985), p. 76: 10 Dec. 1536 (contrast Bush, *Pilgrimage of Grace*, p. 18 n. 68 and p. 412 n. 9).

200 PRO, E36/118 fo. 90 (*LP*, XI 826).

201 'Aske's examination', pp. 571–2 (*LP*, XII i 901); cf. Housley, 'Insurrection as religious war, 1400–1536', pp. 141ff; Shagan, *Popular Politics and the English Reformation*, p. 93.

202 PRO, SP1/109 fos 247ᵛ–48 (*LP*, XI 902 [2]); Hoyle, *Pilgrimage of Grace*, pp. 458–9.

203 PRO, SP1/111 fo. 88 (*LP*, XI 1059 [ii]).

204 PRO, SP1/118 fos 284–84ᵛ (*LP*, XII i 1021 [3]).

205 Not a canon of Bridlington: see D.M. Palliser, *The Reformation in York 1534–1553, Borthwick Papers*, xl (1971), p. 11.

206 PRO, SP1/116 fos 97–97ᵛ (*LP*, XII i 479; *State Papers*, i no. lxxxi p. 538).

207 PRO, SP1/118 fo. 284 (*LP*, i 1021 [3]), reprinted in F.J. Furnivall, *Ballads from Manuscripts* (Hertford, 1873), II ii 304–9.

208 PRO, SP1/118 fos 271–3 at 272 (*LP*, XII i 1019).

209 PRO, SP1/118 fo. 284ᵛ (*LP*, XII ii 1021 [1]).

210 PRO, SP1/118 fo. 280ᵛ (*LP*, XII ii 1021 [1]).

211 PRO, E36/118 fos 63–9 esp. 67–8 (*LP*, XI 956; *State Papers*, i no. liii p. 476).
212 PRO, SP1/111 fo. 21 (*LP*, XI 1014): misdated.
213 *State Papers*, i 498 (*LP*, XI 1064 [1]).
214 Cf. Hoyle, *Pilgrimage of Grace*, pp. 325–7.
215 Ibid., p. 328.
216 PRO, SP1/117 fo. 80 (*LP*, XII i 698 [3]); SP1/118 fos 254, 256ᵛ (*LP*, XII i 1011); SP1/111 fo. 187 (*LP*, XI 1127).
217 PRO, E36/119 fo. 74ᵛ (*LP*, XII i 687 [2]).
218 PRO, SP1/119 fo. 7 (*LP*, XII i 1022).
219 PRO, SP1/119 fos 7–7ᵛ (*LP*, XII i 1022).
220 PRO, SP1/118 fo. 279ᵛ (*LP*, XII i 1021 [1] [i]).
221 PRO, SP1/118 fo. 279 (*LP*, XII i 1021 [1] [i]).
222 John Pickering said that Archbishop Lee broke off from his original purpose of exploring the nature of pilgrimage, and instead then spoke these words once Lancaster Herald appeared: he was implying that if it had been safe to do so, the archbishop would have supported the Pilgrims (PRO, SP1/118 fo. 279ᵛ [*LP*, XII i 1021 (1) (i)]).
223 PRO, SP1/119 fo. 10ᵛ (*LP*, XII i 1022).
224 BL, Cotton MS, Cleopatra E v fos 381–2, variant in PRO, SP1/112 fos 116–17 (*LP*, XI 1245); text reprinted in Strype, *Ecclesiastical Memorials*, I ii pp. 266–8; Wilkins, *Concilia*, iii 812; Dodds, *Pilgrimage of Grace*, i 383–5; and Hoyle, *Pilgrimage of Grace*, pp. 463–4.
225 A.G. Dickens, 'The northern convocation and Henry VIII', *Church Quarterly Review*, cxxvii (1938), pp. 84–102 at 98–101; cf. Hoyle's doubts that clergy who held doctorates of divinity or law could have been representative of parish clergy: *Pilgrimage of Grace*, p. 345.
226 Hoyle, *Pilgrimage of Grace*, p. 463; Shagan, *Popular Politics and the English Reformation*, p. 98.
227 PRO, SP1/117 fo. 214 (*LP*, XII i 789 [ii]).
228 PRO, SP1/112 fos 119–21, another version 122–24ᵛ (*LP*, XI 1246; reprinted in Hoyle, *Pilgrimage of Grace*, pp. 461–3).
229 'Aske's examination', p. 572 answ. 102; Hoyle, *Pilgrimage of Grace*, p. 349.
230 In another version this appears as 'such other heresies anabaptist' (PRO, SP1/112 fos 122–24ᵛ [*LP*, XI 1246]), showing that the reference to 'Anabaptist' was not ignorantly taking him as a person. The authors of this document knew what they were about: what happened here was a scribal error – and if the error reflected ignorance, it was that of the scribe, not that of the northern churchmen.
231 Hoyle, *Pilgrimage of Grace*, p. 351.
232 PRO, E36/119 fo. 94 (*LP*, XII i 901 [1] [17]; 'Aske's examination', p. 567).
233 PRO, E36/119 fos 104–04ᵛ; 'Aske's examination', p. 567.
234 Batesan, 'Aske's examination', p. 571.
235 PRO, E36/119 fo. 109 (*LP*, XII i 901 [1] [17]; 'Aske's examination', p. 570).
236 PRO, E36/119 fo. 99, 'Aske's examination', p. 565.
237 PRO, SP1/117 fo. 80ᵛ (*LP*, XII i 698).
238 PRO, E36/119 fo. 92 (*LP*, XII i 901 [1] [17]; 'Aske's examination', pp. 551–9).
239 PRO, SP1/118 fo. 279ᵛ (*LP*, XII i 1021 [1]).
240 PRO, E36/119 fo. 107 (*LP*, XII i 901 [1]); 'Aske's examination', p. 570.
241 PRO, SP1/119 fos 124ᵛ–25 (*LP*, XI 1086); Shagan, *Popular Politics and the English Reformation*, p. 101.
242 *LP*, XII i 1207 (8) (11).
243 PRO, E36/118 fos 45–45ᵛ (*LP*, XII i 900): questions 30–54.
244 PRO, E36/119 fo. 92ᵛ (*LP*, XII i 901 [1] [19]).

245 PRO, E36/119 fos 94–94^v (*LP*, XII i 901 [1] [31, 36]; 'Aske's examination', pp. 560, 552, 567, 562).

246 PRO, E36/119 fo. 108^v.

247 Ibid. fo. 96^v ('Aske's examination', p. 562).

248 Cf. Aske's instructions 'to inquire of the visitations of Doctor Layton and Doctor Ley and to certify him thereof': PRO, E36/119 fo. 74^v.

249 PRO, SP1/112 fo. 119–21, another version 122–24^v (*LP*, XI 1246; reprinted in Hoyle, *Pilgrimage of Grace*, pp. 461–3).

250 PRO, SP1/119 fo. 146 (*LP*, XII i 1129).

251 PRO, SP1/117 fo. 174 (*LP*, XII i 777); cf. Shaw, 'Papal loyalism'.

252 BL, Cotton MS, Titus B i fo. 441 (*LP*, XII i 1079).

253 PRO, SP1/119 fos 57–57^v (*LP*, XII i 1080).

254 PRO, SP1/117 fo. 206 (*LP*, XII i 788).

255 PRO, SP1/118 fos 138–43^v at 142–42^v (*LP*, XII i 914).

256 PRO, SP1/117 fo. 29 (*LP*, XII i 671 [2 iii]). The manuscript is damaged. Cf. PRO, SP1/115 fo. 244 (*LP*, XII i 384); *LP*, XII i 849 (31); and PRO, SP1/114 fo. 4^v (*LP*, XII i 7) for the violence of the commons on the first occasion, pacified then by Parson Layburne.

257 PRO, E36/119 fo. 72; Davies, 'Popular religion and the Pilgrimage of Grace', p. 75, questions whether this shows 'deep-seated papalism in Kendal', though it is not clear why. PRO, SP1/117 fo. 215 (*LP*, XII i 792).

258 PRO, SP1/107 fo. 143 (*LP*, XI 655; Bush, *Pilgrimage of Grace*, p. 233).

259 PRO, E26/119 fo. 22 (*LP*, XII i 201 [i]).

260 PRO, SP1/109 fo. 14 (*LP*, XI 828 [xii]).

261 PRO, SP1/116 fo. 169^v (*LP*, XII i 536); PRO, SP1/119 fo. 87 (*LP*, XII i 1087); *LP*, XI 1009, after first Doncaster order; PRO, E36/118 fo. 74^v (*LP*, XII i 392) for William Stapleton's account of the commons going to South Cave.

262 PRO, SP1/118 fo. 269 (*LP*, XII i 1018); SP1/120 fo. 175 (*LP*, XII i 1264).

263 PRO, SP1/111 fos 66–67^v (*LP*, XI 1047); Bush, *Pilgrimage of Grace*, pp. 90, 107 n. 166.

264 PRO, SP1/120 fo. 265 (*LP*, XII i 1326).

265 PRO, E36/118 fo. 108 (*LP*, XII i 29 [2]). Cf. Bush, *Pilgrimage of Grace*, p. 43.

266 Hoyle, *Pilgrimage of Grace*, p. 50.

267 PRO, E36/118 fos 82–82^v (*LP*, XII i 392 p. 193); Bush, *Pilgrimage of Grace*, pp. 43–4; PRO, SP1/117 fo. 216 (*LP*, XII i 793).

268 PRO, E36/118 fo. 32 (*LP*, XII i 6 p. 8; 'The manner of the taking of Robert Aske', p. 342).

269 *LP*, XI 481 for leases; cf. Bush, *Pilgrimage of Grace*, p. 43; PRO, E36/118 fo. 75 (*LP*, XII i 392 pp. 185–6).

270 Bush, *Pilgrimage of Grace*, p. 88, from Stapleton's account but not in *LP*.

271 PRO, E36/118 fo. 108 (*LP*, XII i 29 [2]); cf. *LP*, XI 677; Bush, *Pilgrimage of Grace*, p. 163; PRO, SP1/120 fo. 265 (*LP*, XII i 1326). The site and demesnes of Coverham were already being bid for by would-be lessees: *LP*, XI 481; 943 (16); XII i 29 (2).

272 PRO, E36/118 fo. 108 (*LP*, XII i 29 [2]): the site and demesne of St Agatha's were already being bid for: *LP*, XI 481.

273 PRO, SP1/109 fo. 199 (*LP*, XI 879); suppressed in August (*LP*, XI 307). The prioress may have resisted them (Palliser, *Reformation in York*, p. 10).

274 Palliser, *Reformation in York*, p. 10, inferring reoccupation from *LP*, XII i 536 and 1087 (PRO, SP1/119 fo. 87, but badly torn) which refer to the prior taking two trussing bedsteads from Leonard Beckwith, receiver of augmentations, and promising to send them to the rebels.

275 Palliser, *Reformation in York*, pp. 10–11.
276 PRO, SP1/122 fo. 201 (*LP*, XII ii 205).
277 *LP*, XII ii 59 (Wright, *Suppression*, no. lxxvii p. 159); *LP*, XII ii 205; Bush, *Pilgrimage of Grace*, pp. 219–20.
278 PRO, E36/120 fo. 95ᵛ (*LP*, XII i 491).
279 PRO, SP1/108 fo. 180 (*LP*, XI 784 [i]). Hoyle is clearly wrong to say that the movement – the rebellion – did not reinstate them: *Pilgrimage of Grace*, p. 228.
280 PRO, SP1/108 fos 180–80ᵛ (*LP*, XI 784 [i]; Bush, *Pilgrimage of Grace*, p. 223 also cites *LP*, XII i 506 but that is about later matters.
281 PRO, SP1/116 fo. 116 (*LP*, XII i 506).
282 Ibid.
283 *Historical Manuscripts Commission, 6th Report*, p. 445 (*LP*, XI 806; cf. 783).
284 PRO, SP1/108 fos 180–80ᵛ (*LP*, XI 784 [i]); SP1/116 fo. 116 (*LP*, XII i 506); cf. Bush, *Pilgrimage of Grace*, pp. 222–3.
285 PRO, SP1/109 fo. 110ᵛ (*LP*, XI 872 [ii]).
286 PRO, SP1/116 fo. 116 (*LP*, XII i 506).
287 PRO, SP1/108 fo. 183 (*LP*, XI 785); cf. SP1/119 fo. 77ᵛ (*LP*, XII i 1087); E36/118 fos 15–16ᵛ (*LP*, XII i 1034); SP1/118 fo. 265ᵛ (*LP*, XII i 1014); *LP*, XII i 1020.
288 PRO, SP1/108 fos 185ᵛ–86 (*LP*, XI 786; 'The manner of the taking of Robert Aske', pp. 344–5).
289 'The ex-monks must have been together in the vicinity of their houses to have been ready to be restored, and there must be a suspicion, at least in the case of Conishead, they had been urging the commons to help them and defy the king,' says Haigh (*Lancashire Monasteries*, p. 62). Bush goes even further, suggesting the five canons simply returned, but his reference (*LP*, XII i 841 [3]) does not appear to refer to Conishead.
290 PRO, SP1/118 fo. 37ᵛ (*LP*, XII i 849 [1] [29]); cf. *LP*, Addenda, 1112.
291 Haigh, *Lancashire Monasteries*, p. 79, citing *LP*, XII i 841 (3).
292 Haigh, *Lancashire Monasteries*, p. 77.
293 PRO, E36/122 fo. 49 (*LP*, XII i 1088).
294 Haigh, *Lancashire Monasteries*, p. 46.
295 PRO, SP1/110 fo. 89 (*LP*, XI 947 [2]) (*Chetham Society*, xix [1890], p. 45). Presumably, says Bush (*Pilgrimage of Grace*, p. 265), his heart was not in the resistance – earlier he had asked to be relieved from his monastic vows, and he did not wish now to take the rebels' oath.
296 PRO, SP1/115 fo. 209ᵛ (*LP*, XIII i 369).
297 PRO, SP1/112 fos 97–97ᵛ (*LP*, XI 1236); Norfolk on 26 Nov. had pleaded with the king that if he would not agree, then he should come quickly with an army of gentlemen and servants: Hoyle, 'Thomas Master's narrative', p. 74.
298 PRO, SP1/109 fos 248 (*LP*, XI 902 [2] but words quoted not in *LP*; Hoyle, *Pilgrimage of Grace*, pp. 458–9).
299 PRO, SP1/112 fo. 73ᵛ (*LP*, XI 1227); cf. SP1/112 fo. 97 (*LP*, XI 1236).
300 PRO, SP1/112 fo. 120 (*LP*, XI 1246). The possible choice of Nottingham is intriguing: does it envisage movement south?
301 PRO, SP1/111 fo. 61 (*LP*, XI 1045).
302 PRO, SP1/109 fo. 245 (*LP*, XI 902); cf. PRO, SP1/112 fo. 5 (*LP*, XI 1170).
303 PRO, SP1/117 fos 198–98ᵛ (this manuscript is hard to read) (*LP*, XII i 786 [15]); SP1/113 fo. 69 (*LP*, XI 1410).
304 PRO, SP1/112 fos 114–15 (*LP*, XI 1244).
305 PRO, SP1/112 fo. 80 (*LP*, XI 1227).
306 BL, Add. MS 25114 fo. 237 (*LP*, XI 1363).
307 BL, Add. MSS 25114 fos 237–38ᵛ at 237–8 (*LP*, XI 1363).

308 PRO, E36/119 fo. 92ᵛ (*LP*, XII i 901 [1]); 'Aske's examination', p. 559. Bush
    is misleading when he supposes that the post-pardon revolts were intended in
    part to fill gaps in the December agreement: the meeting of parliament would
    have done that: M. Bush and D. Bownes, *The Defeat of the Pilgrimage of
    Grace: a study of the Postpardon Revolts of December 1536 to March 1537
    and their effect* (Hull, 1999), *passim*, esp. pp. 289–97.
309 PRO, SP1/113 fos 78–78ᵛ (*LP*, XI 1410 [4]); Bush and Bownes, *Postpardon
    Revolts*, pp. 186–7.
310 Hoyle, 'Thomas Master's narrative', p. 74. Davies gives just these, and nothing
    more, as the concessions: 'Popular religion and the Pilgrimage of Grace', p. 62.
311 Cf. Dodds, *Pilgrimage of Grace*, ii 18.
312 PRO, SP1/112 fos. 151–3ᵛ 61 (*LP*, XI 1271).
313 Ibid., XII i 98, 302.
314 PRO, SP1/112 fos 151–51ᵛ, 153–53ᵛ (*LP*, XI 1271). The Dodds wondered
    whether the letter was ever sent (*Pilgrimage of Grace*, ii 22), but that is irrel-
    evant to the argument here.
315 Cf. Bush, *Pilgrimage of Grace*, p. 305: 'the king was left in a state of fury
    because none had been reserved for punishment and because, with the restored
    abbeys left standing, the way was now open for a permanent undoing of the
    Dissolution.'
316 PRO, SP1/112 fos 151–51ᵛ (*LP*, XI 1271).
317 PRO, E36/119 fo. 104 (*LP*, XII i 901 [4]).
318 Hoyle, *Pilgrimage of Grace*, p. 358 n. 51; Bush and Bownes, *Postpardon
    Revolts*, p. 16, think 'of the king's farmers' means 'from the king's farmers'.
319 PRO, E36/118 fo. 31ᵛ (*LP*, XII i 6; 'The manner of the taking of Robert Aske',
    p. 341).
320 PRO, SP1/112 fo. 97ᵛ (*LP*, XI 1236).
321 PRO, SP1/109 fos 214–14ᵛ (*LP*, XI 884; *State Papers*, i 495).
322 Cf. Bush, *Pilgrimage of Grace*, p. 398: 'for the rebels the second appointment
    represented a magnificent achievement. For the government it marked a humil-
    iating climb-down'.
323 'The manner of the taking of Robert Aske', p. 340 (*LP*, XII i 6). Bush and
    Bownes read this – I think – as showing that Norfolk had agreed to present
    the Pilgrims' twenty-four articles to the king: *Postpardon Revolts*, p. 16.
324 *LP*, XII i 6; 'The manner of the taking of Robert Aske', p. 342.
325 Hoyle, *Pilgrimage of Grace*, pp. 339, 3.
326 PRO, E36/122 fo. 28 (*LP*, XI 1336).
327 Hoyle, 'Thomas Master's narrative', p. 75; Hoyle thinks Lee got it wrong –
    Lee, he says, wrote 'expressing his pleasure that the king . . . had conceded their
    requests (*which he had not*),' Hoyle adds (*Pilgrimage of Grace*, p. 2). But
    perhaps Lee knew better than the modern historian what he believed had been
    and would be conceded.
328 *Pace* Hoyle, *Pilgrimage of Grace*, p. 362.
329 PRO, SP1/119 fo. 9ᵛ (*LP*, XII i 1022).
330 PRO, SP1/112 fos 206–06ᵛ (*LP*, XI 1319; XII i 16; 28).
331 PRO, E36/118 fo. 159ᵛ (*LP*, XII i 787).
332 PRO, SP1/112 fo. 165 (*LP*, XI 1279); SP1/118 fo. 37ᵛ (*LP*, XII i 849 [1] [26]).
333 PRO, E36/118 fo. 159 (*LP*, XII i 787).
334 PRO, SP1/117 fo. 202 (*LP*, XII i 788).
335 PRO, SP1/117 fos 202–02ᵛ (*LP*, XII i 788).
336 PRO, SP1/112 fo. 165 (*LP*, XI 1279).
337 PRO, SP1/112 fo. 165 (*LP*, XI 1279); SP1/117 fo. 202 (*LP*, XII i 788). Bush
    most misleadingly quotes this in the form: 'prior to the revolt he had pleaded

in vain for the preservation of Nun Monkton Nunnery: and after it he declared to the government: "no abbey should have been suppressed" ': *Pilgrimage of Grace*, p. 180.
338 Though he denied that: PRO, SP1/117 fo. 201^v (*LP*, XII i 788).
339 PRO, SP1/117 fo. 75 (*LP*, XII i 698).
340 PRO, SP1/113 fo. 31^v (*LP*, XI 1372): not just two, as Bush and Bownes suppose: *Postpardon Revolts*, pp. 220–1.
341 *LP*, XI 1399.
342 *State Papers*, i no. lxxix pp. 534 (*LP*, XII i 337).
343 PRO, SP 1/118 fo. 141^v (*LP*, XII i 914); cf. *LP*, XII i 878.
344 PRO, E36/118 fo. 159^v (*LP*, XII i 787); Dodds, *Pilgrimage of Grace*, ii 21.
345 PRO, E36/120 fos 95–6 (*LP*, XII 491).
346 PRO, E36/118 fo. 32 (*LP*, XII i 6; 'The manner of the taking of Robert Aske', p. 342).
347 *Pace* Dodds, *Pilgrimage of Grace*, ii 39. Bush and Bownes read this as a retraction by Aske of a central principle of the Doncaster agreement, namely that houses restored should stand occupied by their monks until parliament reviewed the dissolution. It is much too conditional for that – it is only if anyone comes, force should not be used (*Postpardon Revolts*, p. 146). Shagan uses this to show that Aske was open to compromise and 'tacitly admitted that the dissolution of the monasteries had to be analysed on a case-by-case basis' – which again is highly misleading (*Popular Politics and the English Reformation*, p. 100).
348 *LP*, XII i 306.
349 PRO, SP1/115 fo. 29 (*LP*, XII i 281).
350 PRO, E36/120 fo. 95^v (*LP*, XII i 491).
351 PRO, SP1/118 fo. 19 (*LP*, XII i 847); E36/118 fo. 113 (*LP*, XII i 848 II [13]; SP1/119 fo. 80^v (*LP*, XII i 1087).
352 PRO, SP1/114 fo. 189 (*LP*, XII i 154).
353 PRO, SP1/115 fos 2–3 (*LP*, XII i 192). Davies describes this as 'a rather extreme example of the "clerical plot" theory': 'Pilgrimage of Grace reconsidered', p. 65.
354 PRO, SP1/114 fos 171–2 (*LP*, XII i 141); fo. 173 (*LP*, XII i 142); fos 212–14 (*LP*, XII i 174).
355 PRO, SP1/114 fos 194–7 (*LP*, XII i 157–9); fo. 224 (*LP*, XII i 179).
356 PRO, SP1/114 fo. 167 (*LP*, XII i 138).
357 PRO, E36/119 fos 20–35^v (*LP*, XII i 201 [p. 86]).
358 *LP*, XII i 292.
359 PRO, SP1/118 fos 258–58^v (*LP*, XII i 1011 [1]).
360 PRO, SP1/118 fos 258, 259, 259^v, 262–62^v (*LP*, XII i 1012 [1, 2]).
361 PRO, SP1/118 fo. 259^v (*LP*, XII ii 1011 [1]).
362 PRO, SP1/119 fos 15^v–16 (*LP*, XII i 1023 [ii]); *LP*, XII i 1036 (iv).
363 PRO, SP1/119 fo. 22 (*LP*, XII i 1035 [2]).
364 PRO, SP1/114 fo. 201 (*LP*, XII i 163).
365 PRO, SP1/115 fo. 206 (*LP*, XII i 362).
366 PRO, SP1/115 fo. 191 (*LP*, XII i 337).
367 Bush and Bownes, *Postpardon Revolts*, p. 109.
368 Ibid., pp. 230–88.
369 PRO, SP1/114 fo. 75 (*LP*, XII i 71).
370 PRO, SP1/114 fos 228–9 at 228^v (*LP*, XII i 185).
371 PRO, SP1/115 fo. 115 (*LP*, XII i 281).
372 PRO, SP1/115 fo. 173 (*LP*, XII i 318); cf. PRO, SP1/115 fos 176–76^v (*LP*, XII i 319).

373 PRO, SP1/115 fo. 190 (*LP*, XII i 336).
374 Allegedly slaying many: *LP*, XII i 411. Cf. Bush and Bownes, *Postpardon Revolts*, pp. 258–9, from *LP*, Add. 1261. Evidently at one point things went very badly for the loyalists.
375 PRO, SP1/116 fo. 26 (*LP*, XII i 419).
376 PRO, SP1/116 fo. 49 (*LP*, XII i 439); *LP*, XII i 426.
377 BL Cotton MS, Caligula B iii fo. 287 (*LP*, XII i 1259 [3]); Bush and Bownes, *Postpardon Revolts*, p. 271.
378 *LP*, XII i 426. Bush and Bownes say that the Public Record Office has lost the original (*Postpardon Revolts*, p. 277). Norfolk sent two to Dacre with copies of his letter appealing for his aid: two in case the rebels captured one of them (*LP*, XII i 439).
379 PRO, SP1/116 fo. 33 (*LP*, XII i 427).
380 PRO, SP1/116 fo. 83 (*LP*, XII i 468).
381 PRO, SP1/116 fo. 108 (*LP*, XII i 498).
382 PRO, SP1/116 fo. 49 (*LP*, XII i 439). The *LP* wording is a little misleading in that it could be read as envisaging Dacre's disloyalty rather than simply his not coming soon. Bush and Bownes attribute too much confidence to Norfolk's remarks: *Postpardon Revolts*, p. 277.
383 PRO, SP1/116 fo. 112 (*LP*, XII ii 500).
384 Bush and Bownes, *Postpardon Revolts*, p. 276.
385 Ibid., p. 278.
386 PRO, SP1/116 fo. 72 (*LP*, XII ii 448).
387 Cf. Bush and Bownes's comment that 'The 16th February saw a decisive change in the government's fortunes': *Postpardon Revolts*, p. 116.
388 *LP*, XII i 498.
389 PRO, SP1/118 fo. 237 (*LP*, XII i 992).
390 PRO, SP1/120 fo. 112 (*LP*, XII i 1215); fo. 114 (*LP*, XII i 1216); fo. 117 (*LP*, XII i 1217).
391 Bush, *Pilgrimage of Grace*, p. 268.
392 Ibid. That confusion is characteristic. Elsewhere Bush describes the Lancashire Oversands manifesto as 'failing to mention priories', which he sees as a significant omission, yet he goes on to say that it specifies as the rebels' aim 'the reformation of such abbeys and monasteries now dissolved and suppressed without any just cause' (p. 268). Bush then tries to minimise the place of the monasteries in the commons' grievances by stressing other factors and concludes that 'actual revolt was imported by invading rebels rather than internally generated' (pp. 268–9).
393 But see ibid., p. 334 for the restoration of Seton: the evidence is its farmer's complaints: *Victoria County History, Cumberland*, ii 194.
394 Harrison, *Lake Counties*, pp. 73–4, 79, 135.
395 *LP*, XII ii 1269.
396 PRO, SP1/141 fo. 205 (*LP*, XIII ii 1279).
397 *LP*, XIV ii 186.
398 PRO, SP1/140 fo. 1 (*LP*, XIII ii 960).
399 PRO, SP1/154 fos 79–81 (*LP*, XIV ii 439).
400 PRO, SP1/154 fos 190–3 (*LP*, XIV ii 454).
401 PRO, SP1/154 fos 98ᵛ–99 (*LP*, XIV ii 458).
402 PRO, E36/118 fo. 32ᵛ (*LP*, XII i 6; 'The manner of the taking of Robert Aske', p. 342).
403 Bush, *Pilgrimage of Grace*, p. 107.
404 PRO, E36/119 fo. 91ᵛ (*LP*, XII i 901 [1], no. 9; 'Aske's examination', p. 558).
405 PRO, E36/119 fo. 92 (*LP*, XII i 901 [1] no. 16; 'The manner of the taking of Robert Aske', p. 559).

406 PRO, E36/119 fo. 92ᵛ (*LP*, XII i 901 [1] no. 19; 'Aske's examination', p. 559).
407 PRO, E36/119 fos 96–96ᵛ (*LP*, XII i 901 [2]; 'Aske's examination', pp. 561–2).
408 'In this particular uprising . . . the rebel concern for the church was not simply a religious matter'; 'in the course of October the dissolution of the lesser monasteries emerged as a major grievance in the region but was presented very much as a temporal issue, affecting the commonwealth and resulting from government greed'; 'the case against suppression was thus presented as a material issue: a loss of wealth which would harm not only the church as an organisation but also its lay employees and dependants'; 'behind the Craveners' support for the restoration of Sawley were emphatic temporal and material, as well as spiritual, considerations'; 'What is clear, however, is that the rebels' fears in matters of religion were not confined to religious houses or the wealth of the church – including rights of church, liturgy and taxation (Bush, *Pilgrimage of Grace*, pp. 109, 103, 163–4, 235, 200–2). Oddly, Bush and Bownes do note that if the December agreement had held, the monasteries would have survived, not in totality, but in number, and with them a church based on intercession (*Postpardon Revolts*, pp. 400–1), which makes the Pilgrimage of Grace very much about monasteries and religion.
409 Hoyle, *Pilgrimage of Grace*, p. 48.
410 Davies, *Peace, Print and Protestantism*, p. 205.
411 Shagan, *Popular Politics and the English Reformation*, p. 100.
412 PRO, SP1/112 fos 53–4 (*LP*, XI 1218).
413 PRO, E36/118 fo. 27 (*LP*, XII i 6; 'The manner of the taking of Robert Aske', p. 335).
414 Hoyle, *Pilgrimage of Grace*, pp. 412–14.
415 Ibid., p. 50.
416 Ibid., p. 48.
417 Wood, *Riot, Rebellion and Popular Politics*, p. 54.
418 Ibid., p. 51.
419 Ibid., p. 52.
420 Ibid., pp. 53–4.
421 PRO, SP1/106 fos 301–02ᵛ (*LP*, XI 569); *LP*, XI, 598; cf. the letter of 11 Oct. to Gardiner and Wallop in France: *LP*, XI 656.
422 PRO, SP1/107 fo. 94 (*LP*, XI 611).
423 PRO, E36/118 fos 92ᵛ–93 (*LP*, XI 780 [2]; Dodds, *Pilgrimage of Grace*, i 136–7).
424 Hoyle, *Pilgrimage of Grace*, p. 312, from *LP*, XI 955 (1–3).
425 PRO, E36/118 fos 67ᵛ–69 (*LP*, XI 956; *State Papers*, i no. liii pp. 476–8). Cf. 'To know what abbots, nuns, or canons either set them on or aided them' (*LP*, XI 843 Memoranda).
426 PRO, E36/118 fo. 124.
427 PRO, SP1/107 fo. 94 (*LP*, XI 611).
428 PRO, SP1/108 fos 176–8 (*LP*, XI 783).
429 PRO, SP1/109 fo. 88 (*LP*, XI 856); SP1/109 fo. 89 (*LP*, XI 857).
430 PRO, SP1/109 fos 224–24ᵛ (*LP*, XI 894).
431 Cf. Henry's similar letters of encouragement to Sir Roger Bradshaw, Sir Thomas Langton and Sir William Leyland to press on 'till the said traitors shall be utterly subdued': *LP*, XI 895–7: PRO, SP1/109 fo. 236 (*LP*, XI 897).
432 PRO, SP1/108 fos 14 (*LP*, XI 681).
433 PRO, SP1/108 fo. 187 (*LP*, XI 787); SP1/112 fo. 48 (*LP*, XI 1212 [2]). The latter text followed: the former is illegible in places.

434 The words 'indicted and straight thereupon arraigned and so without further tract out all to execution' in the first draft were 'very properly', according to Elton, replaced in Audley's hand by 'hanged' (*Policy and Police*, p. 322).

435 PRO, SP1/111 fo. 26 (*LP*, XI 1019); Elton, *Policy and Police*, p. 322 reads this as asking Cromwell to intercede for the monks of Norton, i.e. all of them.

436 PRO, SP1/112 fo. 47 (*LP*, XI 1212); SP1/114 fos 154–54ᵛ (*LP*, XII i 130); Elton, *Policy and Police*, pp. 323–4, from *LP*, XII ii 597.

437 *LP*, XII i 1282.

438 Elton, *Policy and Police*, pp. 324–5; *LP*, XII ii 58, 597.

439 PRO, SP1/112 fos 151–6 at 153–53ᵛ and 151–51ᵛ (*LP*, XI 1271).

440 PRO, SP1/110 fo. 1 (*LP*, XI 1002).

441 PRO, E36/121 fos 9–9ᵛ (*LP*, XI 995).

442 *State Papers*, i no. lxvii p. 502 (*LP*, XI 1064).

443 PRO, SP1/111 fo. 177 (*LP*, XI 1120) is Suffolk's reply.

444 PRO, E36/121, fos 20–25 (*LP*, XI 1175).

445 PRO, SP1/112 fo. 9ᵛ (*LP*, XI 1174).

446 PRO, SP1/112 fo. 16 (*LP*, XI 1178).

447 PRO, SP1/112 fos 151–6 at 153–53ᵛ and 151–51ᵛ (*LP*, XI 1271).

448 *LP*, XI 984; cf. PRO, E36/118, fos 116–35 (*LP*, XI 1064) and PRO, SP1/112, fos 71–86 (*LP*, XI 1227) which continue that two-pronged approach.

449 PRO, SP1/112 fo. 64ᵛ (*LP*, XI 1225).

450 PRO, SP1/112 fos 97–97ᵛ (*LP*, XI 1236).

451 PRO, SP1/112 fo. 197ᵛ (*LP*, XI 1306).

452 PRO, SP1/112 fo. 199ᵛ (*LP*, XI 1306 [2]).

453 PRO, E36/118 fos 24–33; fos 35–43 are in part another copy. The text is reprinted by M. Bateson, 'The Pilgrimage of Grace', *English Historical Review*, v (1890), pp. 330–45 (cited in these notes throughout as 'The manner of the taking of Robert Aske'), and summarised in *LP*, XII i 6.

454 PRO, SP1/120 fo. 134 (*LP*, XII ii 1224). According to the untrustworthy *Spanish Chronicle*, Aske was greeted warmly by Henry, made a councillor, given a chain of gold and an annual pension: M.A.S. Hume, ed., *Chronicle of King Henry VIII* (1889).

455 PRO, E36/118 fo. 143ᵛ (*LP*, XII ii 292 [iii]).

456 PRO, SP1/120 fo. 93 (*LP*, XII i 1206).

457 PRO, E36/118 fo. 33 (*LP*, XII i 6 [ii]; 'The manner of the taking of Robert Aske', p. 343; PRO, E36/118 fo. 46 (*LP*, XII i 900 [57]) on burgesses.

458 PRO, SP1/114 fo. 22ᵛ (*LP*, XII i 23).

459 PRO, SP1/114 fos 49, 50 (*LP*, XII i 43 [1, 2]; SP1/114 fo. 51 (*LP*, XII i 44); SP1/118 fo. 39 (*LP*, i 848 I [13]).

460 PRO, SP1/114 fo. 51 (*LP*, XII i 44).

461 PRO, SP1/114 fo. 18 (*LP*, XII i 20); SP1/118 fo. 40ᵛ (*LP*, 849 [1] [43]) (later text noted).

462 PRO, SP1/10 fo. 34 (*LP*, XII i 1175 [1]).

463 *LP*, XI 1397.

464 PRO, SP1/114 fo. 52 (*LP*, XII i 45).

465 PRO, SP1/114 fo. 200 (*LP*, XII i 162).

466 PRO, SP1/115 fo. 119 (*LP*, XII i 271).

467 PRO, SP1/115 fo. 192ᵛ (*LP*, XII i 338).

468 *LP*, XII i 234. Cf. Sir Ralph Eure's report how 'I heard his grace speak that he had not only forgiven by his writing sealed under his great seal but also he hath forgiven them in his heart and willed that all realms christian and also his subjects would take it for a dream for so would his grace': PRO, SP1/114 fo. 68 (*LP*, XII i 66).

469 PRO, SP1/114 fo. 69ᵛ (*LP*, XII i 67).
470 PRO, SP1/114 fo. 128 (*LP*, XII i 103); cf. SP1/118 fo. 16ᵛ (*LP*, XII i 847 [5]).
471 PRO, SP1/114 fo. 127 (*LP*, XII i 102); cf. the government's later note, when Constable was under interrogation, that he was 'trusting then [at the arrival of Norfolk] to have knowledge of the king's pleasure for the reformation of certain articles by parliament and also by convocation, whereby his intent doth clearly appear that they stand yet in their traitor's opinions': PRO, E36/118 fo. 112ᵛ (*LP*, XII i 848 II [8]).
472 PRO, SP1/114 fos 179–79ᵛ (*LP*, XII i 146 [1]). *LP* has 'hand' but the manuscript is far too faded to be sure, though it does not seem likely. PRO, E36/122 fo. 64 (*LP*, XII i 146 [2]) does not have 'king's hand'. PRO, SP1/118 fos 14ᵛ–15 (*LP*, XII I 847 [2]).
473 PRO, SP1/114 fos 164ᵛ–5 (*LP*, XII i 136).
474 PRO, E/322 fo. 3 (*LP*, XII i 26); SP1/114 fos 93ᵛ–94 (*LP*, XII i 84).
475 PRO, SP1/114 fos 164ᵛ–5 (*LP*, XII i 136); cf. SP1/120 fo. 34ᵛ (*LP*, XII i 1175 [1]).
476 PRO, SP1/114 fo. 101 (*LP*, XII i 96).
477 PRO, SP1/114 fo. 166 (*LP*, XII i 137).
478 PRO, SP1/119 fo. 79ᵛ (*LP*, XII i 1087).
479 PRO, E36/119 fo. 21 (*LP*, XII i 201 [i]); *LP*, XII i 201 (iii); i 202; PRO, SP1/114 fo. 64 (*LP*, XII i 64) and fo. 69 (*LP*, XII i 67).
480 PRO, SP1/114 fo. 160 (*LP*, XII i 134).
481 PRO, SP1/114 fo. 142 (*LP*, XII i 115).
482 PRO, E36/122 fo. 36; SP1/114 fo. 162 (*LP*, XII i 135).
483 PRO, SP1/114 fos 192–92ᵛ (*LP*, XII i 155).
484 PRO, E36/122 fo. 34 (*LP*, XII i 156).
485 PRO, E36/122 fos 4ᵛ, 10 (*LP*, XII i 171 [1, 2]); SP1/114 fo. 208 (XII i 171 [3]).
486 PRO, E36/122 fo. 1 (*LP*, XII i 184); SP1/118 fo. 39 (*LP*, 848 I [2]).
487 PRO, E36/119 fo. 65ᵛ (*LP*, XII i 466).
488 PRO, E18/122 fo. 3 (*LP*, XII i 26); E36/122 fos 18ᵛ–19 (*LP*, XII i 84 [2]).
489 PRO, SP1/120 fo. 136 (*LP*, XII i 1225).
490 PRO, E36/122 fo. 51ᵛ (*LP*, XII i 849 [3]). The manuscript is very faded.
491 PRO, E36/118 fo. 111 (*LP*, XII i 848 [II] [4]); SP1/119 fo. 79ᵛ (*LP*, XII i 1087); cf. Dodds, *Pilgrimage of Grace*, ii 38–9, 48.
492 PRO, E36/122 fo. 4ᵛ; cf. copy in SP1/114 fo. 208 (*LP*, XII i 171).
493 PRO, SP1/118 fo. 112 (*LP*, XII i 892). Cromwell had evidently earlier favoured the appointment of the prior, who asked for a delay in paying the final £40 of the £100 he had promised him. His brethren wished to continue and he asked Cromwell's favour (*LP*, X 1234).
494 PRO, SP1/111 fo. 135 (*LP*, XI 1103).
495 PRO, SP1/140 fo. 1 (*LP*, XIII ii 960 quoted); *LP*, XIII ii 702 (1); 830 (5 ii), 876.
496 PRO, SP1/114 fo. 178.
497 PRO, SP1/114 fo. 22ᵛ (*LP*, XII i 23).
498 PRO, SP1/109 fo. 96 (*LP*, XI 864; Dodds, *Pilgrimage of Grace*, i 259–60).
499 *LP*, XI 884.
500 PRO, SP1/112 fos 67–69ᵛ at fo. 68ᵛ (*LP*, XI 1226).
501 PRO, SP1/112 fos 154ᵛ–55 (*LP*, XI 1271).
502 PRO, SP1/115 fo. 10 (*LP*, XII i 198).
503 PRO, SP1/114 fos 103–16ᵛ (*LP*, XII i 98 [1]); E36/118 fo. 173 (*LP*, XII i 302).
504 PRO, E36/118 fos 173–83 at 175ᵛ (*LP*, XII i 98 [2]); SP1/114 fos 108–9 (*LP*, XII i 98 [1] but not including the very last quotation).

505 PRO, SP1/114 fo. 117 (*LP*, XII i 98 [4]) or the virtually identical SP1/114 fos 118–19 (*LP*, XII i 98 [5]).
506 PRO, SP1/114 fos 120–20ᵛ (*LP*, XII i 98 [6]).
507 PRO, SP1/114 fo. 123 (*LP*, XII i 98 [8]).
508 PRO, SP1/114 fo. 122 (*LP*, XII i 98 [7]).
509 Ibid.; cf. Bush and Bownes, *Postpardon Revolts*, pp. 20, 370–1.
510 Haigh notes that the most detailed part of these instructions concerned the attack on the monasteries: *Lancashire Monasteries*, p. 86.
511 PRO, SP1/115 fos 148ᵛ–49ᵛ (*LP*, XII i 98 [1]); E36/118 fos 175ᵛ–76ᵛ is a slightly shorter version; cf. SP1/114 fos 109–10 (a variant version).
512 PRO, SP1/115 fos 148ᵛ–49ᵛ (*LP*, XII i 98 [1]); E36/118 fos 178–78ᵛ (*LP*, XII i 98 [2]); cf. SP1/114 fos 110ᵛ–11 (*LP*, XII i 98 [1]).
513 In another draft 'determinacion': PRO, E36/118 fo. 178.
514 '[B]y reason whereof some ringleaders may percace make some argument for the continuance of the said monks nuns and canons with such sustentation at their liberties': ibid.
515 PRO, SP1/115 fos 150–53ᵛ.
516 Bush and Bownes, *Postpardon Revolts*, p. 373.
517 *LP*, XII i 368.
518 PRO, SP1/116 fo. 20 (*LP*, XII i 416, though the *LP* rendering makes too much of Cromwell's insinuation of some fault to be found in Norfolk over the suppression of the abbeys; cf. Dodds, *Pilgrimage of Grace*, ii 19).
519 PRO, SP1/112 fos 108–08ᵛ (*LP*, XI 1241).
520 PRO, SP1/112 fo. 110 (*LP*, XI 1242).
521 PRO, SP1/115 fo. 240 (*LP*, XII i 381).
522 It is noteworthy that it was the king who showed Norfolk this: Norfolk is treating Cromwell as on his side: PRO, SP1/116 fo. 49–49ᵛ (*LP*, XII i 439).
523 *LP*, XII i 499.
524 PRO, SP1/120 fos 14–14ᵛ (*LP*, XII i 1162); SP1/120 fo. 6 (*LP*, XII i 1157).
525 Herbert of Cherbury, *Life of Henry VIII*, p. 428 (who is sceptical); Hoyle, 'Thomas Master's narrative', p. 79; Dodds, *Pilgrimage of Grace*, i 267.
526 *LP*, XII ii 291.
527 PRO, SP1/120 fos 66–8 (*LP*, XII i 1192).
528 PRO, SP1/120 fo. 108 (*LP*, XII i 1214).
529 PRO, SP1/115 fo. 27 (*LP*, XII i 292).
530 PRO, SP1/115 fo. 194 (*State Papers*, i no. lxxix pp. 534; *LP*, XII i 337).
531 *LP*, XII i 378; cf. Hoyle, 'Thomas Master's Narrative', p. 77 (4 Feb.); cf. *LP*, XI 1399 (this is miscalendared: probably early Feb.).
532 PRO, SP1/115 fo. 206–06ᵛ (*LP*, XII i 362).
533 PRO, SP1/116 fo. 74 (*LP*, XII i 449).
534 PRO, SP1/115 fos 243, 246 (*LP*, XII i 383, 391).
535 PRO, SP1/116 fos 20, 22–22ᵛ; 13–13ᵛ (*LP*, XII i 416 [2]; 410).
536 PRO, SP1/116 fo. 26 (*LP*, XII i 419).
537 *LP*, XII i 439.
538 PRO, SP1/116 fo. 83 (*LP*, XII i 468).
539 PRO, SP1/116 fos 108–108ᵛ (*LP*, XII i 498 [1, 2]); Elton, *Policy and Police*, p. 389.
540 Bush and Bownes, *Postpardon Revolts*, p. 282.
541 *LP*, XII i 1156, 1214 (1, 2).
542 PRO, SP1/116 fo. 116 (*LP*, XII i 506).
543 PRO, SP1/116 fo. 89 (*LP*, XII i 478).

544 PRO, SP1/116 fos 97–97ᵛ (*LP*, XII i 479; *State Papers*, i no. lxxxi p. 538).
545 PRO, SP1/116 fo. 197 (*LP*, XII i 577).
546 PRO, SP1/116 fo. 108ᵛ (*LP*, XII i 498). This manuscript is very faded.
547 *LP*, XII i 546.
548 Ibid. 594: not legible at all on microfilm.
549 PRO, SP1/117 fos 15–16ᵛ (*LP*, XII i 666).
550 *LP*, XII ii 1076.
551 PRO, SP1/113 fo. 31 (*LP*, XI 1372).
552 PRO, SP1/117 fo. 150 (*LP*, XII i 749; cf. XII i 698).
553 S.M. Jack, 'The last days of the smaller monasteries in England', *Journal of Ecclesiastical History*, xxi (1970), p. 122; *LP*, XI 1268.
554 Jack, 'Last days of the smaller monasteries', p. 122; *LP*, XII i 231, 243, 251, 388, 510, 512–13, 571, 572, 638, 728, 747.
555 *LP*, XII i 455.
556 Ibid. 503.
557 PRO, SP1/115 fo. 176ᵛ (*LP*, XII i 319).
558 PRO, SP1/115 fo. 173 (*LP*, XII i 321).
559 *LP*, XII i 353.
560 PRO, SP1/117 fos 75–75ᵛ (*LP*, XII i 698).
561 PRO, SP1/117 fo. 94 (*LP*, XII i 710).
562 PRO, SP1/117 fo. 96 (*LP*, XII i 712).
563 What must Aske have thought in March as Norfolk set about the dissolution of the smaller monasteries? 'It must have been a terrible journey for Aske': Dodds, *Pilgrimage of Grace*, ii 130.
564 *LP*, XII i 846.
565 BL, Harleian MS 282 fo. 203ᵛ (*LP*, XII ii 41).
566 PRO, E36/118 fo. 110 (*LP*, XII i 848 I [2]). Cf. SP1/118 fos 14ᵛ–19 (*LP* XII i 847 [2, 5, 6, 13]); E36/118 fo. 110ᵛ (*LP*, XII i 848 I [5]; E36/118 fo. 111 (*LP* 848 I [13], II [3, 7, 8, 15]).
567 PRO, E36/118 fo. 110ᵛ (*LP*, XII i 848 I [6]); *LP*, XII i 155.
568 PRO, SP1/118 fo. 16ᵛ (*LP*, XII i 847 [5]); cf. E36/118 fo. 113ᵛ (*LP*, XII i 848 II [15]).
569 *LP*, XII i 1207.
570 PRO, SP1/118 fo. 19 (*LP*, XII i 847 [13]; E36/118 fo. 113 (*LP*, XII i 848 II [13]).
571 PRO, E36/118 fo. 44ᵛ (*LP*, XII i 900).
572 *LP*, XII i 1207 (11).
573 Ibid. ii 133, 156.
574 PRO, SP1/119 fo. 61 (*LP*, XII i 1082).
575 PRO, E36/118 fos 143–44 (*LP*, XII ii 292 [iii]).
576 *LP*, XII i 1207.
577 Ibid., XIII i 803, 804 (4); PRO, SP1/139 fo. 20 (*LP*, XIII ii 829); fo. 76 (*LP*, XII ii 831).
578 *LP*, XII ii 228.
579 PRO, SP1/120 fos 136–7 (*LP*, XII i 1125).
580 *LP*, XII i 1227.
581 PRO, SP1/121 fo. 202 (*LP*, XII ii 178).
582 PRO, E36/118 fo. 169 (*LP*, XII ii 133).
583 *LP*, XII ii 156.
584 PRO, SP1/122 fo. 216 (*LP*, XII ii 229; *State Papers*, v no. cccxxii p. 91).
585 PRO, SP1/121 fo. 202 (*LP*, XII ii 178).
586 J. Greenbury, 'Reginald Pole', University of Southampton BA thesis (1988).

587 PRO, SP1/111 fos 134–34ᵛ (LP XI 1101); LP, XI 1353, 1354; XII i 53, 105; XII i 779.
588 PRO, SP1/115 fo. 34ᵛ (LP, XII i 129).
589 Ibid. 444.
590 Ibid. 696.
591 Cf. Ibid. 368.
592 T.F. Mayer, 'A diet for Henry VIII: the failure of Reginald Pole's 1537 legation', Journal of British Studies, xxvi (1987), pp. 305–31 at 305–6 (reprinted in T.F. Mayer, Cardinal Pole in European Context [2000]).
593 LP, XII i 779.
594 Ibid. 865; BL, Add. MS, 25114 fo. 255 (and LP, XII i 817; see Add. MS 25114 fo. 253 for earlier request for Pole's apprehension).
595 LP, XII i 988.
596 BL, Add. MS 25114 fo. 257 (LP, XII i 939) (for warning: LP, XII i 625).
597 BL, Add. MS 8715 fo. 359 (LP, XII i 931).
598 LP, XII i 868. 'Intendo che questo ribaldo di Vincestio ha fattu conto il Rme legate con il Rre di quelli oficii, che si profiono aspettare da Diaboli, e non da huomini.'
599 Ibid. 1135.
600 BL, Add. MS 25114 fo. 263 (LP, XII i 1032: 25 April 1537).
601 BL, Add. MS 8715 fo. 361 (LP, XII i 996).
602 Cf. LP, XII i 1242.
603 BL, Add. MS 25114 fo. 265 (LP, XII i 1235).
604 LP, XII i 1242.
605 Ibid. i 1293.
606 Ibid. ii 552, 619, 620.
607 PRO, SP1/125 fo. 71ᵛ (LP, XII ii 795).
608 LP, XII ii 952. Was Michael Throckmorton a sort of double agent? See e.g. PRO, SP1/139 fo. 2ᵛ (LP, XIII ii 820 [III]): Baynard, a servant of the king's in the Tower, said that 'there was ever in our house prisoner who being delivered thence by the king's favour and sent to the said Poole beyond the sea to show unto him the king's pleasure doth yet there remain and now is one of the greatest in favour with him'. Cf. PRO, SP1/124 fos 76–7 (LP, XIII ii 507) for Michael Throckmorton's deceiving Cromwell and Henry VIII.
609 LP, XII i 1242.
610 Ibid.
611 Ibid., XII ii 174–6, 310, 311.
612 Ibid., XII ii 949.
613 Ibid., XIII i 1115 (42).
614 Ibid., IV iii 6513.
615 Ibid., V app. 33.
616 Ibid., VI 562.
617 H. Pierce, Margaret Pole, Countess of Salisbury 1473–1541: Loyalty, Lineage and Leadership (Cardiff, 2003), pp. 110–11.
618 LP, VII 1368; cf. VI 1164; cf. VIII 750 for Sir Geoffrey telling Chapuys he would like to go to Spain.
619 LP, XII i 313.
620 Ibid., VI 1199.
621 Ibid., 1009, 1041.
622 Ibid., 1126; Cal. S.P., Spanish, iv (ii) no. 1161; LP, VI 1199.
623 LP, VI 1528.
624 Ibid., VI 1126.
625 Ibid., VI 1468.

626 Ibid., VIII 263.

627 Ibid., VI 1164.

628 PRO, SP1/105 fo. 65 (*LP*, XI 93; 92). Pierce, *Margaret Pole, Countess of Salisbury*, p. 217, thinks that this 'could clearly have been delivered in much stronger terms', but that seems implausible. According to Thomas Starkey, 'his own mother which bare him . . . now repenteth of his bringing forth to light' (BL, Cotton MS, Cleopatra E vi fos 384–84ᵛ [*LP*, XI 157]). These letters were evidently discovered when Margaret was arrested in November 1538 (*LP*, XIII ii 855 [2 iii]).

629 PRO, SP1/166 fos 168–68ᵛ (*LP*, XI 451).

630 *LP*, XI 654.

631 C. Höllger, 'Reginald Pole and the legations of 1537 and 1539: diplomatic and polemical responses to the break with Rome', University of Oxford D. Phil. thesis (1989), p. 103.

632 Ibid., p. 105.

633 *LP*, XIII ii 753.

634 PRO, SP1/138 fos 171–72ᵛ at 172 (*LP*, XIII ii 800).

635 Hollger, 'Reginald Pole and the legations', p. 85.

636 1539: *RSTC* 18111.

637 Morison, *Invective*, sig. E ii v. (My italics.)

638 *LP*, XIII ii 232.

639 PRO, SP1/136 fo. 158 (*LP*, XIII ii 392 [2 iv]). Taylor also thought, though with less certainty, that it was from 'Richard Heyre surgeon' that he had heard that Sir Geoffrey Pole 'would send over the sea to his brother at March next': PRO, SP1/136 fo. 159ᵛ (*LP*, XIII ii 393). Cf. PRO, SP1/95 fos 146–7 (*LP*, IX 740); BL, Cotton MS, App. L 82 (*LP*, XIII ii 817); PRO, SP1/139 fos 122–22ᵛ (*LP*, XIII ii 875).

640 BL, Cotton MS Appendix L fo. 71 (*LP*, XIII ii 825); BL, Harleian MS 282 fo. 48ᵛ (*LP*, XIV i 280).

641 *LP*, XIII ii 201. These details were noted by James Gairdner in the preface of *LP*, XIII ii.

642 Ibid. 1280 p. 534.

643 PRO, SP1/138 fo. 180 (*LP*, XIII ii 804 [4]). Pierce, *Margaret Pole, Countess of Salisbury*, p. 116, suggests that Holland had been arrested just before Corpus Christi day, 20 June, but it is more likely that Sir Geoffrey Pole's arrest in late August came very quickly after Holland's arrest and revelations. Pierce also speculates (ibid., pp. 117–18) that Tyndale was Cromwell's spy: but there is no regular correspondence between Cromwell and Tyndale; Tyndale argued openly with the countess of Salisbury's chaplains (when a spy would have been discreet); and, as we have seen, Cromwell was not immediately receptive to what Tyndale (and Ayer) said.

644 BL, Cotton MS Appendix L fo. 71 (*LP*, XIII ii 825).

645 PRO, SP1/138 fos 145–45ᵛ at 145ᵛ (*LP*, XIII ii 772); SP1/138 fos 185–85ᵛ at 185ᵛ (*LP*, XIII ii 804 [II]); SP1/139 fo. 4 (*LP* XIII ii 830 [1] [iv]).

646 PRO, SP1/138 fo. 35ᵛ (*LP*, XIII ii 703).

647 Morison, *Invective*, sigs E iii–vᵛ.

648 PRO, SP1/139 fo. 34ᵛ (*LP*, XIII ii 830 [1] [i]).

649 Morison, *Invective*, sigs E iii–vᵛ.

650 PRO, SP1/138 fo. 14ᵛ (*LP*, XIII ii 695 [2]); SP1/138 fo. 178ᵛ (*LP*, XIII ii 804 [1]); SP1/139 fo. 31ᵛ (*LP*, XIII ii 830 [1] [i]).

651 *LP*, XIV i 191 (3).

652 Ibid. 37 p. 19.

653 PRO, SP1/152 fo. 63 (*LP*, XIV i 1127).

654 PRO, SP1/136 fos 155–56ᵛ, 157–8 at 158 (*LP*, XIII ii 392 [1] and [2]); SP1/136 fos 159–60 (*LP*, XIII ii 393).

655 PRO, SP1/163 fos 4–5 (*LP*, XVI 19).

656 It was decided to commit Sir Geoffrey to the Fleet (*LP*, XVI 32); he was released on condition of agreeing with Gunter (XVI 75).

657 A.G. Dickens, *The English Reformation* (2nd edn, 1989), p. 146.

658 PRO, SP1/138 fo. 14 (*LP* XIII ii 695 [2]); SP1/138 fo. 178ᵛ (*LP*, XIII ii 804 [1]); SP1/139 fo. 31 (*LP*, XIII ii 830 [i]); SP1/139 fo. 67 (*LP*, XIII ii 831 [2 i]); KB8/11/2 fo. 26.

659 PRO, SP1/138 fo. 137 (*LP*, XIII ii 770); SP1/138 fo. 179ᵛ (*LP*, XIII i i 804 [2]); SP1/139 fo. 32ᵛ (*LP* XIII i 830 [i]).

660 PRO, SP1/138 fos 138–38ᵛ but badly damaged (*LP*, XIII ii 770); SP1/138 fos 180–81 (*LP*, XIII ii 804 [4]); SP1/139 fos 33–33ᵛ (*LP* XIII ii 830 [1] [i]).

661 PRO, SP1/138 fo. 181ᵛ (*LP*, XIII ii 804 [5]).

662 Phrasing that was used in the indictment against him and dated to 2 April 1537, and followed by the words 'I trust the world will amende and that we shall have a day upon these knaves' (PRO, KB8/11/2 no. 4 [*LP*, XIII ii 979]).

663 PRO, SP1/138 fo. 181 (*LP*, XIII ii 804 [5]); cf. SP1/138 fo. 139 (*LP*, XIII ii 770 but very damaged).

664 But dated 28 March 1537 to Geoffrey Pole, 27 Feb. to John Collins: PRO, KB8/11/2 fo. 4 (*LP*, XIII ii 979).

665 PRO, SP1/138 fo. 139ᵛ (*LP*, XIII ii 770 but very damaged); SP1/138 fo. 182 (*LP*, XIII ii 804 [5]); SP1/139 fo. 34 (*LP*, XIII ii 830 [1] [i]); KB8/11/2 fo. 4.

666 PRO, KB8/11/2 no. 4.

667 PRO, SP1/138 fos 171–72ᵛ (*LP*, XIII ii 800).

668 PRO, SP1/138 fo. 157; SP1/138 fos 183–84ᵛ; and SP1/138 fo. 193 (*LP*, XIII ii 805 [2]); SP1/139 fo. 35ᵛ; cf. indictment KB8/11/1 no. 6ᵛ).

669 PRO, SP1/139 fo. 17 (*LP*, XIII ii 828).

670 PRO, SP1/139 fo. 6 (*LP*, XIII ii 822); SP1/139 fo. 21 (*LP*, XIII ii 829 [II]); fos 40–3 (*LP*, XIII ii 830 [1] [iii]); KB8/11/1 no. 5.

671 PRO, SP1/139 fo. 17 (*LP*, XIII ii 828).

672 PRO, SP1/139 fos 17–18ᵛ (*LP*, XIII ii 828); fos 20–23ᵛ (*LP*, XIII ii 829 [I]), but top of fo. 21 torn; fo. 40 (*LP*, XIII ii 830 [iii]); *LP*, XIII ii 830 (5 i).

673 PRO, KB8/11/2 fo. 4 (*LP*, XIII ii 979 [7]).

674 John Collins said that 'Morgan once showed him that whosoever did kill the cardinal pole he would kill him again take head what he did': PRO, SP1/139 fo. 37ᵛ (*LP*, XIII ii 830 [1] [ii]). Morgan Wells said that 'he hath said openly that [he] wold kill with a handgun Peter Meotes or any other whom he should know to kill the Cardinal Pole, and that he was going overseas for that purpose: PRO, SP1/139 fo. 19 (*LP*, XIII ii 828 [2]); SP1/139 fos 56ᵛ–57 (*LP*, XIII ii 830 [2] [vi]). The material in this paragraph is combined from PRO, SP1/139 fo. 181 (*LP*, XIII ii 955 [8]; SP1/138 fos 139–39ᵛ (*LP*, XIII ii 770 but very damaged); SP1/138 fos 181–2 (*LP*, XIII ii 804 [5]); SP1/139 fos 33ᵛ–34ᵛ (*LP* XIII ii 830 [1] [i]); indictment: *LP*, XIII ii 979 (11).

675 PRO, SP1/138 fo. 170 (*LP*, XIII ii 170); and in indictment of Sir Geoffrey KB8/11/1 no. 4ᵛ); SP1/138 fo. 159ᵛ (*LP*, XIII ii 170).

676 PRO, SP1/138 fos 159–62 (*LP*, XIII ii 797); SP1/138 fo. 77 (*LP*, XIII ii 743); SP1/138 fo. 179 (*LP*, XIII ii 804 [2]); SP1/139 fo. 62 (*LP*, XIII ii 830 [5] [iii (vi)]); SP1/140 fo. 2 (*LP*, XIII ii 960).

677 PRO, SP1/118 fo. 134 (*LP*, XIII ii 766); SP1/139 fo. 29 (*LP*, XIII ii 829 [3]); SP1/139 fo. 47ᵛ (*LP*, XIII ii 830 [vii]).

678 PRO, SP1/138 fos 77–77ᵛ (*LP*, XIII ii 743); SP1/138 fos 178ᵛ–79ᵛ at 178 (*LP*, XIII ii 804 [2]); SP1/139 fos 31ᵛ–32, last quote at fo. 32 (*LP* XIII i 830 [i]);

for request to be commended to brother see also indictment KB8/11/1 no. 4ᵛ (*LP*, XIII ii 986 [10]).

679 *LP*, XIII ii 772; PRO, SP1/139 fos 45ᵛ–46 (*LP*, XIII ii 830 [v]).
680 PRO, SP1/140 fo. 1 (*LP*, XIII ii 960); SP1/139 fo. 19 (*LP*, XIII ii 828 [2]); SP1/139 fo. 15 (*LP*, XIII ii 827 [3]).
681 According to Morgan Wells 'his right hand': PRO, SP1/139 fo. 19 (*LP*, XIII ii 828 [8]); according to Sir Geoffrey Pole, 'very familiar' with Montagu: PRO, SP1/139 fo. 35 (*LP* XIII ii 830 [(1) (i)]).
682 PRO, SP1/138 fo. 32 (*LP*, XIII ii 702 [2]).
683 Cf. *LP*, XIII ii 959; PRO, SP1/138 fos 28–31 (*LP*, XI II i 702 [1]); SP1/140 fo. 1 (*LP*, XIII ii 960).
684 PRO, SP1/138 fos 28–30 (*LP*, XI II i 702 [1]); SP1/140 fo. 1 (*LP*, XIII ii 960).
685 PRO, SP1/118 fo. 31 (*LP*, XIII ii 702 [2]); indictment: 2 or 25 April 1537: *LP*, XIII ii 979.
686 PRO, SP1/118 fo. 32ᵛ (*LP*, XIII ii 702 [2]).
687 PRO, SP1/138 fo. 32 (*LP*, XIII ii 702 [2]).
688 PRO, SP1/139 fo. 181 (*LP*, XIII ii 955).
689 PRO, SP1/139 fos 25–8 at 27 (*LP*, XIII ii 829 [2]); SP1/139 fos 37–9 at 39 (*LP* XIII ii 830 [1] [ii]); SP1/139 fos 49–52 (*LP*, XIII ii 830 [3]).
690 PRO, SP1/139 fo. 12ᵛ (*LP*, XIII ii 827 [1]).
691 PRO, SP1/139 fo. 61 (*LP*, XIII ii 830 [5] [ii]); SP1/139 fo. 12 (*LP*, XIII ii 827 [1]); *LP*, XIII ii 979; SP1/139 fo. 123 (*LP*, XIII ii 875); SP1/140 fo. 1ᵛ (*LP*, XIII ii 960).
692 PRO, SP1/139 fos 64ᵛ–65 (*LP*, XIII ii 830 [ii]).
693 PRO, SP1/138 fos 132–3 (*LP*, XIII ii 765); SP1/138 fo. 187 (*LP*, XIII ii 804); SP1/139 fo. 44 (*LP*, XIII ii 830 [iv]); SP1/139 fos 64–64ᵛ (*LP*, XIII ii 831 [i]).
694 The marchioness had explained that 'the chief cause why she sent for her was to have her forasmuch as she had had children before which lived not after their birth', and now she thought she was with child again, she wanted Elizabeth Barton to pray for her to Our Lady that she might have issue (PRO, SP1/80 fos 130–30ᵛ [*LP*, VI 1468 (7)]). For her abject submission to the king on 25 Nov. 1533 see *LP*, VI 1464–5. Cf. *Cal. S.P., Spanish.*, IV ii 1149 (p. 857) (*LP*, VI 1419).
695 PRO, SP1/140 fo. 11ᵛ: these are not in *LP*, XIII ii 962.
696 PRO, SP1/140 fos 6–8 at 7ᵛ (*LP*, XIII ii 961 [2]).
697 PRO, KB8/11/2 no. 9.
698 Ibid. nos 9, 9ᵛ, 10 (*LP*, XIII ii 979 [15, 17]).
699 PRO, SP1/138 fos 139–39ᵛ at 139 but very damaged (*LP*, XIII ii 770); SP1/138 fos 181–2 at 181 (*LP*, XIII ii 804 [5]). Cf. SP1/139 fo. 19 (*LP*, XIII ii 828 [2]); SP1/139 fo. 56ᵛ–57 (*LP*, XIII ii 830 [2] [vi]); SP1/139 fos 33ᵛ–34ᵛ (*LP* XIII ii 830 [1] [i]).
700 PRO, KB8/11/2 nos 4, 8ᵛ (*LP*, XIII ii 979 [7]); KB8/11/1 no. 4ᵛ (*LP*, XIII ii 986 [10]).
701 PRO, SP1/140 fo. 10ᵛ, not in *LP*, XIII ii 962. Cf. SP1/140 fo. 3ᵛ (*LP*, XIII ii 961).
702 Repeated in PRO, SP1/140 fo. 11 (but not in *LP*, XIII ii 962).
703 PRO, SP1/140 fos 3ᵛ, 11ᵛ, not in *LP*, XIII ii 962.
704 *LP*, XIV i 37.
705 BL, Harleian MS 282 fos 48–48ᵛ (*LP*, XIV i 280).
706 *LP*, XIV i 37.
707 BL, Cotton MS, Titus B i fo. 140 (*LP*, XIII ii 884).
708 PRO, SP1/138 fos 199–202ᵛ (*LP*, XIII ii 818).
709 BL, Cotton MS, Appendix L fos 77–8 (*LP*, XIII ii 835).

710 BL, Cotton MS, Appendix L fo. 79 (*LP*, XIII ii 855).
711 PRO, SP1/139 fo. 105 (*LP*, XIII ii 855 [2]).
712 PRO, SP1/139 fos 122-22ᵛ (*LP*, XIII ii 875).
713 Cf. Pierce, *Margaret Pole, Countess of Salisbury*, p. 137.
714 BL, Cotton MS, Cleopatra E iv fos 177-77ᵛ (*LP*, XIV i 520).
715 PRO, SP1/139 fo. 6 (*LP*, XIII ii 822: George Crofts); SP1/139 fo. 21 (*LP*, XIII ii 829 [II]); SP1/139 fo. 41 (*LP* XIII ii 830 [1] [iii]).
716 PRO, SP1/105 fo. 65 (*LP*, XI 93; 92).
717 PRO, SP1/138 fo. 77 (*LP*, XIII ii 743); SP1/138 fo. 179 (*LP*, XIII ii 804 [2]); SP1/139 fo. 62 (*LP*, XIII ii 830 [5] (iii [vi]).
718 PRO, SP1/140 fo. 108 (*LP*, XIII ii 1070).
719 PRO, SP1/140 fo. 219 (*LP*, XIII ii 1176).
720 *LP*, XIV ii 627. I cannot trace this in BL, Cotton MS, Cleopatra E iv fo. 267.
721 *LP*, XIV i 980.
722 PRO, SP1/138 fo. 14 (*LP* XIII ii 695 [2]).
723 Ibid.; SP1/138 fo. 178ᵛ (*LP*, XIII ii 804 [1]); SP1/139 fo. 31 (*LP*, XIII ii 830 [i]); SP1/139 fo. 67 (*LP*, XIII ii 831 [2 i]).
724 PRO, SP1/139 fo. 23 (*LP*, XIII ii 829 [III]); *LP*, XIII ii 829 (5) (i); SP1/139 fo. 42ᵛ (*LP* XIII ii 830 [1 (iii)]); SP1/139 fos 67-8 (*LP*, XIII ii 831 [2 (ii)].
725 PRO, SP1/139 fo. 4 (*LP*, XIII i 821); SP1/139 fo. 30 (*LP* XIII ii 829 [4]); *LP*, XIII ii 831 (2 ii); SP1/139 fo. 48 (*LP*, XIII ii 830 [viii]); SP1/139 fo. 68ᵛ (*LP*, XIII ii 831 [2 (iii)]); SP1/140 fo. 13, not in *LP*, XIII ii 962.
726 *LP*, XIII ii 829 (II).
727 PRO, SP1/139 fo. 6 (*LP*, XIII ii 822); *LP*, XIII ii 831 (2 ii); SP1/139 fo. 41 (*LP*, XIII ii 830 [1] [iii]).
728 PRO, SP1/139 fo. 6 (*LP*, XIII ii 822); *LP*, XIII ii 831 (2 ii); SP1/139 fo. 41 (*LP*, XIII ii 830 [1] [iii]).
729 BL, Cotton MS, Titus B i fos 70-70ᵛ (*LP*, XIII ii 968).
730 *LP*, XIII ii 982.
731 Ibid. 1062.
732 Ibid. 1112.
733 Ibid. 1117.
734 Ibid. 979 (17); 986 (7, 15).
735 Hall, *Chronicle*, p. 827.
736 *LP*, XIII II 979 (4).
737 Ibid. 979 (15).
738 Morison, *Invective*, sig. F iᵛ.
739 PRO, E36/120 fo. 35 (*LP*, XIII i 987); *LP*, XIII i 986 (29).
740 Hall, *Chronicle*, p. 827.
741 Morison, *Invective*, sig. F ii.
742 Ibid. 520, 573.
743 Ibid. 988.
744 Ibid. 655, 867 (15); 980.
745 PRO, SP1/153 fo. 171 (*LP*, XIV ii 287).
746 BL, Cotton MS, Titus B i fo. 439ᵛ (*LP*, XIV ii 427). Cf. PRO, E36/143 no. 26 (*LP*, XIV i 1050): 'To remember what shall be done with the lady of Sares and where she shall be kept.' 'What shall be done with the lady marchioness.' 'For the execution of them that be attainted.'
747 *LP*, XIV i 37.
748 BL, Harleian MS 282 fo. 48ᵛ (*LP*, XIV i 280).
749 *LP*, XIV i 290.
750 Hall, *Chronicle*, p. 827.
751 BL, Cotton MS, Titus B i fo. 140 (*LP*, XIII ii 884).

752 PRO, KB8/11/2 no. 4.

753 Ibid. nos 6ᵛ, 7.

754 Dodds, *Pilgrimage of Grace*, ii 286.

755 *LP*, XIII ii 804 (7).

756 Mayer, 'Reginald Pole's legation', p. 322.

757 E.W. Ives, 'Faction at the court of Henry VIII: the fall of Anne Boleyn', *History*, lvii (1972), p. 180.

758 PRO, SP3/6 fo. 112 (*LP*, XII ii 921).

759 Cf. Pierce, *Margaret Pole, Countess of Salisbury*, p. 154.

760 Mayer, 'Reginald Pole's legation', pp. 317, 323, 327. For a neat rejection of Mayer's claim for Fitzwilliam, see Pierce, *Margaret Pole, Countess of Salisbury*, pp. 154–5. Unfortunately Pierce goes on to list what she presents as 'the Poles' connections and *thus* [my italics] their potential supporters': Sir John Wallop, Lord Lisle, Lord Sandys.

761 PRO, SP1/108 fo. 104 (*LP*, XI 737).

762 PRO, SP1/106 fo. 272 (*LP*, XI 556 [1]).

763 PRO, SP1/114 fo. 187ᵛ (*LP*, XII i 152).

764 PRO, KB 8/11/1 no. 7.

765 PRO, SP1/140 fo. 2 (*LP*, XIII ii 960).

766 *LP*, XIII ii 804 p. 317.

767 Ibid. 804 (5).

768 Dodds, *Pilgrimage of Grace*, ii 277.

769 PRO, KB 8/11/1 no. 7.

770 Morison, *Invective*, sig. cvi–vii.

771 BL, Harleian MS 282 fos 47ᵛ–48 (*LP*, XIV i 280).

772 Elton, *Reform and Reformation*, p. 279.

5: The Final Suppression of the Monasteries

1 Knowles, *Tudor Age*, iii 332, endorsed by Haigh, *Lancashire Monasteries*, p. 91.

2 *LP*, VI 1381 (3).

3 Ibid., IX 881 (T. Wright, ed., *Letters Relating to the Suppression of the Monasteries*, Camden Society, [1843], no. xli pp. 90–1).

4 Elton, *Policy and Police*, pp. 290–1.

5 Estgate was the abbot of Sawley's chaplain: he was involved in the abbot's supplication to Sir Thomas Percy: PRO, E36/118 fos 15ᵛ, 16ᵛ (*LP*, XII i 1034).

6 I.e. convicted: cf. Elton, *Policy and Police*, p. 295 on usage.

7 PRO, SP1/116 fo. 251 (*LP*, XII i 630, 632).

8 PRO, SP1/117 fos 18–20; (*LP*, XII i 668; *State Papers*, i no. lxxxii pp. 540–1); cf. Haigh, *Lancashire Monasteries*, p. 91, from Knowles, *Religious Orders*, iii 332; PRO, SP1/117 fo. 72 (*LP*, XII i 695); *LP*, XII i 716; xii 778.

9 *LP*, XII i 581, 734.

10 PRO, SP1/117 fo. 31 (*LP*, XII i 676).

11 *LP*, XII i 639; PRO, SP1/117 fo. 32 (*LP*, XII i 677); PRO, SP1/117 fo. 84 (*LP*, XII i 700) (searching for money and plate); *LP*, XII i 765, 768. Hoyle unnecessarily supposes that Barlings and Kirkstead were dealt with before, rather than at the same time as, Whalley.

12 *LP*, XII i 998.

13 Ibid., XIII ii 1195 iv; XIV i 867; Elton, *Policy and Police*, pp. 350, 359.

14 Elton, *Policy and Police*, pp. 350, 359, esp. n. 4, citing PRO, KB9/542/8, 10, 11.

15 *LP*, XII i 892.
16 Ibid. 706; *State Papers*, i no. lxxxiii pp. 541–2. Probably misdated and 28 rather than 24 March: cf. *LP*, XII i 840.
17 PRO, SP1/118 fos 7, 5 (*LP*, XII i 841 [3 i, ii]; *LP*, XII i 652).
18 PRO, SP1/118 fo. 5 (*LP*, XII i 841 [3]). Cf. *LP*, XII i 842.
19 PRO, SP1/117 fo. 72 (*LP*, XII i 695).
20 BL, Cotton MS, Cleopatra E iv fos 244–5 (*LP*, XII i 840); cf. Haigh, *Lancashire Monasteries*, p. 98.
21 BL, Cotton MS, Cleopatra E iv fo. 246 (Wright, *Suppression*, no. lxxiv pp. 153–4; *LP*, XII i 832, 903).
22 PRO, E322/91 (*LP*, XII i 880).
23 *LP*, XII i 896.
24 Ibid., XIII i 176; 190 (42).
25 PRO, SP1/118 fos 221ᵛ–22 (*LP*, XII i 970). 'Sussex had thus shown once and for all how to deal with the greater abbeys': Knowles, *Tudor Age*, iii 333.
26 *LP*, XII i 896.
27 Ibid., ii 205.
28 PRO, SP1/119 fo. 82ᵛ (*LP*, XII i 1087). Cf. 'the said prior very familiar with Sir Robert Constable': PRO, SP1/117 fo. 75 (*LP*, XII i 698).
29 PRO, SP1/118 fo. 276 (*LP*, XII i 1020).
30 PRO, SP1/119 fo. 82ᵛ (*LP*, XII i 1087, 1088).
31 *LP*, XII i 1285.
32 PRO, SP1/117 fo. 173ᵛ (*LP*, XII i 777c).
33 PRO, SP1/120 fos 26–7 (*LP*, XII i 1172).
34 PRO, SP1/120 fo. 66 (*LP*, XII i 1192).
35 BL, Harleian MS 283 fo. 76 (*State Papers*, i no. lxxxiii p. 541; *LP*, XII i 706).
36 *LP*, XII i 1214; 1218.
37 Ibid. 1237; *State Papers*, v 76.
38 PRO, SP1/120 fo. 166 (*LP*, XII i 1257).
39 *LP*, XII i 1227.
40 Ibid. i 1285.
41 Ibid. i 1264; 1307; accomplished ii 14, 16, 59.
42 Ibid. i 1232, 1233; from Rymer, *Foedera*, xiv 588.
43 *LP*, XII i 1207 (8).
44 Ibid. 1285.
45 PRO, SP1/120 fo. 200 (*LP*, XII i 1285; XII ii 166).
46 *LP*, XII ii 27, 64, 91.
47 Elton, *Policy and Police*, pp. 144–9; C.E. Moreton, 'The Walsingham conspiracy of 1537', *Historical Research*, lxiii (1990), pp. 29–43.
48 Moreton, 'Walsingham conspiracy', pp. 30, 32.
49 PRO, SP1/119 fo. 36 (*LP*, XII i 1056 [1]).
50 Moreton, 'Walsingham conspiracy', p. 29.
51 PRO, SP1/119 fo. 37 (*LP*, XII i 1056 [2]).
52 PRO, SP1/119 fo. 31 (*LP*, XII i 46); Moreton, 'Walsingham conspiracy', pp. 30–1.
53 PRO, SP1/119 fo. 30 (*LP*, XII i 1045 [2]).
54 PRO, SP1/119 fo. 29 (*LP*, XII i 1045); Moreton, 'Walsingham conspiracy', p. 31.
55 PRO, SP1/19 fo. 51 (*LP*, XII i 1063).
56 PRO, SP1/119 fos 141–42ᵛ (*LP*, XII i 1125).
57 PRO, SP1/120 fo. 24 (*LP*, XII i 1171).
58 PRO, SP1/200 fo. 220 (*LP*, XII i 1300).

59 Cf. Elton, *Policy and Police*, p. 151: 'the fact that it was discovered in time saved the government from having to suppress yet another rising, but does not prove that no rising could have come out of these plots.'
60 PRO, SP1/120 fos 179–79ᵛ (*LP*, XII i 1268).
61 *LP*, XII i 1212 (2, 3).
62 Moreton, 'Walsingham conspiracy', pp. 31–2.
63 Elton, *Policy and Police*, pp. 146–50, from PRO, KB9/538/4–8.
64 *LP*, XIV i 186.
65 Ibid., XV 136.
66 E. Hallam Smith, 'Henry VIII's monastic refoundations of 1536–37 and the course of the dissolution', *Bulletin of the Institute of Historical Research*, li (1978), pp. 124–31 at 130–1. An alternative reading is that these refoundations were 'decoys' that were 'intended to persuade his subjects that whole suppression was not envisaged': J.J. Scarisbrick, 'Henry VIII and the dissolution of the secular colleges', in C. Cross, D. Loades and J.J. Scarisbrick, eds, *Law and Government under the Tudors* (Cambridge, 1988), p. 64 n. 45.
67 *LP*, XI app. 4: 12 Aug. 1536.
68 Ibid., XII i 41.
69 Ibid., XII ii 411.
70 Ibid., XIV ii 235.
71 Ibid., XII ii 220: 6 July 1537.
72 As noted by Hallam Smith, 'Henry VIII's refoundations', p. 125.
73 Colvin, *History of the King's Works*, iii 65.
74 *LP*, XII ii 1311 (22); cf. charter of Dec. 1537 (*LP*, XII ii 1311 [22]; cf. 1267).
75 Hallam Smith, 'Henry VIII's refoundations', p. 129.
76 *LP*, XII ii 411.
77 Ibid. 1311 (22).
78 Hallam Smith, 'Henry VIII's refoundations', p. 126.
79 Ibid., p. 127.
80 Ibid., pp. 127–9.
81 Rex and Armstrong, 'Henry VIII's foundations', p. 395.
82 *LP*, XII ii 489.
83 Ibid. 864.
84 Wriothesley, *Chronicle*, i 42–3.
85 PRO, SP1/139 fos 17–17ᵛ (*LP*, XIII ii 828).
86 *LP*, XIII ii 702.
87 Ibid., XIII ii 797, 986 (10).
88 Ibid., XII ii 402; cf. MacCulloch, *Cranmer*, p. 186. An intriguing contrast is offered by comparison with the letter sent to Pope Clement in July 1530 threatening him with dire consequences if he did not satisfy the king over the divorce: only four bishops but as many as twenty-three abbots signed it: PRO, E30/1012a, currently in folder marked E30/1025 (*LP*, IV iii 6513).
89 *LP*, XII ii 409.
90 Ibid. 914.
91 Ibid. 1060.
92 Ibid. 357.
93 Ibid. 800.
94 Ibid. 1101, 1119.
95 Ibid. 1062.
96 Ibid. 1101; J.H. Bettey, *The Suppression of the Monasteries in the West Country* (Gloucester, 1989), p. 76.
97 *LP*, XII ii 1030.

98 Ibid., 1154; valor of Cromwell's possessions at Lewes: XIII i 290; grant to Cromwell: XIII i 384 (74).

99 Ibid., XII ii 1151 (2).

100 Ibid. 1311 (30). One wonders whether the report by some Greyfriars of Lewes that the king was dead was in any way related to the surrender of the priory: any discontent seems to have been nipped in the bud – the friars were punished and took it very penitently: *LP*, XII ii 1185; 1282. But rumours of the king's death were also reported in Reading and in Huntingdonshire: XII ii 1205, 1208, 1256, 1298; XIII i 58; 76, 141; 172; but cf. Elton, *Policy and Police*, pp. 73–4. There had been hints of treason at Lewes, according to Richard Layton, in 1535: *LP*, IX 632.

101 Ibid., XII ii 1311 (40).

102 Ibid., XII ii 1153; XIII i 384 (74).

103 Ibid., XII ii 1159.

104 Ibid., XII ii 1245; cf. 1270; XIII i 19; 20.

105 Ibid., XII ii 1274.

106 Ibid., XII ii 1311 (40).

107 Ibid., XII ii 1171.

108 Ibid., XII ii 1191.

109 Ibid., XII ii 1219; XIII i 85, 86, 101, 102 (PRO, SP1/128 fos 87ᵛ–88), 112; ii app. 3.

110 Ibid., XII ii 1209.

111 Ibid., XII ii 1210.

112 Ibid., XIII i 49.

113 Ibid., XIII i 27, 42; 190 (41) for grant to Edward Seymour, earl of Hertford.

114 Ibid., XIII i 199.

115 Ibid., XIII i 221.

116 Ibid., XIII ii 1187.

117 Ibid., XIII i 102.

118 BL, Cotton MS, Cleopatra E iv fo. 68 (*LP*, XIII i 573). Bettey thinks this was prompted by a frantic wave of leasing: *Suppression*, p. 72.

119 *LP*, XIII i 173, 195.

120 Ibid. 822; 27 Henry VIII c. 28 (*Statutes of the Realm*, iii 575–8).

121 *LP*, X 364.

122 Ibid., XII i 317, 512.

123 Ibid. 1257.

124 PRO, SP1/129 fos 12–12ᵛ (*LP*, XIII i 231).

125 Bury St Edmunds: *LP*, XIII i 192; Boxley: PRO SP1/129 fos 12–12ᵛ (*LP*, XIII i 231), fo. 89 (*LP*, XIII i 339); *LP*, XIII i 348, 754; Wriothesley, *Chronicle*, i 74–6; *Camden Miscellany, Camden Society*, lxxiii (1859), pp. 11–12. Bermondsey: Wriothesley, *Chronicle*, i 77. Ipswich and Walsingham: Wriothesley, *Chronicle*, i 83; *LP*, XIII i 1376, 1407, 1501. Caversham: *LP*, XIII ii 328. Hales: Wriothesley, *Chronicle*, i 75–6, 90; *LP*, XIII ii 347, 409, 709, 710.

126 P. Marshall, 'The rood of Boxley, the blood of Hailes and the defence of the Henrician church', *Journal of Ecclesiastical History*, xlvi (1995), pp. 689–96, esp. p. 693. Note in passing the assumption that Cromwell, rather than the king, is 'the driving force', and see discussion of Cromwell's religion below pp. 512–21.

127 *LP*, XII ii 1190.

128 Ibid., XIII i 225, from Wilkins, *Concilia*, iii 829.

129 *LP*, XIII i 926; ii 1186 'Draft commission for taking the surrenders of the houses of friars and for selling their goods'.

130 R. Whiting, 'Local responses to the Henrician reformation', in D. MacCulloch, ed., *The Reign of Henry VIII: politics, policy and piety* (Basingstoke, 1995), p. 206.
131 *LP*, XIII i 651.
132 Ibid. 1052; Wright, *Suppression*, no. xcvii pp. 193–6 (*LP*, XIII i 1053, 1108–9).
133 *LP*, XIII i 1456, 1457.
134 Ibid. ii 56.
135 Ibid. ii 88.
136 Ibid. ii 41.
137 Ibid. ii 44.
138 Ibid. ii 96.
139 Ibid. i 170.
140 Ibid. ii 200, but he surrendered in Sept.: ii 321.
141 Ibid. ii 49.
142 Wright, *Suppression*, no. xcviii pp. 196–9 (*LP*, XIII i 1484).
143 Wright, *Suppression*, no. c pp. 203–6 (*LP*, XIII ii 92; XIII ii 169).
144 Wright, *Suppression*, no. cii pp. 210–13 (*LP*, XIII ii 200).
145 *LP*, XIII ii 293, 626.
146 Ibid. i 235.
147 PRO SP1/147 fo. 34 (*LP*, XIV i 712, 940, 711).
148 *LP*, X 613.
149 A modern analogy: if a group of employees threatened with early retirement accept it on the terms offered, however reluctantly, in the face of threats of less favourable terms (including the possibility of compulsory redundancy with only minimal compensation) later, then it is hard for the workforce as a whole, and others outside, to support them purposefully or effectively.
150 *LP*, XIV i 988.
151 Ibid., XIII i 1115 (4); R. Houlbrooke, 'Refoundation and reformation, 1538–1628', in I. Atherton, E. Fernie, C. Harper-Bill and H. Smith, eds, *Norwich Cathedral: church, city and diocese, 1096–1996* (1996), pp. 507–9; S.E. Lehmberg, *The Reformation of Cathedrals: cathedrals in English society, 1485–1603* (Princeton, 1988), pp. 81–2, and pp. 81–94 for a more general survey.
152 BL, Cotton MS, Cleopatra E iv fo. 305.
153 Cf. Wooding, *Rethinking Catholicism in Reformation England*, pp. 65–6.
154 Essex – Waltham; Hertford – St Alban's; Bedfordshire and Buckinghamshire – Dunstable, Nowenham, Elnestowe; Oxford and Berkshire – Osney, Thame; Northamptonshire and Huntingdonshire – Peterborough; Middlesex – Westminster; Leicester and Rutland – Leicester; Gloucestershire – St Peter's; Lancaster – Fountains and archdeaconry of Richmond; Suffolk – Bury; Staffordshire and Shropshire – Shrewsbury; Nottinghamshire and Derbyshire – Welbeck, Worksop, Turgarton; Cornwall – Launceston, Bodmin and one other.
155 BL, Cotton MS, Cleopatra E iv fo. 365*.
156 Wright, *Suppression*, pp. 262–5, from BL, Cotton MS, Cleopatra E iv fo. 305; H. Cole, *King Henry the Eighth's Scheme of Bishopricks* (1838), between pp. xxiv and 1; *LP*, XIV ii 428–30.
157 BL, Cotton MS, Titus B i fo. 439 (*LP*, XIV ii 427).
158 Scarisbrick, 'Henry VIII and the dissolution of the secular colleges', p. 64. For a striking defence of Henry's deliberate foundation of Christ Church, Oxford, as 'large, well-endowed and educationally advanced', and as 'part of a rationalization of the funding of higher education' that included the founding of Trinity College, Cambridge, see C. Haigh, '1546, before and after: the making of Christ Church', *Christ Church Record* (1993), pp. 1–16, esp. 16, 6.

159 *LP*, XIV ii 429.
160 Ibid., XV 322.
161 J.G. Clark shows that the abbot in question is not Robert Catton, removed in 1538, but Richard Boreman: 'Reformation and reaction at St Albans Abbey, 1530–1558', *English Historical Review*, cxv (2000), pp. 298–9.
162 Wright, *Suppression*, no. cxxiv pp. 250–1.
163 *LP*, XIII i 1484.
164 Ibid. 981 (1 ii); BL, Cotton MS, Cleopatra E iv fo. 106ᵛ (*LP*, XIII i 981[2]).
165 Wright, *Suppression*, no. lxviii pp. 145–6 (*LP*, XIII i 956).
166 BL, Cotton MS, Cleopatra E iv fo. 107 (*LP*, XIII i 981 (2)).
167 Ibid., 1280.
168 Though not always: e.g. Shaftesbury (for which the wording is purely legal – and in Latin: PRO, E322/211) and Hinton E322/99).
169 PRO, E322/22 (*LP*, XIII ii 421).
170 PRO, SP1/129 fos 143–7 (*LP*, XIII i 396).
171 PRO, E322/10 (*LP*, XIII ii 501); E322/224 (*LP*, XIII ii 565).
172 PRO, E322/279 (*LP*, XIII ii 340).
173 *LP*, XIII i 396.
174 Ibid. ii 56.
175 PRO, E322/10 (*LP*, XIII ii 501). The wording was formulaic: see E322/22 (*LP*, XIII ii 421).
176 PRO, SP1/135 fo. 126 (*LP*, XIII ii 139).
177 *LP*, XIII ii 180.
178 Ibid. 408.
179 PRO, SP1/118 fo. 131 (*LP*, XIII ii 764).
180 *LP*, XIV i 629.
181 BL, Cotton MS, Cleopatra E iv fo. 246 (Cranmer, *Writings and Letters,* pp. 363–4; Wright, *Suppression*, no. lxxxviii pp. 174–7).
182 D. Knowles and T. Dart, 'Notes on a Bible of Evesham Abbey', *English Historical Review*, lxxix (1964), p. 776.
183 *Eighth report of the Deputy Keeper of Public Records*, app. ii p. 3; *LP*, XIV ii 140.
184 *LP*, XIV ii 229.
185 Ibid. 36: Wright, *Suppression*, p. 240.
186 *LP*, XIII ii 528 (2).
187 Ibid., XIII ii 744.
188 Ibid., XIV i 1094; XIII i 1130.
189 PRO, SP1/129 fo. 94 (*LP*, XIII i 347). Cf. Cromwell's remembrance c. 1537: 'to remember the abbot of Hales to be the king's chaplain': PRO, SP1/120 fo. 257 (*LP* XII i 257); SP1/136 fos 221–2 (*LP*, XIII ii 409).
190 *LP*, XIII ii 252.
191 PRO, SP1/139 fo. 17 (*LP*, XIII i 828).
192 PRO, SP1/114 fo. 37 (*LP*, XIII ii 1198).
193 *LP*, XIII i 981.
194 Ibid., XIV i 295.
195 Ibid., XIII i 1117; Bettey, *Suppression*, pp. 87–8.
196 *LP*, XIII ii 306.
197 Ibid., XIII ii 285.
198 Ibid., XIII ii 593, 677.
199 Ibid., XIII ii 1198; cf. XIV i 871.
200 Wright, *Suppression*, no. lxxi pp. 148–50 (*LP*, XIII ii 1036).
201 PRO, SP1/139 fos 114ᵛ–15 (*LP*, XIII i 866); *LP*, XIV i 1191; Wright, *Suppression*, no. lxxxix pp. 177–8.

202 *LP*, XIII ii 394; cf. 650, in which they asked that the churches, or at least one of them, be left standing.
203 Ibid., XIII ii 674.
204 Ibid., XIV i 34, 57; Wright, *Suppression*, no. cxvii pp. 238–9; cf. *LP*, XIV i 1350.
205 Ibid., XIII ii 86.
206 PRO, SP1/140 fo. 126 (*LP*, XIII ii 1092); Bettey, *Suppression*, pp. 178–9, from H. Ellis, *Original Letters illustration of English History* (3 series in 11 vols, 1824–46), III iii 229–31.
207 Wright, *Suppression*, no. xc pp. 178–80.
208 *LP*, XIII i 1330.
209 Ibid., XIV ii 750.
210 Ibid., XIII ii 758; Wright, *Suppression*, no. cxii pp. 229–31.
211 PRO SP1/139 fo. 154 (*LP*, XIII ii 911, which omits the last part of the text quotes).
212 *LP*, XVI i 629.
213 Ibid., XIV ii 26, 27, 646; Bettey, *Suppression*, pp. 86, 92. None of the nuns, however, signed the deed of surrender, and Florence does not appear in the pension lists.
214 *LP*, XIII ii 314, miscalendared at XI 433; Wright, *Suppression*, no. cxxi pp. 244–5.
215 *LP*, XIII ii 315.
216 Ibid., XIV ii 700.
217 Ibid., XIV ii 750 (1, 2); 700.
218 Ibid., XV 25, 125.
219 Ibid., XIV i 145.
220 Ibid. 269; Bettey, *Suppression*, pp. 88–9.
221 *LP*, XIV i 145. Hinton had been surveyed by June 1539; the priest who denied the royal supremacy was described as having been out of his mind and not much recovered (*LP*, XIV i 1154).
222 Bettey, *Suppression*, p. 86: *LP*, XIV i 324, 491 (prior had been obstinate), 664 (surrender of Montacute March and Bruton April 1539: *LP*, XIV i 575, 664.)
223 *LP*, XIV ii 58.
224 Ibid. 79.
225 Wright, *Suppression*, no. cxxvi p. 256 (*LP*, XIV ii 206).
226 *LP*, XIV ii 185; Ellis, *Original Letters*, III iii 247.
227 Wright, *Suppression*, no. cxxvi pp. 255–6 (*LP*, XIV ii 206); cf. the French ambassador Marillac's comments: *LP*, XIV ii 389.
228 Wright, *Suppression*, no. cxxvii pp. 257–8 (*LP*, XIV ii 232).
229 Wright, *Suppression*, no. cxxviii p. 259 (*LP*, XIV ii 272).
230 Wright, *Suppression*, no. cxxx pp. 261–2 (*LP*, XIV ii 531).
231 Wright, *Suppression*, no. cxxix pp. 259–60 (*LP*, XIV ii 530).
232 Cf. Bettey, *Suppression*, p. 102. Mark Stoyle wonders how much other, similar evidence of opposition might have been found if similar searches had been carried out in other monasteries.
233 *LP*, XIII ii 346.
234 Ibid., XIII ii 377.
235 Ibid., XII ii 1205, 1220, 1252, 1256.
236 Ibid., XIV ii 49.
237 Ibid. 136.
238 Ibid. 256.
239 PRO, KB9/548 fo. 4, reprinted by J.E. Paul, 'The last abbots of Reading and

Colchester', *Bulletin of the Institute of Historical Research*, xxxiii (1960), pp. 118–19.

240 *LP*, XIV ii 613; cf. Elton, *Policy and Police*, p. 195.

241 Two associates were executed with him on 14 Nov. 1539 – John Eynon, priest of St Giles's, Reading, and John Rugge, former prebendary of Chichester Cathedral, living in retirement in Reading Abbey. A general commission dated 27 Oct. was sent to the sheriff of Berkshire to try cases of treason, a writ was issued on 3 Nov. summoning a jury for the Thursday after St Martin's day, that is 13 Nov. The indictments are PRO, KB9/458 fos 4–6; cf. KB9/458 fo. 1; cf. Paul, 'The last abbots of Reading and Colchester', pp. 115–21.

242 *LP*, XV 259; cf. 269.

243 BL, Cotton MS, Titus B i fo. 433 (*LP*, XIV ii 399).

244 Elton, *Policy and Police*, p. 305.

245 *LP*, XIV ii 459.

246 Ibid. 458; cf. 45.

247 Ibid. 454.

248 PRO, SP1/154 fos 79–81 (*LP*, XIV ii 439).

249 PRO, SP1/139 fo. 74 (*LP*, XIII ii 887).

250 *LP*, XIII ii 764.

251 PRO, SP1/139 fo. 74 (*LP*, XIII ii 887); cf. Elton, *Policy and Police*, p. 156.

252 *LP*, XIV ii 458.

253 Ibid. 454.

254 PRO, SP1/154 fos 79–81 (*LP*, XIV ii 439).

255 *LP*, XIV ii 459.

256 Ibid. 494.

257 Ibid. 554.

258 Trial is PRO, KB9/545 fos 34–41, cited by Elton, *Policy and Police*, p. 156.

259 PRO, SP1/156 fo. 183 (*LP*, XIV ii app. 45), cited by Elton, *Policy and Police*, p. 160.

260 Elton, *Policy and Police*, p. 159.

261 Ibid., p. 160.

262 See Rex and Armstrong, 'Henry VIII's foundations', pp. 400–7. Norwich had already been converted into a secular cathedral with a dean and chapter in 1538. Winchester, Canterbury, Carlisle, Durham, Rochester, Ely and Worcester would be converted between March 1541 and January 1542.

6: The Making of Religious Policy

1 Cranmer, *Writings and Letters*, p. 98.

2 *LP*, XII ii 410.

3 Wilkins, *Concilia*, iii 830.

4 Cranmer, *Writings and Letters*, p. 470; PRO, SP6/2 fos 102–4 (*LP*, XII ii 618). Cf. *LP*, XII ii 329.

5 *LP*, XII i 457.

6 Ibid. i 1086.

7 Ibid. i 1187.

8 Ibid. ii 289.

9 Lloyd, *Formularies of Faith*, p. 25.

10 J.A. Muller, ed., *The Letters of Stephen Gardiner* (Cambridge, 1933), p. 351.

11 *State Papers*, i 563 (*LP*, XII ii 295).

12 BL, Cotton MS, Cleopatra E v fos 308–9 (*LP*, XV 758).

13 BL, Cotton MS, Cleopatra E v fos 73–101 (*LP*, XII ii 403).

14 Cranmer, *Writings and Letters*, ii 470.
15 PRO, SP6/13 fos 123ᵛ–25.
16 R. Rex, *Henry VIII and the English Reformation* (Basingstoke 1993), p. 151; J. Guy, 'Henry VIII and his ministers', p. 39; MacCulloch, *Cranmer*, pp. 185–6.
17 *LP*, XII i 839.
18 Lloyd, *Formularies of Faith*, p. 23.
19 *LP*, XII ii 790.
20 *Pace* Guy, 'Henry VIII and his ministers', p. 39.
21 PRO, SP6/13 fos 124ᵛ–25.
22 BL, Cotton MS, Cleopatra E v fo. 55 (*LP*, XII ii 293).
23 *State Papers*, i 555–7 (*LP*, XII ii 289).
24 *LP*, XII ii 330.
25 Scarisbrick, *Henry VIII*, pp. 404–5.
26 *LP*, XIII ii 147.
27 PRO, SP6/2 fos 102–02ᵛ (Cranmer, *Writings and Letters*, p. 469; *LP*, XII ii 618 [1]). Kreider wonders whether this draft was ever sent (*English Chantries*, p. 249 n. 38). But the Bishops' Book was printed without a royal preface.
28 British Library, Harleian MS 282 fo. 281ᵛ (*LP*, XII ii 871).
29 November or December, says MacCulloch (*Cranmer*, p. 208).
30 Scarisbrick, *Henry VIII*, p. 403.
31 The count is Haigh's (*English Reformations*, p. 133). Cranmer, *Writings and Letters*, pp. 83–114.
32 *LP*, XII ii 1122 (2), XIII i 187 ('Remembrances to be remembered to the king's highness . . . item, the determination of Mr Day, Heath, Thirlby, and Skip upon the x commandments, justification and purgatory'). It is worth noting that Cromwell is collecting views, not all of them from reformers (the inclusion of John Skip is interesting here), and that he is remembering them to the king.
33 Cranmer, *Writings and Letters*, pp. 358–9.
34 BL, Cotton MS, Cleopatra E v fos 110–10ᵛ (Cranmer, *Writings and Letters*, pp. 358–60; *LP*, XIII i 141); a précis of their responses was prepared (BL, Royal MS 7 C xvi fos 199–207).
35 BL, Royal MS 17 C xxx (Kreider, *English Chantries*, pp. 132–4).
36 Cranmer, *Writings and Letters*, p. 353.
37 Cf. Hughes, *Reformation in England*, ii 36–7.
38 Cranmer, *Writings and Letters*, p. 95; partially cited by Scarisbrick, *Henry VIII*, p. 407; Redworth, *In Defence of the Church Catholic*, p. 172.
39 Scarisbrick, *Henry VIII*, pp. 412–13; Cranmer, *Writings and Letters*, p. 99.
40 Cranmer, *Writings and Letters*, p. 87.
41 Ibid.
42 Ibid., p. 89.
43 Ibid., p. 90.
44 Ibid., p. 91.
45 Ibid., p. 92.
46 Cranmer retorted: 'who liveth as he ought to do?' (ibid., p. 96).
47 Ibid., p. 92.
48 Ibid., p. 94.
49 Ibid., p. 84.
50 Ibid., p. 85.
51 Ibid., p. 86.
52 Ibid., p. 96.
53 Ibid., p. 112.
54 Ibid., p. 107.
55 Ibid.

56 Ibid., p. 93.
57 Ibid.
58 Scarisbrick, *Henry VIII*, p. 417.
59 L.B. Smith, *Henry VIII: the mask of royalty* (1971), p. 100.
60 Haigh, *English Reformations*, p. 133.
61 Ibid.
62 Kreider, *English Chantries*, p. 136.
63 Lloyd, *Formularies of Faith*, p. 111.
64 Ibid., p. 136.
65 Ibid., p. 130; M. Aston, *England's Iconoclasts* I (Oxford, 1988), p. 240.
66 Lloyd, *Formularies of Faith*, pp. 134–5; Aston, *England's Iconoclasts*, p. 241.
67 Lloyd, *Formularies of Faith*, p. 135; Cranmer, *Writings and Letters*, p. 101.
68 Cranmer, *Writings and Letters*, p. 110; Redworth, *In Defence of the Church Catholic*, p. 170.
69 Cranmer, *Writings and Letters*, pp. 100–1; Aston, *England's Iconoclasts*, p. 242, citing J.G. Nichols, ed., *Narratives of the Reformation*, Camden Society, lxxvii (1859), p. 224. Cf. MacCulloch, *Cranmer*, pp. 191–2. In the King's Book the second commandment would be reworded 'thou shalt not have any graven image, nor any likeness of any thing that is in heaven above, or in earth beneath, or in the water under the earth, to the intent to do any godly honour and worship unto them' (Lloyd, *Formularies of Faith*, p. 299).
70 Scarisbrick, *Henry VIII*, p. 419.
71 Hughes, *Reformation in England*, ii 39; Dickens, *The English Reformation*, p. 200; Rex, *Henry VIII and the English Reformation*, p. 152.
72 Lloyd, *Formularies of Faith*, p. 100; Cranmer, *Writings and Letters*, p. 96.
73 *LP*, XII ii 1060. A contrast is offered by the plainness of the obsequies requested in his will by the London merchant Humphrey Monmouth: no hearse, no dirige, no bells, no priests singing, no trental – but rather thirty sermons to be delivered by Bishop Hugh Latimer, Dr Crome and Mr Taylor, parson of St Peter's, Cornhill, together with a *Te Deum* after every sermon to the king, 'who hath caused the word of God to be preached sincerely and truly', for putting down the pope (Wriothesley, *Chronicle*, i 72).
74 *LP*, XII i 789.
75 Ibid., XV 758.
76 Foxe, *Acts and Monuments*, v 379–83; *LP*, XII i 790.
77 Muller, *Letters of Gardiner*, p. 350.
78 PRO, SP6/13 fos 124ᵛ–25: bald summary in *LP*, XII ii 404.
79 Cf. Haigh, *English Reformations*, p. 132, paraphrasing Lloyd, *Formularies of Faith*, pp. 128–9.
80 Lloyd, *Formularies of Faith*, p. 125.
81 Ibid., pp. 127–8.
82 Brigden, *London and the Reformation*, p. 206, approvingly citing *Narratives of the Reformation*, pp. 223–4.
83 M.F. Powicke, *The Reformation in England* (Oxford, 1941), p. 71; T.M. Parker, *The English Reformation to 1558* (2nd ed., Oxford, 1966), p. 91; Duffy, *Stripping of the Altars*, p. 400; Elton, *Policy and Police*, p. 247 n. 2; R. McEntegart, 'England and the League of Schmalkalden, 1531–1547: faction, foreign policy and the English Reformation', University of London Ph.D. thesis (1992), p. 236.
84 Haigh, *English Reformations*, p. 133.
85 Cranmer, *Writings and Letters*, p. 366; Wriothesley, *Chronicle*, i 79; PRO SP1/131 fo. 182 (*LP*, XIII i 863). Cf. P. Marshall, 'Papist as heretic: the burning of John Forest, 1538', *Historical Journal*, xli (1998), pp. 351–74, esp. 354–6.

86 Hughes and Larkin, *Tudor Royal Proclamations*, i no. 168, pp. 275.
87 PRO, SP1/143 fo. 8 (*LP*, XIV i 402).
88 Hughes and Larkin, *Tudor Royal Proclamations*, i no. 186, pp. 275–6; *LP*, XIII ii 848.
89 Hughes and Larkin, *Tudor Royal Proclamations*, i no. 186, pp. 273–4.
90 Ibid., pp. 274–5.
91 Elton, *Policy and Police*, p. 257.
92 Brigden, *London and the Reformation*, p. 296.
93 Elton, *Reform and Reformation*, p. 278.
94 Ibid., p. 279.
95 Ibid., pp. 221, 257. Cf. Aston, *England's Iconoclasts*, p. 237, citing R.W. Heinze, *The Proclamations of the Tudor Kings* (Cambridge, 1976), pp. 139–41; P. Marshall, 'The rood of Boxley', p. 695; MacCulloch, *Cranmer*, pp. 233–4.
96 Haigh, *English Reformations*, p. 152.
97 Ibid., pp. 136–7; Guy, 'Henry VIII', p. 40.
98 *LP*, XIII ii 834, 842; 851; Foxe, *Acts and Monuments*, v 230; Dickens, *English Reformation*, p. 196.
99 Foxe, *Acts and Monuments*, v 249.
100 Hughes and Larkin, *Tudor Royal Proclamations*, i no. 186, p. 272.
101 Ibid. no. 186, p. 273.
102 Ibid. no. 155, pp. 227–8 at 228.
103 Ibid. no. 155, pp. 227–8.
104 Ibid. no. 155, p. 227.
105 Duffy, *Stripping of the Altars*, p. 421.
106 Davies, *Peace, Print and Protestantism*, p. 190.
107 Haigh, *English Reformations*, p. 137).
108 Cf. Dickens, who misleads in seeing Henry's action as a fortuitous response to the needs of diplomacy: 'It so happened that at this moment the King, disappointed in the Lutheran princes, desired not merely to placate Catholic opinion but to gain the friendship of the great Catholic powers . . . [the king's] eagerness to impress Europe with a spectacle of orthodoxy': *English Reformation*, p. 196.
109 Hughes and Larkin, *Tudor Royal Proclamations*, i no. 188 pp. 278–80.
110 Merriman, *Letters of Cromwell*, ii 153 (*LP*, XIII ii 281).
111 Merriman, *Letters of Cromwell*, ii 154 (*LP*, XIII ii 281).
112 Merriman, *Letters of Cromwell*, ii 153 (*LP*, XIII ii 281; C.H. Williams, ed., *English Historical Documents*, v 1485–1558 [1967], p. 812).
113 Merriman, *Letters of Cromwell*, ii 153 (*LP*, XIII ii 281; Williams, *English Historical Documents*, v 812).
114 Duffy, *Stripping of the Altars*, p. 408; Hughes, *Reformation in England*, i 362.
115 Aston, *England's Iconoclasts*, p. 226.
116 Haigh, *English Reformations*, p. 134.
117 Elton, *Policy and Police*, p. 254.
118 Merriman, *Letters of Cromwell*, ii 153 (*LP*, XIII ii 281; Williams, *English Historical Documents*, v 812).
119 Elton, *Policy and Police*, p. 254, citing Merriman, *Letters of Cromwell*, ii 156–7.
120 Brigden, *London and the Reformation*, p. 288.
121 Elton, *Reform and Reformation*, p. 279, citing the proclamation pardoning sectaries. Cf. idem, *Policy and Police*, pp. 221, 257–8 where the proclamations of 16 Nov. 1538 and 23 Feb. 1539 are seen as 'contradictory actions'.

122 Duffy, *Stripping of the Altars*; cf. Elton, *Policy and Police*, p. 258; Hughes and Larkin, *Tudor Royal Proclamations*, i no. 188.
123 Aston, *England's Iconoclasts*, pp. 228–9, 245.
124 Hughes and Larkin, *Tudor Royal Proclamations*, no. 191 pp. 284–6.
125 *LP*, XIV i 402.
126 S.E. Lehmberg, *The Later Parliaments of Henry VIII 1536–1547* (Cambridge, 1977), p. 71.
127 31 Henry VIII c. 13–14 (*Statutes of the Realm*, iii 739–40); Williams, *English Historical Documents*, v 814–16.
128 BL, Cotton MS, Cleopatra E v fos 327–35ᵛ for draft corrected by king (as noted by *LP*, XIV i 868 [9]).
129 Cox, *Writings and Letters*, p. 168.
130 Lehmberg, *Later Parliaments*, p. 57.
131 Elton, 'Fall of Cromwell', pp. 206–7; J.A. Froude, *History of England from the Fall of Wolsey to the Defeat of the Spanish Armada* (12 vols, 1870), iii 195.
132 Elton, 'Fall of Cromwell', pp. 208–9.
133 Elton, *Reform and Reformation*, p. 284. Cf. Rex, *Henry VIII and the English Reformation*, p. 154; Duffy, *Stripping of the Altars*, p. 423; Block, *Factional Politics*, p. 159; Byrne, *Lisle Letters*, v 359.
134 Scarisbrick, *Henry VIII*, p. 420.
135 G. Redworth, 'Whatever happened to the English reformation?', *History Today*, xxxvii (Oct. 1987), p. 35. Cf. Davies, *Peace, Print and Protestantism*, p. 195; Duffy, *Stripping of the Altars*, p. 424; Guy, *Tudor England*, p. 185; idem, 'Henry VIII and his ministers', p. 40; Davies, *Peace, Print and Protestantism*, p. 195; Elton, *Reform and Reformation*, p. 287; idem, 'Fall of Cromwell', p. 224; Scarisbrick, *Henry VIII*, p. 365; St Clare Byrne, *Lisle Letters*, v 363; MacCulloch, *Cranmer*, pp. 237, 246.
136 *LP*, XIV ii p. xxvii.
137 Wriothesley, *Chronicle*, p. 118.
138 Rex, *Henry VIII and the English Reformation*, p. 155, citing *LP*, XIV i 585, 967; Wriothesley, *Chronicle*, pp. 97–101, 104, 106–7.
139 Lehmberg, *Later Parliaments*, p. 302: PRO, SP3/7 fo. 63 (*LP*, XIV i 1015); *LP*, XIV i 1003.
140 *LP*, XIV i 1003.
141 Kaulek, *Correspondance politique*, no. 118 pp. 101–2 (*LP*, XIV i 1091); cf. no. 119 p. 103 (XIV i 1092).
142 BL, Cotton MS, Cleopatra E v fos 327–30 at 329ᵛ–30.
143 So C.R. Trueman is wrong to say that 'with the passing of the Six articles in 1539 transubstantiation was official Church doctrine': *Luther's Legacy: Salvation and English Reformers 1525–1556* (Oxford, 1994), p. 23.
144 Rex, *Henry VIII and the English Reformation*, p. 154, based on texts in Wilkins, ed., *Concilia* iii 845–6, and *Lords Journals*, p. 111.
145 *LP*, XIV i 1035.
146 Ibid. 1004.
147 Trueman, *Luther's Legacy*, pp. 21–2, 11 n. 11.
148 Brigden, 'Fall of Cromwell', p. 274.
149 St Clare Byrne, *Lisle Letters*, v 533–4; *LP*, XIV i 1108.
150 PRO, SP1/152 fo. 18ᵛ (*LP*, XIV i 1065 [3]).
151 PRO, SP1/152 fo. 18 (*LP*, XIV i 1065 [3]).
152 *LP*, XIV ii 400.
153 BL, Cotton MS, Cleopatra E v fos 53–4.
154 Merriman, *Letters of Cromwell*, ii 220; *LP*, XIV i 844.

155 MacCulloch sees two minor concessions to evangelicals – a delay in implementing the order for married clergy to put away their wives; and a narrowing of the conditions under which clerical celibacy was binding: *Cranmer*, p. 249.

156 31 Henry VIII c. 6 (*Statutes of the Realm*, iii 724–5).

157 PRO, SP1/152 fo. 18 (*LP*, XIV i 1065 [3]); BL, Cotton MS, Cleopatra E v fos 328, 330, with revisions in the king's hand.

158 BL, Cotton MS, Cleopatra E v fo. 138.

159 PRO, SP1/152 fo. 18 (*LP*, XIV i 1065 [3]), cited by Lehmberg, *Later Parliaments*, pp. 6–9).

160 Tunstal's memorandum is BL, Cotton MS, Cleopatra E v fo. 133 (*LP*, XIV ii app. 28).

161 BL, Cotton MS, Cleopatra E v fo. 131 (*LP*, XIV ii app. 29). Cf. Scarisbrick, *Henry VIII*, p. 410; MacCulloch, *Cranmer*, pp. 174–5, 177. Hughes (*Reformation in England*, i 349) saw this as the solitary change in dogmatic belief that Henry endorsed: cf. *LP*, X 494.

162 D. MacCulloch, 'Two dons in politics: Thomas Cranmer and Stephen Gardiner, 1503–1533', *Historical Journal*, xxxvii (1994), pp. 1–22.

163 BL, Cotton MS, Cleopatra E vi fo. 232 (Cranmer, *Writings and Letters*, p. 327).

164 Cranmer, *Writings and Letters*, p. 322.

165 BL, Cotton MS, Otho C x fo. 226 (Cranmer, *Writings and Letters*, p. 324).

166 Cranmer, *Writings and Letters*, p. 336.

167 BL, Harleian MS 6148 fo. 20 (Cranmer, *Letters and Writings*, p. 283).

168 BL, Harleian MS 6148 fo. 41 (Cranmer, *Writings and Letters*, p. 309).

169 BL, Harleian MS 6148 fo. 41 (Cranmer, *Writings and Letters*, p. 308).

170 BL, Harleian MS 6148 fo. 1 (Cranmer, *Writings and Letters*, p. 280).

171 BL, Cotton MS, Cleopatra E vi fo. 232 (Cranmer, *Writings and Letters*, pp. 326–7).

172 BL, Cotton MS, Cleopatra E vi fo. 232 (Cranmer, *Writings and Letters*, p. 327).

173 Cranmer, *Writings and Letters*, p. 330.

174 BL, Harleian MS 6148 fo. 23 (Cranmer, *Writings and Letters*, p. 246).

175 Cranmer, *Writings and Letters*, p. 341.

176 Ibid., p. 344.

177 Ibid., p. 372 (*LP*, XIII i 1237; PRO, SP1/133 fo. 174).

178 Cranmer, *Writings and Letters*, p. 375.

179 MacCulloch, *Cranmer*, p. 182.

180 Cranmer, *Writings and Letters*, pp. 349–51 (*LP*, XII ii 846).

181 Cranmer, *Writings and Letters*, pp. 352–3.

182 Ibid., pp. 353–4.

183 Ibid., pp. 355–6 (*LP*, XII ii 846 [iv]).

184 Cranmer, *Writings and Letters*, pp. 349–51 (*LP*, XII ii 846).

185 Cranmer, *Writings and Letters*, pp. 319–20.

186 BL, Cotton MS, Cleopatra E v fo. 110.

187 BL, Cotton MS, Cleopatra E v fos 56–59ᵛ (quotation from fo. 59ᵛ).

188 Cranmer, *Writings and Letters*, p. 323 (*LP*, X 792).

189 G.W. Bernard, 'Elton's Cromwell', *History*, lxxxiii (1998), pp. 587–607, reprinted in G.W. Bernard, *Power and Politics in Tudor England* (Aldershot, 2000), pp. 108–28.

190 Foxe, *Acts and Monuments*, v 403.

191 Dickens, *English Reformation*, pp. 217, 157, 169, 203.

192 Davies, *Peace, Print and Protestantism*, pp. 190, 212.

193 Block, *Factional Politics*, p. 61.

194 Brigden, *London and the Reformation*, p. 220.

195 S. Brigden, 'Popular disturbance and the fall of Thomas Cromwell and the reformers 1539–1540', *Historical Journal*, xxxiv (1981), p. 32.

196 Brigden, *London and the Reformation*, p. 300; Brigden, 'Fall of Cromwell', p. 257.

197 G. Walker, *Plays of Persuasion: drama and politics at the court of Henry VIII* (Cambridge, 1991), pp. 208, 203; Guy, 'Henry VIII and his ministers', pp. 38–9; R. McEntegart, *Henry VIII, the League of Schmalkalden and the English Reformation* (Woodbridge, 2002), p. 223.

198 G.R. Elton, 'Thomas Cromwell redivivus', *Archiv für Reformationsgeschichte* (1977), pp. 192–208 at 201–2 (reprinted in G.R. Elton, *Studies in Tudor and Stuart Government* [Cambridge, 4 vols, 1974–92], iii 373–90); idem, *Policy and Police*, p. 424.

199 Elton, *Reform and Reformation*, p. 172; idem, 'Thomas Cromwell redivivus', pp. 196–7.

200 Only a few have voiced doubts or hesitations. Guy, though seeing Cromwell as firmly in the protestant camp, and saying that he 'showed an increasingly "reformed" outlook after Wolsey's fall, and may have decided that England was best served by a form of protestantism after the Act of Appeals', nevertheless noted that Cromwell never espoused justification by faith alone or denied the real presence in the eucharist, though he does not pause to reflect on the larger implications of this (*Tudor England*, p. 178). S.E. Lehmberg cautioned that 'there can be no other leader of the Reformation whose religious beliefs remain as obscure as Thomas Cromwell's' ('The religious beliefs of Thomas Cromwell', in R.L. DeMolen, eds, *Leaders of the Reformation* [1984], p. 134). Brendan Bradshaw, in playing down Elton's image of Cromwell as an evangelically inspired social reformer, by extension reduced the reach of his supposed religious radicalism ('The Tudor commonwealth: reform and revolution', *Historical Journal*, xxii [1979], pp. 455–76). P.J. Ward questioned Cromwell's reputation as a patron of radicals: (Ward, 'The politics of religion: Thomas Cromwell and the reformation in Calais, 1534–40', *Journal of Religious History*, xvii [1992], pp. 152–71). P. O'Grady sees Cromwell as reflecting the conventional religious platitudes of the day (*Henry VIII and the conforming catholics* [Minnesota, 1994], p. 9).

201 Cf. Brigden, 'Fall of Cromwell', pp. 32–3.

202 31 Henry VIII c. 10 (*Statutes of the Realm*, iii 729).

203 Elton, *Reform and Reformation*, p. 171, from Merriman, *Letters of Cromwell*, i 279: Elton, 'Fall of Cromwell', p. 206.

204 For modern historians' contortions on this, see Elton, 'Fall of Cromwell', pp. 212–13; cf. pp. 206, 224; McEntegart, *Henry VIII, the League of Schmalkalden*, pp. 190–1.

205 Burnet, *History of the Reformation*, iv 417.

206 Ibid. 418.

207 Ibid. 419.

208 Elton, 'Fall of Cromwell', p. 225.

209 *LP*, XV 498 (60).

210 Merriman, *Letters of Cromwell*, i 56, 61; cf. Lehmberg, 'Religious beliefs of Cromwell', pp. 135–6.

211 D. Norris, 'The fall of Thomas Cromwell', University of Southampton BA dissertation (1995), p. 22.

212 Merriman, *Letters of Cromwell*, i 327; *LP*, IV iii 6076. Elton says 'that remark was addressed to Wolsey and meant to please' (*Reform and Reformation*, p. 171; 'Thomas Cromwell redivivus', p. 196), but it seems more definite than anything that mere obsequiousness would have required.

213 S. Brigden, 'Thomas Cromwell and the "brethren"', in C. Cross, D. Lades and J.J. Scarisbrick, eds, *Law and Government under the Tudor* (Cambridge, 1988), p. 37, citing Bodleian Library, Oxford, Jesus College MS 74 fo. 192.

214 Elton, *Reform and Renewal*, p. 40 (*LP*, V 65 [i, ii]).

215 Elton, *Reform and Renewal*, p. 40. The letter is in Merriman, *Letters of Cromwell*, i 335–9 (*LP*, V 248).

216 Elton, *Reform and Renewal*, p. 40.

217 *LP*, IX 275.

218 Ibid., IX 498.

219 Ibid., XIII ii 849.

220 PRO, SP1/162 fos 86, 88ᵛ–89 (*LP*, XV 1029 [6]).

221 Foxe, *Acts and Monuments*, v 402–3; Hall, *Chronicle*, p. 306; Lehmberg, 'Religious beliefs of Cromwell', pp. 138–9. Lehmberg sees Cromwell's prayer as 'suffused with personal conviction that is at once orthodox and reformed'.

222 O'Grady, *Henry VIII and the conforming catholics*, p. 9.

223 *LP*, XII ii 1122 ii.

224 Elton, *Reform and Renewal*, pp. 26–7, n. 61.

225 Ibid., p. 28.

226 PRO, SP1/141 fos 125–26ᵛ (*LP*, XIII ii 1223): *pace* Brigden, 'Cromwell and the "brethren"', p. 41. Most probably this was the same John Oliver who, as chaplain to the king, had in 1530 exhibited answers by the Parisian doctors on whether king could be compelled to appear at Rome (*LP*, V 306 [2, 5], and who was later ordained prior of the Cambridge Blackfriars: he was accused by Cranmer of preaching against the king's great cause and defending the authority of the bishop of Rome (Cox, *Writings and Letters*, pp. 295–6).

227 Elton, 'Fall of Cromwell', p. 224.

228 Rex, *Henry VIII and the English Reformation*, p. 144; Guy, 'Henry VIII and his ministers', p. 40.

229 Elton, 'Thomas Cromwell redivivus', p. 197.

230 Brigden, 'Cromwell and the "brethren"', pp. 34–5, citing *LP*, VII 1618, 923 xxvi, and his will.

231 Norris, 'Fall of Cromwell', p. 21, citing Merriman, *Letters of Cromwell*, ii 241 (*LP*, XIII i 572).

232 Strype, *Ecclesiastical Memorials*, I ii pp. 222–8 (*LP*, XIII i 571; BL, Cotton MS, Cleopatra E iv fo. 58); Burnet, *History of the Reformation*, iv 314–17 (*LP*, XIII i 572), from BL, Cotton MS, Cleopatra E iv 62.

233 PRO, SP1/116 fo. 173 (*LP*, XII i 542).

234 PRO, SP 1/116 fo. 157 (*LP*, XII i 529).

235 PRO, SP1/103 fo. 234 (*LP*, X 804).

236 *LP*, XII i 1001.

237 Ibid., XIII ii 758: Cromwell took her part, it seems.

238 Ibid., XV 545; Merriman, *Letters of Cromwell*, ii 128–31, cited by Norris, 'Fall of Cromwell', p. 21.

239 *LP*, XIV ii 71.

240 Lehmberg, 'Religious beliefs of Cromwell', p. 90 for text from *Lords Journal*, i 128–9 (Burnet, reprinted in his *Studies in Tudor and Stuart Politics and Government* (4 vols, 1974–92), *History of the Reformation*, i 438–9; G.R. Elton, 'Thomas Cromwell's decline and fall', *Historical Journal*, x 216 (1951) p. 216 has his own translation).

241 Foxe, *Acts and Monuments*, v 384.

242 Elton, *Reform and Reformation*, p. 274.

243 Elton, 'Fall of Cromwell', p. 202. Cf. idem, *Reform and Renewal*, pp. 34, 278; Guy, 'Henry VIII and his ministers', p. 40; MacCulloch, *Cranmer*, p. 170, cf. p. 196.

244 *RSTC* 2066.
245 Cranmer, *Writings and Letters*, p. 344 (*LP*, XII ii 434).
246 BL, Cleopatra E v fo. 348 (Cranmer, *Writings and Letters*, pp. 345–6; *LP*, XII ii 512; Foxe, *Acts and Monuments*, v 411–12).
247 Cranmer, *Writings and Letters*, p. 346.
248 BL, Cotton MS, Cleopatra E v fo. 349.
249 Guy, 'Henry VIII and his ministers', p. 40.
250 BL, Cotton MS, Cleopatra E v fo. 349.
251 Ibid. fo. 338ᵛ.
252 Hall, *Chronicle*, p. 771.
253 Scarisbrick, *Henry VIII*, pp. 252–4; see Hall, *Chronicle*, p. 771; *LP*, IV iii 6385.
254 BL, Cotton MS, Cleopatra E v fo. 347.
255 Gardiner, *Letters*, p. 66 (*LP*, VIII 850).
256 Foxe, *Acts and Monuments*, i 277–8.
257 Cranmer, *Writings and Letters*, p. 344 (*LP*, XII ii 434).
258 *English Historical Documents*, v 807; W.H. Frere and W.M. Kennedy, eds, *Visitation Articles and Injunctions of the Period of Reformation, 1536–58* (Alcuin Club Collections, xv, 1910).
259 Haigh, *English Reformations*, p. 130 and p. 368 n. 29; Dickens, *English Reformation*, 1st edn, 1964, p. 131; M. Bowker, 'The Henrician reformation and the parish clergy', *Bulletin of the Institute of Historical Research*, i (1977), p. 31 n. 1. It is, as Bowker says, 'highly improbable' that those bishops would have acted without the support of a royal injunction.
260 *LP*, XII i 98.
261 BL, Cotton MS, Cleopatra E v fo. 340ᵛ (*LP*, XII ii app. 35).
262 *LP*, XII ii 410.
263 Wilkins, *Concilia*, iii 830; *LP*, XII ii 410.
264 *LP*, XII i 98; 302.
265 Ibid. 1158.
266 BL, Cotton MS, Cleopatra E v fo. 340ᵛ (*LP*, XII ii app. 35).
267 Dickens, *English Reformation*, p. 156; Hughes, *Reformation in England*, ii 59.
268 BL, Cotton MS, Cleopatra E iv fo. 109 (*LP*, XIII i 981 [2]; S. Brigden, ' "The shadow that you know": Sir Thomas Wyatt and Sir Francis Bryan at court and in embassy', *Historical Journal*, xxxix (1996), pp. 1–32, at 10–11.
269 *English Historical Documents*, v 807. Cf Bowker, 'The Henrician reformation and the parish clergy', p. 31 n. 1 and Elton, *Policy and Police*, p. 247 n. 3.
270 Merriman, *Letters of Cromwell*, ii 152 (*LP*, XIII ii 281).
271 Cranmer, *Writings and Letters*, pp. 391–2; Merriman, *Letters of Cromwell*, ii 146; *LP*, XIII i 1304 (2).
272 Hughes and Larkin, *Tudor Royal Proclamations*, i no. 186, pp. 273–5.
273 Ibid. no. 191, p. 286: text from BL, Cotton MS, Cleopatra E v fos 313–26ᵛ.
274 F. Heal, *Reformation in Britain and Ireland* (Oxford, 2003), p. 257; see G. Walker, *Persuasive Fictions* (Manchester, 1996), pp. 92–3.
275 St Clare Byrne, *Lisle Letters*, vi 228–9.
276 Ward, 'Cromwell and Calais', p. 170.
277 Merriman, *Letters of Cromwell*, ii 64–5 (*LP*, XII ii 267).
278 *LP*, XII ii 328 (Merriman, *Letters of Cromwell*, ii 65–6; cf. A.J. Slavin, 'Cromwell, Cranmer and Lord Lisle: a study in the politics of reform', *Albion*, ix (1977), pp. 320–5).
279 Notes made by Lord Herbert of Cherbury's secretary Thomas Master from a manuscript once in the Cotton Library record a 'sharp' letter of Cromwell (dated 14 Aug. 1539 or 1540, but most probably, as Brigden has it, 1538) to

Lord Lisle: Oxford, Bodleian Library, Jesus MS 74 fo. 198^v; cf. Brigden, 'Cromwell and the "Brethren"', p. 47. The dating is clinched by Cranmer's thanking Cromwell for his frank admonition of Lisle: *LP*, XIII ii 127; cf. MacCulloch, *Cranmer*, pp. 218–19.

280 *LP*, XIV i 251.
281 Ibid., XIV i 1029.
282 St Clare Byrne, *Lisle Letters*, v 523–5 (*LP*, XIV i 1086).
283 St Clare Byrne, *Lisle Letters*, v 351, 675; cf. v 462–3; Block, *Factional Politics*, p. 142 (though Block apparently puts it before Damplip's arrest); Brigden, 'Cromwell and the "Brethren"', p. 47; idem, *London and the Reformation*, p. 304.
284 St Clare Byrne, *Lisle Letters*, v 525–6.
285 Merriman, *Letters of Cromwell*, ii 226 (St Clare Byrne, *Lisle Letters*, v 523–5; *LP*, XIV i 1086).
286 St Clare Byrne, *Lisle Letters*, v 525.
287 Merriman, *Letters of Cromwell*, ii 139–40 (St Clare Byrne, *Lisle Letters*, v 462–3; *LP*, XIII i 936). This has been misdated: it is from 1539, not 1538.
288 Cf. St Clare Byrne, *Lisle Letters*, v 501 (*LP*, XIV i 1029).
289 *LP*, XIII ii 97.
290 Ibid. 127, cited by P. Morgan, 'The government of Calais, 1485–1558', University of Oxford D. Phil. thesis (1966), p. 222.
291 *LP*, XIII ii 248 (cf. Slavin, 'Cromwell, Cranmer and Lord Lisle', p. 332).
292 *LP*, XIII ii 523, 538.
293 Ibid. 897.
294 PRO, SP3/9 fo. 24 (St Clare Byrne, *Lisle Letters*, v 534; *LP*, XIV i 1108); PRO, SP3/6 fo. 27 (*LP*, XIV i 1152).
295 St Clare Byrne, *Lisle Letters*, v 579 (*LP*, XIV i 1234).
296 *LP*, XIV i 1086.
297 Ibid. 1144, 1139, 1153.
298 PRO SP1/152 fos 209–10, quoted by Morgan, 'The government of Calais, p. 209 (*LP*, XIV i 1298); St Clare Byrne, *Lisle Letters*, v 589–90 (*LP*, XIV i 1299).
299 *LP*, XIV ii 154, 164, 166.
300 Ibid. 496.
301 McEntegart, 'England and the League of Schmalkalden', p. 414. Intriguingly, in his book, the words 'independently of the king' have been replaced by 'within the foreign policy parameters set by the king: McEntegart, *Henry VIII, the League of Schmalkalden*, p. 200.
302 Redworth, *In Defence of the Church Catholic*, pp. 115–16.
303 McEntegart, *Henry VIII, the League of Schmalkalden*, pp. 220, 223.
304 Ibid., p. 15.
305 McEntegart, 'England and the League of Schmalkalden', pp. 63–4; cf. Guy, *Revolution Reassessed*, p. 71.
306 McEntegart, 'England and the League of Schmalkalden', p. 64 n. 107.
307 BL, Cleopatra E vi fos 327^v–28 (*State Papers*, i no. xx pp. 413–14; *LP*, VI 1487).
308 In his book McEntegart backs away from the bold claims earlier advanced in his thesis on this point, and concedes that 'Cromwell was now, as he always would be, the king's servant. Though he might be guiding policy, he certainly was not making it: the king remained the final arbiter': *Henry VIII, the League of Schmalkalden*, pp. 17–18.
309 McEntegart, 'England and the League of Schmalkalden', p. 71. Cf. MacCulloch, *Cranmer*, pp. 113–14: 'this mission [of early 1534] is likely to have been

designed by Thomas Cromwell to promote the evangelical cause in the English church.'

310 *LP*, VII 19.
311 Ibid. 52.
312 Muller, *Letters of Gardiner*, p. 12 (*LP*, IV iii 5476).
313 *LP*, IV iii 6026 (p. 2684).
314 Ibid. 6519.
315 Vienna, Haus-, Hof- und Staatsarchiv, England, Karton 5, Berichte, 1532, fo. 9 (*Cal. S.P., Spanish*, IV ii no. 888 pp. 366–9); *LP*, V 737.
316 *LP*, V 327, 337, 534.
317 Ibid. 711, 791.
318 D. Potter, 'Foreign Policy', in D. MacCulloch, ed., *The Reign of Henry VIII: politics, policy and piety* (Basingstore, 1995), p. 120.
319 *LP*, VII 21; IX 213; X 457.
320 Ibid., VII 211, 147, 17, and cf. instructions to Paget: VII 148.
321 Ibid. 14.
322 McEntegart, *Henry VIII, the League of Schmalkalden*, p. 27.
323 *LP*, VIII 475.
324 Ibid. 892.
325 McEntegart, 'England and the League of Schmalkalden', p. 82.
326 *LP*, VIII 1061.
327 McEntegart, 'England and the League of Schmalkalden', p. 92.
328 *LP*, IX 498 i.
329 Ibid., XII ii 814.
330 McEntegart, 'England and the League of Schmalkalden', p. 86.
331 McEntegart, *Henry VIII, the League of Schmalkalden*, p. 29.
332 *LP*, VIII 1062.
333 As McEntegart appears to concede: 'England and the League of Schmalkalden', p. 84.
334 *LP*, IX 443.
335 PRO, SP1/96 fos 13–14ᵛ (*LP*, IX 213).
336 McEntegart, *Henry VIII, the League of Schmalkalden*, p. 49.
337 *LP*, V app. 7.
338 Ibid., IX 213; cf. IX 979.
339 BL Cotton MS, Cleopatra E vi fo. 294 (*LP*, X 457; Burnet, *History of the Reformation*, vi 158).
340 Quoted by McEntegart, *Henry VIII, the League of Schmalkalden*, p. 100.
341 Ibid., p. 193.
342 McEntegart, 'England and the League of Schmalkalden', pp. 132–3.
343 Ibid., p. 488.
344 *LP*, VIII 1061–2.
345 Ibid., IX 733.
346 Quoted in McEntegart, *Henry VIII, the League of Schmalkalden*, p. 100.
347 Ibid., p. 130.
348 Ibid., pp. 80–4.
349 Ibid., pp. 83–4.
350 McEntegart, 'England and the League of Schmalkalden', p. 484.
351 McEntegart, *Henry VIII, the League of Schmalkalden*, p. 96.
352 Ibid., pp. 97–8.
353 Ibid., p. 100.
354 Ibid., p. 128 (*LP*, XIII ii 164).
355 Ibid., *Henry VIII, the League of Schmalkalden*, pp. 180, 220. It is hardly corroboration to cite evidence that Cromwell had indeed been ill in the spring, or that some bishops were more conservatively inclined.

356 Merriman, *Letters of Cromwell*, i 279.
357 BL, Add. MS 25114 fos 30–1 (*LP* IV iii 6364). This may date from 1536, not 1530.
358 Potter, 'Foreign policy', p. 120.
359 *LP*, XV 825.
360 Cf. R.M. Warnicke's remark: that 'Henry did not expect the Cleves alliance to lead to further religious reform in his kingdom': *The Marrying of Anne of Cleves: royal protocol in early modern England* (Cambridge, 2000), p. 94.
361 *LP*, IV iii 6364.
362 Scarisbrick, *Henry VIII*, p. 368. Cf. Elton's remark that 'the duke of Cleves was a catholic' *Reform and Reformation*, p. 211. Guy is mistaken in supposing that Anne was 'a German Lutheran noblewoman' ('Henry VIII and his ministers', p. 40).
363 St Clare Byrne, *Lisle Letters*, v 362.
364 McEntegart, *Henry VIII, the League of Schmalkalden*, pp. 141–2.
365 Cf. J.K. McConica, *English Humanists and Reformation Politics under Henry VIII* (Oxford, 1965), pp. 175–6; cf. Norris, 'Fall of Cromwell', p. 7.
366 J. Kaulek, *Correspondance politique de MM de Castillon et Marillac, ambassadeurs de France en Angleterre, 1537–42* (Paris, 1885), no. 160 pp. 137–8 (*LP*, XIV, ii 388); Norris, 'Fall of Cromwell', pp. 43–4.
367 *LP*, XIV ii 657–8.
368 Kaulek, *Correspondance politique*, p. 148 (*LP* XIV ii 744); cf. no. 184 p. 154 (*LP*, XV 123).
369 Kaulek, *Correspondance politique*, no. 180 p. 152 (*LP*, XV 76); Norris, 'Fall of Cromwell', p. 44.
370 Norris, 'Fall of Cromwell', p. 44.
371 Bodleian Library, Oxford, MS Jesus 74 fo. 299^v.
372 *LP*, XIV ii 274.
373 Ibid. i 1198.
374 Ibid. 1320.
375 *Cal. S.P., Spanish*, v (i) no. 7 p. 18.
376 *LP*, XIII ii 923.
377 Ibid., XIV i 103 (1).
378 PRO, SP1/142 fos 105–9 (*LP*, XIV i 103 [1] and [2]).
379 BL, Harleian MS 296 fo. 163 (*LP* XIV i 489); cf. *LP*, XIV i 490).
380 *LP*, XIV i 552.
381 Ibid. 920.
382 Ibid. 1193.
383 Kaulek, *Correspondance politique*, no. 143 pp. 124–5 (*LP*, XIV ii 117).
384 Kaulek, *Correspondance politique*, no. 153 pp. 133–4 (*LP*, XIV ii 274).
385 Kaulek, *Correspondance politique*, no. 157 p. 135 (*LP*, XIV ii 328); no. 160 p. 138 (*LP*, XIV ii 388).
386 Warnicke points out that the diplomats negotiating the marriage sent reports to Henry, not Cromwell, and that they were not obviously servants of or connected to Cromwell: *Marrying of Anne of Cleves*, p. 124.
387 MacCulloch, *Cranmer*, p. 262.
388 BL, Cotton MS, Titus B i fos 418–19 (*LP*, XV 822 [1]); Cotton MS, Otho C x fos 241–41^v (much mutilated original draft of questions to be asked of Cromwell, in the king's own hand) (*LP*, XV 822 [3]; x fos 246–7 (copy) (*LP*, XV 822 [2]. For Cromwell's confirmation, see Merriman, *Letters of Cromwell*, ii 268–73, from Hatfield MSS (*LP*, XV 823; Burnet, *History of the Reformation*, iv p. 424); and cf. Otho C x fo. 242, a close variant, but much mutilated (*LP*, XV 824).

389 Burnet, *History of the Reformation*, iv p. 430. BL Cotton MS, Otho C x fo. 240^v is badly damaged. The summary in *LP*, XV 825 does not include the passages quoted here. Burnet presumably saw the document before it was damaged.

390 Strype, *Ecclesiastical Memorials*, I ii 454–5 (*LP*, XV 850 [5]).

391 Strype, *Ecclesiastical Memorials*, I ii 458 (*LP*, XV 850 [8]).

392 Strype, *Ecclesiastical Memorials*, I ii 459 (*LP*, XV 850 [9]).

393 Strype, *Ecclesiastical Memorials*, I ii 461 (*LP*, XV 850 [12]).

394 Strype, *Ecclesiastical Memorials*, I ii 461 (*LP*, XV 850 [13]). Warnicke says this was to show that the king was capable of emitting semen (*Marrying of Anne of Cleves*, p. 205), but there is no reason why it should not be accepted as true.

395 Strype, *Ecclesiastical Memorials*, I ii 460–1 (*LP*, XV 850 [12]).

396 Warnicke disbelieves this: *Marrying of Anne of Cleves*, pp. 139–40. According to other accounts, they had a meal together: *LP*, XV 14, 18.

397 Strype, *Ecclesiastical Memorials*, I ii 456–8 (*LP*, XV 850 [7]).

398 Strype, *Ecclesiastical Memorials*, I ii 453–4 (*LP*, XV 850 [4]).

399 Warnicke, *Marrying of Anne of Cleves*, p. 138.

400 Hall, *Chronicle*, p. 299; cf. Warnicke, *Marrying of Anne of Cleves*, p. 148.

401 Kaulek, *Correspondance politique*, no. 178 p. 151; *LP*, XV 22.

402 Kaulek, *Correspondance politique*, no. 179 p. 151 (*LP*, XV 23).

403 Strype, *Ecclesiastical Memorials*, I ii 462 (*LP*, XV 850 [14]).

404 Warnicke, *Marrying of Anne of Cleves*, p. 234.

405 BL, Cotton MS, Otho C x fo. 241; Titus B i fo. 418 (*LP*, XV 822 [3], [1]).

406 Burnet, *History of the Reformation*, iv 430 (*LP*, XV 825). Cf. n. 389.

407 Strype, *Ecclesiastical Memorials*, I ii 452–5 (*LP*, XV 850 (1–3)).

408 BL, Cotton MS, Titus B i fo. 418^v (*LP*, XV 822).

409 Strype, *Ecclesiastical Memorials*, I ii 455 (*LP*, XV 850 [5]).

410 BL, Cotton MS, Otho C x fos 241–41^v (*LP*, XV 822 [3]); Titus B i fos 418–19 (*LP*, XV 822 [1]); Otho C x fos 246–7 (*LP*, XV 822 [2]).

411 BL, Cotton MS, Titus B i fo. 418 (*LP*, XV 822); *LP*, XV 823 (and BL, Otho C x. fo. 241, damaged).

412 *LP*, XV 823.

413 Strype, *Ecclesiastical Memorials*, I ii 458 (*LP*, XV 850 [7]).

414 Cf. Warnicke, *Marrying of Anne of Cleves*, p. 151.

415 Strype, *Ecclesiastical Memorials*, I ii 458 (*LP*, XV 850 [8]).

416 Strype, *Ecclesiastical Memorials*, I ii 455 (*LP*, XV 850 [4]).

417 Strype, *Ecclesiastical Memorials*, I ii 457 (*LP*, XV 850 [6]).

418 Strype, *Ecclesiastical Memorials*, I ii 454 (*LP*, XV 850 [5]).

419 *LP*, XV 823; 824 for Cromwell's account of the king's discussions of his marital difficulties.

420 Burnet, *History of the Reformation*, iv 430 (*LP*, XV 825) (from now damaged BL, Cotton MS, Otho C x fo. 240^v).

421 Strype, *Ecclesiastical Memorials*, I ii 455 (*LP*, XV 850 [3]).

422 Sketched in personal correspondence by my former colleague the late T.B. Pugh.

423 *LP*, XV 860 for date.

424 Ibid., 823.

425 Warnicke, *Marrying of Anne of Cleves*, pp. 257, 213.

426 BL, Cotton MS, Titus B i fo. 274 (*LP*, XV 776).

427 BL Cotton MS, Titus B i fos 273–74^v (*LP*, XV 776).

428 Redworth, *In Defence of the Church Catholic*, p. 119.

429 Letter to the author, 20 Dec. 1984; Elton, 'Fall of Cromwell', p. 218.

430 BL, Cotton MS, Titus B i fo. 274 (*LP*, XV 776).
431 Strype, *Ecclesiastical Memorials*, I ii 460 (*LP*, XV 850 [11]).
432 Warnicke, *Marrying of Anne of Cleves*, p. 219, thinks Cromwell was taciturn because he had been instructed by the king to keep his decision to inquire into the validity of the marriage secret: 'Wriothesley's testimony, which lacks corroboration, does not ring true; it was likely a fictionalised narrative created to indicate his conviction that Cromwell not only hoped to keep the king trapped in the Cleves marriage but was also incapable of maintaining secrecy about the king's private matters.' It is hard to see why that must be so.
433 Wriothesley, *Chronicle*, p. 119.
434 Bodleian Library, Oxford, Jesus MS 74 fo. 299.
435 BL, Cotton MS, Otho C x fo. 240 (*LP*, XV 825).
436 Anne responded willingly to the investigation of the marriage: *State Papers* i no. cxl pp. 637-8 (*LP*, XV 872). She consented, after at first being much astonished, to the annulment, admitted Henry's 'pure and chaste living with her', and accepted that she should no longer be styled queen: *State Papers*, viii no. dcxii p. 395 (*LP*, XV 881). Cf. Anne's letter to Henry VIII, *State Papers*, i no. cxlii p. 641 (*LP*, XV 891); *LP*, XV 844, 845.
437 *LP*, XV 850 (11).
438 *State Papers*, i no. cxli p. 640 (*LP*, XV 883).
439 *State Papers*, i no. cxliv p. 645 (*LP*, XV 898).
440 *State Papers*, viii 406 n. (*LP*, XV 899); cf. XV 925.
441 *State Papers*, viii no. dcxvii pp. 403-5 (*LP*, XV 908); cf. *LP*, XV 930.
442 Kaulek, *Correspondance politique*, p. 214 (*LP*, XV 976); cf. p. 218 (*LP*, XVI 12).
443 *State Papers*, viii no. dcxxiv pp. 427-8 (*LP*, XV 990).
444 *LP*, XV 943; cf. *LP*, XV 801, 898-9, 908. Wotton continued as ambassador there: Warnicke, *Marrying of Anne of Cleves*, p. 191.
445 Elton, 'Thomas Cromwell's decline and fall', pp. 150-85 and in Elton, *Studies in Tudor and Stuart Politics and Government*, i p. 189. Dickens follows John Foxe in saying that 'the king – no doubt encouraged by the Duke of Norfolk and the conservative bishops' listened to the criticisms directed against his minister by Gardiner and Norfolk (*English Reformation*, p. 201). Scarisbrick reflects how 'at the time, probably, Henry had never fully understood how and why Cromwell was suddenly swept away. The king had been stampeded by a faction bent on a coup d'état and swept along by it, like the suggestible man he was' (*Henry VIII*, p. 383).
446 *LP*, XI 233.
447 Ibid., XI 470.
448 Ibid., XII i 216; cf. Norris, 'Fall of Cromwell', p. 12.
449 *LP*, XII i 252.
450 Ibid., XII ii 101.
451 *State Papers*, v no. cccxxii p. 91 (*LP*, XII ii 229).
452 *LP*, XII ii 1101, 1191, 1030, 1154, 1311 (30).
453 Elton, 'Fall of Cromwell', pp. 196-7.
454 *State Papers*, viii no. dlx pp. 245-52 (*LP*, XV 145).
455 PRO, SP1/157 fo. 146 (*State Papers*, viii. no. dlxiii p. 260 [*LP*, XV 223]).
456 *State Papers*, viii no. dlxxv pp. 295-8 (*LP*, XV 459).
457 *LP*, XV 468-9; cf. Elton, 'Fall of Cromwell', p. 215 n. 4.
458 G.R. Elton, *The Tudor Revolution in Government* (Cambridge, 1953), p. 315 n. 2.
459 *LP*, XV 541; Elton, 'Fall of Cromwell', p. 217.
460 *LP*, XV 540.

461 Ibid. 611 (8).
462 Kaulek, *Correspondance politique*, no. 216 pp. 179–80 (*LP*, XV 567). Brigden sees Cromwell, masterminding parliamentary business in April, 'apparently as much in favour as ever': 'Fall of Cromwell', p. 266.
463 *LP*, XV 598.
464 *State Papers*, i no. cxxxvii pp. 628–9 (*LP*, XV 658).
465 Elton, 'Fall of Cromwell', p. 216.
466 *LP*, XV 746.
467 BL, Cotton MS, Cleopatra E v. fo. 300 (*LP*, XV 758).
468 BL, Cotton MS, Titus B i fo. 267ᵛ (Merriman, *Letters of Cromwell*, ii 266; *LP*, XV 776).
469 Kaulek, *Correspondance politique*, no. 164 p. 142 (*LP*, XIV ii 449).
470 Kaulek, *Correspondance politique*, no. 167 p. 143.
471 *LP*, XIV ii 732.
472 Ibid., XV 248.
473 Kaulek, *Correspondance politique*, no. 171 pp. 144–5 (*LP*, XIV ii 648); no. 181 p. 153 (*LP*, XV i 98).
474 Kaulek, *Correspondance politique*, no. 189 p. 158 (*LP*, XV 155).
475 Kaulek, *Correspondance politique*, no. 209 p. 173 (*LP*, XV 401).
476 Ibid.
477 J.R. Hale, 'The defence of the realm 1485–1558', in Colvin, *History of the King's Works*, iv 367–76.
478 Kaulek, *Correspondance politique*, no. 209 p. 173 (*LP*, XV 401).
479 Kaulek, *Correspondance politique*, no. 206 p. 170 (*LP*, XV 334).
480 Kaulek, *Correspondance politique*, no. 209 p. 173 (*LP*, XV 401); Marillac repeated this on 31 March (Kaulek, *Correspondance politique*, no. 210 p. 174 [*LP*, XV 425]).
481 Kaulek, *Correspondance politique*, no. 215 p. 178 (*LP*, XV 566).
482 Kaulek, *Correspondance politique*, no. 216 p. 179 (*LP*, XV 567).
483 *LP*, XV 735.
484 Kaulek, *Correspondance politique*, no. 223 p. 184 (*LP*, XV 697).
485 *State Papers*, viii no. dlx pp. 245–52 (*LP*, XV 145).
486 *LP*, XV 222; cf. 223.
487 Ibid. 224.
488 Ibid. 233.
489 Kaulek, *Correspondance politique*, no. 220 p. 182 (*LP*, XV 651).
490 Kaulek, *Correspondance politique*, no. 184 pp. 154–5 (*LP*, XV 123).
491 Kaulek, *Correspondance politique*, no. 209 p. 174 (*LP*, XV 401).
492 Kaulek, *Correspondance politique*, no. 212 p. 176 (*LP*, XV 487).
493 Kaulek, *Correspondance politique*, no. 204 p. 167 (*LP*, XV 289).
494 Kaulek, *Correspondance politique*, no. 216 p. 179 (*LP*, XV 567).
495 Kaulek, *Correspondance politique*, nos 217–18 p. 180 (*LP*, XV 625–6).
496 Warnicke, *Marrying of Anne of Cleves*, p. 176: 'Henry had to continue the farce of their marriage until he could be certain that a combined assault against him was not underway.'
497 Elton, 'Fall of Cromwell', p. 214. Warnicke notes that Francis and Montmorency had complained about Cromwell's decisions in the dispute that Montmorency's brother, Rochepot, had over a ship captured in 1538: 'by July 1540 Francis had written three times to Henry about the dispute': *Marrying of Anne of Cleves*, pp. 178–9, 215.
498 Kaulek, *Correspondance politique*, no. 228 p. 191 (*LP*, XV 785).
499 Kaulek, *Correspondance politique*, no. 228 p. 191 (*LP*, XV 785); *Cal. S.P., Spanish*, vi i 539; Norris, 'Fall of Cromwell', pp. 48–9.

500 *LP*, XV 803.

501 *State Papers*, viii no. dcvi p. 377 (*LP*, XV 842); *LP*, XV 792 (I and II).

502 Kaulek, *Correspondance politique*, no. 226 pp. 189–90; *Cal. S.P., Spanish*, vi i 538; Norris, 'Fall of Cromwell', pp. 37–8.

503 Kaulek, *Correspondance politique*, no. 226 pp. 189–90 (*LP*, XV 766).

504 Kaulek, *Correspondance politique*, no. 220 p. 182 (*LP*, XV 651).

505 Kaulek, *Correspondance politique*, no. 240 p. 207 (*LP*, XV 926).

506 Warnicke, *Marrying of Anne of Cleves*, no. 240 p. 215 oddly puts this as: 'the second reason Francis welcomed his fall was that his diplomats had long identified Cromwell as one of Chapuys's special informants.'

507 *State Papers*, viii no. clcxiii p. 396 (*LP*, XV 876).

508 Kaulek, *Correspondance politique*, no. 143 p. 125 (*LP*, XIV i 117).

509 Kaulek, *Correspondance politique*, no. 152 p. 132 (*LP*, XIV i 223).

510 Kaulek, *Correspondance politique*, no. 307 p. 274 (*LP*, XVI 590).

511 Cf. Norris, 'Fall of Cromwell', p. 37.

512 Kaulek, *Correspondance politique*, no. 205 p. 169 (*LP*, XV 306).

513 Foxe, *Acts and Monuments*, v app. vii.

514 PRO, SP1/158 fo. 50 (*LP*, XV 345); cf. Foxe, *Acts and Monuments*, v app. viii; Brigden, 'Fall of Cromwell', p. 264.

515 *LP*, XV 414.

516 Interestingly, Foxe says the same: *Acts and Monuments*, v 433 app. vii. Marillac's account was that in his sermon Barnes duly recanted and asked Gardiner's pardon (Kaulek, *Correspondance politique*, pp. 174–5 [*LP*, XV 425]). It will not do, then, to say of Barnes that 'in 1540 he was once again accused of heresy and this time he was unable to save himself by recantation' (W.D.J. Cargill Thompson, 'The sixteenth-century editions of *A Supplication unto King Henry the Eighth* by Robert Barnes, D.D.*: a footnote to the history of the royal supremacy', *Transactions of the Cambridge Bibliographical Society*, iii [1960], pp. 133–42 at 133).

517 Kaulek, *Correspondance politique*, p. 175 (*LP*, XV 485).

518 Foxe, *Acts and Monuments*, v 434–6.

519 PRO, SP1/158 fo. 124 and BL, Cotton MS, Cleopatra E v 406 (*LP*, XV 414).

520 Foxe, *Acts and Monuments*, v 437.

521 Burnet, *History of the Reformation*, iv 420.

522 Elton, 'Fall of Cromwell', p. 225.

523 *State Papers*, viii no. dxci pp. 349–50 (*LP*, XV 765).

524 *Pace* Brigden, 'Fall of Cromwell', p. 267.

525 *LP*, VII 27, 1026 (7); PRO, SP1/82 p. 445; *LP*, VIII 534.

526 *LP*, VII 530, app. 21; VIII 666; XV 747; J.E. Paul, *Catherine of Aragon and her Friends* (1966), pp. 226–31.

527 *LP*, X 308; Paul, *Catherine of Aragon and her Friends*, pp. 226–31.

528 Kaulek, *Correspondance politique*, no. 241 p. 208 (*LP*, XV 953).

529 Foxe, *Acts and Monuments*, v 438.

530 Ibid. v 438–9.

531 Scarisbrick, *Henry VIII*, p. 383.

532 Elton, *Reform and Reformation*, p. 293. Elton almost simultaneously, on the same page, took a different view: 'it has been suggested that Henry knew little or nothing about these executions and that they should not, therefore, be interpreted . . . as a public demonstration of his impartiality among the parties: and this is indeed likely.'

533 Brigden, 'Fall of Cromwell', p. 268, citing Foxe, *Acts and Monuments*, v 420.

534 Cf. Moreau, *Rome ou l'Angleterre*, p. 297: 'alors le laxisme va très loin et devient diabolique.'

535 Brigden, *London and the Reformation*, pp. 320–22; Redworth, *In Defence of the Church Catholic*, p. 115.

536 Brigden, 'Fall of Cromwell', p. 277, citing City of London Record Office, Letter Book P fo. 219ᵛ; Hall, *Chronicle*, p. 828; Foxe, *Acts and Monuments*, v 451.

537 Kaulek, *Correspondance politique*, no. 307 p. 274 (*LP*, XVI 590).

538 Lehmberg, 'Religious beliefs of Cromwell', p. 90 for text from *Lords Journal*, i 128–9 (Burnet, *History of the Reformation*, i 438–9; Elton, 'Thomas Cromwell's decline and fall', p. 216 has his own translation).

539 Kaulek, *Correspondance politique*, no. 215 p. 178 (*LP*, XV 566).

540 Kaulek, *Correspondance politique*, no. 223 p. 184 (*LP*, XV 697).

541 Wriothesley, *Chronicle*, i 114.

542 *State Papers*, i 627 (*LP*, XV 719).

543 Kaulek, *Correspondance politique*, no. 225 p. 187 (*LP*, XV 736); BL, Cotton MS, Cleopatra E v fo. 308 (Strype, *Ecclesiastical Memorials*, I ii 93; *LP*, XV 758).

544 *LP*, XV 747. Wilson admitted giving relief to Powell, Abel and Featherstone. He had asked Sampson to plead that Powell might be less rigorously treated in prison, but that, he claimed, was only so that Powell might be brought to conform: and it was with that intention, he claimed, that he had spoken to Powell only once, not twice as alleged. He acknowledged nevertheless that he had offended while in prison between April 1534 and May 1537.

545 Kaulek, *Correspondance politique*, no. 225 p. 187 (*LP*, XV 736); cf. p. 187 (*LP*, XV 737) on Sampson. The last quotation is all but untranslatable.

546 Kaulek, *Correspondance politique*, no. 226 pp. 188–9 (*LP*, XV 737).

547 Kaulek, *Correspondance politique*, no. 226 p. 189 (*LP*, XV 737). Details of questions, on the nature of a sacrament, and various bishops' and churchmen's responses, in *LP*, XV 826: some in Cranmer, *Writings and Letters*, p. 115.

548 Lehmberg, 'Religious beliefs of Cromwell', p. 120, citing 32 Henry VIII c. 26; Kaulek, *Correspondance politique*, no. 242 p. 211 (*LP*, XV 954). A committee of churchmen worked to prepare an act concerning 'True Opinions and Declarations of Christ's Religion', 32 Henry VIII c. 26. Is this what Marillac so bitterly criticised? There was, he wrote, a new act of parliament whereby, if two witnesses swore and affirmed before the king's council that they had heard someone say any words against the king's edicts concerning the obedience due to him and the articles concerning religion, the accused person, without any further process, even if absent and unaware of that of which they were accused, would be condemned to death. Everyone was dismayed by the fear that 'malveillans' could easily avenge themselves against their 'malvoluz', and the opportunities given to those who wanted to be false witnesses: Kaulek, *Correspondance politique*, no. 241 p. 209 (*LP*, XV 953); cf. p. 211 (*LP*, XV 954).

549 Wriothesley, *Chronicle*, i 123.

550 Ibid. 147.

551 Ibid. 149.

552 Ibid. 161.

553 Ibid. 163–5.

554 Haigh, *English Reformations*, p. 161.

555 Elton, *Reform and Reformation*, p. 299. 'The expected stamping out of new opinions . . . did not take place': Parker, *English Reformation*, p. 93.

556 Brigden, *London and the Reformation*, p. 320 and 'Fall of Cromwell', p. 273: citing Hall, *Chronicle*, 828, who puts it into 1539, and Foxe, *Acts and Monuments*, v 443–51; though in 'Fall of Cromwell', p. 273 n. 131, she notes that Foxe puts it into 1541: Foxe's editors (v 831) suggest the details are from

several years, including later ones: so it is by no means clear that so many people were arrested in July 1540.

557 Brigden, *London and the Reformation*, p. 322.
558 Duffy, *Stripping of the Altars*, p. 429.
559 Ibid., pp. 427–8.
560 *LP*, XV 772; cf. Rex, *Henry VIII and the English Reformation*, p. 98.
561 Rex, *Henry VIII and the English Reformation*, p. 98.
562 *LP*, XVI 446, 448–9, 450, 452, 535.
563 Foxe, *Acts and Monuments*, v 463.
564 Aston, *England's Iconoclasts*, p. 239. Marshall writes that 'at the end of 1538, the pace of radical change visibly slowed, and the following decade saw no repeat of the iconoclastic spectacles of that year' ('The rood of Boxley, the blood of Hailes and the defence of the Henrician church', p. 695), and in one sense that is true, since the greatest shrines were dismantled in 1538 and few significant shrines remained to be dealt with. But, as what happened in York shows, the thrust of royal policy remained as it was.
565 Hughes and Larkin, *Tudor Royal Proclamations*, i no. 203; *LP*, XVI 1192, 1258; cf. Rex, *Henry VIII and the English Reformation*, p. 94; Duffy, *Stripping of the Altars*, p. 431, Brigden, *London and the Reformation*, pp. 337–8, citing Foxe, *Acts and Monuments*, v 462–3, 832. Haigh notes all this but minimises it by putting it almost as an aside: *English Reformations*, p. 164.
566 R. Hutton, 'The English reformation and the evidence of folklore', *Past and Present*, cxlviii (1995), p. 109, citing BL, Arundel MS 97 fos 20ᵛ, 76. Cf. John Hussee's report to Lord Lisle: 'there shall be no solemn watch in the city this year [1539] on Midsummer night, as the custom hath been; wherewith some of the citizens, having prepared for the same, are not very well pleased' (St Clare Byrne, *Lisle Letters*, v 542 [*LP*, XIV i 1144]): if that had happened in 1539, the instructions of 1541 represent continuity of policy.
567 Hughes and Larkin, *Tudor Royal Proclamations*, i no. 203; Duffy, *Stripping of the Altars*, pp. 430–1.
568 Aston, *England's Iconoclasts*, p. 238; Rex, *Henry VIII and the English Reformation*, pp. 98–9; Marshall, 'Rood of Boxley', p. 696; Cranmer, *Writings and Letters*, pp. 490–1; *LP*, XVI i 1233, 1258, 1262; Foxe, *Acts and Monuments*, v 462–3.
569 J. Bain, ed., *Hamilton Papers* (Edinburgh, 2 vols, 1890), i no. 348 pp. 498–9 (*LP*, XIV i 364).
570 *Pace* Brigden: the last years of Henry's reign were 'of no certain purpose or directive in religion'; 'For all the feuding at Court and in the Council, no faction was able to win lasting favour or ascendancy'; 'The avowed aim of the conservatives, led by Gardiner and Norfolk, was to restore the country to orthodoxy. In order to do this they must overthrow their rivals at court, and permanently': *London and the Reformation*, p. 325.
571 Kaulek, *Correspondance politique*, no. 242 p. 211 (*LP*, XV 954).
572 *LP*, XV 826.
573 Lloyd, *Formularies of Faith*, pp. 215–377: *RSTC* 5168/77. BL, Cotton MS, Cleopatra E v fos 5–35ᵛ.
574 Duffy, *Stripping of the Altars*, p. 432.
575 Ibid., p. 442.
576 Ibid., p. 443.
577 Aston, *England's Iconoclasts*, p. 239.
578 Haigh, *English Reformations*, p. 160.
579 N. Tyacke, *English Historical Review*, cx (1995), p. 469; cf. P. Lake, *Journal of Ecclesiastical History*, xlvi (1995), pp. 110–23.

580 Cf. Lloyd, *Formularies of Faith*, pp. 135–7, 141, 148 and 301, 304–5, 310–11.
581 Ibid., p. 215: cited by Marshall, 'Rood of Boxley', p. 696, and described as 'a heartfelt personal apologia'.
582 Lloyd, *Formularies of Faith*, p. 310.
583 Ibid., pp. 265–6.
584 Rex, *Henry VIII and the English Reformation*, pp. 157–8.
585 Lloyd, *Formularies of Faith*, p. 223.
586 Ibid., pp. 224–5.
587 Ibid., pp. 238–9, 251.
588 Ibid., p. 240; cf. p. 71 (Bishops' Book).
589 Ibid., pp. 359–75.
590 Ibid., p. 359.
591 Ibid., pp. 360–1.
592 Ibid., p. 362.
593 Ibid., pp. 362–3.
594 Ibid., p. 363.
595 Ibid., p. 365.
596 Ibid., pp. 364–5.
597 Ibid., p. 365.
598 Ibid., p. 366.
599 Ibid., p. 370.
600 Ibid., p. 367.
601 Ibid.
602 Ibid., p. 368.
603 Ibid., pp. 371–2.
604 Ibid., p. 373.
605 Ibid., p. 374.
606 Ibid., p. 375.
607 Hughes, *Reformation in England*, ii 56.
608 Lloyd, *Formularies of Faith*, pp. 298 (almost exactly following Bishops' Book), 133.
609 Haigh, *English Reformations*, p. 163; D. MacCulloch, 'Henry VIII and the reform of the church', in D. MacCulloch, ed., *The Reign of Henry VIII: politics, policy and piety* (Basingstoke, 1995), p. 177; Kreider, *English Chantries*, p. 94; P. Marshall, 'Fear, purgatory and polemic in reformation England', in W.G. Naphy and P. Roberts, eds, *Fear in Early Modern Society* (Manchester, 1997), pp. 150–65 at 151; P. Marshall, *Beliefs and the Dead in Reformation England* (Oxford, 2002), p. 77; Duffy, *Stripping of the Altars*, p. 443.
610 Lloyd, *Formularies of Faith*, pp. 237–8.
611 Ibid., p. 375.
612 Ibid., p. 376.
613 Ibid., p. 376–7.
614 Foxe, *Acts and Monuments*, v 534–6; Dickens, *English Reformation*, p. 135. For a linguistic discussion see P. Marshall, 'Mumpsimus and sumpsimus: the intellectual origins of a Henrician *bon mot*', *Journal of Ecclesiastical History*, lii (2001), pp. 512- 20. It derived, as he shows, from Erasmus's tale of the ignorant priest who said 'mumpsimus' when he meant 'sumpsimus'. Mumpsimus became a stock word for humanists and protestants to characterise clerical ignorance, and superstition more generally. Marshall goes on to claim that the king's *bon mot* 'was not quite so even-handed as it would at first appear', because while mumpsimus was 'just plain wrong', sumpsimus was, 'at worst, pedantry' (p. 519). But in fact the juxtaposition might be thought to work in the opposite direction, equating sumpsimus with mumpsimus. And the context

and tone of Henry's speech taken as a whole reinforce the case for seeing it as an eloquent rendition of the middle way that he sought.

615 This paragraph is heavily indebted to R. Bowers, 'The vernacular litany of 1544 during the reign of Henry VIII', in G.W. Bernard and S.J. Gunn, eds, *Authority and Consent in Tudor England* (Ashgate, 2002), pp. 151–78.

616 F. Kisby, ' "When the king goeth a procession: chapel ceremonies and services, the ritual year and religious reforms at the early Tudor court, 1485-1547', *Journal of British Studies*, xl (2001), pp. 44–75.

617 Cranmer, *Writings and Letters*, pp. 414–15.

618 Kreider, *English Chantries*, pp. 173, 175.

619 J. Loach, *Edward VI* (1999), pp. 11–14; Scarisbrick, *Henry VIII*, pp. 474–5.

620 Foxe, *Acts and Monuments*, v 568ff.

621 Ibid., v 553ff; vii 24ff.

622 Loach, *Edward VI*, pp. 17–28; E.W. Ives, 'Henry VIII's will: a forensic conundrum', *Historical Journal*, xxxv (1992), pp. 779–804; R.A. Houlbrooke, 'Henry VIII's wills: a comment', *Historical Journal*, xxxvii (1994), pp. 891–9; E.W. Ives, 'The protectorate provisions of 1546-7', *Historical Journal*, xxxvii (1994), pp. 901–14.

623 R. Bowers, 'King Henry VIII's intended chantry in St George's Chapel, Windsor Castle', unpublished paper; cf. Rex and Armstrong, 'Henry VIII's foundations', pp. 406–7.

Conclusion

1 O'Grady, *Henry VIII and the Conforming Catholics*, p. 13 is a rare exception.

2 Wooding, *Rethinking Catholicism*, p. 271.

3 Rex, *Henry VIII and the English Reformation*, pp. 173–4; idem, 'Henry VIII and his church', *History Review*, xxix (Dec. 1997), pp. 33–7. Cf. P. Tudor Craig, 'Henry VIII and King David', in D. Williams, ed., *Early Tudor England: proceedings of the 1987 Harlaxton symposium* (Woodbridge, 1989), pp. 183–205; J.N. King, *Tudor Royal Iconography: literature and art in an age of religious crisis* (Princeton, 1989), pp. 73–81, 90–3.

4 *Pace* McEntegart, *Henry VIII, the League of Schmalkalden*, pp. 218–19.

5 PRO, SP1/143 fo. 164^v (*LP*, XIV i 368).

6 Most recently by S. Doran and C. Durston, *Princes, Pastors and People* (2nd ed., 2003), p. 199.

7 P. Marshall, 'The other black legend: the Henrician reformation and the Spanish people', *English Historical Review*, cxvi (2001), pp. 31–49, esp. 41–2.

8 Wriothesley, *Chronicle*, i 52. Cf. Armstrong, 'English catholicism rethought?', pp. 723–6.

9 Wooding, *Rethinking Catholicism*. Wooding's analysis is ingenious but it is narrowly focused on elements of theology and doctrine and is not set in a broader context.

10 Shagan, *Popular Politics and the English Reformation*, p. 59.

11 Shagan develops his theme: 'people make bargains with even the most odious regimes in more cases than we would usually care to admit'; 'The English Reformation, like every aspect of early modern governance, depended on the collaboration of the governed'; 'people played an important role in choosing what sort of reformation they experienced and constructing the meanings of that reformation in their communities'; 'religious innovations were not . . . not forced on the population by an all-powerful government but

rather were negotiated through layers of local agents and collaborators'; 'a narrative which acknowledges for the first time that the Reformation was necessarily based, like all aspects of Tudor government, on the collaboration of the governed': ibid., pp. 16, 14, 22–3, 307.

12 The attempt to present the Henrician settlement as 'Lutheranism without justification by faith' (A. Ryrie, 'The strange death of Lutheran England', *Journal of Ecclesiastical History*, liii [2002], pp. 64–8) is strained: that doctrine was at the heart of Luther's message.

13 That makes the analysis offered by Ryrie, 'The strange death of Lutheran England', pp. 64–92, at best incomplete.

14 Cf. A. Ryrie, *The Gospel and Henry VIII: evangelicals in the early English reformation* (Cambridge, 2003), p. 6.

15 I am grateful to Euan Cameron for the formulation quoted and for his comments on this point.

16 Kaulek, *Correspondance politique*, no. 241 p. 210 (*LP*, XV 953).

17 Harpsfield, *Pretended Divorce*, p. 297; cf. L.B. Smith, *Henry VIII*, p. 130.

18 C.S.L. Davies, *English Historical Review*, cxi (1996), p. 168.

19 G.W. Bernard, 'The church of England, c. 1529–1642', *History*, lxxv (1990), pp. 183–206, reprinted in G.W. Bernard, *Power and Politics in Tudor England* (Aldershot, 2000), pp. 191–216.

20 For a closer analysis, see G.W. Bernard, 'The tyranny of Henry VIII', in G.W. Bernard and S.J. Gunn, eds, *Authority and Consent in Tudor England* (Aldershot, 2002), pp. 113–30.

Bibliography

Primary Sources: Manuscript

British Library, London
Cotton MS
Harleian MS
Additional MS

Public Record Office, London
SP1
SP3
PRO31/18
E36

Christ Church, Oxford
Wake MS 306

Vienna, Haus-, Hof- und Staatsarchiv
England, Karton 4–6

Primary Sources: Printed

Allen, P.S. and H.M., eds, *Letters of Erasmus* (Oxford, 12 vols, 1906–58).
Bain, J., ed., *Hamilton Papers* (Edinburgh, 2 vols, 1890).
Bale, J., *A Comedye concernynge thre lawes* (15[4]8) (RSTC 1287).
——, *The Actes of Englyssh votaryes* (1546) (RSTC 1270).
Bateson, M., ed., 'The Pilgrimage of Grace' (the text of 'The manner of the taking of Robert Aske'), *English Historical Review*, v (1890), pp. 331–45, 'Aske's examination', *English Historical Review*, v (1890), pp. 550–73.
Brewer, J.S., J. Gairdner and R.H. Brodie, eds, *Letters and Papers, Foreign and Domestic, of the Reign of Henry VIII* (21 vols in 36, 1862–1932).
Bruce, J., 'Observations on the circumstances which occasioned the death of Fisher, Bishop of Rochester', *Archaeologia*, xxv (1834), pp. 61–99.
Calendar of State Papers, Spanish, ed. G.A. Bergenroth, P. de Gayangos, and M.A.S. Hume (1862–1954).
Calendar of State Papers, Venetian, ed. R. Brown, *et al.* (1864–1947).
Camusat, N., *Meslanges Historiques* (Troyes, 1619).

Cavendish, G., *The Life and Death of Cardinal Wolsey*, ed. R.S. Sylvester, *Early English Text Society*, ccxliii (1959).

Dudding, R.C., ed., *The First Churchwarden's Book of Louth 1500–1524* (Oxford, 1941).

Dwyer, J.G., ed., *Reginald Pole's Defense of the Unity of the Church* (Westminster, Maryland, 1965).

Ellis, H., *Original Letters illustrative of British History* (11 vols in 3 series, 1824).

Foley, S.M. and C.H. Miller, eds, *The Complete Works of St Thomas More: xi The Answer to a poisoned book* (1985).

Foxe, J., *Acts and Monuments*, ed. S.R. Cattley and G. Townsend (8 vols, 1837–41).

Furnivall, F.J., *Ballads from Manuscripts* (Hertford, 1873).

Frere, W.H. and W.M. Kennedy, eds, *Visitation Articles and Injunctions of the Period of Reformation, 1536–58* (Alcuin Club Collections, xv 1910).

Gee, H. and W.J. Hardy, *Documents illustrative of English Church History* (1896).

Guy, J., R. Keen, C.H. Miller and McGuggan, eds, *The Complete Works of St Thomas More: x. The Debellation of Salem and Byzance* (1987).

Hall, Edward, *Chronicle* (1809 edn).

Harpsfield, Nicholas, ed. N. Pocock, *The Pretended Divorce between Henry VIII and Catharine of Aragon*, Camden Society, 2nd ser., xxi (1878).

Hatt, C.A., *English Works of John Fisher, Bishop of Rochester* (Oxford, 2002).

Hay, D., ed., *The Anglica Historia of Polydore Vergil*, Camden Society, lxxiv (1950).

Henry VIII, *Assertio Septem Sacramentorum adversus M. Lutheru* (1521) (*RSTC* 13078).

Herbert of Cherbury, *Life of Henry VIII* (1649).

Hitchcock, E.V. and R.W. Chambers, eds, *Nicholas Harpsfield's Life and Death of Sir Thomas More*, Early English Text Society, clxxxvi (1932).

Hitchcock, E.V., ed., *The Lyfe of Sir Thomas Moore Knight by William Roper*, Early English Text Society, cxcvii (1935).

Hughes, P.L. and J.F. Larkin, eds, *Tudor Royal Proclamations* (3 vols, 1964–9).

Kaulek, J., *Correspondance politique de MM de Castillon et Marillac, ambassadeurs de France en Angleterre, 1537–42* (Paris, 1885).

Joye, George, *George Joye confuteth Winchesters false articles* (1543) (*RSTC* 14826–7).

Latimer, H., *Sermons*, Parker Society (1844).

Le Grand, *Histoire du Divorce de Henry VIII* (Paris, 1688, 3 vols).

Le Labourer, J., ed., *Les mémoires de Messire Michel de Castelnau* (Brussels, 3 vols, 1731).

Lloyd, C., *Formularies of Faith* (Oxford, 1856).

Lords Journals, 1513–1800, vol. i.

Merriman, R.B., ed., *Life and Letters of Thomas Cromwell* (2 vols, 1904).

Mitchell, W.T., ed., *Epistolae Academicae 1508–1596*, Oxford Historical Society, new series xxvi (1980 for 1977–8).

Nichols, J.G., ed., *Narratives of the days of the Reformation*, Camden Society, 1st ser., lxxvii (1857).

O'Donovan, L., ed., *Assertio Septem Sacramentorum* (New York, 1908).

van Ortroy, F., ed., 'Vie du bienheureux martyr Jean Fisher, cardinal eveque de Rochester', *Analecta Bollandiana*, x (1891), pp. 121–365, xii (1893), pp. 97–283.

Pantin, W.A., ed., *Documents illustrating the activities of the general and provincial chapters of the English Black Monks, 1215–1549*, vol. iii, Camden Society, 3rd ser., liv (1937).

Pocock, N., ed., *Records of the Reformation* (Oxford, 2 vols, 1870–1).

Pollard, A.W., *et al.*, *A Short-Title Catalogue of Books Printed in England, Scotland and Ireland, 1475–1640* (revised edn, 1986).

Rogers, E., ed., *Correspondence of Thomas More* (Princeton, 1947).

Rymer, T., *Foedera* (1739–45 edn).

Scheurer, R., ed., *La Correspondance du cardinal Jean du Bellay* (2 vols, Paris, 1969–73).

St German, Christopher, *A Treatise concerning the division between the spiritualtie and temporaltie* (?1532) (RSTC 21586–7).

St Clare Byrne, M., ed., *Lisle Letters* (6 vols, 1982).

State Papers of Henry VIII.

Statutes of the Realm.

Strype, J., *Ecclesiastical Memorials* (3 vols in 6 parts, Oxford, 1820–40).

Surtz, E. and V. Murphy, eds, *The Divorce Tracts of Henry VIII* (Angers, 1988).

Toller, T.N., ed., *Correspondence of Edward, third earl of Derby, during the years 24 to 31 Henry VIII*, Chetham Society, n.s., xxix (1890).

Trapp, J.B., ed., *The Complete Works of St Thomas More: ix. The Apology* (1979).

Wakefield, R., *Kotser Codicis* (*c.* 1534), (RSTC 24943).

Whatmore, L.E., 'The Sermon against the Holy Maid of Kent and her Adherents, delivered at Paul's Cross, November the 23rd, 1533, and at Canterbury, December the 7th', *English Historical Review*, lviii (1943), pp. 463–75 (a modernised text of PRO, SP1/82 fos 73–80v).

Wikins, D., *Concilia Magnae Britanniae* (4 vols, 1737).

Williams, C.H., ed., *English Historical Documents, v 1485–1558* (1967).

Wright, T., ed., *Letters relating to the suppression of the monasteries*, Camden Society, xxvi(1843).

Secondary Sources

Armstrong, C.D.C., 'English catholicism rethought?', *Journal of Ecclesiastical History*, liv (2003), pp. 717–26.

Aston, M., *England's Iconclasts: volume 1 Laws against Images* (Oxford, 1988).

Beckett, N., 'Sheen Charterhouse from its foundation to its dissolution', Univ. of Oxford D. Phil. thesis (1992).

Bedouelle, G. and P. Le Gal, eds, *Le Divorce du roi Henry VIII* (Geneva, 1987).

Bernard, G.W., *The Power of Early Tudor Nobility: a study of the fourth and fifth earls of Shrewsbury* (Brighton, 1985).

——, 'The Pardon of the Clergy reconsidered', *Journal of Ecclesiastical History*, xxxvii (1986), pp. 258–87.

——, *War, Taxation and Rebellion in Early Modern England* (1986).

——, 'The Church of England, *c.* 1529–1642', *History*, lxxv (1990), pp. 183–206, reprinted in Bernard, G.W., *Power and Politics in Tudor England* (Aldershot, 2000), pp. 191–216.

——, 'The fall of Anne Boleyn', *English Historical Review*, cvi (1991), pp. 584–610, reprinted in Bernard, G.W., *Power and Politics in Tudor England* (Aldershot, 2000), pp. 80–107.

——, 'Anne Boleyn's religion', *Historical Journal*, xxxvi (1993), pp. 1–20.

——, 'The making of religious policy, 1533–1546: Henry VIII and the search for the middle way', *Historical Journal*, xli (1998), pp. 321–49.

——, Elton's Cromwell', *History*, lxxxiii (1998), pp. 587–607, reprinted in Bernard, G.W., *Power and Politics in Tudor England* (Aldershot, 2000), pp. 108–28.

——,'Vitality and vulnerability in the late medieval church: pilgrimage on the eve of the break with Rome' in J.L. Watts, ed., *The End of the Middle Ages? England in the fifteenth and sixteenth centuries* (Stroud, 1998), pp. 199–233.

——, 'The piety of Henry VIII', in S.N. Amos and H. van Nierop, eds, *The*

Education of a Christian Society: Humanism and the Reformation in Britain and the Netherlands (1999), pp. 62–88.

——, 'The tyranny of Henry VIII', in G.W. Bernard and S.J. Gunn, eds, *Authority and Consent in Tudor England* (Aldershot, 2002), pp. 113–30.

Bettey, J.H., *The Suppression of the Monasteries in the West Country* (Gloucester, 1989).

Bindoff, S.T., ed., *History of Parliament: 1509–58* (3 vols, 1982).

Block, J.S., *Factional Politics and the English Reformation 1520–1540* (Woodbridge, 1993).

Bowers, R., 'The Vernacular Litany of 1544 during the reign of Henry VIII', in G.W. Bernard and S.J. Gunn, eds., *Authority and Consent in Tudor England* (Aldershot, 2002), pp. 151–78.

——, 'King Henry VIII's intended chantry in St George's Chapel, Windsor Castle', (forthcoming).

Bowker, M., 'The Supremacy and the episcopate: the struggle for control', *Historical Journal*, xviii (1975), pp. 227–43.

——, 'The Henrician Reformation and the parish clergy', *Bulletin of the Institute of Historical Research*, l (1977), pp. 30–47.

——, *The Henrician Reformation: the diocese of Lincoln under John Longland 1521–1547* (Cambridge, 1981).

Bradshaw, B., 'The Tudor commonwealth: reform and revolution', *Historical Journal*, xxii (1979), pp. 455–76.

——, B. and E. Duffy, *Humanism, Reform and the Reformation: the career of Bishop John Fisher* (Cambridge, 1989).

Brigden, S., 'Popular disturbance and the fall of Thomas Cromwell and the reformers 1539–1540', *Historical Journal*, xxxiv (1981), pp. 257–78.

——, 'Thomas Cromwell and the "brethren" ', in C. Cross, D. Loades and J.J. Scarisbrick, ed., *Law and Government under the Tudors* (Cambridge, 1988), pp. 51–66.

——, *London and the Reformation* (Oxford, 1989).

——, ' "The shadow that you know": Sir Thomas Wyatt and Sir Francis Bryan at court and in embassy', *Historical Journal*, xxxix (1996), pp. 1–32.

——, *New Worlds, Lost Worlds* (2000).

Brighton, T., 'Art in the cathedral from the foundation to the Civil War', in M. Hobbs, ed., *Chichester Cathedral: an historical survey* (Chichester, 1994), pp. 69–84.

Brown, K.D., 'The Franciscan Observants in England, 1482–1559', Univ. of Oxford D.Phil. thesis, 1986.

Burnet, G., *History of the Reformation of the Church of England* (3 vols in 6, 1820).

Bush, M.L., ' "Up for the Commonweal": the significance of tax grievances in the English rebellions of 1536', *English Historical Review*, cvi (1991) pp. 299–318.

——, *The Pilgrimage of Grace* (Manchester, 1996).

—— and D. Bownes, *The Defeat of the Pilgrimage of Grace: a study of the Post-pardon Revolts of December 1536 to March 1537 and their effect* (Hull, 1999).

Cargill Thompson, W.D.J, 'The sixteenth-century editions of *A Supplication unto King Henry the Eighth* by Robert Barnes, D.D.: a footnote to the history of the royal supremacy', *Transactions of the Cambridge Bibliographical Society*, iii (1960), pp. 133–42.

Carley, J.P., ed., *The Libraries of Henry VIII* (2000).

Chester, A.F., *Hugh Latimer: Apostle to the English* (Philadelphia, 1954).

Chibi, A.A., 'Henry VIII and his marriage to his brother's wife: the sermon of Bishop John Stokesley of 11 July 1535', *Historical Research*, lxvii (1994), pp. 40–56.

Clark, J.G., 'Reformation and reaction at St Albans Abbey, 1530–1558', *English Historical Review*, cxv (2000), pp. 297–328.

Clebsch, W.A., *England's Earliest Protestants 1520–1535* (New Haven, 1964).

Cole, H., *King Henry the Eighth's Scheme of Bishopricks* (1838).

Collett, B., *Female Monastic Life in Tudor England: an edition of Richard Fox's translation of the Benedictine Rule for women* (Aldershot, 2002).

Colvin, H.M., ed., *History of the King's Works, iii. 1485–1660 (Part I)*, (1975).

——, ed., *History of the King's Works, iv. 1485–1660 (Part II)*, (1982).

Cooper, J.P., 'The Supplication against the Ordinaries reconsidered', *English Historical Review*, lxxii (1957), pp. 616–41.

Croft-Murray, E., 'Lambert Barnard: an English early renaissance painter', *Archaeological Journal*, cxiii (1956), pp. 108–25.

Cunich, P., 'The Dissolution', in D. Rees, ed., *Monks of England: the Benedictines in England from Augustine to the Present Day* (1997), pp. 148–66.

Daniell, D., *William Tyndale: a biography* (New Haven, 1994).

Davies, C.S.L., 'The Pilgrimage of Grace Reconsidered', *Past and Present*, xli (1968), pp. 54–76, reprinted in P. Slack, ed., *Popular Protest and the Social Order in Early Modern England* (Cambridge, 1984), pp. 16–36.

——, *Peace, Print and Protestantism 1450–1558* (1976).

——, 'Popular religion and the Pilgrimage of Grace', in A.J. Fletcher and J. Stevenson, *Order and Disorder in Early Modern England* (Cambridge, 1985), pp. 58–91.

Derrett, J.D.M., 'The trial of Sir Thomas More', *English Historical Review*, lxxix (1964), pp. 450–77.

Dickens, A.G., 'The northern convocation and Henry VIII', *Church Quarterly Review*, cxxvii (1938), pp. 84–102.

——, *The English Reformation* (1st edn, 1964; 2nd edn, 1989).

Dobson, R.B., 'The monks of Canterbury in the later middle ages, 1220–1540', in P. Collinson, N. Ramsay and M. Sparks, eds, *A History of Canterbury Cathedral* (Oxford, 1995), pp. 69–153.

Dodds, M.H. and R., *The Pilgrimage of Grace 1536–7 and the Exeter Conspiracy 1538* (Cambridge, 2 vols, 1915).

Doran, S. and C. Durston, *Princes, Pastors and People* (2nd edn, 2003).

Dowling, M., *Fisher of Men: a Life of John Fisher, 1469–1535* (Basingstoke, 1999).

Duffy, E., *The Stripping of the Altars* (New Haven 1992).

Ellis, S.G., *Tudor Frontiers and Noble Power: the making of the British State* (Oxford, 1995).

Elton, G.R., 'The evolution of a reformation statute', *English Historical Review*, lxiv (1949), pp. 174–97; reprinted in Elton, *Studies*, ii. 82–106.

——, 'A note on the first act of annates', *Bulletin of the Institute of Historical Research*, xxiii (1950), pp. 203–4.

——, 'The Commons' supplication of 1532: parliamentary manoeuvres in the reign of Henry VIII', *English Historical Review*, lxvi (1951), pp. 507–34, reprinted in Elton, *Studies*, ii. 107–36.

——, 'Thomas Cromwell's decline and fall', *Historical Journal*, x (1951), pp. 150–85, reprinted in Elton, *Studies*, i. 189–230.

——, 'King or minister? The man behind the Henrician Reformation', *History*, xxxix (1954), pp. 216–32, reprinted in Elton, *Studies*, i. 173–88.

——, 'Sir Thomas More and the opposition to Henry VIII', *Bulletin of the Institute of Historical Research*, xli (1968), pp. 19–34, reprinted in Elton, *Studies*, i. 155–72.

——, 'The King of Hearts', *Historical Journal*, xii (1969), 158–63, reprinted in Elton, *Studies*, i. 100–8.

——, *Policy and Police* (Cambridge, 1972).

——, *Studies in Tudor and Stuart Politics and Government* (Cambridge, 4 vols, 1974–92).

——, *Reform and Reformation* (1977).

——, 'Thomas Cromwell Redivivus', *Archiv für Reformationsgeschichte* (1977), pp. 192–208, reprinted in Elton, *Studies*, iii. 373–90.

——, 'Politics and the Pilgrimage of Grace', in B. Malament, *After the Reformation* (1979), pp. 25–56, reprinted in Elton, *Studies*, iii. 183–215.

Fenlon, D., *Heresy and Obedience in Tridentine Italy: Cardinal Pole and the Counter Reformation* (Cambridge, 1972).

Fines, J., 'Cathedral and Reformation', in M. Hobbs, ed., *Chichester Cathedral: an historical survey* (1994), pp. 47–68.

Fletcher, A.J. and D. MacCulloch, *Tudor Rebellions* (4th edn, 1997).

Froude, J.A., *History of England from the Fall of Wolsey to the Defeat of the Spanish Armada* (12 vols, 1858–70).

Gasquet, F.A., *Henry VIII and the English Monasteries* (7th edn, 1920).

Greatrex, J., 'St Swithun's Priory in the late middle ages', in J. Crook, ed., *Winchester Cathedral: nine hundred years* (Chichester, 1993), pp. 139–66.

Gunn, S.J., *Charles Brandon, duke of Suffolk 1484–1545* (Oxford, 1988).

Guy, J., *The Public Career of Thomas More* (Brighton, 1980).

——, 'Henry VIII and the *praemunire* manoeuvres of 1530–31', *English Historical Review*, xcvii (1982), pp. 481–503.

——, *Tudor England* (Oxford, 1988).

——, 'Henry VIII and his ministers', *History Review*, xxiii (1995), pp. 37–40.

——, *Thomas More* (2000).

Gwyn, P., *The King's Cardinal: the rise and fall of Thomas Wolsey* (1990).

Haigh, C., *The Last Days of the Lancashire Monasteries and the Pilgrimage of Grace*, Chetham Society, xvii (1969).

——, *Reformation and Resistance in Tudor Lancashire* (Cambridge, 1975).

——, 'Anticlericalism and the English Reformation', *History*, lxviii (1983), pp. 391–407, reprinted in C. Haigh, ed., *The English Reformation Revised* (Cambridge, 1987), pp. 56–74.

——, ed., *The English Reformation Revised* (Cambridge, 1987).

——, *English Reformations* (Oxford, 1993).

——, '1546, before and after: the making of Christ Church', *Christ Church Record* (1993), pp. 1–16.

Hale, J.R., 'The defence of the realm 1485–1558', in Colvin, *History of the King's Works*, iv. 367–76.

Hallam Smith, E., 'Henry VIII's monastic refoundations of 1536–37 and the course of the dissolution', *Bulletin of the Institute of Historical Research*, li (1978), pp. 124–31.

Hamilton, W., ed., *Wriothesley's Chronicle*, Camden Society, 2 vols, cxvi (1875).

Hardy, T.D., *Report upon the Documents in the Archives and Public Libraries of Vienna* (1886).

Harper-Bill, C. *The Pre-Reformation Church in England 1400–1530* (1989).

Harrison, S., *The Pilgrimage of Grace in the Lake Counties, 1536–7* (1981).

Heal, F., *The Reformation in Britain and Ireland* (Oxford, 2003).

Hollger, C., 'Reginald Pole and the legations of 1537 and 1539: diplomatic and polemical responses to the break with Rome', University of Oxford D.Phil. thesis, 1989.

Hoskins, A., 'Mary Boleyn's Carey children: offspring of Henry VIII', *Genealogists' Magazine* (Mar. 1997).

Houlbrooke, R.A., 'Henry VIII's wills: a comment', *Historical Journal*, xxxvii (1994), pp. 891–9.

——, 'Refoundation and Reformation, 1538–1628', in I. Atherton, *et al.*, eds, *Norwich Cathedral: Church, City and Diocese, 1096–1996* (1996), pp. 507–39.

Housley, N., 'Insurrection as religious war, 1400–1536', *Journal of Medieval History*, xxv (1999), pp. 141–54.

Hoyle, R.W., ed., 'Thomas Master's narrative of the Pilgrimage of Grace', *Northern History*, xxi (1985), pp. 53–79.

——, 'The origins of the dissolution of the monasteries', *Historical Journal*, xxxviii (1995), pp. 275–305.

——, *The Pilgrimage of Grace* (Oxford, 2001).

Hughes, P., *The Reformation in England* (3 vols, 1954).

Hutton, R., 'The English Reformation and the evidence of folklore', *Past and Present*, cxlviii (1995), pp. 89–116.

Ives, E.W., 'Faction at the court of Henry VIII: the fall of Anne Boleyn', *History*, lvii (1972), pp. 169–88.

——, *Anne Boleyn* (Oxford, 1986), re-issued as *The Life and Fall of Anne Boleyn* (Oxford, 2004).

——, 'Henry VIII's will: a forensic conundrum', *Historical Journal*, xxxv (1992), pp. 779–804.

——, 'Anne Boleyn and the early reformation in England: the contemporary evidence', *Historical Journal*, xxxvii (1994), pp. 389–400.

——, 'The protectorate provisions of 1546–7', *Historical Journal*, xxxvii (1994), pp. 901–14.

——, 'Henry VIII: the political perspective', in D. MacCulloch, ed., *The Reign of Henry VIII: Politics, Policy and Piety* (Basingstoke, 1995), pp. 13–34.

Jack, S., 'The last days of the smaller monasteries in England', *Journal of Ecclesiastical History*, xxi (1970), pp. 97–124.

James, M.E., 'Obedience and dissent in Henrician England: the Lincolnshire Rebellion 1536', *Past and Present*, lxviii (1970), pp. 3–78, reprinted in M.E. James, *Society, Politics and Culture* (Cambridge, 1976), pp. 188–269.

Katz, D.S., *The Jews in the History of England 1485–1850* (Oxford, 1994).

Kelly, H.A., *The Matrimonial Trials of Henry VIII* (Stanford, 1976, new edn 2004).

Kelly, M.J., 'Canterbury jurisdiction and influence during the episcopate of William Warham, 1503–1532', Univ. of Cambridge Ph.D. thesis, 1965.

——, 'The submission of the clergy', *Transactions of the Royal Historical Society*, 5th ser., xv (1965), pp. 97–119.

Kesselring, K.J., 'A draft of the 1531 "Acte for Poysoning"', *English Historical Review*, cxvi (2001), pp. 894–9.

King, J.N., *Tudor Royal Iconography: literature and art in an age of religious crisis* (Princeton, 1989).

Kisby, F., ' "When the king goeth a procession": chapel ceremonies and services, the ritual year and religious reforms at the early Tudor court, 1485–1547', *Journal of British Studies*, xl (2001), pp. 44–75.

Knowles, M.D., *The Religious Orders in England: vol. iii The Tudor Age* (Cambridge, 1959).

——, and T. Dart, 'Notes on a Bible of Evesham Abbey', *English Historical Review*, lxxix (1964), pp. 775–8.

Kreider, A., *English Chantries: the road to dissolution* (Cambridge, Mass, 1979).

Lehmberg, S.E., *The Reformation Parliament 1529–1536* (Cambridge, 1970).

——, *The Later Parliaments of Henry VIII 1536–1547* (Cambridge, 1977).

——, 'The religious beliefs of Thomas Cromwell', in R.L. DeMolen, ed., *Leaders of the Reformation* (Cranbury, N.J., 1984), pp. 134–52.

——, *The Reformation of Cathedrals: cathedrals in English society, 1485–1603* (Princeton, 1988).

Loach, J., *Edward VI* (New Haven, 1999).

Loades, D., ed., *The Papers of George Wyatt*, Camden Society, 4th ser., v (1968).

——, *Mary Tudor* (Oxford, 1989).

Logan, F.D., 'Thomas Cromwell and the vicegerency in spirituals: a revisitation', *English Historical Review*, ciii (1988), pp. 658–67.

——, 'The first royal visitation of the English universities, 1535', *English Historical Review*, cvi (1991), pp. 861–88.

MacCulloch, D., 'Two dons in politics: Thomas Cranmer and Stephen Gardiner, 1503–1533', *Historical Journal*, xxxvii (1994), pp. 1–22.

——, 'Henry VIII and the reform of the church', in D. MacCulloch, ed., *The Reign of Henry VIII: politics, policy and piety* (1995), pp. 159–80.

——, *Thomas Cranmer* (New Haven, 1996).

Marshall, P., *The Catholic Priesthood and the English Reformation* (Oxford, 1994).

——, 'The Rood of Boxley, the Blood of Hailes and the defence of the Henrician Church', *Journal of Ecclesiastical History*, xivi (1995), pp, 689–96.

——, 'Fear, purgatory and polemic in Reformation England', in W.G. Naphy and P. Roberts, eds, *Fear in Early Modern Society* (Manchester, 1997), pp. 150–65.

——, 'Papist as heretic: the burning of John Forest, 1538', *Historical Journal*, xli (1998), pp. 351–74.

——, 'Mumpsimus and Sumpsimus: the intellectual origins of a Henrician *bon mot*', *Journal of Ecclesiastical History*, lii (2001), pp. 512–20.

——, 'The other black legend: the Henrician Reformation and the Spanish people', *English Historical Review*, cxvi (2001), pp. 31–49.

——, *Beliefs and the Dead in Reformation England* (Oxford, 2002).

—— and A. Ryrie, eds, *The Beginnings of English Protestantism* (2002).

Mattingly, G., *Catherine of Aragon* (1942).

Mayer, T.F., 'A Diet for Henry VIII: the failure of Reginald Pole's 1537 Legation', *Journal of British Studies*, xxvi (1987), pp. 305–31, reprinted in T.F. Mayer, *Cardinal Pole in European Context* (Aldershot, 2000).

——, 'A fate worse than death: Reginald Pole and the Parisian theologians', *English Historical Review*, ciii (1988), pp. 870–91, reprinted in *Cardinal Pole in European Context* (Aldershot, 2000).

McConica, J.K., *English Humanists and Reformation Politics under Henry VIII* (Oxford, 1965).

McEntegart, R., 'England and the League of Schmalkalden, 1531–1547: faction, foreign policy and the English Reformation', Univ. of London Ph.D. thesis, 1992.

——, *Henry VIII, the League of Schmalkalden, and the English Reformation* (Woodbridge, 2002).

Moreau, J.-P., *Rome ou L'Angleterre? Les reactions politiques des catholiques anglais au moment du schisme (1529–1553)* (Paris, 1984).

Moreton, C.E., 'The Walsingham Conspiracy of 1537', *Historical Research*, lxiii (1990), pp. 29–43.

Moyes, J., 'Warham: an English Primate on the eve of the Reformation', *Dublin Review*, cxiv (1894), pp. 390–420.

Muller, J.A., *Stephen Gardiner and the Tudor Revolution* (1926).

——, ed., *Letters of Stephen Gardiner* (Cambridge, 1933).

Murphy, V., 'The debate over Henry VIII's first divorce: an analysis of the contemporary treatises', Univ. of Cambridge Ph.D. thesis, 1984.

——, 'The literature and propaganda of Henry VIII's first divorce', in D. MacCulloch, ed., *The Reign of Henry VIII: politics, policy and piety* (Basingstoke, 1995), pp. 135–58.

Nicholls, M., *A History of the Modern British Isles: 1529–1603* (1999).

Nicholson, G., 'The Act of Appeals and the English reformation', in C. Cross, D. Loades and J.J. Scarisbrick, eds, *Law and Government under the Tudors* (Cambridge, 1988), pp. 19–30.

Norris, D., 'The fall of Thomas Cromwell', University of Southampton BA dissertation, 1995.

O'Grady, P., *Henry VIII and the Conforming Catholics* (Minnesota, 1994).

Palliser, D.M., *The Reformation in York 1534–1553*, Borthwick Papers, xl (1971).

Parker, T.M., *The English Reformation to 1558* (2nd edn, Oxford, 1966).

Paul, J.E., 'The last abbots of Reading and Colchester', *Bulletin of the Institute of Historical Research*, xxxiii (1960), pp. 115–21.

——, *Catherine of Aragon and her friends* (1966).

Pierce, H., *Margaret Pole Countess of Salisbury 1473–1541: loyalty, lineage and leadership* (Cardiff, 2003).

Potter, D., 'Foreign Policy', in D. MacCulloch, *The Reign of Henry VIII: politics, policy and piety* (1995), pp. 101–33.

Powicke, F.M., *The Reformation in England* (Oxford, 1941).

Redworth, G., 'Whatever happened to the Reformation?', *History Today*, Oct. 1987.

——, *In Defence of the Church Catholic: the life of Stephen Gardiner* (Oxford, 1990).

Rex, R., 'The earliest use of Hebrew in books printed in England dating some works of Richard Pace and Robert Wakefield', *Transactions of the Cambridge Bibliographical Society*, ix (1990), pp. 517–25.

——, *The Theology of John Fisher* (Cambridge, 1991).

——, 'The execution of the holy Maid of Kent', *Historical Research*, cxiv (1991), pp. 216–20.

——, *Henry VIII and the English Reformation* (Basingstoke, 1993).

——, 'The crisis of obedience: God's word and Henry's Reformation', *Historical Journal*, xxxix (1996), pp. 863–94.

——, 'Henry VIII and his Church', *History Review*, xxix (December 1997), pp. 33–7.

—— and C.D.C. Armstrong, 'Henry VIII's ecclesiastical and collegiate foundations', *Historical Research*, lxxv (2002), pp. 390–407.

Reynolds, E.E., *Saint John Fisher*, (1955).

Rollison, D., *The Local Origins of Modern Society: Gloucestershire 1500–1800* (1992).

Ryrie, A., 'The strange death of Lutheran England', *Journal of Ecclesiastical History*, liii (2002), pp. 64–92.

——, *The Gospel and Henry VIII: evangelicals in the early English Reformation* (Cambridge, 2003).

Scarisbrick, J.J., 'The conservative episcopate in England 1529–1535', Univ. of Cambridge Ph.D. thesis, 1955.

——, 'The pardon of the clergy', *Cambridge Historical Journal*, xii (1956).

——, 'Clerical taxation in England, 1485–1547', *Journal of Ecclesiastical History*, xi (1960), pp. 41–54.

——, *Henry VIII* (1968).

——, 'Henry VIII and the dissolution of the secular colleges', in C. Cross, D. Loades and J.J. Scarisbrick, eds, *Law and Government under the Tudors* (Cambridge, 1988), pp. 51–66.

——, 'Fisher, Henry VIII and the Reformation crisis', in B. Bradshaw and E. Duffy, *Humanism, Reform and the Reformation: the career of Bishop John Fisher* (Cambridge, 1989), pp. 155–68.

Schenk, W., *Reginald Pole: Cardinal of England* (1950).

Shagan, E.H., 'Rumours and Popular Politics in the Reign of Henry VIII', in T. Harris, ed., *The Politics of the Excluded, c. 1500–1850* (Basingstoke, 2001), pp. 30–66.

——, 'Print, orality and communications in the Maid of Kent affair', *Journal of Ecclesiastical History*, lii (2001), pp. 21–33.

——, *Popular Politics and the English Reformation* (Cambridge, 2002).

Shaw, A., 'Papal loyalism in 1530s England', *Downside Review*, cxvii (1999), pp. 17–40.

Smith, L.B., *Henry VIII: the mask of royalty* (1971).

——, *Land and Politics in the England of Henry VIII: the West Riding of Yorkshire* (Oxford, 1970).

Starkey, D., *Six Wives: the Queens of Henry VIII* (2003).

Stewart, A., *Close Readers: humanism and sodomy in early modern England* (Princeton, 1997).

Summerson, H.R.T., *Medieval Carlisle: the city and the borders from the late eleventh to the mid-sixteenth century* (2 vols, Kendal, 1993).

Tait, M.D., 'The Brigittine monastery of Syon (Middlesex), with special reference to its monastic usages', Univ. of Oxford D.Phil. thesis, 1975.

Thompson, A.H., *The English Clergy and their Organization in the Later Middle Ages* (Oxford, 1947).

Thompson, S., 'The bishop in his diocese', in B. Bradshaw and E. Duffy, eds., *Humanism, Reform and the Reformation: the career of Bishop John Fisher* (Cambridge, 1989), pp. 67–80.

Trueman, C.R., *Luther's Legacy: salvation and English reformers 1525–1556* (Oxford, 1994).

Tudor Craig, P., 'Henry VIII and King David', in D. Williams, ed., *Early Tudor England: proceedings of the 1987 Harlaxton symposium* (Woodbridge, 1989), pp. 183–205.

Victoria County History, Cumberland, ii, ed. J. Wilson (1905).

Victoria County History, Cambridgeshire, ii, ed. L.F. Salzman, *et al.* (1948).

Victoria County History, Kent, ii, ed., W. Page (1926).

Walker, G., 'Saint or schemer?: the 1527 heresy trial of Thomas Bilney reconsidered', *Journal of Ecclesiastical History*, xl (1989), pp. 219–38, reprinted with revisions in G. Walker, *Persuasive Fictions* (Aldershot, 1996), pp. 143–77.

——, 'Cardinal Wolsey and the satirists: the case of *Godly Queen Hester* re-opened', in S.J. Gunn, and P.G. Lindley, eds., *Cardinal Wolsey: Church, state and art* (Cambridge, 1991), pp. 239–60, reprinted with revisions in G. Walker, *Plays of Persuasion: drama and politics at the court of Henry VIII* (Cambridge, 1991), pp. 102–32.

——, *Plays of Persuasion: drama and politics at the court of Henry VIII* (Cambridge, 1991).

Ward, P.J., 'The politics of religion: Thomas Cromwell and the Reformation in Calais, 1534–40', *Journal of Religious History*, xvii (1992), pp. 152–71.

Warnicke, R.M., *The marrying of Anne of Cleves: royal protocol in early modern England* (Cambridge, 2000).

Watt, D., 'Reconstructing the word: the political prophecies of Elizabeth Barton (1506–1534)', *Renaissance Quarterly*, l (1997).

——, *Sectaries of God. Women prophets in late medieval and early modern England* (1998).

Wernham, R.B., *Before the Armada* (1966).

Whiting, R., 'Local responses to the Henrician Reformation', in D. MacCulloch, ed., *The Reign of Henry VIII: politics, policy and piety* (1995), pp. 203–26.

Wood, A., *Riot, Rebellion and Popular Politics in Early Modern England* (2002).

Wooding, L.E.C., *Rethinking Catholicism in Reformation England* (Oxford, 2000).

Woodward, G.W.O., 'The exemption from suppression of certain Yorkshire priories', *English Historical Review*, lxxvi (1961), pp. 385–401.

——, *The Dissolution of the Monasteries* (1966).

Index